Contemporary
Literary Criticism

Guide to Gale Literary Criticism Series

For criticism on	Consult these Gale series
Authors now living or who died after December 31, 1999	*CONTEMPORARY LITERARY CRITICISM (CLC)*
Authors who died between 1900 and 1999	*TWENTIETH-CENTURY LITERARY CRITICISM (TCLC)*
Authors who died between 1800 and 1899	*NINETEENTH-CENTURY LITERATURE CRITICISM (NCLC)*
Authors who died between 1400 and 1799	*LITERATURE CRITICISM FROM 1400 TO 1800 (LC)* *SHAKESPEAREAN CRITICISM (SC)*
Authors who died before 1400	*CLASSICAL AND MEDIEVAL LITERATURE CRITICISM (CMLC)*
Authors of books for children and young adults	*CHILDREN'S LITERATURE REVIEW (CLR)*
Dramatists	*DRAMA CRITICISM (DC)*
Poets	*POETRY CRITICISM (PC)*
Short story writers	*SHORT STORY CRITICISM (SSC)*
Black writers of the past two hundred years	*BLACK LITERATURE CRITICISM (BLC)* *BLACK LITERATURE CRITICISM SUPPLEMENT (BLCS)*
Hispanic writers of the late nineteenth and twentieth centuries	*HISPANIC LITERATURE CRITICISM (HLC)* *HISPANIC LITERATURE CRITICISM SUPPLEMENT (HLCS)*
Native North American writers and orators of the eighteenth, nineteenth, and twentieth centuries	*NATIVE NORTH AMERICAN LITERATURE (NNAL)*
Major authors from the Renaissance to the present	*WORLD LITERATURE CRITICISM, 1500 TO THE PRESENT (WLC)* *WORLD LITERATURE CRITICISM SUPPLEMENT (WLCS)*

ISSN 0091-3421

Volume 131

Contemporary Literary Criticism

Criticism of the Works
of Today's Novelists, Poets, Playwrights,
Short Story Writers, Scriptwriters, and
Other Creative Writers

Jeffrey W. Hunter
EDITOR

Jenny Cromie
Justin Karr
Linda Pavlovski
ASSOCIATE EDITORS

Rebecca J. Blanchard
Vince Cousino
ASSISTANT EDITORS

GALE GROUP

Detroit
New York
San Francisco
London
Boston
Woodbridge, CT

STAFF

Lynn M. Spampinato, Janet Witalec, *Managing Editors, Literature Product*
Kathy D. Darrow, *Product Liaison*
Jeffrey W. Hunter, *Editor*
Mark W. Scott, *Publisher, Literature Product*

Jenny Cromie, Justin Karr, Linda Pavlovski, *Associate Editors*
Rebecca J. Blanchard, Vince Cousino, *Assistant Editors*
Patti A. Tippett, Timothy J. White, *Technical Training Specialists*
Deborah J. Morad, Kathleen Lopez Nolan, *Managing Editors*
Susan M. Trosky, *Director, Literature Content*

Maria L. Franklin, *Permissions Manager*
Edna M. Hedblad, *Permissions Specialist*

Victoria B. Cariappa, *Research Manager*
Tracie A. Richardson, *Project Coordinator*
Tamara C. Nott, *Research Associate*
Scott Floyd, Timothy Lehnerer, Ron Morelli, *Research Assistants*

Dorothy Maki, *Manufacturing Manager*
Stacy L. Melson, *Buyer*

Mary Beth Trimper, *Manager, Composition and Electronic Prepress*
Carolyn Fischer, *Composition Specialist*

Michael Logusz, *Graphic Artist*
Randy Bassett, *Image Database Supervisor*
Robert Duncan, Dan Newell, *Imaging Specialists*
Pamela A. Reed, *Imaging Coordinator*
Kelly A. Quin, *Editor, Image Content*

Library of Congress Catalog Card Number 76-46132
ISBN 0-7876-3206-6
ISSN 0091-3421
Printed in the United States of America

10 9 8 7 6 5 4 3 2 1

Contents

Preface vii

Acknowledgments xi

Preface

Named "one of the twenty-five most distinguished reference titles published during the past twenty-five years" by *Reference Quarterly,* the *Contemporary Literary Criticism* (*CLC*) series provides readers with critical commentary and general information on more than 2,000 authors now living or who died after December 31, 1999. Volumes published from 1973 through 1999 include authors who died after December 31, 1959. Previous to the publication of the first volume of *CLC* in 1973, there was no ongoing digest monitoring scholarly and popular sources of critical opinion and explication of modern literature. *CLC,* therefore, has fulfilled an essential need, particularly since the complexity and variety of contemporary literature makes the function of criticism especially important to today's reader.

Scope of the Series

CLC provides significant passages from published criticism of works by creative writers. Since many of the authors covered in *CLC* inspire continual critical commentary, writers are often represented in more than one volume. There is, of course, no duplication of reprinted criticism.

Authors are selected for inclusion for a variety of reasons, among them the publication or dramatic production of a critically acclaimed new work, the reception of a major literary award, revival of interest in past writings, or the adaptation of a literary work to film or television.

Attention is also given to several other groups of writers—authors of considerable public interest—about whose work criticism is often difficult to locate. These include mystery and science fiction writers, literary and social critics, foreign authors, and authors who represent particular ethnic groups.

Each *CLC* volume contains individual essays and reviews taken from hundreds of book review periodicals, general magazines, scholarly journals, monographs, and books. Entries include critical evaluations spanning from the beginning of an author's career to the most current commentary. Interviews, feature articles, and other published writings that offer insight into the author's works are also presented. Students, teachers, librarians, and researchers will find that the general critical and biographical material in *CLC* provides them with vital information required to write a term paper, analyze a poem, or lead a book discussion group. In addition, complete biographical citations note the original source and all of the information necessary for a term paper footnote or bibliography.

Organization of the Book

A *CLC* entry consists of the following elements:

- The **Author Heading** cites the name under which the author most commonly wrote, followed by birth and death dates. Also located here are any name variations under which an author wrote, including transliterated forms for authors whose native languages use nonroman alphabets. If the author wrote consistently under a pseudonym, the pseudonym will be listed in the author heading and the author's actual name given in parenthesis on the first line of the biographical and critical information. Uncertain birth or death dates are indicated by question marks. Single-work entries are preceded by a heading that consists of the most common form of the title in English translation (if applicable) and the original date of composition.

- A **Portrait of the Author** is included when available.

- The **Introduction** contains background information that introduces the reader to the author, work, or topic that is the subject of the entry.

- The list of **Principal Works** is ordered chronologically by date of first publication and lists the most important works by the author. The genre and publication date of each work is given. In the case of foreign authors whose works have been translated into English, the English-language version of the title follows in brackets. Unless otherwise indicated, dramas are dated by first performance, not first publication.

- Reprinted **Criticism** is arranged chronologically in each entry to provide a useful perspective on changes in critical evaluation over time. The critic's name and the date of composition or publication of the critical work are given at the beginning of each piece of criticism. Unsigned criticism is preceded by the title of the source in which it appeared. All titles by the author featured in the text are printed in boldface type. Footnotes are reprinted at the end of each essay or excerpt. In the case of excerpted criticism, only those footnotes that pertain to the excerpted texts are included.

- A complete **Bibliographical Citation** of the original essay or book precedes each piece of criticism.

- Critical essays are prefaced by brief **Annotations** explicating each piece.

- Whenever possible, a recent **Author Interview** accompanies each entry.

- An annotated bibliography of **Further Reading** appears at the end of each entry and suggests resources for additional study. In some cases, significant essays for which the editors could not obtain reprint rights are included here. Boxed material following the further reading list provides references to other biographical and critical sources on the author in series published by Gale.

Indexes

A **Cumulative Author Index** lists all of the authors that appear in a wide variety of reference sources published by the Gale Group, including *CLC*. A complete list of these sources is found facing the first page of the Author Index. The index also includes birth and death dates and cross references between pseudonyms and actual names.

A **Cumulative Nationality Index** lists all authors featured in *CLC* by nationality, followed by the number of the *CLC* volume in which their entry appears.

A **Cumulative Topic Index** lists the literary themes and topics treated in the series as well as in *Literature Criticism from 1400 to 1800, Nineteenth-Century Literature Criticism, Twentieth-Century Literary Criticism,* and the *Contemporary Literary Criticism* Yearbook, which was discontinued in 1998.

An alphabetical **Title Index** accompanies each volume of *CLC*. Listings of titles by authors covered in the given volume are followed by the author's name and the corresponding page numbers where the titles are discussed. English translations of foreign titles and variations of titles are cross-referenced to the title under which a work was originally published. Titles of novels, dramas, nonfiction books, and poetry, short story, or essay collections are printed in italics, while individual poems, short stories, and essays are printed in roman type within quotation marks.

In response to numerous suggestions from librarians, Gale also produces an annual paperbound edition of the *CLC* cumulative title index. This annual cumulation, which alphabetically lists all titles reviewed in the series, is available to all customers. Additional copies of this index are available upon request. Librarians and patrons will welcome this separate index; it saves shelf space, is easy to use, and is recyclable upon receipt of the next edition.

Citing *Contemporary Literary Criticism*

When writing papers, students who quote directly from any volume in the Literary Criticism Series may use the following general format to footnote reprinted criticism. The first example pertains to material drawn from periodicals, the second to material reprinted from books.

Alfred Cismaru, "Making the Best of It," *The New Republic* 207, no. 24 (December 7, 1992): 30, 32; excerpted and reprinted in *Contemporary Literary Criticism,* vol. 85, ed. Christopher Giroux (Detroit: The Gale Group, 1995), 73-4.

Yvor Winters, *The Post-Symbolist Methods* (Allen Swallow, 1967), 211-51; excerpted and reprinted in *Contemporary Literary Criticism,* vol. 85, ed. Christopher Giroux (Detroit: The Gale Group, 1995), 223-26.

Suggestions are Welcome

Readers who wish to suggest new features, topics, or authors to appear in future volumes, or who have other suggestions or comments are cordially invited to call, write, or fax the Managing Editor:

Managing Editor, Literary Criticism Series
The Gale Group
27500 Drake Road
Farmington Hills, MI 48331-3535
1-800-347-4253 (GALE)
Fax: 248-699-8054

Acknowledgments

The editors wish to thank the copyright holders of the excerpted criticism included in this volume and the permissions managers of many book and magazine publishing companies for assisting us in securing reproduction rights. We are also grateful to the staffs of the Detroit Public Library, the Library of Congress, the University of Detroit Mercy Library, Wayne State University Purdy/Kresge Library Complex, and the University of Michigan Libraries for making their resources available to us. Following is a list of the copyright holders who have granted us permission to reproduce material in this volume of *CLC*. Every effort has been made to trace copyright, but if omissions have been made, please let us know.

COPYRIGHTED EXCERPTS IN *CLC*, VOLUME 131, WERE REPRODUCED FROM THE FOLLOWING PERIODICALS:

African American Review, v. 28, Winter, 1994 for "Angry Arts: Silence, Speech, and Song in Gayl Jones's 'Corregidora'" by Amy S. Gottfried. © 1994 by Amy S. Gottfried. Reproduced by permission of the author./ v. 28, Spring, 1994 for "Gayl Jones's Oraliterary Explorations" by Gay Wilentz. © 1994 by Gay Wilentz. Reproduced by permission of the author./ v. 28, Summer, 1994 for "'These Are the Facts of the Darky's History': Thinking History and Reading Names in Four African American Texts" by Adam McKible. © 1994 by Adam McKible. Reproduced by permission of the author.—*American Historical Review,* v. 97, June, 1992. Reproduced by permission.—*Book World—The Washington Post,* March 29, 1987 for "Almanacs of Urban Decay" by E. F. Bleiler; October 23, 1988 for "Crimes Against Conscience: The McCarthy Era in Fiction" by Bruce Cook; March 26, 1989 for "Marvels and Mysteries" by Michael Dirda; November 25, 1990 for "Citizen Howard Fast" by Christopher Hitchens; January 12, 1992 for "Four Cheers For Liberal Democracy" by George Gilder; September 6, 1992 for "Caught in the Waltz of Disasters" by Thomas Mallon; March 1, 1998 for "Faith in Herself" by Valerie Boyd; May 23, 1999 for "The Trouble with Women" by Elizabeth Ward; May 23, 1999 for "It's A Dog's Life" by Jonathan Yardley; June 13, 1999 for "The End of Amorality" by Michael Kazin. © 1987, 1988, 1989, 1990, 1992, 1998, 1999 Washington Post Book World Service/Washington Post Writers Group. All reproduced by permission of the respective authors./ March 3, 1987; June 12, 1999. © 1987, 1999 Washington Post Book World Service/Washington Post Writers Group. Both reproduced by permission.—*Callaloo,* n. 16, October, 1982 for "A Spiritual Journey: Gayl Jones's Song for Anninho" by Trudier Harris; n. 16, October, 1982 for "Escape from Trublem: The Fiction of Gayl Jones" by Jerry W. Ward. Copyright © 1982 by Charles H. Rowell. Both reproduced by permission of the respective authors./ v. 19, Winter, 1996. Copyright © 1996 by Charles H. Rowell. Reproduced by permission of The Johns Hopkins University Press.—*Chicago Tribune,* January 20, 1991 for "Comrade Novelist Howard Fast Sentimentally Evokes His Life As an American Communist" by Clancy Sigal. © 1991 Tribune Media Services, Inc. All rights reserved. Reproduced by permission of the author./ April 21, 1987. © 1987 Tribune Media Services, Inc. All rights reserved. Reproduced by permission of Knight Ridder/Tribune Information Services.—*Choice,* December, 1986. Reproduced by permission from *Choice,* copyright 1986 by the American Library Association.—*The Christian Century,* v. LXXXV, October 16, 1968. Reproduced by permission.—*Commentary,* v. 78, August, 1984 for "Feminism Ad Absurdum" by Carol Iannone; v. 91, March, 1991 for "About-Face" by Ronald Radosh; v. 93, March, 1992 for "To the 21st Century" by Paul Johnson; v. 108, July-August, 1999 for a review of "The Great Disruption: Human Nature and the Reconstitution of Social Order" by Charles Murray; v. 108, September, 1999 for "Blast from the Past" by Samuel McCracken. Copyright © 1984, 1991, 1992, 1999 by the American Jewish Committee. All rights reserved. All reproduced by permission of the publisher and the respective authors.—*Commonweal,* v. CXIX, June 19, 1992. Copyright © 1992 Commonweal Publishing Co., Inc. Reproduced by permission of Commonweal Foundation.—*The Critical Quarterly,* v. 3, Spring, 1961 for a review of "Let's Have Some Poetry" by Robin Skelton. Reproduced by permission of the Literary Estate of Robin Skelton.—*Critique: Studies in Contemporary Fiction,* v. XXXI, Winter, 1990; v. XXXII, Summer, 1991; v. XXXVII, Fall, 1995. Copyright © 1990, 1991, 1995 Helen Dwight Reid Educational Foundation. All reproduced with permission of the Helen Dwight Reid Educational Foundation, published by Heldref Publications, 1319 18th Street, NW, Washington, DC 20036-1802.—*differences: A Journal of Feminist Cultural Studies,* v. 8, Summer, 1996. Copyright © 1996 by Brown University and *differences: A Journal of Feminist Cultural Studies.* Reprinted by permission of the publisher.—*Dissent,* v. 43, Winter, 1996 for "What Francis Fukuyama Can Teach . . . And Learn" by Robert Heilbroner. © 1996, by Dissent Publishing Corporation. Reprinted by permission of the publisher and the author.—*Encounter,* v. XXIX, November, 1967 for "Recent Verse" by Alasdair Clayre. © 1967 by Alasdair Clayre./ v. XII, February, 1959 for "Poets and Poetry" by John Heath-Stubbs. © 1959 by John Heath-Stubbs. Reproduced by permission of the author.—*Journal of Aesthetic Education,* v. 25, Fall, 1991. Reproduced by permission.—*Journal of Religion,* v. 63, October, 1983 for "An Assessment Reassessed: Paul Tillich on the Reformation" by George Lindbeck. Reproduced by permission of The University of Chicago Press and the author.—*The Los Angeles Times,*

Paul Auster
1947-

American novelist, poet, memoirist, essayist, critic, screenplay writer, translator, and editor.

The following entry presents an overview of Auster's career through 1999. For further information on his life and works, see *CLC,* Volume 47.

INTRODUCTION

A provocative experimental novelist whose work represents an amalgam of several genres, Paul Auster is best known for his *New York Trilogy,* which consists of *City of Glass* (1985), *Ghosts* (1986), and *The Locked Room* (1987). In these novels and others, he combines elements of hard-boiled detective fiction, *film noir,* dystopian fantasy, and postmodern narrative strategies to address the possibility of certain knowledge, human redemption, and the function of language. His ambitious work is distinguished for challenging the limits of the novel form and tackling difficult epistemological concepts.

BIOGRAPHICAL INFORMATION

Born in Newark, New Jersey, Auster was raised by parents Samuel, a landlord, and Queenie on the outskirts of New York City in the North Jersey suburbs. His interest in literature is indirectly attributed to his uncle, translator Allan Mandelbaum, who left a box of books at the Auster home while away in Europe. The teenaged Auster began reading them and soon resolved to become a writer himself. Upon graduating from high school, he attended Columbia University, where he earned a B.A. in English in 1969 and an M.A. in 1970. While still in college, he wrote both poetry and prose and participated in campus protests against the Vietnam War. He then worked as a merchant seaman for several months to fund a move to France, where he remained for four years and worked a variety of odd jobs to make ends meet. In 1974, he married writer and translator Lydia Davis, with whom he shares a son; they divorced in 1979 and Auster remarried Siri Hustuedt in 1981. After returning to New York, Auster published his first two books—the thin poetry collections *Unearth* (1974) and *Wall Writing* (1976). He was awarded Ingram Merrill Foundation grants in 1975 and 1982, as well as National Endowment of the Arts fellowships in 1979 and 1985. Auster continued to labor in relative obscurity as a poet, essayist, and translator of French literature until the publication of his first novel, *City of Glass,* which was rejected by seventeen publishers before

Sun & Moon Press finally issued the book in 1985. The novel was nominated for an Edgar Award for best mystery novel in 1986. The third volume of his *New York Trilogy, The Locked Room,* was also nominated for several awards. Auster taught creative writing at Princeton University from 1986 to 1990. In 1994 he collaborated with director Wayne Wang on the films *Smoke* and *Blue in the Face,* which he co-directed. Auster was awarded the prestigious Chevalier de l'Ordre des Arts des et des Lettres in 1993.

MAJOR WORKS

Though Auster's fiction eludes easy classification, his novels embody several recurring elements: the use of metafictional narrative techniques, textual puzzles, doppelgangers, ironic distancing, and self-reflexivity to underscore the relationship between past and present and the ambiguous nature of language and identity. While instances of confused or mistaken identity are common in the mystery genre, Auster adapts this stock device into a metaphor for contemporary urban life in his *New York*

Trilogy, deliberately blurring the distinction between author and text. *City of Glass,* a grim and intellectually puzzling story, superficially resembles a mystery novel that exploits the conventions of the detective genre. The protagonist, Quinn, is a pseudonymous mystery novelist who assumes the identity of a real detective, named Paul Auster, after receiving a phone call intended for Auster. Lonely and bored, Quinn accepts the case in Auster's place. His assignment is to shadow Stillman, a brilliant linguistics professor whose obsessive quest to rediscover humanity's primordial language compelled him to isolate his own son in a closet for nine years. Newly released from a mental hospital, Stillman poses a threat to his son's life, prompting the need for a detective. In *Ghosts,* the second volume of the trilogy, Auster continues his investigation into lost identity with increasing abstraction, including characters identified only as Blue, White, and Black. The novel's coy tone and austere plot—a detective named Blue is contracted by a client named White to pursue a man named Black—places the action in a cerebral context largely disconnected from reality. The trilogy's concluding volume, *The Locked Room,* is less abstract and more accessible than the previous two. This novel features flesh and blood characters with whom readers can easily identify, including a nameless first-person narrator who ostensibly represents Auster himself. The narrator is summoned by the wife of a childhood friend named Fanshawe who has disappeared and is presumed dead. A fantastically gifted writer, Fanshawe has left behind some unpublished writings as well as instructions for his friend to see them into print. As time passes, the narrator easily moves into Fanshawe's existence, marrying his wife, publishing his work, and eventually engendering rumors that he is actually Fanshawe or, at least, the man who created the works. His deception is finally jeopardized when he receives a communication from the real Fanshawe.

In the Country of Last Things (1987), published the same year as *The Locked Room,* is an epistolary novel depicting a dystopian American city of the future. As in previous works, this novel evinces Auster's abiding interest in the nature of language and reality. The protagonist, Anna Blume, travels from one continent to a large metropolis on another, where she hopes to find her missing brother. Instead, she discovers a city in chaos where criminals brazenly exploit the desperate and homeless, "Runners" trot themselves to death, and "Leapers" jump to their deaths from the city's crumbling skyscrapers. Anna relates her search through this hellish environment in a letter to someone left behind on the other continent. Though Auster seems to have shifted from mystery to science fiction, *In the Country of Last Things* shares many of the narrative devices and thematic preoccupations of his *New York Trilogy,* most apparently the search for identity, also the central theme of *Moon Palace* (1989), a postmodern bildungsroman around the theme of lost family. In this story, the protagonist is Marco Stanley Fogg, an orphan who eventually becomes homeless in New York City after running out of money while studying at Columbia University. After recovering in the care of a college friend and a Chinese

woman, Marco goes to work for an eccentric old man who turns out to be his paternal grandfather. The remainder of the narrative follows Marco's journey of discovery and loss as he encounters his previously unknown relatives and records the fantastic tales of his grandfather's youth. Auster's next novel, *The Music of Chance* (1990), begins as a generative personal journey, bringing to mind such fictional characters as Mark Twain's Huck Finn, John Updike's Rabbit Angstrom, and Jack Kerouac's Dean Moriarty. Protagonist Jim Nashe hits the road in search of self-knowledge after his wife leaves him and he receives an inheritance from his deceased father. His tour of the country winds down at about the same time as his money runs out, whereupon he meets a young gambler, Pozzi, who entices him into a poker game with two eccentric lottery winners from Pennsylvania. The two lose what they have and fall further into debt. In order to pay off the debt, Nashe and Pozzi are forced to build a stone wall for the eccentrics. Auster continued the thematic and stylistic concerns of his previous novels in *Leviathan* (1992), whose title brings to mind the legendary ocean beast and the seventeenth-century political philosophy of Thomas Hobbes. The opening event of this novel is actually its denouement—the death by explosion of a New York writer, Benjamin Sachs. What follows—a reconstruction of precipitating events—is facilitated by Peter Aaron, another New York writer who learns of Sachs's bizarre death and becomes obsessed with writing the story of his friend. Aaron's investigation uncovers a world of secrets, multiple and exchanged identities, and previously unknown connections between characters.

In *Mr. Vertigo* (1994), Auster relates the story of Walter Rawley, also known as "Walt the Wonder Boy" and "Mr. Vertigo." Set in the Midwest of the 1920s, Walt is an orphaned street urchin who is offered a new life by a mystical showman, named Master Yehudi, who teaches Walt to levitate. The two, along with a Sioux Indian woman and an Ethiopian boy, barnstorm the country, growing increasingly famous on their way toward Broadway. However, on the verge of stardom, Walt loses his gift for levitating. He begins to wander and eventually ends up in the mobster underworld of Chicago. *Timbuktu* (1999) revolves around a poignant relationship between a middle-aged homeless man named Willy G. Christmas and his dog, Mr. Bones. The narrative is notable for its unusual dog's-eye perspective, as an omniscient narrator relates the story through the observations of Mr. Bones. In anticipation of his death, Willy travels with Mr. Bones from Brooklyn to Baltimore to establish a new home for his dog and to vouchsafe the manuscript of his epic lifework with a former high school English teacher. After Willy's death, Mr. Bones passes through a succession of new owners—some loving, some cruel—as he traverses rural, suburban, and urban America. Throughout, Mr. Bones is sustained by his continuing love for the deceased Willy and the promise of their reunion in an afterlife destination called Timbuktu. Auster's various volumes of nonfiction and translation further display his diverse literary talents and knowledge of international literature. *The Invention of*

Solitude (1982), a memoir written after the death of his father, details Auster's relationship with and impressions of his father. Through a discursive and fragmented presentation, this book also contains discussions of authors such as Stéphane Mallarmé and Carlos Collodi. In addition, Auster has translated works by Jean-Paul Sartre, Jacques Dupin, and Mallarmé, edited the *Random House Book of Twentieth-Century French Poetry* (1982), and published a collection of essays and interviews entitled *The Art of Hunger* (1992).

CRITICAL RECEPTION

Often regarded as a postmodern writer, a default classification due to his metafictional techniques and ironic posturing, Auster is noted for his idiosyncratic work, which resists simple categorization. His critical reputation rests largely upon his *New York Trilogy,* which was enthusiastically received by reviewers, winning him respect as a formidable new literary talent during the mid-1980s. While *The Locked Room* is judged by many to be the richest and most compelling book of the trilogy, all three volumes have been commended for their facile appropriation—and dismantling—of conventional detective motifs to expose contradictory aspects of reality, literary artifice, and self-perception. Additional genre-defying novels such as *Moon Palace, The Music of Chance, Leviathan, Mr. Vertigo,* and *Timbuktu* won critical approval for tackling difficult themes without sacrificing the pleasures of entertainment or alienating the reader. Though some commentators have dismissed Auster's intellectual game-playing as unconvincing and gratuitous, and others find his wit and symbolism labored, most critics praise his sophisticated narrative structures, lucid prose, and daring forays into the philosophical paradoxes surrounding issues of linguistic self-invention and metaphysical doubt. Auster's innovative work is appreciated by many critics for reclaiming the vitality of contemporary experimental literature, for which he is widely regarded as one of the foremost American novelists of his generation.

PRINCIPAL WORKS

Unearth: Poems (poetry) 1974
Wall Writing: Poems, 1971-1975 (poetry) 1976
Facing the Music (poetry) 1980
White Spaces (prose) 1980
The Invention of Solitude (memoir) 1982
Random House Book of Twentieth-Century French Poetry [editor] (poetry) 1982
City of Glass (novel) 1985
Ghosts (novel) 1986
The Locked Room (novel) 1987
In the Country of Last Things (novel) 1987
Disappearances: Selected Poems (poetry) 1988
Moon Palace (novel) 1989

The Music of Chance (novel) 1990
The New York Trilogy [contains *City of Glass, Ghosts,* and *The Locked Room*] (novels) 1990
The Art of Hunger: Essays, Prefaces, Interviews (essays and interviews) 1992
Leviathan (novel) 1992
Mr. Vertigo (novel) 1994
The Red Notebook and Other Writings (prose) 1995
Smoke and Blue in the Face: Two Screenplays (screenplays) 1995
Hand to Mouth: A Chronicle of Early Failure (memoir, novel, and dramas) 1997
Timbuktu (novel) 1999

CRITICISM

Carolyn See (review date 17 November 1985)

SOURCE: A review of *City of Glass,* in *Los Angeles Times Book Review,* November 17, 1985, pp. 3-4.

[*In the following review, See offers positive assessment of* City of Glass.]

"I have come to New York because it is the most forlorn of places, the most abject. The brokenness is everywhere, the disarray is universal. You have only to open your eyes to see it. The broken people, the broken things, the broken thoughts. The whole city is a junk heap. It suits my purpose admirably. I find the streets an endless source of material, an inexhaustible storehouse of shattered things. Each day I go out with my bag and collect object that seem worthy of investigation. My samples now number in the hundreds—from the chipped to the smashed, from the dented to the squashed, from the pulverized to the putrid."

City of Glass is the first in a New York trilogy, an experimental novel that wanders and digresses and loses its own narrative thread, but with all that, keeps offering bits of dialogue or scenes or "ideas" that make the whole thing much like a very good day for a street scavenger: In among the nondescript junk, there are maybe a hundred little treasures. . . .

City of Glass is about the degeneration of language, the shiftings of identity, the struggle to remain human in a great metropolis, when the city itself is cranking on its own falling-apart mechanical life that completely overrides any and every individual. Our hero, our narrator, has already gone through several lives, several identities. His name, he tells us, is Quinn (which rhymes with *twin* and *bin*). For a while he was "William Wilson," but before that "he had published several books of poetry, had written plays, critical essays, and worked on a number of long translations. . . ."

But quite abruptly, he has changed all that. As Wilson, he took a pseudonym within a pseudonym, and began to write a series of detective novels about a private eye named Max Work: "In the triad of selves that Quinn had become, Wilson served as a kind of ventriloquist, Quinn himself was the dummy, and Work was the animated voice that gave purpose to the enterprise."

Once all this has been established, we are instructed to see Quinn as bereft of a wife and child, a "bachelor" living alone, interested in the fate of the Mets, one of those sad, single guys who eat breakfast alone at lunch counters. The author then allows him to get a phone call (put through by mistake?) asking for Paul Auster (the author of this book). This is a plea for some detective work and Quinn/twin, after hesitating, answers that request.

A loving wife has a crazy husband, who has been locked up in a dark room for the first nine years of his life by a mad dad, who sometimes takes the name of "Henry Dark" to use as a mouthpiece for some of his more revolutionary scholarly ideas about language, civilization, Paradise and child-rearing. This mad dad, whose name is Stillman, has been put in jail some years before for abusing his son, and is just now returning to New York. Quinn/Auster, because of his stories about Max Work, and because he has nothing else to do, agrees to watch for the elder Mr. Stillman.

Except, of course, when Mr. Stillman gets off the train at Grand Central, there are *two* of him—one shabby, one perfectly dressed. Quinn makes an arbitrary decision and begins to shadow the shabby one, starting a long journey through the city to his ultimate destiny.

Walking through the city! This really is a New York novel. Quinn walks the length and breadth of Manhattan Island just for the heck of it, and the elder Mr. Stillman, in *his* walks, manages literally to spell out cryptic messages about the meaning of life. It is Stillman who sees the great Metropolis as a city "of broken people, broken things, broken thoughts," but that falls right in with his theory that we are to return soon to a "prelapsarian" condition: a universal language, a universal state of well-being. Of course, Stillman has cracked completely, as Quinn realizes, as he presents himself to him in a series of interlocking identities.

Quinn, at one point, begins to wonder about the "real" Paul Auster and goes to see *him*—and if you're thinking that Pirandello and Unamuno and a hundred other serious writers and tens of thousands of undergraduates have pondered the relationship between character and author, it really is OK, since those "identities" are only two among 20 or so.

In fact, Auster's laconic, throwaway, often very funny tone keeps this book (and many of its ideas) fresh. If, during the middle of the narrative, the reader entertains a few vagrant thoughts about where this novel is going, what Quinn/Wilson/Work/Auster is up to anyway, that question

is satisfactorily answered in a series of ending scenes that mustn't be given away—except that there's a clue hidden in this sentence.

It's true, in a small town we are born, live and die as more or less one person, because that's the way our family and friends know us. In cities, we either rush to change our identities—or they are changed brutally for us. *City of Glass* thoughtfully and cleverly draws our attention to these questions of self.

E. F. Bleiler (review date 29 March 1987)

SOURCE: "Almanacs of Urban Decay," in *Washington Post Book World,* March 28, 1987, p. 11.

[*In the following review, Bleiler offers positive estimation of* The Locked Room *and* In the Country of Last Things.]

In *City of Glass,* the first volume of *The New York Trilogy,* Paul Auster wrote of his character Quinn/William Wilson that "what interested him about the stories he wrote was not their relation to the world but their relation to other stories." This is perhaps also true of Paul Auster.

In *The Locked Room,* the third volume of the trilogy, Auster builds on *Fanshawe* (1828), Nathaniel Hawthorne's suppressed first novel, which is a secularization of the demon-lover motif with strong mythic elements. *Fanshawe* is generally rated a bad book, but it has one interesting point: After rescuing a fair maiden from the fate worse than death, Fanshawe rejects her and a worldly life because of a spiritual leprosy that gnaws at his soul.

Auster, who is saturated in 19th-century fiction, in *The Locked Room* creates another Fanshawe, who, suffering from spiritual death, withdraws from life and passes the possibility of worldliness on to another, normal man. This, however, is not Auster's only theme; he enriches his story with concepts of metaphysical dual identity and interpenetration of author and work. The narrator both is and is not the great writer Fanshawe, and part of his story is the possibility that he will become Fanshawe.

According to the plot line, which is that of a mystery story, the narrator is summoned by the widow of his childhood friend Fanshawe, with whom he has long been out of touch. Fanshawe, it turns out, has simply disappeared and is presumably dead. His task, set up by Fanshawe, is to act as literary executor and place the novels, short stories, plays and poems that Fanshawe created. Since (ironically) they are all great, the narrator succeeds, but there are complexities when he is commissioned to write a life of Fanshawe.

The narrator (who is both a character and Paul Auster) wanders in and out of Fanshawe's life, compulsively, convulsively, seeking Fanshawe, until a melodramatic climax. Along the way he receives a letter from the sup-

posedly dead man, warning him that if he ever finds Fanshawe, Fanshawe will kill him. The letter urges the narrator to "be who you are," which the narrator unwittingly
alters to "remain who you are."

In summary *The Locked Room* sounds much like one of
Claude Houghton's neglected metaphysical novels of the
1930s, a comparison that is not improper. But there are
differences. Houghton wrote about quests for a self, with
an exuberant, optimistic, yet elegantly styled mysticism,
while Auster is concerned with darker shadows of
personality, and the inevitable conclusion is not enhance-
ment but death.

The Locked Room is well worth reading. It lacks the brilliance and wild imagination of *City of Glass,* but it
conveys a message of somber doom through a rhythmic,
austere (to make a necessary word-play) style and excellent characterizations.

If the members of *The New York Trilogy* are presented as
extrapolations of the detective story, *In the Country of
Last Things* is a similar extension of the dystopia and the
journey through Hell. The subject is "the city," a horrible
place not geographically identified, but certainly the faulty
side of the United States. The author focuses on milieu
more than on individual spiritual downfall, and the book
tends to be an ethnographic survey of death and degradation. Hawthorne, now cited by the author, is again the
historical germ, with perhaps links back to John Bunyan
and forward to the *Land of Darkness* of the prolific
Victorian Mrs. Oliphant.

To describe the city in any detail would be beyond the
scope of this review. Let it be enough to say that it is a
world of entropy, where everything runs down into decay,
and that the central metaphor is cannibalism, both literal
and figurative. The city's ailment is not so much political
(as is most common in such dystopias) as spiritual.
Creation has ended. Life persists by devouring the past
and recycling it in ever more inferior forms. On the
specific, material side, there is no housing, though sharp-
ers survive by selling its non-existence; there is little food,
and that little is obtainable only by violence or an exchange
system based on scavenging. Life is so miserable that the
will to live diminishes, and there are institutionalized ways
of dying. Not just in euthanasia chambers, but with bands
that starve themselves to death, troupes that race until they
drop dead and fanatics that leap in exaltation off high
placcs. (The exact analogies to our world are clear in
Auster's text.) All these horrors are told in a bald style
with little emotional tone, as passionless as an almanac.

The story vehicle is a long letter written in a small
notebook that Anna Blume sends back to her friends across
the sea. Anna, who in addition to being a well-rounded
character is a type representing the will to live and perhaps
Judaism, has come to the city to find her brother, a journalist who disappeared some time before. Her quest, at first
arrogant and ill-planned, is predictably unsuccessful, but

she gradually adapts to the city and survives. She becomes
a professional scavenger; pushing a small cart that is
chained to her to prevent its being stolen, she prowls the
streets looking for things edible or barterable. Her
adventures take her through violence, privation, cold,
disease and hunger.

In the Country of Last Things is a painful, horrible book,
and it cannot be called enjoyable in terms of light reading.
But it is powerful, original, imaginative and handled with
artistry. It is one of the better modern attempts at describing Hell.

Michael Dirda (review date 26 March 1989)

SOURCE: "Marvels and Mysteries," in *Washington Post
Book World,* March 26, 1989, pp. 3, 10.

[*In the following review, Dirda offers positive assessment
of* Moon Palace.]

Hemingway once remarked that "all modern American
literature comes from one book by Mark Twain called
Huckleberry Finn." That story of a boy's passage toward
maturity, told against the astounding dreamscape of
America, has since been repeated in the adventures of
Nick Carraway, Ralph Ellison's *Invisible Man* and countless others. *Moon Palace,* which relates the growing up of
Marco Stanley Fogg, shows that there's a dance in the old
theme yet, especially when a brilliant writer takes the
floor.

After working for many years as a translator of modern
French poetry, Paul Auster rocketed into semi-celebrity
with the publication of his New York trilogy: *City of Glass,
Ghosts,* and *The Locked Room.*

The first of these novels played with the conventions of
the hard-boiled detective story, as a mystery writer finds
himself impersonating a private eye in order to help a
beautiful dark-haired woman. The second, displaying a
more austere Auster, worked a series of Beckett-like
permutations on the relationship between observer and
observed: a p.i. named Blue spends years shadowing a
character named Black. The concluding volume of the trilogy took up the modernist conceit of a shamus-like
biographer compelled to learn the truth about a writer, no
matter what the personal costs.

Chock-a-block with arcana about language, responsibility
and identity, the novels might have been nothing more
than a high-brow snooze were it not for their author's
commanding narrative skills. For all his post-modern
reflexivity, Auster is a masterly, often autobiographical,
storyteller, one whose voice—unruffled, meditative, intelligent—quickly snares a reader. His memoir, *The Invention of Solitude,* points up the personal element in much
of his writing—from the recurrent obsession with fathers
and sons to details about life in Paris and his characters'

refined taste in reading. Anyone who likes, say, the philosophical melodramas of Robertson Davies, the melancholy comedies of Russell Hoban or the intellectual fantasies of John Crowley should try Auster. He's of their company.

His latest book, *Moon Palace,* divides roughly into three main sections. In the first we meet the hero, Marco Stanley Fogg, an orphan—named after three explorers—who has just enough money to finish Columbia University. But, "like all the Foggs, he had a penchant for aimlessness and reverie, for sudden bolts and lengthy torpors." Acting purely out of a kind of existential obstinacy, M.S., as he likes to be called, ends up starving on the street, dimly surviving as a wanderer in Central Park, living on discarded food and sleeping under bushes.

Eventually, though, he is rescued by his old roommate Zimmer and a future girlfriend named Kitty Wu. They nurse him back to health, at which point he finds a job as a companion to a wealthy old man, Thomas Effing. Nearly 90, blind, confined to a wheelchair, the cantankerous Effing is a blend of magus, Ancient Mariner and the invalid Gen. Sternwood of *The Big Sleep.* In a thrilling flashback, lasting nearly a third of *Moon Palace,* he recounts his life from his youthful admiration for the inventor Nikola Tesla and his passion for the paintings of Ralph Albert Blakelock through his disorienting adventures in the Utah desert.

By the time we reach these last, "his narrative," remarks Fogg, "had taken on a phantasmagoric quality . . . and there were times when he did not seem to be remembering the outward facts of his life so much as inventing a parable to explain its inner meanings."

Actually all of *Moon Palace* shares this same phantasmagoric quality, this skirting around the edges of the uncanny, this sense of "subterranean vision."

Where did Effing get his money? How can he predict the exact date of his own death? Why is he excessively thin, while his neglected son is exceedingly obese? The book shimmers with such mysteries, thematic echoes, outrageous coincidences, as well as artfully timed revelations. All three main characters, classic American loners, suffer the same pattern of madness. Allusions to the moon abound, largely as an emblem of man's deepest or most extreme desires. Unexpected paternity plays a major role, as do unwanted babies. By his story's end, the genial and likeable Fogg also manages—indirectly—to kill his grandfather, father and child.

Partly to counter these Jacobean excesses Auster chooses to have Fogg tell his tale in a voice like twilight, serene, after the fact, almost resigned. All of Auster's books follow this pattern of the French *recit,* short, introspective narratives, relying on telling as much as showing, keeping dialogue to a minimum. The effect is to grant this, and Auster's other novels, an air of wistfulness and a certain calm plausibility: I was there, I suffered, I am the man.

Auster also enjoys following a seemly, straightforward narrative line, until everything starts to get tied up, at which point he will let the story go slack, twist and loop back on itself. In *Moon Palace* the last third of the book introduces a new character, an historian named Solomon Barber, who "was born of a madwoman and a ghost." Naturally Barber holds the keys to several mysteries—not all of which are resolved before our hero stands, at the novel's soulful but happy end, on a California beach and stares up at the moon rising above the dark Pacific.

At one point, Fogg mentions the writing habits of his friend Zimmer, habits which clearly apply to his creator as well: "Zimmer's chief concern in life was writing . . . and he spent long, hard hours at it, laboring over each word as if the fate of the world hung in the balance—which is surely the only sensible way to go about it."

If the result is a book as fine as *Moon Palace,* then it is unquestionably the only sensible way of going about it.

Sven Birkerts (review date 27 March 1989)

SOURCE: "Postmodern Picaresque," in *The New Republic,* March 27, 1989, pp. 36-40.

[*In the following review, Birkerts provides an overview of Auster's fiction and evaluation of* Moon Palace, *which he finds promising but ultimately disappointing.*]

Paul Auster has been, until just now, the ghost at the banquet of contemporary American letters. Though unquestionably accomplished (in the last decade he has published a memoir, five novels, several collections of poetry, and a major compendium of modern French poetry, which he edited and partly translated), he has been curiously absent from the debates being waged at the far end of the table. There are reasons for this. For one thing, his work does not fit neatly into the currently active slots. While his prose has tended toward stylistic austerity, it has little in common with the water and wafer fare beloved of the minimalists. In the same way, Auster has narrowly escaped the "postmodernist" tag; for all his concern with the slipperiness of perception and identity, his writing has a solid modernist grounding. He has not given up on the idea that art can discover new meaning from experience.

This has really been the main cause of Auster's marginality: that he has favored the serious and "artistic"—the novel as epistemology—over the democratically accessible. His characters have been embodiments, players in philosophical puzzles (I'm thinking mainly of the three books of his *The New York Trilogy*), or test cases to be subjected to the pressure of extreme situations; his plots, coolly calculated. But now, quite suddenly, comes a change. *Moon Palace,* Auster's new novel, breaks the chrysalis of high seriousness and stretches out its colorful wings. And the retrospective gaze alters everything: we see that his career has been in fact a complex progress toward liberation.

Auster first announced himself with the publication of a two-part memoir titled *The Invention of Solitude* (1982). Section one, "Portrait of an Invisible Man," begins with the author receiving word of his father's death. The prose, as Auster searches himself for his reactions, is remarkably matter-of-fact. Distant. As if the deeper turmoils of life could only be handled with the gloves of intellect. Auster himself is surprised by his response:

> I had always imagined that death would numb me, im-
> mobilize me with grief. But now that it had happened,
> I did not shed any tears. I did not feel as though the
> world had collapsed around me. . . . What disturbed
> me was something else, something unrelated to death
> or my response to it: the realization that my father had
> left no traces.

We then partake of the sustained excavation of the life—of the apparent *non*-life—of a man who was a stranger to himself. A man who hid from all emotion, all responsibility, who donned the proper masks of civility, who confided nothing, gave nothing. "Solitary. But not in the sense of being alone. . . . Solitary in the sense of retreat. In the sense of not having to see himself being seen by anyone else."

A coincidental encounter on an airplane (Auster is, throughout his work, a connoisseur of the serendipitous) eventually puts him on the track of the hidden horror in his family's past. He learns that 60 years before, in a small Wisconsin town, his grandmother shot her husband to death in their kitchen. His father, Sam, then a young boy, was present. The psychological clues begin to fall into place; the memoir becomes a kind of Freudian detective story. Auster steeps himself in ancient newspaper clippings, clarifying the web of circumstance for himself. Now all of the reticence, the blankness, that he remembers in his father can be explained. But explanation is cold comfort: a small compensation for a life with a man who gave nothing, and left nothing behind. Nothing, that is, but a permanent suspicion of appearances.

"The Book of Memory," the second section, is a collage of meditations, memories, and quotations. Auster reflects upon his solitude, and upon his situation as a husband and a father. The piece is not satisfying as a narrative—the fragments gather no momentum—but we come away with a clear sense of the psychic imperatives that drive the writer. We feel the desolation of his small rooms in New York and Paris, as well as the nullifying glare of the empty page. The author struggles to find an expression that will be his own. His last sentences are tense with the effort of bringing a truth up out of the self:

> He finds a fresh sheet of paper. He lays it out on the
> table before him and writes these words with his pen.
>
> It was. It will never be again. Remember.

Auster's next three books, *City of Glass, Ghosts,* and *The Locked Room,* known collectively as *The New York Tril-*

ogy, can be seen as detached, intellectual explorations of some of the core themes of the memoir. Each of these short, elegant books turns on a search of some kind—all of them feature detectives, missing persons, mistaken identities. The moods are of watching and waiting. Personalities and human crochets have no place here. Indeed, Auster seems bent upon pruning the urban detective novel (he has written in the genre under a pseudonym) of all extraneous particulars, in order to reveal the underlying paradigm: that all existence is, at root, a stalking of clues to the self, and to the true relation of that self to everything that is Other.

The premises in these novels are resoundingly French. Auster has absorbed a great deal from the hypervigilant and ultimately self-reflexive practice of the French modernists. (He has translated Mallarmé, Blanchot, and others.) The narration of the search, carried out in the simplest translucent prose, invariably reflects back upon the process of writing itself. Time and again, the characters come to feel that they are being scripted by some higher authority; their ventures come to seem co-extensive with the movement of figments in an author's mind. Take, for instance, this passage from the climactic scene of *The Locked Room.* The narrator has just opened a notebook that he hopes will clarify something about his prolonged quest for a certain Fanshawe:

> I read steadily for almost an hour, flipping back and
> forth among the pages, trying to get a sense of what
> Fanshawe had written. If I say nothing about what I
> found there, it is because I understood very little. All
> the words were familiar to me, and yet they seemed to
> have been put together strangely, as though their final
> purpose was to cancel each other out. . . . Each
> sentence erased the sentence before it, each paragraph
> made the next paragraph impossible.

In some way, this response to the text is designed to mirror our response to the text that encloses it. The prose is thrilling in its reduced precision, its escalating sense of paradox, but it asks of the reader a powerful appetite for cerebration.

The problem with self-reflexive fictions is that they obey a law of diminishing returns. Unable to suspend his disbelief, the reader starts to find the revelations merely academic. Auster appears to have recognized this. In *In the Country of Last Things* (1987), he reasserted the traditional rights of the genre, exploring the "real" (here the word needs cautionary quotation marks) by way of the invented. This is not to say that Auster found his way back to naturalism—he's too much of a modernist for that—but he does allow us to forget that the story is the product of a superintending author.

In the Country of Last Things is a legend of post-apocalypse. A young woman named Anna Blume (the book is her letter to a friend) arrives by ship at a large, unnamed port city. Its location, as well as the historical period, remain unspecified. Her mission is to locate her missing brother. But as she discovers that she has journeyed into a nightmare, the search is suspended; survival becomes her sole imperative.

The city is a place of worst fears. All municipal order has broken down. Gangs terrorize and pillage; those who would eat are forced to spend the entire day scavenging. Before long, Anna is pushing her own scavenger cart:

> Little by little, my hauls became almost adequate. Odds and ends, of course, but a few totally unexpected things as well: a collapsible telescope with one cracked lens; a rubber Frankenstein mask; a bicycle wheel; a Cyrillic typewriter missing only five keys and the space bar; the passport of a man named Quinn . . . but there were certain lines I drew within myself, limits I refused to step beyond. Touching the dead, for example.

Anna does eventually cross all of her inner boundaries, and with each transgression she discovers that she is less bound by her "human" ways than she had thought. Auster's aim is to find what remains after Anna has been systematically divested of the accretions of civilization. What she arrives at, paradoxically—and exaltingly—is an ideal of charity. Beneath brutishness a flame of goodness can live. In our extremity, Auster suggests, something like grace may flourish.

It is almost as if the author needed to put himself through a winnowing process—cutting away at narrative, peeling away the fabric of learned behavior—before he could find a way to begin writing. I don't mean that the prose of these novels is lacking in artistry. But what riches are there on the page have been carefully accumulated. The augmentation comes sentence by sentence, and is the product of great discipline. *Moon Palace* breaks free of such constraint with its opening lines:

> It was the summer that men first walked on the moon. I was very young then, but I did not believe there would ever be a future. I wanted to live dangerously, to push myself as far as I could go, and then see what happened to me when I got there. As it turned out, I nearly did not make it. Little by little, I saw my money dwindle to zero; I wound up living in the streets.

The paragraph continues. But one does not need to quote at great length to show that a change has taken place in Auster's prose. The forward motion is now kinetic; the language feels inhabited from within, is self-propelling. Gone is the studious bricklaying, the sense of mind controlling hand.

In *Moon Palace* Auster sets out to write the fantastic destiny tale of Marco Stanley Fogg. In the manner of all good picaresques, Marco is presented as serious, noblehearted, and (we might think of David Copperfield, Tom Jones, and Huck Finn) orphaned. Born illegitimate—he was never told about his father—Marco lost his mother in an accident while very young. He grew up in the care of his Uncle Victor. (We can compute, by the way, that Marco was born in 1947, the same year as Auster.) Victor is something of an eccentric, an itinerant clarinetist with a love of books and chess. He treats the boy to his theories

and obsessions, making little allowance for his years. Marco—small wonder—grows up a solitary misfit.

Victor uses the insurance payments from his sister's accident to set up a small trust for the boy. He sends him away to boarding school, and later provides tuition to Columbia. When Marco is ready to move to New York. Victor insists that he pack along the dozens and dozens of boxes that contain his library. Marco obliges, though the first use he finds for the books is peculiar; he uses the boxes to build a table, chairs, and bed for himself.

Auster begins the novel with energy and inventiveness, building in layers of allusiveness. There is, for instance, the matter of Marco's name:

> Uncle Victor loved to concoct elaborate, nonsensical theories about things, and he never tired of expounding on the glories hidden in my name, Marco Stanley Fogg. According to him, it proved that travel was in my blood, that life would carry me to places where no man had ever been before. Marco, naturally enough, was for Marco Polo, the first European to visit China. Stanley was for the American journalist who had tracked down Dr. Livingston "in the heart of darkest Africa"; and Fogg was for Phileas, the man who had stormed around the globe in less than three months. It didn't matter that my mother had chosen Marco simply because she liked it, or that Stanley had been my grandfather's name, or that Fogg was a misnomer, the whim of some half-literate American functionary. Uncle Victor found meanings where no one else would have found them, and then, very deftly, he turned them into a form of clandestine support.

Not only will Marco fulfill the promise of his moniker, but he will also become, like his uncle, a man who finds meanings and coincidental flashes wherever he turns. Auster obviously loves to sport with the possibilities. The mention of the moon landing in the first sentence is a case in point: Marco's wanderings will be accompanied at every step by lunar symbols. The word "moon," the orb's painted image, and the orb itself are persistently recurrent in these pages. To what end? Perhaps just to place everything under the aspect of fancy and madness (lunacy). But Auster is also, to some extent, seeding the clouds to make sure that there will be rain. Though the references at times feel artificially planted, they help to promote an atmosphere of uncanniness that makes the myriad coincidences seem less impossible than common sense would judge.

Marco is studying at Columbia and living the fringe life of the late '60s when he learns that Uncle Victor has died. Soon after, compounding his grief, he discovers that his money is nearly gone—he will not be able to make his way through school as planned. Marco faces the problem with profound passivity. Little by little—reading them first—he sells off his uncle's books. When that money is gone, he starts to practice extraordinary economies, giving up one necessity after the next. He all but stops eating. Finally, inevitably, his landlord throws him out. But even when he reaches the street, Marco cannot take initiative. He can only react.

It is as if he must undergo this peculiar rite of passage—turning himself into a vagrant—before he can connect with his fate. Holderlin's lines are appropriate here: "Near, but hard to find, is the God / But where danger is, there the saving power grows." When Marco reaches the far extreme of destitution, everything changes. A beautiful young Chinese woman named Kitty Wu rescues him and becomes his lover. And very soon after, Marco answers a posted ad. The problem of making a living is solved as he signs on as amanuensis and scribe to a wealthy old cripple named Thomas Effing.

The first third of the book, which I have tried to summarize, is enormously compelling. We identify with Marco, share his confusions and pains. The voice is direct and winning. In addition, Auster is skillful in creating the ambience of the times: Marco's urban adventures are played against a backdrop of larger social malaise; change and violence are everywhere on these streets. Our hero is living, exaggeratedly, the life of his times. Alas, with the introduction of Effing comes a shift that weakens the strong surge of Marco's tale.

Effing wants Marco to write his obituary, as well as a lengthy essay that will explain his mysterious life to posterity. For months he retails his deeds and misdeeds: how he was once a promising painter, how he entangled himself in an unhappy marriage, how he traveled to the deserts of the West to paint. The story gets increasingly improbable. Effing is betrayed by his guide, left for dead; he engineers his own disappearance and returns under a new identity. The episodes are piled high. And Marco reports them all in faithful detail. The problem is, it has been Marco's book all along: *his* is the life that has won our attention, and he steps aside for too long. For the marvels of Effing's account come to us from a propped-up figure, and it gets harder and harder to care. Interestingly, Marco at one point makes an observation that inadvertently reflects upon Auster's own failing:

> The major turning points in Effing's life had all taken place in America, in the years before his departure for Utah and the accident in San Francisco, and once he arrived in Europe, the story became just another story. . . . Effing was aware of this. I felt, and though he didn't come out and say it directly, the manner of his telling began to change, to lose the precision and earnestness of the earlier's episodes.

A meta-fictional prescience is expressed here: Auster has, likewise, begun to lose the precision and earnestness of his earlier pages.

I am circumspect about describing the developments in the second part of *Moon Palace,* because the drama hinges upon a series of recognitions as outlandish as anything in Dickens. I will not spoil the reader's pleasure by discharging the central tensions. I will say only that a player even stranger than Effing makes his way onto the stage, and that the discoveries that Marco subsequently makes tie a knot of lineage so bizarre that he ends up poised between madness and enlightenment. In contriving his kinds of

resolutions, Auster takes a risk: the novel that began among portents and promises ends up ominously close to campy self-parody. Too many coincidences overwhelm the ground of plausibility that meaningful coincidences require. While *Moon Palace* never entirely surrenders its charm—the writing is engaging throughout—its animating force slackens at the halfway mark.

One would like to herald Auster's breakthrough without reservations. He has a rare combination of talent, scope, and audacity. And in the beginning of this novel, when all of the elements are working in concert, the narrative achieves an irresistible propulsion. The diminution, therefore, a consequence of overreaching, is doubly disappointing. Still, there is the good news. Auster has served out an exciting apprenticeship. He stands poised to write something momentous about our times.

Alison Russell (essay date Winter 1990)

SOURCE: "Deconstructing *The New York Trilogy:* Paul Auster's Anti-Detective Fiction," in *Critique: Studies in Contemporary Fiction,* Vol. XXXI, No. 2, Winter, 1990, pp. 71-84.

[*In the following essay, Russell examines the patterns of representation and meaning in* The New York Trilogy *based on the theoretical principles of Jacques Derrida. Russell contends that Auster's fiction, with its multiple interpretations and nonlinear movement, resists the conventions of detective fiction and works to "deconstruct logocentrism."*]

Detective fiction comprises a genre seemingly at odds with American experimental writing. The detective story's highly stylized patterns are derivative of the Romance, an extremely conventional literary genre. Recent experimental novelists, however, are taking advantage of these conventions to create what Stefano Tani has called "anti-detective fiction."[1] Pynchon's *The Crying of Lot 49* and Nabokov's *Pale Fire* illustrate this postmodern mutation in their parodic forms and subversions of the end-dominated detective story. A more recent example of anti-detective fiction is Paul Auster's **The New York Trilogy,** a highly entertaining yet sophisticated work, amenable to the deconstructive principles of Jacques Derrida. Auster's novels have attracted the attention of a wide range of readers: *City of Glass,* the first volume of the trilogy, was nominated for an Edgar Award for best mystery of the year, but this recognition by a non-academic community may account for the lack of critical attention given to *The New York Trilogy.* The fact that Auster is known primarily as a poet and translator may also account for his exclusion from recent studies of American experimental fiction. This essay offers a Derridean analysis of Auster's trilogy, which will hopefully attract further academic attention to *The New York Trilogy.*

The three novels comprising the trilogy—*City of Glass,* *Ghosts,* and *The Locked Room*—are essentially retellings of the same story. All three employ and deconstruct the conventional elements of the detective story, resulting in a recursive linguistic investigation of the nature, function, and meaning of language. The trilogy also parodies and subverts the Romance, "realistic" fiction, and autobiography, thereby exploding the narrative traditions associated with these genres. By denying conventional expectations of fiction—linear movement, realistic representation, and closure—Auster's novels also deconstruct logocentrism, a primary subject of Derrida's subversions. Logocentrism, the term applied to uses and theories of language grounded in the metaphysics of presence, is the "crime" that Auster investigates in *The New York Trilogy.* In each volume, the detective searches for "presence": an ultimate referent or foundation outside the play of language itself. This quest for correspondence between signifier and signified is inextricably related to each protagonist's quest for origin and identity, for the self only exists insofar as language grants existence to it.

In *Writing and Difference,* Derrida states that "the absence of [a presence or] a transcendental signified extends the domain and play of signification infinitely."[2] As a retelling of the same story, each volume of Auster's trilogy illustrates this Derridean dissemination; each text denies any one meaning or "solution." Like language itself, the three texts are an incessant play of "différance," which Derrida defines in *Positions* as "the systematic play of differences, of the traces of differences, of the spacing by means of which elements are related to each other."[3] Meaning is deferred in an endless movement from one linguistic interpretation to the next. Auster reinforces this deconstructive effect through the use of other language games, such as intertextual references, mirror images, and puns, thereby exploding the centering and unifying conventions of detective stories. The distinction among author, narrator, and character is increasingly blurred. Similarly, the textual boundary of each volume of the trilogy disintegrates: characters in one book dream of characters in another or reappear in different disguises. For obvious reasons, it may be inappropriate to discuss these books separately, just as it may be equally inappropriate to use the terms "author," "narrator," and "protagonist"; for the sake of convention, however, this approach and these terms will be used to analyze Auster's trilogy.

The title of the first volume, *City of Glass,* is a play on Augustine's *The City of God,* a neoplatonic treatise that suggests that an eternal order exists outside the realm of sense: Augustine's work posits transcendence or, in Derrida's terms, presence. The title *City of Glass* also connotes transparency; thus Daniel Quinn, the novel's detective and protagonist, becomes a pilgrim searching for correspondence between signifiers and signifieds. The search for transparent language is predominantly visual, a characteristic alluded to in the narrator's discussion of the phrase "private eye" in the novel's first chapter.

> The term held a triple meaning for Quinn. Not only was it the letter "i," standing for "investigator," it was "I" in the upper case, the tiny life-bud buried in the

body of the breathing self. At the same time, it was also the physical eye of the writer, the eye of the man who looks out from himself into the world and demands that the world reveal itself to him.[4]

Quinn, as a writer of mystery novels, exists in a world dominated by signifiers and assumed solutions. The first chapter of *City of Glass* describes the function of the writer-detective and reveals the metaphor that will be employed—and deconstructed—in all three volumes of *The New York Trilogy:* "The detective is one who looks, who listens, who moves through this morass of objects and events in search of the thought, the idea that will pull all these things together and make sense of them. In effect, the writer and the detective are interchangeable" (15). This passage offers a multiplicity of orientations, as the detective metaphor applies to Quinn, to Auster, and to the relationship between the two. It is also a "clue" to the mystery of *The New York Trilogy* because Auster is always both inside and outside his three texts. The narrator of the first volume continually denies any one locus of meaning, yet teases the reader with the possibility of one: "The center, then, is everywhere, and no circumference can be drawn until the book has come to its end" (15). By directing our attention to the end of the book and to a possible solution, the narrator forces us to participate in the detective's game.

As a genre, the detective story is end-dominated, and its popularity attests to Western culture's obsession with closure. By denying closure, and by sprinkling his trilogy with references to other end-dominated texts, Auster continually disseminates the meaning of this detective story. The detective story also necessitates a movement backward in time, from the corpse to the crime, so to speak. In *City of Glass,* Quinn's quest for an ultimate referent leads him into an investigation of the origin of logos; his quest becomes a pursuit of paternal authority associated with creation and also a quest for his own identity. In the beginning of the novel, Quinn is described as a mystery novelist who writes stories about the detective Max Work under the pseudonym William Wilson (an allusion to Poe's story about doubles and, later in the novel, to the baseball player Mookie Wilson). The narrator alludes to Quinn's identity crisis by withholding information: "Who he was, where he came from, and what he did are of no great importance" (7). Essentially, Quinn is a paper-Auster, a mere linguistic construct of the author himself: "As a young man he had published several books of poetry, had written plays, critical essays, and had worked on a number of long translations" (9). Although Quinn suspects that he is not real, he is not aware that he is Auster's creation. The novel becomes increasingly comic when Quinn receives middle-of-the-night telephone calls for the Paul Auster Detective Agency. Quinn tells the mysterious caller, "[T]here is no Paul Auster here" (13).

Logocentrism in *The New York Trilogy* is closely associated with paternal authority. Quinn's unconscious denial of his creator's presence suggests the loss of the Father, the ultimate authority and founder of logos—the word. Quinn usurps the role of the Father when he assumes the identity of Paul Auster (of the detective agency)—when he meets his client, Peter Stillman, he thinks of "his own dead son," but "just as suddenly as the thought had appeared, it vanished" (25). Quinn is unable to posit the determinacy characteristic of paternal authority. The interview with Stillman strikes Quinn as strange and unreal, and "as a consequence, he could never be sure of any of it" (23). Significantly, Quinn is hired to find and tail the father of his client, also named Peter Stillman. The elder Stillman had attempted to find God's language thirteen years earlier by keeping his young son in a locked dark room for nine years. As a product of this experiment, the son babbles incoherently to Quinn, unable to affirm his own identity: "For now, I am Peter Stillman. That is not my real name. I cannot say who I will be tomorrow. . . . But that makes no difference. To me. Thank you very much. I know you will save my life, Mr. Auster. I am counting on you" (36-37). Like his language, Stillman himself lacks solidity—he moves like a marionette "trying to walk without strings" and dresses completely in white (25). At one point in their meeting, "Quinn suddenly felt that Stillman had become invisible" (26). Everything about Stillman and the Stillman case lacks substance, for they are fictions within the larger fiction of *City of Glass.*

Quinn's pursuit of the Father is a search for authority and "author-ity." In looking for the creator of logos, he is looking for his own creator as well, but his investigation is subverted by Auster's authorial duplicity. In many ways, *City of Glass* is a reworking of *Don Quixote,* a book that also denies its own authority while claiming to be a true story. When Virginia Stillman tells Quinn that she was referred to the Paul Auster Detective Agency by Michael Saavedra (Cervantes's family name), Quinn becomes the quixotic hero, the unknowing victim of a strange conspiracy. This possible "solution" to *City of Glass* is exfoliated in chapter ten, when Quinn decides to contact the "real" Paul Auster for help with his case. This Auster claims to know nothing about a detective agency. He is a writer, he explains to Quinn, working on an essay about the hoax of *Don Quixote. Don Quixote* "orchestrated the whole thing himself," Auster tells Quinn, duping Cervantes into "hiring Don Quixote to decipher the story of Don Quixote himself" (153-54). This analysis, when applied to *City of Glass,* raises a number of questions about the book's authorship, and results in endless doublings and mirror images. When Quinn meets Auster's young son, also named Daniel, he tells the boy, "I'm you, and you're me." The boy replies, "and around and around it goes" (157).

Quinn's investigation becomes an obsessive search for an ultimate authority, for his research on the elder Stillman leads him to believe that this "father" holds the key to finding a way back to pure logos. He reads Stillman's book, *The Garden and the Tower: Early Visions of the New World,* in which Stillman analyzes *Paradise Lost,* identifying words that embodied two equal and opposite meanings—"one before the fall and one after the fall"

(70). This ironic deconstructive reading of Milton's text results in Stillman's own quest for prelapsarian language: he prophecies a new paradise based upon his reading of Henry Dark's pamphlet, *The New Babel* (75). According to Derridean philosophy, Dark's (and Stillman's) return to pure logos is impossible because of the nature of language. As a play of differences, language offers no basis for attributing a determinate meaning to any word or utterance.

The quixotic Quinn, deluded by Stillman's book, stalks the old man throughout the labyrinth of New York City, recording Stillman's every move in a red notebook (possibly a parodic allusion to Wittgenstein's *The Blue and Brown Books*). By keeping Stillman in his sight, Quinn is attempting to retain "presence," but in rereading his notebook, he "often discovered that he had written two or even three lines on top of each other, producing a jumbled, illegible palimpsest" (100). Words continually fail to produce an absolute meaning for Quinn, for Stillman's movements always remain divorced from the words in the red notebook. Repeatedly frustrated in his attempts to decipher the meaning of Stillman's patterned walks through the city, Quinn decides to confront physically the logocentric father. Presenting himself alternately as Paul Auster, Henry Dark, and Peter Stillman, Quinn discusses language, lies, and history with the old man. Stillman tells Quinn, "A lie can never be undone. . . . I am a father, and I know about these things. Remember what happened to the father of our country" (133). By referring to one of the most popular fictions of American history, Stillman unwittingly subverts his own authority. His attempt to rename the world is doomed to failure.

By the end of the novel, fiction is piled upon fiction, negating any one meaning or solution to the mystery of *City of Glass.* The narrator interrupts his own narrative in Cervantes's fashion, claiming both ownership and authorship of the text: "Since this story is based entirely on facts, the author feels it his duty not to overstep the bounds of the verifiable, to resist at all costs the perils of invention. Even the red notebook, which until now has provided a detailed account of Quinn's experiences, is suspect" (173). The narrator is a self-undermining linguistic agent, offering truth and then subverting the possibility of truth, continually denying his readers any one locus of meaning.

As the novel "ends," *City of Glass* illustrates Derridean dissemination. Quinn literally vanishes from the text when he runs out of space in his red notebook, seemingly imploding into the text of *City of Glass:* "It was as though he had melted into the walls of the city" (178). Similarly, Peter Stillman and his wife have disappeared, while the elder Stillman has supposedly committed suicide. In *City of Glass,* characters "die" when their signifiers are omitted from the printed page. All that remains is the cryptic conclusion of the narrator, who claims to have received Quinn's notebook from his friend, the writer Paul Auster.

> As for Quinn, it is impossible for me to say where he is now. I have followed the red notebook as closely as I could, and any inaccuracies in the story should be

blamed on me. There were moments when the text was difficult to decipher, but I have done my best with it and have refrained from any interpretation. The red notebook, of course, is only half the story, as any sensitive reader will understand. As for Auster, I am convinced that he behaved badly throughout. If our friendship has ended, he has only himself to blame. As for me, my thoughts remain with Quinn. He will be with me always. And wherever he may have disappeared to, I wish him luck. (202-03)

The narrator's conclusion shows this fiction to be a game against itself. His assertion deconstructs itself through references to the indeterminacy of the red notebook. *City of Glass* is a paranoid text in its uncertainty and contradictory frames of reference.

In *Ghosts,* the second volume of the trilogy, Auster presents another version of this detective story. This text, as a repetitive but also differing collection of signifiers, continues to illustrate Derridean différance, both within the text itself and in its differences from *City of Glass.* Like its predecessor, *Ghosts* defers the possibility of a solution or meaning. Again, Auster explores and deconstructs the logocentric quest for origin—the origin of language, but also the origin of "self." The story begins on February 3, 1947 (the author's birthdate), a movement backward in time appropriate to the text's illustration of différance. In *Speech and Phenomena,* Derrida explains that

> différance is what makes the movement of signification possible only if each element that is said to be "present," appearing on the stage of presence, is related to something other than itself but retains the mark of a past element and already lets itself be hollowed out by the mark of its relation to a future element. This trace relates no less to what is called the future than to what is called the past, and it constitutes what is called the present by this very relation to what it is not, to what it absolutely is not; that is, not even to a past or future considered as a modified present.[5]

Thus, in *Ghosts,* we read the narrator's statement, "the time is the present," followed two pages later by a contradicting statement: "It is February 3, 1947. . . . But the present is no less dark than the past, and its mystery is equal to anything the future might hold."[6] *Ghosts* is a "trace" of a past element that was never fully present; therefore, the novel's detective protagonist, Blue, is shown to be increasingly obsessed with "presence." Like Daniel Quinn, Blue's identity is inextricably related to language. Since différance destroys the notion of a simple presence, identity and the origin of self are equally destroyed, for origin is always other than itself.

The title of *Ghosts,* like *City of Glass,* suggests transparency, the ideal logocentric relationship between signifier and signified, but it also connotes a lack of substance. *Ghosts* contains fewer pages, characters, and plot complications than the other two volumes of the trilogy. The book is a "ghost" of *City of Glass* and of the detective story genre: the "meat" of the text is stripped down to a generic level, reinforced by Auster's rejection of nomenclature and his use of Film Noir signifiers. Auster's reduc-

tionist technique in *Ghosts* is in itself a form of deception—it suggests that the details of the story will be presented in black-and-white, transparent facts that will lead to the solution of the trilogy. The opening lines of the book are equally deceptive in their sparing use of language and their structural similarity to Biblical syntax: "First of all there is Blue. Later there is White, and then there is Black, and before the beginning there is Brown" (7). These bare "facts," with their connotations of creation, begin the deconstructive process of the text by illustrating the movement of signification as a distortion of the linear regression to origin.

Ghosts, as an investigation of origin, also suggests the parallel search for truth—truth as measured by visual presence. Blue, the protagonist-detective, is hired by White "to follow a man named Black and to keep an eye on him for as long as necessary" (7). Truth, for Blue, is always limited to that which he can see: "Words are transparent for him, great windows that stand between him and the world" (23-24). Blue dutifully writes his reports on Black for the never present or visible White, but he becomes frustrated with the ineffectiveness of language: "He discovers that words do not necessarily work, that it is possible for them to obscure the things they are trying to say" (25-26).

Blue's obsession with transparency is rooted in the primacy he gives to visual perception. He attends a baseball game, "struck by the sharp clarity of the colors around him," and is fond of movies because "the pictures on the screen are somehow like the thoughts inside his head" (42, 44). When Blue's vision is obscured, language (and therefore truth or meaning) becomes opaque to him: "Without being able to read what Black has written, everything is a blank so far" (11). Significantly, when Blue experiences this failure of language, he begins to think about his dead father and other dead or rejecting father figures. Blue's memories of lost fathers result in the loss of his own identity. He feels as if he is becoming one with Black, "so completely in harmony . . . that to anticipate what Black is going to do, to know when he will stay in his room and when he will go out, he needs merely to look into himself" (38).

Although Blue occasionally ventures out of his room, he exists essentially in a hermetic space. *Ghosts* is a self-enclosed structure of self-mirrorings, but it is also a mirror image, in some ways, of the first and third volumes of *The New York Trilogy.* Much of the book consists of Blue looking out of his window to observe and write about Black, who sits by a window in a building across the street writing and looking back at Blue. Blue reads *Walden* because he sees Black reading *Walden,* but he feels trapped in the process: "He feels like a man who has been condemned to sit in a room and go on reading a book for the rest of his life . . . seeing the world only through words, living only through the lives of others" (57). Blue's description of *Walden* is self-reflexive: "There is no story, no plot, no action—nothing but a man sitting alone in a room and writing a book" (58). Blue becomes trapped in the hermetic world of the text: "How to get out of the room that is the book that will go on being written for as long as he stays in the room?" (58). Blue verges on insanity when Black claims that he, too, is a private detective hired "to watch someone . . . and send in a report about him every week" (73). Experiencing complete ontological instability, Blue tries to recover language by verbally cataloguing objects according to their color, but he realizes that "there is no end to it" (77). The colors blue, black, and white are meaningless distinctions, he realizes, for each can be applied to any number of people, places, and things.

Ghosts is not merely a reductive version of *City of Glass,* despite its stripped-down quality and bared concepts. In many ways, the second volume of the trilogy offers itself as a collection of the signs that make up American culture, taken from baseball, popular movies, and the canonical texts and authors of nineteenth-century literature. These artifacts of our collective identity haunt the pages of *Ghosts,* raising the issue of whether or not original discourse is possible. Just as language is divorced from the things it signifies, texts themselves become divorced from their creators. When Black recounts anecdotes about the "ghosts" of New York City, he provides Blue with a lesson about the flesh and spirit of the writer. Whitman's brain, Black recalls, was removed from his body to be measured and weighed, but it was dropped on the floor: "The brains of America's greatest poet got swept up and thrown out with the garbage" (63). Black is equally amused by Thoreau's visit to Whitman, a meeting that took place next to Whitman's full chamber pot.

> That chamber pot, you see, somehow reminds me of the brains on the floor. . . . There's a definite connection. Brains and guts, the insides of a man. We always talk about trying to get inside a writer to understand his work better. But when you get right down to it, there's not much to find in there—at least not much that's different from what you'd find in anyone else. (65)

Black's anecdotes reveal his concern with the solipsistic existence of the writer's life. He tells Blue how Hawthorne sat in a room for twelve years to write, a situation similar to his own: "Writing is a solitary business. It takes over your life. In some sense, a writer has no life of his own. Even when he's there, he's not really there" (66). The writer is a ghost, a trace. In *Of Grammatology,* Derrida explains that there is nothing outside of textuality, outside of "the temporalization of a lived experience which is neither in the world nor in 'another world.'"[7]

This "problem" is the crux of the mystery in *Ghosts.* Black and Blue are both inside and outside one another, oppositions of what Derrida calls a "violent hierarchy": "one of the two terms governs the other (axiologically, logically, etc.) or has the upper hand. To deconstruct the opposition, first of all, is to overturn the hierarchy at a given moment."[8] Throughout *Ghosts,* Black has the upper hand, as it is he who hired Blue. When Blue decides that he must deny Black's existence in order to prove his own, he sets

out "to erase the whole story" (89). In the novel's final scenes, Blue and Black are intent upon killing one another, and their physical struggle illustrates Derrida's "violent hierarchy." Although Blue appears to be the victor, he is not sure whether the sound of Black's breath is coming from Black or from himself (94).

The final volume of *The New York Trilogy, The Locked Room,* takes its title from a popular motif of detective novels: a murdered body is discovered in a sealed room, the exits of which have been locked from the inside. Auster complicates the conventional puzzle by omitting the corpse in *The Locked Room* (another denial of presence). The third version of this repeating story continues to keep différance in play by rejecting the binary opposites inherent in Western traditions and philosophies. In *The Locked Room,* each side of the dualism is inextricably related to the other; thus, like Black and Blue in *Ghosts,* the narrator (the protagonist of this volume) and his counterpart Fanshawe experience a mutually parasitic relationship.

Binary opposition is deconstructed on a larger scale throughout *The New York Trilogy,* not only because the work is in three parts, but because the texts are linked parasitically: references to Quinn, Stillman, and Henry Dark reappear in *The Locked Room,* just as subtle allusions in the first and second volumes foreshadow events in the third. The oscillation of the dominating term of any hierarchy is also illustrated by the changing hierarchy of the terms "writer" and "detective": Daniel Quinn is a writer turned detective, Blue a detective turned writer, and the narrator of *The Locked Room* a writer turned detective. Since deconstruction rejects the notion of a single self, these three novels, as linguistic constructs, also serve as the selves of Auster.

The logocentric quest in *The Locked Room* differs from that of the preceding volumes in several ways. Quinn and Blue are able to confront Stillman and Black physically, but the narrator of *The Locked Room* is frustrated in his attempts to find evidence of the physical presence of his childhood friend, Fanshawe, who has mysteriously disappeared. He has only the words of Fanshawe, the unpublished novels he inherits as Fanshawe's literary executor. As soon as he gains possession of Fanshawe's manuscripts, he usurps the role—the life—of his friend. He marries Fanshawe's wife, adopts his son, and considers the idea of publishing Fanshawe's books as his own. Unlike Quinn and Blue, the narrator of *The Locked Room* has access only to the language, the signifiers, of his counterpart, never to his physical presence. When he learns that Fanshawe is not dead, he sets out to recover and re-create presence in a search that takes him to Fanshawe's mother and childhood home, to his haunts in Paris, and, finally, to a locked room. His quest for Fanshawe turns out to be a quest for himself, for his own identity, since like Black and Blue, the narrator and Fanshawe are inseparable.

If these novels are linguistic constructs of the author, Paul Auster, their protagonists' quests for an ultimate authority and identity serve as ironic frames for the author's own logocentric quest for origin, a quest he himself continually deconstructs. Early in *The Locked Room,* the narrator wonders "what it means when a writer puts his name on a book, why some writers choose to hide behind a pseudonym, whether or not a writer has a real life anyway."[9] This echo of Black's reference to Hawthorne (*Fanshawe,* ironically, is the title of an early novel by Hawthorne) raises again the question of the writer's nonlife. In *The Locked Room,* Auster suggests that language can destroy identity as well as create it. The narrator, in attempting to write a biography of Fanshawe, realizes that life, the "essential thing," resists telling.

> We imagine the real story inside the words, and to do this we substitute ourselves for the person in the story, pretending that we can understand him because we understand ourselves. This is a deception. We exist for ourselves, perhaps, and at times we even have a glimmer of who we are, but in the end we can never be sure, and as our lives go on, we become more and more opaque to ourselves, more and more aware of our own incoherence. No one can cross the boundary into another—for the simple reason that no one can gain access to himself. (80-81)

This is the problem of the writer, as well as of the reader. *The Locked Room* is a "locked room" for Auster himself: it contains the life of Auster, not only in the sense that it contains his words, but also in its biographical elements. Auster is inside and outside his text, fighting for the upper hand of Derrida's "violent hierarchy." Since the self in the text must die when the story ends, the rewriting of the detective story in *The New York Trilogy* is also a deferment of death for the author. The narrator says, however, that "stories without endings can do nothing but go on forever, and to be caught in one means that you must die before your part in it is played out" (63). The solution for Auster, then, is to posit no one self but many selves.

The narrator's logocentric quest for origin (for his search for Fanshawe is undertaken ostensibly to collect data for a biography of his friend) involves a deterministic single-minded approach to what he sees as a self-contained entity. Instead, he accumulates information and learns that Fanshawe has many lives.

> A life touches one life, which in turn touches another life, and very quickly the links are innumerable, beyond calculation. . . . Faced with a million bits of random information, led down a million paths of false inquiry, I had to find the one path that would take me where I wanted to go. (131)

In Paris, where words become a "collection of sounds" without meaning, the narrator loses the ability to distinguish between signifiers and signifieds: "Thoughts stop where the world begins. . . . But the self is also in the world" (143). In place of stable meaning, he finds what Derrida calls "free-play." He becomes exhilarated by this freedom of language and his ability to name things at random. He usurps the role of the creator of logos and becomes mad with this power: he "names" a girl in a bar

Fayaway and himself Herman Melville, recalling the naming of the narrator in *Moby Dick* (a book the narrator's wife had given him). When the narrator meets a vaguely familiar young man, he decides that this person will be Fanshawe: "This man was Fanshawe because I said he was Fanshawe" (152). The narrator is unable to retain his naming power, however, for the "Fanshawe" claims that his name is Peter Stillman (153). When the two men fight, they reenact the battle for identity between Black and Blue in *Ghosts.* This time the battle also suggests two texts, or versions of the story, grappling for supremacy. In accordance with the oscillating dominance of the "violent hierarchy," the narrator loses the battle, getting pummeled by Stillman before blacking out.

In this same chapter, the narrator claims authorship of *The New York Trilogy* and reveals his own interpretation of the books: "These three stories are finally the same story, but each one represents a different stage in my awareness of what it is about. I don't claim to have solved any problems. . . . The story is not in the words; it's in the struggle" (149). This "author," who intrudes into his narrative to assert his intentions and conclusions, is also a self-undermining linguistic agent within the text. He offers a kind of closure to the puzzle of *The New York Trilogy* but undermines this solution by continuing the story in the following chapter.

The relationship between the narrator and Fanshawe is extremely complicated throughout *The Locked Room.* An examination of the "clues" invites us to infer that the narrator and Fanshawe are one and the same; if so, this person is the victim of the sort of quixotic conspiracy promoted by the writer Paul Auster in *City of Glass.* This solution is subverted in the last chapter of the story, in which the textual boundaries of the trilogy disintegrate: Fanshawe may also be Daniel Quinn, Peter Stillman, and Henry Dark, in accordance with the deconstructive denial of a single self. When the narrator is summoned by Fanshawe, he goes to the locked room in Boston expecting to find a presence outside of himself, a correspondence between his thoughts and external reality. (Significantly, Fanshawe summons the narrator in a letter, implying the possibility of correspondence.) The locked room in which Fanshawe "exists" is located on Columbus Street in Boston—place names associated with the discovery of a new Eden and with the founding fathers of this country. Fanshawe is thus associated with paternal authority, but he denies both his name and his presence to the narrator: they communicate through the door of the locked room.

In an ironic subversion of theistic authority and logocentrism, Fanshawe reveals that he is going to kill himself: "I've proved the point to myself. There's no need to go on with it. I'm tired. I've had enough" (174). The narrator blacks out and wakes up to darkness—the fallen world—holding the red notebook left behind by Fanshawe. The authority of logos is completely deconstructed in this paternal message to the narrator:

> All the words were familiar to me, and yet they seemed to have been put together strangely, as though their

final purpose was to cancel each other out. . . . Each sentence erased the sentence before it, each paragraph made the next paragraph impossible. It is odd, then, that the feeling that survives from this notebook is one of great lucidity. It is as if Fanshawe knew his final work had to subvert every expectation I had for it. . . . He had answered the question by asking another question, and therefore everything remained open, unfinished, to be started again. I lost my way after the first word, and from then on I could only grope ahead, faltering in the darkness, blinded by the book that had been written for me. (178-79)

The red notebook illustrates Derrida's writing "sous rature"—writing under erasure, a ceaseless undoing and preserving of meaning. Even these words are suspect, however, the narrator tells us, leading him to destroy the paternal message: "One by one, I tore the pages from the notebook, crumpled them in my hand, and dropped them into a trash bin on the platform. I came to the last page just as the train was pulling out" (179).

Throughout *The New York Trilogy,* Auster parodies elements and motifs of the Romance in order to bare the formulaic expectations associated with this genre. According to Northrop Frye, in *The Secular Scripture,* "most romances exhibit a cyclical movement of descent into a night world and a return to the idyllic world."[10] Ostensibly, the failure to ascend or return characterizes a failed quest. Ironically, Auster's protagonists, by continually descending into darker and darker worlds, are freed from the tyranny of their logos-motivated quests. In Frye's mythological universe, based upon Judeo-Christian polarities of Heaven and Hell, "themes of descent are connected with the establishing of order, authority, and hierarchy."[11] In *The New York Trilogy,* these concepts of power and control are repeatedly denied to each of the protagonists because they are logocentric ideals, the subjects of Auster's subversions. Quinn, Blue, and the narrator of *The Locked Room* are parodic romantic heroes. Like Don Quixote, they are all bewitched by books, especially books of a romantic nature: "Quinn had been a devoted reader of mystery novels. He knew that most of them were poorly written, that most could not stand up to even the vaguest sort of examination, but still, it was the form that appealed to him" (14); Blue is "a devoted reader of *True Detective* and tries never to miss a month" (16); the narrator of *The Locked Room* reads *Moby Dick, Robinson Crusoe,* and other travel-oriented books (24, 54, 85, 91).

Similarly, the themes and conventions associated with descent in Romance—confused identities, twins, doubles, and mirror images—appear repeatedly in the trilogy: in *City of Glass,* Quinn starts to follow Stillman but sees another man whose face is "the exact twin of Stillman's" (90); Blue, in spying on Black, feels as though he were "looking into a mirror" (20); the narrator of *The Locked Room* reads one of Fanshawe's stories, which hinges on "the confused identities of two sets of twins" (30). According to Frye, "[A]t the lower levels the Narcissus or twin image darkens into a sinister doppelganger figure, the hero's shadow and portent of his own death or isolation."[12]

Auster subverts this binary opposition characteristic of Romance by insisting upon a "both/and" oscillating movement: he denies romantic hierarchization by refusing to privilege permanently one term of an opposition over another. Blue is Black, for example, and also not Black.

The detective story is closely affiliated with the Romance (despite its "gritty" realism) through its solitary quest and in its emphasis on "reintegrating the existing order."[13] The detective in conventional fiction discovers "the truth," but in the deconstructive anti-detective novel, "the inanity of the discovery is brought to its climax in the nonsolution, which unmasks a tendency toward disorder and irrationality that has always been implicit within detective fiction."[14] The lack of any one single solution leaves the narrator, and implied author, of the trilogy free to choose any or none of the potential solutions available to him; he is free to begin another quest in a new world full of possibilities.

The New York Trilogy is in many respects a travel narrative—a semantic journey through fictional space and an ontological voyage for a paradise of pure presence. The implied author of the trilogy, and perhaps Auster himself, crosses the boundaries of fictional zones to rediscover himself through self-exploration. In romantic literature, the hero often returns to his native land; in *The New York Trilogy,* the return to origin is impossible. Each volume serves as a trace or recording of the travel, and each concludes with a reference to other travels: at the end of *City of Glass,* the narrator claims to have just returned from Africa (201); at the end of *Ghosts,* the narrator says he likes to think of "Blue booking passage on some ship and sailing to China" (96); at the end of *The Locked Room,* the narrator stands on the platform waiting for a train (179).

The travel theme of the trilogy is reinforced through references to fictional, nonfictional, and imaginary travel narratives: *Moby Dick, A. Gordon Pym, Robinson Crusoe, Don Quixote,* Raleigh's *History of the World, The Journeys* of Cabeza de Vaca, Peter Freuchen's *Arctic Adventure,* Marco Polo's *Travels,* Fanshawe's *Neverland,* and many others. The protagonists of these books, like those of *The New York Trilogy,* are exiles, pilgrims, and explorers who claim unknown regions through language. The traveler's attempt to name things and to decipher "signs" is also the function of the ontological voyager, for adventures only "exist" in language—when they are told or written down. Since language is unstable and it's meaning indeterminate, no place can be completely claimed or owned by its discoverer. The uncertainty of language also denies the self-exploring traveler access to an absolute origin, or self. As a travel narrative, *The New York Trilogy* is nomadic in nature: the semantic journey never ends but consists of a never-ending loop of arrivals and departures. The Chinese box structure of the trilogy offers vertical, as well as horizontal, travel. The references to historical texts allow travel through time as well as space, as does the trilogy's movement from present to past to present. This plurality of orientations results in endless shifting frames of references that continually deny any one locus, or "place," of meaning for the infinite traveler.

Notes

1. Stefano Tani, *The Doomed Detective* (Carbondale: Southern Illinois U P, 1984).

2. Jacques Derrida, *Writing and Difference,* trans. Alan Bass (Chicago: U of Chicago P. 1978) 280.

3. Jacques Derrida, *Positions,* trans. Alan Bass (Chicago: U of Chicago P, 1981) 27.

4. Paul Auster, *City of Glass* (1985; New York: Penguin, 1987) 15-16. Subsequent references are to this edition.

5. Jacques Derrida, "Différance," *Speech and Phenomena and Other Essays on Husserl's Theory of Signs,* trans. David B. Allison (Evanston: Northwestern U P, 1973) 142-43.

6. Paul Auster, *Ghosts* (1986; New York: Penguin, 1987) 7, 9. Subsequent references are to this edition.

7. Jacques Derrida, *Of Grammatology,* trans. Gayatri Chakravorty Spivak (Baltimore: Johns Hopkins U P, 1976) 65.

8. Derrida, *Positions* 41.

9. Paul Auster, *The Locked Room* (1986; New York: Penguin, 1988) 64. Subsequent references are to this edition.

10. Northrop Frye, *The Secular Scripture: A Study of the Structure of Romance* (Cambridge: Harvard U P, 1976) 54.

11. Frye 182.

12. Frye 117.

13. Frye 138.

14. Tani 46.

Michiko Kakutani (review date 2 October 1990)

SOURCE: "Allusions and Subtext Don't Slow a Good Plot," in *The New York Times,* October 2, 1990, p. C15.

[*In the following review, Kakutani offers positive assessment of* The Music of Chance.]

Paul Auster's new book, **The Music of Chance,** begins like many classic American novels with the hero leaving an old life behind and setting off to invent a new identity for himself. When Jim Nashe inherits a modest fortune from his father, he quits his job as a fireman in Boston, parks his daughter with his sister, sells his possessions, buys a new car and begins driving the highways. He zigzags back and forth from Oregon to Texas, "charging down the enormous, vacant highways that cut through Arizona, Montana and Utah," then turns around and heads back East. Addicted to the idea of motion, he finds himself reluctant to stop and decides to keep driving around the country until his money completely runs out.

A critic as well as a novelist, Mr. Auster is an old hand at cramming literary allusions into his fiction, and Jim Nashe's odyssey of self-invention immediately brings to mind a variety of earlier books. The reader thinks of Huck Finn lighting out for new territory, of Jimmy Gatz transforming himself into the fabulous Gatsby, of John Updike's Rabbit trying to run away from his family obligations, of Jack Kerouac's Dean Moriarty navigating one of his jalopies on the road. In each case, the hero embraces the idea of freedom as his legacy of the American dream, and in each case he tries to leave the past behind in order to start over again, tabula rasa.

As for Jim Nashe, he quickly runs through most of his money, and he soon realizes that without money, he has no real freedom. It is then that his life takes another unexpected turn: he meets an itinerant poker player named Jack Pozzi, who offers him the opportunity to make some quick and easy cash. Nashe takes Pozzi under his wing, buys him some new clothes and installs him in a suite at the Plaza Hotel. In exchange for the use of Nashe's last $10,000, Pozzi will cut him in, 50-50, on a high stakes poker game with a pair of wealthy eccentrics who live in Pennsylvania. Pozzi has played these men before, he says, and he knows they're easy marks. Their names are Flower and Stone.

When Pozzi and Nashe turn up at the Pennsylvania estate, they are given dinner, a tour of the house, and a rambling account of how Flower and Stone made their millions. It seems the two of them bought a lottery ticket many years ago, won and parlayed their windfall into a fortune. The garrulous Flower used to be an accountant; the bashful Stone used to be an optometrist. Now, freed from the need to earn a living, they spend their time pursuing hobbies. Stone is building a miniature model of an elaborate city on a table top; Flower is collecting objects from around the world. Among his most recent acquisitions are a heap of stones from a ruined castle in Ireland: he wants to use them to build a wall in his backyard.

Although Stone and Flower seem benign, even inept during the dinnertime pleasantries, they turn into ferocious competitors once the poker game has begun. Pozzi's brief winning streak quickly ends, and within hours he's lost all of Nashe's money. Desperate to get back into the game, Nashe allows Pozzi to use his car for collateral. He does and promptly loses it. By the time the evening is over, he and Nashe owe their hosts $10,000.

Instead of allowing them to write an I.O.U., Flower and Stone gently but firmly persuade Nashe and Pozzi to work off their debt: they are to stay on at the estate and help build Flower's wall. It's supposed to take them only 50 days to settle their account, but things quickly take a sinister turn, and Nashe and Pozzi soon realize they are being held captive on the estate against their will.

Writing in brisk, precise prose, Mr. Auster lends these events all the suspense and pace of a best-selling thriller. As his last novel, **Moon Palace,** so clearly demonstrated, he can write with the speed and skill of a self-assured pool player, sending one bizarre event ricocheting neatly and unexpectedly into the next. At the same time, he gives Nashe's adventures a brooding philosophical subtext that enables him to explore some of his favorite preoccupations; the roles of randomness and causality; the consequences of solitude, and the limitations of freedom, language and free will in an indifferent world.

Indeed, the reader becomes increasingly aware of the parallels Mr. Auster is drawing between Nashe's story and Beckett's *Waiting for Godot.* Pozzi's name, of course, instantly recalls that of Pozzo in the play; and a small boy, much like the one in *Godot,* makes a brief but crucial appearance later in the story. In addition, Stone and Flower are described in terms reminiscent of Vladimir and Estragon. They seem mysteriously but permanently bound to each other, and they are compared to Laurel and Hardy: the first is tall and thin; the second, short and round.

Instead of belaboring such analogies, Mr. Auster simply plays with them, working variations on some of Beckett's themes while at the same time creating a narrative that continually manages to elude our expectations. The result: a chilling little story that's entertaining and provocative, resonant without being overly derivative.

Guy Mannes-Abbott (review date 22 March 1991)

SOURCE: "Unlucky Jim," in *New Statesman and Society,* March 22, 1991, p. 45.

[*In the following review, Mannes-Abbott offers favorable assessment of* The Music of Chance.]

Paul Auster has produced some of the most remarkable fiction of the past decade in the **New York Trilogy** and **Moon Palace.** Those books combined a formal complexity with sheer imaginative exuberance to produce a particularly distinctive voice. High expectations indeed, then, for **The Music of Chance.**

It begins with ex-fireman Jim Nashe nearing the end of more than a year on the road. A $200,000 inheritance from a long-estranged father began a series of "odd conjunctions of chance", typical of Auster. It enabled Nashe to abandon the life he knew and drift: we meet him waiting for the money to run out. Just as action becomes necessary, he meets a "wiry little runt" called Jack Pozzi who welcomes him into the "International Brotherhood of Lost Dogs".

Impulsively, he decides to gamble his last cent on a poker game that Pozzi has arranged with two reclusive millionaires in Pennsylvania, called Flower and Stone. After testing Pozzi's integrity and ability. Nashe is convinced of

success and volunteers to bankroll the game. They lose badly and, suddenly stranded, agree to work off their debt with 50 days' labour on the millionaires' estate.

Despite its familiar parameters, **Chance** is a departure for Auster. In contrast to his fiction imbued with urban exile, this is a "road" narrative. Much of it is told through dialogue, which proves the weakest element of the book. Unable to luxuriate in the high-minded monologue at which he excels. Auster is constrained to lower the standard of his own prose to that of Pozzi's speech. The result is a rather lightweight, but correspondingly lean, Auster.

Moon Palace finished on the road, at the end of a continent but the beginning of a new life. Nashe picks up from there, finding absolution in the pain of destroying his old life. The "bullet through his head . . . was not death but life". Independence arrived in a miraculous windfall, but is lost in enslavement to Flower and Stone. Their state lottery millions enable them to indulge in various eccentricities evocative of an infantilised *Bouvard and Pecuchet.* In respective playrooms in their shared mansion. Stone builds a model utopia while Flower creates a museum from his collection of historical ephemera.

Nashe and Pozzi's punishment is to build a "Wailing Wall" of 10,000 stones from a ruined Irish castle. Set up in an open prison on the estate and overseen by a man called Calvin, they perform what Stone characterises as "honest work for an honest wage". As a neat Puritanical parable takes shape, it is thwarted by Auster's restless narrative intrigue, built on the veneration of chance. An abrupt ending only adds ambivalence, though leaving a hint of respect for the ridiculous but purposive Flower and Stone.

Auster works over the language of the novel with the eyes of a poet and hands of a storyteller to produce prolonged bursts of joy. **The Music of Chance** sustains the brilliance of his previous writing, providing another rare experience of contemporary fiction at its most thrilling.

Norma Rowen (essay date Summer 1991)

SOURCE: "The Detective in Search of the Lost Tongue of Adam: Paul Auster's *City of Glass,*" in *Critique: Studies in Contemporary Fiction,* Vol. XXXII, No. 4, Summer, 1991, pp. 224-34.

[*In the following essay, Rowen examines Auster's detective-like investigations into the role of language as a medium of representation and the nature of reality in the modern world as portrayed in* City of Glass. *"Throughout the book,"* Rowen notes, *"we are continually reminded of the unknowable nature of this world."*]

When the volumes of Paul Auster's New York trilogy began to appear, reactions were confused. Reviewers were interested and curious, even excited, but puzzled and rather wary. Rebecca Goldstein in the *New York Times Book Review* described *Ghosts,* the second work of the trilogy, as "a mystery novel-of-sorts," a kind of "metamystery" (13); and other reviewers noted the presence of such disturbing elements as complex interplays of doubles and a wilful confusion of fact and fiction that added more mystery to the basic mystery of the detective story form. Some bookstores, on the other hand, showed less readiness to speculate. They simply placed the book on the detective-fiction shelves.

In fact, all three works of the trilogy are examples of the genre now known as the metaphysical detective story, which has been shaped by a number of modern writers from Borges to Pynchon and Nabokov. Its defining characteristic is its transmutation of the traditional detective's quest into something more elusive and complex. In it, the relatively straightforward business of identifying a guilty person, bringing him or her to justice, and restoring social order is ineluctably subverted into a larger and more ambiguous affair. The identity in question becomes as often as not the detective's own, and justice and order dissolve into chimeras in a struggle with a reality that has become increasingly ungraspable. In this postmodernist version of the detective genre, rather than the final working out of the initial puzzle, we are left with what Stefano Tani in *The Doomed Detective* describes as "the decentering and chaotic admission of mystery, of non-solution" (40).

The parts of *The New York Trilogy* are set in such a universe of "chaos and non-solution," and the Auster detectives find themselves decoyed into a quest of a very different kind from the one they contracted for.

But Auster comes up with another and very original twist by adding a crucial language theme. Many who write about the detective story have pointed out that the detective is a kind of reader, a decoder of signs, of the clues that the scenario of the crime throws up. Peter Huhn in his article on this topic characterizes the similarities. "Continual rearrangement and reinterpretation of clues" he says, "is, of course, the basic method of reading and understanding unfamiliar texts" (455). Todorov in *The Poetics of Prose* is even more succinct. "Author:reader = criminal:detective" (49), he states, citing S. S. Van Dyne.[1] In the postmodern world, however, things have become more complicated. Clues no longer point to anything certain; signifiers have drifted away from what they signify; and what Peter Huhn refers to as "a general lack of confidence in the efficacy of reading" has arisen (462).

This "lack of confidence in the efficacy of reading" forms the major theme of *The New York Trilogy.* Alison Russell, in her article "Deconstructing *The New York Trilogy:* Paul Auster's Anti-Detective Fiction," identifies the central "crime," and also the central quest of the three books, as "logocentrism," the search for a Derridean "presence," "an ultimate referent or foundation," which is "outside the play of language itself" (72). Locating such a "presence" may ultimately restore something of the lost efficacy of reading.

Although this search is a major preoccupation of all the New York novels, the first one, perhaps presents this theme with the most force and clarity. In this opening work, the detective's quest becomes overtly and inextricably mingled with the search for the prelapsarian language, the tongue of the innocent Adam by which alone things can be reunited with their right names.

For centuries this quest had been a concern of biblical scholars, who speculated that the prelapsarian tongue might be a form of Hebrew; and as John Irwin has demonstrated in his book *American Hieroglyphs,* it also haunted the works of Poe and Whitman and other nineteenth-century American writers. Whether Daniel Quinn, Auster's twentieth-century representative of American consciousness in *City of Glass,* ever finds the prelapsarian tongue and—perhaps more important—whether he should, are matters that the book leaves open. However, during the search, interesting questions are raised about the capacities of language and the role of story in the postmodern world.

As befits a work centered on language, Quinn, the central questor, is not a detective but merely a writer of detective stories. His obsessive interest in the genre (he is a committed reader of them as well) arises from a profound sense of loss of a rationally ordered universe that the conventional detective story so reliably projects. As Quinn himself explains it:

> In the good mystery there is nothing wasted, no sentence, no word that is not significant. . . . Since everything seen or said, even the slightest, most trivial thing, can bear a connection to the outcome of the story, nothing must be overlooked. Everything becomes essence. . . . The center . . . is everywhere. (15)

Quinn's own world, we soon learn, has been radically decentered. The deaths, some years ago, of his wife and son, unexplained and apparently arbitrary, have dislocated every certainty and have banished forever all idea that the universe makes sense. For him, then, the detective story is a refuge from the metaphysical chaos that he finds around him.

Quinn's broken condition, rooted in the deaths of his wife and child, is in one sense particular to him. But throughout the work, we are made to see that this experience is also representative, one form of a general late-twentieth-century malaise. This is perhaps best illustrated in an early scene in a diner. Quinn converses, with marked fluency and coherence, with the owner, an old acquaintance. The conversation, however, is restricted to baseball, another example of an artificial world of order in a chaotic universe. Subsequently, we learn that the owner has a concentration camp number tattooed on his arm.

Here, then, is the postholocaust universe, in which the only coherent stories, ones with beginnings, middles, ends, and comprehensive solutions, are told in protected, carefully set-up areas of the consciousness, far removed from the terrible heart of contemporary experience.

That such refuge in games and avoidance exacts its price, however, is soon demonstrated. Writing his detective stories has caused Quinn in some measure to disintegrate, to split into a triad of selves whose relationship to each other he can describe only in a curious metaphor of ventriloquism. In his eyes, the actual writer of the works is no longer himself but a kind of double called William Wilson. The speaker of the words is the fictional detective, Max Work. The self closest to Quinn, because it bears his name, is the dummy, the insensate block in the middle. The dangers of this psychological situation are obvious. As a self, Quinn has lost control of his words. They originate with and issue from someone else. He has become a puppet through which they pass, and hence they no longer seem to belong to him. He did not, we are told, "consider himself to be the author of what he wrote" (9).

The relationship to language indicated here gains even more significance as a comment on Quinn's alienated state of mind when we remember that in his earlier days he was a poet, the kind of writer who presumably is very close to his own words and the self from which they issue. Reversing the implications of his first name (the biblical Daniel was a dream reader), he determinedly suppresses his dreams, just as he refuses to deal in the language in which his inner reality might be expressed. Like Paul Auster's own father, as he is described in *The Invention of Solitude,* Quinn has become "a block of impenetrable space in the form of a man" (7).

Quinn is roused from this invisible existence when a midnight phone call gives him a chance, like Don Quixote whose initials he shares, to inhabit and make real one of his own fictions. Don Quixote manages to turn himself into a medieval knight; Daniel Quinn is given the opportunity to play the detective. Like Don Quixote, he is able to do so only by first assuming another identity. The fact that by an amusing trick, this identify is apparently that of Paul Auster himself, the writer of the novel, illustrates the extent to which elements of instability and of self-reflexive fictionalizing have invaded all ideas of self and its manifestations in the postmodern world.

Quinn's case seems at first to take him into the world of Chandler or Macdonald. All the conventional elements of their detective fiction are present. The bizarre crime, in which a member of a rich and distinguished family has locked up and abused his young son, creates an appropriate ambience of money, madness, and damage. A number of familiar genre figures soon make their ritual appearances: the loyal retainer, the voluptuous, ambiguously available wife. Quinn himself moves smoothly into his appointed role, adopting a manner and way of speaking that turn him into a kind of Philip Marlowe:

> Quinn smiled judiciously. . . . "Whatever I do or do not understand," he said, "is probably beside the point. You've hired me to do a job, and the sooner I get on with it the better. From what I can gather the case is urgent. . . ."
>
> He was warming up now. Something told him that he had captured the right tone, and a sudden sense of pleasure surged through him. (41)

Soon, in typical detective style, he is tailing the father, Peter Stillman, Sr., newly released from confinement, through the streets of New York. At this point, however, elements emerge in the case that suggest that a story may be developing that is different from the one that Quinn thinks he is in. To begin with, Stillman's seemingly random wanderings appear to be tracing out hieroglyphic shapes that may or may not make certain words. Second, the motive for the crime is untypical to say the least: The father locked up his son in accordance with an old theory that an infant insulated from the world in this fashion would start speaking the language of unfallen man, thus making it available again. Most disturbing of all, as Quinn follows this strange figure, the trail shifts its nature and direction to lead not outward to the world around him but inward to his own self. All the figures and situations in the case turn out inexorably to be in various ways his own reflections, and his wide divagations through the labyrinth of New York only bring him back to the inner world that he has been so assiduously avoiding.

Thus, the central situation of the case immediately confronts Quinn with an image of his own. Here, too, a son has been lost and destroyed and a father set adrift in the world. Now, however, the situation has taken on a more intense and horrific coloring. In this version of father-son estrangement, the father is unequivocally guilty and the son openly hostile and frightened. Quinn's own situation has been given the dimensions of nightmare.

As individuals, the Stillmans have a reflexive function, embodying aspects of Quinn's own nature and forming part of the complicated interplay of doubles that confront him. Perhaps most important for the themes of the book, they each embody aspects of Quinn's relationship to language. The speeches of Peter, Jr., victim and puppet as he is, reflect Quinn's own estrangement from language. Their reliance on cliché and their contrived and mechanical delivery express in extreme form Quinn's sense, underlying all his fluency, that the language he is using is not his own:

> "No questions please," the young man said at last. "Yes. No. Thank you." He paused for a moment. "I am Peter Stillman. I say this of my own free will. Yes. That is not my real name. No." (26)

Peter Stillman, Sr., seems to represent the other side of the coin. His aim is to find the *non*-alien tongue, the first language of Adam that, by giving everything its right name, will heal this breach between speaker and word, subject and object. In having this attitude, he recalls the earlier Quinn, the poet Quinn. Auster's article on Charles Reznikoff (**"The Decisive Moment"** in *The Art of Hunger*) explicitly connects poetry and the attempt to rediscover the prelapsarian language. In the fallen world, Auster suggests, only through the practice of poetry can this language be regained even momentarily (16).

If Stillman's interest in the prelapsarian language recalls the poet, the uses to which he seeks to put this language reveal him to be another version of the detective. He is seeking a solution, and a solution on a cosmic scale. Fuelled by a biblical sense of the creative power of the word and by the millenarian zeal of his Puritan culture, he sees the recovery of the Adamic tongue as the means by which the whole world can be redeemed and restored to its original order. He had argued for this idea earlier, under the guise of the seventeenth-century clergyman Henry Dark, in his book on the Tower of Babel and the fall of language it involved.

> If the fall of man also entailed the fall of language, was it not logical to assume that it would be possible to undo the fall, to reverse its effects by undoing the fall of language, by striving to recreate the language that was spoken in Eden? (76)

Earlier in this article it was pointed out that in the metaphysical workings of the detective story, the detective-reader often is in difficulties because clues and the things they point to, signifiers and the signified, no longer match up. In repossessing the prelapsarian tongue, Stillman aims to clear up these difficulties. By giving things their right names again, calling back to its signifier the wandering signified, he finally will be able to achieve a reliable reading of the world and formulate, once and for all, the correct, clear, accessible, and unified text of reality. This vision still works in him as, old and broken himself, he now wanders through the city, trying to find the right names for all the broken things he finds there and thus making whole again the fragmented Tower of Babel of the late-twentieth-century cosmos.

Such is the monomaniacal visionary whom Quinn tracks through the wilderness of the city. Quinn, himself a Don Quixote figure, has encountered another one, more obsessive, more powerful, and madder than he, whom, like Sancho Panza, he now must follow and serve. Thus over the next few weeks Quinn reduplicates Stillman's every move, going where he goes and trimming his own stride and behavior to Stillman's. Soon we begin to realize that this shadowing is not only physical. Noting down every detail of his quarry's behavior in a special new red notebook, trying in orthodox detective fashion to penetrate his mind and manner of thinking, Quinn begins to be drawn into Stillman's obsessive world. He starts to perform actions that are hard to explain in rational terms. He insists on always using the pen given him by a deaf-mute. If we remember that one school of thought adhered to the theory that the prelapsarian language was preverbal, a language of signs, we can see that, without perhaps being aware of it, Quinn is becoming involved in Stillman's search. This is further suggested by his obsessive concern about how to hold the red notebook while he tails Stillman. Eventually he hits on a method that will enable him to "[see] the thing and [write] about it in the same fluid gesture" (100-101). This unimpeded melding of subject and object, in which word and thing perfectly coalesce, is again characteristic of language in the prelapsarian world.

Despite these incidental oddities of behavior, Quinn, for the moment, plays the part required of him by the detective story he is engaged in. Then a series of incidents occurs that shatter Quinn. Although for a while he remains unaware of the fact, these incidents cause the story he is in to collapse around him; another story that decisively shifts the direction of the quest takes shape from the wreckage.

The first of these incidents is the disappearance of Stillman; the follower is deprived of what he has been following. The second is Quinn's encounter with another double in the person of "Paul Auster," the character[2] (obviously himself a kind of double of Paul Auster the author of the work) whose identity Quinn had previously assumed. This double, however, works in the opposite way from the ones previously encountered. Unlike the Stillmans, who presented him with nightmare images of his situation as it now is, the "Paul Auster" figure presents an image of his unfallen world, as it was in the idyllic past. The visit to "Auster" brings him face-to-face with Auster's wife and son and poignantly resurrects the warm and close-knit family life, the connectedness that Quinn has lost. The boy, close to the age that Quinn's own child would have been, increases the sense of inexorable doubling by bearing Quinn's own first name, Daniel.

This vision of his past, which also, ironically, is a vision of his present, totally unhinges Quinn. From now on his actions seem completely mad, although at first he advances careful rationales for them. On leaving "Auster's" place he forsakes his home and daily life and stows himself away in a garbage can outside the residence of the junior Stillmans. During the several weeks of his stay there he systematically reduces his bodily needs to almost nothing. His pretext for these actions is that it is his duty as a good private eye to maintain a constant watch over his clients. In fact he has by now lost all contact not only with the case but also with the story of which it was a part. Although at this point he is not yet aware of it, he has started to move into the other story. Viewed from the perspective of this superseding story, his actions make a kind of sense.

Quinn, deeply upset by the vision of his own unfallen world, is taking upon himself the quest that Stillman Sr., left behind. He now is in search of the lost paradise, the world of innocent wholeness that Adam knew, and the prelapsarian language through which it might be recovered. This quest will take over his attention and direct his actions for the rest of the book.

From this context, his immersion in the garbage can has a number of complex meanings. On the simplest level, it is an attempt to make his outward state reflect the inward one, to link up word with thing. After his encounter with "Paul Auster," Quinn realizes that he "was nowhere now . . . he knew nothing, he knew that he knew nothing" (159). By reducing himself to rubbish, Quinn tries to express this nothingness. Deeper motives are also involved. The language of innocence can issue only from the mouth of innocence. Such innocence requires rebirth, and to be reborn one first must die.

Something of this pattern and this necessity is revealed to Quinn by his namesake, "Paul Auster's" little boy. As has been noted, Quinn resolutely forgets his dreams, but this new Daniel is true to the implications of his name. An unconscious revealer and interpreter, he brings to the surface the knowledge and desires that are now beginning to work in the depths of Quinn's psyche. This is what occurs in the incident with the yo-yo. Presented with the toy by the child, Quinn finds he can make it go down but cannot find a way to make it go up. His comments and the child's, however, make clear that one direction may be part of the other.

> "A great philosopher once said," muttered Quinn, "that the way up and the way down are one and the same."
>
> "But you didn't make it go up," said the boy. "It only went down."
>
> "You have to keep trying." (156)

Up and down are parts of the same process; one cannot be without the other. This perception, in part, fuels Quinn's aggressive pursuit of his own nothingness, his determination to seek rock bottom, to throw himself thoroughly away. Only from this near obliteration of the self may a new one arise. Only by becoming garbage can one hope to be recycled.

Quinn's actions in the concluding part of the novel, after he has emerged from the garbage, conform to this death-rebirth pattern. Finding the case in disintegration around him, and the doors of his previous life almost literally shut against him, he moves into Peter Stillman, Jr.'s room. The movement is both physical and symbolic. Physically, he ensconces himself in a room in the now-deserted Stillman apartment and reproduces almost exactly the conditions of Peter's childhood incarceration—the total silence and sequestration in which he spent his first years. Symbolically, he tries to become what Peter then was, the child, the unmarked innocent, pure of all contact with the outer world, through which the language of unfallen man may issue. Thus he divests himself of his clothing, making himself completely naked like the child just emerged, or about to emerge, from the womb.

In this condition we catch our last glimpse of Quinn, sleeping intermittently, eating occasionally, and writing steadily in his red notebook as the darkness falls. A narrator, editor figure, who earlier has given hints of his existence, emerges at this point and takes control of the story. Subsequent investigation, he tells us, has revealed no more of Quinn than the red notebook, left lying on the floor of the room. Quinn himself has completely disappeared.

What are we, as readers and detectives ourselves, to make of this conclusion? Has Quinn found the prelapsarian tongue? Has he achieved anything, or have his endeavors ended in absurdity? The narrator-editor seems to take a gloomy view of Quinn and his life. He refers to him as "a man . . . obviously in trouble," blames Auster (character or author?) for his treatment of him, and ends his comments on a lugubrious note. "My thoughts remain with Quinn," he says. "And wherever he may have disappeared to, I wish him luck" (201). However, in a late-twentieth-century text that continually stresses the subjective element in all experience, we need not take this authorial view as authoritative. Certain aspects of the final phase of Quinn's story require more consideration. During this period he produced writing of a very different kind from his previous detective works. It is described as follows:

> He wrote about the stars, the earth, his hopes for mankind. He felt that his words had been severed from him, that now they were a part of the world at large, as real and specific as a stone, or a lake or a flower. . . . He remembered the moment of his birth and how he had been pulled gently from his mother's womb. He remembered the infinite kindnesses of the world and all the people he had ever loved. Nothing mattered now but the beauty of all this. (200)

Much in this account reminds us of Auster's description of the works of Charles Reznikoff, a poet who he seems to feel came close in his use of language to finding the freshness and creative clarity of prelapsarian speech. Auster sees in Reznikoff's writings such a perfect coalescing of words into things that they seem to "penetrate the prehistory of matter" (*Art of Hunger* 16). As a poet, he seems to be seeing rather than speaking, or speaking "from his eye" (16). Influenced by the imagists, he has learnt from them "the value—the force—of the image in itself, unadorned by the claims of the ego" (18). Into these images the poet disappears. He becomes transparent and "invisible" (19).

Such qualities are recalled in the description of Quinn's final writings. Here are words that turn into things, images of such force and clarity that they seem able to take their place in the world of objects, to become matter. And here, too, is a testament to his invisibility and transparency—in the sense of his words becoming severed from himself. Earlier he felt that his words had become severed from himself because they were not his own. Here, the feeling of severance seems to arise from the fact that he has effaced himself in them.

Perhaps then, in some measure, Quinn achieved his quest. He made his difficult way back to language's unfallen core and gave it utterance. However, he achieved nothing on the scale envisioned by his mentor, Stillman, Sr. He was not able to come up with the correct text of reality. He did not importantly alter reality. Above all, he did not achieve any cosmic solutions. Fragmented, fallen, the world at the end of Quinn's quest remains in much the same plight as it was at the beginning. Quinn's contact with the pure prelapsarian word has been partial, momentary, and personal. He was granted only a series of glimpses. In giving utterance to these glimpses, however, Quinn again laid hold on his vocation as a poet; in the process he became reconciled to the world he could not save and sensitive again to what it has of beauty.

Much in both *City of Glass* and in Auster's other works suggests that this partial, glimpsed achievement of truth is the only possible and genuine one in the difficult world of the twentieth century. Throughout the book we are continually reminded of the unknowable nature of this world. In the Babel of New York, things stream across the eye in a series of disconnected atoms, and subject and object blur each other's image until we feel trapped in a universe of mirrors, a city of glass indeed. As the novel pointed out, in Poe's tale of the journey of Arthur Gordon Pym, the hieroglyphs that the hero discovers and that might be a form of the first tongue of Adam, though undecipherable, are inscribed on solid rock. The hieroglyphs that Stillman's wanderings seem to inscribe upon New York are inscribed in air or may simply be a figment of Quinn's imagination. Over the intervening century, the decipherment of the world has become so much more difficult. To seek for absolute knowledge and final solutions is, therefore, a form of madness. The career of Stillman, Sr., bears this out. The effects of his totalitarian vision are fearful. In the end, they destroy everything human, all connection, all community, and life itself.

Discussing *Hunger* by Knut Hamsun, Auster suggests that a truly modern art, the only one relevant to our current condition, "begins with the knowledge that there are no right answers" and cites Samuel Beckett's statement that this art must "be of such a type that it admits the chaos and does not try to say that the chaos is something else" (***Art of Hunger*** 13). For Auster, the profound and unassuageable metaphysical insecurity of twentieth-century man is symbolized in the condition of the hero of the novel. Perpetually hungry, he obtains only enough food to stop him from starving, never enough to satisfy him. In the same way, modern man can know only enough to see him through the day, to enable him to go on feeling his way along. Metaphysically speaking, in the late twentieth century, there is no such thing as a complete meal. Quinn's crucial understanding of this fact is perhaps demonstrated by his refusal, in his last confinement, to eat more than a small portion of the lavish trays of food that appear before him like mysterious temptations.

At the end the text we are left not with Quinn's final pieces of writing, the examples of vision achieved, but the story of the search for that vision, the novel ***City of Glass*** itself. Perhaps this is a reflection of Auster's sense of the nature of the modern condition. Auster's reworking of the detective story as a quest for the definitive language finally tells us that it is not the correct and final text of reality but a text about the text that is the most appropriate one for the postmodern world. Stories about stories, books not of answers but of questions: these are the forms in which the difficult reality of our time finds its best embodiment.

Notes

1. The view of the reader as a decoder of signs is central to modern theories of narrativity. See, especially, Shlometh Rimmon-Kenan, pp. 117-129.

2. During the course of this paper, I will refer to Paul Auster the character in quotation marks to distinguish him from Paul Auster the author.

Works Cited

Auster, Paul. *The Art of Hunger.* Northants: Menard, 1982.

———. 1985. *The City of Glass.* New York: Viking Penguin, 1987.

———. 1982. *The Invention of Solitude.* London: Faber, 1988.

Goldstein, Rebecca. "The Man Shadowing Black Is Blue." *New York Times Book Review* 29 June 1986: 13.

Huhn, Peter. "The Detective as Reader: Narrativity and Reading Concepts in Detective Fiction." *Modern Fiction Studies* 33 (1987): 451-456.

Irwin, John T. *American Hieroglyphs.* New Haven: Yale UP, 1980.

Rimmon-Kenan, Shlometh. *Narrative Fiction: Contemporary Poetics.* London: Methuen, 1983.

Russell, Alison. "Deconstructing *The New York Trilogy*: Paul Auster's Anti-Detective Fiction." *Critique* 31 (1990): 71-83.

Tani, Stefano. *The Doomed Detective.* Carbondale: Southern Illinois UP, 1984.

Todorov, Tzvetan. *The Poetics of Prose.* Trans. Richard Howard. Oxford: Blackwell, 1971.

Thomas Mallon (review date 6 September 1992)

SOURCE: "Caught in the Waltz of Disasters," in *Washington Post Book World,* September 6, 1992, p. 5.

[*In the following review, Mallon offers positive assessment of* Leviathan.]

Some years ago, in a burst of pre-p.c. phallocentrism, Bernard Malamud responded to an interviewer's question about the supposed death of narration by saying, "It'll be dead when the penis is." There was a certain defensiveness in this outburst, of course. Plots, once the protein of prose fiction, had been shunned by many modern writers as if they were animal fat, a vulgar diet for the poor and unenlightened.

In recent years, however, plots have had a spectacular champion in Paul Auster, who once explained his preference for writing novels rather than plays in this way: "I wanted just narrative, telling the story . . . I think we absolutely depend on [stories] for our survival." In such novels as the marvelous ***Moon Palace*** (1989) he has confected worlds of tremendous complication and bizarre plausibility.

His new work, ***Leviathan,*** contains the following account of a novel being constructed from peculiar, juxtaposed stories: "All of them are true, each is grounded in the real, and yet [he] fits them together in such a way that they become steadily more fantastic . . . you reach a point where you feel the whole thing begin to levitate, to rise ponderously off the ground like some gigantic weather balloon." Though these words might serve as Auster's characterization of some of his own work, they actually belong to *Leviathan*'s narrator, Peter Aaron, who is talking about the work of another novelist, his friend Benjamin Sachs.

Their lives have been intertwined for 15 years when *Leviathan* opens on July 4, 1990, with Aaron telling readers that he is sure a man who recently "blew himself up by the side of a road in northern Wisconsin . . . sitting on the grass next to his parked car when the bomb he was building accidentally went off," was his friend Sachs, an "exhausting" personality, a being "too large-spirited and cunning, too full of new ideas to stand in one place for very long." A draft resister who served time in prison, Sachs created much excitement with a novel called *The New Colossus* and was renowned as an essayist on any number of subjects, though he was largely indifferent to "pursuing what people refer to as a 'literary career.'"

Auster's novel, like Sachs's, is full of stories within stories, driven by a plot that is linear only in the way spaghetti is. What eventually emerges from the brilliant tangle is the story of how Sachs eventually meets his own doppelganger and becomes "a solitary speck in the American night," removed from his wife and friends and work, "hurtling toward his destruction in a stolen car."

In *Leviathan* the Statue of Liberty serves the kind of connective and causative functions that the moon did in *Moon Palace.* When Sachs was a little boy he visited it with his mother, who suffered a panic attack while climbing up its arm. Years later his *New Colossus* is "filled with references" to the Statue, and on July 4, 1986, four years before *Leviathan* opens, Sachs is nearly killed by falling off a fire escape during a rooftop party where guests are watching the fireworks celebration of the Statue's 100th anniversary. This ambiguous accident is the true beginning of the "waltz of disasters" in which Sachs and his friends become caught.

Sachs, we are told, is in love with ironic coincidences, and *Leviathan* is full of them, great and small. The largest involves the manner in which he meets the above-mentioned doppelganger. In most modern novels, plot is so subordinate to character and sensibility that reviewers needn't worry about giving anything away, but with Auster it is different, and it must suffice to say of this biggest coincidence what the narrator says of Sachs's own attitude toward it: It "was in fact a solution, an opportunity in the shape of a miracle. The essential thing was to accept the uncanniness of the event—not to deny it, but to embrace it, to breathe it into himself as a sustaining force." This is precisely how Auster himself works his often strange material.

Leviathan's vivid pivotal characters include Maria, a demi-artist given to arbitrary projects like "following strangers around the streets, choosing someone at random when she left her house in the morning and allowing that choice to determine where she went for the rest of the day." The novel contains occasional patches of gorgeous prose, but more often the style is deliberately spare, a stainless steel string for all the gaudy narrative beads. Aaron is supposedly writing the book over a period of two months, trying to get the whole story down from memory before an expected return visit from two FBI agents investigating the explosion in Wisconsin. The conceit proves effectively unnerving. Convinced of the urgency of Aaron's situation, the reader experiences the narration like the kind of deliberate driving that's done in a rainstorm. *Leviathan* ends with one "last little surprise, the ultimate twist." As it happens, this last twist is among the less compelling ones, but readers will find that it hardly hampers the improbable flight of Auster's beautiful new balloon.

Barry Lewis (essay date Spring 1994)

SOURCE: "The Strange Case of Paul Auster," in *Review of Contemporary Fiction,* Vol. 14, No. 1, Spring, 1994, pp. 53-61.

[*In the following essay, Lewis examines the narrative and thematic characteristics of Auster's "anti-detective" fiction and the elusive authorial presence of Auster.*]

The mystery is this: How can we best classify the works of Paul Auster? Exhibit 1 is a statement he makes about one of his characters: "What interested him about the stories he wrote was not their relation to the world but their relation to other stories."[1] Auster's fictional world is an austere one, composed of reconfigured plots and reworked motifs drawn from the history of American literature and his own back catalog, and this makes it difficult to untangle the many different intertextual threads which stitch his stories together. One consistent theme is that of the detective's search for a missing person, so in this inspection I too shall turn detective and search for the person who is most conspicuously absent from the texts of Paul Auster: Paul Auster himself.

The typical detective story can be divided into three basic components: the presentation of the mystery, the process of detection, and the solution towards which the whole of the narrative moves. The invariability of this formula accounts in large part for the continued popularity of such writers as Arthur Conan Doyle and Agatha Christie and their rituals of ratiocination. Each of the novels in Auster's *The New York Trilogy* follows the pattern by introducing the detective figure and the case he has to solve.[2] In *City of Glass* Daniel Quinn is hired by Virginia Stillman to follow her father-in-law, Peter Stillman, who has been in a mental hospital for fifteen years for keeping his son locked up in solitary confinement throughout his childhood. The mystery centers on Stillman's motives for his bizarre behavior. *Ghosts,* the second novel, introduces the ground situation in a more schematic fashion: "The case seems simple enough. White wants Blue to follow a man named Black and to keep an eye on him for as long as necessary" (161). Unfortunately, Blue is not told why he has to shadow Black, and the case drags on for several months. The third novel, *The Locked Room,* revolves around the unnamed narrator's attempts to find out why his best friend, Fanshawe, has abandoned his wife and child.[3] A series of manuscripts is the only trace which has been left behind for the narrator to investigate Fanshawe's sudden disappearance.

At the beginning of an investigation everything is a potential clue, and both the detective and the reader operate at their height of attentiveness. This is an important lead towards understanding Auster's use of the detective genre, and Exhibit 2 is another comment from *City of Glass* which sheds light on his own methods:

> In the good mystery there is nothing wasted, no sentence, no word that is not significant. And even if it is not significant, it has the potential to be so—which amounts to the same thing. The world of the book comes to life, seething with possibilities, with secrets and contradictions. Since everything seen or said, even the slightest, most trivial thing, can bear a connection to the outcome of the story, nothing must be overlooked. Everything becomes essence; the center of the book shifts with each event that propels it forward. The center, then, is everywhere, and no circumference can be drawn until the book has come to its end.(9)

The process of detection is initiated when the detective assesses the situation and amasses clues, usually by a combination of patient observation and logical deduction. Auster's protagonists are all reluctant detectives who are drawn into the case against their inclination, and in this respect they resemble the second generation of cynical sleuths, such as Raymond Chandler's Philip Marlowe, who obtain financial rather than intellectual satisfaction from their work. Nevertheless, it is to Edgar Allan Poe's character August Dupin—the prototype of the old school of detectives—that Quinn turns to for advice in *City of Glass.* He copies Dupin's dictum that there must be "an identification of the reasoner's intellect with that of his opponent"[4] into his notebook, and follows Stillman for several days as he wanders aimlessly around the city, picking up broken or discarded objects. These random walks puzzle him until he traces the routes out on paper. They spell out the words "TOWER OF BABEL," and this convinces him that the enforced detention of Stillman's son was part of a bizarre, Kaspar Hauser-like linguistic experiment. Quinn identifies himself so closely with his adversary's insane behavior that he himself undergoes a kind of breakdown. In order to keep Virginia Stillman's apartment under continuous observation, he lives like a tramp on the street below and gradually reduces his need for food and sleep. In *Ghosts* Blue cracks up too, suspecting that Black and White are in league and that it is really he who is being watched by Black. Disguising himself also as a tramp, he engages Black in conversation about the ghosts of literary figures, such as Whitman and Thoreau, who haunt the district in which they live. Black tells

Blue the story of Hawthorne's "Wakefield," in which the central character pretends to his wife to go away on a business trip but rents a room close by his house where he spies on her for several days. The days soon turn into weeks and then months, and twenty years go by until he finally returns to his home. This parable does not enlighten Blue, but the person who goes "missing" from everyday life is an important theme in Auster and therefore constitutes Exhibit 3. It is also a potential key for unlocking *The Locked Room.* The narrator in that story slowly steps into the shoes of his friend by marrying his wife Sophie, adopting his son Ben, and acting as executor of his literary legacy, little suspecting that Fanshawe—like Wakefield—is watching his old life from afar. The narrator conducts research for a biography of Fanshawe after the success of the manuscripts he publishes but soon realizes that his friend's identity and the reason for his disappearance will remain a mystery no matter how much information he obtains: "I was a detective, after all, and my job was to hunt for clues. Faced with a million bits of random information, led down a million paths of false inquiry, I had to find the one path that would take me where I wanted to go. So far, the essential fact was that I hadn't found it" (332).

The three novels of *The New York Trilogy* illustrate Hawthorne's moral that "by stepping aside for a moment, a man exposes himself to a fearful risk of losing his place forever."[5] Stillman, Black, and Fanshawe are all Wakefields who have stepped aside from the routines of daily life to follow their own crazy visions, and it is one of the unique ironies of Auster's world that the very figures who look for these missing persons—Quinn, Blue, Fanshawe's friend—are themselves stripped of their former identities during their search. This is a movement which is present in Auster's other work too. *In the Country of Last Things* maintains the investigative frame despite being set in a postapocalyptic future, as Anna Blume hunts among the ruins of a devastated city for her brother William. Her mission soon takes second place to the continuous struggle to find food and shelter, and she becomes one of the Object Hunters, scavengers who make their living by finding goods and materials which can be salvaged or recycled. *The Invention of Solitude,* Auster's autobiographical work, can also be viewed in terms of a search for a missing person: in this case, his dead father, whose life is reconstructed via a series of old photos and random memories. But these scraps cannot help him find his parent, and the project is every bit as futile as the search for Stillman, Black, or Fanshawe: "In the deepest, most unalterable sense, he was an invisible man. Invisible to others, and most likely invisible to himself as well. If, while he was alive, I kept looking for him, kept trying to find the father who was not there, now that he is dead I still feel as though I must go on looking for him."[6]

Perhaps the search for Auster can be advanced by a close examination of his novel *Moon Palace,* which features the elements of mystery and detection familiar from his other books. It opens with the breakdown of a student called

Marco Stanley Fogg, who was brought up by his Uncle Victor, a musician, after his mother Emily died in a traffic accident. He never knew his father. In the summer of the first moon landing, Fogg hears that Victor has died of a heart attack, following an unsuccessful tour of the West with a band called the Moon Men. Overcome with grief, Fogg "began to vanish into another world."[7] He sets himself the pointless task of reading from cover to cover the almost 1,500 books Victor had given him, which had functioned as makeshift chairs and tables in his apartment. As he finishes each volume, he sells it to the local bookstore and so gradually his "furniture" is dismantled: "Piece by piece, I could watch myself disappear" (24). Meanwhile, he casts off his other possessions and develops increasingly bizarre excuses to his friends for his apparent indifference to these discomforts. In fact he exhibits all the typical signs of a severe schizophrenic episode: his behavior becomes increasingly erratic, he loses track of time, he experiences disturbing hallucinations, and his powers of association are considerably loosened. Gazing at the neon sign of a Chinese restaurant opposite his apartment, he ponders the significance of the words **Moon Palace**:

> I would think: the Apollo Project; Apollo, the god of music; Uncle Victor and the Moon Men traveling out West. I would think: the West; the war against the Indians; the war in Vietnam, once called Indochina. I would think: weapons, bombs, explosions; nuclear clouds in the deserts of Utah and Nevada; and then I would ask myself—why does the American West look so much like the landscape of the moon? It went on and on like that, and the more I opened myself to these secret correspondences, the closer I felt to understanding some fundamental truth about the world. I was going mad, perhaps, but I nevertheless felt a tremendous power surging through me, a gnostic joy that penetrated deep into the heart of things. (32-33)

This chain of speculative correspondences is similar to the type of lateral reasoning which a detective cultivates as he commences an investigation. No detail must be rejected; even the most trivial link is worth examining and pursuing to its logical conclusion, no matter how absurd. The slightest thing, to paraphrase Auster, has the potential to be significant. But the steady accumulation of clues and lines of inquiry should result in a gradual ordering of the apparently random set of data, otherwise the investigation is fruitless. The detective "moves through this morass of objects and events in search of the thought, the idea that will pull all these things together and make sense of them" (*New York Trilogy* 9). In the three novels of **The New York Trilogy** the detective figures keep an open mind in the hope of stumbling upon the correct sequence of reasoning which will unravel the mystery. Auster delights in multiplying the connections involved in the investigation. Quinn, Blue, and Fanshawe's friend all skirt insanity as they try to solve an inscrutable riddle, and the process of detection crumbles. In **Moon Palace** the sequence is reversed, and Fogg's breakdown occurs before the investigation is even under way. His manic reading of Uncle Victor's books seems to indicate that he is looking for clues, but the real mystery is the fact that there is, as yet, no mystery to solve. His thinking shows an inability to maintain boundaries between different concepts, and this "Moon Palace" train-of-thought shall be Exhibit 4:

> the fact was that the words *Moon Palace* began to haunt my mind with all the mystery and fascination of an oracle. Everything was mixed up in it all at once: Uncle Victor and China, rocket ships and music, Marco Polo and the American West. I would look out at the sign and start to think about electricity. That would lead me to the blackout during my freshman year, which in turn would lead me to the baseball games played at Wrigley Field, which would then lead me back to Uncle Victor and the memorial candles burning on my windowsill. One thought kept giving way to another, spiraling into ever larger masses of connectedness. (32)

Like other Auster protagonists who have become swamped by possibility, Fogg deteriorates rapidly towards a degree-zero level of existence and lives as a tramp in Central Park when he is thrown out of his apartment for nonpayment of rent. He takes shelter in a cave, where he is later found by his friends Zimmer and Kitty Wu who restore him to health. The book then enters its second phase, which features the mystery Fogg is called upon to solve.

After his recuperation, Fogg is employed as a companion to Thomas Effing, who is old, blind, and crippled. Effing is a strange character who hints about his dark past and forces his bewildered employee to undergo a series of tests before he declares him suitable to take down some notes for an "obituary." Effing claims to have been in his youth a promising artist called Julian Barber, who set off on a painting exhibition into the Great Salt Desert with his topographer friend, Teddy Byrne. Barber had been married for four years and on the eve of his departure enjoys rare sexual relations with his wife. Barber and Byrne hire a guide from Salt Lake City called Jack Scoresby, but the journey turns sour when Barber beats him at a game of cards. Not long after, Byrne has a bad accident after falling down the side of a cliff, and Scoresby cynically abandons Barber to tend to his injuries. The boy dies, and this cruel blow pushes Barber into insanity: "That was the moment when Julian Barber was obliterated: out there in the desert, hemmed in by rocks and blistering light, he simply canceled himself out" (165). On the fourth day of wandering dementedly across the arid plain, he takes shelter in a cave, which—incredibly—contains food and furniture and a corpse. Barber cannot believe his good fortune and for several months lives as a hermit. Then unexpectedly he receives a visitor, a halfwit called George Ugly Mouth who mistakes Barber for the dead man, Tom, and warns him that a group of bandits called the Greshams will be coming shortly to the cave. Barber kills them without remorse, just as they had murdered the cave's original inhabitant, and returns to civilization with their stolen money under the new name of Thomas Effing. So the mystery of Effing's early life is clearly another variation on the "disappearing man" motif, and Hawthorne's judgment of Wakefield is equally true of Julian Barber: "He had contrived, or rather he had happened, to dissever himself from the world—to vanish—to give up his place and privileges with living men, without being admitted among the dead" (160).

Fogg types up the story as a short article called "The Mysterious Life of Julian Barber" and as a longer biography; but Effing's mysterious life is not quite over. He sets himself a day to die, and with the help of Fogg gives away thousands of dollars on the streets of New York before that date as a means of making amends for the money he stole from the Greshams. Effing duly dies on 12 May, and after the funeral, Fogg contacts the historian Solomon Barber in accordance with the old man's last wishes. Solomon is the son who had been conceived the night before Barber departed on the painting expedition, and Fogg arranges to spend a weekend with him. It transpires that Solomon knew Emily Fogg, and this leads up to the revelation that Effing's son is Fogg's father. Auster creates no suspense out of this—indeed, this outcome is hinted at within the first dozen sentences of the book—but it functions as a decoy which deflects attention from the central mystery of the cave. Barber persuades Fogg to help him find Effing's shelter in the Utah desert, but before they even leave Chicago, the historian dies as a result of injuries sustained at the graveside of Emily Fogg. Fogg sets off on the expedition alone, only to find that the whole area has been submerged. This meandering conclusion of **Moon Palace** and the many coincidences in the narrative led one reviewer to describe it as a "spaghetti-junction of omens and congruencies."[8] Here is how Fogg himself describes it:

> It was all a matter of missed connections, bad timing, blundering in the dark. We were always in the right place at the wrong time, the wrong place at the right time, always just missing each other, always just a few inches from figuring the whole thing out. That's what the story boils down to, I think. A series of lost chances. All the pieces were there from the beginning, but no one knew how to put them together. (249)

So the mystery is left dangling, unresolved. In traditional detective fiction, various false trails and red herrings will momentarily complicate the plot, but overall the possibilities will be narrowed down until only one sequence of events remains: the solution. This allows a circumference to be drawn around the action and the center of the story to be located. Auster subverts this familiar progression from chaos to order in **Moon Palace** by concentrating on the breakdown of the detection of the process. From the very opening pages the tale is one of dissolution, not solution, suspension, not suspense. Never was a detective better named than Marco Stanley Fogg: his spirited explorations only take him deeper into the heart of the pea-souper.

Unlike Sherlock Holmes or Hercules Poirot or even Philip Marlowe, Auster's detectives never reach a solution, and the missing persons they pursue are either mad or addicted to motiveless games of cat and mouse. As in **Moon Palace,** none of the novels in **The New York Trilogy** ends conclusively. In **City of Glass** Quinn remains outside Virginia Stillman's apartment for several months without result, and when he returns to his own abode, he finds it is now occupied by a stranger who does not recognize him. He has become a Wakefield, an invisible man, and the case has been forgotten. In **Ghosts** Blue finally confronts Black and threatens him with a gun: "You're supposed to tell me the story. Isn't that how it's supposed to end? You tell me the story, and then we say goodbye" (230). But Black will not play the game, and Blue murders him without finding out what the affair was all about. In **The Locked Room** Fanshawe contacts his friend and arranges to speak to him through the locked door of an apartment in Columbus Square, Boston. He gives his friend a notebook in which his disappearance is explained, but the narrator tears it up on the way back to Sophie, without revealing its contents.

These disrupted endings are Exhibit 5 and suggest an answer to our own enigma: perhaps Paul Auster's fiction can be most accurately defined in terms of the anti-detective genre. This is a term used by Stefano Tani to describe books which employ the trappings of crime fiction to introduce the detective and a mystery only to frustrate the reader's expectation of an acceptable solution.[9] There are several ways in which this can be accomplished. The case might be solved by pure chance or with a solution which is more puzzling than the initial state of affairs. *The Conversions* (1962) by Harry Mathews, for example, begins with three riddles set by Grent Wayl in his will. The anonymous narrator's attempts to answer them involve fortuitous encounters with various secret societies and translingual puns which complicate considerably an otherwise simple detection plot. Alternatively, the narrative may close prematurely before the guilty party has been named or a vital clue revealed. The final pages of Thomas Pynchon's *The Crying of Lot 49* (1966) do not disclose whether Oedipa's conspiracy theory—involving an underground postal network called the Trystero—is rooted in fact or fantasy. Lastly, the mystery might be subsumed under the weight of metafictional games played by the writer with the "detection" metaphor. Gilbert Sorrentino's *Mulligan Stew* (1979) is a good instance of this. The murder which begins the book is really a thin pretext for the elaborate game of hide and seek played with Ned Beaumont, Antony Lamont, and Martin Halpin, characters who have been "borrowed" from the fictions of other authors. In each instance, the case is dissolved before a satisfactory outcome has been reached, and in the absence of an overarching plot to tie the narrative together, it is often the nature of objects themselves which becomes the focus of investigation. This explains Mathews's detailed descriptions of ludicrous machines, the scrupulous attention Pynchon pays to stamps and signs on lavatory walls, and the long lists in Sorrentino which itemize the books and furniture at the scene of the crime. These objects—unlike the stain on the door handle or the ash on the linoleum in the more conventional detective fiction—are no longer signs which point toward the discovery of a solution but opaque "things" resistant to interpretation. Alain Robbe-Grillet describes the mechanics of the anti-detective genre as follows:

> the plot starts to thicken alarmingly; witnesses contradict each other, new factors crop up which had previously been overlooked. . . . And you have to keep coming back to the recorded evidence: the exact posi-

tion of a piece of furniture, the shape and frequency of a fingerprint, a word written in a message. The impression grows on you that nothing else is true. Whether they conceal or reveal a mystery, these elements that defy all systems have only one serious, obvious quality—that of being *there*.[10]

This description fits the works of Auster well. The plots of *The New York Trilogy* and *Moon Palace* branch out disturbingly, without ever returning to their source; characters switch roles unexpectedly; and there is always the primacy of objects, whose quality of "being there" reinforces the chief imperative of Auster's vanishing men: "the need to be here."[11]

The case seemed simple enough. You, the reader, wanted this writer to keep an eye on a man called Paul Auster and to follow him for as long as necessary. But the clues are proliferating already, new factors are coming into play, so let's see what can be gleaned from Exhibits 1-5 before the puzzle eludes us. First, there is the quote from *City of Glass* which seems self-referentially to point to the dynamics of Auster's fiction: his stories are built out of other stories. Therefore we would expect to define his work by its relation to other genres and fictions, and Exhibits 2 and 3 confirm this intuition. The former—a comment about the merits of detective tales, particularly their propensity for galvanizing the reader's attention and distributing it equally throughout the text—places his work in the context of one of the purest of fictional modes.[12] The latter—the recurrent theme borrowed from Hawthorne's "Wakefield"—is an indication of Auster's indebtedness to earlier American writers such as Poe and Melville, and their probings into the frailties of human identity. Exhibit 4, Fogg's "Moon Palace" train of thought, is a pointer towards what is unique about Auster's blending of the detective and "disappearing man" tropes: the breakdown of the detection process is always accompanied by a breakdown of the self. The "disappearances" his books present are mental as much as physical, and it is this focus on the collapse of the self which lends to Auster's works "a narrative style that partakes of both the dryness of a clinical report and the inventiveness of fiction."[13] Exhibit 5, Auster's penchant for deferred endings, is the outcome of this dual preoccupation. The evidence is scanty, that is for sure, but from these isolated trails we have at least constructed a working hypothesis: Auster can best be classified as a late example of the anti-detective genre.

Yet a nagging suspicion remains that this is too simple a solution. It does not take sufficiently into account the ambivalence of Auster's texts and the way in which they play with equal irony upon the conventions of the anti-detective as well as the detective genre. But an examination along these lines would take us deep into the pea-souper and the terrifying possibility that it is Paul Auster who is the invisible man.

Notes

1. Paul Auster, *The New York Trilogy* (New York: Penguin, 1990), 8; hereafter cited parenthetically.

2. Auster's detective figures usually have literary associations. For example, Daniel Quinn in *City of Glass* is a writer of crime fiction under the name of William Wilson. Dan Quin was the pseudonym of Alfred Henry Lewis, who wrote about Western frontier life in the nineteenth century, and William Wilson is the protagonist of the eponymous Poe tale. The web of reference becomes instantly more complex when Quinn is mistaken for a detective called Paul Auster. Have we found our quarry already?

3. The device of the locked room is one of the clichés of traditional detective fiction.

4. Edgar Allan Poe, "The Purloined Letter," in *The Portable Poe,* ed. Philip Van Doren Stern (New York: Penguin, 1977), 451.

5. Nathaniel Hawthorne, "Wakefield," in *The Portable Hawthorne,* ed. Malcolm Cowley (New York: Penguin, 1969), 161-62; hereafter cited parenthetically.

6. Paul Auster, *The Invention of Solitude* (New York: SUN, 1982), 7.

7. Paul Auster, *Moon Palace* (New York: Viking, 1989), 3; hereafter cited parenthetically.

8. Michael Walters, "In Circulation," *The Times Literary Supplement,* 28 April—4 May 1989, 452.

9. Stefano Tani, *The Doomed Detective: The Contribution of the Detective Novel to Postmodern American and Italian Fiction* (Carbondale: Southern Illinois University Press, 1984).

10. Alain Robbe-Grillet, *Snapshots and Towards a New Novel,* trans. Barbara Wright (London: Calder and Boyars, 1965), 56.

11. The phrase is from Paul Auster's essay on the paintings of Jean-Paul Riopello in *Ground Work: Selected Poems and Essays 1970-1979* (London: Faber and Faber, 1990), 176.

12. Michael Holquist has suggested that detective fiction is to postmodernism what myth was to modernism, an ideal vehicle for the exploration of each period's concerns. See "Whodunit and Other Questions: Metaphysical Detective Stories in Post-War Fiction," *New Literary History* 3.1 (1971): 135-56.

13. Again I have taken down Auster's words and used them in evidence against him, as this is a description from his essay on the writings of schizophrenic Louis Wolfson (*Ground Work* 120).

Katharine Washburn (essay date Spring 1994)

SOURCE: "A Book at the End of the World: Paul Auster's *In the Country of Last Things,*" in *Review of Contemporary Fiction,* Vol. 14, No. 1, Spring, 1994, pp. 62-5.

[*In the following essay, Washburn examines the imagery, literary and historical allusions, and narrative design employed by Auster to portray the deterioration of civilization* In the Country of Last Things.]

Transparent, straightforward as speech, and almost entirely innocent of the formal conundrums and cross-referenced allusions for which his **New York Trilogy** is noted, Paul Auster's **In the Country of Last Things** would appear at first glance to take a sharp turn in a new literary direction. Auster's novel, like the long visionary epistle that ends Doris Lessing's *The Four-Gated City,* is written in the shape of a document cast into the void, mailed to some sort of dead letter zone at the end of the world. This, too, is a fictional account of an apocalypse, but where Lessing's Martha Quest is prolix, doctrinaire, and relentlessly literal, the voice of Anna Blume maintains through 182 pages the discipline of a rare sanity contemplating extreme derangement, observing, reporting, and never escaping into the ease of the oracular or the comfort of the grand historical explanation.

A young woman has sailed across the ocean, leaving one continent, where civilization is evidently still intact, for another in a terminal stage of collapse and ruin. Although the text makes no such proposal, we are tempted to substitute the maps of first Europe, then America to chart her voyage. In search of her missing brother, William, Anna discovers she will require all her wits to survive in the rubble of a city governed by assassins, profiteers, and thugs. Years later she writes in a blue notebook of the failure of her quest and describes the history of her wanderings to an unnamed person, some old lover, old friend, or even her former self, still safe in the civility and reason of an older order on the other side of the sea. Anna's lost brother was sent across the same ocean on a journalistic mission, to report what he found in a city where all social and material structures have sunk into that debris which is the central image of this book. His reports soon cease, and it is one of the small ironies Auster folds into his story that it is Anna, in fact, who will send the last dispatch from a universe of "last things."

What Anna finds in a country whose darkened shoreline warns her at her approach of a disaster beyond words—Hawthorne's "City of Destruction" provides the novel's epigraph—is a nightmare place where no children are born, a *univers concentrationnaire* whose inmates toil at the collection of garbage and corpses, where mayhem has replaced the rule of law, where nothing, save for a solitary madman's construction of a miniature fleet confined in glass bottles, is manufactured. Its beggared inhabitants scrabble in the ruins for the shards of material goods, the "last things" which give them their final employment in a brutal, half-criminalized salvaging and recycling operation. There is an official currency, measured in "glots," but Auster, who wears his wide reading lightly, is no doubt playing with a Dickensian trope for the breakdown of industrial society by conjuring up a swarm of Golden Dustmen trafficking in the night soil and corpses which convert into the fuel which still runs the engine of this debased and exhausted world.

Anna Blume never finds her brother and spends her days roaming the blasted landscape of a city which, like Eliot's Unreal City, becomes a score of dying cities in the West. No departure is possible from this place: the city, under some last, mad, military directive, is expending its final resources in building a sea-wall to repel invaders, an echo of a similar enterprise undertaken by Thucydides' Athenians near the end of the Peloponnesian War which ultimately destroyed them. This city, where governments change with the same speed, incomprehensibility, and hostile force as its unpredictable weather, mirrors other cities, other dark times, as it tunnels through twentieth-century history: the Warsaw Ghetto, the Siege of Leningrad (without any redeeming heroic purpose), postearthquake Managua, the last days of Berlin, and, above all, New York City in the present.

Herein lies the enormous irony of Auster's tale. Once more, as in the three volumes of **The New York Trilogy,** it's all done with mirrors. This time, the game is played with, if anything, greater cunning and obliqueness behind the same screen of lucid and uncompromising prose. **In the Country of Last Things** is occupied not with a future dystopia but with a hellish present. Its citizens are no more inhabitants of the future than Swift's Houyhnhnms are native to some unmapped mid-Atlantic island. They belong to the here and now, to its ethical, spiritual, and cultural chaos. The broken objects and decayed relics they dig up from rutted streets and collapsed buildings to trade at considerable sums for a marginal existence are emblematic of a society which has not only ceased to invent and produce but which, for nearly two decades, has inflated the value of real property, objects of art, and fetishistic junk alike. Where productivity and invention fail, any artifact from the recent past becomes a work of art. Where even memory fails, becoming an atrophied faculty of human intelligence, the desire for sensation and novelty is quickly gratified by a highly accelerated recycling of goods, whether damaged or sound. Auster's description of this process gives the word *collector* an almost sinister ring, just as his "Leapers," a group of elective suicides who jump from high buildings, suggest, through a familiar historical association, the shaky financial structure of our own economy.

Some of these correspondences converge in such an inescapable fashion on life in the present in New York City that **In the Country of Last Things** supplies a phantom unit to what is, in effect, Auster's New York Tetralogy. "A house is there one day, and the next day it is gone. A street you walked down yesterday is no longer there today." A bomb crater, a vanished neighborhood, a demolished building unite in the unstable urban landscape of an American city. Few readers will miss these implications, or, when they encounter the book's description of the howling "Runners" who hurl themselves down the filthy streets of Auster's metropolis, running blindly until they attain their end—death by exhaustion—will ever contemplate an urban creature loping along, senses sealed through his electronic apparatus, eyes glazed and vision straining at a distant nullity, in quite the same way.

Part of the book's bleak entertainment lies in the discovery of these manifold and dense connections between the fictional city and present reality. These remain, however, suggestive rather than coercive. Auster parodies the breakdown of law by unionizing his muggers: they organize themselves as "Tollists," patrolling random streets, extorting a fee from every passerby unable to anticipate the presence of their barriers. The vacancy rate in the city is at zero, and streets and subways swarm with sleepers from an underclass of paupers, criminals, and lunatics, although a level of society called "the rich" still coexists with it.

In this climate of endless scarcity, there is continuous talk of food, obsessive reminiscence of meals once eaten, the preparation of meals which might be eaten, the verbal evocations of perfect menus and the sensations they bestow. The speakers in Anna Blume's astonished narrative are, in fact, half-starved, but their preoccupation with food, like the onanistic rush of the Runners, mimics still another cultural vagary of the last decade: the urban sophisticate's absorption in restaurants and cuisine. The parallels become uncanny. Where are we, if not in New York, near the end of the century, in an entrepreneurial capital where nothing indigenous is grown or generated? Children appear twice: one a corpse and the other an unborn fetus. (Anna's pregnancy ends in miscarriage.) Zero Population Growth is at its zenith. And corpses, which can be mined for gold teeth and burned for fuel, have some residual value.

Anna sees and records this world, her pluckiness and intelligence marking her for independent survival, although several calamities make her a candidate for rescue. Losing the shopping cart on which her trade as a licensed scavenger depends, cast out in the streets once more after the death of her dubious protectors, she wanders to the library (a beleaguered monument to high culture in which books must be burned for warmth) where she finds her brother's old colleague Samuel Farr. They fall in love and winter over in the library until Anna, literally barefoot and pregnant, is lured into a shop where corpse-merchants assault their victims. Diving through a window to safety, she's found by the head of a charitable hostel, a woman named Victoria whose rescue operation will end in defeat. Nursed back to health, restored to sanity by salvaging, this time, the sick and starving and through a somewhat unconvincing lesbian relationship with Victoria, she watches the city burn, smolder, and die around them through another frightful winter. Farr rejoins them, and a small pack of survivors prepares an escape from the city. Rejecting various exit points, all treacherous and uncertain, they choose a gate which leads—in hope? in despair?— past the westernmost barrier of the city. (The promise of safety outside the city seems small, and the western exit,

in all the indices of folklore and mythology, is synonymous with death.) Although the close of the novel is ambiguous, Anna's doom seems imminent. The blue notebook will fall into the immense detritus of her world.

Closing the book, we think of Emmanuel Ringelbaum's memoir of the Warsaw Ghetto, buried in the earth and dug up for another generation. Anna's book, however, can address itself to no such hope, for in her catalog of loss the words which would serve her purpose and make intelligible her story are consigned to a rubbish heap from which they will not rise again. When Anna learns that there can be no return voyage by sea to her own country, she alludes to airplanes and learns that not only have airplanes been absent from this country for some time but the very word is extinct. Oceania has always been at war with Eastasia. *There are no more bicycle wheels left in the world.* Memory of the past is fading and Anna in **In the Country of Last Things** is one of its rare agents: perhaps this accounts for her name, borrowed from an obscure poem of Kurt Schwitters which celebrates an eponymous "pale Anna Blume." Auster's Anna, however strong and unfaltering her powers of observation, is a wan ghost of the past astray in an intolerable present.

Auster's naming of his characters, however, points to one of the few flaws in his careful composition. There's a tendency to seed this book, as in his earlier volumes, with Significant Names, without any commitment to integrate them. "Ferdinand and Isabella," "Samuel Farr," and "Mr. Frick" summon associations that come too easily, shortcuts to the unfolding of a narrative scheme which Auster's fine prose is well equipped to avoid. The true force of the book lies in its oblique aim; the feminine narrator has managed an elegant trick of distance without relinquishing the power to move us, and the book does not suffer through the numerous comparisons to be made with the tone and the urgency of Anne Frank's *Diary of a Young Girl.* The strain of recording the gaze of the utterly normal on the totally insane is immense, and that Anna abides her author's severe economy, telling her personal story in precisely the same cadences she employs to detail the wreck of Western culture, is no small achievement.

Auster has succeeded with Swiftian guile and ferocity in constructing a world of demolished things which we are forced, immediately and painfully, to recognize as our own. The antecedents of such fables of an intolerable present, given life by removal to another place, another time, would comprise a long and honorable list. Among these, Orwell's *Nineteen Eighty-Four,* springing from an altogether different literary tradition, is considered to be grounded in the reality of the postwar England in which he wrote it. Here, coming in from a different angle, is an oblique history chronicle of a great city "after the storm," its fall as unaccountable to its narrator as it is to us.

Phil Edwards (review date 8 April 1994)

SOURCE: "Air Head," in *New Statesman and Society,* April 8, 1994, p. 37.

[*In the following review, Edwards offers unfavorable assessment of* Mr. Vertigo.]

Since the *New York Trilogy* in 1986, Paul Auster's style has been unmistakable: erudite, laconic, minutely responsive to changes of light and mood. Auster's characters are beset by patterns and coincidences, driven by the urge to make sense of it all and become the authors of their own lives. The attempt is foredoomed, because nothing means anything: nothing matters beyond the bare fact of survival.

Auster's protagonists carry around thousands of dollars, then spend it all, lose it, gamble it away or simply forget about it. It makes no difference. Sleep rough and spend the day watching the clouds, your life will still be as valuable—will still be the same—as it ever was. When the money's gone. Auster's heroes head off into the blue again, unencumbered, aimless and alone.

Man (sic) as bare animal, condemned to pattern-making; man in search of significance, in flight from involvement. It's a distinctive but chilly way to write, something like a cross between Beckett and Hawthorne. Auster's masterpiece, *The Music of Chance,* was his last unselfconscious work in this mode. In *Leviathan,* his next novel, we saw the protagonist, with his mythic-existential-American baggage, as others see him: self-absorbed, obsessive, unreliable, the adolescent as hero.

Mr Vertigo is something else again. In 1924, aged nine, Walt Rawley is taken into the charge of the mysterious "Master Yehudi". A horrific apprenticeship follows, at the end of which Walt can levitate. "The Master" works out a stage act and takes Walt on tour; then, in 1929, comes adolescence and the loss of Walt's gift.

By then the book is almost over. Walt works for the Mob, runs a nightclub ("Mr Vertigo's"), gets drafted, comes home. A few pages later, it's 1993. Walt is now 78 and writing his memoirs; and yes, it's this book.

Auster has not written a historical novel, any more than Hawthorne did: stock situations are furnished with minimal background detail. Sadly, *Mr Vertigo* also lacks the strengths of Auster's previous work. The young Walt's dialogue is a constant outpouring of bad puns and smart answers, just the kind of linguistic jangle Auster has previously banished from his writing. What's worse, Walt tells his story straight: there are no sudden epiphanies here, no yearnings after significance.

Shorn of the intense self-consciousness of the typical Auster narrator, the book's symbolism seems laboured and arbitrary. If Walt has the same name as the founder of Virginia, so what? If Walt learns his art in the house shared with a Jew, a black and an Oglala Sioux, so what? If Walt flies through the air . . . well, so what? Walt's act is described without any of the numinous quality Auster has previously brought to the most mundane scenes. He might as well have been a tightrope walker. The jacket tells me

that this is "a profound meditation on the nature of creativity" and that it's by the author of *The New York Trilogy.* One of these claims, unfortunately, is true.

James Walton (review date 9 April 1994)

SOURCE: "Facing Fearful Odds," in *The Spectator,* April 9, 1994, pp. 28-9.

[*In the following review, Walton offers tempered assessment of* Mr. Vertigo, *noting shortcomings in the novel's "excessive writerly knowingness."*]

As the standard government comment on the economy has demonstrated over the last three years, the fact that all the elements are in place for something does not guarantee that something will materialise. In *Mr Vertigo,* all the elements are in place for a fine novel.

The book's starting point, for example, is an enticing one—though admittedly the same enticing one as that of Auster's fine and recently filmed *The Music of Chance.* In this case the two outsiders pitched together by accident—or is it fate?—are Master Yehudi, a mysterious middle-aged Hungarian émigré and Walter Rawley, a nine-year-old ragamuffin from the streets of St Louis. The Master then takes the kid off to Kansas and teaches him to fly. Having perfect aerial 'loft and locomotion', Walt the Wonder Boy is—not altogether surprisingly—the sensation of the age (the 1920s) until puberty finishes his career at the end of the decade. He becomes a gangster, a second world war soldier and a figure of Fifties' domesticity, before ending up, in elegaic mood, in the present day. There is, in short, no lack of incident, and much of it is undeniably compelling. Moreover, the decades-spanning nature of the story allows Auster to add to the fictional mix some deeper reflections on The American Century. And the whole is narrated by Walt in authentic *Billy Bathgate* baroque, with a great villain, Uncle Slim, thrown in too. So why does the promised fine novel never materialise?

The problem is the very professionalism of the whole operation. Take the book's first sentence: 'I was 12 years old the first time I walked on water.' Arresting certainly, but in a self-conscious way. This sets the pattern. Too often the novel's oddness feels like a ploy—the product, not of an author who sees life as essentially strange, but of one who has decided to adopt this perspective for his own transparent literary purposes. 'Odd' novels work best when an internal logic dictates events; here the event always seem an authorial imposition. At one point Walt confesses: 'I'm hard-pressed to explain how such a twisted notion wormed its way into my head.' In fact the explanation is obvious—the notion wormed because Auster required it to do so. Similarly, because he required the young Walt to be 'lit up with the fire of life', Auster had earlier made his illiterate nine-year-old speak with forceful erudition. 'The only brink I'm standing on is the brink of perdition,' he tells the Master during a row. The same sense of contrivance, meanwhile, infects the aforementioned deeper reflections, as Walt's progress (the crashing to earth in 1929, the careers which follow) turns out to mirror that of his country rather too neatly.

Mr Vertigo is readable enough, but Auster clearly intends, and in his earlier fiction has accomplished, much more than that. This is a novel which occasionally hovers above the ground. Excessive writerly knowingness prevents it achieving genuine loft and locomotion.

Joanna Scott (review date 31 July 1994)

SOURCE: "Levitate!," in *Los Angeles Times Book Review*, July 31, 1994, p. 2.

[*In the following review, Scott offers positive assessment of* Mr. Vertigo.]

Throughout his career as a novelist, Paul Auster has been making a fictional map of the United States, carefully pinning his characters to real places—to specific city streets, small towns and stretches of highway. In this new novel, Auster takes us to the Midwest in the 1920s and '30s, but this time his map includes a portion of the Kansas sky.

"I was 12 years old the first time I walked on water," begins the narrator of *Mr. Vertigo*. He is Walter Rawley and, though he likes an occasional wisecrack, he's telling us the truth here. "Walt the Wonder Boy," as he is nicknamed, does walk on water in this novel. He flies. He climbs up invisible staircases and over bridges that don't exist. He somersaults in midair, falls, brakes inches above the ground and floats down to earth. He is the supreme vaudevillian, a nearly flawless entertainer and his greatest act is the story he tells us, the story of his life.

Paul Auster has always been intrigued by games, and the fact that he is playing with the rules of realism in this novel seems a natural development, given his earlier sleight of hand. He's a sly realist, a writer who asks us to lose ourselves totally in the illusion of his fiction even as he exposes the artifice. This is part of the joy of reading Auster's work—his stories are absorbing, his insights jolting.

Mr. Vertigo is surely one of Auster's most absorbing tales, written in a prose that is precise, confident in its use of vernacular and sometimes smoothly lyrical, as in this description of a Kansas drought: "The air was so parched, so delirious in its desiccation, you could track the buzzing of a horsefly from a hundred yards away." Reaching from old age back through memory, Auster's narrator recounts his life, miracle by miracle, beginning in 1924, when the mysterious Master Yehudi enters Walt's life. Walt is only 9, an orphan living with a wicked uncle and an indifferent aunt. Master Yehudi offers a rather primal proposition to

young Walt. "If I haven't taught you to fly by your 13th birthday, you can chop off my head with an axe." Since Walt has no better prospects, he accepts the challenge and goes to live with Master Yehudi on a farm in rural Kansas. There he meets Mother Sue, a Sioux Indian, and Aesop, an Ethiopian boy, both of whom are indebted to Yehudi for their lives.

Walt joins this makeshift family weighted down with the burden of provincial bigotry. He identifies Mother Sue as the "Queen of the Gypsies" and Aesop as the "Prince of Blackness." It doesn't take him long to give up his prejudices, though. Walt attempts to escape Master Yehudi's harsh regimen and runs away several times. His last failed attempt ends in illness, and his recovery is marked by a vast shift in attitude. He forgets his earlier prejudices and comes to consider Aesop and Mother Sue his best friends. This improvement—too complete, too convenient, even for Auster's modern fairy tale—may be the one significant weakness of the novel. Walt gives up his dangerous bigotry as easily as an old coat, replacing it with loyalty and deep respect. The snarling, distrustful boy suddenly becomes likable, a transformation that ends up seeming more unreal than his levitations.

That complaint aside, Walt's catalogue of initiating terrors is unforgettable. In order to achieve some kind of psychic control over gravity, he must endure a variety of tortures. "I was flogged with a bullwhip; I was thrown from a galloping horse; I was lashed to the roof of the barn for two days without food or water; I had my skin smeared with honey and then stood naked in the August heat as a thousand flies and wasps swarmed over me. . . ." The list goes on. Somehow Walt manages to survive initiation. And at last, in his moment of deepest despair, he feels his body rise a few inches into the air.

With practice, Walt learns to control his flights, to turn levitation into a graceful dance. But his magical buoyancy has little consequence—it is entertainment, stupendous entertainment. Walt is no more than a boy with an amazing trick up his sleeve. His magic can't help him when the Ku Klux Klan rides in. He cowers with Yehudi behind a tree and witnesses terrors that far surpass the cruelties of his initiation.

The road has always been a useful metaphor for Auster—it is a means of escape and pursuit, as well as an image for the motion of though. Walt and Yehudi take their show on the road and escape the Klan's destruction. At the same time they head out in pursuit of fame, fighting their way into the limelight. Walt the Wonder Boy becomes a national celebrity, though only for a few short years. Levitation, it turns out, is a kind of magic that belongs only to children (and to eunuchs, Master Yehudi intimates). When Walt enters puberty, the effort of flying becomes unbearably excruciating and he is forced to abandon the show.

Walt all but abandons his singular self as well. No longer a curiosity, he becomes a type—a slick nightclub owner obsessed with guns and baseball. If Walt seems less interesting as an adult, it is not a fault of the novel. It is the fault of the culture, which offers the earthbound young man few prospects and no miraculous escape.

"Very slowly. I felt my body rise off the floor. The movement was so natural, so exquisite in its gentleness, it wasn't until I opened my eyes that I understood my limbs were touching only air," Walt says about his first levitation. But as soon as the magic is over, Walt sinks "like a stone to the bottom of the world." *Mr. Vertigo* is a thrilling flight of fancy that never abandons the world. A magical-pertinent book, it gives us a bird's-eye view of the strange, violent, paradoxical century behind us.

Stanley Kauffmann (review date 26 June 1995)

SOURCE: "Tracing Patterns," in *The New Republic,* June 26, 1995, pp. 28-9.

[*In the following review, Kauffmann offers positive assessment of the film* Smoke.]

In *My Dinner With André,* the Shawn-Gregory film of 1981, André tells Wally of his transfiguring experiences in far-off places. Wally replies:

> Why do we require a trip to Mount Everest in order to be able to perceive one moment of reality? Is Mount Everest more real than New York? Isn't New York real? I mean, I think if you could become fully aware of what existed in the cigar store next to this restaurant, it would blow your brains out.

I can't say if Paul Auster knows these lines, but they could almost serve as epigraph for his screenplay of *Smoke* (Miramax), except that a cigar store is only one of the important places in the film and, as in Auster novels, the quest is for something more than reality—it's for parareality, the mysteries that underlie dailiness.

An easy comparison for this film (as for Auster novels) is to a jigsaw puzzle: the pieces are interesting chiefly because they foretell a larger picture they will combine to form. For instance, the cigar-store owner, Auggie, tells us that, five years earlier, a young pregnant woman stopped in for something. He gave her exact change for her purchase. She left and, a minute later, was accidentally killed in a criminal shoot-out down this Brooklyn street. The tragedy crushed her husband, Paul, a novelist, who, five years later, when the film begins, has long been unable to write. Chatting with Paul, Auggie mourns the fact that he had exact change for Paul's wife that day. If only it had taken him a little bit longer to make change, if he had delayed her a few seconds. . . .

Yet—without implying that it compensates for Paul's loss—if he were not now alone, he would not have invited a vagrant black teenager to crash in his place for a few days. The invitation then creates twists that enable the

youth, Rashid, to find the long-lost father for whom he has been searching. This is only one example of the film's interweavings; and, once we get past Rashid's superficial reminders of *Six Degrees of Separation,* we see that his story and the others that it crosses are meant to dramatize a stark theme.

Patterns. All of us love patterns. Auster, in his fiction and in this screenplay, explores that love intensely. As in *The Music of Chance,* which was exquisitely filmed two years ago, Auster shows us that patterns are not divine, but man-made. We find, we insist on finding, patterns in everything: tornadoes, auto crashes, slaughters in restaurants by maniacs with Uzis. But the blunt fact is that most experience, no matter how grotesque, is sooner or later absorbed into human history; and after that happens, we retrospectively find some point in the disaster. Or, if it's a bright eventuality, we find some deep prior justification for it. Auster shows us how our penchant for pattern-making cossets us in the midst of chaos.

The director, Wayne Wang, is, we're told, in some measure responsible for the screenplay. A few years ago, Wang read a Christmas story of Auster's on the op-ed page of *The New York Times,* sought out Auster and suggested that they develop it into a screenplay. This they did, working backward from the original story, which is a wry account of how a deception made a Christmas cheerful. A theft in that story suggested a major segment of the finished film. (At the end of *Smoke* Auggie tells Paul that Christmas story. Paul doubts it. Then, under the closing credits, we see the story actually happening—in black and white.)

Wang is a Chinese-American whose first two films, *Chan is Missing* and *Dim Sum,* showed more promise than achievement. He made four subsequent pictures, of which I saw one, *The Joy Luck Club.* There's no stylistic connection between Wang's previous work, which was at best good ethnic celebration, and *Smoke,* which is crafted with subtle artistic intelligence. As Philip Haas did with the previous Auster film, Wang immediately sets a tone that seems a cinematic equivalent of the author's prose; patient, considerate, companiable yet sharp. Amused, almost, as it watches the antics of human beings.

Early on, in the cigar store, Paul tells some of the cigar store's usual crowd how smoke can be weighed. In an arch way, that story is symbolic of the film—paradoxically—because it symbolizes absolutely nothing about the film, other than mankind's hunger for symbology as for patterns. Wang treats the episode with just the right mixture of gravity and wit.

Paul, here and throughout, is simple and strong. He is played by William Hurt, bearded and surprisingly excellent. The surprise is in the way that Hurt speaks Auster's lines, without his customary ponderousness and conceit but with true thoughtfulness, keen inflection.

As Auggie, Harvey Keitel surprises, too. Instead of slicing off one more Keitel performance, saran-wrapped at the source, he looks for colors, shades, verity. Harold Perrineau plays Rashid with touching bravado, and Forest Whitaker is tremendous as his father. Stockard Channing has an easy part as a tough former girlfriend of Auggie's, but she avoids the usual clichés in playing toughies. Ashley Judd is vitriolic in her brief role as Channing's—and perhaps Auggie's—18-year-old daughter.

The story has a few glitches. (How did Rashid's aunt find out that he was staying with Paul?) But they fade in the film's generally quiet embrace. The idea of quiet means much to Auster and Wang. Instance: the reunion of Rashid and his father at a country garage. It's stormy. Paul and others struggle to part the fighting pair. Cut. All the parties are now sitting around a picnic table behind the garage. Silence. Paul offers the father one of his small cigars. The father offers Paul one of his large ones. More silence. Cut. It's delightful. It trusts us to supply the unseen and unsaid, and we enjoy doing it.

Steven E. Alford (essay date Fall 1995)

SOURCE: "Mirrors and Madness: Paul Auster's *The New York Trilogy,*" in *Critique: Studies in Contemporary Fiction,* Vol. XXXVII, No. 1, Fall, 1995, pp. 17-33.

[*In the following essay, Alford examines the identity and function of the narrator in* The New York Trilogy *and the use of shifting perspectives to juxtapose contradictory aspects of self-identity, textual meaning, and relationships between author, narrator, and reader.*]

> My true place in the world, it turned out, was somewhere beyond myself, and if that place was inside me, it was also unlocatable. This was the tiny hole between self and not-self, and for the first time in my life I saw this nowhere as the exact center of the world.
>
> —*The Locked Room*

Among the many puzzles in Paul Auster's remarkable *New York Trilogy,* a persistent one involves the identity of the narrator(s) of these novels. In answering the question, Who narrates these three stories? I will demonstrate that thematically the novels develop the problematic of self-identity. Along the way I will show how questions of identity flow into questions about textuality, and undermine the ontologically distinct categories of author, narrator, and reader. Thematically, *The New York Trilogy* argues that the self—within the novels and without—is a textual construct, and subject to the difference and deferral inherent in language. The novels enact a series of binary oppositions—between characters engaged in dramatic psychological and physical confrontation—that demonstrates the impossibility of a pure opposition between self and other. From within every conflicted doubling a triad emerges, challenging our common-sense notions of the self.

Previous scholars have examined *The New York Trilogy* from different angles. Alison Russell linked the novels to Derrida's analysis of polysemy and the problems such polysemy produces for our senses of identity and unity, and for the ability of language to refer truthfully to the world. In addition, she briefly explored the relation between *The New York Trilogy* and the romance (including the detective story), as well as noting the connection between it and travel literature. Norma Rowen's 1991 essay focused exclusively on *City of Glass,* arguing that the novel concerns the madness involved in the search for absolute knowledge, symbolized in the book (among other ways) as Peter Stillman's search for a prelapsarian language. While relying on their excellent work, I am concerned here to explore the issue of the identity of the narrator(s) of these stories.

The New York Trilogy is nominally a collection of detective stories that, within the generic constraints of detective fiction, engage in a series of self-oriented metaphysical explorations.[1] These tales could be characterized accurately as postmodern, in that they employ a pop culture form to reflect on issues more profound than "whodunit," but postmodern detective fiction did not originate the concern with metaphysical issues. Julian Symons offers some examples of metaphysical detective fiction at virtually the beginning of the genre. We can see, for example, a predecessor of Auster's Daniel Quinn-William Wilson-Max Work triad in Frederick Irving Anderson's *Adventures of the Infallible Godahl* (1914): "Godahl, a criminal who always succeeds, is the creation of a writer named Oliver Armiston. In one of the best stories the two become confused in a Borgesian manner, as Armiston is duped into using Godahl's talents to provide the means of committing an actual crime" (83). And Maurice Leblanc's Arsène Lupin poses "in the novel *813* (1910) . . . as the Chef de la Sureté for four years, and arrests himself during the investigation" (84), echoing in fiction the experiences of the real-life Vidocq, whose own *Mémoires* were thought to be largely fictional (32). These latter dramas that reveal the border between lawfulness and criminality as nonexistent echo the erasure of the borders between one self and the other that we find between Black and Blue in *Ghosts,* and between the narrator and Fanshawe in *The Locked Room.*

Closer to our own time, Dashiell Hammett's Continental Op is not innocent of a metaphysical flavor. As Steven Marcus has noted

> [The detective] actively undertakes to deconstruct, decompose, and thus demystify the fictional—and therefore false—reality created by the characters, crooks or not, with whom he is involved. . . . His major effort is to make the fictions of others visible as fictions, inventions, concealments, falsehoods, and mystifications. When a fiction becomes visible as such, it begins to dissolve and disappear, and presumably should reveal behind it the "real" reality that was there all the time and that it was masking. Yet what happens in Hammett is that what is revealed as "reality" is still a further fiction-making activity . . . Dashiell Hammett, the writer, is continually doing the same thing as the Op and all the other characters in the fiction he is creating. . . . He is making a fiction (in writing) in the real world; and this fiction, like the real world itself, is

coherent but not necessarily rational. What one both begins and ends with, then, is a story, a narrative, a coherent yet questionable account of the world. (xxi)

What Stephen Marcus is suggesting here about Hammett's text could be asserted about Auster's works as well. Unlike Hammett, however, Auster recognizes that whereas detective stories are "coherent yet questionable," the same could be said about any story about the world, including those nominally regarded as nonfictional. And given that the "real" authors of stories are themselves a part of the world, the making of the author, as well as the narrator is the making of a fiction, both inside and outside the text.[2] Hence, in Auster's work, the solution to the mystery is not the discovery of the criminal "other," but how the other is implicated in the self-constitution of the investigator. In turn, just as Lupin claims that detection involves "an identification of the reasoner's intellect with that of his opponent" (qtd. in Auster 65), the author's intellect can be identified with that of his narrator. But the connections between author, narrator, character (and the character's relation with other characters, as well as the relation between these entities and the reader) are not as simple as a string of binary associations.

The names and interrelations of the narrators of the three books of *The New York Trilogy* are complex and paradoxical. Characters' names are twinned, characters are revealed to be imaginary beings invented by other characters, characters appear in one book, only to maintain their name, but switch to another identity, in another book, and so forth. This makes for not only complexity, but outright contradiction.

CITY OF GLASS

Told in the third person by an unnamed narrator, *City of Glass* follows Daniel Quinn, who at the prompting of a wrong number, impersonates Paul Auster of the Auster Detective Agency (who seems to exist only in the imaginations of Virginia and Peter Stillman, Junior, because Quinn fails to find him). The Paul Auster Quinn does find is a Manhattan author, whose name is identical to the "real" author of *The New York Trilogy*.[3] This Paul Auster tells Quinn he is working on a book of essays, currently a piece about *Don Quixote,* concerned "with the authorship of the book. Who wrote it, and how it was written."[4]

Don Quixote claims the text was originally written in Arabic by Cid Hamete Benengeli. Chancing on it in the Toledo market, Cervantes arranged to have it translated, and then presented himself as the editor of the translation. Because Cid Hamete neither appears in the novel, nor ever claims to be present during Quixote's exploits, the character Paul Auster argues that Cid Hamete is actually a pastiche of four people—the illiterate Sancho Panza and only witness to all Quixote's adventures, the barber and the priest (who transcribed Panza's dictated story), and Samson Carrasco, the bachelor from Salamanca, who translated it into Arabic. Cervantes then discovered the book, and had it translated and published.

Why should these men go to such trouble? According to Auster, to cure Don Quixote of his madness. "The idea was to hold a mirror up to Don Quixote's madness, to record each of his absurd and ludicrous delusions, so that when he finally read the book himself, he would see the error of his ways" (118-19). But Auster adds one last twist to his argument. Don Quixote was not mad, as his friends thought. Because Quixote wonders repeatedly how accurately the chronicler will record his adventures, he must have chosen Sancho Panza and the three others to play the roles of his "saviors." In addition, Quixote probably translated the Arabic manuscript back into Spanish. That is, Cervantes hired Quixote to translate Quixote's own story.

Why, according to Auster, would anyone do anything so complex and bizarre?

> [Quixote] wanted to test the gullibility of his fellow men. Would it be possible, he wondered, to stand up before the world and with the utmost conviction spew out lies and nonsense? To say that windmills were knights, that a barber's basin was a helmet, that puppets were real people? . . . In other words, to what extent would people tolerate blasphemies if they gave them amusement? The answer is obvious, isn't it? To any extent. The proof is that we still read the book. (119-20)

As we shall see, *The New York Trilogy* holds a mirror up to our own madness—the assumption of our hermetic individuality.

City of Glass is told in the third person. However, after the bulk of the novel is rendered in the third person, the final two pages shift to the first person, when the narrator returns from a trip to Africa and calls his friend, the writer Paul Auster. Auster has become obsessed with Quinn (who himself was obsessed with the Stillmans), but has lost track of him, and also cannot find Virginia Stillman. Auster and the narrator visit Virginia Stillman's apartment, where Auster finds Quinn's red notebook and gives it to the narrator for safekeeping. The narrator then confesses that he has followed the red notebook as closely as possible in telling his story and has "refrained from any interpretation" (158).

Like "editors" of previous fictions (*The Sorrows of Young Werther* and *Notes from Underground,* for example), the confident professions of editorial thoroughness and sincerity lack foundation. The narrator has never met Quinn, the subject of his story, and has only two sources of information about him, Auster and the red notebook. Auster's knowledge of his narrator, Quinn, actually emerges only from Quinn's account, because the only time he and Auster met was in Auster's apartment (and Quinn's account to Auster may or may not have been distorted). Hence, the narrator's only two sources are the hearsay of Auster and a text, Quinn's notebook. The narrator has no direct experience of or information about the story he tells.[5]

Returning to the account of Quixote by the character Auster, we can observe some parallels.[6] If we were to say provisionally that the narrator is {Paul Auster} (bracketing, for now, his ontological status),[7] we could say that the story {Auster} tells has been invented for him by some concerned friends, presumably a real-life Quinn (who would parallel Sancho Panza) and the Stillmans (who would parallel the other three friends). Presumably, {Auster} has been having difficulty with his sanity, and his friends have concocted *City of Glass* to hold up a mirror to his madness. However, continuing to follow the lines of the Quixote argument, we could argue as well that {Auster} has engineered the entire enterprise and chosen Quinn and the Stillmans as his "saviors," so that he could spew out lies and nonsense for people's amusement. Hence, Paul Auster, the writer in *City of Glass,* is a character invented by {Paul Auster}, narrator, the same way that the character "Don Quixote" was engineered by Don Quixote.

Of course, Don Quixote never existed, but was invented by Miguel de Cervantes Saavedra of Spain. By association, {Paul Auster} never existed, but was an invention of the "real" Paul Auster, of Manhattan.[8] Hence, we have three Austers, not two: author, narrator, and character, each ontologically distinct.

The twinning has uncovered a triad, which has its corollary in *City of Glass.* Daniel Quinn, detective fiction writer, had taken on the pseudonym of William Wilson. "William Wilson, after all, was an invention, and even though he had been born within Quinn himself, he now led an independent life. Quinn treated him with deference, at times even admiration, but he never went so far as to believe that he and William Wilson were the same man" (5). "William Wilson" has authored a series of books featuring a private-eye narrator, Max Work. "Whereas William Wilson remained an abstract figure for [Quinn], Work had increasingly come to life. In the triad of selves that Quinn had become, Wilson served as a kind of ventriloquist, Quinn himself was the dummy, and Work was the animated voice that gave purpose to the enterprise" (6).

Note the surprising role assignment in this conceit. Ordinarily, we would consider Quinn the ventriloquist, Wilson the dummy, and the words of the dummy Work's story. As the audience, we would then attend to the dummy's words, failing to notice Quinn moving his lips, owing to our absorption in the tale. By this account, however, *Wilson* is the ventriloquist and Quinn is the dummy. This textual analogy suggests that Quinn exists only insofar as the words he invents give him life.

To tell the story that is *City of Glass,* {Auster's} only sources are a text and one person's second-hand account. But, in terms of self-knowledge, what does Paul Auster, author, have to go on? In his daily life, Paul Auster tells himself stories about himself (as we all do, by engaging in interior dialogue), and others tell him stories about himself. He creates a text (whether it be *The New York Trilogy* or his other works) and through that text gains self-

knowledge. But what kind of knowledge of self can one acquire by inventing stories, which are, by definition, untrue?

Auster's trilogy dramatizes the assertion that the self can gain knowledge only through language because, in a strict sense, the self is language. Anthony Paul Kerby argues that other views of the self, such as the Cartesian, originate in three fundamental misconceptions: (a) "that there is a doer before the deed," that the "I" causes narration, rather than being implied by it; (b) that intentions or thoughts exist prior to their linguistic expression; and (c) that "language has a certain neutrality or transparency with respect to what is expressed" (65). On the contrary, "the self is a social and linguistic construct, a nexus of meaning rather than an unchanging entity" (34). One further misconception should be mentioned: that our originary experience of the world occurs in perception. Although no one would question that we do have extra-linguistic bodily experiences involving perception and sensation, the self, in its genesis and self-understanding, is a construct.[9]

In the wake of Benveniste and Michel Foucault, such an insight may approach a commonplace. However, when we ally the notion of the linguistically constructed self with the Saussurean/Derridian notion of language as a differing/deferring process, the real drama begins. Two problems with self-knowledge arise.

First, if the self is a text, and if text's knowability is endlessly deferred, referring within the cognitive process only to other texts (be they physical texts or other selves), then "true" self-knowledge is impossible. We understand our self as the locus of our identity by telling ourselves stories, yet these stories' criterion of correctness is not truth, but what we might call the adequacy of a meaningful narrative sequence. Kerby explains, "this identity . . . is not the persistence of an entity, a thing (a substance, subject, ego), but is a meaning constituted by a relation of figure to ground or part to whole. It is an identity in difference constituted by framing the flux of particular experiences by a broader story" (46).

Second, we should recognize also that once truth is abandoned as the transcendental criterion of self-knowledge, we find ourselves in a vertiginous intellectual space in which the distinction between narrative and its traditional certifying element (truth, whether that term be understood as a Kantian *adequatio* or in some other sense) collapses. In practical terms, if I assert that "true" self-knowledge is impossible, what is the guarantor of the truth of *that* statement? In discussing Lyotard, Lacoue-Labarthe, and Foucault, Linda Hutcheon recognizes the implicit paradox of such a position. "These [positions] are typically paradoxical; they are the masterful denials of mastery, the cohesive attacks on cohesion, the essentializing challenges to essences, that characterize postmodern theory" (20). Hence, we must proceed to the next step of the argument fully conscious of the paradox involved: *I* am asserting the truth of an argument that assumes the unavailability of a truth-based certification.

Each of Auster's stories features a character who awakens to the ongoing deferral of the possibility of self-knowledge. {Auster} cites Baudelaire: "Wherever I am not is the place where I am myself" (132). In *The Locked Room,* the narrator suggests

> We all want to be told stories, and we listen to them in the same way we did when we were young. We imagine the real story inside the words, and to do this we substitute ourselves for the person in the story, pretending that we can understand him because we understand ourselves. This is a deception. We exist for ourselves, perhaps, and at times we even have a glimmer of who we are, but in the end we can never be sure, and as our lives go on, we become more and more opaque to ourselves, more and more aware of our own incoherence. No one can cross the boundary into another—for the simple reason that no one can gain access to himself. (292)

The particular contribution of *The New York Trilogy* is that in each story, we see the realization of the "substance-lessness" of the self in its psychological dimension.[10] The characters and narrators of these stories respond to their evolving insight into the "nature" of their selves with fear, violence, and despair. Self-knowledge becomes a narrative agon, a contest in which there can be no declared winner. Or, to put it another way, the loser is whoever quits writing first.

One of the more interesting scenes in *City of Glass* has already been alluded to, wherein {Auster} and Auster visit the Stillman's apartment, only to find that Quinn has disappeared. Where is he? Alison Russell notes: "In *City of Glass,* characters 'die' when their signifiers are omitted from the printed page" (75). Quinn has "died" because he filled up his red notebook with signifiers. When he came to the last page, *he* himself came to an end.

GHOSTS

Within the free realm of imaginative invention, an author's characters can, of course, do anything the author wants, including violating laws of logic and nature, in particular those involving paradox and identity. Also, they can easily breach ontological categories, as has already been shown with the three Paul Austers. These thematic threads run through this trilogy. However, what does the quandary of identity the characters experience imply for Paul Auster, the author of *The New York Trilogy* (or any writer, for that matter)? His work suggests that no clear dividing line exists between the characters' predicament and his own, that he is beset by the same paradoxical problems of identity in his "real" life. As Blue says in *Ghosts,* "Writing is a solitary business. It takes over your life. In some sense, a writer has no life of his own. Even when he's there, he's not really there" (209). As we shall see, these problems will emerge for the readers of his texts as well.

In *Ghosts,* a certain detective Blue is hired by White to shadow Black.[11] The narrator says the location is unimportant, "let's say Brooklyn Heights, for the sake of argument. Some quiet, rarely traveled street not far from the bridge—Orange Street perhaps" (163). Blue moves into the third floor of a four-story brownstone to shadow Black, who lives in a third-floor apartment opposite. Blue is a detective self-conscious about his social role. He reads *True Detective* and *Stranger Than Fiction* with devotion. Owing to a peculiarity of his client, White, Blue is consigned to remain in his room and write weekly reports, which he mails to White. Observing Black, Blue notes that Black is composing a manuscript. Hence, Blue spends his days writing a report about someone who spends his days writing.[12]

For Blue, things are not going well:

> He feels like a man who has been condemned to sit in a room and go on reading a book for the rest of his life. This is strange enough—to be only half alive at best, seeing the world only through words, living only through the lives of others. But if the book were an interesting one, perhaps it wouldn't be so bad. He could get caught up in the story, so to speak, and little by lit the begin to forget himself. But this book offers him nothing. There is no story, no plot, no action—nothing but a man sitting alone in a room and writing a book. That's all there is, Blue realizes, and he no longer wants any part of it. But how to get out? How to get out of the room that is the book that will go on being written for as long as he stays in the room? (202)

A series of events complicate Blue's life. He discovers his fiancee is seeing another man. He tries to meet White in the post office, but White eludes him. Black continues to scribble. Blue's anxiety mounts. "It seems perfectly plausible to him that he is also being watched, observed by another in the same way that he has been observing Black. If that is the case, then he has never been free. From the very start he has been the man in the middle, thwarted in front and hemmed in on the rear" (200). Like Quinn, the dummy, whose words were generated by the ventriloquist, his narrator, William Wilson, Blue's words are being generated by the person controlling him, but that person is neither himself, nor White, but Black. From the twinning of Blue and Black, Blue has uncovered a triad, one beyond his control.

Like Quinn, who in his three meetings with Peter Stillman, Senior, adopted the "disguises of Quinn, Henry Dark, and Peter Stillman, Junior" (88, 95, 100), Blue adopts a series of disguises to get closer to his quarry, Black.[13] Like Quinn, who visits Paul Auster, Blue gathers the courage to take the next, "inevitable" step and confront Black directly in his apartment. The narrator notes, "To enter Black, then, was the equivalent of entering himself, and once inside himself, he can no longer conceive of being anywhere else. But this is precisely where Black is, even though Blue does not know it" (88).

Black is not home, and Blue steals the papers on Black's desk before returning to his apartment. With a creeping sense of horror, Blue reads Black's papers, recognizing that they are nothing more than Blue's own reports to White. Blue is both scared of and angry with Black because he thinks that Black has somehow stolen his freedom and autonomy. The narrator comments, "For Blue at this point can no longer accept Black's existence, and therefore he denies it" (226).

Blue's error is an intellectual one with emotional consequences. As an individual, he thought he possessed the freedom one ordinarily ascribes to individuals. As a detective, as a type of private contractor, he thought he independently took the job of shadowing Black, and in a sense he did. But he now realizes that his metaphysical assumptions about his freedom, both personal and professional, were wrong. He responds with fear and projected anger. He denies Black's existence. What he doesn't understand is that "autonomy, freedom, and identity . . . are not pregiven or a priori characteristics but must be redefined within the context of the person's appearance within the sociolinguistic arena" (Kerby 113-14).

In his analysis of Derrida, Kerby further suggests that

> If auto-affection is the possibility of subjectivity, this subjectivity finds its release, its expression of itself, in acts of signification. The feeling of subjectivity that we have more or less continually, . . . is quite simply the possibility of signification, of expression, what might be called *vouloir dire* or a wanting and being able, in most cases, to say or express. But this subjectivity does not know itself outside the fulfillment of its desire to express. (77)

Blue's selfhood emerges as his Self in his "reports." But the reports themselves are not a discrete product of an autonomous, isolated self; they emerge as even feasible only through the possibility of the other's existence. In denying Black's existence, Blue is denying his own.[14] For, "One cannot become 'I' without an implicit reference to another person, an auditor or narratee—which may be the same subject qua listener. 'I' functions in contrast to 'you' in much the same way as 'here' refers linguistically to 'there' rather than any fixed location" (Kerby 68). Hence, Blue's freedom, a consequence of his self-understanding, is contingent on Black's existence.

A further level of Blue's misunderstanding involves his notion of the "job," namely that one begins a job, carries it to an end, and moves on to the next. He assumes that the persistent element linking one job to the other is his ongoing, Cartesian self, one which remains apart and exempt from whatever "case" he is under contract to pursue, in this instance, Black. Blue is, in this sense, denying the historical and hermeneutical dimension of self-constitution. "Interpretation, like understanding, is a continuous process with no precise starting point. . . . interpretation has always already started" (Kerby 44). Blue denies this "always-already" underway aspect of self-understanding and, when he sees himself mirrored in Black (or more precisely, mirrored in Black's text), he responds violently.

Blue enters Black's apartment, and Black awaits him, masked and armed with a revolver.[15] Blue disarms Black and attacks him, rendering him unconscious, possibly dead.

Blue muses, "There seems to be something [breathing], but he can't tell if it's coming from Black or himself" (231). Blue returns to his apartment with Black's manuscript, reads it, and leaves. The narrator explains, "For now is the moment that Blue stands up from his chair, puts on his hat, and walks through the door. And from this moment on, we know nothing" (232).

Quinn ceased to exist when he completed the red notebook. Blue ceased to exist when he completed reading Black's manuscript, which, we are told, Blue already knew by heart. When the words of the other ceased, the self ceased to exist. In Quinn's case his other was himself, which he masked from himself by filling his red notebook with observations about Stillman. In Blue's case his other was himself, which he masked from himself by filling his pages with observations about Black.

Who narrated *Ghosts?* I adduced the identity of the narrator in *City of Glass* from the story of Don Quixote. However, ferreting out the narrator of *Ghosts* is complicated by the difference in narrative time between the two books. *City of Glass* occurs in the narrative present and, based on copyright and publication information, we can date the narrative present of that book as the mid-eighties.[16] *Ghosts,* on the other hand, occurs approximately thirty-five to forty years before *City of Glass,* beginning on 3 February 1947, with the action continuing through midsummer of 1948 (203).[17] Based on the evidence in *City of Glass,* Daniel Quinn and {Auster}, the narrator, are approximately the same age, and Quinn's age is given as thirty-five (3). Hence, {Auster} would have been born around the beginning of the narrative time of *Ghosts.*

Scouting ahead a bit, however, I note that the first-person narrator of *The Locked Room* talks about having written both *City of Glass* and *Ghosts* (346). Neither horn of this dilemma yields much satisfaction if we consider the world(s) of these stories to be governed by empirical laws. If {Auster} narrated both books, then he is either approximately thirty-five-years-old in *City of Glass,* or a new born infant in *Ghosts.* Both contradictory possibilities have equal textual evidence. But let us consider the passage in *The Locked Room* immediately following his admission that he wrote *City of Glass* and *Ghosts:* "These three stories are finally the same story, but each one represents a different state in my awareness of what it is about" (346). Given the paradox, given the imaginative arbitrariness of proper name and geographic place assignments in *Ghosts* (everyone's name is a color; the narrator confesses the place names originate in narrative convenience), it seems reasonable to assume that the narrator of *Ghosts* is {Auster}, who is establishing for himself an imaginative narrative space around the time of his birth. This allows him to metaphorically explore the complex issues of the relation of selfhood to language, but not as a self-reflecting, on-its-own constitution (as in *City of Glass*), but as one reflecting on its origin.

Further support for this position can be gleaned from the final paragraph, where a series of curious semantic shifts occur. The paragraph is worth quoting in full.

Where [Blue] goes after that is not important. For we must remember that all this took place more than thirty years ago, back in the days of our earliest childhood. Anything is possible, therefore. I myself prefer to think that he went far away, boarding a train that morning and going out West to start a new life. It is even possible that America was not the end of it. In my secret dreams, I like to think of Blue booking passage on some ship and sailing to China. Let it be China, then, and we'll leave it at that. For now is the moment that Blue stands up from his chair, puts on his hat, and walks through the door. And from this moment on, we know nothing. (232)

Ghosts began in third person omniscient. Like *City of Glass,* it closes with a shift into first person. But unlike *City of Glass,* the narrator does not assume the role of another (albeit unnamed) character. Instead, the reader is included along with the author, using the first person plural: we must remember, *our* earliest childhood.

At this point it becomes clear that the search for a narrator, the search itself, has been swallowed up into the anti-metaphysical[18] (or metaphysical detective) terms of the novel(s). Just as Blue could not be Blue without including within himself Black, the narrator cannot exist without our inclusion into him, and he into us. "For in spying out at Black across the street, it is as though Blue were looking into a mirror, and instead of merely watching another, he finds that he is also watching himself" (20). Paul Auster, author, establishes the sense of his identity by projecting himself into the narrator, {Auster}, and holding the textual mirror up to himself. With *Ghosts,* we can now understand that the identity of the narrator lies in that ontologically indistinct realm of textuality, a linguistic black hole in which our common sense understanding of the proper separation of ontologically discrete categories—fiction, history, speculation, the empirical world of common, personal identity, as well as the conventional distinctions between author, narrator, and character—collapses. So, to answer the question of who narrates *Ghosts,* we can reply: you, me, and Paul Auster, all of whom are elided into an entity known, for the convenience of the narrative, as the narrator, or in our (!) terms, {Auster}.[19]

THE LOCKED ROOM

We can answer the question about the narrator's identity in *The Locked Room* right away. He is {Auster}, narrator of *City of Glass* and *Ghosts,* so long as we understand both the terms "narrator" and "author" as standing for what we might call a locus of textual space, one which nominally includes you, me, and Paul Auster, author. (Note that in the course of our discussion, this additional triad has been spawned.)[20] We would do well to investigate this pattern of triads emerging from binary oppositions, wherein the self and other confrontation engenders a third entity.

Narrated in first person, *The Locked Room* opens in May 1984, with the disappearance of {Auster's} childhood friend, Fanshawe. {Auster} is summoned by Sophie, Fanshawe's wife, and he learns that Fanshawe has named {Auster} executor of his unpublished literary works, in the instance of Fanshawe's death or disappearance. He accepts the job and arranges for Fanshawe's works to be published with a calculated schedule of publication that, following wide acceptance of Fanshawe's first novel, engenders both Fanshawe's literary fame, and fortune for both Sophie and {Auster}. {Auster} and Sophie fall in love, and he moves in with her and her child by Fanshawe. Fanshawe's works make {Auster} and Sophie rich, and all seems to be going well until {Auster} receives a letter from Fanshawe, thanking him for his help and claiming that Fanshawe will never contact him again.

{Auster} is intrigued, but more so when he contracts to write Fanshawe's biography. He gains access to Fanshawe's childhood works from Fanshawe's mother, with whom he begins an affair. At this point, for {Auster}, "everything had been reduced to a single impulse: to find Fanshawe, to speak to Fanshawe, to confront Fanshawe one last time" (317). He is confused: he wants to kill Fanshawe; he wants Fanshawe to kill him; he wants to find Fanshawe and then walk away from him.

Fanshawe's trail leads to France, and {Auster} locates him in a Paris bar. Confronting him, however, Fanshawe says, "My name isn't Fanshawe. It's Stillman. Peter Stillman" (349). Fanshawe/Stillman leaves the bar and {Auster} follows him. They have a bloody fight and Fanshawe/Stillman wins.

Three years pass. Sophie and {Auster} have a child, Paul. In the spring of 1982, {Auster} receives a letter from Fanshawe, saying they must meet in Boston.

Fanshawe, armed behind a door, confronts {Auster}. At this point, a blizzard of twinning occurs: like Stillman, Fanshawe claims to have been followed by a detective, Quinn; like Black, he says he traveled in the West; like Quinn, he claims to have camped outside Sophie's apartment for months, observing Sophie, {Auster}, and the child; Fanshawe uses the name Henry Dark in his travels, and so forth. Fanshawe has lured {Auster} to give him an explanation of why he left; and there {Auster} picks up a red notebook, filled with text. Back in the New York train station, {Auster} reads the notebook.

> All the words were familiar to me, and yet they seemed to have been put together strangely, as though their final purpose was to cancel each other out. I can think of no other way to express it. Each sentence erased the sentence before it, each paragraph made the next paragraph impossible. It is odd, then, that the feeling that survives from this notebook is one of great lucidity. . . . I came to the last page just as the train was pulling out. (370-71)

In her discussion of the postmodern novel, Linda Hutcheon has argued that the self-other opposition is what we could call a modernist moment along the way to postmodernism, a way-station through which our thought must pass (and conceivably return) in our understanding of postmodern texts. She writes, "The modernist concept of a single and alienated otherness is challenged by the postmodern questioning of binaries that conceal hierarchies (self/other)" (61). Instead of binary oppositions, she suggests it is more useful to think of *difference,* and the chaining movement of signifiers (originating in Saussure's insights and developed further by Derrida) that describes not only the movement of meaning-constitution within language, but self-constitution as well. "Difference suggests multiplicity, heterogeneity, plurality, rather than binary opposition and exclusion" (61).

Whenever a binary, self-other opposition is erected (as is the case in *The New York Trilogy*), it establishes a hierarchy that is both arbitrary and illusory. When Blue imagines his control of his case, or when {Auster} asserts control over Fanshawe through the decision to write his biography, both characters employ the self-other opposition and privilege the self as the controlling origin of the "job" (surveillance, writing) and of the discourse that constitutes the larger tale. Along the way, however, confidence in their autonomy is undermined, and they increasingly see themselves as being controlled and, ultimately, constituted as themselves by the other. This second movement, then privileges the other, rather than the self. The consequence is projected anger and violence: Blue assaults Black; {Auster} assaults Fanshawe/Stillman, and {Auster} wants to engage in some sort of violence toward Fanshawe near the end of the novel, although his confusion renders his exact aim unclear.[21]

The final pages of *The Locked Room* embody these arguments. The character Fanshawe evolves from his oppositionary role as {Auster's} other into an "Everycharacter," wherein his own experiences suggest that he is the "same" character as Quinn, Stillman, Blue, Black, and Henry Dark.[22] {Auster}, standing on the train station platform, realizes that in the end, there is text, and only text, and that each text (or, in this case, sentence, or paragraph) cancels out the previous one, establishing not the truth of identity, whether that be one's self-identity or the identity of the other, but simply another text, an experiential description of the differing/deferring movement of language.

I suggested earlier that our identity, far from originating within a soul or mind, has its origin in text. But if, "reality only exists in function of the discourse that articulates it" (Thiher 27), our attempts at truth-making are doomed to irrelevance. Instead we are left with the adequacy of a meaningful narrative sequence.[23] In discussing Nabokov, Allen Thiher argues,

> Freud appears to be a quintessential modernist insofar as the unconscious, with its storehouse of time past, can be compared to the modernist domain of revelation, waiting to be seized in the form of iconic symbols. By contrast Nabokov's self-conscious play with ironic doubles exults in the arbitrary relations that obtain between signs. There is, for Nabokov, no other discourse than this manifest play of autonomous language. There is nothing beneath this verbal surface. The novel's surface is all that the novel is: a self-enclosed structure of self-mirrorings, offered as so

many language games, with only an occasional catastrophe to recall the void that waits on the other side. (100)

This description could well be applied to Paul Auster's *New York Trilogy.*

Hence, in Auster's work we have moved from the modernist, alienated fiction of the other, exemplified in Hammett and others of the hard-boiled school, to a postmodern fiction of difference.[24] In Michael Huhn's discussion of the hard-boiled novel, he argues that the contest between detective and criminal is one for control over interpretation of the clues, a control over the text that defines the reality of their linked situation:

> The main difficulty of the reading process is occasioned by the criminal's attempts to prevent the detective from deciphering the true meaning of his text. This is, basically, a contest between an author and a reader about the possession of meaning, each of them wishing to secure it for himself. (The contest within the novel is repeated on a higher level between the novelist and the actual reader.) (456)

The detectives and searchers in Auster's fiction, by contrast, realize that possession of meaning invariably lies in becoming one with the other, the object of their surveillance or search. What they do not realize, and what carries the main thematic weight of these texts, is that they have failed to take the next step, the movement from the violent confrontation of the self-other to the realization that both figure in a larger whole, that of a set of texts, whose shifting relations of difference and deferral form what we know as the world.

Having reached the end, let us return to the beginning, and the story of Don Quixote. Cervantes wrote a novel narrated by Cid Hamete Benengeli about Don Quixote, which is read by you and me. Because Cid Hamete is ultimately a "fiction," we understand that only Cervantes is "real." However, {Auster} argues that Quixote wrote a novel narrated by his friends about Quixote, which is read by you and me. {Auster's} argument suggests that Cervantes is generated by the text as much as the characters and that ultimately, he *is* Quixote. If this argument is itself a meaningful narrative sequence, then the readers of Quixote are themselves Quixote, insofar as their self-constitution is implicated in the texts they read. *The New York Trilogy* is a work written by Paul Auster, narrated by {Paul Auster} about, among other characters, Paul Auster, which is read by you and me. If this analysis of *The New York Trilogy* parallels that of {Auster's} of Quixote, then we can close best by echoing the words of {Auster's} child, Daniel: "Goodbye, myself!"

Notes

1. As Michael Holquist notes, the term "metaphysical detective story" was coined by Howard Haycraft in his 1941 book, *Murder for Pleasure,* to describe G. K. Chesterton's work. (Holquist 154, n.8)

2. Paul Auster (the real Paul Auster) has been a student of Jean Paul Sartre's works and translated Sartre's

Life/Positions. We owe to Sartre's *The Transcendence of the Ego* the notion that "there is no ego 'in' or 'behind' consciousness. There is only an ego *for* consciousness. The ego is 'out there,' in the world, an object among objects. . . . consciousness is a great emptiness, a wind blowing toward objects. Its whole reality is exhausted in intending what is other. It is never 'self-contained,' or container; it is always 'outside itself'" (Williams and Kirkpatrick 22). What distinguishes Sartre and Auster in this respect is Auster's focus on language as constitutive of the self and world, and the rendering problematic of any notion of an originary intentionality, a la Husserl, Auster rejects the autonomy of consciousness Sartre so ardently defends (in *The Transcendence of the Ego*), and places in between self and world (or other) language. This interposition problematizes the notion of self-knowledge, because if everything is text, the notion of autonomy (which would ground self-knowledge) is suspect.

3. Of course, the author featuring himself as a character is not new, and is an almost *de rigueur* trope for postmodern fiction. In this context, Auster is echoing Cervantes, in which a certain Saavedra is featured in the Captive story (1:42), as Robert Alter notes (17). Note also Alter's comments about Cervantes' Brechtean impulse: ". . . Cervantes' principal means for [drawing the reader into the narrative and then wrenching him away] is to split himself off into a fictional alter ego, the Moorish chronicler who is supposedly the true author of the history; Don Quixote himself is another kind of surrogate for the novelist, being prominent among the characters of the novel as an author manqué, who is impelled to act out the literary impulse in the world of deeds, to be at once the creator and protagonist of his own fictions" (21).

4. Paul Auster, *The New York Trilogy: City of Glass, Ghosts, The Locked Room* (New York: Penguin, 1985-86), 116. All subsequent references will be to this combined edition of the novels.

5. Alison Russell's comment on the narrator of *The Locked Room* is interesting in this context. "Unlike Quinn and Blue, the narrator of *The Locked Room* has access only to the language, the signifiers, of his counterpart, never to his physical presence" (79-80). In fact, Quinn, as this sentence seems to imply, doesn't narrate *City of Glass*. The unnamed narrator, who is, as I will suggest {Paul Auster}, has no direct access to the character whose story he tells either.

6. Here I would disagree with Alison Russell, when she says that "This [Quxitoean] analysis, when applied to *City of Glass*, raises a number of questions about the book's authorship, and results in endless doublings and mirror images" (74). As I hope to demonstrate, the linguistic quandaries the characters experience imply a notion of selfhood in

which the possibility for self-knowledge is endlessly deferred, the doublings and mirror images are themselves not "endless." One can take the Quixote model and apply it to *City of Glass* (and other texts-within-the-text as well, such as the film *Out of the Past,* featured in *Ghosts*) without the danger of an argumentative mise-en-abyme.

7. In subsequent references to the narrator, Paul Auster, I will adopt the convention of referring to him as {Auster}, to distinguish him from Paul Auster, author, and Paul Auster, character.

8. As Robert Alter notes, however. "If the Quixote calls into question the status of fictions and of itself as a fiction, it also affirms a new sense of the autonomy of the artist who has conceived it" (15). As we shall see, *The New York Trilogy,* far from affirming the autonomy of the artist, calls into question his very selfhood: its origin, constitution, and capacity for originary linguistic intentionality.

9. "Perception" can be understood here in two senses, in the scientific, biological sense of the activity of light on the eye, optic nerve, and brain; and in the phenomenological sense of that which is present to consciousness. The problems with grounding experience in biological perception are well known. The problems with phenomenology have been amply examined by Jacques Derrida, in his critique of presence. In this context, the problem with phenomenology's account is phenomenology's grounding of the investigation into Dasein's being in consciousness's (presumed) interiority.

10. If we follow the lessons of the text, we would have to abandon the notion of psychology as the investigation of some "interior," dimension of a single human subject, and instead focus on how self-construction occurs in the public, narrative arena in which selves, both those of the "individual" and "others," are constructed.

11. The studied arbitrariness of these names is emphasized in *The Locked Room,* when the narrator describes his experiences as a census taker involved in inventing families to fulfill his quota. "When my imagination flagged, there were certain mechanical devices to fall back on: the colors (Brown, White, Black, Green, Gray, Blue)" (Auster 294).

12. Russell notes the continuity among the three stories: "Daniel Quinn is a writer turned detective, Blue a detective turned writer, and the narrator of *The Locked Room* a writer turned detective" (79).

13. The similarity between Quinn and Blue is highlighted by detail: when {Auster} opens the door to Quinn. Quinn finds "In his right hand, fixed between his thumb and first two fingers, he held an uncapped fountain pen, still poised in a writing position" (Auster 111). When Blue, in his Fuller Brush Man disguise, visits Black, Black is "standing

in a doorway with an uncapped fountain pen in his right hand, as though interrupted in his work" (Auster 218).

14. In their final confrontation, Black says to Blue. "I've needed you from the beginning . . . to remind me of what I was supposed to be doing. . . . At least I know what I've been doing. I've had my job to do, and I've done it. But you're nowhere, Blue. You've been lost from the first day" (Auster 230).

15. This mask is the same one "White" wore in the post office when Blue attempted to confront him, suggesting either that White and Black are the same person, or that White has given his mask to Black to wear. In either case, Blue's paranoia is justified.

16. Internal evidence, such as Mookie Wilson's tenure on the New York Mets, also supports this assumption.

17. Having spent this much time on the Trilogy, I have reason to believe that 3 February 1947 is author Paul Auster's birthdate.

18. As we will see below, preceding a term with "anti" establishes a binary opposition that, within the developing argument, is illegitimate.

19. We should keep in mind, however, that such insights are not equivalent to claims such as "People qua people are merely the consequence of a grammatical reference *simpliciter,*" or "The World is a fiction," or "Everything is a text." Fiction qua fiction relies for its understanding on the distinction, however imprecise, between "reality" and "fiction". To conflate this important distinction into a comprehensive claim about the fictionality of persons or "reality" would be to empty the term of any meaning. For a traditional and common sense discussion of such issues, see Crittenden 158-174.

20. Like the binary oppositions, the number and type of triads are dizzying, but here are a few to support the idea. *City of Glass*—Quinn talks about the three senses of the term "eye," in "private eye": "investigator" "I" and "physical eye of the writer." Quinn had a triad of selves: Quinn, Wilson, and Work. Stillman, Senior, had a wife and child; Quinn had a wife and child; and Auster, the character, has a wife and child. In Peter Stillman's book, *The Garden and the Tower: Early Visions of the New World,* he refers to the builders of the Tower of Babel: those who wanted to dwell in heaven, those who wanted to wage war against God, and those who wanted to worship idols. Paul Auster occurs as author, narrator, and character. Quinn has three meetings with Stillman: where Quinn is Quinn. Henry Dark, and Peter Stillman, Junior. *Ghosts*—The three primary characters are White, Blue, and Black. Among the three books Black recurs as Walter J. Black, editor of *Walden,* black Jackie Robinson, and Black as an arbitrary name. Mr. White occurs in all three books, under differing

auspices. Mr. Green occurs in *City of Glass;* and, in *The Locked Room,* two characters are called Green: Stuart Green, editor, and Roger Green, Stuart's brother and the narrator's friend. Columbus is mentioned in Peter Stillman's book, and New York's Columbus Square serves as a meeting place in *Ghosts,* as does Boston's Columbus Square in *The Locked Room.* In this inquiry I have uncovered two sets of three: first, Paul Auster, author; the narrator {Auster}, and the reader of the Trilogy. Second, myself as the author of this, article, the text, and you, the reader. I'm confident more can be uncovered.

21. In that final confrontation in *The Locked Room,* Fanshawe himself (or someone we assume is Fanshawe, hidden behind a door) threatens violence, again either toward {Auster} or toward himself if {Auster} does not do his bidding.

22. We learn in *City of Glass* that Henry Dark wasn't a "real" person anyway, but one imagined by Peter Stillman, Senior, for the purposes of his argument.

23. As Hutcheon observes, "Narrative is what translates knowing into telling, and it is precisely this translation that obsesses postmodern fiction" (121).

24. See Hutcheon, 62.

Works Cited

Alter, Robert. *Partial Magic: The Novel as a Self-Conscious Genre.* Berkeley: U of California P. 1975.

Auster, Paul. *The New York Trilogy City of Glass, Ghosts, The Locked Room.* New York: Penguin, 1985, 1986.

Crittenden, Charles. *Unreality: The Metaphysics of Fictional Objects.* Ithaca, N. Y.: Cornell UP, 1991.

Holquist, Michael. "Whodunit and Other Questions: Metaphysical Detective Stories in Post-War Fiction." *New Literary History* 3 (1971): 135-56.

Huhn, Peter. "The Detective as Reader: Narrativity and Reading Concepts in Detective Fiction." *Modern Fiction Studies* 33 (1987): 451-56.

Hutcheon, Linda. *A Poetics of Postmodernism: History, Theory, Fiction.* New York: Routledge, 1988.

Kerby, Anthony Paul. *Narrative and the Self.* Bloomington: Indiana UP, 1991.

Marcus, Steven. Introduction. *The Continental Op.* By Dashiell Hammett. Ed. Steven Marcus. New York: Vintage Books. 1974. vii-xxix.

Rowen, Norma. "The Detective in Search of the Long Tongue of Ariel: Paul Auster's City of Glass." *Critique* 32 (1991): 224-35.

Russell, Alison. "Deconstructing The New York Trilogy: Paul Auster's Anti-Detective Fiction." *Critique* 31 (1990): 71-84.

Symons, Julian. *Bloody Murder: From Detective Story to the Crime Novel.* London: Faber & Faber, 1972.

Thiher, Allen. *Words in Reflection: Modern Language Theory and Postmodern Fiction.* Chicago: U Chicago P, 1984.

Williams, Forrest, and Robert Kirkpatrick. Introduction. *The Transcendence of the Ego: An Existentialist Theory of Consciousness.* By Jean-Paul Sartre. Tr. Forrest Williams and Robert Kirkpatrick. New York: Farrar, 1987. 11-27.

Toby Mundy (review date 14 November 1997)

SOURCE: "What's the Point?," in *New Statesman,* November 14, 1997, pp. 54-5.

[*In the following review, Mundy offers unfavorable assessment of* Hand to Mouth.]

"We're talking about your life," proclaims a character in Paul Auster's first novel, *Squeeze Play.* "There's nothing more important than that."

Hand to Mouth left me with the uneasy feeling that it would have been more enjoyable if I'd shared the speaker's selfless priorities. The book is outwardly about Auster's attempts to become a writer and the travails he suffered in realising this cherished ambition. It concludes with three huge appendices: the first reproduces three sub-Beckettian dramas written by the young Auster; the second comprises colour plates of a card game that he was unable to exploit commercially; the third gives us *Squeeze Play,* a modestly impressive hard-boiled detective novel. After *The Red Notebook* and *Groundwork,* this is Auster's third consecutive collection of his juvenilia.

Indeed it is so crammed with traces of what is to come that at times it reads like an Ur-text for dedicated Auster fans: we learn that the man who blew himself up on the first page of *Leviathan* resembles Auster's college friend, Ted Gold, who destroyed himself with a home-made bomb; Casey and Teddy, two eloquent tatterdemalions Auster encounters while working in a hotel, remind us of Stone and Flower, the lottery-winning poker players in *The Music of Chance;* and Quinn, the metaphysical detective in *The New York Trilogy,* is revealed here to be Auster's *alter ego,* a pseudonym used for his early articles. I could go on.

In the enigmatic worlds evoked by the novels, characters strive to understand what is happening to them, slowly building up understanding piece by piece, as one would a mosaic. Each snatched fragment of conversation, each serendipitous moment is slotted carefully into place in the hope that an overall pattern will emerge. Usually something then happens that undercuts all that the character thinks is true. At times in this book I felt like one of Auster's characters. Reading it has caused something to crash, rock-like, into my admiration of his writing. Indeed, *Hand to Mouth* made me wonder what exactly has been quite so pleasing about Auster's work all these years.

His writing seems to have an easy intimacy with the reader—the lightness of tone, the beautifully weighted prose, a sense of relaxed familiarity—but scratch the surface and it reveals itself as rather po-faced and self-important. This book is really not about writing at all but about the mythic status of the writer. Throughout, Auster persistently neglects to connect his attempts to be an artist with the romantic myth of how an American author learns his craft: he goes to live and write in Paris, but doesn't mention the illustrious American literary figures who had done so before him; he goes to sea, like Melville, Poe and, if legend be believed, Pynchon, and yet makes no mention of how often this has served as a literary rite of passage.

Hand to Mouth causes us to reassess the opacity of the previous books. What is enigmatic is its very pointlessness, which leaves one marvelling how such an accomplished writer can be reduced to plundering, yet again, the notebooks in his bottom drawer. The terrible sense at the end is that Auster has run out of things to say and is more interested, for the time being at least, in the type of immortality that comes from giving undergraduates a corpus of work to dissect.

Cressida Connolly (review date 29 November 1997)

SOURCE: "Get Better Soon," in *The Spectator,* November 29, 1997, pp. 46-7.

[*In the following review, Connolly offers unfavorable assessment of* Hand to Mouth.]

I hope that this book doesn't mean that there's something the matter with Paul Auster. He is the most distinguished American writer of the generation below Updike and Bellow, indeed their only author under 60 with any claim to greatness. Posterity will doubtless smile upon Edmund White, David Mamet, Sam Shepard, Mark Doty, but it will positively beam at Paul Auster. Since the publication of his acclaimed New York trilogy almost a decade ago, he has received reviews ranging from the admiring to the ecstatic. Even so, the arrival of this collection of juvenilia—or not quite juvenilia, being mostly the labours of his late twenties—seems premature. Nothing Auster writes could be boring, but some of this material comes perilously close. Notwithstanding its introductory essay and a short crime novel tacked on to the end, the book doesn't amount to a heap of beans. The rest—three short plays and an incomprehensible card game—are the sort of material that irresponsible literary executors might put out after a writer's death. That's why *Hand to Mouth* made me worry about Auster's health. This is a collection with 'posthumous' written all over it.

> In my late twenties and early thirties [the book begins] I went through a period of several years when everything I touched turned to failure. My marriage ended in divorce, my work as a writer foundered, and I was overwhelmed by money problems.

The memoir goes on to recall the odd jobs which Auster took in attempts to stave off indigence—working on an oil rig, as a translator, a game inventor. He travelled to Paris and Dublin, suffering from poverty, a romantic disposition and ingrowing toenails. But he never wavered in his desire to write, never for a moment considered an alternative profession. As is now known, his doggedness paid off.

Few writers enjoy overnight success; fewer still chronicle their early failures as honestly as Auster has here. Such candour is admirable, and will be encouraging to young, aspiring authors. So too will the inclusion of the early plays: copying Samuel Beckett is a phase that all junior writers go through, and reading Auster's attempts to imitate the master of the meaningful pause will help a new generation to see the folly of their own attempts. The play in which Laurel and Hardy build a stone wall in heaven, with its heavy debt to *Waiting for Godot,* is especially salutary on this point. But the inclusion of the card game Auster made up as a young man—reproduced in colour—is mystifying. The game is called Action Baseball; misleadingly, since a card game is, by definition, neither a ball game nor an active one. Perhaps American readers, with their understanding of and affection for baseball, would get it, but Faber would surely have done better to have dropped this from the English version. If ephemera are what is on offer, I'd rather read Auster's shopping lists.

Much the best part of the book is saved till last. *Squeeze Play* is a whydunnit in the Raymond Chandler vein, which deservedly found a publisher in New York in the early 1980s. This being at the tail-end of Auster's run of bad luck, the company folded almost as soon as they had printed it, leaving most of the edition to moulder in a warehouse in Brooklyn. Both Auster fans and thriller-lovers will find much to enjoy here. Using all the tricks in the *noir* book—the retired mafia boss, the pair of hoods, the mysterious, chain-smoking brunette, wisecracks and pithy one-liners galore—he inverts the usual murder story to create a modern moral fable. In this, *Squeeze Play* resembles Martin Amis's recent *Night Train,* the best existential novel since Sartre or Camus (and a lot funnier than either). Both Auster and Amis use the conventions of the genre, its quick wit and slow revelations, to provide a glimpse into the darkness of the human condition. Now that students no longer have to confine themselves to the classics—I met a young man studying contemporary pop lyrics at Leeds the other day—someone can have fun writing a thesis comparing the two.

The rest of the book will be of more interest to Paul Auster's future biographers than anyone else. The introductory essay does contain a few eccentric characters, but characters without a story look very self-conscious. There's a woman who tips beer over her boyfriend's head, a fat Fundamentalist, a sadly eloquent drunk: all grist to the novelist's mill, but insufficient entertainment in themselves. His novels—*Moon Palace* and *Mr Vertigo* in particular—are original, touching and funny. Let's hope nothing ails him, so that he can produce more such mature, wise, delightful work.

Jonathan Yardley (review date 23 May 1999)

SOURCE: "It's a Dog's Life," in *Washington Post Book World,* May 23, 1999, pp. 1-2.

[*In the following review, Yardley offer positive assessment of* Timbuktu.]

To say that Paul Auster's new novel is a departure from his previous work is true but inadequate, for each of his novels has been a departure; he is one of our most inventive and least predictable writers, forever exploring new territories and taking unexpected risks. Still, there is nothing in his other books—nothing, at least, of which I am aware—to prepare us for a novel the protagonist of which is a dog, "a hodgepodge of genetic strains—part collie, part Labrador, part spaniel, part canine puzzle": a creature that thinks human thoughts yet remains dog to the core.

His name is Mr. Bones. He is 7 years old and has spent all but a few weeks of his life as companion to William Gurevitch, aka Willy Christmas, "a flawed creature . . . a man riddled with contradictions and inconsistencies, the tugs of too many impulses," part "purity of heart, goodness, Santa's loyal helper," part "loudmouthed crank . . . nihilist . . . besotted clown." Willie is now in his mid-forties, nearing the premature end of a life at once misspent and holy, putting Mr. Bones in a state of "pure ontological terror" because of his apprehension that "subtract Willy from the world, and the odds were that the world itself would cease to exist." Mr. Bones fears that Willy is soon to leave this world:

> Once your soul had been separated from your body, your body was buried in the ground and your soul lit out for the next world. Willy had been harping on this subject for the past several weeks, and by now there was no doubt in the dog's mind that the next world was a real place. It was called Timbuktu, and from everything Mr. Bones could gather, it was located in the middle of a desert somewhere. . . . It didn't matter how hot it was there. It didn't matter that there was nothing to eat or drink or smell. If that's where Willy was going, that's where he wanted to go too. When the moment came for him to part company with this world, it seemed only right that he should be allowed to dwell in the hereafter with the same person he had loved in the here-before.

As that passage indicates, the novel is told by an omniscient narrator but from the point of view of Mr. Bones. Auster accomplishes this without a trace of the cloying anthropomorphism to which decades of Disney cartoons and animated features have accustomed us. The reader accepts without question that although Mr. Bones cannot speak, save to bark, he can think and understand as keenly as can any human creature; he and Willy are "boon companions," Mr. Bones is "not just Willy's best friend but his only friend," and what exists between them is not merely friendship but also love.

As the novel opens the two have made their way from Brooklyn to Baltimore, where Willy hopes before he dies to find a new home for Mr. Bones and to track down his old teacher, Mrs. Swanson, to whom he intends to entrust the several dozen notebooks he has filled with "poems, stories, essays, diary entries, epigrams, autobiographical musings and the first 1800 lines of an epic-in-progress, *Vagabond Days,*" the unpublished work that constitutes, in sum, the evidence that his life has not been lived in vain. Mr. Bones dreams of a meeting between Willy and Mrs. Swanson, but reality moves faster than dreams; suddenly the ailing Willie has been spirited off the streets of Baltimore in an ambulance and Mr. Bones, knowing that Willy's end has come, is left to fend for himself: "He was on his own, and like it or not, he would have to keep on moving, even if he had nowhere to go."

For a time he finds affection and protection with an 11-year-old boy, Henry Chow, with whom he briefly enjoys "an exemplary friendship." Henry is an admirer of the Baltimore Orioles and decides to name the dog in honor of one whose "name was Cal, and although he was no more than a ball-playing oriole, he seemed to embody the attributes of several other creatures as well; the endurance of a workhorse, the courage of a lion, and the strength of a bull." Baseball being beyond the ken of Mr. Bones, he does not entirely comprehend this honor, but since Henry loves him, he accepts it as being "as good a name as any other."

The idyll with Henry soon ends, when the boy's dog-hating father discovers the dog, but not before Mr. Bones understands the novel's central theme: "For Mr. Bones, Henry proved that love was not a quantifiable substance. There was always more of it somewhere, and even after one love had been lost, it was by no means impossible to find another." Mr. Bones is determined to leave Baltimore, "a place of death and despair," but he heads west into the countryside in the serene belief that he will find love somewhere else, as well as understanding that Willy will be with him forever:

> He watched the sun as it continued to sink behind the trees, his eyes struggling to stay open as the darkness gathered around him. He didn't hold out for more than a minute or two, but even before weariness got the better of him, Mr. Bones's head had already begun to fill up with thoughts of Willy, fleeting pictures from the bygone days of smoke rings and Lucky Strikes, the goof-ball antics of their life together in the world of long ago. It was the first time since his master's death that he had been able to think about such things without feeling crushed by sorrow, the first time he had understood that memory was a place, a real place that one could visit, and that to spend a few moments among the dead was not necessarily bad for you, that it could in fact be a source of great comfort and happiness.

Mr. Bones's travels take him to a new family and a new place, a green lawn in the new America "of two-car garages, home-improvement loans, and neo-Renaissance shopping malls." Willy "had always attacked these things, railing against them in that lopsided, comic way of his," but "now that Mr. Bones was on the inside, he wondered

where his old master had gone wrong and why he had worked so hard to spurn the trappings of the good life." There, in the plush suburbs of northern Virginia, Mr. Bones has found love once again; though his loyalty to Willy is as deep and strong as ever—Willy tests the dog's love from the beyond, and is pleased with what he finds—he knows that it is not the only love offered to him, and he embraces his new family with gratitude and joy.

One need not be a lover of dogs to be enchanted (for that is the only appropriate word) by the story of Mr. Bones, but it helps. As one who talks to dogs every day and has done so for years, I am confident that they know whereof I speak and that they would reply to me if only they could. Mr. Bones, through Paul Auster's words, confirms me in the conviction that anything they might say would be sensible, wise and compassionate. "If God had sent his son down to earth in the form of a man," Auster asks, "why shouldn't any angel come down to earth in the form of a dog?" Mr. Bones, "wholly and incorruptibly good," is just such an angel.

Auster includes no epigraph at the beginning of this lovely novel, but as I read it the words of Konrad Lorenz kept echoing in my mind. "The fidelity of a dog," he wrote, "is a precious gift demanding no less binding moral responsibilities than the friendship of a human being. The bond with a true dog is as lasting as the ties of this earth can ever be." It is hard to imagine more touching evidence of the truth of those words than the story Paul Auster tells in *Timbuktu.*

Jim Shepard (review date 20 June 1999)

SOURCE: "This Dog's Life," in *New York Times Book Review,* June 20, 1999, p. 11.

[*In the following review, Shepard offers positive assessment of* Timbuktu, *though finds fault in lapses of self-consciousness and overstatement in the novel.*]

At least since Alexander Pope, literature has been drafting dogs into service as metaphysical guides: "I am his Highness' Dog at Kew; / Pray tell me Sir, whose Dog are you?" The protagonist of Paul Auster's latest novel, *Timbuktu,* may be a "hodgepodge of genetic strains" who's all burrs and bad smells, with a "perpetual bloodshot sadness lurking in his eyes," but he carries on that tradition. Unable to speak (though he can passably render the anapest of his three-syllable name: "woof woof *woof*"). Mr. Bones opens the novel in a state of near-pure ontological terror, mostly because Willy G. Christmas, the homeless man who has been his boon companion and spiritual adviser, isn't long for this world, and in such a case, what's a poor dog to do? "Every thought, every memory, every particle of the earth and air was saturated with Willy's presence. . . . Subtract Willy from the world, and the odds were that the world itself would cease to exist."

Together Willy and Mr. Bones have walked to Baltimore from Brooklyn in the hopes of persuading Willy's high school English teacher, out of touch for 17 years, to provide a new home for Mr. Bones and become the literary executor of Willy's lifework: 74 notebooks crammed into a locker at the bus terminal. Willy considers himself an "outlaw poet prowling the gutters of a ruined world." Primed by a lifetime of voluntarily ingesting "enough toxic confections to fill a dump site in the Jersey Meadowlands," he experienced, years earlier, a mystical encounter with blessedness in the form of a television Santa excoriating him and exhorting him to goodness, as if in a Best version of "A Christmas Carol." Since then, he's been trying to make the world a better place, with Mr. Bones as sidekick.

Now, coughing up blood, Willy is clearly headed for the next world, "an oasis of spirits" where you become "a speck of antimatter lodged in the brain of God." He names that world Timbuktu, the colloquial site of the unimaginably exotic and distant. To his dog, the word alone seems "a promise, a guarantee of better days ahead." But will poor Mr. Bones take the trip too, when his time comes? Willy expires before he makes this clear; his friend will have to figure it out for himself. But this is only fitting, given that he's named for the comedian at the end of the line in the minstrel show who gets peppered with questions from the straight man.

Fans of Auster's work will recognize some familiar themes in *Timbuktu:* the nature of solitude and memory; the lost father and abandoned son; the power of contingency; the confrontation between the individual and the void. Here, as in his *New York Trilogy,* the forms of popular culture are enlisted in the service of the most weighty sorts of meditations.

At times, the book flaunts the fairy-tale simplicity of its plot. "Thus began an exemplary friendship between dog and boy," we're told after Willy's death leaves Mr. Bones free to find another companion. A "new chapter in Mr. Bones's life began," we're informed at another stage in his adventures. Angelic benefactresses appear as needed to shelter both man and dog. It's as if everything that might clutter our perception of the central issues has been pared away or simplified.

Yet this particular fairy tale is also constructed with cultural detritus, since nowadays there's all this gunk gumming up the imaginative works. A little girl, reacting to Mr. Bones's general dilapidation, exclaims, "There's nothing wrong with him that a little soap and water can't fix," and "We've just got to keep him, Mama. I'll get down on my hands and knees and pray to Jesus for the rest of the day if it'll make Daddy say yes." In the meantime, we're provided with persistent hints of a self-conscious design at work: "What was true, what was false? It was difficult to know when dealing with a character as complex and fanciful as Willy G. Christmas." "Pure corn will cure porn," Willy remarks. Later he confesses that "it feels good to let the purple stuff come pouring out sometimes."

Mr. Bones becomes an actual fly on the wall to witness an important moment. There are references to dreams within dreams. And Paul Auster as a character peeks out, sometimes half-hidden, sometimes not, from within the machinery of the plot. The book even provides its own operating instructions. "The thing I look like is the thing I am," the television Santa tells Willy. "This unlikeliest of fictions . . . this absurd display of hokum," we learn, "had sprung forth from the depths of Television Land to debunk the certitudes of Willy's skepticism and put his soul back together again. It was as simple as that."

Unfortunately, gunk is still gunk, and however self-conscious the intent, the reader still must negotiate the occasional sentence like "How could a man of his ilk propose to don the mantle of purity?" or endure the Norman Rockwellish brio of archetypal collisions between boy and dog: "The little fellow howled with laughter, and even though the thrust of Mr. Bones's tongue eventually made him lose his balance, the rough-and-tumble Tiger thought it was the funniest thing that had ever happened to him, and he went on laughing under the barrage of the dog's kisses even as he thudded to the ground on his wet bottom."

Things also get thematically insistent for those of us slow to make connections. "Dog as metaphor, if you catch my drift, dog as emblem of the downtrodden," Willy lectures our hero. And later: "People get treated like dogs too, my friend." Such moments seem more committed to providing answers than to fully interrogating questions.

Ultimately, though, *Timbuktu* is much smarter than either of its seekers of wisdom, and there are periodic flashes of gorgeous prose to prove it. For Mr. Bones, we're told, the word "Tucson" bears "the scent of juniper leaves and sagebrush, the sudden, unearthly plenitude of the vacant air."

On his own, Mr. Bones samples urban, suburban and rural America, and after being partly seduced—especially by the "splendor and well-being" of a yuppie household—he decides to go his own way, understanding that his own health is failing. When the departed Willy suggests in a dream that his friend transmute Sparky, the humiliating new name he's been given in suburbia, into Sparkatus (the dog who sought to free Rome's slaves?), we begin to see where all this is headed. Throughout his story, Mr. Bones has been demonstrating the ways in which we're both haunted by and find solace in memory, and as he comes to understand the uses of memory in the construction of dreams, he begins to move into the presence of a beauty "beyond the boundaries of hard fact," a place where our solitude is alleviated—the Timbuktu he's been seeking. Its threshold is "a spectacle of pure radiance, a field of overpowering light."

Mr. Bones has earned his election. He's convinced us that he harbors a divine presence, possibly first and foremost because he is the thing he appears to be: a dog unshakably devoted to his longtime companion. Their connection has allowed them both access to a world beyond themselves, a glimpse of a kind of continuum that puts their own mortality into perspective. Contemplating Willy's death, Mr. Bones is better armed to face his own, and vice versa. Unable actually to speak, he has communicated all he hoped to and more: "He was painfully aware of how far from fluency these noises fell, but Willy always let him have his say, and in the end that was all that mattered."

Jonathan Levi (review date 27 June 1999)

SOURCE: "His Master's Voice," in *Los Angeles Times Book Review,* June 27, 1999, p. 2.

[*In the following review, Levi offers positive assessment of* Timbuktu.]

On the cover of Paul Auster's latest novel, **Timbuktu,** half the face of a dog peers out at the prospective buyer, daring him or her to take it home. The face is blurry, the focus as indistinct as the pedigree—a mutt of a photo. A book about a dog, it seems to say. And yet, there are dog books and there are dog books—hearty canines from Jack London, over-bred varieties like *Millie's Book: As Dictated to Barbara Bush* and kennels full of child-friendly puppies, from Eric Hill's *Spot* to Sheila Burnford's classic *The Incredible Journey.* Some of the finest writers in the English language have paper-trained their dogs, from Virginia Woolf with her story of Elizabeth Barrett's "Flush" to John Berger and his "King." Everyone, as Geoffrey Rush's Elizabethan producer says in *Shakespeare in Love,* likes a bit with a dog.

But Auster's entry is a mixed breed that defies easy categorization.

Timbuktu opens on a gloomy Sunday morning. A mutt who answers to the name of Mr. Bones waits patiently on the edge of a road between Washington, D.C., and Baltimore, while his master, Willy, coughs up bloody sputum onto his wild beard. Willy G. Christmas né Willy Gurevitch is a former Columbia University student who, like an unfortunate few in the Leary-sparked '60s, ended a youthful acid trip with a descent into debilitating schizophrenia. Discovered by his roommate (Willy can't remember whether his name was Auster or Omster) "buck naked on the floor—chanting names from the Manhattan phone book and eating a bowl of his own excrement," Willy was sent to a hospital, from which he was released into the care of his aging mother. Six months later, weaned from drugs to alcohol, Willy had his epiphany. Bleary-eyed from too much TV and bourbon, Willy was flipping through the channels one Christmas Eve when Santa Claus came on and spoke directly to him, to his soul.

Taking on the new surname (and a tricolored tattoo of Mr. Claus on his right arm), Willy set off on the road to preach the gospel of Christmas. After a few seasons of saintly heroism, tempered by the scars of knifings and beatings, Willy adopted a four-legged companion. Thanks to Willy's

manic logorrhea, Mr. Bones has not only heard enough of his master's voice to dictate a passable biography but has learned enough "Ingloosh" to understand the human race, if not how to communicate on the level, say, of Doctor Dolittle's canine friend, Jip.

Willy not only speaks to Mr. Bones but believes that his dog understands and that that understanding means he has a soul. Willy reasons that "if, as all philosophers on the subject have noted, art is a human activity that relies on the senses to reach that soul, did it not also stand to reason that dogs—at least dogs of Mr. Bones' caliber—would have it in them to feel a similar aesthetic impulse? . . . If dogs were beyond the pull of oil paintings and string quartets, who was to say they wouldn't respond to an art based on the sense of smell? Why not an olfactory art? Why not an art for dogs that dealt with the world as dogs knew it?"

And so Willy spends an entire winter constructing a Symphony of Smells for Mr. Bones to perform, painting scents on sequences of cardboard boxes, urine-soaked rags and "a tunnel whose walls had been smeared with the traces of a meatball-and-spaghetti dinner." Like all Willy's projects, the Symphony of Smells fails to bring in the fame and fortune that Willy expects. "It might not have served any purpose," the straight-shooting *philosophe* Mr. Bones opines, "but the truth was that it was fun."

But Willy's masterwork is words. These words survive in 74 notebooks of writings, including the first 1,800 lines of an epic-in-progress titled "Vagabond Days," which themselves are living in a rental locker in the Greyhound bus terminal in Baltimore. Within his delusion, Willy understands that his best chance at immortality requires that he deliver the key to the locker to Mrs. Bea Swanson, Willy's former high school English teacher, whom he hasn't seen in 25 years. And it is to find Mrs. Swanson that Willy and Mr. Bones make their hajj to Baltimore.

Willy's pilgrimage finishes short, however, as he collapses only 2 1/2 blocks from the Greyhound station, at 203 N. Amity St., for three years of the 19th century the residence of Edgar Allan Poe. To Mr. Bones' semi-educated ear, there is little difference between the Poland that nurtured Willy's Gurevitch ancestors and the Poe-land where the dying Willy will breathe his last. Yet there is one word that Mr. Bones is certain he understands—Timbuktu.

Timbuktu is the Big Rock Candy Mountain of this late-century breed of hobo, the never-never land to which the tubercular Willy is inevitably bound. Following logic, Mr. Bones reasons that "it seemed only right that he should be allowed to dwell in the hereafter with the same person he had loved in the here-before. . . . [I]n Timbuktu dogs would be able to speak man's language and converse with him as an equal. That was what logic dictated, but who knew if justice or logic had any more impact on the next world than they did on this one?"

Mr. Bones soon has an opportunity to investigate the justice and logic of this world as he escapes from the police who are bent on evicting the unconscious Willy from his Poe-land stoop. He gallops off on an incredible journey of his own through the suburbs and countryside surrounding the nation's capital. Along the way, Mr. Bones is taken in by the 10-year-old son of a Chinese restaurateur and, later, the 12-year-old daughter of a depressed suburban housewife. As he receives kindnesses and cruelties from his new masters, Mr. Bones comes to learn how complex and dangerous is the highway that separates the lives of the well from the lives of the ill; how wonderful and terrible is the navigation of that road, in that "venerable, time-honored" sport of dogs, dodge-the-car.

Auster has made a big-hearted search throughout his career for the poetry in the lost souls of his contemporaries, from Columbia and other parts, who came of age in the '60s at the cost of their minds. His sense of smell has been matched only by his fearless ear for the sad truths of the fragile—that they ultimately have no greater gift for language than the healthy. And yet, as he shows so simply in *Timbuktu,* their need for words in their imprisoned monologues and their capacity for love may be as unbounded and unspoken as, say, a dog's.

FURTHER READING

Criticism

Adams, Robert M. "Cornering the Market." *New York Review of Books* (3 December 1992): 14-6.

> Offers tempered evaluation of *Leviathan* and *The Art of Hunger.*

Alford, Steven E. "Spaced-Out: Signification and Space in Paul Auster's *The New York Trilogy.*" *Contemporary Literature* XXXVI, No. 4 (Winter 1995): 613-32.

> Examines the function of three categories of space—pedestrian, mapped, and utopian—and their association with the search for selfhood and meaning in *The New York Trilogy.* Alford contends that such fictive "spaces" in Auster's novels serve as a forum for his characters to explore, confront, and evade their various fears and misunderstandings.

Barone, Dennis. Review of *The Art of Hunger,* by Paul Auster. *Review of Contemporary Fiction* 13, No. 2 (Summer 1993): 259-60.

> A positive review of *The Art of Hunger.*

Barone, Dennis. Review of *Leviathan,* by Paul Auster. *Review of Contemporary Fiction,* 12, No. 3 (Fall 1992): 193-4.

> Summarizes the central themes and concerns of *Leviathan.*

Bell, Madison Smartt. "Poker and Nothingness." *New York Times Book Review.* (4 November 1990): 15-6.

> Offers tempered assessment of *The Music of Chance,* which he concludes "is not Paul Auster's best novel" but "still a very good one."

Birkerts, Sven. "Reality, Fiction, and *In the Country of Last Things.*" *Review of Contemporary Fiction* 14, No. 1 (Spring 1994): 66-9.

> Examines the narrative structure and archetypal themes of *In the Country of Last Things.*

Creeley, Robert. "Austerities." *Review of Contemporary Fiction* 14, No. 1 (Spring 1994): 35-9.

> Discusses associations between author, language, and meaning in Auster's writing and Creeley's personal reaction to Auster's work.

Denby, David. "Curls of Smoke." *New York* (19 June 1995): 74-5.

> A favorable review of the film *Smoke.*

Edwards, Thomas E. "Sad Young Men." *New York Review of Books,* (17 August 1989): 52-3.

> A positive review of *Moon Palace.*

Kakutani, Michiko. "A Picaresque Search for Father and for Self." *The New York Times* (7 March 1989): C19.

> A positive review of *Moon Palace.*

———. "How Ben Sachs Came to Blow Himself Up." *The New York Times* (8 September 1992): C14.

> Kakutani offers unfavorable assessment of *Leviathan,* which he concludes is "a disappointing novel by a dextrous and prolific writer."

———. "My Life as a Dog: In His Master's Death, a Dog Feels Life's Vagaries." *The New York Times* (25 June 1999): E39.

> Offers tempered praise for *Timbuktu.*

———. "Shamed by Excess, Then Shamed by Too Little." *The New York Times* (2 September 1997): C14.

> An unfavorable review of *Hand to Mouth.*

Lavender, William. "The Novel of Critical Engagement: Paul Auster's *City of Glass.*" *Contemporary Literature* XXXIV, No. 2 (Summer 1993): 219-39.

> Examines Auster's subversion and deconstruction of literary theory, traditional genres, and narrative representation in *City of Glass.*

Little, William G. "Nothing to Go On: Paul Auster's *City of Glass.*" *Contemporary Literature* XXXVIII, No. 1 (Spring 1997): 133-63.

> Examines Auster's use of detective techniques and minimalist prose in *City of Glass* to deconstruct and neutralize limited, value-laden representations of reality and experience. "The narrative's ascetic aesthetic,"

writes Little, "reflects th[e] desire to construct a perfectly decontextualized text."

Malin, Irving. Review of *The Music of Chance,* by Paul Auster. *Review of Contemporary Fiction* 11, No. 1 (Spring 1991): 315-6.
Summarizes the central themes and narrative features of *The Music of Chance.*

McCaffery, Larry McCaffery, and Sinda Gregory. "An Interview with Paul Auster." *Contemporary Literature,* XXXIII, No. 1 (Spring 1992): 1-23.
Auster discusses the relationship between his fiction and life, the themes and construction of his novels, his artistic and theoretical perspective, and his work as a critic and poet.

Nealon, Jeffrey T. "Work of the Detective, Work of the Writer: Paul Auster's *City of Glass.*" *Modern Fiction Studies* 42, No. 1 (Spring 1996): 91-110.
Examines metafictional and metaphysical aspects of *City of Glass,* drawing attention to the limitations, rather than the open-ended possibilities, of language, space, and time in Auster's anti-detective postmodern novel.

Towers, Robert. "Enigma Variations." *New York Review of Books* (17 January 1991): 31-3.
A positive review of *The Music of Chance.*

Yardley, Jonathan. "Above the Fruited Plain." *Washington Post Book World* (28 August 1994): 3.
Offers favorable assessment of *Mr. Vertigo.*

Howard Fast
1914-

(Full name Howard Melville Fast; also wrote under the pseudonym E. V. Cunningham) American novelist, short story writer, biographer, nonfiction writer, memoirist, playwright, and screenplay writer.

The following entry presents an overview of Fast's career through 1996. For further information on his life and works, see *CLC,* Volume 23.

INTRODUCTION

A prolific and politically controversial author, Howard Fast has written numerous works of popular fiction, biographies, plays, and film scripts, though is best known for his historical fiction and the novel upon which the 1960 movie *Spartacus* was based. In a career that extends over the greater part of the twentieth century, Fast has demonstrated a talent for writing fast-paced, engaging narratives and an ability to provide realistic historical backdrops to his stories. Often violent and sometimes sentimental, his novels display a respect for personal courage and a desire for social justice. At one time a devoted Communist—and then a repentant one—Fast is almost as well known for his political life as he is for his novels, which have introduced millions of readers to his liberal vision and interpretation of America's historical legacy.

BIOGRAPHICAL INFORMATION

Fast was born in New York City to immigrant parents; his father was from the Ukraine and his mother from Lithuania. Fast grew up in poverty and his mother died when he was eight. His older sister soon moved out to get married, leaving his father to take care of Fast and his two brothers. His father held a series of low-paying jobs, forcing Fast and his older brother to earn money from a newspaper route and sometimes to steal food from their neighbors. Fast worked various odd jobs while in high school, from which he graduated in 1931. He won a scholarship to the National Academy of Design, but after selling a story to a science fiction magazine, he dropped out the next year. He ran away from home and traveled through the South with a friend, but had to return home after failing to secure a job. Fast managed to have his novel *Two Valleys* (1933) published at the age of eighteen. The book was well received but its successor, *Strange Yesterday* (1934), was not similarly welcomed. While his next novel, *Place in the City* (1937), failed to sell, Fast's career was strengthened when in 1937, *Story* magazine published his short story,

"The Children." Several New England cities, including Boston, banned the story, which centers on a Halloween lynching, no doubt aiding sales. The rapid publication of several successful novels followed: *Conceived in Liberty* (1939), *The Last Frontier* (1941), *The Unvanquished* (1942), and *Citizen Tom Paine* (1944). Fast wrote Voice of America broadcasts to occupied Europe from 1942-44. The following year, he served as a war correspondent in the China-Burma-India theater. He joined the Communist party in 1944. Fast appeared before the House Un-American Activities Committee (HUAC) and in 1950 was briefly imprisoned on contempt charges leveled against him by HUAC. Inspired by his time in prison, Fast wrote *Spartacus* (1951). Unable to find a publisher due to interference from J. Edgar Hoover's FBI headquarters, Fast finally published the novel himself, producing a great popular success. Politically active, he worked for the Progressive party in 1948 and in 1952 attempted to run for Congress. The subsequent year, Fast was awarded the Stalin International Peace Prize. In 1954 he joined the permanent staff of the Communist party newspaper the

Daily Worker. However, he finally resigned from the party in 1956 after Khrushchev's speech on the horrors of Stalin's regime was released. Fast was once again welcomed by mainstream publishing and released such novels as *April Morning* (1961) and *The Hessian* (1972), as well as numerous science fiction and detective novels under the pseudonym E. V. Cunningham. At the end of the 1970s, Fast's popularity enjoyed a renaissance with the publication of the series that began with the novel *The Immigrants* (1977). Since then, Fast has continued his pattern of publishing frequently, including the memoir *Being Red* (1990).

MAJOR WORKS

Fast's career can be roughly divided into three periods, during which his writing was affected by his political leanings. His first novels, published during an initial period of devoted liberalism, often focus on early American history, specifically the fight for freedom. His first novel, *Two Valleys,* is a frontier adventure set during the American Revolution. *The Last Frontier* looks at a group of Cheyenne Indians who attempt to leave their reservation in Oklahoma for their homeland in North Dakota while being pursued by cavalry. *The Unvanquished* provides a human portrait of George Washington during the American Revolution's darker days. *Citizen Tom Paine* offers an interesting portrayal of one of the revolution's most important political leaders.

The next period in Fast's literary development revolves around his membership in the Communist party, a time in which his novels reflected not only his political beliefs but the influence of party leaders as well. *Freedom Road* (1944) presents a vision of Reconstruction as a period in which southern blacks and whites worked together to construct a new society. *The American* (1946) features a profile of John Peter Altgeld, the governor of Illinois who pardoned three anarchists in the 1886 Haymarket bombings, while *Spartacus* details the mainly fictitious revolt conducted by Roman slaves. During this time, Fast also wrote partisan works of nonfiction that demonstrated his political concerns, including *Peekskill, U.S.A.* (1951), *Spain and Peace* (1952), and *The Passion of Sacco and Vanzetti* (1953). In *The Naked God* (1957), Fast's refutation of Communism, the author described his growing disenchantment with the Communist party and his renunciation of Communist affiliations. Fast would return to this subject in *Being Red,* in which he attempted to explain his experience as a member of the Communist party.

In the period following his disavowal of Communism, Fast's writings demonstrate a more compassionate philosophy than what his Communist-influenced writings provided. *April Morning* describes a teenage boy's coming of age during the Battle of Lexington, while *The Hessian* depicts the struggles of a Quaker family and a doctor during the American Revolution when a young Hessian soldier faces hanging. This period also features the novels Fast

wrote under the pseudonym E. V. Cunningham, in many of which he explores his attraction to Zen Buddhism. Fast's most recent popular success has been *The Immigrants,* the title referring both to the 1977 novel and to the series which now comprises several novels—*Second Generation* (1978), *The Establishment* (1979), *The Legacy* (1981), *The Immigrant's Daughter* (1985), and *An Independent Woman* (1997). Beginning in turn-of-the-century San Francisco, the first installment focuses on an Italian fisherman named Dan Lavette who marries a Nob Hill heiress and builds a shipping empire, yet finds happiness only with his Chinese mistress. *Second Generation* centers upon Lavette's daughter, who endeavors to come to terms with her double heritage of immigrant and upper-class backgrounds. Along with the publication of these novels, Fast continued to release many additional works of fiction, notably *Max* (1982), *The Dinner Party* (1987), *The Pledge* (1988), and *Seven Days in June* (1994).

CRITICAL RECEPTION

Fast's reputation with critics has not, unfortunately, kept pace with his prolific output. His earlier novels, in fact, have tended to receive the most praise among his works. *Two Valleys* was welcomed as an exciting start for a promising beginner. Within the following decade, Fast's compelling novels of the early American frontier established him as a talented writer of historical fiction; many of these books became standard reading for high school students. Highly praised among Fast's early novels was *Citizen Tom Paine,* which reviewers commended for providing a convincing portrait of Thomas Paine set against an expressive wartime background. The popularity of these historical novels among both critics and the reading public was fostered by the atmosphere of patriotism that the United States experienced as the nation entered World War II. The critical esteem that Fast received during his career peaked with this group of historical novels, which also includes *The Last Frontier* and *The Unvanquished.* While many reviewers and public figures such as W. E. B DuBois and Eleanor Roosevelt lauded *Freedom Road* as a significant novel on race relations, it was also criticized for showing little resemblance to reality.

The writing that Fast released during his most active years as a Communist tended to receive negative comments, not surprising during the Cold War. In these works, Fast was accused of being a party hack, allowing his Marxist themes to intrude on his storytelling and proving himself unable to maintain an adequate distance from his subject. While *Spartacus* returned Fast to mass popularity, reviewers were left unimpressed by the novel. Today, the fame of *Spartacus* rests perhaps less with the novel than with the 1960 movie starring Kirk Douglas. Though *The Naked God,* Fast's contemporaneous look at his rejection of Communism, was dismissed as badly written and lacking in analysis, *Being Red* was received as a more balanced account of American Communism, though criticized for its lack of introspection and historical accuracy. With the novels *April Morning* and *The Hessian*, Fast was credited as having demonstrated a more mature vision. While Fast's fame was renewed with the popular series *The Immigrants*, his critical standing was not rejuvenated. Critics applauded Fast for demonstrating that he could still tell a good story, but otherwise were not much impressed by the work, citing a lack of subtlety as well as pointing to Fast's tendency toward didacticism. While Fast has continued to publish much since the 1970s, none of his more recent works have had the critical or popular appeal of *Citizen Tom Paine*, *Spartacus*, or *The Immigrants*. Fast, however, has consistently shown himself capable of producing engrossing works of fiction, causing some critics to call for serious reevaluation of his massive oeuvre and literary significance.

PRINCIPAL WORKS

Two Valleys (novel) 1933

Strange Yesterday (novel) 1934

Place in the City (novel) 1937

Conceived in Liberty: A Novel of Valley Forge (novel) 1939

Haym Salomon (novel) 1941

The Last Frontier (novel) 1941

Lord Baden-Powell of the Boy Scouts (novel) 1941

The Romance of a People (novel) 1941

The Unvanquished (novel) 1942

The Tall Hunter (novel) 1942

The Picture-Book History of the Jews [with Bette Fast] (nonfiction) 1942

Goethals and the Panama Canal (nonfiction) 1942

Citizen Tom Paine (novel) 1944

Freedom Road (novel) 1944

The Incredible Tito (nonfiction) 1944

Patrick Henry and the Frigate's Keel and Other Stories of a Young Nation (short stories) 1945

The American: A Middle Western Legend (novel) 1946

The Children (novel) 1947

Clarkton (novel) 1947

My Glorious Brothers (novel) 1948

Departure and Other Stories (short stories) 1949

Intellectuals in the Fight for Peace (nonfiction) 1949

The Hammer (drama) 1950

Literature and Reality (nonfiction) 1950

The Proud and the Free (novel) 1950

Tito and His People (nonfiction) 1950

Peekskill, U.S.A.: A Personal Experience (nonfiction) 1951

Spartacus (novel) 1951

Thirty Pieces of Silver (drama) 1951

Fallen Angel [as Walter Ericson; republished as *The Darkness Within*, 1953; republished under Howard Fast as *Mirage*, 1965] (novel) 1952

Spain and Peace (nonfiction) 1952

The Passion of Sacco and Vanzetti: A New England Legend (nonfiction) 1953

Silas Timberman (novel) 1954

The Story of Lola Gregg (novel) 1954

The Last Supper and Other Stories (short stories) 1955

George Washington and the Water Witch (drama) 1956

The Naked God: The Writer and the Communist Party (memoir) 1957

Moses, Prince of Egypt (novel) 1958

The Winston Affair (novel) 1959

Spartacus [with Dalton Trumbo; based on Fast's novel of the same title] (screenplay) 1960

Sylvia [as E. V. Cunningham] (novel) 1960

April Morning (novel) 1961

The Edge of Tomorrow (short stories) 1961

The Crossing (drama) 1962

Phyllis [as E. V. Cunningham] (novel) 1962

Power (novel) 1962

Alice [as E. V. Cunningham] (novel) 1963

Shirley [as E. V. Cunningham] (novel) 1963

Agrippa's Daughter (novel) 1964

The Hill (screenplay) 1964

Lydia [as E. V. Cunningham] (novel) 1964

Penelope [as E. V. Cunningham] (novel) 1965

Helen [as E. V. Cunningham] (novel) 1966

Margie [as E. V. Cunningham] (novel) 1966

Torquemada (novel) 1966

The Hunter and the Trap (novel) 1967

Sally [as E. V. Cunningham] (novel) 1967

Samantha [as E. V. Cunningham; republished as *The Case of the Angry Actress*, 1985] (novel) 1967

Cynthia [as E. V. Cunningham] (novel) 1968

The Jews: Story of a People (nonfiction) 1968

The Assassin Who Gave Up His Gun [as E. V. Cunningham] (novel) 1969

The General Zapped an Angel: New Stories of Fantasy and Science Fiction (short stories) 1970

The Crossing [based on his drama of the same title] (novel) 1971

The Hessian (screenplay) 1971

What's a Nice Girl Like You? (screenplay) 1971

The Hessian [based on his screenplay of the same title] (novel) 1972

Millie [as E. V. Cunningham] (novel) 1973

A Touch of Infinity: Thirteen Stories of Fantasy and Science Fiction (short stories) 1973

The Ambassador (screenplay) 1974

Time and the Riddle: Thirty-one Zen Stories (short stories) 1975

21 Hours at Munich [with Edward Hume] (screenplay) 1976

The Art of Zen Meditation (nonfiction) 1977

The Case of the One-Penny Orange [as E. V. Cunningham] (novel) 1977

*The Immigrants (novel) 1977

The Case of the Russian Diplomat [E. V. Cunningham] (novel) 1978

**Second Generation* (novel) 1978

The Case of the Poisoned Eclairs [as E. V. Cunningham] (novel) 1979

**The Establishment* (novel) 1979

The Case of the Sliding Pool [as E. V. Cunningham] (novel) 1981

*The Legacy (novel) 1981

The Case of the Kidnapped Angel [as E. V. Cunningham]
  (novel) 1982
David and Paula (drama) 1982
Max (novel) 1982
The Case of the Murdered Mackenzie [as E. V. Cunningham] (novel) 1984
The Outsider (novel) 1984
*The Immigrant's Daughter (novel) 1985
The Wabash Factor [as E. V. Cunningham] (novel) 1986
Citizen Tom Paine (drama) 1987
The Dinner Party (novel) 1987
The Novelist (drama) 1987
The Pledge (novel) 1988
The Confession of Joe Cullen (novel) 1989
Being Red (autobiography) 1990
The Second Coming (drama) 1991
The Trial of Abigail Goodman (novel) 1993
War and Peace: Observations on Our Times (essays) 1993
Seven Days in June (novel) 1994
The Bridge Builder's Story (novel) 1995
*An Independent Woman (novel) 1997
Redemption (novel) 1999

*All part of the "Immigrants" series.

CRITICISM

George Mayberry (review date 10 May 1943)

SOURCE: "Journeyman of Revolution," in *The New Republic*, May 10, 1943, p. 646.

[*In the following review, Mayberry offers positive assessment of* Citizen Tom Paine, *though notes the work's limitations.*]

To his growing portrait gallery of the American Revolution Howard Fast now adds a full-length, unvarnished picture of the man whom Theodore Roosevelt in arrogance and ignorance once called a "a filthy little atheist." With adequate recognition of the warts upon Paine's character, Fast presents sympathetically this sometime staymaker, resident of Gin Alley, editor, soldier, inventor, politico and always pamphleteer and journeyman of revolution. Particularly good are those passages in which the disheveled and frequently drunken Englishman arouses the American colonists to transform their uprising into revolution and then sustains them by his writing and example to carry through to victory. Less successful are the episodes of Paine's last years when a bewildering succession of scenes and characters flit through the book. Fast, however, has blocked in the background of a turbulent era with an understanding of its historical complexity, and the figure of Paine is never lost in the carpet of social and intellectual forces which embraces it. It is a masterful drawing done in a prose as sharp and clean and as loving of its medium as the pen of a Daumier or an Ingres.

But it remains a line drawing, with all the virtues and limitations of the medium, whereas we have long needed a full-dress oil of the man and his age—a Life and Times by a master that will rectify, illuminate and refurbish the vituperative, pedestrian and outmoded work of Paine's earlier biographers. Possibly the difficulty lies with the subject; for Paine the writer is far more alive than the man, indeed is the man, and although his personality and his story are fascinating, it is in "Common Sense," "The Rights of Man" and "The Age of Reason" that his enduring importance lies. Although Howard Fast's fictionalized biographies are not the bastard things such products usually are, his method raises questions to which there are no satisfying answers, and I am by no means certain that he gains in not accepting the limitations (and the possible riches) of straight-forward biography. The novel is one of man's greatest achievements, but there is no reason to believe that it transcends biography, which has an older and equally honest place among the arts of creation. To reply with Shakespeare and Tolstoy is no answer; for if Fast is to deal with historical characters after their fashion, we might require from him an Enobarbus or a Natasha.

Irving Howe (review date 16 December 1957)

SOURCE: "A Captive Not Quite Freed," in *The New Republic*, December 16, 1957, pp. 18-9.

[*In the following review, Howe objects to Fast's Communist loyalties and offers unfavorable analysis of* The Naked God.]

The first though not least important thing to be said about *The Naked God* is that simply as a piece of writing it is extremely shabby: incoherent in structure, florid in diction, inflated and hysterical in tone. Since books of this kind are generally treated as "documents," they seldom meet with such criticism; but I am enough of a literary man to believe that Fast's ineptitude is a significant fact in estimating the political meaning and value of his book.

It is true of course that other people, including many who were never Communists, also write badly; but the particular kind of badness found in Fast's book is not that of an amateur or novice: it is a learned badness, the heritage of that corrupt Popular Front rhetoric which makes precise thought impossible and emotional candor unlikely. Even when Fast was most deeply involved with Stalinist politics, his literary inclinations were toward those middlebrow values which, being pervasive to our time, are not the monopoly of any political movement. And the middlebrow in Fast may yet survive the Old Stalinist, bringing him success of a kind parallel to that which he enjoyed during the past two decades. Popular tales about American heroes can be tailored to any bias; mass culture undercuts all opinions.

Nevertheless, *The Naked God* does contribute a few items to the documentation of the psychopathology of Stalinism.

There is the *Pravda* correspondent whom Fast quotes as saying angrily: "Howard, why do you make so much of the Jews? Jews? Jews? That is all we hear from you! Do you think Stalin murdered no one but Jews?" There is Joseph Clark, then foreign editor of *The Daily Worker*, telling Fast: "If you and Paul Robeson had raised your voices in 1949, Itzik Feffer [a Yiddish poet murdered by the Stalin regime] would be alive today." There is Boris Polovoy, head of the Union of Soviet Writers, reassuring Fast that another Yiddish writer, Kvitko, was well and alive ("at present living in the same apartment as he, Polovoy"), though as it turned out, Kvitko "had been dead for years." And, most pitiful of all, there is Fast himself, being ordered by "a petty Party functionary . . . in terms of savage vindictiveness . . . to change the third act" of a play he had written. "I made the changes."

Beyond such bits of information, and a few shrewd observations about life inside the Communist party, such as a description of the sadistic glee with which the leader prepares to be "sharp" in treating a dissident within the ranks, there is little to recommend in **The Naked God.** My objection, I should stress, is not that Fast hesitates to condemn his allegiance of yesterday: no one could charge that against a man who writes that to join the CP is to "sell one's soul" or who says that he found Eugene Dennis less humane in his treatment of Communists than the warden of the prison in which he, Fast, was unjustly confined during the McCarthyite hysteria. But on the level of analysis, and still more important, of self-confrontation, the book is a failure.

Fast never explores the crucial question: what was it that held him, and others like him, for so long a time in a condition of intellectual bondage? The question matters not because it may reveal something about his personal psychology or because it comes as a thrust from hostile critics like myself, but because it helps us get at a major political and intellectual problem. At one point Fast does sidle up to it:

> . . . the simpletons say, "But we have always known the truth about the Party. Why did it take you so long?"

> *What truth?* Even in this brief book, I have put down a picture that few people outside actually understood . . . [emphasis added.]

One finds it hard to suppose that this is anything but disingenuous. Fast's picture of the Communist movement, far from being something that a few outsiders understood, is essentially the same that hundreds of writers have drawn for the past few decades. "What truth?" cries Fast as if he were Pilate himself. Very simply the truth that Communist Russia is a brutal dictatorship, that the Stalin regime murdered millions of innocent persons and that the Communist parties are dupes of this regime. The truth which Fast so violently refused to credit when it was told by honest men like Andr Gide or John Dewey or Sidney Hook, he finally did believe when he heard it from Khrushchev, a self-confessed participant in mass murder. Had Khrushchev not spoken, Fast would probably still be a loyal Stalinist. Now surely this presents an interesting political and moral problem that a person in Fast's position ought to consider and perhaps even find a bit troubling. And if to suggest this makes one a simpleton, well—call me a simpleton.

Fast's book is written with a high and exalted moral tone, almost as if he were the first—instead of the most recent—to be discovering what is by now the common property of decent men. When Trotsky or Victor Serge used this tone in writing about Russia 25 years ago, they had earned it, for they were battling against widespread illusions among "progressive" intellectuals in the West. But while Fast, like any other human being, has earned his right to sorrow and pain, he might have taken a more modest tone had he kept asking himself the question which he neither can nor should wish to avoid: why so late?

For it is a question that brings us to the heart of a major distinction in the analysis of Communism and its relationship to intellectuals. A few decades ago the average Communist or fellow-travelling intellectual suffered from ignorance and illusions. He generally believed that Russian society conformed to his vaguely libertarian and socialist desires; he felt himself to be identified with a movement that was weak and a country that was besieged; he thought he was casting his lot with the oppressed and powerless of the world. Once he was forced to compare the reality of Stalinism with the ideals he confusedly held, he could often be broken from the party.

During the last ten or fifteen years, however, men like Fast were identifying themselves not with a besieged outpost of revolution, but with one of the two most powerful nations on earth Communism was persecuted in America, but on a world scale it had become enormously strong. Loyalty to Russia now rested not primarily (though, in some cases still partly) on humanitarian illusions, but upon a corruption of values: Communism, inhumane as it might be, came to be regarded as the wave of the future. By now the Communist intellectuals could hardly help knowing at least some of the truth about Russia—for them to deny this would be as credible as the claim of the Germans that they did not know what was happening in Buchenwald. Those who remained faithful to the party learned to look the other way they, became masters at the art of deadening their sensibilities.

Between, say, 1932 and 1948 the whole nature of Communist politics and psychology changed significantly, and among American intellectuals Fast was one of the few who stuck it out through the climax of Stalinist horror. The question, "why so long," therefore becomes more than a personal reproach; it is a request for an analysis of political morality which men like Fast cannot avoid if they are to finish the painful task of earning their freedom.

As it is, Fast has broken loose from Communist belief but not from the style of thought behind it. Let me cite one example, apparently trivial yet very revealing. The writer in America, says Fast, faces "the Communist party on his left, the fleshpots of well-paid mediocrity on his right; but I make no judgments. . . . Ours is an old and honorable craft, and perhaps someday it will be that again."

Now, by its tacit elimination of a large number of choices other than the CP and the fleshpots, is this not the kind of offensive nonsense that characterizes the style of Communist thought? There are no doubt plenty of writers in America who have sold their souls, but there are also many who, whatever intellectual disagreements one may have with them, remain honest and free. These are writers who find no difficulty in foregoing both the Communist party and the fleshpots, and who pursue their craft as honorable men. Being fallible and human, they are open to many criticisms, but I doubt that Fast is the one to make them. Besides, does he really suppose that writing for *The New Republic* or any number of similar journals is exactly equivalent to dipping into a fleshpot?

The Naked God, like many bad books before it, may prove to be a useful book. For if politics requires men to refight battles that a disinterested intellect considers to have been settled long ago, then the need remains for hammering away at the deceit of Communism. If Fast's book is widely circulated in France and India, it may do some good. If it is read by those sections of crypto-Communist opinion in America which, though horrified by the Khrushchev report, still think that some sort of "progress" or even "socialism" can be found in Russia, it may do some good. For we had better recognize that pro-Russian sentiment is far more significant than the present collapse of the Communist party would indicate: those for whom Dnieperstroy was an adequate reply to the slave camps in Siberia will now find Sputnik a brilliant reply to what happened in Hungary.

Kenneth Fearing (review date 23 April 1961)

SOURCE: "A Meeting at Concord," in *New York Times Book Review,* April 23, 1961, p. 38.

[*In the following review, Fearing offers positive assessment of* April Morning.]

Two meanings are attached to the title *April Morning.* The first is a literal reference to the action that took place throughout the Middlesex countryside in 1775 when the British forces marched out to capture certain stores in Lexington and Concord. The second is a symbolic dramatization of the turning point in the life of a 15-year-old boy, forcibly becoming a man in the course of a single day.

Neither point is labored and events move swiftly along in a nimbus of historic color and detail. The reader always knows which turnpike he has reached without being too heavily forewarned, at the same time, of precisely what action is coming up next. When the curtain rises for the juvenile Adam Cooper, who can't understand why his

disputatious father is always picking on him, a lone horseman has ridden out of the night with the alarm that the redcoats are coming. The message may be a little crude, but it can't be misunderstood. No matter what happens, it can't be all bad, and for the Cooper family, it needn't be all good. Or at least, not too good.

A veteran at this sort of historical re-creation, Howard Fast has admirably recaptured the sights and sounds, the religious and political idioms, the simple military tactics and strategies of that day—maneuvers that foreshadowed the painful development of a professional army. Adam Cooper has seen his father shot down on the village common, where the local Minute Men had assembled for a peaceful debate with the British regulars. He has witnessed the dismay of the naive local militia, fleeing the massacre. Then he hears the plan of a veteran fighter of the Indian wars:

"It seems plain to me that the redcoats are going to march down that stretch of road. * * * All that five miles to Lexington, and ten miles more to Charlestown, we'll give them no peace whatsoever. At least half the stretch of that road is lined with stone walls. We'll lie down behind those walls and make them mighty uncomfortable." Whereupon Adam is forced to take another giant stride forward in his blind pilgrimage to maturity: "I wondered. Could you be shot down and run away in such fear as we had on the common, and then fight and win—and all of it on the same day?"

That prolonged, bloodstained and yet disciplined retreat is portrayed with an eye to the innocence that obtained—on both sides—at the time it occurred. While it would be too much to say the Continental Army came into being at that time, it is only logical to assume that mature staffwork grew out of it. And in that connection, the seasoning of the armed forces in that baptism of fire greatly resembled the tempering also undergone by Adam. At day's end an orphan, a duly mustered-in militiaman, the betrothed of a childhood sweetheart, he could already look back upon a 24-hour past that was like an abyss:

"Then, falling asleep, I said farewell to a childhood, a world, a secure and sun-warmed existence and past that was over and done with and gone away for all time."

R. Z. Sheppard (review date 7 November 1977)

SOURCE: "Reds to Riches," in *Time,* November 7, 1977, pp. 120-2.

[*In the following review, Sheppard offers unenthusiastic assessment of* The Immigrants. *"Unfortunately," writes Sheppard, "Fast's life contains more dramatic and moral conflict than his new novel."*]

There is something basically unpatriotic about F. Scott Fitzgerald's contention that American lives have no second acts. The tainted blessing of early success ("the victor belongs to the spoils") and a guilty sense that character is fate may have accounted for his bitter judgment. But the fact remains that the world's best-advertised nation of immigrants was built on second—even third and fourth—acts.

Howard Fast's novel *The Immigrants* is yet another pop epic to underscore this fact. The life and writing career of the author follow a familiar script as well. Fast, 62, was once the U.S.'s best-known literary Communist. In the '40s he wrote throbbingly about American history: the Revolutionary War in *The Unvanquished* and *Citizen Tom Paine,* Reconstruction in *Freedom Road.* As a political activist of the far left, he spent three months in jail during 1950 for failing to comply with a House Un-American Activities Committee subpoena. He was a columnist for the *Daily Worker,* a 1952 American Labor Party candidate for Congress, a 1953 winner of a Stalin Peace Prize and the most popular American author in the U.S.S.R. "There is no nobler, no finer product of man's existence on this earth than the Communist Party," he said in 1949.

In 1957, the year of Sputnik, Fast declared his disenchantment with Soviet Communism in a book called *The Naked God.* It ensured his distinction as American letters' slowest study in Stalinism. Like the immigrants of his new novel, the author looked to California, where some of his earlier novels, including *Spartacus,* had been turned into film scenarios. He wrote science fiction and mysteries under the name E. V. Cunningham, eventually acquired a house in Beverly Hills, a Porsche and a yen for Zen Buddhism.

Unfortunately, Fast's life contains more dramatic and moral conflict than his new novel, *The Immigrants.* It is the first book in a projected trilogy that will follow a number of families from 1888 into the present. Universal already plans to film the saga as a 36-part TV series, for which Fast should gross $975,000. The paperback rights have been sold for $832,000.

As an entertainment package, *The Immigrants* could easily be read, and eventually seen, under the title *Uphill, Downhill.* The principal setting is San Francisco, where Daniel Lavette battles his way from crab fisherman to business tycoon. "He had come out of nothing and he had made himself a king, a veritable emperor," writes Fast with stagy solemnity. "He ruled a fleet of great passenger liners, an airline, a majestic department store, a splendid resort hotel, property, land, and he dispensed the food of life to hundreds of men and women who labored at his will."

This handsome hulk of a capitalist-benefactor was born in a boxcar, son of an Italian immigrant mother and a French-Italian father en route to a railroad job in California. Mama and Papa Lavette perish in the San Francisco earthquake of 1906. Daniel is left with his father's small boat and a shockproof will to rise in the world. He is a tough, practical, democratic cuss who cares little for racial, religious or class barriers. To keep track of his profitable fishing venture, he hires a Chinese bookkeeper and later takes a Jewish business partner. An unself-conscious climber, he woos, and wins the hand of, a beautiful Nob Hill heiress.

Need one go on? Only to say that Daniel Lavette is always in the right place at the right time—getting into shipping for World War I and out of it before the armistice gluts the seas with empty freighters; that he hedges his private happiness by keeping a wise, patient Oriental mistress in reserve; and that he is neither too proud nor too dissipated to return to his nets when the Depression shatters his empire.

Fast, too, leaves no base uncovered as he once again demonstrates his knack for soap history. The old Marxist reveals a genuine enthusiasm for the rugged values of laissez-faire enterprise in his energetic descriptions of Lavette's schemes and deals. Lest one think that this hero escaped from an Ayn Rand novel, appropriate lip service is paid to such issues as war profiteering and the passive wisdom of ancient Chinese philosophy.

The author is still a pro at milking emotions out of his characters' complicated personal relationships, and still a hacker when it comes to pumping life into his historical props. An overripe description of the Statue of Liberty, for example, ends with the line, "Across the water, there was the mass of buildings on the battery, but the lady of liberty was something else." It is a long way from Emma Lazarus' New York to Howard Fast's Beverly Hills, where descendants of immigrants cater to huddled masses yearning for TV.

Merle Rubin (review date 30 September 1984)

SOURCE: "A Rabbi Ponders Social Justice," in *Los Angeles Times Book Review,* September 30, 1983, p. 4.

[*In the following review, Rubin offers a qualified endorsement of* The Outsider.]

In 1946, gentle, conscientious young David Hartman, formerly a U.S. Army chaplain, comes to a small Connecticut town to serve as rabbi to an even smaller Jewish congregation. He is accompanied by his bride, Lucy, who is also Jewish, but who does not share his religious beliefs or his idealism.

Howard Fast's latest novel follows the rabbi's story from his arrival up to 1977. Hartman suffers through the Rosenberg trial and execution, the ugliness of McCarthyism, repeated bouts of local anti-Semitism. He participates in freedom marches in the early days of the civil rights movement and later takes part in demonstrations against the war in Vietnam. But while he always seems to do the right thing, he spends much of his time feeling guilty and worried, which, alas, may well be the fate of many decent people in the world today.

He is sustained by his friendship with a Congregational minister and by the support of some good people in his own congregation, but he is undermined by his wife, whom *he* considers refreshingly frank and clever, but who, in fact, is basically unsupportive of his goals.

In the same years that find the rabbi pondering questions about social justice, the nature of evil and his own fitness to be a rabbi, one member of his congregation, Jake Osner, rises to a position of power in the federal government. Osner's career—in direct contrast to Rabbi Hartman's—seems intended to serve as an almost allegorical model of how far someone without a conscience can travel.

The novel as a whole, despite its focus on recent history, has an air of unreality rising from such literary flaws as sketchy characterization, stagy dialogue and generally lackluster writing—surprising flaws from an author who has written more than 40 books in his long career.

Fast is one of those popular writers who profess not to understand why critics do not admire their work. He handles his worthy themes with a clumsy simple-mindedness. Readers who are tired of sleazy sagas may welcome an uncomplicated story that at least tries to ask some ethical questions. But those in search of a subtler and more thoughtful treatment of such questions would do well to look elsewhere.

Christopher Lehmann-Haupt (review date 9 February 1987)

SOURCE: "Books of the Times," in *The New York Times*, February 9, 1987, p. C16.

[*In the following review, Lehmann-Haupt offers positive evaluation of* The Dinner Party, *though he finds fault in Fast's lack of literary sophistication.*]

An old-fashioned Ibsenesque moral drama is what Howard Fast has undertaken in his latest novel, *The Dinner Party,* about a wealthy liberal United States Senator who is forced to confront his own limitations.

Honoring Aristotle's prescription that a tragedy should occur "within a single circuit of the sun," *The Dinner Party* begins with Senator Richard Cromwell waking up on his estate in the suburbs of Washington early in the morning, and ends with his retiring to bed late the same night. Between these moments, a great deal happens.

Cromwell gets up, goes for a run and makes an appointment with his secretary—who is also his mistress—to do some work on a Senate bill he is preparing. His wife, Dolly, sets the household in motion to prepare for an important dinner party to be held that evening, at which the Secretary of State and his assistant are to be the guests of honor. Later in the day, the Senator and his wife reconcile certain differences and make passionate love together for the first time in several years.

The Cromwells' son, Leonard, comes home from Harvard Law School with a black classmate, Clarence Jones, who turns out to be his lover. During a talk the two have together, it becomes apparent that Leonard has AIDS. Later in the day, he will reveal this fact not only to his sister, Elizabeth, who is, of course, devastated by the news, but also to his parents, for whom it becomes the final blow in a series of unhappy events.

Dolly Cromwell's parents, Augustus and Jenny Levi, arrive. Augustus, the billionaire head of an engineering firm (and the source of the Cromwells' affluence), is the point of the coming dinner party. As Augustus tells Senator Cromwell, the Secretary of State wants him to quit work on a road he has contracted to build across Central America, linking the oceans, because the United States won't be guaranteed control of the road.

Later, in the afternoon, the Senator will ask his father-in-law to make a deal with the Secretary of State to stop work on the road only if the Government will protect the rights of refugees seeking sanctuary in American churches from Guatemalan and Salvadoran death squads. Augustus will answer that sympathy and compassion are "not my line. . . . I don't bleed for anyone, not here, not in Africa, not in Asia. I'm in this to have fun and make money."

Finally the dinner guests gather. After politely slicing one another up over lamb and Lafite-Rothschild, the women will withdraw and the men will try to come to a meeting of minds. Augustus, out of sheer contempt for the Secretary and his assistant, will reverse himself and try to bargain for his son-in-law's sanctuary deal. The Senator will withdraw and try to comfort his stricken son.

Mr. Fast, writing sparely and trying always to register his points through his plot and his dialogue, succeeds here in dramatizing many of the major moral dilemmas of our age. His after-dinner showdown crackles with tension, and the daylong drama is heightened by the choruslike commentary of the black couple who run the Cromwells' household.

Indeed the polish of the entire exercise raises the question in the reader's mind why it was ever necessary, historically, for drama to evolve from the well-made play. Why shouldn't the eternal questions that the novel grapples with always be treated in the old-fashioned form that Mr. Fast has chosen to cast *The Dinner Party* in?

Looking at the novel in this light, one begins to wish that Mr. Fast had availed himself of certain modern literary techniques. One wishes, for instance, that he had made use of symbolism, so that the various characters could stand for something more than the mere categories they now seem to represent: blacks, liberals, Jews, women and homosexuals ranged against the brutal and bigoted representatives of the American establishment.

One wishes that Mr. Fast had made use of the techniques of irony and ambiguity so prevalent in modern literature, if only so that the main message of **The Dinner Party** weren't so blatantly didactic: that the maintenance of the Cold War military economy inevitably obviates such humane priorities as protecting refugees from foreign tyrannies or researching a cure for AIDS.

As crusty old Augustus Levi tells the Secretary of State and his assistant: "You and your mirror image in the Kremlin could have stopped this lunacy years ago, but neither of you had the brains or the guts. There's no way to rectify it now. You've doomed this lovely little planet of ours. Sure we're enemies. You damn fool, it's not communism that's going to destroy us—it's plain, old-fashioned ignorance and stupidity."

All the same, considering the artistic limitations he has set himself, Mr. Fast has produced a powerful and absorbing drama. If its characters are types, they are richly illustrated ones. And in addition to Cold War politics, it concerns itself with an issue that isn't narrowly ideological, the problem of coming to terms with death in a secular world.

At the end of the book, after Senator Cromwell has gone to bed and wept "for his son and for himself," we get a final glimpse of the doomed Leonard, alone in his bedroom meditating. "He sat cross-legged on a small round pillow, watching the rise and fall of his breath, listening to the question, Where were you before you were born? For this moment, his fear was gone."

Diana McLellan (review date 17 February 1987)

SOURCE: "Washington's Power Eaters," in *The Wall Street Journal*, February 17, 1987, p. 32.

[*In the following review, McLellan offers unfavorable assessment of* The Dinner Party.]

Recently, an attractive woman told me of attending a Washington dinner party with a lobbyist beau. During the evening, she met a bigwig she had once expressed a fleeting desire to know.

Next morning, her lover mailed her a bill: "For Introduction: $600."

Romantic, no? No. Romance is never invited to Washington dinner parties; the lingering glance and secret touch are out of place. Introduction is the main course: "Persuasion, meet Power."

Over snowy napery and gleaming silver, their faces magically softened by candlelight and their wits sharpened by

wine. Washington's great, near-great, and Oh-God-if-I-pull-this-one-off-I'll-be-great gather for their kind of dinner party.

It is the kind where you hustle clients, push causes, and, after careful premeditation, pass, share and relish the tastiest dish of the night, inside Washington gossip. Austin Kiplinger, renowned newsletter mogul and guest, remarked that in Washington. "At any given party it's hard to know who's paying the bill, and for what motive you happen to be invited."

These days, fun comes to an end sooner rather than later. Washington's curfew has become earlier and earlier. For the past year or so, Washington hosts have bade their last dinner guests adieu as early as 10 p.m. Some say It's because of the advanced age of top administration figures. Others point out that Power Diners of the late '80s expect to rise at dawn for the obligatory game of Power Tennis that precedes their Power Breakfast. (That will be at the Hay Adams near the White House, La Colline on Capitol Hill, or Joe and Mo's downtown.)

"Since fitness hit," crows one athletic lobbyist, "the backstage bonding that once took place exclusively over cigars and brandy—the bonding with your White House person, your senator, your powerful journalist, your diplomat—now, it all happens in the mornings."

It is not too late, though, for author Howard Fast's novel **The Dinner Party,** which is about a senator's dinner party and that purports to show how power, pelf and push interact over the lemon mousse.

Mr. Fast seems like a man keenly tuned to trends. He served a three-month jail sentence in 1950 for taking the Fifth before the House Un-American Activities Committee; he won the Stalin International Peace prize in 1953; was blacklisted in Hollywood along with the very nicest people; and he repented, writing of communism as **The Naked God** in 1957. In season, his passions have been pricked by Zen meditation, Jewishness, Sacco and Vanzetti, immigrants, Hessians, Thomas Paine (his play **Citizen Tom Paine** will hit the Washington stage this spring) and Spartacus. Many of his 50-odd works are standard biographies used in high schools.

This, his latest, is, well, weighty. We learn, for example, that the senator who hosts the dinner party is 30 pounds overweight at 190 pounds—at least 50 pounds heavier than his gay son, Leonard, who has AIDS. In this corner, the senator's wife, Dolly, weighs in at 122 pounds. Joan his mistress and secretary, tips the scale at 130. Mother-in-law Jenny is 30 pounds overweight at 150 pounds. (A handy size for a referee if wife and mistress ever go for each other. But they don't.) The senator's father-in-law, a billionaire whom some of the guests wish to dissuade from building a road clear across Central America, appears "large but not fat" at 240 pounds.

Obsessional as he is about the results of eating, Mr. Fast is surprisingly inaccurate about the details of dinner itself.

Food and clothing are of very limited interest at Washington dinner parties—what comes out of people's mouths being far more important than what goes in. Few Power-Circuit Washingtonians would insist, or notice, that beans and chopped spinach are hotsy-totsy veggies, as Mr. Fast does. Nor would they think white tuxedos are particularly grand. Oh, they appear occasionally, like peregrine falcons over the Pentagon, but vanish as quickly. Once last year, George Shultz sported a white brocade dinner jacket to a fete at the Canadian Embassy. Washington Post publisher Kay Graham, was far more stricken by Shultz's get-up than she was by the now-notorious slapping scene that was about to occur. "Oh my God, a white tuxedo! I think I'll go home," she told a chum. The jacket has not reappeared.

Nobody in Mr. Fast's book gets what he wants from the dinner party. Well, except the billionaire. I guess that's pretty true to life. Most of the other characters, regardless of weight, are constantly fumbling through a ragbag of fashionable issues and, with Mr. Fast's help, treating them as matters of ethics and morality.

No matter how sleazy their acts, how primitive their consciences, how witless their talk and how inexplicable their motives, we are definitely supposed to know that this senator and his family think right.

Well, they can't come to dinner at my house.

David Savage (review date 22 February 1987)

SOURCE: A review of *The Dinner Party,* in *Los Angeles Times Book Review,* February 22, 1987, p. 6.

[*In the following review, Savage offers negative assessment of* The Dinner Party.]

A Washington dinner party could make for a good novel. Politicians are calculators, and the best of them know how the figures will come out before all the numbers are punched in. An ostensibly social occasion—a dinner or a reception—is among the best places to watch a politician at work. He seeks information, asks what others think about an issue, tries out an argument on one side—analyzing, calculating. Put another politician there too, and you might want to listen in.

But not at a dinner party created by Howard Fast. Rather than ideas, issues, names and witticisms, you get a couple of college kids sounding off about Buddhism and meditation—reverberations of the worst of the 1960s. "I mean, to me," the senator's son tells the secretary of state, "taking a human life is an act of murder." His daughter, equally given to profundity, tells the secretary about "mushroom-like clouds" that will "blow us all away."

Her father, Sen. Richard Cromwell, is silent at dinner, and silent through most of the novel. He is shown to be vaguely liberal. He is angry about the arrest of the Tucson activists who gave sanctuary to Salvadorans. And he's against nuclear war.

But other than that, we get "Dallas" or "Dynasty" in the Washington suburbs. We see him jogging in the morning, cruising in his Mercedes sports coupe, swimming in his pool, setting up a rendezvous with his female assistant, discussing wines with his butler. He is surrounded by a cardboard cast that includes a son at Harvard Law, tall and handsome but with AIDS, and a wife with family wealth but aging and unhappy. And guess what? She is seeing an analyst.

"She realized that there was a true mythic connection in what was happening this evening," Fast tells us about the impending dinner party. "Two of the most powerful people in all of mankind's history on Earth were coming to her pleasant old country house. They represented a power that dwarfed the Alexanders and Caesars and Napoleons and Hitlers. They could press a button and extinguish not only mankind, but all that lives on Earth."

Guess who's coming to dinner? Not Reagan and Gorbachev. It's the secretary of state and an assistant secretary. An assistant secretary with his finger on the button?

My suggestion is, don't wade through another 100 pages waiting for this dinner party to begin. Skip the book, call a few friends who are good conversationalists, and meet them for dinner.

Jacqueline Trescott (essay date 3 March 1987)

SOURCE: "Fast and Furious," in *The Washington Post,* March 3, 1987, pp. D1, D4.

[*In the following essay, Trescott provides an overview of Fast's life, literary career, and critical reception, including Fast's own comments on these subjects.*]

Howard Fast, one of the world's most prolific writers and four decades ago one of the country's best-known Communists, is cordially mad. His anger over politicians and other people who he feels have little respect for history keeps his flame of intolerance going.

"The actual fact of the matter is that the United States is like no other country," he says. He sits in a leather armchair, this man of memory, his thin body seeming about to propel itself forward but held back by the dignity of his 72 years. From the president to the expression "page-turner," Fast can move from impatience to indignation.

"When you get a group of thugs like you have in the White House today with a semi-senile actor playing the part of the president, then it is possible to wipe the entire consciousness of the country into a state of knowing nothing about their country. In particular, I guess the most outrageous example of that is when [President] Reagan compared the men around George Washington to the contras. This is like comparing them to the Mafia."

The author of 44 books, many of them historical novels such as **Citizen Tom Paine, Freedom Road, Spartacus** and **The Immigrants,** thinks Americans shortchange their history. He doesn't feel that when Reagan said in 1985 of the contras that "they are the moral equivalent of the Founding Fathers and the brave men and women of the French Resistance," that many people were as angry as he.

So the volley against the president is fired, the dry wit and biting passion are there, but for an aging leftist, the volleys are aimed in large measure at the darkness. He's written like a causist "all my life," he says, but "it doesn't do much good, believe me."

Fast is one of the survivors of the blacklisting of the 1940s and 1950s, a popular writer who was a member of the Communist Party for 14 years and refused to name names to the House Un-American Activities Committee. In 1950 he spent three months in a federal prison for contempt of Congress, and there finally finished reading his favorite book, *War and Peace.*

When publishers wouldn't touch his work, Fast published his own books, and later he wrote successfully under such pseudonyms as E. V. Cunningham and Magnus Erickson. He survived, he says, "because all through that time my books sold tremendous quantities in Europe."

Since the late 1970s, Fast has been enjoying a renaissance of attention and financial rewards. **The Immigrants,** the first of a five-volume saga, was made into a television miniseries, and his latest book. **The Dinner Party,** is receiving respectable notices.

This week **Citizen Tom Paine,** a drama based on a book Fast wrote 43 years ago, opens at the Kennedy Center, starring Richard Thomas.

Fast detests most adaptations of his work. "The people who adapt them are very often idiots and the producers who produce them are very often illiterates. And so the product is very often a frightful travesty of what I wrote," he says.

But he is lavish in his praise of **Paine.** It was first revived with a script written by Fast at the Williamstown Theater Festival in the summer of 1985. "There never was in my experience so beautiful an equation as Richard Thomas and Tom Paine. Richard is an indestructible bundle of energy. He is not only a brilliant actor, I think one of the fine actors of our time . . . but Richard is an intellectual, which is not too common among actors." As for director James Simpson, Fast tags him "the most gifted director since [Elia] Kazan."

While Fast talks, this clear winter day in his homey Fifth Avenue apartment overlooking Central Park, he looks

downward, his chin almost buried in a sleeveless pullover. But his dry humor filters up through the wool, even with occasional fading of his strong voice. "If I don't remember, I talk softly," he laughs. But he fairly shouts about politics.

The evening news is his video B-12 shot, entertaining, agonizing and infuriating. General U.S. dismissal of Soviet reforms under Mikhail Gorbachev, Fast finds, is part of "the infantile approach to history that permeates overstuffed American commentators . . . These pompous idiots know nothing about history and nothing about politics. They write such things off as public relations gestures, and they are not. They are gigantic movements, and Gorbachev is simply the apex of the movement."

Though his renaissance of the last few years has made him prosperous, Fast grew up in poverty on New York's Lower East Side. His grandparents had immigrated from Fastov in the Ukraine. His father was a working man with stretches of unemployment during which the family lived off the children's earnings. Fast and his brothers had newspaper routes, and Fast worked in the Harlem branch of the New York City library.

His first novel, **Two Valleys,** was published in 1933, and for the next 20 years Fast was a regular on the bestseller lists. At the same time, his success was tempered by frustration over the minimal social impact of his books.

"In 1944 I wrote a novel about black Reconstruction in the South, **Freedom Road.** It became the most widely read novel of the 20th century. It was reprinted in 82 languages. It is a record that as far as I can find out no other book matches. There was a tribe in Africa . . . where a few members of the tribe had been educated in England, and they created a [written] language and it was the first book ever published in their language. For all that I could see, it didn't shake America one bit. The liberation of black people was still 20 years in the future," he says.

Fast was one of the headliners in the 1950s in the famous anti-Communist hearings spearheaded by Sen. Joseph McCarthy. He had joined the Communist Party in 1943 and in 1950 was elected to the honorary presidium of the Congress for the Struggle for Peace Committees in Romania, along with Paul Robeson and Josef Stalin.

When he was called before the House Committee on Un-American Activities, he refused to answer the question that symbolized the inquiry and the era: "Are you now or have you ever been a member of the Communist Party?"

"The first thing, they asked me if I was an agent of a foreign power and I said 'Yes.' They said, 'Is this a conspiratorial power?' And I said, 'Yes.' They asked, 'Are you in the service, do you take orders from this power?' and I said, 'Yes.' They said, 'Are you ready to name this foreign power?' At that point they were so excited they were having orgasms in their seats. They were ready to embrace me. They said, 'Very well, name the power.' And I said, 'God.' And I went to jail. But I got in a good one-liner."

Six years later, he was called to testify before McCarthy's Senate committee, and after the session, he recalls, "I walked over to where Senator [Everett] Dirksen was. I said, 'Senator Dirksen, take a few minutes. I want to explain something to you.' And he was so taken aback. He stopped and said, 'All right.' I said, 'We are not a conspiracy. These are people who are trying to help the country. We are trying to bring a little more freedom, a little more this and that into it.' I said, 'If you would read your history, if you would read about Eugene Debs . . . you would understand these things better.' And this silly man just stood there and nodded his head and said, 'Yes sir, I'll try.' And he walked off . . .'"

"It was so important," he says, "to talk back and not be afraid."

Why did he buttonhole Dirksen? "We used to buy his records. He would sing country songs," the author recalls, launching into a little Dirksen discography.

Fast has never written about that period, but says, "I will, if I live long enough. It is very personal and I would not know how to tell it except in nonfiction."

But there are aspects of the McCarthy era he doesn't want people to forget: "The fact that in our beautiful country, the same thing could happen that happened in Nazi Germany. That you could terrify an entire nation to the point of hysterical fear . . ."

"I was terrorized, my kids were threatened. I expected it. I had nothing to hide. The real terror was among people who had something to hide. Those people—I could walk down the street and meet three people I had known for years, and they would all walk past me pretending not to see me for fear of what might happen to them if they said hello."

In *The Naked God,* published in 1957, Fast explained his involvement with the Communist Party. After Nikita Khrushchev revealed details about the murders of writers under Josef Stalin without promising reforms, Fast left the party. Later he was denounced by the Soviets as a "deserter under fire."

"Why can't they say the book is a pleasure to read or a delight to read or a bore to read?"

This year Fast and his wife Bette, a sculptor, will have been married 50 years. They have two children, Rachel, a psychologist, and Jonathan, a novelist. In recent years Fast has adopted Buddhism. He once called it "the only nonexclusionary religion on Earth, and therefore the only one I feel at ease with."

Fast thinks audiences at the Kennedy Center will be able to connect with Citizen Thomas Paine's crusade to convince the Founding Fathers that a new experiment and new country could be created. "The enormously energetic, enthusiastic Paine in the first act is something that any young person would find great rapport with," he says.

But he remains troubled that history, both in and out of school, remains terribly neglected in the United States. "If this country had a consciousness of history, such as exists in Great Britain, they would have been much more outraged at Reagan's comparison of Washington to the contras . . . an explosion of such incredible ignorance that . . . he is not fit for public office of any kind."

But with all his strong opinions, Fast still respects his readers. He remains grateful to them. And at times, he even spies on them. Occasionally, he says, he hangs around a bookstore at 82nd and Madison. "They sell a great deal of my books there, and sometimes I see the people buying and no one under 30 comes in there and buys a book." This reader-browsing gives him energy. "You do it out of curiosity. If you do a play, you see the audience, you watch their faces, you go in the lobby and circulate and listen to what they say. You write a book, you cast it into the wind, and who knows what anyone says?"

Howard Fast with Mervyn Rothstein (interview date 10 March 1987)

SOURCE: "Howard Fast in a New Mode with Latest Novel," in *The New York Times,* March 10, 1987, p. C16.

[*In the following interview, Fast discusses his life, political concerns, and* The Dinner Party.]

"It's been said," Howard Fast remarked, "that I am the most widely read writer of the 20th century. The number of books I've sold runs into untold millions. *Freedom Road* alone we calculated at one point years ago had sold over 20 million copies. The only complete bibliography of my work was done by a Russian scholar who came up with 82 languages and something in the neighborhood of 30 million books, but that was in 1952, so it's more than 30 years ago. I always tell myself that someday I'm going to try and add this up, but there's really no way I can do it."

Mr. Fast, 72 years old, the author of *Spartacus, Citizen Tom Paine, April Morning, Freedom Road, The Immigrants* and more than 60 other novels, was sitting in his Fifth Avenue apartment getting ready to discuss his latest book, *The Dinner Party,* a work that is a departure from his best-selling immigrant saga of recent years. The cast of characters includes a United States Senator and his wife; the Secretary of State; the Senator's billionaire father-in-law; the Senator's homosexual son, and the son's black lover. The topics include Zen meditation, AIDS, quantum mechanics, and the church-related sanctuary movement that has helped illegal aliens from Central America enter this country.

Critics have said that **The Dinner Party** reads like a well-made play. Mr. Fast has written nine plays; his most recent, an adaptation of **Citizen Tom Paine,** is being done in Philadelphia and Washington, and there is a possibility that it will come to Broadway. "The play is a marvelous form," he said. "But it demands less than a novel. A really fine novel to me is the highest form of literature we have today. On the other hand, the theater is direct and intimate, and I wanted that quality in this book—a direct confrontation with the audience."

Some critics have lamented that Mr. Fast did not use in the novel certain techniques of modern fiction, such as irony and ambiguity. "I think I used a good deal of irony," Mr. Fast said. As for ambiguity, he said, he's not an ambiguous person—"An opinion, any opinion, unless it's voiced tentatively, is in black and white."

A 'Stain' on Honor

"**The Dinner Party** is a direct result of my being unable to get over my problem of indignation," he said. "I get indignant too easily. I had been following this sanctuary business. To me, this was the kind of stain on the honor and decency of America that had never happened. To wire an informer and send him into a church to record conversations, and then to use those recordings to threaten priests, a minister, a nun and other people with five years' imprisonment?"

"I began brooding over this," he said. "What happens," I asked myself, "if a United States Senator is equally horrified by this sanctuary business? What could an honest man do in the face of this abomination? Or could he do nothing? Is a man in the Senate, the highest deliberative body we have, as powerless as I am?" These are interesting questions. The book is my attempt to explore these questions—not to answer them, because I don't know the answers. And I thought the exploration of these questions was terribly important.

Mr. Fast was born in New York City, into poverty. "I began to work when I was 11 years old, to help support our family," he said. "When I got out of high school there was no way I could even dream of going to college, so I got up at 6 in the morning and wrote for two hours and then went down to the garment district to work in a factory. I sold my first story when I was 17, to Amazing Stories magazine. When I was 18 I sold my first novel."

Three Months in Prison

A successful writer, Mr. Fast joined the Communist Party—a move he attributes at least in part to the poverty of his youth. Appearing before a Congressional committee investigating Communism, he refused to name names, and served three months in prison in 1950 for his refusal. Then, from 1950 to 1960, he was blacklisted.

In 1956, Mr. Fast denounced and left the Communist Party. "It was one thing after another," he said, and it culminated "when Khrushchev gave that speech before the 20th Party Congress" exposing the horrors of the Stalinist era. Another reason, he said, was the growing realization "that anti-Semitism had taken root and had grown in the Soviet Union."

After the blacklist, Mr. Fast of course went back to being a best-selling novelist, and his books have sold millions of copies.

"I've been very fortunate," he said. "No question about it. Because even during the blacklist years my books were selling by the millions all over the world. There were always enough royalties for us to live decently. I was very lucky, very fortunate. But I was born and grew up in the greatest, the noblest achievement of the human race on this planet—which was called the United States of America."

Michael Kilian (review date 21 April 1987)

SOURCE: "Tom Paine Returns to Life—Briefly—on Stage," in *The Chicago Tribune,* April 21, 1987, p. 3.

[*In the following review, Kilian discusses Fast's stage version of* Citizen Tom Paine *and actor Richard Thomas's lead performance as Paine.*]

Tom Paine lives.

He has been brought back to life by Richard Thomas, an actor of intellect and range who gained fame playing John-Boy in "The Waltons," and playwright Howard Fast, the iconoclastic and prolific left-wing author of **Freedom Road, Spartacus, The Immigrants** and more than 40 other books, who was jailed and blacklisted in the 1950s for membership in the Communist Party (from which he subsequently resigned).

Their collaborative efforts have produced **Citizen Tom Paine,** a two-act patriotic play adapted from Fast's novel of the same title. It is a tour de force for Thomas, who nearly exhausts himself in an energetic 2 1/2-hour re-creation of the life of the brilliant and unkempt firebrand and pamphleteer whose words helped inspire America's independence from Britain and the survival of George Washington's beleaguered Continental Army.

Paine, who died in poverty and disgrace in New York in 1809, is brought back to life twice in the play. The drama had originally ended with a deathbed scene, but a clever addendum by Thomas and Fast has Paine talking, lambasting and blaspheming past his own expiration.

If Paine lives, *Citizen Tom Paine* is unfortunately in limbo. It played to packed houses in Philadelphia and last week completed a successful seven-week run at Washington's Kennedy Center. But its future is uncertain as it has not received another booking.

Although he intends to return to television for a time, Thomas is disappointed that *Paine* is without another audience, if only temporarily. "I think it's a show the heartland would enjoy a great deal," said Thomas, 35. "It's more important than getting it into New York. In the heartland, people won't be expecting this kind of fun thing. That's the audience it's really meant to reach. It's a popular show with a populist appeal, just as Paine himself was."

"Of course, he breaks all the rules, and he's a very disagreeable person. He has no manners. But people enjoy seeing that on stage every now and then. I think they enjoy seeing me raise a little hell."

To call *Paine* a patriotic play is not to imply a Fourth of July tableau. The unshaven, brandy-swigging, ink-stained journalist and propagandist gave short shrift to the pomposity and upper-class arrogance exhibited by many of the Founding Fathers, including such gentlemen as Thomas Jefferson and James Monroe. Fast—and Thomas—bring forth this radical and sometimes roguish disrespect with force and hilarity.

Washington, for example, is not the noble general of "Crossing the Delaware" fame. His big moment with Paine comes in a drinking scene in a very cold tent, which is much closer to the real man. In the actual crossing of the Delaware, Washington sat huddled in a cloak and is reported to have spoken only the words, "Shift your arse, Knox, and trim the boat."

Paine has received decidedly mixed early reviews from local critics. Local television's Arch Campbell, probably Washington's most popular critic, gave it a rave review. *The Washington Post*'s David Richards called it "instructive, picturesque and well-intentioned," but added it was "stuffed with pomposity, pretension and dialogue so ripe that, were it fruit, you wouldn't be able to see the stage for the flies." Still, Joe Brown of the *Post*'s "Weekend" section gave it a plus, saying Thomas "packs such fireworks into his portrait of Paine that it seems like a one-man show with a few human props."

It is a one-man show in that the play would be absolutely impossible without Thomas, whose fire and gall keep the show going at times when it might otherwise collapse. As with Hal Holbrook and his famous portrayal of Mark Twain, Thomas has put his own stamp on the character so indelibly that one cannot imagine anyone else in the part.

Thomas Paine spends a lot of time stepping out of scenes to talk to the audience. In fact, he spends part of the time among the audience, swaggering noisily down the center aisle and up on stage at the beginning.

But rather than a flawed play, perhaps, *Paine* is simply a strange one. Modern critics who fault the dialogue forget how archly 18th-Century men of position spoke, and if there ever was a man for ripe invective, it was Tom Paine.

The plot is odd and occasionally disappears, but essentially it consists of Paine's life, one of the more melodramatic in history. The first act deals with his arrival in colonial America in 1774 from England, the revolutionary struggle that prompted him to write "Common Sense" and "Crisis" and his personal triumph at Revolutionary War's end.

The second half depicts the long misadventure that was his involvement in the French Revolution, his imprisonment and exile and ultimately, his death in New York, where his body was forbidden burial because of his deist tract "The Age of Reason," which was almost universally condemned as atheistic.

If the scenes are episodic, there is really no other way to present 35 years of a man's life and confrontations with the historic likes of Benjamin Franklin and Washington, Robespierre and Napoleon. Besides, most of these scenes are rousers.

"I like to play it," said Thomas, who read all of Paine's works in preparing himself for the part. "I like to bring this man's ideas out to the public. It's not just that one is doing a play that's fun to do and fun to see. He (Paine) is reminding us of what our roots as Americans are and letting us know that radicalism is part and parcel of every great central earthquake that takes place. Certainly this country is the result of a great one."

Thomas, a veteran stage actor whose television credits also include the lead roles in "All Quiet on the Western Front" and "The Red Badge of Courage," may have the ideal solution for "Paine's" future.

"This play, I think, would work splendidly on television."

Bruce Cook (review date 23 October 1988)

SOURCE: "Crimes Against Conscience: The McCarthy Era in Fiction," in *Washington Post Book World*, October 23, 1988, p. 10.

[*In the following excerpted review, Cook praises the authenticity of* The Pledge, *though finds fault in Fast's literary ability.*]

To their everlasting discredit, American novelists, most of them, have conscientiously avoided the big subjects since the war. All exceptions granted, those whom we hold in highest esteem today seem to work small.

Take, for example, the red witchhunt period of the '40s and '50s, otherwise known as the McCarthy era. (Actually, it was well under way before Tail-Gunner Joe made his appearance.) Although relevant histories and biographies appear every season, few works of fiction by established writers have dealt with this period. It was a theme, one of a few, in Lionel Trilling's *The Middle of the Journey*. It formed the plot of Frederick Buechner's *The Return of Ansel Gibbs,* which not many remember now. But of the important novelists of the postwar period, only Norman Mailer has given it serious attention—in two novels, *The Barbary Shore* and *The Deer Park.*

But now, practically simultaneously, two novels about this shameful period have been published. One, **The Pledge,** by Howard Fast, was predictable, perhaps even inevitable. The other, *The Big Nowhere* [by James Ellroy], comes as something of a surprise. . . .

Howard Fast has done something quite different. His novel, **The Pledge,** takes the red witchhunt following World War II directly as its subject. He meets it head-on, just as the witchhunt once met Howard Fast himself. Today's best-selling author of chronicles depicting upwardly mobile protagonists in their battles to get to the top (books such as **The Immigrant** and **The Outsider**) was himself jailed for contempt of Congress during that period. He refused to give the House Committee on Un-American Activities names it already had. At the time he was already well established as a novelist, with at least a couple of bestsellers to his credit—**Citizen Tom Paine** and **Spartacus.**

Bruce Bacon, the young hero of **The Pledge,** is not quite so well known. A reporter, and a good one, he had earned a solid reputation for himself as a war correspondent in Europe. We pick him up in Calcutta, post VE Day, where he has gone to finish out the war. (Why there and not the South Pacific is anybody's guess.) There is a rice famine: millions are dying in Bengal. Local communists prove to him that there is rice enough to feed the starving population. The Muslim merchants are holding it back with the connivance of the British colonial authorities. Bacon tries to get this story out and gets kicked out of the China-Burma-India Theater for his trouble. Back in New York he starts to write a book about the war that will include the famine story. That's when his troubles really begin.

A word about Bruce Bacon. Simply put, he's a stiff. People are always telling him how innocent he is, saying he's an Eagle Scout. Well, he is, sort of—but he is also rather thick-headed, all too confident that his reputation as a reporter and his comfortable upper-middle class background will see him through every sort of test.

As a matter of fact, the reader may find himself rather bored with Bruce (that awful WASP name!) and will welcome the entrance of Molly Maguire on page 77. This is a woman with some style. An Irish-Catholic from Boston, she has become a communist without giving up her religion; she is passionately both a Catholic and a communist. She also becomes Bruce Bacon's passionate lover. A reporter for *The Daily Worker,* she is well-informed about the threat to the reds posed by the HUAC and the FBI. She is not in the least surprised when personal pressure from J. Edgar Hoover forces publisher after publisher to turn down Bruce's book. Nor is she astonished when he is brought before the Committee to answer questions on his contracts with communists in India and New York. Although he is not then and never was a member of the Communist Party, Molly of course is. Her name comes up, and he refuses to name her as a communist.

(Another word here: Howard Fast presents his communists realistically in **The Pledge:** there are careerists and tunnel-visioned true believers among them, just as there are idealists who need a dream to hold onto. Fast himself was a Communist Party member until 1956, when he broke with it over Soviet repression of the Hungarian revolution.)

Bruce is convicted on charges of contempt of Congress and sentenced to a year in prison. The section of **The Pledge** covering Bruce's imprisonment—roughly the last hundred pages—is wonderfully written, as though it were from a different book entirely. But it's from no book at all; it's written from life—Howard Fast's own. Bruce Bacon comes out of prison a better man, as I suspect the author also did, having learned a lot about himself and common humanity.

If the rest of the book could only have been written as honestly from the well of personal experience, **The Pledge** might have been that novel on the witchhunt that we still look for. We may never find it. Those best prepared by experience seem unequipped as writers.

Rhoda Koenig (review date 5 November 1990)

SOURCE: "Party Time," in *New York,* November 5, 1990, pp. 124-5.

[*In the following review of* Being Red, *Koenig provides an overview of Fast's life and literary career.*]

Novelist, playwright, biographer, detective-story writer—Howard Fast has been all these, but we know the author of more than 70 books best as a former Communist.

As the title of his autobiography indicates, he knows we do, too **Being Red** stops in 1957, several years after Fast ended a prison sentence for refusing to name names to the House Un-American Activities Committee and a few months after he left the party, when Khrushchev revealed the crimes of Stalin. The story he has to tells is a lively and gripping one, and better written than Fast's preachy excursions into other people's histories, though there are lapses: "A writer is a strange creature. He is a delicate sheet of foil on which the world prints its impressions. . . ." Like the imprisoned Oscar Wilde remarking that the writer who should have been locked up was Marie Corelli, a character in a Mordecai Richler novel set in the fifties says that Howard Fast should stay in jail for "violence to the English language."

Left-wing activism was part of the Fast family tradition. In 1898, his father, a Ukrainian immigrant, "and a few other Jewish boys working at the tin factory organized regiment to fight in Cuba and thereby revenge themselves for the expulsion of the Jews from Spain in 1492." Unfortunately, there was also a tradition of dissension in the ranks: The worker who collected money for uniforms, sabers, and horses ran off with it. Barney Fast, "a man who always had both feet planted firmly in midair," married and fathered five children (Howard was born in 1914), a poor but close-knit family that was shattered when Fast's mother died and his father sank into depression.

Eight years old at the time, he went to work soon after, delivering newspapers and hiring himself out to a cigar-maker. (Later, his jobs, such as reclaiming overdue library books from whorehouses, became more interesting.) Worse, his father, in a shortsighted attempt to help the family, moved them from the Lower East Side to the Upper West, where they were the only Jews. After being attacked again and again, Fast "put the largest kitchen knife we had in my belt, walked down the stairs and into the street, and as four kids advanced on me, I presented the butcher knife and stated that I might get only one of them, but that one would be dead." He was eleven. When not working or fighting, Fast read his way through the public library and started to write. At seventeen, he sold a short story. At eighteen, he sold a novel, his sixth. Shortly before that, thumbing his way through the South, he saw police set on other vagrants with clubs and haul them off, and only his plea to phone his father for bus fare home, he believes, saved him from a chain gang.

The brutality of Fast's background, he says, and his awareness of the misery caused by the Depression, made him a socialist. "And because I came to believe that the only serious socialist party in America was the Communist Party, I was bitterly attacked and slandered for fifteen years of my life." The ironies alone of Fast's persecution would be enough to make him bitter. Not only was he the author of such advertisements for America as *Citizen Tom Paine* and *Freedom Road* (the story of a slave who becomes a congressman), he also wrote the government's daily shortwave broadcast to occupied Europe on the progress of World War II. Also during the war, Fast organized a Communist-sponsored reception for Harry Truman (who, Fast says, knew who his backers were) and was invited to the White House as a reward for his contributions to the 1944 Democratic campaign. The lunch was somewhat less glamorous than Nancy Reagan's affairs: Eleanor Roosevelt explained that while combat GIs were eating cold C rations, she didn't think it right to serve a meal costing more than 30 cents.

The money and influence Fast's career brought him, however, were no use against the anti-Communist mania of the postwar period. He brings alive the days of parochial-school children carrying signs that read KILL A COMMIE FOR CHRIST, of the moronic and vicious editorials that justify his lurid metaphor "dogs sniffing a trail of blood," and of the Peekskill concerts of 1949, where local rednecks, assisted by local police, burned peace pamphlets and beat and stoned the "white niggers" who had come to hear Paul Robeson. The persecution did not stop with Fast's conviction and imprisonment; magazines and book publishers rejected his work, some of them simply afraid, some directly threatened by the FBI, which also sent an agent to the New York Public Library with an order to destroy his books.

Against this, of course, one must set the fact that even if Communism was no threat to America, it was evil. Fast's defense concerning his ignorance of the party's crimes is that he heard so much anti-Communist nonsense it was hard to believe that some of the accusations were true. But the censorship and interference he suffered from the party higher-ups, too, was a comic distortion of the grimmer restrictions of freedom in the Soviet Union. (Of course, much about the American Communist Party was strange: One wonders what Lenin would have made of *The Daily Worker*'s Broadway-gossip column.) When a play of his was put on by the Communist-backed New Playwrights group, he was told that the part of one son in a Jewish family would be played by James Earl Jones and was reprimanded for his "white chauvinism" when he protested.

Explaining his disenchantment with the party, Fast says, "When you find that a priest can be a selfish bastard and a rabbi a lecher and a judge a cold-blooded murderer . . . and in your Communist Party, the same lechers and mindless jerks and egotistical power-hungry bastards, then something washes out of you and you are cold and empty inside." To put it another way, you are grown-up and free of illusions about a perfect substitute family. But that is by the way. Oscar Wilde also thought that it was not as bad to be immoral as to be mediocre, but about that he was wrong. What the strongest nation on Earth did to its woolly thinkers was a lasting shame and a permanent warning. It is good to have this sordid and salutary tale told again.

Christopher Hitchens (review date 25 November 1990)

SOURCE: "Citizen Howard Fast," in *Washington Post Book World,* November 25, 1990, p. 5.

[*In the following review of* Being Red, *Hitchens praises Fast's engaging recollections, though he finds fault in his writing.*]

Murray Kempton once told me what he called the only really funny story about American Communism, adding that unlike many such stories it had the merit of being true. In the early 1950s, Howard Fast was walking along a New York street when he encountered the cultural attaché of an Eastern European mission. Bidding good day to Comrade Fast, the attaché asked if he would be attending next week's special caviar-and-culture soiree, to be held at the mission in the interests of peace and brotherhood. Stiffening slightly, Fast replied that if the comrade read the newspapers he would know that fascism was coming to the United States and that, as a direct consequence he, Fast, would be in prison by the following week. He therefore had no choice but to decline the kind invitation. "All right then," returned the Pole or Czech or Hungarian envoy, "Come when you get out."

This memoir brought that tale back to mind. Like the tale, the memoir is modern history as it affected Fast. But like the tale, the memoir is also true. Fast *did* go to jail for his convictions (one of the few Stalinists who did) and he has led a life rich in incident. Moreover, his **Spartacus** and his **Citizen Tom Paine** are still on many a shelf, and once set the blood coursing through the veins of men and women who are now safe, staid liberals. Fast also differs from the classic pattern of the ex-Communist stereotype, made notorious by James Burnham and Whittaker Chambers. He left the Communist Party for the same reason that he joined it—which is to say he left it because he was interested in social justice and historical truth.

Love him or hate him, it's very difficult to read him. "There is no way to tell the story of the curious life that happened to me without dealing with the fact that I was for many years what that old brute Senator Joseph McCarthy delighted in calling 'a card-carrying member of the Communist Party.'" Hold it right there, one wants to exclaim, except that this is the opening sentence. Do you intend to include any punctuation? Will *all* your passages and periods be so exhaustingly informal?

Things improve a little, though it's not as if one hasn't read other accounts of being a Jewish proletarian, kicked around by poverty and the police, happening suddenly upon the work of Jack London and John Reed. After about 50 pages, however, Fast tells us of being turned down by a white street gang because he was an "unwanted Jew bastard," thus missing the fight where "They took one of the black kids prisoner, driving away the others, and in imitation of stories they had read in the tabloids and movies they had seen, they lynched the little boy—he was thirteen—putting a rope around his neck and pulling him up on a tree branch in the woods to the south of Macomb's Bluff."

A hell of a story, you'll have to admit, and later fictionalized by Fast as part of his astounding output.

The most moving and effective parts of this book show Fast's engagement in the battle against racism. There is an outstandingly graphic eyewitness description of the near-pogrom at Peekskill, where a crowd that wanted to hear Paul Robeson was set upon by a mob which acted with all the courage guaranteed it by police complicity. The other accounts of rallies, picket-lines and causes long past are small beer compared to this, and could have benefited from the blue pencil. I hope it's not churlish to say the same about his confrontation with the House Un-American Activities Committee, which except for some two-fistedly

Fastian details is the story of bovine, philistine persecution as we have come to know and accept it.

Published as it is at the beginning of the post-Communist era, Fast's book seems even more dated than many narratives that emerged considerably earlier. There is, however, one episode that might tickle the historians. In 1946, the famous French Communist physicist Frederic Joliot-Curie came to New York. During a conversation with Fast, he revealed that the Soviet Union already possessed atomic bombs and that he had seen and worked on the weaponry. He gave an approximate timetable for the growth in Soviet nuclear capacity. To Fast's astonished questioning, he replied calmly that there was nothing to be surprised about, except that all Americans thought Russians were primitives. Fast printed the claim in the Daily Worker, expecting to elicit some official response, and was surprised at the resulting silence. Three years later, when Truman and Omar Bradley made the announcement for themselves, there was hysteria. How does this anecdote alter the fabled "atom spy" controversy?

Everyone, they used to say, has his Kronstadt—his breaking point with the mixture of Utopianism and cynicism that was American Communism. For Fast, it was anti-Jewish mania in the Soviet Union that broke the main spring. But, as this rambling first-person stream of consciousness makes plain, if it hadn't been that, it would assuredly have been something else. How fortunate we are to live in a time when this book will arouse no controversy.

Leo Braudy (review date 9 December 1990)

SOURCE: "Rolling Up the Red Carpet," in *Los Angeles Times Book Review*, December 9, 1990, pp. 2, 13.

[*In the following review of* Being Red, *Braudy commends Fast's insight into political history, though he finds fault in his reticence concerning his personal life and motivations.*]

Howard Fast published his first novel in 1933 at age 18. He was part of a generation of up-from-poverty writers who came of age in the 1930s, working a multitude of odd jobs while they read their way through the library stacks. It seemed almost inevitable that he would also join the Communist Party.

Fast's first great successes were in historical novels that looked at American values from the vantage point of the rebel, the outsider and the slave. They reflected the revisionary view of what was truly "American" that animated both Popular Front politics and the then-embryonic academic interest in American history and literature. **Conceived in Liberty** (1939), **The Unvanquished** (1942), and **Citizen Tom Paine** (1943) recounted in Fast's plain-spoken passionate prose his story of the American Revolution.

The story of *The Last Frontier* (1941) was the desperate Cheyenne march from Oklahoma to their native lands on the Yellowstone. The hero of *Freedom Road* (1944) was a freed slave and of *Spartacus* a Roman gladiator. And when Fast wrote a novel called *The American,* his central character was not some Jamesian American abroad but John Peter Altgeld, the governor of Illinois who freed the anarchists accused in the Haymarket riots in Chicago.

In 1957, after Khrushchev's revelations at the 20th Party Congress, Fast left the party and wrote *The Naked God* to describe his disillusionment as a Communist writer. Since then, his writing has been as prolific as before. His series of novels about the immigrant Lavette family brought him to the best-seller list several times (although perhaps no single book of his has sold as well in the United States as did his brother Julius' *Body Language*).

But as far as his new memoir, *Being Red,* is concerned, the years since 1957 have been primarily a lengthy postscript to his life in a movement and at a time when moral commitment and political engagement really counted. "We are romantics," he says, "like a priesthood," and a good deal of his attitude evokes the sustaining feeling of being embattled for a good cause, what Fast at another point calls "the burden of morality," that was assumed by so many party members, confirmed in their beliefs in part because of their persecution by the obviously fiendish and evil. As Fast remarks later, he would not mind leaving his FBI report behind as a testament for his grandchildren of his commitment to human rights.

The image of himself that Fast presents in *Being Red* is that of a heterodox and independent writer who believed in the Communist vision of a better future at the same time that he chafed under party discipline. As the most prominent American writer who remained a party member during the hard days of the blacklist, he was allowed a certain latitude, although he recounts being attacked for his "I Write as I Please" column in the *Daily Worker* by John Howard Lawson and here, as in *The Naked God,* he details the attacks made on his novels by party functionaries for their doctrinal deviations.

The issue of artistic independence was always a vexed question, especially for the writers in the party. In memoirs and other books about the period, Fast often appears as a staunch defender of the party's political authority over errant artists. But by his own account, he is just as frequently a victim. In one incident, he is threatened with expulsion for his refusal to change "boys and girls" to "youths" in a passage describing a group of black and white teenagers. Yet, when he complains about the CP's tyranny over artists and praises the moral conscience of Albert Maltz (with whom he was in prison in 1951), the reader has no way of being reminded (except by omission) that in 1946 when Maltz complained in the New Masses of the aridity and constriction of party artistic life, Fast attacked him roundly a few weeks later for his "reactionary" point of view.

Fast made an anguished apology in *The Naked God* for the attack on Maltz. But despite his growing misgivings,

Fast remained in the party until Khrushchev's speech. His general disaffection from the party leadership and his disillusionment over the increasing evidence of Soviet anti-Semitism drove him out. Unlike many who recanted their old allegiances, Fast never named names, and even now he carefully avoids incriminating those who might still wish to be anonymous.

On the whole, his account of the faults and virtues of American Communism is more balanced than it was 23 years ago in *The Naked God.* But the basic question still remains: What was the bargain that Faust had struck with his own demons and his ideals that allowed him to stay in the party so long as its most prominent apologist in the arts, and then to leave with an equally strenuous denunciations?

Some aspects of Fast's political history will need a historian's care to verify and interpret. He recounts, for example, how in 1949 he carried to the Paris Peace Congress a formal charge of anti-Semitism brought by the Communist Party of the United States against the Communist Party of the Soviet Union. According to Fast, the charge was summarily rejected by Alexander Fadeyev, the head of the Soviet Writer's Union, the same man who a short time before (in a story told fully in *The Naked God* and only alluded to here) had assured Fast and others that Soviet Jewish writers were flourishing, when they had in fact been tortured and executed.

It's hard not to see Fadeyev as a kind of Soviet doppelganger for Fast—the writer as political operative. But, while Fadeyev coolly offered up historical necessity in place of truth, Fast's own commitment to the party line held a precarious rein on his passions. With Khrushchev's revelations, Fadeyev committed suicide. Fast, the American literary commissar, curiously compounded of totalitarian and anarchist impulses, left the party.

But in general there is a peculiarly disjointed quality to Fast's view of himself in *Being Red.* Like the revolutionary heroes in his best novels, Fast has more gift for action than for introspection. There are gestures toward his personal psychology (he remarks that his childhood was so tormented that he has been virtually unable to write about it), but they are largely abortive. The little fragments of personal psychology and peevishness and over-explanation that might help the reader to put together a picture of him are there, but it is difficult to make a meaningful mosaic.

We never really learn what writing means to him beyond a way of getting out of the ghetto. Nor do we finally understand what the party meant to him, and why by the early 1950s he "was steadily and sometimes obsessively destroying a career that had started off only ten years earlier as one of the most promising of the time." His books were selling by the millions abroad, while they were being banned from libraries at home (he had to publish *Spartacus* on his own). But finally both the lionized Communist hero and the despised Communist traitor were equally unreal to him.

In essence, *Being Red* is exactly what its title says. It is a memoir of his political nature and its involvement with American Communism, where the political and the personal always had uneasy commerce. Although Fast's wife, her cooking, her sculpture and their children do get mentioned, along with a few enigmatic arguments, *Being Red* is less an autobiography than a moral testament, an implicit self-exoneration with enough *mea culpa* to keep away the shadows but not enough light to dispel them.

Perhaps it is the testament that he hopes he will leave to his grandchildren—like his FBI file. But another version of himself seems equally valid:

When Fast is in prison, he works on a fountain sculpture of the famous Prince of Essen, the lost young boy who is immortalized as he is discovered urinating. Others will have to sift through the facts of the history of American Communism and decide how *Being Red* contributes to them. But for Fast, who wore his politics on his sleeve while his heart remained more hidden, the Prince of Essen may be his own sardonic emblem.

Stefan Kanfer (review date 10-24 December 1990)

SOURCE: "Fast Backward," in *The New Leader,* December 10-24, 1990, pp. 21-3.

[*In the following negative review of* Being Red, *Kanfer condemns Fast's "disingenuous" account of his life and the Communist Party.*]

Thanks to such works as Lillian Hellman's memoirs, Vivian Gornick's *The Romance of American Communism* and now Howard Fast's *Being Red,* an elaborate new myth is flourishing on college campuses and in salons afflicted with political amnesia. It goes like this:

Once upon a century there were two ogres, one with a small moustache and one with a big moustache.

There was never a doubt about Small Moustache. He was evil incarnate. He was an absolute ruler who believed in terror as a political means. He was psychotic. He was responsible for the deaths of millions. Hate underlay his actions, especially toward the Jews.

Big Moustache was different. He was evil incarnate. He was an absolute ruler who believed in terror as a political means. He was psychotic. He was responsible for the deaths of millions. Hate underlay his actions, especially toward the Jews.

But everyone knew the sins of Small Moustache, and no one knew the flaws of Big Moustache. After all, he had helped defeat Small Moustache, and his followers were forever trumpeting the benefits of freedom and equality. How could he stand for anything bad? Thus the minstrels and the scribes were completely taken in.

Then, long after Big Moustache had passed into legend, a minor ogre revealed his ancient and hidden crimes. Imagine the surprise of the True Believers! They ran from the shadow of Big Moustache into the sun, never to be deceived again.

If Bill Moyers ever decides to produce *The Power of Myth II* on PBS, he should aim his cameras at Fast. The author's 47th book is the most fabulous of them all. He rushes to tell us that he grew up in New York, Jewish, poor, hungry, and filled with compassion for the down-trodden. After fellow-traveling through the '30s he finally made his allegiance official—but not without some internal swaggering: "You don't join the Communist Party without carrying a burden of morality. . . ."

Thousands took the same path: writers, performers, intellectuals, politicians. Somewhere along the line, though, they realized that the burden was outside the party; that official American Communism was false to the minorities it said it would protect, and injurious to the workers it promised to represent; and that below all it apotheosized the century's second greatest mass murderer, Josef Stalin.

Not Fast. Like one of those guests who get loaded and immobile in the first hour, he hung around at the party until no one was left but his uncomfortable hosts. Only after cold water was splashed in his face did he rise and wobble to the door, loudly announcing that he was just about to depart.

Fast claims to have been dismayed by the Moscow Trials of 1936: "In August of that year, 16 of the true old Bolsheviks, men who had participated nobly in the making of the Revolution only 20 years earlier . . . were put on trial, forced to confess, and then executed." Many others took this as a symptom of the Soviet Union's malaise and got out.

Not Fast. He dealt with Stalin's lethal farce by looking the other way for eight years. "During that time, I educated myself, went on with my task of learning to write. . . ." The autodidact pursued a fool's course. In 1944 he joined the CP. Without a trace of irony, he describes his colleagues as "a galaxy of talent and national distinction and international fame." Assuming the posture of a man on the witness stand, he refuses to name names, perhaps wisely. Richard Rovere, who had his own youthful adventure with the party, once described the esthetics of the Old Left: "The American intellectuals who fell hardest for Communism were men . . . of tastes at once conventional and execrable. Many of them, of course, had no literary tastes of any sort. The reading matter of Communists was the dreariest kind of journalism. If they read poetry at all, it was likely to be Whittier and Sandburg, not Rimbaud and Ezra Pound . . . the cultural tone they set in the '30s was . . . deplorable because it was metallic and strident. Communist culture was . . . cheap and vulgar and corny."

For good old-fashioned self-delusion like mother used to make, Fast's chapter on the '40s is indispensable. "Most of us," he testifies, "had never been to the Soviet Union [Fast, 75, has yet to visit the USSR] and we knew little about it and less about Stalin. I don't believe our leadership lied to us; I think they knew as little as we did. . . ." He could have come up with a whomping working hypothesis from a re-examination of the Moscow trials, a look at the 1939 Stalin-Hitler Pact, a reading of Orwell's *Animal Farm* ("'Ah, that is different!' said Boxer. 'If Comrade Napoleon says it, it must be right.'") Alternatively, he might have flipped through the observations of Irving Howe or Murray Kempton or Richard Wright or Ignazio Silone, or, just for laughs, the arrogant and premonitory comments of Josef Stalin: "One death is a tragedy. A million deaths is a statistic."

Not Fast. He and his colleagues were in business to deceive each other first and the public second. Some 50 years later he cannot let go of the legends that sustained them. "F. Scott Fitzgerald had been ready to embrace the party, I was told, but whether he actually joined or not, I don't know." That is Fast talking. Here is Fitzgerald sneering, *in re* Dorothy Parker's radical babble in the *New Masses:* "Dotty has embraced the church and reads her office faithfully every day, [but it] does not affect her indifference."

In 1949 came the Scientific and Cultural Conference for World Peace, held at the Waldorf-Astoria Hotel in Manhattan. Fast proclaims: "Subsequent histories and the newspapers of the time indicate that it was Soviet-inspired and backed with Soviet money. Let me put that to rest. It was my idea."

The Conference occurred at the apogee of the shameful blacklisting epoch in Hollywood, and the cusp of the McCarthy hysteria in Washington. Many significant personalities showed up at the Waldorf in a defiant mood, and the idea man used their presence to publicize his own agenda. He is still using them: "I do believe that it brought home to the Truman Administration that its carefully orchestrated campaign of terror had not yet reduced everyone to the point of abject cowardice and indifference."

In fact, the Conference was designed to encourage that master of terror and promoter of abject cowardice, Josef Stalin. No one critical of the Soviet Union was invited to participate. On various platforms the ideals of peace were boomed at a time when the USSR was blockading Berlin, when purges (i.e. executions and one-way voyages to labor camps) were taking place in Eastern Europe, and when the falsities of Lysenkoism (acquired characteristics are inherited) were being forced on Soviet scientists. None of this, naturally, is of concern to Fast; he has other flesh to fry.

Whenever he mentions Soviet processes, the writer trots out his notions of political parity. A friend is involved in a Soviet-American TV project when he finds himself tailed. Since this is a co-operative venture, the man wonders, why the KGB? Fast gives an official explanation: "If the

KGB did not ask for more money each year, their budget would be cut. But when the money was forthcoming, they had to use it, and that meant more operatives, and having an American film crew here in Moscow was a golden opportunity to use up the excess. . . . I imagine it's no different in the FBI." Just so; and the Gulag was merely a snowbound version of Leavenworth.

Other malicious tales are set down without a shred of supporting evidence. The Truman Administration, Fast reports, had "a list of 300,000 people . . . [who] would immediately be interned in case of war with Russia, and a number of large concentration camps had already been built (and are still in existence, for all know)." As for the President himself, a lawyer informed Fast "that the biggest and best fix in the city was at the White House . . . and then went on to explain, with a good deal of admiration, that Harry Truman was totally honest and dependable, that when he was Senator, his price was $3,000, when he was Vice President, his price was $3,000, and when he became President, his price was still $3,000—and he always delivered. There are enough men still alive who know that I am writing the truth. I am not trying to trash the memory of Harry Truman. I am telling what I know. . . ."

Having scattered the field with his unique amalgam of smear, rumor and innuendo, Fast prepares for the confessional. In 1949 he heard of horrific anti-Semitic purges in the USSR. During yet another Old Left conference, this time in Paris, he confronted Aleksandr Fadeyev, head of the Soviet Writers Union. The accusations were categorically denied, and the plaintiff dropped the subject. Four years later—just about the time Fast was accepting the Stalin Peace Prize—nine Jewish doctors were framed in a "Zionist plot" against the Soviet State. Fast told a colleague about the earlier conversation with Fadeyev.

> "Oh, my God," exclaimed the listener. "Why haven't you written about this?"
>
> "Because the party asked me not to."
>
> "Because the party asked you not to? My God, Howard, what are you saying to me?"
>
> "You know I'm a Communist. I can't write about this unless they agree. I spoke to Fadeyev as a disciplined party member. . . ."

In 1956, Nikita S. Khrushchev went public with the crimes of Stalin, safely dead for three years. Thousands rushed for the doors. Fadeyev took a pistol and blew his brains out.

Not Fast. The disciplined party member continued to write for the *Daily Worker* and to skirmish, in the way that professional wrestlers do, with his conscience. Irving Howe recalls that period in *A Margin of Hope*: At Brandeis, "I debated Howard Fast, the popular writer who in a month or two would break with the Communist Party, but was still defending Stalinism. I lashed Fast without kindness or mercy. . . . Students could not understand the bitterness some of us felt toward Fast, and when he appealed to their sense of 'fair play'—hack that he was, defender of the Moscow trials, defamer of the Yiddish writers murdered by Stalin!—they responded sympathetically. I could only reply that the spectacle of Fast asking for 'fair play' was like a man who kills his mother and father and then asks for mercy on the ground that he is an orphan."

But that is a hostile memory. What about a friendly one? Here is the lapsed *Daily Worker* editor John Gates, who was expelled from the party, recalling the comrade who could not bring himself to resign from the CP until 1957: "Fast . . . defended everything Communist and attacked everything capitalist in the most extravagant terms. It was to be expected that he would react to the Khrushchev revelations in a highly emotional manner. . . . Later, when he announced his withdrawal and told his story, party leaders leaped on him like a pack of wolves and began that particular brand of character assassination which the Communist movement has always reserved for defectors from its ranks."

It has been suggested that Fast recently wrote a critique of Leninism in the New York *Observer* not out of conviction, but because of those character assassins. I am not attempting to trash the image of Howard Fast. I am telling what I know. . . .

"The Leninist structure became a prison and a church," the lecturer harrumphs. "As a church, it paraded Marxism as a religion, a new earthly religion given as new knowledge, and as a prison it sealed the minds of its believers. . . . At the very beginning the men who took power in Russia forgot that dissent, disbelief, questioning and doubt are the only roads to the stars. The devil has two names—orthodoxy and righteousness."

I would add a third, disingenuousness: "*adj.*" says the dictionary, "not straightforward; not candid or frank; insincere." That marks Fast's combination of chutzpah and mendacity from bottom to bottom—there is no top. There is, however, an exchange worth nothing in *Being Red.* During the convention of the Progressive Party in 1948, H. L. Mencken saw through the Communist agitprop and warned Fast to cut loose:

> "I can't put politics aside."
>
> "'Put it aside?' Hell, no. Henry Louis Mencken is a party of one. Do you understand me? You're a party of one. You don't put politics aside; you taste it, smell it, listen to it, and write it. You don't join it. If you do, these clowns will destroy you as surely as the sun rises and sets."

Why would Fast quote such damaging dialogue? Manifestly because he hopes, even at this late date, to shift the *culpa* away from *mea* and onto "those clowns"—the men and women who were once his mates at the pulp barricades. It is not a bad strategy. A lot of readers were not alive during the later Revolutionary era, and they may very well be taken in. The sharper ones will discern that Mencken was wrong. No conspiracy of buffoons could

ever destroy Howard Fast. That demolition was an inside job, as evidenced by *Being Red,* composed by a mythmaker who got along, went along, stayed too long, and has lied happily ever after.

Clancy Sigal (review date 20 January 1991)

SOURCE: "Comrade Novelist Howard Fast Sentimentally Evokes Himself as an American Communist," in *Chicago Tribune Books,* January 20, 1991.

[*In the following review of* Being Red, *Sigal commends Fast's accounts of his persecution, though finds fault in his sentimentality and lack of insight.*]

We American ex-Communists sometimes find it hard to tell the truth about our Party experiences, partly because being hunted like animals isn't always nice to recall. The United States is the only western democracy that has not been able to live with its native Reds. In Britain, France and Italy, even Canada and Mexico, indigenous Communists are accepted as part of a political scene. People pass in and out of the Party in those countries as Democrats and Republicans do here. Although a million or more Americans have been Communists since the 1920s, the memoirist's tone has tended to be either celebratory, defensive or disillusioned: Howard Fast is all three, but he's also illuminated by a serious attempt to be straightforward.

Fast's look back at his Party days—from his bitterly poor New York childhood to his fame as the Communists' best-selling writer and internationally acclaimed "cultural" figure—is, by turns, warm, cozy, angry and informative (if not always informed). He is not one of the world's great political thinkers. Except, sometimes, as a byproduct of his research on historical novels like *Freedom Road* and *Citizen Tom Paine,* Fast is not predisposed to cool analysis. His strength has always been a tremendous faith in ordinary people to move social mountains—a slightly fulsome love of an American ideal as exemplified in its radical dissidents. Nobody can beat him at establishing historical credentials, in the popular novel vein, of such figures as Illinois' great liberal governor John Peter Altgeld, in *The American,* or Rome's immortal slave rebel, Spartacus.

But even thoughtful Communists like *Daily Worker* editor John Gates used to brood that Fast "was not noted for his depth of characterization or historical scholarship." I'm not sure that's what we want of a populist writer "whose genre falls somewhere between Harold Robbins (without the sleaze) and James Michener (without the historical bulk)," as Fast likes to quote an admiring reviewer. In fact, Fast succeeded in his earlier novels at doing what not even Hollywood's left-wing screenwriters were able to do: put real Communist propaganda into work that passed the censor and sold brilliantly. (Later mainstream books like

The Immigrants carried on his historical obsessions but with less slanting.)

As Fast makes clear in this unashamedly affectionate, irk-somely egocentric portrait of his young Party self, he—like thousands of Communists—saw absolutely no contradiction between pro-Soviet agitation and a strong, even fanatic, American patriotism. That's the way it was back then. If you were poor in the Depression, you wanted to overthrow capitalism for a socialist utopia, where kids didn't have rickets and black people weren't lynched; a lot of the time it seemed as bald as that. And if you were Jewish and felt Hitler had to be fought, Russia seemed the best hope of the "anti-fascist struggle."

In other words, you had to have a fairly simple heart to stay a Red. It helped if, like Fast and other non-religious Jews, you "felt a sense of identity with the early Christians" and were, as a more or less full-time activist, "a sort of priest." The problem is that Fast wasn't a simple rank-and-filer. He was up here with the cultural elite, a big name and a front man. He knew—when he wanted to know—where the bodies were buried.

Those bodies had little or nothing to do with being Soviet agents or spies, as Fast makes clear. With the possible exception of Julius and Ethel Rosenberg—Fast only lightly touches on their ticklish "atom bomb espionage" case—"the issues that Communists fought for were issues that people of good will believe in," such as anti-racism, affordable housing and labor struggles. The real dead body was the American Communist leadership.

For reasons best left to radical scholars and argumentative old men, the U.S. Communist Party was cursed with leaders considerably more stupid than the membership. Fast finally couldn't tolerate these "arrogant, thickheaded people," as he calls them. He left the Party in the late '50s and wrote his apologia, ***The Naked God.***

The present book is different in tone and aim from his previous exculpatory and perhaps even obligatory anti-Red confession. (Remember, in those days, "re-entry" for blacklisted artists often was possible only by informing on one's friends or "making a clean breast of it.") ***Being Red*** may be partly an apology for ***The Naked God*** or just Fast's way of tying up loose ends. He is still very angry at the witch-hunters, especially the FBI's J. Edgar Hoover (who personally intervened with publishers to ban Fast's novels), and almost embarrassingly warm toward his old comrades. But then what can you expect of an adult who can say, with a straight face, that "[f]or the most part, writers are gentle and sensitive creatures"?

The chief value of ***Being Red*** is Fast's first-person evocation of what it felt like to take your whacks in the public eye. The episodes are vivid and plausible, including the nearly forgotten Peekskill, N.Y. riot, when townspeople, including local cops and American Legionnaires, attacked an audience assembled to hear Paul Robeson; his brief

spell at a "country club" prison for refusing to tell government inquisitors who had donated to the Joint Anti-Fascist Refugee Committee; and the experience of seeing publishers like Alfred Knopf bend to Hoover's pressure and reject Fast's manuscripts.

But Fast is a sentimentalist at heart. He buys into an essentially unreal picture of what people really are like and won't deal with anything that doesn't fit into a worldview he first developed as the gutter-smart son of a horribly depressed, low-wage steel-and-garment worker. He credits two people with saving his life, his older brother Jerry and his wife of 53 years, Bette, and lavishes a rich stream of compliments upon them. But praise is no substitute for insight. The only people written about with real care in this book are Fast himself and some of the famous people he met, especially the Frenchmen Joliot-Curie and Jean-Paul Sartre.

"Today," Sartre intones, "how else can a man confirm his right to existence and his membership in the human race" except by being a Communist? Fast reports this, as so much else, without irony. The author has many fine qualities, and a talent for comradeship is not the least. Few writers have conveyed as successfully the thrill of standing side by side with Communist comrades against a common enemy. But he lacks a sense of humor about anything having to do with himself—and in this book that means almost everything.

Ronald Radosh (review date March 1991)

SOURCE: "About-Face," in *Commentary,* Vol. 91, No. 3, March, 1991, pp. 62-4.

[*In the following negative review of* Being Red, *Radosh criticizes Fast's involvement in the Communist Party and discrepancies in his recollection of such activities.*]

Howard Fast is best known as the author of a score of historical novels which epitomized what the Old Left liked to call the true spirit of "progressive" America—***Citizen Tom Paine, Freedom Road, The American,*** and ***Spartacus.*** He was also one of the last writers in America to give his allegiance to the American Communist party, of which he was a member from 1944 through 1957.

Now, in a memoir of that period, Fast offers us a very strange book indeed. It is a book which Rhoda Koenig in *New York* magazine called a wonderful remembrance of "the anti-Communist mania of the postwar period," and which inspired Christopher Hitchens, in the Washington *Post Book World,* to describe Fast as one who "left the Communist party for the same reason that he joined it . . . because he was interested in social justice and historical truth." Yet, as is clear from a comparison of ***Being Red*** with the book Fast wrote in 1957, ***The Naked God: The Writer and the Communist Party,*** the one thing he is not devoted to is historical truth, not even about his own experiences in the Communist movement.

Fast's earlier memoir was a strong indictment of American Communism. In that volume, for example, he declared:

> There was the evil in what we dreamed of as Communists: we took the noblest dreams and hopes of mankind as our credo; the evil we did was to accept the degradation of our own souls—and because we surrendered in ourselves, in our own party existence, all the best and most precious gains and liberties of mankind, . . . we betrayed mankind, and the Communist party became a thing of destruction.

Now, nearly thirty-five years later, Fast has produced a new memoir in which he keeps telling us that the Communist version of events, which motivated people like himself to join the party, was essentially correct. For Fast, the enemy of enemies is still Harry Truman, whom he blames for both the cold war and McCarthyism. As for the Soviet Union, whose internal faults he readily acknowledges, it is seen as having had no responsibility for the international tensions of that age.

So too with the American Communist party. After all, American "Communists had laid down their lives" fighting "for the hungry and the homeless and oppressed," and they had a well-deserved "reputation for integrity and decency and honor." Moreover, Fast now asserts, "a very substantial number of the best minds and talent in these United States were party members." It is a pity, he tells us, that their identities cannot be revealed, because their very names would "refute the uncounted slanders hurled against the Communist party." Why, having once strongly renounced the party, Fast now seems so eager to rehabilitate it, he never makes clear.

Fast informs us that he joined the party in 1944 with full knowledge of the Nazi-Soviet pact and the purge trials of the 30s. But those episodes were "part of the past," something to be forgotten at a time when Soviet troops were destroying Nazism and restoring hope to humanity. In any case, "Stalin was no great presence in our thoughts," and the lies being told about the party were so severe that there was simply no way of "winnowing out the truth about Russia and Stalin from the mass of manufactured indictments." No way? What about the writings of Anton Ciliga, or Victor Serge, or Walter Krivitsky, or George Orwell? In continuing to act as though such writings did not exist, Fast shows that he has still not learned to deal with the truth.

Nor is this the only example. Thus, attempting to nail what he considers crude slanders about the party, Fast recalls that once, at Indiana University, when he commented that the novelist James T. Farrell was "one of the finest social realists of our time," a member of the English department announced that Fast could not say such things and be a Communist, "since any party member would face expulsion if he dared to praise Farrell." Fast offers this as typical of "the arrant nonsense" that was spread about the party.

Is Fast simply being disingenuous here, or has he suffered a complete lapse of memory? For he himself played a major part in the famous Albert Maltz affair. Maltz, a well-known author and screenwriter, once published a piece in the Communist magazine *New Masses* in which he called James T. Farrell (then a Trotskyist) a great writer even if ideologically incorrect. In response, Fast accused Maltz of, among other sins and crimes, perpetrating "the ideology of liquidation," while Maltz's Hollywood party cell called a special meeting at which scores of his closest comrades and associates denounced him. Finally, two months later, to save himself from expulsion, Maltz published a humiliating retraction.

In *The Naked God,* Fast admitted his own role in the Maltz affair. Maltz, he then said, was "a writer of talent and unshakable integrity," who had been "denounced by his own comrades as one seeking to strike a death blow at man's holiest hopes and aspirations . . . he had sinned, and the aim was to make him submit to a process of total degradation." In 1957 as well, Fast was able to acknowledge that he himself was "among those who blew up [Maltz's] criticism all out of proportion to its intent; a matter for which I have never forgiven myself." Yet today he can dismiss an "arrant nonsense" the idea that "any party member would face expulsion if he dared to praise Farrell."

Another discrepancy between *The Naked God* of 1957 and *Being Red* of 1990 concerns the so-called Waldorf Peace Conference in 1949. Anti-Communist intellectuals like Sidney Hook and Mary McCarthy correctly saw this event as part of a Communist-controlled attempt to win the minds of the world's intellectuals, while participants in the conference, like the playwright Lillian Hellman, claimed, then and later, that it was not run by the CP. On this point Fast confirms the anti-Communists (whom he and so many others attacked at the time for "Red-baiting"): "Over 500 of the nation's leading intellectuals were willing to put their careers and names on the line for a conference created by the Communist party . . . the lines were clearly drawn, and no one at the conference had any illusions as to who the organizers were."

Yet the official conference booklet, published by the National Council of Arts, Sciences, and Professions, stated that the meeting included sponsors who "ranged in their political orientation and social philosophy from a half dozen outspoken Communists to another handful of persons barely Left of the political Center. . . . The majority were . . . merely New Dealish liberals." In other words, the party then engaged in its usual attempt to make it appear that the conference was the effort of a broad front, in which only a few Reds participated. Moreover, the conference brochure noted that a campaign had been waged in advance to discredit the meeting. How? "The Red label was to be pinned on the meeting."

This makes it all the more puzzling when Fast now writes that the intellectuals "rallied to the cause of peace with the

Soviet Union," as if that were the conference's purpose, when, as he well knows, it really was to defend Soviet policy and build up a movement against America's response to Soviet aggression.

In another change of tune, Fast also ridicules Mary Mc-Carthy's attempt at an intervention (she "was neither a supporter nor was she invited, but she appeared, umbrella in hand, striding fiercely down the center aisle . . . where the literary panel was in session," at which point Fast "took the wind out of her sails" by helping her onto the platform).

Here, by dramatic contrast, is how he described the same incident in *The Naked God:*

> It should also be noted that when . . . [Fadeyev, the Soviet Cultural Commissar] was asked directly by Mary McCarthy and some of her friends to explain what had happened to a number of Soviet writers, whom they carefully named, he not only gave his solemn word as a Soviet citizen that all of the named writers were alive and well, but he brilliantly ticked off the titles and description of the work that each particular writer had engaged upon. He . . . even repeated details of their merry reaction to the "capitalist slander" that they were being persecuted. So smooth and ready was his rejoinder, so rich was the substance of his quickly supplied background, that one might as well credit him with more creative imagination than he had ever shown in his own books. As chairman, . . . I was quite naturally provoked that Miss McCarthy . . . should so embarrass this fine and distinguished guest. His conviction and meticulous sincerity were above suspicion . . . how could they possibly have believed that a man would create such a monstrous and detailed lie and expect it to hold water? . . . Yet this is precisely what it was . . . and all of the men Fadeyev had spoken of so casually and lightly and intimately were, at the time he spoke, either dead from the torture chambers of the secret police or by firing squads, or lying in prison, being tortured and beaten.

The Rosenberg case provides yet another instance of Fast's inability to deal with historical truth. He writes that "with all the books and articles about the Rosenbergs, no one ever questioned why the important atomic physicists of the time were not brought in as witnesses." But in *The Rosenberg File,* Joyce Milton and I show that the defense had indeed approached the major scientists—including sympathetic fellow-travelers—and they all responded that the information supplied by David Greenglass could well have been of value to the Russians.

Again, Fast accurately notes the party's reluctance to enter the case, and he claims credit for persuading it to change its mind. The evidence, however, strongly indicates that the American party went in only after it was sure that the Rosenbergs would not cooperate with the government, and after French CP chief Jacques Duclos began an international campaign around the case, meant to deflect the West's attention from the anti-Semitic Slansky purge trial going on in Czechoslovakia. The Rosenbergs, Duclos proclaimed in Paris, were being sentenced to death because they were Jews, while the Slansky group had received a death sentence because they were traitors.

Fast's own contribution to this propaganda campaign was to paint a picture abroad of a United States in the grip of fascism, with Truman and then Eisenhower playing the role of Hitler. Today, instead of repudiating that version, he endorses it: "The terror was not slackening," he writes incredibly of those years in *Being Red,* "the Rosenberg case had been orchestrated to an anti-Communist frenzy that matched the exuberant hysteria of the Nazi horror."

In general, Fast seems intent on propagating the myth of moral equivalence—in particular the idea (also espoused by Carl Bernstein in *Loyalties*) that America too had its gulag and reign of terror. Yet Fast once knew better. In his earlier account, Fast acknowledged that although he himself went to prison for contempt of Congress and was forced to become his own publisher because his books had been dropped by his commercial house (as well as being removed from library shelves), he nevertheless "continued to write" and "continued to live," while his Soviet counterpart "was silenced . . . [and] cruelly tortured and . . . put to death."

Today, amazingly, he seems unaware even that the McCarthy era is over. He says that the Communist Control Act of 1954—which, due to Supreme Court decisions, became inoperative—is "still part of the criminal code of the United States," and writes that "there is no law extent in any country . . . as all-embracing and terrifying." He even says that, for all he knows, the internment camps set up under the act still exist. Does he not know that these camps, which were kept intact but never used, were finally closed down by the hated Nixon administration?

Years ago, Fast co-authored a polemical article with his comrade Paul Robeson called **"We Will Never Retreat."** Events forced Fast to make precisely such a retreat, and when he did, his old comrades spewed their venom on him. Lester Cole, a Communist screenwriter and one of the Hollywood Ten, gave his own reason for Fast's quitting the party: "The swimming pool and house on the hill in Hollywood . . . are now his at last." Now, nearly thirty-five years later, it almost sounds as though Fast wants to end his days winning back the admiration of those unreconstructed Communists—"some of the noblest human beings I have ever known."

How ironic that, when Communism is collapsing everywhere, one of the earliest defectors from the American party should look back to reaffirm the "nobility" of that lost cause, and to condemn the anti-Communist American administrations of the 40s and 50s which repelled Stalin's advances in Europe. And how ironic too that, in our strange culture, a book written from that point of view should be so warmly received.

Gerald Meyer (review date Spring 1993)

SOURCE: "Howard Fast: An American Leftist Reinterprets His Life," in *Science & Society,* Vol. 57, No. 1, Spring, 1993, pp. 86-91.

[*In the following review, Meyer discusses Fast's political involvements and offers tempered assessment of* Being Red, *which he describes as "readable and useful" though "inaccurate" and evasive.*]

The publication of **Being Red,** Howard Fast's account of his association with the Communist Party, should be a valuable addition to the growing list of memoirs and historical studies about the CPUSA. Unfortunately, Fast is unable to separate his primary role as a novelist from his less familiar role as memoirist.

Fast is an unusually prolific writer: his corpus includes more than 80 books, including 50 novels, ten plays, and 20 books of nonfiction. Worldwide sales of his novels have exceeded 80 million. His writings have been translated into 82 languages and many observes—including Fast—insist that he may be the most widely read writer of the 20th century.

From 1943, until 1956, while Fast was a Party member, the Party and indeed the world movement lionized him. It was during this period that the vast circulation of his books occurred. In his popular historical novels—*Citizen Tom Paine, Freedom Road, The American,* (about John Peter Altgeld), *The Last Frontier,* and *Spartacus*—protagonists from the oppressed classes—craftsmen, freed slaves, immigrant workers, Native Americans, and slaves—dramatized the class struggles, with its tragic setbacks yet somehow certain ultimate victory. Fast was a major figure in the Party's remarkable enterprise of developing a complex and almost complete popular "progressive" American culture.

As a result, Howard Fast entered the Party's pantheon. At home he was ranked together with Paul Robeson and W.E.B. Du Bois. When he traveled to the 1949 World Peace Conference in Paris, he entered "a world where Communists were honored, not hunted down and imprisoned." He sat on the stage next to Louis Aragon. Pablo Picasso kissed him on the mouth and offered him any painting he chose. Later, Pablo Neruda wrote a poem to him. In 1954, he received the Stalin Peace Prize.

At home, the system visited on Howard Fast every punishment it had devised to persecute and obliterate the Communist movement. In April 1946, the House Committee on Un-American Activities subpoenaed Fast and 15 other members of the executive board of the Joint Anti-Fascist Refugee Committee, an organization supporting medical facilities for Spanish Republican refugees living in Southern France. The House Committee demanded the names of the Joint Committee's 30,000 donors. (Fast tells us they included Eleanor Roosevelt, José Ferrer, Ruth Gordon, Stella Adler, Leonard Bernstein, Van Wyck Brooks, Mark Van Doren, and Lucille Ball.) The board refused and, by a Congressional vote of 262 to 56 eleven of its members became the first group to be cited for contempt of Congress for refusal to cooperate with the Congressional inquisition. In 1950, after the Supreme Court refused to issue a writ of certiori, Fast and ten other members of the executive board were imprisoned for three months.

In 1949 *Citizen Tom Paine* was removed from New York City's libraries. Fast was barred from speaking at City College and many other campuses. He was under constant surveillance by the FBI (his file ultimately reached 1100 pages), and he was refused a passport until 1961. Publisher after publisher (Little Brown, Viking, Scribners, Harper, Knopf, Simon & Schuster, Doubleday) rejected his new historical novel, *Spartacus,* which, published privately, ultimately sold 50,000 copies.

After resigning from the Communist Party, it was not until 1977 that Fast found a new audience and a new identity with the publication of **The Immigrants,** the first in a highly successful series that has been characterized as a San Francisco family saga. One critic noted: "I'm sure [**The Immigrants**] has some overriding social purpose, but happily it never gets in front of the relentless pace of events. In short, you can enjoy this book without a thought in your head. . . ." Ironically, the most significant literary event in Fast's career after leaving the Party was his 1960 collaboration with Dalton Trumbo on the screenplay for *Spartacus,* which represented a major breakthrough in overcoming the Hollywood blacklisting.

Fast was never again to attain the same degree of fame he had enjoyed as a Communist. The most important prize he ever received was the Stalin Peace Prize and he is remembered as the writer who converted the genre of the historical novel to the requirements of Popular Front culture. *Freedom Road, The Unvanquished* (Fast's novel about George Washington and the American Revolution), *Citizen Tom Paine,* and *The American* encapsulate Party Secretary Earl Browder's understanding that if Communism was to become 20th-century Americanism it had to have historical antecedents.

Fast chaired the 1949 Peekskill concert, sponsored by the Civil Rights Congress, where mobs of rock-hurling youths screaming "Kill a Commie for Christ" prevented Paul Robeson from singing. One week later, 15,000 attended the rescheduled concert, protected by 3,000 trade unionists. After a most successful program, mobs attacked the concert-goers' cars and buses as they left routed by police through narrow back roads, causing many severe injuries. Recently while interviewing an elderly woman who had been present at the affair, I mentioned that I was writing this review. With great vehemence she said: "Don't you go and say anything bad about Howard Fast. I saw him in Peekskill with a Coke bottle in each hand fighting back."

Being Red then is the story of the best years of Howard Fast's life. "I don't know anything in life so satisfying and nourishing as the sense that you are doing what you were put on earth to do, fighting for things you believe, for the poor, the oppressed and against racism. It gives one a feeling of being, of consciousness, and connection." This is what Fast now remembers he found in the Party.

Fast also refutes all the major criticisms of the Party. He insists that the Party was not dominated by the Soviet Union and, in any case, that it was "Russia [which] had paid a price of twenty million human lives to destroy the Nazis . . . and moved three million Polish and Ukrainian Jews eastward beyond the reach of the Nazis." He states that the *Daily Worker* "never compromised with the truth as it saw truth. . . ." Again and again he returns to the theme that the Communists were "priests in the brotherhood of man. When I joined the Communists Party, I joined the company of the good." Fast also reminds the reader that the Party was the group which best knew how to conduct the anti-Fascist struggle, and that Communists "fought and often enough died for black freedom." He also recalls the Party's leading role in the organization of the Progressive Party and speaks of the famous people who joined its ranks.

Similarly, Fast provides vivid and often touching descriptions of his early life, a life which could logically lead a thinking person toward the Communist movement. He ascribes his "sense of identity with the poor and oppressed of all the earth" to his working-class father, a Jewish immigrant from the Ukraine. The extreme poverty experienced by Howard and his brothers was overcome only through their cooperative efforts. This too must have led him to believe in the possibilities of collaboration among the oppressed.

But apparently Fast's need to glorify his past prevents him from accurately remembering a number of critical events. Most egregious is his account of an incident at the World Peace Conference in Paris in 1949. He says he was carrying instructions given him by Paul Novick, leader of the Jewish Commission of the CP, from the Central Committee of the Communist Party, USA. He claims to have been instructed to inform the head of the Soviet delegation that the CPUSA was bringing charges against the Communist Party of the USSR because of anti-Semitism in the Soviet Union! The implausibility of this story is total. Nowhere in the public record is there any instance of the CPUSA criticizing the CPSU, much less "levying charges" against it. Moreover, none of the many memoirs of or interviews with Party leaders or ex-Party leaders has ever mentioned this extraordinary event.

Even more significantly, Fast himself never mentions this episode in his earlier memoir, *The Naked God* (New York: Fredrick Praeger, 1957) which does deal with Soviet anti-Semitism. Indeed although it covered much of the same ground as *Being Red* from a very different viewpoint, Fast never mentions *The Naked God* in this autobiography. It is even omitted from the "Books by Howard Fast" listed in this volume. Clearly, *The Naked God* is something he wants to forget, and amazingly the reviewers of *Being Red* have allowed it to be forgotten.

Being Red is the autobiography of an old man who wants to be remembered as a man of the left. After all, everything that happened to him before joining the CP seemed to lead

to that decision, and his fame and feelings of self-worth were at their height when he was a member. He has recently reestablished his connections with the left by becoming a columnist for the *New York Observer*, writing trenchant and militant critiques from a strongly left perspective.

The Naked God served as a questionable passport used to gain reentry into the capitalist publishing world. Its account of many events greatly contrasts with those in *Being Red. The Naked God* stated that communism was based on "naked terror, awful brutality, and frightening ignorance." It goes on to say that the evil Communism did "was to accept the degradation of our own soul," and that in joining the CP "one sells his own soul." At the same time, it underplays Fast's own persecution by the United States government.

To be sure, *The Naked God* also contains glowing descriptions of party members: "Never in so small a group have I seen so many pure souls, so many gentle and good people. So many men and women of utter integrity." But its *leitmotif* is that the CP is an "oriental temple of organization [led by a] dogma-ridden priesthood. . . ." Although all his best work was written during his Party years, Fast writes about the Party's destruction of his muse, claiming he had to leave the Party in order to become a better writer.

Fast's resignation from the Party was announced in a front-page *New York Times* interview with the extreme anti-Soviet reporter, Harry Schwartz. And while there is no record that Fast ever named names, Natalie Robins reports in *Alien Ink: The FBI's War on Freedom of Expression* that Fast's FBI file indicates he contacted the FBI to report that his just completed book would "assist the anti-Communist cause" and gave its agents a set of galleys.

Intellectuals remaining within and close to the Communist Party filled the pages of *Mainstream*, the Party's cultural journal, with angry and sad comments. Walter Lowenfels queried:

> Where are your wound stripes? Your torn and battered uniform? Your badge in the fight for the clean word? . . . I expected a battle scarred front line dispatch from you. Instead, you give us a political report on the Russian situation. What I was expecting was not your farewell to Russia but your salute to the people of the U.S.A.

However, it was Joseph Starobin who drew the most blood. He depicted Fast as the Party's Frankenstein:

> In the CP Fast found adulation. . . . And he reveled in what he should have resisted. . . . For Howard became in the CP the oracle on every issue from Negro rights to socialist realism . . . he headed every conceivable committee, took the floor each time without saying too much, refused the pleas of his best editors to revise his first drafts, published the best novel of the year every year. . . . But throughout it all he neither grew as a writer nor gained wisdom as a man. . . . [He lived] in a left which had lost all sense of proportion about Howard Fast.

It is understandable that Fast may want to forget all this, but *Being Red* is finally only as important as it is accurate. It would seem that Fast invented his mission to the 1949 Paris Peace Conference, in order to bury the memory of having uncritically supported a movement which at that time glorified a regime obliterating Yiddish culture. Similarly, in *Being Red* Fast accuses Morris U. Schappes of having threatened to bring him up for expulsion from the Party on charges of Jewish nationalism because of the publication of *My Glorious Brothers,* a novel about the Maccabees. Schappes pointed out in *Jewish Currents* that although Fast had mentioned his name in *The Naked God,* he did not there connect Schappes to this report of a threatened expulsion. In a somewhat similar though less damaging way, Angus Cameron has rejected Fast's explanation that he resigned as editor-in-chief and vice president of Little, Brown in protest against Little, Brown's refusal to publish *Spartacus.* Cameron insists that the question of *Spartacus* was only peripheral to his decision, which was prompted more by the general retreat of the company in the face of the intensifying repression.

Despite these serious weakness, *Being Red* is both readable and useful. It helps the reader to understand the attractions of the Communist Party in the 1930s and 40s, as well as its many accomplishments. It also effectively documents the as yet not fully acknowledged depredations of what has become known as the McCarthy Era. But it fails as autobiography, because Fast is still unable to integrate not only his leaving the Communist Party but also the nature of his attacks on it in his earlier book, with his life as he now chooses to remember it. There remains a discontinuity, which must always be unexplained as long as it is unacknowledged.

Howard Fast with Alan Wald and Alan Filreis (interview date 1995)

SOURCE: "A Conversation with Howard Fast, March 23, 1994," edited by Thomas J. Sugrue, in *Prospects: An Annual of American Cultural Studies,* edited by Jack Salzman, Vol. 20, Cambridge: Cambridge University Press, 1995, pp. 511-23.

[*In the following interview, Fast discusses his life, literary activities, the Communist Party and his involvement in that organization, and his memoirs* The Naked God *and* Being Red.]

[*Alan Wald]: When we read your memoir that came out in 1990,* **Being Red,** *many of us had also read an earlier book called* **The Naked God** *in 1957—and our impression of your experience was represented by* **The Naked God** *until we read* **Being Red.** *There seems to many of us to be a big difference between the two books and it is also noticed by some of us that in your long list of books in front of* **Being Red** *you don't mention* **The Naked God,** *and in* **Being Red** *you don't talk about* **The Naked God.**

So we are wondering whether or not **Being Red** *is sort of a new version of the past that is appropriate for some reason. Is there something inadequate, perhaps, about the earlier version or some political need now to rethink and reform your ideas? What are the differences between the two books? Why did you write the second?*

[Howard Fast]: The chief difference is thirty-five years—which is a big difference. When I wrote *The Naked God,* I was very angry. I was furious with what I considered a betrayal of people of good will by a large part of the leadership of the Communist Party. You see, I do not look upon the destruction of the Soviet Union and the careers of the men who led the Soviet Union as an attempt to establish a tyranny. I look upon it as a betrayal of the long struggle of man to create an equitable society. If, if—and like all "ifs" it is rather unthinkable—but if the leadership of the struggle of the Soviet Union had not fallen into the hands of Stalin and the people around him, would it have been any different?

Well, after an experience of twelve years as a member of the Communist Party of the United States, I can say it would have been no different. The structure—Leninist concept—of a party that was incorruptible was as fallible as all other dreams. All parties are corruptible, and Lenin created a form of party that was even more corruptible than any of the capitalist parties. So, when I wrote *The Naked God,* everything had come up to hit me in the face, and particularly the report of Khrushchev to the 20th Congress of the Soviet Union. Now people said to us—by us I mean people in the Communist movement, the many, indeed hundreds of thousands of people who were associated, with it as fellow travelers and friends—they said to me and to all of us: "How could you not know what was happening?" The answer is that at least half of the people who were gathered in the hall of the Supreme Soviet listening to Khrushchev also did not know what was going on. There was a cloak of secrecy that had never been penetrated until Khrushchev made his speech.

The list of people who saw in the Soviet Union the salvation of mankind goes from George Bernard Shaw and Sean O'Casey and Bertrand Russell to so many others. All of us believed that the torrent of anti-Soviet propaganda was without foundation. This is something that will be studied by future scholars, and they will ask how is it possible that you were willing to die? And so many of us did die, and so many of the boys I knew who went to Spain died there, all of them believing what Lincoln Steffens had said was true, "I have seen the future and it works." Was that the future?

It did not work. And when we saw it collapse, our anger was enormous. In those few weeks . . . by the way I should say that I hope you know what I am referring to when I speak about the Khrushchev speech to the 20th Congress of the Soviet Union. It was a twenty-thousand-word document read in a secret session to representatives of the Communist Party from all over the world. And, as a matter of fact, in historical hindsight, it is the Khrushchev speech at the 20th Congress that destroyed the world organization of the Leninist Party as it existed. Now, there was a Hungarian delegate there who took his copy of the speech (they were all given copies) and sold it to the CIA. The CIA had it translated and gave it to the *New York Times*. The editorial board of the *Times* called us at the *Daily Worker* and said, "Look, we have a copy of Khrushchev's speech to the 20th Congress. We are satisfied, totally satisfied, that this is a verbatim and totally honest copy." (Which as it turns out it was.) "Do you want it?" We said, "Send it right over." So the *Times* copied it and sent it right over to us.

There was a meeting in the editorial rooms of the *Daily Worker* that somehow has not been mentioned here this afternoon, but I must mention that in its thirty-five-year history this paper never retreated, never hesitated. It printed the truth as we saw the truth for every one of those thirty-five years. Every measure of force and legality that the United States could garner was used against us. I say "us" because, on and off through a period of twelve years, I worked without pay as both a correspondent and a columnist for the *Daily Worker*. We gathered there in the editorial rooms and for the next several hours listened to the collapse of our world, the collapse of our dreams, the collapse of what people who are beloved of us, our dearest friends had died for. And willingly died for. All of it crumbling there. Then we did what no other Communist newspaper in the world did. We published the entire text of the Khrushchev speech in the *Daily Worker*. It took a whole expanded edition to do it. We were the only Communist Party in the world that had the courage to do that. For the next two weeks, we launched a series of attacks on the Soviet leadership. Not the kind of attacks that a capitalist press had been launching against them in the past half-century. We said, "You have betrayed us. You have betrayed the human race. You have betrayed everything that man believed in."

[Wald]: *So one of the big differences—to you—between the two books* [**The Naked God**] *and* [**Being Red**] *is that the first is written in the anger of betrayal?*

In rage. **Being Red** is written in reflection.

[Wald]: *There is something here in this version that you see in the past that you want to pass on to the younger generation as positive. Is that more than rage?*

Perhaps more that is positive. Perhaps less that is rage. Because when I wrote **The Naked God** there was no perspective. We did not understand. How could men who accepted the brotherhood of man—how could such men betray us? How could they do it?

[Alan Filreis]: *In that era of frustration and anger, you wrote a letter, which I have here, in which you said, "I guess I am over the worst of it." This is after you left the Party. It is dated October 1, 1957: "All of those with just*

a few exceptions whom I loved and honored in the Party have left it. Many of us keep thinking how lucky we are. I know I often have that thought. There were many nights of heartsickness and fear but that is mostly done with now. The problem now is not to hate out of a subjective sense of tragedy, but I suppose that has always been the problem with those who left."

Can you tell us a little more about the "heartsickness and fear"?

The Communist Party ran a training school up on the Hudson River. It was in a summer hotel. They would take fifteen or twenty—most of us veterans, people who had come out of World War II—and subject us to a fantastically compressed course of philosophy and socialism and Marxism, and the whole rest of it. It was a great experience for me. It lasted only two weeks, but the people I met there, all of them, were steelworkers and coal miners. It was just a marvelous experience to be with them for those two weeks. All of them veterans and at least a half-dozen of them veterans of the Spanish [Civil] War. And a question came up that sounds completely cynical: "Suppose the Party instructed you to go to the top of the Empire State Building and jump off? What would you do?" My answer was I'd tell them to go to hell. But there were people there—working people there—who said, "If it was necessary for the victory of the working class I would do it." And they would. And they believed it. So when you ask about the heartsickness, think about what these men would do.

[Wald]: *This raises an important question for us. If it's true, as you and as many other people have written about the Communist Party say, that the flaw in the American Communist Party was its dependence on and delusions in regard to the Soviet Union, how much of the heroism and self-sacrifice were dependent on that belief? Would all those people—such as the three thousand Americans who went to Spain to fight, with two thousand of them dying because they had very few weapons and so on—have made great sacrifices if they had not really believed that the Soviet Union was the first step forward? Would people have resisted McCarthyism so heroically if they had not believed that somewhere people had really created socialism?*

That's a good question. Think of what the position of the Soviet Union was. If you know the history of the Spanish War, you know that to some extent—and I think to a very large extent—the Soviet Union betrayed the Spanish Republic, because Hitler sent his dive bombers and Mussolini sent his Blackshirts, and all sorts of aid was given to the Franco forces, but the Soviet aid to the Republic was minimal. And yet it was not enough to shake us. We made excuses. The Soviet Union had to do this. They were in a position where they could not give us the aid that the Republic needed to be victorious, even though a victory in Spain would have changed the whole course of events that led to World War II.

On the other hand, I have to say this: We had the best party in the world. We had the best of America, the best of American know-how. With this little party, we worked wonders. And if the Soviet Union had not been there, there still would have been a working-class party, but it would have taken a different direction and would have been a different kind of a party. There has always been a socialist movement of sorts in America going way back to the middle of the 19th Century. No such measures were taken against the socialist forces in Europe or England, for example. Why this sudden outburst of murderous fury against the Communist Party of the United States?

[Filreis]: One of the things that Alan's [Alan Wald's] work has led me to is an enormous appreciation of the Left's antiracism activities and policy in this period. One of your most remarkable activities was the "We Charge Genocide" petition to the United Nations for "relief from crime of the U.S. government against the Negro people."

It was my idea.

[Filreis]: It was your idea. It's astonishing when you think about it. A number of Americans appealed to the United Nations for "relief from crimes of the U.S. government against the Negro people." I would like you to think about how that looks to you now—years later—after the Khrush-chev revelations [that] a party that did or did not know what is going on in the Soviet Union was charging genocide that was perpetrated by the United States against some of its own people. How complicated is that?

The Soviet Union, the leaders of the Soviet Union—and this I know from personal experience—never understood "the Negro question" and in those days we called it "the Negro question." This was a very pertinent focus, a chief focus of the Communist Party here. I will get to that in a moment. There was a man called Willy McGee who was unjustly sentenced to life imprisonment, I believe, or perhaps death . . .

[Wald]: He was executed.

He was executed. My memory goes. Just before he was executed, the Party asked for volunteers to go to Washington, D.C., and make a rather unique protest. So this group went to Washington and I went with them to write about it for the *Daily Worker*. They went to the Lincoln Memorial. Half of the men there were Spanish vets. They chained themselves to the Lincoln Memorial—to the pillars of the Lincoln Memorial. I think there were about ten men chained in a circle around each pillar. Fortunately I was not chained. I was standing at the side with my little notebook—which is always an advantage a reporter has—to be out of the direct line of fire. We had every expectation that the Washington police would simply come and open fire against these men. They didn't. They came and cut the chains and they didn't even put us in jail.

But to get back to your question. Afterwards I was discussing this with Bill Patterson, who was one of the leading

black Communists at the time. This was when the drive of the Negro people was integration, not separation, and the drive of the Party was toward integration. We were discussing what had happened in Europe—the Holocaust. I said, "Bill, if we put together every unjustified murder—the death of a black in the South—you would have a Holocaust. You would have the material for it. Could you get the records?" He thought he could. That is how the book appeared which was titled *We Charge Genocide*. Then I said, "Let's take it to the United Nations."

*[Wald]: I want to ask you something about the cultural activity in the 1950s. Again, I don't ask these questions merely out of curiosity about the past, but many young people today would like to be cultural workers who participate in antiracist struggles and pro-union struggles, and use their talents to forward our contemporary social-ist values, but they are uncertain as cultural workers how they can relate to a political party. So I want to look back at the Communist experience about what is recuperable and what could be rejected. You talk in both **Being Red** and in **The Naked God** about the cultural section of the Party. You talk about your relations with [Lionel] Berman and [V.J.] Jerome. And you describe a situation in which it seems that you are continually being watched for the pos-sible misuse of a word or for writing something that could be misinterpreted, or for creating an ending of **Spartacus** that is not quite right. And yet you have a lot of freedom, too, because no one is forcing you to submit your manuscripts in advance and no one is telling you what to write in advance, but there is a feeling of somebody watch-ing over your shoulder. I think you gained a lot of freedom from having a connection with the radical movement in terms of giving you themes and inspiration, but there are constraints at the same time. What can we learn today in terms of the relationship of the artist to political struggle and political organizations?*

Well, to begin with, aside from my rage and grief and anger, there is also part of me that was very happy that the Communist Party of the United States came to its end. It was constructed as the Soviet Party was constructed. I understood everything that happened in Russia because I saw the same thing happening in a minuscule fashion in our Party. And here you heard some nice things said about V. J. Jerome. I always looked upon V. J. Jerome—who was the cultural czar of the Communist Party—as a hor-rible, rigid little monster who never knew what he was do-ing. In the Soviet Union, the things I did would have been, I suppose, punishable by death or by being put away in one of the camps or whatever. But, here, the Party lacked the power. They lacked the power to inflict any punish-ment on a member of the Party except expulsion from the Party. They would have liked to have expelled me on many occasions, but they were afraid to because so many had left. I was one of the few remaining. On one occasion, I wrote a piece about a meeting in Boston and I said there were white boys and black boys and white girls and black girls. And, for this, they brought me up on expulsion for using the term girl in connection with a black person.

They were rigid. They were stupid. And I am talking now about the top leadership of the Party. When I wrote **My Glorious Brothers** in 1948, they brought me up for expulsion. Jewish nationalism. Thank God there was a man in the leadership named Jack Statchel who said any Jew here in 1948 who is not a Jewish nationalist is an idiot. So they dropped that.

Now, the cultural things we did as individuals, we did. There was very little the Party could do about it except to criticize it. And I am not talking in this sense about the great proletarian, the great anti-institutional novelist writers we have in this country: a man like [Samuel] Ornitz writing *Haunch, Paunch and Jowl* as a Communist, Mike Gold writing *Jews Without Money,* or Cliff Odets writing *Awake and Sing.* These were not subject in any sense to the Party. The Party had enough sense to know that they had to keep hands off. But in certain cases where the Party made something possible, they thought that they had the right to have hands on.

[Wald]: You tend to use "they" to refer to officials such as Jerome, yet in the case of Albert Maltz, who wrote about the need for more freedom, you yourself were one of the people who jumped on Maltz.

Yes, yes I did.

[Wald]: And you would not regard yourself as one of the "idiots" at the top?

At the time, yes. Jack Lawson—John Howard Lawson—who was the cultural commissar of the Party on the West Coast was writing a history of Western culture and, when certain things happened in terms of World War II, he began to revise it. Maltz attacked him severely and Maltz was a beloved friend of mine. (It was one of the consolations of being in prison that I was in prison with him.) When [Lawson] felt that events forced him to change much of what he had written, Maltz said, "No, if you write honestly and truly, you should not have to change it." And, in a sense, Maltz was right. I thought Maltz was all wrong because at that time I believed wholly in anything that John Howard Lawson or V. J. Jerome would say.

[Wald]: But the article that Maltz wrote—"What Shall We Ask of Writers?"—was not about Lawson. It was arguing that we cannot judge writers by their political commitments. He particularly pointed to James T. Farrell, whom you yourself admired very much, as an example of a writer whose writing was criticized because he had gone over to Trotskyism.

Maltz was right.

[Wald]: You and others such as [Samuel] Sillen and Gold—even though Sillen is a very nice man and Gold is a charming loveable guy—jumped on Maltz viciously until he finally capitulated and said he was wrong and that art is a weapon and people have to be judged by their politics.

That is absolutely true.

[Wald]: So there was something more than stupid guys at the top. There must have been some kind of culture that encouraged the judgment of art by political positions.

It was more than a culture. It was a dogmatic part of the Party's existence. Let me give you an even more horrible example—where, thank God, I was at that point where you grow and you change unless you have a rock mind. I wrote a play [**The Hammer**] about a family that had three sons and one became a wealthy businessman and war profiteer. It was a Jewish family, obviously. An actor, Michael Lewin, a skinny little guy with thin red hair and one of those pasty white skins, played the father. And this was to be a great surprise for me when I came out of prison. I come out of prison. I go down with my wife to watch. And who do I see walk onto stage as the third son, but James Earl Jones. With a voice that shook the place. Six feet tall, built like a mountain.

"Oy!" I said, "Herb! What the hell are you doing? This is a Jewish family.[1] The father is a skinny, little redheaded Jew. What are you doing?"

He said, "We are carrying out a decision of the Party that the validity of what the theater calls the suspension of disbelief is more valid than casting according to type."

I said, "But everyone is going to see Jimmy Jones. They will not see the suspension of disbelief. Nobody has that much suspension of disbelief."

They came down on me with great force and either I accepted it or all sorts of things would lead up to my expulsion—which was always the case. The first night—the opening night—was sold out to an organization that no longer exists, a Jewish garmentworkers organization called the Jewish People's Organization or something of that sort.[2] It was one of those working-class mutual-insurance groups. And they filled the theater. Everything is going nicely and all of a sudden Jones walks onto the stage. And I hear all over, in Yiddish, *"Was tut de shvartze?"* Well, the rest of the show was a nightmare. And the *Herald Tribune* critic who was there came to me afterward and said, "Fast, I admire you and I'm gonna do you a favor and not review this."

*[Filreis]: This is an example of unintentional Party high hilarity. In **Being Red,** you describe at least one story that I found wonderful, which suggested intentional Party high hilarity. Something that you did that was outrageous and funny to you and part of some kind of protest activity. I am recalling the story where you and a friend rented a room, put up a speaker, locked the door on the way out. You had moments like that which were not moments of super seriousness that were creative and innovative.*

When Truman recalled MacArthur, they were going to have a great parade up Park Avenue for MacArthur. One of my friends who was a Lincoln [Brigade] veteran, Irv Goff, a wonderful man, came to me and said, "Look, I talked the Party into it. We will rent a room in the Waldorf and put so much magnification in there and we'll play a record that can be heard all over Manhattan Island denouncing MacArthur, denouncing Truman: 'Bring the boys back! Why did you bring MacArthur back?!'" So I wrote this thing, a very passionate little piece, and I recorded it. I had a friend who was a bond salesman who used to sell phony bonds, but in his heart he was all left-wing. And he rented a room in the Waldorf facing Park Avenue. Then there were electricians and radio men in the Party. They got these giant speakers that we had to fold up to put into suitcases, and all sorts of amplifying material put into suitcases.

There were fifty secret service men and over a hundred G-men, not to mention five hundred New York cops around that building and in every floor of it, and we had to walk about a thousand pounds of electronic material through them. If ever there was a testimony of the stupidity of the Secret Service and the Justice Department! We brought it all into this room and we set it all up there and we were ready to go. We closed the door and worked the key back and forth and snapped the key in the lock, so the only way to open the door was to take the lock out. After that, we discovered that the Waldorf had direct current—they did not have alternating current.

So, Goff went down to the Party headquarters on 13th Street and explained the situation. They asked him, "How do we know that you and Fast aren't government agents and deliberately screwed it up? There is only one way to prove you're not. That's two thousand dollars worth of material that the Party put out for. You've gotta go up there and bring it out." You have to explain to fifty secret service, G-men, and cops . . . They said, "Either do that or you're both out." Then we had to find a locksmith who was a Communist, and we found him. He took the lock off, Secret Service and all. And we put two thousand dollars worth of amplifying machinery back into the suitcases and took it out of the Waldorf. And no one was caught and no one was punished for it.

[Wald]: *I would like to ask a question about the literary impact of the Cold War in terms of your writing style and strategy. One of the most remarkable novels you ever wrote is* **The Proud and the Free,** *which came out just as you were going to prison. It is a remarkable novel for me because, as someone who follows the New Left revisions of U.S. history, I have noticed all the revisions about slavery and the Civil War. But you take up the American Revolution and argue that in fact there was a class struggle within the American Revolution between what you call the foreign brigades, the Pennsylvania Line, made up of basically poor people—children of indentured servants, blacks, Jews, and so on—and the gentry officers. When I look at all the revisionist historians of the New Left generation, I do not see anybody else who has yet to take up that question. I think you were way ahead. I wonder whether the crisis of the Cold War forced you to go more deeply and critically into U.S. history than you had before. Did the*

Cold War force you to take up new literary tasks and projects that you might not have?

Actually not. The story of **The Proud and the Free** begins with Carl Van Doren. He had taken me under his wing before I ever joined the Party. Carl Van Doren wrote a marvelous book called *Mutiny in January,* and he suggested that I write a novel about [the American Revolution] years back and finally I got around to it and I wrote this novel about the Foreign Brigades of the Pennsylvania Line. This was the beginning of the enlistment of Irish immigrants, blacks, some Hungarian and Polish immigrants, a handful of Jews, into what were called the Pennsylvania Foreign Brigades. They became the backbone of the struggle. They were the best troops in the American Revolution and they were actually removed from history—taken out of history—and, until Carl Van Doren dug this up, there was no mention of them in any history course taught in North American schools.

But I don't think [my interest in history] was a result of the Cold War. It has been a passion of my life to try to dig out the truth about the American past. I did it in **The Last Frontier.** I did it again in the book called **Unvanquished** and **Tom Paine.** And, in October, a new book of mine is being published called **Seven Days in June.** I am telling the truth in this book of what we call the Battle of Bunker Hill. It is the first time any book I know of has told the truth about what happened there. So, I have always been intrigued by the past. This is what happened with **Freedom Road,** too—why I became so fascinated by **Freedom Road.**

[Wald]: *In* **Literature and Reality,** *you argue that the interpretation of the past is something that is always conditioned on the present moment. You wrote* **The Proud and the Free** *in 1950-51, so surely the form and focus and emphases might have been influenced by 1951.*

That is absolutely true. We reinterpret the past according to this moment and someday there will be a reinterpretation—I say very softly so as to speak of the role of Abraham Lincoln and it would be very difficult because gods are hard to destroy. But these things go on when you reach a part of history that clarifies a certain issue. When we take up the question—"Should there have been a Civil War (the bloodiest war in the history of the world up to that time) or should there not have been a Civil War?"—people will write books about the Civil War that have never been written before.

[Filreis]: *You endured bitter poverty as a child and I wonder if you would tell us a little about that and its effects on your subsequent politics, your attitudes about writers and American literature, and its effect on your career as a radical writer.*

I can say a great deal about that. I am one of the few American writers who achieved prominence—Jack London is another one; there are not too many more—who came from the working class. My father was an ordinary working man. He started life—his great dream was to be an ironworker—because in those days when he was a kid the city was festooned with rolled iron. If you had been in New York in my childhood, you would have seen this twisted, rolled iron everywhere you looked: balconies, fences, millions of tons of it all through New York. It's mostly gone today. So, at the age of fifteen—sixteen, he became an ironworker. When that gave out, he got a job as a crimper on a cable car running south from 42nd Street on Seventh Avenue. Then he went to work in a tin factory in Long Island. He and all the other young Jewish workers there trained with an officer of the Civil War who was going to lead them as a Cavalry Regiment in the war in 1898 to avenge themselves on Ferdinand and Isabella for expelling them from Spain! They put half their salary into the kitty to buy horses, and of course the Civil War guy walked away with the kitty and no horses and they never got there.

This was a man who married a wonderful woman who grew up in England, and for the first eight years of my life I lived under the aegis of this marvelous woman. She died leaving three little boys. And my father, all his life, was a wonderful man with two feet firmly planted in midair—and it was a terrible time: it was the Depression. He tried to keep a job as a cutter or something in the garment factories. He was always out of work, on strike, or something else. I went to work at age eleven with my brother selling newspapers. We always worked and very often the family kept alive on what we brought home. My brother and I said to my father, "We are not going to live in this filthy, miserable slum apartment anymore." My father said, "I can't move. I do not know where to go." So we rented another apartment. We moved him out of there. We adored him. We worshipped him. But, after my mother died, he could never take hold of anything. It was a hellish, terrible, hungry existence. For some reason—my brother and I—we supported each other and got through it.

The thing that got me through it was the New York Public Library, where I read everything passionately. Over the weekend when I wasn't working, I would read from morning to night. And so I came to [writing and politics] on my own in the public library—with some guidance from a wonderful librarian there. When I became a teenager, she gave me George Bernard Shaw's *Intelligent Woman's Guide to Socialism and Capitalism.* It's a wonderful book. Much better than Karl Marx's *Capital,* I think it is the best book on socialism that has ever been written. Then I began to read Shelley, who is a tremendous revolutionary influence. *Men of England* is one of the most passionate revolutionary songs ever written. Here and there, I was being restructured into a socialist, eventually into a Communist.

People ask, "Would you do it all over again?" Of course I would do it all over again. There is no question about it. It was a point in my life when I did not feel that a decent person had any right to exist in this society if he were not a member of the Communist Party. Today, I think very differently. Now I am eighty years old next November, so

you learn, and you think, and you change. But that was my only childhood. It was a bitter childhood. My only joy was when it ended, when I finally realized that we could take something into our own hands.

[From the audience (Eric Cheyfitz)]: Since you talk about changing and you talk about your own critique of the Communist Party and its failures, I wonder what you see today in the United States and the world that might represent or coalesce into a progressive social politics?

You see, the destruction of the American Communist Party, as I said, was a deliberate thing. I don't think the ruling class ever acts unintelligently. They will act unintelligently in every way except the maintenance of their own power. And they certainly knew that the trade union movement in America, the Congress of Industrial Organizations was . . . well, it could not have been possible without the Communist Party. The Communist Party lived for that and they created it. The Communist Party created trade unions and built that great sixteen-million person force. So when they killed the Communist Party, and they killed it dead (I should say, they created the situation for its destruction—and it also destroyed itself). Then they went after the trade unions.

Up to the point where Ronald Reagan did something that was astonishing and horrible. He fired the entire union of plane guidance workers (PATCO). When he did that, it struck the death knell to the American labor movement. After that, one by one, every union in this country is being broken, and the unions that still survive—great unions like the municipal unions in New York, the teachers' union, and certain industrial unions—they are going to be broken too. This is death battle that the American ruling class is fighting. They are "leaning down" as they say, making themselves cleaner, more productive, more profitable, and they are firing thousands of people. They are cutting down the sustenance level of the working class. With all of the intelligence, the brilliant advice of John Maynard Keynes, they have cast Keynes aside, and they are back to what Marx described as "the relative and absolute impoverishment of the working class." And this impoverishment is taking place all over America. Executives, vice-presidents, second vice-presidents. I live in Greenwich, Connecticut. Our town is filling up with the CEOs of various industries who are now out of a job, with no hope, no future, nowhere to turn—cast down from the upper middle class to working-class stature. Good luck if they can get a job in one of the supermarkets or one of the big general stores that are opening up all over.

So what do I see in the future? I see a worsening of this, because this is a process that is shipping our work out to the Far East, to other countries, to cheap labor. The latest thing—cheap labor in Mexico—shipping work to Mexico. They have forgotten a simple proposition than you cannot manufacture anything unless you have someone to buy what you manufacture. We are racing into a condition where the American working class—or what is left of it—

the American working people—cannot buy back what the industries here are making. It does not matter whether they make it in China or Japan. The American people cannot buy it back. And what will come next? I cannot forecast it, but it will come. It will be the most explosive thing in the next twenty years.

Notes

0. Thanks to Dan Traitser and Beth Wenger for editing advice and to Jason Busch for research assistance.

1. Fast refers here to Herb Tank, co-founder of New Playwrights with Howard Fast, who produced Fast's *The Hammer.*

2. Jewish Workingmen's Circle—ed.

George Traister (essay date 1995)

SOURCE: "Noticing Howard Fast," in *Prospects: An Annual of American Cultural Studies,* edited by Jack Salzman, Vol. 20, Cambridge: Cambridge University Press, 1995, pp. 525-41.

[*In the following essay, Traister provides an overview of Fast's life, literary career, political consciousness, and popularity, drawing attention to the need for critical reevaluation of Fast's numerous works and their significance.*]

I. INTRODUCTION

In 1933, Dial Press in New York published *Two Valleys,* the first novel by a very young man named Howard Melvin Fast. The publisher's blurb noted that *"Mr. Fast is not yet nineteen."* (He had been born in 1914.) In 1995, *The Bridge Builder's Story,* the most recent of Howard Fast's novels, appeared.[1] Sixty-two years lie between *Two Valleys* and *The Bridge Builder's Story.*

During this interval, Fast has produced an uncommonly large oeuvre for an American writer with claims on serious attention. He has written books in several genres; stories equally varied and numerous; plays; scripts for radio, television, and the screen; and much occasional prose, journalistic and otherwise. Some of this productivity results, no doubt, from sheer longevity. But Fast has also written with a rapidity and a level of energy that were remarked upon even relatively early in his career.[2] Many of his works were published to considerable acclaim, had excellent sales, and quickly entered public consciousness. Several—among them, *The Last Frontier* (1941), *The Unvanquished* (1942), *Citizen Tom Paine* (1943), *Freedom Road* (1944), *Spartacus* (1951), and *April Morning* (1961)—still retain whatever place in popular awareness is reserved for books widely assigned as texts in high schools and universities.

Almost as uncommonly for a serious American writer, Fast has also followed an active public career. He has

been, among other things, a wartime and, later, political journalist and activist; foreign correspondent; candidate for public office; publisher; worker for the government's Office of War Information; newspaper columnist; and inmate at a federal penitentiary. Fast has actually lived what, for many people, has seemed one of the great literary myths of our time: he *is* the artist as *l'homme engagé.* On the other hand, of course, his politics have been distinguished not only by his leftist orientation but also by actual Communist Party membership, complicated by a very public 1957 withdrawal from the Party. He has been engaged, in short, on the "wrong," indeed, the losing, side of one of our century's great political wars.

Fast's politics, his productivity, and his popularity all combined to do his reputation little good. America's critical establishments have been predisposed to mistrust Fast himself for his political activities, his works for their political stance,[3] or (on occasion) both for their subsequent departure from those activities and that stance. These establishments tend also to suspect books that are produced as quickly and sell as well as his. Perhaps this generalized distrust explains the almost complete lack of attention paid Fast by the literary historical and critical communities.[4] No matter that he is highly prolific; no matter that his books, often popular with readers, are also often taught; and no matter that he is, finally, someone who has been (if nothing else) part of America's literary and political scene for a period of time longer than most people have been alive. Fast is nonetheless very nearly invisible. Alan Wald's extremely brief article in the *Encyclopedia of the American Left* summarizes Fast's career. He has also written a short critical review of Fast as a writer. These are among the very few studies that try to offer anything resembling an overview of either the man or his career. The present essay offers a somewhat fuller survey than Wald has provided and suggests that both Fast and his work deserve new attention. In passing, as it were, it also indicates a few specific topics to which attention might profitably be paid.

The essay is based largely on a reading of many (but by no means all) of Fast's own works and on the criticism and history cited herein. I have also relied heavily on the resources of the Howard Fast Collection. Housed in the Department of Special Collections, Van Pelt-Dietrich Library, at the University of Pennsylvania, the Fast Collection contains Fast's literary works in printed form (in the English language, in reprints, and in foreign-language translations); manuscript notes and drafts of published and unpublished works; printers' galleys, many with revisions that reveal how Fast worked on his books; his political and journalistic writings; his children's, genre, and pseudonymous works; and family, public, and political photographs and ephemera. The collection is still growing, thanks to assistance from Fast and his family, and continues to add such examples of his literary, personal, business, and political correspondence and papers as survive. It documents the literary and public career of a writer both *read* and *red* whose very considerable presence in American letters, from the 1930s through the present, has yet to be assessed. Indeed, it seems not yet even to have been noticed.

II. STARTING OUT

The 1933 publication of Fast's *Two Valleys* announced the arrival of a new American writer of real interest. By the time *The Unvanquished* appeared nine years later, Fast was an established presence in the American literary firmament. *The Unvanquished* was quickly reprinted for Bennett Cerf and Donald Klopfer's Modern Library (1945), then the commercial equivalent of admission to literary canonization. (The Modern Library also published *The Selected Work of Tom Paine and Citizen Tom Paine* as a Modern Library Giant [1946].) Fast's books were not only praised, they also sold well. As a result, Fast found ready and frequent access as a writer of short stories to such pulp magazine markets as *Romance* and to such slicks as the *Saturday Evening Post* and *Women's Day*. He was able to earn a living sufficient to marry and start a family.

Fast was writing his way out of a background that he remembered as impoverished both financially and emotionally. On the one hand, he could recall, with some pride, a friend once telling him that, "since Jack London, I was the first American writer to emerge from the working class" (*Being Red* 63). On the other hand, however, the anguish with which Fast described his background when he tried to evoke it (and he tried at some length for readers of *Being Red*) is palpable. That anguish may help to explain why, from the very outset of his career, he wrote as much and as quickly as he has. The painful memory of early poverty seems to have been a prod to exertion for Fast, just as it was for others whose memories of poverty were formed later, during the Depression. Perhaps Fast would have agreed (as Hicks, Rideout, and Wald have all argued [see note 2]) that haste had unfortunate consequences for the artistic success of many of his individual works. Nonetheless, in fleeing an impoverished background, he may have felt unable to worry about artistry as an end in itself. He may instead have felt that no individual work mattered as much as the economic cushion they were, all together, placing between him and the dread memories of the conditions of his own past.

The Children was first published as a very long short story in Whit Burnett's *Story* (March, 1937) and appeared ten years later as a short novel.[5] It evokes Fast's background as clearly—and as bleakly—as anything else he was ever to write (including *Being Red*). Concise, powerful, and grim, the book seems never to have found an audience (not, at any rate, since its initial appearance; I find no evidence that it has affected anyone's estimation of Fast's career). *The Children* deals with a lynching. It is set, not in some distant, imagined, and benighted South, but in Fast's own well-known and well-remembered Manhattan. The lynching it depicts, racially directed but complexly motivated, is perpetrated not by warped and horrifying adults but by deprived and thoughtless urban street children, very much the sort of children among

whom Fast recalled himself as having grown up. Indeed, the plot is based on an incident that has gnawed at Fast all his life. He would retell the story yet again, but as memoir rather than fiction, in *Being Red,* where he also recalled that he got the idea for the voice he used in the story from Henry Roth's 1934 novel, *Call It Sleep* (*Being Red,* 42-43, 64).

Fast's fame and reputation, such as they are, now rest largely on his historical novels, the most frequently adopted for classroom use of all his books; and on his various evocations of immigrant and American Jewish life, best-sellers in the 1970s and 1980s. *The Children,* however, is quite a different kind of work. Its first enthusiastic reception by Whit Burnett and by *Story*—at least as Fast, many years later, was to remember that reception (*Being Red,* 65-68)—must have contributed to the writer's early reputation; it surely seemed a work of real importance when it originally appeared. Despite its present neglect, it provides evidence that at least something of Fast's early critical reputation depended on work that (like Roth's *Call It Sleep*) could be valued as proletarian fiction. Alan Wald has criticized Fast for "the shallow eclecticism and lack of clarity reflected in his political thought" ("Legacy," 99). Relying on the difference between realism and naturalism, as these approaches are distinguished by George Luk cs, Wald finds Fast "disappointingly" naturalistic, evasive of complex and multilayered human drama, and the victim of a Popular Front approach to the creation of a progressive literature for "the masses" ("Legacy," 97-98). These strictures may seem valid to current readers as generalizations about Fast's best-known works, yet *The Children* represents a different aspect of Fast's early work. Here, at least, Fast crafts a fiction that evades many if not all of the limitations to which Wald points.[6]

During the late thirties and early forties, claims on Fast's time increased. Some resulted from his marriage to Bette Cohen and the start of their family, others from the governmental and journalistic positions that he took up after the United States entered World War II, and still others from his increasingly complicated political activities. Yet Fast produced numerous books during this period, and they continued to receive good notices and were frequently reprinted both in hardbound and paperback editions. Some even appeared in Armed Services editions for distribution during and immediately after the war to American servicemen and servicewomen. Not only his well-known novels but also some less well-known shorter works circulated in this manner.[7] They spread Fast's name to a vast potential readership. All of these books and reprints helped to solidify and extend a literary reputation that, moving from success to success, appeared to have nowhere to go but up.

On the dust jacket of the 1943 first edition of *Citizen Tom Paine,* his publisher wrote that Fast "has long been a name on the critics' lips." The blurb goes on to say that, with this book, Fast becomes "one of the few major American novelists." Any of Fast's readers in that year possessed of even a modicum of cynicism might well have paused over this phrase to consider the promotional nature of a publisher's puff, yet few of even the most cynical would ultimately have found much hyperbole in these laudatory words. They appeared to be but the sober truth. They were soon to seem, however, quite wrong.

III. POLITICS

Fast has told and retold stories about his engagement in the political battles of his time. *Being Red,* his 1990 autobiography, is the most recent version of this tale. He has also written others, such as *The Naked God* (1957).[8] Several of them reveal his anger and lingering pain.

Fast lavished time from his working life as a writer on leftist causes in general and the Communist Party (which he joined in 1943) specifically. He helped staff the *Daily Worker.* He wrote for the *Masses* and other leftist or Party journals. He attended various world congresses called to consider one issue or another. He worked for Henry Wallace's 1948 presidential campaign. He was tried on federal charges and then imprisoned in 1950 after failing to overturn his conviction. Two years later, he ran for public office in his own name. In addition to works of literary imagination, he also wrote political journalism, articles, and tracts. The differences between these forms were not always vast. Novels about strikes (*Clarkton* [1947]) or about *The Passion of Sacco and Vanzetti*(1953) appeared more or less concurrently with books of reportage such as *Peekskill, U.S.A.: A Personal Experience* (1951), about the riot when Paul Robeson tried to perform. Fast wrote many short political pieces, as well. A pamphlet about the Warsaw Ghetto uprising illustrated by William Gropper appeared the year after the war ended (*Never to Forget: The Battle of the Warsaw Ghetto* [1946]). An article about the Peekskill riot—an event that affected him deeply— appeared in the *Masses* of October, 1949, two years before his book on the same subject was published. He published a barrage of articles and pamphlets opposing the Korean War. A tract about literature—*Literature and Reality* (1950)—tried to connect his literary and political ideals; it appeared the same year he went to prison.[9] All of this reportage—articles, pamphlets, and tracts—was a major part of his output during the forties and fifties. Not often collected or reprinted, it is, nowadays, almost completely unread. Even without reference to this enormous amount of writing, however, it would be difficult to overestimate the time, energy, and commitment that Fast gave to leftist, Party, and Party-related causes. It would be equally difficult to overestimate the effect of such commitments upon his work as a writer of imaginative fictions.

The two great political traumas he experienced were, of course, first, his trial and imprisonment, and, second, his later resignation from the Party. Unwilling to provide the House Committee on Un-American Activities with the names of contributors of financial support for a hospital caring for wounded Spanish Republicans, Fast lost several appeals of his subsequent conviction for contempt of Congress. In 1950, he served a three-month sentence in a federal penitentiary.[10] With the energy that he seems always to have shown, he was able to work on *Spartacus* while he was in prison. Within two years of his release, Fast ran for a Bronx Congressional seat as an American Labor Party candidate (1952). He remained a member of the Communist Party for several more years, until, in 1957, he finally broke from it in a public departure that caused considerable public stir. Many newspapers and magazines took note; Fast himself commented in several media, explaining his disenchantment with the Party and resignation from it.[11]

This resignation cost Fast several friendships, and some regard, from former colleagues on the Left, while bringing him no new companionship or regard from the Right. Following his public resignation, he had (also publicly) to forge a new and independent political stance. Simultaneously, he faced widespread opprobrium and serious threats to his ability to pursue his livelihood, to neither of which, of course, he was by this time a stranger. Since the later 1940s while he was still in the Party, as well as in the late 1950s after he had left it, such problems had made supporting himself and his family a much more pressing issue than Fast must have expected to encounter during the days of his early successes. He saw his problems as a consequence of his involvement with a Party which, he now felt, had betrayed the very ideals that had originally attracted him to it. His sense of betrayal parallels the feeling of many in his generation who, once able idealistically to view their own leftist political activities as a search for social justice, saw themselves instead as dupes whose idealism had allowed them to be manipulated by people for whom "social justice" was a fig leaf covering up other, less noble goals. Unlike numbers of his contemporaries, however, Fast, even after leaving the Communist Party, continued to proclaim that such justice could only be sought from a politics of the Left. Nonetheless, he was himself seen as a betrayer by some who regarded his departure from the Party and subsequent activities as a sellout. Both his memoir, *The Naked God,* and its numerous journalistic relatives, and his immediate move to Hollywood and screenwriting, could be seen in this light, and were.[12] The Right had never trusted Fast; it did not now begin to do so. The Left, despite his protestations of ongoing commitment to leftist ideals, ceased doing so.

Several of Fast's novels—*Silas Timberman* (1954) and *The Story of Lola Gregg* (1956) are among the most powerful[13]—represent issues that dominated this period of Fast's life. *Silas Timberman* concerns an academic community under attack by people who seek to purify the university of carriers of tainted thoughts. A non-Communist English teacher at a mid-Western state university, Silas Timberman winds up in prison as the result of his disinclination to support local civil defense measures. His institution's leadership and the majority of its personnel do not assist Timberman to fight the charges of Communism to which this disinclination gives rise. Instead, the majority collapse ignobly and cooperate with those who seek, first, Timberman's dismissal and prosecution, and, second, evisceration of the practices of intellectual freedom for which a university supposedly stands.[14] *Lola Gregg,* a closely related novel, also looks at what happened to ordinary people caught in the swirl of political emotionalism as America entered the Cold War and "the Great Fear." Lola Gregg's husband is, only slightly less than Silas Timberman, a political naïf. Both his world and, ultimately, his life, are disrupted beyond repair.

Since his emergence from the political wars of the 1930s, 1940s, and 1950s, Fast's distance from organized politics has increased, yet his concerns for the political life of the society in which he lives show no corresponding tendency to decrease. Sixty years after his first novel appeared, Fast published not only another novel but also a collection of newspaper columns, *War and Peace: Observations on Our Times* (1993).[15] He began to write these columns in December of 1988, originally for the *New York Observer,* and then for subscribers to the newspaper syndicate that picked up the column for national distribution. They have continued his lifelong critical engagement with American society through their author's eightieth year. So, of course, do the fictions he continues to write.

IV. TROUBLED TIMES

THE BLUE HERON PRESS

In *Being Red,* Fast describes how, as the 1940s drew to a close, his normal trade publishing outlets also closed down. Publishers rejected his new books, despite the critical and popular acclaim his earlier works had received—and despite the sales those earlier works continued to attain. This turnabout was a result, in part, of the relatively poor sales of his postwar books.[16] More importantly, Fast felt, it reflected pressures analogous to those simultaneously affecting the broadcasting, screen, and theatrical media and known collectively as "the blacklist." Fast cites the direct intervention of the Federal Bureau of Investigation as a major source of this blow to his career (e.g., *Being Red,* 246).

After the manuscript of Fast's novel *Spartacus* had received multiple rejections, including some from publishers who had published earlier books he had written, a person at Doubleday urged Fast to publish it himself. George Hecht felt strongly that Doubleday had rejected a major commercial prospect. He guaranteed to purchase numerous copies of any edition of the book that Fast published for distribution through Doubleday's chain of bookstores. Thus discouraged, on the one hand, and encouraged, on the other, Fast responded by turning himself into the self-publisher of *Spartacus* at the Blue Heron Press, the imprint he established in order to follow Hecht's advice. Operating out of their home—then at 43 West 94th Street in Manhattan—Fast and his wife published the book and sold (as he recalled) more than 48,000 copies of it in three months (*Being Red,* 294). Its sales made it "the only self-published best-seller in recent history" (Wald, "Legacy," 94).[17]

Other books followed over Fast's Blue Heron imprint. Among them were his own *Passion of Sacco and Vanzetti, Silas Timberman,* and *Lola Gregg.* The press also published other writers who, in the peculiar atmosphere of that time, were unable to receive normal publication and distribution in the United States. W.E.B. Du Bois's classic *The Souls of Black Folk* and a work by radical poet Walter Lowenfels were among the books by writers other than Fast that Blue Heron printed and distributed in both hard and paper covers. Fast's own books, however, were Blue Heron's staples for both new publications and the backlist.

GENRE WRITING

Fast has written fictions in a great variety of genres. If we except his novels with generally "contemporary" settings, the genre for which he is best known is the historical novel. Within that rubric, some of his historical tales—most notably *The Last Frontier*—have Western settings and themes. So do a few of Fast's short stories, some of which have been anthologized in collections of Western tales. Fast seems, however, less a writer of Westerns than of historical fictions, some of which are set in the old West. He has also written for children since the 1930s, but these books seem a relatively minor part of his output. Neither the books set in the West nor his children's books give Fast the appearance of anything other than the author of mainstream fictions. Historical novels, themselves generally regarded either as a subset of mainstream fictions or indistinguishable from them, are rarely marginalized in quite the same consistent way that some other fictional genres routinely experience.

In fact, however, Fast has also published fictions in two very conventional, generically ghettoized literary forms—mystery and science fiction—although his work in these kinds remains less well known than his mainstream historical novels and best-sellers. Yet these works are by no means a minor nor even a numerically insignificant part of his literary output. The mysteries appeared with two pseudonyms:[18] Walter Ericson and E. V. Cunningham. Some of the Cunningham titles have recently begun to reappear over Fast's own name. *Sylvia,* for instance, was republished in 1992. It now has a dust jacket that not only names Fast as its author but also tells prospective readers that "Fast . . . had written the book at a time when he was hounded by J. Edgar Hoover and the FBI for his then radical views. . . . But Fast could not stop writing." As a science fiction writer, Fast was able to use his own name.

Clearly, Fast turned to both forms for a variety of reasons. He had begun to write science fiction as early as the late 1930s—that is, at a time well before his "then radical views" were out of fashion. After the end of World War II, however—as the *Sylvia* dust jacket remarks—among the most important reasons he wrote works of science fiction was that his ability to publish books of the kind through which he had first established his reputation was severely hampered by the political interdiction beneath which he had fallen. But Fast also needed to work in forms that gave him latitude to try things that would have taxed the limits of more ordinary novels. (His interest in Zen meditative techniques, for example, plays an important role in one of his mystery series.)

Science fiction, as a highly marginalized literary form, has also been traditionally less conservative than mainstream fiction. Both its formal properties and its range of permissible political points of view vary far from what is ordinarily allowed in popular fictions—and these variations were particularly characteristic of the genre during the 1950s. Science fiction editors also offered Fast outlets that enabled him to keep his own name when he published stories with them. Indeed, several magazines in which his stories appeared made much of his turn to science fiction, using his name and what they supposed to be its literary and status associations to raise the status of their own venture.[19] More importantly, they enabled Fast a venue in which he could explore political themes. The self-consciously speculative nature of the science fiction genre has long enabled the presentation even of oppositional viewpoints with only slight allegorical protective coloration.

V. Popularity

Popularity and good sales are a serious writer's dream—but they may also prove a curse. Many of Fast's books have become best-sellers. Many have been adopted for use in schools. Many have attained notable paperback sales. Many have enjoyed considerable foreign and foreign-language sales. In all these ways, they demonstrated Fast's power to win audiences.

Fast achieved such success with relative speed. *Two Valleys,* his first novel, appeared in 1933. An English edition appeared that same year. It signified critical rather than financial benefits for the young writer. (When, a few years ago—as Fast has told me in conversation—he saw a copy of the first American edition for sale for five hundred dollars, he told the bookseller that five hundred dollars was more than he had earned for *writing* the book.) But by 1942, only nine years after the publication of *Two Valleys,* Fast writes, "I was sitting right on top of eighteen pots of honey." He continues, "My third novel, *The Last Frontier,* . . . had been greeted as a 'masterpiece' . . . and my new novel, just published, called *The Unvanquished,* a story of the Continental Army's most desperate moment, had been called, by *Time* magazine who found in it a parallel for the grim present, 'the best book about World War II.' . . . [At this time, too,] I finished writing a book I would call *Citizen Tom Paine*"—a book that would bring Fast even more praise and high (and still ongoing) sales (*Being Red,* 2).

Other major historical fictions, such as *Freedom Road* and *April Morning,* would also prove to be popular with the general public. As school texts, they would become, as they remain, consistent sources of income for their author. Between these two books, the self-published *Spartacus*

would bring Fast still more success. Eventually, through its 1960 release as a movie, it would also help to puncture the pretensions of the Hollywood Blacklist. Its success would help Fast return to ordinary commercial publishing venues. Slighter works, such as *The Winston Affair* (1959), would yield income from both their various printed and their movie versions. *The Winston Affair* became *Man in the Middle* (1964), with Robert Mitchum and Trevor Howard.

Fast's extensive publications in foreign-language translations offer a specific instance of his broad popularity for which the evidence is almost more overwhelming than that of his English-language sales. Worldwide interest in Fast's work developed rapidly. His political views, of course, were well suited to the Depression era in which he began to write. Moreover, his books were exceedingly popular in the Soviet Union and the satellite nations of Eastern Europe. Walter Felscher, now a professor at Tübingen but raised as a youth in East Germany, from which he eventually fled, remembers (without the slightest bit of pleasure) Fast's works as ubiquitous in bookstore windows in East Germany.[20] A prominent American Communist Party member, Fast attained to a popularity in the Soviet Union and Eastern Europe that, occasionally, translated not only into sales but also into royalties—somewhat unusual for Americans whose works were published in those places. (It was a popularity that also translated itself into the award of a Stalin Prize in 1954.)

In fact, however, his works had attained transatlantic interest, and not only in the Communist-dominated East, from the very first. *Two Valleys,* published in England in the same year it first appeared in this country, established a pattern of English interest in Fast's work that continues to this day. His books have also appeared in French, Italian, Rumanian, German, Spanish, Catalan, Portuguese, Greek, Czech, Croat, Hebrew, Bengali, Chinese, and Japanese, among many other languages. He was and remains proud of this evidence of popularity. The 1953 Blue Heron reprint of Fast's own *Last Frontier* lists on its title-page verso the twenty languages into which that novel had, by then, been translated.

The range and variety of foreign editions and translations of Fast's works, as well as their sales, indicate that Fast is among the most widely read of living American authors. So geographically widespread a readership is itself another reason for paying Fast increased critical attention. In addition, however, even as he was being ignored at home, Fast represented "American literature" to millions of readers throughout the world. How he was presented to them and how they received him are both questions that need investigation. Such inquiries will help us better to understand the complexities of how the idea of America and its literature have been constructed in our time.

In the 1980s and 1990s, Fast continues to attract audiences, as sales of his series of novels on the American immigrant experience attest, but he rarely finds the critical acclaim, or even the notice, that his earlier works achieved (see note 4). This change may result from ordinary shifts in literary taste and fashion. It may result from an aversion to Fast's perceived or actual political views and behavior, or it may result from a general mistrust of broad popularity itself, Fast's or anyone else's. Whatever the explanation, Fast continues to write and to be read despite this context of general lack of attention or outright critical dismissal. His books continue to be used in classrooms and to sell well in bookstores, yet scholars and critics routinely notice other contemporary writers while ignoring Fast. Best-seller status is not always its own reward.

VI. LATER WORK

Blacklisting, political disillusionment, imprisonment: there seem few modern public pitfalls, *including* popularity, that Fast has not encountered. Yet his ability to keep on writing and to produce at a prolific pace has, from all outward signs, not been affected by these difficulties in ways an ordinary reader would notice. He has produced successful books despite the most awkward personal situations. The first of the novels that his postwar circumstances required him to self-publish, *Spartacus,* became a huge seller, despite its mode of publication and the general dismissal or utter lack of notice accorded the book by the media. *Freedom Road,* a fictional introduction to the experience of African Americans in the Reconstruction era, appeared while Fast was still working his way out of the aftereffects of his 1957 resignation from the Party. It became another of his hugely successful historical novels and, like several of its predecessors, entered numerous classrooms.

Fast's series of novels concerned with the immigrant experience in America began with *The Immigrants* (1977) and continued through *Second Generation* (1978), *The Establishment* (1979), *The Legacy* (1981), and *The Immigrant's Daughter* (1985). Using immigration and subsequent successful acclimatization to the United States as its frame, the series—a "family saga dramatizing both personal and epoch-making struggles against white supremacy, war, fascism, anti-Semitism, industrial exploitation, McCarthyism, and the subjugation of women"—achieved consistent bestsellerdom (Murolo, "History," 23). The Jewish-American experience, long a major theme for Fast, is heavily emphasized in this series. Fast had previously published several nonfiction historical essays about Jewish history, including the 1942 armed forces pamphlet on U.S. Jewry mentioned previously and a more broadly focused history, *The Jews,* of 1968. Even as he was finishing *The Immigrants* series, he revisited Jewish themes in another novel, *The Outsider* (1984). This book concerned a rabbi's experiences in a small Connecticut town. Both *The Immigrants* series and his books on Jewish themes brought Fast considerable financial but few critical rewards.

Unnoticed among the books of his later period—Murolo, in fact, writes that Fast "did not . . . return to the historical novel" and adds that, as a writer of "historical epics,"

he "dropped out of sight" ("History," 23)—is *The Hessian* (1972), the novel that Fast himself once called (in conversation with the author) his best. *The Hessian* appeared when Fast was well beyond the initial period of working his way through the personal and political difficulties that resignation from the Party had raised for him. He had once again resumed a commercially successful career, but he had not returned to critical favor. Perhaps as a result of critical inattention, *The Hessian*—in this respect very much like *The Children*—has never found an audience. Quintessential Fast, it seems a pure historical tale, yet the relationship of its purely historical tale to current issues is strikingly clear. Fast imagines a tiny military incident and its aftermath during the American Revolution. The book begins with the killing of an American by a band of Hessian mercenaries traveling inland from Long Island Sound on Connecticut's High Ridge Road. (Fast lived for many years in Greenwich, not far from High Ridge Road, which can still be found in Fairfield County.) The Hessians take the American, who follows them, for a spy. No spy, the American they kill is instead a local simpleton whose death inspires the neighborhood to revenge. The Americans ambush the Hessians, killing all but one of them. What happens to the one whom they do not kill, a boy, is the burden of the rest of the novel, which is beautifully realized. Fast views his characters with clear-sighted sympathy and objectivity. The novel itself is utterly rooted in its time and place, yet few of its first readers could have failed to relate *The Hessian* to the defining political problem of the moment when it was published, the American war in Vietnam. The power of this book, by itself, reveals a writer who deserves critical reevaluation.[21]

The Dinner Party (1987), *The Pledge* (1988), and *The Confession of Joe Cullen* (1989) are among Fast's later overtly political novels. Each is highly critical of certain aspects of American life. *The Pledge,* for example, finds the older Fast meditating upon some of his own youthful public experiences—experiences whose personal nature Fast has indicated elsewhere (*Being Red,* 120-28, 131-32). In *The Pledge,* Fast recalls how, as a war correspondent, he encountered British misrule in India and American attitudes toward a wartime, and then Cold War, ally that made disclosure of British brutality impossible. A few years later, in *The Trial of Abigail Goodman* (1993), Fast looked with a dubious eye upon efforts to restrict women's right to abortion.

One might have expected an aging Fast to have slowed his pace of writing or moderated the critical perspective from which he views American public life. True, the stridency of some of his earlier work is gone, yet Fast had never really adopted a "root-and-branch" critical stance in his fictions, perhaps as a result of his early acceptance of a Popular Front aesthetic. This is the aesthetic which, Wald argues, vitiated much of his radical potential (see "Legacy" generally and note 13). Fast continues on as he has always done, dramatizing "excesses and abuses" but looking only obliquely, if at all, at "process." By and large, Fast writes anything but "analytical" fictions. Not only does he seem not to have slowed his pace of production, but also he shows few signs in his later work of having moderated his critical perspective.

VII. *BEING RED*

Being Red (1990) is a remarkable memoir. In many ways, although Fast claims otherwise (*Being Red*, 63), it is his political "Apologia pro vita sua." Like many of his novels and short stories, it is available in paperback. (A second paperback edition has recently appeared.) Like many of those other works, it, too, has quickly achieved a classroom career. It is eminently readable. And it is worth reading.

It is true that *Being Red* goes over some of the same ground Fast had earlier traversed in *The Naked God.* In that book, Fast had similarly dealt with the impact of his involvement with the Communist Party. In 1957, however, his perspective was perhaps not yet quite distant or calm enough.[22] Fast therefore gave its concerns a second try, after thirty-odd years of additional reflection. In the later book, his tone has become more moderate and his range broader than either had been in 1957, yet, in *Being Red,* Fast still conceives of his life and the shape his career has taken in terms of the Party. Its ideals, its betrayal of those ideals, and his own entry into, work for, and departure from it: all these remain among the determinants of the life Fast depicts. But *Being Red* is more than political self-exploration. A much longer book than *The Naked God,* it also has a range that the first book cannot match. It provides an unusually detailed entrée into the life and work, as well as the political activities, of an American author. This author's career took him into several fields, in addition to politics, that most of his contemporaries rarely experienced; even those who experienced some of them, almost never experienced as many of them as Fast. Notable among these, as it would be for any novelist and writer, is self-publication. Journalism; investigation, trial, and jail; a political candidacy: these, too, are notable. But, more generally, *Being Red* illuminates the experiences, the issues, and the perspectives (the worldview, if you will) in terms of which Fast chose to adapt and tell the stories that constitute the bulk of his work throughout his long and highly productive career. The record his book provides is all the more important because so many of his contemporaries, if they had similar experiences (perhaps *especially* if they had similar experiences), tried as hard as they could deliberately to forget them.

Being Red is far from a perfect history of its time (as if any such thing could be imagined). Its frequent omissions, distortions, and lapses—even, in fact, its tone—are, nonetheless, often as significant as what Fast deliberately and accurately includes, at least, for any reader interested in recovering the temper of the period through which its author lived and wrote. Its view of the impact of one of the great intellectual and political movements of our time on a sensitive, responsive, prolific, and influential American writer, however partial that view necessarily is, makes its documentary value incalculable. *Being Red*

sheds a bright and a raking light on Fast's career and on his era. Because of its self-absorption and partiality, it cannot be the last word on either. But insofar as it provokes its readers to further recovery of hitherto suppressed memories, it is certainly a propaeduetic to thought about both.

If Fast had written nothing else, this one book would give him an abiding claim on our attention. In fact, he has written much more that begs for renewed attention to his career and his work. A survey such as this one succeeds insofar as it encourages just such a second look.

Notes

1. I quote the publisher's comment about Fast's youth from the dust wrapper preserved on a copy of the first edition of *Two Valleys* in the Howard Fast Collection, Department of Special Collections, Van Pelt-Dietrich Library, University of Pennsylvania. This collection is described briefly below. M.E. Sharpe (Armonk, NY) published *The Bridge Builder's Story.*

   For a brief survey of Fast's career, see the article (s.v. "Fast, Howard [b. 1914]") by Alan Wald, in *Encyclopedia of the American Left,* ed. Mari Jo Buhle, Paul Buhle, and Dan Georgakas (New York: Garland, 1990), 219-20; hereafter cited as *Encyclopedia.* I have also used Fast's own autobiographical writings, especially *Being Red* (Boston: Houghton Mifflin, 1990). As my text makes clear, I have also benefited from the opportunity of speaking about his life and career on several occasions with Fast.

2. Alan Wald comments on this productivity, but not warmly, in "The Legacy of Howard Fast." Fast, he writes, "paid a heavy price for his machine-like production of books and screenplays." This essay appeared originally in *Radical America* 17 (1983); it is reprinted in Alan M. Wald, *The Responsibility of Intellectuals: Selected Essays on Marxist Traditions in Cultural Commitment* (Atlantic Highlands, N.J.: Humanities, 1992), 92-101. I quote from the later text (99) and cite this essay hereafter as "Legacy." Wald recalls that Granville Hicks wrote in 1945 to warn Fast that high-speed productivity might well depend on a degree of carelessness and inattentiveness from which his work would suffer. In 1956, Walter B. Rideout also spoke of the same problem (with somewhat more sympathy) in *The Radical Novel in the United States, 1900-1954: Some Interrelations of Literature and Society* (rept. New York: Columbia University Press, 1992), 275-85.

3. The general disinclination of American literary historians and critics not only to valorize but even to pay attention to writers emerging from the political Left is discussed by Cary Nelson. See his *Repression and Recovery: Modern American Poetry and the Politics of Cultural Memory, 1910-1945,*

Wisconsin Project on American Writers (Madison: University of Wisconsin Press, 1989). Yet even those for whom such a generalization seems valid may, perhaps, doubt its *specific* applicability to a writer such as Fast, whose prolific approach to his writing career has produced works of distinctly uneven quality. In any event, it is difficult at best to propose an explanation for neglect; there are so many possibilities. But consider the exemplary diction of Mark Shechner, writing that "the emergence of Jews as major contemporary writers had to await the 1940s, when a prevailing fiction of documentary realism and proletarian romance, produced by the likes of Cahan, Fuchs, Gold, Howard Fast, and Albert Halper, gave way to the subtler and more evocative writing of Delmore Schwartz, Saul Bellow, Isaac Rosenfeld, and Norman Mailer, and a significant advance in articulateness, power, and modernity appeared to be at hand" ("Jewish Writers," in *Harvard Guide to Contemporary American Writing,* ed. Daniel Hoffman [Cambridge: Harvard University Press, 1979], 193). I suppose some readers may not feel that anything other than the "mere" passing of literary judgments—and certainly nothing that might, perhaps, be thought *political* ("the likes of")—is at work in this passage even when they encounter the names of the five writers whom Shechner defenestrates. In truth, however, I fail to have an imagination capacious enough to envisage such readers.

4. Priscilla Murolo writes that the "rave reviews" accorded the book in which Fast first explained his departure from the Communist Party, *The Naked God,* in 1957 "signalled . . . [Fast's] reacceptance by the cultural establishment" ("History in the Fast Lane," *Radical History Review* no. 31 [1984]: 23; cited hereafter as "History"). I cannot agree, seeing no evidence that Fast has been "reaccepted" by any "cultural establishment" whatsoever. The Modern Language Association of America (MLA) maintains an online database that records scholarly and critical work undertaken by those who teach literature in our colleges and universities (and who, in current political mythology, are mostly demonized as the sort of left-wing subverters of accepted cultural norms for whom the Fasts of this world ought to be bread and butter). A search of this database for works that have Howard Fast as their subject yields, as of February, 1995, seven items. The database is retrospective and presently extends back to 1963. To put this figure into some perspective, contrast it with the number of scholarly books and articles that the same database lists that, published during the same thirty-two-year period, concern other modern American writers of varied stature and status: for example, Flannery O'Connor, 850; John Crowe Ransom, 146; Stephen King, 120; Isaac Asimov, 60; and Ross Macdonald, 52. Macdonald, a popular mystery writer and the *least* studied member of this

group, is the subject of *more than seven times* the number of publications devoted to Fast. In fairness, I should note that the MLA database does not turn up the articles on Fast by Wald or Murolo published in history journals that MLA does not index. Nonetheless, these figures reliably indicate the degree of "reacceptance"—that is, virtually none—Fast has attained since he left the Party.

Alan Wald notices this lapse of scholarly attention when he comments in passing that "we have not even made a rudimentary beginning of an examination of the major contributions of leftist writers to the historical novel (for example, . . . Howard Fast)" (*Writing from the Left: New Essays on Radical Culture and Politics* [London: Verso, 1994], 79).

5. As a novel, *The Children* appeared over the Duell, Sloan and Pearce imprint (New York, 1947). It was reprinted once again in *The Howard Fast Reader: A Collection of Stories and Novels* (New York: Crown, 1960).

6. This is a view that deserves expansion; I hope to expand it in a different framework than that permitted by a survey such as this one. One might nonetheless note that, in *Being Red,* Fast bathes the book in false and partly misleading bathos. In the memoir, he writes that *The Children* "was the only time, in all my long life as a writer, that I wrote of my childhood"; but since then, he concludes, and "even in a dispassionate telling in my old age, I find that walls separate me from the intensity of the suffering of those three more or less abandoned children, myself and my brothers" (43). Readers who know no more of *The Children* than what the self-absorbed memoirist says of it here may decide on this basis that it sounds like a book they can easily live without. If so, they will miss a book at once more coldblooded, dispassionate, yet attuned to others, than its own author remembered in 1990.

7. See, for instance, Howard Fast, *The Story of the Jews in the United States,* Jewish Information Series, no. 1 (New York, 1942), "for Jews in the Armed Forces of the United States"; and his *Patrick Henry and the Frigate's Keel* (n.p., 1945; the Armed Services edition reprint).

8. Daniel Aaron writes, briefly and perceptively, about some of the limitations of *The Naked God* in his *Writers on the Left: Episodes in American Literary Communism* (1961; rept. New York: Columbia University Press, 1992), 311.

9. Wald calls this work simply "a vulgar treatise on Marxist criticism" (*Encyclopedia,* 219). That may well be a justified criticism. Nonetheless, anyone who, considering the small number of representative articles, pamphlets, and tracts cited in the text as examples of Fast's occasional writings (and among which this reference to *Literature and Reality* is found), and who has even a slight sense of the vast

number of other such ephemeral pieces Fast produced, may well suppose that, however vulgar any of these pieces may be, getting them controlled bibliographically would benefit all students of leftist thought in Fast's era. A serious bibliography of Fast's entire output would be even more valuable; he used many names and published in an enormous variety of venues. Questions such as the one Wald asks (see note 4) about the reception of Fast's historical fictions simply cannot receive a serious answer without this preliminary basic information.

10. Walter Goodman provides a brief overview of the background to this affair in *The Committee: The Extraordinary Career of the House Committee on Un-American Activities* (New York: Farrar, Straus and Giroux, 1968), 176-81, as does David Caute, *The Great Fear: The Anti-Communist Purge Under Truman and Eisenhower* (New York: Simon and Schuster, 1978), 177-78.

11. Fast wrote several times to explain his resignation from the Communist Party: see, for example, "An Exchange with Howard Fast," *Mainstream* 10; 3 (March 1957): 29-47 (Fast's "My Decision" followed by the Editors' "Comment"); "On Leaving the Communist Party," *Saturday Review* 40; 46 (November 16, 1957): 15-17, 55-58; and "The Writer and the Commissar," *Prospectus* 1; 1 (November 1957): 31-57.

12. The resentments that Fast's conversion elicited among his former comrades on the Left must have been at least slightly exacerbated because of his former and fairly prominent role as a sort of "enforcer" of Party discipline. His participation in the correction of Albert Maltz, who fell into ideological error with respect to the question of the potential independence of the artist from adherence to political orthodoxy, is an oft-told tale (see, for example, Aaron, *Writers on the Left*, 386-90). This affair took place in 1946. Earlier still, Fast played a role in keeping Joseph Freeman's 1943 novel *Never Call Retreat* from being filmed because Freeman, who had broken with the Party in 1939, was regarded as a renegade; this matter is mentioned in Joseph R. Starobin, *American Communism in Crisis, 1943-1957* (1972; rept. Berkeley: University of California Press, 1975), 253-54 (n. 32).

13. Wald ("Legacy," 96) notes that the "left-liberal doctrine" with which Fast infuses these books "is not just simplified but fatally trivialized" by Fast's failure "to address the civil rights of those who were real 'subversives' in the eyes of the witch-hunters." Instead, he portrays only simple innocents who are framed by McCarthyites. Fast criticizes "excesses and abuses," not "the entire process."

14. Fast was no academic; but neither were the issues he raised in *Silas Timberman* matters he could afford to find "purely academic." Ellen W. Schrecker usefully recalls Fast's experiences as a speaker barred from appearances at various universities in *No Ivory Tower: McCarthyism and the Universities* (New York: Oxford University Press, 1986), 91-93.

15. One of these columns provided an occasion for one of the relatively rare bits of knuckle-rapping notice Fast can still attract from the right (*Being Red* was to provide another occasion, of course). See William F. Buckley, Jr., "Mr. Fast Explains," *National Review* 41; 3 (February 24, 1989), 62-63, where Buckley explains how Fast, writing about abortion, fails to grasp significant distinctions between a fetus's right to life and the forfeiture of claims to the same right by a person convicted of a capital crime.

16. Wald writes that books such as *Clarkton, Silas Timberman,* and *Lola Gregg* were "less successful and . . . explicitly more radical" than Fast's earlier novels. He says that *Freedom Road, The American* (1946), and *Spartacus* were the "most successful" of Fast's books while he was a Party member (*Encyclopedia,* 219).

17. Since Wald wrote these words in 1983, a few other self-published bestsellers have appeared. They remain uncommon enough to warrant notice in the *New York Times* (see, for example, Edwin McDowell, "The Rise of the Self-Published Best Seller," July 9, 1990, D6).

18. Fast used other pseudonyms, as well. In *Being Red* (159-61), for instance, he tells of his use of the name Simon Kent for a story whose title he remembered as "A Child is Lost," published and then often reprinted under that name at a time when his own name would have killed sales. "The Day Our Child Was Lost," by Simon Kent, appears—"Condensed from *This Week* magazine"—in *Catholic Digest* 15; 4 (February 1951): 38-40 at a time when that magazine would have reprinted nothing "by Howard Fast."

See my comment at the end of note 9. Until Fast's vast output has been given basic bibliographical attention, we remain unclear about both its extent and its reception, even when (perhaps especially when) those who were "receiving" it were uncertain or simply wrong about whose work they were reading.

19. Thus they unwittingly betrayed their vast distance from the arenas in which literary status was conferred—arenas where, for all practical purposes, Fast no longer had any reputation proximity to which could enhance the status of their own product. Nonetheless—to cite three literally random examples—Fast is prominently named on the covers of the March, 1959; November, 1959; and February, 1960, *Magazine of Fantasy and Science Fiction;* two of those covers also give the title of the story to be found within.

20. I owe this recollection to a private communication from Professor Felscher.

21. Like *The Children,* this is a book to which I hope to return on another occasion. I would, however, draw attention, if to nothing else, at least to the restraint Fast shows in developing the characters in this novel. His use of ellipsis, his refusal to "explain" them, is masterful. Fast never opens up the relationship of his narrator—a Roman Catholic physician—to his Puritan neighbors (and his Puritan wife) or to the Quakers also resident in the neighborhood. These relationships, and that between the narrator and his wife especially, remain among many sources of fruitful mystery in this book—and, I think, among the sources of its power.

   As Wald, among others, has noticed (see note 2), Fast *is* too prolific. He is thus easy to underestimate. Not only has he written too much (who has read it all?), but also his most interesting books are not always his best-*known* books. The reader who concentrates on the latter may not invariably meet the former. On the other hand, of course, the ways in which Fast's various books have been received is itself a topic that would repay further study; it might by itself offer a kind of roadmap to U.S. literary politics over a large chunk of the 20th Century.

22. Barbara Foley is not alone in distinguishing between Fast's earlier and his later versions of this tale of disengagement. See her *Radical Representations: Politics and Form in U.S. Proletarian Fiction, 1929-1941* (Durham: Duke University Press, 1993), 220 n. 6.

Andrew Macdonald (essay date 1996)

SOURCE: "Howard Fast: An American Life," in *Howard Fast: A Critical Companion,* Westport, CT: Greenwood Press, 1996, pp. 5-35.

[*In the following essay, Macdonald provides an overview of Fast's life, literary career, and numerous published works, drawing attention to the recurring preoccupations and unifying themes that link the author's biography and fiction.*]

> I've been very fortunate, no question about it, because even during the blacklist years my books were selling by the millions all over the world. There were always enough royalties for us to live decently. I was very lucky, very fortunate. But I was born and grew up in the greatest, the noblest achievement of the human race on this planet—which was called the United States of America.
>
> —Howard Fast, quoted by Mervyn Rothstein in "Howard Fast in a New Mode," *New York Times,* March 10, 1987.

All writers create out of their life experiences, and their biographies—biographies in the larger sense of what they read, thought about, and learned, as well as what events happened to them—are vital to our understanding of what shaped their fictional work. The influence of life experience clearly varies from writer to writer, with some using the fictional world as an escape from a grim past or present, some following the events of their own lives as a general guide, and others indulging in virtual autobiography disguised as fiction. In the case of a writer like Howard Fast, much of whose early and best work was based on historical research, biographical information may seem beside the point, for surely the overwhelming weight of historical fact and the inescapable patterns of verifiable event must guide the fiction. What chance can the writer's own experience have against the known circumstances of, say, the American Revolutionary War?

In fact, although Fast has said he is "too close" to the incidents of his life "to be able to separate the important from the unimportant" (*Something about the Author* 81), much of his work, even the historical fiction, is autobiographical. When Fast writes from research, he chooses his central characters with great care; protagonists such as Tom Paine, whose life and work have been well established in documented sources, parallel elements in Fast's own personality and worldview, elements clearly related to his personal history. The historical figures thus provide a kind of psychological biography of Fast, a duplication and validation of his own philosophy and personal leanings in someone known to have existed earlier. When the protagonist of a Fast historical novel is purely fictional—an amalgam of real figures, perhaps, but not a historical personality—Fast again puts together a character who is recognizably a product of forces familiar to Fast from his own life. The central figures from books such as **Conceived in Liberty** and **April Morning,** for example, though fictional and very different from their creator in age, education, religion, geographic origin, vocation, and so on, nevertheless share key values, attitudes, and assumptions that firmly link Fast, the urban New York literary figure and political activist, with rural farm boy or uneducated soldier.

In addition, some nonhistorical Fast works are thinly disguised autobiographies. **The Pledge,** a straightforward account of a young journalist's experience in post-World War II India and the United States, culminating in a jail term for contempt of Congress, is virtually true, at least if Fast's accounts of his own experiences are to be trusted. More commonly, echoes and parallels of Fast's life occur throughout the novels—reminders of real characters encountered, locations visited, events and situations experienced, political and social happenings confronted. The lines between biography and fiction are often parallel but at times diverge, depending on the kind of fiction being written, but the lines generally move in the same direction, as we would expect. It is thus helpful to know the shaping factors of Fast's long and event-filled life, an exciting and very American life that tells us much about what it was like to be in the thick of things politically and socially in the mid- to late-twentieth century, the period of America's greatest power and influence.

This is not to say that the value of Fast's work lies in conscious or unconscious revelations about his own life. Biographical readings are useful when we know enough about a writer's life to see what has been done to turn reality into art; our emphasis should be on Fast's fiction, on the patterns, themes, and characters that have intrigued and captivated several generations of readers who know nothing of the writer's history. For that reason, the biographical material in this chapter should be seen as a guide to what motivated Fast rather than as a key to unlocking meaning.

The discussion is based mainly on Fast's excellent 1990 memoir, *Being Red*. A second, less detailed source for the discussion is *The Naked God: The Writer and the Communist Party*, published in 1957; this book began as a magazine article about Fast's departure from the Communist party and focuses almost entirely on his political life. Apart from incidental facts culled from various standard references, the final source of material for this chapter is Howard Fast himself, in the form of brief discussions with me.

Fast's entrance on the American scene in November 1914 was uneventful enough, probably hardly noticed outside his own family, for he was the son of working-class, first-generation immigrants, Barney Fastov, the name shortened to "Fast" by immigration officials, and Ida Miller. His parents were from the Ukraine and Lithuania, respectively. Barney Fast seems to have been something of a romantic rebel before marriage to Ida, apparently seriously planning to join a cavalry regiment invading Cuba in 1898 during the Spanish-American War as a means of revenge for the expulsion of the Jews from Spain in 1492. The military escapade never materialized, however, and after five children were born, Howard being the fourth, Ida Fast died in 1923, when the author-to-be was eight and a half years old.

His mother's death left Howard's father with four children (Arthur, the second child, died of diphtheria in 1912) and a limited means of earning a living, as his original trade as a wrought-iron worker disappeared because of changing construction methods and his second livelihood as a gripper man on a cable car fell prey to new means of transportation in New York. The elder Fast became a dress factory cutter, a dead-end job never paying more than forty dollars a week. The eldest child, Rena, left to marry soon after her mother's death, and the three younger boys were thrown, according to *Being Red*, pretty much on their own resources as their father slipped in and out of depression and employment, a distant parent who left at eight in the morning and returned to their tenement as late as midnight. Jerome, known as Jerry, was one year older than Howard, and the two took over the household. Fast says their poverty, both financial and emotional, was unchanging. Significantly, what did change, the author says in *Being Red*, was his "ability to face and alter circumstances. I ceased to be wholly a victim" (31).

One need not be a Freudian analyst to see in this grim childhood history patterns later emphasized in Fast's work: the distant, somewhat unreliable father/authority figure, well meaning but ineffectual; the mother figure, absent and possibly idealized by childhood memory; the need to confront all problems actively; the power of brotherhood, as Jerry and Howard, almost the same age, confronted the hostile world of the ghetto and paid their own way with a constantly changing series of jobs, beginning at age ten for Howard. Throughout the Fast canon, we see protagonists in rebellion against authority, often an authority unaware of and uninvolved with the main characters, who soon learn to depend on themselves and on their own true "brothers," always a limited group against the world. Brotherhood abounds in Fast's books, both literal, as in *My Glorious Brothers,* about the rebellious Jewish brothers who become leaders of ancient Israel, or metaphorical, as in the union of mine workers in *Power.* And until a notable change in the 1960s when Fast turned to novels about women, the group is male, for women, though often well drawn, are subsidiary in the early works. Perhaps paralleling his mother's "desertion" of Fast and his brothers through her death and then his sister Rena's escape into marriage, the elegant, somewhat older female figure who is either distant or unreachable and sometimes leaves the protagonist is a familiar figure in the earlier works.

Fast's childhood also inculcated two formidable though contrasting shaping elements: the anti-Semitism of his rough immigrant neighborhoods and the uplifting power of the written word, the latter located most conveniently in the New York Public Library. After leaving the East Side Jewish ghetto, Fast's family moved to 159th Street, just west of Amsterdam Avenue, where Italian and Irish immigrants predominated. This was young Howard's introduction to racial and religious hatred, and although the Fasts had never kept a kosher household or felt any particular Jewish identity, the accusations of "Christ-killing" by the neighborhood children helped create a new unity among Howard and his brothers, a closed circle against hostile outsiders. Thus, in spite of his lack of early training in Judaism as religion or culture, Fast came, presumably beginning at this point, to entertain a lifelong interest in his heritage, even writing a novel, *The Outsider,* about a rabbi married to a nonpracticing Jew and struggling with his role in a Christian-majority society. Apart from *Moses, Prince of Egypt,* and *My Glorious Brothers,* both wholly on Jewish history, many Fast novels include Jewish characters, often in contexts such as the American Revolution or Reconstruction in which Judaism is usually given little or no credit for having a role. In *Citizen Tom Paine,* for example, it is a Jewish moneylender who finances one of Paine's revolutionary screeds, while in *Freedom Road,* Gideon Jackson's first mentor is Jewish. Doctor Gonzales, a Jewish physician, accompanies the main character of *Seven Days in June.* A Jewish family, the Levys, figures importantly in The Immigrants series. The struggles of Bernie Cohen, and later of his son Sam, over the proper place of a Jewish heritage in an "American" identity become important in the later novels of the family saga.

Apart from summer vacations in the Catskill Mountains when young Howard spent time with his aunt and uncle in Hunter, New York, childhood provided few pleasures. Even these escapes from big city poverty were tempered by family conflict with aunt and cousins, although Fast loved the mountains, forests, and wild animals, an appreciation of nature we see again throughout his work, even in the fictional descriptions of Mill Point Prison in West Virginia in *The Pledge,* where Fast in reality served time for contempt of Congress. We see a big city boy's love of open spaces in *Max,* whose hero, like Fast, moves from New York to California, and again in incidental descriptions of the American landscape, from *Freedom Road* to *Power* to more recent works like The Immigrants series, where the Napa Valley near San Francisco receives loving description. But New York did have one overwhelming formative influence: the availability of free books from the New York Public Library.

Fast reports reading everything and anything from the shelves of this wondrous collection of texts, and any serious reader of his novels believes him. Fast is complimentary enough about the public education he received, acknowledging that for all its rigidity and lack of imagination—he was forced to write with his right hand though he was born left handed—it might have been superior to more modern approaches that produce poor or few results. However, it is clear that his real education came through omnivorous reading—of the classics of American literature, of fiction that was mentioned or recommended, of whatever else took the fancy of the boy and the young man. We can imagine Fast's remembering himself when he wrote about Gideon Jackson, the semiliterate slave of *Freedom Road,* discovering books and the huge new world they offered, of Tom Paine's similar self-taught odyssey, and of myriad other scholars and readers who pull themselves up in his novels. Again and again the point is made that nonreaders are confined to the experiences of their own place and time. For the ambitious who are excluded from formal education, books are like wondrous time travel and space travel devices, machines that permit local experience to be compared to universal human practice. Education, always the key to the city on the hill for immigrants, came to Fast through a library card.

The evidence reveals varying experiences in Fast's early life—some very harsh, some, as in his relationship with his brothers, less so. His biography speaks of poverty and a fierce struggle for a decent life in a ghetto, of brutal street toughs and gangs that had to be fought for survival. Yet there must have been good times as well. A photograph of Howard at age three in *Being Red* shows a solemn straw-hatted and bespectacled toddler with toy spade and pail, on holiday in Hunter, New York, an image a bit at odds with the grim self-portrait in words of the same book. The photograph of his father, Barney Fast, shows a fairly well-dressed, even dapper man at ease, and the photos of brothers Jerome and Julius, as well as of Howard at twenty-one, show healthy and vigorous- looking young men of their time, looking out at the camera with

adolescent confidence. The depression years were grim and New York street life violent, of course, and it would be churlish to question memories held so firmly, but it is at least clear that Fast's intellectual development as a child and youngster were completely out of character with the tenement housing, the street victimization, and the generally gritty physical environment he describes surrounding him. In this intellectual development, books from the New York Public Library played an important role in producing a writer, but Fast was also lucky in his teachers and in his literary models and influences. Even for poor boys from the ghetto, the times were rich with stimulants to the artistic and intellectual sensibility.

Fast's career as an author began with a number of different factors shaping his imagination. Jack London's prose was a recurring pleasure (now Fast finds it too flowery and mannered), and from London's *The Iron Heel,* Fast learned how the "wild word" *bolshevik* could be used to condemn a work of art even when the librarian in question had not read the book, a lesson of great importance later in his life when Communist party censors attacked his own works. An English teacher from Texas named Hallie Jamison is remembered fondly, a one-time friend of O. Henry who imbued Fast with a love of the lore of the American West and praised his gift for writing. She urged him to read Robert Louis Stevenson, George Bernard Shaw, and Shakespeare; Shaw's *The Intelligent Woman's Guide to Socialism and Capitalism* was a Pandora's box, leading Fast to Thorstein Veblen's *The Theory of the Leisure Class,* Bellamy's *Looking Backward,* and Engel's *The Origin of the Family.* The movement away from the narrow world of poverty and provincialism had begun.

Captivated by these models of rigorous thought, Fast decided to become a writer at age fifteen, not so much by conscious decision but by default, for other avenues were closed to him due to his indifference to academic subjects other than literature and ideas. He describes himself as neither quiet nor contemplative as a child, but as "one of those irritating, impossible, doubting, questioning mavericks, full of anger and invention and wild notions, accepting nothing, driving . . . peers to bitter arguments and . . . elders to annoyance, rage, and despair" (*Being Red* 48). He says dryly that he probably had some good points as well, and then seriously and significantly claims that he and his brothers, in spite of their rough upbringing, had no hate of others different from themselves, hate being something picked up along the way, surely a key to understanding his later work. From this perspective, hatred is not part of the innocent young human but rather "picked up," learned or acquired from society as one grows older; human nature, he implies, is a blank tablet written on by experience, at least as far as this destructive emotion goes, with youthful decency poisoned by environment. The suggestion is of human perfectibility. Hatred, simply one of the characteristics of social organization, can be eliminated by reorganizing society, much as one could eliminate smoking or drinking by doing away with opportunities to learn about them. This question of the origin of hatred and prejudice is wrestled with throughout the canon.

The fledgling literary man was unenrollable in most colleges because of his spotty academic record, and at age seventeen he chose the National Academy, a prestigious New York City art school, to instruct him in how to illustrate his own writing. Each morning he would arise at 6:00 A.M. and write for two hours before art school. After learning two-fingered typing (which he still uses) and banging out a few dozen stories, he finally sold one, **"Wrath of the Purple,"** to *Amazing Stories* magazine for thirty-seven dollars, a good deal of money in 1931. Now working for the public library, Fast was assigned to pick up overdue books checked out by prostitutes at a huge nearby brothel, an experience with temptation overcome by fear of syphilis that shows up in **Max.** In spite of such distractions, Fast still managed to write two novels, to try to read *Das Kapital,* to read *The Communist Manifesto* and John Reed's *Ten Days That Shook the World* with pleasure, to drop out of art studies at the National Academy, to fall in and out of love with various young women his age, to resign from the public library job, to begin to meet other intellectuals and political folk interested in leftist ideas, and to work for a hat maker. None of these activities necessarily had any causal relation with the others, but he was learning that he was a writer and a thinker, not a student, that he enjoyed the company of women, and that his great interest was in the politics of the left. One young woman, Sarah Kunitz, was a member of the Communist party but discouraged the seventeen-year-old Fast from joining as well, and his designs on both Sarah and party membership gradually faded.

Next, in 1933, footloose and unencumbered by any formal obligations, Fast joined a friend on a hitchhiking tour of the South, catching rides down the eastern part of the country, through Richmond, Winston-Salem, Savannah, Tampa, and Fort Lauderdale all the way to Miami. These southern experiences gave him good background for **Freedom Road,** he says, and, one suspects, colored his attitudes toward that whole section of the country thereafter, since most of his contacts with southern officialdom and the general populace were negative—"jails and guns," he remembers—although a few individuals and the picturesque and romantic scenery are recalled fondly. On return to New York, the young Howard went to work as a shipping clerk and wrote six to eight hours a day, completing novels number four and five, both, like the first three, unpublishable. Then he wrote his sixth novel, **Two Valleys,** and found a publisher, Dial Press, in 1933. At nineteen he received the Bread Loaf Writers Conference Award. His next works were the novels **Strange Yesterday** (1934) and **Place in the City** (1937), but though he was being published, Sarah Kunitz, with whom Fast had stayed in contact, criticized his work, pointing out that his stories were "fairy tales" written by a legitimate working-class writer, while middle-class writers were writing about the depression and the life of the poor. In reaction, Fast tried a story about a street boy from his neighborhood, which he found so painful to write about that after publishing it as **The Children** he turned to research on the American Revolution, in part to "try to find out what had actually happened" and to avoid another "fairy tale" or the pain of writing about his own life (**Being Red** 65).

The scorn of Sarah Kunitz for his escapist tales was a watershed event, for Fast thereafter relied on research, to greater or lesser degrees to be sure, but for the most part avoiding "fairy tales" coming purely out of his own imagination until much later in his career. He was also temporarily lionized by the left and the John Reed Society for **The Children,** whose politics agreed with their own. Fast, however, was put off by the show trials and executions of old bolsheviks in Russia in 1936, and he had no further contact with the Communist party until the end of World War II. What he describes as the most important event of his young life occurred at about this time: his meeting with Bette Cohen, a young woman from New Jersey with whom Fast fell immediately in love and who became his wife. Their life as a young married couple was one of poverty, for Fast gave up factory work to write freelance for magazines such as the *Saturday Evening Post* and the *Ladies Home Companion.* A jaunt in an old jalopy to Valley Forge, then undergoing historical reconstruction, led to **Conceived in Liberty,** an interesting if harrowing book written in the realistic style of Erich Maria Remarque's *All Quiet on the Western Front.* The Revolutionary War had never been approached in this way, and **Conceived in Liberty** was well received, including a very positive review in the *New York Times* by the American realist author James T. Farrell.

A trip to the American West, including Oklahoma, Arizona, New Mexico, the Rockies, and Mexico, led to an enthusiasm for the history and lore of the American Indian, and especially the Cheyenne. Fast, a quarter of a century before it became fashionable, was interested in telling the American Indian story from the Indian point of view. **The Last Frontier** (1941) received particular praise as a taut and moving story of the abuse and extermination of three hundred Cheyenne. The manuscript was ill received precisely because of its innovative viewpoint, but after a lengthy revision, it was published and praised by critics, including Alexander Woollcott, Rex Stout, and the eminent Carl Van Doren.

The early 1940s were eventful years for Howard and Bette Fast. **The Tall Hunter** came out in 1942, followed by **The Unvanquished,** in the same year, about the lowest point for the Continental army, and *Time* magazine called it the "best book about World War Two," seeing in it a parallel to the current struggle. Also in 1942, at the suggestion of Louis Untermeyer, Fast joined the Office of War Information (OWI) and worked for the Voice of America. He began to write **Freedom Road** and received, through a work colleague, an invitation to stay with an anti-Semitic family of southern aristocrats in Charleston, South Carolina, to do background research. Fast's visit shows up in **Freedom Road** in his evocative descriptions of old Charleston mansions and the waterfront, and especially in the descriptions of the dinner parties his central character Gideon Jackson attends, social gatherings equally notable for elegance and bigotry.

In this same period Fast and Bette were slowly drawn into the circle of New York communists. Fast is somewhat defensive about his ignorance of the true face of Stalin (he admits to being disturbed by the Non-Aggression Pact with Hitler), and he points out the stalwart Americanism of his Communist party compatriots, their decency and integrity. Fast asserts that the American Communist party led the struggle for the unemployed, the hungry, the homeless, and the oppressed, and he offers as evidence the known names of the best and the brightest who were party members, an honor roll of writers and thinkers of the time: W.E.B. Du Bois, Albert Maltz, John Howard Lawson, and Dalton Trumbo. (Much later, Trumbo would write the screenplay for the film version of Fast's novel *Spartacus.*) Many others were secret members of the party, and, of course, were trapped by their "premature anti-Fascism," in the euphemism of the McCarthy years, when U.S. policy shifted quickly from embracing the Soviet Union as an ally to defining itself against the U.S.S.R. as its mortal enemy.

These years leading to Fast's identification as a "card-carrying member of the Communist party," as the rhetoric of the time termed it, were clearly painful and difficult for him to deal with, even decades later. He was a successful writer, with both critics and the public, now financially secure and newly married. But with the war, all carefully laid plans for the future were disrupted. Bette Fast miscarried their first child, and there were apparently strains in the marriage over her depression and the prospect of Howard's possibly serving abroad; however, a job with the OWI offered a compromise in which Fast could help the war effort yet remain in New York. His work with the OWI turned out to be not just a temporary stopgap but rather another turning point; he would become ever more involved in politics, and his novels based on wartime and postwar experiences would eventually take him in new political and artistic directions.

Fast's OWI work was writing propaganda. Initially hired because he knew something about the American Revolution and might therefore produce patriotic pamphlets, he was recommended as a newswriter by the eminent theater producer John Houseman, who had read the proofs for *Citizen Tom Paine* and thought Fast could write good, clean political prose. The young novelist, still in his late twenties, became the wordsmith for the still-forming Voice of America, writing daily fifteen-minute scripts to be read by actors in English and a wide variety of European languages. The irony of the future communist's being chosen as mouthpiece of the U.S. government and the army is not lost on Fast's retrospective view of his work. Millions of Europeans of different nations enslaved by the Nazis heard Fast's words and formed their mental images of the United States on that basis. Generals, bureaucrats, representatives of shipbuilders and the State Department, of the U.S. Chamber of Commerce and the Merchant Marine: a full contingent of unlikely folk beat a path to Fast's office trying to get their story told on the Voice of America. The opening words to his news show, "Good morning, this is the Voice of America, and here is the situation today," still deeply affect Fast: "this is the voice of mankind's hope and salvation, the voice of my wonderful, beautiful country, which will put an end to fascism and remake the world" (*Being Red* 14). Fast's political beliefs brought him to many criticisms of American culture, yet the pure and idealistic patriotism expressed here is consistent throughout his long career as an author.

A measure of how innocent the future communist was about things Russian is captured in an amusing Voice of America story. One day the State Department told Fast that President Roosevelt wanted the entire broadcast for that evening—and it was already 6.00 P.M.—devoted to the virtues of a Russian soldier, an Ivan Ivanovich. Roosevelt assumed that Fast knew that "Ivan Ivanovich" was the nickname for the typical Russian infantryman, the counterpart to the American G.I. Joe, but Fast and his staff, in blithe ignorance, spent two hours calling around trying to find information about this particular Soviet before learning from the Russian news agency TASS that there was no such individual. Far more troubling was the necessity of watching battlefield film clips from the Allies and enemy forces in order to make the radio reports realistic; the films made war real and hateful to Fast in a way that prose could not, and he found his early antiwar sentiments reconfirmed. We might note also that throughout his seventy-odd novels, scenes of war are always realistic, engrossing, and horrifying; the wartime battle footage he viewed, unedited for the public, must have shaped his later descriptions.

Under Fast's direction, the Voice of America broadcasts became polished and successful, and during this period of fourteen months or so of broadcasting, *Citizen Tom Paine* came out and garnered rave reviews. Fast applied for the overseas VOA position in North Africa but was told that the State Department, on the advice of the Federal Bureau of Investigation, would not issue him a passport because of his communist sympathies and Communist party connections. Fast says that he had neither, only a fair-minded appreciation of the sufferings of the Soviet Union in its struggle against Nazism and a refusal to advance the anticommunist agenda. In January 1944 Fast resigned angrily, admitting much later to intemperance in his speech (a lifelong characteristic) but never in his actions, which were entirely loyal and proper.

At this time, Fast took his first trip to California to discuss a possible film of *Citizen Tom Paine.* (Images of California in this era abound in *Max.*) The deal fell through, as have most other arrangements to film Fast's works, but he met many movie people, including Paul Robeson, the African-American singer and actor. He discovered in the Hollywood community a number of communist sympathizers, and, when again in New York, he and Bette were asked to join the party. They did so that year, 1944, and he says that there were no party cards involved, simply a self-identification: we are with you.

Ironically, this was also the moment of Fast's greatest success as a novelist, for *Freedom Road* had won enthusiastic adherents, including Eleanor Roosevelt and W.E.B. Du Bois. A Soviet bibliography counted its publication abroad at eighty-two languages; another Soviet estimate called it the most widely printed and read book of the twentieth century. Fast was receiving requests for publication forty-six years after the original publication, and pirated editions were in the millions at least. One African scholar was inspired by the book to create a written language for his tribe, in which the first work printed was *Freedom Road.* During this period Fast received the Schomburg Race Relations Award (1944), the Newspaper Guild Award (1947), and the Jewish Book Council of America Award (1948). But irony abounded: as soon as word of Fast's communism began to spread, his literary reputation began to disintegrate, just as, over a decade later, his name was obliterated from Soviet literary journals and courses once he quit the party.

Fast's memories of the party in the postwar period are of a benign, almost mainstream group, one very much in the American socialist tradition dating back to the Levelers in colonial days, through the labor movement of the nineteenth century, the International Workers of the World (the Wobblies), and on into the Socialist party of Eugene V. Debs. Fast claims the party did believe in violent revolution in the nineteenth century but gave it up for labor and community organizing in the twentieth, a position in accord with party dogma but in dispute among historians. In fact, Fast's descriptions of his first party meeting, held in the New York brownstone of an upper-class aristocrat, make it sound like a discussion group sponsored by the Democratic party: how could the participants help reelect Franklin Delano Roosevelt? Fast insists that he never heard a single call for the overthrow of the government by violence. Of the sixty thousand or so party members in the United States at the time, Fast asserts that the vast majority were decent, honorable people of great talent and idealism. In fact, Fast met Harry Truman, then vice president, and later was invited with his reelection committee to the White House for lunch with the Roosevelts. Mrs. Roosevelt chatted with Fast about *Freedom Road.*

The next great adventure shaped a number of novels. Fast received an offer from *Coronet* magazine to go to the China-Burma-India theater as a war correspondent. In fact, the war was virtually over, and Fast was moved from one public relations office to another in places where the battles had been won long before. In Casablanca he was impressed by the easy, luxurious life led by officers and troops far from the front lines, the palatial quarters and picnics at the beach with champagne and caviar. In contrast, in Benghazi, he was taken into the desert to see miles of wrecked military vehicles—German, American, and British tanks, jeeps, and so on—piled together in testimony of the enormous waste of war. The experience, says Fast, made him a pacifist at that moment. (In fact, he has made this statement about a number of experiences.) In Cairo he saw human misery unparalleled even by that in Calcutta, which he was to see later. He flew over the Negev and Sinai, then over Iraq, Iran, Abadan, Bahrain Island, and Palestine,

absorbing images of the "terrible mountains and desert" that would show up in *My Glorious Brothers.* In Saudi Arabia his huge C-46 cargo plane put down to pick up empty Coca Cola bottles in a desert airstrip where the thermometer read 157 degrees Fahrenheit. The plane lumbered back into the air but could not gain altitude in the desert heat because of its load of empty soft drink bottles. Fast yelled for the crew to dump cases out to save all their lives, but they refused, explaining that while military equipment might be sacrificed, they would be in deep trouble for "messing around with Coca Cola." The plane, flying just above the ground, landed on its belly at an emergency air field with no loss of life and no broken bottles, but was ruined. Both *Coronet* and *Esquire* refused to write the story, which eventually appeared in *The Howard Fast Reader,* where most readers took it as fiction.

In India, Fast encountered the British, a people who generally come off very negatively in all his writing, from *Citizen Tom Paine* to *The Pledge,* the fictional version of this trip. A severe critic of colonialism, Fast blames the British for their toleration and perhaps encouragement of Indian poverty under the raj, the rule by the British empire, and, even worse, their personal indifference to the humanity of their colonial subjects. Two events from this trip sum up this dehumanizing attitude, both of which show up as incidents in *The Pledge,* in slightly different form. First, Fast sees two British officers being dried after a shower, their Indian servants toweling off their private parts to the complete indifference of the officers, as if the servants were not human. A second story was told to Fast, that when the British high commissioner at New Delhi learned that poor people were using a lamppost as an open air night school to learn reading, the commissioner acted quickly to help this literacy effort: he had a larger light bulb installed!

Fast saw Gandhi from a distance at a train station, but the greatest influence on him, apart from the negative effect of the snobbish, class-conscious British officers and official-dom and the self-indulgence of the American military in essentially peacetime circumstances (the front-line fighting was far away), was the Indian communists and their seriousness about fighting poverty and misery among their people. The chief of the Delhi Communist party sent a message through Fast to his opposite number in the United States: four hundred million Indians have been learning to spit together, and they will wash the British into the sea. A journey from Delhi to Calcutta by train revealed all the wonders and horrors of India, including unknown tribes, a man dying of starvation, wild exoticism, and appalling poverty—topics too alien for the conventional *Coronet* magazine, which had sent Fast. Many of these impressions would end up in *The Pledge,* observed by his character Bruce Bacon, a stand-in for Fast. Barbara Lavette of The Immigrants series also serves as a correspondent in Calcutta, as depicted in *Second Generation. Being Red* and the two fictional works describe the huge numbers of the homeless—people living outdoors permanently, with streets set aside for sleeping and possibly for dying from starvation. Fast was told that six million people had died, at least in part because the British authorities had arranged with Muslim rice dealers to withhold food in order to weaken the will of Indians who might support the Japanese.

This story is central to the plot of *The Pledge,* and as in the fictional version, Fast gets second-hand confirmations but never enough direct evidence to break the scandal into the mainstream media. Again as in *The Pledge,* Fast met with Indian communists and dined at a Jewish restaurant founded in Calcutta two hundred years before the birth of Christ. He traveled by bicycle with a communist organizer into neighborhoods so poor that the organizer would read the one-page party newspaper to residents, who would pay, if they could, with a single grain of rice—scenes of poverty so wretched that Fast compares them to Dante's *Inferno.* This is one of the most affecting portions of *The Pledge* and makes understandable Fast's belief in the self-denial and commitment to the poor of the party. Fast was well aware that change was unlikely and that ordinary human common sense leads people the way of self-protection and self-interest. Yet the "saintliness" of Sind, the Communist party organizer, remains shimmering in the memory, his gestures toward reform perhaps absurd and futile, but clearly the only right thing to do.

Back in the United States, Fast delivered the message from the Delhi party secretary to Gene Dennis, head of the American party, and was very let down by the man's coldness and lack of interest in his Indian colleagues. As in *The Pledge,* no mainstream American paper would touch Fast's story on the British-caused famine, not even the leftist *New Masses.* In Fast's mind the allegations of British culpability constituted proof, and the issue ended there. The twice-told famine story (thrice told, if we count Barbara Lavette's version) is a window on Fast's strength, his ability to feel the suffering of others deeply and to render their misery in dramatic example and detail, but also on his weakness, a tendency to shoot from the hip that can deny moral complexity and varying shades of responsibility. To call the British action the moral equivalent of Hitler's Holocaust, a charge made by the Indian communists that Fast repeats without comment, was sure to provoke counterclaims and countercharges at a time when the British were firm U.S. allies. In a self-revealing anecdote in *Being Red,* Fast is talking with a sympathetic lawyer when a professional red baiter walks by. Fast calls the anticommunist a "sonofabitch," and the Philadelphia lawyer chides him, "Come on, Howard, you only hate him because he's their sonofabitch. If he were our sonofabitch, you'd cover him with roses" (28).

Fast's trip to India served him well as a writer, for it resulted in a powerful novel and a good repertoire of story material. As a reporter, however, Fast made a good advocate but not an objective investigator ferreting out evidence of the truth, an activity that was perhaps denied him by circumstances but that also seemed to interest him

less. *Coronet* may well have been correct in rejecting some of his reports (some were later written up as effective stories). We should note, of course, that these versions of events, in *Being Red, The Pledge,* and *Second Generation,* were published long after the fact, when the distorting mirror of time and memory must have had some effect. Their consistency with each other, however, suggests that Fast is sure in his own mind about his experiences and has, with all his skill as a storyteller, shaped them for maximum effect. And this, of course, is his forte.

Fast met and got along well with Jean-Paul Sartre, then visiting New York, and found much in common with the French philosopher and party member. Both were ignorant of the atrocities of Stalin and the party in Russia. Fast notes the excesses and contradictions of the American Communist party in these postwar years but also its distinguished membership and good intentions. In a way, the U.S. government's increasing intolerance of the left in general and of communists in particular caused Fast to harden his position and to explain away the antidemocratic and arbitrary practices he saw in the party as simply responses to oppression.

And the left was increasingly being isolated and persecuted in the immediate postwar years. The House Un-American Activities Committee, known later as HUAC, and Senator Joseph McCarthy's Senate committee were particular goads and tormentors, with their listing of communists and leftists in various institutions and their requiring of loyalty oaths as a condition for membership or employment, as the Taft-Hartley Labor Act of 1947 had done for labor union leaders. Fast was called up before HUAC because of his support of the Spanish Refugee Appeal, an innocuous enough organization raising money for food and medical supplies for displaced persons in Spain. Nervous (the eminent Clark Clifford had abased himself before the committee for sending out fifty copies of *Citizen Tom Paine* to friends, claiming he did not know it was "communist propaganda") but convinced that Congress did not send people to jail for their beliefs, Fast testified along with other members of the Appeal executive committee and was called back alone to answer charges that the record shows were clearly trumped up. The record does show, however, that Fast was impolitic in the extreme, calling the committee members names and pointing out their stupidities to them.

Tolerance of any views outside the mainstream was shrinking. While living under the threat of a jail term, Fast wrote a play, *Thirty Pieces of Silver,* about a White House staff member who betrays a colleague; it was never produced in the United States but was successful in Europe and Australia. Another event indicated the changing climate in the postwar years. A friend's temporarily lost child stimulated a Fast story, **"A Child Is Lost,"** scheduled to be published in *This Week,* a nationally distributed Sunday newspaper supplement, but Fast's literary agent asked that he publish under a pseudonym, since his own name would not be acceptable. A movie deal for this short story failed for the same reason, as the witch hunt for communists infected Hollywood, led in part by actor Ronald Reagan. A measure of the increasing attention from the government was that Fast's FBI file eventually reached eleven hundred pages, costing over $10 million to compile; he says that he is proud of every incident reported, none being immoral, illegal, or indecent but rather just the opposite. After a trial in 1947, Fast and other members of the board of the Joint Anti-Fascist Refugee Committee were found guilty of contempt of Congress for refusing to name the contributors to their cause. Appeals delayed the serving of Fast's three-month prison sentence until the spring of 1950.

In 1948, Fast became involved in the rebirth of the Progressive party, with Henry Wallace as presidential nominee. At pains to show the Progressive party as centrist, Fast traces its history back to Theodore Roosevelt through the Farmer-Labor party of 1924 led by Robert La Follette of Wisconsin. However, at the Philadelphia party convention, Fast was sought out by H. L. Mencken, who, after praising Fast's recent book about Altgeld, *The American,* asked Fast bluntly "what in hell" he was doing with the "gang" that formed the Progressive party (*Being Red* 192). Fast, a great admirer of the iconoclastic Baltimore journalist and scholar, mumbled in reply that he did not have a better place to be in the Republican or Democratic parties. Mencken answered that there was indeed a better place—"with yourself"—adding that he, Mencken, was a "party of one," an observer rather than a participant, and that Fast should be too. Fast should not join the party, for if he did, "these clowns will destroy you as surely as the sun rises and sets" (*Being Red* 193).

These were prophetic words, for the Progressive party failed, winning only 2 million votes nationwide in 1948, marking, as Fast points out with great accuracy, the end of the left-liberal-labor alliance that had been a major force in American politics since Eugene V. Debs before the turn of the nineteenth century. Labor distanced itself from the left in order to prove its patriotism and "Americanism"; liberal intellectuals were cowed and defensive, both groups defeated by the anticommunist fervor of Richard M. Nixon and J. Edgar Hoover, head of the FBI. The Communist party shrank steadily until by the end of the 1950s, it numbered only ten thousand or so members and had lost all its previous influence with movers and thinkers. Fast kept publishing, with *Clarkton* coming out in 1947, but his next book brought him trouble on two fronts. *My Glorious Brothers,* about the heroic Jewish Maccabee brothers in biblical times, appeared in 1948; it received the Jewish Book Council of America annual award, but Fast's name was removed from all subsequent lists of the award. Fast was banned from speaking at fifteen colleges and universities. In 1949, J. Edgar Hoover tried to remove *Citizen Tom Paine* from New York school and public libraries, as well as from libraries in other cities.

Fast blames almost all of these shameful happenings on the FBI, HUAC, and the generally conservative (and cowardly) times, but even his own testimony shows some culpability on the part of the party itself. As the U.S. government moved to censor ideas it disliked, so too did the party. For example, *My Glorious Brothers* was widely read in the just-formed state of Israel as a well-told historical parallel to Jewish aspirations for freedom but was panned by some party members as "Jewish nationalism." The party enforced political correctness thirty years before the term became current: Fast was criticized widely for using the word *wolfish* to describe a nonwhite, and for other linguistic offenses. Fast dutifully covered the trials of the party leadership for the *Daily Worker* but admits that many individuals were "arrogant" and "thick-headed"; he uses these words to describe his own "stupid" behavior in driving off his own nonparty friends because of the party's dictates, including the eminent Moss Hart.

Yet even forty years after the fact, Fast's testimony in *Being Red* reveals conflict about the true nature of the Communist party. He defends his assertion about the decent and principled nature of most party members he knew, listing a series of outstanding luminaries who participated in the Scientific and Cultural Conference for World Peace, a meeting rejected by the party leadership but promoted by Fast and others to support the ideas of the left. Participants included poet and critic Louis Untermeyer; poet Langston Hughes; writers John Lardner, Dalton Trumbo, Dashiell Hammett, and Thomas Mann; composer Leonard Bernstein; and other notables of the time (including writers Mary McCarthy and Norman Mailer as rump speakers). But while many of these figures surely had motives above reproach and while Fast states unequivocally that there was no Soviet money or influence on the conference, the role of the Russians in the American left in general remains murky, at least if recent information from KGB archives is to be trusted. The final chapter is yet to be written about these years.

At the International Peace Congress in Paris where he was embraced by everyone from taxi drivers to Chilean poet Pablo Neruda and Pablo Picasso (who kissed Fast full on the mouth, he notes), Fast secretly delivered a charge of anti-Semitism against the Communist Party of the Soviet Union, a charge made by the American Party. Alexander Fadeyev, the head of the Soviet delegation, repeated over and over, even in the face of Fast's listing of facts and evidence, that there was no anti-Semitism in the Soviet Union. Fast found himself irritated and angry but even in the retelling tries to explain away Fadeyev's stonewalling as honest ignorance. He never fully acknowledges the deep corruption that suffused the Soviet system not just in the party leadership but also the winked-at anti-Semitism that was so much of the normal way of doing things, and the inherent dishonesty that it created in those who could see beyond the Potemkin village of ethnic, religious, and racial harmony. Like one of his own literary characters— Tom Paine, or Ely and Jacob in *Conceived in Liberty,* or the Maccabee brothers—Fast's compass points stubbornly in one direction only, and he refuses even forty years after the event to admit wholeheartedly that this commitment was wrong. (In some ways the angry denunciations of ideological betrayal in *The Naked God* are more revealing than the sometimes defensive autobiographical explanations four decades later.) Yet literary commitments to truth are easy; real-life relationships to organizations are shaded in all the grays of ambiguity. As always, Fast wrote the plots of his stories far more neatly than the sometimes messy scripts of his own life.

A watershed event occurred when Bette Fast took a trip to Europe, and Howard, with a newly hired nanny to replace the Japanese woman who had taken care of the children in the past, repaired to Mt. Airy in Croton, New York, for some weeks in the country. The singer Pete Seeger contacted him about a peace meeting near Peekskill in Westchester Country, New York, including a concert by the great Paul Robeson. The event was a disaster, with rural hoodlums surrounding the entrance and yelling, "Kill a Commie for Christ" and "white niggers" at the concert-goers, then attacking them with fists, clubs, rocks, and even knives. Fast organized, the forty-two men and boys among the peace contingent into a defense force, which held off repeated charges by hundreds of drunken tormentors. He reports that the experience was important to him, and it is easy to see the Peekskill defense as a metaphor for Fast's view of his relation to society: a band of diverse believers, bonded into brotherhood by an ideal, holding off superior forces and triumphing by enduring. *My Glorious Brothers* fits this pattern, but so do all the books about the American Revolutionary army, and a number of other works as well. Peekskill had all the elements that define the Fast hero, his immediate surroundings, and society at large. Shortly after retelling the Peekskill story, Fast even says that people in the Cultural Section of the Communist party felt, because of their persecution, an identity with the early Christians!

In June 1950, after all appeals had failed, Fast began to serve his prison sentence, an experience told vividly in fictional form in *The Pledge.* (Barbara Lavette also goes to jail for contempt of Congress, but on Terminal Island, not far from Los Angeles.) After being held briefly in a Washington jail, Fast was transferred to a federal prison in West Virginia, Mill Point Prison, a minimum security institution where he lived with moonshiners from the Kentucky mountains and blacks convicted of relatively minor crimes. This "prison without walls" was established by Franklin Roosevelt and run by Kenneth Thieman, a civilized and humane man, and while it would be a distortion to say that Fast talks of his time there with pleasure, he calls the prison the best-run institution he had ever seen, prison or otherwise, and views his three months there as less a punishment than an indignity. Fast gave reading lessons and provided Bible exegesis for the moonshiners, met novelist-screenwriter Albert Maltz and director Edward Dmytryk there, both victims of the purge of Hollywood by HUAC, taught himself to cast a concrete statue (of a little boy urinating), began to think about his plan for *Spartacus,* one of his best-known novels, and in general fared a lot better than he expected to.

Back in New York, friends had produced a Fast play called *The Hammer,* about a Jewish man with three sons. The Communist party Cultural Section leader had arranged for James Earl Jones, the physically imposing black actor with the booming voice, to play one of the sons. When Fast saw the father, played by a slight, pale, fair-haired man and the huge Jones playing his son on the same stage, he reacted in horror: the audience would be confused at best by this genetic unlikelihood and might even think it comic. The cultural commissar accused Fast of white chauvinism, an absurdity Fast thinks indicates precisely what was wrong with the party: its inability to deal with reality in place of its elaborate theory. Fast also criticized the party for its unwillingness to defend the Rosenbergs in the famous spy case, and he pushed party officials to take action.

Fast by this time had finished *Spartacus,* a controversial treatment of the great slave revolt of 71 B.C. as a metaphor for all oppressed people's struggle to throw off the shackles of their inhuman oppressors. Though it was well reviewed by Little, Brown Publishing, J. Edgar Hoover had given express directions to the president of the company not to publish any books by Fast. One by one other publishing houses rejected the book: Viking, Scribner's, Harper, Knopf, Simon and Schuster. Finally, Doubleday, though afraid to publish the novel, agreed to sell copies through its bookstore chain if Fast published it himself. This led him into the adventure of self-publishing, which began the slow process of making *Spartacus* a success; he sold 48,000 self-published copies and untold numbers abroad, both legal and pirated. By the end of the 1950s, hundreds of thousands of paperback copies were sold. *Spartacus* won Fast the Screenwriters Award in 1960. From 1952 to 1957, still unable to find a publisher, he founded the Blue Heron Press (a word play on a friend's suggestion that he call it the Red Herring Press) and published *The Passion of Sacco and Vanzetti, Silas Timberman,* and a collection of short stories. During this controversial period in the 1950s, Fast founded the World Peace Movement and served as a member of the World Peace Council. While denied the freedom to publish under his own name by the blacklist, he began to write under the pseudonym of Walter Ericson, first with a detective thriller, *The Fallen Angel,* which was later made into a film, *Mirage,* starring Gregory Peck as the amnesiac hero.

Ever since Mill Point Prison, Fast had experienced cluster headaches, an excruciating condition then untreatable. While vacationing at White Lake resort, owned by the Fur and Leather Workers Union, a friend suggested that the headaches resulted from frustration about his inability to strike back and that Fast should take drastic action to relieve this stress: he should run for Congress. Thus began Fast's quixotic run for office in the Twenty-third Congressional District on the American Labor party ticket, an experience reflected long after in *The Immigrant's Daughter.* Fast amusingly calls his affliction *candidatitus:* the conviction that one can win office against impossible odds. An incident with another symbolic candidate, a rich man's son, illustrates what Fast thinks of as an almost unbridgeable gap between wealth and poverty, a chasm of understanding that divides so completely that the rich can never think or understand life as the poor do. His fellow candidate invited him over for dinner and allowed a full gallon of ice cream to melt away while they talked, oblivious as the nervous Fast agitated over the waste of food. The incident appears in several Fast novels as a touchstone of the difference between rich and poor. In the election, Fast polled only two thousand votes, to over forty thousand for the Democratic candidate, but he clearly enjoyed the experience of running for office.

Fast's cluster headaches worsened, and he took oxygen for partial relief, and learned mediation that would eventually take him to the study of Zen Buddhism. He was awarded the Stalin International Peace Prize in 1953 (later renamed the Soviet International Peace Prize; he and Paul Robeson were the only Americans over to receive it) and reports that the Russians frequently consulted him because of their ignorance of and bewilderment about the United States, *Pravda* reporters believing that, for example, in the American South any person disapproved of by the majority would be hanged. As with Fadeyev, Fast seems to take straight these assertions of Soviet ingenuousness, but the reader can be forgiven some skepticism: why would Russian reporters with access to superb KGB sources of information go to a New York novelist for advice? Fast had always viewed the American South negatively, and one must wonder about the motives of journalists' asking tendentious questions. For all his growing frustrations with party discipline, Fast seemed to give too much credence to the purity of Soviet intentions, which were no doubt less than absolutely pure.

The Fasts spent two months in Cuernavaca, Mexico, as a temporary refuge from the red-baiting and harassment by FBI phone tap and surveillance that were becoming more and more oppressive. He met the famous artist Diego Rivera, who told him that artists *must* offend, a sentiment Fast definitely agreed with. Significantly, though Fast loved the sensual and beautiful landscape of Mexico, the Mexican people, and the American communist exiles from Hollywood and the rest of the United States, he quickly grew bored, unable to write or even to live fully without the opposition that had been so long a part of his daily life. Cutting short their intended three-month stay, the Fasts planned to return to the United States, only to face the newly passed Communist Control Act, a piece of legislation he claims turned America into a police state. As Fast points out with considerable self-understanding, creative artists (and others) living abroad, separated from their country and culture, lose all perspective. They begin to think like refugees and therefore frequently exaggerate their oppression to justify their new lives as refugees. The Soviet ambassador to Mexico offered refugee status in Russia, which Fast turned down, remarking later to Albert Maltz, his old colleague from Mill Point Prison who had exiled himself to Mexico, that they had no roots in the country and they did not have their native language: "Our lives are our language" (*Being Red* 342).

The Communist Control Act was never used or even much noticed. Back in America, the Fasts lived in the suburbs, in Teaneck, New Jersey, and Howard joined the *Daily Worker* as a permanent staff member. By 1956 the stories of life under Stalin had become undeniable, and a conflicted Fast struggled to maintain his ideological faith. When Nikita Khrushchev's secret speech detailing his predecessor's horrors became public, as John Gates, executive editor of the *Daily Worker,* notes in *The Story of an American Communist* (1958), Howard Fast, "the only literary figure of note left in the Communist Party," was one of those most shaken. Gates points out that Fast had gone to jail for his beliefs and had stuck his neck out more than most others, defending everything communist and attacking everything capitalist "in the most extravagant terms." He adds, "It was to be expected that he would react to the Khrushchev revelations in a highly emotional manner, and I know of no one who went through a greater moral anguish and torture" (*Being Red* 351-352). Gates goes on to describe party leaders leaping on Fast like a "pack of wolves" when he formally quit the party, though no leader bothered to discuss the problem with Fast when it might have done some good. He also went from being one of the foremost American writers read and taught in the Soviet Union to being a nonentity, his literary reputation ruined almost overnight by his change in politics.

Although *Being Red* was published in 1990, it ends with this leave-taking from the Communist party in 1957, when Fast was forty-two. He clearly feels that a major phase of his life ended here, though in the next thirty-odd years he published scores of books, pushing his total number of publications to somewhere around one hundred, most of them substantial. (Even Fast is not completely sure of the total number of publications; title changes and his own pseudonyms have confused the issue. Given the huge number of his books that have been translated and published abroad, many without benefit of legal permission, the total number of sales may be as high as 80 million copies.) In the midst of this phenomenal production, Fast also became a writer of detective stories and novels about strong women, completed a highly successful series of popular novels (The Immigrants series), moved to California and back to the East Coast, to Connecticut, traveled the country and the world, studied Zen Buddhism, and, as always, wrote. He has kept these decades out of the newspaper headlines and lived privately, enjoying a life free from government and media harassment. He gives occasional interviews but has generally stayed out of public notice. Writing under the pseudonym of Walter Ericson and later as E. V. Cunningham, under which name he produced twenty books, Fast reinvented himself as a writer of detective fiction, creating the character of the Japanese-American detective Masao Masuto and enjoying the writing of this form of popular fiction immensely. As he says in *Contemporary Authors Autobiography Series,* he underwent what he calls an "explosion" of creativity repressed until after he left the Communist party; and his bibliography shows he does not exaggerate. He has published almost sixty novels and major works since his departure. The Fasts moved to Los Angeles in 1974, where they lived until 1980; although only one of his screenplays from this period was eve produced, residence in California paid off in The Immigrants series, especially in the unforgettable portrayals of Los Angeles, San Francisco, and, in particular, the fictional Napa Valley winery called Higate.

Despite his comparative reticence about this period, his writing reveals much about his interests. In the 1960s, Fast built a series of novels around extraordinary women, some criminal, some instigators of crime, and others co-investigators with a male detective. This was a new emphasis; apart from *Agrippa's Daughter* (1964) and a handful of characters in other early works, Fast had focused on male protagonists. The potential had always existed, for female characters in even the earliest novels were consistently well drawn. These later books, however, constitute a near full turn in perspective: they are tributes to the intelligence, courage, resourcefulness, and wit of women and a reprimand to the husbands, lovers, and friends who underestimate their capabilities and pluck. Shirley (*Shirley* 1964) is a tough, wise-cracking Bronx diamond-in-the-rough, who exasperates the tough cops she deals with, while Sylvia (*Sylvia* 1960), once an abused child and then a teenage prostitute, has, through sheer guts and determination, read voraciously, taught herself several languages, and fought her way into polite society. Penelope (*Penelope* 1965), an independently wealthy socialite, bored by male pretensions and her banker husband's arrogant complacency, plays Robin Hood to the local parish and associated charities, stealing from rich acquaintances whose sentiments and values offend; even when the police commissioner and district attorney confront irrefutable evidence of her activities, their preconceptions prevent their accepting the truth of her wit and professionalism. The unflappable Margie (*Margie* 1966) is an innocent mistaken for a thief and then for an oil-rich countess, her whole adventures comic and resolvable despite serious negative possibilities. Other heroines from this set of novels face more sinister dangers and threats. For instance, Phyllis's mother is brutally beaten to death (*Phyllis* 1962), Lydia's father is forced into suicide (*Lydia* 1964), and Alice's child is kidnapped and terrorized (*Alice* 1963). Helen (*Helen* 1966) faces sexual sadists, as does Samantha (*Samantha* 1967), a would-be star, who is raped by a half-dozen young men on a Hollywood set and seeks bloody revenge, while Sally (*Sally* 1967), thinking she is dying of an incurable disease, hires a professional gunman to end her pain quickly, only to learn the original diagnosis was incorrect and to have to battle an assassin she herself is paying. Some of Fast's usual villains show up in these works: German ex-Nazis, still loyal to Hitler's memory, hypocritical military and political leaders (a general and a senator heading a heroin smuggling operation), and international terrorists. However, the main thrust of these novels, whether comic or deadly serious, is a paean to women. Although their characters move around a great deal in familiar Fast settings, a number of these books have a California setting. Fast clearly became fascinated

by the state, the new goal for immigrants searching for the American dream, and much of his best work in the 1970s and after has a California setting or at least includes a few scenes in the West. The tension between the new lifestyles and personal philosophies on the coast, summed up by the competition between Los Angeles and San Francisco, was clearly a deeply felt personal issue, and its working out in fiction, sometimes as tragedy, sometimes as high comedy, constitutes much of the pleasure in the works of this period.

In The Immigrants series, Los Angeles comes off comparatively badly, a diffuse Johnny-come-lately town, offering opportunities and excitement of a kind but also being a place populated by con men and vulgarians. Fast's depiction of the movie industry is especially caustic: Martha Levy commits suicide as a result of exploitation by a sleazy producer; Sally Levy finds one honest man, her director and mentor, but no emotional satisfaction from movie industry life; the filmscript of Barbara Lavette's first novel is taken out of her hands though she has been hired as a screenwriter. Portraits in other books, such as the Masao Masuto series and *Max,* Fast's novel about the development of the movie industry, depict Los Angeles more positively, or at least neutrally. But the contrast remains: Los Angeles can be summed up by the powerful Devron family, opportunists who trace themselves back to frontiersman Kit Carson. San Francisco has the Lavettes, perhaps just as opportunistic, but driven by nobler motives than the struggle for filthy lucre. The Devrons watch their fiscal bottom line; the Lavettes know the value of a dollar but are also capable of the grand gesture, such as when Dan supports Bernie Cohen's quixotic trek to Israel or Jean gives a huge amount of money to Barbara in support of a cause Jean has no part in. Los Angeles is driven by profit, in other words, while San Francisco, for all its gold rush origins, has a romance and a nobility of style that Fast regards with approval.

Even the contrasting climates show Fast's preference for the Bay Area. For all the perfections of the southern California weather as described in *Second Generation, The Legacy,* and *The Immigrant's Daughter,* readers will almost certainly retain stronger impressions of San Francisco's bracing chills or of its fogs cut through with rays of bright sunshine. The tactile imagery—of color and light, smell and temperature, the texture of daily life—in The Immigrants series is the most pronounced and effective in Fast's extensive canon. Readers of these glowing portraits of San Francisco and the Napa Valley might assume that Fast lived in the Bay Area, for the descriptions seen through the eyes of Barbara and others suggest a longing for home, the nostalgic ache for the place that defines normality of climate, of sight, smell, and sound. In fact, the Fasts were simply visitors to the area, taking driving tours of Napa, with San Francisco as a temporary base for travel. Perhaps the six years Fast spent in Los Angeles account for his ambivalence about that city, and especially for his dislike of the hypocrisies of the movie industry. However, Fast insists that a writer's personal setting is irrelevant to his work; where he lived, he says, had little or no effect on his fiction. During the Los Angeles period Fast wrote screenplays for three films, only one of which was produced; he turned his novel *Citizen Tom Paine* into a theatrical play (produced in Williamstown, Massachusetts, and later at the Kennedy Center in Washington, D.C., in 1987, starring Richard Thomas), and he wrote a charming, intuitive play, *The Novelist,* which was based on the life of Jane Austen and was staged at Williamstown, at Theater West in Springfield, Massachusetts, in Mamaroneck, New York, and in New York City. *The Novelist* postulates a Ms. Bennett-Mr. Darcy style encounter between the British writer Jane Austen and a dashing, vigorous, but also highly intelligent navy captain, who has fallen in love with her through reading her books and who sees beneath the quick-witted and distancing repartee to find the strong but romantic woman behind the facade.

While much of Fast's work includes settings he has known intimately from residence in them, the Bay Area portraits, seemingly so personal and complex in their links of character and setting, give credence to his assertion: a good writer simply needs the appropriate mental imagery and an understanding of how people live in a place and what they feel about it in order to describe their lives credibly. Readers of The Immigrants series may be forgiven for identifying Fast and California, but his comparatively brief residence in Los Angeles and his brief excursions in the Bay Area are in fact typical of his other travels earlier in his career to the Middle East and India, travels that produced a whole series of books notable for their sense of place. Throughout his career, Fast has absorbed information through research and setting through travel, fusing both into convincing stages and backdrops for his characters.

The post-Communist party years were not simply characterized by a retreat from the newspaper headlines into private family and professional life for the Fasts. Although the California years were clearly enjoyable and stimulating at the time, Fast recently remarked that he has never missed the West Coast because the California he knew then is dead and gone; in fact, every time he has visited there since leaving, he has disliked it more, a result of overpopulation, pollution, and a rape of the natural beauty and purity that attracted people there in the first place. But one influence has remained with Fast, and it is related to his split with the party: the influence of Zen Buddhism.

After rejecting communism, Fast studied Zen formally for eight years. That philosophy, of course, is not necessarily related to a particular place, but the Masao Masuto books illustrate the connection of the discipline with California. Fast calls his study "very important" even now, living long after in the environs of New York City. Zen provides a context for the moral issues that have consumed Fast's attention all his life. Also, Zen stresses a form of unconventionality—the student of Zen is not allowed to give an expected or conventional answer to an assigned *koan*, or

puzzle—that is an obvious Fast characteristic. But Fast stresses that after living much of his adult life with the socialist framework providing direction and answers to the puzzling questions of existence, one does not simply give it over and move on easily. Zen provided an "ability to focus, to center . . . [his] life" that was invaluable then, in the difficult years after the party, and now. Fast clearly still believes in the humanist principles that underlie a good deal of socialist thought, but the loss of party discipline and structure must have involved a true crisis for a writer fond of clarity and order. Zen provided such a focus, and we may not be reading too much into the Masao Masuto books if we think of both their hero (a lean, six-foot-tall Nisei attached to the Beverly Hills Police Department) and their author as outsiders, somewhat alienated by perspective from the majority culture in which they must operate, but finding their center through Zen meditation.

Masuto, like Fast, finds in the Zen meditative philosophy the calm, the self-assurance, and the introspective insights necessary to carry out his work, and, again like Fast, he empathizes with the common worker, despite the wealthy environment in which he works. Like Fast, Masuto cultivates the yin and the yang, loves roses and the exquisite calm of the tea ceremony, and has fond memories of the peaceful and productive farm life of the San Fernando of bygone years, the romantic agrarianism that runs through so many of Fast's books. Like his creator, Masuto has an American maverick streak beneath his surface Zen serenity: his independent thinking and contempt for overbearing authority. Reflecting his creator, Masuto says, "I try not to respond to fools" (*The Case of the Russian Diplomat* 65). Masuto speaks Spanish as well as Japanese (Fast does not), and he sometimes faces cruel taunts about his nisei heritage, but just as Fast survived similar attacks because of his Jewish background, he has learned to cope with the crass lifestyles and acid tongues of southern Californians.

Fast says that he enjoyed writing the Masuto detective novels because the use of a pseudonym (E. V. Cunningham, a name suggested by his agent, Paul Reynolds) gave him a sense of freedom that allowed him to toy with ideas for pleasure and to write in a style and with a focus quite different from what he had done before; he describes the experience as "captivating" and his results "half-serious." He could have his hero share his pet peeves (for instance, California funeral homes in *The Case of the Murdered Mackenzie*), battle his favorite villains (the S.S. in *The Case of the One-Penny Orange,* former Nazis in *The Case of the Russian Diplomat,* and the CIA, which fixes evidence and phony charges and condones double murder, in *The Case of the Murdered Mackenzie*), and reflect values dear to him, including a deep distrust of any group that tries to repress the individual, force the human into mechanical categories, or deny genuine emotion.

The detective hero Masuto combines Buddhist meditation with Holmesian ratiocination to make intuitive leaps of both reason and imagination that leave his colleagues and superiors puzzling over the assumptions that further investigation, physical evidence, and testimony confirm. The close observation that allows the Buddhist in Masuto to see beauty where others see ugliness also allows him to see the mundane, the corrupt, and the repulsive behind the beautiful facade of Beverly Hills. These stories look at the wealthy California scene from the perspective of an outsider, racially, culturally, and economically. Masuto can bring Asian perceptions to unraveling the mysteries of his adopted community and counters the mainstream disintegration of family values with his own deep-seated commitment to home and family. His son and daughter are quiet, obedient, and respectful, and his Japanese-American wife, Kati, though at times truly Californian (she participates in consciousness-raising sessions), observes traditional Japanese customs and rituals (providing hot baths, fine cuisine, and soothing solace) to help him recuperate from the conflicts of his job.

Fast's mystery plots, which occupied his thoughts throughout the late 1970s and early 1980s, are amusing puzzles, but they have political undercurrents. In *The Case of the One-Penny Orange,* for example, Masuto penetrates the link between seemingly unconnected events (a local burglary, a murdered stamp dealer, and a missing S.S. commander) with an 1847 Mauritius one-penny stamp worth half a million dollars and a revenge ritual that originated in the bitterness of the Holocaust, while in *The Case of the Russian Diplomat,* fascistic Arab and East German terrorists assassinate a Russian diplomat and plan to sabotage an airplane full of Soviet agronomists, all to undermine the Jewish Defense League. In *The Case of the Sliding Pool,* powerful financial and industrial speculators play games with people's lives, impede Masuto's investigation, and break rules with impunity, while *The Case of the Poisoned Eclairs* explores the uglier costs of wealth in marriage and divorce. Fast's Masuto believes that crime encapsulates the general illnesses of humanity and is an affront to human dignity and conscience. A Buddhist involved with humanity but faced with the materialism, corruption, and inhumanity of the Beverly Hills rich, he must constantly battle external political pressure to limit or even end his investigation and the internal hatred that discovering evil makes him feel. His family is vital to providing the moral and emotional foundation necessary for Masuto to carry on in a society and culture that attacks his values.

Fast's later life has not all been Zen meditative calm. When asked about his key interests in the mid-1970s, Fast cited, "my home, my family, the theater, the film, and the proper study of ancient history. And the follies of human kind" (*Something about the Author* 82). It is the "follies of human kind" that have dominated his journalism and writing in general. For instance, Fast calls *The Dinner Party* a "direct result" of his being unable to get over his "problem of indignation" (Rothstein 16). He brooded over the question of sanctuary, particularly as related to helping illegal Central American aliens enter the country, and the moral questions involved in sending a wired informer into a

church to record conversations that could later be used to threaten priests, a minister, a nun, and others with five years of imprisonment. And he found himself posing questions about the responses of an honest man, particularly one who might have a certain amount of clout from a position of authority, like that of U.S. senator. *The Dinner Party* is an exploration of such questions of responsibility and duty, infused and driven by righteous indignation. Critics compared it to a well-made play. This is an appropriate comparison, for Fast's strengths as a writer often involve dramatic confrontations. His political essays written for the *New York Observer* include provocative attacks on drug dealers, political hacks, anti-Semites, racists, arms traffickers, women bashers, and presidents Reagan and Bush. In other words, he has used his political commentary to carry on the liberal politics that have consumed his interest all his adult life.

The Fasts moved back to the East Coast in 1980 and lived quietly, with Fast still producing on the average about one major work every year through the 1990s. He wrote a weekly column for the *New York Observer* from 1989 until his wife's illness in 1994 and collected a number of these essays in a book entitled *War and Peace.* The Fasts moved to Connecticut in the early 1990s. Bette Fast pursued sculpture and art until she died in 1994. Fast's tribute to Jane Austen in his play *The Novelist* is to a great degree also a tribute to the charm, intelligence, and talent of Bette Fast, with whom Fast fell in love at age twenty, with whom he had two children and three grandchildren, and to whom he was married for over fifty-six years.

Fast resides in Connecticut not far from his native New York, living the life of a writer, with *Seven Days in June* published in 1994. *Seven Days* represents five years of work, and though the novel was not marketed effectively, it marks a return to Fast's earliest successes, the Revolutionary War works. Fast says of his reasons for this reprise that "so much of our early history is pure invention, pure lies." The fire of the reformer still burns hot: Fast writes a column on politics for a local newspaper and takes vigorous daily walks, preferably in company that will stimulate lively conversation. Fast believes that books "open a thousand doors, they shape lives and answer questions, they widen horizons, they offer hope for the heart and food for the soul." Another novel, *The Bridge Builder's Story,* concerning the Holocaust, was published in 1995.

Modern criticism teaches that every biographer is also a creative artist, and Fast's memoir, *Being Red,* is a good example, for his autobiography sometimes reads like one of his own novels. His indisputably modest beginnings were the start of a very American life, with a child of recent immigrants fitting the mythic American model of pulling oneself up by one's bootstraps; he is a kind of bad boy Horatio Alger hero, an unsentimentalized rags-to-riches character and a member of the loyal (in the eyes of the House Un-American Activities Committee, *disloyal*) opposition. In this sense Fast was a generation or two ahead of his time, for his jaundiced but pro-American point of view would not become common until the last decades of the twentieth century. As with his pro-and anti-Americanism, contradictions abound: while he values working-class heroes, his own life has been lived as a creative writer and as an intellectual commentator, under varying but apparently comfortable material circumstances. The best model for Fast is the newsman in *Power,* a sympathetic observer of the labor movement rather than a constantly involved participant.

But his story is American in other ways, a conflict between the big city urbanism of his youth and the California mellowness of his later years, between the lure of success and wealth and the call of conscience, between writing what the public wants and saying what one feels must be said. Fast says of himself, "No matter what direction my writing took, I could never give up a social outlook and a position against hypocrisy and oppression. This has been a theme that runs through all of my writing" (*Contemporary Authors Autobiography Series* 184).

FURTHER READING

Criticism

MacDonald, Andrew. *Howard Fast: A Critical Companion.* Westport, CT: Greenwood Press, 1996.

  The only book-length study of Fast's life and literary works, including extended analysis of his major novels and a bibliography of his writings.

Additional coverage of Fast's life and career is contained in the following sources published by the Gale Group: *Authors and Artists for Young Adults,* **Vol. 16;** *Contemporary Authors,* **Vols. 1-4R;** *Contemporary Authors Autobiography Series,* **Vol. 18;** *Contemporary Authors New Revision Series,* **Vols. 1, 33, 54;** *Dictionary of Literary Biography,* **Vol. 9;** *DISCovering Authors Modules: Novelists;* **and** *Something About the Author,* **Vol. 7.**

Francis Fukuyama
1952-

American nonfiction writer.

The following entry presents an overview of Fukuyama's career through 1999.

INTRODUCTION

Social scientist Francis Fukuyama touched off a maelstrom of controversy with his provocative essay, "The End of History?," published in the small-circulation journal *The Public Interest* in the summer of 1989. In this sixteen-page treatise that captured international attention, he proposed that the collapse of Communism in the Soviet Union and Eastern Europe signaled the end of historical progress and the de facto victory of liberal democracy over all other forms of political ideology. Fukuyama's essay, revised and expanded in *The End of History and the Last Man* (1992), attracted an outpouring of critical commentary and debate in both academic and mainstream media circles. In subsequent works, *Trust* (1995) and *The Great Disruption* (1999), he similarly attempted to elucidate and anticipate the grand forces at work behind the major social, political, and economic developments in the contemporary world.

BIOGRAPHICAL INFORMATION

Fukuyama was born in Chicago, Illinois, and raised in New York City by his Japanese parents. His father, Yoshio, was a Congregationalist minister and professor of religion. Fukuyama attended Cornell University, where he majored in classics and studied philosophy under professor Allan Bloom, author of the 1987 bestseller *The Closing of the American Mind*. Graduating with a B.A. from Cornell in 1974, Fukuyama began graduate work in comparative literature under Paul de Man at Yale University, then spent six months in Paris where he visited the classrooms of preeminent literary theorists Roland Barthes and Jacques Derrida. Dissatisfied with postmodern criticism, Fukuyama returned to the United States and shifted his interest to government and foreign policy. He enrolled at Harvard University and studied Soviet and Middle Eastern politics, earning a Ph.D. in political science in 1981. Fukuyama worked for the Rand Corporation in Santa Monica, California, until 1989, with a brief period in Washington, D.C., as a member of the policy planning staff under the Reagan Administration. In 1989 Fukuyama was named deputy director of the U.S. Department of State Policy Planning Staff, a position he held until 1990. After the 1989 publication of "The End of History?," Fukuyama

turned to full-time research, writing, and lecturing. He subsequently took a position as the Omer L. and Nancy Hirst Professor of Public Policy at George Mason University. His *The End of History and the Last Man* won the Premio Capri International Award and the *Los Angeles Times* Book Critics Award in 1992. Fukuyama has authored many papers for the Rand Corporation and published numerous articles in both professional and popular periodicals. He married Laura Holmgren in 1986, with whom he shares several children.

MAJOR WORKS

Fukuyama's reputation centers primarily upon the ideas presented in "The End of History?" In this essay, he attempts to establish a conceptual framework in which to view the end of the Cold War and dramatic liberal reforms in the Soviet Union, Eastern Europe, and China during the late-1980s. Drawing upon the historiographic perspective of nineteenth-century German philosopher Georg W. F. Hegel, Fukuyama suggests that "history," viewed as a struggle between competing ideologies, has reached its terminus in liberal democracy. Hegel, as Fukuyama recalls, proclaimed that history had come to an end in 1806 with Napoleon's victory over the Prussian monarchy at the Battle of Jena, signaling the ascendancy of democratic ideals borne of the Enlightenment and French Revolution. Along these lines, Fukuyama asserts that the chief rivals to liberal democracy—Fascism and Communism—have run their course and ended in disrepute; Fascism was vanquished with the defeat of Germany, Italy, and Japan during World War II, and Communism has been disaffirmed by recent political and economic concessions in the Soviet Union and China, and the reunification of Germany. Thus, as Fukuyama asserts, in the world of ideas, Western liberal democracy has emerged as the unchallenged victor over all other competing ideologies, with only religious fundamentalism and nationalism remaining as potent, though inferior, adversaries. Despite this apparent "triumph of the West," Fukuyama notes that international conflict will by no means cease, but that future wars, uprisings, and regional disputes will pit "historical" factions (those who still cling to outmoded, discredited ideologies) against the "post-historical" embodiments of liberal democracy. From this perspective, Fukuyama contends that it is not necessarily important that all societies develop into healthy, prosperous liberal democracies, but that none seriously upholds the pretense that it can offer a superior, viable alternative to liberal democracy. Far from extolling this prospect, Fukuyama laments the passing of "history," which he concludes will usher in "a very sad time." In this post-historical era, Fukuyama notes, the excitement of revolutionary fervor and ideological possibility will give way to the sterile solving of economic, technological, and environmental problems, and the perpetual boredom of consumerism. Fukuyama does, however, hold out the hope that such interminable boredom will eventually give rise to the rebirth of "History." In *The End of History and the Last Man,* Fukuyama defends and further elaborates his original thesis, again drawing upon the insights of Hegel as well as twentieth-century Hegel scholar Alexandre Kojève. Fukuyama identifies two principal "mechanisms" of historical change—man's effort to master nature through scientific progress and *thymos,* a Greek term adopted from Plato that refers to the individual's desire for recognition. Noting the universal Judeo-Christian moral code that undergirds democratic egalitarianism, Fukuyama attacks contemporary moral relativism and multiculturalism. The "last man," a concept borrowed from nineteenth-century German philosopher Friedrich Nietzsche, refers to the spiritless inheritors of modern liberal democracy who, in a world devoid of ideological causes, languish in self-satisfaction and mediocrity.

In *Trust,* Fukuyama examines the relationship between culture, social behavior, and economics, particularly the importance of trust as essential "social capital" that determines the level of economic activity between individuals and groups. According to Fukuyama, high levels of social trust permit the organization of large, multilevel corporations and economies of scale, as evident in prosperous countries such as the United States, Germany, and Japan. However, in nations such as China, Italy, and France, where trust is either insular, provincial, or weakly linked to the state, the ability to expand beyond small, family-owned businesses into the global marketplace is hampered. Fukuyama also asserts that increasing mistrust breeds corresponding increases in crime, litigation, and corruption. In the United States, Fukuyama observes, declining rates of participation in voluntary associations indicate a weakening of social commitment in general, and thus an erosion of valuable social capital that is difficult to replenish and without which society suffers detrimental effects. Fukuyama takes up this subject in *The Great Disruption,* in which he trains his focus on the deterioration of morality and civic values in America and other developed countries between the 1960s and 1990s. His analysis, supplemented with much statistical data and graphs, suggests that the troubling vices—such as divorce, illegitimacy, sexual promiscuity, violent crime, and drug abuse—that have eroded social capital are indicative of a rise of selfish individualism and a lack of regard for traditional authority. Such rampant amorality, Fukuyama notes, is historically cyclical and typical of periods of great economic change—in the present case, the move from a post-industrial to an information society. Fukuyama suggests that the women's liberation movement, though ultimately a positive force of social transformation, was also a major source of the "disruption." Drawing upon research in anthropology, evolutionary biology, game theory, psychology, and moral philosophy, Fukuyama contends that humans by nature tend to self-organize and self-regulate in beneficial ways, leading to his optimistic conclusion that a new era of spontaneous, popular reform is on the horizon, a period during which people will likely demand higher standards of morality and responsibility among themselves, others, and institutions.

CRITICAL RECEPTION

Fukuyama's "End of History" thesis attracted heated controversy among a wide range of historians, journalists, and social observers, prompting a flurry of published responses, rejoinders, and editorial commentaries that continued to appear in periodicals and newspapers even several years after the essay's first appearance and the publication of its book-length elaboration. While most critics either refuted or dismissed Fukuyama's contention that human consciousness had evolved to its highest form in liberal democracy and that historical progress had ceased, many found his ideas compelling and erudite, particularly among those on the political right. The fact that this obscure article—written by a then-little-known foreign policy analyst and heavily-laden with complex Hegelian philosophy—captured so much attention was itself a source of wonder among critics. Many reviewers note that Fukuyama's essay and book *The End of History and the Last Man* reflect the heady mood and uncertainty immediately following the collapse of Communism and the end of the Cold War. Fukuyama's critics, on both the left and right side of the political spectrum, leveled strong objections to his lack of concern for persistent warfare, political oppression, genocide, and fundamentalist insurgence throughout the world—all evidence, according to such critics, that history is alive and well. On the reputation of his "End of History" publications, *Trust* and *The Great Disruption* received much critical interest, though far less controversy. Many reviewers praised Fukuyama's impressive grasp of world history and sociology in these works, and welcomed his ambitious effort to distill the grand significance of contemporary social and economic trends. However, others found his comprehensive approach unconvincing and overly deterministic, undermined in many cases by the overwhelming scope of his subject and Fukuyama's tendency to refute his own assertions with contradictory qualifications and omissions. Yet, despite the limitations of Fukuyama's wide-angle worldview and criticism stemming from his neoconservative political perspective, he is respected as an subtle intellectual and engaging social commentator.

PRINCIPAL WORKS

The Soviet Union and the Third World: The Last Three Decades [editor; with Andrzej Korbonski] (nonfiction) 1987
*"*The End of History?*" (essay) 1989
The End of History and the Last Man (nonfiction) 1992
Trust: The Social Virtues and the Creation of Prosperity (nonfiction) 1995
The Great Disruption: Human Nature and the Reconstitution of Social Order (nonfiction) 1999

*First published in *The National Interest*, Summer, 1989, pp. 3-18.

CRITICISM

James Atlas (essay date 22 October 1989)

SOURCE: "What Is Fukuyama Saying?," in *New York Times Magazine,* October 22, 1989, pp. 38-40, 42, 54-5.

[*In the following essay, Atlas provides an overview of Fukuyama's professional background, historical perspective, and critical controversy surrounding "The End of History?"*]

The year 2000 fast approaches, and millennial doom is in the air. Global warming, nuclear proliferation, chaos in Eastern Europe. Even the notion of *post* is over. Postmodernism, post-history, post-culture (to borrow the critic George Steiner's term)—we're beyond that now. "The sun is about to set on the post-industrial era," declares the economist Lester C. Thurow in *The New York Times.*

What follows *post?* Samuel P. Huntington, Eaton Professor of the Science of Government at Harvard, has a name for the latest eschatological craze: "endism." The critic Arthur C. Danto theorizes on "the end of art." Bill McKibben, a former staff writer for *The New Yorker*, issues a dire report on "The End of Nature." Clearly, it's late in the day.

On the face of it, the lead article in the summer issue of *The National Interest*, a neoconservative journal published in Washington, seemed like more bad news. "The End of History?" it asked. The author, Francis Fukuyama, a State Department official, was unknown to the public, but his article was accompanied by "responses" from Irving Kristol, Allan Bloom, Senator Daniel Patrick Moynihan and others notable for their gloomy prognostications.

The magazine's readers were in for a surprise. What was Fukuyama saying? That the end of history is *good* news. What is happening in the world, claimed his eloquent essay, is nothing less than "the triumph of the West." How else to explain the free elections in Poland and Hungary? The reform movement in China? The East German exodus?

In Fukuyama's interpretation, borrowed (and heavily adapted) from the German philosopher G. W. F. Hegel, history is a protracted struggle to realize the idea of freedom latent in human consciousness. In the 20th century, the forces of totalitarianism have been decisively conquered by the United States and its allies, which represent the final embodiment of this idea—"that is, the end point of mankind's ideological evolution and the universalization of Western liberal democracy." In other words, we win.

Within weeks, **"The End of History?"** had become the hottest topic around, this year's answer to Paul Kennedy's phenomenal best seller, *The Rise and Fall of the Great Powers.* George F. Will was among the first to weigh in, with a *Newsweek* column in August; two weeks later, Fukuyama's photograph appeared in *Time.* The French quarterly *Commentaire* announced that it was devoting a special issue to **"The End of History?"** The BBC sent a television crew. Translations of the piece were scheduled to appear in Dutch, Japanese, Italian and Icelandic. Ten Downing Street requested a copy. In Washington, a newsdealer on Connecticut Avenue reported, the summer issue of *The National Interest* was "outselling everything, even the pornography."

"Controversial" didn't begin to cover the case. Unlike that other recent philosophical *cause célèbre,* Allan Bloom's "The Closing of the American Mind," Fukuyama's essay was the work of a representative from what is often referred to in academic circles as the real world. This was no professor, according to the contributor's note that ran in the magazine, but the "deputy director of the State Department's policy planning staff."

It wasn't just the message, then; it was the source. Maybe there was an agenda here. . . . By mid-September, Peter

Tarnoff, president of the Council on Foreign Relations, could speculate on the Op-Ed page of *The New York Times* that. **"The End of History?"** was "laying the foundation for a Bush doctrine." Not bad for a 16-page article in a foreign-policy journal with a circulation of 6,000.

You have to pass through a metal detector to get to Francis Fukuyama's office in the State Department, and the silver plaques beside the doors—INTERNATIONAL NARCOTICS MATTERS, NUCLEAR RISK REDUCTION CENTER—confirm that this isn't a philosophy department. But the elegant private dining room on the 8th floor, overlooking the Potomac, could easily be mistaken for an Ivy League faculty club. Plush carpets, chandeliers, a sideboard out of Sturbridge Village, oil portraits of 19th-century dignitaries on the walls—an environment conducive to shoptalk about Hegel.

It's mid-September, and the arrival of Soviet Foreign Minister Eduard Shevardnadze for meetings with Fukuyama's boss, James A. Baker 3d, is less than a week away. "It's a busy time," says Fukuyama, apologetically. Apart from assisting in the preparation of "talking points" for the Secretary of State, he's been besieged with telephone calls from book editors and agents eager to cash in on his famous article.

How does he account for the commotion? "I don't understand it myself," Fukuyama says quietly, sipping a Coke. "I didn't write the article with any relevance to policy. It was just something I'd been thinking about."

He does seem an unlikely celebrity. (But so was Paul Kennedy. So was Allan Bloom.) His khaki suit has an off-the-rack look about it, and he speaks in a tentative, measured voice, more intent on making himself clear than on making an impression. A youthful 36, he emanates a professorial air—an assistant professorial air.

Fukuyama doesn't quite fit the neo-conservative stereotype. Whatever ideological direction he has gone in lately, he's still a child of the 60s. He belongs to the Sierra Club; he's nostalgic for California, where he worked for the Rand Corporation; he worries about pesticides in the backyard of the small red-brick bungalow in the Virginia suburbs where he lives with his wife and infant daughter.

"The last thing I want to be interpreted as saying is that our society is a utopia, or that there are no more problems," he stresses. "I simply don't see any competitors to modern democracy." In short, he's a liberal neo-conservative.

Fukuyama grew up in Manhattan's Stuyvesant Town, a middle-class housing development on the Lower East Side. His father was a Congregational minister who later became a professor of religion, and Fukuyama's own direction in the beginning was toward an academic career. As a freshman at Cornell in 1970, he was a resident of Telluride House, a sort of commune for philosophy students; Allan Bloom was the resident Socrates. They shared meals and talked philosophy until all hours, living the good life Bloom would later evoke in "The Closing of the American Mind," the professor and his disciples sitting around the cafeteria discussing the Great Books.

Fukuyama majored in classics, then did graduate work in comparative literature at Yale, where he studied with the deconstructionist Paul de Man (who would achieve posthumous notoriety when it was discovered that he'd published pro-Nazi articles in the Belgian press at the height of World War II). "It was kind of an intellectual side journey," Fukuyama says.

After Yale, he spent six months in Paris, sitting in on classes with Roland Barthes and Jacques Derrida, whose abstruse and fashionable *discours* would become required reading for a generation of American graduate students. Fukuyama was less than impressed. "I was turned off by their nihilistic idea of what literature was all about," he recalls. "It had nothing to do with the world. I developed such an aversion to that whole over-intellectual approach that I turned to nuclear weapons instead." He enrolled in Harvard's government department, where he studied Middle Eastern and Soviet politics. Three years later he got a Ph.D. in political science, writing his thesis on Soviet foreign policy in the Middle East.

Fukuyama's first job out of the academic world was at the Rand Corporation in Santa Monica. Then, in 1981, Paul D. Wolfowitz, director of policy planning in the Reagan Administration (and also a former student of Bloom's), invited him to join his staff. Fukuyama worked in Washington for two years, then returned to Rand.

For the next six years, he wrote papers for Rand on Soviet foreign policy, speculating on such weighty matters as "Pakistan Since the Soviet Invasion of Afghanistan" and "Soviet Civil-Military Relations and the Power Projection Mission." In "Gorbachev and the Third World" (published in the spring 1986 issue of *Foreign Affairs*), Fukuyama claimed that Soviet foreign policy was still expansionist, and that despite efforts to economize at home and act conciliatory abroad, Gorbachev was quietly "trying to stake out a more combative position" in client nations like Angola and Afghanistan, Libya and Nicaragua. The message of these heavily footnoted articles was clear. The cold war is still on.

Last February, shortly before he returned to Washington to become deputy to Dennis Ross, the new director of policy planning. Fukuyama gave a lecture at the University of Chicago in which he surveyed the international political scene. It was sponsored by his former professor, Allan Bloom. "My whole life has been spent in organizations that prize technical expertise," says Fukuyama. "I was anxious to deal with larger and more important issues"— what Bloom calls "the big questions."

As it happened, Owen Harries, co-editor of *The National Interest*, was looking around for a think piece on the current situation—a piece, as Harries explains it, that would "link history with the great traditions of political thought." Harries got hold of Fukuyama's lecture and instantly recognized that it was "a provocative, stimulating essay, just what the times needed."

Harries, a donnish, pipe-smoking Welshman whose desk is piled high with books—he was educated at Oxford and was for many years a professor of politics—belongs to a type that exists only in Washington. Leon Wieseltier, literary editor of *The New Republic*, calls them "policy intellectuals." In New York, people talk about the latest issue of *Vanity Fair*; in Washington, they talk about the latest issue of *Foreign Policy*.

Some of these policy intellectuals are in government; Carnes Lord, the author of a highly regarded translation of Aristotle's *Politics*, is national security adviser to Vice President Quayle. Others are "fellows" or "scholars" at the Heritage Foundation or the Brookings Institution. Often, they have grand titles: Michael Novak, for instance, is the George Frederick Jewett Scholar in Religion and Public Policy at the American Enterprise Institute. Many are fugitives from academic life. "A lot of people around the office came up to me after the article appeared," Fukuyama says. "Hegelians who hadn't gotten tenure."

The political orientation is well to the right. "We hold to a traditional view of foreign policy," says Owen Harries. And what does he mean by "traditional"? "The belief that power politics is still in business. A belief in the efficacy of force."

The National Interest is clearly a well-heeled outfit. It's funded by the Lynde and Harry Bradley Foundation, a prominent neo-conservative organization; the John M. Olin Foundation, established by a wealthy manufacturer who made his fortune largely in munitions, and the Smith Richardson Foundation—which, says Harries, "supports a number of good causes around the place."

The magazine's quarters, in a modern office building on 16th Street in Washington, are a far cry from the grubby cubicles one associates with political journals on the left (if there still are any). The floors are carpeted and the phones ring with a muted chirp. The elevator has piped-in Mozart instead of Muzak. Directly across the street, behind a wrought-iron fence, is the Russian Embassy.

The National Interest, now four years old, is the creation of Irving Kristol—listed on the masthead as its publisher. His desk at the magazine is sort of in the lobby area; but then, he occupies many desks. Apart from his two magazines (he's also publisher of *The Public Interest*), Kristol is a distinguished fellow at the American Enterprise Institute. Last year, he gave up his professorship at New York University and moved to Washington.

New York was no longer the nation's intellectual center, he wrote in *The New Republic* a few months later, explaining his decision. The intellectuals had disappeared from the universities. The culture of Washington was just as "nasty and brutish," in Kristol's Hobbesian view, as anywhere else. "But there is one area in which Washington *is* an intellectual center, and that is public policy: economic policy, social policy, foreign policy, today even educational policy."

Living in Washington doesn't make Kristol any less a New Yorker. The cigarette, the rumpled seersucker jacket, the shrewdly self-deprecating wit are more congenial to a seminar room at the City University of New York's graduate center on 42nd Street than to a Washington think tank. Why did **"The End of History?"** make news? "I'd like to think it's because my coming to Washington from New York has raised the level of discussion," Kristol says with a laugh. And Fukuyama's thesis? "I don't believe a word of it."

Neither did a lot of other prominent opinion-makers around town. "At last, self-congratulation raised to the status of philosophy!" sneered Christopher Hitchens, a Washington-based Englishman who writes a column for the *Nation*. "The Bush years have found their Burke, or their Pangloss." For Strobe Talbott, editor at large for *Time* magazine, **"The End of History?"** was "The Beginning of Nonsense."

It if wasn't nonsense, Fukuyama's basic thesis wasn't exactly news, either. For months, conservatives had been gloating over the demise of Communism. "The perennial question that has preoccupied every political philosopher since Plato—what is the best form of governance?—has been answered," wrote Charles Krauthammer in *The Washington Post* last March, before anyone had ever heard of Francis Fukuyama. "After a few millennia of trying every form of political system, we close this millennium with the sure knowledge that in liberal, pluralist, capitalist democracy we have found what we have been looking for." Essentially, that was Fukuyama's message, but it didn't draw swarms of reporters to Krauthammer's door.

So how did **"The End of History?"** become such a big event? It was the Hegel that did it. Not only is American winning, Fukuyama claimed, but the flourishing of democracy around the world is the fulfillment of a grand historical scheme. The end of the cold war and the disarray of the Soviet Union reflected a larger process—the realization of the Idea. History, Hegel believed (or Fukuyama says he believed), "culminated in an absolute moment—a moment in which a final, rational form of society and state became victorious." And that moment, it just so happens, is now.

A weird thesis, utterly speculative and impossible to prove. But **"The End of History?"** was a stylish performance, erudite and written with a rhetorical flair rare in the somber prose of Washington policy journals; it possessed intellectual authority.

Fukuyama's respondents greeted the piece with open arms. "I am delighted to welcome G. W. F. Hegel to Washington," declared Kristol. Senator Moynihan, himself a Harvard government professor before he discovered politics, confessed that his grasp of Hegel was shaky; but he dusted off his European history, tossing in a few references to Marx and Rousseau. "It is not often that one has the opportunity to argue about Hegel in *The National Interest* (or anywhere else, for that matter)," noted the historian Gertrude Himmelfarb, who is the wife of Irving Kristol. Soon after the article appeared, there was a conference held to discuss it at something called the United States Institute of Peace. Kristol, Himmelfarb and Krauthammer were in attendance, along with the Sovietologist Richard Pipes. The rest is . . . history?

It's not hard to see why Fukuyama's essay won favor among this community. It's not only the high-flown references to Kant and Hegel, not only the message that Western democracy beat out he competition. **"The End of History?"** has a polemical edge familiar to readers of "The Closing of the American Mind."

Like Bloom, Fukuyama doesn't have much patience for non-Western cultures. ("For our purposes," he writes, "it matters very little what strange thoughts occur to people in Albania or Burkina Faso.") And like Bloom, Fukuyama's no booster. The West isn't so hot either. At the heart of his critique is a veiled contempt for the very culture whose triumphs in the politic sphere it purports to celebrate.

What distinguishes Fukuyama from the crowd of conservative pundits elated by Gorbachev's troubles is his curled-lip attitudes toward the victorious party. Say the West *has* won, that fascism and Communism are dead, that no significant ideological challenges are on the horizon then what? There's an "emptiness at the core of liberalism," Fukuyama maintains. What does American have to offer? "Liberal democracy in the political sphere combined with easy access to VCRs and stereos in the economic." The society Hegel envisioned at the end of history, a universal state in which the arts flourish and virtue reigns, is nowhere to be found. Instead we're stuck with a "consumerist culture" purveying rock music and boutiques around the world.

So the end of history may not be such a good thing after all. In fact, Fukuyama concludes, it will be "a very sad time." Why? Because the meaning of life lies in the causes that we fight for, and in the future there won't be any. "The struggle for recognition, the willingness to risk one's life for a purely abstract goal, the worldwide ideological struggle that called forth daring, courage, imagination and idealism, will be replaced by economic calculation, the endless solving of technical problems, environmental concerns and the satisfaction of sophisticated consumer demands." Put plainly, we're heading for a time of "boredom."

As a Washington cab driver said when I tried to explain why I was in town, "*Give me a break!*" Does Fukuyama really believe all this? "I guess I prefer not to answer that," he said one afternoon, talking in his State Department office—"Leave it ambiguous. All I can say is, if people can't take a joke. . . ."

That he meant to be provocative is obvious; but it's clear from his rational, erudite prose that he wasn't fooling around. As a political theorist, Fukuyama is more in the tradition of Bentham or Locke than of pop futurist Alvin Toffler. "All I meant by that last paragraph," he says "was that there's a tension in liberalism that won't go away. There are all kinds of reasons for being a liberal: the security and the material wealth it provides, the opportunity for spiritual and intellectual development. But it fails to address some fundamental questions. You know, what are the higher ends of man? Should we just be content with having secured the conditions for a good life, or should we be thinking about what the content of that good life is?"

If liberalism still has a few kinks to work out, Communism is finished, although "there may be some isolated true believers left in places like Managua, Pyongyang or Cambridge, Massachusetts," writes Fukuyama with characteristic acerbity.

In Cambridge, the contempt is mutual. Even in that citadel of 1960s subversion, there aren't too many Communists left, but there is an inordinately dense concentration of people around Harvard Square who know their Hegel, and the summer issue of The National Interest sold out there virtually overnight. By and large, the Cambridge intelligentsia is dubious about **"The End of History?"** The distinguished Harvard government professor Judith N. Shklar didn't even have to read Fukuyama's piece in order to dismiss it as "publicity." Her colleague Daniel Bell, who did, pronounced it "Hegel at third remove . . . and wrong." (Bell's classic book, *The End of Ideology*, anticipated Fukuyama 30 years ago.)

The historian Simon Schama, author of *Citizens: A Chronicle of the French Revolution*, is more tolerant. Himself an idiosyncratic practitioner of the genre, he found the piece "spirited and lively," but wonders how Fukuyama could have failed to address the revival of religious fundamentalism or the conflicts that could arise out of nationalism. "It's more of a theological document, don't you think, a work of prophecy," he says. "I mean, nobody really believes in the end of history."

It's not too hard to think of scenarios that would spoil Fukuyama's end of history. Who's to say what would happen in the Soviet Union if glasnost and perestroika collapse? What new dangers might a reunified Germany pose? Or a newly industrialized China? And what about the nuclear threat? That would put an end to things, the political scientist Pierre Hassner observed, "in a more radical sense than he envisages."

Gertrude Himmelfarb's response in *The National Interest* was perhaps the most damaging refutation of all. To begin with, Hegel never said that history would end in a literal sense; it's a continuous process in which "the synthesis of the preceding stage is the thesis of the present, thus setting in motion an endless dialectical cycle—and thus preserving the drama of history." And what about black poverty, the poverty of the underclass? asked Himmelfarb. In southeast Washington, where young blacks are dying nightly in the front lines of the drug war, history doesn't seem over, it seems to be just beginning. As Irving Kristol tartly put it, "We may have won the cold war, which is nice—it's more than nice, it's wonderful. But this means that now the enemy is us, not them."

Liberals complained that Fukuyama ignored the third world. Conservatives weren't too enthusiastic about his dour assessment of the winning team. Where is it written that government should provide for the spiritual needs of its citizens? Michael Novak wondered in *Commentary*. Democracy promises freedom from tyranny, it doesn't promise to make us happy. "The construction of a social order that achieves these is *not* designed to fill the soul, or to teach a philosophy, or to give instruction in how to live," Novak wrote. Democracy isn't a required course; it's an elective.

A number of commentators have compared **"The End of History?"** to the famous article published by George F. Kennan in *Foreign Affairs* in July 1947 and signed with an anonymous "X." Kennan's essay warned of Moscow's expansionist tendencies and called for a policy of "firm and vigilant containment," thus supplying the term that would come to characterize America's foreign policy in the postwar era.

In an article in *Policy Review* last summer, "Waiting for Mr. X," Burton Yale Pines, the magazine's associate publisher, called for an update. The cold war was over, Pines agreed; only what was the United States doing about it? How to deal with the turmoil Gorbachev's reforms have provoked? What should be our policy toward Eastern Europe? "Needed, in essence, is another 'X' article," wrote Pines—an article that would encourage the United States to seize the initiative. Given this hunger for a sequel, it's not surprising that Fukuyama is being touted as our "X."

But is he? It's tempting to dismiss the whole thing as a media phenomenon. "Each year needs a new sensation," says Daniel Bell. "It encapsulates a mood that people feel and gives it a vocabulary."

The practical consequences have been more difficult to measure. In the wake of Shevardnadze's visit, interpreters of foreign policy were busy scrutinizing speeches for evidence of endism. Did Fukuyama's article reflect President Bush's thinking? Was it a high-level policy paper in disguise? Senator Moynihan, for one, is skeptical. "The minute you announce that the cold war has ended and history is over," he notes, "a lot of people are going to say, 'Hey, wait a minute, we're out of a job.'" If only for bureaucratic purposes, then, history is still a going concern.

As for the article's actual influence, "there's no connection between this piece and what the Government does," Kristol says flatly. "No one in the Administration has read it."

Everyone else has. Whether or not we've reached the end of history, we haven't reached the end of **"The End of History?"** The fall issue of The National Interest featured more "responses," and you still can't pick up a magazine or a newspaper without stumbling across some reference to Fukuyama. "I don't see much of a future for liberal democracy here in Peru's Shining Path country, but people would be pretty excited about VCRs if they only had electricity," the journalist Tina Rosenberg reported with laconic irony in *The New Republic*, writing from Baja Collana, Peru. "But that's just one of those technological problems Francis Fukuyama says we'll have to spend our time grappling with now that there are no more ideological conflicts to keep us busy."

In a way, though, the question mark in Fukuyama's title has pre-empted criticism. History, after all, is only a way of making sense of things. Human beings depend on narrative to create an illusion of order, the literary critic Frank Kermode has argued in his profound book, *The Sense of an Ending*. "To make sense of their span they need fictive concords with origins and ends, such as give meaning to lives and to poems."

"The End of History?" is a poem. (No wonder no one in the Administration has read it.)

Even if we *have* come to the end of history, that may not be the end of it. As the historian Jerry Z. Muller observed, writing in *Commentary* last December, "After late capitalism comes more capitalism." And after the end of history comes more history.

Richard Bernstein (essay date 10 December 1989)

SOURCE: "The End of History, Explained for the Second Time," in *The New York Times*, December 10, 1989, p. E6.

[*In the following essay, Bernstein discusses Fukuyama's defense and elaboration of "The End of History?" in* The National Interest.]

The debate about the "end of history" has not come to an end. Francis Fukuyama, the State Department official who declared the end of the ideological struggle between East and West in an article last summer in *The National Interest*, has responded to his critics, and taken the argument a step further.

Not only has history ended, Mr. Fukuyama argues in a crisply written eight-page essay to appear in the journal tomorrow, but human nature itself has changed. History has ended because our "democratic-egalitarian consciousness," the highest form of political thought, has become "a permanent acquisition, as much a part of our fundamental 'natures' as our need for sleep or our fear of death."

Mr. Fukuyama's argument is in most respects an extension, and a defense, of the one he made several months ago when he resurrected certain notions of the German philosopher Hegel, particularly his view that history is not much the record of events as it is the progress of ideas. History has ended, Mr. Fukuyama said, because there is not going to be any further evolution in human ideology. The dissolution of the cold war in particular reveals that the liberal-democratic idea has permanently triumphed over its Communist rival, he said. And while, to be sure, there will be events, even dramatic ones, disturbing ones, violent and exciting ones, such as the exploration of space, the essential elements of human consciousness will no longer evolve.

"The end of history then means not the end of worldly events but the end of the evolution of human thought," Mr. Fukuyama writes in his defense. He notes ruefully that his original article served the rare function of creating consensus across the political spectrum. Virtually none of the many writers and commentators who reacted to his thesis agreed with it, whether they were writing in *The Wall Street Journal* or *The Nation*.

The major objection of these writers is that the Fukuyama hypothesis is divorced from the real world, which remains fraught with anti-democratic ideas, tension, violence and the threat of renewed war, all of which belie the notion that a happy post-historical era is dawning. Their point is that Mr. Fukuyama, arguing within his closed Hegelian system, may be right that history has ended, but only in a very abstract way, since the possibility of turmoil and war remains strong.

In the fall issue of *The National Interest*, the Harvard political scientist Samuel P. Huntington argued that the passing of the cold war does not mean the end of superpower conflict. The Soviet Union, he agreed, could well revert to being "just another great power," devoid of Marxism-Leninism. But even when Russia was "just another great power," he said, it created plenty of history, deploying its troops in Europe and suppressing uprisings in neighboring states. In the future there are likely to be new and unpredictable manifestations of such things as nationalism, religious fanaticism and just plain human foolishness to keep history going.

"To believe in the end of history," Leon Wieseltier, the literary editor of *The New Republic*, wrote in the same issue, "you must believe in the end of human nature, or at least of its gift for evil." Or, as Jean-François Revel, the French political analyst, put it, "In politics I don't much care about the long run: it's the short one that counts, after all, since human life is short."

In his reply, Mr. Fukuyama divides his critics into two groups: those who, he says, understood his original thesis and those who did not. The second group, he says, failed to grasp the Hegelian definitions. Mr. Fukuyama is trying to give back to ideas the central importance he feels they merit in human affairs. Thus, future tragic events do not discredit the end-of-history idea. The important issue is not the events themselves but whether the ideas that inspire them offer real competition to the liberal democratic idea.

"A nuclear war between India and Pakistan—horrible as that would be for those countries—does not qualify, unless it somehow forced us to reconsider the basic principles underlying our social order," he writes.

It is toward those who, he believes, understood his argument but still disagreed that Mr. Fukuyama directs his notion of an altered human nature. Again arguing from Hegel, he contends that even if future conflicts take place, they are unlikely to produce anything that will supersede the liberal democratic idea, in part because that idea has become so inherent to our makeup. Hegel, he says, believed that human nature itself is "self-created by man in the course of his historical evolution." The direction of that evolution, Mr. Fukuyama adds, is inevitably in the direction of "democratic egalitarianism."

And so, to those who say, for example, that the Soviet Union could well intervene in European affairs again, Mr. Fukuyama replies that history as Hegel saw it would in no way be resurrected. The important element of the recent Soviet threat was its link to Communism's "messianic mission," to a "universalist idea that was inimical to our way of life." Even if dictatorship is restored in the Soviet Union, Mr. Fukuyama writes, Marxism-Leninism as an ideology will remain defunct. The idea competing with liberal democracy will have disappeared.

George Gilder (review date 12 January 1992)

SOURCE: "Four Cheers for Liberal Democracy," in *Washington Post Book World*, January 12, 1992, pp. 1, 6.

[*In the following review, Gilder offers favorable evaluation of* The End of History and the Last Man.]

Amid all the timid tomes and hollow debates of the day, ruminating on the moral codes of the Palm Beach Au Bar, the fiery bellyaches of the New Male, or the platoons of CIA officials and Watergate burglars now widely identified with heavy weapons blazing away on the Grassy Knoll, Francis Fukuyama has launched a countercultural blitzkrieg. Despite a cumbersome title, ***The End of History and the Last Man*** unleashes an awesome barrage of some 200,000 well-boned words at all the multiculturalism, ethical relativism and pseudomarxist economics that now addle the American liberal-arts campus and political establishments.

According to Fukuyama, the American system is not a flawed and failing order about to give way before a global upsurge of more vigorous and populous Third World cultures, ethnic demands, relativistic ethical codes, and racialist or tribal politics. Liberal democracy, capitalism and Judeo-Christian morality are not ethnocentric figments of American or European pride in a culture of "dead white males." Rather, in all its crucial fundamentals, the U.S. constitutional order of liberal democracy and economic system of entrepreneurial capitalism define the end point of human political history, the very end of teleological time. This is it: the goal of several millennia of human groping and searching and dying in the dark—through wars, utopian experiments, eugenic pogroms, authoritarian bureaucracies, philosopher kingdoms, nationalist frenzies, revolutionary purges, totalitarian horrors—looking for the one true way, the way according best with the real intrinsic nature of the human being.

In the mastery and scope of its case, ***The End of History and the Last Man*** may be seen as the first book of the post-Marxist millennium—the first work fully to fathom the depth and range of the changes now sweeping through the world. According to Fukuyama's relentless argument, even the realist view that "war is eternal," feeding on "man's natural instinct for aggression," is fallacious. Fukuyama points out that war was a product of the zero-sum strivings of aristocracy and totalitarianism; over the last 200 years no liberal democratic state has ever attacked another. As all nations turn toward the positive-sum spirals of democratic capitalism and world trade expands at a pace of some 14 percent a year, he boldly asserts, war will disappear.

Along with war, nationalism too will wither away. Fukuyama dismisses as "parochial and untrue" the idea that nationalism is a deep-seated human trait. Most of these so-called nations with allegedly deep cultural imprints and primal human allegiances are in fact recent and transitory inventions affording far less powerful ties than kin or class.

Fukuyama scorns the United Nations as a reactionary alliance in defense of the falsehood of "sovereign equality of all its members." National self-determination has no foundations outside of democratic theory. Yet the most essential message of the U.N. Charter is the legitimacy of non-democratic nations. Fukuyama implicitly dismisses also the "new world order" of President Bush, which apparently accepts the notion that non-democratic regimes have sovereign rights. On the other hand, Fukuyama supports as profoundly realistic and important the campaigns for human rights which many foreign policy "realists" disdain.

Just as he spurns as a "total illusion" the idea of a "humane" middle way between communism and capitalism, he denounces the notion of a deep cultural propensity for authoritarianism. Except in the case of Somoza in Nicaragua, the recent authoritarian governments, left and right, fell of their own contradictions and inner divisions, often voluntarily, not because of revolutionary violence. Authoritarians saw that they needed legitimacy and the

only source was the democratic process. History has refuted all the sociological hokum about the "naturally" totalitarian Soviet citizens or the "naturally" theocratic and feudal Iberians or naturally traditionalist Poles and shows a truly natural trend toward democracy everywhere.

Not only cultural relativism but also moral relativism falls before his remorseless scythe. "Apparent differences between people's 'languages of good and evil' will appear to be an artifact of their particular stage of historical development." The universalist moral codes of the Judeo-Christian tradition, with their revolutionary claim of basic equality and moral autonomy for all individuals, are the foundation of liberal democracy and the new global system.

The driving force behind this global trend is the cumulative logic of natural science and technological enterprise, bringing the world into an "information age." "Evolution in the direction of decentralized decision making and markets becomes a virtual inevitability for all industrial economies that hope to, become 'post-industrial'," Fukuyama writes. "While centrally planned economies could follow their capitalist counterparts into the age of coal, steel, and heavy manufacturing," Marxism-Leninism "met its Waterloo" in "the highly complex and dynamic 'post-industrial' economic world."

"In particular," be continues, "President Reagan's Strategic Defense Initiative (SDI) . . . threatened to make obsolete an entire generation of Soviet nuclear weapons, and shifted the superpower competition into areas like microelectronics and other innovative technologies. . . ." He argues that when Mao attacked the technocrats in the Cultural Revolution, he "set China back a generation."

Nonetheless, as Fukuyama understands, "Modern science may explain why history unfolds as it does, but science itself does not explain why men pursue science." Modern science may explain the move to capitalism, but it does not explain the move to democracy. Many analysts who accept Fukuyama's argument for the necessity of capitalism will balk at his case for the inevitability of liberal democracy throughout the Third World.

Fukuyama, however, does not shrink from the more difficult claim. Devoted to the profound roots of the inevitability of liberal democracy, the second half of the book ingeniously reconciles the competing claims of democracy, capitalism, science and freedom, and at the same time transcends the Lockean and Jeffersonian roots of the liberal democracy he reveres.

Fukuyama sees that the secular, rationalist "Last Man" of modern liberal democracy could have neither created it nor defended it. Indeed, the modern scientific view of man tends to render incomprehensible the entire historic struggle by which the human race reached its current emancipation—the long saga of men and women who imposed an edifying imperialism around the globe, launched revolutionary technologies in the face of expert pessimism, tested rival philosophies and scientific paradigms, and evangelized for the Judeo-Christian revelations of human equality and freedom.

In many of these struggles, the scientific intelligensia was on the wrong side. "In our grandparents' time, many reasonable people could foresee a radiant socialist future in which private property and capitalism had been abolished, and in which politics itself had somehow been overcome." This fantasy of intellectuals prepared the way not for liberal democracy but for a century of atavistic horrors.

Beset by Marxist, Third World, and environmental claims, Western intellectuals still suffer the severe crisis of confidence that "left liberal democracy without the intellectual resources with which to defend itself . . . and led to serious doubts about the universality of liberal notions of right." Under the influence of environmentalism, the intelligensia still tends to believe that humanity is merely part of nature—that natural science itself disproves all the transcendent claims that drove human achievement to the current pinnacle. As Fukuyama puts it, "Modern natural science seems to show that there is no natural difference between man and nature, that man is simply a better organized and more rational form of slime."

Fukuyama sees that this twisted vision of modern science would have been less likely to consummate history than to leave it stalled in some communist or Nazi cul de sac. Liberal democracies, he writes, "are not self-sufficient: the community on which they depend must come from a source different from liberalism itself." To define this source, he returns to the concept of the First Man in a "state of nature" or "original condition" that is the foundation of much political theory.

According to the argument, there are two traditional First Men. One belongs to the school of Locke and Hobbes that is motivated chiefly by the rational impulse of self-preservation. This First Man created human communities to assure his survival in a world where life is otherwise, as Hobbes put it, "solitary, poor, nasty, brutish, and short." According to Fukuyama, it is this Hobbesian or Lockean man motivated by rational self-preservation that has evolved into the secular rationalist Last Man of today. Having achieved self-preservation and comfort, he is a complacent and self-absorbed member of the "me-generation." Indeed, facing cultures based on duty, discipline, and transcendence, the Lockean "pursuit of happiness" may be the fatal flaw of Western society. Sliding down the determined gradients of our reason and desire, we become less than autonomous human beings, incapable of defending our freedoms against relativistic assaults.

Fukuyama dismisses this prevailing Lockean image in favor of a First Man from Nietzsche. Fully aware of the perils of citing this alleged father of fascism, Fukuyama

rejects Nietzsche's moral relativism. Indeed, it was his moral relativism that allowed his work to be abused by Nazis. But Fukuyama declares that the Nietzschean First Man is indispensable to explain the triumph of liberal democracy.

Rather than a pursuer of happiness, Nietzsche's First Man is a valiant fighter for recognition and esteem. In order to assert his moral autonomy and prove his superiority to the beasts, he risks his life in battle. Because this act is irrational, it projects him beyond the determinist sway of natural forces. No longer a mere function of nature, he can be a master of it. Risking his life, he becomes a man of moral autonomy who can drive history to a new summit rather than a slide down into a murk of materialism.

It is this proud first man, mastering nature in the name of transcendent ideals, not the Lockean man succumbing to nature in the name of self-preservation, who is the bulwark of democracy. It is this proud first man, "ruddy cheeked, full chested," asserting his moral value, rather than a reasonable first man, prone to relativism in his desire for self-preservation, who impelled the human struggle up from the slime. As Fukuyama writes in the last chapter of this landmark work: "Relativism—the doctrine that maintains that all values are merely relative and attacks all 'privileged perspectives'—must ultimately end up undermining democratic and tolerant values as well . . . If nothing can be true absolutely, if all values are culturally determined, then cherished values like human equality have to go by the wayside as well." This is the lesson of Nietzsche and Nazism.

Ultimately, the belief in equality stems from neither the Lockean nor the Nietzschean first man but is founded on the universalist Judeo-Christian assertion of the worth of every individual before God. But even this claim expresses what Fukuyama calls *thymos,* a Nietzschean demand for recognition and a mandate for transcendence of nature. It accords with every individual's hunger not merely for self-preservation and pleasure but for recognition and moral dignity.

Such recognition is also at the heart of democracy. Through the equal vote, the equal access to political power, the equal right to express views and see them reflected in the political process, the nominally equal participation in the clash of opinions, the citizen gains the recognition for which human nature hungers. Fukuyama makes a persuasive case that this Nietzschean lust for recognition is the crucial driving force of the triumph of democracy around the globe. He powerfully documents his case that it suffices to make liberal politics, as well as capitalism, the inevitable destination of human history.

It is a supremely timely and cogent work, discernibly unbalanced only by a strange Fukuyama fudge on free will. He seems to entertain the sophomoric view that free will is a "tortured issue," an "abyss of philosophy" that it is prudent to avoid confronting. But without free will, as

Fukuyama himself implies, not only philosophy but science as well becomes nonsense, since it reduces scientists themselves to mere functions of forces that they cannot transcend and reduces their findings to mere figments of false consciousness. As chemist-philosopher Michael Polanyi has shown, a natural determinism that includes the scientist is so much gibberish. It takes a philosopher or logician to deny or even unduly complicate free will; no ordinary persons entertain the notion for a minute that their human wills are predetermined.

Only someone who finds the case for free will precarious, however, could imagine that the best way to assert it is to risk death in Nietzschean status struggles. Although understandable as a forensic strategy, Fukuyama's stress on Nietzschean swashbuckling as the test of human dignity rings false amid the perfect pitch of most of his argument.

The test of freedom is human creativity. In Michael Novak's aperçu, humans were made in the image of their creator—to be creative. Any creative endeavor is as palpably and undeniably free as the imagination is free. As manifestations of creativity, Fukuyama speaks first of art and letters. But just as any scientific theory that denies the free will of the scientist falls into gibberish, so does any economic theory that denies the free creativity of the entrepreneurs—that reduces them to production functions and consumer demands. Capitalism itself consists chiefly of creative entrepreneurship and in this way fully satisfies the thymos of its protagonists without bloodshed. In the cause of launching new businesses and technologies, entrepreneurs may not risk their lives but they risk their work, wealth, and esteem.

As Fukuyama understands, entrepreneurial competition and creativity are prime outlets for the hunger for recognition in democratic capitalist societies. The chief threat to his vision, as he recognizes, is the conflict between citizens seeking recognition through creative and productive entrepreneurship and seekers of recognition through litigation and bureaucracy at the expense of entrepreneurs.

Democratic thymos increasingly takes the form of a hunger for recognition as an enemy of the "rich" and the capital gains that embody the very essence of their creative efforts. Capital gains are the only form of wealth that is not explained or captured by determinist models of capital accumulation, retained earnings and return on investment. The fruit of innovation, capital gains are the unexpected yields of entrepreneurial thymos; their reinvestment in new ventures is the real reason for the triumph of capitalism. A capitalist system that expropriates capital gains is scarcely superior to socialism.

In a successful system, both forms of recognition—economic and political—must be granted. The drive for power needs free outlets no less than the impulse to create. Without democracy, the power seekers stifle the capitalist creators or transform them into mercantilist arms of the state, more feudal fiefs than free enterprises. While socialist regimes suppress creativity, authoritarian capitalist regimes block the no less imperious expression of political thymos and divert it into the economic sphere. Fukuyama ascribes the failure of Latin American economies, nominally capitalist, to their neo-feudal mercantilist character.

In this pathbreaking work, Fukuyama shows that both kinds of authoritarianism will ultimately and inevitably fail. All systems that deny either human impulse will lose military and economic power vis a vis liberal democracies. Indeed, as Fukuyama shows, democratic capitalism achieves such a good balance—a balance that accords so closely with the psychic balance of mankind—that it will end the long historic search for ways to organize human society and thus allow a new golden age of creativity and freedom for all.

Walter Russell Mead (review date 19 January 1992)

SOURCE: "The Theory That May Be History," in *Los Angeles Times Book Review,* January 19, 1992, pp. 2, 7.

[*In the following review, Mead offers tempered assessment of* The End of History and the Last Man, *which he describes as "a book of murkily vast ambitions and limited successes."*]

"The End of History?" was the provocative title of an essay published in the summer 1989 issue of *The National Interest.* It was written by Francis Fukuyama, then the deputy director of the State Department's Policy Planning Staff. The article made the point that, with the collapse of communism, there were no worldwide ideological rivals to western style democracy as a form of government. History, said Fukuyama following the German philosopher G. W. F. Hegel, is at bottom the story of ideological struggles between opposing ways of life. Feudalism, fascism, and communism: they had all fought democracy and they had all lost. Democracy had now won its last battle with communism: Could we now say that history was finished?

Fukuyama's essay ignited an international media firestorm as other intellectuals grappled with the issues he raised. Criticism from both the left and the right was harsh and often misplaced.

Fukuyama has now returned with *The End of History and the Last Man,* a fuller statement of his views.

So: Is history over? Fukuyama's answer is anticlimactic. History *might* be over, he says, but then again maybe it isn't. There's no way we can know for sure. Or, as "Saturday Night Live's" Emily Litella might have put it, "Never mind."

The End of History and the Last Man turns out to be a kind of philosophical bait-and-switch. For more than 300 pages Fukuyama tells us about Universal History, about

Hobbes, Locke, Hegel, Nietzsche and a 20th-Century French lecturer on Hegel named Alexandre Kojeve. For most of the book he carefully lays the groundwork for a claim that history is over—only to back away at the end and admit that the framework he lays out can't answer the question he poses.

A famous 19th-century cartoon in *Punch*, the British magazine of satirical humor, once showed a very meek young curate (a low-ranking member of the Anglican clergy) eating breakfast at the home of a very intimidating bishop. "I'm afraid," said the bishop, "that your egg is bad."

"Oh, no, my Lord," said the curate. "Parts of it are excellent."

This is what we have here—a curate's egg of a book. Parts of it are excellent, and parts of it are best pushed under the toast and out of sight. At his best, for example in his discussion of Nietzsche, Fukuyama shows himself to be a talented and thoughtful writer who is able to explain even the most recondite philosophical issues with grace and style.

But this is also an honest book. Lesser writers would have tried to make their conclusion sound more definite; Fukuyama doesn't have a clue whether history is over and he won't, to please his publisher, pretend that he does.

Another point in Fukuyama's favor, and one which some of his critics have missed: Fukuyama is no cheerleader for the status quo. He is happy to see the downfall of communism, but does not go on, as so many do, to argue that if communism is bad, capitalism must therefore be perfect.

One must also admire Fukuyama's intellectual ambition. There are few subjects in intellectual history as complicated as the relationship of Hegel in particular, and German philosophy in general, to the Anglo-American philosophical tradition that runs from people like Locke and Hobbes to Adam Smith and James Madison. In fact, Karl Marx once said that his life's work was to reconcile English political economy with German philosophy.

What Karl Marx tried—and failed—to do over a lifetime, Fukuyama tries to do in a few chapters. Fukuyama also fails, but American culture desperately needs people who will at least take on the big issues. We have plenty of professors who turn out narrow little monographs that are impeccably mediocre and of no importance whatever. Fukuyama is at least trying to engage important contemporary issues in the light of our intellectual heritage, and for this he deserves a sympathetic and attentive hearing.

Fukuyama's real subject is not so much whether history is over as whether it has a plot. Is history going anywhere, or are we just sitting around? Cultural relativists say we are sitting around. Western civilization, they maintain, is different from but not necessarily better than other civiliza-

tions and cultures of the present and the past. Progress is an ethnocentric illusion.

Fukuyama, an ardent disciple of Allan Bloom, thinks this is a dangerous idea. He wants to take Hegel's complex and supple philosophy of historical progress and human freedom and bring it into the field against the postmodernists and deconstructionists. He believes that these thinkers, in abandoning "metanarratives" and universal values, are undermining liberty and civilization itself.

This is a noble but difficult project; Fukuyama has philosophical enemies on all sides, and his struggles to fight them off provide all the drama and excitement to be found in his book. On one side he has the Marxists, whose historical philosophy begins with their own interpretation of Hegel. Fukuyama identifies with Hegel's philosophical idealism against Marxist materialism, and argues that the original Hegelian concepts make more sense than Marx's recasting of them.

On the other hand, Fukuyama stands with the Marxists against the postmodernists and the pure relativists in his belief that progress exists and that there are universal values that apply to all human beings. This, he believes, puts him on the opposite side of the fence not only from people like Lyotard, Baudrillard and Derrida, the three horsemen of postmodernist France, but also distinguishes him from the Anglo-American tradition rooted in the thought of Hobbes, Locke and Adam Smith. Anglo-American democratic thought, Fukuyama believes, is inherently vulnerable to relativism.

These are deep waters, and Fukuyama does not always keep his head in them. The few people who actually read Allan Bloom's *The Closing of the American Mind*—as opposed to the many who bought it—will find that Fukuyama's book is largely a remake of Bloom's: Nietzsche's challenge to the Enlightenment project of freedom; the inability of Anglo-American liberal/libertarianism to meet it; the need for an idealist philosophy to save society from the consequences of Nietzschean nihilism.

This is Bloom; it is also Fukuyama. It is also, in the opinion of this reader, dead wrong. It underrates both the Anglo-American tradition and the philosophical traditions represented today by anti-communist Marxists like Oxford's David Harvey and critical philosophers like Jurgen Habermas.

Conservatives and neo-conservatives will like Fukuyama's attacks on cultural relativism, but many will bridle at his wholesale dismissals of Christianity—"a slave ideology"—and of the conservative as well as the liberal roots of Anglo-American thought. Edmund Burke and Samuel Johnson would hate this book as much as Jacques Derrida and Alexander Cockburn.

Neither will this book be popular among the politically correct. Fukuyama suffers from the neo-conservative urge to *épater les proles*—to get in a few sly digs against Afro-centrists, radical environmentalists and other lefties who drive him crazy. A predictable but pointless debate is likely to follow. Passionate voices from the cultural left will denounce Fukuyama as racist and all kinds of other nasty things. He and his neo-conservative allies will deny the charges with irritating calm. Fukuyama and his defenders will be right. He isn't a racist. But baiting one's opponents in this way is neither the wisest nor the most charitable course for an author bent on persuasion and hoping, if possible, to heal and renew an impoverished American intellectual climate.

The End of History, then, is a book of murkily vast ambitions and limited successes. It is more provocative in the questions it poses than it is interesting in the answers it suggests. Given the subject matter, it cannot always be a good read, but it is usually a clear one. Like the curate's egg, and the optimist's glass, it is partly excellent and half full.

For many readers, such is the sorry state of American intellectual life that it will be their introduction to a world of important philosophical and political reflection, and this is reason enough to congratulate Fukuyama on what he has accomplished with this book, and to wish him better success in his future endeavors.

William H. McNeill (review date 26 January 1992)

SOURCE: "History Over, World Goes On," in *New York Times Book Review,* January 26, 1992, pp. 14-5.

[*In the following review, McNeill approves of Fukuyama's serious concerns though dismisses* The End of History and the Last Man *as "silly" and "reactionary."*]

"Back to Hegel" is not a rallying cry many Americans are likely to find plausible, yet this is what Francis Fukuyama advocates in this quixotic and tightly argued work of political philosophy. Actually, Mr. Fukuyama—a consultant at RAND and the former State Department official who caused a stir three years ago with his essay **"The End of History?"**—does not really recommend Hegel, but an interpretation of Hegel by a French intellectual named Alexandre Kojève (to me, entirely unknown), who explained in 1947 that History with a capital "H" had reached its logical end with the emergence of liberal democracy. In *The End of History and the Last Man,* Mr. Fukuyama adds a dash of Nietzsche to this strange cocktail, which is where the Last Man in his title comes from.

Mr. Fukuyama's invocation of German political philosophy aims to correct what he sees as a serious defect of Anglo-American political thought. Hobbes, Locke and Madison, he says, based their political theory on a topsided view of human nature. By appealing only to reason and desire, their liberalism left out a third element of human nature, which, according to Mr. Fukuyama, is of special impor-

tance for politics. This he calls *thymos,* a term borrowed from Plato that he translates as "spiritedness" or "desire for recognition." When properly satisfied, *thymos* arouses pride; when frustrated it results in anger. A failure to assert it brings a sense of shame.

Thymos, Mr. Fukuyama argues, is the principal motor of politics, impelling some men, throughout history, to assert personal mastery over others. But the genius of liberal democracy, dating from the American and French Revolutions, is that *thymos* could now begin to find universal satisfaction in shared citizenship. Freedom, in short, was perceived as a goal for all, and the struggle for mastery that had dominated the past now reached its logical and necessary conclusion. History (capitalized to signify a "meaningful order to the broad sweep of human events") came to an end.

To be sure, not all the countries of the world have yet achieved liberal democracy. But Mr. Fukuyama argues that they are all bound to get there sooner or later, since human nature requires it. Until that time, history continues in the old way in the illiberal parts of the globe, and the End of History affects only Europeans, Americans and the inhabitants of a few other nations, such as Japan.

Moreover, even after the End of History has become global, Mr. Fukuyama observes in the final pages of his book, we cannot know for sure that human beings will rest forever content with the imperfect satisfactions of human nature that our political institutions permit. In the future, people may become confused about what is possible for them to enjoy. "If it is true," he says, "that the historical process rests on the twin pillars of rational desire and rational recognition, and that modern liberal democracy is the political system that best satisfies the two in some kind of balance, then it would seem that the chief threat to democracy would be our own confusion about what is really at stake." Clearing up that confusion is, of course, the purpose of this book. It is therefore an immensely ambitious work, and a reviewer must ask whether Mr. Fukuyama has succeeded.

His book deserves respect. It is clearly written, discusses important questions and contains pithy sayings (as well as some silly remarks). As a professional historian, however, I am bound to point out that Mr. Fukuyama is so eager to address the grand sweep of History that he does not bother much with the details of history (without a capital letter) Thus, for instance, he asserts that Hobbes profited from the ideas of Newton, who was all of 11 years old when *Leviathan* was published. He also tells us that the English civil wars of the 17th century were fought between Catholics and Protestants, thereby administering a posthumous conversion to some of the antagonists in those all-Protestant conflicts.

Yet such errors, however egregious, are really beside the point. As a thinker and theorist of politics, Mr. Fukuyama deserves to have his argument taken seriously. Trying to do so, I find myself quite in sympathy with his effort to base politics on something more than the calculus of material self-interest. Ever since economists achieved the status of national soothsayers through their success in generating new concepts and statistics for maximizing war production during World War II, economics has pervaded public discourse in the United States far more than it deserves to. Americans, like other human beings, clearly do respond to noneconomic motives; and what Mr. Fukuyama refers to as *thymos* does, in fact, frequently outweigh material self-interest, impelling individuals to engage in acts of collective self-assertion or to display behavior that sometimes puts their lives at risk.

Nonetheless, the lesson Mr. Fukuyama derives from his reading of History seems to me fundamentally false. His argument that all the human past was no more than a fumbling progress aimed at the perfection of liberal, capitalist democracy, as exemplified here and in a few other countries, simply reformulates a longstanding vision of the United States as embodying an earthly perfection toward which all other peoples have been expected to aspire. The exotic Germanic garb in which Mr. Fukuyama expresses this self-flattering image may give fresh life to this myopia. But when Asian models of social and economic efficiency seem to be gaining ground every day, and when millions of Moslems are at pains to sustain the differences, great and small, that distinguish them from Americans, it is hard to believe that all the world is destined to imitate us.

My basic difference with Mr. Fukuyama is this: I do not believe that human nature is uniform and unchanging. Rather, whatever penchants and capabilities we inherit with our genes are so malleable that their expression takes infinitely diverse forms. Personal identification with a group of fellows is the basic guide for most behavior; and groups define themselves by marking the ways they differ from outsiders. This, I believe (in contrast to Mr. Fukuyama), assures permanent institutional diversity and cultural pluralism among humankind.

Mr. Fukuyama is not entirely blind to these dimensions of social life, but he only considers nationalism, which, he holds, can "fade away as a political force" by becoming "tolerant like religion before it." Oddly, he says nothing about race feeling, which appears to be on the rise in Europe as well as in the United States. He likewise skips over religiously defined identities and rivalries so prominent in the Middle East, which he presumably thinks will eventually sink toward the sort of political marginality that Protestantism and Catholicism have attained in this country and in most of Western Europe. Similarly, he says nothing about class conflict, perhaps because he thinks that Marxism has now been so discredited that refutation of one of its primary doctrines is unnecessary.

Another, related defect of Mr. Fukuyama's view of human nature, I believe, is that he fails to recognize that *thymos* is not always (or perhaps even usually) individual. Human beings are capable of transferring their desire for recognition to a collectivity, and surely this is the most effective form of political action. Often, a real sense of freedom results from deliberate and habitual submission to an external authority; soldiers frequently experience this phenomenon. And the freedom that follows from total surrender to God's will is the theme of innumerable religious discourses.

Finally, it seems worth pointing out that Mr. Fukuyama's philosophical approach entirely omits the biological and ecological setting within which human society and politics inevitably exist. Even if his End of History were to arrive, the enduring equilibrium he attributes to liberal, democracy, because it "gives fullest scope to all three parts" of the human soul, would confront serious outside disturbances arising from the instabilities in the natural environment created by our technology and ever increasing numbers. Under such circumstances, tumults like those of the past would surely continue, even if, from Mr. Fukuyama's point of view. History had somehow lost its right to a capital letter.

Ultimately, this sort of word game seems silly rather than illuminating. I conclude that "Back to Hegel," glitteringly refracted through the mind of Mr. Fukuyama though it may be, is reactionary in the true sense of the word.

Paul Johnson (review date March 1992)

SOURCE: "To the 21st Century," in *Commentary*, Vol. 93, No. 3, March, 1992, pp. 51-4.

[*In the following review, Johnson provides analysis of* The End of History and the Last Man *and refutes Fukuyama's thesis. According to Johnson, "History does not end; it simply becomes more complicated."*]

Educated people have an extraordinary appetite for absolute answers to historical questions, answers which wise historians know cannot be forthcoming. It is astonishing that Hegel's reputation survived his absurd declaration that history had ended with Bonaparte's victory over Prussia at Jena in 1806. Yet Hegel went on to hold what was then the most enviable academic post in Germany, the chair of philosophy in Berlin, and to write much more clever and influential nonsense. In due course his thoughts were transmuted by Marx not merely into a set of absolute answers about where history was heading but into a program for accelerating the process. Until recently this moonshine was believed by millions of comparatively well-educated people, and indeed there remain corners of university campuses where it is still upheld and taught.

There was a time, too, especially in the 1920's, when Oswald Spengler's *Decline of the West* was the ultra-fashionable text for historical determinists, and that was succeeded, a decade or so later, by Arnold Toynbee's *A Study of History*. It sold in prodigious quantities, despite its offputting length, and I am old enough to remember a time when it was still taken seriously, even though Toynbee changed his entire theory fundamentally, halfway through it.

The latest intellectual entrepreneur to supply the appetite is Francis Fukuyama, whose 1989 article, **"The End of History?,"** with its notion that the collapse of Soviet Communism had opened the era of total liberal triumph and brought history to a stop, was a sensation in the United States and elsewhere, and so got the 1990s off to a thoroughly muddled start. No doubt anxious to consolidate his perhaps fragile reputation as the guru of the decade, he has now produced a volume of 400 pages which says the last word on—well, everything, more or less.

Fukuyama here restates his original contention in less exalted, and therefore more acceptable, terms than in his original essay:

> As mankind approaches the end of the millennium, the twin crises of authoritarianism and socialist central planning have left only one competitor standing in the ring as an ideology of potentially universal validity: liberal democracy, the doctrine of individual freedom and popular sovereignty.

This proposition is, at any rate, worth debating. The only trouble is that its assumption of the imminent triumph of liberalism was a 19th-century commonplace, shared alike by John Stuart Mill and Woodrow Wilson, Mazzini and Kossuth, Gladstone and Thiers; indeed, it was pretty generally held, among "enlightened" people, as late as the Versailles Conference in 1918-19. Unfortunately, such complacency was succeeded by the totalitarian era, from which we are only just beginning, rather tentatively I would say, to emerge. Even in its watered-down form, Fukuyama's optimism appears presumptuous.

Moreover, it gets him only as far as page 42, and he still has more than 350 pages to fill. Fukuyama is himself a Hegelian, and the thoughts of the Master keep popping up in his text, rather as King Charles's head intrudes into the memorandum which Mr. Dick, in *David Copperfield,* is writing to the Lord Chancellor. To make matters worse, Fukuyama is also bedazzled by a now-obscure French philosophy expert, Alexandre Kojève, here described as "Hegel's great interpreter," and he too keeps popping up, behind and sometimes in front of Hegel, rather like Sancho Panza squiring Don Quixote.

As I say, the book goes on to cover a lot of ground, and the author enjoys conjuring up fancy chapter headings, such as "The Mechanism of Desire," "The Beast with Red Cheeks," and "The Coldest of All Cold Monsters." But these promise more than they perform, and much of the book is anodyne in effect, ranging through conventional poli. sci. to standard futurology, with a tendency to waffle at critical points. Perhaps the fairest comment I can make is to recall the exchange between the High Court Judge and the sharp-tongued barrister F. E. Smith. Judge: "I have listened carefully to your exposition, Mr. Smith, and I am none the wiser." "Possibly not, my lord, but considerably better informed."

Alas, "considerably" would be out of place here: Fukuyama does not deal widely in facts, and the key table he presents, "Liberal Democracies Worldwide," tracing their increase through the years 1790, 1848, 1900, 1919, 1940, 1960, 1975, and 1990 seems to me a minefield of misunderstandings, both historical and contemporary. In the bound reviewers' galleys of this book, Yugoslavia was rated as a "liberal democracy"—that country riven by half-a-dozen civil wars, with a million homeless refugees, its rump still run by a heartless Communist dictatorship; in the nick of time, the listing was removed from the final published version. But is it right to call Romania a "liberal democracy"? Or Paraguay? Or genocidal Sri Lanka? There are a dozen other countries Fukuyama complacently lists in his "end of history" column which do not belong there.

The truth is that though Fukuyama repeatedly refers to "the recent worldwide liberal revolution," it is at present one of aspiration rather than reality. What is true is that, for the first time in history, every single nation in Western Europe is now, theoretically at least, a democracy under the rule of law, and there has been a strong movement toward political and economic freedom in Eastern Europe, too. But with some exceptions, much the same could have been said of Europe in 1918-19, and look what followed.

Even in Western Europe, the credentials of some countries need examination. In France, for instance, the ability of citizens, either as individuals or through their puny parliament, to resist the overweening power of the state is minute—though perhaps Fukuyama, as a Hegelian, and so a state-worshipper, would approve of that. In Italy, only last year, the special anti-Mafia prosecutor told parliament in despair: "Whole provinces of Italy and Sicily are now beyond the law." Moreover, as Britain, where liberalism originated and which has been a country under the rule of law since at least the mid-17th century, is discovering to its cost, the European Community is slowly enmeshing twelve nations in a labyrinth of bureaucratic regulations which is profoundly undemocratic and illiberal.

Elsewhere, the outlook is much darker. The likelihood of working democracies, where all are equal under the law, emerging in any part of the Muslim world is not great, and Fukuyama's listing of Turkey as a "liberal democracy" seems to me quite false, as the author would discover for himself if he went there in the guise of a Kurd or an Armenian. The only successful democracy in the Arab world was Lebanon—it worked well when I first visited it in the 1950's—and it was so by virtue of its Christian majority, which has since vanished, along with democracy and law. The first free elections ever held in "liberated" Algeria, after 30 years, produced an overwhelming first-round victory for Islamic theocracy—the negation of liberal democracy—at which point the experiment was aborted.

The one liberal democracy in the African continent, the Republic of South Africa, has a parliamentary democracy, albeit limited to the white race, and a rule of law which extends to all; it is now threatened by black power under an unreconstructed Stalinist-type party. There *are* democratic stirrings in Africa, after a long night of Marxist and collectivist failure, but they are no more than stirrings.

In South America (if not in Central America), the skies are a little lighter, at any rate for the present, though that part of the world specializes in false dawns. And it must be pointed out, as Fukuyama half-admits, that the present wave of economic liberalism is almost entirely due to the success of the seventeen-year military dictatorship of General Pinochet in Chile. The freeing of what had been an economy strangled by collectivist regimentation and bureaucracy could only have been achieved by a masterful man of his stamp, able to do as much as he pleased by virtue of his bayonets. And, though many neighboring countries currently going through a democratic, parliamentary phase—such as Argentina—have taken courage to follow suit, it remains to be seen whether their governments have the stamina to go on with it. In the Latin American context. I fear, democracy and economic liberalism tend to be mutually exclusive, a point not lost on that wise old Pole, Joseph Conrad (cf. *Nostromo*).

As for Asia, who will be bold enough to predict the political future of the three key peoples, the Japanese, the Indians, and the Chinese? Believing, as I do, that political freedom and economic freedom are ultimately indivisible, and that if you embark on one the other must eventually follow suit, I assume that if the Beijing regime reverts to its program of commercial liberalization, as it seems inclined to do, moves toward political democracy must follow. But I would not bet one Kuomintang dollar on it. Again, India has now practiced a form of democracy—by no means a liberal form, despite what Fukuyama's table states—for nearly half a century, thanks to a useful foundation of British institutions. But its survival, amid all the stresses of race, region, and religion, is a kind of daily miracle, a gift from God.

Then there is Japan, another half-century-old democracy. Fukuyama classifies it as a liberal one, and so in certain technical respects it may be; but in other, much more important respects, it is not, or not yet. To me, Japan is the most elusive and impenetrable nation on earth, which in some ways has more in common with the Middle Kingdom of ancient Egypt than anything in contemporary society. Far more than Stalin's Russia, it fits Churchill's description, "a riddle wrapped in a mystery inside an enigma." Japan, so far, has clung to democracy because it is convenient, and safe, and has proved mighty profitable. If these conditions should change, will Japan, a country with a large and now-affluent population and few natural resources, look elsewhere for political salvation? Has democracy, let alone liberalism, struck deep, self-sustaining roots in Japanese civic habits and attitudes? How can we

possibly say? The Japanese, or so many of them tell me, do not even know themselves; or if they do know, are not saying.

This *tour d'horizon* leaves out North America, and the United States in particular. Fukuyama assumes that America is intrinsically and incorrigibly liberal-democratic, the *fons et origo* of the concept. Of the 64 countries in his table, it is the only one to score full marks all the way through from 1790 to 1990. Yet because a state may formally qualify for the status of a liberal democracy, it does not follow that all its inhabitants enjoy the benefits. Can we say a society is democratic if democracy is not in fact practiced, or is under the rule of law if law is not, in reality, available?

One problem Fukuyama does not consider is the way in which liberal democracy, or liberalism *tout court*, breeds its own nemesis. Let us take an illustration from a recent examination of the state of the U.S. economy, *The Great Reckoning*, by J. D. Davidson and William Rees-Mogg. They cite Dodge City in 1871 as an example of a primitive, pre-civil society, without representative government, police, courts, or justice of any kind. Its murder rate was, accordingly, high. But it was only half, per capita, of the murder rate in Washington, D.C., the nation's capital, in 1990. In large parts of Washington today, fewer than one in ten adults vote; one person in sixteen will be murdered over a life-span, and among children under twelve murder is now the leading cause of death. To a lesser degree, such conditions apply to portions of other major cities in the richest, most democratic, and most liberal country on earth. To someone in a U.S. ghetto, or for that matter in a big-city housing complex in Britain or France, the consequences of liberalism may themselves be a tyranny, and life for many is liable to be, in Hobbes's words, "solitary, poor, nasty, brutish, and short."

History does not end; it simply becomes more complicated. Whereas capitalism, judged by its historical performance over two centuries, is a self-correcting system, being a form of economic activity which tends to occur at a certain stage in human development unless you do something specific to stop it, liberalism is an intellectual concept which to some extent has to be imposed on societies by its better-educated elites: no large democracy, for instance, has ever abolished capital punishment by referendum. That, of course, is why liberalism tends to be self-defeating—because it often runs across the grain of popular sentiment, based on harsh experience. Similarly, such concepts as racial equality and nondiscrimination, buttressed as they usually are by practical measures like quotas, busing, and positive law, are imposed by elected elites, often responding to pressure groups or "expert opinion" rather than being demanded by mass opinion.

Ordinary men and women favor freedom of speech and movement; all want the right to sell their labor in the highest market, to spend their money as they please; they welcome the right to vote, and most support freedom of the press, and even religion. But the more sophisticated forms of liberalism are less popular, and some are downright unpopular. If countries like the United States and Britain had government by referendum—something which is now technically possible on a day-to-day basis—they would become radically less liberal in a short time. Over a huge range of issues, from what is taught in the schools and how, to the treatment of criminal offenders, public opinion, so far as one can see, would insist on a harder, harsher society, but also one which would become more industrious, and safe. Such are the orders of human priorities in the mass.

In short, it is not only in South America that there tends to be a conflict between democracy and liberalism. In fact, "liberal democracy" is to some extent a contradiction in terms. The more democratic it is, the less liberal; and vice versa. I cannot, for instance, honestly call Britain a democracy, though it is certainly a liberal-led society. There, 30 years ago, capital punishment—an issue on which virtually every adult has, and is entitled to have, strong opinions—was abolished, not indeed by referendum but by parliamentary vote. On the evidence of polls, public opinion has continued to demand its return, usually by majorities of 80 percent; parliament has continued to ban it, by almost equally large majorities.

It occurs to me, then—and it is the sort of point which Fukuyama, were he not such a blinkered Hegelian, might have considered—that over the next twenty years or so, the advanced societies will move further in the direction of liberalism, or will become more democratic; but not both. I foresee all kinds of tensions developing, as our cities grow richer, more violent, more hedonistic, and, if not more liberal, then more libertarian, and our countrysides (therefore) more threatened. As history grows in complexity, it becomes more fascinating, as well as more difficult to predict. *Pace* Fukuyama, we face new nightmares in the 21st century, as well as realized dreams, and the really disturbing prospect is that they will be nightmares of a kind we have never before experienced.

Stephen Holmes (review date 23 March 1992)

SOURCE: "The Scowl of Minerva," in *The New Republic*, March 23, 1992, pp. 27-33.

[*In the following review of* The End of History and the Last Man, *Holmes provides analysis of Fukuyama's historical perspective and postulations, and cites contradictions in his theoretical assumptions and inattention to historical reality.*]

I.

The collapse of communism has brought dizziness and disorientation across the political spectrum. For the barbarians, as the poet Cavafy wrote, were a kind of solution. But no longer: the East-West confrontation has lost its power to threaten and to clarify our lives. Even the distinction between left and right, which has underlain all European politics since 1789, has been shaken. Throughout the post-Communist world, from the Baltics to Albania, and now in Russia itself, we are observing waves of radical change that look so far like a *liberal* revolution. The strangeness of the notion suggests the unprecedentedness of the change. But how else to describe the ground-up reorganizations occurring, with varying degrees of haste and success, across the post-Leninist world? Is liberal revolution not the most significant fact of contemporary political life?

An immense task of reconceptualization lies before us. Scholars and politicians alike are wondering how to bring this complex and novel world into focus, how to comprehend its new powers for good and ill. A first avalanche of answers to these questions came cascading into print two years ago. The man who threw the stone that loosed the avalanche was Francis Fukuyama: his essay **"The End of History?"** appeared in 1989 in *The National Interest,* and the colloquium of rejoinders organized by the journal was only the beginning of a worldwide outpouring of reactions.

Most of these responses, as Fukuyama has boasted, were negative, if not jeering. They also had real force. History is unpredictable, so why speak of its end? Why describe a movement from the frozen to the fluid, from riveted bipolarism to unsettled multipolarism, in these eschatological terms? What has died is not history but Marxism, and Marxism was precisely an eschatological philosophy that distorted history by forcing it into a procrustean scheme with a predetermined direction and a happy end. But Fukuyama was unmoved by these early animadversions, and now he invites the world to stir for a second time. His book appears not only to answer his many critics, but also to amplify and to enlarge his account of politics and history. This time around he will "[take] into account the experience of all peoples in all times."

Though he might not admit it, Fukuyama has accepted many of the criticisms leveled against him and incorporated them into his narrative, sometimes suavely, in the main text, at other times clumsily, in the footnotes. But still he sticks obstinately to his original claim. His stubbornness does not appear to be based on a need for recognition (a need that figures prominently in his new analysis of human affairs) or reputation. He seems sincerely to believe that in some sense all the "major problems" in world history have now been solved. We are facing, he says, "the end of all large disputes"; we are on the threshold of "a world where struggle over all of the large issues has been largely settled."

Fukuyama sees a new agreement in world politics, "a remarkable consensus concerning the legitimacy of liberal democracy." In 1932 or 1942, liberal democracy was besieged by ideological enemies on the right and the left. Many Western intellectuals heard the siren songs of fascism or communism; disagreement raged about the direction in which contemporary societies should move. In 1992, however, these old controversies have vanished. The two great totalitarian temptations of the twentieth century have gone down, one with a bang, the other with a whimper. And so a quietus has descended on history's long storm. "Everyone" now recognizes that the ideal of liberal democracy cannot be improved upon. It is worshiped even in those underdeveloped countries where the possibility of putting it into practice seems remote. To be sure, debates continue about the extent of government regulation or the size of the public sector within advanced liberal states, but the differences between liberal regulators and liberal marketers pale against the background of their underlying agreement. All parties now accept private property, economic competition, juridical equality, the separation of powers, competitive elections, freedom of the press, religious toleration, and so on.

This new consensus spells the termination of ideological debate (or, to coin a phrase, the end of ideology). That is the phenomenon that Fukuyama wants to capture with his metaphor—if it is a metaphor—about history's culmination. Obviously he has a point. But how much of a point? And is this the most precise and the most intellectually responsible way to make it? If Fukuyama were simply registering a narrowing of ideological differences among secular Western elites, or the recent collapse of long-standing tyrannical regimes, he would be on fairly safe ground. But he is grander. The collapse of our major rival for the past forty-five years, he claims, tells us something essential about nothing less than the overall course of world history—about "a broader historical process leading to the spread of liberal democracy around the world."

In some places Fukuyama sets forth his chronicle of the human story with the authority of a mastermind holding the key to the universe; in other places he offers it tentatively, as a *façon de parler,* as a hypothesis, worth considering, maybe. In any case, his description of "the historical process" conflates many different claims. Here, world history is described as coherent or intelligible; there, it is called irreversible. Here, history is cumulative (all past achievements are retained); there, history is directional (headed toward perpetual peace or the convergence of political and economic systems). And everywhere history is described as meaningful and having a plot, as beginning with a problem that, after much travail, it solves. The sheepish version of this thesis is that secular Western intellectuals now agree that history has a goal. The knock-'em-down version is that the world, or some of it, already has arrived at this goal.

All these claims are jumbled together, though they are analytically quite distinct. (History can disclose irreversibilities without containing any meaning and without having any overarching goal.) By slipping around among different conceptions of historical change, however, Fukuyama achieves a tactical advantage: he presents his critic with a moving target. Consider his double-talk about

progress. In some passages, he claims that the overarching pattern has no moral content: history marches on, but it may well make things worse instead of better. This is a defensible view. But it is a view that flies in the face of Fukuyama's own thinking; for if history is not a process of improvement, then he cannot define the end of history as the end of improvement, which he repeatedly does.

In transcribing into his book many of the best arguments made against his original essay, Fukuyama walks into other contradictions as well. He now admits that history is unpredictable: "some new authoritarian alternatives, perhaps never before seen in history, may assert themselves in the future." And he says that old tyrannies may return: "We have no guarantee and cannot assure future generations that there will be no future Hitlers." Moreover, "we can expect a higher degree of nationalist conflict in Europe with the end of the cold war." And cultural wars are just about to begin: if, in one mood, perpetual peace is supposed to come about thanks to "an increasing homogenization of all human societies, regardless of their historical origins or cultural inheritances," in another mood "persistent cultural differences between ostensibly liberal democratic capitalist states will prove much harder to eradicate."

Fukuyama does not seem to understand that all these pre-emptive concessions amount to an admission of defeat. Indeed, the most important sentence in his book is this one: "No regime—no 'socioeconomic system'—is able to satisfy all men in all places." With this fine observation, however, he stands himself on his own head. He flatly, and rightly, contradicts the idea of an end of history: if liberal democracy, too, is unsatisfying, then it, too, cannot represent the climax.

And the sentence illustrates something else, perhaps the most profound of Fukuyama's divisions against himself. Switching from cheerleading to doom-saying, he laments "the banalization of life through modern consumerism." Fukuyama begins as an anti-Jeremiah, announcing that "good news has come" and urging us "to shake off our acquired pessimism," and ends up as just another Jeremiah, denouncing "some kind of internal rot" at the heart of the West. In short, he celebrates and deplores the West in the same breath: that is the real plot of his book. (When he wants to explain how unsatisfying liberal democracy is, he calls it "bourgeois society.") He is an optimist and a pessimist, without worrying the logical and moral contradictions. He praises the Soviet debacle and damns our alleged degeneration; he waves a flag of victory and hangs his head in despair. His strong cultural pessimism is reflected in the second half of his title, "the last man," a phrase borrowed from Nietzsche: the inhabitants of Western-style liberal democracies are last men, emptied of ambition, satisfied with mediocrity, bereft of high ideals, unwilling to make sacrifices.

Fukuyama's argument rests on three fundamental and closely related premises that have been characteristic of a particular variety of conservatism. First, the battle against communism is the heart and soul of world history. Second, Western liberal democracies are vulgar and corrupt and rotten. (We won the cold war because of the inner weaknesses of Communist states, not because of any great strength of our own.) Third, the only thing that prevented corrupt liberal states from sinking to the ultimate depravity was the moral struggle against communism. Our final victory, therefore, is our final defeat. Having vanquished communism, we have nothing to fight for except security, wealth, and comfort—but those are not ideal values, they are materialist temptations. Thus history after the struggle will be flat and without interest. Indeed, there will be no history worthy of the name.

But it is obvious, or it should have been obvious, that communism was neither our only important problem nor our only ideological enemy (how some conservatives will miss it!). To the forms of antiliberalism that exist today, others will surely be added in the future, due to human ingenuity and human evil. It should also be obvious that liberal democracy is flawed but not rotten. Despite its shortcomings, liberal democracy has enormous internal strengths, and will remain a fairly stable political and economic system, offering much to different people across the globe without draining their lives of moral meaning.

Fukuyama borrows his idea of the end of history from Alexander Kojève, the Russian émigré philosopher and cult figure who taught an influential seminar on Hegel in Paris in the 1930s. (Among the many things Fukuyama undermines is his own admiration for Kojève: my favorite understatement in this overstated book is his admission, which is hidden in the footnotes, that "there are certain problems in seeing Kojève himself as a liberal, insofar as he frequently professed an ardent admiration for Stalin and asserted that there was no essential difference between the United States, the Soviet Union, and China of the 1950s.") Kojève's thesis was that the pivot point of world history was the transition from separate class societies to a single classless society encompassing the whole of mankind, that hierarchical and particularistic societies have gradually given way (or are gradually giving way) to "the victory of the universal and homogeneous state." The transition from aristocracy to egalitarianism was simultaneously a revaluation of values and an abandonment of violence and war for perpetual peace. Citing Hegel, Kojève asserted that this Great Transition became inevitable in 1806, when Napoleon (or more generally the force that Kojève called "Robespierre-Napoleon") defeated the Prussian army and prepared the way for the spread of Enlightenment ideas throughout the world.

As a moment's reflection makes clear, however, the transition from a class society to classlessness, or from pre-Enlightenment ideals to Enlightenment ideals, has nothing to do with the end of the cold war. Intellectually, the cold war was an internecine conflict, a battle between two Enlightenment ideologies. The end of that intellectual and political struggle certainly does not signal the defeat of the premodern by the modern. Kojève was concerned with the victory of an egalitarian ideology over its inegalitarian rival; but the occasion for Fukuyama's speculation is the victory of one egalitarian ideology over another. This difference is fundamental, yet it is never mentioned.

It is true that Communists and liberals give contrary answers to a whole range of important questions (Does the march of History guarantee the triumph of justice? How great a threat to freedom is posed by state power? What are the consequences of private property for the worst-off members of society?). It is also true that the schismatic war within the Enlightenment is done. But for all their differences, liberalism and communism share egalitarian and cosmopolitan presuppositions. Both favor in principle the emancipation of the individual and the development of his potential. Both are secular. (Communists wish to eradicate religion, liberals to depoliticize it.) Both admire technical advance and economic growth. (They even cooperated in the great struggle against fascism, which was the real revolt against modernity.) Like all family quarrels, their confrontation was especially intense, but it is now ended, and it can be asserted with some confidence that the antiliberalism of the future will not be Marxist, or in any way a child of the Enlightenment. But does even this extraordinary development amount to the end of "large issues" and ideological conflict? I doubt it.

How can Fukuyama claim that the battle between liberalism and non-Communist forms of authoritarianism is not ideological in the customary sense? (He also claims the opposite, but let's ignore the inconsistency this time.) Are not ideas clearly at stake in these other confrontations? Is it really correct to say that the end of the cold war means the replacement of ideological conflict by ethnic conflict? Will the battle of grand universalism against grand universalism really be replaced by the battle of petty particularism against petty particularism? Or to put it differently, are not particularisms also informed by grand and dangerous ideas?

Religion and nationalism are rising, not falling, and they often take the form of ideological beliefs that prefer History to history. And what the West stands for in its struggle against, say, Islamic fundamentalism or Baathist dictatorship are precisely the central values and institutions of liberalism: individual freedom, tolerance for diversity, rights of minorities, impartiality of the law, government by consent, competitive elections, freedom of the press, wide-open public debate, and so on. So why should confrontation with a form of authoritarianism that has been culturally untouched by the Enlightenment be less ideological than confrontation with a bastard child of the Enlightenment itself? Why should the coercive imposition of a public conception of virtue on all citizens be any less ideologically repulsive to liberals simply because it is ethnocratic or theocratic rather than egalitarian?

Fukuyama is a fierce critic of cultural relativism, but he is oddly a cultural relativist on this point. He thinks that the

West has every reason to impose its own political norms on Eastern Europe and Russia, but not on East Asia or the Muslim world, because we inhabit a different cultural space or tradition. Multiparty democracy cannot be exported to Japan, for example, because Japanese culture abhors wide-open public debate in the liberal manner:

> There are several respects in which one could say that Japan is governed by a benevolent one-party dictatorship, not because that party has imposed itself upon society in the manner of the Soviet Communist Party, but because the people of Japan *choose* to be ruled in that fashion. The current Japanese system of government reflects a broad social consensus rooted in Japan's group-oriented culture that would feel profoundly uncomfortable with more "open" contestation or the alternation of parties in power.

Because of Asia's Confucian traditions, in other words, the Japanese voter is grateful to have no real choice on election day. Autocratic rulers in Europe, of course, always invoked their society's low tolerance for disagreement as a fundamental justification for their monopoly on power. The LDP does the same in Japan today. But it is a little shocking to find Fukuyama furnishing those places in the world where history did not end with a historical excuse.

II.

Fukuyama is not content with merely describing the pattern of history. That is the work of mere historians. He wants to explain history, to show why it *necessarily* moves in the direction he detects. His explanation fails, but it is interesting. There are two basic motors, he says, that drive the historical process: science, or the rational domination of nature, and pride, or the demand for social recognition.

Fukuyama calls modern science "the Mechanism that gives history its directionality." The ancient conception of history as a repetitive cycle has been retired by the relentless and irreversible advance of science. Once unleashed, its power is unstoppable: technology, the major outgrowth of the scientific worldview, has swept the world. And science—here is the rub—"in some way makes capitalism inevitable." The argument is admittedly and a little amusingly Marxist: the forces of production develop according to a logic of their own, and at a certain point the old relations of production become a fetter on the further use and development of technology, and then the old social system crumbles and is replaced by a new one. Applying this deterministic scheme to 1989, Fukuyama reasons that the Stalinist system, while perfectly compatible with industrialization, became a shackle on the development of computer technology: when the microchip was ripe, the Communist system went down.

Technical rationality does not, however, guarantee the triumph of political democracy. Science may flourish in an atmosphere of freedom, but neo-Confucian authoritarianism, not democratic individualism, is the best system for exploiting the forces unleashed by science and technology. Unlike the free-wheeling, individualistic, and consumption-oriented societies of the West, the tradition-bound culture of Japan promotes pride in one's work and group loyalty, which are the optimal conditions for uncorking the potential of modern technology and a rational division of labor.

If we think only of economic development, therefore, the end of history lies not with "unimprovable" individualistic democracy but with "market-oriented authoritarianism" on the Asian model. The obvious implication is that, if science alone moved history, then the future would belong to group-think. So what accounts for the supremacy of liberal democracy? Enter the second major force in Fukuyama's Universal History: human pride, or the desire for recognition.

Democratic politics—as opposed to mere market capitalism—becomes inevitable because of this yearning deeply planted in the human soul. As Hegel explained, man desires more than food, shelter, sex, and sleep: "He desires the desire of other men, that is, to be wanted by others or to be *recognized*." Most of life is dominated by this non-materialistic need for respect. The end of history has arrived, in Western liberal democracies, because man has found here what he has been seeking from the beginning of time: recognition.

Fukuyama means this aspect of his analysis to be a protest against the reductionist picture of human motivation characteristic of neoclassical economics. Departing from his usual praise of "cumulative" scientific advance, he laments "the successful 'economization' of our thinking that has occurred in the past 400 years." Economics, having forgotten Plato's wisdom about irrational passions, has made much of human behavior unintelligible. For if man were an economic animal (or a rational pursuer of material advantage) he would never, as he sometimes does, throw away his life in pursuit of something so utterly useless as an enemy flag. To understand the course of human history, we need to grasp such non-economic motives as pride, ambition, indignation, and anger.

Fukuyama's intentions here are admirable. But it is not enough merely to assert the existence of non-material motives and non-calculating styles of action. There are important distinctions among the many non-materialist and non-economic motives, that is, among the passions, which Fukuyama fails to make. He does not even distinguish between material and non-material goals, on the one hand, and calculating and non-calculating styles of behavior, on the other. But this is an essential distinction, since we can easily pursue non-material goals in a perfectly rational and calculating manner.

At first Fukuyama draws a sharp contrast between the rational desire for economic prosperity and the prerational desire for the recognition of others. He uses the Greek word *thymos* or "spiritedness," from Plato's *Republic,* to stand for this second desire. Thus, he argues that "the self-assertion arising from *thymos* and the selfishness of desire are very distinct phenomena." But while he asserts that they are "very distinct," he also says that they are one and the same. In fact, capitalism is a product not of material self-interest, but of pride: "The wants created by modern consumerism arise, in other words, from man's vanity." *Thymos* is not repressed in economic life, it is merely demilitarized. Fine; but this claim is repeatedly contradicted by Fukuyama's assertion that *thymos* is wholly eliminated in economic man.

Many of Fukuyama's problems stem from his decision to elide the Platonic idea of *thymos* with the Hegelian idea of recognition. There are some interesting parallels, but the two concepts are not so easily conflated as Fukuyama assumes. And other muddles result from fusing Hegel's historicism with Plato's antihistoricism. Sometimes Fukuyama claims that *thymos* is a permanent feature of the human mind. At other times he claims that it can be extinguished, and perhaps has been extinguished, in bourgeois societies. Sometimes he says that *thymos* is an unsatisfiable desire. At other times he says that it can be satisfied, and perhaps has been satisfied, in bourgeois societies.

Fukuyama's complaint that the economist's idea of "utility" has no explanatory value because it is used tautologically to "encompass any end actually pursued by human beings" may be appropriately directed at his own notion of *thymos*. This desire for recognition is "the origin of tyranny, imperialism, and the desire to dominate" as well as "the psychological ground for political virtues like courage, public-spiritedness, and justice." It explains anger and pity, duty and disobedience, religious piety and aggressive ultranationalism, pride in one's work and shame at one's looks, extreme self-confidence and its total lack. It is the source of eccentricity as well as conformism, fierce individualism as well as subordination to the group. It is the passion that engenders affection for a heroic leader as well as contempt for pitiful weaklings. It produces the striving for excellence and the acceptance of one's worm-like nullity.

It never occurs to Fukuyama that a concept that may explain so much might not explain anything at all. He should have distinguished more carefully among the passions, and more generally among passions, interests, and norms. Instead, he adheres confusingly to a crude opposition between the economistic and the non-economistic, employing the general category of non-materialistic motivation to cover both moral ideas and irrational impulses. But surely norms and passions—say, the idea of justice and the feeling of envy—should be kept distinct. Similarly, Fukuyama fails to distinguish between the man who risks his life "for the sake of higher, abstract principles and goals" and the man who does so "for the sole purpose of demonstrating that he has contempt for his own life." But attachment to moral norms is quite different from existential daredevilry. (Fukuyama does not worry about the relationship between irrational impulses and the higher ends of life.) And both of these motives are distinct from the impulse to prove one's superiority to another human being at risk of life and limb.

If democratic governments are everywhere replacing non-democratic ones, argues Fukuyama, it is because only democracy provides citizens with recognition from their government. Only democracy allows people to escape the humiliating status of dependency and to achieve the self-respect of autonomous adults. Fukuyama's presentation of this central point is vague. Did communism collapse because it was a fetter on the forces of production or because it failed to provide the moral recognition that individuals need and seek? (He sometimes advances the materialist claim, sometimes the non-materialist one.) And surely the desire for recognition does not necessitate the total victory of democracy: socialism may hurt human pride, but it may also gratify human envy. Moreover, there are many kinds of recognition. Some are liberal, some are not liberal. Fukuyama himself argues that Japanese culture offers workers recognition as team players, a highly stable kind of recognition that differs from the individualistic recognition granted in the West.

III.

Fukuyama first announces that liberal democracy satisfies every important longing in the human soul, and then explains that liberal democracy does not satisfy the most vital longing of all, which is *thymos*. The reason for that failure lies in the nature of *thymos*: it contains two contradictory drives—a desire for equal recognition and a desire for unequal recognition. In opposing the desire to be recognized as a superior with the desire to be recognized as an equal, Fukuyama draws a distinction that introduces a fundamental confusion into the meta-narrative he borrows from Kojève.

Following Kojève's analysis of the transition from aristocratic to egalitarian societies, Fukuyama describes the shift from "inherently unequal recognition" to "universal and reciprocal recognition" as a logical necessity. The desire for recognition-as-a-superior is irrational or internally incoherent, because who wants to be recognized by underlings and nobodies? Recognition as an equal by equals, by contrast, is wholly satisfying and wholly rational. This is an excellent point, although Fukuyama does not seem to appreciate its force as a democratic response to Nietzsche's aristocratic ideal.

Alexander Kojève was an egalitarian and a universalist. Fukuyama, finally, is not. The reason is that Leo Strauss (whose student, Allan Bloom, was Fukuyama's teacher) was not. Strauss was opposed to egalitarian ethics, as well as to any cosmopolitan weakening of national borders. Fukuyama, you might say, is stretched to the breaking point between Kojève and Strauss. For his larger argument, this is the most fatal tension of all.

Following Strauss, and in opposition to Kojève, Fukuyama expresses his deep and rather disturbing disapproval of "liberal democracy's tendency to grant equal recognition to unequal people." Treating unequals as equals is not at all rational, whatever Kojève may have claimed; and Strauss, convinced of the baseness of equality, opposed Kojève on these grounds. Fukuyama adopts this pose, emphasizing "the inherent contradictions in the concept of universal recognition." And he adopts the Straussian strategy of disguising his opposition to the norm of equality as outrage at "moral relativism." But then he also seems to take over Kojève's sincerely egalitarian position. Fukuyama-the-KojŠvian stresses the way universal education (a key feature of economic modernization) encourages people to demand recognition as moral beings. Fukuyama-the-Straussian despises this demand, declaring it an irrational request for the equal recognition of unequals.

Fukuyama presents himself at times as a cosmopolitan, like Kojève, adducing the European Community as a symbol for the borderless liberal world of the future. But he also appears as an anti-cosmopolitan, like Strauss, pointing out the political necessity of morally unjustifiable borders. He repeats the Jekyll-and-Hyde routine when discussing war. (What has been the main cause of war throughout all of human history? Why, *thymos,* of course.) In some passages, Fukuyama celebrates the end of inhuman and wasteful war. In others, he deplores pacification as a moral disaster, since armed confrontationalism tightens sinews and gives meaning to life.

In any case, warfare, too, has now become a thing of the past, because bourgeoisification has cooled man's original hot-bloodedness; the addiction to security and comfort accounts for "the fundamentally un-warlike character of liberal societies." It also explains why the planet is headed inevitably for perpetual peace. Why is deterrence no longer necessary in Western Europe? Why has the "realist" logic of power politics been suspended in the posthistorical zone? "Because most European states understand each other too well. They know that their neighbors are too self-indulgent and consumerist to risk death." Remember, our happy present moment is owed less to the strength of freedom than to the weakness of tyranny: liberal societies are weak-kneed appeasers. (This is contradicted by the history of wars between liberal states and nonliberal states, but never mind.) We are entering a world of sissy states, which will be a world of perpetual peace.

But all this is based on a fundamental misunderstanding of social life in a liberal order. In such an order, it must be recalled, not every complication is a contradiction. The existence of contrary urges, the coexistence of egalitarian impulses and anti-egalitarian impulses, the appetite for security and the desire for dignity, do not necessarily spell tragedy, or even instability, because a liberal society may be complex enough to admit both equalities and inequalities.

The typical pattern in liberal society is a combination of public equality and private inequality. Just as liberalism encourages self-assertion without violence, so it encour-

ages private and domesticated attempts to prove one's superiority so long as no coercive authority over others is the consequence. Seen this way, liberal democracy does not look eschatological. It is merely stable, and more fair. It satisfies both pride and envy. It allows individuals to be both equal and unequal. And this particular arrangement, for all its failure to satisfy those who hunger for an end, seems to be just about as admirable and as durable as any imperfect and rickety creation of human beings can hope to be.

The melancholy truth about Fukuyama is that in the end he fails to appreciate the higher values protected by liberal society. Quite the contrary. He asserts that the battle to throw off Communist tyranny was much more fulfilling than the life that will be achieved once liberal democracy is reliably installed in the ex-Communist states. The Chinese students "who stood up to tanks," the Romanian revolutionaries who battled Ceausescu's Securitate, the Lithuanians who fought the Russian black berets, the Russians around Yeltsin's White House: they enjoyed a high that is not available to the inhabitants of normal bourgeois societies. When bravely confronting their armed oppressors, they "were the most free and therefore the most human of beings." But what have they achieved? Not much. They may get VCRs and even passports, but their life will be void of drama and significance. In fact, their hard-won liberation totally destroys "the possibility of their ever again being as free and as human as in their revolutionary struggle."

In sum: becoming free is everything, being free is nothing. How can Fukuyama preach such a message to the millions of men and women still groaning under the bitter legacy of decades of totalitarian rule? Welcome, he tells them, you have just been released from Communist unhappiness into democratic meaninglessness. Welcome to the vacuum at the heart of liberal society, where life is no longer worth living. You are no longer admirable prisoners. You are now contemptible last men.

"Human life," Fukuyama observes from some point very high above human life, "involves a curious paradox: it seems to require injustice, for the struggle against injustice is what calls forth what is highest in man." How should we respond to this sagacity? We might advise Fukuyama, for a start, to have a look at the world around him. It contains ample pain and evil. It confronts human beings with multiple inner and outer struggles. Some are even ideological. Fukuyama may be right, of course, that Communist totalitarianism became a perverse crutch for some Western conservatives, but surely a respect for the all-too-real sufferings of those who lived for decades under that colossal lie rules out anything resembling nostalgia for it. As for Fukuyama's "deeper" suggestion that we need tyranny and war and struggle to make our lives worth living, that peace will bring emptiness and a collapse of meaning, suffice it to say that, whether or not history has ended, there is more to living humanly than living historically.

Alan Ryan (review date 26 March 1992)

SOURCE: "Professor Hegel Goes to Washington," in *New York Review of Books*, March 26, 1992, pp. 7-8, 10-3.

[*In the following review of* The End of History and the Last Man, *Ryan provides an overview of Fukuyama's historical and intellectual perspective and the book's appeal to conservative critics. Ryan objects to Fukuyama's historical determinism and assumptions about the nature of and inevitability of liberal democracy.*]

Francis Fukuyama's discovery of the end of history first came to the public's attention in the summer of 1989. The essay he wrote for *The National Interest* on **"The End of History?"** made the headlines in *Time, Newsweek,* and elsewhere; it was for a short time a truly global sensation. The news that history had ended aroused much disbelief. Even those who were glad that Fukuyama had declared that democracy was in no further danger from its rivals were not persuaded that this was because history had stopped. Indeed, the suggestion struck many readers as more or less mad; this seemed to be a time when history was happening everywhere and happening particularly fast. The announcement of the end of history coincided with the bloody repression of the Chinese democratization movement in Tiananmen Square, and only briefly preceded the fall of the Berlin Wall and the overthrow of Ceausescu.

Other readers, familiar with the work of Hegel, Marx, Nietzsche, and their interpreters, knew that what Mr. Fukuyama had in mind was not history but History, not the "tale told by an idiot, full of sound and fury, signifying nothing" that Macbeth railed against, and Henry Ford dismissed as "bunk," but "History as a Whole." They were less surprised by Mr. Fukuyama's discovery than by the furor it aroused. They remembered Herbert Marcuse announcing the end of history in *One Dimensional Man,* and Daniel Bell discovering "the end of ideology" some years before that. Mr. Fukuyama candidly admits that the tale he tells is an old one. Its author was a Russian emigré philosopher, Alexander Kojevchnikoff, better known as Alexandre Kojève, who in the mid-1930s began to lecture to the students of the Ecole Pratique des Hautes Etudes on Hegel's *Phenomenology of Spirit.* It was in these lectures that he first laid out Hegel's account of the end of history, an account he made his own, and one that Mr. Fukuyama has now popularized with a few modifications of his own.

Kojève's lectures evidently had a considerable charm; Raymond Aron, Sartre, and Merleau-Ponty attended them along with Georges Bataille, Jacques Lacan, Eric Weil, and many others. In 1947 the French novelist Raymond Queneau turned Kojève's lecture notes into a book entitled *Introduction . . . la lecture de Hegel.* Given Queneau's other work and Kojève's intellectual skittishness, I have always regretted that it wasn't called *Zazie dans la dialectique,* but one can't have everything.

The book seems not to have been well known in the United States—it was better known in Canada[1]—until it was partially translated in 1968. This version was edited by Allan Bloom, better known for *The Closing of the American Mind,* and one of Mr. Fukuyama's teachers at the University of Chicago. On the other side of the Atlantic, Kojève provided many students' first introduction to Hegel, even though he dealt with only one of Hegel's major works—the *Phenomenology of Spirit*—and seduced students into concentrating on only one section of that dense volume, the so-called "dialectic of lordship and bondage" or the "master-slave dialectic."

There were many reasons for the book's popularity. It was written with great panache, while Kojève made Hegel seem both intelligible and exciting, even if pretty far gone in megalomania. He picked out those aspects of Hegel that led most naturally to Marx on the one hand and to Heidegger on the other; he played down Hegel's philosophy, narrowly considered, and played up the historical sociology that was latent in his work. And he said a lot of strikingly implausible things about the politics of the twentieth century.

Kojève was a Marxist, but he spent the postwar years working for the greater glory, of corporate capitalism and the capitalist welfare state in the French Ministry of Economic Affairs, and then as a senior civil servant of the European Community; he died in Brussels in 1968. In what sense he was a "Marxist" is a bit mysterious. Perhaps his most famous opinion was that postwar America is a classless society which has little labor and high consumption, and therefore has realized Marx's aspirations.

> One can even say that from a certain point of view, the United States has already attained the final stage of Marxist "communism," seeing that, practically, all the members of a "classless society" can from now on appropriate for themselves everything that seems good to them, without thereby working, and the USSR gave me the impression that if the Americans give the impression of rich Sino-Soviets, it is because the Russians and Chinese are only Americans who are still poor but are rapidly proceeding to get richer.

So much for the cold war.

The End of History and the Last Man is not just warmed-over Kojève, nor is it just an inflated essay. It is a long book, and tackles a large number of questions—from staples of the op-ed pages such as the differences in American and Japanese work habits and the prospects for nationalism in Eastern Europe, to staples of undergraduate sociology such as the plausibility of an "economic interpretation of history." What makes it distinctive is its attempt to connect such issues with the two large themes gestured at in the title. Has History—*Weltgeschichte* with a Big H—come to an end? If it has, has it created a world in which only the projects of the *bons bourgeois* are possible? Are we doomed to be what Nietzsche dismissed as "last men," animals whose horizons are limited to securing their creature comforts?

The End of History and the Last Man is an easy book to summarize, and Fukuyama does it very well in his introduction. History has ended in the sense that there is no more room for large ideological battles. Liberal democracy is not merely triumphant, it is simply what there is, and all there can be. There is literally no more room for debate over fundamentals. What Kojève called the "universal and homogeneous state" has arrived, and it is liberal democracy. There are two reasons for its triumph. First, the growth of science and our increasing ability to dominate nature means that societies that are technologically effective dominate societies that are not. Part of the technique of dominating nature efficiently is to be properly organized, and the market, the capitalist firm, and the capitalist entrepreneur have proved to be uniquely efficient forms of organization. This is sociologically commonplace and amounts to the common coin of Marx and Weber.

Still, this does not explain how the modern organization of the economy happened, or how it ended in democracy. The second element is the irrational component in economic behavior that the sociology of Marx and Weber doesn't explain. This is "the search for recognition." We do not want only to satisfy our needs for food, shelter, sex, and comfort; we much more powerfully wish to establish ourselves as people to be reckoned with. Achilles sulked in his tent while the Achaean army failed to make any headway against the Trojans, not because the slavegirl Briseis was important as an item of consumption, but because he had lost face surrendering her to Agamemnon. Mankind is much more powerfully driven by the desire for recognition than by desires for a high standard of living. The mastery of nature owes more to the spirit of conquest than to economic calculation. A society, like our own, in which economic calculation holds sway is the by product of a history driven by the demand for recognition.

Why does this yield liberal democracy? Because this is the form of social order in which the desire for recognition can be satisfied by everyone. Each is recognized by all. It is stable, immune to subversion by outgroups who desire to be recognized but are not recognized. It is this that was Hegel's message. But the result is ambiguous. Nietzsche's complaint, echoed by Heidegger, was that the terms on which this was achieved destroyed the whole point of the search for recognition. As has rather too often been said. "If everybody's somebody, nobody's anybody." Worse yet, if there are no projects that are worth risking our lives for in the search for recognition, what is most distinctive in human life has gone. For Kojève, following Heidegger following Nietzsche, Americanization is a return to animal mindlessness. Fukuyama converted that hardly optimistic observation into the conclusion that history had ended in the triumph of the West.

In the two years since his original article appeared, Fukuyama has taken heed of the many critics his essay attracted. In the process, he has stripped his argument of much of its empirical content. The most obvious complaint against the view that the whole world is committed to liberal democracy is that most of it is not. Much of Asia is committed to some form of democracy, to the idea that

governments are accountable to their subjects, and must maintain constitutional rather than merely personal authority. But this is not *liberal* democracy; it is neither built on nor friendly to the moral individualism that underpins liberalism.[2] It is not concerned with our anxieties about the boundary between the private and the public; it is not worried as we are about keeping government authority out of our sexual, religious, intellectual, and moral allegiances. Lee Kuan Yew has called the system he has built "East Asian Confucian capitalism."

Fukuyama agrees and disagrees almost simultaneously. He has a chart of liberal democracies on which Singapore appears, and two discussions in the text in which Singapore is treated as an authoritarian and nonliberal political system. Japan gets the same contradictory treatment. This incoherence is hard to account for; it may be because he does not know what he really believes.

This suspicion is reinforced by the discrepancy between the bold statements of the beginning of the book and the hesitant tone he strikes three hundred pages later. To begin with. Fukuyama is sure that liberal democracy is the wave of the present and the future, and that any disturbances to the liberal hegemony will be brief localized, and unimportant. But in the last three chapters of the book, History threatens to begin all over again. Western societies are unsatisfying to their own members because they offer too little sense of community, the point on which Asiatic societies are strongest. Since he has already agreed that liberal democracy may not be as good for economic growth as a more authoritarian and more communalist social and political order. Fukuyama cannot but agree that more communitarian and authoritarian societies may succeed in the global competition, after all. But then where is the end of history? The "universal and homogeneous state" is not dictated by "rational desire" and "rational recognition" after all, or if it is, it manifests itself as nonliberal democracy.

He acknowledges, too, what the Berkeley political scientist Ken Jowitt has been arguing much more vividly, that the vast gap between the increasingly rich first world and a resentful but possibly nuclear-armed third world may lead to any amount of twenty-first-century violence, with unpredictable consequences.[3] Fukuyama is unable to decide whether this outcome would still be a triumph for the end of history thesis—since what the resentful third world resents is not being like the modernized first world—or a genuine departure for a different destination. If the third world isn't the source of something new, Fukuyama nonetheless wonders whether internal strife may undo countries like the United States. Indeed, he ends the book wondering whether we may not first converge on liberal democracy, and then head off in entirely new directions after all.

He spins an elaborate metaphor: history is like a pioneer wagon train heading for a distant town, with different wagons at different points, but all heading for the same place. But he ends uncertainly:

Alexandre Kojève believed that ultimately history itself would vindicate its own rationality. That is, enough wagons would pull into town such that any reasonable person looking at the situation would be forced to agree that there had been only one journey and one destination. It is doubtful that we are at that point now, for despite the recent worldwide liberal revolution, the evidence available to us now concerning the direction of the wagons' wanderings must remain provisionally inconclusive. Nor can we in the final analysis know, provided a majority of the wagons eventually reach the same town, whether their occupants, having looked around a bit at their new surroundings, will not find them inadequate and set their eyes on a new and more distant journey.

This last thought is simply inconsistent with what purports to be the philosophical basis of the end of history thesis.

Read unsympathetically, *The End of History and the Last Man* is a string of op-ed page speculations. No subject receives more than a page or two of discussion. While every issue is interesting, and Fukuyama writes agreeably enough, his treatment rarely rises above the banal. Yet the book comes encrusted with tributes to its brilliance from George Will, Charles Krauthammer, Irving Kristol, and Tom Wolfe, none of whom is especially stupid or easily deceived. It is easy enough to see that George Gilder has misread the whole thing[4] and believes that it is a hymn to laissez faire; but George Will at least should know better than that. There must be something going on whose attractions are not immediately visible.

One attraction is that Fukuyama likes asking Big Questions, and much of the world likes Big Questions, too. Fukuyama doesn't just argue that liberal democracy is the only political option now open; he argues that liberal democracy is the meaning of history. The authority for this claim is Hegel-as-filtered-through-Kojève. It is an odd place to turn for metaphysical reassurance, however. Anyone who has read any Hegel knows that Hegel did not think that liberal democracy was where history would end. Hegel thought that the ultimate form of political association was a rational legal state, but it would be explicitly antidemocratic, and liberal only in its attachment to the rule of law. Crucially, Hegel had no time for the individualism that Americans regard as the very heart of liberalism. He insisted on the priority of the state to the individual, insisted that individuals had no rights against the state, said that the common people should be "simultaneously respected and scorned," and offered as the most rational form of modern political association something much more interesting than Fukuyama, namely the corporate state.

Pace Kojève and Fukuyama, the Hegelian state was not "homogeneous," that is, classless, other than in the sense that the rule of law applied to everyone—which was also the only sense in which it was "universal." Hegel was explicit about the need to balance the marketplace with legally recognized corporations, about the need for a hereditary, agrarian element in the state, about making representation corporate rather than individual, and about doing what could be done to control capitalism as well as

allow its modernizing effects full play. Fukuyama says that few Americans read Hegel, because he is thought to be difficult and metaphysical. Fukuyama appears to be among their number, for the truth is that Hegel's *Philosophy of Right* is not in the least difficult; it just happens to say pretty much the opposite of what he claims.

Fukuyama, like Kojève, rests his case on the *Phenomenology of Spirit*. The *Phenomenology* is difficult, partly because Hegel finished it in a hurry, and it is unclear whether it says what he wanted to say or not. It is in fact hard to say just what the book is about. At one level it seems to be the autobiography of God, insofar as God manifests Himself in human culture. At another level, it is a history of human consciousness, both the way individual minds develop and the way cultures develop characteristic ways of thinking. Politics occupies a fairly lowly place in such an enterprise; art, religion, and philosophy are much more salient. Kojève somewhat vulgarizes the entire project by turning it into sociology; Fukuyama vulgarizes it entirely. Having taken the high ground by insisting that we need to give an account of History as a Whole, a project that Hegel called "the true theodicy." Fukuyama reassures his readers a dozen pages later that the philosophy of history has nothing to do with religion. This is either incoherent or disingenuous.

In the first place, it misrepresents the driving force behind the philosophy of history, even on Fukuyama's own account. Fukuyama himself observes that the philosophy of history, in the sense in which it is concerned with the "meaning" of the entire historical process, is a secular holdover from Christian eschatology. Greek and Roman philosophers thought history was cyclical and repetitive just like any other natural process; Machiavelli, whom Fukuyama mysteriously believes to have been the founder of modern historicism, followed his classical masters in thinking the same. The Judeo-Christian tradition was anticlassical in thinking that history had a definite dramatic shape, with a beginning, a middle, and a conclusion. It was the Christian image of History as a three-act play— Fall, Suffering, Redemption—that found its way into Kant's philosophy of history, into Hegel's and eventually into Marx's supposedly empirical and sociological "materialist conception of history." President Bush tells us that it was with God's help that America won the cold war and defeated Saddam Hussein; Fukuyama's God is History-with-a-Big-H.

Disclaiming any religious intention misrepresents Hegel's philosophy. There is an old tradition, started immediately after Hegel's death, that Hegel was an atheist whose talk of God was simply a ruse to deceive his Prussian employers, and Kojève subscribed to that view. Much of his *Introduction . . . la lecture de Hegel* is devoted to the idea that Hegel's atheism consists in his treating God as a sort of allegory for Man. But all the evidence we have tells us that Hegel was a Lutheran who thought that the truths presented pictorially and imaginatively in religion needed to be represented plainly and rationally in philosophy if they were to be rationally discussed. The point of the philosophy of history was theodicy, to justify the ways of God to man, or, more philosophically, to show people that they could not rationally wish the world to be other than it is. As Hegel says at the end of *The Philosophy of History,* thus we see that this process is not only not without God but is always and everywhere God's work. Passing off the *Phenomenology* as sociology misses the point of Hegel's Idealism. Unless the *Phenomenology* can explain history as the work of Spirit, history is one damned thing after another, an empirical, not an intelligible, process.

Hegel did after a fashion present the modern world as coming "at the end of history." But Fukuyama is deaf to the multiple ambiguities in Hegel's account. Hegel claimed that history was the history of freedom. The freedom in question was not political freedom, but the "rational self-direction" that Isaiah Berlin has baptized "positive liberty." Freedom was not a matter of indeterminacy or randomness—a child who replies "nine" or "six" or "five" at random, when asked to add four and three, is not displaying freedom but mathematical incapacity. A mathematician knows that "seven" is the only thing to say, but "seven" is not forced upon him; it is not an external reality to which he has to conform. Rather, when counting properly there is only one route to go. How this rationalist view of freedom is to be applied in each sphere of life is hotly debated; what is not open to dispute is that Hegel's conception of freedom is "rational freedom." One reason why he never captured the hearts of English commentators was that he thought English "laissez faire" mistook chaos for freedom.

Fukuyama knows this, I think, though he has nothing to say about the ways in which liberal democracy does (or more plausibly does *not*) sustain rational freedom. His interest is exhausted by the claim that the achievement of freedom means the end of history. Even here, he is deaf to nuance. Hegel's view that history had ended rests on a simple triadic account of the history of freedom. Once, there was prehistory, when mankind lived in something other than organized political society, nomadic tribes, scattered families gardening in the bush, and so on. History began with Persian despotism. Here the discovery of the human will took place. *One* person, the despot, was free. Freedom had arrived in the world, but as the possession of one man, and manifested as arbitrary rule. Its next manifestation was in the Greek polis, which was law-abiding, self-governing, and independent of other states, but which restricted freedom to a small number of its inhabitants—citizenship was confined to free, adult, native-born males, who were capable of fighting for their country, and whose independence was guaranteed by their ownership of enough land to live on.

Like most German philosophers Hegel had hankered after the classical republics in his youth, and as a young man he had gone off with Schiller to plant a "freedom tree" in celebration of the outbreak of the French Revolution. But by the time he wrote the *Phenomenology of Spirit* and even more so when he wrote *The Philosophy of Right* and *The Philosophy of History,* he had decided that classical citizenship represented a form of freedom that was beneath the moral and intellectual level of the modern world. The truth represented by the modern world was that "man as such is free." It is this slogan that Fukuyama latches on to.

But when did mankind discover that "man as such is free"? Kojève identified the end of history with the work of the French Revolution, and claimed that "Robespierre-Napoleon" was a world-historical individual whose tyrannical eruption into European history paved the way for the "universal and homogeneous" state. On that view, the battle of Jena at which Napoleon defeated the combined forces of Austria and Prussia in 1806 really was the end of history, and when Hegel saw Napoleon ride into the captured city of Jena he really had "seen the Spirit of the World crowned and riding on a horse." For Kojève it was a comforting creed, since it suggested that Stalin and Hitler, too, were just quirky ways in which the "cunning of reason" had chosen to work out the implications of Napoleon's victory over the *ancien régime.* Matters had been settled at Jena, and were merely ratified by Stalingrad and Hiroshima.

But this is a peculiar rendition of Hegel's ideas. Hegel frequently claimed that the discovery that freedom was the human essence became a world-historical doctrine with Martin Luther and the Protestant Reformation. He sometimes traced it back much earlier than that. He suggested that Socrates' appeal to the dictates of his own individual daemon against the common opinion of Athenian democracy first launched the thought; and Nietzsche's distaste for Socrates certainly rested on the view that conscientious dissent was destructive of the solidarity of the Greek polis. Hegel also suggested that Roman law manifested a commitment to individualism in that every individual was treated as a legal person, subject to and protected by the law. His taste for contradiction, of course, was gratified by the way the Roman Empire simultaneously reduced the value of citizenship by subjecting everyone to the power of the emperor and elevated individuality by insisting on the omnipresence of the law.

The rights of conscience, legal individuality, and the capacity to own property all form elements of modern freedom, and Hegel thought modern society could, in principle, realize them, though only insofar as its members were taught to demand their rights within its limits. Was this the end of history? In one sense, yes. The history of the concept of freedom must come to an end once "man as such is free"—the triad "one, some all" extends no further. But this is a purely verbal point. It does nothing to settle the question whether our exploration of rational freedom itself has any boundaries. Socrates died twenty-three centuries ago, and it would be hard to deny that fundamental changes have taken place since then: Luther died four centuries ago, and changes almost as fundamental have taken place since then; even the hundred and sixty years since Hegel's death have been rich in fundamental changes. All of which makes one wonder quite what Hegel had in mind, if he thought that further fundamental transformations were out of the question.

My own view is that Hegel was much more ambivalent and ambiguous than Fukuyama supposes. Hegel's vision of philosophy as an ascent to Absolute knowledge meant that serious philosophy had to represent itself as summing up all previous thought, all human history, all cultural achievement; but there was a pathos about this, since any serious philosopher also understood that previous philosophies had been superseded in ways their creators could not have foreseen. By the same token, any philosophy of history is retrospective, viewing the historical process as leading up to the present, and refusing to predict the future. In his introduction to *The Philosophy of Right* Hegel famously declared that "the Owl of Minerva only flies at dusk." Philosophy paints in "grey on grey"; it looks backward, and "paints a form of life grown old." This is far from triumphalist, and suggests that Hegel's view was that new forms of life might arise, but that it was not up to philosophers to predict them.

What of the "last man" in Fukuyama's title? Kojève and Fukuyama both make much of the passage in *Phenomenology* in which Hegel raised the question of how human beings distinguish themselves from the outside world. Characteristically, Hegel thought that eating things, burning them to keep warm, using them in general, made a metaphysical point: conscious beings were more important than mere nature. The dialectic of master and slave starts from the thought that we are inclined to treat other people as if they were part of nature, too; we want to use them. But since they are people, not mere things, we want to make a particular kind of use of them. We want them to acknowledge that our purposes are their purposes, that we count and they do not. This sets up an obvious conflict—for they see us in the same light. It is a conflict with no room for negotiation; either I am the one who matters or *You* are. It seems clear that Hegel had in mind the heroic ethos represented in Homeric poetry as an example of what it was like to be driven by this urge to impose one's will upon all comers.

This conflict of aspirations leads to a struggle to the death. Since it is our life that gives us value, we are not serious unless we risk it. But, a fight in which both parties die is no good; nor is one in which one party dies, since what we are after is recognition, and you can't get that from a corpse. The struggle must divide mankind into masters and slaves. The slave is defined by his fear of death, the master by his willingness to hazard his life. Which holds the key to the human future? Paradoxically, the slave. The slave owner is typically idle, perhaps a splendid beast, exciting to watch in battle, but otherwise conservative and unimaginative. The slave has to work, and in the process learns what human creativity is capable of. He also knows what it is like to be recognized as a person, since he recognizes the master as one. The slave thus knows what recognition of one another as equals would be like.

To abbreviate Hegel's very long story, human freedom is achieved in a society whose members recognize each other as free and equal citizens. This freedom and equality is, once more, not that of liberal individualism, but that of the corporate state—the Napoleonic ideal. What Hegel does not ask—or Kojève for that matter—is whether the end results are particularly attractive. Kojève observes in passing that if human beings were made human by the historical struggle, they will cease to be human once the struggle is over. With the Americanization of the world, we shall become superior animals; strictly speaking, we shall have no culture, no art, no romantic love, and none of the passions that once drove history. The heavily ironic tone of much of the *Introduction* makes it hard to know what we are supposed to make of it all. It is made harder by a footnote which Kojève added after visiting Japan in 1959. Here he says that an alternative to American mindlessness is Japanese snobbery—equally unhistorical, formal, and empty, but undeniably a human achievement. Again, it is hard to know what to make of the thought, all the more so when Kojève assured an interviewer who raised the matter just before Kojève's death in 1968 that he was merely playing when he wrote it, and was playing with his interviewer now.

Fukuyama knows what he makes of the thought. Unlike those who read him as a simple triumphalist, he is alarmed by the idea that the end of history will produce people who only want high levels of consumption, enjoyable leisure activities, and security. He mentions the possibility that Wall Street traders, makers of Donald Trump-like deals, and similar heroes of the acquisitive culture may find enough challenges in such activities to keep the appetite for heroic risk-taking satisfied. He doesn't believe it; he thinks graduates troop into law schools like sheep. He is well read enough to know that for Nietzsche nothing would do except risking one's life. If the test of character is the ability to face annihilation without flinching, all other forms of risk-taking are surrogates; conversely, if risking your life is simply a leisure activity, as it is in rock climbing or hang gliding, it simply can't matter in the way courage in battle did for Hector and Achilles. Those who complain that victory in the cold war is less exciting than it ought to be have their answer. It is as exciting as the end of History allows—not very exciting at all.

Although Fukuyama's *éclat* comes from the way he throws Hegel and Nietzsche into the post-cold war debate, much of his book is sociological rather than philosophical. This is especially true of the long argument to the effect that industrialism is inescapable, and that capitalist industrialism is a lot more efficient than the alternatives. On all this, his views are orthodox and sensible. Where it is hard to know what really causes what, he is properly reticent. Thus, he considers explanations for the economic troubles of Latin America—Catholicism rather than the Protestant ethic, feudal assumptions among both the elites and the workers, misguided attempts at self-sufficiency rather than specialization for the international market—but does not settle for any one in particular.

The same readiness to canvass all possibilities comes out in his discussion of the prospects for international peace and security. Observing that no liberal democracies have ever fought each other—the British burned Washington in the War of 1812, but that hardly counts—he is sanguine about a future in which the world is full of liberal democracies. Whether they will fight the third world he cannot say. He notices in passing that one prospect is vast population movements as third world and recently emancipated second world peoples try to get into Western Europe and the United States; but whether this will result in mayhem is again too hard to predict.

It is hard to quarrel with such reticence. If History is at an end, particular events certainly are not, and only a fool would risk his reputation by predicting the course of either domestic or international affairs over the next ten years. It is much easier to quarrel with the extraordinary analytical looseness with which Fukuyama tackles the issue on which he is decisive, namely the irreversibility of the liberal-democratic solution to our ills. Part of the problem is that he seems to have a complete contempt for history in the usual sense, and part is that he seems to have no imagination.

So far as history goes, the text suggests that he believes that Britain was a "liberal democracy" in 1848, and the US in 1790, even though he defines democracy in terms of full adult suffrage—which Britain did not achieve until 1928 and even the US only in 1919. Turn to his footnotes, and he points this out himself, arguing that we can still call them "democracies" when they do not fit his own criteria. This is impossible, since it ignores the central question raised by the horrors of the twentieth century—whether mass democracy is consistent with liberal values, and whether capitalism can work smoothly in anything other than a corporatist environment. That Fukuyama does not see this is not surprising, for analytically, he seems to have no idea what "liberal" means.

The index of the book is a giveaway: Tocqueville is well represented, Jefferson hardly appears, and Mill not at all. Nobody who took liberalism seriously could think that the best guides to liberalism are the illiberal Hegel and the Stalinist Kojève—in the footnotes Fukuyama does his not very convincing best to claim Kojève as a liberal, but the task is hopeless. When the question confronting Americans today is whether the chaotic but undeniably liberal democracy that they have inherited from the Founding Fathers is any match for the corporatism of Japan and a united Europe, it won't do to lump all regimes other than centrally planned Communist dictatorships together and call them liberal democracies. It is only from an altitude so great that most of human life is invisible that Japan and the United States could be passed off as examples of the same socio-political system.

As to the longer future, how can we tell what novelties mankind might come up with? Only nine years ago Jean-François Revel made a great hit with *Why Democracies*

Perish. At the time, many people pointed out that they weren't perishing in any great number, but M. Revel was not much deterred. The logic of democracy was to perish, and if communism somehow failed to be the cause of their perishing, something else would show up to do it. Now we have Mr. Fukuyama telling us that democracies not only do not perish, but are inscribed in History. Economic, political, and cultural divergence is ruled out for ever. This claim is made at a time when world population is growing far too fast, when religious fundamentalism is increasing, and when we have no idea how to resolve our environmental problems at a reasonable cost, to name only a few of the central issues of which Fukuyama hardly seems aware. Innumerable problems will surely demand new institutional, cultural, and psychological resources to adapt to them, and it takes an astonishing smugness to think that "more of the same" will be enough, and an extraordinary lack of imagination to believe that we are incapable of thinking of something new.

Nor is it so clear that spontaneous cultural divergence has become impossible. It was not History that imposed a sort of democracy on Japan, but two nuclear attacks and an American occupation. It was not the inefficiency of Nazism that brought multiparty democracy and welfare capitalism to the Federal Republic of Germany, but millions of dead and wounded at Stalingrad and in Hamburg, Dresden, and Berlin. These were not societies whose inhabitants spontaneously gave up on them and turned to "the West." They were bombed, beaten, and occupied into democracy. Why should we think the People's Republic of China is going to develop into a larger version of the US? There will be technological convergence, but why should there be cultural convergence? Of course, it's hard to imagine what dramatic changes will take place. But history has always taken us by surprise.

It remains, in the end, a puzzle that Mr. Fukuyama is such a darling of American conservatives. It's not as though the US were Britain where conservative intellectuals are a rare breed; they are to be found in droves in think tanks, on newspapers, and on television programs, interning away for conservative politicians, and word processing in assorted foundation offices. Still, they are usually employed to comment on matters of the day, rather than deliver the judgments of world history. What is puzzling is why the idea that "Professor Hegel goes to Washington" has become popular. Why should people sleep more soundly for thinking that a dead Prussian philosopher and his eccentric French interpreter have certified them as the final products of History as a Whole?

The only explanation I can think of comes from Voltaire's *Candide*. Candide's tutor, Dr. Pangloss, held that this was the best of all possible worlds, and every evil a necessary evil. *Candide* is an outraged satire on the very idea that this could be the best of all possible worlds, and a savage commentary on the idea that its evils are necessary. Mr. Fukuyama is the conservative's Dr. Pangloss. If what we've got is what History with a capital H intends for us, then we, too, live in the best of all possible worlds, and if it remains a bit of a mess, this is a necessary mess. Meanwhile the comfortable and conservative may bask in the thought that their privileges come with the blessing of History; they can display high seriousness by writing elegant essays on the low cultural level of consumer society, and display a decent compassion for those who have fallen off the historical bus before it ever got to the consumer society. But above all, they can settle for the politics of business as usual. It used to be said that the Church of England was "the Tory Party at prayer." The United States has never had an established church, and conservatives may have felt the lack of it. Mr. Fukuyama has provided them a Hegelian prayer book, for which they are properly grateful.

Notes

1. See Tom Darby's discussion of Kojève in *The Feast* (University of Toronto Press, 1982; 1990); the preface to the 1990 edition contains some acerbic criticism of Fukuyama's 1989 essay, which Darby sees as a simple ideological exercise in celebrating the triumph of Western liberalism. Darby's view is that "there are no winners."

2. This point has been made with some authority by Li Xianglu, the former secretary for economic reform in the government of the reformist Chinese prime minister Zhao Ziyang. In an essay in the Winter 1992 number of *New Perspectives* he says of Singapore that "its core values are not Western liberalism or individualism and it may yet evolve into a system posing a challenge to the West. China is likely to follow this alternative path." (p. 15).

3. His *New World Disorder: The Leninist Extinction* (University of California Press, to be published in April 1992), has some very sharp and anxious things to say about the dangers to world peace posed by "American liberal absolutism," and the seeming incapacity of American politicians to embrace the idea of sharing global influence with Japan and a united Europe, as well as the prospects of continued disorder in an impoverished and bitter third world.

4. Reviewing Fukuyama in *The Washington Post*, Gilder even contrives to include a plug for a capital gains tax cut in his essay.

John Gray (review date 11 May 1992)

SOURCE: "Cleopatra's Nose," in *National Review*, May 11, 1992, pp. 46-8.

[*In the following review, Gray offers unfavorable assessment of* The End of History and the Last Man.]

In his brilliant, ingenious, but nevertheless deeply unhistorical and ultimately absurd book, Francis Fukuyama argues that History—understood, in Hegelian-Marxist terms, to mean ideology—is over. With the collapse of Communism, there remains no legitimate alternative to liberal democracy, which is therefore the final form of human government. Wars and revolutions, tyrannies and dictatorships, may yet come and go, so that history understood as the events historians study will doubtless drag on; but History as the contestation over economic and political systems has come to an end. Only liberal democracy can satisfy the universal human need for self-recognition, or *thymos*—the Platonic virtue of spiritedness. Fukuyama acknowledges fundamentalism and nationalism to be powerful forces currently at large in the world; but he interprets them as reactive phenomena, responses to oppression or to over-rapid modernization, with little power of their own. We need not fear another century of global wars, as we creep nervously into the new millennium. We have more to fear, according to Fukuyama—following Nietzsche and perhaps Weber—from the boredom that flows from the rationalization of the world. It is Nietzsche's Last Men, not his blond beasts, that herald the mild and gentle Apocalypse to come.

Fukuyama is right that we are seeing the end of ideology—that is to say, of those secular religions, or political faiths, that we inherited from the Enlightenment and from its nineteenth-century followers, such as Marx. He does not notice, however, that the end of ideology encompasses the euthanasia of liberalism—that tottering political faith his book is devoted to propping up. The post-Soviet peoples have not shaken off one nineteenth-century ideology, Marxism, to adopt another, liberalism; none of them ever accepted the former, and few the latter. They have instead returned to their immemorial ethnic and cultural identities, national and religious, with all the ancient enmities they carry with them. The post-Communist peoples do not express their *thymos* by wishing to become producers and consumers in a global market, or rights-bearers in a universal liberal democracy; they express it by the demand for nationhood, as Armenians or Georgians, Lithuanians or Russians, and by the reassertion (as in the former Soviet Central Asia) of their traditional religious identities. For the post-Communist peoples, history has not ended. Instead, after decades of interruption, it has been resumed.

Our author—referred to in Japan, pointedly, as "the American writer Fukuyama"—is able to pass over these evident facts because, despite himself, he is propounding a secular theodicy, a directional and teleological interpretation of history—in which history's *telos* is, of course, *us*. The notion that human history has a goal or *telos*, and the related notion that it is possible to write a Universal History of Mankind, makes sense, if at all, only when based on religious suppositions, such as the Christian idea of Providence that animates Edmund Burke's whiggish interpretation of history. Yet religion is wholly absent from Fukuyama's thought, except as an inconvenient (and ephemeral) impediment to the global tranquilization he thinks is our fate. (The banal and insipid quality of the godlessness that pervades Fukuyama's book is in stark contrast with the atheism of one of his mentors, Nietzsche, which is—rightly—suffused with anguish and despair.) Fukuyama tells us that "liberalism vanquished religion in Europe"—a statement that will come as a surprise to the ordinary denizen of Belfast, but may be unsurprising coming from one who, in his lectures in Britain, referred to the English Civil War as a conflict between Protestants and Catholics. The idea that religious faith has been domesticated and privatized, and thereby nullified as a force in political life, may well have some plausibility in England today; but it is not true of contemporary Germany, say, and it is ludicrously false in respect of the United States, whose public and political life is pervaded by religious ideas and values.

The Mechanism (his term) that Fukuyama invokes to sustain the directionality of history is, in fact, a compound of two ideas: Hegel's morality tale of the dialectic of Master and Slave, as interpreted by Fukuyama's other mentor, and interpreter of Hegel, Alexandre Kojève; and what Fukuyama himself describes as "a kind of Marxist interpretation of history that leads to a completely non-Marxist conclusion"—namely, an economic interpretation of history that explains the growth of human productive powers by the development of scientific knowledge and its exploitation by human beings to satisfy their desires.

The trouble with this Mechanism of Fukuyama's is the trouble with Marxism—it is monocausal and overly deterministic. It is true that the Communist regimes fell partly because of the ruinous poverty they presided over, but it is also true, as the author himself admits, that they fell because their subject peoples perceived them as illegitimate, and their rulers had lost the will to rule by terror. The same point may be put in more general and more philosophical terms. While it is true that human history exhibits tendencies and perhaps even cycles, these are always subject to contingency, to the forces of chance and accident. (Would the Bolshevik regime have survived if the bullet fired at Lenin by his would-be assassin, Fanny Kaplan, had in fact killed him?) Cleopatra's nose is a better guide to history than Fukuyama's Mechanism.

Whatever slight plausibility the Mechanism might possess derives entirely from the truly fantastic abstractness of Fukuyama's account of recent history. Accordingly, in a table plainly designed to overwhelm the reader with a sense of the virtually irresistible charm of liberal democracy, we learn that among the 61 liberal democracies that existed in 1990 are Rumania and Japan, Bulgaria and Great Britain, Sri Lanka and Papua New Guinea—all listed as examples of a single form of government. It is hardly necessary to comment on the Monty Pythonish character of this categorization. Rumania certainly, and Bulgaria probably, remain ruled by manipulative Bolshevik cliques; Britain retains (so far) an adversarial parliamentary system, but Japan has single-party rule, and the most significant decisions are not taken in the political realm at all; and so on. Again, our author tells us that "Contemporary liberal democracies did not emerge out of the shadowy mists of tradition. Like Communist societies they were deliberately created by human beings at a definite point in time." But the world's genuine liberal democracies have very different histories: democracy in England *did* "emerge out of the shadowy mists of tradition," as it did in the Low Countries and perhaps also in Scandinavia. As at many other points, Fukuyama here implicitly deploys the United States as a paradigm, when it is in truth a limiting case.

It would be easy, but mistaken, to write of Fukuyama's treatise as an exercise in a genre as charmingly dated as heraldry or metaphysical history, and as practically irrelevant. This would be a grave error, since Fukuyama's Panglossian (or Pollyannaish) vision has undoubted appeal to some sectors of conservative opinion, and it has real and dangerous implications for policy. Consider his account of universal convergence on democratic capitalism. This implies that the "systems debate"—the debate about which economic and political institutions' are best for modern industrial societies—is over, when in fact one such debate has merely replaced another. The model of the socialist command economy has indeed been removed from the political and intellectual agenda, and a consensus reached on the indispensability of market institutions as vehicles for the self-reproduction of modern societies. The debate now is over *which variety* of market institution is to be adopted in the post-Communist states and in the developing world. Is the model of market institutions that of Anglo-American democratic capitalism, or is it that of German neo-corporatism, or East Asian *dirigisme* under authoritarian political auspices? If present trends are any guide, the new systemic debate is going against the model of democratic capitalism, with China opting for authoritarian development on the Japanese and South Korean models, and Russia oscillating uncertainly between a more or less Chilean model of capitalist development and the East Asian example. The Olympian abstraction of Fukuyama's account obscures this important debate.

Or consider the implications of Fukuyama's tranquilly apocalyptic vision for strategic and security policy. If fundamentalism is transitional and transitory and has no long-range political importance; if nationalism is fated to become a matter of private cultural preference, like tastes in ethnic cuisine; if we can expect a universal convergence on liberal democratic institutions, and these are inherently non-aggressive—if these premises are all granted, what need will the Western powers then have for national defense? If we are entering a world whose chief evil is boredom, it would seem not at all unreasonable to cut defense expenditure to the bone—as is, in fact, currently the trend, especially in the United States. All this assumes that the world after the unraveling of the postwar settlement will be a peaceful world, and it panders to the hopes and illusions of democracies, such as the United States, that lack strong martial traditions. Worse, Fukuyama's argument supports the groundless claim that modern states are by nature post-military societies in which national defense is unnecessary or optional. It is hard to think of a more perilous or debilitating idea.

A far truer, and much darker, picture of our likely future is given in the recent book *Le nouveau monde de l'ordre de Yalta au chaos des nations* (Paris: Gasset, 1992), by Pierre Lellouche, foreign-policy advisor to Jacques Chirac, leader of the Gaullist opposition in France. For Lellouche, the undoing of the postwar settlement inaugurates a desperately dangerous period for the world—a period in which the United States retreats as a global power and exhibits ever more of the traits of the Latin American states, in which the mirage of a federal superstate in Europe is dissipated by the re-emergence of immemorial national rivalries, and in which most of the post-Communist countries, including Russia, turn to forms of dictatorship and authoritarianism.

If this is so, the coming century looks to be, not the end of history, but a tragic epoch in which history is resumed along traditional lines, but on a far vaster scale—an epoch of Malthusian wars and religious and ethnic convulsions, of ecological catastrophes, forced migrations, and mass deaths overshadowing those of our century. It will be an epoch in which the uncontrolled proliferation of technologies of mass destruction shifts the balance of advantage of nuclear deterrence from the North to the anarchic South and in which (because of their economic success, and because neither of them is emulating the unilateral military self-emasculation of the Western powers) Japan and China are set to overturn the Occidental supremacy of the past few centuries. It is hard to avoid the suspicion that, with these great geopolitical changes afoot, and with the United States seemingly bent on repeating on a grander scale the historical experience of Argentina, but in a context in which the crumbling Leviathan of the Federal Government presides over a Hobbesian anarchy of warring ethnicities, Fukuyama's book will have to endure the mockery of fate, as we shuffle, exhausted and blinking, back onto the classical terrain, harsh but familiar, of history and human tragedy.

Peter Fritzsche (review date June 1992)

SOURCE: A review of *The End of History and the Last Man,* in *American Historical Review* Vol. 97, No. 3, June, 1992, pp. 817-9.

[*In the following review, Fritzsche provides analysis of Fukuyama's argument in* The End of History and the Last Man.]

Francis Fukuyama would not be at the RAND Corporation if he were an avowed postmodernist. But the implication of his thoughtful essay point in just that direction. Like many cultural theorists today, Fukuyama argues that there are no longer any overarching plots or designs that give prescribed meaning to our political endeavors. History with a capital "H" has come to an end, although the lower-case history of births and deaths and private aspirations persists. This is the case because the twentieth century has knocked out all the ideological challengers to the principles

of the liberal democratic order. "The last man" left standing is a democrat and a capitalist. And once there is a winner, there is no longer a contest. This Last Man has concluded History.

In similar fashion, postmodern critics in the 1990s have taken pains to distinguish themselves from their modernist counterparts of the 1890s, who still sought some order in the grand narratives and unified subjects of History. That Marxism, with its story-line of class struggle and its well-known proletarian subject, has crumbled as an intellectual tool in the academy is a striking indication of the present-day postmodernist sensibility. Both Fukuyama and postmodernists agree that the recent past is different from the present because yesterday was experienced as a dramatic contest of ideologies in a way that today is not. The only difference is that Fukuyama believes the contest to have been won while postmodernists argue that it was all theater to begin with. In either case, today, tomorrow, and the day after will simply proceed without a new or believable narrative in place to give events any coherence, a predicament of drift that is both novel and terrifying and poses once again Nietzsche's questions about the diminution of the human spirit.

Moreover, Fukuyama implicitly questions the further usefulness of historians since any meaning invested in the reading and writing of history depends in large part on the validity of grand narratives, partisan purposes, and good causes. Without these, history books become aimless, antiquarian, merely interesting. The end of History is thus the end of a genre, although not the foreclosure of events themselves.

The end of History rests on the victory of liberal democracy and capitalist economics. According to Fukuyama, no other competing system of thought has survived the twentieth century. The key dates denoting liberalism's triumph are 1945, the year the Allies defeated Nazism, and 1989, the year that marked the collapse of communism. Whatever the misgivings about democracy or capitalism, misgivings that Fukuyama is willing to concede, no one today imagines a radically better future that is not essentially democratic and capitalist. To be sure, the delights of the liberal order have yet to reach everybody, a process that might take several generations. But even if they do not, the incompleteness of liberalism is not necessarily its invalidation. According to Fukuyama, who in turn leans on Hegel and Alexandre Kojève, history only moves forward when the contradictions of one system give way to basic alternatives.

All the crushing poverty and bruising political tyranny around the world does not add up to an alternative order. If the rest of time is simply testimony to the incompleteness or slow implementation of liberalism's promises, it would still be the case, for Fukuyama, that History has ended. This is a point most of Fukuyama's critics have misunderstood. The idea of the end of History is not an argument for the rightness of all things. Fukuyama is not replaying Pangloss, even if he is too strident in his applause for Western politics and Western economics. Rather, Fukuyama's news is that we have stopped thinking about what might lie beyond capitalism and democracy. All that goes on now is tinkering with a system that variations such as Swedish-style social democracy and Reaganomics leave basically intact. In a fundamental way, Fukuyama asserts that we have all become neoconservatives; even leftists are mostly lapsed Marxists who are now simply social democrats. This disenchantment might be sad, but it rings true.

There are powerful reasons for the triumph of the liberal order. Fukuyama argues that 400 years of military and mercantile competition required states in Europe and elsewhere to adhere to rational and scientific principles. If this revamping of structural-functionalism and modernization theory explains the victory of capitalism, it is not sufficient to explain the ultimate triumph of democracy, which Fukuyama argues is the endpoint of humanity's species-unique struggle for recognition or *thymos*.

Fukuyama insists that the origins of democracy are to be found in the willingness of men and women to risk comfort and security in order to attain liberty and dignity, a point he makes by profitably comparing Hobbes with Hegel. Both philosophers agreed that people often act to gain prestige as individuals. These irrational endeavors lead to unfortunate episodes of imperialism and domination. It is precisely this self-proclaimed ethic of aristocratic mastery that Hobbes saw as the barrier to well-ordered government. Once citizens agree to live rationally by submitting to the laws of the monarch, they avoid the horrors to which irrational vanity leads. For Hegel, the Hobbesian submission to the state is little more than slavery, and vanity's contempt for this "mere life" is the beginning of freedom. The conditions of liberty are secured only once the slaves conceive in universal and this-worldly terms the freedom that nobles had once acquired one-by-one. History ends with the final revolt of the slaves, which Hegel identified as the French Revolution.

If all this sounds familiar it is because Fukuyama overstates the originality of his argument and, in fact, closely follows "the march of progress" that is still embedded in many modern history courses. Remember the class? German and Russian misdevelopment accents the righteous path of France, Britain, and the United States. For all the wrenching pessimism about the authenticity of progress that Fukuyama laments in post-Holocaust thought, the story of the twentieth century is told from what Michael Geyer has termed a North Atlantic or NATO perspective that invariably leads to a happy ending. It was in this North Atlantic realm that weak feudal traditions, more languorous industrialization, and strong civic traditions supposedly favored the advance of political democracy and measured social reform. By contrast, Germany's rise to nationhood after 1870 was turbulent in the extreme and turn-of-the-century Russia faced even more difficult social and economic circumstances. The price paid for the

disfavors of history was Nazism in Germany and Bolshevism in Russia.

The story of the progress of liberal democracy depends on declaring fascism and communism exceptional and thus illegitimate challengers. Fukuyama, for example, argues that fascism was an aberration generated by "hothouse" industrialization and post-World War I chaos. A similar compound of bad luck left Russia vulnerable to communism. What this line of argument ignores, however, is the degree to which fascism and Marxism emerged out of the intellectual mainstream in Western Europe, and therefore they cannot so easily be separated from democratic thought.

It was the coldness and shallowness of the very rationalist forms of capitalism and bureaucracy that Fukuyama sees triumphant at the end of the twentieth century that spurred the search for new political communities at the end of the nineteenth century. Solidarities based on class, blood, nation, or generation seemed to offer more social intimacy and more spiritual purpose than did free-market liberalism. Political modernism after the 1890s was the composition of this emotional foundation to public action. It did not just prosper in those nations (such as Germany) that were scarred by rapid industrialization and the remnants of the feudal order. A glance at France at the turn-of-the-century moment of the Dreyfus Affair, for example, provides plenty of evidence for the widespread appeal of integral nationalism, strident racism, and exclusively working-class syndicalism.

The point is not only that racists or fascists or Marxists have much deeper roots in nineteenth-century thought than Fukuyama allows, but that they shared with liberalism basic assumptions about progress as well. It would be nice to think of fascists, for example, as improbable types, resentful antimodernists and the executors of history in its most extreme conditions. But their appeal was surprisingly broad and often rested on democratic or populist appeals, and their programs were technocratic and forward looking. Indeed, it is striking to see how unquestioningly most political groups in this century have invested in the vocabulary of modern science, diagnosing sickness in the population, deploying interventionist therapies to restore "health," classifying and sorting out physiognomic types, and doing so in the name of progress. The eugenic imagination is in the name of progress. The eugenic imagination is an excellent example of the commonalities among liberals, fascists, and communists. This common ground should give pause to those such as Fukuyama who dismiss any necessary link between modernism and the Holocaust. By the same token, total war in 1914-18, with its awesome mobilization of bodies and hearts and minds, was not an irksome German or Russian invention but the consequence of the democratization of war, a process that implicated each belligerent. Fukuyama stumbles across all sorts of history when he tries to separate the righteous aspects of the democracies from the sinful ones of the dictatorships.

It is precisely because the twentieth-century order has witnessed the menace of Nazis and Stalinists and also the menacing effects of technological protocols, scientific classifications, and popular nationalisms that thoughtful observers have become skeptical about progress. It is simplistic to accuse Western philosophers of being unduly pessimistic in the face of the Holocaust or Hiroshima. What leaves observers "speechless," as Fukuyama somewhat crudely puts it, is not the existence of evil as revealed by the Holocaust but overconfidence in the ability of science and rationalism to remake the social world, an arrogance on which no one side has a monopoly. The recognition of the fragile and destructive aspects to civilization is not out of place.

Fukuyama's collapse of modernism into well-ordered democracy has the unfortunate effect of sanitizing Western history. Fukuyama distinguishes a liberal telos from illiberal pathologies with unjustified rigor. At a certain point the menaces cannot be explained away as either exogenous aberrations or mere growing pains that do not impinge on the underlying principles—otherwise the ideal adds up to little more than ideology. Indeed, Fukuyama's distinction between democracy and totalitarianism rests on a total misreading of Kojève, the French philosopher and interpreter of Hegel on whom Fukuyama relies. For Kojève, the historical function of Stalin and Mao was to introduce the Napoleonic code to Russia and China, the severity of their methods being a function of tardy deployment rather than essential illiberalism, a view whose ironic statement and political implications a more attentive Fukuyama, for one, would certainly abhor.

None of this really compromises Fukuyama's central point: there are no robust ideological alternatives to liberalism, which enjoys broader worldwide acceptance than at any time this century. And Fukuyama is right in insisting that those constituencies who already enjoy the fruits of capitalist economics and liberal democracy do not intend to roll back this "progress." Modern history has taught us many lessons, Fukuyama maintains, with the result that we appreciate the modest successes of the present and remember the disastrous results of hubris in the past. This collective memory guards against history repeating itself. But if we remember, what do we forget? What are the irretrievable losses that have been incurred in the twentieth century? Another way of putting this question is to consider progress not simply from the point of view of the living but also of the dead.

I suspect that the nineteenth century would have been appalled at the twentieth century. Most nineteenth-century intellectuals did not endorse democracy as Fukuyama suggests. On the contrary, democracy was widely regarded as the vulgar rule of averages, a despotism of the masses to which fascism and communism attested. This perspective is rather different than Fukuyama's. Nineteenth-century thinkers also assumed that men and women would make use of new ideas and new tools in an effort to become more able and more worthy of their god. They could not

easily have imagined a culture of passive spectators and consumers. If the twentieth century is happy not to have to live in the nineteenth, which was without anaesthesia, ice cubes, or indoor plumbing, the nineteenth century, in turn, must regard the twentieth as a nightmare of complacency. Fukuyama completely lacks the irony of Kojève, who acknowledged that the End of History is not accompanied by the fullness of wisdom. Perhaps progress exists only as the conviction of each present, plausible because the dead do not speak, credible because we have forgotten more than we have remembered. Is this not the cunning of History?

Patrick J. Deneen (review date 19 June 1992)

SOURCE: "It Ain't Over 'Til It's Over," in *Commonweal*, June 19, 1992, pp. 25-6.

[*In the following review of* The End of History and the Last Man, *Deneen provides an overview of Fukuyama's historical postulations and critical reaction to his thesis.*]

Francis Fukuyama's 1989 article **"The End of History?"** in *The National Interest* caused a sensation in both academic and nonacademic circles of a magnitude unprecedented since Allan Bloom's *The Closing of the American Mind* in 1987. The resemblance of the sound and the fury is not coincidental: Fukuyama—a former student of Bloom's—veered from the well-worn discursive paths within the field of international relations with as much aplomb as did Bloom in domestic fields. Fukuyama's book—fundamentally a lengthy extension of his original article—should continue to infuriate as well as stimulate debate as the West finds itself somewhat lost in a new but no less frightening international arena.

Fukuyama's thesis is grand, even brash at times, deriving as much from the subtle and difficult theories of Hegel and Nietzsche as from recent developments on the front pages. History—conceived here not as a pastiche of disjunct events, but in broad, panoramic strokes from which developmental stages can be discerned—has reached its logical conclusion with the worldwide embrace of the "universal and homogeneous" state of liberal democracy. Fukuyama contends—and, one would have to admit, correctly—that no other political arrangement contains the legitimate and ethical components found in the liberal democracies of Europe and the United States. Fukuyama provides ample historical evidence demonstrating the decline of alternative political arrangements, notably fascism and communism; but the display of evidence is secondary to his larger contention that it is the *idea* of liberal democracy that has prevailed, and that localized exceptions merely continue to play out the necessary conflict that will inevitably drive each nation to similar liberal arrangements.

Such a cavalier dismissal of contradictory historical evidence is grounded in Fukuyama's supporting thesis that there are two forces which impel the course of History. First, the exigencies of national defense will inevitably require a country to pursue a policy of a scientific research, and thus foster economic development that supports—materially and educationally—continued military competitiveness. The result of this first force in its most developed form is market capitalism. Nevertheless, Fukuyama acknowledges, a capitalist economy does not necessarily result in a democratic polity, and thus a second force is introduced: the struggle for *recognition*. In perhaps the most original and controversial part of the book, Fukuyama links the Hegelian notion of "recognition" (*Annerkenung*) with the Platonic source of honor, *thymos*—translated alternately as "heart" or "spiritedness." Described as the "psychological seat" of the human desire for recognition, *thymos* is the inegalitarian impulse that drives the human person to struggle for recognition of his or her human dignity; writ large, that worldwide individual struggle ironically results in democracy, the only political system in which each person is both accorded recognition by, and is in turn required to recognize the dignity of, fellow citizens.

Yet this very solution contains the seeds of its own dissolution: recognition, by its very essence, requires, on the one hand, inferiors to whom one can compare oneself advantageously; and alternatively, those in a superior position whose esteem is worth seeking. Egalitarian democracy leaves the individual's *thymotic* desires unsatisfied, akin to "the Last Man" scenario described by Nietzsche in which mankind is left materially contented but spiritually bereft as an equal if mediocre democratic citizen. The "End of History" is by no means to be celebrated in Fukuyama's estimation; in fact, given the inevitability of humanity's continuing search for recognition, the end of History may simply result in a condition of such overarching discontent that human beings will once again struggle—this time against equality itself—thereby jeopardizing the stability of liberal democracy and starting the march of History anew.

Fukuyama's conclusions are certain to provoke an angry response by those on the Left, particularly Marxists, who will be disturbed by the supposed configuration of the economy at the end of History, and liberals who will object to the Nietzschean conclusions that Fukuyama draws from the dynamics of egalitarianism. The vehemence of their response should be indicative of the threat they perceive from Fukuyama's thesis—and justly so. Ultimately, these opposition camps share an uncomfortable similarity with Fukuyama's approach, namely a belief in the progressive course of History. They will object, then, not necessarily with the premises of Fukuyama's analysis, but with its *conclusions,* rather seeking alternative explanations that will result in a more benevolent future. Such debates should prove amusing: for, if the forces of History must inevitably result in a single tableau, then arguments over its likely appearance should prove quite irrelevant.

Notwithstanding these critics, significant (and *consequential*) questions should remain for those not wholly satisfied with Fukuyama's thesis, yet sympathetic with some of his criticisms of modern liberal democracy. While at first glance it seems apparent that the two forces of History can be divided into a material explanation (scientific capitalism) and a *moral* explanation (*thymotic* democracy), further contemplation should force us to conclude otherwise. In fact, by calling attention to the *philosophical* origins of the scientific method—namely, in the writings of Francis Bacon and his Renaissance contemporaries—Fukuyama indicates that scientific and capitalistic development was, and to some extent still is, subject to moral considerations. Alternatively, the individual's craving for recognition has been a *natural* feature of the human psyche, at least since the first chapters of Genesis. The inherent contradiction described by Fukuyama concerning the egalitarian result of humanity's *thymos* and the individual's subsequent dissatisfaction, suggests no more than the longstanding Judeo-Christian belief that solutions to the cravings of the human soul are not available in wholly secular—including political—terms. Fukuyama, while recognizing the paradox of the individual's desires, nevertheless appears to accept without perturbation Hegel's thesis that Christianity is the culminating "slave-morality" of world history, and that its replacement by liberal democracy has made the individual's inferiority to God unnecessary. Yet, only through "recognition" originating from a higher source can mankind achieve both meaningful equality (as mutual subjects) *and* recognition (through worship and imitation of the divine). Otherwise—following to its conclusion the argument originally shared by both Hegel and Nietzsche, and acknowledged by Fukuyama—the sole secular source of recognition in a world of liberal democracy is through participation in the glories of warfare. And given the destructive forces that we now wield against one another in this potential struggle for wholly earthly recognition, we may quite literally find ourselves at the end of History, but this time with no one to lament its passing.

Gregory Bruce Smith (essay date 1994)

SOURCE: "The 'End of History' or a Portal to the Future: Does Anything Lie Beyond Late Modernity?," in *After History?: Francis Fukuyama and His Critics,* Rowman and Littlefield, 1994, pp. 1-21.

[*In the following essay, Smith provides an overview of Fukuyama's "end of history" thesis and examines the sources of its critical controversy. Smith contends that "the End of History debate" is more properly an "End of Modernity debate."*]

This is a significantly enlarged and transformed version of an essay that initially appeared in *Perspectives on Political Science,* Vol. 22, Fall 1993, under the title "Endings, Transitions or Beginnings."

Rarely does one see so many take so much trouble responding to the arrival of a new book—and what for many was a new idea—as with the release of Francis Fuku-yama's *The End of History and the Last Man,* especially in light of the almost universally critical, occasionally hyperbolic, nature of the responses. This was perhaps predictable in light of the controversy generated earlier by the article that launched the book. But prediction and explanation are two different things, and an explanation is harder to come by. However, I think they clearly protest too much.

If Fukuyama's argument impacted only one side of the contemporary political spectrum to the exclusion of the other, an easy explanation might present itself. Needless to say, liberal progressives were not intrigued by having the idea of History co-opted only to be told that liberal individualism and free markets represent its terminus.[1] And conservatives were less than thrilled to be told that the victory of the liberal West in the cold war might eventuate in the moral decay and spiritual hollowness of the Nietzschean last man. Since the negative responses cut across the political spectrum, it is reasonable to suppose that there may be more here than meets the eye; Fuku-yama has apparently struck a nerve. I believe that there are several explanations of this phenomenon and that they tell us something of importance about our contemporary moral, intellectual, and political environment.

I

On one level the End of History debate points to the frequent parochialism of the American academy. Similar debates, with far less fanfare, had already been conducted in France, Canada, and elsewhere. For American academics, one part of the scandal was that this debate traced its roots to a German philosopher and one of his left bank Parisian commentators.[2] The continental roots of an argument are indictment enough in some circles. But the heat generated by the present debate, even in theaters where it had already played, indicates there is far more to the matter than American parochialism. Needless to say, playing out the End of History debate at the end of the cold war was significant. The liberal West could no longer define itself simply as the demonstrably superior of two available options. The liberal West now has to look at itself in the mirror and define itself in relation to intrinsic, substantive goals and ideals—that is, articulate what we are *for* rather than take our bearings by what we are *against*. Therein lies one of the significant problems; neither the right nor the left seem well equipped at present to join that discussion.[3]

The End of History debate also came at a time of declining faith that History could be understood as linear and one-directional.[4] For a long time it has simply been assumed that the present is in principle superior to the past merely by having come later. That premise had worked its way out until it seemed like sound common sense for a series of generations.[5] But the commonsense belief in linear history is by no means obvious when one looks at the actual grist of history. Empirically, the past presents a spectacle of random occurrences. The faith that history has a meaning and direction requires a theoretical critique; it does not rest on empirical evidence. A theoretical frame must be brought to the empirical data from outside. It is precisely the status and origin of such frames—especially in the late modern world—that is at issue.

As I will argue throughout this essay, the fundamental issue with which we are confronted in the End of History debate is theoretical, not empirical. But after Hegel and Marx it has become increasingly difficult to accept the theoretical premises that underpin the notion of linear history. Nonetheless, political and moral life in the modern world has increasingly been driven by ideas. Many of those ideas lost theoretical credibility in previous generations; yet political and moral life continues to be driven by them. The premises that underlie our actions can remain suppressed for some time, but not indefinitely. When they are eventually brought to the light and seen as questionable a complicated situation arises. We live in one of those complicated times.

On the basis of a past theoretical faith in the linear, unidirectional movement of history, it was possible simply to begin from the prejudice that the past is a chronicle of ignorance and vice. To that could be added the gratifying notion that the present generation starts on a moral and political promontory simply by coming later. By extension, it was possible to adopt the conclusion that the future should in principle be superior to the present with or without reactualizing necessary antecedent virtues and circumstances that made the present what it is. If we lose our faith in linear history, our easy-going faith in all manner of commonsense opinions will be unhinged as well.[6] This is where we had arrived prior to the End of History debate, without having publicly admitted it. "We" expected further progress, perhaps indefinitely, and Fukuyama suggested that we had more or less arrived at a terminus. Without History to support our aspirations we would have to defend our idea of the good far more explicitly. But at present, no one is in a particularly strong position to do so.[7]

An adequate rejoinder to the End of History thesis would require that one furnish a substantive discussion of the good that the future *should,* rather than *inevitably will*—or at present does—offer, along with the ways in which it is plausible to believe that it can be actualized. If History does not somehow underpin the movement toward the good, substantive argument or capitulation to the status quo is all that is left. No self-respecting progressive can ever publicly accept the status quo and most are loathe to turn to nature to underpin their arguments because the left generally does not like to admit that intransigent matter, human or otherwise, might limit its utopian agendas. The left prefers instead to believe in the relative indeterminacy and malleability of human beings, as well as material reality, at the hands of clever social manipulation, education and technological mastery.

But without a fixed nature that presupposes its own end or perfection, or an inevitable history that moves only in the desired direction, one is in a very awkward position in trying to justify one's idea of the good. The left is not alone in this predicament. Most conservatives sneak in a linear conception of history along with their various "invisible hands." Invisible hands have the effect of making it equally unnecessary to discuss substantive ends and explicitly justify them. Likewise, one need not consciously foster the political prudence and moral virtue that are the only alternatives to faith in mythical inevitability.[8] Fukuyama's thesis put many in the position of the emperor with no clothes. Being forced by Fukuyama to confront their substantive nakedness was not met with gratitude by either the left or the right.

That said, it was liberal progressives who were most discomfited. Theoretically, many had backed themselves into a corner by arguing for several generations that liberalism does not rest on a substantive teaching or point to distinctive liberal virtues.[9] According to this argument, liberalism is neutral as regards ways of life and substantive ends. It is fundamentally a set of procedural norms open to a diversity of ends. This fashionable "antifoundationalism" is frequently secured by elements drawn from even more fashionable postmodern*ism* in a way that yields an entirely jury-rigged contraption.[10] However secured, this view represents the cul-de-sac that most on the present-day left have decided to colonize. Hence being forced either to accept the End of History or to be nudged into a substantive debate was particularly annoying in these circles.

Granted, arguing that history ends precisely where many neo-conservatives would wish it to end—in modern, commercial individualism—had the look of a "reactionary" maneuver. For many it was difficult to respond other than with outrage to the notion that history would not continue to progress even further in what had been assumed to be not only the desired but also the inevitable direction. The central point is this—and it is precisely the point Hegel made—one cannot know that history is linear and progressive except in light of the end toward which it moves. One cannot know of or about the end unless is has been, or soon will be, actualized. Without an End of History thesis the idea of a progressive linear history cannot stand.[11] It is impossible to conceptualize History progressing indefinitely. More to the point, if one rejects the End of History thesis, the only alternative is to show that we can somehow stand outside the flux of temporality at some fixed point. Only by standing at that atemporal point could we then presume to measure temporal movement. That atemporal standpoint is what is traditionally meant by the concept *nature*. Without being willing to openly accept the End of History, and refusing to accept nature, antifoundationalists are in a difficult position. The only consistent move they have left is to valorize "our own" as the good—and since at least Aristophanes, that has been the most traditional and conservative of maneuvers.[12]

II

While most on the left proceed from the assumption of the malleability and indeterminacy of man, Fukuyama has also been attacked by many, from both the right and the left, for not realizing that human nature does *not* change. History, they argue, cannot end because human nature will never allow itself to be satisfied by any substantive outcome, even prosperous liberal democracy. But that argument substantially begs the question. First, even such seeming absolutists on this question as Aristotle make clear that our nature requires completion by education and habit—that is, cultural variables—and those are obviously not static. It begs the question further by failing to mention that modern philosophical fellow travelers from John Locke and Jean-Jacques Rousseau to Robert Nozick and John Rawls have told us we must quit the natural condition because the good for man exists only within an artificially constructed human arena. Debate in the modern era has focused explicitly on the relation between nature and the good and by and large has concluded that the human good requires quitting the natural condition. To simply assert nature as if it operated qua efficient causality in human affairs as it does for beavers, bees, ants, and other social species does not hit the mark. The fact that there is a natural fabric to human existence does not immediately prove that it conduces to the good. The substantive question of the human good still has to be addressed even if we mechanically invoke nature.

Another variety of responses to the End of History thesis which invokes something empirically pregiven as an indication that history cannot end focuses on the renaissance of tribalism in Eastern Europe, the former Soviet Union, and elsewhere as clear evidence that secular, Western, liberal, technological commercialism has not been, and will not be, globally victorious. In a similar vein, rising Islamic fundamentalism is put forward as empirical counterevidence to the possibility of the End of History. This approach also begs the question. The modern moral, political, and technological juggernaut has confronted revealed religion before and an accommodation has been reached—and without the total secularization of religion. Someone would have to explain why Islam, which shares sacred texts and multiple principles with Judaism and Christianity, so differs that accommodation will be impossible. Is not political marginality far more accountable for the frustration that presently finds vent in Islamic fundamentalism, for example, than simple moral outrage at the Western understanding of justice and the good? If that is the primary ground of frustration, there is no reason why accommodation is not possible. Otherwise, it would be necessary to explain why, even if a radical choice for or against Islam develops, the realities of the modern world would not force a decision for modern technological civilization.

As regards the hegemony of parochialism, ethnic tribalism, and nationalism, what leads us to believe that present manifestations of tribalism will have greater staying power in their Russian, Eastern European, and Asian manifestations than they did in Western Europe? Has not the former Soviet experience demonstrated that one cannot ultimately retain any national autonomy in the modern world without at least free markets, and probably liberal freedoms as well? And even if we anticipate a relative withering away of the modern nation-state, and the movement toward a more homogeneous, cosmopolitan, global civilization, there would predictably still be states competing to maintain their place in the cosmopolitan market. Kant's vision of a cosmopolitan federation of states is probably more plausible than any simple world state. Further, the tribal traditions to which our contemporaries turn in desperation represent a response to *present* difficult circumstances and resultant apprehensions. But such traditions emerged under entirely different concrete circumstances than those of increasingly global, modern technological civilization. As modernity consolidates, the future world will become increasingly foreign to the traditional world of the past. What leads us to believe that ancient traditions have any chance of maintaining themselves in a radically transformed environment?

Any tradition is born of an attempt to explain reality and support a shared conception of the good. It must be consistent with its concrete present, at least to some significant degree. The real question is, is not the modern world intrinsically at odds with the generation of stable customs and habits and hence with living additions to traditions generated in the past? If so, old traditions will become increasingly stale and out of touch. Why will the attempt to hold on to old traditions not become more and more of a parody with each passing generation? The mere fact that something is old does not make it good. It must also be reasonable. But will reason be able to substitute something in the place of decaying traditions? This latter question is another way of asking, will universal Enlightenment ever be able to take the place of a shared ethos in giving solidity to our lives?[13]

There is no doubt that we have habits in the modern, Western world. But our habits are ones that accommodate us to constant change.[14] There has never been a greater mechanism for constant change than free markets, conjoined with modern technology. This is especially true when they are likewise conjoined with an increasingly global mass media supported by ever expanding information technologies. What could plausibly bring this mechanism to a grinding halt? Is this not a steamroller that will crush everything that tries to congeal in its path, along with any remnants of past traditions? Put another way, is it possible for new traditions to form in this whirlwind?

Needless to say, near-term political and economic collapse in the former Soviet Union and elsewhere is a very real possibility, but how would it do anything but postpone the eventual march of modernity? Will Russia or its former satellites in Eastern Europe continue to turn to old traditions when they have become more successful at being modern, as seems a likely outcome sooner or later? To presume to prove empirically that History cannot end because of present manifestations of tribalism, fundamentalist religion, or any other "facts," one would have to give persuasive answers to these questions and many more, not simply make empirical assertions. The real issue is, what sovereign *theoretical* understanding leads us to believe in the imperviousness of present empirical givens in the undeveloped world, in an age of cascading global technological homogenization? Have we not created a world that will inevitably destroy old traditions without providing the circumstances for the generation of new ones? Are there any rational principles that can plausibly be thought to replace the shared *ethoi* that bind classes and generations together? If there were such rational principles, has our experience in the modern world heightened or destroyed our faith in universal Enlightenment?

If we have created a world of constant, monotonous change, history could end with ongoing, monotonous agitation. We would not have proved that history was some inevitable process. But we might be forced to conclude that our unique present obliterates past possibilities and simultaneously makes unique future possibilities unlikely.[15] After a certain point humanity could very well arrive at a moment of *irreversibility*. The End of History need not require Hegelian *inevitability*. If we arrive at a moment of irreversibility, and movement forward seems implausible, we may at the very least have arrived at an extended hiatus of history. The question is, is there some nexus of variables that makes liberal, commercial, technological civilization both plausible as a global outcome and difficult, if not unlikely, to transcend—at least for a very considerable period of time? And if transcended, would our movement be in the direction of "down" or "back"? That too would prove the End of History thesis; all novel possibilities have already been seen, while repetitions of past moments are still possible.[16] If one is opposed to the possibility of historical novelty—opposed to the possibility of the generation of novel ideals and ends not yet longed for—then one should accept the End of History.[17] Either there is the possibility of historical novelty or we have seen all possibilities in morality, religion, poetry, art, and politics played out at least once already.

III

It could be argued that even if human nature, understood primarily qua efficient causality, is not simply operative, human imagination and creativity are indomitable. Here we arrive at an argument that is in its own way Hegelian; it rests on the premise that genuine, concrete historical change is preceded by the generation of novel ideas. When we generate new aspirations, goals, and ideals we act differently and that eventually has concrete consequences in the world we share. But this approach also begs the question. The Hegelian point is that ideas and ideals sequence themselves in a way that leads from less comprehensive and more contradictory ideas to the most comprehensive and least contradictory ones, at which point the process of fundamental change stops because idea-novelty stops. When idea-novelty stops, and the latest ideas have been actualized in concrete institutions, history ends. Again, the only compelling empirical proof that this position is wrong would require the production of a novel ideal.[18] There simply is no evidence that has occurred since Hegel.

There have been post-Hegelian thinkers who have operated on a very high philosophical level—I have in mind especially Nietzsche and Heidegger—but they are fundamentally negative or merely hopeful. The central question is, what ideal is possible beyond a world devoted to universal equality (hence the pursuit of equal dignity and recognition), prosperity for all individuals, a secure, long, fear-free life, etc.? That ideal may not be fully-manifested in present concrete reality, but what *ideal* could conceivably replace it that would win substantial acceptance? If no such ideal is imaginable, history could be at an end. If no novel ideals are possible, our only alternative—other than to continue to globally actualize the reigning ideal—is to engage in sorties through past ideas and forms in acts of remembrance. Or we could try to patch old ideals and forms together into novel pastiches (i.e., practice the ironic eclecticism of postmodern*ism*). The possibility of idea and ideal completion or exhaustion points in the direction of another fairly recent "end of" thesis—the end of political philosophy. There has surely been revived interest in the history of political philosophy in recent years, and political theory abounds—that is, working out the ramifications of already manifest ideals—but where is the evidence of a novel speculative political philosophy? Much of fashionable postmodernism seems devoted to proving both the impossibility and the undesirability of efforts to generate such political philosophies. What is at stake is the possibility of the generation of novel speculative political philosophies.

The proof that speculative political philosophy remains a possibility is an empirical one. But anyone trying to produce a truly novel speculative ideal will immediately see the difficulty. Again, precisely what is it one would wish for that we do not already have in theory? And is there an interesting, nonatavistic faction in the world that wishes something other than a long, comfortable life, self-interested and self-sufficient, devoted primarily to an industrious acquisitiveness, freedom from pain and fear of violent death, with secularized institutions, great latitude of moral belief, and so on? Where is the longing that lies beyond that modern dream? And even if there are a few who have such a longing—and they would need someone to articulate it in a theoretically serious fashion—what is the likelihood of it gaining public manifestation rather than remaining a shared private fantasy?[19] Is not the modern, bourgeois longing precisely what the majority of human beings desire everywhere and always? Other ideals are those of the few. What chance do the ideals of the few have of gaining ascendancy in an increasingly homogeneous, egalitarian age?

The two greatest philosophers of the post-Hegelian era, Nietzsche and Heidegger, give us no specific political philosophies, and Heidegger's thought, like much of contemporary philosophy, moves further and further away from concrete discussions.[20] Nietzsche, conceding Hegel's point, brings his thought to a culmination in willing the eternal recurrence of the same; in other words, Nietzsche simply wills a rerunning of history, not a novel moment. Heidegger, again conceding an Hegelian point, argues that at least an extended historical hiatus has arrived. He waits for a new god or a new dispensation of Being, neither of which, he admits, may come for a long time if at all. The record to date should not occasion great optimism about the early arrival of a genuinely *post*modern idea of justice and the good. Hence the End of History thesis is not as simple to dismiss as many on both the right and the left would lead us to believe. Simply to confront it would require that a different set of questions be addressed than those that have occupied most of Fukuyama's respondents.

It is certainly true that we have been witnessing the theoretical disintegration of faith in the principles that provide the foundation for the modern civilization that seems to be consolidating its gains globally.[21] But that fact only proves the ironic nature of our situation, not that counter-ideals exist. And when we are repeatedly told that modern liberal principles do not ground moral meaning, while allowing that meaning to intrude from a variety of traditional sources, we again see the irony of our situation. Will past traditions and norms become extinct and new ones become impossible, leaving global modern liberalism spiritually hollow—albeit materially comfortable and perhaps thereby acceptable to the majority?

Needless to say, the irony of our situation has caused more than a little shared inarticulate anxiety. The energetic responses Fukuyama has aroused are related to this pool of anxiety. But anxiety does not prove the possibility of a counter-ideal either. We should recall that the End of History thesis is just one of a series of parallel theses that we have witnessed as the twentieth century has unfolded. We could begin by pointing to the earlier twentieth-century preoccupations with the end or decline of the West, add to that the far more academic discussions of the end of ideology or the end of political philosophy and make ourselves fashionably current by pointing to the various discussions of postmodern*ism* that will undoubtedly preoccupy us into the twenty-first century. Add to these, terms like postindustrial society, poststructuralism, the end of man, the decline of logo-centrism, and like phrases that are all too familiar and one would have an odd mélange that seemingly shares only one idea: there is a more or less inarticulate sense that something out of the ordinary is occurring around us.

Beyond that vague sense, it remains unclear whether that which is occurring points toward a long period of stasis, a relatively quick transition to something novel, or the early stages of a novel future already deploying itself. Ambiguity always leads to uneasiness. Only a few, rare intellectuals could revel in irony and ambiguity as a way of life. Hence, anyone who revivifies an inarticulate uneasiness will run the risk of the kinds of responses Fukuyama received. But none of this proves the possibility of a novel postmodern ideal.

IV

Many of Fukuyama's critics have been generous enough to recognize that his book-length treatment adds depth and subtlety to the initial articulation of his thesis. The price one pays for subtlety is frequently the introduction of new ambiguities. In the latest account, Fukuyama offers several different engines that move the dialectic of history. There is the dialectic of modern science and technology, which overlaps with and informs a dialectic of capitalist market economies. Something similar to the Heideggerian analysis of the inevitable and unidirectional march of modern technology seems to take hegemony in this part of the account—albeit in modern fashion, technology is seen by Fukuyama as primarily emancipatory rather than alienating. There is also the spiritual or psychological dialectic of recognition, which is given two by no means identical articulations, one in *consciousness*—and here we come in contact with its modern Hegelian manifestation—and one in the *instinctive* love of honor—here we are confronted with Plato's discussion of *thymos*.[22] The spiritual dialectic leads Fukuyama to a reflection on the banality of bourgeois culture—shared substantially by authors from Tocqueville to Nietzsche, Reisman, and many others. This part of the argument is in tension with the fundamentally optimistic faith in the emancipatory goodness of technology and markets. Many of the ambiguities of Fukuyama's account come from a failure to differentiate these different engines of history, or to explain how they might converge.

Fukuyama's technological engine of history moves unavoidably in the direction of a global economy in which nation-states play a diminished role in the face of large-scale global, multinational institutions. This effect is magnified by the existence of the mass media, which increasingly give everyone access to the same culturally homogenizing influences. In this fashion Western influences consolidate their hold globally. No nation can afford not to modernize or it will lose any chance for even minimal national autonomy, whether conceived in tribal terms or in some other fashion. Despite the growing global tribalism many of his critics glory in reciting, Fukuyama concludes that the parochial—whether conceived ethnically or religiously—is on a more or less gentle and extended slippery slide toward the universal. (Fukuyama clouds the issue somewhat by observing that this outcome may be mitigated in various Asian nations by Confucian traditions. Why that would be true requires further articulation.) Brute nature itself seems to pose the only potential barrier to this outcome, since limited resources might lead to the inevitability of a zero-sum economic game. While it would be imprudent to predict with certainty the near-term outcome of the simultaneous globalization and tribalization which at present confront each other, the globalizing tendencies seem to have the upper hand.

As regards the dialectical movement of consciousness (recognition), Fukuyama openly follows Hegel—passed through the mediating lens of Alexandre Kojève.[23] The fundamentally modern turn to *consciousness* that Kojève resolutely developed,[24] shared by many of Fukuyama's critics, is that man is not primarily a fixed, determinate being but a consciousness that changes and evolves and at each stage "outers" itself, achieving thereby various concrete manifestations in different religions, art forms, cultures, constitutions, and eventually the technological transformation of the natural world. Having passed through a multitude of stages and seen the various forms of narrowness of each successive stage, humanity would return to a previous stage only on the basis of forgetfulness rather than choice.

Through an extended period of trial and error, which must be recorded in detail—and our historically conscious age is amazing in its ability to record and preserve—consciousness reaches ever more comprehensive and allegedly less contradictory states. Eventually it arrives at a point with which there is at least relatively high satisfaction on the part of the majority—taking into account the effects of the unavoidable pettiness, envy, and jealousy that would remain—having transformed the external world to correspond with its internal consciousness. In the process of its journey, consciousness not only produces ideas, but acts upon them and concretely actualizes them. In this way consciousness transforms the external world, and any adequate theory of human reality must account for our ability to do this. Eventually the world we occupy bears primarily the stamp of a human creation. Consequently, the dialectic of consciousness should ultimately dovetail with the technological dialectic. Living in a humanized world, human beings allegedly achieve a satisfaction they could not achieve in the natural world. Again, this is the modern premise par excellence, whether we take Hobbes, Locke, Rousseau, Hegel, or whomever as our favorite exemplar.

It is certainly true that Fukuyama adds a potential confusion by trying to synthesize the Hegelian discussion of recognition—a phenomenon primarily of consciousness—and Platonic *thymos*—primarily a phenomenon of fixed, instinctive being. As a result, Plato and Hegel cease to present us with fundamental alternatives. Further, Fukuyama's psychological dialectic eventually comes up against the empirical fact of significant if not universal alienation from modern, urban, global, technological civilization. That alienation can be accounted for in one of two more or less exclusive ways. Either the ideal that awaits at the end of the evolution of consciousness has not yet been perfectly manifested empirically on a sufficiently global basis, or man is not so much an evolving consciousness as a fixed being with a nature, suppression or sublimation of which within a technological civilization is necessarily alienating or dissatisfying. If the latter, nature could always rebel given the chance (barring the transformation of that nature by modern biological science). History might be irreversible, but it is never simply at an end as long as something deep in our being can repeatedly reassert itself.[25] History could be both irreversible and a terminus only if man was primarily a consciousness or if that part of his being which is fixed was irreversibly transformed.[26]

V

The central issue raised by the End of History debate has simply not been addressed by Fukuyama's critics: Is Fukuyama's point primarily theoretical or empirical? If both, how are the two related and/or which takes priority? By way of an answer, I would make the following fairly simple observation: To know on a purely theoretical level that history, or anything else, had ended would require us to know how the entirety of the human things—which is the subject matter of History—is integrated into the nonhuman. In other words, we would have to have complete knowledge of the Whole to make definitive statements about how any of the parts, particularly the human, fit into the Whole. We should admit that we will never have perfect knowledge about the Whole; hence we will never have finished knowledge about how the parts are articulated into the Whole. Likewise, we will never have final knowledge about the sense in which any of the parts could reach a terminus beyond which there is no novelty. Consequently, we cannot know with theoretical certainty whether history has or has not reached a terminus. But we can know that empirical evidence is never adequate to dispose of the issue. Where does that leave us?

This points to the fact that we should expect all articulations of the Whole to be partial. One would therefore expect a spectacle of repeated attempts to articulate the Whole, none of them perfectly adequate, with different ones publicly persuasive at different times and with the reasons that account for persuasiveness being somewhat unpredictable. If each attempt gives rise to various interpretations or "disseminations," with their own distinctive deferred ramifications and unpredictable practical consequences—as is reasonable to predict—one would expect novel ways of living to emerge. If we do not see evidence of that and see instead what looks like snowballing global homogenization, some at least temporary impasse or hiatus can legitimately be thought to have settled in and require explanation.[27] That explanation will be theoretical even though it can never be apodictic. Since it is unlikely that we will ever grasp the Whole, or if we did adequately grasp it—through some direct noetic act of apprehension—that we could articulate it comprehensively in some final form of public speech, it is unlikely we will ever arrive at the comparatively prosaic knowledge of the exact relationship between human consciousness or thought and our determinate natural being.[28] Hence perfect knowledge of precisely what we are as human is likely to remain a mystery—which is not to say that since we do not know everything, we do not know anything.

Further, as a theoretical matter it is necessary to state precisely what kind of terminus it is at which we are asserting history arrives when we say it ends. Is it the kind of end beyond which there is one or another form of nothingness or indeterminacy, or is it the kind of end that is understood as a perfection? In a significant way, Fukuyama thinks that something literally ceases in the sense that something that was part of the human scene hitherto

will not be seen in the future. In another sense, Fukuyama wants to say that a form of perfection is reached, although the message is mixed, since a certain impoverishment is also possible, and the end of the possibility of novel ideas and ideals is posited as well. It would be helpful if Fukuyama could clarify the relationship between end understood teleologically and as terminus beyond which there is one kind of nothingness or another.[29] While it is plausible to project a terminus of history qua extended hiatus, it is not theoretically possible to project an end qua perfection given that we are not simply determinate beings moved only by efficient causality. If we were, there would be no History in any interesting sense.

These clarifications to the contrary notwithstanding, it should be admitted that one can "clarify" even a compelling idea out of existence and not thereby attend to what is truly compelling in it. What is it that is truly compelling in the End of History thesis? No empirical evidence exists separate from some theoretical frame, which we all use in our approaches to reality. That said, it should be recognized that it will be difficult to develop—or to mysteriously find ourselves equipped with—a post-Hegelian theoretical frame, here understood as a genuinely postmodern frame. Hence present empirical circumstances may be settling in for a long period. On this level, the End of History thesis can be *compelling* without being *conclusive*.

The End of History thesis presents a picture of an increasingly global, egalitarian, commercial, technological civilization emerging, one that at the very least may have great staying power. Yet two issues remain open: (1) Is it good? (2) If not, what is implied in the possibility of transcending it? Having arrived at those two questions, I would argue that the End of History debate would be better posed as an End of Modernity debate in which one seriously reconsiders the modern dream, the arguments in its favor and those against it. Such a reconsideration would occasion an explicit discussion of fundamental questions concerning the nature of justice and the human good. It would also require an explicit reflection on the place of the human within the larger Whole, knowing in advance that we cannot arrive at a definitive conclusion as a result of those reflections. Reflections of this kind are necessary and ones which an increasingly technological and utilitarian civilization has tried to bury in the dustbin of History—while implicitly presupposing distinct answers.

I would argue that we should engage in a fundamental questioning of modernity not with an eye to premodernity as an alternative to the possibility of a late modern hiatus of History, but with an eye to the possibility of the genuinely *post*modern.[30] As long as a fundamental, essential kind of thinking of this sort remains possible and can find some public manifestation in the concrete world—in other words, as long as thinking does not choose, nor is forced, to retreat to some epicurean garden—History cannot end in any strong sense.[31] But if such essential reflection ceases to have a public echo we would have no right to glibly dismiss the End of History thesis. The End of History thesis points toward the need for—and reflections on the possibility of—speculative political philosophy. If it remains possible, all horizons are still open.

Notes

1. What progress means cannot be explained without some notion of History. In other words, progressives always presuppose some "metanarrative" about the course of human events, and that metanarrative rests on a theoretical picture of history as linear and one-directional.

2. The operative texts are G. W. F. Hegel, *Phenomenology of Spirit,* trans. A. V. Miller (New York: Oxford University Press, 1977), and Alexandre Kojève, *Introduction to the Reading of Hegel,* trans. James H. Nichols Jr. (New York: Basic Books, 1969).

3. The End of History debate also comes at a time when there is increasing suspicion about the meaningfulness of traditional left-right or progressive-conservative dichotomies. Progressives frequently label everything that differs from their view as "reactionary," usually on the basis of a hidden End of History premise. They know they represent the cutting edge of history, hence only movement in the same direction they desire is legitimate. Anything that differs from the direction in which they wish to move must be a form of going back because there is nothing beyond their position that could come in the future. In this way the progressives become the defenders of the status quo. It is the conservatives who want change—either back or in some unclearly specified direction. The role reversals of progressives and conservatives may indicate the approaching end of the line for such distinctions. Terms that emerged as part of the fight for and against throne and altar, even when revamped for use in the confrontation between Marxist collectivism and liberal capitalism, will not retain their force indefinitely.

4. This can be seen clearly in the work of Nietzsche. However, history still retained a somewhat predictable circularity or repeatability for Nietzsche. It was Martin Heidegger who, in radically attacking the premises that support the Enlightenment faith in progress, opened the door to the historically random and mysterious. Heidegger presents an account of the Whole (Being) dominated by various fated historical dispensations that are altogether unpredictable. In its comings and goings, presencings and absencings, Being is simply beyond human comprehension; consequently so is history. French epigones such as Michel Foucault and Jacques Derrida build on these Heideggerian premises to the same end. Man can no longer predict and control existence as the modern thinkers had hoped. Fellow Frenchman Jean-François Lyotard codifies these efforts and announces the end of the age of "metanarratives." See, especially, Jacques Derrida, *Writing and Difference* (Chicago: University of Chicago Press, 1978); Michel Foucault, *The Order of Things* (New York: Vintage Books, 1973); and Jean-François Lyotard, *The Post-Modern Condition* (Minneapolis: University of Minnesota Press, 1984).

5. What we call "common sense" is never something autonomous that we can use as a yardstick to measure theoretical frameworks. Today's common sense is the diluted, deferred ramification of a theory from the past.

6. Obviously, progress in limited individual areas would remain possible; together with simultaneous retrogression in others. But the larger notion of simultaneous, linear progress scientifically, morally, politically, socially, technologically, psychologically, etc., would be lost.

7. For example, if we think greater egalitarianism is necessary, then it must be defended substantively on the basis of an explicit discussion of such things as the nature of justice and the human good. In such a discussion, all manner of suppressed premises would have to be made explicit. Then we would immediately see the difficulties involved in enjoining the substantive debate.

8. One can accept the wisdom of unleashing human spontaneity from bureaucratic manipulation without falling prey to a mythic faith in an "invisible hand"—one permutation of which is not that far from Hegel's notion of the "cunning of reason."

9. One exception is William Galston's *Liberal Purposes: Goods, Virtues and Diversity in the Liberal State* (New York: Cambridge University Press, 1992). Fukuyama may still be correct that the kinds of virtues Galston catalogues are an uninspiring ensemble ill-equipped to hold the spiritual attention of the brightest and best, or even the majority.

10. Elsewhere I have differentiated what I believe could legitimately be called postmodern from postmodernism. The latter is a straightforwardly late-modern phenomenon. See my *Between Eternities: Deflections Toward a Postmodern Philosophy* (Chicago: University of Chicago Press, 1994).

11. The not so subtle irony is that many of those who attacked Fukuyama had been operating upon their own furtive, usually suppressed, End of History theses.

12. This is precisely what a self-styled "postmodern, bourgeois ironist" like Richard Rorty does. See especially *Contingency, irony, solidarity* (New York: Cambridge University Press, 1991).

13. The central issue we confront at this point is one that cannot be adequately dealt with at present: What is the relation between reason, habit, and

tradition? The End of History thesis is the ultimate outcome of the Enlightenment faith that reason could replace habit and tradition completely. That was a fantastic hope from the beginning. But through acting upon that faith we have gone a long way toward destroying the habit background that is needed by any functioning society. Reason always requires law and habit as allies.

Even if reason is sufficient to grasp eternal questions and problems, that does not prove that reason can be immediately manifested in the conventional arrangements needed for everyday life. Indeed, reason can be adequately manifested in more than one set of conventional arrangements—the doctrinaire, modern, absolutist faith to the contrary notwithstanding. That is substantially what Aristotle meant when he asserted that justice is natural even though it changes.

The relation between philosophic insight and the traditions and *ethoi* that support daily existence is complicated. Unless one retains an unbounded faith in Enlightenment, shared *ethoi* are needed and must be allowed to evolve slowly over many generations. We cannot simply will traditions even if we could grasp the Whole exhaustively. We always need to find the way to articulate the truth for our time and place. How that could be accomplished in our time of unprecedented simultaneous changeability and creeping homogeneity remains the open question.

Even if we concluded that Plato, Aristotle, Aquinas, or whomever had grasped the truth, it still has to be articulated publicly and manifested in laws, customs, and habits. And the truth must be presented in ever renewed poetic articulations. Where are the poetic articulations, habits, and traditions for our time—the time at the end of the persuasiveness and plausibility of many *modern* beliefs and premises?

14. Consider in this regard, Alexis de Tocqueville, "How the Aspect of Society in the United States is at Once Agitated and Monotonous," *Democracy in America,* trans. George Lawrence (New York: Doubleday, 1969), pp. 614-16.

15. Of course, we can always believe in—or will—some version of the eternal recurrence. Even then we would be forced to explain what circumstance might return us to the beginnings. For us, the possibility of such a "return" probably would imply an apocalypse no sane person would wish for. But this would still not disprove the End of History thesis which claims only the impossibility of future novelty, not the impossibility of retrogression.

16. The collapse of Western (a.k.a. American) liberalism would in and of itself prove nothing. Likewise, natural catastrophes that reduce us to a more barbaric situation would prove nothing. The question would be, did we move to a novel set of historical possibilities, or "back" to ones that had already been lived? Having been pushed back to such a prior state, would we long for something novel in the future or would we then strive to get back to where we had already been? Everything comes back to the question, is there something novel—beyond late modernity—to long for? If not, the End of History thesis is plausible. The only point at which empirical evidence would be interesting is the empirical production of a novel ideal. We have seen none since Hegel.

17. If one accepts the argument that human nature is fixed and that there are a finite number of fundamental questions and human longings capable of playing themselves out, at some point history should have played out its finite possibilities. At that point only repetition or stagnation are possible.

18. It is no good saying that changes in material circumstances precede all changes in ideas, for one must still conceptualize, using ideas, what that change is/was. Worrying about the relation between ideas and material circumstances, one quickly gets drawn into an unsolvable chicken-egg conundrum. Rather than be drawn into this useless discussion we should bring ourselves back to more manageable observations, such as the observation that ideas have concrete consequences and no ideas are formed in a vacuum. We should add to this the understanding that truly novel ideas are rare.

19. The same response can be made to those who say that "philosophy" represents a satisfactory response to present dissatisfaction with the moral and political contours of the late modern world. "Philosophy" is hardly an alternative for any but a few—to believe otherwise is Enlightenment at its silliest. Further, if philosophy exists only in some Epicurean garden, of what public interest is it? We may grant that philosophy should not be turned into a public weapon as it has in the modern world, but as an entirely private affair of the few it would be publicly irrelevant and hence irrelevant to the present discussion. Were the privatization of philosophy to occur, we would have the Nietzschean picture of free-spirited over-men tripping quietly across the anthills that pass for civilization—what Nietzsche also termed the timeless "tombs of death." A deeper response would go to the nature of philosophy itself. Must not philosophy, in Socratic fashion, remain in the cave, and begin from speeches in the political community? If so, the Epicurean alternative is destructive for philosophy itself. Once we recognize the need to speak, we recognize simultaneously the need to be persuasive. Then we are led back to the issues we have been discussing—what novel ideal can be persuasively argued for at present—surely not the universalization of philosophy?

20. This is not to say that in unhinging old presuppositions Heidegger's thought may not eventually have concrete, deferred ramifications. See in this regard my *Between Eternities,* especially Part

3, "Heidegger's Critique of Modernity and the Postmodern Future."

21. It is not at all easy to explain what accounts for the disintegration of faith in a moral or political dispensation—unless, of course, one turns to Hegelian premises. It is far too easy to say that it is because the old dispensation came to be seen as false. Does that mean that the reason for its initial persuasiveness was precisely its falsity? It seems to me that a dead end lurks in that direction. It is unlikely that reason is ever *fully* adequate to "prove" or "disprove" the persuasiveness of a political and moral dispensation. To claim that it is gets us in the awkward position of arguing that the "irrationalists" had, at one time, the stronger "reasons." And once again, even if we are capable of a noetic apprehension of the truth, it must still be put into speech, and unless you are Hegel, there is more than one way to do that. There is no reason to believe that what some of us might see as a compelling articulation of the truth will be publicly more persuasive than what some of us perceive to be false.

22. The idea that our fundamental humanity is to be found in our ego or consciousness rather than in our instinctive materiality is one of the central modern premises from Descartes to Hegel. It was not a premise shared by, for example, Plato. By the time this modern idea had worked its way out to Kant and Hegel, our fundamental humanity was to be found not only in consciousness, but in conscious opposition to or negation of our instinctive materiality. This consciousness/instinct dichotomy is a distinctively modern invention.

23. Many critics of the End of History thesis have dismissed Kojève as a quaint and curious volume of increasingly forgotten lore. But the customary basis for those rejections is far from weighty—usually boiling down to the observation, correct if banal, that Anglo-American academics have paid him almost no attention. But Kojève is one of those rare individuals who truly deserve to be called thinkers. He knew how to take a theoretical premise, isolate its key concepts, and follow them resolutely to wherever *they* might lead, regardless of personal rooting interests. That kind of philosophical honesty is rare. It does not prove that Kojève is correct, but it does prove he deserves respect. By the same token, that most Hegel scholars dismiss Kojève's reading of Hegel does not prove that he is wrong. It is rare to find scholars who are honest brokers. One cannot fail to see the extent to which Hegelian scholarship gives us a liberal, socialist, conservative, or simply boring Hegel.

24. This could also, to use a term coined by Rousseau, be designated our "metaphysical freedom." This is *the* premise of late modernity—shared by Rousseau, Kant, Hegel, Marx, existentialism, critical theory, etc. This is the idea upon which late modernity must make its stand. See in this regard my *Between Eternities,* Part One, "The Essence of Modernity." According to this understanding, our metaphysical freedom is based on the fact that we are unlike all other species in that we are instinctively underdetermined. This allows us to determine ourselves, to a greater or lesser extent and more or less consciously, depending on the author. Unfortunately, the competition to determine man becomes increasingly hypothetical, abstract, and artificial, at which point one senses that this line of argument has more or less reached its terminus. For an Anglo-American example of this artificiality consider John Rawls, *A Theory of Justice* (Cambridge: Harvard University Press, 1971) and his "Original Position."

25. For reasons I will indicate shortly, I don't believe we should become overly delighted with the premise that human nature can always reassert itself. We live in a time when the mentality of limitlessness has taken hegemony. We are simultaneously equipped with techniques that allow us to assault natural limits—e.g., genetic engineering—and the desire to transcend all natural limits. Even if we could articulate what is fixed in our humanity, we are in a position to eradicate it. Hence the central question is one of ideas: should we or should we not continue further on the path to overcoming natural limits? We are then led right back into the kinds of issues we have been considering.

26. In my opinion, we are not confronted here by an either/or situation: The relationship between evolving consciousness and determinate materiality is complex. Fukuyama needs to work out more explicitly how the two are related. Perhaps he will return to this issue in the forthcoming sequel. The End of History debate confronts us with a version of the traditional nature/convention distinction. Is man primarily shaped by education, environment, culture, etc., or is he a genetically fixed and determinate being? This is in turn a version of what I would argue is an unsolvable chicken-egg problem of whether ideas cause changes in material reality or whether material changes prefigure changes in ideas. I believe it is best to conclude that the relationship is complex and that an either/or answer is not available. We have a fixed being that must be completed by habit—i.e., in a variety of different ways, albeit not an infinite variety. Our changing ideas have a significant influence on how that is accomplished.

Even here we are not confronted with a fundamentally empirical issue. Every modern "science" that presumes to speak about reality presupposes theories prior to the act of approaching empirical data; it would be naive to think that those theories were morally and politically neutral. To try to deduce anything from scientific "facts" is simply to dig up what was presupposed from the very

beginning. No science is morally, politically, or metaphysically neutral. We should dismiss the contrary early modern faith as a myth. Given that modern science cannot mediate the nature/convention issue, it is probably the case that we will never get beyond the conclusion that the relationship between evolving consciousness and determinate materiality is complex. Put another way, we will never get around the need to do speculative political philosophy.

27. As mentioned above, even if we find dissatisfaction by a few—or any minority—with the present world and the prevalent articulation of the Whole, justice and the good, it need not be interesting if global satisfaction by the majority remains. Because we live in a mass democratic age it would be unclear what ideas could come along to delegitimize the hegemony of the tastes, perceptions, and desires of the majority. Who thinks there is a plausible basis for a newly legitimate aristocracy, and from what direction might we expect its approach? Therein one may see one of the more compelling reasons why an extended hiatus of history is plausible.

28. This means we will never put to rest the fundamental nature/convention question and should be cautioned not to accept any simple invocation of either side of the equation.

29. For an important reflection on this subject see Joseph Cropsey, "The End of History in an Open-Ended Age?" in *If History Is Not Over, Then Where Is It Going? Reflections on Progress and Democracy*, eds. Arthur Melzer, Jerry Weinberger, and Richard Zinnman (Ithaca: Cornell University Press, 1994).

30. I have undertaken such a discussion in *Between Eternities*.

31. In other words, philosophy must always remain primarily dialectical political philosophy, for its own sake as well as that of the rest of the world. The retreat to some garden of shared noetic apprehension—which always raises the question of whether or not one is engaged in some subjective fantasy—points toward an ultimate alogon, "blindness." Here we should recall the Socratic metaphor of trying to grasp Being directly as an inevitably blinding staring at the sun. Religion always runs the same risk of blindness as any simply noetic philosophy. Our noetic visions, whether based on grace or otherwise, must be brought to speech. Even faith in the words of the prophets raises the question of how to tell true from false prophets. All of our endeavors require dialectical speech. There is no way to transcend the dialogue which is intrinsic to being human. As dialectical, philosophy must be of and part of its shared world, and that ultimately means it must engage in shared public speech.

Barry Gewen (review date 5-19 June 1995)

SOURCE: "Contradicted by the Facts," in *The New Leader*, June 5-19, 1995, pp. 5-7.

[*In the following review, Gewen offers unfavorable evaluation of* Trust.]

Not since Ray Bolger went dancing down that yellow brick road has there been a more popular straw man than Francis Fukuyama. In a sense, it's his own fault: By titling his provocative 1989 article **"The End of History?"** and then repeating the phrase in his 1992 book, *The End of History and the Last Man,* Fukuyama gave every lazy editorialist and Op-Ed writer in America the chance to pontificate about how wars and other disasters were going to continue to plague humanity despite the collapse of the Soviet Union. "Contrary to Francis Fukuyama, history has not come to an end," the pieces usually began, before going on to talk about Bosnia or Rwanda or whatever, and though they made Fukuyama famous, they probably left those people who had not bothered to read him with the impression that he was a complete idiot.

In fact, he is a highly intelligent and erudite man who, in his article and book, was attempting to extract some philosophical implications from the West's victory over the Soviet Union. Liberal democracy, he said, had proved superior to every competing ideology and was spreading around the world. Atavisms like ethnic nationalism and militant Islam were still possible—and tragic—choices in some regions, but Western principles of liberty and equality represented the highest level of social thought, indeed the "end point of man's intellectual evolution." Civilization had progressed to the stage where "all of the really big questions had been settled."

Fukuyama conceded that serious internal problems remained in the democracies. These, he maintained, were due to a failure to implement Western ideas, not to shortcomings in the ideas themselves. Anticipating the criticism that was sure to come, he stressed that his arguments had a worthy pedigree, deriving from Hegel (as well as Hegel's French proselytizer, Alexandre Kojeve). They were certainly open to question, whatever their source, but they deserved more than a thousand flicks of the editorial wrist.

Now, undaunted, Fukuyama is back with *Trust: The Social Virtues and the Creation of Prosperity.* He is just as wide-ranging, just as abstract and contemplative as before; only this time it is not Hegel he is serving up, it is Max Weber. In his new book Fukuyama takes issue with neoclassical economics, insisting that the rational, calculating, profit-seeking "economic man" beloved by Milton Friedman and his ilk is a distortion of reality, an incomplete picture of why human beings behave the way they do. People do not look simply to maximize utility, he says; they act for a whole host of reasons—many grounded in culture, belief and tradition—that cannot be fit into the economists'

models (one of the book's chapters is called "The Spiritualization of Economic Life").

Perhaps as a concession to the dismal scientists, Fukuyama does try to quantify these reasons, and he comes up with figures of 80 per cent for rational self-interest and 20 per cent for culture and habit. The numbers are silly, but the key insight is not. The author correctly warns that economists and, more important, societies as a whole ignore the nonrational origins of human motivation at their peril.

In particular, Fukuyama argues, successful nations—as measured by their economies—require a significant degree of trust. "Spontaneous sociability is critical to economic life because virtually all economic activity is carried out by groups rather than individuals." Trust not only enables persons to come together to solve problems, it gives them the flexibility to reorganize themselves to deal with the novel and the unexpected. "People who trust each other and are good at working with one another can adapt easily to new conditions and create appropriate new organizational forms." Trust also allows societies to form relatively large productive units to take advantage of economies of scale.

Some of the strongest pages of the book detail the economic inefficiencies caused by a lack of trust (and it is no accident that these will sound familiar to most Americans). Crime rises, requiring more investment in police and prisons. Law suits proliferate, making attorneys happy but sending insurance rates through the roof and imposing a tax on consumers. Corruption drains resources. In labor relations, every detail of the work process has to be contractually spelled out because neither side is willing to give the other any breathing space. "There is usually an inverse relationship between rules and trust," Fukuyama writes. "The more people depend on rules to regulate their interactions, the less they trust each other, and vice versa." Clearly, it seems, countries with high levels of trust are likely to do better in the global rat race than those with low levels.

The bulk of *Trust* is taken up with comparisons of different societies, and no one can accuse Fukuyama of not doing his homework. He examines trade unions in the United States and Germany, small business in France and Taiwan, family life in China and Japan. He tells us about samurai ethics, Sicilian sharecroppers, Christianity in South Korea, Frederick Taylor's management theories, and the size of Roger Smith's bonus after he practically drove General Motors off the road in the early 1980s. Mainly, Fukuyama draws distinctions between high-trust nations like Japan and Germany and low-trust ones like China, South Korea, France, and Italy.

Rather surprisingly, he finds that societies with strong family structures tend to develop low levels of trust, "because unrelated people have no basis for trusting one another." In China, for instance, and in places influenced by Chinese culture such as Singapore, Taiwan and Hong Kong, businesses function successfully at a Mom-and-Pop level, yet they never expand into large-scale enterprises since the owners are unwilling to place responsibility in the hands of managers who are not related to them. A company may survive into a second generation, when the sons take it over, and sometimes into the third generation, but it falls apart after that. Fukuyama notes that one consequence of this "Buddenbrooks phenomenon" is a dearth of recognizable Chinese brand names.

In a trust society like Japan, by contrast, family ties are much weaker and the impulse to reach out beyond next-of-kin much stronger. Voluntary associations in Japan are common, whether in archery or finance, and loyalty to the group is esteemed. Because their culture encourages large bureaucratic units run by professional managers, the Japanese were quick to adopt the corporate form of organization developed in the United States, and to make the most of it. The result has been all of those familiar names—Toyota, Mitsubishi, etc.—that have given American businessmen and a succession of American Presidents fits.

So far, so convincing. But as Fukuyama extends the argument to encompass France, Germany, Italy, South Korea, Taiwan, Hong Kong, and a large part of Latin America, he gets into trouble. South Korea, he tells us, is a low-trust society influenced by Chinese culture. Yet it has huge business organizations that are, if anything, more concentrated than those in Japan. How come? Because, Fukuyama remarks, the government has stepped in to create an economy based on the Japanese model, and it has succeeded splendidly, even if the Koreans don't much care to associate with one another. Untrusting South Korea is booming.

Or take Italy, another low-trust land. Sure enough, families are tight and businesses are small there; and in the south the economy is languishing. In central Italy, however, thousands of family enterprises are busily churning out shoes, machine tools and apparel for a highly competitive international market. Fukuyama observes that a lack of trust limits the size of these firms—none will ever become General Motors—yet why should the prosperous shoemakers of Tuscany care? Small can obviously be better, especially in labor-intensive industries with rapidly fluctuating consumer demand. And when Fukuyama concludes that "smallness of scale is . . . no more of a constraint on aggregate gross domestic product growth in Italy . . . than it is in Taiwan or Hong Kong," a reader begins to wonder just how important trust is anyway.

Matters are not helped when Fukuyama goes on to point out that high-trust nations have their downside. Tolerance and openness do not come naturally to them. "The egalitarianism in communally oriented societies," he explains, "is often restricted to the homogeneous cultural groups that tend to comprise them and does not extend to other human beings, even if they share their society's

dominant cultural beliefs. Moral communities have distinct insiders and outsiders; insiders are treated with a respect and equality that is not extended to outsiders." Fukuyama reminds his readers—if they need reminding—that high-trust Germany and high-trust Japan became notorious in the past for their treatment of conquered peoples and other "inferiors." Apparently it is the rule-bound societies, that is to say the low-trust ones, that accept differences among groups and adhere to universal codes of law protecting everyone.

Where does the United States fit in? Is it a high-trust or a low-trust country? According to Fukuyama it is a high-trust society on its way to becoming a low-trust one. There is all that crime, all those law suits. He also cites statistics showing that Americans are not the joiners they once were. The Lions, the Elks, the Masons, the Boy Scouts, and the American Red Cross have all lost members over the last 20 years. Parent-teacher associations have seen their rolls drop from 12 million in 1964 to 7 million today. And individuals apparently feel the difference. In 1960 a survey asking whether "most people" could be trusted elicited a "yes" from 58 per cent of the participants; in 1993 only 37 per cent answered affirmatively.

Fukuyama offers several reasons for this decline, ranging from the community-destroying effects of capitalism to the rise of the welfare state; most of his causes are drawn from the standard neoconservative litany (even if he does have to tap dance around a bit while bemoaning the weakening of the American family). The crucial question is whether any of this is pertinent. It would be nice, of course, to be able to leave our homes unlocked when we go out or to walk through our parks at night, but Fukuyama has been taking economic well-being as his standard, and by that measure the level of trust in American society appears largely irrelevant.

Compared to most other countries, the high-trust ones included, we seem to be doing all right. Fukuyama himself says: "From the perspective of the middle of the last decade of the 20th century, the economic prospects of the United States look very good indeed. . . . There have been few other periods in recent decades when American economic prospects looked brighter." Maybe they would look even more promising if we all became Elks and attended our local PTA meetings, but that is an awfully tough case to make.

In the end, a reader of *Trust* is likely to be somewhat puzzled. Low-trust societies are supposed to produce small enterprises—yet South Korea's are enormous. Low-trust societies, it is implied, do less well than high-trust ones— yet South Korea and central Italy are humming away, and the United States, declining on every sociability graph, is poised to take off once again economically. No doubt if he had wanted to, Fukuyama could have trotted out a few high-trust societies whose cupboards are bare. Britain, perhaps? Ireland? Egypt, maybe? Surely, they are out there. To his credit, he is honest with his evidence, and does not shrink from any of the exceptions or counterexamples to his thesis.

Actually, Fukuyama is so honest that by the final pages of his book he is left practically without any conclusion at all, as if the study he had undertaken to produce had turned out to be contradicted by the facts he accumulated. Limply, he writes: "What we can say is that the impact of cultural differences in the propensity for sociability will have a large, but at the moment indeterminate, impact on economic life." Max Weber would have done better.

Fareed Zakaria (review date 13 August 1995)

SOURCE: "Bigger Than the Family, Smaller Than the State," in *New York Times Book Review,* August 13, 1995, pp. 1, 25.

[*In the following review, Zakaria offers tempered assessment of* Trust, *which he describes as "a fascinating and frustrating book."*]

In 1989, as Communism teetered on the brink, Francis Fukuyama wrote a now-legendary essay extravagantly titled **"The End of History?"** In it, he argued that the global movement toward democracy and capitalism had brought to a final conclusion the centuries-old ideological debate over the ideal form of government. Now Mr. Fukuyama has shifted his attention from the state to society; the result is a fascinating and frustrating book, ***Trust: The Social Virtues and the Creation of Prosperity.*** We have settled on the structure of the state, he writes, but "liberal political and economic institutions depend on a healthy and dynamic civil society for their vitality."

In the world of ideas, civil society is hot. It is almost impossible to read an article on foreign or domestic politics without coming across some mention of the concept. And "civil society" has bipartisan appeal; from Hillary Rodham Clinton to Pat Buchanan, politicians of all stripes routinely sing its praises.

At the heart of the concept of civil society lie "intermediate institutions," private groups that thrive between the realm of the state and the family. Alexis de Tocqueville famously observed during his sojourn in this country that America was teeming with such associations—charities, choral groups, church study groups, book clubs—and that they had a remarkably salutary effect on society, turning selfish individuals into public-spirited citizens.

The renewed interest in civil society first emerged in Eastern Europe after Communism crumbled. Leaders like Vaclav Havel wanted to go beyond establishing new governments and create a culture that could sustain political and economic liberalism. They looked for help to those private groups beyond the reach of the state—citizens' associations, churches, human-rights chapters, jazz clubs— that had nourished dissident life. Around the same time, the victorious Western democracies found themselves confronting sagging economies, a fraying social fabric and the loss of national purpose. Here too, the experts and statesmen agreed, revitalizing civil society would overcome our malaise.

Mr. Fukuyama, a social scientist and former State Department analyst who is now a scholar at the Rand Corporation, pushes Tocqueville's argument a step further. The art of association is good not just for politics, be asserts, but for economics too: association inculcates the habit of working together with ease and therefore increases productivity; it makes rigid rules and complex legal contracts unnecessary. In short, it smooths the frictions of capitalism. Since Tocqueville, we have assumed that Rotary Clubs help democracy; Mr. Fukuyama tells us they help capitalism as well.

The ability to form the kind of groups that will help, Mr. Fukuyama argues, depends on trust. If a society has a culture of trust, and particularly if its members have the capacity to trust people outside their families, it generates "social capital," which is as useful as financial capital to its economic wellbeing. "Social capital is critical to prosperity and to what has come to be called competitiveness," he says.

Or that is what he says sometimes. Mr. Fukuyama has almost written two books in one. The first is his argument, interleaved throughout his 457 pages, for the virtue of trust, social capital and intermediate groups. The second, the bulk of the book, contains well-researched case studies of three "high-trust" countries—Germany, Japan and the United States—and three "low-trust" countries, France, Italy and China. In a discussion that is dazzling in its intelligence and complexity, he explains how trust and culture have affected the economic and political life of these six countries. Mr. Fukuyama ranges widely across civilizations and subjects, writing with as much originality and insight about Confucianism as about corporate structure. This very richness and nuance, however, undermines his book's general arguments.

Mr. Fukuyama's central assertion is that the strength of civil society strongly affects the industrial structure of societies. Far from being three distinct forms of capitalism, the American, Japanese and German economies, he says, bear a striking resemblance to one another. All three are dominated by large, private, professionally managed corporations, like the General Electric Company, the Toyota Motor Corporation and Siemens. France, Italy and China, on the other hand, have many small, family-run companies and a few giant, state-owned or subsidized corporations, like Renault and Italy's large banks. Mr. Fukuyama makes a persuasive case that this difference in industrial structure stems from differences in levels of trust within these societies. In France, Italy and China, people appear little able to trust anyone outside their families and form few intermediate organizations. The United States, Japan and Germany, by contrast, are societies of joiners, filled with organizations that bring strangers together in various ways. In a striking example, Mr. Fukuyama recounts how Wang Laboratories, "the one Chinese brand name familiar to many Americans," collapsed because its founder could not bring himself to trust professional managers and instead handed the company over to his incompetent son.

The correlation between trust and industrial structure is unimpeachable. But does it matter? Mr. Fukuyama admits that large professional corporations are not necessarily better for a country's growth or productivity. (The three fastest-growing industrialized nations in the postwar period have been Japan, France and Italy—one high-trust and two low-trust countries.) In fact, some economists argue that in the post-industrial age, small companies have the flexibility to outwit their larger, lumbering competitors. Small businesses have produced most of the jobs in the industrial world in the last two decades. In the end, Mr. Fukuyama reverts to a best-of-both-worlds prescription: the ideal economy, he says, would have small companies that are linked together, thus gaining both flexibility and size. Yet it is not clear why high-trust societies would be better at creating such arrangements. Indeed, linkages among small firms have already begun flourishing in low-trust Italy and China.

Social capital, then, is *not* critical to prosperity. Mr. Fukuyama mentions some ways that it might be useful economically, in positioning a country in key technological sectors, maintaining domestic control of arms industries and so on. But in truth, he seems to believe that civil society and social capital are good, not for their economic consequences, but rather for their noneconomic benefits. The "more important consequences," he writes, "may not be felt in the economy so much as in social and political life." Civil society breeds sociability, community and citizenship, and bolsters liberal democratic government; in other words, we are back to Tocqueville.

But even Tocqueville may have been wrong, not in his empirical observation that intermediate institutions bolster the American system of government, but in his generalization that such institutions are the key to democracy. Much of the current scholarly interest in intermediate institutions has been based on a study of Italian politics by the distinguished social scientist Robert D. Putnam, who argues that the rich civil society of northern Italy has fostered better government than the group-poor society of southern Italy. The book is brilliant, but its title, "Making Democracy Work," is utterly misleading. The Italian north has been better run than the Italian south for hundreds of years, during which time the country was, to put it mildly, not always democratic. One might more reasonably conclude from Mr. Putnam's research that social capital makes any regime work, whether monarchical, democratic or fascist. Democratic theorists, in fact, have typically disliked efficient government because it increases the power of the state vis-à-vis society, which is why James Madison consciously designed the Government of the United States to be unwieldy.

Behind much of the new interest in civil society, on the part of communitarians as well as social conservatives, is the idea that culture and society shape the nature of government. Obviously, there is some truth to this. But there is a tradition much older than Tocqueville's, running from Aristotle to Montesquieu, that asserts that fundamentally the state shapes society, not the other way around. Mr. Fukuyama claims that deep (and relatively unchanging) cultural traditions create trust, but his empirical sections suggest that culture is quite malleable. He argues—persuasively—that the growth of an overly centralized, regulatory and legalistic American state in the last 25 years has crowded out our once-flourishing civil society. Similarly, he shows that the reason the French, Italians and Chinese seem unwilling to trust people outside their families in business activities is a simple one. All three countries experienced long periods of centralized, arbitrary and domineering government with little respect for property rights and business contracts.

From East Asia to Africa, states that hit the right balance between order and liberty create successful nations and societies. (Even the Czech Republic will succeed more because of what Vaclav Klaus, the conservative economist who is Prime Minister, does to its state than what Vaclav Havel, the philosopher and playwright who is President, does to its society.) Consider Russia today, whose success or failure surely depends more on getting its political and economic fundamentals right than on the number of soccer leagues that spring up in Moscow. This is because the structure of the state has powerful effects, for good or for ill, but also because not all Russia's private groups will be soccer leagues. The Mafia is, after all, an intermediate institution. The Middle East, to take another example, is currently experiencing a renaissance of intermediate institutions, but the citizens' groups forming there are often intolerant, politically and religiously extreme, and advocate violence and terror. It is difficult to believe that the emergence of more groups like these will lead to genuine democracy there.

We have come to think of civil society as being full of Rotary Clubs, Red Cross chapters and social workers' groups. Such organizations, of course, help bolster liberal democracy. But the space between the realm of government and that of the family can be filled with all kinds of associations, liberal and illiberal. Historians have amply laid out how the Nazi Party made its first inroads through infiltrating local groups. On a less extreme note, many of the small groups that have formed in America over the last two decades have been thoroughly illiberal in spirit: victims' groups that have discouraged individual responsibility, minority clubs that have Balkanized the campus and the workplace, pseudoreligious cults with violent agendas. Will more of these save American democracy?

In the economic realm, some private groups can actually hurt economic growth. Mr. Fukuyama is well aware that historically "medieval producers following the economic doctrines of the Catholic Church," as well as some unions and small special-interest groups, have created the deadlock and stasis that are inimical to energetic capital-

ism. Social capital, he says revealingly, "is likely to be helpful from an economic standpoint only if it is used to build wealth-creating economic organizations." Exactly. We like intermediate institutions when they have good effects and dislike them when they have bad ones. What we want, it would seem, is not civil society, but civics—what the Romans called *civitas;* that is, public-spiritedness, sacrifice for the community, citizenship, even nobility. But not all of civil society is civic minded.

In a thoughtful essay at the beginning of this year, Mr. Putnam argued that America's social capital is dwindling dangerously, membership in Rotary Clubs, P.T.A.'s and the Boy Scouts is dropping. As a symbol of the problem, he noted that while more Americans are bowling, fewer are bowling in leagues and groups. With its haunting title, "Bowling Alone," the piece won applause across the spectrum, from George Will to President Bill Clinton.

Less noticed was a report in *The New York Times* four months later on Timothy J. McVeigh, the accused bomber of the Federal Building in Oklahoma City. It turns out that Mr. McVeigh and his buddies, Terry and James Nichols, would go to a bowling alley some evenings. The group seemed to perform all the functions of a good intermediate institution, creating a sense of community, fostering comradeship and facilitating the planning of group projects. But perhaps we would all have been better off if Mr. McVeigh had gone bowling alone.

Philip Green (review date 25 September 1995)

SOURCE: "History: To Be Continued," in *The Nation,* September 25, 1995, pp. 318-22.

[*In the following review, Green offers an unfavorable evaluation of* Trust.]

How is it that some people become famous while others do not? Of course, it smacks of sour grapes for one of the latter to ask this about one of the former, but Francis Fukuyama's career begs for the question. How exactly do you get ahead by boldly making one of the worst predictions in the history of social science? In case anyone has forgotten, six years ago he wrote that, with the fall of Communism, we've reached an "end of history," marked by a "worldwide convergence in basic institutions around liberal democracy and market economics," in which "the broad process of human historical evolution culminates not, as in the Marxist version, in socialism but rather in the Hegelian vision of a bourgeois liberal democratic society." This is also a world in which "modern technology . . . shapes national economies in a coherent fashion," so that "the world's advanced countries have no alternative model of political and economic organization other than democratic capitalism to which they can aspire."

He's got to be kidding. The American economy (or the South Korean or Italian or Chinese or British economy) is "coherent"? The aspirants to "democratic capitalism" (Margaret Thatcher, Ronald Reagan, Pat Robertson, Patrick Buchanan, Charles Pasqua, Silvio Berlusconi) are trying to adopt *liberal* democratic political institutions? "Human societies . . . around the world" are restricted to a handful of nation-states, mostly in Western Europe and North America? How much effort does it take to notice that elites in one after the other of the "advanced countries" have sought to shed liberal institutions as fast as they can, in order to crush rebellions bound to arise as "the global capitalist division of labor" integrates all of us into a two-class world of unrelenting rigidity?

And what of Hegel, to whom Fukuyama explicitly compares himself? Yes, Hegel thought that a world of independent nation-states might reach the "end of history," but only by manifesting the triumph of *reason* in their institutions. It doesn't take more than a cursory reading of *The Philosophy of Right* to discover that he didn't have in mind anything remotely like governments in thrall to organizations of multi-armed paranoiacs or neofascist thugs or (especially!) religious sectarians; or governments that deny a general duty to maintain the welfare of the poorest-off. Hegel notoriously toadied to the Prussian regime, but his euphemistic account still makes it sound a lot better than the Tory regime of 1995, or what we can expect for the United States by 1997. Bourgeois liberalism? If only. Any socialist nowadays would gladly settle for that. How about John Stuart Mill for President? Jefferson? Kant? Adam Smith? Lincoln? One is reminded of Gandhi's famous response on being asked what he thought of Western civilization, that "it would be a good thing."

How to demonstrate this alleged convergence, as opposed to simply asserting it? The trick is methodological, assiduously perfected by Fukuyama in the more than 400 pages of *Trust,* almost all of which he borrows from other people's sociology or economics—Alice Amsden on South Korea, Ronald Dore on Japan, Michel Crozier on France, Charles Sabel and Michael Piore on the new regime of work, Alexis de Tocqueville on the United States and the *ancien régime,* Edward Banfield on Southern Italy, Max Weber on the Protestant Ethic and Confucianism, Mary Ann Glendon on rights, Samuel Huntington on the excesses of democracy . . . and on and on. Replace Marx's emphasis on historical materialism with Weber's on culture; "culturalism" then does the lion's share of the work. ("Cultural relativism," the more familiar term, is an ethical stance; what I prefer to call "culturalism" is purely sociological.)

From a culturalist perspective, there are no inherent contradictions in capitalism that cry out for resolution; instead, there are many capitalisms, each based on a national culture, and each successful or not depending on how congruent the culture is with a lifeworld of market exchange—the best lifeworld available. Progressive economic life is based on a culture of generalized "trust," or what Fukuyama calls "spontaneous sociability." The best index of such sociability turns out to be widespread

corporate conglomerations, monopolies, cartels, the *zaibatsu,* all of which indicate that their host-societies (Japan, Germany and the United States) have cultural understandings that generate trust in non-kin, most importantly, in professional corporate managers and engineers. Conversely, Confucian familism in China and Korea limits the spread of the impersonal corporate form, obliging the relatively inefficient state to take over the role of general entrepreneurship, while British class contempt dictates a destructive split between financial and industrial capital, and "amoral familism" in Southern Italy makes progressive economic development there all but impossible.

We are told that this spontaneous sociability is rooted in precapitalist political decentralization and in concomitant institutions of an elaborated civil society, such as the well-known web of reciprocal obligations in Japan that led to the post-World War II trust-based exchange of lifetime employment (*nenko*) for labor peace; or, in Germany, feudal guilds and the universal work ethic they fostered, which ultimately made possible an immensely elaborated welfare state; or, in the United States, Protestant sectarianism and its correlative, communal activism, which until recently balanced out a hypertrophied individualism.

It's helpful to compare this basically static account of capitalist development with such neo-Marxist versions of the same phenomenon as those of Rodney Hilton, Barrington Moore, Perry Anderson and Robert Brenner. Brenner's analysis of the transition from feudalism to capitalism in England, France and Poland describes social actors (lords and peasants, landowners and agricultural laborers), significant events (peasant rebellions in times of economic crisis) and transformative outcomes—different political settlements of these class struggles, resulting in different patterns of land tenure with consequently different implications for later economic activity. In Moore's account (from which Brenner took off), top-down transformations resulted in fascism (e.g., in Japan and Germany). Overall, these "historical materialist" approaches to change emphasize the role of struggles for power among social classes, rather than socially neutral abstractions such as "decentralization" or "communitarianism."

Fukuyama's culturalist explanations, in contrast, are devoid of historical struggle, and tend to vanish into dust at the first sight of it. For example, the web of obligation in Japan, based on a cultural proclivity for "spontaneous sociability," does almost the whole work of the Japanese "miracle"—until, that is, "the bursting of the bubble economy of the late 1980s." Now, it appears, economic recession has put "tremendous pressures on the lifetime employment system," so that "some large corporations have in fact resorted to layoffs." And in Germany that same recession "created high and seemingly intractable levels of unemployment, and in the view of many observers it was precisely the communitarian aspects of the German postwar *Sozialmarktwirtschaft* that was to blame." Just as in Japan, "the general intensification of global competition . . . will continue to put a great deal of pressure on German communitarian economic institutions," and the welfare state may have to be downsized considerably. The Old Mole under Highgate Cemetery is surely saying at this point: Well, that's what I told you, isn't it? Cutthroat competition, a falling rate of profit, the need to maintain surplus value through a sloughing off of labor and a lowering of the average wage—what did you expect? The chapters on Japan and Germany, in fact, both end on an almost elegiac note: Hey guys, this communitarian stuff was nice while it lasted, but now let's get with global capitalism.

What is the point of these cross-cultural comparisons that come to nothing, especially since, as Fukuyama assures us, cultural patterns are not exportable? On the face of it, they seem to have nothing to do with Fukuyama's legendary convergence. Actually, though, the culturalist analysis makes his point, which is that there are many roads to capitalism, and some of them are communal rather than (liberal) individualistic or *state-oriented*. And so, "a corollary to the convergence of institutions at the 'end of history' is the widespread acknowledgment that in post-industrial societies, further improvements cannot be achieved through ambitious social engineering." Put simply, the United States could stand some communitarianism of the old style (German, Japanese or American Puritan); what it doesn't need are strong *public* institutions.

The target of these 457 pages of other people's sociology is educated, prosperous and powerful American elites, who receive a simple and helpful message: Nothing painful or costly has to be done, because nothing can be done. Install Japanese production techniques ("lean manufacturing") in your workplaces to produce company loyalty in the place of job-productive trade unionism, provide in-house flexible training, and that's about it. Your taxes needn't go up, and the state won't bother you because the state can't accomplish anything worthwhile. We philosophize; you are philosophized. *Your* history has ended, buddy; mine has just begun. Back to Chiapas with you. Or to inner-city ghettos, whose inhabitants, per Fukuyama (out of Thomas Sowell) are "deracinated," without entrepreneurial spirit or institutions of communal self-help; and thus beyond *other people's* help.

It's impossible to tell if Fukuyama *intends* this book to be read as an essay in political negativity, but that's certainly how it will be read by those who matter. This is especially so since he peddles the usual line of American nostalgia ("The Way Things Never Were," in Stephanie Koontz's wonderful title), according to which we were a trusting, communal bunch until—guess what?—yes, the 1960s. (The nostalgicists should all be forced to read an entertaining book on early twentieth-century labor struggles by Louis Adamic called, simply, *Dynamite*. Or any book on slavery or Reconstruction. Or . . .) Then came the welfare explosion, the litigation explosion, the rights explosion and abortion, and so—here he appropriates the recent work

of Robert Putnam—Americans stopped being communal, stopped joining voluntary organizations. And it's all our fault!

Well, if Putnam and Fukuyama insist on looking at bowling clubs and P.T.A.s, that's what they'll find. But have they heard of the N.R.A. and the Christian Coalition? It's not community that's lacking, but civility and a respect for equal justice. Putnam uses the decline of union membership as an index of failing communalism, but somehow he and Fukuyama have missed the development of corporate unionbusting as one of the major American growth sectors of the past two decades. Do workers distrust managers because of too much individualism? Actually, most of the participants in "the rights explosion" whom I know belong to many voluntary associations and are intensely communal, though it's true they don't go bowling much. Does standing in vigils count?

Fukuyama (like his source Mary Ann Glendon) does not consider the possibility that our unending racial and sexual confrontation is a cause as well as an outcome of communal breakdown. Nor does he notice the savage class warfare that capital (not labor) has been waging for two decades. Nor the way in which social decay in the face of global redistribution has produced the distorted sociability of superpatriotism ("We're Number One!"). Nor the enveloping culture of greed, hyped not by "inner-city African-Americans" or tort lawyers but by good old-fashioned economic elites and their pet Presidents. That is, he doesn't notice much because he keeps looking for "culture," instead of looking for people who are doing things to other people.

In a throwaway that sums up his critique of liberal individualism, Fukuyama remarks that Asians—especially the familistic Chinese—have difficulty understanding American insistence on human rights because of the abstract universalistic principles on which such rights are based. I pondered this notion. What might it mean? The best I could come up with is that people with Confucian rather than Christian traditions think that it's perfectly O.K. to torture nonkin. Do they really? And let's see, was the embrace by Jeane Kirkpatrick and *Commentary* magazine of Argentine torturers due to some defect in Irish Catholic or Jewish culture? What culture trains all those Latin American torturer/murderers at Fort Benning? When the U.S. Air Force decided that the best way to prepare female pilots for rape was by raping them, whose cultural tradition was that? Men's?

The world over, a depressingly large number of people will torture and murder in the pursuit of power, or out of the desire to maintain it ("maintaining order" is what this is usually called), and if we are among those people it appears that our only internal constraint will be the urgency of our need. External constraints, on the other hand, are considerably more important. There's plenty of abuse of rights in the United States, but a lot less than in China, and the reason is not some kind of communitarianism but because we have created a variety of institutions to restrain such abuses, and China hasn't. On the other hand, we're not nearly so good as the Germans at creating institutions to prevent and alleviate economic despair. Of course, cultural patterns do count here, as this comparison suggests; a one-sided economic materialism (as Weber put it) cannot by itself explain the differences. But the overemphasis on culture is worse, because it justifies a cop-out on action, on taking as much responsibility as one can reasonably manage for the state of the world. That's why when I see the word "culture" these days, I reach for my eraser.

Actually, no one will really read **Trust,** except reviewers like me, because it's 200 pages too long and repeats every point many times. But everyone in a certain milieu will talk about it, because as a crash course in comparative political economy and sociology it enables them to think they know what they're talking about when they chit-chat about lifetime employment in Japan or the high cost of the German welfare state. And it fits perfectly with the dominant political consciousness of the day.

Anthony Giddens (review date 13 October 1995)

SOURCE: "Keeping the Family Firm," in *New Statesman,* October 13, 1995, pp. 30-1.

[*In the following review, Giddens offers positive assessment of* Trust.]

The End of History and the Last Man was always going to be a hard act to follow. Much criticised in the social-science community, Francis Fukuyama's book was actually a major work that captured the mood of 1989 and after. It deservedly projected the author to global fame, and one might suspect a few sour grapes in the dismissive attitudes of some academic critics. His new book isn't going to set the cash registers ringing as his first did and it has nothing like the same originality. Yet it is a work of considerable intellectual substance, engagingly written and ambitious in content.

We're back on the familiar terrain of the end of history. Right up to 1989, there were deep cleavages between different ideologies; but these have been replaced, Fukuyama notes, by a "remarkable convergence" of opinions and institutions. Societies which have liberal democracy and capitalism can see nothing beyond those which haven't got them want them.

The global triumph of democracy and capitalism, however, doesn't mean that there's an even playing field, even in the advanced countries. There are different types of capitalism; some are gaining in strength while others are threatened.

Writing nearly a century ago, the great German sociologist Max Weber sought to answer the question: why did capitalism first develop in the west, and not in the eastern civili-sations? Criticising both Marx and orthodox economics, Weber argued that economic development is strongly affected by social habits and ethical codes, especially those contained within religion. Weber was interested only in the origins of capitalism. He accepted that once a capitalistic system had come into being, it might not develop in the same way elsewhere. Capitalism could not have emerged spontaneously in the east, but it might be transplanted there. And this is just what has happened, with the coming of the "Asian miracle".

But what accounts for that "miracle"? Many current observers have drawn upon Weber to seek an answer—and so does Fukuyama. The economic competitiveness of Japan and the other "Asian tigers", Fukuyama says, comes from some of the traits Weber identified. Rather than the capitalist spirit as such, Fukuyama emphasises what he calls "social capital" or the "social virtues".

In the early years of western capitalism, Weber pointed out, Protestantism provided a moral context for business activities. Businessmen travelling across the US would introduce themselves to new contacts as Christian believers: shared beliefs served as a guarantee of mutual trustfulness.

Capitalistic enterprise needs an undergirding of trust in others, and that can't be delivered by the economic contract alone. In the terminology of another founder of sociology, Emile Durkheim, there is a non-contractual element in all contracts.

Economic activity isn't carried out by individuals, Fukuyama says, but by people acting in association. In small groups and large organisations, cooperation depends on shared values, a property of culture rather than the economy. And social capital is a precondition for the effective building of economic capital. Fukuyama is putting forward a sort of historically based communitarianism.

The family is one obvious form of moral community generating trust relations. Hence "it is no accident"—a phrase he uses often—that most businesses, in current as well as earlier times, are family businesses. The influence of the family over economic enterprise links apparently divergent societies. Southern China and northern Italy, both hotbeds of rapid development, are each characterised by the extended family. Familialism alone, he admits, is not enough, as southern Italy shows. Families are a fount of economic activity only if they are dynamic and outward-looking.

Capitalistic societies with strong families but fairly weak bonds of community between strangers are marked by the predominance of small businesses. The resources of trust needed for larger enterprises are difficult to create. These countries have weak intermediary associations between families and the state: Italy, Spain and France in Europe; China, Taiwan, and Singapore in the east.

Japan, Fukuyama suggests, is different from all of these; the Asian miracle isn't cut of single cloth and Japan resembles Germany more than it does the other successful Asian economies. No surprises there—the more inventive part of his argument lies in the claim that Japan and the US resemble one another. Japan is usually thought of as a society oriented towards the group, the US as the home of rampant individualism. In Fukuyama's view these perceptions are wrong. Americans may dislike big government, but they are great joiners. They aren't individualists at heart: witness their dense networks of voluntary organisations. These are part of the social capital responsible for the robustness of the US economy.

The state pays a larger part in Japanese society than in the US, but it isn't, Fukuyama says, the prime force in Japan's impressive development. Japan also boasts a large network of voluntary groups—more hierarchical than in the US, but not based upon kinship. The social capital they generate allows for the creation of bigger enterprises than those in kinship-dominated trust systems. Hence, in both Japan and the US, large corporations are much more prominent than in, say, Italy, France or Taiwan.

The US today, however, finds itself in trouble; its fund of social capital is being depleted. Here Fukuyama echoes authors such as Robert Bellah and Robert Putnam. Individualism is winning out over more collective styles of social life. The pre-existing balance between individual rights and community obligations has tilted too far in favour of the former. Thus membership of voluntary groups has dropped over the past two decades.

Fukuyama comes close to endorsing the "Singapore critique" of the US, as offered by that state's leader, Lee Kwan Yew. Family life in the US, says Fukuyama, "has deteriorated markedly since the 1960s" and civic mistrust has grown. The US is living off past glories, drawing on an historical fund of social capital that isn't being renewed.

Fukuyama's book has many virtues, not least its boldness in attempting such a vast comparative sweep. Yet he is no Max Weber and a host of objections or qualifications springs to mind. The key terms "trust" and "social capital" aren't discussed at any length, although both are problematic. "Trust" in particular has a large role to play; but Fukuyama doesn't refer to the seminal work done on the topic by writers such as Niklas Luhmann or Diego Gambetta.

Fukuyama's comparison of Japan and the US is thought-provoking, but scarcely persuasive. In spite of his attempts to downplay it, the state has been much more important in Japanese society than in the US. One can't help but feel that Fukuyama wants to stress similarities to accommodate a preconceived argument.

Japan was and is a much more hierarchical society. Voluntary associations have long been well-developed in the US, but this is *because* of the high degree of individualism rather than in spite of it. "Individualism" is itself a complex term—Steven Lukes, if I recall, once distin-

guished 17 different meanings—but isn't analysed by Fukuyama. Individualism in certain senses is advancing in Japan. Moreover, the idea that the family and "community life" in the US (and in the UK?) are threatened with breakdown is much more controversial than Fukuyama suggests.

His main claim is that economic modernity depends on sources of social capital that are not themselves modern. To function effectively, capitalistic enterprise presumes traditional solidarity. Arnold Gehlen made much the same argument many years ago. Jurgen Habermas developed this theme in proposing that capitalism tends to destroy the sources of its own moral legitimacy, since the expansion of markets attacks tradition. Fukuyama should have confronted these and similar ideas.

He might be right that "social capital" is relevant to economic success—although I don't think that the book even comes close to demonstrating this. Yet western and eastern societies alike will have to search for new sources of solidarity, because detraditionalisation is advancing apace almost everywhere. In the east, as elsewhere, time will show that economic modernity and tradition are an unstable mix.

Robert Heilbroner (review date Winter 1996)

SOURCE: "What Francis Fukuyama Can Teach . . . and Learn," in *Dissent,* Vol. 43, No. 1, Winter, 1996, pp. 109-14.

[*In the following review, Heilbroner provides an overview and critique of Fukuyama's historical, political, and social perspective in* The End of History and the Last Man *and* Trust.]

Francis Fukuyama's **The End of History** predictably earned him a skeptical response when it appeared a few years ago, especially from critics on the left, many of whom, one suspects, had not read the book. (There are some notable exceptions, such as Perry Anderson's "The Ends of History," a brilliant treatment, at once critical and admiring, in *A Zone of Engagement.*) Our daily exposure to Yugoslavian chaos, Russian anarchy, Chinese instability, African decay, and not least, United States retrogression offered ample reason to jeer at what seemed to be the smug conservatism of his title. Having myself harbored similar sentiments at the time (and for the same reason), I would like to begin this consideration of that infamous book, and of *Trust,* its newly published successor, by examining what they actually say. For I believe that Fukuyama has something of value to teach the left, not the least part of which is the necessity to discover what the left may be able to teach him.

The thesis that underlies these books is nothing less than an effort to discover the meaning of human history, which is to say, the core of significance behind the tragedies, disappointments, and occasional successes that assail us daily in the newspapers or that we find retrospectively in the great narratives of Thucydides, Gibbon, and the like. Lest this only deepen our suspicion of Fukuyama's work, it may be helpful to recall that many of us have begun from, or still harbor, such an ambitious overview of history as the gradual movement from the alienating and exploitative life of a class-stratified society to the emancipated existence of a democratic socialist one. This derives, of course, from Marx's view, celebrated in his much quoted description of a communist society as one in which one could "hunt in the morning, fish in the afternoon, rear cattle in the evening, criticize after dinner . . . without ever becoming hunter, fisherman, shepherd, or critic."

There is no need to criticize this famous flight of fancy, which stands in sharp contrast to the meaning of history that informs Fukuyama's work. Fukuyama treats Marx with all due respect, but he finds his own inspiration in Marx's own source, Georg Wilhelm Friedrich Hegel. This is a view of history not merely as a vehicle for emancipation from oppression, but as a process by which humanity gradually becomes aware of a deeper need. In Fukuyama's paraphrase of Hegel:

> Men seek not just material comfort, but respect or recognition, and they believe that they are worthy of respect because they possess a certain value or dignity. A psychology, or a political science, that did not take into account man's desire for recognition, and his infrequent but very pronounced willingness to act at all times contrary to even the strongest natural instinct, would misunderstand something very important about human behavior.

Fukuyama employs the Greek term *thymos*—roughly *dignity* or *self-respect*—for this crucial need. *Thymos* plays a central role for him, as it does for Hegel (who does not, however, use its Greek name), because the transcendent importance of dignity leads both to ascribe to political liberty a primary place in the development of complete human beings, ultimately more important for their self-realization even than the satisfaction of "natural"—that is, material—wants. It goes without saying that this stress on *thymos* also serves to separate Hegel and his followers from Marx, who assuredly valued human self-respect, but rather too easily assumed that political liberty would naturally follow economic emancipation.

It is here, however, that Fukuyama himself departs sharply from a mere restatement of Hegel's views. Specifically, for Hegel, the mechanism for the historical transformation of personhood has a heroic, even mystical quality—"The individual, who has not risked his life, may, no doubt, be recognized as a person; but he has not attained the truth of this recognition as an independent self-consciousness." With Fukuyama, the development of full personhood has a much more matter-of-fact character. We find it set forth in the opening chapters of *The End of History,* where he identifies the transformative Mechanism (with a capital "M") as the growing embrace of natural science, with its

enlargement of material abundance. This is a far cry from Hegel's heroic awakening, but it is equally—perhaps much more—effective. Fukuyama writes: "Apart from fast-disappearing tribes in the jungles of Brazil or Papua New Guinea, there is not a single branch of mankind that has not been touched by the Mechanism, and which has not become linked to the rest of mankind through the universal economic nexus of modern consumerism."

As this passage makes clear, the historic process for Fukuyama is driven primarily by much less inspiring means than is the case with Hegel, but there is, nonetheless, a specifically Hegelian emphasis in Fukuyama's treatment. This is the importance of the idea of freedom. With Hegel this idea is finally instantiated in a state governed by an upper class that protects and values the *thymos* of its citizenry. In Fukuyama the historic process leads to the recognition that democratic institutions are the only possible template for the political life of an advanced society. However much reality may depart from this ideal, the ideal itself is now everywhere acknowledged. "That is to say," Fukuyama writes, "for a very large part of the world, there is now no ideology with pretensions to universality that is in a position to challenge liberal democracy, and no universal principle of legitimacy other than the sovereignty of the people."

Finally, capitalism completes the picture as the economic expression of liberalism. Fukuyama defines capitalism pragmatically, with emphasis on the relative strengths of the public and private sectors: "It is evident," he writes, "that there are many possible interpretations of this rather broad definition of economic liberalism, ranging from the United States of Ronald Reagan and the Britain of Margaret Thatcher to the social democracies of Scandinavia and the relatively statist regimes in Mexico and India. All contemporary capitalist states have large public sectors, while most socialist states have permitted a degree of private economic activity . . . Rather than try to set a precise percentage, it is probably more useful to look at what attitude the state takes *in principle* to the legitimacy of private property and enterprise."

As we shall see, this seemingly uncritical approach to capitalism ultimately leads Fukuyama into serious difficulties. But it is enough for the moment to complete the argument. A triad of science, political liberalism, and capitalism constitutes the elements of a social order that qualifies as the End of History. In the author's words:

> It is not the mark of provincialism but of cosmopolitanism to recognize that there has emerged in the last few centuries something like a true global culture, centering around technologically driven economic growth and the capitalist social relations necessary to produce and sustain it. Societies which have sought to prevent this unification, from Tokugawa Japan and the Sublime Porte, to the Soviet Union, the People's Republic of China, Burma, and Iran have managed to fight rearguard actions that have lasted only for a generation or two. Those who were not defeated by superior military technology were seduced by the glittering material

world that modern natural science has created. While not every country is capable of becoming a consumer society in the near future, there is hardly a society in the world that does not embrace the goal itself.

Not very long ago such a thesis would have been laughed out of court, or at the very least asked to take its place in line behind socialism. I need hardly add that these views have changed as a consequence of the disasters in the Soviet Union, China, and Cuba. As a result, one can see why Fukuyama's claim deserves to be taken seriously. Science, liberal democracy, and capitalism do in fact constitute an uncontested center of gravity for institutional design in our day, and in the foreseeable future. To repeat, Fukuyama is not blind to the presence of fundamentalist beliefs, dictatorial governments, and anticapitalist mentalities. His point, rather, is that the force of science, the political frame of liberal democracy, and the energizing impetus of capital accumulation and competition have today become ideas beyond which it is very difficult— Fukuyama might even say impossible—to think. As we will see, I am doubtful that the triad, as it is defined in Fukuyama's book, constitutes an end to history, but I think he is right that it has created a resting point that may endure for a considerable while.

Having paid my tribute, I must state my reservations. The first concerns an issue whose centrality for Fukuyama I have only indicated in passing. It is the importance of *thymos* as an indispensable requirement for any envisioned "end of history." Fukuyama's commitment to *thymos* is passionate, which does not prevent him from a keen awareness of its potential for conversion into *megalothymos,* or the desire for collective recognition that leads easily to nationalism or ethnic aggressions. In the same reflective vein, he admits that it is uncertain whether the inequality associated with capitalism may not pose a serious threat to the attainment of a society of mutual recognition, as critics on the left would maintain; while also giving ear to the fears of the right that any such hoped-for equality may simply founder before the reality of human differences.

Thus Fukuyama offers hopes, but no assurances, with regard to the attainment of *thymos* in the liberal capitalist setting he favors. To me that candor, itself very typical of this bold but modest thinker, only strengthens his central placement of political and psychological concerns as the underlying requirement for a durable and workable historical model. But there is also something here that critics can teach Fukuyama. It is that his depiction of *thymos* smacks too much of an adult struggle for virtue and rationality. Dignity may well be a necessary condition for a good society, but the character and intensity of that need—not to mention the ease with which it is turned into racial and other intolerances—does not reflect only the spiritual strengths and weaknesses of mature individuals. Rather, it mirrors the fact that, like all behavior, *thymos* is formed in the gauntlet through which all must pass—the long and painful passage through childhood into early adolescence. If it lies within our capabilities to create a good society—by no means an assumption to be easily granted—the lesson-

books will have to be those that help us strengthen the psyches of infants and children; and the teachers to whom we must turn not the dramatists of the adult spirit, but the explorers of the infantile imagination—not Hegel or Kojeve or Nietzsche, but Sigmund Freud.

There is none of this in Fukuyama's book. Indeed, there is an amusing indication of its absence: in the extensive index to *The End of History* there is one entry for Freud, but when we turn to the indicated page, his name does not appear there (nor on any other page). Neither is any work of Freud's, or of other students of the unconscious, cited in the long list of sources. In a word, whatever we know about the process of personality formation is left out in a book in which personhood is given center stage.

A second criticism is much more predictable. It is the inadequate treatment of the dynamism of capitalism. To be sure, capitalism is described as deeply and by no means always constructively transformative, but somehow this recognition is never fully realized. Instead, capitalism appears as an essentially static framework within which disruptive developments, such as trends toward automation and globalization, appear but are never linked to the momentums and hungers of a social order dependent on ceaseless accumulation. In similar fashion, even when Fukuyama acknowledges the relation of capitalism's dynamism to the question of *thymos,* his treatment lacks vitality. For example, in assessing its negative effects he writes:

> The possibility of strong community life is also attacked by the pressures of the capitalist marketplace. Liberal economic principles provide no support for traditional communities; quite the contrary, they tend to atomize and separate people . . . [L]ives and social connections are more unstable, because the dynamics of capitalist economies means constant shifts in the location and nature of production and therefore work. . . . The sense of identity provided by regionalism and localism diminishes, and people find themselves retreating into the microscopic world of their families which they carry around with them from place to place like lawn furniture.

This is a strong presentation of the economic pressures of a market system on community life. Yet, where are the impacts of falling real wages, of disappearing employments, of the stupefaction of relentless advertising on the capacity to cultivate one's own dignity, much less to respect that of others? Perhaps more telling, the passage occurs a mere fourteen pages before the book's conclusion, in which the gravest danger to the End of History is seen as the *political* uncertainty as to "what constitutes man and his specific dignity." Thus, unaccountably, Fukuyama acknowledges but then forgets the role of capitalism as a powerful agency in forming man's conception of his self. Having given lip service to the possibility that capitalism may well undermine the attainment of a society of mutual concern and respect, in the end Fukuyama allows himself to be carried away by a conception of that ultimate desideratum as a process determined by high moral and political considerations, to the neglect of lower, but perhaps more powerful, psychological and economic ones.

This brings me to Fukuyama's second book, *Trust: The Social Virtues and the Creation of Prosperity,* which he describes as an economic sequel to his first. To his credit I should add that it bears little resemblance to the abstract economics we learn in the standard textbooks. "Economics," he tells us on the first page, "is grounded in social life and cannot be understood separately from the larger question of how modern societies organize themselves." This leads Fukuyama into an analysis of the social relationship that constitutes the title of his book—a relationship that clearly has its roots in *thymos,* although that key word no longer appears in the text, perhaps because the sociologist Max Weber now becomes more of a tutelary figure than Hegel. Trust is vital to the success of capitalism, Fukuyama explains, because it constitutes the ultimate basis of its productive capabilities. In conventional economics, success *is* attributed to the vast structure of capital that the system accumulates, together with the immense division of labor that this makes possible. In Fukuyama's economics, the secret lies in the growth of "social capital"—the ability of people to work together—and this social capital, in turn, derives from the capability of individuals to share norms, to respect the dignity of others, and to join hands in common goals—in short, from the system's capacity to generate trust.

As a consequence, we find a spectrum of capitalisms whose varying performances reflect, more than anything else, the levels of social capital they can generate. Economies in which there is a high degree of mutual regard develop smooth management-labor relations, flexible and adaptive work teams, and highly effective networks of suppliers; countries that lack this capability do not. Fukuyama cites modern-day Japan and Germany, and the United States in its nineteenth-century heyday, as examples of high trust societies; and (Southern) Italy, France, and China as examples of the opposite.

The bulk of *Trust* consists of an analysis, part historical, part contemporary, of both ends of the spectrum. Rich in examples and argument, it will amply repay study, but I will not attempt to summarize this portion of the book here. For my own main interest, and I imagine that of most readers of this essay, concerns the connections that Fukuyama finds between trust and the institutions and dynamics of contemporary capitalism.

As we must have divined from his earlier treatment of capitalism and the development of *thymos,* Fukuyama is ambivalent in his assessment. On the positive side, he argues convincingly that capitalism initially breaks down the barriers of kinship orders, the suspicions characteristic of peasant communities, and the rigidities of precapitalist command societies. All these social formations are obviously inimical to the development of a climate of generalized trust. Thus the market serves at first as a great social force for redirecting the search for dignity away from acts of valor or violence to those of material attainment, while at the same time encouraging the development of informal associations of capitalists and, to a lesser extent, of workers.

Fukuyama is not, however, a simplist in this belief. "[T]he larger theme of this book," he writes, "is that sociability does not simply emerge spontaneously once the state retreats. The ability to cooperate socially is dependent on prior habits, traditions, and norms, which themselves serve to structure the market." Capitalisms thus inherit varying degrees of precapitalist propensities to form relatively more or less trusting societies. Not surprisingly, here Fukuyama mentions Tocqueville's amazement at the network of civil associations he saw in America, so different from the French system of carefully determined place and privilege. Fukuyama is quick to note, however, that although initial social givens are important, these capabilities can change over time. Indeed, he notes that Tocqueville himself feared that the individualistic basis of American gregariousness could easily become an egotism that would "[dispose] each member of the community to sever himself from the mass of his fellows."

How is this tension between individualism as a force for and against trust resolved? In Fukuyama's view, there are powerful tendencies in both directions. On the one hand, the expanding exercise of economic activities gradually changes the motivation of its participants from a drive for power to the milder purpose of expressing their roles, of finding their place in society. In a word, acquisitiveness loses its combativeness and becomes the more matter-of-fact, although no less important, expression of one's *thymos,* one's dignity. Wealth is thereby "spiritualized"—not perhaps the most fortunate term, but one that dramatizes the point Fukuyama wants to make with regard to capitalism as a source of increased mutual respect.

On the other hand, Fukuyama recognizes that individualism also destroys trust. We have already seen his recognition of the fact that the inner dynamic of capitalism reduces individuals to "a microscopic world" of family relations. This brings me once again to note the incompleteness with which Fukuyama assesses the economic system that he has made one of the legs of his triadic end of history—in this case, his unwillingness to consider the degree to which the dog-eat-dog necessities for survival in the marketplace can coexist with the trusting patterns of live-and-let-live. It is surely to the point, as Fukuyama himself points out, that the highly trust-directed relationships of Japanese capitalism, with its lifetime employment, have been seriously challenged by its recession of 1992-3, while the frail *ententes* of American labor-management relations have been ruthlessly discarded under the pressures of ever more fierce world competition.

Fukuyama remains distanced before this contest of forces. So, too, with the fact that the favorable influences of capitalism seem to be associated with its initial appearance, and the unfavorable effects with its later development—a matter that is mentioned but never pursued. Even more important is his treatment of another economic development that, were it fully examined, could seriously, perhaps even fatally, challenge his fundamental vision. In the background of both his books Fukuyama perceives the growing presence of a vaguely defined, but unmistakably real entity called the World Economy—an entity that begins to surround and overshadow even such powerful national economies as our own, much as ours surrounds and overshadows the state economies of Illinois and California and New York.

Here the question that remains unasked is whether this emerging supranational aspect of capitalism does not call into question the plausibility of an end of history posited on the triad of science, democratic government, and capitalism. Surely the last two of these constitutive forces depend on strong and stable national entities within which to exert their social influence. But if the world economy continues its self-generated growth, the consequences for both democratic politics and capitalist economics are likely to be disastrous. What will be left of the relevance of liberal political structures for an end of history if the world economy makes ever more irrelevant the boundaries of the nation-state—massive ecological effects and unmanageable immigration pressures as examples? What is left of the relevance of capitalist national economies if their real-world counterparts are increasingly defenseless against economic penetration, to the point at which they can no longer even exercise effective control over so fundamental a means of self-regulation as the quantity of money within their national control? The world economy, in a word, is an entity whose sole unifying attribute is a commitment to an economic system that erodes the longevity of its presently constituted members. The self-consuming aspects of such an institutional framework seem ill-suited to serve as the setting for Fukuyama's vision.

These prospects are still distant, save for the already manifest pressures of international finance and migration. Nonetheless, the contradictions of a world economy of capitalisms suggest that at some imaginable time in the future another set of institutional structures may become necessary to create a durable setting for humanity's journey. Perhaps wishfully, I can imagine one in which each of the three legs of Fukuyama's design have been changed in significant fashion. In place of science guided to an important degree by economic and military incentives, I could picture it guided by the need to protect the fragile ecosphere against further deterioration. In place of political structures concerned with the rights of individuals within their national boundaries, I could picture the addition of transnational rights—the protection of immigrants as a case in point, the outlawing of international exploitation as a second.

And in lieu of our present range of capitalisms, I could even see a range of "socialisms" that sought to combine the flexibility of markets and the protection of individual property with safeguards against the many negative side-effects of markets and the asocial consequences of both the absence of property among the lower portion of the population and its excessive possession among the topmost portion. Some such an amended triad might form the basis of an End of History better suited to cope with the

problems generated by its present supposed terminus. I should add, however, that I suspect even such a much-hoped-for future will be not so much an end to human history as another resting place.

John Lloyd (essay date 23 May 1997)

SOURCE: "Interview: Francis Fukuyama," in *New Statesman,* May 23, 1997, pp. 26-7.

[*In the following essay, Lloyd discusses Fukuyama's views on contemporary social, economic, and gender issues, as addressed in his writings and a recent interview with Fukuyama.*]

The most influential of public-policy intellectuals, who are most attended to by politicians and their advisers, are those who search for the modern holy grail of contemporary social policy: how to secure the values and security of a community without reproducing the intolerances and exclusivity that communities habitually produced? Can it be done within the framework of a liberal state?

This is a large part of the new Labour project. To new Labour Britain, in its second week of existence, came one of the most prominent public-policy intellectuals of our times, to give lectures in London and Oxford.

Francis Fukuyama transformed himself from an analyst of Soviet foreign policy at the Rand defence think tank in Los Angeles to a global guru, with the publication in 1990 of his *The End of History,* which claimed—with the assistance of Hegel—that the implosion of Soviet communism left the world with no alternative to what he called "liberal capitalism".

His reputation was buttressed—though some reviewers thought it was tarnished—by a second book, *Trust,* published in 1995.

The key concept in *Trust* was "social capital", a commodity close to trust which resides in the relations set up within families, but also in institutions such as churches, voluntary societies, trade unions, company structures. Social capital can be saved; it can also be wasted.

Courteous, contained, scholarly and worldly at once, Fukuyama is the very model of the modern conservative-liberal. That is, he approaches the study of society with an unencumbered mind: at least one unencumbered by notions of political correctness, or with a list of no-go areas that might inhibit observation and prescription.

He believes that since the 1960s we have been living through a "great disruption". This is comparable to the transition from a largely agricultural to a largely industrial society which consumed much of the 19th and early 20th centuries. In our case it is the shift from industrial to post-industrial society, which means a shift in ethical values as much as in the nature of work.

At times, in his talks, he gives the impression that the great disruption is coming to an end. Asked if he thinks so, he replies, "I don't know," and gives an example, which is clearly one that impresses him a good deal.

"What is a little bit frightening is that, if you look at the US, the blacks have led the whites by about 20 to 30 years. In this sense, when Daniel Moynihan wrote his famous *Report on the Negro Family* in the mid-1960s, the black illegitimacy rate was 28 to 29 per cent. Now that rate is up to 66 to 67 per cent, and the white rate is up to around 25 per cent."

"I'm not sure where that ends. It may be in another couple of decades the majority of kids will be born out of wedlock in society as a whole. On the other hand we may be at the tail end of a big hump and things will start to come down. Certainly the cultural mood of the society is much more conservative now."

"The position of the poor has deteriorated very badly. In fact, among blacks who make up a good part of that underclass there is a kind of nostalgia—not for discrimination, but for the effects of discrimination, when they were all forced to live in the same neighbourhood. They had stronger community ties and vastly lower rates of crime and family breakdown—much more social capital."

He sees the 1960s as a time not just of excessive liberations, or Liberations, but of excessive and destructive social engineering. "Social engineering was undertaken in a completely wrong-headed way in the 1960s and 1970s, in ways that had unanticipated consequences. They made things worse, cost the taxpayers a lot of money and made them distrust government."

Asked where he stands on the most controversial work of social policy in recent years—Charles Murray and Richard Herrnstein's *The Bell Curve,* whose stormy reception was a result of its contention that, on average, blacks are less intelligent than whites—Fukuyama marks clear water. "Most biologists I've seen will not agree with Murray and Herrnstein. They will say that race's effect on intelligence is pretty minor."

However, where he shocks is on gender. At a lecture he gave in London last week, and at a dinner after that, the largest and most urgent questions came from the women present. That is because, in researching and thinking about his next book, probably to be called The Origins of Order, he has identified the changing role of women as the most dynamising and disturbing part of the great disruption.

He is thus poised to insert himself into the centre of a debate acquiring an ever-wider moral resonance. In the week in which he was speaking in the UK, *Newsweek* carried a cover story under the title "No Time for the Kids?

How Working Parents Cheat their Children". It jangles every nerve in the body not just of the new female professionals, but of men, too, beginning to believe that their parental responsibilities do not end with conception. Fukuyama, by luck or judgment, is bringing his own brand of social-philosophic theorising into the heart of a contemporary anxiety.

"Biology is making a stunning comeback. Through most of the 20th century the social sciences did not believe that you could explain any kind of important phenomena by reference to any kind of biological imperative or instinct. In fact, 20th-century social science was to an extent founded on this, because in the 19th century you had all of these racist theories."

"But what's happening now is that attention has focused not on race but on gender. There's a lot of empirical work coming out now which seems to show that things are much more genetically determined than we had thought before—not by race, but by gender."

"This is an ideologised sore point. Many women will assert there's no psychological difference between men and women, and to the extent that people think there is, it's a result of living in a repressive, male-dominated society. The interesting thing about the latest work is that it's empirical, and you can bring real evidence to bear."

"The really important differences are gender differences. This is one of the big policy problems for the US—that gender difference has been treated like race discrimination. There is no basis for race discrimination. There is of course no basis for any discrimination—but the fact remains that there are serious biological differences between the sexes while there are no serious biological differences between the races."

"At present the official tide is against that. For example I think it's really lunatic to take 18-year-old men and women, put them in uniform and send them off to fields to train together—and then to punish sexual misbehaviour with great severity. It's one of these things we'll do for some time, it will degrade performance, and then we'll stop it and people will shake their head and say—why ever did we do it?"

The key problem caused by working women is the breakdown of the family. Fukuyama is relatively unambiguous about this, tracing the steeply rising curve of crime against the steeply rising curve of women working since the 1960s.

Women's work is in part to compensate for the drop in male incomes. It has meant that household incomes have held up, but that child care has not. The rise in one-parent families, especially among blacks, has meant a huge rise in the number of fatherless children who have no male close to them to teach them life's limits and possibilities from a man's standpoint.

Will *The Origins of Order* present solutions? No: it will point out the areas of deepest malaise, and invite consideration of why the malaise has happened or worsened. Laws can do something: Fukuyama instances laws on civil rights as helpful in changing moral perceptions. But there is no longer any hope from a social democratic state setting in place a strong framework of support.

"The social democratic ideal of the state sector acting as a motor for egalitarianism is completely dead. The countries that have gone farthest down that road, such as Germany and Sweden, are now in the deepest trouble, and will have to undo their pasts. Political stability in many European countries, the UK excepted, depends on the ability of their politicians to manage the deconstruction of the excessive parts of their welfare states without having a political blow-out—and that's going to be terribly difficult."

"In the US the problem is so much less. The unemployment rate is now 4.5 per cent and the real debate is whether you can push it much lower without getting wage inflation. There are a lot of arguments that, because of globalisation, workers will not push that hard through fear of losing their jobs."

"There was a lot of talk in the press about downsizing and how awful it was. I think it was overdone because most people got other jobs very quickly. But it has had the happy outcome that people are now so worried and anxious that they are not pushing for higher wages, which means you can push the unemployment rate to historically unprecedented low levels."

Politicians can give some assistance. Fukuyama noted that both Bill Clinton and Tony Blair have been criticised for occupying the centre, even centre-right ground: for him, this is inevitable and vindicates his *End of History* thesis that modern politicians are extremely tightly constrained in what they can do. But they can be something of a moral exemplar.

"The Clinton strategy has been to stress moral values. He has a little bit of a harder time [than Tony Blair] of holding his own as a family model, but he certainly makes plenty of speeches on the theme. I wish his own family ties were a bit stronger because people tend to laugh when he says these things—yet it's also true that he's the first Democrat who has stood up and said that it's not right to raise a child you can't support outside of marriage. There's a role to that: but the solutions lie outside of the things politicians can do."

The "solution" to our present disorder is, in the end, to build social capital. "Social capital comes from all sorts of sources—some of which are traditional and some of which can be socially constructed. Traditionally it has come from such things as religion and culture and social mores handed down from one generation to another. Ralph Dahrendorf has a book called *Life Chances* in which he says there is a trade-off between what he calls ligatures and options—ligatures being the ties which bind people, options the choices they have."

"Society had been all ligatures and no options; then, gradually, options increased, first for men and then for women. These have come at the expense of ties which bind people to other groups. Some of these ties are good to see go—obscurantist religions, ties which were built purely on religious or ethnic identity. The real question is whether that can be replaced by voluntary sorts of ties which can be undertaken freely but still tie people to norms which allow people to live in communities."

This is, to be sure, the real question. Yet it is one posed by many—by the communitarian writer Amitai Etzioni (to whom Fukuyama is close); by the new Democrats and new Labour; by priests and policy wonks. Fukuyama has moved far from reflections on the end of the cold war which became *The End of History*—into other areas, where, say his critics, he shows less mastery. His reflections so far fall into the conservative-communitarian camp: to produce a framework for order in a liberal society still seems to elude him, as it does everyone.

Francis Fukuyama with Melanie Rehak (interview date 2 May 1999)

SOURCE: "The Unselfish Gene," in *New York Times Magazine*, May 2, 1999, p. 24.

[*In the following brief interview, Fukuyama comments on the human need for connection and cooperation and the causes of social fragmentation.*]

[*Rehak*]: *In your new book, you present the contentious view that on some fundamental, genetic level, human beings are built for consensus. Can you explain that?*

[Fukuyama]: We're programmed to cooperate in groups, to be joiners, to feel accepted. This is one of these things that people believe common-sensically, and that social scientists tell us is wrong. Economists begin with this understanding that human beings are selfish and just want to make money. Even many religious conservatives view humans as essentially sinful. But people feel intensely uncomfortable if they live in a society that doesn't have moral rules.

Are you saying that every human being prefers law to lawlessness?

Not everyone will obey them, but over a large population, there is a tendency to spontaneously generate rules to control deviance and set limits on individual behavior.

Is there an example of how this tendency toward moral order manifests itself in daily life?

All the companies scrambling to dissociate themselves from the Salt Lake City Olympics because of a possible bribery scandal. Now, you can say that all of this is self-interested behavior, but from a social standpoint it doesn't make much difference. A market society promotes honest behavior because it is in people's self-interest to develop reputations for honesty. So even Wall Street sharks or whatever kind of predatory animal will generate order and rules, and therefore a certain kind of socially constructive behavior.

You also talk about some fundamental human need for ritual.

The more that modern economic life strips that stuff out of the workplace and the family, the more intensely people want it. In the United States, the only real secular ritual that we've managed to create that has a lot of meaning for people is Thanksgiving. We worship individualism, yet at Thanksgiving it's all about sharing and communal values.

So you're saying that that's not enough? Is the modern world diminished in some ways?

People's lives used to be full of Thanksgivings and now we're reduced to just this one. I think ritual will never disappear, but there's a kind of privatization, a tendency toward rituals that involve, in my language, a much smaller radius of trust—you and people like you.

Like what, for example?

Watching "Ally McBeal." Well, you don't want to get too silly, but even something like that still draws together people and allows them to relate to a common set of experiences.

Is gossip also a kind of ritual?

I wouldn't call it a ritual, but it's one of the most important things that people do to establish communities and maintain informal moral norms. It involves this very basic human ability to make judgments about other people: who naughty, who's nice, who can be relied upon, who's a rat. They're essential to the functioning of any society.

Technology must have a big impact on that sort of functioning. Are people getting more isolated?

It's not that people associate with one another less, it's that they belong to a range of communities and want complete freedom to enter and exit each one. The Internet is a perfect example: you can go to a chat room anonymously, have what feels like a community experience and if you don't like it, you walk away. That's modern individualism. We seek to associate, but we want no restrictions on our behavior. Group membership becomes more superficial.

You trace a lot of these ills—the breakdown of the family unit, a rise in crime, a loss of community—to the social disruptions of the 1960s and 1970s. Have they affected your own life?

I lived in California in the 1980s and by the end of the decade there were hardly any of my colleagues who hadn't gone through a divorce or a family breakup, sometimes a couple of times. But my family has actually been kind of boringly stable. My parents stayed together their whole lives, and I've never been divorced, so I can't really talk about the instability part of the story from my own experience. It's more the stories of people I've seen around me.

How did you end up on such a stable course? What great epoch-making forces missed you?

I don't know the answer. Part of it is your family, what precedents or expectations they set, and part is your environment. But a lot of it has to be luck.

Walter Kirn (review date 7 June 1999)

SOURCE: "The Sweetest Science," in *New York,* June 7, 1999, pp. 88-9.

[*In the following review, Kirn offers skeptical assessment of* The Great Disruption, *finding fault in Fukuyama's faith in human nature and preference for stability.*]

Francis Fukuyama's **The Great Disruption** comes at a peculiar moment. In a season of school shootings, spy scandals, and "collateral damage" from errant cluster bombs, it's tempting to regard as wishful thinking a book that argues, using graphs and diagrams and lessons from economics and anthropology, that our present state of social turmoil will, in time, be naturally replaced by a new, benevolent moral order. But that is precisely Fukuyama's prediction, not merely his hope. A resurgence of grassroots goodness. A spontaneous regeneration of civic-mindedness. The dark days are almost behind us, he asserts. At a time when the average news watcher might mistake America for a rich but failing empire, unable to keep the peace at home, abroad, or in the marbled corridors of government. Fukuyama is bullish on human nature.

That's right: human nature. We haven't heard that phrase used seriously lately, but Fukuyama is out to revive it, rescuing from the deconstructionists, multiculturalists, and sundry relativists the notion that we are all in fact the same—rational, system-building social animals who, by virtue of genes and long experience, are programmed to do the right thing in the end, by ourselves, one another, and our children. It's another sweeping thesis from the man (a professor of public policy and former State Department staff member) who gained fame when he wrote that the end of the Cold War represented "the end of history," meaning the death of ideological struggle and the rise of near-universal democracy and market capitalism. Whether history has truly ended I'll leave to the Serbs, Chinese, and NATO to answer, but Fukuyama's was a bold analysis, highly understandable and discussable. It held special appeal for maturing American baby-boomers, who've never met a tribute to the distinctiveness of their own, privileged role in human history that they didn't like.

The Great Disruption is a home-front version of the earlier book. Its subject is domestic, not foreign, affairs, and its findings are just as broad and optimistic, styled in the sort of bleached-out, bottom-line prose favored by CIA officers and corporate management consultants: "Social order, once disrupted, tends to get remade once again, and there are many indications that this is happening today." The tone is a major tip-off. This is science, not opinion, we're reading, founded on facts and comparative analysis, with none of the fashionable European obscurity that has lately crept into cultural commentary. Fukuyama is a throwback here, a time traveler from the age of certainty. His theme—that the past 30 years of social confusion contain in themselves the seeds of a new clarity—is strikingly reflected in his prose, which is almost Victorian in its tidy positivism.

Before he can give the good news, of course, Fukuyama has to give the bad news. He has to outline how It All Went Wrong. Assumption No. 1 is that it did go wrong. Crime rose. Trust fell. Families disintegrated. The social stitches that knit up marriages, neighborhoods, schools, and community organizations decayed in an acid bath of individualism. At fault were a range of overarching trends. As industrialism gave way to the information age and as longevity and wealth increased, people sprinted selfishly from the pack, abandoning commitment and tradition for Pepsi-generation freedom and novelty. Women in particular fell for the Aquarian bait, victimizing themselves in the process. Lapsing into stridency, he writes: "One of the greatest frauds perpetrated during The Great Disruption was the notion that sexual revolution was gender neutral, benefiting women and men equally, and that it somehow had a kinship with the feminist revolution." Take that, Erica Jong!

It's hard not to feel that when Fukuyama mentions "The Great Disruption," he really means the sixties, just as when he wrote of "history," he really meant the Cold War fifties. What distinguishes him from talk-show-circuit ideologues such as William Bennett, however, is his fondness for complicated graphs plotting everything from fertility rates to crime and divorce statistics. He takes pains to distance himself from social conservatives. Religious values, for Fukuyama, are merely one form among others of "social capital," a respectably secular, ivory-tower term whose meaning I struggled to get a handle on. Team spirit among league bowlers, affection between parents and children, and the presumption of honest dealings between businesspeople are all examples of social capital. But whatever it is precisely, a lot of it has been lost, apparently, especially down at ground level, where ordinary citizens work and live.

Fukuyama is no alarmist—he's too cool for that, too academic and wedded to the sociological long view—but now and then he spins a nightmare scenario. His vision of the lives of aging baby-boomers, bereft of family ties and social structures linking them to the wider world, is bleak. It also seems unnecessarily baroque, the voice of a hothead lurking inside the scientist. The typical boomer, "twice or thrice divorced, will pass his or her waning years living alone in a house or apartment, visited occasionally by a son or daughter who are themselves past retirement age and seeking ways to deal with their own deteriorating health. The connection with these relatives will be tenuous, because the long and tumultuous personal lives they led when younger—the different marriages and sexual partners, the separated homes . . . have left their descendants with a sentimental but slightly detached relationship."

Fukuyama's best-selling Theories of Everything have always had a faint ring of manic grandeur, as though they were first scribbled out on dozens of napkins on a park bench. In passages like the one above, he seems to know too much and know it too surely. Is it really programmed in our brains that we will eventually reform society, peacefully and from the bottom up, in a triumph for justice, compassion, and stability? Fukuyama draws on a dozen disciplines, from game theory to genetics, to make his case that stable states arise naturally from chaotic interludes the way Sunday morning follows Saturday night. He seems to confuse stability with goodness, though. Things may indeed get better all on their own, but what is better? Quieter? Faster? Slower? Fukuyama simply puts his chips on human nature, suggesting that however we spin the wheel, we'll come out winners. It's a risky bet.

Michael Kazin (review date 13 June 1999)

SOURCE: "The End of Amorality," in *Washington Post Book World*, June 13, 1999, pp. 1, 3.

[*In the following review, Kazin credits Fukuyama as a "subtle, learned thinker," though finds shortcomings and contradictions in* The Great Disruption.]

Are you worried about the rise of violent crime, the illegitimacy, the child abuse, and the pervasive cynicism that seem to have dominated public life over the past three decades? Then Francis Fukuyama has good news for you: We are, he maintains, on the verge of a new era in which ordinary people will strive to live morally and insist that their institutions and leaders do the same. An ethic of collective responsibility will gradually replace that of rampant individualism.

Armed with so bald a thesis, Fukuyama might sound like a right-wing polemicist straining to be a prophet. But the author who burst into prominence in the early 1990s with a remarkable argument about "the end of history" is a subtle, learned thinker who shares little with tub-thumping moralists like William Bennett and Charles Murray beyond a generally conservative worldview. Fukuyama is one of the few American intellectuals of any ideological bent capable of training a knowledge of world history and a grasp of social theory on topics of undeniable contemporary significance.

But the loftier the ambition, the greater the risk of failure. In **The Great Disruption,** Fukuyama has written two different books, each of which takes up roughly half the volume. The first and more successful half is an historical essay that interprets the decline of moral order since the 1960s and its sprouts of revival through the lens of "social capital." This is a concept, currently fashionable among academics, that Fukuyama defines as "a set of informal values . . . shared among members of a group that permits cooperation between them." "Social capital" is the fuel that runs the institutions of civil society; it depends on a culture of trust (subject of the author's last book) that exists to different degrees in every postindustrial society.

To his credit, Fukuyama avoids blaming the problem of diminished social capital on any ideological faction or bundle of policies. He points out that, from the mid-1960s to the mid-'90s, champions of the individual unbound reigned across the political spectrum and in nearly every developed nation. "To put it simplistically," he writes, "the Left worried about lifestyles, and the Right worried about money."

Such ubiquity can only be explained by a larger phenomenon: the instability that accompanies the shift from an industrial to an information society. Fukuyama argues that amoral behavior has gained legitimacy during every transition from one economic order to another. He points to the rise of intemperance and sexual promiscuity during the early change from agrarianism to industrialism. And he indicates, with a brief statistical survey, that "negative measures of social capital" increased from the late '60s into the '90s throughout Western and central Europe as well as the United States. The strength of family discipline in Japan and South Korea evidently protected those nations from the same ordeal.

Such a comparative perspective is valuable in rescuing debates about moral concerns from the verbal skirmishes of culture warriors on both left and right. But by presenting only the skeleton of an argument, Fukuyama skates over matters that could undermine it. For example, in a provocative chapter, "The Special Role of Women," he argues that the related upsurges of feminism and sexual liberty frayed social bonds from the mid-20th century on. Liberation movements targeted the oppressive aspects of monogamy and paternalist families but neglected to substitute an equally effective way to rear the young.

Fukuyama has swallowed one of the more popular myths of social history. In fact, the "traditional" order never existed for most women; they had to care for the kids while toiling, inside and outside the home, at a myriad of paid and unpaid tasks. And his worry about the impact of falling fertility in the United States and Europe neglects the possibility that adults with fewer children or none at

all should have more time to participate in the types of associations, from churches to political parties, that make up civil society. Of course, whether they are motivated to do so is a different question.

But the first half of **The Great Disruption** is a model of originality and clarity compared to the second. Instead of fleshing out his historical claims and predictions, Fukuyama launches into a rambling survey of what a hefty roster of scholars has written about the "genealogy of morals." His capsule summaries do serve a purpose—to reveal the roots of cooperative behavior in both evolutionary biology and the networks and hierarchies every culture needs. But the result is an unhappy marriage of the banal and the abstract. "Thus, to say that human beings are by nature social animals," Fukuyama concludes one chapter, "is not to argue that they are inherently peaceful, cooperative, or trust-worthy. . . . Rather, it means that they have special facilities for detecting and dealing with deceivers and cheaters, as well as for gravitating toward cooperators and others who follow moral rules." I think we all learned that in kindergarten.

The lengthy digression into other people's research seems to contradict the very title of Fukuyama's book. If biologists and social scientists have come to agree that "the capacity to create social capital through elaborate forms of social cooperation" is integral to human nature, was "the great disruption" that big a deal? The author who once announced the end of history now implies that it never really mattered. Thus does Pollyanna get dressed up in the verities of sociobiology.

Virginia Postrel (review date 13 June 1999)

SOURCE: "The Big One," in *Los Angeles Times Book Review,* June 13, 1999, pp. 4-5.

[*In the following review, Postrel offers favorable assessment of* The Great Disruption, *which she concludes is "an important and ambitious work."*]

Francis Fukuyama likes big subjects and bold claims. In 1989, he burst into public consciousness with his provocatively titled National Interest article, **"The End of History?,"** later expanded into a book, **The End of History and the Last Man** (1992). His thesis: Liberal, democratic capitalism represents the final stage in the Hegelian evolution of governing regimes, and the fall of the Soviet Union settled the debate. When the musical group Jesus Jones hit the pop charts with a 1991 song lauding the post-Cold War joys of "watching the world wake up from history," Fukuyama achieved a cultural penetration few intellectuals—let alone Hegel interpreters—dream of.

So what do you do after History? In his book, Fukuyama glumly imagined a boring, bourgeois life for the "last man": passive VCR-watching, perhaps enlivened by the pursuit of artistic perfection à la the Japanese tea ceremony. Life after History seemed to offer little to those once fired by high-stakes ideological struggle.

But Fukuyama is far too curious to stay bored. Market liberalism poses plenty of interesting challenges to the inquiring mind—not the least of which is what makes it tick. In his 1995 book *Trust,* Fukuyama explored the role of "social capital" in creating prosperity. To flourish, he argued, economies need people who can spontaneously form communities, extending trust beyond the clannish bounds of kinship or the formal claims of contract.

Trust was an intelligent but rather conventional conservative-communitarian paean to the black box called "culture." It celebrated the Protestant ethic, hinted at the superiority of Japanese lifetime employment and declared that "the ability to obey communal authority is key to the success of the society"—an ability that contemporary American individualism was eroding. The message was troubled: America seemed to have lost the social habits that had made it a flourishing society. Fukuyama warned readers that "once social capital has been spent, it may take centuries to replenish, if it can be replenished at all."

In his new book, Fukuyama continues his emphasis on social capital. But *The Great Disruption* represents an important break with his earlier message and with the cultural pessimism that grips Washington intellectuals. "Social order, once disrupted, tends to get remade once again, and there are many indications that this is happening today," writes the upbeat author.

Fukuyama now explicitly rejects the idea, a commonplace among neoconservatives, that social capital is finite and static. It is not, he writes, "a rare cultural treasure passed down across the generations—something that, if lost, can never again be regained. Rather, it is created all the time by people going about their daily lives. It was created in traditional societies, and it is generated on a daily basis by individuals and organizations in a modern capitalist society." From "it may take centuries to replenish" to "it is generated on a daily basis" is quite a change of tone.

Before we get to the innovative, positive half of *The Great Disruption,* however, Fukuyama takes readers through an eight-chapter section on what he argues are related social ills: increasing crime, family instability, a general decline in trust. Through a host of statistics and graphs, he seeks to demonstrate that a Great Disruption in norms—a breakdown of existing social order—did in fact occur, not just in the United States but in other developed countries. His international perspective avoids the trap of attributing general trends to country-specific events, such as the Vietnam War. He also undermines the conservative assumption that the '60s caused the disruption. The cultural upheavals of that period, he suggests, were a symptom rather than a cause.

Family life appears key to the Great Disruption's origins, at least if you believe that we learn how to relate to others first in the home. But Fukuyama notes that crime rates don't match up with the rise in divorce or unwed births. Crime shot up too soon: "There was evidently something beneath the surface of family domesticity in the 1950s that wasn't entirely right, since the generation growing up in it proved more than ordinarily vulnerable to a variety of temptations when they came into adulthood. . . . The onset of the Great Disruption needs to be traced to a factor common to both crime and family breakdown."

That factor, he argues, is disregard for traditional authority: "the rise of moral individualism and the consequent miniaturization of community." When individuals make their own moral decisions and insist on exercising the choices that market economies and advanced technologies enhance, the existing social order is disrupted. (Oddly, Fukuyama does not address the postwar expansion of education, which encourages individuals to think for themselves even as it enhances the knowledge economy.)

This argument gives the book's first section a conservative tone reminiscent of *Trust,* especially in the chapter called "The Special Role of Women." For the first time in history, women in the West (and to a lesser extent in Asia) have the economic power and reproductive technologies to live independently of men—and even to support their children. As Fukuyama notes, this change is a product not primarily of government policy but of the economic shift from brawn to brains. The ratio of female-to-male earnings started rising in the mid-1960s. Not coincidentally, he suggests, this period "is a good starting date for the beginning of the Great Disruption." The emancipation of women, he implies, is at the root of social disorder.

Fukuyama is no misogynist, and the changing role of women is undoubtedly crucial to the social transformations that interest him. But his discussion of women's opportunities is unduly negative. One reason lies in his tendency toward determinism: Throughout the book, he treats "technology" and "the economy" as forces largely independent of important human goals. Yet technology by itself is not an explanation for change; it is only a vehicle for solving problems. New technologies do create options once foreclosed not just by authority but by practicality; individuals, however, must choose to exercise those options. What latent dissatisfaction, we're left to wonder, led people to make those choices? What was wrong with the world before the Great Disruption?

This blind spot leads Fukuyama to ignore the keen desire of women to escape their vulnerability to the whims of nature and of men, a desire that any search for the sources of new social capital must take into account. The evolution of the family in an individualist age must be one that allows women to feel that they and their children are secure, not trapped.

But just when you think *The Great Disruption* is only a more rigorous version of the usual conservative gripes, it veers into its second section, and entirely new vistas open up. In seven wide-ranging chapters, Fukuyama lays out his theoretical case for social optimism. Order breaks down, yes, but it also reemerges, because "we human beings are by nature designed to create moral rules and social order for ourselves." The answer to current problems is not "a full-scale retreat into one of the traditional cultures of the past" but a bottom-up dynamic process of developing new habits and institutions under changed circumstances Just as we adapted to the move from farm to city, from the integration of home and work to their separation, we will adapt to the effects of contraception and a knowledge economy (and, Fukuyama might have emphasized more, to increasing longevity).

This engaging section is the heart of the book, its contribution to the cultural debate. It is informed by a rich body of important scholarship that is virtually unknown among not only East Coast intellectuals but also Wired-style exponents of the "New Economy." Drawing on serious empirical and theoretical work from fields ranging from evolutionary game theory to animal behavior, Fukuyama provides a lucid course in what he rightly argues is "one of the most important intellectual developments of the late twentieth century": "the systematic study of how order, and thus social capital, can emerge in a spontaneous and decentralized fashion." It is a mark of the book's sophistication that political scientist Elinor Ostrom and economic historian Douglass North, a Nobel laureate, loom larger than management gurus and "complexity" popularizers.

Self-organization, as Fukuyama depicts it, is what individuals do without hierarchical direction: It includes the informal norms that prevail in small groups of the sort in which human beings, and their primate ancestors, lived throughout most of our existence. He opens the section with the story of commuters from the Washington suburbs who line up at a local restaurant every day to take rides with complete strangers. By picking up two or three of these "slugs," a driver can use the carpool lanes and considerably shorten the trip into D.C. Over the years, Fukuyama reports, rules have evolved: "Neither cars nor passengers may jump the line; passengers have the right to refuse to get into a particular car; smoking and the exchange of money are forbidden." The system works because people trust each other as fellow government workers and because people voluntarily obey sensible rules. It is a small-scale model of self-organization and evolving norms. It illustrates how human beings naturally create social order and thus suggests the process through which the Great Disruption might be repaired.

In Fukuyama's version, self-organization does not account for what economist and social theorist F. A. Hayek called "the extended order"—the impersonal relationships that allow culture and trade to flourish among strangers. (Fukuyama attributes the term to Hayek but defines it as "the sum total of all the rules, norms, values, and shared behaviors that allow individuals to work together in a capitalist society." He thereby misses Hayek's crucial distinction between the extended order and small-group

norms, which can be quite hostile to outsiders.) For extended orders, Fukuyama maintains, you need hierarchy. The rules are not instinctive and have depended on the authoritative lawgivers of religion and politics: "Culture with a capital C . . . does not have spontaneous roots."

No matter. Today's problems, he argues, come not from the absence of formal authority, which we have in abundance but from a breakdown of quotidian morality: "The reconstitution of social order for the United States and other societies in a similar position, then, is not a matter of rebuilding of hierarchical authority. It is a matter of reestablishing habits of honesty, reciprocity, and an enlarged radius of trust under changed technological circumstances."

He's right about the current situation but wrong to oppose hierarchy (or Culture) to spontaneity. If "human beings by nature like to organize themselves hierarchically," as he argues, leadership itself must often emerge spontaneously. The issue is one of levels: A leader proposes a hierarchy (an organization, strategy, plan of action, etc.) that must win converts, just as any new "slug" rule must. The emergence of new hierarchies is itself part of the spontaneous process of self-organization. The important contrast is not hierarchy versus spontaneity but persuasion (including competition) versus imposition.

Fukuyama, for instance, calls organized religions (as opposed to traditional folk religions) hierarchical without considering their evolution or, for that matter, their variety. This omission hurts his ability to imagine the sources of new order. What accounts for the development, within recent history, of the Mormon church or Pentecostalism, one hierarchical in organization and the other radically decentralized? Both were in fact spontaneous orders, rallying followers who felt moved by their spiritual insights, communal values and modes of worship.

These two movements were arguably responses to the last "great disruption," the social and economic changes of the 19th century. In his final section, a scant two chapters exploring life "After the Great Disruption," Fukuyama sets great store by the Victorian era's ability to transform a society of crime, grime and extraordinarily heavy drinking into the quintessence of propriety. We did it before and, he believes, we will do it again: The divorce rate has peaked, as have out-of-wedlock births. Welfare rolls and crime rates are dropping. Laura Schlessinger's "often censorious tone" has replaced feel-good pop psychologizing. The Million Man March and Promise Keepers have affirmed men's familial responsibilities.

All true, and undoubtedly a bottom-up response to social excesses. But Fukuyama's contribution would have been greater if he had extended his imagination beyond the comfortable conservative litany. Youth culture is full of indications of a new moral consciousness. If you're looking for meditations on "honesty, reciprocity, and an enlarged radius of trust," (not to mention awesome responsibility, and problematic parenting), you can learn at least as much from "Buffy the Vampire Slayer" as from Dr. Laura.

Nor have traditionalist men been the only ones gathering on the Washington mall. By some counts, the 1993 gay rights march attracted as large a crowd as the ones inspired by Nation of Islam leader Louis Farrakhan and the Promise Keepers, and it, too, had marriage as a central theme. The push for gay marriage—for the freedom to make commitments—marks a dramatic change not merely from the pre-Great Disruption days of the closet but from the aggressive libertinism of the 1970s. Whatever happens legally, a new order is already evolving in the lives of individuals, with the sanction of voluntary institutions, including many churches and employers.

Discovering such evolving orders requires a combination of journalism and cultural studies, not social science. That would not suit Fukuyama's preferred methodology and would take him into uncomfortable territory. And though such explorations would make the book more interesting and perhaps more convincing, they would not necessarily make it more influential.

The Great Disruption is an important and ambitious work. It promises to communicate unconventional ideas to political intellectuals bound by convention and thus to inject much needed vitality and realism into stale and stylized debates. In a nonthreatening and serious way, Fukuyama is making another bold, and I believe correct, claim: that the trial-and-error processes of a free society lead not to decay but to discovery, not to disorder but to new and ever-evolving forms of order.

Bryan Gould (review date 14 June 1999)

SOURCE: "Moral Panic," in *New Statesman*, June 14, 1999, p. 46.

[*In the following review of* The Great Disruption, *Gould offers positive assessment, though finds fault in Fukuyama's lack of concern for the increasing concentration of money and media power among a small number of individuals.*]

If you are interested in a guided tour of current intellectual fashion, Francis Fukuyama's latest book is just the ticket. It offers overnight stops in anthropology, economics, moral philosophy, psychology, neuro-physiology and other attractive locations. As with all good tours, it offers a combination of the exotic and the familiar. There are enough new names to suggest that we are breaking new ground, but there are also comfortingly established names—from Schumpeter to Margaret Mead, from Socrates to Hayek.

The tour has the merit, too, of being a round trip. We are taken through some disturbing and challenging terrain but eventually arrive back at the point we started. The theme of the tour is the breakdown of social order, the rise in crime, the weakening of trust and morality. This is familiar territory, but Fukuyama does not seek to minimise its challenges. He takes a studiedly neutral view of the various arguments from left and right as to why what he describes as the "great disruption" has happened. But in the end his message is a reassuring one.

Fukuyama tells us that while things may seem bad, they are not as bad as they have been on previous tours. We (by which I think he means what used to be called western society) have been over this course before. Human society is always likely to follow this track, as one social order breaks down and another takes a little time to re-establish itself. But, he assures us, a re-establishment will happen. Human nature, both individually and in society, ensures that some new form of order will be arrived at, even though it may seem unfamiliar and unattractive in prospect. We arrive at the end of the journey with a sigh of relief, perhaps bemoaning our bad luck in having lived through the period of the disruption, but confident that our successors will complete the job of social reconstruction.

I learnt much from and enjoyed the book. But the package tour left me dissatisfied in one major respect. I couldn't help but think about that which seems to have been deliberately skirted around. There is, it is true, a brief discussion at the end of the book which takes us into some of this region. This is the chapter asking, "Does capitalism deplete social capital?" Fukuyama offers a tentative negative answer but seems hardly aware that the capitalism about which this question has sometimes been asked in the past has now been transformed into a different and much more powerful beast.

There are, in other words, major aspects of the modern global economy that Fukuyama fails to take into account. One does not need to be a Marxist to understand that the shape of that modern economy has huge implications for societies across the globe. The mere fact of the single global economy; the concentration of economic power in fewer and fewer hands; the increasing importance of technology and the corresponding decline in the value of labour; and the rapidly growing significance of the privately owned media as a means of shaping social values are all new phenomena which raise in a serious form, for the first time, the question of whether or not an acceptable social order will or will not be allowed to reassert itself this time. It is at least arguable that these global forces are now so powerful that the efforts of individuals or of whole societies to negate or reverse them will come to nought. The great disruption and the breakdown of social order may not be the cyclical phenomena that Fukuyama comfortably identifies. They may be, on this occasion, the outcome of forces so powerful that they can actually prevent the operation of the expected self-righting mechanisms.

What is odd about the book is not that it provides no answer to this sort of question, but that it appears to ignore it altogether. In averting his gaze from this part of the territory, in his apparent belief that everything is for the best in the best of all possible worlds, Fukuyama exhibits that same Pollyanna-ish optimism that we saw in Anthony Giddens' Reith lectures. So Fukuyama's package tour is an enjoyable and reassuring experience for the small number that can afford it. It seems scarcely relevant to those thousands of millions who inhabit the territory that the package tour avoids.

George Lucas (essay date 28 June 1999)

SOURCE: "Francis Fukuyama," in *New Statesman*, June 28, 1999, pp. 18-9.

[*In the following essay, Lucas discusses Fukuyama's burdensome reputation as a prognosticator and his concerns in* The Great Disruption.]

Beware beatification. Few things must disturb the soul more than sudden conscription as a global guru. A decade ago this was the fate of Francis Fukuyama, a US government Soviet foreign policy specialist who wrote an article, **"The End of History?"**, for fellow policy-makers. His piece predicted an end to competing ideologies, and no sooner did it hit the stands than Egon Krenz and other comrades began the demolition of communist eastern Europe. Suddenly Fukuyama had shot to planet-wide superstardom. He had, however bizarrely, defined his era.

But since then, fêted by heads of state, policy wonks and dinner-party hard-nut professionals alike, he has suffered his fair share of brickbats. It is not even certain that he has relished the fortune life has forced on him; to his lasting credit, he looks almost in physical agony when on chat shows he is asked for the third time in a minute: "What can you *foresee?*" His own quandary, in a world that, as his critics rightly point out, reveals history moving again, is over what to do next. More seminars. Lectures. Appearances. Shows. And books. Well, what's a guru to do?

As marooned by circumstance as Monty Python's Brian or Tony Hancock's Rebel, Fukuyama, now 47, has responded with fair honour. His latest work, *The Great Disruption,* is striking in its earnestness and assuredly sincere intentions. But it also betrays a weariness with the whole charade of foretelling humanity's destiny. Fukuyama is no longer—if he ever was—the gleeful young prophet; rather he is exhausted, a fading player on another dead evening on another summer season at the pier.

All too readily he betrays his doubts in his argument, which reasons that, given the precedent of 19th-century recoveries from widespread vagrancy to restored social order in both Britain and America, a recent slight tempering of several leading measurements of social upheaval indicates that a similar improvement is now under way. He says that, because people have a biological tendency to cooperate and to make rules, the upheavals of the 1960s,

1970s and 1980s may be set to abate. Disturbingly, though, he also readily agrees that we could instead face, like the Romans in AD 300 or 400, several centuries of Dark Age barbarity. "It's perfectly possible. I am not a soothsayer. I really don't know. My argument is just out there. It could easily be proved wrong." Human beings like "societies where they have morals and are related to each other at a community level". There are "some empirical grounds for thinking that might have happened, but who knows?".

But these doubts have not prevented his publishers from aiming his book squarely at the fears of the airport bookshop victim. The design is dark and threatening: lightning forks cut across the cover to add yet more volts to every reader's worst nightmare of social collapse. The actual text—like its author, well expressed, gracious and informed—provides a comparatively undistinguished trawl through a mountain of statistics and, more sadly, an often repetitive secondary meander through the work of others. Certain near-lethal doses of the worst of social science jargon (one especially cringe-making new term is the "New Hamelin", so named because we'll get there *without* the Piper) truly jar.

He is on far more comfortable territory when it's time to shock: having warned that the introduction of the pill for Japanese women would do more for east-west convergence than the Internet, he admits sheepishly to intentional provocation: "That article? Well sure!" So the pill *isn't* as large a shockwave to hit Japan as the net? A cheeky, you've-caught-me grin. "Well, you know, that, I think, may have been a little bit of an overstatement."

Beyond that, what remains is a series of all-too-blatant assaults on the headline writers' barricades. Having vanquished communism, he has turned his fire on the feminists—though women in their fifties and sixties, he says, have been the "most hostile". He feels it is easier now to have a "more intelligent discussion" than ten or 15 years ago. Other than that, certain purple patches cause anxiety. Any religious revival is dismissed as one driven by a need for ceremony, not sincere belief. There are brisk pot-shots at Mediterranean Catholic states, but other faiths are barely mentioned. And the music plays on; in Britain last week, with no eye, surely, on current UK debates, he expressed special fears of rampaging biotechnology. It is "potentially very scary stuff", he says. "Don't mess with human nature."

If these antics create anxiety, the subjects about which Fukuyama is more serious trouble for good reason. Although the new book tackles important themes that deserve full debate, it smacks horribly of being written mostly about America, a tiny touch covering Europe, with precious little for the rest of an expectant planet. On top of that, the admission is too instant that the slight recovery of American social order is greatly dependent on a runaway economic boom. "There is a real vulnerability there," he says. The last few years have indeed, he says, provided a "gigantic job creation engine". So, what if the stock-market music stops? Then there'll be "very bad consequences". After all, "no society does well in a correction".

Not even fleeting prosperity is open to the many. Fukuyama shows little sympathy for those older workers downsized out of their livelihoods by large firms. Indeed the great thing about the 1991-92 recession was that it gave some firms "an excuse" for lay-offs.

Beyond US borders, his seeming lack of concern is often frankly terrifying. What about the failures of South-east Asian states which tried to join the west's economic party? "One of the great things" about the Asian crisis, he says, was that certain investors "got burned". Was it an error that the Russians were inveigled into starting their rush for the capitalist goal line too quickly? Well, they had an "inability for cultural and various political reasons to get their own act together". How did Central African states stand in his version of events? Sadly, political inadequacies meant they were just, it seems, non-starters in the great globalisation steeplechase. "How can you have economic growth in Zaire [its name, in fact, altered some years ago] or Rwanda . . . [or in] a state like Nigeria, where the whole place is such a kleptocracy?"

So not everyone can join. Apart from that, for the lucky ones who were within the perimeter fence, would his favoured restored world of stable families, neighbourhoods and greater order not be, well, a little stale, a little *boring?* What of the more outlandish people, the great entrepreneurs, inventors and iconoclastic thinkers, any number of whom could easily be crushed under the re-emboldened conformism?

He admits that having such guru status carries responsibilities: "I obviously feel the responsibility if I tell people things that I think lead them to make wrong choices." He has, to his credit, admitted errors made a decade ago, although he does also have an apparent instinct sometimes to flee the scene of the crime. "Nobody was listening to me particularly," he says. "I don't have anything, I think, particularly to apologise for."

The far darker reality for him is that his worldwide fame has become a vicious curse that generates a daily appetite for more truths, more insights, more profundity. He is, if you like, the King Midas of best-selling futurology; a little trapped, a little transfixed by the cameras, he is more victim than victor in his own micro-fragment of history.

He is not, however, in jail. He is free to leave whenever he wishes. He could just walk away to a life with no more TV, no more books, no more ceaseless tramping the boards, year in, year out. He must dream of those less pressured days when all he did was prepare obscure State Department papers on the Soviet Union's latest moves. But if he walked out now . . . oh, those fears, that dread that curdles the blood so monstrously: what if he left and then they never allowed him *back?*

Decisions, decisions. Let's hope he gets it right.

Charles Murray (review date July-August 1999)

SOURCE: "Big Picture," in *Commentary,* Vol. 108, No. 1, July-August, 1999, pp. 80-3.

[*In the following review, Murray offers a positive evaluation of* The Great Disruption.]

Francis Fukuyama likes to paint on a big canvas. He came to international attention in 1989 with an article in the *National Interest,* **"The End of History?,"** controversially proposing that liberal democracy might constitute the end point of our political evolution. This was followed by two books, ***The End of History and the Last Man*** (1992) and ***Trust*** (1995), in each of which, calling upon all the social and behavioral sciences, he grappled with the meaning of life in a world grown (hypothetically) rich and peaceful.

He has not scaled back. In his new book, ***The Great Disruption,*** Fukuyama takes it upon himself to explain the sudden downward slide on a wide variety of social indicators that began in the mid-1960s and in some ways is still with us: what happened, why it happened, and whether we might hope for a Great Reconstruction to follow the Great Disruption. Fukuyama has considerably broadened the many previous treatments of this topic by bringing to bear an international perspective and, still more ambitiously, by grappling with what he sees as the underlying aspects of human nature that govern large historical swings.

Fukuyama groups the social problems that characterized the Great Disruption under the headings of crime, family, and trust. The indicators for crime and family are by now familiar: steep rises in violent and property crime, a soaring divorce rate, illegitimacy ratios that went from a few percent of live births at the end of the 1950s to a third or more in the 1990s. What may be less familiar to readers is the extent to which these same problems have plagued not just America but Western Europe.

For more than a decade now, peaceful, civil England has had a property-crime rate higher than the crime-ridden U.S. In Sweden, the Left's one-time model, the rate of violent crime is now as high as in the United States—far fewer murders, to be sure, but just as many assaults, robberies, and sex crimes. The breakdown of the family is also far advanced in most of Western Europe. England has leapfrogged America's illegitimacy ratio, going from one much lower than ours in the 1970s to one considerably higher in the 1990s. In Sweden, marriage appears to be a dying institution. Added to these indicators is a plunge in fertility, with many European countries now far below the replacement rate.

Fukuyama's treatment of the theme of trust draws on his 1995 book of the same name and is intimately linked with a central construct of ***The Great Disruption,*** social capital. Social capital is the "set of informal values or norms shared among members of a group that permits cooperation among them." These shared norms facilitate one's trust that another person will act reliably and honestly, while trust itself acts "like a lubricant that makes the running of any group or organization more efficient."

Social capital, lubricated by trust, is what has let the Japanese sustain their extraordinarily low crime rate without a lot of prisons; the lack of social capital is what has saddled southern Italian villages with amoral familism (in Edward Banfield's term). Social capital makes the free market work in the United States; the lack of social capital makes a free market impossible, so far, in the former Soviet Union. During the period of the Great Disruption, Fukuyama tries to demonstrate, trust deteriorated, including trust in one's fellow citizens and trust in government; and so, inevitably, did social capital.

Turning to causes, Fukuyama lists four alternative explanations of the Great Disruption, each identified with a particular point of view. The contemporary Left has blamed rising crime figures and the breakdown of families on the persistence of economic and social inequality, while a smaller group of theorists, straddling the political divide, has found the culprit to be greater wealth and security. Then there are libertarians like me who concentrate on mistaken government policies. Finally, social conservatives point a finger at cultural values.

Fukuyama finds something unsatisfactory in each of these explanations, preferring instead to focus on the way many factors work in tandem to produce certain effects. For example, family breakdown has clearly had an adverse impact on the socialization of children, and that in turn has had much to do with rising crime, which in turn has fostered distrust, of neighbors in particular and of the world in general. Family breakdown similarly promotes what Fukuyama calls the "miniaturization of community," the displacement of affiliation with large institutions (a labor federation, for example) by smaller, more local institutions (aerobics groups, Internet chat rooms) sporting a smaller "radius of trust." As for the causes of family disorder itself, they too are multiple and variegated—but the special role of the feminist revolution has been crucial, and Fukuyama devotes one long and important chapter to it.

In the end, however, what makes this book so valuable is neither Fukuyama's description of the Great Disruption nor his analysis of its proximate causes. Rather, it is his prolonged meditation on what comes next.

Where do norms come from? How do cooperation and trust emerge from them? How, once disrupted, can they be expected to reemerge? Such questions, framed in other vocabulary, were the stuff of social analysis from the Greeks to the 19th century. Is man, by nature, fitted for society? But then, for most of this century, the question virtually disappeared. The renewed interest in it is one of the happier trends in today's social science, and Fukuyama does a masterly job of surveying and synthesizing what has been learned.

He begins by laying out a useful conceptual framework. Briefly, it consists of a horizontal axis anchored on one side by pure hierarchically-generated norms (the Qu'ran's proscription of alcohol, California's proscription of smoking in restaurants) and on the other by pure spontaneously-generated norms (the incest taboo, the price of a commodity). Along the vertical axis is a continuum ranging from "rational" on the top ("rational" merely in the sense of deliberately chosen) and "arational" (meaning socially inherited) on the bottom. The four quadrants in this scheme (hierarchical/rational, spontaneous/arational, etc.) represent four basic types of norms, and Fukuyama sets out to explain how each comes about.

Here, he draws on a wide and vivid set of examples from the sociobiological and anthropological record to demonstrate a few basic points. Most basically of all, human beings are naturally gregarious. They do not behave as the ruthlessly profit-maximizing model of *Homo economicus* would have us believe. Reciprocity, generosity, and loyalty are integral parts of human nature. Humans are not entirely trustworthy—not angels, Fukuyama repeatedly reminds us—but everything we have learned from modern behavioral and biological science gives us sound reason to think that they are indeed fitted for society.

To be sure, most of these new "findings" about human nature have also been stated in other terms, by thinkers from Aristotle to Adam Smith. But it is important at the end of our century to have the imprimatur of science on them, and I suppose we can also be said to have learned a few new things along the way, or at least to have stated old truths with greater precision. Certainly we have acquired a better understanding of the biochemical origins of behavior, and that understanding may be expected to increase. In any case, these chapters of ***The Great Disruption*** are uniformly fascinating.

Shifting gears abruptly, the book takes us into the world of organizational theory, which, as Fukuyama sees it, is increasingly in sync with the sources of human cooperation. The 20th century began with Max Weber telling us that the essence of modernity was bureaucracy. It ends with bureaucracies everywhere in decline, replaced by spontaneous, self-organized markets and networks.

These two things are not identical, Fukuyama explains. In a market, agreements and cooperation require only a minimal set of shared values. That minimal set includes some exceedingly important items, especially a common agreement to engage in voluntary, good-faith transactions. But in every other aspect of their lives, the members of a market can be highly individualistic. They do not even need to like each other.

By contrast, a network is defined by larger shared values. The members of the Sierra Club are part of a network, and so are members of a kinship group or a religion. For that matter, organizations that are putatively market-driven routinely take on some of the characteristics of a network, as in the development of corporate cultures that shape behavior far beyond the narrow terms of a job description.

Fukuyama, putting distance between himself and libertarians, is careful to note the limits of markets and networks alike. Although their spontaneity and flexibility give them great range and vitality, some degree of hierarchy, he believes, is necessary, especially in large social units. Gossip, for example, can be a wonderful mechanism of control in a community of 50 to 100 people; in an anonymous urban neighborhood, it needs to be replaced by more formal systems. And besides, Fukuyama notes, people *like* to organize themselves hierarchically. What they dislike, he observes trenchantly, "is not hierarchy in principle, but hierarchies in which they end up on the bottom." Hierarchies, including powerful government hierarchies, we will always have with us.

Where, then, are we left? Fukuyama urges us, as a first step, to reject the notion that the engine of our destruction is, as some on both Left and Right would have it, capitalism itself, relentlessly eating away at our social capital. Quite the contrary. Although he seldom says anything unequivocally, on this point Fukuyama is unequivocal:

> Montesquieu and Adam Smith were right in arguing that commerce tended to improve morals; [Edmund] Burke, Daniel Bell [in *The Cultural Contradictions of Capitalism*], and [the British social critic] John Gray are wrong to assert that capitalism necessarily undercuts its own moral basis or more broadly that the Enlightenment is self-undermining.

It is not capitalism that worries Fukuyama but the state. Governments, he believes, can help generate social capital—the American public educational system in the first half of this century is his example—but they can also destroy it. Are modern liberal states ineluctably drawn to promote individualism at the expense of social capital? Not necessarily, Fukuyama tells us, but he does not sound wholly confident. For government, the trick is not to contrive artificial ways of restoring social capital but to provide an environment in which the natural human tendencies to create norms and values can reassert themselves.

About the likelihood of this happening, Fukuyama is refreshingly sanguine. In the 1820s, he reminds us, the United States was mired in a slough of alcoholism and crime; a few years later, it had been turned around by the Second Great Awakening. Similarly, 19th-century England was caught in the grip of the most wrenching national economic transformation in history: within a matter of decades, it shifted from a country of agrarian hamlets to an urbanized industrial power suffering from all the severe social ills that Charles Dickens would make notorious. But by the second half of the century, even as the economic transformation continued at full force, Victorian middle-class values had been propagated so relentlessly that crime dropped to the very low levels that would remain characteristic of English society all the way through the first two-thirds of the 20th century.

We have seen the pendulum swing many times before: from license to prudery, from profligacy to thrift, from social chaos to social order. Social capital will be regenerated in the natural course of things: that is the central theme through which Fukuyama draws together the many strands of his argument. Maybe all we need to do is wait.

Fukuyama's historical reconstruction is persuasive, and his understanding of human nature is one with which I emphatically agree. My reservations lie primarily in his tendency to use society as a whole as his unit of analysis. Where he tends to aggregate, I would often prefer to disaggregate.

Doing so tempers his picture in interesting ways. A strong case can be made, for example, that even as trust of fellow citizens was deteriorating appallingly in some parts of America—like inner cities—in others, both trust and civil institutions were continuing to function largely unchanged. Similarly, the loss of trust itself needs to be disaggregated. When it comes to government, a loss of trust in the courts is palpably bad because the rule of law is at stake, but what about a loss of trust in the efficacy of government programs? To me the latter sounds like part of the solution, not part of the problem.

Disaggregation is especially important in thinking about the future, where Fukuyama's wide-angled focus may yield too bright a picture. As it happens, I see harbingers of a Great Reconstruction everywhere—for the middle class on up. We may even be entering a golden age, recovering from the destructive intellectual fads of the recent past and rediscovering our attraction to the beautiful and the true, with technology providing wonderful new possibilities—for the middle class on up. But meanwhile there is the other part of American society—the part often called the underclass—that was the source of many of the statistical trends that define the Great Disruption.

America, after the Great Disruption, is split in a way that it was not split prior to 1965. The underclass is not just a traditional lower class, eager to climb the ladder to middle-class respectability, but a segment of society that is acquiring a code, structure, and culture of its own. It has the ability, through its own underground economy and through the assistance extended to it by government policy, to exist independently of the rest of society. It is increasingly white, and it is increasingly making inroads into the working class.

Added to this is one of the most potent variables that will shape social structure in the 21st century: intelligence. Any attempt to think through the question of where technology and the information economy are taking us must come to grips with the radically different ways this process will play out depending on an individual's IQ. The smart are going to do extremely well. The average will do all right. Those of low intelligence are going to be excluded from many more social goods than we can now imagine. They are in danger of becoming economically and, worse, socially superfluous. Combine this with the presence of a sizable underclass, and even in the face of a regeneration of social capital of the kind Fukuyama foresees, America is likely to be a markedly different place from the country we knew prior to 1965.

These, at least, are the strictures of one who has been working some of the same territory as Fukuyama. But put them aside. **The Great Disruption** takes on questions that go to the heart of social policy writ large. It is written with never-failing lucidity, brings together vast and disparate literatures, and makes one think in new ways about the prospects of post-industrial society. That is quite enough for one book.

FURTHER READING

Criticism

Alter, Jonathan. "The Intellectual Hula Hoop." *Newsweek* (9 October 1989): 39.

> Discusses Fukuyama's background and the central issues and critical interest surrounding "The End of History?"

Aoudjit, Abdelkader. Review of *The End of History and the Last Man,* by Francis Fukuyama. *Clio: A Journal of Literature, History, and the Philosophy of History* 22, No. 4 (Summer 1993): 377-82.

> An unfavorable review of *The End of History and the Last Man.*

Bernstein, Richard. "Judging 'Post-History,' The Theory to End All Theories." *The New York Times* (27 August 1989): E5.

> Discusses "The End of History?" and critical reaction to Fukuyama's thesis.

Brogan, Hugh. "Hegel in Blue Jeans." *History Today* 42 (December 1992): 58.

> An unfavorable review of *The End of History and the Last Man.*

Dunn, John. "In the Glare of Recognition." *Times Literary Supplement* (24 April 1992): 6.

> An unfavorable review of *The End of History and the Last Man.*

Elson, John. "Has History Come to an End?" *Time* (4 September 1989): 57.

> Discusses the controversy, Hegelian underpinnings, and implications of Fukuyama's "The End of History?"

Galston, William A. "Trust—but Quantify." *The Public Interest* No. 122 (Winter 1996): 129-32.

> A positive review of *Trust.*

Hage, Jerald. "The End of History, or a New Crisis?" *Contemporary Sociology* 22, No. 2 (March 1993): 199-202.

> Provides a summary of Fukuyama's thesis and attendant sociological issues in *The End of History and the Last Man.*

Hartley, Anthony. "On Not Ending History." *Encounter* LXXIII, No. 3 (September-October 1989): 71-3.

> Hartley summarizes Fukuyama's argument in "The End of History?" and disagrees with his conclusions.

Lindsay, Peter. "Trust and the Bottom Line." *Review of Politics* 58, No. 4 (Fall 1996): 829-31.

> A review of *Trust,* in which the critic objects to Fukuyama's assertions concerning the relationship between trust and market values.

Marwick, Arthur. Review of *The End of History and the Last Man,* by Francis Fukuyama. *History* 79, No. 255 (February 1994): 83-4.

> An unfavorable review of *The End of History and the Last Man.*

Roth, Michael S. Review of *The End of History and the Last Man,* by Francis Fukuyama. *History and Theory* 32, No. 2 (1993): 188-96.

> Discusses Fukuyama's historical thesis and intellectual debts to G. W. F. Hegel, Friedrich Nietzsche, and Alexandre Kojève in *The End of History and the Last Man,* finding fault in Fukuyama's nostalgic perspective.

Shell, Susan. "Fukuyama and the End of History." In *After History?: Francis Fukuyama and His Critics,* edited by Timothy Burns, pp. 39-46. Lanham, MD: Rowman and Littlefield, 1994.

> Examines Fukuyama's "end of history" thesis in the context of the historical theory of earlier philosophers Immanuel Kant, G. W. F. Hegel, and Alexandre Kojève.

Talbott, Strobe. "Terminator 2: Gloom on the Right." *Time* (27 January 1992): 31.

> Summarizes and refutes Fukuyama's theoretical postulations in *The End of History and the Last Man.*

Thomas, Hugh. "The Valley of the Shadow of Liberalism." *The Spectator* (7 March 1992): 26-7.

> Discusses the intellectual origins and contradictions of Fukuyama's ideas in *The End of History and the Last Man.*

Wright, Esmond. "Hegel for 1992." *Contemporary Review* 261, No. 1519 (August 1992): 105-6.

Discusses Fukuyama's historical thesis in *The End of History and the Last Man,* finding fault in his "too-comfortable philosophy."

Additional coverage of Fukuyama's life and career is contained in the following sources published by the Gale Group: *Contemporary Authors,* **Vol. 140;** *Contemporary Authors New Revision Series,* **Vol. 72.**

Germaine Greer
1939-

(Also has written under pseudonym Rose Blight) Australian nonfiction writer, critic, essayist, and editor.

The following entry presents an overview of Greer's career through 1999.

INTRODUCTION

A controversial feminist critic and scholar, Germaine Greer emerged as a maverick spokesperson for women's liberation with the publication of *The Female Eunuch* (1970). This sensational best seller, distinguished for its frank, iconoclastic discussion of female anatomy, sexuality, and irreverence toward mainstream feminist views, established Greer as a compelling public intellectual and celebrity. In subsequent books, such as *Sex and Destiny* (1984), *The Change* (1991), and *The Whole Woman* (1999), Greer similarly combined scholarly analysis, personal observation, and high rhetoric to produce thought-provoking commentaries on the social status of women in contemporary society.

BIOGRAPHICAL INFORMATION

Greer was born near Melbourne, Australia, to parents Reginal "Reg" Greer, a newspaper-advertising manager, and Peggy Greer. The eldest of three children in a home lacking artistic or cultural stimulation, Greer early on displayed a talent for languages, developing fluency in French, German, and Italian. She won a scholarship to attend a convent school near Melbourne, where her intellectual abilities were further encouraged, as well as the nuns' disdain for marriage. Her unhappy relationship with her parents compelled her to leave home permanently upon receiving a scholarship to attend the University of Melbourne. There she studied English and French literature and earned a B.A. with honors in 1959. After completing an M.A. in English at the University of Sydney in 1961, she taught at a girl's school and tutored at the university. In 1964 she won a Commonwealth scholarship to study at Newnham College, Cambridge University, in England, where she earned a Ph.D. in 1967 with a doctoral dissertation entitled "The Ethic of Love and Marriage in Shakespeare's Early Comedies." Greer subsequently taught English at the University of Warwick in England from 1967 to 1973, during which time she was involved in the theater, appeared on television shows, and published articles in well-respected periodicals. Greer married Paul du Feu in 1968, but the relationship was short-lived, ending in divorce in

1973. A self-described "supergroupie," Greer also entered the circles of rock stars and the British counterculture. She wrote for the underground magazine *Oz* and cofounded *Suck,* a radical pornographic magazine in whose pages nude photographs of Greer once appeared. With the publication of *The Female Eunuch,* Greer won international fame, including numerous guest appearances on television and radio shows in Britain and the United States and a now-famous debate with Normal Mailer in New York City. After purchasing a rural home in Tuscany, Italy, and traveling to Africa, Asia, and India, Greer took a teaching position at the University of Tulsa, Oklahoma, where she founded the Tulsa Centre for the Study of Women's Literature in 1979 and served as its director until 1982. At age forty, Greer learned that she was unable to conceive children, a painful disappointment that colored her feminist perspective; her infertility was induced by several earlier abortions and gynecological surgery. Greer has appeared as a lecturer at Newnham College, Cambridge, since 1989, and is a professor at the University of Warwick. She was awarded a J. R. Ackerley Prize and the Premio Internazionale Mondello for *Daddy, We Hardly Knew You* (1989).

MAJOR WORKS

In *The Female Eunuch,* a trenchant feminist polemic that resonated among millions of readers, Greer rails against the social and psychological oppression of women in modern society. She encourages women to reclaim their independence and vitality, or "woman energy," by eschewing monogamy, heterosexual marriage, and traditional child-rearing. Greer advocates open relationships, sexual freedom, and communal parenting as an antidote to female passivity, repressed desire, and debilitating dependence on men for security and the false promises of romantic love. While criticizing other feminist writers for being either too middle-class or militant, Greer expresses uncharacteristic sympathy for men as victims of their own power structures, suggesting that at least some of their hostility toward women is caused by women themselves. In *Sex and Destiny,* a much longer and heavily researched work, Greer criticizes Western consumer society and interrelated attitudes toward reproduction, contraception, and family. Reversing her position on several key issues, in this work Greer diminishes the importance of sexual pleasure and promiscuity, holding up motherhood and the traditional family unit with veneration while advocating chastity and coitus interruptus as preferred modes of birth control. Greer suggests that the preference for nonreproductive sex in the West reflects an attitude of hostility toward children. In contrast, she extols the cultural values, kinship, and child-rearing practices of various indigenous, non-Western societies. Denouncing the efforts of international bureaucracies to control population growth in the Third World, Greer defends the viability of nontechnological birth control techniques and condemns the importation of unsafe contraceptives by which exploitative pharmaceutical companies profit and prejudicial Western fears are allayed.

The Madwoman's Underclothes (1987) contains selections of Greer's journalism from 1968 to 1985, including early columns published in *Oz* and commentaries on various topics such as feminism, world politics, sexuality, cosmetic surgery, and abortion. *Daddy, We Hardly Knew You* chronicles Greer's arduous and personally distressing effort to uncover her father's dubious origins, a quest she initiated after his death in 1983. Alternating between memoir, detective narrative, and digressive travelogue and national history, Greer reconstructs her father's life through painstaking research in archives and libraries throughout Britain, Australia, and elsewhere. To her surprise, she learns that her father was not born to respectable English parents in South Africa, but was the illegitimate child of a servant, born and raised in a humble, lower-class Australian foster home. His military service in Malta during World War II is also proved an exaggeration, as he was prematurely discharged due to an anxiety disorder. In the end, Greer attempts to come to terms with his deceptions and the feeling that her remote, unaffectionate father did not

love her. In *The Change,* Greer examines the physical, emotional, and social implications of menopause, which she prefers to call the "climacteric." Drawing attention to the cultural overvaluation of youth and fertility, Greer condemns the pervasive negative stereotypes attached to post-menopausal women, whom Greer contends are often jettisoned by men as undesirable crones. Greer strongly criticizes the ignorance of the medical community concerning menopause, noting the past use of harmful treatments and the mixed results of hormonal replacement therapies. Greer recommends a number of herbal and homeopathic remedies and suggests that aging women simply enjoy their freedom from physical self-obsession and refrain from sex altogether.

In *The Whole Woman,* Greer reexamines the social condition of women thirty years after the publication of *The Female Eunuch,* concluding that things have not improved and that renewed anger is in order. Citing a litany of anecdotal evidence culled from newspaper reports and the popular media, Greer contends that post-1960s feminism has produced legal equality without real liberation and, despite apparent professional and personal advances among many women, the oppressive forces of male power and desire remain largely intact. While denouncing international efforts to ban female genital mutilation in the Third World, one of the most controversial aspects of the book, Greer also argues that birth control, cervical and breast cancer screening, and legalized abortion are evidence of the male-dominated medical establishment's effort to control women's bodies. Greer has also published a number of scholarly works, including: *The Obstacle Race* (1979) a study of women painters; *Kissing the Rod* (1989) an anthology of seventeenth-century poetry by women; and literary criticism in *Shakespeare* (1986) and *Slip-Shod Sibyls* (1995). *Slip-Shod Sibyls* offers a revisionist study of women poets from antiquity to the present, including Sappho, Aphra Behn, Christina Rossetti, Elizabeth Barrett Browning, Sylvia Plath, and Anne Sexton, among others. In this work Greer challenges the canonical status of such luminaries and a number of minor figures by arguing that women poets have too easily succumbed to flattery, manipulation, neurosis, and suicide, often diminishing the seriousness of their work and inflating their actual literary significance by the spectacle of their decline.

CRITICAL RECEPTION

Since the publication of *The Female Eunuch,* a book considered by some a classic feminist text, Greer has won both admiration and notoriety as an idiosyncratic icon of the women's movement. Critics often cite the enormous popularity and influence of *The Female Eunuch* during the 1970s as evidence of Greer's powerful insight into the female condition and sex relations. Commentators note, however, that many of Greer's ideas in this work were not original in light of earlier works by Simone de Beauvoir and Betty Friedan. Nevertheless, Greer is credited with making radical feminism appealing and accessible for a large general audience of both women and men. Critics further acknowledge that Greer's savvy media persona and passionate heterosexuality stood in contrast to other feminist writers who, at that time, were unjustly stereotyped as either angry man-haters or lesbians. Reviewers consistently praise Greer's intelligence, sharp humor, and rhetorical powers, particularly in *The Female Eunuch*. However, many find fault in her combative tone and tendency toward self-contradiction, hyperbole, and romantic antimodernism. While *The Female Eunuch* is still regarded as her most significant work, *The Change* and her memoir *Daddy, We Hardly Knew You* have received positive evaluation, as have her several works of literary criticism. As is typical of critical analysis of her work, reviewers single out passages of brilliance and clarity for praise, though dismiss much of the work for its scattered approach and Greer's antagonistic assertions. *Sex and Destiny,* for example, received pointed criticism for its social conservatism and uncritical alliance with Third World cultural practices. Likewise, *The Whole Woman* was faulted by many reviewers for its bleak view of women's liberation and near total mistrust for the medical establishment, as well as her defense of female genital mutilation, condemned by many critics as patently unethical. Greer's continuing ability to elicit such strong reaction—both positive and negative—is recognized by many critics as a reflection of her great strengths and limitations as a feminist visionary and provocateur.

PRINCIPAL WORKS

The Female Eunuch (nonfiction) 1970
The Obstacle Race: The Fortunes of Women Painters and Their Work (nonfiction) 1979
Sex and Destiny: The Politics of Human Fertility (nonfiction) 1984
Skakespeare (criticism) 1986
The Madwoman's Underclothes: Essays and Occasional Writings, 1968-1985 (essays) 1987
Daddy, We Hardly Knew You (memoir) 1989
Kissing the Rod: An Anthology of Seventeenth-Century Women's Verse [editor; with Jeslyn Medoff, Melinda Sansone, and Susan Hastings] (poetry) 1989
The Change: Women, Aging, and the Menopause (nonfiction) 1991
Slip-Shod Sibyls: Recognition, Rejection, and the Woman Poet (nonfiction) 1995
The Whole Woman (nonfiction) 1999

CRITICISM

Anne Richardson Roiphe (review date 17 May 1971)

SOURCE: "Of Mothers and Sisters," in *The New Leader,* May 17, 1971, pp. 8-10.

[*In the following review of* The Female Eunuch, *Roiphe objects to Greer's disavowal of motherhood, family, and monogamy.*]

Germaine Greer is a charming, spunky, honest woman; I admire her direct style, and enjoy her pleasure in words and ideas. She achieves a vital fusion of intellect and passion in her book that places it among the best of Feminist literature—neither a cold tract, cataloguing male abuses, nor a fervid call for revenge on mankind. Her energy, female energy, is strong and free and, like the center-forward on the field-hockey team, she urges us all on to victory. For Germaine Greer is a sexual person who has understood that the vagina is a source of pleasure and pride, and she wants her sisters to share her sensuality of body and spirit. She pushes them to renounce passivity, to exorcise crippling romantic illusions, and to reject plastic images of femininity.

Many of this Englishwoman's views are fairly common in this country. Kate Millett, Ti-Grace Atkinson, Betty Friedan and others have already opened the Pandora's box of woman's misery. But Germaine Greer, while complaining much the same complaints, fairly sings with the joy that love and work can bring to the liberated woman.

How my mother (who thought I should hold my virginity as bait for a desirable male) would have cringed to read this book. How the matrons of middle America will recoil in horror at the mention of tasting menstrual blood (I was shocked, too, but I shouldn't have been). Germaine Greer runs like a Gilbert and Sullivan operetta through the linguistic and other comedies and tragedies of cunt-hatred, ending with a fierce kind of hope in a new tomorrow when all our daughters—yes, yours too, Tricia Nixon—may dance like Isadora Duncan beside the moonlit Parthenon.

Now, although I am a sister in arms, I have some major quarrels about the direction of Germaine Greer's campaign. I am concerned that in our desire not to be slaves we do not sever loving connections to each other and to the next generation.

Despite discussing menstruation and its meaning for women at great length, Germaine Greer fails to give equal time—or, in fact, any time—to pregnancy. She speaks gaily of children bringing themselves up, not needing to be *brought* up. In the event of her own maternity, she says, she would purchase a house in the country for herself and many others, where the father might visit the child and she might or might not admit to being the womb mother, but responsibility for the child's needs would be corporate. She does not support the institution of marriage, and graphically describes the boredom, malfunction and dwarfing of spirit that often occur as husband and wife structure their lives around security.

Her numerous arguments against the nuclear family are not novel, but they do describe its failures accurately. Endless articles on the bliss awaiting the bride in the white gown and the raptures of baby care have so romanticized the relationship between mother and child that the woman who has bought the whole package can only feel cheated. Still, there are certain gratifications and exhilarating adventures that even the most burdened reader of *Family Circle* or *Redbook* is privy to, and I am anxious that the lifestyles we may adopt not destroy or abort the few known good things we already have.

In the chapter devoted to the body, Germaine Greer minimizes the male-female differences by attributing them all to one microscopic "Y" chromosome. Yet this single impertinent "Y" does make a difference in biological reality—a reality that does not shape itself to social fashion. It is particularly important in the inner space of the woman, the origin of life.

Certainly, pregnancy is not all serenity; there are nauseous months and tired months, aches in the back and legs, bulging veins and hernias. But these do not spoil the extraordinary wonder of creating life. When at four-and-a-half months the baby kicks, a woman knows she is at the heart of the mystery. This event, announcing death and age as it announces the next generation, is glory.

Natural childbirth methods now allow many women to control their labor contractions and to consciously push the baby's head through the vagina as both parents watch. For my husband and me it would have been a deprivation, not a liberation, to miss those moments. While I do not believe in the moralistic injunction that women should have babies because that's what they're made for, etc., I do believe that women should not be made to feel enslaved or inferior for wanting to enjoy and fulfill their biological potential.

Delivering the baby, however, is only the beginning. The drudgery, the guilt, the restrictions on personal freedom increase with the poundage of the infant sucking at the breast. (Nursing is another female function Germaine Greer ignores. I remember the months I had a baby sleeping, nursing at my breast as an especially warm and peaceful time. That experience is an important part of me.)

Germaine Greer reports an experiment in which children raised without a specific mother and given complete freedom climbed ladders at the age of eight months. (What is so desirable about an eight-month-old on a ladder I don't know.) I think it is dangerous to go from caring so much about the child that the needs of the mother are ignored to ignoring the child for the supposed benefit of the mother. If we do that, the next generation will be even more isolated, psychotic and vicious than today's. Children do not need less love and attention but more, of the right kind. I am not saying women should spend their lives pregnant and rinsing diapers, repressing their energies in martyrdom to their children. I believe children can receive the love, support and guidance they need while the mother balances her maternal interests with other personal and intellectual ones.

Our nuclear-family isolation is painful, and maybe a commune would supply some of the answers. But we have to remember that historically we all lived in tribal communes and emerged eagerly to seize our individuality and privacy. Although I feel we must explore all the alternatives, I am not certain if going back to the tribe is a step forward.

Germaine Greer has earned her doctorate in Shakespeare; that is surely an achievement of worth and dignity. But the woman who has taught her child not to bash in the head of his brother has also achieved something, and the woman who might accomplish both would be doubly enriched.

Reading **The Female Eunuch,** which makes so little of motherhood, I thought about myself as a mother. I suspect I am similar to most others—my involvement with the physical and emotional well-being of my children is intense and sometimes terrifying, a grand passion of its own sort. My feeling for my children may be narcissistic, but so is writing a book. It may be ambitious, but so is writing a book. Depriving me of my young would be no liberation.

I am not one who sees motherhood in pastels of pink and blue. Yet as a mother I have experienced the danger, fear, occasional despair, and overflowing love that involves me intimately with another life. Mothering is not smothering, not just Mrs. Portnoy and her Alex. As almost any woman can tell you, there is something more, something exciting behind the everyday nurturing of the child. It reeks of life, and Germaine Greer cannot ignore it without peril to the very fullness of experience she is trying so hard to achieve.

My second major disagreement with the author has to do with monogamy. She states that some 19 million English housewives are working without a salary—unpaid slave laborers. What a strange way to look upon a life of shared responsibility. Ideally, the man and woman have set up house together out of love and tenderness and desire for each other. The man brings home money that buys food, clothing and shelter; the woman maintains the home and the young. The woman's work may be the more restricting, and she may lose some of her intellect and energy in this arrangement—as will a man in a dull job. I agree with Germaine Greer that if men share more of the woman's work so that women may share in the man's pleasures and burdens, both will benefit.

Unlike her, though, I accept a long love relationship as a possibility for most people; I think tenderness, compassion and bonds of deep affection can exist with vital sex and real desire. Only exceptionally strong, individualistic women do not need or want familiar arms around them in their different nights. Most women will reach toward one man in hopes of building a temple in which they can eat, drink, copulate, propagate, guard the light of their love, and age together.

This is not, as Germaine Greer describes it, a sordid search for security; for television sets and lawn-mowers. It is the fundamental stuff that moves most of us closer in bed. If she is free of the need for lasting love, she must at least see that most of the world cannot follow her.

Claudia Dreifus (review date 7 June 1971)

SOURCE: "The Selling of a Feminist," in *The Nation,* June 7, 1971, pp. 728-9.

[*In the following review, Dreifus offers negative evaluation of* The Female Eunuch, *which she describes as "shallow, anti-woman, regressive."*]

Early last year, when the high priests of publishing began to discover that their female readers were insatiably curious about the women's liberation idea, there was much discussion as to which of the bountiful crop of feminist authors would become the big femme lib superstar. Betty Friedan had no appeal for the literary lions—she was too old, too bourgeoise, too organization-conscious. Shulamith Firestone, the author of *The Dialectic of Sex* and organizer of New York Radical Feminists, was strikingly attractive; but alas, anti-love, perhaps even anti-men. Ti-Grace Atkinson, an advocate of extra-uterine birth, was considered too far out for a whirl through the major networks. For a while it seemed as if the brilliant and beautiful Kate Millett, whose *Sexual Politics* was for a short time on the best-seller list, might be star material. But she made the mistake of openly asserting her bisexuality. *Time* took due note of this state of affairs, and that finished Millett. So who was left to launch on the Dick Cavett-Johnny Carson-Virginia Graham-*Time-Life* circuit? American feminists, with their dogged determination to be themselves, were a publicity man's nightmare. Someone more palatable would have to be found.

Or even imported. On a warm spring day, Germaine Greer, the author of the English best-seller, *The Female Eunuch,* jetted into New York from London. Miss Greer was everything those messy American feminists were not: pretty, predictable, aggressively heterosexual, media-wise, clever, foreign and exotic. Her background was fascinating. At 32, she was an accomplished actress, a Ph.D. who lectured in Shakespeare at Warwick University, editor of the European pornographic journal, *Suck,* and contributor to various London underground newspapers. Her philosophy, as outlined in *The Female Eunuch,* could be expected to appeal to men: women's liberation means that women will be sexually liberated; feminism equals free love. Here was a libbie a man could like.

Full-page ads announced that Miss Greer had written the women's liberation book of the year, and that despite this achievement, she was "a feminist leader who admittedly loves men." Six feet tall, fashion-model beautiful, Miss Greer was the toast of *The Tonight Show.* Dick Cavett was enthusiastic about her. Norman Mailer suggested that her book was worth reading.

There is a catch to this fairy tale. Germaine Greer is not the feminist leader she is advertised to be. Back home in London she has no active connections with any women's liberation group. And the book she has written is hardly feminist. True, *The Female Eunuch* does contain an obligatory enumeration of the many economic and psychological horrors that women are subjected to. But Miss Greer's information is hardly new, and could be gleaned from a half-dozen other books. What's more, the whole tone of *The Female Eunuch* is shallow, anti-woman, regressive, three steps backward to the world of false sexual liberation from which so many young women have fled.

Miss Greer quite rightly asks women to abandon the institution of marriage, but she means to replace it simply with the dehumanizing, anonymous, and spiritually debilitating thrusting that men call sex. In her view, sex is something to be collected—like money. The more of it you get, the richer you are. The difficulty is that many feminists have been to that movie before. Many of the younger women in the movement recall a period, four or five years ago, when in order to qualify as hip, emancipated females, their alternate-culture brothers insisted they perform as sexual gymnasts. Resentment at this treatment is one powerful motive for the current women's movement.

The author's insistence that "sexual liberation" is the prerequisite for women's liberation has a lot to do with the fact that she thinks like a man. She has done very well in the male world, and she has yet to identify herself with the essential condition of women. From her book, one learns that Germaine Greer has rarely (except during a miserable youth) had to suffer the kinds of misfortune that most women endure. She was always accepted in the world of men. She was always treated as an equal. That good fortune just about disqualifies her for writing a feminist book. She has had no experience of what it means to be adult and female in the world inhabited by most women, and she does not have the gift of imagination that could make up for that lack. Indeed, she consistently takes a viewpoint that is not merely male but inimical to women. Her book is littered with unkind and unfeminist snipes at her sisters. Most of the women in her book are described as whiny, simpy and boring. "As a female lecturer at a provincial university," she complains in a typical passage, "I have to tolerate the antics of faculty wives, but they are strikingly easy to ignore." What separates Germaine Greer from women's liberationists is that a sensitive feminist would regard a faculty wife's failings as the end product of a useless, oppressive and unfulfilling life. A feminist would feel sisterly sympathy for the faculty wife, and be interested in working with her to help change her condition.

Aside from the author's obvious misogyny, she exhibits very little respect for those women who are organizing against sexual oppression. Her chapters on "Rebellion" and "Revolution" are packed with contradictory ranting about how the women's revolution must be part of The Bigger Revolution, how the feminist movement is not militant enough, how the movement is too middle class. On the one hand, she exhorts the women's liberationists to be more militant in their fight against sexism. On the other, she suggests that women make love, not war. "Women cannot be liberated from their impotence by the gun. . . . The process has to be the opposite: women must humanize the penis, take the steel out of it and make it flesh again."

If Miss Greer has no patience with the state of the feminist movement, she has even less love for the literary women who have aligned themselves with it. Betty Friedan is described as middle class and boring. Kate Millett "persists in assuming that [Norman] Mailer is a cretin." Anne Koedt, author of the important Women's Liberation pamphlet, "The Myth of Vaginal Orgasm," is dismissed this way: "One wonders just whom Miss Koedt has gone to bed with."

On the whole, *The Female Eunuch* is a grossly inconsistent book. Yes, Germaine Greer says all the right things about the economics of sexism. Yes, she is extraordinarily observant about some of the physiological results of our sexual conventions. Her chapters on female anatomy are brilliant. Where she falls down is in her inveterate dislike of women, her idiotic exhortations to revolution and nonviolence alike, and her passionate identification with all things male.

Throughout history there have always been a few women who have been able to fight and seduce their way to the top of the patriarchy. In pre-revolutionary France, these women were highly educated, highly cultivated courtesans who provided intellectual and sexual stimulation for the male nobility. (What self-respecting noble would try to carry on an intelligent discussion with his wife?) Germaine Greer is the closest thing we have to this old-world, old-style courtesan. Nor would she be offended by this description. By her own admission, she is a groupie, a supergroupie—which means that she is a sexual and intellectual consort to the royalty of rock music. On television programs she has made comments like: "I'm really just an intellectual superwhore!"

The Female Eunuch is designed to provide intellectual and sexual thrills to those men who would like to see a feminist revolution because it would take that *one* woman off their back and make a lot more women available to them. How nice to be told that women's liberation will mean the liberation of more women for bed service! One reading of *The Female Eunuch* suggested to me that it had been written to assuage the fears of jittery male chauvinists. A second reading convinced me that if Germaine Greer didn't exist, Norman Mailer would have had to invent her.

Barbara Ehrenreich (review date 21 May 1984)

SOURCE: "Feminism Interruptus," in *The New Republic,* May 21, 1984, pp. 32-5.

[*In the following review, Ehrenreich offers unfavorable evaluation of* Sex and Destiny.]

Apostasy is the last resort of the political writer. Angry, provocative best-sellers do not lend themselves to sequels, for, as editors and agents are quick to remind us, it is novelty that oils the wheels of commerce. So writers who would like to sell books and at the same time hold on to their followings are driven at least to revisionism. For example, four years ago Betty Friedan published *The Second Stage,* in which she announced—a bit prematurely for some of us—a dtente in the battle of the sexes. Then last year, Susan Brown-miller, author of the powerful 1974 treatise on rape, *Against Our Will,* came out with a far fluffier book, *Femininity,* which allowed her, among other things, to express her ambivalence about shaving (or not shaving) her legs. Extrapolating from this trend, we might have expected Gloria Steinem to publish her beauty secrets, or Ellie Smeal to rethink the E.R.A. What is far more astounding, Germaine Greer, who is best known for the ebullient sexual radicalism of *The Female Eunuch,* has come out with a book that dismisses orgasms, condones the chador, and advocates chastity as a means of birth control.

Anything with as grandiose a title as *Sex and Destiny* should deserve a less flippant introduction. Greer tells us in the preface (aptly entitled "Warning") that she did not write this book "for fun or for profit," and I am ready to believe that this clever and venturesome woman has already enjoyed a surfeit of both. Here she writes in a tone of high moral purpose, without a trace of her former wit, and on themes that should command the most solemn attention: motherhood, sexuality, the relations between rich and poor nations, human evolution, and Western culture. Yet the result is so jumbled and idiosyncratic that it is not the moral purpose that shines through so much as the perverse and cranky pleasure of the apostate.

The core argument of the book is intelligent enough and, if not exactly new, it still bears repeating. Greer contends that population control efforts, whether undertaken by international agencies or local governments, do more damage than good, if good is indeed intended. Sometimes they merely miss the mark, as in the case of the I.U.D.s that end up being worn as amulets, or the diaphragms dispensed to people who lack indoor plumbing and privacy. Very often they do violence to local customs and cultures, if not to the physical health of the "target populations." High estrogen birth control pills have been dispensed in vast quantities to the malnourished, underweight women of Bangladesh; unsterile and otherwise hazardous I.U.D.s still lodge in the wombs of thousands of Third World women; surgical sterilizations have been performed on large numbers of the unwilling as well as the uninformed. In almost all cases, population control efforts have been shaped by Western values—which, she argues, are profoundly antinatalist and even antichild—and tainted by Western technocratic arrogance.

If Greer's argument stopped there she would have succeeded in offending, or at least provoking, a great many well-meaning people, but she would still have remained in good company. Many thoughtful people, mostly of a left or feminist persuasion, have challenged the meaning of "overpopulation" in a world where the necessities of life are so unequally apportioned, have questioned the chauvinist and racial biases of the population controllers, and have done their utmost to expose particular horrors, like the drug companies' practice of dumping hazardous contraceptives in the Third World. But the last thing Greer seems to want is company. Not only does she fail to acknowledge any likely allies or ideological predecessors, she often goes out of her way to antagonize them.

One small but telling example: feminist groups in the United States and England have campaigned long and hard against the distribution of unsafe contraceptives in the Third World. One of these drugs is Depo-Provera, which is valued by population control agencies because it is injectable and requires little conscious effort on the part of those who use it. Depo-Provera has not been approved for use as a contraceptive in this country because it causes what one physician has called "menstrual havoc," and may cause sterility and cancer. Does Greer, then, who finds something sinister about almost every known method of contraception, have a kind word for the anti-Depo campaign? No, she asserts that the side effects of Depo-Provera are relatively benign ("inconveniences rather than major health hazards") and that the efforts to ban it are "downright crackpot."

In general, the forward motion of *Sex and Destiny* derives less from the strength of its arguments than from Greer's efforts to scamper ahead of the reader and pop out, almost maliciously, from unexpected places. Usually she does this by engaging in a kind of hyperbolic rampage, in which it seems that no bath water can be disposed of without stuffing a few babies down the drain after it. Thus it is not enough to condemn the coercive or reckless imposition of contraceptives on people of other cultures; we are invited to throw out all "mechanical and pharmacological methods." But a few chapters later we find that even this isn't enough. The problem is "recreational sex," presumably another Western capitalist invention like rubber condoms and plastic I.U.D.'s, and aimed, like them, at luring the world's innocents from the proper goals of "land, family, and children" to "orgasms and consumer durables." At this point, Greer peeps out momentarily to acknowledge that "such an attack upon the ideology of sexual freedom, usually, and quite correctly, called permissiveness, must seem shocking coming from a sexual radical, as the present writer professes to be."

Indeed. And it is on the subject of sex that Greer seems most determined to disconcert us, switching suddenly from Falwellian to Sadeian themes. She starts, as she often does, with a point well taken: that Western (and, I would guess, much non-Western) sexuality focuses unduly on the kind of genital encounter most likely to lead to pregnancy. Hence our dependence on contraception. There are alternatives, however, to the old vaginal in-and-out, and at this point my imagination leapt to homosexuality, masturbation, and varieties of heterosexual attention to the clitoris. But Greer has no brief for these innocent and familiar practices. Clitoral sexuality bothers her because it is "masculine," because it lets men off the hook for "any ineptitude in the phallic department," and finally because "it leaves no irritating surplus of orgastic potency . . . in woman"—which, I would have thought, is its strongest selling point. What Greer promotes, instead, is coitus interruptus, a practice she recklessly insists is a reliable method of birth control, and heterosexual anal intercourse, which she seems to feel quite militant about. Well, *chacun . . . son go–t,* but when it comes to intercultural sensitivity, I think most of us would be more comfortable offering a weary Third World multipara a Lippes loop rather than a jar of vaseline.

There are, however, themes that give a certain tortured consistency and, eventually, predictability, to *Sex and Destiny.* One of these is antimodernism, which is more or less of the quotidian, pro-family type popularized by the new right, except that the new right's lost Golden Age is the capitalist suburban culture of the 1950s, while Greer's is represented by the world's embattled peasantry. Whether they are the farmers Greer knows through her part-time residence in Tuscany, or members of the intact preliterate cultures preserved in anthropological accounts, peasants can do no wrong.

Nor, it seems, can their counterparts in the world's metropolitan centers do anything right, from sex to child raising. While this may be a commendably humble stance for a writer of Anglo-Saxon descent, it creates some awkward conflicts with her extreme pronatalist bias. Greer would like the peasants to be as pronatalist as she is—to have sex for the sake of reproduction and to welcome each baby with spontaneous affection. But the truth is that pre-industrial people almost universally have shown remarkable ingenuity—and sometimes coldbloodedness—in contracepting and otherwise reducing the birth rate. They have devised pessaries, douches, magical remedies, and both mechanical and herbal methods of abortion; and—not uncommonly—they have resorted to infanticide.

Greer gets around this in a most peculiar way. First she simply ignores—or is ignorant of—the wealth of folk methods of contraception, which she regards as a rather recent Western invention. (Except for coitus interruptus, which is favored by her Tuscan neighbors.) One might have expected infanticide to be more daunting, especially after her attack on the industrialized West for failing to love its children. But even infanticide turns out to be an act of affection when performed by a suitably brown and weathered hand. In fact her argument in defense of infanticide is the same one that has been used to defend the most callous and coercive schemes of population control: "if you will not feed them, do not condemn them to life. . . ." She finds female infanticide especially "merciful," since girl babies are less valued and more likely to suffer from neglect anyway!

There is a real case to be made against the West, but the grounds are not anti-modernist, as Greer insists in her woolly-minded way; they are anti-imperialist. Before contact with the West, most indigenous peoples managed to live in some kind of rough equilibrium with their food supply, using a variety of means to limit births when necessary. When Europeans arrived on the scene, they did not initially bring condoms and pills, but drastic disruption: slavery, epidemics, forced dislocations, extermination, and—in all cases—an end to the old ecological balance between food and population. Traditional food sources gave way to cash crops, and traditional birth control, especially prolonged lactation, became impractical. Some populations dwindled toward extinction, but others increased rapidly, in no small part because of the disruption of traditional birth-spacing methods. If there is overpopulation—and there certainly is relative to 1800 or even 1900—then the only cure we know is the one Europe and North America themselves underwent: raise the standard of living so that people have some reason to believe that their children will survive and that they themselves will not starve in old age. Hence the message from most critics of population control as it is usually practiced: offer contraceptives (and, preferably, the best we have to offer, not the discards), but offer also health care and some chance for genuine economic development.

But Greer does not analyze the world in terms of nations and classes and their economic interests, for the other great organizing theme of *Sex and Destiny,* in addition to antimodernism, is sociobiology. Individuals are slaves to their genes, which aim only to reproduce; and whole cultures also turn out, by some mystical leap, to be mere carriers for the genes of their members. Sadly, the West is a tired, "subfertile" culture that has gotten too lazy to propagate as fast as its collective genes would like. Hence it resorts to suppressing the genes of more vigorous, child-loving cultures, and it does this by barraging them with contraceptives and alluring images of recreational sex. From Greer's sociobiological vantage point, population control turns out to be just one more skirmish in the D.N.A. wars that have been raging since our ancestral molecules emerged in the primordial soup.

This is not the place to attempt a refutation of the tenets of sociobiology (interested readers are referred to the recent *Not In Our Genes,* by R. C. Lewontin, Steven Rose, and Leon J. Kamin), nor to question what genetic unity defines "the West," nor to inquire into what miracle of genetic transcription impels an official of the International Planned Parenthood Federation to foist I.U.D.s on the peoples of the southern hemisphere, and so on. But I will underscore a point that may already be obvious: Greer's sociobiology of cultures justifies all the abuses and tragedies she decries. If population control at its most arrogant and imperious is only an expression of our genes, why buck nature? Why not root for the home team? Sterilize the wretched of the earth, and, while we're at it, add a few more babies to the greedy legions of the West.

In the end I can't imagine that Greer is any happier with the morass of *Sex and Destiny* than the reader is likely to be. While she never tells us directly what path led her from the good-humored lucidity of *The Female Eunuch* to this strange destiny, the book is littered with clues. She emerges, in her first-person persona, as an affluent white tourist on sabbatical in the Third World, where she discovers that all her fame, knowledge, feminist insight, etc., are as nothing compared to the simple joys of motherhood. Among the peasantry she finds women who are "unequivocally successful," who have not succumbed to "a masculine sense of self," and who are living out their late and middle years surrounded by loyal progeny. In their eyes, she imagines that her own childlessness is tragic and inexplicable, that her life is "shapeless, improvised, and squalid."

Well, this is sad. Sad that Greer doesn't have her own children, if that's what she now wants. Sadder still that she has not chosen to expend her maternal energies on the spiritual progeny she has earned in her years as a feminist spokeswoman. They deserve something better than this burst of midlife petulance.

Linda Gordon (review date 26 May 1984)

SOURCE: "Bringing Back Baby," in *The Nation,* May 26, 1984, pp. 645-6.

[*In the following review, Gordon offers unfavorable assessment of* Sex and Destiny.]

Because this book about fertility was written by a woman suffering from infertility it elicited my sympathy even before I opened it. I would not mention Germaine Greer's personal situation had she not reported it herself in *The New York Times* and in several other interviews. And that too—her openness about a painful and stigmatized subject—won my respect. Nevertheless, and despite Greer's opinion, the pain of infertility is *not* biologically determined; instead the meaning and experience of "barrenness" are created by culture, have changed historically and will undoubtedly change further.

Although improved health care in industrial societies has increased fertility in general, the current practice of postponing childbearing ten or twenty years has itself become a cause of infertility. And perhaps this—the knowledge that some infertility results partly from choice, from prolonged singleness or education or work—has worsened the agony of women unable to conceive. Medical intervention can help many such women, but for others the hope for a cure may simply postpone a necessary coming to terms.

It is also possible that the contemporary reaction to infertility has been intensified through its symbolic connection with other anxieties: fears about ecological imbalance; suspicions of the technological society; and feelings of loneliness resulting from the decline of kinship and community ties. But the connections between biological infertility and overall personal, cultural and societal malaise are *only* symbolic. Expressions such as "intellectual fertility" or "artistic sterility" are *only* metaphors. Germaine Greer is entitled to grieve for her own childlessness, and to turn that grief into a bit of contemplative literature to generate understanding of the problem. But she can be criticized for generalizing on the basis of what seems to be her personal response—her anger at the very freedom that led her to postpone childbearing—and presenting it as an objective critique of the ills of sexual and familial life.

Sex and Destiny launches two arguments at once: the first is a criticism of sexual and familial behavior in modern industrial societies; the second is an attack on population control in the Third World. Greer's case against population control is strong, if not new. But her legitimate criticisms are situated in an overall argument that is both antifeminist and condescending toward people who aspire to greater wealth and more independence than they now enjoy. (One is often reminded here of those privileged advice givers who like to tell the poor how morally and culturally superior the simple life is.) In this respect she has placed herself in that long tradition of women writers who have built careers telling other women to be content with domesticity.

Greer charges industrialized societies with having produced child-hating cultures, in contrast to the child-loving values of traditional societies. The examples of child-loving societies come from her visits to and reading about India and Africa, and from her periodic residence in rural Tuscany. She further believes that there is an indestructible human drive for procreation and that attempts to repress it can only be futile and productive of neurosis. Greer argues that in developed societies the attempt to substitute "orgasm for babies," or nonreproductive sexual pleasure for the pleasures of raising children, has impoverished life, particularly for women; human sexuality, she believes, is so essentially an aspect of a larger drive that the separation of sex from reproduction may be destructive. Her book offers up chastity as a preferred form of birth control and affirms the superiority of family bonds, defined primarily as mother-child bonds, to any other human ties.

No doubt the criticisms of "junk sex" and of dangerous and coercive birth control policies have their merits, but they don't constitute evidence for the overall arguments of *Sex and Destiny,* all of which are either historically or ethically wrong. In arguing that ours is a child-hating culture, Greer ignores a large body of historical literature which suggests the opposite: that children used to be treated far more callously than they are today. And whatever criticisms she might level at it, our treatment of children is easily matched by cruelties to children practiced by the simpler societies she admires.

Regarding the drive for fertility, there is no evidence that frustrated longings for children have generally deleterious

effects. And Greer makes no case whatever on the dangers of nonreproductive sex. Her nervousness about appearing antisexual makes her argument slippery, but her attitude is clear in passages like these:

> Human libido is the only force which could renew the world. In allowing it to be drawn off, regularly tapped in domestic ritual, we are preparing the scene of our own annihilation, stupefied by myriad petty gratifications, dead to agony and to ecstasy. . . . Having fun means having recreational sex: recreational sex means no fear of pregnancy, a wife who is always available and who is content with orgasms in place of land, family and children—orgasms and consumer durables.

> There is no logic in a conceptual system which holds that orgasm is always and everywhere good for you, that vaginal orgasm is impossible, that no moral opprobrium attaches to expenditure of semen wherever it occurs . . . [since the system also holds that] "normal" heterosexual intercourse should always culminate in ejaculation within the vagina.

Whose norm is this? At a time when feminists and other sexually enlightened people are arguing against such a norm with significant success, Greer writes a book which entirely ignores their efforts. In her chapter on "polymorphous perversity," the missionary position is taken as a given (if women don't enjoy it as much as men, the moral is to have less sex); feminists are criticized for their emphasis on clitoral stimulation; and lesbianism does not exist.

Her critique of commercial society, of the transience of all relationships other than the maternal, resonates with modern insecurity. And her sketches of the good life, often drawn from images of rural Tuscan families, erases from that landscape all evidence of poverty and drudgery, of women's often brutal oppression and of female longing for adventure, knowledge and power.

Greer's discussion of modern birth control similarly minimizes the importance of women's autonomy. Apart from chastity, her favorite birth control methods are *coitus interruptus* and the use of condoms, because they involve no health hazards. But both devices must be controlled by men, a fact Greer does not discuss. Indeed, nowhere can one find the discussion of the *politics* of reproductive rights which is certainly relevant here. One would assume from reading this book that men's and women's interests in sex and reproduction are always identical, that no one had yet noticed that sexual transactions involve inequities of power, that no one had yet pointed out that women are often forced into sex or conception.

The attack on population control seems at first glance more compelling, but a closer look reveals that here, too, issues of power and inequality are ignored. Greer is right of course to challenge the notion that birth control rather than the redistribution of resources can combat poverty. And her examples of the coerciveness of population control programs are persuasive. But her vision of the Third World as peopled by men and women living in equality and sexual harmony, jointly oppressed by Western norms, is absurdly romantic. She seems not to understand that victims of imperialist oppression can themselves be the perpetrators of sexual cruelty.

The central contribution of *Sex and Destiny* is no more then a New Right perspective on sex and birth control, a profamily line in the name of women's best interests. There is nothing new about this maneuver: Jean Elshtain has been doing it, and it has also crept into Betty Friedan's work Like Elshtain, Greer appropriates feminist ideas, for example critiques of competitive individualism, and uses them to attack the women's movement.

Greer's social analysis resembles New Right thinking in its method as well. It is moralistic rather than historical. The version of social change offered here is like a young child's notion of history: there were the "old days," secure, simple, satisfying and restful, and there is now. There is no doubt that sexual permissiveness has become a new orthodoxy and a new kind of conformity and that contraception is often coercive and dangerous. It doesn't follow that reattaching sex exclusively to reproduction is the appropriate remedy.

Greer's passion in this book is for fertility, not for actual children—another position similar to that of the New Rightists, who defend the fetus's "right to life" but advocate cutting support for child care, education and child abuse prevention programs. Children figure in this book only as assets which parents have or don't have; there is very little feel for the actual enjoyments of parenthood. On the contrary, the accusation that our culture is child-hating is not a defense of children, but reveals Greer's hostility toward adults:

> Drinking and flirting, the principal expressions of adult festivity, are both inhibited by the presence of children. Eventually our raucousness wakes them and they watch our activities through the stair rails and learn to despise us. . . .
>
> So much adult amusement stems from matters ribald or malicious that even lighthearted conversation is censored for the younger generation.

As if adult conversation in "traditional" society was neither ribald nor malicious!

Greer's value system, to give credit where credit is due, is more consistent than that of the New Right. The New Rightists employ what they call a "fusionist" perspective, uniting traditionalism on "social" issues (such as sex, abortion and women's rights) with a progrowth, big-capital economic policy. Greer is a bit more old-fashioned in her conservatism, romanticizing rural life and condemning commercial as well as feminist values.

It is irritating to read and wearying to review a book so careless and bitter. Still, two aspects of it are provocative: its popularity and its relation to Greer's past work. The positive reception of the book illuminates those areas where New-Right thinking, repressive and pessimistic, has

influenced even the liberal gentry. Greer has been a feminist media star noted for her defense of women's sexual and professional achievement. Her arguments in *Sex and Destiny* are patent rejections of her earlier positions. Yet it is hard to avoid noticing a certain political continuity. *The Female Eunuch* articulated the aspirations and frustrations of women who had considerable resources and opportunities in their lives; it had little connection with the aspirations and frustrations of women without money, education or status. Greer formulated her feminist demands in the direction of the individual's right to achievement. Perhaps it is logical that the extreme emphasis on individualism in her earlier stance would eventually produce a conversion experience. But what we need now is not one more wild swing of the pendulum back toward social conservatism but a recognition of the tension between individual freedom and nurturing bonds, a tension by no means always destructive.

Peter Singer (review date 31 May 1984)

SOURCE: "Sex and Superstition," in *New York Review of Books,* May 31, 1984, pp. 15-6, 18.

[*In the following negative review of* Sex and Destiny, *Singer finds fault with Greer's cultural relativism, inconsistencies, and "absurdities."*]

Germaine Greer's *The Female Eunuch* was perhaps the most brilliant, and certainly one of the most influential, of the wave of feminist books that appeared in the early 1970s. As the title suggested, Greer pictured women as pressured into a stereotypical female role which effectively castrated them, forcing them to deny their sexuality and to see themselves as wives and mothers, ministering to the needs of others instead of being true to their own natures. It was a polemical work, but a persuasive one. It caught the mood of the times and led many women to assert their own sexuality, shattering the bonds of convention that had repressed their mothers and grandmothers.

Greer's new book deals with our attitudes to reproduction, with particular attention to attempts by Western scientists and population agencies to persuade other nations to use the new fertility control methods recently developed in the West. As an offshoot of this theme, Greer argues that Western society places too much importance on "recreational sex" and has become positively hostile to children. It is because of these attitudes that we are so committed to devices like oral contraceptives and IUDs. If we were less concerned about recreational sex and more concerned about children, we might regulate our having children by the rhythm method, by coitus interruptus, or even, like the Dani people of Irian Jaya, by sexual abstinence for a period of four to six years after the birth of a child.

Like *The Female Eunuch, Sex and Destiny* is a polemical work, and much of it is concerned with sex, but there the resemblance ends. It is far longer than *The Female Eunuch*, but not nearly so persuasive. The wit and brilliance displayed in the earlier book now struggle vainly to surface amid a seemingly endless series of scholarly quotations, mixed with anecdotes drawn from Greer's travels in India and Italy. More striking still, however, is the contrast between the conclusions of the two books. On the basis of *The Female Eunuch*, Greer was acclaimed as one of the leaders of feminist thought. But if feminism stands for the belief that women should not be inferior to men in the power they exercise over their own lives and over the community in which they live, *Sex and Destiny* makes it hard to see Greer as a feminist at all. She has become, instead, an apologist for social institutions that keep women in their place: at home with the children.

Here is one revealing and characteristic passage, taken from the first chapter of the book. Having described the isolation from the family in which Western children are allegedly born and reared, Greer cites a description of child rearing in Bangladesh:

> In Bangladesh children under the age of five or six are looked after by the whole family. All the children of the joint family are looked after together. They are taken to the pond for a bath perhaps by one daughter-in-law. . . . Perhaps the youngest daughter-in-law has cooked the meal. Another woman feeds them. . . . Maybe there is a favourite aunt, she tells them [fairy] stories. But at night when they get sleepy they always go to their mother and sleep in her embrace.

Greer refers to this as a "rosy picture" and while acknowledging that "the system does not always work as well," she seems in no doubt of its superiority to modern Western methods of child rearing. She appears not to notice that this description of children being looked after "by the whole family" is in fact an account of children being looked after entirely by women. This is all the more extraordinary because only a few pages earlier Greer had criticized northwestern European civilization for its tendency to separate children from parents: "The most privileged people in protestant Europe have traditionally seen least of their children." Clearly the most privileged people in Bangladesh are men, and from the account cited, they see even less of their children than the most privileged people of Protestant Europe.

It is entirely consistent with the themes of her book that Greer should take no notice of the blatantly sexist assumptions about child rearing made by her informant on family life in Bangladesh. For Greer now rejects the common feminist assumption that women are conditioned into seeing motherhood as their prime function in life. To the contrary, she regards modern Western society as fundamentally opposed to childbearing:

> It used to be a truism of feminist theory that women were railroaded into motherhood by the expectations of their parents and their in-laws. In the view of this writer, such forms of persuasion and pressure as the kin group can bring to bear pale into utter insignificance next to the powerful disincentives which are offered by the actual social context in which the would-be child-bearer lives.

Nor does Greer agree with feminists who see the role of motherhood as a restrictive one:

> We have at least to consider the possibility that a successful matriarch might well pity Western feminists for having been duped into futile competition with men in exchange for the companionship and love of children and other women.

The reader is left wondering whether Greer believes that having given up the "futile" competition, women will be able to rely on the compassion and nobility of males as a bulwark against repression. But then, perhaps even repression does not matter too much, because Greer later suggests that "the fact that women are not free to follow their own inclinations and preferences in sexual matters may not be experienced by the woman as a restriction, for she is not encouraged to internalize the repressive mechanism or to cultivate an image of herself as powerless or passive." In support of this claim, Greer tells us of Hindu and Tamil beliefs about the dangerous powers women possess, and the need for them to be kept under control by puberty rites, menstrual taboos, and widow restrictions.

There is something slightly absurd about the solemn respect with which Greer treats these exotic superstitions. If they were Western doctrines, every feminist—even the author of *Sex and Destiny*—would denounce them as transparent devices for maintaining male dominance. (Have feminists ever regarded the myths surrounding the importance of motherhood in Western society as any compensation for the fact that it is so much harder for women than for men to achieve leadership in Western society?) When these beliefs are the beliefs of a mysterious non-Western culture, however, Greer accepts them as ingenious ways of overcoming problems inherent in the human condition.

This humility before the wisdom of the East, or the South, or the Tuscan peasant, stands in sharp contrast to the views expressed in *The Female Eunuch*. There, in her section "The Wicked Womb," Greer asserted that we still are ignorant and wary of the female reproductive organs, and described our attitude to menstruation as part of the "atavistic fear" surrounding the womb. Hindu, Moslem, and Jewish beliefs that a menstruating woman is unclean were cited as evidence of this pervasive fear, although Greer found some evidence that "enlightenment is creeping into this field at its usual pace."

The Greer of *Sex and Destiny* must have changed her mind about menstruation, for in addition to her newfound respect for Hindu menstruation rituals, she is quite prepared to sneer at the very Western attitudes that she previously characterized as enlightened: in a section attacking the "tremendous sexual orthodoxy" of modern Western society, she scoffs that "refraining from sexual intercourse during menstruation is deemed fainthearted."

In this obeisance before the folk wisdom and the religious superstitions of every culture but her own, we can find the clue to Greer's break with feminism. She has embraced some muddled form of cultural relativism, according to which we in the West have no right to criticize any other culture. "What is our civilization," she asks, "that we should so blithely propagate its discontents?"—and she continues with other, presumably equally rhetorical, questions, such as "Why should we erect the model of recreational sex in the public places of all the world?" and more pointedly still, "Who are we to invade the marriage bed of veiled women?"

There is no denying that our civilization is far from ideal; but if we seriously believe that feminist principles have no application to the women of non-Western societies, our feminism cannot run very deep. Since most cultures are sexist, to refuse to criticize the beliefs and practices of other cultures is equivalent to acceptance of sexist beliefs and practices.

This is exactly what we find in *Sex and Destiny.* For instance, Greer finds that the Islamic religion treats "the lowest and least prestigious groups as deserving of the same respect as the highest" and that, accordingly, in veiling its women, Moslems are "conferring upon them a new kind of value and, hence, self-respect." She appears to admire the "heroic determination" of Yanomamo Indian women, who submit themselves to a method of abortion that consists of the pregnant woman lying on her back while a friend jumps on her belly. And perhaps most oddly of all, whereas the author of *The Female Eunuch* poured her fiercest vitriol on the Western tendency to deny female sexuality and misrepresent it as "passivity," the new Greer has nothing to say against the "value systems" of Mediterranean societies like the Greek Sarakatsani shepherds, who believe that "intercourse must occur in darkness, without speech, and the woman must remain motionless and passive." This value system, Greer tells us, is a way of "promoting the importance of sexuality." She doesn't tell us if it is specifically female sexuality that it is so effective in promoting.

Greer's form of cultural relativism is misconceived. It may arise out of a well-meaning and sensible desire to avoid ignorant Western tampering with social practices that have important beneficial consequences. For instance, as Greer points out in her discussion of infanticide, many societies have used infanticide as a means of spacing dependent children, who would become an impossible burden if there were too many at any one time. Westerners encountering this practice for the first time may find it shocking, and try to stamp it out, without realizing that in the absence of any alternative method of spacing dependent off-spring, the results will be disastrous both for the children and for their mothers. A better understanding of the practices of any society may lead us to see virtue in what at first seemed horrific.

From this simple truth, however, it certainly does not follow that all cultures are equally good, or that we are never justified in criticizing the social practices of a different culture. Sometimes social practices will not benefit the society as a whole, but only one section of it, and at great cost to another section of the society. Slave societies are obvious examples, but a feminist would not need to be reminded of the fact that some social practices exist for the exclusive benefit of the dominant group. We must sometimes choose between, on the one hand, the principles of sexual equality that are expressed in feminism, and, on the other, our desires to avoid the cultural imperialism that seems to be implicit in suggesting that the traditional ways of doing things are not always the best. On the evidence of this book, Greer has not chosen feminism.

Greer's unthinking acceptance of an untenable form of cultural relativism is one major reason for rejecting many of her conclusions. But even without this, her book is so riddled with inconsistencies, errors, and downright absurdities that it cannot stand as a serious work.

First, some examples of the inconsistencies. The theme of the first chapter of *Sex and Destiny* is that we in the West do not like children: "modern society," Greer tells us, "is unique in that it is profoundly hostile to children." Greer suggests, as we have already seen, that Western society offers powerful disincentives to childbearing, and that it is "anti-child." As evidence she offers an English restaurant which advises patrons to "leave under-fourteens and dogs at home."

If these claims do not strike a responsive chord, and the evidence cited seems insufficient, there is no need to take the trouble of finding counterinstances. Greer does it for you. In the second chapter she writes of our extreme reluctance to tolerate involuntary sterility, and in the third chapter she tells us that "Western women may spend a fortune and masochistically undergo repeated surgical procedures in an attempt to bear a child." If this does not create confusion enough, she also throws in the suggestion that our attempts to regulate the fertility of others derive from our fear that the exploding populations of the world will challenge our own subgroup and "compromise our survival as the biggest, richest, greediest and most numerous group on earth." Greer apparently sees no need to reconcile this suggestion with the fact that she has just been belaboring Western society for its hostility to children and the difficulties it puts in the way of childbearing.

For a second example of Greer's confusion about what she really wants, consider her attitude to eugenics. She devotes a forty-six-page chapter to retelling the story of the eugenics movement, from the Social Darwinists through Francis Galton and Hermann Muller to William Shockley. The tone, as might be expected, is one of contempt and horror:

> Practical eugenics denies all the values which justify our civilization. When we have a clearer idea of our own ignorance, we shall see that eugenics is more barbarous than cannibalism and far more destructive.

In preferring cannibalism to eugenics, Greer was no doubt influenced by the assumption that eugenics is a Western idea, while cannibalism belongs to those other cultures that are so much wiser than our own. Unfortunately she has forgotten that in an earlier chapter, discussing infanticide, she came to precisely the opposite conclusion: there she praised infanticide as practiced by non-Western societies, describing it as a method of "culling the newborn." In unfavorable contrast to such practices, she describes modern man (yes, "man") as having a greater chance of "bearing genetically incompetent children" and yet still being morally bound to keep children alive as long as is humanly possible.

These unreconciled contradictions suggest that the book was written with insufficient care. It appears to have been researched in the same style. There is, for instance, a brief account of the development of in vitro fertilization—"test-tube babies" as the press likes to describe it. The discussion appears to be based on a two-page article that appeared in *Science* in 1978, and even this article has not been properly taken into account. Greer describes Patrick Steptoe as working at Cambridge on the fertilization of animal ova in a petri dish, and then "sneaking" off to "Royston" to try out the technique on human patients. She also asserts that "his experiments were the outcome of millions spent on luxury research."

This account is garbled from beginning to end. Patrick Steptoe never worked at Cambridge and never did experiments on animal ova in petri dishes. Steptoe is a gynecologist whose major contribution to in vitro fertilization was his skill at laparoscopy, a then-novel technique for seeing inside a patient's abdomen. This technique made it possible to recover ripe eggs from the ovary, for fertilization in the laboratory. The work on animal ova was carried out by Robert Edwards, a Cambridge scientist. It was modestly funded and did not receive "millions" (though in any case it is not easy to see why Greer, who considers fertility to be of such paramount importance, should consider this "luxury" research). Edwards did not "sneak" away to conduct experiments on human patients. He contacted Steptoe after reading a paper Steptoe had written on laparoscopy, and suggested that they team up in an attempt to help some of Steptoe's infertile patients. The work was done at Royton (not "Royston") near Oldham, because that is where Steptoe had his practice and his research facilities, and there were no funds available to set up similar facilities in Cambridge.

This instance is enough to suggest that the reader should not take Greer as a reliable authority when she discusses recent developments in fertility research—and large sections of the book discuss just that. It also seems that Greer is unreliable on other subjects. She criticizes Ferdinand Mount, "that champion of the nuclear family," for failing to notice that Jesus Christ had no brothers or sisters. Had Greer read the Gospel according to Matthew, she would have known that Jesus had at least four brothers, and sisters too. (Or were they only stepbrothers and stepsister? But this fine point would scarcely help Greer. See Matthew 13:54-57; see also Matthew 12:46-47 and John 7:1-10.)

Even with respect to the subject of her doctorate—Shakespeare—Greer is disappointing. She commits the common but nonetheless deplorable error of using the quotation "a custom more honored in the breach than the observance" as if it meant simply that the custom was more often broken than observed. Hamlet meant, rather, that the custom that had been mentioned was one that it would be more honorable to break than to observe.

Finally, Greer makes statements that are not so much errors as absurdities. What is the reader to think when confronted with a flat statement that in our society "the role of mother is socially marginal"? How about: "Common morality now treats childbearing as an aberration; there are practically no good reasons left for exercising one's fertility." Perhaps the limits of silliness are reached with this comment on voluntary sterilization: "Sterilization is not a substitute for contraception because it is the destruction of fertility: it makes as much sense as blinding a man who needs glasses." Vivid prose is one thing, but this kind of nonsense can only irritate the reader and discredit the writer.

All of this is a pity, because struggling within the fat of *Sex and Destiny* is the skeleton of a good book waiting to be written. No doubt there is much wrong with the way in which Western population experts go about trying to persuade people in other countries to control their fertility. It would be valuable to have a careful study of the mistakes that such experts have made, and the ways in which we need to be more sensitive to the cultures of other people. Greer might have even been able to make plausible her startling contention that the best forms of birth control for most people are those that require no technology at all—the rhythm method, coitus interruptus, and sexual abstinence—backed by easy access to safe abortion. She might even have been able to say something challenging about the importance that Western society places on sex, as compared with the importance we place on enjoying our children. This would have been an interesting and provocative book.

Unfortunately *Sex and Destiny* is not that book. In her preface—which she dramatically entitles "Warning"—Greer says that the function of polemical writing is to stimulate creative thought and to break down "settled certainties." To challenge orthodoxy successfully, however, it is necessary to argue carefully, accurately, and consistently. This Greer has not done. The only conventional opinions that *Sex and Destiny* is likely to change are those about Greer's argumentative skills, and her commitment to feminism.

Carol Iannone (review date August 1984)

SOURCE: "Feminism Ad Absurdum," in *Commentary*, Vol. 78, No. 2, August, 1984, pp. 71-2.

[*In the following review, Iannone offers unfavorable assessment of* Sex and Destiny.]

Anyone reading this book might find it hard to believe that its author also wrote one of contemporary feminism's pioneering texts. *The Female Eunuch* (1970) was a racy, radical, best-selling manifesto that posited sexual freedom as the key to women's liberation. Germaine Greer, with her disheveled Anna Magnani-style sexiness and sharp dry Cambridge wit, became a talk-show and counterculture celebrity, shocking her then perhaps eager-to-be-shocked audiences with outrageous ideas, such as the obsolescence of marriage and the dispensability of underwear.

Times of course have changed, but even changing times cannot fully account for what appear to be the violent reversals of her newest book. To be sure, Miss Greer has not lost her power to shock. Where *The Female Eunuch* deplored every inhibition placed on women by the patriarchal West, the present book manages a good word for such Third World practices as the veil, menstrual segregation, and even polygamy. Where *The Female Eunuch* preached spontaneous self-realization against the oppressive forces of civilization, the present book speaks glowingly of the self-sacrificing collectivity of extended families in underdeveloped countries. Where *The Female Eunuch* suggested that we find ways to deepen our sexual delight (because "the sexual personality is basically anti-authoritarian"), the present book decries the cooptation of sex by consumer society and tersely recommends chastity as a form of birth control.

In Miss Greer's current view, the West is now oversexed, subfertile, and hopelessly materialistic. Our skimpy nuclear families are centered on the consumer-oriented "copulating couple," who indulge in "recreational sex" and barely manage to turn out a child or two as they contend for orgasmic bliss. In addition, because of our insistence on genital sex without conception, we have accepted the dangerous pharmacological hardware of modern birth control, and lost the ability to remain chaste or to employ the healthy varieties of anal sex and coitus interruptus.

Moreover—and this is the second theme of the book—we are, true to our imperialist selves, enforcing our own corrosive arrangements all over the world. Miss Greer excoriates Western efforts at birth control in developing countries. Declaring that overpopulation is a myth concocted by elderly right-wing millionaires, she argues that we are imposing our own hatred of children, together with our fevered consumerism, on countries where children are loved and enjoyed—all to insure that the darker races not inherit the earth.

Sex and Destiny contains so many startling shifts in thought that one might expect they would be accompanied by deep soul-searching and lengthy explanations. In fact, they are barely acknowledged. A few superficial admissions here and there cannot disguise the profound lack of self-insight that is one of the book's presiding deficiencies. Nowhere in this 500-page harangue, for instance, is there any speculation on how Miss Greer's own former beliefs helped prepare the ground for the state of affairs she perceives today. Traditions she attacked and helped destroy in *The Female Eunuch* still receive from her nothing like the sympathy she now extends to traditions supposedly threatened by the advance of imperialist capitalism.

The book's weighty scholarship is suspiciously one-sided in its deployment. Miss Greer catalogues anything incriminating she can find in Western practices and omits anything that might serve as balance. One needs to read between the lines to surmise that great numbers of women in developing countries are gladly availing themselves of birth-control devices, Miss Greer's rehearsal of the horrors associated with them notwithstanding. After hearing idealized stories of the tender care afforded the elderly in traditional societies, one is startled to be reminded (in a separate context, of course) that there are far fewer old people in these countries than in our own—a factor that might well influence differing approaches to the problem.

In truth, despite plentiful research, most of *Sex and Destiny* is simply an angry, impressionistic, and tendentious tirade against the Western way of life. Traditional societies are described at their best; ours at its worst. Sunny Third World moppets disport themselves with loving female kin while irate Western mothers stuff sweets into the mouths of their screaming young to quiet their greed. Stately, beloved matriarchs are contrasted with our own lonely "blue-rinse widows." When Miss Greer speaks of the hapless Indian surrounded by children he cannot afford, she compassionately invokes the mysterious powers of sensuality under which he has struggled and lost. Our own failures at chastity, however, are simply due to selfishness, laziness, and irresponsibility. Even the book's one or two tender moments are edged and sharpened by disdain for the West. She remarks on the sweetness of children, but cannot resist adding that this sweetness is more apparent to people worn out from toil than to our own "smooth-skinned, overfed selves."

The West, then, is utterly worthless, and Miss Greer cannot use the word democracy without putting it in quotation marks. We have, according to her, no values; what values we think we have, we have no right to promote. She openly declares that the annihilation of our whole civilization would be of little consequence. A feminist counterpart of those starry-eyed Western travelers to totalitarian dictatorships, Miss Greer praises or condones practices in underdeveloped countries—abruptly dismissing clitoridectomy and the unbelievably barbaric practice of female circumcision—that she would never tolerate in her own.

Miss Greer thinks as little of the natural processes which gave her life as she does of the civilization that nurtured her. Despite, or perhaps because of, her own prodigious and much chronicled sexual indulgence, her hatred of sex, men, and biology itself runs deep. She remarks with irritation on the wastefulness of the human reproductive process: "billions of sperm are doomed to struggle and die completely pointlessly." But sperm at least call up some admiration in her for being "lively," while their female counterpart, the blastocyst, earns Miss Greer's contempt: "torpid," "passive," "lumbering." In her promotion of anal sex, one senses a scorn of the womb; despite her frenzied enthusiasm for large families, she commends the Marquis de Sade for calling this form of sex "'*la plus délicieuse*' of the ways of cheating nature." In the insistent way in which she argues for coitus interruptus, one senses a disdain for male potency (she characterizes male ejaculation as the "trivial spasm," although elsewhere she is forced to concede that it is this "spasm" that produces life).

Ironically enough, given her "liberation," Miss Greer does not really seem capable of handling the immense freedom of Western women; certainly she praises more prohibitive arrangements as superior. Although she reasserts in this book her old sentimental belief that it is only the consumerization of sex she deplores, and that human libido can renew the earth, she means by this nothing so definite as the urge to reproduce. This libido, rather, appears to be an ideological construct, Miss Greer's vague and fitful version of the God she cannot bring herself to believe in.

In the end, after one has considered the startling reversals of Miss Greer's earlier views, a certain demented continuity emerges. For what **Sex and Destiny** most clearly reveals is that feminism—at least in its messianic, world-transforming manifestations—was less a rational program with fixed goals than an irrational shriek of hatred against the human condition itself, one that will not be silenced until every aspect of life, with its attendant irregularity, imperfection, and inequality, has been eradicated. This book is a reversal of feminism only if one assumes that feminism is the humane movement it purports to be. In fact the book is no reversal at all, but a logical, if absurd, conclusion.

Sara Maitland (review date 21 November 1986)

SOURCE: "Her Own Thing," in *New Statesman,* November 21, 1986, pp. 29-30.

[*In the following review, Maitland offers unfavorable assessment of* The Madwoman's Underclothes.]

When I was an undergraduate I heard Germaine Greer speak: she was indeed weird and wonderful and, as it turned out, the evening transformed my life. A short while later I bought a copy of **The Female Eunuch** and pored over it—alone and with others—and thus she was the instrument, if the image may be so pressed, of my birthing into feminism. I owe her a debt of gratitude which I suspect is shared by many women, even though I am sure that if I read the book again I would be appalled by its contents and amazed at the impact that it had on me.

I relate all this anecdotal stuff only because it explains how I come to approach **The Madwoman's Underclothes** with the sort of tolerance that is normally reserved for beloved but slightly senile old ladies. I truly want to do the best I can for her, as I attempt to make something coherent out of this collection of her 'essays and occasional writings, 1968-1985'. Because, dear God, she really is *bonkers.* What we see in the progression through these 50 or so pieces of, predominantly, journalistic writing is libertarian individualism running amok and ending up not in anarchic chaos, as our elders and betters once feared, but in a manic individualism which is frequently charming, occasionally brilliant and fundamentally arrogant and patronising. Right from the beginning in the *Oz* pieces of the late 1960s she conflated 'doing your own thing' with 'political revolution'. 'To kill a man is simply murder: it is revolution to turn him on.' (Go tell that to the ANC or, indeed, any serious revolutionary, even a feminist one.)

Perhaps it is not really fair to hold such youthful expressions against anyone but, first, Greer has chosen to reissue these burblings and, second, in them lie the seeds of her improbable present conviction: that she is the only person in the world who has got it right. These papers cover an enormous diversity of subjects, from vaginal deodorants to the distribution of aid in Ethiopia, with underclothes, premenstrual syndrome, cosmetic surgery and transexualism thrown in, and in none of these articles does anyone, by name or by ideology, come in for any praise (except possibly the Cuban women's organisation who, they'll be glad to hear, are doing more or less okay). Well, not no one—there is one person who knows where it's at and will be pleased to correct you, and that is Dr Greer herself. Most recently she has taken up the causes of various victim groups, as she sees them, in the Third World. It is not her sincerity that is in doubt here; it is her conviction that no one else in the whole of the West is sincere. And interestingly she ends up speaking of them exactly as Victorian men spoke of women: they are purer, nobler in their suffering and poverty than we can ever be; they are 'closer to nature' and able to teach us moral truths so long as we do not contaminate them with our evil materialism; they are too innocent to know what they really need, but luckily they have Greer to tell them.

Despite my delight in her stunt acts, my old debt and my agreement with so many things she says, none of this is enough. Feminism was born out of libertarianism and has had to struggle to grow out of it, to replace manic individualism with solidarity and discipline itself with political analysis. Of course we need that crazy flamboyance too, but Greer does not write like someone who is auditioning for the role of Court Jester, more like someone applying for the job of God. Frankly, despite the mess we are in—which she so often notes perceptively—this career opportunity is not currently being advertised.

Linda Blandford (review date 11 October 1987)

SOURCE: "Notes of a Nag and a Roisterer," in *New York Times Book Review,* October 11, 1987, p. 14.

[*In the following review, Blandford offers positive assessment of* The Madwoman's Underclothes.]

Germaine Greer has never truly been a writer. Her spirit has illuminated her written word as if the very act of expressing herself were but a brief, rushed gathering-up of her living. She is, perhaps, one of the marvelous letter writers of an age that no longer trifles with them much. Her essays, columns and books—transcripts as they are of a heroic heart and intellect—seem to have been dashed off in the fire and dispatched to her many sisters. Feminism as a literary family.

To come unawares upon *The Madwoman's Underclothes,* a collection of her essays from 1968 to 1985, is to intrude unexpectedly into another's family reunion. All those private jokes, shared memories, intimate confidences, demands and contradictions: a noisy, emotional, overbearing, lusty family, loving and cursing across the dinner table. Incomprehensible, or simply an embarrassment, to those who are not of it and hungering for its warmth. It is not, after all, the madwoman's collection of hats that is at stake here but her underclothes. ("In Australia," Ms. Greer has said elsewhere, "if you leave your room in a terrible mess, your mother says: 'Look at this room . . . it's like a madwoman's underclothes.'" The journey of woman's life defies order and good taste—if she is lucky.)

It is not possible, in short, to read these essays dispassionately, to approach this as a book per se. Here are our history, our gladdened days, our shame and disappointments. Germaine Greer is nearing 50 now. She lives in a farmhouse in the English countryside: rain boots by the back door, everything wind-weathered and drizzle-gray. Her public and youthful randiness settled into bigheartedness, perhaps.

This collection—arbitrary, quixotic, untidy—starts when Germaine Greer was a lecturer in English at Warwick University, a dull and worthy town, a good third choice for the best undergraduates. She was Australian—a synonym then in middle-class, prim-lipped parlors for being brash, vulgar, easy. Being an outsider gave her freedom, however. She wrote, largely unpaid, for *Oz* (as in Ozzie, Aussie, Australian), an underground paper in England that was then being prosecuted under the obscenity laws and became a famous counterculture rallying point.

In 1970 came *The Female Eunuch*—denouncing the image of woman unable to love, only to bargain, worship or be worshipped, an object, a sexual marionette. It was a clarion call and was followed by the debates in New York's Town Hall with Norman Mailer—much of the tension of which, we see now in wiser days, hinged on her sexuality. It mattered that she was so desirable, he so used to desiring.

There were many such battles over the years, most of which are chronicled here: about abortion, rape, pornography, seduction as "a four-letter word." She wrote for *The Sunday Times* of London at its most trendy, before Rupert Murdoch. There was, most of the time, a sexual roistering to her writing. But also, apropos of abortion: "The compelled mother loves her child as the caged bird sings. The song does not justify the cage nor the love the enforcement."

Her strengths and weaknesses, successes and failures are all here; they are the human stumblings of feminism itself, wanting it all while wanting none of it. There was the lure of becoming a celebrity, a television personality, a pop expert and thereby colluding with the censors about The Acceptable. *The Sunday Times,* in the end, started to spike her riskier, more controversial columns. She was a nag when she was meant to amuse. She still is. Fortunately.

It is hard to quote much of her early writing here: her usual expletives could hardly be Acceptable. It is the language not of the family breakfast table but of the women's baths. In truth, much of her early writing is also irritating. How innocent it seems now, gamboling over naked bodies and others' beds. How irrelevant after AIDS, how childish after Chernobyl.

Unlike most collections of journalism, it is the later writing that is the finer. Here is what she did not grow into: a whiner or wimp, embittered, tired, smug or even very rational (a point with which she might disagree). She, as others, in the end turned to embrace the wider world. Vietnam, briefly, but later Brazil, Ethiopia (drawn by disgust at "the media binge on pictures of the dead and dying").

It will be said, of course, that she is politically naïve. ("The Cubans are involved after all in a much bigger adventure than sex, speed and smack could possibly supply. Their morale is towering.") But at heart, she is on the side of neither regimes nor ideology but of individuals. The best essay of all describes, in the long introduction, her time in a poor village in the south of Italy: Mariuzz', her 8-year-old "escort"; Rosetta, the young unmarried woman waiting for marriage; the Mafiosi bombing the fish. Not a word of invective and each word convincing.

The Madwoman's Underclothes, like the feminist movement, is nevertheless about being white, middle-class and well-educated. The empathy with those who are poor, black, brown, in terror or dying is, in the end, that of a traveler from another, bountiful land. We cannot help it. It is the condition of privilege. At least, let it be said that Ms. Greer is not afraid to look, to care. Poverty, hunger, oppression, despair: here is Death's dominion. And to attack Germaine Greer would be to betray one's own to the enemy.

Hermione Lee (review date 26 March 1990)

SOURCE: "Mother Country," in *The New Republic,* March 26, 1990, pp. 33-5.

[*In the following review, Lee offers positive evaluation of* Daddy, We Hardly Knew You.]

The real problem is Mummy. "Reg Greer" is called Daddy by his middle-aged daughter, even after his death, because she would still like to love him, and would like him to have loved her. But Mummy, very much alive, is never called anything else but "Mother," a word, we are told at the outset, "admirably adapted for saying through clenched teeth." As the world's most famous feminist sets out, teeth clenched, across the world in search of her father's true life story, she is balked, mocked, and misled by her terrible mother, who sits perpetually tanning her aged body on her sunbed in a Melbourne suburb, made up to the nines and shrieking with demonic laughter.

It's an Australian version of Conrad's grimly knitting ladies, placed like Norns or "tricoteuses" at the gateway of Marlow's journey toward the fraudulent Kurtz. To account for the catastrophic ill luck and frustration that dog her quest toward her own particular heart of darkness, Greer evolves a fantasy of a primal elder's curse, like Noah's curse on his sons for uncovering his nakedness. One myth tends to leak into another with this global thinker, so the biblical curse turns into a pact with an Indian goddess and a pursuit by the Eumenides. These Furies bear a marked resemblance to one inescapable figure. Who forced the father to plead and sob, who "foamed at the mouth" like a "mad dog," who took all the old man's possessions and threw him out to die, who never cared enough to find out who he really was? Who called the daughter a foul-mouthed liar and told her that everything she ever achieved was rubbish? Why, mother, mother, mother!

It might seem surprising that Germaine Greer, whose life as a performer and writer has been dedicated to establishing a coherent system of values for women, should present us with "mother" as the embodiment of sadism and stupidity. In fact, the combination of terrible mother and fraudulent daddy is the key to her life's work. *Daddy, We Hardly Knew You* is an autobiography (and a detective novel, and a travelogue, and a history of Australia, and a collection of the usual breathtakingly opinionated Greerisms) that reveals the autobiographies inside the earlier "public" works.

Greer introduced her 1988 collection of essays, *The Madwoman's Underclothes,* with a euphoric reminiscence of her first experience, twenty years before, of peasant life in Calabria. Like *Daddy* . . . , it is a story of pride before a fall: one of Greer's most endearing characteristics is that she never minds looking a fool. Arriving with a baggage of hip Western prejudices about freedom, independence, and sexiness, she began to learn the virtue of traditional communal life from her neighbors' extended families. The son of the shepherd next door was embarrassed for her that she had no husband and no mother:

> His voice would drop to a whisper, as if he was asking something deeply shameful, "Why did your mother send you away?" I tried a hundred ways of answering that one, but to Mariuzz, not loving your mother above all earthly things was unimaginable. If I tried to explain that I left home at eighteen and neither my mother nor

I ever tried to make contact, his face became haggard with trying to understand such a nightmare.

The memory culminates in an emotional celebration of "the only perfect love . . . not sexual love, which is riddled with hostility and insecurity, but the wordless commitment of families, which takes as its model mother-love."

This early education in nontechnological, extended family living was the basis, she says, of all her writing. Lately, Greer has been accused of betraying her past. Those who cut their teeth on the radical liberationism of *The Female Eunuch* were dismayed by *Sex and Destiny*'s reactionary and sentimental preference for matriarchal peasant families over the liberated, "child-hating" West. Certainly the tone has changed from the raunchy outrageousness of Greer's sixties style: the voice of the *Oz* trial and the Town Hall Mailer duel and the Amsterdam Wet Dream Film Festival and *Suck* ("the first non-sadomasochistic sex paper"), telling us to drink our own menstrual blood, abandon the missionary position, and throw away our underwear. Now it's all heartfelt polemic about the evil effects on the underdeveloped world of Western technology, or the inadequate international responses to the Ethiopian famines.

Still, she is right to insist on her consistency. She has always taken a high moral tone on the nastiest effects of capitalism, from cultural imperialism to pornography. "It is curious," she says in *The Madwoman's Underclothes,* "to find myself an architect of the permissive society, when all the time I was one of its bitterest opponents." Her romantic attraction to Third World matriarchies provided her from the start with an antidote to the sexual narcissism of the West. Now we can see the roots of the argument.

Daddy . . . is full of alternative family models, like the calm, graceful (and wholly idealized) Brahman household of her hosts in India, or the good-humored friendliness of a Queensland country party. What they contrast with, of course, is "mother." After her first visit to a rural Australian family home, at fifteen, Germaine told her father that "these country women were real people":

> If we lived in the country I reckoned Mother's energy would be absorbed, and not frittered away in flightiness. "I didn't know women could be like that," I said. "Like what?" Resourceful, straightforward, capable, funny, proud, independent, you know." I might have said, "Not vain, capricious, manipulative, unreliable, girlish, affected, infantile."

That unspoken reply became *The Female Eunuch.*

Since so much of her writing consists of prescriptions for family life, Greer's own childlessness is a bitter irony, which this book touches on with dignity. (I was less moved by her compensating soppiness about animals, from the red Essex cat who shares her moods to the squashed kangaroos on the Queensland roads.) "A woman with neither father, husband, nor son," she sets out, in a sense, to give birth to her own father, to re-create him, to take possession of him: "I wanted to find my own father, not my mother's husband." Giving birth to the real "Reg Greer" is a process as painful, mentally, as parturition, and comes to feel more like a death than a birth. But it involves a more positive form of re-creation, too, a subversive rewriting of the male history that created female eunuchs like "mother" and failed fathers like "daddy." So the book takes an exhilarating revenge, not only on a father and mother, but also on a mother-country.

Revenge, though, is embroiled with the need to know and the need to forgive. (These mixed motives are compounded, as "mother" is the first to observe, by the need to earn back a large advance from Heinemann. At times, as Germaine tours the world, appears on chat shows, and consults famous friends in her pursuit of the Greers, the whole thing takes on the look of a canny promotional package: great locations, great plot, and all that *human stuff*.)

There seems to have been a great deal to forgive. What she remembers about Daddy is, first, that he wasn't there. When she was five, he came back from the war, looking old and ill. That was in 1944. Thereafter, he kept his clever, aggressive, curious daughter at bay. He never hugged her. He never praised her. He favored her brother. He made silly jokes when she asked him questions. He told her nothing about himself. He despised everything that was beginning to interest her: books, music, culture, the wider world. She "hardly knew him"—and then she left home.

Forty years after his return from the war, she went back to Australia because he was dying, and found him, abandoned and pauperized, in a horrible derelicts' hostel: "In every subtle and crazy detail the work of my mother." Rescuing him, and watching him die, her ignorance of him began to obsess her. In an article written before this book, she described (with a typical mixture of vulgar sentimentality and urgent curiosity) "a certain expression" that she found in his face in the last few months of his life, "an almost indescribable look which contained elements of trust and puzzlement, of skepticism and innocence. It was as if all the veils of social attitudinizing and defensiveness had been stripped away and for an awful moment I could see into my father's soul." What was in there?

She knew a few things. Reg Greer was a newspaper advertising salesman, but he was "posh": dapper, leisured, condescending to his peers. He was supposed to be English, born in South Africa to parents passing through Natal on their way to a "temporary sojourn" in Australia, and brought up in Launceston, Tasmania. In 1937, when he was thirty-two, he married Peggy LaFrank, a part-Italian Catholic nineteen-year-old would-be model, whose family, in true Australian style—"no names, no pack drill is the Australian way"—didn't bother to find out anything more about him than that he seemed "a good bloke." In the war, he worked on secret "cipher duties" in Cairo and Malta. He told everyone he had endured the terrible siege of

Malta in 1942. Invalided out for "bronchial catarrh" and "anxiety neurosis," he came home via India, which he hated. For the rest of his life, he resisted any attempts to fill in the gaps in this patchy and dubious biography.

"Reg Greer" turns out to be a hollow man, a set of ignominious secrets. One of the few true facts, his war work for ULTRA, the Allied operation for decoding German signals, seems too good to be true, since Germaine's decoding of Reg Greer's ciphers begins and ends with misleading documents. She has a passion for libraries—places where Reg Greer would never have set foot—and (hence) takes a naive and touching pleasure in describing herself in them. She forges through bureaucracies worthy of an Australian Dickens: the Registrar-General's Offices in Hobart and Melbourne, the Archives Office of Tasmania, the Melbourne Veterans Affairs building. Like the RAF intelligence officers in wartime ("our deception people," as the bosses called them), she "sinks up to her armpits in bumf": her parents' marriage certificate, back issues of Tasmanian newspapers, passenger lists of ships, her father's RAF forms, his repatriation file. . . . What she can't track down is his birth certificate. As she tours the world and comes back full circle on her "demented pilgrimage," "Daddy" falls apart.

His war illness, it transpires, was anorexia—a pitiable and "girlish" disease—not the strain of the Malta bombardment, which he in fact missed by several weeks. Like the faked-up war record, the "posh" manner, the "English" background were all an act. There *were* no English Greers going from Natal to Australia, no Greers in Tasmania, no Greer journalist on the Launceston paper, no "Reg Greer" at all. "Daddy" was the illegitimate child of a domestic servant, who was the daughter of a farm laborer, granddaughter of convicts, and he was fostered, along with numerous adoptive siblings, by a remarkable woman (also from a family of convicts and laborers) called Emma Greeney, whose name, family, and upbringing Reg Greer entirely repudiated. It's this betrayal of the true mother, the extended family, the working-class Australian history, that his daughter cannot forgive.

By the end of the quest, no piece of him seems real to her. He smoked a pipe to make himself look more distinguished. His "beautiful teeth," which he said were lost in the war through poor diet, were a false set. His dark hair and mustache, which made him look so like the English actor Basil Rathbone, were dyed. He is like Edgar Allan Poe's "The Man That Was Used Up," an impressive-looking military man who, deconstructed piecemeal by the amazed narrator, turns out—chest, scalp, voice box, and all—to be a total artifact: the "real man" is, horrifyingly, a squeaky little lump of blubber.

Poe's story makes a grotesque satire on male heroism. Greer wanted her father to be a hero, not a bounder, but she recognizes the desire as a weakness. Her quest is, in the end, not merely personal. It sabotages the official male version of war and colonization, and rewrites her father's history as "herstory," "puncturing" the false ideology that made him pretend to be toff, a hero, and an Englishman. The deconstruction of Daddy involves, too, a demystification of Australian facades: genteel pretensions, suburban domestic respectability, picturesque tourist spots, and un-ecological agriculture are all vociferously exposed.

The tone is bossy and enraged. Germaine Greer loves to lecture, she is relentlessly moralistic, and she has a passion for educative details. So there are energetic sermons on the Australian ecology and some splendid effusions, for instance on pioneering life in a small Tasmanian town, circa 1910:

> They arranged fêtes, bazaars, raffles, contests, made cakes, garments, bibelots, etc. for the fêtes, bazaars and so forth, attended race meetings, cricket matches, regattas, football, cycling, hockey, rifle shoots, lectures on theosophy, hypnotism, spiritualism, exotic religions, gave parties for engagements, weddings, anniversaries, visitors from the mainland, retiring dignitaries, grew things, cooked, embroidered and preserved things for the local show, and competed in practically every human activity including rabbit-skinning, sheep-shearing, and the wood-chop.

If her research takes her to a 1919 Launceston menswear shop, we get a lip-licking list of the fabrics on sale ("the taffetas, in fashion shades of mole, mastic, putty, nigger and bottle"); if to a local theater, we get the full program of shows and artistes. No opportunity is lost for a display of horticultural or culinary know-how. Maltese goat an unpalatable wartime diet? No problem!

> If the goats' meat had been properly hung or marinaded in a smidgen of garlic and oil in sour goats' milk or yogurt, or rubbed with pepper, it would not have smelled so disgusting that only the starving dogs and cats would eat it.

But fear and dread underlie the bustling energy; and that's what makes this an impressive and troubling document. Greer says of the book's heroine, Emma Greeney, that she knew that "the doctrine of inherited moral defect was a doctrine of despair." She herself emphasizes all the points of difference between herself and her father. But these differences may, rather, be reactions: because he was secretive, she won't put up with anything "hush-hush"; because he obscured himself, she became an exhibitionist. "There is no bucking the genes." And if she is like Daddy, she may also—a much worse thought—be like Mother. The specter of determinism, the "doctrine of despair," looms over this superstitious narrative. One of the contemporary world's most redoubtable, self-invented public characters confronts the possibility that she has had no choice. She looks in the mirror, and sees the staring face of a woman possessed.

Nancy Mairs (review date 8 April 1990)

SOURCE: "Germaine Greer as Dogged Daughter," in *Los Angeles Times Book Review*, April 8, 1990, p. 8.

[*In the following review, Mairs offers unfavorable assessment of* Daddy, We Hardly Knew You.]

"The Quest," Germaine Greer titles the opening chapter of ***Daddy, We Hardly Knew You,*** a memoir of her search for her father's past begun after his death in 1983, as if to lift her pursuit to mythic heights. But the premise of the heroic quest is that its object possesses unique, often mysterious, even sacred, value, capable of transforming at least the searcher and generally the wider world as well. In these terms, Greer's is an anti-quest: "a classic example of her-story [sic], puncturing the ideology" of the hero.

Although she knew her father for more than 40 years, Greer learned almost nothing about his background, and what little information he released, she discovers, was fabricated. Reticence this absolute seems all but implausible, but apparently the "anxiety neurosis" with which Reg Greer returned from World War II effectively barred all inquiry.

"You will be wondering why I did not simply ask my mother," Greer says. Yes, indeed, that's exactly what I was wondering. "Suffice it to say that for Mother language is a weapon rather than a means of communication." Two less appealing creatures than Reg and Peggy Greer, as seen through their daughter's eyes, would be hard to imagine. But at least their singularly uncooperative natures provide her the pretext for a book.

And a book of sorts she produces: part childhood reminiscence, part travelogue, part genealogy, part history, part social commentary. Unfortunately, the lack of something meaningful at the center (Daddy, I believe) prevents these elements from coalescing. Greer is a skillful writer, and there are plenty of terrific passages here: quick insights ("Our whole lives are lived in a tangle of telling, not telling, misleading, allowing to know, concealing, eavesdropping and collusion"); painterly descriptions of landscape from Tasmania to Tuscany; a breathtaking evocation of conditions during the siege of Malta. Too often, however, the insights are facile.

This clutter becomes especially troublesome with regard to the book's central purpose: the revelation of the "truth" about Reg Greer's life, which his daughter confounds with the knowledge of his origins and antecedents. Now, as the popularity of Alex Haley's *Roots* demonstrated some time ago, many people are fascinated by their lineage; at least half a dozen of my friends and relations pursue their forebears with varying degrees of preoccupation. But it seems a queer sort of obsession for a feminist to take up with scant reflection; and really this author of an early and influential feminist text, ***The Female Eunuch,*** has given herself over to her patrilineal search with far fewer and less sophisticated questions than readers might reasonably hope.

Instead, with prodigious expenditures of money, time and energy, she amasses and recounts quantities of genealogical detail. She is nothing if not the "doggedest of daughters," and the descriptions of her research methods, frustrations and victories may prove instructive to other genealogists. The rest of her readers must simply slog along in her wake (wondering, perhaps, why she perseveres until they read: "I cannot go backward. I've spent too much of the advance." Ah, Knopf has paid for a book, and a book they shall have).

For naught, it turns out. Because, after transforming herself into "a Greer-ologist, a Greerographer, a Greeromane" and summarizing one Greer pedigree after another (perhaps so that her readers can experience the same sense of wasted time she endured), she turns out to be "not a Greer" at all but a Greeney by adoption, a Hamilton by birth. Her father's lies and evasions masked no "prince in disguise"; he was simply ashamed to have been an illegitimate child reared by poor but honest folk whom he left without looking back.

"No matter how I try," Greer writes, "no matter how loyal I feel, I cannot make this man a hero." And perhaps it's this incapacity that dooms the book. Perhaps, if you're going to set out on a quest (itself conventionally considered a heroic undertaking), its object must be rare and precious in some way. Perhaps it—in this case he, Reg Greer—can't be a "liar," a "bounder" an "office masher," snobbish and cowardly and small-minded. Perhaps the failure lies in the unworthiness of the object.

"Daddy, we hardly knew you," Greer complains. "Why would we even want to?" the reader may sadly ask.

Sara Maitland (review date 11 October 1991)

SOURCE: "Hagiography," in *New Statesman and Society*, October 11, 1991, p. 23.

[*In the following review, Maitland offers positive evaluation of* The Change, *though finds fault in Greer's lack of practical instruction.*]

I am 41 years old; my menstrual cycle, which for over 20 years has behaved with discreet but impeccable regularity, has recently turned funny on me; I have odd pains in my wrist, and attacks of savage ill temper; my lovely daughter has left school, started being kind to me and departed for Paris. I am full of strange regrets (that I didn't have eight children, that I didn't become a contemplative nun) and strange desires (to live alone in the country, to scream very loudly in supermarkets). Last week I bought the shortest skirt I have worn since 1970. A woman not just of a "certain", but of a "dangerous" age.

Now what? I ask, along with others who entered female adulthood to the trumpet blasts of liberation and the revolution, and read *The Female Eunuch* in 1970. And there are not a lot of answers, frankly, even if we can bear to ask the right questions. Not even medical answers, if Dr

Greer is right; or rather, there are masses of answers, mainly contradictory, ill-proven, male-biased, and frequently dangerous to women's health.

The depth of ignorance and prejudice and guilt-inducing psychopoop ought to stagger us. It does not, of course, because we have had the same business with contraception and fertility and orgasm and childbirth and lesbianism and menstruation. Given how obsessed by women's bodies men are, it is continually fascinating how unbelievably ill-informed they remain: imagine a train spotter who couldn't distinguish between a steam engine and an Intercity 125.

In short, no one knows anything useful about the menopause at all: not what it is, what is going on, what helps, what is "healthy". There isn't even an agreed list of symptoms, or a clear distinction between what is menopausal and what is, more simply, ageing.

Well, I shouldn't say no one. Germaine Greer, none of us will be surprised to discover, knows *lots* and tells it to us at considerable length (over 400 pages). This is Greer's best book for years: she is just right for the subject. At her best, she has always had a savage truculence, and at her worst a strident self-righteousness, combined with a maudlin romanticism. But the situation of the menopausal woman in western society calls for both truculence and self-confidence, and in the absence of almost any positive images of ourselves, a strong dollop of romanticism goes not amiss.

At the core of Greer's argument here lies her belief that sex is overrated. This flies in the face of modern orthodoxy, which preaches that heterosexual penetrative sex is good for you. Not to have it is bad for you, and not to want it proves that you are bad. Much treatment for menopausal symptoms is to keep your sexual bits, physical and psychological, in good working order for your man, who, against statistical odds, is dreamed into existence for everywoman. For example, the increase of both rage and independence found by some researchers is deemed pathological, instead of a sensible response to a grim reality.

The reality is that:

> "The tiny nuclear family built about the copulating couple is unsafe for women and children. It is arguable that it is unsafe because of the primacy given to the sex relation between the couple, the maintenance of which may be thought to justify all kinds of distorted behaviour and certainly conflicts with the demands of small children."

Women who want hormone replacement therapy and silicon breast implants, women who can't or won't live without sex, who refuse to grow up, all play into the hands of a self-defeating and degrading anophobia (irrational hatred of old women) which re-imprisons women at the very moment when they could be free.

"Don't buy it," Greer tells us, which is good. And she is so good at telling us: funny and quick on the trial of double-think and self-satisfaction; sharp in the analysis of both ignorance and silence; full of information, perception and energy.

But then, she goes on. "Instead, be like *me*", which is more dubious. Because, although she paints a rosy picture of herself as crone and witch, invisible on the street and strong in her head, renewed, freed, joyful ("Before I felt less on greater provocation; I lay in the arms of young men who loved me and felt less bliss than I do now"), she singularly fails to tell us how she got there. Her pages of excoriating contempt for Simone de Beauvoir's fear and hatred of age, for Marquez' sentimentalisation of geriatric intercourse, for medicos and silly women, for Joan Collins and Jane Fonda, are not matched with better strategies.

We need practical strategies at this point, and narratives. The witch and crone remain only archetypes, until they are placed in stories. We know the story of the witch: its moral is that "it is better to marry than to burn". Greer claims to know a better story. I wish she would tell it; we get the happy ending, but not the plot. A few pages less on other women's failures to negotiate this passage, a few pages less of damning everyone everywhere, a few pages less of ecstatic utterance, and a little more about the nitty-gritty could have changed a useful book into a precious one.

Natalie Angier (review date 11 October 1992)

SOURCE: "The Transit of Woman," in *New York Times Book Review,* October 11, 1992, pp. 1, 32-3.

[*In the following review, Angier offers favorable analysis of* The Change, *though finds fault in Greer's "loose and flippant" medical recommendations and attacks on the healthcare establishment.*]

This is a brilliant, gutsy, exhilarating, bruising, exasperating fury of a book, broadly researched, boundlessly insightful and yet so haphazardly presented that this reader was driven more than once to slam shut the volume and curse the author for what seemed like a willful lack of discipline. It may not be fair to judge Germaine Greer for having failed to produce the book one wishes she had written, but *The Change: Women, Aging and the Menopause* is so tantalizingly close to being a potential feminist classic on a par with *The Female Eunuch* (1970) that one cannot help seeing its repeated lapses into muddiness as almost tragic.

For many of us baby-boomer women who are tottering uncomfortably on the rim of middle age, the 53-year-old Ms. Greer might have been the perfect guide to leaping gorgeously to the other side, an antidote to the sorry nail biting of books like Gail Sheehy's best-selling "Silent Passage." But perhaps in keeping with the underlying message of her text, Ms. Greer refuses to make our lives easy. Menopause, or, as she prefers to call it, the climacteric, is a huge and complicated event, one perhaps best experienced by facing the storm of change head on. In that sense, then, reading *The Change* is probably as good a rehearsal as any.

Unlike other books about menopause, which focus on such particulars as hot flashes, thinning vaginal walls and the debate over hormone replacement therapy, Ms. Greer's seizes on everything directly or even peripherally affecting the middle-aged woman. Seeking any mention of the aging female, she has rummaged through historical accounts, memoirs, correspondence from the court of Louis XIV, old medical textbooks, anthropology tracts, novels and poems both familiar and obscure.

Ms. Greer discusses the role of the matron in non-Western societies and, to some degree, romanticizes the power these women command once they have survived the dangerous years of childbearing. She talks with unvarnished candor about the invisibility of the middle-aged woman in our own culture the unfairness of a system that lionizes the silver-haired male while scorning his female counterpart as beyond use, pathetic, desiccated, desexualized, a crone. On occasion she uses herself and her friends to make a point, describing, for example, a sad lunch she had in France with a woman her own age. Both had sailed through their 40's barely noticing the passage of time, but now, at 50, they could ignore it no longer. Sitting near their table were two older men and their lithe young female companions, prompting Ms. Greer's friend to begin bitterly railing against the injustice of it all.

"'It's bloody unfair. Those men can have their pick of women of any age. They can go on for years, and here we are, finished. They wouldn't even look at us.' The unkind sunlight showed every sag, every pucker, every bluish shadow, every mole, every freckle in our 50-year-old faces. When we beckoned to the waiter he seemed not to see us."

Ms. Greer will provide no illusions for anybody expecting soothing reassurances that the middle-aged woman really isn't finished as a marketable commodity, and that she can find love and fulfillment at any age if she only keeps her spirits buoyant and her genitals moist, with either estrogen or drug-store lubricants. Being an older woman in this society is damned difficult, Ms. Greer says, and to pretend otherwise is an act of pathetic self-deception.

"There can be no suggestion that feeling tired and disillusioned at 50 might be the appropriate response and that convincing yourself that you are happy and fulfilled might be self-deluding to the point of insanity," she writes. Not that complaining is likely to do any good; a woman fretting about menopausal symptoms or her fears of getting old alone is likely to be blamed for her own misery. "If you haven't managed to get a husband, let alone keep him alive and by your side until you are 50, if you haven't borne any children or have been unable to get the ones you have brought up to treat you decently . . . then you'll probably make a hash of the menopause as well."

The author views menopause as an enormous turning point in a woman's life, seeing it as so important she dislikes calling it "menopause"—a word that she argues "applies to a non-event, the menstrual period that does not happen." She prefers "climacteric," from the Greek word meaning critical period. And because no formal celebration or ceremony has ever been devised to mark a woman's transition from fecundity to infertility, Ms. Greer suggests that women will have to invent one of their own. If it is honest, the ritual will undoubtedly be solemn, an acknowledgment that one is mortal and that the climacteric is "the entry into the antechamber of death." But even with the realization that "summer is long gone and the days are growing ever shorter and bleaker," one can move beyond morbid preoccupations to a more profound sense of life and one's place in it. "Only when the stress of the climacteric is over can the aging woman realize that autumn can be long, golden, milder and warmer than summer, and is the most productive season of the year."

Ms. Greer sees the medical profession as offering scant help and potential harm to the aging woman, and she snidely refers to physicians who attempt to treat the symptoms of the climacteric as "Masters in Menopause." Gathering evidence from old medical texts, she lists the sometimes dreadful therapies the masters have prescribed. "They have let blood, prescribed violent purgatives, sent women to spas and mountain resorts, dosed them with bromide, mercury, sulfuric acid, belladonna and acetate of lead. . . . Everything, and nothing worked." Only with the isolation of natural estrogens in the 1920's could a more rational approach be designed for treatment of the sharp drop in hormone production that accompanies menopause.

It is on the difficult subject of hormone replacement therapy that the weakness of Ms. Greer's elliptical and fidgety style becomes most evident. On the one hand, she is scathingly critical of the medicalization of middle aged women and menopause, and she attacks those who have relentlessly promoted lifelong estrogen treatment as a cure, not only for such temporary menopausal symptoms as hot flashes and mood swings, but also for aging itself. She faults the medical establishment for its ignorance about many of the details of menopause, and the pharmaceutical industry for hawking pills and patches indiscriminately. On the other hand, she seems to support the use of estrogen replacement in many cases, at one point saying, "What cannot be denied is that patients usually do feel better on estrogen, a great deal better, so much better that they realize for the first time just how unwell they had felt before estrogen. . . . One is obliged to question the morality of withholding estrogen, rather than the wisdom of prescribing it."

The reader is likely to be equally confused by the book's lengthy discussion of traditional treatments like henbane, a coarse and foul-smelling plant historically associated with the practice of witchcraft. Taking on her multicultural-research mantle, Ms. Greer seems to view the famous little plant as a useful sedative for menopausal symptoms, but she also describes it as highly poisonous—it is a member of the nightshade family—and in need of a dilution that she fails to explain. In addition, she blithely repeats questionable theories with little scientific evidence to support them, like the idea that liquor is bad for an older woman because alcohol will burn up what little stores of estrogen she has left, and that the aging woman should take up gardening as a way of breathing in native estrogens found in many types of plants. Ms. Greer is no fool, but she is sometimes as loose and flippant with her medical reporting as she accuses the established health-care system of being.

In the end, though, much is redeemed by Ms. Greer's glorious final chapter, called "Serenity and Power," which is so rich with song and wisdom that it alone is worth the price of admission. Here we read Emily Dickinson ("Our Summer made her light escape / Into the Beautiful") and Elizabeth Bishop ("The art of losing isn't hard to master; / so many things seem filled with the intent / to be lost that their loss is no disaster") and we are given hope—not that we can remain forever and fatuously young, but that we can surmount with our minds and our senses the choke hold of self and self-pity.

Here Ms. Greer talks about the chance that aging gives a woman to step outside the prison of the ego and its "illusions of omnipotence and perfectability," and instead to rejoice in the abundance of the moment, to walk out one fine day and suddenly see the "great boil-up of cloud" and "the green snouts of the crocuses poking through the snow." She suggests that the middle-aged woman take a cue from her newfound invisibility and become invisible to herself, to shuck off at last her desire to please, her endless obsession with her own skin, lips, breasts and buttocks, and to take in the theater of life, "to be agog, spellbound."

The boundaries of body and skull remain, of course, and we can never help thinking of ourselves as the starring actors in the minor plays of our lives; yet a truly wise actor learns to savor with calm delight the displays of others on the stage. "The discontent of youth passes when you realize that the music you are hearing is not about you, but about itself," Ms. Greer writes. "Only when a woman ceases the fretful struggle to *be* beautiful can she turn her gaze outward, find the beautiful and feed upon it."

Rhoda Koenig (review date 12 October 1992)

SOURCE: "Cronehood is Powerful," in *New York,* October 12, 1992, pp. 74-5.

[*In the following review, Koenig provides a summary of* The Change *and Greer's unconventional ideas. Koenig concludes, "it's unlikely that many readers will march behind Greer's custom-made banner."*]

No one following Germaine Greer's work would expect her to go gently into that good night—or anywhere else—

but even her most devoted readers may not be prepared for the way she takes leave of her youth. "The stereotype of the snowy-haired granny beaming affectionately at her apple pie," she says, "needs to be balanced by her dark side, with 'tangled black hair, long fingernails, pendulous breasts, flowing tongue between terrible fangs.'"

A witch may be a daunting model for the average rider of the IRT, but Greer has plenty of others: philosopher, artist, menopausal femme fatale. In *The Change,* she not only upsets the applecart of received wisdom but uses its scattered contents to pelt the media, the medical establishment, and others who give the aging female a view of herself that is unrealistic and depressing. "The purpose of this book," Greer states, "is to demonstrate that women are at least as interesting as men, and that aging women are at least as interesting as younger women." At 53, she has written a lively, provocative, and funny guide for the baby-boomers wondering nervously about life on the other side of the hill.

Greer has less than no time for those who protest "ageism": Calling *old* a dirty word, she says, is offensive in its assumption that there is no value in aging, just as those who insist there is no difference between men and women demean inherently female qualities. Worse than the practitioners of Newspeak are the Jane Fondas, Joan Collinses, and Helen Gurley Browns, so many stretched and painted and grimacing corpses dangled before us as examples of how boundless expenditure and tireless energy can procure eternal youth.

Worse still are the doctors, male and female, who treat menopause as a terrible disease rather than as a natural transition (one surgeon Greer quotes says that women of that age "are no longer women") and prescribe painful, extreme, and often irrelevant (though not necessarily inexpensive) treatments. Nineteenth-century patients were treated with electric shocks to the uterus, early-twentieth-century ones with a bombardment of X-rays. Today, women nearly twenty years past the safety limit are prescribed oral contraceptives; they are given hormone-replacement therapy, about which too little is known; and, at the first sign of trouble, they are often told to have their wombs carved out.

While Greer does not deny that menopause can bring with it many distressing physical symptoms, she feels that hysteria over the change has been induced by our patriarchal and sex-mad society. To the worry that older women are not attractive to men, Greer has a two-part response: Yes, they are, and If not, so what. In a chapter entitled "Sex and the Single Crone," Greer considers the cases of Colette (who at 51 met the 36-year-old man with whom she lived until her death 30 years later) and George Eliot (who at 58 married a man 20 years younger). Elsewhere, she tells us about Diane de Poitiers, who was two decades older than her lover, Henri II, and Ninon de Lenclos, the seventeenth-century courtesan who, in middle age, seduced the son of one of her former conquests.

If your personal charms are not up to those of a French king's mistress, however, Greer counsels you not to be envious of menopausal women with husbands or boyfriends. She sees the emphasis on sex in the twilight years as emanating from men, who believe that the main purpose of women is to gratify their own sexual needs. But, Greer asks, do men care that much about making women happy? "If [a woman] is one of the many women who have been f———ed when they wanted to be cuddled, given sex when what they really wanted was tenderness and affection, the prospect of more of the same until death do her part from it is hardly something to cheer about." Greer says that the menopausal woman's fractiousness and instability may result not from hormonal changes or unhappiness at losing her sex appeal but from "justifiable rage too long stifled and unheard," anger at the years of self-sacrifice and repression of desire that bursts forth when a woman finally decides to put her own wishes first.

Instead of pills, plastic surgery, and other remedies designed to make them more pleasing to men. Greer advises women to enjoy the company of other women, to take up gardening, religion, and homeopathy, and to brood less about their pimples and more about the mystery of existence. "Women who do not adhere to a particular creed will nevertheless find that in the last third of their lives they come to partake of the 'oceanic experience' as the grandeur and the pity of human life begin to become apparent to them. As one by one the Lilliputian strings that tie the soul down to self-interest and the short view begin to snap the soul rises higher and higher, until the last one snaps, and it floats free at last."

While writing as spirited as this is itself exhilarating, many of Greer's attitudes are self-interested, her premises contradictory. Greer's descriptions of older men as smelly and ugly (and, therefore, unfair in demanding that their mates be alluring) partake of the same sort of sexual materialism for which she criticizes them. She will also inspire few readers with her examples of menopausal success stories—all more remote than Hollywood harpies. For Greer, a woman who takes a new career path is not someone who designs stationery or goes to law school, but Baroness Blixen, who at 48 became Isak Dinesen. Nor does Greer acknowledge that the rising of the soul—not to mention prolonged bouts of contemplation and gardening—is considerably assisted by the serenity and free time that accrue from a large bank account. Essentially, Greer's program for the good life after 45 seems to be women for friends and a boy for sex, one that will not suit those who don't share her allure, money, or misandry. As polemics go, *The Change* is bright and brassy, but it's unlikely many readers will march behind Greer's custom-made banner.

Katha Pollitt (review date 2 November 1992)

SOURCE: "The Romantic Climacteric," in *The New Yorker,* November 2, 1992, pp. 106-12.

[*In the following review, Pollitt provides analysis of* The Change *and commends Greer's provocative observations and intelligence, though finds fault in the book's disjointed and one-sided arguments.*]

It seems only yesterday that Germaine Greer was exhorting young women to throw away their inhibitions, their engagement rings, and their underpants. With the publication of *The Female Eunuch,* in 1970, Greer burst into international celebrity—an inescapable media presence, brash, brilliant, and beautiful, as exotically plumed as some wild Australian bird, and equally given to preening. Her love affairs were legendary, her admonitions—Flaunt your tampons! Taste your menstrual blood! Stop expecting men to take care of you! Live!—a heady mixture of rebellion and flirtatiousness. While the press, then as now, delighted to portray the women's movement as motivated by hatred of men and led by frumps and neurotics, it made an exception for Greer. She was, as *Life* put it, the "saucy feminist even men like," and the one who never let men forget how much she liked them.

Well, that was then; this is now. Having publicly mourned her inability to get pregnant in her forties—and having produced *Sex and Destiny,* an anti-contraception polemic and paean to Third World motherhood—Greer has passed through menopause and emerged, in her early fifties, on the other side. It was hardly to be expected that she would experience the transition calmly: rage and passion have always been her strong suits. (Indeed, since *Sex and Destiny* they have sometimes seemed to be her only suits.) Still, among the millions of female baby boomers now moving toward middle age there must be many whose hearts leaped up when they beheld the publisher's announcement of *The Change: Women, Aging and the Menopause.* Who better than Greer to deploy a fiery contrarian sword against society's contempt for older women, drug-company hormone pushing, and the hand-wringing to be found in Gail Sheehy's best-selling *The Silent Passage,* in which woman after woman mops her hot-flashing brow and wails "Why can't I be me anymore?"

Greer does brandish a fiery contrarian sword in *The Change.* But something has gone terribly wrong. Perhaps she dashed the book off too quickly: repeated sentences, haphazard organization, the grab-bag inclusion of irrelevant material (a five-page bone-dry synopsis of Iris Murdoch's novel *Bruno's Dream,* for instance) all suggest a rush to publish. Or perhaps she was overwhelmed by the scope of her task—disputing just about everything that has been thought, said, written, and done regarding women and age for the last two hundred years—and lost the thread of her arguments in the general contentiousness. That would explain why she could spend pages excoriating doctors for handing out estrogen like candy and then, noting that the hormone does seem to make women feel better, reverse gears and "question the morality" of withholding it. In any case, *The Change* is a maddening and frustrating book, in which passages of brilliance, wit, and lyricism alternate with murky and carelessly reported science, crackpot health advice, and a portrait of modern female aging that goes well beyond the evidence in its gloom and despair. And that, given the real difficulties that women face as they get older, is saying a lot.

The Change begins promisingly, with a rousing indictment of modern attitudes toward older women. Greer notes with some bitterness that our supposedly youth-crazed culture is really a girl-crazed culture: men acquire social power along with wrinkles and gray hair, and often a young bride or mistress, too, while their female contemporaries are often consigned to the sexual scrap heap, if not, indeed, the poorhouse. She quotes a friend on the May-November couples around them in a restaurant. "'It's bloody unfair. Those men can have their pick of women of any age. They can go on for years, and here we are, finished. They wouldn't even look at us.' The unkind sunlight showed every sag, every pucker, every bluish shadow, every mole, every freckle in our fifty-year-old faces. When we beckoned to the waiter he seemed not to see us."

Greer has a word for what that waiter feels: "anophobia," the irrational fear and hatred of old women. In many pre-industrial societies, she argues in a somewhat hedged reprise of *Sex and Destiny,* older women are vigorous and respected members of extended families, and, while ultimately subject to men, wield a good deal of informal social power. It is only in the modern West, where women are valued primarily as sex objects, families are small and isolated, and "hostility to the mother . . . is an index of mental health," that the aging woman is an outcast—expected to be unobtrusive, compliant, and grateful for any crumbs of attention that fall her way. Eventually, when he has nothing better to do, that waiter will amble over to her table.

Surrounded as women are by the negative stereotypes of popular culture—harridan mothers-in-law, strident shoppers, comical grandmas—and facing, moreover, the actual fact of their declining value in the sexual marketplace, it's hardly surprising that many regard the prospect of aging with anxiety, or that a vast beauty-exercise-surgery-quackery industry has arisen to exploit their fears while seeming to soothe them. Today, women are told that with enough effort, time, and, of course, money the years need hold no terrors: celebrities like Jane Fonda, Cher, and Joan Collins are touted—and tout themselves—as proof. But, as Greer shrewdly points out, the cult of these bionic sexpots only reinforces the prejudice against the aging female. To urge women to ape youth with an "imitation body" is to declare unacceptable the body they really have.

No wonder the male-dominated medical establishment regards menopause as a trauma and a tragedy. It marks the end of a woman's usefulness to men, and since in Greer's view society permits her no other purpose, doctors are quick to offer, and some women to accept, alarming remedies. (Greer has a scary chapter on the history of useless, painful, and sometimes even fatal treatments for menopause: electric shocks to the womb, X rays, animal-gland extracts, hysterectomy, hormone cocktails.) A woman who finds menopause rough going is invariably blamed for her symptoms: she had no children or was "over-invested" in maternity; dulled herself with domesticity or masculinized herself in the workplace; staked all on romance or failed to make hay while the sun shone. Declining sexual interest in middle-aged marriages is perceived as the woman's problem: if her husband withdraws, it's because she is sagging and nagging; if she does, it's her hormones. Why not, Greer pointedly inquires, ask if the man is a sensitive lover, an affectionate and respectful partner? Maybe *he* has let himself go: "Many a man who was attractive and amusing at twenty is a pompous old bore at fifty." If intercourse has become painful (at menopause the vaginal walls become thinner and drier), why dose the woman with potentially dangerous hormones so that she can have more bad sex, instead of proposing more imaginative ways of lovemaking—or just letting her call it quits?

That, in fact, is Greer's suggestion to women: Give up. It's degrading to turn yourself into a geisha for a man who thinks he's doing you a favor by sticking around. Anyway, it won't work. No one mistakes a chemical peel for the rose-petal skin of youth. To the plaintive question "Is one never in this life to be allowed to let oneself go?" Greer offers a bold answer: Yes! Right now! Today!

Greer wants women to welcome menopause—she prefers the old-fashioned term "climacteric"—as a sweeping natural transition. Yes, it is physically turbulent: like Sheehy, Greer dismisses women who pass through it easily—the vast majority, actually, although you'd never know it from either writer—as anomalous, if not liars. And, yes, it is sad: a time to take stock, to mourn old losses, and to come to terms with death. But it also holds out the promise of freedom and tranquillity: "Autumn can be golden, milder and warmer than summer, and is the most productive season of the year." Rejected by men, and thus freed from "the white slavery of attraction duty," the female eunuch can become, at last, "the female woman": a sibyl, a witch, a crone.

Greer's portrait of cronehood is so charming, so spirited, so seductively rendered—especially when it's contrasted with the situation of the wistful wives, desperate party girls, and breast-implanted exercise addicts which for her constitutes the only alternative—that the reader may find herself barely able to wait. Why *not* take up nature study, herbal medicine, travel, contemplation? Make women friends—and a fuss if you're ignored by the waiter! One notes a certain class bias here, an assumption of leisure and posh tastes: no bowling, or volunteering at the local hospital—or, apparently, earning a living, either. There's an anti-intellectual bias, too: the graying Eternal Feminine is not to sign up for courses at the New School. Still, who wouldn't like to sink into the Bath for Melancholy she cites from an Old English receipt book ("Take mallowes pellitory of the wall, of each three handfulls; Camomell

flowers, Mellelot flowers, of each one handfull; hollyhocks two handfulls")? Or stroll beside the sea with a girlhood chum, like the Sicilian matrons who, before the days of tourism, had the island beaches to themselves? Or start a huge garden, like Lady Mary Wortley Montagu—or Greer, a famous gardener herself? Greer calls us to middle age as to a grand spiritual adventure, and one with distinguished literary antecedents, too. This must be the only book ever written on women's health that illustrates its advice with seventeenth-century poetry and the letters of Mme. de Svign.

But there's a catch—several catches, actually. The would-be crone must become her own doctor—a dangerous prospect if she uses Greer's incomprehensible chapters on herbal and homeopathic medicine as a guide. (Henbane, for example, is a sedative on one page and a poison on another.) She must follow a diet that seems punitive in its frugality. (Giving up smoking and hard drinking makes sense, but red meat, cheese, coffee, tea, wine, beer, and chocolate?)

And—but perhaps you suspected this was coming—barring a miracle, she must give up sex. Now, this is indeed strange, because Greer herself presents a whole gallery of celebrated women who, without benefit of plastic surgery, found romance in mid-life and beyond. It is almost as though she began *The Change* with the idea of championing mature female sexuality—a casual reader might even think she has done so—and suddenly reversed herself in mid-book. One way or another, she dismantles her shining examples: in Colette's last years, her much younger husband never saw her "devastated body" or her face without its "powdered mask"; George Eliot's husband jumped out of the window on their honeymoon; Elizabeth Barrett Browning grew disenchanted with her Robert; Simone de Beauvoir's mid-life affair with Claude Lanzmann "fizzled out" after ten years. "Fizzled out" seems an odd term in this context—a decade is not exactly a summer romance—but it shows how determined Greer is to take a negative view of middle-aged sexuality. For men and women alike, it is unaesthetic and faintly grotesque, but for women it is also potentially tragic, because it exposes them to humiliation and exploitation at the hands of layabouts, philanderers, bisexual flirts, and neurasthenics. Who else, the clear implication runs, would even pretend to be interested? The women whose libido vanishes with menopause are, for Greer, "the lucky ones."

Could it be that Greer is a bit of an anophobe herself? Certainly she seems in a hurry to hustle women out of the bedroom and into the herb garden: by the end of *The Change,* she is lauding peasant cultures in which women don the black dress of matronly celibacy at thirty-five. One waits in vain for her to make the obvious rejoinder to our culture's hard view of older women's sexuality, to challenge the equation of female attractiveness with youth. Why, after all, should not a lined face and gray hair connote in women, as they do in men, experience, strength, staying power, character, sexual self-knowledge? Must older women give up being sexual subjects because Hollywood casting directors do not regard them as sexual objects? Greer cannot challenge the dominant masculine view because, in her heart, she shares it. The best she can do is caricature middle-aged men as "fat, beefy, beery, smelly, tobacco-stained" satyrs and recommend that older women who absolutely can't do without sex take boys (or women) as lovers.

How accurate is the picture of contemporary female middle age presented in *The Change?* Although Greer's books are packed with data, she has never let inconvenient facts stand in the way of her enthusiasms. In *The Female Eunuch,* sex had to hold no dangers, and so she pooh-poohed domestic violence as mostly idle threats that the occasional foolhardy woman drove her man to carry out. (The basis of this extraordinary assertion? Greer's affairs with two young roughnecks, who, despite their criminal records, behaved like perfect gentlemen.) *Sex and Destiny*'s romantic portrait of Third World womanly life dismissed clitoridectomy—inflicted on millions of African, Asian, and Middle Eastern girls each year—in a single sentence. *The Change,* too, ignores reality when it contradicts theory—only this time it's the good news, not the bad, that gets left out.

So, for the record, numerous studies demonstrate that most menopausal women do not, as Greer thinks, regard the cessation of ovulation with anguish or dread, do not undergo bouts of irrationality and rage, and do not lose their libido, their partner, or both. Middle-aged women are actually a fairly cheerful group—perhaps because few of them are living the contracted, empty-nest, husband-focussed domestic life that Greer imagines is still the contemporary norm. Nor is middle-aged and elderly married sex typically the quasi rape Greer imagines, in which a dirty old man subjects his estrogen-drugged wife to beastly practices while he fantasizes about young girls. According to one recent study, couples who make love after sixty are the happiest in America, and the more they make love—and not just in the missionary position, either—the happier they are.

It is curious that Greer, who began her career as a sexual swashbuckler, should end up preaching celibacy. There are doubtless many who will see this intellectual trajectory as a powerful rebuke to feminist hopes of equality. If biology is the culprit—if men are programmed to desire only youth and fertility, and if estrogen, as Greer claims in a particularly paranoid passage, is the "biddability" hormone that keeps women under the male thumb during their child-bearing years—then sexism really is destiny, from which menopause is the sole hope of escape. But a feminism that can envision freedom and self-determination only at the margins of the female life cycle—before twelve and after fifty—has surely taken a wrong turn somewhere.

Yet Greer has never really been a feminist, although the media labelled her one. She has no interest in political action or collective solutions to individual problems, no

skepticism toward essentialist accounts of sexual difference, and no hope that men can change their personal priorities or that women can obtain an equal share of economic or political power—the "spiritual" power of cronehood is the best women can manage. What she is is a romantic egotist—a dramatizer of her own exemplary life—and a critic of modernity. In the former capacity, she resembles no one so much as her old antagonist Norman Mailer; in the latter, the Mexican priest and sociologist Ivan Illich, whose attacks on Western medicine and Western feminism her own work closely parallels. She has never been able to hold all the aspects of women's lives—sex, maternity, work, love, domesticity, passion, reason—in her mind at the same time. She has always seen femininity through the lens of her most recent life crisis, and called on all women to jettison whatever hopes and behaviors have just proved problematical for her. When she was a sexual freebooter, monogamy and children were traps. When she wanted a child, contraception and sexual egalitarianism were suddenly rationalist plots against nature's plan for true female happiness. Now, as she has repeatedly announced, she's through with the whole business—sex, romance, men—and so we must all hang up our spurs and join her in a nice cup of henbane. *The Change* is an original and provocative book. But the only woman who is fully reflected in its pages is the one who wrote it.

Fleur Adcock (review date 6 October 1995)

SOURCE: "Killed with Kindness," in *New Statesman and Society,* October 6, 1995, pp. 37-8.

[*In the following review, Adcock outlines and analyzes Greer's theses in* Slip-Shod Sibyls.]

This long, scholarly book seems destined to be received simply as another instance of Germaine Greer putting the boot into feminists, this time by firing at some of their icons and questioning the place in the literary canon of most poetry by women before the present. Sappho is a myth; Katherine Philips, the "Matchless Orinda", let her work be rewritten by male advisers; Aphra Behn was not a self-sufficient woman of letters but a victim; Christina Rossetti and Elizabeth Barrett Browning, like many 20th-century successors, were neurotic self-destroyers.

These are over-simplifications—mine, not Greer's. In fact, her book offers several distinct theses about the difficulties under which female poets laboured. This is not a unified survey but a series of separate monographs held together by a prologue and an epilogue. There is a chapter on the Muse, one on "The Transvestite Poet" (androgyny and cross-gender impersonation on and off the page), and several devoted to individual cases, including Sappho's textual history and a long study of Letitia Elizabeth Landon, billed as "the story of the exploitation and destruction of an extremely talented but uneducated young middle-class woman at the hands of the London literary establishment of the 1820s and 1830s".

On the whole, Greer is sympathetic to her and her like. If they were under-educated that was not their fault; if they messed up their careers and led miserable lives, that is understandable. Success went to their heads, and they were culturally conditioned to be easily manipulated by their mentors.

The status of the woman poet varied. In 16th-century Italy, Vittoria Colonna was praised without condescension. English-speaking societies were more sexist; and the more women wrote, the greater the threat. "It is only when women begin to make inroads on the male preserves", writes Greer, "that sophisticated strategies of devaluation begin to be employed."

In the 17th century the Duchess of Newcastle was a figure of fun. Pepys called her "a mad, conceited, ridiculous woman". Her contemporary versifiers took more care over their self-presentation, apologising humbly and irrationally for publishing at all. Many burned their juvenile poetic efforts. Poetry was seen as an excusable indiscretion in the young, to be avoided later—in the 18th century, most known poetry by women was written in their youth. The approved subject was religion; meekness was all. Those who stepped outside the boundaries got into various kinds of trouble.

It is not news that for centuries women poets have been undervalued, misrepresented and exploited by men—although the case histories here make grimly fascinating reading. More controversial is the other main strand in Greer's argument: her claim that women poets cooperated in their own downfall. They took bad advice; they fell for flattery; they wrote too fast and without revising sufficiently; and they failed to understand "what was involved in making a poem". Their difficulty was not in finding a publisher—hundreds of them were published, some to enormous acclaim—but in "taking poetry seriously". Hence their work seldom reached the high standards aspired to by dedicated male poets.

There's plenty to argue with here (these failings were not confined to women, for example). But it is the epilogue that is perhaps calculated to provoke the greatest outcry. Greer complains that: "Too many of the most conspicuous figures in women's poetry in the 20th century not only destroyed themselves . . . but are valued for poetry that documents that process." She'd rather have them alive, without the poetry.

As a lead-in to her roll-call of suicides—Charlotte Mew, Sara Teasdale, Amy Levy, Anna Wickham, Robin Hyde, Marina Tsvetaeva, Sylvia Plath, Anne Sexton—she cites Elizabeth Barrett Browning, who went about the process gradually. Self-starvation and drug abuse killed her off in a more socially acceptable fashion. (The deterioration of her marriage dated from the publication of her passionate *Son-nets from the Portuguese,* written for her husband but concealed from him until three years after the wedding. Such a typically "female" outpouring of emotion was too much for him: "That was a strange, heavy crown, that wreath of Sonnets," he wrote to a friend.

Then follow the 20th-century examples. The list is selective, but it certainly carries weight. Greer does not forget the male "confessional" poets who went in for self-destructive behaviour, but only one, John Berryman, happened to die by his own hand. Women were less cautious; we get Anne Sexton's famous account of how she and Plath, sitting over drinks after classes with Lowell, "talked of death with burned-up intensity, both of us drawn to it like moths to an electric light bulb". As Greer more or less admits, two such self-obsessed individuals were hardly likely to settle into contented normality, poets or not.

Surely, then, poetry was merely a chance instrument? (Think of all the self-destructive women in Hollywood or the music industry). But no: "I would argue", says Greer, "that poetry as presented by the male literary establishment . . . enticed the woman poet to dance upon a wire . . . and ultimately to come to grief".

Others will argue back. No consensus will be reached, and Greer will enjoy the hubbub. On the earlier poets, though, she has dared to say what most of us secretly believed: there was never a female Milton, Donne or Pope (let alone Shakespeare). This book illuminates some of the reasons why: the ebb and flow of pressures on women poets, the rise and fall of reputations. But they will stay in the canon, and perhaps we may read them with greater understanding.

Christine Wallace (essay date 1998)

SOURCE: "The Female Eunuch," in *Germaine Greer: Untamed Shrew,* Faber and Faber, 1998, pp. 155-74.

[*In the following essay, Wallace provides analysis of the feminist perspective, mass appeal, and critical reception of* The Female Eunuch.]

The 'advocacy of delinquency' among women was Greer's chief purpose in **The Female Eunuch.**[1] We have to question the most basic assumptions about 'feminine normality,' she argued, when for so long female sexuality has been denied and misrepresented as passivity. 'The vagina is obliterated from the imagery of femininity in the same way that the signs of independence and vigour in the rest of her body are suppressed,' Greer wrote. 'The characteristics that are praised and rewarded are those of the castrate—timidity, plumpness, languor, delicacy and preciosity.' Physically and psychologically the suppression and deflection of women's energy had rendered them eunuchs in modern society. It was time to revolt.

Some women were already well along the path to liberation. Grass-roots feminist activism had emerged throughout the urbanized West as the 1960s progressed. Betty Friedan had articulated middle-class American women's dissatisfaction with their suburban lives as early as 1963 in *The Feminine Mystique*. In 1966 Friedan founded the National Organization for Women (NOW) to campaign for equal rights for women. At the same time many Western women were involved in the burgeoning array of activist movements that blossomed, intersected and overlapped in the 1960s—the civil rights and anti-war movements, the student protest movement, the New Left and the counterculture. Radical political groups and the counterculture proved fertile ground for feminism: small groups of women began meeting to discuss and analyze their unsatisfactory experiences as women in these movements and elsewhere. 'Men led the marches and made the speeches and expected their female comrades to lick envelopes and listen,' Anna Coote and Beatrix Campbell note in their history of the women's movement, *Sweet Freedom*. 'Women who were participating in the struggles to liberate Blacks and Vietnamese began to recognize that they themselves needed liberating—and they needed it now, not "after the revolution".'[2]

There was nothing new in women talking to each other, Coote and Campbell point out. What was different was that women were beginning to draw political conclusions from their experiences. At the same time, there were some isolated protest actions drawing attention to society's sexist foundations. In 1965 two women chained themselves to a public bar in Brisbane, protesting against the exclusion of women from front bars in Australian hotels.[3] In 1968 women demonstrated at the Miss America Pageant in Atlantic City, throwing bras and girdles into a bucket—without setting fire to them, contrary to media reports—to draw attention to the event's intrinsic sexism. Two years later a hundred British women would disrupt the Miss World competition at London's Albert Hall.

By 1969 the New York Radical Feminists and the New York Redstockings were publishing feminist manifestoes; Kate Millett was writing the doctoral thesis that would be published in 1970 as *Sexual Politics;*[4] and Gloria Steinem had given her first major speech, 'After Civil Rights—Women's Liberation,' to the Women's National Democratic Club in Washington. In Britain Juliet Mitchell was running a course on 'The role of women in society' at the 'Anti University' launched by radical academics. Sheila Rowbotham published *Women's Liberation and the New Politics,* linking housework with unequal rights at work, making explicit the objectification and silencing of women, and challenging Marxists to confront male hegemony.[5]

The new sexual orthodoxies accompanying the counterculture's 'free love' ethos were also being undermined. Feminists on both sides of the Atlantic were reading the Redstocking Anne Koedt's paper, 'The Myth of the Vaginal Orgasm,'[6] which identified the clitoris rather than the vagina as the center of women's specific sexual pleasure. In attacking the notion that the penis was the only possible—indeed, according to Reich, the only legitimate—source of sexual satisfaction, Koedt weakened the struts buttressing 1960s counterculture-style permissiveness which, as Coote and Campbell put it, 'kidnapped' women and 'carried them off as trophies' in the name of liberation. 'In the era of flower-power and love-ins, of doing-your-own-thing and not being hung up (especially about sex), "girls" were expected to *do it*, and impose no conditions. The more they did it, the more "liberated" they were deemed to be.' Young women were beginning to rebel against being set up 'in their mini-skirts and mascara, alongside the whole-foods and hippy beads and hallucinogens, in a gallery of new toys with which men were now free to play.'[7] The implication of Koedt's work was clear: when it came to women enjoying orgasms, men were an optional extra.

The industrial sphere was another key site for early second-wave action. In 1968 women machinists at Ford's Dagenham plant in Essex and the Halewood plant in Liverpool went on strike to have their work reclassified from unskilled to semi-skilled. The following year in Melbourne activist Zelda d'Aprano chained herself to a government building to protest against institutionalized pay discrimination. Women campaigning for equal pay boarded Melbourne trams and insisted on paying only 80 percent of the fare, in line with the lesser wages to which they were legally entitled.[8]

By the time *The Female Eunuch* was published in October 1970 the women's movement was rapidly gathering pace, its public forays often reported in the media. At the level of activism, though, the movement was still relatively small. In the course of their daily lives the mass of women did not often run across the paths being beaten through the patriarchal thicket by the early second-wave feminists. Others lacked a sense of commonality with the women in the movement's vanguard. Others again, many of them interested and potentially willing to embrace change, found feminist polemics too remote to move them.

Then came *The Female Eunuch*. Greer may have been 'last with the latest,' as Beatrice Faust puts it, but her book had the virtue of being magnificently accessible. It was bawdy, witty, provocative, dotted with intimate personal testimony and delectable historical titbits. Women *wanted* to read *The Female Eunuch,* relishing its daring and derring-do. 'I myself did not realize that the tissues of my vagina were quite normal until I saw a meticulously engraved dissection in an eighteenth-century anatomy textbook,' Germaine wrote, for example, at the beginning of a fascinating historical assemblage of snippets on women's genitalia in which she highlighted the fact that women had not always been so reluctant to discuss their sexuality.

Her approach was different. Many, many women responded to the book in a way they were not responding to other feminist literature—if, indeed, they had access to any at all.

Apart from anything else, Greer's language caused a sensation. The Australian feminist Anne Summers says it is hard today to describe the dimensions of the book's impact in the early 1970s. 'The [*Sydney Morning*] *Herald* had only just started using the word "pregnant" and "virgin,"' she recalls. There were no sexual references of any kind. 'In the underground press there would have been a bit of stuff around, and some of that was pretty confronting, but this was in a mainstream book—not something sold on street corners at midnight.' Women read Greer, listened, and noted her example well. Promoting the book in Australia, she mentioned she never wore underpants. 'So we all stopped wearing pants for a while,' says Summers. 'It was a bit breezy! We were all trying to be incredibly free. That was a much bigger deal than not wearing a bra, I can tell you.'

Greer's style was both a strength and a weakness. Structurally, there is little sense of a developing idea in the book, which is more a series of restatements of her core analysis from a variety of thematic vantage points. This is a quibble, though, when one considers the power with which she could cast common experiences in a shattering new light. Greer could really see, and Greer could really write. Take, for example, her compelling description of the dynamic of many miserable twentieth-century marriages:

> The real theatre of the sex war. . . . is the domestic hearth; there it is conducted unremittingly. . . . The housewife accepts vicarious life as her portion, and imagines that she will be a prop and mainstay to her husband in his noble endeavours, but insidiously her unadmitted jealousy undermines her ability to appreciate what he tells her about his ambitions and his difficulties. She belittles him, half-knowingly disputes his difficult decisions, taunts him with his own fears of failure, until he stops telling her anything. Her questions about his 'day at the office' become a formality. She does not listen to his answers any more than he heeds her description of her dreary day. Eventually the discussion stops altogether. It just isn't worth it. He has no way of understanding her frustration—her life seems so easy. She likewise feels that he cannot know how awful her days can be. Conversation becomes a mere power struggle. She opposes through force of habit. Why should he be always right? Ever right?[9]

Another of *The Female Eunuch*'s strengths is its convincing revelation of the dark ambivalence of men toward women that is embedded in everyday social practices, many of which were taken for granted at the time of the book's publication, and to a significant extent still are. 'Because love has been so perverted, it has in many cases come to involve a measure of hatred,' Greer contended. In extreme cases it takes the form of loathing and disgust, manifesting itself in sadism and guilt, hideous crimes on the bodies of women, and abuse and ridicule through casual insult and facetiousness.[10]

At the same time, she argued that women had to stop collaborating in their own oppression. If women were to be better valued by men, they had to value themselves more highly: 'They must not scurry about from bed to bed in a self-deluding and pitiable search for love,' she wrote, 'but must do what they do deliberately, without false modesty, shame or emotional blackmail. As long as women consider

themselves sexual objects they will continue to writhe under the voiced contempt of men and, worse, to think of themselves with shame and scorn.'[11] The belittling of women would not diminish until women stopped 'panhandling': 'In their clothes and mannerisms women caricature themselves, putting themselves across with silly names and deliberate flightiness, faking all kinds of pretty tricks that they will one day have to give up.'[12]

Greer made the clarion call to change in such emotionally appealing, idealistic terms that it was virtually irresistible. 'Sex must be rescued from the traffic between powerful and powerless, masterful and mastered, sexual and neutral,' she wrote, 'to become a form of communication between potent, gentle, tender people, which cannot be accomplished by a denial of heterosexual contact.'[13] She made the social 'delinquency' she sought to provoke so delectably inviting that few who read the book could fail to feel its attraction, in theory at least. 'The woman who realises that she is bound by a million Lilliputian threads in an attitude of impotence and hatred masquerading as tranquillity and love has no option but to run away, if she is not to be corrupted and extinguished utterly,' her argument ran. 'Liberty is terrifying but it is also exhilarating.'[14] The book closed with the confrontational question: '*What will you do?*'[15]

The Female Eunuch triggered a shock of recognition in tens of thousands of Western women who read it, and in hundreds of thousands of women who received Greer's analysis via the media. It was feminism's smash-hit bestseller, generating scores of photographs, television and radio interviews and thousands of column-inches of newspaper and magazine copy, and making Greer popularly synonymous with women's liberation across the Western world. It prompted an untold number of women to rethink their self-perceptions, their relations with men, the entire basis of their existence. 'It changed my life' is the most common anecdotal response when the book is mentioned to women who read it in the early 1970s. Middle-class dinner parties broke up in bitter arguments on the book's contentious themes. Some women bought *The Female Eunuch* and hid it from their husbands, fearing the consequences of being found with such an inflammatory tract.

Gloria Steinem recalls the book's impact on two artist friends. While the woman artist's work was as good as her male partner's, he got the profile, the attention, and was generally taken more seriously. He returned home one day to find his partner reading *The Female Eunuch,* which suddenly came whistling through the air aimed at his head. The couple's professional and personal relativities were drastically reordered as a result.

Yet *The Female Eunuch*'s influence on the women's movement itself was in inverse relation to the book's popular impact. While it can still be readily bought from airport bookstands, it is essentially invisible on reading lists for women's studies' courses, hardly referred to in the annals of second-wave feminism and seldom rates even an isolated footnote in the vast literature generated by the women's movement. In later works that traverse similar territory, it gets such passing references that it might almost not exist at all. It is as though, as far as the women's movement is concerned, the book is lost in space.

MacGibbon & Kee published *The Female Eunuch* in 1970. The title was unmissable in bold block letters—dayglo pink on a white background. The blurb on the inside flap announced that the book would offend many, including conventional psychologists, economists, moralists and the 'conventional woman—the female parasite.' Women themselves were clearly going to be among the targets to whom Greer would assign blame. Quotes from the book on the back cover contained reader-grabbing hooks under such headings as 'Love,' 'Marriage,' 'Misery' and 'Revolt.' The first heading, 'Upbringing,' was followed by: 'What happens to the Jewish boy who never manages to escape the tyranny of his mother is exactly what happens to every girl whose upbringing is "normal." She is a female faggot.' Inside, Greer continues the comparison: 'Like the male faggots she lives her life in a pet about guest lists and sauce barnaise.'[16] Greer never made clear in the book why she gave campery such a flogging, why homosexual men produced in her such obvious disdain.

Sales of the book began slowly, then took off. MacGibbon & Kee printed a second run in 1970, but by the beginning of 1971 there had to be monthly reprintings to keep up with demand. Paladin published the paperback version later that year. In the ensuing two decades it was the imprint's biggest and most consistent seller, reprinted a score of times and earning a twenty-first anniversary edition with a new foreword by Greer.

John Holmes's front cover illustration for the Paladin edition was one of the most intriguing and instantly recognizable images in post-war publishing. A naked, headless, legless mature female torso with a handle sprouting from each hip hangs by the shoulders on a pole like some fibreglass cast on an industrial production line. Holmes's first effort, never used, showed a naked woman from the abdomen up, breastless and faceless but unmistakably Germaine from her 'Universal Tonguebath' period, hair fashionably afro-frizzed, waist-deep in a pile of stylized breasts, presumably amputated in the creation of a 'female eunuch' based on an assumed equivalence of testicles and mammary glands.

The Female Eunuch is both exhilarating and exasperating to read. Greer's rhetoric soars, inspires; many insights are sharp, potent and motivating. Yet the book is so studded with political naiveties and passing shots at other women that it is difficult to reconcile as a whole. Its grand sweep, pacy prose and telling revelations encourage the reader to skate over the jagged edges and ride forward on Germaine's romantically anarchistic vision of assertive women in hot pursuit of pleasure, independence and spontaneity. In its popular consumption, this is precisely what happened.

The Female Eunuch contains six sections. Four of them—'Body,' 'Soul,' 'Love' and 'Hate,' each containing numerous mini-chapters, some just two or three pages long—are sandwiched between two free-standing sections, 'Summary' at the beginning and 'Revolution' at the end. Germaine began by declaring *The Female Eunuch* part of the second feminist wave, gently deriding the first wave, whose evangelism she said had withered into eccentricity. The old suffragettes had served their prison terms and lived through the gradual admission of women 'into professions which they declined to follow, into parliamentary freedoms which they declined to exercise, into academies which they used more and more as shops where they could take out degrees while waiting to get married.' The cage door had been opened but the canary had refused to fly out, she claimed, going on to suggest that organizations such as the National Organization for Women (NOW) in the United States were the modern, and by implication equally ineffective, incarnations of the old suffragettes.[17]

Greer noted the daily exposure of women's liberation in the media: everyone was suddenly interested in women and their discontent. 'Women must prize this discontent as the first stirring of the demand for life; they have begun to speak out and to speak to each other,' she wrote. 'The sight of women talking together has always made men uneasy; nowadays it means rank subversion. "Right on!"'[18] Yet in the next breath she dismissed the likely impact of the 'organized liberationists,' who she said were a well-publicised minority, the same faces appearing every time a feminist issue is discussed. Thus, only a few pages into the book, Greer began the gratuitous trashing of activists and their practices that would all too often be a feature of her public forays. She devalued the grinding techniques for promoting grass-roots change, arguing that 'demonstrating, compiling reading lists and sitting on committees are not themselves liberating behaviour.' 'As a means of educating the people who must take action to liberate themselves,' Greer continued dismissively, 'their effectiveness is limited.'

There was an alternative for the woman alienated by conventional political methods: 'She could begin not by changing the world, but by re-assessing herself.'[19] Consciousness-raising was an important practice for the early second wavers: in 'CR' groups women shared their problems, experiences and insights *together* and drew conclusions accordingly. Right from the outset, however, Greer chose the risky course of encouraging women to locate the problem within themselves, without positioning the challenge in a wider framework. This was at best necessary but insufficient, at worst reactionary and individually destructive. For what could be less likely to wreak revolution than a series of individuals contemplating the problem *in them,* in the absence of a wider framework for change?

Some in the women's movement were more generous about Greer's book than she had been about the work of the movement and its prominent figures. Anna Coote and

Beatrix Campbell later judged her book 'powerfully written and often wise . . . widely publicised and wildly popular.' *The Female Eunuch* dug a channel, they argued, from the 'Love Generation' through to the women's movement, introducing many thousands of women to a new sense of self.[20] At the same time, Coote and Campbell drew attention to the reactionary potential of what they termed 'heterosexual chauvinism,' for which they considered Greer set the tone.

As well as developing fault lines over issues of class and political strategy, the women's movement was already beginning to be split by a futile disagreement about whether or not women should consort with men. Greer, herself becoming a public symbol of rampant heterosexuality, argued explicitly that sexual liberation could not be achieved 'by a denial of heterosexual contact.'[21] To be whole, to be liberated, was conditional on having active heterosexual relations. 'At its most glamorous and flamboyant, heterosexual chauvinism appeared like a revamped *femme fatale,*' according to Coote and Campbell. 'It was the kind of feminism men liked best. It slapped their knees for being sexual slobs and chastised women for being sexual slovens. Above all, it promised the superfuck.'[22]

Greer might have had faith in the socially disruptive possibilities of sexual liberation, Coote and Campbell argued, but *The Female Eunuch* was really protecting the conventions of heterosexuality rather than changing them. Greer's insistence that 'genuine gratification' must involve the vagina 'did not identify any difference between the vagina as *a* place of pleasure and *the* place;' the hierarchy of sexual values remained intact.[23]

Lynne Segal, originally a Push libertarian herself, acknowledges the book's widespread influence, but considers it 'surely a pre-feminist text or at the very least an unusual feminist text,' given its tenuous connection to the women's movement. 'Despite popular opinion,' Segal says, '*The Female Eunuch* is unrepresentative of women's liberation in its early days; the movement predominantly dismissed Greer's individualistic anarchism and dismissal of collective action.'[24]

The Female Eunuch is less a sermon from a high priestess than the call of the Siren's song—alluring provided one is prepared to accept her dictum that sexual liberation, which Greer used as a synonym for women's liberation, 'cannot be accomplished by a denial of heterosexual contact.' Nor did Germaine's book allow for the possibility that a lesbian could be liberated, for example, or that a celibate woman could be liberated, or that a woman content simply with self-pleasuring could be liberated. In this respect *The Female Eunuch* is one of the prescriptive extremes of second-wave feminism, every bit as wrongheaded as the other extreme dictating that only lesbians could consider themselves true feminists.

So was this all that liberation required—giving up one's panhandling ways, forsaking false modesty, shame and emotional blackmail, slashing away the ties that bind and pursuing potent, tender heterosexual relations? After Greer's pungent, meandering, often brilliantly written catalogue of insights into the position of women, the solution she prescribed was negated by a dose of empiricism about the sexual revolution. Germaine trounced her own Utopia by describing how the old malign forces had already adapted to the new sexual freedoms that had been brought by the contraceptive pill in conjunction with the 1960s protest movement, the counterculture and mass media.

> The permissive society has done much to neutralize sexual drives by containing them. Sex for many has become a sorry business, a mechanical release involving neither discovery nor triumph, stressing human isolation more dishearteningly than ever before. The orgies feared by the Puritans have not materialized on every street corner, although more girls permit more (joyless) liberties than they might have done before. Homosexuality in many forms, indeed any kind of sex which can escape the dead hand of the institution—group sex, criminal sex, child-violation, bondage and discipline—has flourished, while simple sexual energy seems to be steadily diffusing and dissipating. This is not because enlightenment is harmful, or because repression is a necessary goad to human impotence, but because sexual enlightenment happened under government subsidy, so that its discoveries were released in bad prose and clinical jargon upon the world. The permit to speak freely of sexuality has resulted only in the setting up of another shibboleth of sexual normality, gorged with dishonesty and kitsch.[25]

This analysis was typically Germaine, highlighting the intellectual influences which underpinned *The Female Eunuch.* There is the conjunction of the Push's anarchistic pessimism and Leavisism as she blames the bleakness of relations under the new social mores on her claim that sexual freedom had increased under 'government subsidy,' leading to 'bad prose.' Neither idea is explained, but the implication is clear: the state and inferior writing are doing their wicked damage again. There is the lumping in of homosexuality with the crime of pedophilia and undefined 'criminal' sex; and there is the Push's correct-line Reich, in which homosexuality is contrasted adversely with 'simple sexual energy,' for which read heterosexuality. There is the lack of interest, too, in reconciling key parts of the thesis she is developing with other parts of her analysis and conclusion—or even in acknowledging the gaps and disjunctures that exist in it.

Three other serious problems in *The Female Eunuch* were largely neglected at the time of its publication: its contradictory position on marriage, Greer's analysis of male violence and her treatment of her mother.

The book is premised on the Push's inherent disposition against marriage. Given the personal reflections and anecdotes dotted through *The Female Eunuch,* the chapter on 'The Middle-Class Myth of Love and Marriage' might have been expected to draw on Greer's tear-drenched three-week-long marriage to Paul du Feu. Instead it is the vehicle for what look suspiciously like off-cuts from her doctoral thesis. There is far more on the Renaissance and Shakespeare in the chapter than on modern matrimony and the tyranny of Mills and Boon.

The most significant element of the book's chapter on marriage is Greer's renewed endorsement of the Petruchio-Kate model from *The Taming of the Shrew*. Kate has the 'uncommon good fortune to find Petruchio who is man enough to know what he wants and how to get it,' she wrote in a reprise of her doctoral thesis. 'He wants her spirit and her energy because he wants a wife worth keeping. He tames her like he might a hawk or a highmettled horse, and she rewards him with strong sexual love and fierce loyalty. . . . The submission of a woman like Kate is genuine and exciting because she has something to lay down, her virgin pride and individuality.' She continued at length, giving legitimacy to Kate's defence of Christian monogamy on the grounds that 'It rests upon the role of a husband as protector and friend, and it is valid because Kate has a man who is capable of being both, for Petruchio is both gentle and strong. . . . The message is probably twofold: only Kates make good wives, and then only to Petruchios; for the rest, their cake is dough.'[26] Neither the thoroughly patriarchal nature of the Petruchio-Kate relationship, nor its contradiction of her call for women to slough off the Lilliputian ties that bind them to their men, emerged as a critical issue in the book's consumption. This conflict remained at the heart of Greer's life and subsequent work.

There was also a strange disjuncture between her insights into misogyny and her views on male violence, where she assigned the blame to women themselves. 'It is true that men use the threat of physical force, usually histrionically, to silence nagging wives: but it is almost always a sham,' she wrote. 'It is actually a game of nerves, and can be turned aside fairly easily.' Germaine claimed that she had lived with men of known violence, two of whom had convictions for it, but they did not subject her to violence 'because it was abundantly clear from my attitude that I was not impressed by it.' Most women are fascinated by violence, she argued: 'they act as spectators at fights, and dig the scenes of bloody violence in films. Women are always precipitating scenes of violence in pubs and dance-halls. Much goading of men is actually the female need for the thrill of violence.'[27]

To blame women for inciting male violence was at best naive and, arguably, something much worse. Lynne Segal cites Greer's view as encapsulating the 'nonchalance' of many liberals, and sexual radicals in particular, toward questions of male brutality—an expression of the denial and public tolerance of men's violence to women.[28] In Greer's case the stance was particularly strange given that she had been the victim of male violence herself. Surely she did not think *she* had incited her rape back in Melbourne in the 1950s? Or did she not consider rape a manifestation of male violence?

Greer's deep-seated antagonism toward her mother Peggy is the other striking aspect of the book. Not far into *The Female Eunuch,* Germaine presented her mother and grandmother literally trying to contain her. She recalled her grandmother begging her mother to corset her as a teenager on aesthetic and health grounds, to counteract her youthful ungainliness and support her back, which Liddy feared might not be able to bear Germaine's ultimate six-foot height. There was no sign that Peggy took the advice. She warned Germaine instead against emulating Australia's famous female swimmers, claiming their training regime produced broad shoulders and narrow hips.[29] This is the only neutral comment on Peggy in the book.

The first substantial discussion of mothering in *The Female Eunuch* comes in the chapter on 'Altruism.' As children, Greer wrote, we 'could see that our mothers blackmailed us with self-sacrifice, even if we did not know whether or not they might have been great opera stars or the toasts of the town if they had not borne us.'[30] Then in the chapter on 'Misery' comes damnation for women—specifically Peggy—pursuing education to overcome the unhappiness of their situation at home:

> The idle wife girds her middle-aged loins and goes to school, fools with academic disciplines, too often absorbing knowledge the wrong way for the wrong reasons. My own mother, after nagging and badgering her eldest child into running away from home (a fact which she concealed for years by talking of her as if she were present, when she knew absolutely nothing of what she was doing), took up ballet dancing, despite the obvious futility of such an undertaking, studied accountancy, and failed obdurately year after year, sampled religion, took up skiing and finally learnt Italian. In fact she had long before lost the power of concentration required to read a novel or a newspaper. Every activity was an obsession for as long as it lasted—some lasted barely a month and those are too numerous to list.[31]

Peggy's efforts to educate herself were valiant attempts at just the sort of delinquency *The Female Eunuch* was supposed to be promoting. Yet in Peggy Germaine portrayed this behavior as pathological rather than liberating.

The chapter called 'Resentment' explores the use of children as weapons in domestic in-fighting at its most sinister. Greer depicted Peggy as more desperate than other mothers, muttering to Germaine as a child that Reg was a 'senile old goat.' Women promote their children's dependence as insurance against any attempt to disown them, according to Greer; they attack their husbands for ignorance of children's needs and are jealous of their children for enjoying more freedom than they themselves experience.[32] Without supporting evidence, Greer described it as 'very common' for mothers to enlist their sons in acts of violence against their fathers, especially in poorer families where the father's inadequacies can be 'ruthlessly underlined.' In Greer's argument, the son 'accepts mother's account of her suffering at the hands of her brutal father, and endeavours like Saturn to displace him in his own house.' Germaine claimed that her brother, as a three-year-old, was brutally deployed by her mother against her father in a 'less intense Oedipal' twist on the phenomenon: 'my mother knelt on my small brother's chest and beat his face with her fists in front of my father and was threatened with violent retaliation, the only instance of my father's rising to her bait that I can recall.'[33] She wrote of being beaten by her mother for giving away all her toys at the age of four when she no longer wanted them—probably a reference to the punishment that followed her giving her trike to the needy Pammy in Elwood.[34] Peggy's horror of the schoolgirl affair between Germaine and Jennifer Dabbs is graphically described, as is Germaine's capitulation.

The villain of *The Female Eunuch,* her portrait woven subtly through its pages, is Peggy Greer, depicted by Greer as physically brutal, manipulative, an emotional black-mailer and homophobe. Reg Greer, barely present in the text, has a bit part as victim. Without self-consciousness, Germaine nevertheless noted in the chapter 'Family' that when dealing with the difficulties of adjustment 'children seize upon their parents and their upbringing to serve as scapegoats.'[35]

How did she manage to elicit such interest and sympathy among general readers even as she did such unsympathetic things as attacking her mother, blaming women for male violence, and endorsing a patriarchal marriage model? Some clues to the power of Greer''s book can be found in a paper by Rodney Miller subjecting *The Female Eunuch*'s last chapter, 'Revolution,' to a linguistic analysis.[36]

Miller reveals the traditional rhetorical ploys driving the verve and persuasiveness of Greer's writing. Germaine alternated between active and passive voice and welded the colloquial imaginatively into her prose. She created an ebb and flow by combining extremes of abstract and everyday language. 'This balance between extreme formalism and colloquialism can be seen in other public figures seeking a wide audience,' according to Miller, who also cites Bob Hawke's 'peculiar mix of extremely formal sentence structures with colloquialisms and a nasal almost "ocker" voice.'[37] Hawke went on to become Australia's longest-serving Labour prime minister. While still president of the Australian Council of Trade Unions (ACTU) in the 1970s, he bettered Greer in a television debate—virtually the only occasion in memory when she has come off second-best.

Greer also relied on rhetorical questions and parenthetical clauses to create a sense of cut-and-thrust in her writing. The question-and-answer form surges forward and then arrests the reader's attention. These rhetorical features often occur in the middle paragraphs, 'which to the casual reader may appear merely to be outlining matter that incorporates only a slight amount of rhetorical organization,' writes Miller. 'Although one must look more closely at certain paragraphs to observe their rhetorical components, the extensive occurrence of these features . . . reflects the constant presence of Germaine Greer as *rhetor.*'[38] The lasting power of *The Female Eunuch*'s final paragraph, according to Miller, comes from the close combination of emotional forcefulness with prescription, setting up Greer's ultimate rhetorical question: 'What *will* you do?'

But there was more to it all than appealing to reader emotion, deploying personal pronouns and the like. Miller notes that the higher the proportion of verbs to nouns and adjectives in a piece of prose, the more interesting and persuasive the writing is perceived to be. On this criterion, Greer's style is vigorous and highly verbal. 'Dr Greer's language is forceful and her argument is aggressively competent,' he concludes. 'Perhaps this is the most important model that she provides.' Greer's style, by Miller's analysis, represented a significant departure from the norm for women writers, who had often been associated with a more passive style, relying heavily on nouns and adjectives: 'By integrating language features once characteristic of males, Dr Greer is requiring readers to reassess how they view male and female.'[39] Ever the iconoclast, Germaine managed simultaneously to use traditional rhetorical techniques, to offend against them, and sometimes to transcend them altogether.

The conventions of rhetoric were originally developed in part to establish fair rules for discourse—to ensure, among other things, that speakers addressed each other's arguments rather than engaging in personal attacks. Greer used the techniques of traditional rhetoric to great effect in her polemic while breaching the form's *politesse,* attacking—as Australians put it—the player, not the ball. On top of this she incorporates intimate comment and stories, personalizing the polemic rather than confining it to the abstract space constructed by conventional rhetoric. Greer rooted her rhetoric in the body—through anecdote, often her own body.

Drawing on Plato's *Gorgias,* Iris Young points out the erotic dimension in communication, the fact that 'persuasion is partly seduction.' The most elegant and truthful argument may fail if it is boring: 'Humour, word play, images and figures of speech embody and colour the arguments, making the discussion pull on thought through desire.'[40] Greer understood this implicitly and used it brilliantly.

Her deployment of personal testimony—*with* the traditional tools of rhetoric rather than instead of them, as was the case with most other feminists using the testimonial form—created a massive multiplier effect, heightening the power of her prose. Her story-telling technique carried 'an inexhaustible latent shadow . . . that there is always more to be told,' as Iris Young describes it.[41] This lifted *The Female Eunuch* from earth and made it fly.

At the time of its publication, *The Female Eunuch* did not receive the close critical analysis it deserved. There were honorable exceptions—the English feminist Sheila Rowbotham, for example, and the Australian feminist Beatrice Faust—but they were confined to book reviews. Arianna Stassinopoulos, at Cambridge a little after Germaine, replied with the book-length work, *The Female Woman,*[42] but it was essentially a light-weight vehicle for anti-feminist backlash. Lynne Segal later took issue with Greer's flawed analysis of male violence. However, the only lengthy analysis to appear relatively close to the time of *The Female Eunuch*'s publication came from Juliet Mitchell in her book *Psychoanalysis and Feminism*—though even this was not much longer than a substantial book review.[43]

Mitchell was responsible for stimulating a re-examination of Freud among English-speaking feminists after his comprehensive trashing at the hands of Greer and Millett, among others. One need not agree with Mitchell's stance on Freud to recognize her insights into the lesser side of Greer's polemical style. Mitchell referred to Greer's 'disarmingly cavalier attitude' to mistakes in *The Female Eunuch.* 'She compounds many errors—with facility and wit,' says Mitchell. In the first paragraph of one chapter alone, Mitchell showed Greer referring without differentiation twice to psychoanalysis, six times to psychology and twice to psychiatry, before moving on to begin the next paragraph with: 'So much for the authority of psychoanalysis and the theory of personality.'[44]

Mitchell criticized Greer for setting up a false polarity in Freud between creation and destruction, aggressors and victims, Eros and death. She noted *The Female Eunuch*'s tendency to self-serving intellectual sloppiness as well as the combative implications of even Greer's most ostensibly peace-loving goals: 'If she accepts (and simplifies) Freud's notion of eternal Eros at war with his immortal adversary the death-drive, and then makes Eros (or rather Eros denied) equal women, and death equal men, so that the only way to save the world is for Eros-women to overcome death-men, then surely that accords a very aggressive role to Love?'[45]

One feminist had raised a warning flag about Germaine's warrior ways even before *The Female Eunuch* was published. In April 1970, *Oz* ran a piece written by 'Michelene' called 'Women on the Moon . . . Or the End of Servile Penitude, a Reply to the Slag Heap Erupts and particularly Germaine (Cunt Power) Greer.'[46] The piece responded to Germaine's anticipation of the imminent publication of an edition of *Oz* containing a 'positive statement of Cuntpower' which would expand on her view that the 'cunt must take the steel out of the cock.'[47] (The eventual edition was titled, much more satisfactorily from the censor's standpoint, 'Female Energy Oz.'[48] Michelene took exception to Germaine's barely latent aggression, and objected that the women's movement did not want to replace 'penis-power by Cunt-power, or any generalised power.'

On the whole, in contrast with her strong public identification as a women's movement leader, Greer missed out on serious critical engagement with other feminists. Her loose logic and rhetorical excesses, her occasionally obvious impatience and condescension toward women who did not conform to her own notions, were not polished by critical interaction with informed peers. This set the pattern for her future work. It could be one reason why there is so little sense of growth and development in her later think-

ing and writing. In its absence, Greer would largely extrapolate in her writing from the particular life passage through which she was traveling at the time.

Oz unwittingly pointed to a key aspect of the way *The Female Eunuch* would be read in the two reviews it ran side by side. 'Reading *The Female Eunuch* I felt that there was not one Germaine Greer but several,' wrote Sheila Rowbotham. 'There was one I liked a lot, who had the defiance, the controlled, if sometimes desperate dignity, of revolutionary feminism. . . . But in the midst of the defiance and the irony there's a gawky, forlorn girl, miserably dragging sanitary towels about in her school satchel, uneasily moving into an unhappy adolescence, not liking her mother, self-conscious about being tall and dreaming of crushing her nose into a giant's tweed suit.' Rowbotham confessed that she had her own version of the tweed-suited giant fantasy—though in her case he was leather-clad and swept her off to the hills on his motorbike—but, like Michelene, she identified Germaine's general disconnectedness from the women's movement as a problem. Greer's analysis had 'an external quality,' Rowbotham argued; she lacked the passion and self-criticism of the women working within the movement. As a result she had missed out on learning from working alongside other women, being forced to re-examine preconceived notions, often painfully and painfully often.

'Oh wow it's been done before Germaine,' Rowbotham wrote:

> Ever heard of scarecrow radicals? They frighten the sparrows a bit at first until they get used to them. Scarecrows can look very impudent but they can't do anything. There have been lots of scarecrow feminists, lots of bold women who resisted the servile lot of other women, who made a great flurry and a show, and who ended up like George Sand rejecting the feminist socialist groups to perform for a male audience. You avoid the stiff tense humourless tightness you see as a feature both of feminism and of the revolutionary groups, and you suddenly find yourself becoming a sophisticated brand of titillation on the media. It's a trap that destroys people ruthlessly.[49]

Tim Harris in the accompanying *Oz* review argued that most people lacked the energy or capacity to live their lives in accordance with Greer's blueprint for freedom. Yet his reaction to *The Female Eunuch*'s essence echoed one that can still be heard today from women not involved in the movement recalling their first encounter with the book: 'suddenly one becomes conscious of a whole area of experience previously blinded by habitual response. To have altered our perceptions, enlarged our world, and amused us in the process, that is a brilliant feat.'[50]

In its inimitable style, *Oz* managed to capture the divergence in the review headlines: 'How to Get Your Man . . .' over Harris's review, and over Rowbotham's '. . . The Book That Men Love and Women Hate.' It was almost right. Many men did love the book, but so did many women. It was just that the less a woman had had to do with the women's movement at the time, the more likely it seemed she was to be impressed by **The Female Eunuch.** Women who were already active feminists read it with far more guile and could see the problems in it.

The Female Eunuch is arguably *the* book of the television age. It is not the most brilliant, the best-written, the best-selling or most insightful book; but it exemplifies so many key features of writing, publishing and reading in the mass-marketing era. If one had to choose just one book through which to illustrate the path post-war writing, publishing and popular thinking has traveled, this book would be a good choice. Take a great title, arresting cover artwork, a promotable, quotable author, add sex and install liberally in airport bookstands, stand back, enjoy the controversy and watch it sell its paperback cover off: it is a trite but true formula for modern publishing success. The book's author became a celebrity on three continents, and the man who contracted it eventually went on to New York to head one of the most prestigious publishing houses in the world.

Other elements also speak of its time. The style combines journalese and anecdote with the quasi-academic. It is studded with pull-out quotes, anticipating the drive to break up blocks of text as the march of computer graphics and MTV-length attention spans proceeds. It is a polemic of personal change whose influence attested to the powerful conjunction of ideas and the modern media; and it is an item designed for mass consumption. Its only atypical trait is, perhaps, its long shelf life. The book is still in print and widely available more than a quarter-century after publication.

Representing it like this in purely commercial formulaic terms is not meant to trivialize the book but rather to expose its business brilliance in pure, stripped-back form. **The Female Eunuch** is much, much more than the sum of its considerable commercial parts, more than a text tweaked into shape by the changing moods of Sonny Mehta's eyes. Its success in the marketplace and Greer's success as its author vastly expanded the scope and scale of her opportunities for 'delinquency' in Britain and abroad. Germaine Greer was launched. The world, for which read New York, was about to acclaim her the star that feminism was waiting for.

Notes

1. Greer, *Female Eunuch,* p. 25.

2. Anna Coote and Beatrix Campbell, *Sweet Freedom,* 2nd edition (Basil Blackwell: Oxford, 1987), p. 5.

3. Gisela Kaplan, *The Meagre Harvest: The Australian Women's Movement 1950s-1990s* (Allen & Unwin: Sydney, 1996), p. 32.

4. Kate Millett, *Sexual Politics* (Touchstone: New York, 1990, first published 1970).

5. Sheila Rowbotham, *Women's Liberation and the New Politics* (Spokesman: London, 1969), pamphlet no. 17.

6. Anne Koedt, 'The Myth of the Vaginal Orgasm,' paper presented to the Women's Liberation Conference in Chicago, Thanksgiving 1968, reprinted in *Notes from the Second Year* (Radical Feminism: New York, 1970).

7. Ibid., pp. 11-12.

8. Kaplan, *Meagre Harvest,* p. 32.

9. Greer, *Female Eunuch,* pp. 322-3.

10. Ibid., p. 20.

11. Ibid., p. 300.

12. Ibid., p. 304.

13. Ibid., p. 21.

14. Ibid., p. 22.

15. Ibid., p. 371.

16. Ibid., p. 86.

17. Ibid., pp. 13-14.

18. Ibid., p. 15.

19. Ibid., p. 16.

20. Coote and Campbell, *Sweet Freedom,* p. 12.

21. Greer, *Female Eunuch,* p. 21.

22. Coote and Campbell, *Sweet Freedom,* p. 240.

23. Ibid., p. 241.

24. Lynne Segal, *Is the Future Female? Troubled Thoughts on Contemporary Feminism,* 2nd edition (Virago: London, 1994), p. 88.

25. Greer, *Female Eunuch,* pp. 50-1.

26. Ibid., p. 234.

27. Ibid., pp. 354-5.

28. Segal, *Is the Future Female?,* pp. 84-5.

29. Greer, *Female Eunuch,* p. 36.

30. Ibid., p. 169.

31. Ibid., p. 316.

32. Ibid., p. 324.

33. Ibid., p. 325.

34. Ibid., p. 364.

35. Ibid., p. 266.

36. Rodney G. Miller, 'After the Evolution? Language for Social Comment in Germaine Greer's Book, *The Female Eunuch,*' a paper delivered at the 4th National Congress of the Applied Linguistics Association of Australia, University of Sydney, 27 August 1979, p. 3.

37. Ibid., p. 11.

38. Ibid., p. 12.

39. Ibid., pp. 20-1.

40. Iris Young, 'Communication and the Other: Beyond Deliberative Democracy,' in Margaret Wilson and

Anna Yeatman (eds.), *Justice and Identity: Antipodean Perspectives* (Allen & Unwin, Sydney, 1995), pp. 146-7.

41. Ibid., p. 147.

42. Arianna Stassinopoulos, *The Female Woman* (Davis-Poynter: London, 1973).

43. Juliet Mitchell, *Psychoanalysis and Feminism* (Penguin: Harmondsworth, 1990), first published 1974.

44. Ibid., p. 340.

45. Ibid., p. 345.

46. *Oz* 27, April 1970, pp. 18-19.

47. Greer, 'The Slagheap Erupts,' p. 19.

48. *Oz* 29, July 1970.

49. Sheila Rowbotham, '. . . the book that men love and women hate,' *Oz* 31, November-December 1970, p. 18.

50. Tim Harris, 'How to Get Your Man . . . ,' ibid.

Ferdinand Mount (review date 19 March 1999)

SOURCE: "Still Strapped in the Cuirass," in *Times Literary Supplement,* March 19, 1999, pp. 6-7.

[*In the following review, Mount provides a summary of* The Whole Woman *and unfavorable evaluation.*]

"She's back and she's angry"—thus the *Daily Telegraph* puffed its extracts from Germaine Greer's new book. Can one imagine house-room being given in such a quarter to a serious enemy of comfortable society—Marx or Foucault, say? This kind of mock-alarming reception is normally reserved to drum up custom for an ageing boxer or tennis star whose legs have gone but who can still gouge an ear or terrorize an umpire. Despite her best efforts, Professor Greer has always been held in some affection by those whose certainties she purported to undermine. In my experience, middle-aged tycoons are particularly responsive to her charms, much in the same way that Masters of Foxhounds often have a penchant for the ballet. For a British audience, being Australian helps in this respect. We find it difficult to take umbrage at the foulest language if hurled at us in a North Queensland accent, let alone shrilled in Germaine's pleasant Melburnian mezzo. Greer also lays about her so vigorously, belabouring weak sisters and feminist backsliders with as much vim as she belabours brutal and cloddish men, so that no one group of her victims can feel unfairly singled out. *The Whole Woman* is no exception to her usual practice, and it follows naturally at another decade-and-a-half interval from her earlier works, *The Female Eunuch* (1970) and *Sex and Destiny* (1984), to form a remarkable trilogy.

Those who aspire to chart an alteration, even a repentance in her, are, I think, picking and choosing from her work, taking discourse A from one book and contrasting it with discourse B from another, when in fact A and B are to be found, perhaps in varying dosages, in most of what she writes. No *pentita* she, except in her willingness to denounce her former comrades.

If we are honest, what many of us remember best about *The Female Eunuch* is that soft cuirass on the dust-jacket, representing the burden of femininity strapped on woman by oppressive man. This prosthetic device has a brilliant ambiguity: who exactly designed it? Can you put it on yourself? What are we to imagine lying under it? Another woman-shaped body with all its attendant inconveniences and miseries? Or some untrammelled physique, simultaneously angelic and feisty, which is equipped to enjoy life at its richest—children, sex, art, sun-dried tomatoes—without any of the old inconveniences? Sometimes Greer embraces the warm, smelly, blood-soaked physical destiny of being a woman. Sometimes she dreams of women escaping from their fleshly burdens and living in sisterly bliss with their children. In *The Female Eunuch,* for example, she imagines communes where children are free to choose their parents, while grown-ups stroll from one weightless love to the next.

All her major books (*Sex and Destiny* much less so, being the least showy, least remembered and, I think, best of the three) are peppered with these inconstancies. But that is part of their appeal, their vivacity. And inconsistency is not the kind of accusation likely to slow the author down. As Walt Whitman pointed out, that's the only way to sing the *Song of Myself:*

> Do I contradict myself?
> Very well then I contradict myself
> (I am large, I contain multitudes).

The Whole Woman is made up of four sections—Body, Mind, Love, Power—each divided into half-a-dozen "chapterkins" averaging ten pages each and devoted to specific topics, such as "breasts", "shopping", "sorrow", "wives" and "emasculation". It has not, I think, been much noticed that *The Female Eunuch* follows exactly the same pattern, uses several of the same headings and, alas, quite a few of the same arguments. Still, every page she writes is never less than readable and sometimes fizzes with sardonic aperçus, but taken as a whole this method doesn't work too well. The array of topics is so overwhelming and the chapters so short and packed with statistics and chunks from teen 'zines, interspersed with boxed quotes from feminists, most of whom are a good deal wilder or sillier than Dr Greer, that the total effect is filling but curiously unsatisfying, like a meal in a Chinese restaurant. Arguments are pursued with great ferocity, then undercut or dropped.

This choppiness also prevents any coherent historical analysis of what has happened to women, let alone to men, over the past thirty years. There is a curious reluctance to mention the most obvious landmarks since

1969—the advent of women priests, the appearance of women prime ministers all over the place (Margaret Thatcher is mentioned only as the victim of a "sexist" putsch—after eleven years in power, surely a rather slow-burning sort of sexism). In some cases, Greer actively refuses to take note of change in the real world, continuing to assert, for example, that newspapers are all run by older men, when in fact Rosie Boycott, among other things has edited the *Independent,* the *Independent on Sunday* and the *Daily Express,* and tabloids have been edited by women, not to mention the phalanx of younger female deputy editors on the broadsheets. The truth is that achieving too much reform is bad for business. For rage and indignation must be maintained at boiling-point. Greer has a reputation to keep up. The victims' club accepts only life members. It is hard not to feel that she is a victim herself, a victim of success, and that her supple mind has been prostituted to the need to keep her audience whooping.

More damaging still, we are left with the impression that the "women's movement" or the "feminist revolution" started more or less from scratch in 1969. There is no mention of Simone de Beauvoir, let alone of the suffragettes or Marie Stopes. This short perspective is no accident, since to refer back to that earlier movement would be to recall a struggle which really did have implacable declared enemies.

The eerie thing about the post-60s feminism is that it has had few proper opponents willing to show themselves. The gates of each decayed Bastille turned on their rusty hinges—the colleges of Oxford and Cambridge, the Stock Exchange, the Jockey Club—to reveal only a handful of frightened middle-aged men falling over themselves to show their new colleagues around.

The only serious fight that could be picked—and Greer is nothing if not a scrapper—was within the sisterhood, with men as bemused bystanders. This ideological equivalent of female mud-wrestling (an analogy Greer herself uses in **The Whole Woman**) was not exactly new. Its terms of engagement had changed little since the days of the New Woman and Mrs Humphry Ward. In the red corner, there was the insistent and uncompromising quest for equality between the sexes always and everywhere. In the blue corner, there was the claim that women were deeper, more creative, closer to the mysteries of life, in harmony with the moon and the tides, singled out not by a curse but by a wise wound, white witches, goddesses. These two driving principles, one of absolute sameness, the other of profound difference, do not have to be driven very far before they come into conflict. Nor is either of them entirely unfamiliar or even uncongenial to some of the male bystanders: gender equality has been part of the egalitarian ideal from 1789 onwards, and it has been a central theme among authors from Goethe to Graves, men who would no more have dreamed of joining the women's movement than of taking up ice hockey, that only *das ewig weibliche* can revivify the poor dried-up male and reconnect men to the roots of being.

Greer herself wobbles a bit here. Now and then, she rehearses the standard line that there is a natural condition of "femaleness" which has been overlaid by a false and oppressive social construct of "femininity" (the same for men, of course, except that both the natural condition and the social construct seem to be pernicious). But as the book goes on, femaleness seems to envelop almost everything, leaving only flirting and a taste for frilly underwear as the affectations of femininity. Women, it seems, by nature love more passionately, bear pain more uncomplainingly, work harder, are averse to violence, are endlessly forgiving. Towards the end, even conventional feminist assertions about the ill effects of gendered upbringing—boys are demand-fed, potty-trained later—give way to a resigned admission that "no matter how gender-free their upbringing, children will invent gender for themselves".

Greer frequently sneers at the sort of "feminists everyone can like" who are content to work for mere equality. Women, she says, should not waste their lives trying to imitate men and clawing their way into those oppressive male hierarchies, such as Parliament or the Armed Forces. Yet, of course, a good deal of what she demands depends on just those dowdy campaigners for equality in pay, in political representation, in access to the professions and so on. If they expect any gratitude from Dr Greer, they can forget it. Some of these campaigners happen to be men. If they expect any recognition of this fact, they can forget that too.

She can write acutely and touchingly and does so here now and then, about motherhood and children, for example, or in her chapterkin on the necessary place of sorrow in life. But even there she feels duty bound to go over the top: every woman has to learn that men will *never* admit her to true comradeship, we are living "in a poisoned world that becomes crueller and more unjust every day", in which "there is no longer any free space where individuals might develop alternative cultural and social systems".

Turn over to the next chapterkins, of course, and you will find little parenthetical admissions that, on the contrary, women's lives are better, if more challenging now, "the forces of darkness having been by and large routed", that women *are* carving out free spaces for themselves and that quite a lot of machinery to remedy discrimination against women is now in operation—although naturally she has to complain that it is warped and inadequate.

But these qualifying asides are brief, and the diatribe quickly picks up steam again. The chapterkin on daughters is almost entirely taken up with the subject of father-daughter incest. "These behaviours", we are told, "are less aberrant than normal. They may be outlandish, but they are manifestations of the governing principle that runs the everyday."

The only fathers who have not yet got around to doing a bit of manifesting are, it seems, those who have already deserted the nest to avoid their obligations—or those who are too busy beating up their wives. The chapter on fathers is entirely composed of horror stories about violence and delinquency.

Not that staying home to help raise the kids will earn you any remission of guilt. You will merely be perpetuating the oppression of women and adding to the laundry bills. Perhaps Greer's fiercest condemnation—fiercer even than her fury against cosmetic surgeons and the "fertility moguls"—is reserved for housework in general and the washing machine in particular. Far from these domestic appliances being a boon to the "housewife"—"an expression that should be considered as shocking as 'yard nigger'"—they have made cleaning more time-consuming than ever. Yes, and switching on the heating is so much more exhausting than chopping firewood.

The Whole Woman shares with other great dogmatic texts—Marx, Freud, Foucault—the quality of being irrefutable. Any instances that might on the surface seem to weaken or contradict the teachings of liberation feminism can be shown in reality to reinforce them. You might think, for example, that because female genital mutilation is now condemned as a violation of human rights by every international organization, while male genital mutilation is ignored, women for once were better off. Not a bit of it. The campaign against female circumcision merely shows Western man's determination to impose control on women in the Third World. Again, the obsessive determination to improve screening for cervical cancer, while prostate cancer is neglected, is not a sign that we care more about women's health but rather one more example of the determination of men to control the sexuality of women. Nor should you imagine that male doctors are attempting to bring joy to childless women by inventing new fertility treatments. On the contrary, "fertility treatment causes far more suffering than it does joy", and the "fertility magnates" are simply exploiting women for their own gain and glory.

I would not advise any male suffering from our sex's deplorable excess of testosterone to retort that women continue to live on average five years longer than men, that five times as many young men as women commit suicide, that men are twice as likely to be unemployed and find it twice as hard to get another job, that men are infinitely more likely to suffer industrial accidents and diseases which may destroy their lives. None of these apparent disadvantages begins to compare with the misery—Greer's favourite word—daily endured by women, and in any case men deserve it.

Men can't win and shouldn't. Who needs them anyway? Greer entertains a suspicion that "if heterosexuality is not in future to be buttressed by law and religion and family pressure, it will collapse". Not that Greer cares that much for gays; to her they look just as violent as and rather more promiscuous than other men. She is not even very enthusiastic about lesbians, and she is positively contemp-

tuous of transsexuals' blundering efforts to deny their biological nature.

But there remains, of course, one small problem in a world where men are properly marginalized and left to stew in the pub and the locker-room. How are children to be brought up? Even after we have consigned to history's dustbin "the ghastly figure of the Bride", there remains the awkward fact that, in her words, "A woman without a partner and with children is usually a woman in trouble." Greer, in a significant shift, concedes that "In *The Female Eunuch* I argued that motherhood should not be treated as a substitute career; now I would argue that motherhood should be regarded as a genuine career option." And now that they have this licence to breed professionally, women should be paid enough to raise a child in decent circumstances.

But who is to pay them? Who is to be the "partner"? Not, of course, a man, though every social statistic screams that a child brought up by two parents does better in life. Not the extended sisterhood of traditional society, the loss of which she mourns now as in 1969. Sisters may provide a network of comfort and support, but they cannot be expected to win the bread. Naturally the answer is the age-old one of all utopians: the State must be the new father.

The State doesn't snore or get drunk, the State doesn't beat you up or waste its weekend gawping at muddied oafs or torturing fish, the State doesn't call out "nice tits" as you walk past, and it never says "how like a woman". And if it seems a touch paradoxical that a movement that yearns for total liberation from oppression and commitment should end up by shackling itself to the railings of Whitehall, that would not be the first time this has happened. Egotism has a habit of drifting into statism. That is why egotism is not enough, as I am sure Nurse Cavell would have said if she had survived to see the women's movement in full flow.

Everything that Greer argues—and in places she argues so magnificently, with such wit and zap—leads, it seems to me, to precisely the opposite of the conclusion that she sets out to draw. Ghastly as men are—in fact, precisely because they are so ghastly—the only hope of even half-civilizing them, and their male children, must lie in some social institution, some pattern of shared obligations, which looks remarkably like old-fashioned marriage, looser, more equal, purged of its grosser patriarchal aspects but none the less recognizably marriage. Many marriages are unhappy and most marriage have their unhappy patches, but Greer's insistence that, at the deepest level, women today are no happier than they were thirty years ago does not suggest that she has found a better option.

Camille Paglia (review date 9 May 1999)

SOURCE: "Back to the Barricades," in *New York Times Book Review*, May 9, 1999, pp. 19-20.

[In the following review, Paglia provides a summary of Greer's life and career through evaluation of Christine Wallace's biography of Greer and offers negative assessment of The Whole Woman.]

After a year of divisive White House scandals, the feminist movement in the United States has been struggling to regain its bearings. Reminiscence rather than innovation is the trend, as memoirs and biographies of older feminists pour from the presses.

Two books arrive as timely reminders that feminism is a world movement. The first, by Christine Wallace, an Australian journalist, is a biography of Germaine Greer, author of the 1970 feminist classic, *The Female Eunuch.* The second, by Greer herself, is the "sequel" she vowed she would never write.

Wallace pursued her biography under fire from her displeased subject: Greer called her "a dung beetle" and "flesh-eating bacteria" and blocked access to key sources. Suspicion was probably warranted: *Germaine Greer: Untamed Shrew* veers into partisan sermonizing when it rebukes Greer for being insufficiently feminist (as the term has been narrowly defined by what feels like a shadowy female collective breathing down Wallace's neck).

Wallace should have just stuck to her story, which is spellbinding. Many of today's young feminists outside Britain, where Greer has lived as a formidable public presence since 1964, have never heard of her and badly need a primer in feminist history. Middle-aged feminists, on the other hand, still relish Greer's swash-buckling 1971 American book tour, which was as provocative as Oscar Wilde's 1882 visit.

Though she wonderfully illuminates Greer's early life in Australia, Wallace too often impugns Greer as a faux feminist who latched onto the women's movement for publicity. The facts show the contrary: that well before Betty Friedan's 1963 manifesto, *The Feminine Mystique*, the young Greer was boldly challenging conventions of feminine speech and behavior. She exemplified the revolutionary spirit of the generation rising after World War II.

Born in "conservative, Anglophile, stultifyingly predictable" Melbourne in 1939 to a dapper advertising representative and his "headstrong" wife, Greer was rigorously educated in Roman Catholic schools. She was "terrorized" by her mother, who beat her with a stick or toaster cord. Her "distant, sometimes tortured" father, absent overseas in the Royal Australian Air Force, was in Greer's opinion "weak, craven, feeble" for not protecting or praising her.

Greer's seething sense of defraudation and her stinging portrayals of men as cheats and parasites appear rooted in her disappointment with her father. She would cross the world in obsessive quest of his true identity: *Daddy, We*

Hardly Knew You (1990) charts her sleuthing into her murky, shame-filled family origins.

"Lanky and clever," Greer was an awkward six feet tall by adolescence. She took up fencing and had an affair with another girl. Arriving at the University of Melbourne in 1956, Greer already had "intellectual arrogance" with a persistent "Catholic intensity." "Bullying and obnoxious in argument" but with "a palpable vulnerability," she sank into misery and made "a melodramatic gesture at suicide" by flinging herself down a cliff.

Greer's shocking language and odd dress got her satirized by a student newspaper as "Germaniac Queer." She aspired to a male sexual freedom, and there were abortions and gynecological problems, whose scarring affected her fertility when, in maturity, she longed for a baby.

Wallace examines Greer's rape at a football club barbecue, a trauma that she later publicized as emblematic of male oppression. A witness raises questions about Greer's judgment and actions at the time and insists, contrary to her claims, that sympathetic male students came to her defense.

Wallace gives an invaluable overview of the bohemian coteries and intellectual trends of Melbourne and Sydney University, where Greer received her M.A. in English literature. The combination of anarchism, moralism, and libertarianism in Greer's thinking is deftly traced to such disparate influences as the sex theorist Wilhelm Reich and the critic F. R. Leavis. But Greer's devotion to Byron, her thesis subject, is badly handled by the uncomprehending Wallace. At Sydney, Greer dabbled in theater and fell in love with a libertine male philosopher—the most serious relationship of her life.

Leaving Australia for doctoral study at Cambridge University, Greer found a female mentor in the Renaissance scholar Muriel Bradbrook. Greer's thesis, on love and marriage in Shakespeare's early comedies, is distorted by a hostile Wallace, who can't reconcile Greer's real-life "sexual braggadocio" with the male conquest in *The Taming of the Shrew*—when in fact Greer was asking searching questions about virility and female desire that feminism still cannot answer.

Wallace vividly documents Greer's rise to celebrity. A tour with Cambridge's Footlights Club, where Greer starred in musical revues, led to television offers that introduced her to the booming British rock scene. Greer's life was split between swinging London and the University of Warwick, where she taught for five years.

In London Greer spotted the rugged, hard-drinking Paul du Feu, a well-educated construction worker whom Wallace describes as "the heterosexual equivalent of a rough trade fantasy come true." Du Feu was captivated by what he called Greer's "frizzed-out soul-sister hair," "pre-Raphaelite beauty" and "tough-guy" sexual style. Their hasty marriage lasted three weeks. Greer's new "theology," according to du Feu (who later posed nude for a *Cosmopolitan* centerfold), was sexual promiscuity, as espoused in underground periodicals like *Oz* and an Amsterdam-based, radically pro-pornography magazine Greer co-founded.

Wallace is scathingly negative about Greer's 1969 manifesto, *The Universal Tonguebath*, a paean to rock groupies and group sex. Her political disdain for popular culture is a salient weakness in this biography; Wallace should have noted the striking parallelism between the 1960's Greer and the resurgent pro-sex wing of 1990's feminism, which embraces rock-and-roll instead of condemning it as sexist. Mocking the *Oz* Greer as "grooviness personified," Wallace droningly indicts her "anachronistic passivity" and "hegemonic heterosexuality." Yet Greer's vitality and wit leap off those pages.

The genesis of **The Female Eunuch,** Greer's trenchant analysis of the modern female condition, is ascribed to a woman agent and to Greer's Cambridge friend Sonny Mehta, now the editor in chief of Alfred A. Knopf. Wallace's wholesale rejection of the criticisms of feminist activists in Greer's famous best seller misses Greer's prescience about what would indeed go badly wrong with second-wave feminism.

But Wallace's chronicle of Greer's American tour, notably her tumultuous debate with Norman Mailer at Town Hall in New York City, is a major contribution to cultural history. Wallace unfortunately talked only to feminist leaders—thus committing the same "elitist" sin she accuses Greer of. In attacking Greer for belittling Kate Millett's *Sexual Politics*, Wallace fails to realize that that 1970 book, with its stridently anti-male premises about art, split feminism down the middle. The cultivated Greer was right about Millett's philistinism.

Wallace hurries through Greer's later career—her four years at the University of Oklahoma, her residence in Italy, her active support of third world causes and her books on art and poetry. Though she charts Greer's reversals—"disengaging from sex in her middle 40's" and abandoning concern for her looks—Wallace lacks psychological insight into the Greer who declares "I don't have any enduring relationships of any sort except with animals and plants." But despite its hatchet-grinding and its mundane literalism about esthetics, this biography is a treasure trove of information about one of the world's leading intellectuals—whom women's studies programs, as Wallace observes, have outrageously neglected.

The Whole Woman gave Greer a golden opportunity to retake center stage by reassessing feminist history in her own terms. Alas, the book, which reads as though it was rushed into print to counter Wallace's biography, is exasperatingly disjointed and scattershot. It is overconcerned with Greer's British opponents and provincial feuds. Most American readers, for example, will be baffled by Greer's dark allusions to her angry resignation from Cambridge over the appointment of a male-to-female transsexual astrophysicist to a woman's college. And there are cryptic references to Greer's clash with catty women journalists who falsely claimed that she had had a hysterectomy and whom she charged in turn with excessive, brain-rotting use of lipstick. That battle, showing Greer's rejection of vixenish post-feminism, cries out for fuller detailing.

Like its precursor, **The Whole Woman** is structured in four parts: "Body," "Soul," "Love" and "Hate" (in **The Female Eunuch**) have become "Body," "Mind," "Love" and "Power." Is Greer acknowledging that the sexes must get beyond mutual recriminations and that women have made slow but substantive advances in public life? Not at all: she insists that she never called for "equality" but only "liberation," and she dismisses as inconsequential women's professional gains. "It's time to get angry again," she proclaims about "the false dawn of feminism."

The book is shot through with unhelpful and pass invective against men. "Patriarchal authority," we are told, strangles medicine, the stock market, and media and entertainment. Men are portrayed as filthy, lazy louts, sponging off women's labor. Greer bizarrely claims that "our culture is far more masculinist than it was 30 years ago."

Though she says that "the identification of feminism with the United States has dishonored it around the world." Greer freely borrows without attribution from American writers, as in her critique of the sexual revolution for having liberated men but exposed young women to exploitation and infection.

Among Greer's questionable assertions: ultrasound scanning of pregnant women may cause dyslexia in infants; the Pap smear is "the dragooning and torturing of women"; the "real powers" behind *Roe v. Wade* were male doctors, judges and mobsters who made "fortunes" in "the abortion industry," unleashing "a tide of feticide" that swept the world. In Greer's grisly scenarios, modern medicine is simply "300 years of male professionals lancing women's bodies as if they were abcesses."

Too much of the book consists of citations from recent magazine articles. Tantalizing points are raised but not developed—for example, Greer's attack on post-modernist gay theorists for making the vagina and rectum equivalent or her fascinating juxtaposition of African genital mutilation with Western plastic surgery and breast augmentation. Her gibes at recent pop music and the Internet have a third-hand quality, and she makes breathtaking misstatements—like saying that women's studies faculty members have been "regularly refused tenure" (what planet does she live on?).

The tone of this book is seriously unbalanced: Greer's normal humor and oratorical propulsiveness seem lost in her orgy of contemptuous sardonicism. I miss the mature, contemplative voice of celebration of nature in *The Change,* Greer's 1992 meditation on menopause. *The Whole Woman,* in short, does not give us the whole Greer. Ironically, Greer emerges with more dignity and stature from Wallace's acid-etched biography, which is also a far better read.

Michiko Kakutani (review date 18 May 1999)

SOURCE: "The Female Condition, Re-explored 30 Years Later," in *The New York Times,* May 18, 1999, p. E10.

[*In the following review, Kakutani offers negative assessment of* The Whole Woman.]

When Germaine Greer's swaggering call for sexual liberation, *The Female Eunuch,* appeared in 1970, it created a sensation. The book urged women to embrace their sexuality, to become self-reliant and to repudiate the passive roles in which they have traditionally been cast. It laid out these dictums with a rollicking sense of humor and a marked sympathy for men, two qualities in decidedly short supply among feminist theorists of the time. Indeed, Ms. Greer's book anticipated the thinking of later feminists like Naomi Wolf who would treat men not as adversaries but as potential partners.

Now, some 30 years later, Ms. Greer has written a sequel of sorts to *The Female Eunuch.* It's a book that is as sour as *Eunuch* was exuberant, as dogmatic as *Eunuch* was original, as slipshod in its thinking as *Eunuch* was pointed. Instead of drawing upon her readings in psychoanalysis, literature and cultural history as she did in that earlier book, Ms. Greer relies in these pages on highly selective anecdotal evidence (from newspaper stories, court cases and polls) to support her assertions. Instead of drawing her disparate observations together into a coherent thesis, she settles for giving the reader a scattershot—and often highly contradictory—series of reactions to an assortment of phenomena, including sexual discrimination legislation, deadbeat dads, anorexia, self-mutilation and the rise of Madonna and the Spice Girls.

Throughout this messy volume, Ms. Greer tries to argue that things are worse than ever for women. Although she acknowledges that "feminist consciousness now leavens every relationship, every single social and professional encounter," she insists that our culture is "less feminist than it was 30 years ago."

"When *The Female Eunuch* was written our daughters were not cutting or starving themselves," she writes. "On every side speechless women endure endless hardship, grief and pain, in a world system that creates billions of losers for every handful of winners. It's time to get angry again."

Perhaps one reason Ms. Greer is so pessimistic has to do with her willful—and often perverse—insistence on seeing

developments most feminists would embrace as signs of progress as symptoms of some vague male conspiracy. Modern contraception, she suggests, does not give a woman greater control over her body, but turns her into "a manmade nonmother": it is another instance of "male interference with conception and birth." Reproductive technology, in her view, does not exist to offer unfertile women the hope of having babies but to make women subsidiary to the process of reproduction. Screening for cervical and breast cancer, she declares, "is many times more likely to destroy a woman's peace of mind than it is to save her life."

"Women are driven through the health system like sheep through a dip," she writes in a typically dogmatic passage. "The disease they are being treated for is womanhood."

As for the legal right to have an abortion, Ms. Greer sees it as a reflection of the power of "the masculine medical establishment and the masculine judiciary": "there were fortunes to be made in pregnancy termination," she writes, "at a time when advances in the technology were making a risky procedure fool-proof." In her opinion, all that women won with *Roe v. Wade* was "the 'right' to undergo invasive procedures in order to terminate unwanted pregnancies, unwanted not just by them but by their parents, their sexual partners, the governments who would not support mothers, the employers who would not employ mothers, the landlords who would not accept tenants with children, the schools that would not accept students with children."

While Ms. Greer noisily assails the Western establishment for forcing women to conform to stereotyped standards of beauty, she denounces Western efforts to stamp out female genital mutilation in Africa as "an attack on cultural identity." Although she admits that genital mutilation "represents a significant health risk," she argues that "it must also be a procedure with considerable cultural value because it has survived 50 years of criminalization and concerted propaganda campaigns." Although the brutal procedure is frequently performed on girls who have no say in the matter, Ms. Greer writes that "we should be considering the possibility that F.G.M. acts in a similar way" to tattooing and body piercing "to assert the individual woman's control over her genitals and to customize them to her specification."

Such patronizing, ill-considered remarks do nothing to inspire confidence in Ms. Greer. Nor do her hectoring denunciations of men as lazy beasts who increasingly prefer masturbation to "the services of actual women" or her churlish reluctance to regard male-to-female transsexuals as women.

As for her recommendations for change, they not only sound impractical but often loony as well. She suggests that women "should consider the possibility of deploying grief as a subversive force"—as a means of protesting, even stopping Governments from making "war on a helpless civilian population." She also argues that women—who, she now believes, will always be ignored or treated as sex objects by men—should "make a conscious decision not to want men's company more than men want women's," even if that results in a segregation of the sexes.

While reporters have already made much of the fact that in the 30 years since *The Female Eunuch* Ms. Greer has changed her mind about everything from motherhood as a career option to sex as a liberating (or enslaving) force, she would argue that "women's changeability" can be a "corrective to masculine rigidity."

What is unfortunate about *The Whole Woman* is less that she has changed her views than that she has done such a weak job of articulating her evolving vision and that her writing—and thinking—have grown so vituperative and shrill. None of the thoughtful insights into male and female psychology that animated *The Female Eunuch* are to be found in this volume, just as none of that earlier book's intellectual analysis is to be found in its pages.

The Whole Woman is a castrated book.

Elizabeth Ward (review date 23 May 1999)

SOURCE: "The Trouble With Women," in *Washington Post Book World*, May 23, 1999, p. 8.

[*In the following review, Ward offers unfavorable assessment of* The Whole Woman *and Christine Wallace's biography of Greer.*]

"It's time," announces Germaine Greer in the preface—or "recantation"—to her new book, "to get angry again."

Oh. Had she stopped? According to her biographer, Christine Wallace, "Dr. Grrrr" has been angry with the world since she was a child in 1940s Melbourne: with her parents, with men, with other women (especially other feminists, from the suffragettes to the ERA campaigners) and ultimately with society in all its multiple oppressive manifestations. After the great whip-crack of *The Female Eunuch,* Greer can hardly be said to have sat back paring her fingernails while the tyrants and traitors got on with it. Perceived transgressions large and small have regularly called forth trumpet blasts of Greerian ire, although not such sustained ones. Lately, she has been very angry indeed with her compatriot Wallace, whom she has rather intemperately compared to a "dung beetle" and "flesh-eating bacteria" for having presumed to write an unauthorized and, what is worse, ungrammatical biography of her.

Anger, in short, is Greer's shtick; she makes an art form of it, albeit more street theater than literature. Had she been born a couple of generations earlier, she might well have found herself a real Sunday-afternoon soapbox at London's Hyde Park Corner rather than the virtual soapbox she has constructed out of her academic and polemical

publications and her talent for deploying the media to her advantage. She is an English professor at Warwick University and a longtime occasional journalist but so much more besides: performer, prophet, avenging angel, lash of the ignorant, scourge of the complacent, foe of despots. If this sounds less like a c.v. than a litany, it is only appropriate to the near-religious sense of mission informing Greer's entire career. "I am an anarchist, basically," she told a British interviewer recently, which—given the scope of her rage—is really her way of saying that she, too, brings not peace but a sword. People with such lofty aspirations tend to wobble on the knife-edge between brilliance and battiness. It is to Greer's credit that, through the years, she has tumbled off on the wrong side somewhat less often than she has found herself on the side of the angels.

So, *The Whole Woman:* not a new anger, then, but an old anger taken to a whole new level. Readers of *The Female Eunuch*—and there were literally millions of them back in the '70s—will recognize its ghostly influence here, right down to the cosmic chapter headings ("Body" and "Love" are back, but "Soul" has become "Mind" and "Hate" has mutated into "Power") and inset boxes of poetry and other quotations. The opening "recantation" is simply Greer going back on her vow never to write a sequel to that first, furious, infuriating, oddly inspiring, ultimately quixotic book. Things have not worked out as she had hoped—or prescribed—so, at the age of 60, she is taking another tilt at the windmill. *The Female Eunuch,* she points out, was "one feminist text that did not argue for equality." It argued for liberation, for doing "as much for female people as has been done for colonized nations." Looking about her nearly 30 years on, Greer saw women everywhere continuing to bend and attune themselves to a male-ordered world, laboring under crushingly "contradictory expectations" in everything from health care to housework to sexual harassment. That, she said, is what the spurious notion of equality had amounted to: equality with slaves, freedom "to live the lives of unfree men." Hence her rekindled anger; hence this book.

Without question, the world Greer paints for us, brush stroke by sweeping brush stroke, is a desolate one, almost apocalyptically so. We Western women, it appears, still have not shucked off male ideas of female beauty; the voluntary mutilation of plastic surgery bears witness to our thralldom. We continue to buy into the myth of male-pleasing penetrative sex, locking ourselves into a cycle of hazardous contraceptive practices, abortions that we ludicrously celebrate as "a right" (rather than mourn as "a sad and onerous duty"), and exploitative fertility treatments. We fight for the right to be soldiers and boxers and CEOs; certainly we should have those options, she responds, but why would we want to? Armies are bastions of "conscientious inhumanity." Professional boxers are little better than performing animals, promoters' commodities—an opinion shared by Muhammad Ali. And a woman who succeeds in business (or politics) usually ends up doing it, Thatcher-like, over the bodies of other women.

In an extraordinary chapter on "Sorrow," at the literal center and philosophical heart of the book, Greer berates us for confusing our real, rational feelings of sadness with illnesses to be medicated or outbreaks of hysteria to be shushed and apologized for. "Disturbed animals in the zoo are given Prozac too," she writes, "not for the misfortune of being [a tiger] but for the misfortune of being in a zoo; female depression could as likely be a consequence not of being female but of an inhuman environment." (What other feminist, by the way, would risk her PC credentials by starting such a chapter with an invocation of the Mater Dolorosa herself, "Mary the mother of Jesus"?)

On and on she goes, cataloguing the injustices and misguided aspirations that diminish and embitter our lives. Not just ours, either: Scouring the earth for "a glimpse of a surviving whole woman," Greer found everywhere, from Africa to China, from rural Oklahoma to Central Australia, the insidious encroachment of the Western feminine stereotype, with its sad baggage of high heels, lipstick, contraceptives, baby formula and eagerness to please.

Of course, demurrals bubble up as one reads. The bleakness is so absolute it matches the experience of no woman I know on four continents. There is a curious absence of compassion for men: If they are so unfree and oppressed themselves, what about their rational feelings of sadness, bitterness and inadequacy? "To be male is to be a kind of idiot savant—" We know what she means, but we also know that it is unfair and untrue. What about the patient, humorous, gentle, generous men who have as little time for the sexist jocks and violent jerks as women do? The fact is, Greer's jeremiad is so sweeping it scarcely allows for such nuances and often pushes her over the edge into outright silliness. The solution to the housework problem is not to advise a woman to pack up her stuff and become an "apple-cheeked bag lady" on a park bench. Revulsion at plastic-surgery abuses in Western societies does not somehow put the Third World practice of female genital mutilation in a better light. Nor would there seem to be much of a future for the human race in all-female communes.

And yet *The Whole Woman* remains a marvelous performance. Certainly it is dark, but Picasso's "Guernica" and Tennyson's "In Memoriam" are dark, too, and we recognize those as true, if partial, representations of our complex human experience. Besides, like them, it is oddly exhilarating. Greer may have grim things to say, but she has a rip-roaring time saying them—the soapbox syndrome again. No feminist writer can match her for eloquence or energy; none makes us laugh the way she does. "Feminism," she quotes deluded optimists as saying, "has served its purpose and should now eff off." "Men are no more likely to submit their testicles to official care and attention than they are to wear their muffler when it is cold and keep their feet dry." "Women are to be taken care of whether they like it or not." "Women are worker bees; males are drones." "When cultivation is done with mattocks and hoes, women do it; when a tractor comes along, men drive it."

Again and again, too, she interrupts some tirade or lament with a jolt of profound wisdom or glancing poetry, like that great central paean to female sorrow, which throws us back onto her side all over again. Provided, of course, one can even keep hold of her "side" on this intellectual and emotional roller-coaster ride.

Nobody has ever found it easy to pin down Germaine Greer—and that includes her biographer. True, Christine Wallace's much-resented attempt has resulted in a diligent, intelligent and in many ways enlightening book. It is useful to know, for instance, of Greer's longtime hostility toward her mother, her rape as a university student, her single, three-week fiasco of a marriage and her unsuccessful attempts in later life to have a child. It is helpful to learn of her anarchist "training" (as Wallace dubiously insists on calling it) as a member of the Sydney bohemian and libertarian group known as the Push. Wallace's view of *The Female Eunuch* as essentially a mirror of Greer's own "psychic wounds" is thought-provoking, and at least one sharply worded sentence should be borne in mind in any assessment of *The Whole Woman:* "Testimonial feminism has an important and honorable role in the history of the women's movement, but extrapolating social theory from a statistical sample of one is a dangerous enterprise."

Still, though the portrait of Greer as a disturbed, manipulative, inconsistent, self-promoting, genius-tinged maverick is persuasive, one is not persuaded that it is complete. Perhaps because Wallace was unable to talk to her subject, aspects of Greer that show up in all her books are missing here: notably her humor, her sadness and her odd likableness. More than anywhere, though, the temperamental mismatch of biographer and subject is evident in Wallace's style. If there is one thing Greer handles beautifully, it is language. She must have found it particularly galling to have her life laid bare in English as graceless and lumpy as this: "Far from being a matter of inconsistency, her stance was often a result of her adherence to anarchistic pessimism—which provided a framework within which seemingly contrary positions could have their own internal consistency"—a typical, though by no means the worst, example of Wallace's prose.

In the end, a reader can probably glean more of the essential Greer from one chapter of *The Whole Woman* than from all of this conscientious, plodding biography.

Margaret Talbot (review date 31 May 1999)

SOURCE: "The Female Misogynist," in *The New Republic,* May 31, 1999, pp. 34-40.

[*In the following review, Talbot offers negative evaluation of* The Whole Woman, *citing serious faults in Greer's "men-are-dogs" perspective and contradictory arguments that undermine the well-being of women.*]

I.

Whatever else Germaine Greer's new book will be called, it will almost certainly be called a work of feminism. There are reasons for this, but they have almost nothing to do with the book itself, which is a sour and undiscriminating litany of charges against men—all men, men as nature created them—wrapped around the willfully obtuse argument that little or nothing has improved for American and European women over the last thirty years. *The Whole Woman* presents men as irredeemable and equality as a hoax. For this reason, the book is just a sideshow, a shrill distraction from the humane and transformative and exhilarating vision of justice that has animated the enterprise of feminism since the late eighteenth century.

In that vision, let us remind ourselves, the struggle for equal dignity, equal possibility, and equal worth was supposed to change and to benefit men, too. Women's rights were thwarted by culture, not by nature; by cruel social arrangements, not by timeless male troglodytism. "We do not fight with man himself," the nineteenth-century feminist Ernestine Rose observed, "but only with bad principles." In the great feminist vision, neither men nor women were to be defined by, let alone reduced to, their anatomy. For liberal feminism, as Martha Nussbaum has argued, sex, like caste and rank, was a "morally irrelevant characteristic" that acquired its significance historically and not biologically—through law and custom, which are amenable to moral and historical agency. Otherwise politics are meaningless, and women have reason only for despair.

In Greer's view, however, men are "doomed to competition and injustice, not merely towards females, but towards children, animals, and other men." The concept of doom never served much of a purpose in feminism, which is, at its core, hopeful and ameliorative; but Greer presses it into service. After all, she writes, men are "freaks of nature . . . full of queer obsessions about fetishistic activities and fantasy goals." They are single-minded, and "single-mindedness produces hideously anti-social behaviors, from paedophile rings to waging war." They are slothful and sponging—and irredeemably so, because their "anthropoid ancestors" were slothful and sponging, too. A woman who burdens herself with a man in the form of a husband will likely find that "the cost of feeding him, grooming him, humouring him, and financing his recreation is way out of proportion to the contribution that he makes in return."

The home truth is that men hate women. And "there is no point in trying to establish" why. (Why think, when you can rage?) "Men bash women because they enjoy it; they torture women as they might torture an animal or pull the wings off flies. . . ." So repelled are they by their girlfriends, their wives, their sisters, their mothers, and their daughters that they are doing their malevolent best to eradicate us altogether. As Greer barmily puts it, "If state-of-the-art gestation cabinets could manufacture children and virtual fetishes could furnish sexual services, men

would not regret the passing of real, smelly, bloody, noisy, hairy women." (Smelliness and bloodiness and noisiness and hairiness being the signal qualities of "real" women.) If that is what you really believe, what is the point of any concerted movement for social reform? The answer is simple: Greer sees no point in it. The only tattered hope that she holds aloft is her own naïve enamorment with the gender apartheid of certain Middle Eastern cultures. "I gazed at women in segregated societies," she writes, "and found them in many ways stronger than women who would not go into a theatre or a restaurant without a man." The "dignified alternative" for women in the United States and Europe would be to segregate themselves, perhaps in "matrilocal families." Purdah-hood is powerful!

Why, then, will such fatalistic claptrap be dignified with the good name of feminism? Why, for that matter, is *The Whole Woman* a bestseller in England? Why does the Knopf catalogue praise the book as a "shattering critique" and a "call to arms?" (Even PR should show a little decency.) One reason, certainly, is Greer's reputation as a fire-starter of 1970s feminism, a writer who galvanized and outraged. Another reason, a more alarming one, is the insidious reach of an attitude that we will call Men-Are-Dogs-ism. This increasingly popular sensibility represents a convergence of influences: the animal determinism of evolutionary psychology; essentializing bromides of the sort made famous by *Men Are from Mars, Women Are from Venus;* sitcom-style girl-bonding; the frightened, triumphalist rage of a certain strain of women's rock-and-roll. In the end, it is this way of thinking—or rather, this escape from thinking—that Germaine Greer exemplifies. *The Whole Woman* is empty-headed vehemence of a discouragingly familiar kind.

II.

In 1970, *The Female Eunuch* made Germaine Greer famous, and it made feminism famous, too. "Every self-respecting woman on the Left owned a copy or still owns a copy somewhere around the house, dog-eared and coffee-stained with use," Lisa Jardine recently recalled in the London *Observer.* "[F]or women born in the immediate postwar years, there was 'before Greer' and 'after Greer'; the book, and Germaine's attention-grabbing brand of stand-up comic, in-your-face assertiveness taught us all how to behave badly and take control of our lives." *The Female Eunuch* was the sort of book that wives read in defiance of their husbands, copping a thrill of insurrection. It was the sort of book, according to Christine Wallace's informants in *Untamed Shrew,* her new biography of Greer, that broke up dinner parties, sending fondue sets crashing to the floor. (The copy that I recently took out of the library—the original hardback with Greer in a feather boa on the back and her name on the front in bloopy purple letters—contained this time-capsule inscription: "Sheila the Peela: Don't tell Pat about this. We decided a little lib would be good for you.")

Greer herself was a 31-year-old Cambridge Ph.D. in 1970, transplanted from Sydney and living the Boho life in

London. Within a year of publishing *The Female Eunuch,* she had debated Norman Mailer in a truculent disputation at Town Hall in New York, turned up on the cover of *Life* magazine as the "saucy feminist that even men like," and inspired innumerable women to stop wearing underpants. She was, in short, the "libbers'" first real celebrity, a crossover-hit, with one Mary Quant-ified leg firmly in the counterculture and one firmly in the bestseller lists.

It must be said, though, that *The Female Eunuch* has not aged especially well. In this regard, it is quite different from, say, *The Feminine Mystique,* whose thick description, scrupulous reporting, and acute diagnosis of the social and psychological costs of restricting women's orbit make it, even now, illuminating to read. Betty Friedan's book even has a very particular utility today, as an antidote to Nick-at-Nite nostalgia for an era in which suburban housewifery really was the dominant outlet for female talent and Donna Reed really was the model. All those conservative women who wax rapturous about stay-at-home-momdom (while pursuing ambitious writing careers themselves) should be obliged to re-read it annually.

The Female Eunuch, by contrast, is thoroughly steeped in the patchouli-scented idiosyncrasies of its time and its place, and especially of its author. It is written with vigor, certainly; but its vigor is what hobbles it. There is a great deal of hectoring of women for cooperating in the suppression of their own libidos (Greer was under the sway of the Reichian religion of sexual energy) and adopting the characteristics of the castrate: "timidity, plumpness, languor, delicacy, and preciosity." There is a certain amount of head-girl disdain for lesser—and especially less sexually liberated—females. This privileged sisterly snobbery seems a bit off-point for a time when women still faced institutionalized job discrimination, a criminal justice system preoccupied with the sexual purity of rape victims, a general disregard of, and lack of resources for, women who were beaten by their husbands, and other unglamorous barriers to just bucking up and getting on with things.

The Female Eunuch, like *The Whole Woman,* is dismissive of organized feminism past and present, and bored by political solutions. Still, it is flushed with a sense of possibility—dizzy at times, but inspiriting—that is almost entirely missing from the new book. In 1970, Greer writes stirringly of female independence, of "joy in the struggle" for it.

> Joy does not mean riotous glee, but it does mean the purposive employment of energy in a self-chosen enterprise. It does mean pride and confidence. . . . To be emancipated from helplessness and need and walk freely upon the earth: that is your birthright. To refuse hobbles and deformity and possession of your body and glory in its power, accepting its own laws of loveliness. To have something to desire, something to make, something to achieve, and at last something genuine to give. To be free from guilt and shame and the tireless self-discipline of women. To stop pretending and dissembling, cajoling and manipulating, and begin to control and sympathize. To claim the masculine virtues of magnanimity and generosity and courage.

It was a humane vision; but so much of this vision of new womanhood was to be achieved, in Greer's view, by specifically sexual means: by smashing monogamy, by promoting the commitment-free fuck, and so on. Greer's self-satisfied hedonism crippled her manifesto. In the first place, there were the Greerian idiosyncrasies that made it unlikely to mobilize a real following: she doted on the vagina, at a time when other feminists were cheering the rediscovery of the clitoris. For Greer, the real significance of her favorite female organ resided not so much in its capacity for pleasure as in its capacity for power, since it actively "embraced and stimulated the penis instead of taking it." A minor distinction, you might say—ever hear of Kegel exercises?—but a distinction that promised, for Greer, nothing less than emancipation. More importantly, the Greerian dream of sexual liberation had little relevance for the spheres of life in which women spend most of their days and define much of their identity—work, family, citizenship.

At the time, though, Greer's high-minded randiness—and her gleeful exhibitionism, as when she posed nude for *Screw* magazine, called herself a "super-whore," and wrote paeans to pornography and to the joy of sex with rock stars—had a kind of propagandistic purpose. It signaled that feminism need not mean sexlessness. At a cultural moment when flaunting one's sexual attractiveness and seriously committing oneself to women's advancement really were regarded as contradictory acts (as they no longer are, the latest round of complaints against feminist puritanism notwithstanding), this was probably useful. Indeed, what has been so odd about Greer's incarnation of the last fifteen years or so—during which she has written at least two books (*Sex and Destiny* and *The Change*) in which she broadcast her disgust with promiscuity and argued that intercourse itself degrades women—is that she has made no attempt to explain her reversal, or even to acknowledge it.

There is nothing wrong with changing one's mind in the light of experience. Greer is hardly the first feminist to recognize that the sexual revolution was not an unmitigated blessing for women. What is striking about Greer is that she is so unwilling to take responsibility for her earlier positions, and so averse to arriving at a middle ground. Most feminists—most women—have little difficulty with the notion that neither rock groupiedom and the "zipless fuck," nor the renunciation of intercourse and contraception as so much pandering to men's "penetrative" agenda, hold much promise. Lots of people in their forties and fifties look back with a wince or a smirk on their own days and nights of Aquarian bed-hopping—but they do not devise an entire theory of gender relations on the basis of it. Greer, though, is a creature of absolutes. The substance of her ideas matters less to her than their radicalism. And so her internal gyroscope is permanently out of whack.

She is in the outrage business. In England, Greer's lurchings from hyperbole to hyperbole—combined with her polemical flair in countless television and radio appearances—are often taken as signs of genius. Her more bizarre and offensive positions—such as her defense of female genital mutilation, which may be found in *The Whole Woman*—are met with argument, but not with disgust. Her spiteful attacks on other women—she assailed the journalist Suzanne Moore for her "hair bird's-nested all over the place, fuck-me shoes and three fat inches of cleavage," and remarked of the novelist Fay Weldon, "I know she has had a facelift, and I know she's on HRT, but would that have such a devastating effect on the cerebellum?"—elicit the sort of nervous titters with which you might flatter a formidable and eccentric aunt. Greer may be eccentric, but she is also, as one British journalist put it, "dangerously close to becoming a national treasure." This sort of indulgence presupposes that Greer is still producing something resembling real and original analysis. But what is remarkable about *The Whole Woman*—Greer's particular crotchets aside—is that it has so much in common with the general run of Men-are-Dogs-ism. She is no longer travelling to the beat of a different drum. Her stunts have become banal.

III.

In the men-are-dogs theory of life, anatomy is destiny. Men always have been, and always will be, loutish, messy, insensitive, and helplessly programmed to spread their seed far and wide. Women always have been, and always will be, the moral betters of men, and also their dupes. Real women sometimes talk this way, of course; but it is in television humor and other artifacts of mass culture that this line of thinking receives its fullest elaboration. In pop fiction, it is the language of bitch sessions at the wine bar. ("Bastards!" yells one of Bridget Jones's friends in the eponymous diary, "pouring three-quarters of a glass of Kir Royale straight down her throat. Stupid, smug, arrogant, manipulative, self-indulgent bastards. They exist in a total Culture of Entitlement. Pass me one of those mini-pizzas, will you?") In pop psychology, it is the language of Mars and Venus. You hear it in you-go-girl jokes about Lorena Bobbit. You see it in those posters hanging in dorm rooms that say "10 Reasons Why a Dog is Better than a Man." You see it in Must-She TV and in commercials where wives joke smugly about how "well-trained" their husbands are, and in the explanatory use to which pundits put testosterone.

Lately, Men-Are-Dogs-ism has acquired some intellectual respectability from the pop psychology of our day, which is evolutionary psychology. The new Darwinists are strangely obsessed with the supposedly deep and constitutive and ineradicable difference between men and women—differences that are allegedly "hard-wired" by the machinery of natural selection. Since the most successful of our tree-swinging ancestors were those males who propagated their genes most widely, men today are more promiscuous than women. They just can't help it. They also have stronger sex drives, and seek out the sort of dewy-skinned, dewy-eyed (read: young) partners likely to provide a happy uterine home for their seed. And women,

whose tree-swinging ancestors cared for little else but finding a nice papa monkey for their young, have lower sex drives and prefer the kind of hominid who can give them stability—the older and the richer, the better. (By this calculus of genetic self-interest, as Natalie Angier has pointed out, baldness ought to be a real turn-on for women.)

There is plenty of empirical evidence to complicate and to counter these generalizations, not least our own experiences of women and men who fit neither mold. There is a preponderance of studies that show that most psychological sex differences are small to moderate, and exceeded by variation within each sex. In few other aspects of life, certainly, would we regard animal behavior or the behavior of our anthropoid ancestors as inescapable blueprints for our own actions. (Indeed, as Angier puts it in her delightful new book, *Woman: An Intimate Geography,* "many nonhuman female primates gallivant about rather more than we might have predicted before primatologists began observing their behavior in the field—more, far more, than is necessary for the sake of reproduction.") Most importantly, it is a fundamental lesson of human history that a change in cultural norms can effect a change in sexual behavior—so that, for instance, when women are given the social opportunity and the cultural sanction, many of them will not feel it necessary to hide their libidos (and their thongs). For the evo-psycho school of misogyny (and it *is* misogyny, whether it is delivered in liberal or conservative voices), it is enough that we have all known men and women who resemble the evolutionary stereotypes. But in truth it is *not* enough. The reality of biological differences is undeniable, but it is also not the only reality, or the most significant reality. Yet Darwin brings so much comfort to unregenerate males. . . .

Men-Are-Dogs-ism finds other support in the culture as well. It draws on the sort of "difference feminism" in which women are seen as morally superior creatures—more empathetic, kinder, better listeners, and so on. This tradition of feminine self-congratulation extends from the subset of suffragists who argued for the sweetly civilizing consequences of the women's vote to Carol Gilligan and Deborah Tannen in our day. It need not rest on a theory of innate difference, and many of its adherents explicitly say that they are talking about socialized characteristics; but their accounts have a way of slipping into essentialism—all the more so since they place so much value on the traditionally feminine virtues. These feminists restore women to the pedestal that they set out to destroy.

The difference feminists could have argued that there are jerks of both sexes, and that men in general are prodded by a variety of social clues to express their jerkiness in one way—by crushing beer cans on their heads, say, or by pummeling people—while women in general express their jerkiness in another way—by emotional manipulation or verbal abuse; and they could have argued that both these tendencies are subject to change as cultural expectations change, though they will in all probability never be interchangeable. But that is not what the difference feminists wish to argue. They are not especially struck by the infinite variety of human beings. Like the evolutionary psychologists, they prefer to believe that men are one way and women are another way, and so it has been and so it shall be. And what point is there in social and political reform, if the problem is biological? Genes are impervious to legislation.

From the early chapters of **The Whole Woman,** it is clear that Germaine Greer's feminism has devolved into Men-Are-Dogs-ism. She likes to explain obnoxious male behavior by reference to animal behavior. If men are reluctant to do their share of housework, it is because they inherited from their "anthropoid ancestors" a resentment of work and "a positive ambition to do nothing, which women do not share . . . Females, be they gorillas or worker bees, are naturally busy." (Does Greer forget the Queen Bee? Oh, well.) "Lionesses do the hunting to feed their cubs and their father." "Male animals are conspicuously less busy than females, yet somehow the human male has convinced the human female that he not she is the worker." Never mind the accuracy of Greer's zoology. What on earth does it have to do with the chores of living? Are we really compelled to divide our labors as lions or penguins or cockroaches divide theirs?

Another clue is Greer's tendency to elevate minor complaints about men to the status of gender oppression. Not only are men bellicose and competitive and slovenly. They also "pay less heed to traffic lights" and "brake harder and later." Oh, and they fish too much. Greer has a real bee in her bonnet about fishing, which I must say would seem to be rather a benign pursuit, unless you are a trout. Yet she sees it as yet another male plot to escape us. She insists, darkly, that "women of any age are not welcome on the riverbank." The danger is everywhere.

Then there is Greer's rush to condemn with whatever opprobrium springs to mind, however contradictory or baffling. Men are obsessed with penetrating women—but they are also obsessed with evading women, and therefore with masturbation. This is one of Greer's dicta on the subject: "Masturbation is easy; relationships are difficult." It is not quite as devastating as Lenny Bruce's remark that the nice thing about masturbation is that you don't have to send your hand home in a cab. Or consider the following assertions, at once absurd and unfalsifiable: "In some British circles, women are now expected to perform fellatio on demand." "In the last third of the twentieth century more women were penetrated deeper and more often than in any preceding era." "There are many, and more and more each day, who think a rectum has more character [than a vagina] and that buggery is more intimate than coitus." What British circles? How does Greer know? Why the syntax of social science, as if "deeper and more" were amenable to some sort of statistical proof? If men are perpetually fleeing intimacy, why would they seek a more "intimate" kind of sex? And why the preoccupation—and take my word for it, it is a preoccupation—with the supposed eclipse of the vagina by the rectum?

To establish her case that men in the United States and Western Europe (as opposed, say, to Afghanistan) are engaged in an unprecedented assault on womanhood, Greer defines all manner of medical interventions as attempts by "male-dominated governments" or the "patriarchal medical establishment" to subdue unruly females. "Women," she writes, "are the stomping ground of medical technology, routinely monitored, screened and tortured to no purpose except the enactment of control." (Notice the easy slide from "screening" to "torture.") Contraception is bad because it allows men to keep penetrating women, exposing them to "male hyper-fertility." If we are not actively involved in conceiving a child, we ought to be celibate or to have sex without intercourse, thus avoiding the "wastage of so many embryos." Our wombs, in other words, should determine the way we have sex. Again and again, anatomy is destiny. The only explanation that Greer can offer for the persistent popularity of intercourse (this is a mystery?) is its "symbolic nature, as an act of domination." Pity the woman who experiences sex symbolically.

There is more. Screening for cervical cancer is bad because cervical cancer is not all that common, and also because the pap smear is not a fool-proof test: it returns a lot of false positives and women worry when they have to go back to their doctors for a second time. Or as Greer puts it, "the result is an epidemic of terror." Why this should be regarded as a misogynist assault on the womb, as opposed to a medical procedure open to improvement, is left unsaid. Even a seemingly neutral medical instrument such as the speculum is an instrument of oppression. In Greer's dire description, "it's usually cold, extremely hard-edged and hurts, even if it does not pinch the tissues of the vaginal introitus. What hurts physically can also hurt psychologically. . . ."

There is still more. Episiotomies—the minor incisions made to women's perineums during labor to avoid a tear—are bad, because they are terrifically painful and the pain can last for months or even years. (This is certainly not the experience of anyone I know, but maybe they are too intimidated by the patriarchy to speak of it.) Cesarean sections and hysterectomies are also bad—which is a more substantiated and fair enough charge; journalists have been reporting for years that the rates of both operations are going up, and for reasons that have as much to do with medical economics (fear of malpractice suits, for instance) as with good medical sense. But Greer depicts women who choose hysterectomies as victims of "a female predilection for self-mutilation," hopelessly out of touch with their essential wombitude. Women who want the operation because they have been truly uncomfortable or inconvenienced and want no more children will find this sort of uterine fetish patronizing in the extreme, and who can blame them? Greer is a hysteric about hysterectomies.

I do not mean to say that medicine is blameless, or free of biases, or undeserving of criticism. Indeed, feminists have long been among the most intelligent critics of the practices with which doctors have sometimes infantilized women. In this way feminists have helped to win welcome reforms, such as the establishment of alternative birthing centers in hospitals and the opening up of delivery rooms to fathers, and they have encouraged more women to become doctors. In 1998, 43 percent of entering medical school students in the U.S. were female, a fact that seems to undercut the idea of medicine as an unrelenting masculine citadel.

But Greer plays fast and loose with facts. She claims that "there is no pressure group within the medical profession lobbying for the right to save men's lives by regularly examining their prostate." This is wrong. Prostate cancer, like breast cancer before it, has become one of America's trendy diseases. And Greer's comparison rests on an odd notion of fair treatment. "Men have the right to take care of themselves, or not, as they see fit," she writes, "but women are to be taken care of, whether they like it or not." So men have the right to die young, but women do not? (Some patriarchy.) Nowhere is there any sense that in many parts of the world advances in medicine have helped eradicate one of the most oppressive fates imaginable for a woman: dying in pain and in fear, giving birth to a child whose conception was not her choice.

Greer exaggerates the coercive power of the medical profession. Nobody is obliged to get a pap smear. I doubt that any women in the United States or England are "pressured" by "the health establishment" and "the state" to have abortions. They are certainly not "required" to undergo "investigations of their pregnancies for which there is no treatment but termination." If a pregnant woman has "the tests, say for Down's syndrome," Greer claims, "and refuses the termination she will be asked why she had the test in the first place. And she will probably be talked into the termination." This is nonsense. For one thing, some doctors in England and America will now do surgery in utero for conditions such as spina bifida that have been diagnosed in a fetus. Moreover, some people would prefer to know in advance whether the baby that they are carrying has a birth defect, even if they would not have an abortion. And far from pressuring women to have an amniocentesis or to terminate a pregnancy on the basis of it, most doctors are reluctant to issue a direct recommendation of any kind on the subject, if only because they do not want to be held responsible for a decision that a woman may regret.

It is true that the availability of new medical tests makes it likelier that they will be used and even overused, and that they will encourage unreasonable or unethical expectations of our own perfectibility. Technology always creates its own imperatives. It is also true, as Greer says, that the aggressive expansion of the fertility industry means that many women will undergo expensive, protracted, and even painful fertility regimens that are ultimately disappointing—and that some of those women would have been happier had they never been given the option. And it is also true that we now have tests that diagnose diseases (in both sexes, I might add) for which there is no cure and no clear course of action, such as tests that detect the gene for Huntington's disease.

These are all fair and important points. So why does Greer caricature them? Her intensity is hardly an excuse for her demagoguery. Does fertility treatment really "cause far more suffering than it does joy?" Not if you are one of the many thousands of patients each year who end up with a healthy baby. And Greer's indictment of the medical profession is suffused with an offensive condescension toward women themselves. In her account, women who opt for hysterectomies for whatever medical reason are deluded self-mutilators who are allowing themselves to be "spayed." Women who have abortions have submitted themselves to "the gynecological abattoir." Infertile women who want a child ought to be purged of the notion through hypnosis. And women in general, she avers, "are driven through the health system like sheep through a dip." Like sheep? Through a dip?

IV.

In a way, Greer's deprecation of women's minds, her denial of the capacity of women for intelligent choice and personal agency, is not so surprising. The logic of Men-Are-Dogs-ism demands, after all, that women be earth angels, and earth angels can easily be mistaken for ninnies. The womanly qualities that they display must always be qualities of the heart, not the head. And they must always be self-sacrificing. "Love of the father, love of the partner, love of the child, all remain for the vast majority of women, unrequited," Greer writes. "A woman's beloveds are the centre of her life; she must agree to remain far from the centre of theirs." This is the Tammy Wynette view of the world. It is certainly not a mature or nuanced picture of the twists and the turns of real love between real people. (In real marriages, even in good and lasting marriages, wives sometimes hate husbands and husbands sometimes hate wives.) Nor does Greer's line of thought comport particularly well with the fact that it is women who initiate more divorces, and who report greater levels of happiness afterwards.

"Women love all kinds of things, places, animals and people." We are to infer that men love no kinds of things, places, animals, and people. "They can love animals with such tenderness that they will die for them, whether in a burning home clasping an old cat or under the wheels of a lorry loaded with live calves for export. They love undaunted by ill-treatment, abandonment or death, returning good for evil. They do not kill the things they love but cherish them, feed them, nurture them, remaining more interested in them than they are in themselves. They do not come to love the objects of their love by fucking them." And so on and bathetically on.

It is not enough to point out that women commit many fewer homicides and other violent crimes than men do, which is manifestly true. Greer must also explain away the behavior of women who do commit such crimes, arguing that their brutality toward others is only "an outgrowth of self-destructive behavior." (This was the point sometimes made about Susan Smith, who was going to kill herself along with her two little boys but decided against it.) Aren't many male criminals also self-destructive? Don't men commit suicide—literally self-destruct—at a much higher rate than women do? Well, yes and yes, but never mind. We left the real world long ago.

Greer is not content to rehearse the familiar argument that women often feel pressured by advertising to buy useless beauty products and to fret about the adequacy of their appearances. She must also refuse to acknowledge that clothes and make-up can ever be a source of pleasure or creativity for women, to contend dolefully that "preoccupation about her appearance goes some way towards ruining some part of every woman's day." Even having our teeth fixed is a coerced concession to false gender consciousness that starts us down the slippery slope to plastic womanhood.

Sometimes Greer must flatly deny that women do certain things that, in fact and to no great shame, they do. "I suspect that even if fertility clinics offer significant sums for oocytes women will not respond, not simply because being farmed of oocytes is painful and dangerous but because women do not regard their seminal material as light-heartedly as men do, and have no ambition to spread their genes through the ecosphere." But many women appear to harbor precisely such an ambition: egg donation is one of the fastest growing sectors of the fertility business. When a wealthy couple recently offered $50,000 for an egg from an Ivy League-educated woman, two hundred women responded within a day. When I interviewed the "egg donor administrator" at a fertility clinic in L.A. a year or so ago, she claimed that many women who give eggs are motivated in part by the desire to spread what they regard as their superior genetic goods.

Liberal feminists and egalitarians of both sexes have usually made it a premise of their thinking that none of us can know precisely the essence of womanhood in the absence of social conditions. "What is now called the nature of woman," John Stuart Mill observed, "is an eminently artificial thing—the result of forced repression in some directions, unnatural stimulation in others." American women in 1999 are no longer such constricted houseplants, clipped to bend in one direction and unable to grow in another direction, but neither do they exist in a sexless utopian zone. Surely humility on the subject of what constitutes a whole, a real, an essential woman is in order.

But not for Greer. She is quite sure of what a real woman is. The secrets are in her possession. "Real" women are women who live in sexually segregated societies. Chinese women were real before Western marketing distorted them. The post-menopausal woman is authentic, too, because menopause "burns off the impurities," which is a strange way of referring to the capacity to bear children. But the "whole woman" is also, confusingly, a woman who is acutely aware of her uterus at all times—to the point of embracing the old canard about the wandering womb as the cause of hysteria and the barrier to women's intellectual achievement.

The whole woman is certainly not a woman who seeks to compete with men, to enter professions in which men have previously dominated. For she can have no hope of changing such male enclaves, and the men lying in wait for her there will humiliate her. Still less is she the woman who buys convenience food, wears make-up or otherwise enters with any enthusiasm into the capitalist marketplace. Greer's "whole woman" is just a sentimentalization of the natural woman. Her quarrel is finally with civilization.

This leads her to some very dotty ideas. On the harmless side, there is Greer's nostalgia for chicken-plucking, chip-frying, and the like, and her confident assertions that laundry was easier before the washing machine (you only did the washing one day a week, though a whole day a week), and that women were appreciated and respected more when they had to do all the cooking and therefore exerted a kind of authority as food providers. "That female role has now disappeared. It could only last as long as there was not a shop on the corner selling things more delicious than mother could ever make." It was just a matter of time, I suppose, before the shop on the corner metamorphosed into advanced monopoly capitalism.

But not all of Greer's nostalgia is quite so harmless. Her glorification of preliterate societies, and of female illiteracy in general, is very disturbing. "The preliterate woman lived within a self-validating female culture that was to be obliterated by the authority of the printed text. It is not until women learn to read that they internalize the masculine schema. When women become literate they are brought up sharply against the prevailing misogynies. They will only accept them if they are in the process of swallowing the masculinist cultural package of which they are a part." Oh sister, go and read A Room of One's Own, with its desperate yearning for the wide vistas of the word. Read The Mill on the Floss, with its unforgettable picture of what it is like to be a girl whose mind has always been called "quick" but who will never be permitted to set that mind to a task worthy of it. Read only the epigraph to Sex and Society by Martha Nussbaum, in which a Bangladeshi woman named Rohima explains how learning to read transformed her life:

> If there had been no change, then how could I have learned and understood all this? . . . Mother asked: 'What do you see in the books?' I said, 'Ma, what valuable things there are in the books you will not understand because you cannot read and write.' If somebody behaves badly with me, I go home and sit with the books. When I sit with the books, my mind becomes better.

It is astoundingly naïve to think that illiterate women have no way of being "brought up sharply against the prevailing misogynies." In societies in which women are veiled, kept in purdah, stoned for adultery, infibulated, chronically underfed, burned for their dowries, or cursed when they bear girl-children, they know a thing or two about misogyny. I would venture to say that women also knew a thing or two about misogyny in early Europe, where they were persecuted and tried as witches and generally thought more susceptible to deviltry, where their suffering in childbirth was complacently regarded as the price they had to pay for Eve's apple.

Yet Greer's idealization of miserable women—which is to say, her denial of their misery—is worse than naïve. It is cruel. Consider her defense of female genital mutilation—the ritual, practiced in a number of African countries, whereby young girls are subjected to the forcible amputation of their clitorises (and in some cases of the inner lips of their vaginas as well). These disfigurements have devastating results, which range from life-threatening hemorrhages and infections in the immediate aftermath of the operation to chronic infection and infertility later. Genital mutilation also makes it unlikely that a woman will ever be able to experience sexual pleasure. That is the point of the ghastly procedure. It is designed to make women more tractable.

Greer contends that the "criminalization of FGM can be seen to be what African nationalists since Jomo Kenyatta have been calling it, an attack on cultural identity." But this coarse outburst of multicultural romanticism assumes that cultures are monoliths, and that the only objection to FGM comes from outside African societies—from the World Health Organization or from pampered Western feminists. In fact, there are passionate critics of genital mutilation in all of the countries in which it is practiced; and they have been sufficiently influential to have gotten it officially outlawed in some of those countries. Moreover, there is no reason to consider African opponents of FGM—such as the valiant young women who have sought asylum in Europe and the United States to avoid being cut—any less authentically African than those who uphold it. And even if you could establish a reliable scale of authenticity, the moral value of protecting human beings from forcible mutilation must take precedence over the preservation of cultural customs. Mustn't it?

Ever eager to denounce the West, Greer asks how we can possibly condemn FGM when we countenance plastic surgery, genital piercing, and the circumcision of male infants. "If an Ohio punk has the right to have her genitalia operated on, why has not the Somali woman the same right?" A right to FGM! But circumcision is not comparable to clitoridectomy; the comparable operation for a male would be the removal of most of the penis. Unlike FGM, circumcision is generally regarded as medically neutral or mildly beneficial. And unlike FGM, it is not practised in the absence of adequate sanitation or anesthesia. Plastic surgery in the West is not forced on very young girls. (Greer insists on referring to "women" who undergo FGM, when it is usually children between the ages of five and twelve, who have no choice in the matter.) And even if you want to argue that women who

choose plastic surgery are constrained to choose it by the "beauty myth," a reasonable person would still recognize that being pinned down, screaming, by four adults with a knife is not quite the same as reading a copy of *Vogue*.

Nor is Greer satisfied with her cultural relativism. She insists also upon a positive good for FGM, even if it flies in the face of her own pronouncements on women in the West. "Certainly in many of these cultures tightness in the vagina is prized by both men and women . . . penetrating a tight, dry vagina causes pain but pain can be indistinguishable from pleasure in a state of high arousal." I see. Only Western women ought to be renouncing intercourse. Only Western medical practitioners are to be reviled if they suggest that an episiotomy can help to restore vaginal muscle tone. FGM cannot be bad for women, Greer contends, because women are the ones who perform it. But you don't have to be a man to mistreat a woman.

The problem with Germaine Greer is not only that she is no friend to men. It is also that she is no friend to women. What friend of women could have written this apology for their forced mutilation? What friend of women could have written most of this ugly and loveless book? When we are "brought up sharply against the prevailing misogynies" of our own time and place, we will have to number this famous feminist's misogyny among them.

Susie Linfield (review date 3 June 1999)

SOURCE: "Compelling, If Sloppy, Feminist Manifesto," in *The Los Angeles Times*, June 3, 1999, p. E3.

[*In the following review, Linfield offers tempered assessment of* The Whole Woman.]

Germaine Greer may be a lunatic. But after years of cautious, tepid yuppie-feminism—of being told that women do, or at least can, have it all, and that "it" is well worth having—a lunatic may be just what we need. Many of Greer's more bizarre opinions will probably bewilder, if not appall, large groups of readers. (While she considers mammogram programs sadistic, she supports female genital mutilation.). Yet though too much of **The Whole Woman**—Greer's follow-up to her 1970 manifesto **The Female Eunuch**—is sloppily argued, badly sourced and easy to mock, it is, in its essentials, right on.

First, a rightfully angry Greer argues, feminism is international and egalitarian, or it is nothing; the prosperity of a few select women in developed countries cannot rest on the poverty of others.

"A 'new feminism' that celebrates the right (i.e. duty) to be pretty in . . . little suits put together for starvation wages by adolescent girls in Asian sweatshops is not feminism at all," Greer writes. "Lifestyle feminism has been a sideshow. The main event, the worldwide feminization of poverty, is a tragedy that is moving inexorably and unseen to an unimaginably terrible denouement."

Second, Greer argues, feminism must be pro-mother and pro-child. But Greer severs the welfare of mothers and children from that of the nuclear family, an institution that in her view is clearly failing. All children must be guaranteed a decent standard of living *regardless* of whether they live with one or two (or no) parents, and regardless of the economic situation of those parents. Governments and their constituents must make an unbreakable commitment—not just ideological, but financial too—to every child's education, health and safety.

Third, Greer insists that feminism always assumed a radical critique, and radical transformation, of the repressed, inegalitarian, violent, compartmentalized world that men have created.

"If we accept that men are not free, and that masculinity is as partial an account of maleness as femininity is of femaleness, then equality must be seen to be a poor substitute for liberation. . . . If women can see no future beyond joining the masculinist elite on its own terms, our civilization will become more destructive than ever."

Greer reminds us of several other things that are usually ignored in popular-press discussions of feminism. It is true that more and more women have paid jobs, but it is to "the deconstructed work force of the '90s"—characterized by low-paid, part-time jobs with zero security—that women have been so warmly welcomed. And all over the world it is women who perform the bulk of unseen, unappreciated, unpaid work—from shopping to raising children—upon which every culture depends. "Women are worker bees; males are drones," Greer writes. "Yet somehow the human male has convinced the human female that he, not she, is the worker. His work is real work; her work is vicarious leisure."

As the above quote suggests, Greer does not feel particularly cuddly toward men. But in response to charges of man-hating she points out that it is woman-hating—sexism, patriarchy, call it what you will—that's the real problem and, furthermore, that this problem is systemic. Individual women may hate individual men, but nowhere in the world do women as a group physically or sexually terrorize men; nowhere in the world do women control wealth and deprive men of it; nowhere in the world do women deny men economic, reproductive or legal rights.

Greer's outlook is neither pessimistic nor triumphal; *The Whole Woman* seeks not to depress women (a clearly redundant task) but to alert them to how and why things are still so bad.

"On every side we see women troubled, exhausted . . . lonely, guilty, mocked by the headlined success of the few," she writes. "Every day we are told that there is nothing left to fight for. We have come a long way, but the way has got steeper, rockier, more dangerous, and we have taken many casualties."

Jennifer Frey (essay date 12 June 1999)

SOURCE: "Germaine Greer's Trouble With Men," in *The Washington Post,* June 12, 1999, pp. C1, C5.

[*In the following essay, Frey discusses Greer's views on men, the Clinton-Lewinsky scandal, children, and relationships.*]

Germaine Greer is in a bit of a fuss over a man. Not *men* as a universal group, although she has quite a few issues with them, too. Greer is plenty clear in her new book, *The Whole Woman,* what she thinks about men. "To be male," she writes, "is to be a kind of idiot savant." Men are "freaks of nature." They are slothful. They are spongers. They are mean.

But this fuss isn't about *men,* it's about A Man. The Man. The man she gave—*oh dear, how embarrassing*—a tape of her voice so he wouldn't miss her too much during her current American book tour. She's desperate to get that tape back now that she's dumped him. That's right, she "blew him out," to use her exact words. She had to, after all. He had her in "a tumult."

How can she work if she's worrying about when he's going to call her, if he's going to call her, what he's going to say when he calls her, what she's going to say back? Impossible! She can't be wandering around the world giving lectures about the failures of feminism, or the evils of the male-run medical system, or men's tendency to be hateful to women, while wondering why all she gets is that vile recording when she calls his cell phone.

"He was deliberately keeping me on short rations," Greer confides over lunch at the Four Seasons Hotel. "It's a power play. Always a power play. So in the end I just thought, 'I can't be doing this.' I have too much work to do, it's making me crazy, and of course I began to be worried about the motivations."

"So I blew him out. Stopped. Gone."

For good?

"Oh," she says, in a long exhale, "I shouldn't be so lucky. It's not over. There's a bit of shouting to go on, I think. Shouting is left." Greer sighs. "It's one of the hardest things I've ever done."

Greer is 60 now, and still furious at the world. "It's time to get angry again" is the anthem of her new book—a book she swore, years ago, that she'd never write. But a lot has changed in the 28 years since she became a feminist icon with the publication of *The Female Eunuch,* a smart, witty book that brought a fresh analysis of the modern female condition. A lot has changed and, in Greer's opinion, not enough has changed. Not nearly enough.

"Even if it had been real, equality would have been a poor substitute for liberation," Greer writes in the introduction to **The Whole Woman**. The book is not **The Female Eunuch**—not as sharp, and not likely to have anything approaching the first's impact. She makes some astute points and, as reviewers have noted, she also makes some outrageous points: She compares an episiotomy to female genital mutilation in Third World nations. She declares *Roe v. Wade* to be a tool of a greedy male medical system eager to make money off women's suffering. She suggests that excessive ultrasound tests during pregnancy cause dyslexia in children.

In other words, she's still Germaine: fascinating, opinionated and more than a little outlandish.

CLINTON'S COME-ON

[O]urs is a culture in which elevated testosterone levels are sought, prized and rewarded, no matter how destructive the consequences. Consider the vogue of road rage.

—From the chapter titled "Testosterone" in **The Whole Woman**

Greer is contemplating Mike Tyson. Tyson and his history of rape and violence and, most recently, road rage. Tyson, who appeared recently on the cover of Esquire kissing his young son during a prison visit. It was the Father's Day issue. Greer finds this a bit hypocritical. Which brings her, quickly, to the Clintons.

"It's a bit like Hillary and Bill groping each other for the cameras, which I find disgusting," she says, cringing a bit to emphasize her distaste. "The meaty hands on the shoulder. The holding hands getting out of the plane. Ah, you want to drop him, don't you? You want to drop them both."

Greer had a somewhat infamous run-in with President Clinton years and years ago, when he was studying at Oxford and she was lecturing there. In her oft-told and reported recollection, she was talking about how men marry women of a lower class, for comfort, while women try to marry up—to marry their rivals. What women really need, Greer explained, was to marry for comfort as well. That's when Clinton stood up and said, as Greer recalls it, "Would a middle-class boy from Arkansas be in with a chance?" She was floored.

"I couldn't believe," she says now, "he was coming on to me in front of *500 people*."

Greer is amused by Clinton and the whole Monica Lewinsky thing. She watched Jon Snow interview Lewinsky on British television and was fixated on the way that Snow, in her opinion, stared at Lewinsky's mouth throughout the interview.

But Lewinsky bores Greer. To tears. "Monica has nothing to say except 'poor me,' and as far as I'm concerned, yes, poor her, I agree," she says. "She was abused, but she did most of it to herself like we usually do. She told herself it was not squalid and not impersonal and that it was something that it wasn't."

She saves her venom for Hillary.

"I never liked Hillary," she confides, leaning in as if this is some kind of confession. Then she sits back and smiles.

"The nicest thing about Hillary," she continues, "is her [rear end]. Because it's big and fat and close to the ground, and there's [nothing] she can do about it."

No one ever accused Greer of being tactful.

HER SOFT SIDE

It may be that persecution of mothers is a permanent feature of patriarchal societies, but at the end of the millennium contempt for the mother seems to have assumed a new dimension.

—From the chapter "Mothers"

Greer is enraptured. There is a baby in the restaurant, a tiny little girl, 2 months old at most, wearing a frilly white dress and a matching headband dotted with pink rosebuds.

"A baby," she says, almost breathily. "All that cuddling."

Greer wanted a child. She attempted fertility treatments without success, and she angrily attacks reproductive technology in general in **The Whole Woman**. On the subject of babies, though, she melts.

"Babies can handle all the love you can give them," she says. "That's what is so great about them. They let you love them. They put no obstacles in your way. When they do those things that they do, like when they rub their hands up and down your ribs, or they put their hands on your face, ah, it's heaven. Just heaven."

This is her soft side, a side sometimes lost in her humor, intelligence—and anger. She adores her dogs. She adores her filly. "I don't care how she races—and this is a very womanly thing—I just want my horse to be happy."

Greer is also a godmother. In fact, she has 13 godchildren, by her latest count, and several other children she considers "good friends." Like Matthew and Oliver, two 12-year-olds who drove her nuts over a recent game of pool. They told her what to do, how to play. She rolls her eyes.

"I potted three balls on one break, and they still didn't think I knew how to play pool," she says. "It's because they're boys. Boys think they have a right to criticize anything females do." She says this with affection, but underneath she is completely serious.

LOVE IS HELL

From the beginning feminists have been aware that the causes of female suffering can be grouped under the heading "contradictory expectations." The contradictions women face have never been more bruising than they are now.

—From the chapter "Recantation"

Greer is her own bundle of contradictions. She has been widely quoted as saying that lipstick rots women's brains, yet she wears makeup. In her book *The Change: Women, Aging and Menopause,* she longs for a time when older women can let their bodies settle into their natural shapes, yet she admits going on a diet for this book tour. And she pulls at her Issey Miyake blouse to demonstrate how it will "hide anything."

She complains about men ruling women's lives, then she agonizes over her soon-to-be ex-boyfriend (whom she declined to name) and how his failure to phone affects her day-to-day existence.

And she refuses to call him. Outright refuses. Well, she called twice. That was it.

"He wanted me to ring him," she says. "It was that simple."

And now, it's over—maybe, probably—and she's doing that typical girl thing. She's pining. Missing him. Missing it. Telling herself she'll never find another man.

"I'm 60 years old, girl," she says. "The miracle was that this man responded."

She says she's taking "precautions" so that she won't let it happen again.

"It's been hell," she explains, sounding for all the world like a teenager jilted by her first lover. "Five minutes of bliss for 50 hours of hell. Isn't that what love is? Oh, damn! I can't stand it anymore."

She left him because that's how she keeps her sense of power and control. It's also how she makes her life fit her philosophy. Dating him was a feminist act. She made him better at being a man.

And booting him?

"If he regrets my sudden departure," she says, "let him regret. It will teach him a lesson, and some other woman may be the beneficiary someday."

Samuel McCracken (review date September 1999)

SOURCE: "Blast from the Past," in *Commentary,* Vol. 108, No. 2, September, 1999, pp. 65-6.

[*In the following review, McCracken offers a summary of Greer's "so-called" arguments in* The Whole Woman.]

Three decades ago, the English writer Germaine Greer erupted into the world with *The Female Eunuch,* a cleverly titled book whose core argument, as she recently summarized it, was that "every girl child is conceived as a whole woman but from the time of her birth to her death she is progressively disabled." As summary, that is accurate enough, but it fails to capture the qualities in the book that provoked such a remarkable mixture of admiration and outrage when it was published. The radical, erudite, witty Greer was then, as she is now, a *sui-generis* feminist—*mutatis mutandis,* a kind of Camille Paglia of the 70's.

Greer has been reasonably prolific over the past 30 years, but other authors have come along to shock while she has gradually acquired the patina of an object surviving more or less unaltered from a previous age. This clearly could not be allowed to continue. Although she explicitly forswore any sequel to her first book—on the grounds that, when the time came, a younger woman would have to write it—now, like a congressional supporter of term limits discovering the virtues of experience, she has decided that "it's time to get angry again." And so *The Whole Woman*—a title that invites confusion with Marabel Morgan's antithetical *The Total Woman* (Morgan advises doting on one's husband 24 hours a day)—picks up where *The Female Eunuch* left off.

The reason for Greer's current anger is, in a nutshell, that feminism has not worked out the way it was intended. Women have attained legal equality, but they have not attained liberation. Instead, men have been the primary beneficiaries of the sexual revolution. If this suggests a possible change of mind on Greer's part—perhaps feminism *misread* what women need, or want?—nothing could be farther from the case: "The old enemies, undefeated, have devised new strategies, new assailants lie in ambush," she writes, meaning, by enemies, men and the social arrangements they have invented. "We have no choice but to turn and fight."

There follows a series of tractates organized under the rubrics of Body, Mind, Love, and Power and adding up to a catalogue of how women have either failed to become better off or have actually become worse off since the 1960s. Wherever Greer looks, she finds evidence—whether it exists or not.

Sometimes the problem as she sees it is simply the continuation of an old evil, like women's male-imposed obsession with their own bodies, a/k/a "beauty." But sometimes the problem is the new rights that women have fought for and now *think* they enjoy, like the right to be soldiers, which turns out to be only the right to one long course of abuse by men (except, Greer is quick to add, in guerrilla armies, which provide women with the requisite political "education" to understand why armed struggle is necessary). And sometimes it is technology—that is, male technology.

In-vitro fertilization, for example, is a process leading to "man-made mothers." Mammography is particularly perverse, in Britain because it is free only to women over the age of fifty, elsewhere because it is painful, especially for younger women. Abortion, too, exemplifies the exploitation of woman by man; pregnancy, after all, occurs because of inadequate contraception, and what is that but a consequence of the male demand for, as Greer puts it, access to the cervix during intercourse?

The subject of bodily mutilation gets an entire chapter, one that finely illustrates Greer's attitude toward sex in general and toward her own, female sex in particular. There are, it emerges, two kinds of mutilation. The *bad* kind comprises caesarean sections, hysterectomies, and episiotomies: the good, believe it or not, includes genital piercing and the clitoridectomies widely performed on infants and young girls in Africa. Both, to Greer, are examples of women asserting control over their own bodies—female technology, in other words—whereas efforts to end clitoridectomy, whether led by men or by their female patsies, are simply one more subcategory of the male will to dominate.

And speaking of the will to dominate, what about shopping? First the male-run corporations show their enmity toward women by making available in supermarkets the raw foodstuffs historically provided by women themselves. Next comes the insult of processed and frozen foods. And now you can buy ready-to-serve meals prepared in in-store kitchens. The final infamy is that women still must do all the shopping themselves—this last being one of the myriad pristine assertions in **The Whole Woman** that appear never to have been sullied by simple empirical testing.

A fair amount of ink has been spilled by earnest reviewers taking issue with the arguments, so-called, of this book; the *New Republic* devoted almost 7,000 words to a solemn rebuttal. But what is there, really, to say? The *Encyclopaedia Britannica* wrote better than it knew in describing Germaine Greer in a recent edition as an "Australian-born English writer and feminist who championed the sexual freedom of women." Assuming the statement was ever true, the past tense says it all.

FURTHER READING

Criticism

Chisholm, Patricia. "Greer's Call to Arms." *Maclean's* (24 May 1999): 53.

> An unfavorable review of *The Whole Woman.*

Dinnage, Rosemary. "Happy Cronehood!" *Times Literary Supplement* (25 October 1991): 6.

> A positive review of *The Change.*

Pickering, Sam. "Back Roads to the Self." *Sewanee Review* XCVIII, No. 3 (Summer 1990): lxxxii-lxxxiii.

> A positive review of *Daddy, We Hardly Knew You.*

Robinson, Lillian S. "Consciousness Lowering." *Women's Review of Books* X, No. 4 (January 1993): 11-2.

> An unfavorable review of *The Change.*

Additional coverage of Greer's life and career is contained in the following sources published by the Gale Group: *Authors in the News,* **Vol. 1;** *Contemporary Authors,* **Vols. 81-84;** *Contemporary Authors New Revision Series,* **Vol. 33; and** *Major 20th-Century Writers.*

Elizabeth Jennings
1926-

(Full name Elizabeth Joan Jennings) British poet and essayist.

The following entry provides an overview of Jennings's career through 1998. For further information on her life and works, see *CLC*, Volumes 5 and 14.

INTRODUCTION

Jennings is a highly regarded British poet whose lengthy career has been typified by the steady publication of critically acclaimed poetry on such subjects as religion, mental illness, and childhood. She is best known for her membership in "The Movement," a group of poets and writers who achieved fame in the postwar period for their rejection of pretentiousness and decoration and their call for simplicity in literature. Jennings is known for her subtle, yet skillful, use of language and a strong interest in form that has sparked comparisons with Christina Rossetti, Edwin Muir and Robert Frost.

BIOGRAPHICAL INFORMATION

The daughter of a physician, Jennings was born in 1926 in Lincolnshire, England. She attended private Catholic school before transferring to and graduating from Oxford High School. As a teenager, she discovered a passion for classic poetry when she was introduced to G. K. Chesterton's poem "Lepanto." She began to compose her own verse, exhibiting traits that would remain with her throughout her career: simple language, an interest in form, and the use of rhyme and meter. She graduated from St. Anne's College, Oxford, in 1949 earning an M.A. with honors in English. While at university, Jennings achieved success as a writer, publishing in *Oxford Poetry* in 1948 and 1949, as well as meeting and befriending writers such as Kingsley Amis, Philip Larkin, and Thom Gunn. Nine of these writers formed "The Movement." Scholars have noted that Jennings differed from the rest of the writers as the only woman and devout Catholic. Nonetheless, Jennings writes that she felt a close compatability and common purpose among the members. After graduating, she worked for a short time in the advertising business, which she credits for tightening her writing. She served as a librarian at the Oxford City Library from 1950 to 1958 where she maintained close contact with Oxford students such as Donald Hall. In 1953, Fantasy Press published a small volume of her poems; it was the press's first poetry collection. She earned an Arts Council award for it,

increasing her critical attention and approval. Jennings's subsequent travels in Italy and her battle with mental illness, for which she was institutionalized several times in the 1960s, are prominent subjects in her poetry. During the last four decades she has published numerous collections of poetry, earned praise for her children's poetry and essays on poetics, and edited volumes of verse.

MAJOR WORKS

Critics note that there is a strong strain of continuity in Jennings's poetry, both in regard to form and subject matter. Jennings established her voice in her youth and has not deviated from it greatly throughout her career. In common with the other members of "The Movement," Jennings writes simply and directly without academic pretense or heavy adornment. In her early writing she employed set forms, regular meter, rhyme, and preferred iambic pattern. However, as her career progresses, she primarily uses free verse and unrhymed poetry. Most of her poems are written in a few short stanzas; rarely does her poetry exceed one page. She favors startling line breaks, gaining impact by beginning a line with a strong verb. Throughout her career, Jennings has written about personal subjects, although she is not an autobiographical poet. Much of her work is about religion, particularly Catholicism, and her struggles with faith. In *Recoveries: Poems* (1964) and *The Mind Has Mountains* (1966), she considers her own mental illness and institutionalization. In addition, she composed several books of children's poetry, such as her well received collection *Let's Have Some Poetry!* (1960.)

CRITICAL RECEPTION

From the beginning of her career at Oxford in the 1940s, Jennings has enjoyed critical approval. Looking for new and mature verse, Kingsley Amis included six of Jennings's poems in the 1949 edition of *Oxford Poetry*. In critiques of her early books, reviewers praise her lucid, simple language, citing her as a strong voice and a poet to watch. She received almost universal praise for her two collections of poetry *Collected Poems* (1967) and *Selected Poems* (1979), which provide an overview of her career. However, critics have found fault with Jennings too. Commenting on her collection *In the Meantime* (1996), Clive Wilmer remarks that "(s)he has been prolific without interruption, but the quality of her writing from book to book is strikingly uneven." Other reviewers state that at times her poetry is too coy, her language wooden and uninspiring, that she fails to make connections, and that her work lacks energy. The most common criticism is that Jennings fails to vary her work enough, that her poetry is too similar. However, scholars agree that much of Jennings's poetry is first rate. Samuel French Morse praises her lack of pretension, the freshness of her language, and the high quality of her devotional poetry in *Song for a Birth or a Death and Other Poems* (1961). Robert Sheppard argues that she is the least well-known, but the best in quality, of "The Movement" writers.

PRINCIPAL WORKS

Poems (poetry) 1953

A Way of Looking: Poems (poetry) 1955

A Sense of the World: Poems (poetry) 1958

Let's Have Some Poetry! (poetry) 1960

Every Changing Shape: Mystical Experience and the Making of Poems (essays) 1961

Song for a Birth or a Death and Other Poems (poetry) 1961

Recoveries: Poems (poetry) 1964

The Mind Has Mountains (poetry) 1966

Collected Poems, 1967 (poetry) 1967

The Animals' Arrival (poetry) 1969

Lucidities (poetry) 1970

Relationships (poetry) 1972

Growing-Points: New Poems (poetry) 1975

Consequently I Rejoice (poetry) 1977

Moments of Grace (poetry) 1979

Selected Poems (poetry) 1979

Winter Wind (poetry) 1979

A Dream of Spring (poetry) 1980

Italian Light and Other Poems (poetry) 1981

Celebrations and Elegies (poetry) 1982

Extending the Territory (poetry) 1985

In Shakespeare's Company: Poems (poetry) 1985

Collected Poems, 1935–85 (poetry) 1986

Tributes (poetry) 1989

Times and Seasons (poetry) 1992

Familiar Spirits (poetry) 1994

In the Meantime (poetry) 1996

A Poet's Choice (poetry) 1996

A Spell of Words: Selected Poems for Children (poetry) 1997

Praises (poetry) 1998

CRITICISM

Horace Gregory (review date Fall 1956)

SOURCE: "The Poetry of Suburbia," in *Partisan Review*, Vol. XXIII, No. 4, Fall, 1956, pp. 545-53.

[*In the following excerpt, Gregory praises Jennings for her unique and strong voice.*]

The recent *Zeitgeist* in American culture is of suburban colors, manners, dress. Those who are currently publishing verse are affected by its daily habits and ambitions, and more than a few have mistaken its presence for a visitation of the Muse. The importance of the suburban *Zeitgeist* may not be enduring, but since the end of the Korean War, its influence has spread cross-country from the suburbs of Boston to the state of Washington, far beyond the toll-gates of large cities; and it can be heard and seen as vividly on a college campus as in Westchester or nearby Long Island. It is nourished by the magazines I find in my dentist's office: *The New Yorker, Life*, and *Time*. It may seem strange that popular culture should invade, and so thoroughly and quickly, the landscapes of academic life; it may not (I am sure it does not) represent academic thinking at its centers, yet on the fringes of the campus it is very much alive, geared to the speed of a two-toned—strawberry-pink and gingham-blue—station wagon. It is well known that most of the verse published today is brought forth in the temporary shelter of universities. Suburban culture has spread its wings over all the activities that surround the campus, and verse written in this atmosphere cannot help reflecting the surfaces of everyday experience.

Another factor influencing the spirit of the verse written today was the belated "discovery" of Wallace Stevens. Of course, he had been "discovered" long ago; but in the postwar years it was not only the wit and inventiveness of Stevens' work, it was the *image* of his success, both as an executive of an insurance company and as a poet, that caught and held the admiration of young men and women who wrote verse. It was rumored that he was rich, very rich, rich enough to escape all minor economic misfortunes and turns of chance. In the United States there has never been any sustained disrespect for wealth; roughness and the "homespun" manner are often enjoyed, but always with the hope of finding "a rough diamond" or "a heart of gold." So far as the best of Stevens' verse revealed him, he was a pluralist and a skeptic; and certain external features of his legend had become attractive to emulate. The new *Zeitgeist* quickly absorbed whatever it understood of this legend; then it acquired an air of "difference" from the forty years that separated it from the first publication of *Harmonium*. It disregarded conscious bohemianism and "sexual freedom," as well as the Left Wing politics of the 1930's, and the "academic" irony fashionable in the 1940's that was best represented by the little magazine *Furioso*.

The conventions of the new *Zeitgeist* were being formed. The more "advanced" younger poets had become instructors and lecturers and behind academic facades embittered laurels were being watered and cultivated; old-fashioned excess (if any) and toasts drunk to the memory of F. Scott Fitzgerald were reserved for holidays, or discreetly converted into weekend faculty cocktail parties. These younger poets began to use the word "elegance" in praising each other's writings, and if twenty years ago it had become fashionable to be "proletarian" in spirit, in the early 1950's, it had become a virtue to say that one could not live on less than ten thousand a year, that if one did not have hidden sources of wealth, it was a disgrace to live at all. Stevens' "elegance" was of mind and temperament, yet it was one that seemed easy to imitate in terms of the more garish advertising pages of *Harper's Bazaar, Vogue* and *The New Yorker,* the kind of literature that for a brief, wholly deceptive moment makes the reader feel like a luxury product himself, ready to join the "International Set," to be severe with middle-aged, wealthy American patronesses in Rome, and to drink at Harry's Bar in Venice. The word "elegance," like so many transitory usages of language in the United States, has become the choice of copywriters to sell everything the suburban matron wears. One might suspect collusion between the poets of *Harper's Bazaar* and the shopkeepers of Westchester.

One effect of the suburban influence has been to revive a kind of writing that had been forgotten since 1914. What used to be called "magazine verse" forty years ago is back in print again, decorously written, and admirably fitted to fill empty spaces between fiction and feature articles. One might call it the *New Yorker* school of verse.

Though the offices of *The New Yorker* are in New York, its heart is in the suburbs. The magazine is certainly the handbook of the suburban matron throughout the country. *The New Yorker* publishes a quantity of light verse, which is nothing to be ashamed of; but light verse that lives beyond the moment is extremely rare. It is rare because poetic wit itself is a rarity; what often passes for it is something "cute," something coy, something pleasant, harmless, or naughty-bitter. It should be well-formed; and not—by the same poet—reiterated too frequently in the same phrases. The cutting edge too frequently wears dull. Large indiscriminate doses of it tend to cloy. These truisms are probably known in the offices of *The New Yorker* and regretted—therefore, it has fallen back on publishing quasi-serious verse as well, constructed according to current formulas: certain verse forms used with enough caution to be recognized at once, certain images within the verses that recall the "happy-bitter" experience of childhood, the joy of collecting toys and the discovery that toys are perishable, the country places visited at home, the holiday from suburban security in Europe. The great discomfort in reading too much *New Yorker* verse is that the formula continually wears thin; it is not as cheering as it hoped to be—or as light and witty as Sandy Wilson's parody of the 1920's in his musical *The Boy Friend.* Reading too much *New Yorker* verse becomes a bore.. . .

To be derivative is not a crime; no poet lives in a literary vacuum. The question is: How derivative can you be and yet show the reader you have something to say that is your own—your own language, your own look at the world, your own music? If these remains are worth publication, well and good.

An example of divorce from the *Zeitgeist* is Elizabeth Jennings' *A Way of Looking*, a book of forty well-selected

poems. (Miss Jennings, by the way, has contributed to *The New Yorker,* but is untouched by its formula.) Miss Jennings is English—and the curse of contemporary British verse is an imageless run of too many toneless words, in which, at their worst, these poems share. At her best, Miss Jennings knows her own mind; free of her instructors, her voice is heard in **"Mirrors"**:

> Was it a mirror then across a room,
> A crowded room of parties where the smoke
> Rose to the ceiling with the talk? The glass
> Stared back at me a half-familiar face
> Yet something hoped for. When at last you came
> It was as if the distant mirror spoke.
>
> The loving ended as all self-love ends
> And teaches us that only fair-grounds have
> The right to show us halls of mirrors where
> In every place we look we see our stare
> Taunting our own identities. But love
> Perceives without a mirror in his hand.

I think Miss Jennings has written a directly inspired poem that deserves respect and admiration from her contemporaries; she has set herself distinctly apart from other poets, and may, if all goes well, make her own world, the enduring "something new" that critics always hope to find, the place beyond the *Zeitgeist.*

John Heath-Stubbs (review date February 1959)

SOURCE: Review of *A Sense of the World,* in *Encounter,* Vol. XII, No. 2, February, 1959, p. 74.

[*In the review below, Heath-Stubbs argues that Jennings is not disciplined enough in her writing and produces work with a flat, muted tone.*]

Miss Jennings's work has received so much praise from those whose judgment one must respect, that one hesitates to dissent. One recognises the sensibility and the intelligence, but there is a curiously muted quality about her poetry. It is as if one was listening to someone murmuring to themselves in their sleep. Granted that this is, in Mr. Eliot's phrase, essentially poetry overheard rather than heard, yet one longs for her to wake up and speak out. Her technique does not seem to help. Her rhythms are generally flatly iambic, and blank verse or rather unambitious stanza forms predominate. This leads her, too often, into a weak, meandering syntax, which the discipline of either more adventurous, or stricter verse forms, or indeed of prose, might mitigate. Furthermore, it is time it was said that the scrupulous adherence to the prose order of the words (which has become almost *de rigueur* for poets today) can lead to results as awkward, if you're not careful, as the clumsy use of inversions. For if a pronoun is separated from its verb or an adjective or a preposition from its following substantive by the break at the end of the line, it requires some very special emphasis of meaning not to give the effect of a stutter. This is the kind of thing I mean:

> *Yet there was*
> *Such distance between words and what they*
>   *spoke*
> *About, the marvels would not stand but broke*
> *Away.*

It is curious to find Miss Jennings translating Claudel, of all people, and making quite a good job of it too. Her own exercise in a kind of Claudelian prose poetry at the end of the book, **"Teresa of Avila,"** is quite unlike any of her other poems, and seems to me much better. It suggests that her talent may one day take a new and fruitful turn, though perhaps this may be in the direction of prose rather than of (what then is the opposite?) verse or poetry.

Robin Skelton (review date Spring 1961)

SOURCE: Review of *Let's Have Some Poetry*, in *Critical Quarterly*, Vol. 3, No. 1, Spring, 1961, pp. 89-90.

[*In the following review, Skelton argues that Jennings's penchant for simplifying and her coy tone weaken an otherwise admirable work.*]

The annual P.E.N. *Anthology of New Poems* usually contrives to achieve a high level of competence without being in the least exciting, and the latest in the series is no exception to the rule. There are 64 poems by 51 contributors, and, if one ignores the presence of Edith Sitwell's ridiculous and pretentious *La Bella Bona Roba*, one could fairly say that every poem deserves its place. Nevertheless, doubts cross one's mind. Are there no young poets nowadays attempting to break new ground? Were none of the editors captivated by an eccentric poem, or tempted by an unfashionable one? It is good to see more work by such admirable and as yet uncollected poets as Graham Hough and Zofia Ilinska, but did 1960 produce no new good poems from George Barker, W. S. Graham, Norman MacCaig, Thomas Kinsella, or Robert Graves? This Anthology pretends (by its very title) to be some sort of survey of the poetic output of a year, but the 1960 volume, like all the others, leads one to suspect that the title should be changed to "Poems that Three People Could Agree About". It appears to be nothing more.

Thomas Blackburn's Anthology is not a survey either, in spite of the title. It is a "Programme Anthology", which is intended to illustrate certain attitudes of the editor. These attitudes, which are rather blunderingly and speciously expressed in the Introduction, are based upon the conviction that, "Poetry is concerned with the dark interior engines of the psyche". In this post-Freudian Age, once we have got used to "such terms as the Unconscious, the Super Ego, the Collective Unconscious, or the Id, these abstractions have to be restored to the turmoil of emotional experience they have been distilled from, and known by the whole being." In short, "poets are trying to give a local habitation and a name to the mysterious and savage fauna that are within us." Whether or not this is an accept-able thesis, the consequences of believing in it could be exciting, but the choice of poems is not always understandable in terms of the thesis they are supposed to illustrate. Auden's "The Shield of Achilles" fits, but "The Willow and the Stare" seems a little out of place. Larkin's shorter poems fit, but does "Churchgoing", admirable poem though it is? Moreover, thinking along the lines Mr. Blackburn indicates, one wonders at the absence of work by such explorers as Constantine Trypanis, Terence Tiller, and Norman MacCaig. One also wonders why many of the poems were thought suitable for inclusion, in particular the four quite dreadful poems by John Pudney, who would have served the book better if he had, as a Director of Putnams, devoted his time to seeing that the pages were larger, the print less cramped, and the whole production less sloppily set out.

If Mr. Blackburn deserves castigation for a sloppy job, Miss Jennings must be faulted for her cosiness. Her book (which is garnished with a peculiarly silly dust cover) is, in the main, a thoroughly admirable introduction to both the making and the reading of poetry, and should be in every school library. But it *is* at times far too cosy and simplified. An almost coy note appears in her voice when she discusses (very properly) some of her own experiences as a poet, and by the time one has reached the last chapter the vast simplifications have piled up so high as almost to disguise the fact that this is really a quite intelligent book. In the section on "Poetry in the Fifties", however, a more serious flaw appears: the list of poets awarded certificates of contemporaneity is fashionable rather than perceptive. The expected names turn up with mechanical efficiency—Amis, Wain, Davie, Larkin, Gunn, Enright. To these are added Muir, R. S. Thomas, Ted Hughes, Jon Silkin, David Wright, and Jonathan Price. One wonders why poets such as (again) MacCaig, W. S. Graham, Tiller, Fuller, Norman Nicholson, who are now at the height of their powers, and who, in sober fact, published all their best work during the fifties, never seem to get a mention in these surveys. One has many such moments of doubt in this book. (How, for example, dare Miss Jennings refer to the "Eighteenth century calm concern with generalities?" Can she have forgotten about those angry and passionate men?) Still, this is a worthy book, and some of those who listen to Aunt Elizabeth on the Children's Hour may well be tempted to stay tuned in for the sterner realities of The News.

Samuel French Morse (review date August 1963)

SOURCE: Review of *Song for a Birth or a Death*, in *Poetry*, Vol. CII, No. 5, August, 1963, pp. 330-34.

[*In the following excerpt, Morse praises the quality and content of Jennings's poetry, arguing that she is gaining authority in her work.*]

For the poets of the fifties and after, the veterans of the thirties as Donald Davie calls them, were concerned with "agonies" that have become "highbrow thrillers, though historical", and their feats are "quite strictly fabulous." "And yet," he adds, "it may be better, if we must,/ To find the stance impressive and absurd/Than not to see the hero for the dust." Davie's own poems do not disguise their admiration for some of the heroes of the thirties, and they may be the better for it. But the young poets whose books are at hand belong not only to another age but to a different world. Elizabeth Jennings, it is true, reminds one here and there of Anne Ridler; and Norman MacCaig has an eye as sensitive to the colors of the commonplace as Louis MacNeice's. The tones, however, are very different, as they should be. The somewhat detached intimacy of Miss Jennings is delicately contrived. She publishes nothing that is clumsy or embarrassing, and *Song for a Birth or a Death* immediately attracts one because of its lack of obvious pretense. Her devotional poems, such as the **"Notes for a Book of Hours, A Confession"**, and **"The Resurrection"**, are as moving for their workmanship as they are for their substance. The sequence of six poems called **"The Clown"** shows what she can do with a conventional symbol simply by recognizing that what is conventional can be useful. Miss Jennings's new book also allows one to take a tentative measure of her accomplishment as one of the most highly praised writers of the past decade. The freshness apparent in *A Way of Looking*, which showed signs of becoming a mannerism in *A Sense of the World*, has begun to deepen into poetry of quiet authority.

Alasdair Clayre (review date November 1967)

SOURCE: Review of *The Mind Has Mountains*, in *Encounter*, Vol. XXIX, No. 5, November, 1967, p. 76.

[*In the review below, Clayre argues that these experimental poems do not reflect Jennings's skill or her voice.*]

Miss Elizabeth Jennings, in *The Mind has Mountains*, takes the reader through an English mental hospital, after her attempted suicide. These poems keep close to a single consciousness, which we see re-establishing, in alien territory, the unassuming, observant kindness of its everyday life. The poems are compassionate. In certain lines we can hear Miss Jennings' voice:

> *There should be peace for gentle ones, not pain*

But the versification in this volume is often limp, and produces shapeless effects which I do not think the author can want:

> *Because of all of this, it was a shock*
> *to find that you*
> *were really bad, depressed, withdrawn from me*
> *more than I knew.*

And her experiments in broken verse-forms at the end of the book do not seem to be exactly in her own voice—a voice that in visionary poems like **"A Dream of Birth"**

has spoken with complete assurance, in a technique that seems to have grown out of a given rhythm of feeling, rather than out of the conscious decision to write in lines of ten syllables or of irregular patterns.

Also about madness, but from a very different point of view, is *Mishaps Perhaps*, a book of prose and verse-fragments by Carl Solomon. In the 'fifties Allen Ginsberg dedicated *Howl* to him. At the age of twenty-one, he went into a mental hospital and asked voluntarily for a lobotomy. By travelling without the suitcases of dignity, he has moved through territories not often mapped in this way—worlds of mental hospital jargon, bureaucratic language, and post-beat prose—maintaining always the gentle and ironic speech-rhythms that form the continuity of his work. Here he sees himself being interrogated by a "sane" society:

> *Do you love your mother? Your finger-nails show dirt. Your breath is bad. Do you like girls?*

> *And I have lost my credentials. I liked a girl but she left me for another man. Was she of good character? I thought so in the beginning.*

From hospital, he does not write as a patient waiting for cure, but as a stylist and chronic victim rejecting, in the name of the homosexual world and of his own lucidity, the psychiatrists who give him shock treatment:

> *I couldn't understand what they (who drove me into madhouses twice) thought. I have never yet seen an attractive psychiatrist.*

And of the way of life that the world seems to require of him (**"Relationships"**):

> I am utterly unconcerned with the necessity
> for producing offspring
> And have no need for happiness which is the
> primary obsession of our day.
> Are you happy?
> Being of Jewish descent and
> consequently
> Unhappy of visage
> I have no need for such contentments
> As produce the gleaming smile
> And the sonorous voice.

Michael Mott (review date May 1971)

SOURCE: Review of *The Animals' Arrival*, in *Poetry*, Vol. CXVIII, No. 2, May, 1971, pp. 110-11.

[*In the following review, Mott contends that Jennings exhibits power and bravery in her work.*]

Elizabeth Jennings has been accused at times of quietness, if not tameness, but it would be grossly unfair to accuse the poet of *The Animals' Arrival* of any such thing. Like Abse's recent poems, if these are not shrill, they are bravely concerned with harrowing experience and a still more harrowing vision of it:

> My inward needs and fears still stir and grow
> Into a hideous and nightmare form.
>
> **"Hospital Garden"**

Seeing disorder within and without, Elizabeth Jennings seeks courageously for order. In such poems as **"A Pattern"**, she achieves it at least in the high standard of her own art. But where order is not to be had outside her poetry she admits it. A child can respond to sickness in a simple way; she cannot, projecting one illness far beyond the dimensions it would have for the child:

> Illness for me has no true absolute
> Since so much of my daily action is
> Dressed up in pain. Why am I lying here,
> Voice gone, lips dry, chest fiery, mind quite wild
> Begging the past back, longing to be a child?
>
> **"A Simple Sickness"**

There is a restrained power here, but our responses are diminished indeed if we cannot recognize it as power.

John Lucas (review date 15 November 1985)

SOURCE: Review of *Extending the Territory*, in *New Statesman*, Vol. 110, No. 2851, November 15, 1985, p. 28.

[*In the review below, Lucas finds fault with* Extending the Territory, *arguing that the poetry is vapid, the language unvaried, and the subject matter uninteresting.*]

With Elizabeth Jennings's **Extending the Territory** we are, I fear, back with the kinds of experiences which ask to be taken on trust. 'But six years of my childhood are precise', she says in **'An Absolute'**, and goes on: 'I see the berries // On bushes as imperial as music, / Poised as poetry'. She may be able to, but I'm damned if I can. Nor can I summon up much interest in **'The Circuses'** where downs are said to be 'energetic' and horses 'sprightly'. And the 'untarnished marvel' of **'A Sky in Childhood'** doesn't do a great deal for me, either.

When she gets beyond the world of children ('before time takes their lands / And lowers the sun'—now where have heard that before?) matters improve, but not to any great extent. Even the pain of **'Anger'** and **'Certain Lesson'** and **'A Death Alive'** drains away through the smooth, unvarying grid of language, stanza and metric norm. 'Will all that glowing joy, those long / Excited conversations be the past?' It seems unfair that so much raw, wounding experience should turn into verse of such vapidity, but then you feel, 'Well, but surely if she cares as much as she says she does she could have found *some* way of getting it across?'

J. D. Brophy (review date December 1986)

SOURCE: Review of *Collected Poems, 1953-1985*, in *Choice*, December, 1986, p. 625.

[*In the following review, Brophy outlines Jennings's importance as a poet.*]

Jennings is an original member of the British literary movement disarmingly called "The Movement," which appeared in the early 1950s in part as reaction to what its founders thought were the excesses of Dylan Thomas and his romantic ilk. Philip Larkin was the best known group member; to readers in the US, Jennings was and remains the least familiar member. This collection is not a "Complete Poems," but a selection by the poet of all the work she wishes to preserve from her 17 books that have appeared between 1953 and 1985. An earlier *Collected Poems* was published in 1967. Since her best work is considered to be her earlier poems—the British critic Anthony Thwaite speaks of the "thinning away" of her later work—some libraries that already own a selection of her previous books may not wish to order this one. But no academic library should be without some of her lucid, dignified poetry, and this present collection would be an excellent choice for libraries that have too little or none of her work.

Sandra M. Gilbert (review date May 1987)

SOURCE: Review of *Collected Poems*, in *Poetry*, Vol. CL, No. 2, May, 1987, pp. 106-09.

[*In the review below, Gilbert argues that while Jennings's culture is foreign to Americans, her work is of great merit and importance.*]

Though she not only thinks about the significance of history but, as one of Britain's more important recent poets, she *has* a significant personal and literary history, Elizabeth Jennings hardly seems to inhabit the same language, much less the same world, as the one in which Caroline Finkelstein and Lynda Hull dwell. Indeed, the Atlantic that divides the lives and works of these writers seems not only miles but centuries wide, a gulf in time as well as a gap in space. Beautifully—even, as I shall suggest, *too* "beautifully"—articulated, conceived in a mode of high formalism, Jennings's poems appear at first to be artifacts of a culture so distanced from the varieties of American minimalism that it is difficult to imagine her as our contemporary. And, drawing on powerful monuments of unaging intellect, deploying Yeatsian lines and metaphysical references, citing Traherne, elegizing Auden, and translating Michelangelo, Jennings herself seems like a sort of theatrical relic, an exemplar of what history means as well as an interpreter of its meanings.

Nevertheless, history is not just what Jennings incarnates; it is also her theme: personal history, literary history, Christian history. Her collection opens with a preface in which she declares that "Art is not self-expression while, for me, 'confessional poetry' is almost a contradiction in terms." Yet many of her works use the strategies of what we have lately called the "confessional" in order, as the Catholic church would have it, to explore the (implicitly public) moral implications of private experience. "Family Affairs," she points out in one poem, "can sever veins," and in another piece called **"My Grandmother,"** she describes an antique shop that her grandmother kept, "—or it kept her," admitting that "when she died I felt no grief at all, / Only the guilt of what I once refused": the history of the antique shop, the antique history of the family.

Similarly, Jennings writes poems which recount her experiences in a mental institution and then, both through overt and covert allusion, contextualize such experiences in simultaneously metaphysical and modernist cadences. Her best poems, however—and those which, to my mind, most fully engage with literary and, in a sense, political history—are religious pieces in a half (T. S.) Eliotian, half (Christina) Rossetti-esque mode. On this continent, right now, we rarely see such work, a point that is in itself historically fascinating. For this reason, perhaps, it is in a curious way heartening to think that someone can still write, as Jennings did in **"A Christmas Suite in Five Movements"** (1980), a litany that both echoes and transcends the famous "Lady of silences / calm and distressed" passage of **"Ash Wednesday"**:

> Girl of the fountains, come into our desert.
> Mary of broken hearts, help us to keep
> Promises. Lady of wakefulness, take our sleep.
> You hold God in your arms and he may weep.

For Jennings, in fact, it is as urgent as it was for Christina Rossetti—or, in different ways, for T. S. Eliot and, more skeptically, Emily Dickinson—to clarify her relationship to theological origins. Indeed, in a poem entitled **"Clarify,"** she prays for a solution that would illuminate the future by releasing her from the guilt of the past. I quote the poem in its entirety:

> Clarify me, please,
> God of the galaxies,
> Make me a meteor,
> Or else a metaphor
>
> So lively that it grows
> Beyond its likeness and
> Stands on its own, a land
> That nobody can lose.
>
> God, give me liberty
> But not so much that I
> See you on Calvary
> Nailed to the wood by me.

When I consider that this text was first collected in 1985, I am myself bemused by the vagaries of literary and intellectual history. And charmed by them. The Rossetti-esque intensity of Jennings's faith, or desire for faith, is not something I would wish to lose in the bleakly existential world over which Finkelstein's and Hull's "tide of voices" incoherently washes.

Yet there is, of course, something deeply alien to us, at least to us in the United States, about Jennings's beauti-

fully formed and formulated phrases. I don't think we believe in most of them, much as we'd like to, and therefore I don't think we trust a lot of what she has to say. In an early poem, **"Answers"** (1955), she intuits "all the great conclusions coming near," and thirty years later, in **"A Class-Room,"** she remembers experiencing a "high call" that is no longer available to many of us, certainly not to modest, somewhat muddled writers like Finkelstein and Hull, and she casts her memory in diction that seems as excessively high-flown as the idea of a "high call":

> . . . from a battle I learnt this healing peace,
> Language a spell over the hungry dreams,
> A password and a key. That day is still
> Locked in my mind. When poetry is spoken
> That door is opened and the light is shed,
> The gold of language tongued and minted fresh.

At the same time, however, Jennings is a woman who can write a really glowing line like "Leaves fall / As if they meant to rise." Her notion of history, with its oddly anachronistic evocations of a nineteenth-century Christian teleology, may not be ours, yet it is surely one to which we ought to attend, if only because its complex attention to enduring desires and ancient difficulties is so compelling.

Robert Sheppard (review date 21 August 1987)

SOURCE: Review of *Collected Poems*, in *New Statesman*, Vol. 114, No. 2943, August 21, 1987, p. 22.

[*In the following review, Sheppard compares Jennings's career with fellow* Movement *members, contending that her work exudes greater seriousness and mysticism.*]

The poetry of the Movement orthodoxy won't go away: Larkin's death clearly wasn't the end of it. Indeed, in some of these recent books, Larkin is an excuse for pious, elegiac production by some of his followers. They mourn him, rightly, as a more consummate poet. 'I do not want him to be dead!' pleads Vernon Scannell, as if the whole thing might not function without Larkin. But, obviously, it does.

As one might expect, these poets broadly share a faith in a poetry of anecdote and measured tone, in which irony is used to both project and shield a reserved self. There is an ambivalent respect for traditional form: Anthony Thwaite has a 'sort of ballade' and Gavin Ewart produces a 'so-called sonnet'. Themes recur, too. These poets are all getting on a bit and can celebrate a pivotal birthday—whether 52 or 61—with ironic resignation. Schooldays become a source of nostalgic epiphany (those fragrant schoolmarms who first stirred the male poets' sexuality!); elderly relatives offer easily exploitable pathos. Dying—not death—is popular, particularly terminal illnesses in dehumanised hospitals (a Larkin prop). When this personal vein is exhausted, there's a mine of information in newspapers (particularly in headlines and personal ads) to provide epigraphs, odd lines and even whole poems. However, explanatory footnotes are generally more interesting than the poems which trump up facts into style.

Of the poets here, Elizabeth Jennings is the most serious, even drearily so. Eclipsed by her fellow male Movement poets, and separated from them by a lyrical and mystical streak, it is right that a new **Collected Poems** should redress the injustice. Her work has shown various attempts at escaping the Movement style, although the vatic sweep of the early **'Song for a Birth or a Death'** still strains in its rhythmical and tonal prison.

> Last night I saw the savage world
> And heard the blood beat up the stair;
> The fox's bark, the owl's shrewd pounce,
> The crying creatures—all were there,
> And men in bed with love and fear.

Her Catholicism was allowed full expression in such poems as **'To a Friend with a Religious Vocation'** but, within a few years, the release from social decorum in subject matter led to the more 'confessional' **'On a Friend's Relapse and Return to a Mental Clinic'**. However, she is not a Lowell or Plath. The middle poems, which deal with mental illness, maintain a cool compassion while negotiating fear, dread and oblivion. These subjects, which Larkin addresses from the outside, are addressed repeatedly by Jennings from the inside, as it were, and they remain thematic throughout the book. In the face of a retiring deity, opportunities for epiphany are few: 'Even in spring I see an elegy.' Later poems display a rhythmical variety, allowing a more relaxed voice, but it is often Movement through and through in its use of 'we' as a rhetorical-moral embrace that can pre-empt a reader's free response:

> We are nothing, we are
> A dream in a cosmic mind,
> We are a solitude, an emptiness,
> We only exist in others' thought . . . Why
> Are we set here, frightened of our reflections,
> Living in fear yet desperate not to die?

Glyn Maxwell (review date 5 May 1989)

SOURCE: "Faith in Form," in *Times Literary Supplement*, No. 4492, May 5-11, 1989, p. 495.

[*In the following review of* Tributes, *Maxwell praises Jennings's subtle use of simile and her successful use of form.*]

This is a craftswoman working, so watch the vowels;

> It is not only great stars or the sun
> I owe so many debts to. I now state
> A poet here, a painter there, a place
> That's altered all I do. So I relate
> My debt and give back what I've taken, grace.

Lyric poets, if honest and well practised, know enough to let the sounds run towards them and gather. Elizabeth Jennings is here writing a poetry of A's, with all the light, the aye-saying, the openess and the admission— both confessional and a letting-in—which that vowel affords.

"Tributes" (the poem quoted) strikes, naturally, the keynote of the collection, which includes paeans to Goya, Caravaggio, Turner, George Herbert and Larkin ("Your secret self, the self that exposed itself / To believe in nothing after death" . . .) along with a good deal of breathless awe of Rome, several descriptive lyres the least valuable: phrases such as "a delicate softness", "music of colours" and "magic of love" need strong opponents these days and have nothing to fight here), and the formal sighing-at-passing-Time that this poetess does almost too often and too seamlessly, but not quite.

The "confessional" quality of **Tributes** is ideally suited to Jennings's quiet faith in form. Inside the strict frame and limits (the apparent absence of which seems almost to be a principal of art she says "However inward; it must come. To keep off sprawl and chaos") she emmciates with clarity the honest failure to get it quite right and the calm indestructible sense of having learned:

> You loved the monosyllable and it
>   Runs through your music, I
> Can hear between its graces music yet
>   More deep and much more high.
> You have released my spirit, sent it on
> Audacious flights by what you've said and done.

The line-breaks after "I", a gracious pause before a large assertion, and, after "high", a deep breath (which chimes with "spirit") and the use of "Audacious"—which is audacious—express, as much as the words do, the debt, the reason for tribute, and its strength and depth, which stem naturally from the imperative need not to dis"grace" Herbert's memory.

"Grace" seems to be to Elizabeth Jennings what "Luck" is in the early Auden: a concept of light and worth peculiarly personal, but universal in the sense of its infusing all that the poet values. Therefore the "lyric grace so rare now" which she praises in Charles Causley, holds a much more expansive and affirmative value than the knackered old phrase itself, and it's also a much brighter (in all senses) and quite contemporary light. In **"Tate Gallery"**, Warhol, Pollock and Hockney are described as "bearers / Almost of ungrace" but are, slowly and with some difficulty, absorbed; Jennings accepts "the difficult sturdy beauty in all unlikeliness".

Similes ought to cast sunlight, not, as so often nowadays, striplight, a cleverness of angles. They are less charming than metaphors, but much more honest (metaphors along with exaggerations, euphemisms and poems themselves, being versions of the thing that is not). In these lines of Jennings's—

> I met
> So much kindness from simple Italians and some
> English priests and poets. It was as if
> An unhappy childhood was handed back and altered

—one almost has to look twice to notice that the simile springs from nowhere, but it seems natural, and it casts light.

Where Jennings's translations of *The Sonnets of Michelangelo* (first published in 1961) fail, they fail for noble reasons, as an English lady brings proud masculine endings to the great artist's verses, which are of failure and humility. This, however, produces its own intriguing echo, as Jennings's own tributes—not to mention the tribute of translation itself—reflect, through a veil of time and language, these devotions of genius to deity:

> Thus, in a thousand years all men shall see
> How beautiful you were, how I was faint
> And yet how wise I was in loving you.

Lawrence Sail (review date Autumn 1990)

SOURCE: Review of *Tributes*, in *Stand Magazine*, Vol. 31, No. 4, Autumn, 1990, pp. 48-50.

[*In the following review, Sail cautions that Jennings risks bordering on mannerism in some of her work but proclaims that she is one of the greatest poets at capturing childhood.*]

Like Roy Fuller, Elizabeth Jennings knows the strength of 'energy leashed in', as she writes in one of the poems in *Tributes*. This new collection continues the reflective notes of her *Collected Poems*, sustaining a meditation on the nature of poetry and the other arts, especially music, and on love, faith, joy, sorrow, friendship, childhood and the passage of time. The preoccupation with music is dominant, so to speak, and there is a strong religious element in her affirmation of the artist as an instrument of God's glory. The poems are entirely accessible, often intensely human in their vulnerability, and set firmly within the context of gratitude explicit in the book's title. This underlying sense of joy, despite a real darkness that cannot be ignored, beautifully informs the sequence **'A Happy Death'**, about the death at 57 of one of the poet's friends, a Dominican priest. These four poems cover the same ground and ought to be repetitious merely, but mysteriously they are not—indeed they are very moving. They might be taken as representative of the Jennings method at large—that is, a series of variations which seem to plane away surface after surface in search of a defining core. The danger of the method, to which some of these latest poems also fall prey, is a misleading impression of a writer almost at ease in unease, or else an overworking of stylistic plainness to the point where it falls flat. Occasionally, too, such pronounced tendencies as beginning a number of poems with 'It' or with a question can come close to man-

nerism. Nonetheless there are enough really impressive poems to bring the poet's intentions to life and, as in previous collections, the poems about childhood are particularly strong. Jennings is surely one of our most acute writers when it comes to embodying the immediacies of childhood, as here in **'Psalm of Childhood'**:

> Children are adept and swift at praise undivided
> From the lion's wild ways to the zebra's astonishment
> at
> Its audacious stripes that it can never hide.
> I lay in the humming grass or hay, I hid among shrubs
> and hedgerows
> And smelt the rain on the wind and plucked the vetch
> and convolvulus
> And saw its shrinking with tears.

Here and elsewhere the reader may assent to the proposition about poetry in one of several poems about philosophers, **'Thinking about Descartes'**, which ends—'So maybe poems sing out the greater questions / But questions which expect the answer yes'.

Jerry Bradley (essay date 1993)

SOURCE: "Elizabeth Jennings," in *The Movement: British Poets of the 1950s*, Twayne Publishers, 1993, pp. 87-100.

[*In the excerpt below, Bradley provides an overview of Jennings's career, placing her work in the context of other Movement writers.*]

Elizabeth Jennings is unique in two particular ways: she is the Movement's only woman and its only Catholic. Born Elizabeth Joan Jennings in Boston, Lincolnshire, on 18 July 1926, she was the daughter of Henry Cecil Jennings, a physician. As a teenager she studied poetry in school and was swept up by G. K. Chesterton's battle poem "Lepanto." She wrote an essay on the work and soon was eagerly studying the great romantics—Wordsworth, Coleridge, Keats, and Shelley. Her godfather-uncle was a poet, and he encouraged Elizabeth to write poems herself. She recalls that her first one came to her almost automatically at 13 while she was waiting at a bus stop. From the start Jennings was intrigued by the fascinating variety of poems that could be produced from formal metrical patterns, so she turned her interest to sonnets, ballads, and odes, though she admits that only one four-line poem of her juvenilia warrants preservation. At 15 she began sending out her verse with no success, but she was encouraged by a handwritten rejection from the now-defunct *New English Weekly*, which affirmed, "These poems show talent."[1]

Even in Jennings's earliest poems a sense of form predominates, and the primary characteristics of her mature verse—regular rhyme and meter—are evident. Moreover, they frequently display the simple vision of childhood in an emotionally honest, clear manner.

Jennings moved to Oxford as a child and was educated at Oxford High School and later St. Anne's College, taking an M.A. in English language and literature with honors in 1949, having earlier failed her B.Litt studies, which concentrated on Matthew Arnold as both a romantic and classical poet. At Oxford she met Philip Larkin and John Wain and enrolled in a court handwriting seminar with Kingsley Amis. Despite his youth Amis already held strong opinions on literature and art, and he introduced Jennings to jazz. They spent hours together in record shops and cinemas, but he was never critical of her conventional preference for classical music. Amis also read and admired her poetry, and both had poems in the 1948 Oxford anthology. When Amis and James Michie edited it the following year, they looked for hard, modern poems to print. They selected six of Jennings's poems for publication.

After graduation her verse began to appear in various magazines, including the *Spectator*, the *New Statesman*, and the *Poetry Review*. Jennings worked for a short time as an advertising copywriter, employment which she believes made her style increasingly slick, relaxed, and more publishable. But Jennings was fired from the agency, and in 1950 she hired on as an assistant at the Oxford City Library, where she worked until 1958. Oxford undergraduates interested in her poems or in writing poetry themselves visited her there regularly and often invited her to dinner and the theater. Among those students were Geoffrey Hill, Adrian Mitchell, Anthony Thwaite, and Alan Brownjohn and Americans Donald Hall and Adrienne Rich, all of whom were to achieve their own recognition as poets and critics.

When Jennings had assembled enough poems for a book, she sought a publisher. In time she was introduced to Oscar Mellor, a private printer living in the small village of Eynsham outside Oxford. Mellor issued a pamphlet of her work, thus beginning the Fantasy Press Poets Series, which would come to include works by Gunn, Davie, Larkin, Amis, and Holloway among its distinguished contributors. The success of this inaugural volume prompted Mellor to put forth a full-length book of Jennings's verse, *Poems*, which included three of her poems from *Oxford Poetry 1949* and earned her an Arts Council prize in 1953. Fantasy Press also issued the first full-length books of poems by Gunn (*Fighting Terms*, 1954) and Davie (*The Brides of Reason*, 1955).

As a result of her Arts Council award Jennings was interviewed and photographed by local and London reporters and became one of the first Movement writers to have her fame established primarily through poetry, although Amis and Wain had both published novels by then, and Davie's *Purity of Diction in English Verse* had received considerable critical attention. She began to feel that she should have at least one poem or book review a week in the important journals. She nearly succeeded. *Time and Tide* and the *Spectator* asked her to contribute articles and reviews, and Stephen Spender asked her for poems for his new magazine, *Encounter*. John Lehmann's *New Sound-*

ings radio program had included a poem by Jennings in its first broadcast, and he included three more by her in the first issue of *London Magazine*, prominently placing her work alongside that by Thom Gunn and T. S. Eliot, who wrote a special introduction for the issue. And she was included in Enright's *Poets of the 1950s* and Conquest's *New Lines* anthologies, the two collections that fixed the roll of membership in the Movement, although Conquest humorously claimed that Jennings's relationship with the Movement was comparable to that of a schoolmistress with a bunch of drunken marines.

From the outset her lyrics were distinguished by their brevity (usually fewer than five stanzas in length) and simplicity. Her vocabulary resists strange and unusual words, and there is a noted absence of proper nouns in her work. Preoccupied with the themes of the individual's fears and essential loneliness, her poems became noted for their wit, lyrical innocence, and exploration of nuances of the spirit.

"Delay," the opening poem in the volume, exhibits the tentativeness and rationality commonly found in Movement verse. The poem is one of her best; Jennings chose it for her **Collected Poems** and **Selected Poems** and Larkin included it in *The Oxford Book of Twentieth Century English Verse*. The poem, a short formal lyric, seems well suited to Jennings's talent as she fashions an analogy that compares the speed of light to the speed of love. Despite its emotional subject, the poem's regular stanzas and exactness of language enhance its logic. Jennings emphasizes the colossal distance between lovers by springing from the first stanza to the second on the word love.

> The radiance of that star that leans on me
> Was shining years ago. The light that now
> Glitters up there my eyes may never see,
> And so the time lag teases me with how
>
> Love that loves now may not reach me until
> Its first desire is spent. The star's impulse
> Must wait for eyes to claim it beautiful
> And love arrived may find us somewhere else.
>
> (Jennings *CP*, 3)

Her diction is plain and exacting, yet the understatement in the poem's last line is both tender and poignant.

Jennings's preference for such emotional and syntactic spareness is consistent with the erudite attitudes of other Movement poets, although she was the only member of the group who never worked full-time in academia. While her poems occasionally seem detached in their attempts to demystify emotions, Jennings did not wish to be limited by an intellectual aesthetic. A cradle Catholic, she maintained a lifelong faith in Christianity, which Enright failed in doing, and poems of religious belief always occupied an important place in her work.

Jennings published her second volume, *A Way of Looking*, two years later in 1955. Its 40 poems also display the cool, natural, uncontrived style found in *Poems*. As its title suggests, the volume is interested more in probing ways of looking than in developing particular subject matter. Even when her topics are factually based and drawn from historical record, she rarely employs detailed settings and considers actuality merely a point of departure from which self-understanding may be abstracted. Physical reality serves more as a speculative premise in these poems than as a reminder of verisimilitude. **"Not in the Guide Books,"** from the book's last section, is one such lyric, a travel poem in which public experience gives rise to private understanding. The formula is comparably employed in **"For a Child Born Dead"** and **"The Recognition."** And in **"Tribute"** she directly acknowledges the importance of poetry to this associative process:

> The poem is enough that joins me to
> The world that seems far to grasp at when
> Images fail and words are gabbled speech:
> At those times clarity appears in you,
> Your mind holds meanings that my mind can read.
>
> (Jennings *CP*, 35)

In their reviews of *A Way of Looking*, some critics denounced the unfulfilled potential promised by Jennings's first collection. She reflected, "A second book of verse is always a hazard. Critics are waiting to pounce and declare, 'It doesn't live up to the promise shown in her first book.' If you have enlarged your scope in the matter of theme and form you are unlikely to win even then, for journalists will say, 'She is uneasy with her new subject matter'" (*Contemporary*, 110–11). Nevertheless, the book won the Somerset Maugham prize for 1956; the award stipulated that the recipient must spend at least three months abroad in a country of her choosing. The financial remuneration of 400 pounds enabled her to spend three months in Italy, which she declared to be the happiest and most worthwhile time of her life, and to return to England with 80 pounds left over.

The poems she wrote in Rome became the basis of her third book, *A Sense of the World* (1958), and naturally many of them, such as **"Fountain," "St. Paul Outside the Walls,"** and **"Letter from Assisi,"** contained Roman themes. The poems record her love for Italy and her Catholic heritage, but they are more than postcards intending to conserve the itinerary and topography of her travels. The settings also provide juxtaposition for her spiritual dislocation. Jennings's poetry was becoming decidedly less confessional, and her concerns turned to children, old men and women, storms, religious motifs, and the passage of time. Unlike her Movement colleagues, Jennings never felt comfortable writing poems about popular issues and current events, believing that successful poems absorb writers wholly and completely and not just for the moment. While she admitted that good poems might be written about such matters as nuclear warfare, modern art, popular advertising, and scientific experimentation—all of which had served as topics for Conquest, Larkin, and other Movement writers—she found those subjects generally less compelling than the familiar themes of love and death with which poets had traditionally dealt. "The best poets writing today are those who are most personal, who are trying to examine and understand their own emotions, behaviour or actions, or those of other people" ("Comments," 32). By writing about familiar subjects in orthodox ways Jennings felt she was participating in the proud English tradition of Chaucer, Shakespeare, Wordsworth, and Eliot.

Moreover, satisfied with no single political party, Jennings was not interested in writing political verse, though unlike her *New Lines* colleagues she was devoutly committed to exploring themes of Roman Catholicism. Her Catholicism is especially conspicuous in *A Sense of the World*. While her religiosity and absence of social correctives may at first glance appear uncharacteristic of Movement verse, she explains their relevance. "I believe firmly that every poet must be committed to something and, if his religion or political convictions mean anything to him at all, I do not see how they can fail to affect his poems" ("Context," 51).

Although the verses in *A Sense of the World* are primarily lyrical, she began to experiment with other poetic forms, including free verse, the prose poem, and a good deal of terza rima. She returned to England but visited Rome again in February 1957; she then quit her job, and in April 1958 returned to Rome for 13 weeks.

Upon coming home she became a general reader for Chatto and Windus, the publishers of William Empson and F. R. Leavis, and the position afforded her the opportunity to attend literary teas with T. S. Eliot and Edith Sitwell. Her reputation grew, earning her a membership in the Royal Society of Literature in 1961, and her work was included in the first Penguin Modern Poets series, published in 1962, which also contained the work of Lawrence Durrell and R.S. Thomas. The book went through three additional printings in the next five years and spawned subsequent volumes in a long-running sequence of titles.

In her second year at Chatto and Windus, Jennings suffered a severe mental breakdown and attempted suicide. She consequently left Chatto's and would eventually write two books devoted to her struggle with depression, which are discussed later in the chapter. But during her recovery she completed work on *Every Changing Shape*, a book about mysticism and poetry, reviewed novels for the *Listener*, and worked on four other books: a new book of poems, *Song for a Birth or a Death*; a poetry book for children, *Let's Have Some Poetry*; a translation of Michelangelo's sonnets; and a pamphlet she was editing for the British Council, *An Anthology of Modern Verse 1940–60*.

Song for a Birth or a Death (1961) was composed in Italy, and it deviates from the Movement themes of insularity and secularity. The poems are profoundly religious, at times even mystical, and they display a distinct lack of irony. In **"To a Friend with a Religious Vocation,"** she struggles to articulate her religious vision:

> I see
> Within myself no wish to breed or build
> Or take the three vows ringed by poverty.
>   And yet I have a sense,
> Vague and inchoate, with no symmetry
> Of purpose.
>
> (Jennings *CP*, 114)

In **"A World of Light"** she basks in "A mood the senses cannot touch or damage, / A sense of peace beyond the breathing word" (Jennings *CP*, 92), and in another poem she derives a calming tranquility from a Roman mass, even though she does not understand Latin. Though mystical experiences are by nature fundamentally private, Jennings suggests in **"Men Fishing in the Arno"** that they can become the basis for a whole community with

> Each independent, none
> Working with others and yet accepting
> Others. From this one might, I think
>
> Build a whole way of living.
>
> (Jennings *CP*, 117)

Jennings justifies religion's close connection to her art, believing that the host, wine, and offering contribute to a sacrosanct vision "of art as gesture and as sacrament, art with its largesse and its own restraint" (Jennings *CP*, 104).

Jennings laments that the sense of the sacred is vanishing from modern life, "so the poetic gift, which still remains something mysterious and inexplicable has tended to be ignored along with many other intangible things."[2] Her obeisance to the idea of salvation through art prompted Wain to dedicate his "Green Fingers" to her, claiming "Your art will save your life, Elizabeth."[3]

In contrast to *Song for a Birth or Death*, her anthology seems a clear celebration of Movement virtues. Beginning with the publication of Eliot's last great poem, *An Anthology of Modern Verse 1940–60* (1961) covers "twenty years of suffering, restlessness and uncertainty,"[4] a period marked by an urge for formal order and clarity in verse in defiance of the chaos and confusion of postwar society. Most of the poets she includes were children or adolescents when World War II began. "The war was for them, therefore, little more than a rather vague, unhappy memory. They began to write their mature poems in an atmosphere of political and, indeed, cosmic uncertainty. Yet, paradoxically, it is in their work that we can see the most striking evidence of the desire for form, style and order, and also of a wish to stress the dignity of human personality" (*Anthology*, 9).

Believing that such ruthless honesty and underlying passion had been best exemplified by poets whose love of simplicity and disdain for poetic artifice were common to her own work, Jennings selected all nine Movement poets for inclusion in her anthology: two poems apiece from Amis, Conquest, Davie, Enright, Holloway, and Wain, three from herself (one each from her first three volumes,

including her favorite poem, **"Fountain"**), and four from Larkin and Gunn.

But *An Anthology of Modern Verse 1940–60* notwithstanding, Jennings's gradual dissatisfaction with the characteristic Movement style was becoming apparent. Writing in *London*, she paid homage to the past but also declared her intention to break with its traditions:

> I don't myself always want to write the rhyming lyric of thirty-odd lines. Indeed, I do at times feel positively inhibited and exasperated by the form. At the moment, I am extremely eager to write longer poems, dramatic verse (I would, for example, like to write the libretto for an opera), and prose poems. But I am still as fascinated as I was when I was thirteen by the marvellous variety within strict English lyric verse. As for the "poetic language" of today—there are times when I feel that it is too dry, too intellectual, sometimes, even, too facile. Maybe it needs a little rough treatment, though I can see absolutely no virtue in confusion or obscurity for their own sake.
>
> (**"Difficult,"** 51)

Jennings worried that she was becoming too slick and feared that her talent might dry up before she mastered her craft. She sought to be less an observer and commentator and more a vehicle for her personal experiences, perhaps as a curative for her mental illness. Her tortuous recovery from depression through hospitalization and analysis was detailed by Jennings in **Recoveries** (1964) and **The Mind Has Mountains** (1966). The verses in these two collections are remarkable, given their subject matter, for their lack of sentimentality; they are not the ravings of a broken spirit, nor do they display an open sense of self-pity. Rather she views all those in the mental hospital—patients, doctors, and nurses—with detached compassion, and they are hardly the type of commonsense poems on which the Movement was established.

Jennings's best poems always seem contemplative in nature, and the hospital setting was appropriate for her meditations on psychological pain. The remarkable stillness in these poems is achieved by her clear, spare language. She concentrates meaning in the poems' fluent final lines as momentary stays against disorder, allowing her to transcend for a time the hurt that prompted the utterance. In this way Jennings uses her art to exorcise the demons of her breakdown by transforming the chaos of her dark dreams into a kind of serenity. In **"Works of Art"** she asserts that, although art so often "appears like an escape We want more order than we ever meet / And art keeps driving us most hopefully on" (Jennings *CP*, 137). Though these poems are frequently disquieting, Jennings retains control in them. She examines her illness lucidly and without resorting to self-confession or linguistic confusion.

The Mind Has Mountains, which won the Richard Hillary prize, derives its title from Gerard Manley Hopkins's explorations into the abyss of mental despair. Identifying with other creative artists who have suffered extreme mental distress, Jennings proclaims in **"Van Gogh"** that madness may be an important component of art's tranquility:

> There is a theory that the very heart
> Of making means a flaw, neurosis, some
> Sickness; yet others say it is release.
> I only know that your wild, surging art
> Took you to agony, but makes us come
> Strangely to gentleness, a sense of peace.

(Jennings CP, 176)

Jennings's sympathy with her fellow sufferers and patients is strong. She insists in **"Madness"** that

> It is the lack of reason makes us fear,
> The feeling that ourselves might be like this.
> We are afraid to help her or draw near
> As if she were infectious and could give
> Some taint, some touch of her own fantasies,
> Destroying all the things for which we live.

(Jennings CP, 173)

Jennings was hospitalized on several occasions, and she attempted to gain some peace through the efficacy of poetry, believing "the act of writing a poem is itself an implicit affirmation of the possibility of order" (**"Difficult,"** 30). The composure which she sought in her own verse and valued in that of others became the goal of her personal life, and her poetry often seems a courageous effort to discover a sense of order within, although she confesses in **"In a Mental Hospital Sitting Room"** that "It does not seem a time for lucid rhyming" (Jennings *CP*, 171), and she laments in **"On a Friend's Relapse and Return to a Mental Clinic"** that "It is the good who often know joy least" (Jennings *CP*, 188). *The Mind Has Mountains* displays a heroic dedication to return to the placidity of the poems she wrote before her breakdown. She bravely tries to come to terms with her turbulent illness, but some poems offer little more than pious pronouncements. And while the poems are highly personal in nature, they retain a formality antipodal to their subject and are never particularly revealing in an autobiographical kind of way.

Jennings's *Collected Poems* was issued in 1967, drawing its material from the seven books she had written over a 14-year period. The collection reprints 207 of her 243 previously issued poems. Its publication renewed critical interest in her work, and it was reviewed widely as critics used it as a benchmark to assess her artistic development. Anthony Thwaite noted her "steady and persistent contemplative gift"[5] and appreciated her unsentimental lyrical verses. He proclaimed that the volume "shows a remarkable unity of tone and theme, repetitive and yet gaining strength from that very fact. The most notable development has been one of giving greater prominence to the immediate and circumstantial, and yet clearly the later poems of mental agony and illness come from the same person who wrote such pure and clear lyrics and meditations as the early **'Delay,' 'Reminiscence'** and **'The Island.'**"[6]

Julian Symons praised her ingenuity and wit and remarked favorably on her ability to construct metaphysical conceits. He found sources for her organization and technical clarity in Robert Graves and A. E. Housman. Although he charted little stylistic development in Jennings's verse, Symons observed a change in her subjects. Even the mental illness poems "are composed with the cool firmness of the early poems. Nobody can have written less hysterically about hysteria, yet the sense of personal involvement is always there."[7]

The themes of her next book, *The Animals' Arrival* (1969), are decidedly shopworn, however, and the verses themselves shrill as Jennings sought to emerge from the writings about her breakdown by creating what seemed to her more vital poetry. The book is dedicated to her friend poet Peter Levi, but her concerns here are less personal and more aesthetic. In **"Of Languages"** she demands a new poetic, believing that the hour is nearing when language must be made sudden and new and images sharp and still. A call for honesty also appears in **"Resolve,"** where she vows not to write so glibly of the ill, choosing instead warmth, sanity, and health. But on the whole, the poems are not especially engaging.

Jennings's poetic decline continued in *Relationships* (1972), which Alisdair Maclean labeled "catastrophic."[8] He blames the decrement on her use of Emily Dickinson for a poetic model. Although the resemblance of Jennings's verse to Dickinson's had been approvingly noted by John Thompson in his review of *A Sense of the World*, Maclean complains that "for Emily Dickinson's apparent simplicity, however, Miss Jennings too often supplies bathos, and for phrases like 'zero at the bone' substitutes a language colourless to the point of invisibility. The trouble seems to be a lack of any real pressure in the creation of these poems" (Maclean, 389). He also faults her language as stilted, inverted, and awkward, as in "Simply because they were human, I admire"[9] (**"In Memory of Anyone Unknown to Me"**). Only her pain and vulnerability, best articulated in **"Sympathy,"** keep the poems from seeming overly didactic.

A stronger Jennings emerged in *Growing-Points* in 1975, one admittedly determined to gather strength from her pain. She continued to experiment technically with a variety of verse forms, and the volume seems aptly named. The poems themselves have grown longer, thereby freeing up her diction from the restrictions of regular meter while still remaining essentially pure, and her poetic line has been lengthened as well (though sometimes leading to irksome runons, as in **"An Abandoned Palace,"** where the lines sometimes exceed 20 syllables). Experiments with free verse and prose poetry alternate with traditional poems in an attempt to bring a new force to her work. The poems still frequently end in aphorisms, but the volume shows just how far Jennings had begun to stray from Movement dictum. Her trademark homilies and quiet lyricism are still visible, but her realizations are more labored, muddled, wistful, and complex than before.

Her divergence from Movement themes and techniques is quite evident in her myth poems on Orpheus, Persephone, and the Minotaur and in her muted, unfocused imagery, which all too often falls into clichés and stereotypes—sunsets, falling leaves, and the like. Her poems of tribute and direct address to famous artistic, literary, and religious figures are on the whole sanctimonious and sentimental. The volume includes poems to Mozart and Hopkins, homage to Van Gogh, Thomas Aquinas, Mondrian, Rembrandt, Wallace Stevens, and Auden. And there is a bold but ill-considered monologue projected by Christ on the cross.

Religious themes compose the dramatic substance of *Consequently I Rejoice* (1977), an ample collection of 88 meditations on Jennings's Christian faith. As in *Growing-Points*, she records the pain and suffering of a convalescing Catholic, and there are again dramatic monologues from religious figures, here Christ and Mary. While still an intensely personal, lyric poet, in *Consequently I Rejoice* Jennings turns a bit abstract in her longing for faith, for the book attempts to universalize her campaign against despair. It begins similarly to her previous collections by documenting her nightmares, and there are the familiar lines of self-flagellation, as in **"Elegy for Aldous Huxley"**—"You put away / The novels, verses, stories where the 'I' / Dominates, makes us masochists"[10]—and of pleading, as in **"Cradle Catholic"**—"O take my unlove and despair / And what they lack let faith repair" (*Consequently*, 36). But she expands the scope of her study beyond the personal as she traces her spiritual and intellectual development through a year-long cycle. Seasonal and cyclical patterns (poems of parents and infants, images of sun and moon and night and day) accent the soul's passage until at the cycle's end the last nightmares are no longer uniquely hers but everyone's—especially the elderly, who either dwell in or remain bereft of lasting spiritual peace. Her **"Old People's Nursing Home"** is mindful of Larkin's "The Old Fools"; though her poem is more compassionate and intuitive than Larkin's, it surely lacks his distinctive irony.

By compressing the journey of the soul into one year's time, Jenning's book invites comparison to *In Memoriam*, though it was certainly conceived on a smaller scale. Tennyson's "swallow flights of song" are designed to chart the soul's passage. Jennings too avails herself of bird metaphors, for her poems are haunted by auguries of flight and birdsong meant as hopeful reminders that her spirit may one day again soar. "Wisdom is in our bloodstream not in brain," she affirms in **"Song for the Swifts"** (*Consequently*, 15).

Throughout the poems Jennings equates religious doubt with her self-doubt as a writer, and in penning poems of tribute to other artists (Huxley, Edward Thomas, D. H. Lawrence, Paul Klee, Cézanne, and Virginia Woolf her examples here) she actually seeks self-illumination and understanding; the artists' identity seems consequential to her own. Tennyson felt himself a lesser artist than Hallam, but for Jennings it was Thomas (**"For Edward Thomas"**) who embodied the quiet, principled, amiable nature she wished to capture in her verse. Her meditations on other artists are but another form of self-reflection, and it is instrumental to both her faith and poetic achievement in that she views the relationship between the individual soul and God akin to that between artist and creation.

The title of her next offering, *Moments of Grace* (1979), refers to those brief occasions when despair and frustration are eclipsed by moments of spiritual transcendancy. Jennings's religious verse consistently subscribes to the Wordsworthian notion that daily human experience is laden with potential revelations. Suspending the soul between the natural and supernatural seems her aesthetic goal, but all too often she depicts her aloneness and sorrow without achieving that measured balance. Jennings openly acknowledges that prayer and the sacraments of her faith have not always sustained her. That her devoutness could not allay her religious dismay proved especially troubling; a lifelong Catholic, she struggled perpetually for the protection and blessings of God.

Moments of Grace is not about her mental illness, and it includes Jennings's first poem to address a public issue, **"Euthanasia."** More than in her earlier works, she attempts to witness the unification of God and nature. As a result the strong lyricism of prior volumes is diminished by her emphasis on what is essentially more ponderous, philosophic matter. Perhaps she had previously been afraid to explore such deep, ruminative questions, but in *Moments of Grace* she is ill at ease with her speculative subject matter. She confesses her awkwardness and alienation, and is uncertain when probing the grace afforded by the natural world. Undoubtedly Jennings believed the Wordsworthian premises articulated in her verse, but she is a gentle arguer and seems envious of those able to overcome their estrangement and attain those rare "moments of grace."

Perhaps her reticence is strategic, meant to suggest that she is unworthy of spiritual consolation, that she is to remain in awe forever before God. In any case, the poems are often interrupted by mild interjections that reverse the course of her ideas but allow her to adhere to her metrical pattern (her fondness for terza rima persists). She seems as restive with her fellow humans as she does with herself, and is at times overly apologetic and colloquial, as if her vicarious experiences were more important than her personal ones.

Selected Poems appeared in the same year as *Moments of Grace*. Ninety-one poems from her *Collected Poems*, three with slight verbal changes, appear in *Selected Poems*. That few changes appear in the poems is unsurprising, for 12 years earlier she conceded in an interview with John Press that she wrote swiftly and revised little. Surprisingly, though, three-quarters of the poems written between her *Collected* and *Selected Poems*, that period of her great mental torment, were omitted presumably because Jennings felt they lacked the impact of her earlier work and thereby did not warrant inclusion.

In the 1980s Jennings was again drawn to Italy and southern travel, issuing **Italian Light and Other Poems** in 1981 and the Bibbiena poems, **Celebrations and Elegies**, the following year. Her Lincolnshire childhood is the subject of her fourteenth book of poems, **Extending the Territory** (1985). Her more recent poetry, like that in her first books, is marked by restraint and understatement. Elizabeth Jennings "is not the kind of poet who is likely to find it acceptable to 'say something a bit more interesting' than she means."[11] She has remained a quiet, readable poet preoccupied with suffering and pain, and she has a musical ear, a talent fashioned out of decades of plumbing her own ephemerality and isolation. Her growth as a poet has been modest, though she is still craftsmanlike in her approach to verse and continues to prefer rhyme and traditional meters as ways to balance form and content. A lyrical writer who shuns lengthy descriptions, Jennings is more a temporal than spatial poet; her romanticism and imagery tend toward intellectualization and allegory and away from plot.

Consequently, she continues to receive the complaints, long leveled against Movement verse, that her work is emotionally diffident and self-conscious, that it is frequently too literal, didactic, and banal, and that it lacks vivid descriptive appeal.

William Blissett assesses her contribution to the period as follows: "The student of literary history will discern in Elizabeth Jennings the marks of her generation and The Movement—the continuity of rhyme and reason, of syntax and stanza (as if Ezra Pound had never lived), the easy rhythms, the eschewing of decoration, the control of metaphor; but he will also notice how the one woman and the one Catholic stands apart from the others, in the special insights given her by the enjoyment of Italy and the suffering of illness, by her librarian's nonacademic love of literature, and by her lifelong religious concern."[12]

Notes

1. Elizabeth Jennings, "Elizabeth Jennings," in *Contemporary Authors Autobiography Series* (Detroit: Gale, 1987), 107; hereafter cited in text as *Contemporary*.

2. Elizabeth Jennings, "The Difficult Balance," *London Magazine*, November 1959, 28; hereafter cited in text as "Difficult."

3. John Wain, *Letters to Five Artists* (New York: Viking, 1969), 55.

4. Elizabeth Jennings, *An Anthology of Modern Verse 1940–60* (London: Methuen, 1961), 7; hereafter cited in text as *Anthology*.

5. Anthony Thwaite, *Twentieth-Century English Poetry: An Introduction* (New York: Barnes and Noble, 1978), 44.

6. Anthony Thwaite, "Elizabeth Jennings," *Contemporary Poets* (London: St. James, 1970), 559–60.

7. Julian Symons, "Clean and Clear," *New Statesman*, 13 October 1967, 476.

8. Alisdair Maclean, "Marble Fun," *Listener*, 22 March 1973, 389; hereafter cited in text.

9. Elizabeth Jennings, *Relationships* (London: Macmillan, 1972), 19.

10. Elizabeth Jennings, *Consequently I Rejoice* (Manchester: Carcanet, 1987), 54; hereafter cited in text as *Consequently*.

11. John Matthias, "Pointless and Poignant," *Poetry*, March 1977, 350.

12. William Blissett, "Elizabeth Jennings," in *Dictionary of Literary Biography*, vol. 27 (Detroit: Gale, 1978), 170.

Will Eaves (review date 15 January 1993)

SOURCE: "Ceremonial Forms," in *Times Literary Supplement*, No. 4685, January 15, 1993, p. 23.

[*In the following review of* Times and Seasons, *Eaves discusses Jennings's use of time, form, and language.*]

Time is a continual, if not quite perpetual, worry for Elizabeth Jennings. At its crudest, it represents distance from God—a mechanical, clockwork intrusion into the Garden. At its best, as she refers to it in a poem from her collection, **Extending the Territory** (1985), it is an elemental art that "moves within / The discourse of the learned heart". But while the second condition is clearly the one to which her poetry aspires, the combination of primal faith and "learned" love that is supposed to get her there makes for a God with a rather complicated set of responses to culture and the gods of unruly nature.

Concluding an Advent poem in the new collection's Christmas sequence, she voices the conventional metaphysical *non placet*: "It is a mystery / How God took time and entered history". The language is always innocent, but ambivalently so. Her Catholicism asks for awe at the prospect of the Incarnation and Passion, knowing that God is too various for awe, sensing that His Easter festivals are quickened by the proximity of seasonal rite: "Let us blossom and believe. / Risings are everywhere".

In few other contemporary poets is this tension between the multiform spirit and the single creed pausibly resolved. Jennings's God is attractive because one senses that He is the sort of humanist God who reads His horoscope. There are celebrants who share Jennings's star-gazing persona, but almost none, apart from her fellow Oxford poet Anne Ridler (from whom a Collected Poems is urgently required), for whom poetry as "The poise of time. The history of speech. / Articulation. Subject brought to heel" can still tackle the big questions so directly—and make them new, as Jennings does, on a regular basis. The main thrust of the new book develops this credo: that poetic form can be restorative, providing a ceremony in which the impulses of solstice, season and sacred ritual are to be renewed.

As ever, the *genius loci* of this ceremony is to be found in the Jennings sonnet:

> Spirit of place. Spirit of time. Re-form
> The rugged oaks and chestnuts. Now they stand
> Naked and pallid giants out of storm
> And out of sorts. It is the Autumn's end
>
> And this is Winter brought in by All Saints
> Followed by All Souls to keep us in
> Touch with chill and death. Each re-acquaints
> Us with the year's end.

Characteristically, the first line's invocations melt into meditation, though the wintry heart of the poem is in the rhythmical ellipsis that freezes the metre momentarily after "Touch"; Jennings is a great believer in leaving doors open to "Allow, admit the brave, attentive verb", even if it turns out to be the silent harbinger of "chill and death".

Silence is also germane to verse which takes time to reflect on the pause between good linguistic intention and imperfect expression. Unspoken potency—the erotic impulse of most creation—informs **"In the Beginning"**, which recasts a well-documented sympathy for the Virgin in primordial terms: "The child was small among / All angry drifts but Mary kept her work / And it grew in her womb". Linguistic purpose is conceived in a fallen landscape which awaits seasonal redemption; like the Gawain poet (and Christ's many appearances as the Green Man reinforce the comparison), Jennings anticipates "a meaning that's delayed" by waiting for the natural cycle to take her "back to the start and to the source".

But Elizabeth Jennings's silences have a hard classical edge as well; and the secondary note of loss in this collection has more to do with Platonic regret than it does with a green eschatology. The old comforts are still in evidence (art, nature, childhood, innocence, dreams, embattled optimism), but the distance she maintains from her work—her insistence that each poem is written away from the self—is growing more strained; and the sense that form endures while words can only point to what has already been lost deepens the grief shed in the book's core sequence, **"For My Mother"**.

> Nothing is innocent,
> Nothing unable to alter, to carry a word
>   Of yours. Each element
> Is charged with a copy of you or carries a chord
>   Or echo of something you said.
> Today in a blackbird's joyful cry I heard
>   You speaking from the dead.

That feeling of ambivalent innocence, it is suggested, is probably the best you can hope for in poetry; God's "purposes out of time" may provide the ineffable inspiration, but language still has to do the leg-work. And so it's hard to take Jennings's metaphysical astronomer entirely seriously when she faces the stars and claims. "Our words make them grow less / As we waylay them to define". The stars are surely not so vain as to snub one of contemporary English poetry"s major sublunary assets.

Michael O'Neill (review date 25 December 1998)

SOURCE: Review of *Praises*, in *The Times Liteary Supplement*, No. 4995, December 25, 1998, pp. 28-9.

[*In the following review, O'Neill argues that although there is a repetitive quality to Jennings"s work, her writing deserves praise.*]

At one stage in **Praises**, Elizabeth Jennings asserts, "Stars are a bright simplicity", reaffirming her affinity with Henry Vaughan for whom "Stars are of mighty use". The points of likeness and difference between the twentieth-century Catholic poet and the Metaphysical mystic are fascinating. Like Vaughan, Jennings values intimations of "An unfallen world". Unlike him, she is "not after visions or prayers". Like him, she places emphasis on childhood. Unlike him, she finds in childhood a forecaste of adult suffering. Like him, she has become an elegist, entitling the collection's opening poem **"For my Sister, now a Widow"**. Unlike him, her elegy is this-worldly in its recollections of "The way he washed up the breakfast, hoovered the floor". Yet if the grave dazzle of "They are all gone into the world of light" lies beyond Jennings, it is the case that for her, as for Vaughan, "strange thoughts transcend our wonted themes". She has a gift for making something unparaphrasably individual out of what may seem, initially, to work at the level of a proposition. In **"Myths within Us"**, she claims that "All the great myths that were whispered / Into our childhood ears / Stay with us somehow somewhere." The poem persuades through the rhythmic skills that ensure Jennings's poetry is close to song yet in touch with the flow of speech. Occasionally, her preference for a plain style gives her language a shopworn air, as when she writes "you know how to make magic happen". But the next line, "It's here before me with the curtains open", rides to the rescue, its disciplined music suggesting that "magic" is, indeed, possible. **Praises** treats interconnected subjects (the mysteries of religion, the significance of the apparently insignificant, the reality of transience and pain, the power of art), until the different poems seem to merge into a single, endlessly self-modifying work. This is not an adverse comment, even if there is a degree of repetition between poems. On the contrary, Elizabeth Jennings's poetic inexhaustibility is a matter for gratitude—and praise.

Additional coverage of Jennings's life and career is contained in the following sources published by the Gale Group: *Contemporary Authors*, Vol. 61-64; *Contemporary Authors New Revision Series*, Vols. 8, 39, 66; *Dictionary of Literary Biography*, Vol. 27; *Major 20th-Century Writers*, Vol. 1, and *Something about the Author*, Vol. 66.

Gayl Jones
1949–

American novelist, poet, short story writer, and essayist.

The following entry presents an overview of Jones's career through 1998.

INTRODUCTION

A highly regarded and innovative voice of African-American women, Jones shot to literary fame in the 1970s with the publication of her critically acclaimed novels *Corregidora* (1975) and *Eva's Man* (1976). After a twenty-year hiatus, Jones published two additional novels, *The Healing* (1998), which was nominated for the National Book Award, and *Mosquito* (1999). In her first person accounts, Jones describes the sexual and racial violence perpetrated against African-American women, chronicling these female characters' varied responses. She is credited as one of the first writers to focus extensively on sexual violence and its relationship to African-American women. While her perceived focus on feminism over racism and the brutality of her subject matter have sparked negative responses in some readers, Jones has earned the praise of fellow writers such as Toni Morrison, James Baldwin, and John Updike. Jones is also known for her poetry.

BIOGRAPHICAL INFORMATION

Jones was born in Lexington, Kentucky, on November 23, 1949. She credits her mother's aspirations to be a writer with her own career choice. As a shy student in high school, she earned the praise and respect of her teachers, one of whom helped Jones secure a scholarship to Connecticut College. After graduating in 1971, she earned an M.A. in 1973 and a D.A. in 1975 from Brown University. While there, Jones published her first novel, *Corregidora*, under the tutelage of Toni Morrison, at that time an editor at Random House Publishers. The novel earned Jones instant critical acclaim. The following year she published *Eva's Man*, which cemented her reputation as an innovative and dramatic new literary voice. A very shy person, Jones was uncomfortable with the publicity and fame that accompanied her status as a rising literary star. She accepted a teaching position in the English Department at the University of Michigan, where she led a quiet life encouraging student writers. While in Ann Arbor, Jones began an association with Bob Higgins, who was convicted in 1983 of weapons charge after he threatened gay rights advocators. The couple fled the country before the trial, but Higgins was convicted in absentia. Five years later, the couple, who had married, returned quietly to the United States to care for Jones's ailing mother. The publicity from the publication of Jones's third novel, *The Healing*, served as the catalyst for a showdown between Lexington Police and the couple in 1998. As a result of a book review, the police determined the true identity of Higgins, who had once again been making threats against members of the community. In an attempt by police to serve the original warrant, Higgins killed himself and Jones attempted suicide. The author was institutionalized. Subsequent reviews of her novels *The Healing* and *Mosquito* were read against the dramatic events of her own life, despite her lifetime efforts to distance her life from her writing.

MAJOR WORKS

Jones's novels center upon strong and articulate African-American females. She writes in the first person, often in a nonsequential order. Jones claims that her first two novels were based on the blues form with an emphasis on the wrongs men commit against women and the ways in which women suffer. *Corregidora* is the story of Ursa Corregidora, a blues singer and descendant of women raped and enslaved by a Portuguese slave owner in Brazil. Her ancestors carried down the tradition that their lives must be living testimonies to the violence, incest, and brutality that they suffered. In the novel, Jones explores the limitations that this type of victimization creates as well as the negative consequences Ursa suffers upon trying to break free of the perpetuated victimization. In her next novel, *Eva's Man*, Jones continues to explore these themes. The novel consists of the unordered and, at times, inconsistent ramblings of Eva Canada, who has been institutionalized in a psychiatric hospital for the strange poisoning and dismemberment of her lover. Jones discusses the varied ways in which Eva and other women respond to extreme sexual and racial violence. In her collection of short stories *White Rat* (1977) and her volumes of poetry published through the first half of the 1980s, Jones discusses and describes the many aspects of sexism and racism from a woman's perspective, coloring all with a dark and disturbing tone. However, Jones stated with the release of her third novel, *The Healing*, that she intended to depart from her earlier form. Her tone is happier and more hopeful, the book ends on a positive note, and the characters make choices to pursue avenues out of their victimization. In her novel *Mosquito*, Jones creates a strong, personable character in truck driver and illegal immigrant smuggler Sojourner Johnson, allowing her to explore a stable and healthy relationship with the kind-hearted and gentle philosopher Ray.

CRITICAL RECEPTION

From the publication of her first novel, Jones earned extensive critical and public attention, much of it positive. Writers such as John Updike and James Baldwin praised her first groundbreaking novels; Toni Morrison championed her. Scholars have credited Jones with being one of the first writers to focus on the violence of sexism and racism from a feminist perspective. Her attention to brutality and its effect on the identity of African-American women has earned her the reputation of a distinct and important literary voice. Critics note that her use of first person narrative is reminiscent of slave accounts and that her use of vernacular language and speech patterns is outstanding. However, some readers have objected to her description of intense violence and brutality, arguing that it is gratuitous. In addition, critics have charged that her writing remains outside the Black Aesthetics Movement objectives and, that by focusing on the divisions between African-American men and women, that she has diverted attention from the more important issue of racism. However, critics responded to *The Healer* positively, praising her positive ending, her focus on timely events, and her superb character development. As Jill Nelson writes "Jones's ability to create bizarre yet believable characters is magical, requiring a subtle act of faith between writer and reader."

PRINCIPAL WORKS

Chile Woman (play) 1974
Corregidora (novel) 1975
Eva's Man (novel) 1976
White Rat (short stories) 1977
Song for Anninho (poetry) 1981
The Hermit-Woman (poetry) 1983
Xarque and Other Poems (poetry) 1985
Liberating Voices: Oral Tradition in African-American Literature (essays) 1991
The Healing (novel) 1998
Mosquito (novel) 1999

CRITICISM

Trudier Harris (essay date October 1982)

SOURCE: "A Spiritual Journey: Gayl Jones's *Song for Anninho*," in *Callaloo*, Vol. 5, No. 3, October, 1982, pp. 105-11.

[*In the following essay, Harris outlines the plot and themes in Jones's narrative poem* Song for Anninho.]

In Gayl Jones's long poem, *Song for Anninho*, Almeyda, whose narrative voice we hear, undergoes a spiritual journey which highlights both theme and character. In her explorations of memory and history, Almeyda moves beyond her individuality to represent the destiny of the African descendants who were brought to Brazil in the seventeenth century. Through Almeyda's sights and values, we come to see the strength of her people, and we come to hope—with her—that they might one day establish a spiritual and physical unity which will withstand all oppressors.

Almeyda tells us of the Palmares settlement of Africans who escaped from slavery in Brazil in the 1690s and who, through non-violent raids upon slaveholders, rescued others who were either too timid or otherwise prevented from escaping. Almeyda had been brought to Palmares through such a raid. Jorge Velho, a Portuguese field-master, eventually leads a successful attack against Palmares, reenslaving most of the inhabitants and scattering the others through the hilly forests of Brazil. Among those to escape are Almeyda and her lover Anninho, who voluntarily came to Palmares because he could be useful to the settlement as a trader and a spy.

Song for Anninho combines personal and communal history in recounting the love of Almeyda and Anninho and their separation through the war with Velho's regiments. There is a strong suggestion that the survival of Palmares depends upon the fate of Almeyda and Anninho; their health reflects community health. Where Almeyda is, therefore, and how she came to be there is of primary importance. As she and Anninho had wandered through the forests, they were attacked by a group of Portuguese soldiers; during the attack, Almeyda's breasts were cut off and thrown into a river. She awakens from her pain to discover that Anninho is gone and that she is recuperating at the home of Zibatra, a "wizard woman" who lives high in the mountains. Whether or not she will regain her health and become reunited with Anninho underscores the searching in the poem. A short exchange between the two women establishes the mood as well as the nature of Almeyda's quest:

> Did you see Anninho
> when you found me?
> "No. Only the globes of your breasts
> floating in the river.
> I wrapped them decently and hid them.
> The mud on the riverbank
> had stopped the bleeding.
> I put you in a blanket and
> brought you here . . .
> I cannot find him for you.
> It is you who must make the discovery"
>
> (p. 11).

Almeyda recreates in associative connections, therefore, the events which have brought her where she is. As the wizard woman applies herbs and other healing agents to Almeyda's wounded chest, Almeyda remembers the history of her people as well as her personal history and her relationship to Anninho. Her love for Anninho, and the love and health of her people which is symbolized by her cut-off breasts, provided the dramatic development for the possibility of reunion with Anninho as well as the healing/re-birth of the African settlement of Palmares. Though Zibatra is a wizard woman ("—no witch—") who could guide Almeyda to her lost lover, she does not, insisting instead that Almeyda find Anninho her "own self"; the poem is that seeking. Almeyda is immobilized by her wounds, but her thoughts fly back in time and create a poem of many actions and intriguing occurrences. She undertakes a spiritual journey which has parallels in the physical journey of escape and which often ignores restrictions of temporality and mortality. Zibatra does not take over the process of seeking for Almeyda, but she is there to ask prodding and provocative questions and to offer politely insistent encouragement when Almeyda would blur a vision or hesitate at what she sees.

The poem is composed of three sections. The first and longest, comprising fifty-one pages of the volume, recounts what has happened in the battle, the history of the settlement's fight for freedom, the role of the women in the society, especially those like Almeyda's grandmother, and the escape of Almeyda and Anninho from the battle, an escape so urgent that there was little time for love. Revelation of this information is intertwined with Almeyda's spiritual search for Anninho and, at times, her desire for a metaphysical union which will dissolve the earthly separation; there are remembered scenes of her with Anninho as well as envisioned ones. Section two, slightly over twenty-one pages long, concentrates more on Almeyda and Anninho. As her health improves, she thinks/dreams of some future time when she can relate to him what has happened to her, and she reflects upon past tender moments between them as well as upon those moments when she has been jealous. But there are still memories of other characters and past events in this section. Section three is only six pages long and deals exclusively with Anninho and Almeyda—together again in the past, the present and/or the future, and with a dream she has about Zumbi which emphasizes again the transcendence of mortality.

As the substance of section three suggests, Jones's poem is built upon a series of opposites and oppositions, which are central to Almeyda's search. The most prominent of these are man and woman, love and hate, war and peace, life and death, slavery and freedom, change and stasis, language and silence, hurt and health, seeing (eyes) and seeing (knowledge, clairvoyance), and past and present (with their variations of past/future, present/future, and memory/reality). Some of the oppositions are controlled by time, and others go beyond it; that concept is also central to the poem.

Almeyda's tale illustrates perfectly Plato's theory that men and women are incomplete in themselves and must seek each other for wholeness. We see in Almeyda a very traditional female role of woman expressing need for and

desire to be with her man. That seeking is intensified as we learn in the first few pages that Anninho is not just any man; he is very special indeed. We are given no indication that Zibatra has met Anninho, but her "seeing" ability ("I have seen with a third eye,/and a fourth one, and yet another"—p. 14) enables her to know, after initial skepticism, that he is unusual: ". . . . A woman/such as this one should have/a man as that one" (p. 11).

The seeking for union with Anninho is set against the war with the Portuguese. War by its nature provides no time for gentle love between man and woman; it replaces unity with separation. There can be no gentle caressing, no passionate love-making when the enemy is in pursuit. That opposition underlies Almeyda's desire for expressions of love from Anninho as they are trying to escape and his urgency that they continue on their journey, that they try to reach a place where another Palmares can be founded. Woman's desire to pause—for life, health, and love—as opposed to man's knowledge that wars do not allow pauses, is conveyed vividly in the following passages from Almedya's memories:

> *That was the question, Almeyda*
> *how we could sustain our love*
> *at a time of cruelty.*
> *How we could keep loving*
> *at such a time. How we could*
> *look at each other with tenderness.*
> *And keep it, even with everything.*
> *It's hard to keep tenderness*
> *when things all around you are hard*
>
> (p. 32).

*   *   *

> "That wind is cool here, Anninho; can we stand
> here a moment?"
> He slows down, then stops. It is a short moment
> we stand there. He keeps his back to me, then
> we start up again.
> "It won't be good to stand longer than this,"
> he says, and then we move on.
> I watch his back. If it was a different time,
> I could relax in my watching. It is a tense
> watching. We walk through a tunnel of trees
>
> (p. 65).

Almeyda knows danger, but her need and hope for love is stronger. That need is intensified in section two, when she is apparently picturing herself as not very young anymore ("I said It's been years since the flesh of man/flowed into me. And since that river of blood/stopped and the big wound closed"—p. 64). Here, Anninho represents for her perhaps the last possibility for love in this life, but even the imagined embrace remains beyond physical attainment as long as the war goes on.

Searching through memory and vision. Almeyda has several recurring images of wounds. One such scene vividly ties together the oppositions between man and woman, war and separation, life and death. In it, Anninho makes clear his recognition that one's mistakes can bring about destruction; he teaches that lesson to Almeyda. As he and Almeyda travel, she hurts her foot, opening a bleeding wound which also symbolizes the fate of her people. Anninho remembers Zumbi, the king of Palmares, relating to his people a painful lesson:

> "But Zumbi said . . ."
> "He said that there is always a last day,
> when the blood of the hunted
> serves as a guide for the hunters"
>
> (p. 20).

Zumbi's realistic vision, passed on to Anninho, forces the urgency he insists upon with Almeyda, forces him to deny love in order to prevent destruction and death.

The opposition between life and death can also be seen in the attitude Almeyda has toward King Zumbi's death; it becomes part of her search to transcend temporal limitations. Velho raided Palmares, and Zumbi was captured and killed:

> "I am told that after they killed Zumbi
> they cut off his head and put it in
> a public place to prove to the others
> that he was not immortal."
> "Eh, they think that is proof?"
>
> (p. 56).

but his spirit, Almeyda maintains, did not die. Her belief is almost comparable to that the Bourne Islanders hold toward Cuffee Ned's death in Paule Marshall's *The Chosen Place, The Timeless People*. The spirit of unrest and the desire for freedom will form a new rebellion in Bourne Island just as it will form a new Palmares. We are led toward the conclusion that the nation of ex-slaves will be healed in the same way that Almeyda's chest will be healed. The continuum of human experience will transcend the confines of death.

Almeyda often speaks of transformation in the poem, how states change. In her search for Anninho, she tells of her grandmother, also a woman of more than natural power. The grandmother has told Almeyda that she has "links with the invisible world" (p. 34); those links allow her to go "beyond time" (p. 27) and to see Anninho in "another time and place . . ." (p. 14). Defining the specific source of Almeyda's power and her inheritance of the ability to change, the grandmother says:

> . . . You are the granddaughter
> of an African, and you have
> inherited a way of being.
> And her eyes stayed on mine, Anninho,
> until all her words and memory
> and fears and tenderness
> ran through me like blood . . .
> That was the moment when I became
> my grandmother and she became me
>
> (pp. 32–33).

Her cut-off breasts are also significant in change and transformation. The enemy, by slicing off the symbol of nourishment for future generations, expects to stifle and destroy the Palmareans. But Almeyda is stronger than they. She searches out Anninho, who has the power to give "the long kiss that heals, or that persuades healing" (p. 83). She believes in love and in "transformation through love and tenderness" (p. 43). Though her wound is comparable to that of the woman "who mutilated herself, so she wouldn't have to have any man at all" (p. 44) to keep from having babies in a time of war and slavery, Almeyda has found a way to transcend that limiting political statement. She begins in section two to feel her breasts swelling:

> Anninho, my breasts are swelling.
> I feel them swelling.
> They are gone but I feel them swelling.
>
> My breasts are heavy, Anninho, and she is curing me.
> I am bread soaking in milk.
> She says my breasts were globes floating
> in the river, and that it is only
> memory and desire that replaces them;
> makes them feel heavy.
>
> (pp. 67–68).

Yet, it is that stronger than natural desire which contains hope for the Palmareans. And Almeyda *is* getting better; she is well enough to ease her restlessness by going for walks. There is much in her seeking reunion with Anninho to represent the future and the possibility for happiness.

That future is also represented in the report Jorge Velho makes to the king of Portugal in 1695:

> "It is indeed true that the force and stronghold of the Negroes of Palmares in the famous Barriga range is conquered . . . and that their king was killed (by a party of men from the regiment of the petitioner, which came upon the said King Zumbi on the twentieth of November, 1965) and the survivors scattered. Yet one should not therefore think that this war is ended. No doubt it is close to being terminated if we continue to hunt these survivors through the great depths of these forests, and if the regiment of the petitioners is kept along the frontier. If not, another stronghold will suddenly appear either here in Barriga or in any other equally suitable place. . . ."

Even the enemy recognizes the unquenchable thirst for freedom that slaves have. And if such slaves are accompanied by the Almeydas of their tribes, their journeys will ever lead toward hope for further rebellion and ultimate freedom.

With Zibatra as an encouraging, spiritual guide, Almeyda shapes for herself an understanding of her past with Anninho and a vision of the future. Continuing her preference for having a woman character relate a history of pain, love and suffering through contact with another woman, Gayl Jones offers in *Song for Anninho* a tale which is intense, historical, at times exotic, always pleasantly and painfully engaging. In it, Almeyda, through links with the invisible world, journeys from the past and separation to the hope of reunion with Anninho and the hope for a new Palmares.

Jerry W. Ward Jr. (essay date 1984)

SOURCE: "Escape from Trublem: The Fiction of Gayl Jones," in *Black Women Writers (1950-1980): A Critical Evaluation*, edited by Mari Evans, Anchor Press, 1984, pp. 249-57.

[*In the essay below, Ward discusses the importance of the characters' thoughts and acts of thinking in* White Rat, Eva's Man, *and* Corregidora.]

In the American penal system, female prisoners are often subjected to more psychosexual abuse than their male counterparts. The same condition obtains, according to our most perceptive writers, in American society outside the prison walls. The abuse of women and its psychological results fascinate Gayl Jones, who uses these recurring themes to magnify the absurdity and the obscenity of racism and sexism in everyday life. Her novels and short fictions invite readers to explore the interiors of caged personalities, men and women driven to extremes. Her intentions seem less analytic than synthetic, the strategies of her fictions themselves being indices of contemporary disorder as norm rather than deviation. Throughout Jones's fictions, prisons and asylums function as settings for problematic narratives and as clues for the interpretation of outsideness. In the very act of concretizing these fictions as aesthetic objects, readers find themselves caught. The pleasure of experiencing such irony, and of gradually coming to know how accurately it confirms our habitation of an invisible penal colony, is justification for attending to Gayl Jones's achievement.

The unpredictable structures of **Corregidora** and **Eva's Man** and of the short fiction of **White Rat** provoke questions about how we construct meaning from allowing our minds to play through the texts. The author invites us into semantic realms for which we may have no guides other than cultivated literary competence, previous knowledge of other texts. We cannot begin to speak of the value of the experience until we understand how we have been seduced. Indeed, we may find ourselves posing unusual questions. What does it mean to think in fiction? Does thinking in a fiction lead us to experience states of mind ostensibly *represented* in the fiction? And how does one distinguish thinking in fiction from its mimesis? Where does such inquiry lead us? Does it offer any insights about qualitative differences between fictions by male and by female writers?

Definitive, universal answers to such questions are unlikely. Yet raising them encourages us to think seriously about the verbal entrapment that is so pervasive a quality of modern fiction. Like the magic of Circe and Faust, modern fictions can transform us—while we permit their influence—into the beings that our humanity disguises. As readers we begin to grasp that neither man nor woman is immune to the siren song of Jones's fictions.

When we say we are thinking, we mean we are processing verbal and non-verbal symbols; if we say we are thinking in fiction, we are claiming to manipulate fictions as the basic elements of an associative process. Perhaps an analogy will provide some clarity: thinking in fiction is like thinking in sculpture. The sculptor does not think in material (stone, metal, plastic, clay, wood) but in space and in the possible distributions of spatial form. Likewise, fiction writers do not do their major thinking in words. Lexical items are servants to configurations of action, feeling, event, situation, visions. The sculptor's aim is the realization of spatial concepts in the physical world. The writer attempts to make temporal abstractions derived from human behaviors comprehensible in a text. Fictive configurations, like stone, are givens. The determining process of thinking in fiction elaborates what we assume to be true about human beings and their environments on a symbolic level. Thinking in fiction is at the very core of intertextuality, for the writer is using previous "texts" of human action to fable yet another text. The primal motive of modern fiction is not to conceal this technique; on the contrary, the technique is left so undisguised as to implicate the reader.

That is to say, the reader is forced to imitate the creative process. Once the fluid process of thinking has been frozen into a verbal structure, the writer's thinking *in* becomes the reader's thinking *with* and *about*. The ice cube of fiction is again reduced to liquid. We think with characters as we perform the task of recreating the text. We think about the implied narrator, who may or may not be identical with the writer of the narrative. Why do we let an absent voice speak to us? We think about the insights we gain from the pleasure or discomfort occasioned by the reading. We perform a secondary thinking in fiction, using our minds and the assumed intelligence behind the text as agents.

The chief agents, of course, may be the minds within the narrative, because characters think, and we think *with* them. The assertion that characters think does not require prolepsis. The fact is implicit in our most casual talk about fictions, especially soap operas, and in the sophisticated language of literary analysis. We are given to making contracts with narrative and its contents. In that sense, religion has no monopoly on transubstantiation. Whether we are reading narratives about Odysseus, Sula, Bigger Thomas, or Teacake, we pretend that words have become flesh and intelligence. By our pretending, we empower characters with the ability to think and act. Our judgments are bound by character development, the quantity and quality of traits exposed through description and dialogue. Often these traits are located in represented thought. In Faulkner's *As I Lay Dying* or Joyce's *Ulysses*, for example, much of the narrative is contained in mental operations. Our success with these novels depends on grasping why members of the Bundren family and Bloom, Stephen, and Molly think as they do. The more thoroughly we suspend disbelief, the more fully we think with characters. We adopt their patterns of thought, walking a tightrope between what they think and what we think we know to be real.[1]

There is more than a grain of truth in Frank Kermode's claim that modern readers have discontinued the assumption "that a novel must be concerned with the authentic representation of character and milieu, and with social and ethical systems that transcend it. . . ."[2] As modern writers know perhaps too well, there are no shared conventions about what constitutes authenticity or proper representation. The widespread belief that all systems are random (everything is everything) precludes the existence of authentic representation. Even in fiction, we grant authenticity only to the constituting agent, the mind.[3] As modern readers, we overthrow character for consciousness. We are self-conscious readers, pretending that thought represented in fiction is a key for unlocking repressive doors and thereby freeing the forces imprisoned in the underground of what is real. Gayl Jones's fictions provide rich opportunities for such pretense, because her texts guarantee nothing more than the fact of their existence. We trust thinking in fiction to provide escape from trublem, and that trust is a refraction of our historical dilemma.

Thinking in the fictions of Gayl Jones concerns itself largely with how women and men conceptualize their victimization, with how awareness of one's condition can render the self incapable of transcendence. Within the traditions of African-American and American fiction, her work can be classified as literature of departure; paradoxically, her work does not depart as far from the prototype of the slave narrative as a mere glance at the stylistic surface might suggest. No matter how far Jones ventures away from the naturalistic models of James Weldon Johnson, Richard Wright, Zora Neale Hurston, and Ralph Ellison, the experience of her texts lets us know we are participating in discourse about the slavery of limits. Under the influence of the texts, readers become for a time as enslaved and as psychotic as the characters they think with.

Corregidora, Eva's Man, and *White Rat* are attempts, to borrow words from Clarence Major, "to resolve the artificial representation problem of the realistic tradition and to reestablish a nonlinear view of the world or at least a view that is not confined to the dogma of a particular identity and its ideology."[4] They are also attempts to promote empathy with the diverse causes for abnormal functioning of the ego. In the reading experience, the thinking with and about, the depiction of Black women's suffering under the double yoke of racism and sexism is a simulacrum for the psychological battering that we all feel in varying degrees. It can be nothing more, however, than a simulacrum, a trace of the wasteland produced by the actions of other people, by the course of history, by the process of thinking itself. Thinking shapes personal and public identity. Women and men are their thinking.

Two of the stories in the collection *White Rat* provide excellent examples of thinking in fiction and its consequences. In **"White Rat,"** Rat, the self-named "white-looking nigger," thinks within Kentucky hill country and Black folklore, and within the *social fictions* of race. Rat is imprisoned in the myth of God's retribution for the breaking of priestly vows, especially the vow of celibacy. If the priest is Black, God places a curse on him unto the second generation; his child is born with a club-foot. If the priest is white, his child is born Black. Jammed by history into the fiction of the tragic mulatto, Rat compounds the absurdity by failing to recognize that his language (identifying his wife as the yellow woman with chicken-scratch hair and his son as the club-footed little white rabbit) is the source of domestic discord. As we mediate between Rat's first person narrative and our sense of what it means for a "white nigger" to talk about other "niggers," we begin to appreciate the prisonhouse of language. Just as Rat's acceptance of fictions confines him to a narrow social role, a failure to recognize the consequences of his language would make us as ignorant as he is. **"White Rat"** is a clever game of semantics, a net to catch the reader not attuned to how the codes of fiction operate in literature and in life.

Even should one be very aware of literary codes, Gayl Jones hints in **"The Return: A Fantasy,"** the possibility of being trapped by the consequences of fiction is very strong. In this story, Jones thinks out the probable results of digesting too well the fictions of Kafka. As Stephen must explain to his sister Dora about her husband Joseph Corey.

> He's made himself both the doctor and the patient, the curer and the ill. He has made himself the priest figure, working his own magic

As Joseph commented to Dora before their marriage, referring either to Gregor or Kafka or both

> "The man became a bug," he said. "Men can become bugs. There's no *as if*. You don't conduct your life *as if* you were Christ. You become Christ."[5]

Much of this story about the triangle of Dora, Stephen, and Joseph concerns Joseph's progressive descent into the Kafkaesque world of irreality, his becoming a character worthy of Kafka's imagination. The detrimental potential embodied in the forms and language of these short fictions is fully shown in the novels *Corregidora* and *Eva's Man*.

In *Corregidora*, a blues singer consciously relates selected facts about her life history between the ages of twenty-five and forty-seven. Ursa Corregidora begins with the end of her first marriage, and she ends with a description of the vindictive sexual act that makes reconciliation with her first husband possible. It is not peculiar that the initial and terminal segments of the novel involve the Woman's sexual life, nor that the middle of the book concerns sexual failure and emptiness, encounters with lesbianism, and sexual behavior on a nineteenth-century Brazilian plantation. Obsession with the sexual aspects of the self and of the self's relations with others is appropriate for a woman conditioned to believe procreation is a duty not a choice.

The basis for Ursa's thinking is a special case. It is not located purely in cognition of the status assigned women in society nor in a highly developed awareness of the procreative potential of Woman's anatomy. The sexual monomania that dominates Ursa's thinking is rooted in the ego's acceptance of a predetermined historical role. Unlike the narrator of the short story **"The Women"** Ursa does not exercise the option of not imitating her mother. She accepts the limits set by her great-grandmother and her grandmother, the limits that destroyed her mother's marriage. As Ursa thinks out her autobiography, her great-grandmother's words frequently resound in the depths of consciousness:

> . . .*The important thing is making generations. They can burn the papers but they can't burn conscious, Ursa. And That's what makes the evidence. And That's what makes the verdict.*[6]

In her great-grandmother's view the sole function of a woman descended from slaves is the leaving of evidence (children) against a vaguely defined they (the descendants of slave owners? all European peoples?). Ursa is imbued with this primitive belief in the duty of a Black woman, connected as it is to a circumscribed vision of Woman's possible development. Ursa never rebels, never seeks alternatives, never breaks free of the constrictive role ordained by others. An arrested personality results from failure to revolt against values received during maturation, and the consequences are devastating.

If Ursa's thinking represents the slavery of consciousness, the thinking in **Eva's Man** shows paralysis of consciousness, the inability to make certain decisions that is so vividly portrayed in Buñuel's *The Exterminating Angel*. Eva is forty-three, an inmate of a psychiatric prison, and she tries to account for her condition by remembering portions of her life before she committed a bizarre crime. Eva is the victim of her own passivity, her tendency to accept the Playboy fantasy of what a woman is. Her life history contains a series of sordid, dehumanizing sexual encounters. Although the encounters are linked, neither the pattern nor the debilitating effects of the experiences become meaningful to Eva until abuse drives her to momentary insanity. Putting the puzzle together, saying why she killed Davis Carter after spending five days in his hotel room, is difficult. Even as an unreliable narrator, Eva is aware that honest explanation depends on accurate facts:

> Sometimes they think I'm lying to them, though. I tell them it ain't me lying, It's memory lying. I don't believe that, because the past is still as hard on me as the present, but I tell them that anyway.

> [p. 5]

The psychiatrists think that Eva's lying, but Eva knows one can lie with words but not with the unarticulated contents of memory. Language is not sufficient. It has to be extended as visual thought—woman is queen bee, for

example, because visual thinking allows Eva to grasp meaning more completely. Ghetto socialization did not prepare Eva to master the linguistics code, but she is an expert in sensual conceptualizing.

In the novels, the main characters think in ways we hesitate to call typical. But their thinking, patterned by the manipulative requirements of engaging fiction, provides insights about how and why people think in atypical fashion and cause us discomfort.

It is not unusual to find thinking about slavery and history and the burden contemporary Blacks bear in modern fiction. To suggest, however, as Jones does in **Corregidora**, that a quaint idea about the Black Woman's role in Western history can be the dominant factor in thinking is to introduce a new use of history, since one is now urging that an historical institution may be incorporated as thought's structure rather than its object.

Ursa exercises a modicum of free choice in selecting a career, although the fiction that grows around the lives of blues singers may suggest becoming one is to conspire with one's enslavers. The master-slave relationship underscores Ursa's consciousness at crucial points: when she is recuperating from her operation (anatomical and psychological loss), when she has occasion to discuss mixed ancestry with husbands and others, when she considers that intercourse will be a mere physical act, during the years when she is an unattached woman making her lonely way in the world. Because skewed preconceptions and values are brought to every experience, experience will only serve to reaffirm the rightness of the fixed mind. What is a man? A stud. If he is a husband, a stud who has proprietary rights. What is a woman? A whore who produces evidence. If she is a wife, a sexual possession. From Ursa's perspective, all that is involved in the way men and women relate to one another is lust and mutual suffering. Should love occur, its expression will be perverse. Human feeling is severely limited, paralleling the slight affection between the master and the slave. And what is the self? The victim of history, but more specially of language, the medium in which mind conducts one kind of thinking.

Eva Medina Canada's *a posteriori* understanding of how self relates to others derives from references to specific events in her life. At a very young age she is fascinated by conversations between her mother and Miss Billie about the queen bee, the kind of woman who "kills" every man with whom she is intimate. Eva is deflowered with a dirty popsicle stick. Her ideas about sex are got from the street, from the example of a mother who openly has an affair with a musician, from an endless number of propositions. She learns that marriage is a sadistic-masochistic arrangement by observing the behavior of her neurotic cousin and his wife. Having married a man three times her age when she was seventeen, simply because she had tender feelings for him, she learns that marriage can be a prison. From the university of the streets, Eva learns that sex is fucking and women are bitches and men are eternally on the watch for a good lay. She has the will to resist sexual abuse, but the will is stunted.

Eva does not acquire a whole sense of personhood in her formative years. Woman merely responds to the terms presented by the environment in which she is located at any given time.[7] Thinking of this kind is typical for people who feel the effort to become human (in a restricted Western understanding of what humanity is) is meaningless, absurd. They exercise the dangerous freedom of following biological, and randomly acquired, impulses. Society and its fictions have convinced them that they are detritus; they think and behave accordingly. Low valuation of self is implicit in the vocabulary Eva uses to describe sexual experience, in the way her mind symbolizes womanhood in blood and bread, in private correlatives (man/owl; orgasm/river; power/the Medusa) and establishes resemblances between food and defecation

As one thinks in, with, and about the perspectives offered by Ursa and Eva and the characters that people Jones's short fiction, the fog begins to disappear from the horizon toward which thinking in fiction pushes us. In her novels in particular, Gayl Jones draws attention to fictive thought as it destroys all sense of human worth and dignity, as it destroys human beings who fail, for whatever reasons, to reject certain dimensions of language in their cultivation of innate potentials. Focusing on the sexual aspects of self, minimizing other features of being-in-the-world, the narratives of Ursa Corregidora and Eva Medina Canada intensify the reader's sense of the terror in fictions, and in unqualified acceptance of the fictions in which we costume social norms. Tricky, exotic, grotesquely aesthetic, thoroughly modern, Gayl Jones's fictions offer momentary escape from trublem, the trouble and problem of what is commonplace. On the other hand, the very fictionality of her fiction reimmerses us in man's struggle with the greatest demon in his mind: language.

To return to the initial questions. Thinking in fiction is accepting or rejecting the validity of verbal configurations which claim to explain anything about man, the shared activity of author, text, and reader. The point of offering us tangents and fragments is to induce the represented state we have no more guidelines in dealing with fiction's language than characters have in dealing with language itself. Thinking in fiction is like the dancer and the dance, an integration of means and ends. Qualitative differences between fictions by male and female writers are critical impositions, gender-readings.

The more carefully we attend to our thinking in, the more we recognize that the social norms and correspondences of the "real" world by which we once measured "character" in fiction are now restored to language, to the character's consciousness. Wolfgang Iser's observation about narrative strategies and the relative position of the narrator highlights what Gayl Jones is attempting to mesmerize us into admitting.

Even the narrator, despite his apparent position of superiority over the characters, deprives us of the guidance we might expect by neutralizing and even contradicting his own evaluations. This denial of orientation can only be offset by attitudes the reader may adopt towards the events in the text, which will spring not so much from the structure of the perspectives but from the disposition of the reader himself. The stimulation of these attitudes, and the incorporation of them into the structure of theme and horizon, is what characterizes the echelon arrangement of perspectives in novelists ranging from Thackeray to Joyce.[8]

And, one might add, from Ishmael Reed to Gayl Jones. Hers is fiction as critical, insinuative communication. Thinking in, with, and about can no longer rely on the protection of traditional conventions of reading. The very text of Jones's fictions destroys the usual barriers between text and reader, between original and parasitic speech acts. Whatever we think of her achievement in the context of African-American literary history, the fact remains that her fictions preclude vulgarized simplicity, our asking that fictions illustrate anything more than infinite variety of mind.

Notes

1. Hans Robert Jauss, "Levels of Identification of Hero and Audience," *NHL*, 5 (Winter 1974), 287. In Jauss's terms, thinking with is the "prereflective level of aesthetic perception."

2. Frank Kermode, *Novel and Narrative* (Glasgow: The University Press Glasgow, 1972), p. 6.

3. Some forty years ago, Georg Lukacs sensed that a clearly drawn intellectual physiognomy of character was disappearing from modern literature. What he did not predict was our acceptance of an intellectual electrocardiograph of character as we must with Gayl Jones's work. See Lukacs's comments in "The Intellectual Physiognomy of Literary Characters," *Radical Perspectives in the Arts*, ed. Lee Baxandall (Baltimore: Penguin Books, 1972), pp. 89–141.

4. Clarence Major, "Tradition and Presence: Experimental Fiction by Black American Writers," *American Poetry Review*, 5, iii (1976), 34.

5. Gayl Jones, *White Rat* (New York: Random House, 1977), pp. 132 and 105. Four other stories in this collection—"The Women," "Jevata," "The Coke Factory," and "The Roundhouse"—warrant closer examination. The others are better taken as warm-up exercises for comprehending techniques used in the major fiction.

6. Gayl Jones, *Corregidora* (New York: Random House, 1975), p. 22. Further references to this novel and to *Eva's Man* (New York: Random House, 1976) will be cited in the text.

7. Since *Eva's Man* treats the idea of "the black-woman-as-whore" from a Black female perspective, the novel does not allow us to dismiss this "male" fiction as inaccurate. Eva's complicity in that fiction, like Rat's complicity in racial myth, under the pressures of closed community is the real

issue. It is a matter of selecting at what point on the hermeneutic circle we wish to deal with it. Cf. Saundra Towns, "The Black Woman As Whore: Genesis of the Myth," *The Black Position*, No. 3 (1974), pp. 39–59.

8. Wolfgang Iser, "Narrative Strategies as a Means of Communication" in *Interpretation of Narrative*, ed. Mario J. Valdes and Owen J. Miller (Toronto: University of Toronto Press, 1978), p. 117.

Claudia Tate (interview date 1986)

SOURCE: "Gayl Jones," in *Black Women Writers at Work*, edited by Claudia Tate, Continuum, 1986, pp. 89-99.

[*In the interview below, Jones discusses her writing method, her intent in writing, and the differences between men and women writers.*]

Gayl Jones was born in 1949 in Lexington, Kentucky where she lived until she attended Connecticut College and Brown University. Her first novel, **Corregidora** *(1975), appeared when she was twenty-six years old. It is a bizarre, romantic story exposing the intimate family history of three generations of black women in rural Kentucky from early to mid-twentieth century.* **Eva's Man** *(1976) is a young Woman's recollections of the events leading up to her confinement in a mental institution. A collection of short stories,* **White Rat** *(1977), depicts brief encounters with seemingly ordinary black people, also in rural Kentucky, Jones's latest work,* **Song for Anninho** *(1981), is an extended lyrical ballad about a slave revolt in eighteenth-century Brazil.*

All of Jones's works are carefully wrought narratives developed from her determination to relay a story entirely in terms of the mental processes of the main character, without any authorial intrusion. While this has made many reviewers uneasy, Jones insists her task is to record her observations with compassion and understanding, but without judgment. Her style and method reflect her mastery in combining improvisational storytelling and sophisticated formal techniques, so that the stories do not appear contrived or to be relying on obtrusive narrative devices.

In addition to being a writer, Gayl Jones is a professor of English at the University of Michigan.

CLAUDIA TATE: *Gayl, in your discussion with Mike Harper[1] you said you didn't know what mysterious act Great Gram had performed on old man Corregidora until you got to the end of the novel. Does this mean that your writing is somewhat spontaneous, somewhat open-ended? Would you describe your writing process?*

GAYL JONES: In the interview with Michael Harper I said I didn't know what Great Gram had done to Corregidora when I first mentioned her "mysterious act" in the novel. When I asked myself that question, I didn't know what it was going to be, or even if I was going to resolve it in the book, or whether it was going to remain a "mysterious act." But in the process of writing the question was resolved. Or rather it was resolved in the process of the character Ursa acting out a new situation.

My writing is mostly open-ended, though I make loose outlines of items I want to include: lists of events, themes, situations, characters and even details of conversations. I make notes before and while I'm writing. I find I make more of these notes now than when I was writing *Corregidora* or *Eva's Man*, though this kind of "loose" outlining started with these novels. I like the word "improvisational" rather than "spontaneous"; I think it best describes my writing process.

Corregidora, as it appears in the Random House edition, is mostly my first version as I've made a minor revision. It consists of my adding information about Ursa's past, her relationships with Mutt and her mother. My revision method generally consists of asking questions, and then trying to answer those questions *dramatically*. In the case of *Corregidora*, my editor, Toni Morrison, asked an unanswered question: what about Ursa's past? This question required that I clarify the relationships between Ursa and Mutt and Ursa and her mother. So I added about one hundred pages to answer it. Now before I submit anything, I'll ask myself the questions that have not been answered in the course of the manuscript or perhaps pose new questions, which I then answer. Of course, I prefer to answer them dramatically rather than just to make statements.

Eva's Man went through several rewritings. It was first a kind of lyrical novel, then it was a short "dramatic" story, and then it was the *Eva's Man* as printed in the Random House edition. The handling of time, the ordering of events in this novel were primarily improvisational. I wanted to give the sense of different times and different personalities coexisting in memory. I was also trying to do something else I don't think came across very well. I was trying to dramatize a sense of real and fantastic episodes coexisting in Eva's narrative. The question the listener would continually hear would be: how much of Eva's story is true, and how much is deliberately not true, that is, how much of a game is she playing with her listeners, psychiatrists, and others? And, finally, how much of her story is her own fantasy of the past? I try to suggest this in the manner the story begins, and also by the repetition of the same events and situations but with different people involved.

C. T.: *The process you just described seems especially well suited for someone who is* telling *a story because a story seemingly doesn't have to concern itself with extreme formal aspects. The story seems to unravel. Do you consider yourself to be primarily a storyteller? If so, what then does that involve in terms of your listener, the evolving story, and especially your narrator for whom you shape ideas?*

JONES: I think of myself principally as a storyteller. Most of the fiction I write that seem to work have been those in which I am concerned with the storyteller, not only the author as storyteller but also the characters. There's also a sense of the hearer as well as the teller in terms of my organizing and selecting events and situations.

At the time I was writing *Corregidora* and *Eva's Man* I was particularly interested—and continue to be interested—in oral traditions of storytelling—Afro-American and others, in which there is always the consciousness and importance of the hearer, even in the interior monologues where the storyteller becomes her own hearer. That consciousness or self-consciousness actually determines my selection of significant events.

C. T.: When I read **Corregidora***, I sensed that I was hearing a very private story, one not to be shared with everyone. I felt that the narrator was consciously trying to select events in order to relay her story to me. I also felt it was not just my job to listen to her, but to become so involved in her story that I would somehow share her effort to understand and accept the past. In* **Eva's Man** *I sensed that Eva's character was not going to be violated by anyone, not even by her selected listener.*

JONES: I think that in the Corregidora story I was concerned with getting across a sense of an intimate history, particularly a personal history, and to contrast it with the broad, impersonal telling of the Corregidora story. Thus, one reason for Ursa's telling her story and her mother's story is to contrast them with the "epic," almost impersonal history of Corregidora.

In *Eva's Man* there is not the same kind of straight confiding, the telling of a history as in *Corregidora*. Although Eva renders her "intimate history," she chooses to do so only in terms of horrific moments, as a kind of challenge to the listener. I wanted the sense of her keeping certain things to herself, choosing the things she would withhold. But I also wanted the reader to have a sense of not even knowing whether the things she recalls are, in fact, true. She may be playing a game with the listener.

C. T.: In first-person narratives, especially those concerned with self-revelation of experience, the process of characterization is dynamic. A lot of stories, especially those by black males—I think of Invisible Man, *I think of the* Autobiography of an Excolored Man—*never tell you anything about the intimate self. They tell you about the self in conflict with external institutions. Your work, and also most of that by women, seems to be concerned with revealing the character's intimate sense of self through very complex relationships. Like those by many black women writers, your stories seem to focus on the revelation of inner character rather than on reporting head-on confrontation with social issues. Do you think that black men write differently from black women in terms of characterization, dramatized themes, elements of craft?*

JONES: Yes I've been thinking about that mainly in terms of something I call "significant events" in fiction. There is a difference in the way men select significant events and relationships, and the way women make these selections.

With many women writers, relationships within family, community, between men and women, and among women—from slave narratives by black women writers on—are treated as complex and significant relationships, whereas with many men the significant relationships are those that involve confrontations—relationships outside the family and community. In the slave narratives by women, for instance, one often finds personal, particular, "intimate" relationships; whereas those by men contain "representational" relationships. Even when men create heroines, often the relationships selected or given significance are representational rather than personal. For example, let's compare [Ernest] Gaine's *Autobiography of Miss Jane Pittman* and [Margaret] Walker's *Jubilee*. In the former the relationships given attention have some kind of social implication. On the other hand, we really don't have a sense of any kind of personal history for Miss Jane. Her attention is always directed outside of herself, and those events which are described in detail have social, rather than personal or intimate implications. You don't really have any sense of her relationships, let's say with her husband.

The question of one's identity, the power to act seem to determine these differences. Women writers seem to depict essential mobility, essential identity to take place within the family and community. But perhaps for male writers that "place" as well as those relationships are insignificant, restrictive, circumscribed. The questions we are asking are: generally, would the women's actions be considered significant by men? Would the consequences of a man's actions be different from those of a woman? Have the historical consequences of men's and women's actions carried similar weight, and how are these reflected in the works? If you compare the slave narratives written by men with those written by women, you see very delicate and complex interpersonal relationships in the latter, whether they be among members of the same race or between races. With men the focus is on social grievances, with little sense of intimate relationships among the slaves, precluding the desire for freedom.

The question of significant events/actions/relationships in fiction and how one's sex, history, culture, and geography influence them has been something that has interested me—not only in terms of writing, but in terms of how it affects one's critical response to a work. I wrote a story in which a man and a woman participate in the same action, and the consequence for the man is, let's say, death, whereas for the woman it isn't. Although I don't really want to say that women's actions have not carried similar weight, history seems to insist that the burden of consequence rests more heavily on men than on women.

C. T.: Who or what has had the greatest influence on your work?

JONES: My mother, Lucille Jones; my writing teachers, Michael Harper and William Meredith; and the "speech community" in which I lived while I was growing up have had the most important influence on my storytelling writing style. Although I can never really say the particular ways writers have influenced my work, I can name some writers I especially like: Hemingway, Joyce, Gaines, Cervantes, [Jean] Toomer, Chaucer. They were probably my first influences. Hemingway, Gaines and Chaucer for me are the "storytellers"; Joyce and Toomer, the "fictioneers"; Cervantes, both. I say "in terms of writing" because now a new kind of concern has been added: teaching, particularly the course in Afro-American literature that I teach. As a teacher, I have to look at writers, their work, and literary traditions in a way I didn't have to as a reader or writer. As a result of this different perspective, certain themes and concerns crystalize in ways they otherwise would not have for me. For example, classroom discussions about psychohistorical influences on characters is a case in point. This is particularly so when I discuss how these influences enter Zora Neale Hurston's and Jean Toomer's works, or in Alice Walker's or Toni Morrison's. So having to discuss works in this manner forces me to see them very differently.

When I wrote *Corregidora*, psychosexual ambivalences and contradictions in the American experience weren't self-conscious themes, but now they are; these exist in works by Baldwin or Walker or Toomer. Cervantes also has different implications now. When I read Cervantes now, I connect *Don Quixote* with the picaresque Afro-American slave narratives; consequently, *Don Quixote*—which is a favorite book—becomes even more important. Hurston interests me because of her use of folklore and her storytelling; I also think she's important if one wants consciously to crystalize an idea of a heroine, not in a self-conscious way, but in a conscientious way. None of my women are really heroines except in the sense they're storytellers and central figures.

There are also unconscious ways by which people are influenced by speakers and writers, or by an environment or landscape. I realize I'm rambling, and that is because I hesitate to "analyze" influences. The earlier writers—the ones I read at an earlier age—influenced me more stylistically and perhaps the influences now go beyond style to how style can manifest theme, how it contributes or enhances an idea.

C. T.: Does your writing follow a definite pattern or commitment, or are you telling stories that happen to be in your head?

JONES: Well, I'm mainly telling stories that happen to be there. But I can look at things I've written up to now and see a pattern in terms of ideas I have been interested in: relationships between men and women, particularly from the viewpoint of a particular woman, the psychology of women, the psychology of language, and personal histories.

C. T.: Reviewers of **Corregidora** *talk incessantly about sexual warfare. What is your response to that? I don't see*

sexual warfare. I see something I'll call, for lack of another term, the dialectics of love—a synthesis of pleasure and pain. Do you observe this dialectic at work in your novel?

JONES: I didn't think Ursa was involved in sexual warfare. I was and continue to be interested in contradictory emotions that coexist. There is probably sexual tension in *Corregidora* both in the historical and in the personal sense.

C. T.: Do you find that relationships which involve contradictory emotions reveal more about human character?

JONES: Yes. I also think people can hold two different emotions simultaneously.

C. T.: Do your works attempt to make sense out of the chaos of life or do they just record the chaos?

JONES: They attempt to record that chaos, but at the same time the artistic process is one of ordering for the storyteller and also a way of dealing with experience.

C. T.: Can you say what inspired you to write **Corregidora** *and* **Eva's Man***?*

JONES: Aside from my seeing myself outside of the conventional roles of wife and mother, my interest in Brazilian history, and my wanting to make some kind of relationship between history and autobiography, I cannot. As for **Eva's Man**, I can never really think of any reason why I wrote it. It is easier to talk intellectually about *Corregidora* than about *Eva's Man*. I generally think of *Eva's Man* as a kind of dream or nightmare, something that comes to you, and you write it down. The main idea I wanted to communicate is Eva's unreliability as the narrator of her story.

C. T.: When I read **Eva's Man***, I was immediately aware of three pervasive symbols: Queen Bee, Medusa, and Eve biting into the apple. These three symbolic personages have been very detrimental to men in our cultural history. How did you happen to select them?*

JONES: Well, they're the kind of images that worked themselves naturally into the story as I was writing it. When I began writing the novel, I focused on Eva's concern that she is different from the way others perceived her. She is bothered by the fact that men repeatedly think she is a different kind of woman than who she actually is.

C. T.: They think Eva's a whore.

JONES: Yes. She begins to feel she is, and eventually associates herself with the Queen Bee [the local whore] and the Medusa symbol. I put those images in the story to show how myths or ways in which men perceive women actually define women's characters.

C. T.: When you selected Eva to tell her story, obviously in a rather incoherent fashion, did you think a character who was not bound by sane responses could tell a story of her relationship with a man, something about life in general, with greater sensitivity than a sane character?

JONES: An ordinary sane teller might treat a particular incident as insignificant, brush over it, or compress it into a brief narrative package. The person who is psychotic, on the other hand, might spend a great deal of time on selected items. So there might be a reversal in the relative importance of the trivial and what's generally thought of as significant.

In Eva's mind, time and people become fluid. Time has little chronological sequence, and the characters seem to coalesce into one personality. It was an "irrational" process of selecting incidents to be related in the story. In this regard, there was one critic who talked about my not including incidents to round out Eva's life, to make it into less of a horror story. Those things might have happened in her lifetime, but they wouldn't, given her circumstances, have been the things she would choose to tell you.

I'm also interested in "abnormal" psychology and in the psychology of language. Abnormal psychological conditions affect sensitivity to certain things, change the proportions, affect significant events, relationships. . . .

There are some critics who can't or who don't want to separate the character's neurosis/psychosis from the author's psychological autonomy. They feel the character's preoccupations are those of the author's. I don't think this would be as true if the stories were written in the third person, and if there were some sense of the author's responding to experiences, directing how they're to be taken, or if the author wasn't also female and black. There have also been more responses to the neurotic sensuality in the books than to lesbianism. I don't recall lesbianism entering into any critical discussions except as part of the overall sexual picture.

I think the critics are responding to the absence of authorial "judgment." When I write in the first person, I like to have the sense It's just the character who's there. Judgments don't enter unless they're made by a particular character. And oftentimes that character's responses may not be what mine would be in the same situation. Also, I like to have that character as the storyteller without involving myself. It would be, perhaps, more interesting if my position were known. But there would be the same kinds of problems in terms of critics who do not want authorial intrusion. Maybe some of these problems could be avoided if, in my case, there weren't also elements of identity between the characters and myself as a black female. Critics frequently want to make certain correlations.

C. T.: What kind of responses have you gotten from readers concerning your writing about characters who do not conform to positive images of women or black women? Do

they want to castigate Eva and Ursa as some sort of representative black female?

JONES: Yes. And even if they're not bothered by those things, they're bothered by the fact that the author doesn't offer any judgments or show her attitude toward the offense, but simply has the characters relate it. For example, Eva refuses to render her story coherently. By controlling what she will and will not tell, she maintains her autonomy. Her silences are also ways of maintaining this autonomy. I find the term "autonomy" easier to use with her than "heroism." I like the idea of a heroine, though none of my characters are. That's something I can see working with.

I like something Sterling Brown said: you can't create a significant literature with just creating "plaster of Paris saints." "Positive race images" are fine as long as they're very complex and interesting personalities. Right now I'm not sure how to reconcile the various things that interest me with "positive race images." It's important to be able to work with a range of personalities, as well as with a range within one personality. For instance, how would one reconcile an interest in neurosis or insanity with positive race image? Ernest Gaines can create complex, interesting personalities who are at the same time positive race images. But these can also be very simplistic, so too can negative ones.

*C. T.: When I read your short stories in **White Rat**, I thought about the manner in which James Baldwin tried to vindicate homosexuality. In your works, however, there is no effort to vindicate lesbianism. That it exists seems to be the only justification needed for artistic attention. Is this assessment accurate?*

JONES: Yes. Lesbianism exists, and That's the only way I include it in my work. I'll have characters respond to it positively or negatively, or sometimes the characters may simply acknowledge it as a reality.

C. T.: Do you feel compelled to relate certain themes or just to dramatize situations?

JONES: I mainly dramatize situations. My main interest is in characters in relationship with other characters. Theme for me now is a kind of background thing but not something I'm overly concerned with.

What comes out in my work, in those particular novels, is an emphasis on brutality. Something else is also suggested in them that will perhaps be pursued in other works, namely the alternative to brutality, which is tenderness. Although the main focus of **Corregidora** and **Eva's Man** is on the blues relationships or relationships involving brutality, there seems to be a growing understanding—working itself out especially in **Corregidora**—of what is required in order to be genuinely tender. Perhaps brutality enables one to recognize what tenderness is.

C. T.: Do you take delight in the unusual, or does the unusual event just sort of happen?

JONES: It's something that happens, but I'm also interested in characters who are unusual. I'm not interested in normal characters. This is related to the whole question of positive and negative images: what does a black writer do who is not interested in the normal?

C. T.: How does it feel to know critics are dissecting your works?

JONES: Well, my first response to interviewers and critics was difficult because of the kinds of questions I was asked. The questions seemed to have very little to do with what was for me the process of telling a story. They were curious about my personal life because I have characters who are lesbians.

It feels strange to have people dissect my stories. There's something about it I'm not sure about. I don't know what possible path my writing might have taken had there not been critics. They do make me think of my work in a more self-conscious way. As I write, I imagine how certain critics will respond to the various elements of the story, but I force myself to go ahead and say, "Well, you would ordinarily include this, so go ahead and do it." But I do have a sense of how certain people will take aspects of character, style. Also, I find myself, though not directly, but maybe dramatically responding to certain kinds of criticism, not in ways you might recognize as responses, but in terms of certain kinds of themes. I'm probably taking more notes now than I did when I first started writing. In some ways I like that better. I think some conscientiousness is always necessary when you're writing. This seems even truer now.

C. T.: What is your most recent work?

JONES: I've just finished a new novel, *Palmares*. It's about a man and woman, and it takes place in Brazil in the seventeenth century.

C. T.: Are you working on any short stories?

JONES: A few, but most of them still need a lot of work.

C. T.: Do you write them, put them down and then revise them?

JONES: Yes. There are some stories I've had for more than four or five years now. I recently revised a couple of them. That's pretty much my method. I generally keep the stories for a long time before I decide they are publishable.

C. T.: Do you want to have a reputation, a recognizable name?

JONES: The writers whom I would most like to be like are those whose works have a reputation, but the person, the writer, is more or less outside of it. I would want to maintain some kind of anonymity, like J. D. Salinger. That's the kind of reputation I'd like, where you can go on

with what you're doing, but have a sense that what you do is appreciated, that There's quality to what you're doing.

Note

1. Michael Harper, "Gayl Jones: An interview," *The Massachusetts Review* XVIII (Winter 1977), pp. 692–715.

Sven Birkerts (essay date 1992)

SOURCE: "Writing Black," in *American Energies*, William Morrow and Co., 1992, pp. 168-73.

[*In the following excerpt, Birkerts argues that while Jones raises interesting questions about the distinctive form of African-American writers, her theories are flawed and she fails to take into account the issue of authority.*]

The basic premise of Gayl Jones's **Liberating Voices: Oral Tradition in African American Literature** is as follows: that modern African-American writers did not begin to realize their true literary identity until they either rejected the dominant modes of the European American tradition, adopting instead the forms and approaches suggested by their own oral and musical traditions, or else found ways to transform the received patterns through the deep incorporation of indigenous elements. Jones is highly discriminating in tracing the evolution of the various strategies of adoption and incorporation—of dialect speech, say, or the structures and idioms of blues, spirituals, and jazz—in the poetry, short fiction, and novels of isolated practitioners. Her discussions hew close to her chosen texts. She shows, for instance, the gradual liberation of dialect usage from Langston Hughes to Paul Laurence Dunbar to Sterling Brown to Sherley A. Williams, and the increasingly sophisticated implementation of musical modes from Jean Toomer to Ann Petry to Amiri Baraka. But her procedure of working with isolated texts, and of assuming a high degree of familiarity on the reader's part (with Toomer's story "Karintha," Baraka's "The Screamers," etc.), is likely to keep her study out of the hands of the interested lay reader. This is a book for the library stacks.

And this is a shame. Jones has targeted a topic rich in issues and implications, but she has taken it on with the scholar's narrow range of focus. For all its local acumen—and Jones is a skillful close reader with a sure sense for the symptomatic textual turn—**Liberating Voices** is neither particularly liberating nor revelatory. Certainly not the way it might have been if Jones had addressed certain core questions, most pressingly that of authority.

To get to this authority question, I must first take up what I see as the central problem of Jones's study. And this is, simply, that to set up her thesis, she also decides to set up a straw-man figure called the "European and European American traditions," and, alternatively, "Western literary forms." This shorthand seems tenable enough at first glance—we have a reflex sense of what she means—but on closer inspection it crumbles away. In that crumbling, certain deeper and more vexing issues are disclosed.

When I hear the words "European and European American traditions," I do not, like Göring, reach for my revolver. But I do reach into the banks of my literary memory and try to figure out exactly what this means. Given the context, African-American literature, and the title's telltale "liberating," I cannot but pick up certain trace elements of the pejorative. And though Jones never spells out her conception of these traditions—which she absolutely should—I sense throughout that she has them construed as essentially upright (or uptight), formal, prescriptive, exclusionary, and canonically oriented in their references, and altogether unsuited to the expressive needs of the African-American culture—indeed, of any Third World culture.

This is important. What is Jones talking about when she conjures up this monolithic entity? What underlies the conjuring? Is she suggesting that there is some general way in which these traditions prescribe what literature ought to be and proscribe everything else, or is she referring only to specific forms and conventions? If the latter, then which ones does she have in mind: naturalism, rhyme and meter, symmetrical construction of narrative, standard orthography in the transcription of dialogue, certain norms of "Standard" English—what? Jones never makes this clear, and by not doing so she leaves the impression that they, whatever *they* were, remained closed to the kinds of expression that African-American writers found imperative.

Leaving such an impression, which is bound to have its truths, Jones effectively preempts any discussion of European and American modernism, which was not only contemporaneous with the careers of most of the writers under discussion, but which was also entirely given over to cutting ancient boundary wires and opening up aesthetic options of every sort. *Liberating Voices* gives almost no inkling that this was a revolutionary era within the white European tradition. It makes little sense to posit the restrictiveness of white forms—Jones never calls them that, but she might as well—when writers like James Joyce, William Carlos Williams, Gertrude Stein, Ezra Pound, Virginia Woolf, Guillaume Apollinaire, Hermann Broch, and a phalanx of others were turning them into Plasticene pretzels. Jones does, to be fair, mention Dada and Surrealism, but she does not linger to assess their artistic implications.

My question, then, is not why the African-American writer should look to the oral and musical heritage of his culture for inspiration—there were certainly good reasons for this—but rather why Jones should present this as a choice made necessary by the limitations of the available forms. That is, the available *white* forms. The obvious implication is that these forms were in some way analogous to, or even a continuation of, the societal institutions and ideologies that have wreaked such injury upon the African-American people. It is tempting to draw the link, but it is also inaccurate.

There are two questions that must be asked. First, whether it is true that the available models did not allow the necessary expressive options? And second, whether there is some way in which forms or modes (naturalism, formal meter, etc.) are *intrinsically* value-laden? The answer to both is no. The entire aesthetic spectrum was open to the informed modern artist. James Joyce himself exploited many of its possibilities, including the unmediated incorporation of dialect and the experimentation with musical structures. As for the values that might be felt to inhere in any given form—these are clearly the result of accumulated historical associations. One is not a monarchist because one writes in regular meters.

I would argue that the African-American writer's turn to the oral and musical traditions was not due to the insufficiency of existing forms, but that it was, rather, an essential founding gesture that was vitally bound up with authority. Literature, like any art, requires above all else a secure cultural grounding. Without such a grounding it is a peacock's fan of aesthetic gestures, nothing more. Adjacent terms for this authority are *history* and *tradition*. Indeed, what is a tradition but cultural identity as it is established in and through historical circumstance, and what is authority but tradition revealing itself in a work? This is why the academic debate over the canon is creating such divisions and animosities. Opponents of the multicultural agenda fear more than anything else the leaching out of the substrata of tradition and the inevitable divestiture of authority that would follow. A tradition is, after all, a kind of deed establishing the history of ideological ownership. And in terms of the artistic culture it ends up being a record of prior use.

The point is that while the African-American writer might very well have developed a wide and useful expressive idiom from available models, the expression itself would necessarily carry the taint of prior use. A work could manifest every artistic excellence and still lack the authority conferred by a sustaining cultural connection. It makes perfect sense that the African-American writers should have sought to anchor their production in what are widely felt to be the wellsprings of African-American culture—oral narrative and music.

This turn, toward music in particular, raises certain questions, and Jones could have added some speculative weight to her book by taking them up. For instance, what does it *mean* to appropriate elements from the blues or jazz tradition for a literary work? Is it merely a way of expanding the stylistic reach? It strikes me that there is also a sense in which such a move signals an insufficiency of the usual linguistic tools; and signals, too, that the affective core of the subject or experience is more readily accessible through musical reference. The function of the musical incorporation, in other words, may be to root the credibility of the enterprise in a genre that is closer to the authentic stuff of African-American culture. The paradoxical result—this is at least open to serious questioning—is that while such a strategy can enhance the work with diverse textures, rhythms, and structural possibilities, it may in some subtle way also depreciate the original literary genre. This is, of course, one of the key questions in the debate over postmodernism: whether the cross-pollination of genres and breakdown of distinctions between "high" art and "popular" art does not ultimately take away from the expressive power of the art. This is not an issue, as some believe, of snobbism versus egalitarianism; it has more to with the origins and evolutionary necessity of distinct genres. At what point do borrowings stop counting as artistic enrichment and begin to indicate a crisis in the genre?

But this is not a debate I want to engage in here. Let me resume my contention: that it was not an unsuitability of available forms that directed the African-American artist to oral and musical traditions, but that it was a desire to acquire some of the authority embodied by these traditions. The decision had political, even legalistic, overtones. For the problem with those "European and European American" forms did not have to do with ownership but with prior use. Ownership is a synchronic phenomenon—one either owns something or not, and that thing can be taken away. Prior use, seemingly less binding, in fact is far more of a threat. It is diachronic, and thick with psychological implication. It means that no matter what the latecomer does, it will always be *after*. To be after is to be deprived of the historical claim—that one was there as witness, maker, or participant. All the good will in the world, and all the excellence of subsequent accomplishment, cannot undo it. Symbolic parricide is not the answer. The better way is to change the game, or find a new game—and in the process establish a new authority base.

We can think of the issue by way of analogy, taking the case of white singers and musicians setting themselves up as performers of the blues. There has always been a sense, on the part of whites and blacks alike, that this represents a trespass of sorts. And many white blues artists, recognizing this, have sought the sanction of some mentor from the "real" blues tradition—witness Bonnie Raitt hooking up with Sippie Wallace and Canned Heat cutting records with John Lee Hooker. Many people believe that the form itself, its basic patterns and variations, belongs to the African-American. Does it? That is, does it any more than the sonnet *belongs* to the white European? Or is it just that the African-American artists have stamped it so tellingly through prior use that any white adoption cannot but seem imitative and lacking authority? Where does the authority originate—in having shaped and refined the form, in the tradition of powerful expressions registered using the form, or in having experienced the suffering that is the content? Interestingly, nearly all white blues musicians have paid some lip service to initiation through suffering or social disenfranchisement that runs parallel to what the African-

American has known—perverse irony intended—as a birthright. "you've got to pay your dues—you've got to suffer if you want to sing the blues."

At issue, with blues as with literary forms, is the authority of the artist. You can mimic the outer forms—anyone can—but they mean little without the sanction of tradition. You have to have *had* the blues in order to sing them right—the listener will know if you have not. But wait—if you are white, even if you have paid your dues, you still cannot sing the blues. Not *really*. You may have the private authority—earned through hard living—but you will never have the cultural authority. If you are white, you are a latecomer to the blues, and you will always be a latecomer. It cannot be undone.

We might now consider the same notion, authority of prior use, as applied to traditional (European etc.) forms, and ask whether the same principle—the "blues principle"—applies. That is, whether in order to use one of these forms a writer must in some way *be* a vested member of the cultural tradition? If the writer is *not* a member, will the use, no matter how accomplished, be classed as an imitation? If so—and I will leave these questions dangling—wouldn't we have to say that there is an ineradicable color line running through literature no less than music, and that the African-American writer has had to found a literature by reaching to one side and the other but without stepping over the line? The liberation of voice, then, would have to be seen as a reaching inward, and the successes of the literature as a vindication of a larger sort. Gayl Jones's study raises many of these questions implicitly. I wish that she would have taken some of them on.

Amy S. Gottfried (essay date Winter 1994)

SOURCE: "Angry Arts: Silence, Speech, and Song in Gayl Jones's *Corregidora*," in *African American Review*, Vol. 28, No. 4, Winter, 1994, pp. 559-70.

[*In the following essay, Gottfried posits that Jones addresses an unusual topic for an African-American woman author by examining the roles of power in sexual ownership and political empowerment.*]

Gayl Jones's **Corregidora** (1975) painfully, often brutally, explores rigid definitional boundaries of the self. Dealing with four generations of black Brazilian-American women who are strictly defined initially by a slaveholder/procurer and then by themselves, the novel challenges us to think about how the system of slavery reifies a concept of black women as hypersexual by regarding them as property. Great Gram Corregidora charges her family to "bear witness," to have children who must memorize her old slavemaster CorregiDora's atrocities and recite them at Armageddon, "*when the ground and the sky open up to ask them that question That's going to be ask*" (41). Hence, sexual commodification is supplanted by a deliberate, political self-definition. But as Ursa (a childless blues singer and the youngest Corregidora) discovers, this political move has a double-edged drawback: The Corregidoras' agenda severely limits their sexual identities, a limitation which in turn provokes domestic violence.

Marked by their family history, Mama and Ursa can neither accept nor refute their mothers' belief that all men are rapists. Their ambivalence finally pushes their husbands to the point of violence. Although this violence stems from CorregiDora's sexual abuse, it is not excused by it. Through the framework of blighted sexuality and domestic assault, Jones argues that political self-objectification is a vital yet problematic step toward the empowerment of these women.[1] Not solely focused upon violence and retribution, *Corregidora* also asks how a woman can renegotiate her sexual desire when she descends from a long line of abuse and rage.

In effect, Ursa CorregiDora's sexuality has been silenced first by her family's outrageous history, and then by its vow of retribution. She breaks this silence, as Keith Byerman argues, when she achieves an "epiphany" of self-realization, discovering her own voice and art through the African-American tradition of the blues (180). The blues performer "is not only the victim but also, by virtue of the performance itself, the ultimate power" (179). This kind of dialectic extends to Gayl Jones herself, who resists the silencing identity of a "representative" black woman writer by expanding her depictions beyond what she has called "positive race images" (Tate 97), and by arguing that "There's a lot of imaginative territory that you have to be 'wrong' in order to enter" (Jones, "Work" 234). In applauding but also criticizing certain techniques for black female self-empowerment, Jones enters that territory.

In *Corregidora*, mothers perpetuate as well as suffer from violence. It is therefore important to ask: When are mothers' and daughters' bodies both a private and a public space? How are the bodies of mothers as well as of other women politicized within *Corregidora*? In what ways might their politicization betray women?

Ursa's familial project of passing judgment infuses her very name. As Melvin Dixon notes, *corregidore* means 'judicial magistrate' in Portuguese: "By changing the gender designation, Jones makes Ursa Corregido*r*a a female judge charged by the women in her family to 'correct' (from the Portuguese verb *corrigir*) the historical invisibility they have suffered" (239). Additionally, *Ursa* in Latin means 'bear,' a word whose associative meaning is undeniable here. Rendered sterile when her husband pushes her down a flight of stairs, Ursa must bear witness through her art, the blues. She also bears witness that she has a place beyond retribution and vengeance.

Old Corregidora not only turns Great Gram's sexuality into a product, but also fathers her daughter and her granddaughter, who thus become living emblems of both violence and survival. Each "Corregidora woman" gives

birth to a daughter who must memorize and "leave evidence" of this family history shaped by slavery and rape. Telling of the official abolition of slavery in Brazil, Ursa's grandmother explains the need for this human evidence: The officials burned all written documentation of slaveholding "*cause they wanted to play like what had happened before never did happen*" (79). What had happened, of course, was the violent reduction of women to objects of exchange. In the abusive economy of CorregiDora's Brazilian plantation, Great Gram and her daughter are "'gold [valuable] pussy'"; a Woman's vagina equals her economic value and that economic value equals her essence (124). As CorregiDora's favorite "'*little gold piece*'" (10), Great Gram is used for both his profit and his pleasure until she flees to Louisiana, temporarily abandoning their daughter to the same treatment. The text reinforces her identity as an abused "piece" of goods and her daughter's identity as incest victim; the only formal name Jones gives these women is their rapist's surname.

CorregiDora's definition of slave women crosses time and place, surfacing in Ursa's first marriage. Ownership based on sexual relations informs her relationship with Mutt Thomas, who identifies Ursa as "*his* pussy," a term that signifies for him a faithful and loving wife (46). Possession is as important to Ursa's husband as it was to her great-grandfather: "'*Ain't even took my name. You CorregiDora's, ain't you? Ain't even took my name. You ain't my woman*'" (61). Ursa remembers Mutt's "asking me to let him see his pussy. Let me feel my pussy" (46). Great Gram's identity as CorregiDora's "gold piece" resonates in Ursa's identity as Mutt's "pussy." Caught up in her mothers' political agenda, Ursa initially allows Mutt to own her body and soul; according to Corregidora rules, a woman is wholly defined by her vagina and her womb.

How can "Corregidora rules" still apply in the mid-twentieth-century United States? Working towards self-realization, Great Gram and Gram transform—but do not abandon—CorregiDora's objectifying code. In their philosophy, a Woman's body is never her own, and a child is never a person in her own right. Exploring the problems of self-definition through motherhood, Missy Dehn Kubitschek notes that "Ursa loses her identity with her womb" (180). CorregiDora's victims unknowingly continue his abuse in their injunction to "make generations." These "self-appointed griots" tell and retell an invariant history whose "power to obliterate personality" is remarkable half a century later (Kubitschek 146–147). The Corregidora women respond to their early enslavement by defining themselves and their daughters as wombs intended for the literal bearing of witnesses. Sexual violence doubly limits desire and pleasure for these women. First defined as "pussy," they are now *self*-defined as womb. The function of Woman's body, therefore, is single-minded still: No longer a sexual commodity, it has become a political commodity. Using Ursa's reclamation of desire and sexuality as an example, Gayl Jones argues that political commodification is a stepping stone toward self-empowerment but not an end in itself. Ursa must realize her sexual self in order to resolve her legacy of abuse. As Patricia Hill Collins notes, supplanting "negative images with positive ones can be equally problematic if the function of stereotypes as controlling images remains unrecognized" (106). The empowering mantle of an avenger can become a straitjacket.

Perhaps *Corregidora*'s readers are made most uncomfortable by Jones's refusal to submerge desire under a history of abuse. Gram and Great Gram speak vengeance through their memories, but their stories also resurrect the memory of their abuser. While *Corregidora* works against smothering sexuality beneath a political veil, we must remember that Jones does not exonerate the slavemaster's atrocities. Neither does she depict rape as anything but vicious. Rather, she is concerned with locating sexual pleasure in the lives of the victimized. Mama tells Ursa that Martin, her husband and Ursa's father, "'had the nerve to ask [Great Gram and Gram] *what I never had the nerve to ask. . . .* How much was hate for Corregidora and how much was love?'" (131; italics added). Desire's fusion with hatred is made clear in Melvin Dixon's identifying Corregidora as "the lover and husband of all the women" (241). While the deliberately raw narratives of Great Gram and Gram dispel, for me, the image of Corregidora as romantic "lover," Martin's question still forces Jones's readers to examine the highly disconcerting coexistence of desire and abuse.

It is no coincidence that Ursa can voice her desire through the blues; Jones has explained that *Corregidora* is a "blues novel" because "blues talks about the simultaneity of good and bad. . . . Blues acknowledges all different kinds of feelings at once" (Harper 700). While Ursa's mothers speak freely about sexual abuse, sexual desire appears only in the seams of their narrative. Ursa muses about the possibility of their pleasure: "And you, Grandmama, the first mulatto daughter, when did you begin to feel yourself in your nostrils? And, Mama, when did you smell your body with your hands?" (59)

Corregidora is at its riskiest in hinting that desire can exist in even the most abusive situations. Jones notes that her readers are often "bothered by the fact that the author doesn't offer any judgments or show her attitude toward the offense, but simply has the characters relate it" (Tate 97). Like Jones, Ursa does not judge her mothers, but only puzzles over Grandmama's and Great Gram's "desire":

> *Corregidora was theirs more than [Mama's]. Mama could only know, but they could feel. They were with him. What did they feel? You know how they talk about hate and desire. Two humps on the same camel? Yes. Hate and desire both riding them. . . . Still, there was what they never spoke . . . what they wouldn't tell me. How all but one of them had the same lover? Did they begrudge [Mama] that? Was that their resentment?*

> (102–03)

These questions are enormously difficult, perhaps unanswerable, and Jones's insistence upon asking them reveals the inevitable confusion resulting from linking sexuality with personal and political revenge. More importantly, Jones delineates the extent to which Ursa's mothers have been cheated.

The text shows that desire may sprout between the cracks of a thwarted life, but the plant will never be strong and healthy. No one can forget CorregiDora's identity as rapist and slave-breeder, yet he also provides Great Gram and Gram with their only sexual experience: an experience of fear, rape, and incest. In a twisted sense Corregidora is the only "lover" they ever have, yet their memories of him have maimed their desire as surely as Mutt has maimed Ursa's body. She cannot conceive a child while her mothers cannot conceive of sexual love: Corregidora "'*made them make love to anyone, so they couldn't love anyone*'" (104).

The Corregidora women's repression of desire for political reasons can be read as a response to slavery's capitalist control of black women's sexuality: They bear witnesses rather than human units of labor (see Collins 76). Furthermore, as Collins and Hazel Carby have noted, the justification for "breeding" black slaves is inextricable from nineteenth-century ideologies of white and black womanhood. The "cult of true womanhood," with its required suppression of sexuality, did not simply exclude black women, but also—in labeling them Jezebels or whores—used them as a contrasting backdrop for white women's "purity" (see Carby 23–31, 34–35, 38). This strategy virtually sanctioned the extensive sexual violence black women suffered at the hands of white men. The sexually aggressive "matriarch" and the morally inferior "welfare mother," two images of black women fabricated by contemporary white culture, continue this association (see Collins 77, 78).

In dealing with black female sexuality, *Corregidora* stands apart from much of nineteenth- and early twentieth-century black women's fiction. When black women writers (for example, Jessie Fauset) grappled with the ideology of true womanhood, they sought to dissociate their bodies from "a persistent association with illicit sexuality," and so deleted sexuality entirely from their representations of black women (Carby 32; see also 167–68, 174). *Corregidora*, in challenging instead of fleeing that association, reclaims the erotic as a realm of human agency (see Collins 164, 166, 192). Ursa's struggle to voice her own desire inevitably leads her to that realm.

Although she does not wholly renounce her familial identity of woman-as-womb, she does acknowledge pleasure in a limited way. Certainly, CorregiDora's violent legacy has circumscribed Ursa's sensation of desire; she initially changes the terms of her self-definition by focusing her sexuality upon her clitoris rather than her womb. Unlike her mothers, who try to substitute rage for gratification, Ursa localizes her desire, at one point realizing that "' . . .those times he didn't touch the clit, I couldn't feel anything'" (89). The work of Gayatri Spivak and Hélène

Cixous, each with her own emphasis on the specificity of the body, is helpful in evaluating this localized reclamation of sexuality. In "French Feminism in an International Frame," Spivak describes the clitoris as something suppressed or effaced in the interest of defining "woman as sex object, or as means or agent of reproduction" (151). Since female sexual pleasure has nothing to do with reproduction, the clitoris is what Spivak calls "women's excess in all areas of production and practice" (82). Ursa centers her pleasure precisely on the point that "exceeds" both CorregiDora's racist appropriation and her mothers' political objectification of the female body. In doing so, she takes her first step toward reclaiming her entire body from an initially racist, politically motivated agenda.

Like Spivak, Hélène Cixous also discusses desire; however, Cixous locates female sexual pleasure all through the body rather than focusing on a "phallic" point—i.e., the clitoris. While Cixous's biological and racial essentialism cannot be ignored,[2] we can use her work to further understand the search for desire in **Corregidora**. As long as Ursa confines her pleasure to a singular, finite location, she is still *limiting* her desire, still defining her sexual self in narrow terms. Cixous's emphasis upon the multiplicity of female pleasure is relevant to my discussion precisely because it works *against* that narrowing definition. Cixous visualizes a "Woman's body, with its thousand and one thresholds of ardor" and its "profusion of meanings that run through it in every direction" (315), while Ursa's limited sense of desire leads to her difficulty in "feel[ing] anything" sexually. That difficulty haunts her through the novel, and is largely responsible for destroying her two marriages. More importantly, it reinforces her belief that she is somehow flawed as a woman, and feeds into her family's code of objectification. In the logic of her mothers, without a womb, how can she function as a woman? Ursa's sterility tortures her with the knowledge that she can no longer fulfill her "purpose." She cannot forget the "'*space between [her] thighs. A well that never bleeds*,'" and bemoans the "'*silence in [her] womb*'" (99).

Corregidora's emphasis upon the body ties in with Cixous's and Spivak's perspectives on female desire, which work against what Elizabeth Spelman calls white feminism's somatophobia: "fear of and disdain for the body" (126). Alluding to Simone de Beauvoir's observation that women have been "regarded as 'womb,'" Spelman connects feminism's "negative attitude toward the body" with "white solipsism in feminist thought" and, significantly, with "the idea that the work of the body and for the body has no part in real human dignity" (127). From Jonathan Swift's scatological poetry to Claude Levi Strauss's research on the significance of women's menstrual cycles in "primitive" cultures, women (but not most men) are indeed represented as having lives "determined by basic bodily functions. . . . Superior groups, we have been told from Plato on down, have better things to do with their lives" (127). As Spelman rightly points out, when this disdain for bodies divorces "the concept of woman . . . from the concept of Woman's body," it posits a kind of ahistorical woman, one who

has no color, no accent, no particular characteristics that require having a body. . . . And so it will seem inappropriate or beside the point to think of women in terms of any physical characteristics, especially if their oppression has been rationalized by reference to those characteristics.

(128)

In short, there would be no difference between the lives of a black woman of 1892 and a white woman of 1992.

Biological determinism can be a treacherous landscape for any feminist discussion. Nonetheless, Gayl Jones's physically oriented focus upon female pleasure necessitates a careful look at the body.

The Corregidora women's consistent self-identification with reproductivity is a stunning variation upon Gayatri Spivak's location of women within a Marxist framework of production. While women biologically "produce" children, Spivak notes that, socially speaking, "the legal possession of the child is an inalienable fact of the property right of the man who [biologically, yet also legally] 'produces' the child" (79). I do not want to recreate Spivak's entire Marxist argument here; what interests me is her statement that, culturally, "the man retains legal property rights over the product of a Woman's body."[3] This emphasis upon property and production intersects with the experiences of black slave women squarely at the crossroads of reproduction and desire. As Spivak notes, a system of product/ownership leaves no room whatsoever for sexual pleasure. Naturally, she adds,

One cannot write off what may be called a uterine social organization (the arrangement of the world in terms of the reproduction of future generations, where the uterus is the chief agent and means of production) *in favor of* a clitoral. The uterine social organization should, rather, be "situated" through the understanding that it has so far been established by excluding a clitoral social organization.

(152)

That is, recognition of women's sexual desire *alongside* their "value" as (re)producers is one way of empowering them as subjects of pleasure rather than passive objects of exchange, and women's "pleasure-as-excess" finds an appropriate sign in the clitoris—a sign that Ursa acknowledges in her rejection of her mothers' imposed self-definition.

That sign also defies women's relegation to an inferior status in Freudian terms. When Hélène Cixous attacks the notion of what she calls "the supreme hole," she refers to both the "lack" of a phallus in women, as perceived by Freud, and the literal cavity of the vagina and womb. Focusing upon Woman's "lack" results in the consistent identification of the "female" with "the negative"—an absence and a deformity. Instead, Cixous focuses upon female desire through her location of pleasure *throughout* the body, and argues for the "nonexclusion either of the difference or of one sex" and "the effects of the inscription of desire, over all parts of my body and the other body" (314). In contrast, the Corregidora women see a chance to create a *tabula rasa* upon which they can inscribe their story of sexual violence and rage. But is that all they see? The enforcement of a singular, fixed meaning upon their sexuality would seem to eliminate desire from their lives. Still, Jones's careful and persistent questioning about their "hate and desire" suggests that the issue of vengeance is not so clear-cut as it first appears.

En route to reclaiming her sexuality from this political agenda, Ursa recognizes her family's rigid code of binary oppositions between male and female. Their history categorizes each sex, both black and white. All men are rapists; all women, victims who sustain themselves upon their anger.

Fashioning CorregiDora's sexual commodification of their bodies into political self-commodification, Ursa's mothers do turn his racist, oppositional perspective to their own advantage. In doing so, however, they insist upon what Keith Byerman calls a "dualistic universe" of victims and rapists (180). Historically, this mode of "either/or dichotomous thinking" has fed racist as well as sexist objectification; both Collins and Christian have observed how easily white culture's concept of black women as "Other" leads to forms of manipulation (see Collins 68–69; and Christian, *Perspectives* 160). Additionally, Toni Cade Bambara writes that "stereotypical definitions of 'masculine' and 'feminine'" oppose "what revolution for self is all about—the whole person" (qtd. in Collins 184–85). The men who marry Mama and Ursa try to fight against their imposed definition as rapists. As CorregiDora's legacy wins out, however, their frustration leads to domestic violence against their wives. Martin beats Mama until her face is swollen and discolored. Mutt Thomas drunkenly pushes Ursa down a flight of stairs, killing her fetus and leaving her sterile. Ursa must resolve both the racist brutality of her mothers' lives and the limitations of their response to that brutality. Until she can do so, she is subject to the violence engendered by CorregiDora's atrocities. Familial memories distort her sense of self, and both her husbands victimize her in part (but only in part) because she sees herself as a victim. Ursa needs to transcend the cycle of violence that her mothers have unknowingly passed on to her. To some degree, she can do so by fully understanding her *sexual* self.

Ursa's identity as a daughter is pivotal to this understanding. She must "'*go on making dreams . . . till [she] feel[s] satisfied that [she] could have loved*'" Mutt, and realizes that she "'couldn't be satisfied until [she] . . . had discovered [Mama's] private memory'" of Martin (103–04). With her accident and two failed marriages behind her, Ursa visits her mother to learn about her parents. She needs to see herself as a child born of love rather than of rape. Asking about her father for the first time in her life, she tells Mama that what "'happened with you was always more important [than Corregidora]. What happened with you and him'" (111).

Mama is not a victim of rape or incest when she marries Martin. Identified as a walking womb, however, she still categorizes her husband as a tool for vengeance, telling Ursa, "'. . . I knew I wasn't looking for a man'" (117), but "'. . . my whole body *wanted* you . . . and knew it would have you, and knew you'd be a girl'" (114; italics added). Because Mama's body wants a *daughter*—not a man, not a lover—that body enacts an emotional form of parthenogenesis: Needing a man to conceive a daughter, Mama does not want "'*his fussy body, not the man himself.*'" Ursa reflects that Mama had "'*gone out to get that man to have me and then didn't need him, because they'd been telling her so often what she should do*'" (101). Denied a sense of herself as a private and sexual being, Mama always hears the angry voices of her mothers and their rapist when she closes her eyes. Aware of her own complicity in this denial, she remembers her first sexual experience: "'. . . all of a sudden it was like I felt the whole man in me, just felt the whole man in there. . . . *I wouldn't let myself feel anything*'" else (117–18; italics added).

The pernicious legacy of slaveowners like Corregidora extends not just to Ursa's mothers. Sexual violence committed against black women also affects black men; as Carby notes, "Black manhood . . . could not be achieved or maintained because of the inability of the slave to protect the black woman in the same manner that convention dictated the inviolability of the body of the white woman" (35). Although Mama and Martin have never been slaves, this ideology of black sexuality permeates their relationship. Her identity as angry victim not only thwarts her sexuality, but also reinforces Martin's sense of powerlessness and frustration as a black man in twentieth-century North America.[4]

Living with him in her grandmother's three-room shotgun house, Mama rarely sleeps with Martin:

> "'. . . he wasn't getting what he wanted from me. . . . I kept telling him it was because they were in there that I wouldn't. [But] even if they hadn't been. . . . "What do we have to do, go up under the house?" he kept asking me.'"
>
> (130)

Mama's familial agenda comes full circle, sketching a self-fulfilling prophecy of abuse and victimization as Martin's angry frustration leads first to his disappearance, then to violence. Believing that the only relationship between men and women by Corregidora standards is that of prostitute and client, he beats his wife badly when he next sees her, saying: "'I wont you to go on down the street, lookin like a whore'" (121). Her response is, tellingly, no response at all:

> "'. . . I knew there wasn't nothing I could do if he did [beat me]. I know I wouldn't do nothing even if I could. . . . I carried him to the point where he ended up hating me, Ursa. And That's what I knew I'd keep doing. That's what I knew I'd do with any man.'"
>
> (120–21)

Mama's self-identity as inevitable victim is thus even more malignant, because more powerful, than Martin's rage.

Frustration and violence reemerge in Ursa's own marriage when Mutt pushes her down a flight of steps. Certainly, Mutt is accountable for his behavior, but Ursa also recognizes the indirect operations of her familial agenda. Her mothers' histories thwart her own desire and infect her marriage until Mutt cries that he's "'tired a hearing about CorregiDora's women. Why do you have to remember that old bastard anyway?'" In part, Mutt's own slave ancestry explains his possessiveness, but it is also Ursa's inability to "feel anything" sexually that drives him to wild speculations about "'them mens watching after you'" (154). Ursa's sexual focus is limited because, like her mothers, she is held captive by the raging memories of her ancestry. Corregidora established this captivity, but Ursa's mothers are partially culpable for its reinforcement. Mutt, referring to her slave ancestors as well as his, tells Ursa, "'Whichever way you look at it, we ain't them'" (151). But Ursa *is* them, and will *be* them for as long as their memories confiscate her body as a witness.

Often she wonders just whose body she inhabits: hers, or the collective body of the Corregidora women? Great Gram and Gram re-tell their history so effectively that Ursa's mother "learned it off by heart"; in fact, "it was as if their memory . . . was her . . . own private memory" (129). At one point her mother's narrative merges so strongly with Great Gram's that "'it wasn't her that was talking, but Great Gram. . . . she wasn't Mama now, she was Great Gram'" (124). Staring at a photograph of herself, Ursa realizes: "I'd always thought I was different. . . . But when I saw that picture, I knew I had it. What my mother and my mother's mother before her had. The mulatto women. Great Gram was the coffee-bean woman . . ." (60). *It* refers to CorregiDora's blood, but also to the horrific remembered lives of Ursa's mothers. She is so forcibly identified with her family that she has no privacy from their relentless memories: *"My mother would work while my grandmother told me, then she'd come home and tell me. I'd go to school and come back and be told"* (101). These stories—terrible and essential—become her mothers' wedding gift to her.

To resolve her legacy of abuse, Ursa must relocate the site of her desire and embrace a multiplicity of sexual pleasure. She also needs to recognize her own potential for ruthlessness in what Gayl Jones explains is the "blues relationship" between men and women:

> Although the main focus of Corregidora . . . is on the blues relationships or relationships involving brutality, there seems to be a growing understanding—working itself out especially in Corregidora—of what is required to be genuinely tender. Perhaps brutality enables one to recognize what tenderness is.
>
> (Tate 98)

Tenderness and brutality coalesce in the text's ambivalent closing scene between Ursa and Mutt. Twenty-one years after Ursa's accident, Mutt appears and the two reunite. Still, Ursa's initial thoughts are violently retributive even during a moment of intense sexual intimacy:

> I got between his knees. . . . It had to be sexual, I was thinking, it had to be something sexual that Great Gram did to Corregidora. . . . "What is it a woman can do to a man that make him hate her so bad he wont to kill her one minute and . . . can't get her out of his mind the next?" In a split second I knew what it was. . . . A moment of pleasure and excruciating pain at the same time, a moment of broken skin but not sexlessness, a moment just before sexlessness, a moment that stops just before sexlessness, a moment that stops before it breaks the skin. . . .
>
> (184)

During fellatio Ursa retreats from "broken skin" to stopping just before"—she does not castrate Mutt. The point is that she *could* have done so.[5] She empowers herself in this sexual union, however violently, by becoming an active agent ("I wanted it too. . . . I got between his knees"), not the passive one who must always *"say I want to get fucked"* (89; emphasis added; see also Kubitschek 150). In this pivotal scene Ursa slowly begins to reclaim her desire and her body from her family narrative of abuse.

Ursa reevaluates her role as victim by acknowledging her own power to hurt, a power that is a point of connection for her and Mutt: ". . . was what Corregidora had done to [Great-Gram] any worse than what Mutt had done to me, than what we had done to each other, than what Mama had done to Daddy, or what he had done to her in return . . . ?" (184) By recognizing herself and Mutt in these "others," Ursa also recognizes the pattern of mutual abuse that she must break to reclaim desire (see also Byerman 180–81). Through realizing that the power to hurt lies not only in the victimizers but also in the victims, she empowers those victims. Here, reclaiming desire means first recognizing the potential for mutual abuse between men and women. Locating the other in oneself involves acknowledging that violent possibility, not repressing it. Through this realistic acknowledgment, Gayl Jones breaks a destructive pattern: Ursa opts not for pain, but for pleasure. The text closes with Ursa's realization of her own potential as an abusive agent. It also points toward another potential: that of a woman who can reclaim her body *and* her desire.

Of course, objectification not only sexually constrains but also silences—a silencing that ***Corregidora*** undermines through the blues song and the oral narrative. When a Woman's voice and power are equated solely with her reproductive capacity, she is rendered silent and powerless if she will not or cannot bear children. Because she is sterile, Ursa becomes a cipher in her familial code of vengeance. But Jones's deliberate choice of an oral art form for her narrator shatters the silence of a peculiarly "female" identity. Ursa's artistry is separate from "making generations" yet equally valid when she finally sees herself not as an empty womb, but instead as a powerful blues singer. Jones thus contributes to Black feminism's "overarching theme of finding a voice to express a self-defined Black women's standpoint"—a theme prevalent in other feminist contexts as well (Collins 94).

The Corregidora women's political agenda offers this choice: Sing either the note of vengeance or not at all. Addressing these issues of speech and silencing through an oral narrative, *Corregidora* weaves a pattern out of the blues and colloquial speech. Jones calls this pattern a "ritualized dialogue": "You create a rhythm that people wouldn't ordinarily use . . . [by taking] the dialogue out of the naturalistic realm" (Harper 699; see also Bell et al. 285; and Byerman 3, 7). Ritualized dialogue calls attention to speech itself, emphasizing the ways in which language can transcend a rigid, calcifying identity. For Ursa, two ways out of her repetitive familial narrative are the blues song and her verbalized anger.

Corregidora consists of an improvisational duet of rage and the blues. Mama calls the blues "devil's music," a label whose associations with sinful chaos evoke Ursa's nearly hysterical anger after her accident. Her delirious cursing heralds her refusal to be hemmed in by the violence of both her family and her husband. Just as Mutt's violence forever alters Ursa's ability to bear witness, her ensuing fury transforms her singing voice. As Cat Lawson tells her, "'. . . it sounds like you been through something. Before it was beautiful too, but you sound like you been through more now'" (44). Infusing her art with rage, Ursa's voice becomes the medium through which she empowers and redefines herself.

When Mutt Thomas's act of violence dovetails with the violence of her mothers' histories, Ursa's identity is circumscribed even more tightly than before. Conceived to bear witness to a brutal past that she herself cannot claim, Ursa is now bereft of both child and purpose. She has been groomed for one kind of role in the theatre of her mothers' past, only to discover that she cannot play—or sing—it. In order to sing at all, she must move through her anger toward an artistry of unlimited possibility. Gayl Jones thus uses the extemporaneous quality of the blues to improvise on her protagonist's rage, ending with an ambivalent yet hopeful ritualistic dialogue between Ursa and Mutt.

Even before that exchange Ursa confronts her own desire and conflicts of power and powerlessness in a dream. She and Mutt voice a repetitive pattern of imperative, pleading, and response. Mutt's lines appear in the following order, punctuated only by Ursa's concise "'*Naw*'": "'*Come over here, honey*'"; "'*I need somebody*'"; "'*I said I need somebody*'"; "'*I won't treat you bad*'"; "'*I won't make you sad*'"; "'*Come over here, honey, and visit with me a little*'"; "'*Come over here, baby, and visit with me a little*'" (97–98). The novel's final dialogue is also ritualistic. Three times Mutt and Ursa chant, respectively: "'I don't want a kind of woman that hurt you'" and "'Then you don't want me.'" The pattern changes slightly but powerfully with Ursa's last reply: "'I don't want a kind of man that'll hurt

me neither'" (185). Jones's use of repetition and rhyme is deliberate; in focusing on the *sounds* of these dialogues she focuses upon Ursa's verbal nature. Ritualized dialogue reminds us that Ursa's art form is the blues song and that the novel is also "about a woman artist who sings the blues." Painting a "portrait of the artist as a young woman," Jones both acknowledges and moves beyond Ursa's roles as "hysteric" and black female victim, thus moving beyond a cultural and literary stereotype (Harris 5, 2).

Jones does not quite turn her sword into a plowshare when she turns Ursa's rough language into art; *Corregidora* does not entirely refute violence. Instead, Ursa uses it to transform violence into violent art, while acknowledging the brutality in both her mothers' lives and her own. Her rage becomes more personalized after she undergoes the hysterectomy that destroys her fetus as well as the only sexual identity she has ever known. Her resulting fury is so virulent that her second husband, Tadpole, observes, "'. . . you had those nurses scared to death of you. Cussing them out like that. Saying words they ain't never heard before'" (8). The singer's capacity for invective is apparent throughout her deliberately raw narrative.

Violent words like *fuck* and *cunt* are "taught" to the novel's victimized women by their abusers. Early in their marriage, Mutt's use of these words alarms and embarrasses Ursa. Yet soon she learns to "flare back at him with his own kind of words," telling him, "'I guess you taught me. Corregidora taught Great Gram to talk the way she did'" (153). Great Gram's stories are repeated so that her daughters will memorize them and absorb her identity, but Ursa uses her history to create new voices and new songs. She uses speech, voice, and the blues to undermine objectification, but refuses to deny the violence that has created that objectification. Furthermore, without Corregidora, Gram, Mama, and Ursa would not exist at all. As Janice Harris writes, without Corregidora "she would have nothing to bear, no past or present to sing about, no notes, no lyrics. She is and is not one of CorregiDora's women" (4). Ursa therefore cannot deny the violence of her familial history. Rather, she works against the political agenda that silences all voices except the one screaming for retribution.

Ursa regains her tongue in her art form. She relocates her creativity from her womb to her throat, an act of redemption foreshadowed in her reflections on sterility: "The center of a Woman's being. Is it? No seeds. Is that what snaps away my music, a harp string broken, guitar string, string of my banjo belly. Strain in my voice" (46). In this way, Ursa's art becomes far more important than her ability to "make generations." A singer who sees herself as a broken harp string, Ursa must eventually abandon her damaged self-definition in order to sing at all.

Jones herself works against an imposed definition of herself as writer through her honest treatment of Ursa's familial politics. Unwilling to be pigeonholed as a speaker for her race, Jones agrees with Claudia Tate's observation that many readers object to her depiction of characters "who do not conform to positive images of women or black women," and that "they want to castigate Eva [of *Eva's Man*] and Ursa as some sort of representative black female" (Tate 97). *Corregidora* anticipates this question posed by Jones in a later essay:

> Should a Black writer ignore [problematic black] characters, refuse to enter "such territory" because of the "negative image" and because such characters can be misused politically by others, or should one try to reclaim such complex, contradictory characters as well as try to reclaim the idea of the heroic image?
>
> ("Work" 233)

Certainly, Jones does not deny that political strategy may be helpful to a writer, but she is alarmed by its potentially rigid constraints, warning that an agenda can also "tell you what you cannot do . . . tell you that There's a certain territory politics won't allow you to enter, certain questions politics won't allow you to ask—in order to be 'politically correct.'" As *Corregidora* makes clear, Jones places herself on the side of risk.

Jones's choice to write about a blues singer is double-edged, enabling her to depict "the simultaneity of good and bad," since blues music "doesn't set up any territories. It doesn't set some feelings off into a corner" (Harper 700). Here she foreshadows Houston A. Baker's 1984 observation about the blues, whose "instrumental rhythms suggest change, movement, action, continuance, unlimited and unending possibility" (8). Jones is careful to separate herself from narrators like Ursa Corregidora, but the sign of the blues singer—a woman who often asks the "wrong" questions—does evoke the author's presence as story-teller and blues singer herself. As Janice Harris notes, "Blues singing permits a remarkably open expression of being oppressed . . . in its linguistic license and freedom to improvise" (4–5). Jones "sings the blues" when she insists upon improvising, creating characters who are not inherently "positive race models." Although she argues that she does "not have a political 'stance,'" her writing *is* political in its refusal to be compartmentalized as "positive" African American work, and in its denial that an African American woman writer can only be one kind of artist (Jones, "Work" 234).

Corregidora's system of slavery and prostitution depends upon the silence of women. Also silenced for and by Ursa's mothers, however, are the voices of desire and love—any voice, in fact, that does not speak vengeance. In this way, Jones argues that women as well as men are agents of silencing. Ursa shatters her enforced muteness by singing the blues, an act echoed by Jones's creation of a "blues novel" whose multiple forms of orality and acceptance of both "good and bad" allow the author to speak freely. *Corregidora*'s deliberately colloquial narrative evokes what Jones calls an "up-close" perspective, a direct relationship "between the storyteller and the hearer" (Harper 692, 698). That relationship is perhaps the most appropriate vehicle for Jones's courage in asking such difficult, even unpopular questions about how the political commodification of women's bodies forecloses the real simultaneity of "correct" and "incorrect" desires.

Notes

1. In doing so, she centers her work firmly within certain traditional American quests for self-definition. Patricia Collins offers a cogent analysis of the "journey from internalized oppression to the 'free mind' of a self-defined, Afrocentric feminist consciousness" in black women's writing (93–106).

2. Cixous's (and Irigaray's) theories ignore the impact of race and class by not asking "to what extent the body—whether male or female—is a cultural construct, not a 'natural' given" (Suleiman 14). See also Barbara Christian's "The Race for Theory" (225–37).

3. She cites the "current struggle over abortion rights" as proof of "this unacknowledged agenda" (79–80). See also 78 and 81–83 for her entire complex and qualified Marxist analysis.

4. Collins has a provocative section regarding abusive relationships between black women and men. The section culminates in an excellent analysis of Zora Neale Hurston's *Their Eyes Were Watching God*, which illustrates "the process by which power as domination . . . has managed to annex the basic power of the erotic" in black heterosexual relationships (179–89).

5. Published one year after *Corregidora*, *Eva's Man* takes this moment to its brutal conclusion: Eva Medina murders, then orally castrates her lover.

Works Cited

Baker, Houston A., Jr. *Blues, Ideology and Afro-American Literature: A Vernacular Theory.* Chicago: U of Chicago P, 1984.

Byerman, Keith. *Fingering the Jagged Grain: Tradition and Form in Recent Black Fiction.* Athens: U of Georgia P, 1985.

Carby, Hazel V. *Reconstructing Womanhood: The Emergence of the Afro-American Woman Novelist.* New York: Oxford UP, 1987.

Christian, Barbara. *Black Feminist Criticism: Perspectives on Black Women Writers.* New York: Pergamon, 1985.

———. "The Race for Theory." *Gender and Theory: Dialogues on Feminist Criticism.* Ed. Linda Kauffman. New York: Blackwell, 1989, 225–37.

Cixous, Hélène. "The Laugh of the Medusa." *Signs* 1 (Summer 1976). Rpt. in *Critical Theory Since 1965.* Ed. Hazard Adams and Leroy Searle. Tallahassee: Florida State UP, 1986, 309–20.

Collins, Patricia Hill. *Black Feminist Thought: Knowledge, Consciousness and the Politics of Empowerment.* Boston: Unwin Hyman, 1990.

Dixon, Melvin, "Singing a Deep Song: Language as Evidence in the Novels of Gayl Jones." Evans 236–48.

Evans, Mari. ed. *Black Women Writers (1950–1980): A Critical Evaluation.* Garden City: Anchor, 1984.

Harper, Michael S. "Gayl Jones: An Interview." *Massachusetts Review* 18.4 (1977): 692–715.

Harris, Janice. "Gayl Jones's *Corregidora.*" *Frontiers* 5.3 (1981): 1–5.

Jones, Gayl, "About My Work." Evans 233–35.

———. *Corregidora.* 1975. Boston: Beacon, 1986.

Kubitschek, Missy Dehn. *Claiming the Heritage: African-American Women Novelists and History.* Jackson: UP of Mississippi, 1991.

Spelman, Elizabeth. *Inessential Woman: Problems of Exclusion in Feminist Thought.* Boston: Beacon, 1988.

Spivak, Gayatri Chakravorty. *In Other Worlds: Essays in Cultural Politics.* New York: Routledge, 1988.

Suleiman, Susan Rubin, ed. *The Female Body in Western Culture: Contemporary Perspectives.* Cambridge: Harvard UP, 1986.

Tate, Claudia. *Black Women Writers at Work.* New York: Continuum, 1983.

Gay Wilentz (review date Spring 1994)

SOURCE: "Gayl Jones's Oraliterary Explorations," in *African American Review*, Vol. 28, No. 1, Spring, 1994, pp. 141-45.

[*In the following review of* Liberating Voices *and* White Rat, *Wilentz states that while Jones's academic writing may be flawed, her commitment to first-person narrative has allowed her to discuss aspects of identity and experience perviously unexplored.*]

Gayl Jones is one of the most forceful voices in contemporary African American literature, but until recently her major works were out of print. Her violent use of language and sexual/scatological images have challenged notions of what women write, and when first published, critical reception was based on shock. Acceptance of the multivocal nature of Black women's experience as well as a post-structuralist age which is more open to the language of fragmentation have led to renewed interest in Jones's work in critical circles. And now her 1977 collection **White Rat** has been reissued by Northeastern University Press, joining her two novels, **Corregidora** (1975) and **Eva's Man** (1976), both of which were reprinted in 1986. In addition, Harvard University Press has recently published a work of her criticism written in 1982. Unlike the collection of short stories, which is as impressive as when it was first published, the critical collection **Liberating Voices: Oral Tradition in African American Literature** would have been much more useful and appropriate had it been published when it was first written.

Liberating Voices, as its subtitle suggests, examines the oral tradition, which Jones and others have seen as the basis of African American literature. The book is separated into three sections: "Poetry," "Short Fiction," and "The Novel." Each section begins with early writers, mostly from the Harlem Renaissance, and then moves chronologically to contemporary writers. Jones sees a development from the early pioneers of "dialect" like Paul Laurence Dunbar and Zora Neale Hurston, who were trying to break from Du Bois's "double-consciousness," to modern writers who have more authoritatively freed the voice. In her introduction, she identifies the Harlem Renaissance as the moment when "folklore or oral tradition was no longer considered quaint and restrictive, but as the ore for complex literary influence" (9). Relating this tradition to Euro-American authors such as Mark Twain, she ends her introduction with the concept of an African American "multilinguistic" text which is an admixture of literary and oral genres, both "spoken and musical" (13–14).

The first section begins with Dunbar's reinterpretation of the Plantation tradition as a necessary step to freeing the voice. She examines Dunbar and the later poets in light of the influence of blues and spirituals. Jones focuses on the "multi-voiced blues" of Sherley Anne Williams's poetry and the "jazz modalities" of her mentor, Michael Harper. The second section explores the short fiction of Dunbar, Hurston, Toomer, Petry, Ellison, Baraka, and the lesser known Loyle Hairston. She sees Hurston as an important transition to a freer voice, in which the oral tradition "enters, complements, and complicates character" (67). The rest of this section relates aspects of language and dialect to African American music, especially jazz. The final section deals with novels from Hurston's *Their Eyes Were Watching God* to contemporary works like Ernest J. Gaines's *The Autobiography of Miss Jane Pittman* and Alice Walker's *The Third Life of Grange Copeland.* Jones's conclusion raises some questions about how literary criticism would change if standards of excellence were taken from the oral tradition. Finally, she includes a postscript explaining that the work was originally written in 1982, and gives nominal reference to contemporary critics like Henry Louis Gates, Jr., Houston Baker, and Abena Busia. She then appends a glossary of terms.

Although the reality of an unrevised work presented ten years after its composition poses a problem I examine later, there is much to be gleaned from the book. Jones's chronological exploration of the oral voice of the African American writer is generally satisfying. Statements concerning the relationship of oral and written modes, producing a "composite" novel or poem (13), help expand our concept of the oraliterary quality of the text. Furthermore, Jones, like others since her, relates the African American's search for self-definition to the use of oral modes in the written text, "in which both form and content merge to solve or complicate the questions of language, art, reality, morality, and human value. Thus, in this central concern, the many voices in this book cohere as one voice" (3).

Throughout the work, Jones offers insights into specific writers that respond to the concerns addressed above. In a discussion of Sherley Anne Williams's poem "Someone Sweet Angel Chile," Jones links the author's "multi-voiced blues" to earlier dialect poems. Unlike Dunbar, Williams allows the principal narrator, the blues singer Bessie Smith, to speak for and identify herself. In doing this, Williams relates the singer/storyteller to a cultural history which has been liberated by a contemporary "voice." According to Jones, Williams, as an "individual talent, prepared for and spurred on by the discoveries of earlier literary generations and the resources of classic oral tradition, can give a new vitality to poetic language as speech and music, transfiguring a developing tradition" (43).

In the section on "Short Fiction," Jones also focuses on the aural/oral modes of the speech/music literary tradition. Her chapter on Amiri Baraka's short story "The Screamers" is intriguing not only for its detailing of the relationship between the oral modes of jazz aesthetics and social morality, but also because Jones has chosen to look at Baraka's short fiction instead of his poetry. In the final section, Jones centers her discussion on the novel. Her analysis of extensively critiqued novels, such as Ralph Ellison's *Invisible Man* and Toni Morrison's *Song of Solomon*, is not as enlightening as her examination of less criticized works, like Walker's *The Third Life of Grange Copeland*. In this chapter, Jones identifies the novel's movement from a blues ritual (such as Jones uses in her own work) to a liberating spiritual. Placing the novel within an oraliterary and historical context, Jones perceives that, in Walker's powerful first work, "the precedents of [Richard] Wright and Hurston gain a sense of a formed whole" (154). According to Jones, Walker uses oral modes to "reinforce the spirit of this achievement" (155). In the conclusion, Jones addresses the need to contextualize "freeing the voice" in African American literature, and in her short postscript, she mentions some of the critics who have begun this process.

Jones's postscript, which states what a careful reader might have already guessed—that this work of criticism was written in 1982—identifies the crux of the problems in the text. In the last ten years, much has changed in the state of African American criticism, and many of the questions that Jones ponders in the work have been addressed from various viewpoints, and often been answered. Jones's aim in the work appears to be to justify the oral tradition as a base for African American letters, but at this point, we really don't need a justification of this sort. The use of the orature, from African-based practices to folk elements in African American culture, has not only been identified by contemporary critics but has been developed into a theoretical position of its own. Moreover, the lack of attention to critics, both cursorily named in the postscript and unnamed, seems to deny what has transpired in the last decade. Creative writers often write critical works with their own impressionistic style, but in this case, the work of criticism is an extremely conventional one and therefore needs to be appraised in this context.

Another problem, which also may relate to the lapse of ten years between the writing and the publishing of the work, concerns Jones's use of European models and Eurocentric practice to critique the literature. This is particularly disturbing because Jones's main point is to liberate the African American voice from dominant literary tradition. The overwhelming attention to how Chaucer, Twain, and T. S. Eliot have integrated voice into their work tends to disturb her narrative, because it appears gratuitously inserted to validate her points. The valorization of these models raises concerns about how free Jones's critical voice is. Moreover, the questions raised by this kind of discussion of influence and quality are not articulated in the text, so that, in the chapter "Dialect and Narrative: Zora Neale Hurston's *Their Eyes Were Watching God*," Jones poses contradictions without examining them. Jones quotes Robert Stepto who, in an early article on the novel, points out Hurston's lack of skill in shifting "awkwardly from first to third person" (137), a viewpoint actively challenged by feminists and Afrocentric critics. Jones perceives this shift not as Hurston's intention but as a flaw as well. Accordingly, Hurston does not go far enough in "breaking the frame and freeing Janie's whole voice" (134). Later on in the chapter, she comments that what is "innovative in one tradition may appear conventional in another," challenging the concept of one qualitative standard; yet, ironically, she also compels us to examine Hurston within the literary stylistic framework of T. S. Eliot's *Wasteland*. Unfortunately, the interesting dialectic that could have been explored by a comparative approach is lost because Jones appears unaware of her simultaneous resistance to and acceptance of Eurocentric models.

Another kind of dialectic is posed by examining Jones's critical and creative work together. Often we look at critical writings to gain insight into the author's own work, but in this case, her choices in formulating her own creative writings, including the short stories examined in this review, implicitly influence Jones's critical judgments. In the informative foreword to **White Rat**, Mae Henderson comments that, for Jones, the "technique of first-person narration . . . is 'the most authentic way of telling a story' because it implies 'direct identification of the storyteller with the story'" (xiv). For Jones, the "authenticity" of this form of her own writings is also validated by her critical judgments. In this regard, Ernest Gaines has a much "freer" voice than Zora Neale Hurston because his Jane, unlike Hurston's Janie, never gives up her narrative voice to third-person. One may disagree with this evaluation of the two works, but it tells us something about the dialectical relationship between creative and critical judgments. For Jones, the first person's voice is the voice of the storyteller, a voice from the oral tradition.

Jones's attention in her work to oral voicing, and to those who have been rendered voiceless, is the basis of **White Rat**, a powerful collection of short stories, as volatile and impressive now as when it was first published. Through her use of dialogue and first-person narration, stripped of description and euphemisms, Jones continues her interest in people on the edge. As witnessed in her two novels, this collection addresses abnormal psychology, sexual disruptions, the historical trauma of slavery, and the social basis of silence and madness. These stories tell the lives of people in a "liminal zone"—those who have chosen not to speak, and those whom society has silenced. The collection reflects African orature, in that each story is a dilemma tale, and Jones has left many gaps and silences for her readers to enter into—if we dare. The power of her narrative is that Jones gives us strength to examine on a literary level stories that usually find themselves in tabloids or dry casebook studies.

The title-story is that of a young man, the **"White Rat"** who identifies with Black culture, but because of his blond hair is taken for white. His first-person narration is told to a white bartender and raises the question of color versus culture—if *who you are* is constantly contradicted by *what people think you are*. It is the passing story in reverse, but it also exposes the complexities of a society that refuses to acknowledge its history. This piece reflects one of Jones's themes in the work—one's personal historicity in relation to the larger historical tragedy of slavery and its repercussions. **"Legend"** tells of a Black man hung for "raping" a white woman, but we find out through the dead man's narrative that, in fact, he was forced into sex by her father. As one of Jones's trademarks, violence surrounding sex is also evident in these stories. In one of her most often anthologized tales, **"Asylum,"** a gynecological exam is a horrific violation, with undertones of rape:

> He comes in and looks down in my mouth and up in my noise and looks in my ears. He feels my breasts and my belly to see if I got any lumps. He starts to take off my bloomers.
>
> I aint got nothing down there for you.
>
> (78)

This familiar scene, told within the confines of a psychiatric ward, is defamiliarized to expose how women are abused under the name of medicine. Moreover, the emphasis on the all-powerful white-male doctor and the resisting but powerless Black woman patient serves as a trope for the various violations in a racist, patriarchal society.

Other stories deal with different kinds of violations, and the individuals who suffer or resist through silence. As Henderson notes, many kinds of silences are "at the heart of Jones's stories" (x), a few of which concern taciturn young African American women at privileged white colleges. In the most autobiographical story in the collection (xi), **"Your Poems Have Very Little Color in Them,"** the protagonist comments, "There are two kinds of people, those who don't talk and those who can't talk" (18). For both kinds in this collection, there are others who try to make them talk and pressure them in other ways. In two of the college stories, **"A Quiet Place in the Country"** and **"Persona,"** the young women are silenced not only by the obvious separations of race and class, but also by subtle sexual pressure from professors, both male and female. In **"A Quiet Place,"** however, the protagonist gains her voice by speaking to the Black gardener at a wealthy white professor's summer home. In **"Persona,"** one can identify a concealed attack on lesbianism, since the women—much like the men—prey on the innocent student. Moreover, the story **"The Women"** is virulently homophobic, with the unfit mother apparently unresponsive to her daughter because of her lesbian activities. Yet most sexual, affective relationships are abusive in the world view presented by Jones; the only characters who even come close to an affectionate relationship are the pair in **"The Round House."**

Jones's interest in sexual abuse and abnormal psychology, most decisively articulated in her second novel, *Eva's Man,* is related to the historical trauma of African Americans and the abuses of women. Jones, as a storyteller, focuses on the lives of those silenced by historical and social trauma, who often sink into insanity. It is these voices—finally allowed to speak to the reader, if not within the confines of the tale—which reflect Jones's writing at its most compelling. Ricky, the young mentally disabled boy in **"The Coke Factory,"** makes us aware, in his powerful dialect, of the lack of sympathy his adopted mother and others in his community have for him, as well as his comprehension of his environment: "I'm fifteen. She says when I get eighteen she gon send me out to eastern state that the mentle hospital . . . That's where they put all the mently tarded" (98). In this story, Ricky talks to us, but not to those around him, who call him "bad"; and, in the end, he gets his reward for his one independent act—returning his empties for a new bottle of soda. In a more disturbing pair of stories, **"Return: The Fantasy"** and **"Version Two,"** we are exposed to the breakdown of a young Black intellectual and the woman who allows him to control her in her aim to protect him. The first story is narrated from her point of view, and the second is compiled of his oracular ravings. Joseph, in **"Version Two,"** the last story in the collection, leaves us with a prophetic note: "My words will work your magic. Are you starting to go? Yes, I know you. Everything you told me. I'll help you find your way out" (178).

For Jones, for us, for her characters, words are a way to find one's way out of oppression, silence, and historical and sexual trauma, but words are also part of that nightmare. Unfortunately, the words of her explicitly rendered first-person narratives also limit the use of her writings in college classrooms, because of the scatological and linguistic violence she so expertly exposes. Nonetheless, these stories, like her two novels, present for us an exposed world that we can no longer refuse to see. Jones expands our knowledge of both "normal" and "abnormal"; her commitment to telling stories situates her firmly into the African American literary tradition; and this collection—more than her critical work—emphasizes the importance of writing for defining self and recording history.

E. Patrick Johnson (essay date Spring-Summer 1994)

SOURCE: "Wild Women Don't Get the Blues: A Blues Analysis of Gayl Jones' *Eva's Man*," in *Obsidian II*, Vol. IX, No. 1, Spring-Summer, 1994, pp. 26-46.

[*In the essay below, Johnson develops the thesis that Jones employs Blues structure and content in* Eva's Man *as a means of describing problems particular to African-American women.*]

> When I was a little girl, only twelve years old
> I couldn't do nothing to save my doggone soul
> My mama told me the day I was born
> She said sing the blues, chile, sing from now on
> I'm a woman
> I'm a rushing wind
> I'm a woman
> Cut stone with a pen
> I'm a woman
> I'm ball of fire
> I'm a woman
> Make love to a crocodile
> Spelled W-O-M-A-N
> That means I'm grown
>
> —"I'm a Woman," Koko Taylor

In amazement, I watched blues singer Koko Taylor perform the preceding song in a small nightclub several years ago. Belting every note, Taylor never faltered: she performed each verse as if for the first time and as if she had lived the life about which she sang, for this was the celebratory side of the blues—a Black Woman's blues.

Today when I think about Taylor's performance, I often wonder if the audience, who were mostly White, really understood the message of her song. Did they comprehend the significance of a Black woman singing "I'm a Woman" given the social realities of her life? Undoubtedly, there were those who felt the song was "powerful" because of the singer's spirited performance. From my perspective, however, there is a difference between "powerful" and "empowering." The former, at least in this context, connotes a commitment to audience to give one's all, while the latter suggests a personal catharsis where the self as subject enables a space of visibility, pride, and dignity. Consequently, I believe the song was "empowering" for Taylor because she sang from a tradition of not only women singers, but of Black women in general like my mother and grandmother, who also show the world what it means to be a woman and an African American. I felt this same sense of empowerment when reading Gayl Jones' *Eva's Man*.

Commentary on the fiction of African-American women writers focuses on literary rather than performance traditions. While it is important to point out the significance of literary traditions peculiar to African-American women writers, other avenues of artistic expressions available to and incorporated by these women also deserve attention. Performance traditions such as jazz, the gospel and the blues are aesthetic, artistic, and cultural expressions found in the writing of African-American women which they share with their male counterparts, but are also those used to speak about their different experiences as women.

The blues tradition in particular offers African-American women writers a voice from which to explain their experiences in ways that signify both on European American literary traditions and the writings of African-American males. It is through the blues that the African-American woman writer, like the blues performer, can empower herself, her sister writers (singers), as well as her audience, for blues performances serve as codifiers, absorbing and transforming discontinuous experience through the formal expression of song. Moreover, blues performances resist final or stable meaning—the blues singer's rhythms suggest change, movement, action, continuance, unlimited and unending possibilities. This is the style Eva Medina Canada, the protagonist of Gayl Jones' *Eva's Man*. I argue that this same style offers the African-American woman a kind of feminist discourse that names her individual experience as a marginalized person; it also offers readers of African-American women texts a new and distinctive critical method with which to analyze these works. Because the blues tradition and all of its defining characteristics are unique to African-American culture, it provides if not a critique of mainstream critical discourse, then a viable alternative source from which to distinguish the oppression of African Americans—one that incorporates race and class. Therefore, in this essay, I wish to illuminate the ways in which Gayl Jones transforms the blues as an oral performance into a literary performance and how that transformation reveals new possibilities for analyzing African-American women's writing.

Gayl Jones wrote her two novels, *Corregidora* (1975) and *Eva's Man* (1976) as blues narratives. In the former the protagonist is literally a blues performer in a night club, in the latter the blues performer is more metaphorical or at the level of the narrative itself. Both novels, however, offer a new way of looking at women's oppression, because within the blues tradition the oppression is named and made tangible. In the process of that naming, however, the blues performer simultaneously distances herself from that oppression to hold it up for scrutiny in order to decide on a course of action or to transcend it.

Jones draws on the blues in a way that enables the voice of her protagonists and her reading audience. Finding and speaking from that blues voice in many cases encourages power and change. For Ursa of *Corregidora*, that power and change result from her reconciliation with her slave heritage, and for Eva they follow from her exploring lesbianism. Jones draws from the blues legacy to address a "different" audience—that of contemporary African-American women as opposed to European Americans. Jones uses the novel, a Western form, and incorporates the blues as a way of explaining it to enable her commentary on the lives of African-American women.

How does Jones go about transforming the blues from an oral to a literary performance? She begins by incorporating those elements characteristic of the blues within the narrative. For example, according to Sherley Anne Williams, one defining quality of the blues is that it is analytical. In the blues analysis, a situation, mood, or feeling is expressed where it is described, commented upon and assessed (125). Because the reader has exposure to Eva's inner thoughts, she or he witnesses her analytical process as she makes life decisions throughout the novel.

Moreover, blues lyrics most often follow the a/a/b patterning also found in jazz, where the first two lines are the same and rhyme with the third line, a variation on the first two. These lines taken from Victoria Spivey's "Blood Hound Blues," are an example of this pattern:

> Well, I poisoned my man, I put it in his drinking cup,
> Well, I poisoned my man, I put it in his drinking cup,
> Well, It's easy to go to jail, but lawd, they sent me up[1]

Concomiztantly, there are several passages in **Eva's Man** that resemble a blues song through the use of the same a/a/b line patterning and/or repetition of lines. Variations on this pattern include a/a/b and a/a/a/b. In addition, the blues incorporates "melisma, intentional stutters and hesitations, repetitions of words and phrases and the interjection of exclamatory phrases and sounds" (Williams 125). The use of these features is most apparent in the last third of the novel, where Eva fails to distinguish between fantasy and reality. In this sense, these blues techniques help create the incoherence of Eva's discourse in addition to making the narrative take the form of a blues song. Finally, **Eva's Man** ends on the same note as an oral blues performers', with a signature coda. This coda serves as the personal signature of the performer, which distinguishes her style from other blues performers'. Eva's "Now" at the end of the narrative functions in much the same way.

Beyond particular aesthetic criteria of oral blues performance, Jones also explores some of the same themes as the blues. Eva's "blues," for example, center on themes of imprisonment, sexual innuendo, broken-heartedness, poverty, racism and sexism. While these themes are those most commonly cited in blues analyses, there are others that Jones uses in the novel that are rarely discussed, particularly homosexuality. Accordingly, Eva tells the reader early on in her narrative about Elvira, her cellmate, who makes sexual advances toward her, but to no avail. By the end of the novel, however, Eva succumbs to Elvira's advances by allowing her to perform oral sex on her. This controversial ending, which functions in the same fashion as a blues signature in oral performance, distances the reader from the narrative, while at the same time causes her to reflect on her own sexual identity and experience. The lesbian theme as used within the blues paradigm, then, is of significant importance to feminist readings of the novel.

Jones uses all of the preceding characteristics of the blues to transform her novel into a blues text. Indeed, these components enable the reader to "hear" Eva's narrative as a blues song and, in some instances, the narrative begs to be read aloud. Jones craftily constructs this novel by infusing an oral tradition with a literary one, the success of which depends upon how well the two converge. In the following pages, I attempt to demonstrate Jones' successful use of blues ideology.

As stated earlier, the blues is analytical. Unlike the gospel performance tradition, the blues does not prepare one to "wait on the Lord," to remove the obstacles of life; rather, they prepare one to take stock of his or her situation and ponder the next course of action." This "analysis" certainly holds true for Eva, as she assesses her situation with Davis, who holds her as his sexual prisoner. Confronted with a situation in which she must make a decision, Eva decides to kill Davis. Eva's plan is thought out carefully, however, as she determines when and how she will commit the murder. In the following scene, Davis plans a trip to the store. Eva then realizes that this is her opportunity to devise a plan of action, so she decides to poison Davis:

> 'I'm GOING OUT,' he said. 'Bring home some brandy. I feel like that instead of beer.'
>
> I hadn't meant to call the place home. He must have noticed it, because he laughed and said he would.
>
> I nodded. He went out. The door closed hard.
>
> I went into the janitor's closet and got the rat poison. I tore a piece of sack and made an envelop and shook some powder in and put it in the pocket of my skirt, then I went back and sat on the bed.
>
> (122)

The exchange between Davis and Eva before she gets the rat poisoning is reflective of dialogue between two cordial lovers. But Eva's actions after Davis leaves lets the reader know that all is not well between the two. This kind of irony is reflected in many blues songs. Williams contends that "analytic distance is achieved through the use of verbal and musical irony . . ." and gives an example of this technique with a line from Billie Holiday's "Fine and Mellow":

> Love is like faucet
>   it turns off and on
> Sometimes when you think It's on, baby
>   it have turned off and gone

The persona pointedly reminds her man that her patience with his trifling ways has its limits at the same time that she suggests that she might be in her present difficulties because she wasn't alert to the signs that her well was going dry. The self-mockery and irony of the blues pull one away from a total surrender to the emotions generated by the concreteness of the experiences and situations described in the song. Even where the verbal content of the song is straightforward and taken at face value, the singer has musical techniques which create ironic effects.

(125)

Like Holiday, Eva gives the illusion (to the reader and to Davis) that their relationship is amicable and although she has in some ways been complicitous in her own captivity by not leaving the hotel room when she has had the opportunity, she comes to the critical realization that she cannot remain captive. Thus she plots Davis' murder. According to Harrison, the analytical nature of the blues is an example of "blues as life, identifying the source of the pain, acknowledging its effect, then taking a step to deal with it. In this instance, the blues is a purgative, or aesthetic therapy (101). Eva articulates her burdensome life, having been "done wrong" by the men in her life, until she comes to the point where she cannot deal with the pain anymore. She evaluates her situation as Davis symbolically comes to represent every man who has ever abused her.

Characteristically, the blues most often does not transcend problems, as in the spirituals, but is a call to action.[2] The blues does not look for a resolution in heaven or feel that "the Lord will make a way"; rather, it searches for answers in the tangible realities of life. Accordingly, the solution that Eva finds is to kill Davis. She does not wait for God to deliver her; rather, after analyzing the situation, she takes it upon herself to do what she feels is in her best interest. Eva's behavior is consistent with the ideology of the blues in that if a man has "done you wrong" then he must "pay." Davis is the "sacrificial lamb" so to speak, as he comes to represent, in Eva's mind at least, all of the men who sexually abuse her. Whether we condone or even understand Eva's behavior, her narrative identifies the source of her oppression, and because she tells her narrative within the blues tradition, she must take action in whatever form. "For some women [blues singers] self-reliance was not enough to fulfill their emotional and physical needs; distrust of men pushed some of them toward forms of antisocial behavior that isolated them from the group" (Harrison 102). Eva is pushed further and further to her limit with each experience with a man such that she moves closer and closer toward "antisocial" behavior. This shift in behavior, however, reflects Eva's move from passive receiver of abuse and objectification to active defier of patriarchy and male control.

The blues' text reflects the conditions and experiences of African-American women as they are positioned on the bottom rung of class and race—a position that motivates thought and action. What Eva's action represents, then, is an active mode of Black feminism. Eva takes on the role of the novel's character, Queen Bee. But unlike Queen Bee, who actually becomes a martyr for her last lover, Eva takes on the queen bee role in its extreme—she uses it to gain control over her male oppressors. She leaves the male-dominated world by leaving the scene of the crime, but re-enters as a "reigning" queen bee. Eva's actions are reflective of another of Koko Taylor's songs, entitled "Queen Bee":

> I'm a Queen Bee, baby, buzzin' all night long,
> I'm a Queen Bee, baby, buzzin' all night long,
> When you hear me buzzin', There's some stingin' going on.

The "sting" in this instance is a metaphor for sex, but it may also refer to the fatal sting of a woman pushed to her limit. Eva is empowered then, for a queen bee suggests power, fertility, and creativity.

Eva's narrative also exemplifies techniques such as hesitations, repetition, and exclamatory phrases and sounds. Jones uses this pattern consistently in *Eva's Man* such that the novel can be categorized as a "speakerly" text, for the blues is meant to be heard rather than read silently. The following passage provides an example of this technique:

> I said I didn't know how anybody else was going to vote. I said I just knew how I was going to vote. He said there were ten percent more black people there since he was foreman, and that he liked people that showed gratitude. I said I didn't know how anybody else was going to vote. I said I knew how I was to vote. He said he had some money for me if I want it. I said I didn't know how anybody else was vote. He said never mind that. He said he didn't mean that.
>
> (75)

Therefore, when read aloud, one can hear the text's musicality.

The lyricism of the text points to the oral nature of African-American culture, as it intersects with and produces the blues tradition. Language becomes the focus in Jones' text as she places the emphasis not so much on what is said but how it is said. Language, then, is ritualized to find meaning in the musicality of speech (grounded in the blues) and to explore its capacity to convey meaning. The task of discovering the meaning or meanings is left up to the reader or blues listener. The reader must make sense out of the language and apply it to her or his own experience. In *Eva's Man* the reader must wade through the musical nature of the text to get to the deeper underlying meaning:

> We are in the river now. We are in the river now. The sand is on my tongue. Blood under my nails. I'm bleeding under my nails. We are in the river. Between my legs. They are busy with this woman. They are busy with this woman now. They are busy with this woman. . . .
>
> (176)

As one discovers from this passage, grasping that deeper meaning is no easy task, for the tendency is to get "caught up" in the music, but there is just enough distance between the text's musicality and the performer/reader that the subtext is not lost. Eva's mixing fantasy and reality, then, is not a symptom of "madness"; rather, it resembles the repetition of sounds and words found in the blues aesthetic as she incorporates disjointed and seemingly disconnected phrases:

> Nothing you wouldn't know about. Nothing you wouldn't know about. Nothing you wouldn't know about.
>
> (135)

> An owl sucks my blood. I am bleeding underneath my nails. An owl sucks my blood. He gives me fruit in my palms. We enter the river again . . . together.
>
> (176)

Eva moves in and out of fantasy and reality using the a/a/a blues rhyme patterning in the first three lines and then to a general repetition of phrases in the last six. This kind of image switching is common in the blues and has the same effect when used as a literary device. On one hand, it draws the reader into the text through the musicality of the words, while on the other, it distances her through the juxtapositioning of two discontinuous images. Thus "a member of the blues audience [the reader] shouts 'Tell it like it is' rather than 'Amen' or 'Yes, Jesus' as a response to a particularly pungent or witty truth, for the emphasis is on thinking not tripping" (Williams 126). Moreover, this kind of technique has implications that extend beyond the immediacy of the blues performance, for "when language is drawn from the musical and sexual idiom and shared with the reader in a ritualistic cadence of speech rendered like a song or incantation, there is a chance that painful wounds may be healed" (Ward 255). For African-American women, those wounds often include self-hatred, sexism, and racism.

Unlike some critics, I see Eva's murder of Davis as a self-empowering experience rather than a nihilistic one. For instance, Melvin Dixon argues that

> Eva confuses Davis with Alphonse, Moses Tripp, and James Hunn. When she finally decides to be active in lovemaking with Davis by making 'music hard, deep, with my breath,' it is too late. She has already poisoned him. Eva's behavior here is demented and pathetic, a travesty of the successful coupling Ursa [of *Corregidora*] finds with Mutt.
>
> (119)

The implication here is that a "successful coupling" is one between a man and a woman.

Eva's blues narrative—reliving, reexperiencing, and reshaping of her life—facilitates in her a rebirth that critically analyzes and identifies her source of oppression and lack of fulfillment. Ultimately she discovers that she does not need a man and that lesbian sex is a viable source of fulfillment. Accordingly, Jones says that critics rarely discuss the lesbianism in the novel. Jones comments, "There have also been more responses to the neurotic sensuality in the books than to the lesbianism. I don't recall lesbianism entering into any critical discussions except as part of the overall sexual picture" (97). Yet, the lesbian theme occurs throughout the novel, the first of which is seen through Eva's relationship with Charlotte, Miss Billie's 27-year-old daughter. Eva meets Charlotte during a visit with her mother to North Carolina. Miss Billie worries that Charlotte will never marry, a subject that Charlotte discusses with Eva:

> 'Have you ever done it?' she asked.
>
> 'Done what? Twist Tobacco.'
>
> It was cool in there laying back against the wall. I didn't answer.
>
> 'I asked you have you ever been with a man.'

> 'No. Have you?'
>
> 'No'.
>
> She closed her eyes, her mouth was hanging open a little, then she made a sucking sound.
>
> 'Mama keeps asking me when am I going to get a man,' she said. 'I don't want a man.'
>
> (88–89)

Eva and Charlotte have several conversations like this in the garage while lying together on a mat or while walking through the woods. On one occasion, Charlotte even touches Eva on the waist and comments on its size: "She touched my waist and said that I had a little waist. She kept her hand on my waist and then she walked out of the garage" (90). While nothing explicit ever happens between the two, their interactions reflect sexual tensions.

Moreover, lesbianism as a viable sexual avenue is symbolically foreshadowed three-fourths through the novel after Eva castrates Davis:

> I got the silk handkerchief he used to wipe me after we made love, and wrapped his penis in it. I laid it back inside his trousers, zipped him up. I kissed his cheeks, his lips, his neck. I got naked and sat on the bed again. I spread my legs across his thighs and put his hand on my crotch, stuffed his fingers up in me. I put my whole body over him. I farted.
>
> (129)

At this moment in Eva's sexual history, she assumes control, situating herself in the dominate position by mounting Davis. Eva exemplifies sexual agency here my making love to a "feminized" body instead of being "fucked" by a man. Indeed, Eva conquers the phallus, symbolized in the novel as an apple in reference to the Eve myth and the fall of man: "My mouth, my teeth, my tongue went inside his trousers. I raised blood, slime from cabbage, blood sausage. Blood from an apple. . . . My teeth in an apple" (128). By making the connection between the phallus—the source of male domination—and the Eve myth symbolized through the apple, Jones points to the archetypal discourses responsible for the oppression of women and then rewrites that discourse in ways that enable rather than disable.

Eva/Eve takes a bite of the apple/penis, which also causes the "fall of man," but this time the act castigates or demonizes her only from a White, patriarchal and/or fundamentalist perspective. But within a blues framework, which has its own set of ethical and logical standards that some would even consider amoral, Eva's actions remain extreme, yet permissible.

The consummation of Eva's lesbianism in the literal sense comes at the novel's end when Elvira performs oral sex on her:

> 'Tell me when it feels sweet, Eva. Tell me when it feels sweet, honey.'

I leaned back, squeezing her face between my legs, and told her, 'Now.'

(177)

Lovemaking or "fucking," as Eva knows it, has never been "sweet" until this point. Fulfillment and satisfaction is the subtext of "Now." Eva's voice at this point is drawn from "margin to center" as she punctuates the signature of her blues narrative. Eva's sexual fulfillment is different than Ursa's in *Corregidora*, even though they engage in the same sexual act. In *Corregidora* for example, Ursa performs fellatio on Mutt:

'You never would suck it,' he was saying. 'You never would suck it when I wanted you to. Oh, baby, you never would suck it. I didn't think you would do this for me.' He came and I swallowed. He leaned back, pulling me up by the shoulders.

(184–185)

In this final scene in *Corregidora*, Ursa remains subordinate to her lover, performing fellatio while on her knees and holding his ankles. And like the men in Eva's life, Mutt has been abusive to Ursa, causing her to fall down a flight of steps and lose her unborn child. And after years of separation, Ursa goes back to him, consummating their reconciliation through fellatio. While some may argue that Ursa and Mutt act out the blues destiny, the reader still gets the sense that Ursa will suffer abuse and remain subordinate to Mutt, although her final words to him are "I don't want a kind of man that'll hurt me neither" (185).

While Elvira's performing cunnilingus on Eva is no different than Ursa's act, one senses that Elvira's and Eva's sexual activity will help heal Eva's wounded psyche and self-esteem. I fear, however, that Eva still has a long way to go before she is completely released from the hold of internalized sexism, racism, and homophobia. But like the character John in Baldwin's *Go Tell it on the Mountain* (1953), "[She's] ready. . . . [She's] coming. [She's] on [her] way" (221).

Unlike Ursa, in *Corregidora*, Eva is not a blues singer in the literal sense; rather, her narrative is her song, and we as readers are her listening audience. Some critics view Eva's refusal to speak to other characters in the novel who could presumably help her—the patriarchal police and male psychiatrist—as defeatist and as ultimately leading to her "failure to achieve refuge and redemption" (Dixon 117). To the contrary, Eva's silence is important to the ideological framing of African-American women's oppression and self-empowerment in the novel. On one hand, Eva is defeated by words. On the other hand, her silence may symbolically represent the silencing of African-American women institutionalized by a White, racist, patriarchal society. Like many singers, Eva only confides in those who know and understand the conditions of her life. Singing the blues is certainly one of these coping strategies. It makes sense, then, that Eva does not seek the advice of a White, male psychiatrist—she would rather sing her experience through the blues.

In this way, Eva is the one who is in control. Empowerment for Eva comes from an internal spirituality rather than from an external, prescriptive society, especially one that reinforces the status quo. If Eva speaks to those in the novel who seemingly want to "help" her, she will collaborate in her own dehumanization—she will be "treated," which implies that something is wrong with her in the first place. Her behavior, then, would have to conform to what society considers "normal" or acceptable. In other words, the hegemonic forces that lead Eva to prison would remain intact. Conversely, Eva does not give the reader a "confession"; rather, she tells her story as a story, be it true or not, for "truth" is not the issue. Eva tells the reader:

At first I wouldn't talk to anybody. All during the trial I wouldn't talk to anybody. But then, after I came in here, I started talking. I tell them things that don't even have to do with what I did, but they say they want to hear that too. . . . I know when I'm not getting things straight, but they say That's all right, to go ahead talking. Sometimes they think I'm lying to them, though. I tell them it ain't me lying, It's memory lying. I don't believe that, because the past is still as hard on me as the present, but I tell them that anyway. They say they're helping me. I'm forty-three years old, and I ain't seen none of their help yet.

(5)

Consequently, the matter-of-fact style in which Eva renders her tale is problematic for many readers, particularly because there is no sense of moral judgment from the author. Jones, however, purposefully withholds authorial judgment, for she believes in her characters' autonomy when they narrate their lives:

. . . they're [critics] bothered by the fact that the author doesn't offer any judgments or show her attitude toward the offense, but simply has the characters relate it. For example, Eva refuses to render her story coherently. By controlling what she will and will not tell, she maintains her autonomy.

(1983, 97)

Because of Eva's autonomy and unreliability as a narrator, we are still no closer to a rational explanation for her behavior; yet, as audience to this blues tale, we hear a story of human experience that is refashioned, retold, and rethought as Eva, a blues woman, would have it be told. It is for these reasons that she tells the doctor not to explain her. What she is really saying is "do not define me or tell me who I am." This is not to say, however, that Eva does not pay a price for her autonomy and eccentricity, for she remains a prisoner at the novel's close.

Eva also mixes reality and fantasy (the literal and the metaphorical) in accordance with the blues tradition. Her narrative is not language that has "atrophied from disuse," as critics suggest. Eva uses language to her advantage because she is in control—she tells her story (sings her song) to and for whom she wants. It is the expression of the self more than the content of the narrative that matters because the narrative is reexperienced and re-created by the performer. Eva's blues, then, "are a means of articulating experience and demonstrating a toughness of spirit by creating and re-creating that experience" (Harrison 65). She is in control of her discourse and necessarily monitors what she says to those whom she cannot trust. Her "toughness" is also apparent as she tells us that the past is still "hard" on her and that she must rely on herself rather than others.

Melvin Dixon argues that Eva's refusal to speak keeps her "imprisoned literally and figuratively" and that she "is unable to gain the larger historical consciousness to end individual alienation" (118). However, the fact that the narrative is told from a prison cell speaks more to the common setting of blues songs than to imprisonment as discipline or punishment. Many of the blues songs sung by early blues women were about their experiences in jail. Take, for instance, Bessie Smith's "Sing Sing Prison Blues":

> You can send me up the river or send me to that mean ole jail,
> You can send me up the river or send me to that mean ole jail,
> I killed my man and I don't need no bail.

Like the vengeful woman in Smith's song, Eva is in jail because she committed murder and "lost her man," which is also a common theme in blues songs. But Dixon's conclusion about her "individual alienation" misses the feminist implications of Eva's choices. Given how Eva is treated by her environment, both sexually and physically, her choice to alienate herself from others is a sign of self-determination and self-preservation. Eva's alienation is symbolic of the blues woman singing her song in isolation, not acknowledging self-defeat, but proclaiming self-definition.

There are, of course, psychological answers for Eva's choice. Eva is exposed to and affected by child molestation as early as the age of five. She witnesses the sadistic/masochist relationship between Alphonse and Jean, the sexual abuse of her mother by her father, and experiences sexual abuse from Freddy Smoot, Alphonse, Tyrone, Moses Tripp, and James Hunn. Eva's sexuality is shaped by her environment—an environment inundated with abusive men. Her negative experiences with men cause her to withdraw within herself. When she does speak, then, her discourse emerges as a blues narrative. And somewhere in that song, Eva comes to the conclusion, like the character Sula, that "a lover [is] not a comrade and [can] never be—for a woman" (Morrison 121). Consequently, her coupling with Elvira at the end of the novel reflects Eva's discovery of lesbianism. Dixon believes Eva's cry at the end "emphasizes her failure to escape claustrophobic interiors or to utter anything more significantly than the chilling 'Now' announcing her solo orgasm at the novel's close" (119). Alternatively, Eva's "Now" may signify a rebirth into a new self that subverts the hetero-sexist, sexist, and to an extent, racist society of which she is a part. Eva, cast in the blues tradition, has the option of singing about an alternative sexual orientation,

for "sex between men and women was not the only topic in women's sexual blues. Homosexuality, though generally frowned upon by the Black community, was also sung about" (Harrison 103). A classic example of "lesbian" blues is Ma Rainey's song, "Prove It on Me Blues":

> Went out last night, had a great big fight,
> Everything seemed to go on wrong;
> I looked up, to my surprise,
> The gal I was with was gone.
>
> Where she went, I don't know,
> I mean to follow everywhere she goes;
> Folks said I'm crooked, I didn't know where she took it,
> I want the whole world to know:
>
> They say I do it, ain't nobody caught me,
> Sure got to prove it on me;
> Went out last night with a crowd of my friends,
> They must've been women, 'cause I don't like no men.
>
> It's true I wear a collar and a tie,
> Like to watch while the women pass by
> They say, I do it, ain't nobody caught me,
> They sure got to prove it on me.
>
> Say I do it, ain't nobody caught me,
> Sure got to prove it on me;
> I went out last night with a crowd of my friends,
> They must've been women, 'cause I don't like no men.
>
> Wear my clothes just like a fan,
> Talk to the gals 'just like any old man;
> 'Cause they say I do it, ain't nobody caught me,
> Sure got to prove it on me.

Ma Rainey's song affirms lesbian love and sexuality as well as suggests that lovemaking is a private act, for no one has actually seen her "do it." Because they have not seen her in the sexual act (although she openly "Talk[s] to the gals just like any old man"), they will have to "prove" their suspicions about her being a lesbian. Eva, on the other hand, represses her lesbian feelings throughout her narrative. Unlike the woman in "Prove It on Me Blues," Eva does not brag about her attraction to women; indeed, she resents Elvira for making advances toward her. It is not until the end of the novel when Eva tells Davis, "Last night she got in bed with me, Davis. I knocked her out, but I don't know how long I'm going to keep knocking her out . . ." (176), that Eva begins to acknowledge her closeted feelings. Hence, the lesbian theme in **Eva's Man** is less about being boastful about one's sexuality as in some lesbian blues and more about coming to terms with one's sexuality. Eva's coupling with Elvira at the end of the novel, then, breaks Eva's silence and offers her a new beginning and may offer one for her listeners.

Another way of looking at Eva's last word is as the signature to her blues narrative. The blues performer has her own style that distinguishes her from other performers.

She also has her own signature that personalizes her performance. For Eva that personal signature is the chilling "Now." Here lies the possibility for Eva's blues to empower her readers (women in general, but particularly African-American women) to find their own voice. I do not suggest, however, that Eva asks the reader to "become a lesbian," but that Eva discovers that lesbianism or even "performing solo" is an option in a Woman's sexual expressiveness. While it is questionable whether Eva reaches some kind of resolve at the novel's end, the ending may help women with similar experiences come to terms with their own sexuality. Houston Baker suggests that the signature of a blues narrative leaves a "space"—the Black (w)hole—to be filled by the audience:

> . . . What emerges is not a filled subject, but an anonymous (nameless) voice issuing from the black (w)hole. The blues singer's signatory coda is always a topic, placeless. . . . The 'signature' is a space already 'X'(ed), a trace of the already 'gone'—a fissure rejoined. Nevertheless, the 'you' (audience) addressed is always free to invoke the X(ed) spot in the body's absence. For the signature comprises a scripted authentication of 'you' feeling. Its mark is an invitation to energizing inner subjectivity. Its implied (in)junction reads: Here is my body meant for (a phylogenetically conceived) you.
>
> (5)

Put in simpler terms, the blues performer's signature articulates the personal (through the body), but at the same time leaves a space for the audience to make its own connections to the narrative or even to discover its own inner subjectivity in ways that empower or move it to action. As Williams says, "both poet (singer) and audience share the same reality" (127). Hence, *Eva's Man* can serve as an affirmation of sexuality for readers who are closeted and/or women who are abused.

Because Eva's Man fits into the blues tradition, it is possible that the novel also facilitates a feminist discourse that subverts racism, sexism, and homophobia. These possibilities lie in the connection between what is allowed within the blues tradition and Eva's action in the novel.

Call to action and victimization are predominate themes not only in the blues tradition but in the lives of African-American women. Consequently, there is a tendency on the part of some critics to glorify struggle or to romanticize the notion of the "strong Black woman," based on sexist and racist theories. There is nothing intrinsic to African-American women that makes them strong; rather, their conditions are such that they are *required* to be strong. Deborah Gray White debunks the myth of the Black superwoman in her book, *Ar'n't I A Woman*, when she writes:

> Slave women have often been characterized as self-reliant and self sufficient because, lacking black male protection, they had to develop their own means of resistance and survival. Yet, not every black woman was a Sojourner Truth or a Harriet Tubman. Strength had to be cultivated. It came no more naturally to them than to anyone, slave or free, male or female, black or white. If they seemed exceptionally strong it was partly

because they often functioned in groups and derived strength from numbers.

(119)

African-American women, then, "cultivate" a strength that is necessary to their survival. They not only rely on themselves, but each other for support, like the blues performer who performs "solo" and who also feeds off the call-and-response relationship with her audience. Thus an occasional "Sing it, girlfriend!" or "Tell the truth!" encourages and supports the performer. The blues performance is a communal ritual that thrives on audience participation, similar to the relationship between a preacher and his/her congregation in African-American church services. In both instances, the relationship between performer and audience punctuates, heightens, and seals the message conveyed. A literary text, then, may also facilitate a communal ritual and call-and-response relationship between the reader and the author/protagonist when framed within the blues performance paradigm. Women readers of the text may identify with Eva's experience, however similar to or different from theirs, which in return may lead them to their own personal discoveries of self.

Eva's Man as a blues text also challenges the sexism and homophobia of Black men and the Black community in general. Eva acts out the blues destiny by identifying Black males as the source of her sexual and mental anguish. Facilitated by the blues tradition, she literally and symbolically paralyzes the weapon (the phallus) responsible for her pain. And somewhere in her reexperiencing through the blues narrative, she discovers an alternative to heterosexuality. Furthermore, the lesbian theme in *Eva's Man*, defined through the blues idiom, subverts and critiques Black male homophobia. Homophobia is inherent in the discourse of some male critics who describe Eva's behavior as "demented" and "pathetic" because she never has "active" lovemaking with a man. Because the blues creates its own morality with regard to sex, it facilitates a way to subvert the imperialism of heterosexuality or sexual propriety.

Like Eva Canada's life, the lives of African-American women are complex. Specifically, their lives are not necessarily bound between the binary relationship of sexism and racism; rather, they are caught in a liminal state "betwixt and between" meaning and experience that is constantly negotiated from within and outside African-American culture. The blues idiom provides a way to talk about that complexity of experience. The music of African Americans is sophisticated in composition and structure and writers sophisticated in composition and structure and writers incorporating this form must strive toward making their texts meet those same criteria. When they do, it provides for an in-depth look at experience through a different medium:

> . . . to get to the height of structural and psychological complexity of the music, black writers, when they [begin] to experiment with their own artistic traditions, [begin] to look to the music as a significant—indeed the most significant—extraliterary mode.
>
> (Awkward 92)

Jones masters this "extraliterary mode" in a way that provides for new possibilities for articulating the concerns of African-American women.

Concentrating more on the graphic language and "gratuitous" sex, previous critics rarely speak of this novel as a blues text. Placed within the blues tradition, however, this novel moves beyond a simple experiment with words on a page, for it takes this musical tradition, transforms it into a literary one, and, by doing so, weaves a tale of human experience that gives voice to a sector of our society that is traditionally silenced. Eva emerges as the reigning queen bee because her song (the narrative as blues text) empowers her to do so.

Eva's Man, when read through the blues filter, provides a new way for listening to the "other," for through the creation of the blues text itself, the performer re-creates her experience. But when she sings it for us, not only do we share her pain, sorrow, joy, *and* idiosyncrasies, we also are distanced enough to realize how her experience or position in society is different from or in contradiction to our own. Dialoguing in this call-and-response fashion provides for a better understanding of the issues that concern African-American women and facilitates more understanding on the part of White women, as both of these groups combat the colonizing effects of patriarchy and paternalism. Finally, the blues remains a vital means of communicating experience, particularly for African-American women, reflecting their ethos and culture:

> We all know something about blues. Being about us, life is the only training we need to measure their truth. They talk to us, in our own language. They are the expression of a particular social process by which poor Black women have commented on all the major theoretical, practical, and political questions facing us and have created a mass audience who listens to what we say, in that form.

> (Russell 130)

Koko Taylor engenders this "particular social process" of Black womanhood in her performance of "I'm a Woman" and Eva Medina Canada through her storytelling in *Eva's Man*. It is my hope, however, that audiences of both women stop not only to listen, but to hear the words of these "wild" blues women—"NOW."

Notes

1. EDITOR'S NOTE: More often, however, the second line is a variation of the first, as

   Well, I poisoned my man, I put it in his drinking cup.
   Yes I poisoned my man, put it in his drinking cup,
   Well, It's easy to go to jail, but lawd, they sent me up.

   See also Erskine Peters' "Blues Cycle" on pages 99–102, this issue.

2. Like other African-American musical forms, there are more similarities than differences, with regard to themes and style. Specifically, there is an intertwining of the sacred and the secular in the black community, particularly between the blues and gospel music. Thus there are instances where the blues serves a cathartic and/or transcendent function. In this essay, however, I focus more on the blues as a form of agency. For more on the transcendent function of the blues, see Ellison.

Works Cited

Awkward, Michael. *Inspiriting Influences: Tradition, Revision, and Afro-American women's Novels*. New York: Columbia University Press, 1989.

Baker, Houston A., Jr. *Blues, Ideology, and Afro-American literature: A Vernacular* Theory. Chicago: University of Chicago Press, 1984.

Baldwin, James. *Go Tell it on the Mountain*. New York: Dell, 1953.

Dixon, Melvin. *Ride Out the Wilderness: Geography and Identity in Afro-American Literature*. Urbana: University of Illinois Press, 1987.

Ellison, Ralph. *Shadow and Act*. New York: Random House, 1964.

Harrison, Daphne Duval. *Black Pearls*. New Brunswick: Rutgers University Press, 1988.

Holiday, Billie. "Fine and Mellow." Commodore 24405-A, New York 1939.

Jones, Gayl. *Corregidora* New York: Random House, 1975.

———. *Eva's Man*. New York: Random House, 1976.

———. Interview. *Black Women Writers at Work*. Ed. Claudia Tate. New York: Continuum, 1983. 89–99.

Morrison, Toni. *Sula*. New York: Knopf, 1973.

Rainey, Ma. "Prove It on Me Blues." Paramount 12668–D, Chicago 1928.

Russell, Michele. "Slave Codes and Liner Notes." *All the Women are White, All the Blacks Are Men, But Some of Us Are Brave: Black Women Studies*. Ed. Gloria T. Hull, Patricia Bell Scott, and Barbara Smith. New York: The Feminist Press, 1982. 129–140.

Smith, Bessie. "Sing Sing Prison Blues." Columbia 14051–D, New York 1924.

Spivey, Victoria. "Blood Hound Blues." RCA Victor V–38570, October 1929; reissued by RCA Victor on *Women of the Blues*, LP534, 1966.

Taylor, Koko. "I'm A Woman." Alligator 471 I-D, Chicago 1978.

———. "Queen Bee." Alligator 4740, Chicago 1985.

Ward, Jerry W. "Escape from Trublem: The Fiction of Gayl Jones." *Black Women Writers 1950–1980*. Ed. Mari Evans. New York: Doubleday, 1984. 244–57.

Washington, Mary Helen, ed. *Black-Eyed Susans/Midnight Birds: Stories by and about Black Women*. New York: Doubleday, 1990.

White, Deborah Gray. *Ar'n't I A Woman: Females Slaves of the Plantation South*. New York: W.W. Norton & Co., 1987.

Williams, Sherley A. "The Blues Roots of Contemporary Afro-American Poetry." *Chant of Saints: A Gathering of Afro-American Literature, Art, and Scholarship*. Ed. Michael S. Harper and Robert B. Stepto. Urbana: University of Illinois Press, 1979. 123–135.

Adam McKible (essay date Summer 1994)

SOURCE: "'These Are the Facts of the Darky's History': Thinking History and Reading Manes in Four African American Texts," in *African American Review*, Vol. 28, No. 2, Summer, 1994, pp. 223-35.

[*In the following essay, McKible analyzes the definitions of power and identity in the context of naming in Jones's* Corregidora, *Toni Morrison's* Beloved, *Octavia Butler's* Kindred, *and Sherley Anne Williams's* Dessa Rose.]

> In every era the attempt must be made anew to wrest tradition away from a conformism that is about to overpower it. . . . Only that historian will have the gift of fanning the spark of hope in the past who is firmly convinced that *even the dead* will not be safe from the enemy if he wins. And this enemy has not ceased to be victorious.
>
> (Benjamin 255)

> We are rooted in language, wedded, have our being in words. Language is also a place of struggle. The Oppressed struggle in language to recover ourselves—to rewrite, to reconcile, to renew. Our words are not without meaning. They are an action—a resistance. Language is also a place of struggle.
>
> (hooks 28)

> "I know Mammy didn't know a thing about history."
>
> (Williams 124)

At the conclusion of Sherley Anne Williams's *Dessa Rose*, the title character narrowly escapes being recaptured by Adam Nehemiah, the writer who has followed Dessa since her flight from slavery and imprisonment. Dessa eludes Nehemiah with the aid of Aunt Chole, who reads Dessa's body differently than does Nehemiah, and she is helped by "Rufel," her white accomplice and putative mistress. Dessa, Rufel, and a number of escaped slaves had been running a scam through the South by selling the runaways and then arranging to meet them before their new "owners" have a chance to take possession of them; Dessa's brush with Nehemiah has threatened to undo an otherwise smooth operation. With "Nemi's" allegations discredited, Dessa leaves the jail, thinking:

> Nemi was low; and I was the cause of him being low. He'd tried to play bloodhound on me and now some bloodhound was turning him every way *but* loose. He knowed me, so he said, knowed me very well. I was about bursting with what we'd done and I turned to Miz Lady. "Mis'ess," I said, "Miz—" I didn't know

what I wanted to tell her first. And it was like I cussed her; she stopped and swung me around to face her.

> "My name Ruth," she say, "Ruth. I ain't your mistress." Like *I'd* been the one putting that on her.

> "Well, if it come to that," I told her, "my name Dessa, Dessa Rose. Ain't no *O* to it."

> (232)

Insisting on the validity of their own experiences and the integrity of their own names, Dessa and Ruth resist and rewrite the Master narrative of antebellum slavery as represented by Adam Nehemiah. This dynamic of resistance and naming can be found in a number of contemporary adaptations of the nineteenth-century African American female slave narrative[1] but in this essay I will concentrate on four such texts—*Corregidora* by Gayl Jones, *Beloved* by Toni Morrison, *Kindred* by Octavia Butler, and *Dessa Rose* by Sherley Anne Williams. In these texts, certain names function as emancipatory mnemonic devices that simultaneously disrupt and revise the Master narrative—or dominant historiography—within and against which central characters must define themselves. These characters, caught in dilemmas of discursive oppression, find themselves at the crossroads of race, class, and gender—and usually at the bottom of one or more of these hierarchies. The "privilege" of this marginalization is a consciousness that defies the purported truthfulness of History, a perspective that envisions Truth as a fictionalized assemblage and erasure of events rather than as a factual representation of actual social or historical relations. The following discussion will be divided into three sections: a brief analysis of historiography, a discussion of the emancipatory impulse and the development of a trope suitable to it, and, finally, a discussion of naming as literary technique.

Representations of historiography play an important and thoroughly problematized role in the texts under consideration. The same holds true for depictions of history itself, which Butler, Jones, Morrison, and Williams portray as fields of contestation that persist into the present rather than as a series of past, finished events. Marx's description of history in *The Eighteenth Brumaire of Louis Bonaparte* is helpful here: "Men [and women] make their own history, but not spontaneously, under conditions they have chosen for themselves; rather on terms immediately existing, given and handed down to them. The tradition of countless dead generations is an incubus to the mind of the living" (13). That is, the jaws of history maintain a chokehold on the present by offering ideologically invested storytelling posing as commonplace fact. what's more, as Walter Benjamin rightly suggests, the historical account given the greatest credence always belongs to the ruling culture.[2] Thus, history is the Master narrative a dominant culture tells about itself. This narrative effaces as much contradiction as it can, destroying certain records, highlighting others, and creating heroes and villains generally convenient to it. Historiography, then, is a place of struggle, and indeed this is the case in *Beloved*, *Dessa Rose*, **Corregidora**, and *Kindred*.

In *Dessa Rose*, Adam Nehemiah, the author of *The Master's Complete Guide to Dealing with Slaves and Other Dependents* and the uncompleted *The Roots of Rebellion in the Slave Population and Some Means of Eradicating Them*, functions as the scribe of antebellum culture. His first name implies his role as archetypal namer and controller of language, and *Nehemiah*, the name of the Old Testament prophet who rebuilt the wall around Jerusalem and awakened the religious fervor of the Jews, implies the guardianship of traditional culture and values. Nehemiah takes upon himself the writing of Dessa's history and attempts to contain her meaning within the language of slavery. In the novel, after approximately thirty pages largely taken up by Dessa's stories of the plantation and her love of Kaine, the husband debased and killed by their owner, Nehemiah writes his version of Dessa's life:

> These are the facts of the darky's history as I have thus far uncovered them:
>
> The master smashed the young buck's banjo.
>
> The young buck attacked the master.
>
> The master killed the young buck. The darky attacked the master—and was sold to the Wilson slave coffle.
>
> (39)

Nehemiah grounds everything he writes about Dessa in fact; he is, after all, a man of "'Science. Research'" (232), "'a teacher man'" (66). But Nehemiah's compilation of data proves itself a methodology of distortion and—for Dessa—a disabling construction of the truth. His pared down "facts" convey nothing of Dessa's experience; as Deborah McDowell notes, "Nehemiah's account actually essentializes Dessa and attempts to fit her into a recognizable proslavery text" (148). In *Dessa Rose*, Adam Nehemiah, the Southern historiographer, weaves a narrative designed to trap Dessa and unwrite her humanity.[3]

Similarly, Schoolteacher in *Beloved* acts as a man of science who works to control the lived and written lives of the novel's black characters. Along with reading and writing, Schoolteacher instructs his nephews in the proper management and classification of slaves. One day, Sethe comes across Schoolteacher during one of his lessons:

> He was talking to his pupils and I heard him say, "Which one are you doing?" And one of the boys said, "Sethe." That's when I stopped because I heard my name, and then I took a few steps to where I could see what they was doing. . . . I heard him say, "No, no. That's not the way. I told you to put her human characteristics on the left; her animal ones on the right. And don't forget to line them up."
>
> (193)

Schoolteacher extorts Sethe's labor—in this case, the ink she makes for him—in order to write "scientific" analyses of Sethe that justify or obscure the intolerable relations of production under which she must live and work. Controlling the written word, Schoolteacher portrays Sethe as an animal, all the while erasing his own cruelty and the bestiality of his nephews, who at one point hold down the pregnant Sethe while they feed from her breasts and rape her.

Finally, in *Corregidora*, hegemony effaces its earlier criminality through the destruction of incriminating records, (". . . when they did away with slavery down there they burned all the slavery papers so it would be like they never had it" [9]), and in *Kindred*, when Dana travels to twentieth-century Maryland to search through newspapers and legal documents for records of her black ancestors, she finds only a notice of sale, nothing else. Like *Corregidora's* Ursa, Dana learns that the written records of her family history have also disappeared. Not coincidentally, the Maryland Historical Society's remaining records of its antebellum past are housed in "a converted early mansion" once owned by a member of the slavocracy (264).

Considering the brutal experiences of the black and female characters in *Corregidora*, *Beloved*, *Kindred*, and *Dessa Rose*, how is it possible—in the texts and in our readings of them—for these characters to achieve any sort of liberation, or even distance, from the oppressive practices and discourses defining their positions? Angela Davis, in developing a black feminist Marxism, suggests that the very intensity and positioning of the black Woman's marginalization (particularly the slave's) leads to her resistance and to the oppositional strength of her consciousness. The perspective of the black female slave, who finds herself at the bottom of the hierarchies of race, class, and gender within a society otherwise characterized by the "equality" of "free" wage-labor,[4] can in fact become a powerful site of rebellion and self-assertion, and any portrait of her "must simultaneously attempt to illuminate the historical matrix of her oppression and must evoke her varied, often heroic responses to the slaveholder's domination" (Davis 4). This is indeed the case for the central characters in the texts under consideration.

In a provocative analysis of *Dessa Rose* and Morrison's *Sula* entitled "Speaking in Tongues: Dialogics, Dialectics, and the Black Woman Writer's Literary Tradition," Mae G. Henderson offers a valuable critical methodology for the present study. Drawing upon "Bakhtin's notion of dialogism and consciousness" and Gadamer's conception of the "I-Thou" relationship, Henderson describes black female subjectivity as constituting simultaneously" a multiple *dialogic of differences*" and "a *dialectic of identity*" (18–19). This complex subject position experiences gender from a "racialized" position and race from a gendered position; any notion of the unified self is thus challenged from both without and within. "If Bakhtin's dialogic engagement with the Other signifies conflict, Gadamer's monologic acknowledgement of the Thou signifies the potential of agreement. If the Bakhtinian dialogic model speaks to the other within, then Gadamer's speaks to *the same within*" (20). For Henderson, then, black female subjectivity is at the crossroads of harmonic and competing discourses.

Henderson further proposes "a tradition of black women writers generated less by neurotic anxiety or dis-ease than by an emancipatory impulse which engages both hegemonic and ambiguously (non)hegemonic discourse" (37). These writers, then, incorporate into their texts the racist and sexist discursive practices employed by both dominant and subdominant social groups, while their characters dramatize various efforts to undo or elude these practices. Thus, the "emancipatory impulse" Henderson describes consists of two theoretically discrete moments. First, "the initial expression of a marginal presence takes the form of disruption—a departure or break with conventional semantics and/or phonetics." Next, "this rupture is followed by a rewriting or rereading of the dominant story, resulting in a 'delegitimization' of the prior story or a 'displacement' which shifts attention to the other side of the story." These double actions are charged with revolutionary potential, and they "represent a progressive model for black and female utterance" (35).

Henderson also suggests a trope for this model, the "'womblike matrix' in which soundlessness can be transformed into utterance, unity into diversity, formlessness into form, chaos into art, silence into tongues, and glossolalia into heteroglossia" (36; emphasis added). The words *womb* and *matrix* provide a lexical explosion of linguistic possibilities and critical applications, and the following discussion of representations of emancipatory consciousness in *Beloved*, **Corregidora**, *Dessa Rose*, and *Kindred* constitutes a borrowing and expansion of Henderson's useful trope, primarily as it applies to disruptions of hegemonic discourse by black female characters.

The term *matrix* presents an array of suggestive contradictions. It is the solid matter in which a fossil or a crystal forms—in this context, the fossil of an undead, murderous past, as well as the crystal of a future Utopia. And *matrix* denotes the intersection of input and output, encoding and decoding, the site of competing discourses. In a matrix, monologues of power and dialogues of difference collide with each other and with the conversations of the self. External oppression becomes the threat or reality of implosion and self-destruction; self-empowerment explodes or disrupts that which would contain it.

Two examples from the texts will demonstrate this dynamic. In **Corregidora**, Ursa, whose "veins are centuries meeting" (44), must contend with the memory of her foremothers' Portuguese owner. As a blues singer, if one uses Houston Baker's formulation in *Blues, Ideology, and Afro-American Literature*, Ursa stands as a sign of interpretation at the intersection of social, historical, and subjective forces. "The singer's product," according to Baker, "constitutes a lively scene, a robust matrix, where endless antinomies are mediated and understanding and explanation find conditions of possibility" (7). Ursa, a crossroads of resistance and repression, seeks the creation of "a song that would touch me, touch my life *and* theirs. A Portuguese song, but not a Portuguese song. A new world song" (59). Her consciousness and creativity point

at once to past and future, to the violence of memory and the violence of expression; her music contains both Old man CorregiDora's fossilized memory and the assertion of Ursa's own pure song:

> *I am Ursa Corregidora. I have tears for eyes. I was made to touch the past at an early age. I found it on my mother's tiddies. In her milk. Let no one pollute my music. I will dig out their temples. I will pluck out their eyes.*

(77)

Ursa attempts, like Walter Benjamin's historical materialist, to extract tradition from the cultural victors her great-grandfather/grandfather represents.

Dessa Rose also serves as a decoding matrix of social hierarchies. After the attempted rape of Rufel, the wife of a plantation owner, by Oscar, a plantation owner himself, Dessa realizes that gender significantly mediates class and race, creating a possibility for unity where one did not seem to exist:

> The white woman was subject to the same ravishment as me. . . . I hadn't knowed white mens could use a white woman like that, just take her by force same as they could with us. . . . Cause they could. I never will forget the fear that come on me when Miz lady called me on Mr. Oscar, that *knowing* that she was as helpless in this as I was, that our only protection was ourselfs and each others.

(201–02)

Equally open to rape by white men regardless of their status within the structures of race and class, Dessa and Rufel must join forces if they wish to survive. Throughout her text, Williams places Dessa at conflicting matrices of social forces, thus deconstructing the privilege of any one category or position as a self-sufficient perspective.

A matrix can also be the situation within which something must develop—that is, a matrix can also be a womb. Positing the womb as a figure for consciousness in fiction by African American women introduces the impossible contradictions of love and hate, perpetuation and eradication, resistance and complicity, and the nightmares of the past as well as the faint, nearly imperceptible glimmer of the future. Of course, a danger here lies in the reduction of female consciousness (of any race or class) to a biological function, and that is not my intention. Rather, I would argue that black women's fictive discourse considers race as well as gender when representing material and ideological reproduction. In such representations, the surplus-labor value of the enslaved black woman includes the fruits of both material production and human reproduction. In addition, the reproduction of an exploited labor force is depicted as including the potential reproduction of conscious resistance against hegemonic configurations. The womb, therefore, necessarily becomes a site of ideological struggle regardless of any supposedly "natural" relationship between consciousness and biology.

Using the womb as a trope for emancipatory consciousness calls into play an analysis of the role of biological reproduction within a particular mode of production, thus opening onto a vital critical debate that has much to gain through an inclusion of black women's discourse. Marxist feminists have argued at length about the specific relationship between capitalist modes of production and reproduction. In *women's Oppression Today*, Michele Barrett writes: "Attempts to combine an analysis of social reproduction with an analysis of patriarchal human reproduction represent the fundamental problem Marxist feminism faces" (29). Barrett notes "three analytically distinct referents of the concept—social reproduction, reproduction of the labor force and human or biological reproduction" (21). The specific interrelationship of these referents and their role(s) in capitalist production have not been satisfactorily resolved. Novels by black women, which incorporate theoretical machinery and overt political content generally avoided by the canonical Masters (or downplayed by subsequent critics), intervene strategically in this debate through their reconstitutions of historical narrative.

In the texts under discussion, the interplay of maternal reproduction and hegemonic practices and discourses intensifies around reproductive issues. In *Kindred*, Octavia Butler consistently delineates pregnancy and birth within the socioeconomics of slavery. For example, when Carrie and Nigel, twoof Rufus's slaves, have a child, Rufus rewards the parents with a few household items. "'See,' Nigel told [Dana] later with some bitterness. 'Cause of Carrie and me, he's one nigger richer'" (161). More importantly in the text, Dana contributes to the increase of Rufus's wealth in slaves by assisting him in the rape and concubinage of Alice Greenwood. Although Dana resists her complicity with Rufus as much as possible, she must aid him in order to insure the birth of Hagar Weylin, the first inscriber of Dana's family history. In other words, Alice's rape and continued brutalization constitute a precondition of Dana's existence. The rapes that lead to the conceptions of Alice's children unavoidably mediate her love of them; Alice's feelings as a parent collide with her anger and resentment at her victimization. But she also regards their births as the possible destruction of the foundations of their paternity. "'If Hagar had been a boy,'" Alice tells Dana, "'I would have called her Ishmael. In the Bible, people might be slaves for a while, but they didn't have to stay slaves'" (234). Dana carries this wisdom with her back into the twentieth century, but it is a wisdom she gains at great cost, and a wisdom that cannot save Alice; toward the end of the text, she hangs herself, the only resistance left open to her being self-destruction.

Names in Butler's *Kindred*, Morrison's *Beloved*, James's **Corregidora**, and Williams's *Dessa Rose* are constant reminders of resistance and the will to freedom.

In *Dessa Rose*, "'that breeding business'" (12) clearly links the maternal reproduction of the slave labor force and the material production of capital. At the beginning of William's text, the pregnant Dessa is confined in a root cellar, awaiting execution. Dessa had participated in a

slave uprising on a coffle headed south, but unlike her fellow rebels, who were hanged almost as soon as they were caught, Dessa's captors postponed the date of Dessa's execution until after the birth of her (saleable) child. Dessa carries her child fully aware of the contradictions that decision entails; her husband Kaine had reminded Dessa that their child would most likely be sold away from them, and he asked Dessa to get the medicaments necessary to abort the fetus: "'Kaine not want this baby. He want it and don't want it. Babies ain't easy for niggas, but still, I knows this Kaine and I wants it cause that'" (46). Dessa intends to bring their child to term because she loves Kaine and his memory, all the while knowing that Kaine did not want to be the father of a slave. Of course, Kaine could not know that Desmond would be born outside of slavery, that his child's very existence embodies Dessa's resistance and the possibility of future redemption.

Similarly, Sethe is also enmeshed in the involuntary production of human capital, and she discovers herself caught between love for her children and hatred of the system that would enslave them. Her own birth is situated uneasily between complicity and resistance: Sethe's mother bore several children fathered by white slavers, but she killed or abandoned them as soon as they were born. She kept and protected Sethe, however, because Sethe was conceived in an act of love, not rape; and she gave her child a name commemorating that act, *Sethe* being a feminization of her Father's name. Further, all of Baby Suggs's children with the exception of Halle were sold away (23); within the economy of slavery, her value and Sethe's derive primarily from their potential as "property that reproduced itself without cost" (228). When Sethe attempts to kill all of her children rather than allowing them to be returned to slavery, she does so because she finds the intersection of love and resistance impossible to navigate.

Reproduction also plays a central role in **Corregidora**. Ursa's foremothers want to preserve the oral history of their former owner so that his crimes do not go unremembered:

> "Corregidora. Old man Corregidora, the Portuguese slave breeder and whoremonger. . . . He fucked his own whores and fathered his own breed. . . . My grandmama was his daughter, but he was fucking her too."

> (8–9)

Accordingly, they teach Ursa that . . . "*the important thing is making generations. They can burn the papers but they can't burn conscious, Ursa. And that what makes the evidence. And That's what makes the verdict*" (22). Ursa's foremothers urge her to have children so that the story of their bondage will not disappear. The loss of Ursa's biological reproductive capabilities, however, forces her into a critical dialogue with this position, leading her to wonder, "pussy. The center of a Woman's being. Is it?" (46) Ursa's physical loss produces a perspective gained through distance, intensifying the contradictions of procreation as both sexual love and the perpetuation of brutality.

Corregidora exemplifies a related concern shared by all four novels. The insistence in many African American women's texts on the contemporaneity of history suggests that the relations of production experienced by black women under slavery continue to have force in the twentieth century, that the lived experience in a "free" wage-labor system and a slave-labor system are more similar than not. In the following passage from *Corregidora*, Ursa listens to her friend Cat describe an incident at the home of Cat's employers:

> . . . she was telling me about Mr. and Mrs. Thomas Hirshorn and something that happened in the kitchen. She was a young woman, about my age. She lived in during the week and every morning at six o'clock she had to get up and get Mr. Hirshorn's breakfast because he was the supervisor in a plant, and his wife stayed in bed sleeping. He always waited till she called him, but one morning he was sitting at the table while she was fixing coffee. "You pretty, Catherine, you know that? You pretty, Catherine. A lot of you nigger women is pretty." . . . She was saying nothing and then when she'd got the can of coffee grounds down and was opening it to pour in the pot, he was behind her, touching her arm, and she dropped the can, and it banged and rolled across the kitchen floor spilling grains. He jumped back, and she was stooping trying to clean it up when his wife came in. "What happened, Tom?"

> "That clumsy nigger. I won't have time to eat breakfast this morning, sweetheart."

> While she was bending, she could see him bending to kiss his wife's mouth, then he went out the kitchen door, stepping over coffee grounds.

> "You made a mess," his wife said, and went back to bed.

> (65–66)

With a few stylistic modifications, these events, although they were written in the 1970s and take place in the mid-twentieth century, could easily be part of a nineteenth-century slave narrative: Mr. Hirshorn, the owner of the means of production (slaveholder/employer) exploits the labor of a black woman and makes unwanted sexual advances toward her; Mrs. Hirshorn (Southern belle/middle-class wife) and Cat become polarized rather than recognize that the social constructions of race and gender benefiting Tom inform both Cat's oppression and Mrs. Hirshorn's "uselessness" (I employ this term with reservations). A peculiar institution is at work in the Hirshorn house. Similarly, in *Kindred*, Dana calls her twentieth-century employer—a "casual labor agency" that relies on surplus labor ("winos trying to work themselves into a few more bottles, poor women with children trying to supplement their welfare checks, kids trying to get their first job, older people who'd lost one job too many")—a "slave market" (52). And in Morrison's text, the "free" blacks in Ohio uniformly hold the lowest paying jobs.

What does the persistence of a historical relation of production have to say about the present mode of reproduction? What do these novels have to offer to a Marxist feminist debate? I would argue that they provide an expanded representation of production that recognizes the gendering and racializing of reproduction. In African American women's fiction, with its deconstructive sense of history and constructive assertion of personal narration, the exploitation of slave women as the producers of surplus value—children—and the exploitation of "free" black women as low-wage producers and surplus-labor reproducers amount to very nearly the same form of exploitation; the reproduction of a wage-labor force by black women constitutes the production of capital. The perspective gained through this particular marginality expands conceptualizations of production and reproduction so that they begin to conflate and include each other. This conflation does not eviscerate the necessary Marxist feminist differentiation between production and reproduction; each of course has its own discrete theoretical status. However, this formulation does help challenge the deceptive conception of the actuality of separate spheres—one public, male, valuable, and productive; the other private, female, worthless, and somehow "outside" capitalist production. The exploitation of gender and race is integral to the machinations of capitalism, and it extorts profit from the womb as surely as it does from the field or factory.

Gayatri Spivak makes a similar argument in "Feminism and Critical Theory." In the first part of her essay, Spivak argues that traditional Marxism has not adequately theorized human production:

> I would argue that, in terms of the physical, emotional, legal, custodial, and sentimental situation of the Woman's product, the child, this picture of the human relationship to production [specifically here the Marxist conception of alienation] is incomplete. The possession of a tangible place of production in the womb situates the woman as an agent in any theory of production.

> (79)

Spivak goes on to suggest that her earlier formulations were inadequate because she did not take into account "the dimension of race" (81). Warning against the tendency in American critical debates to equate all racism with racism in the United States, Spivak analyzes feminist concerns in relation to postcolonial and multinational practices. Toward the end of "Feminism and Critical Theory," she makes a claim well worth mentioning here: "However active in the production of civilization as a by-product, socialized capital has not moved far from the presuppositions of a slave mode of production" (91). The interdependent constructions of racialized and gendered subjectivities vis-à-vis capitalism must therefore also be understood in terms of imperialism.

This argument deserves further consideration and development. For example, the actual utility of African American *fiction* (or any fiction, for that matter) in a discussion of material (re)production and ideology must be addressed; bell hooks and Michele Barrett would be of use here. And Lise Vogel's concern that a "linguistic similarity of terms" between *production* and *reproduction* does not constitute the basis of a theoretical discussion (139) deserves a reply. Also, a more detailed comparison of the slavocracy and the wage-labor system would be needed. However, I hope I have at least demonstrated that the womb as a trope for the emancipatory consciousness offers manifold literary and theoretical applications.[5]

Morrison, Williams, Butler, and Jones encapsulate the dynamic interrelationship of historiography and the "womblike matrix" of emancipatory consciousness in their texts through the technique of naming. Names, according to Louis Althusser, indicate that "ideology has always-already interpellated individuals as subjects, which amounts to making it clear that individuals are always-already interpellated by ideology as subjects, which necessarily leads us to one last proposition: *individuals are always-already subjects*" (176–77). Certain names in the four novels under discussion lead to a similar and perhaps potentially more useful conclusion than one that could be drawn primarily according to Althusserian lines of thought, for besides suggesting the pervasiveness of material conditions and the persistence of the conditions of history, names in these novels also offer connotations of resistance and Utopian futurity.

In Morrison's *Beloved* and Jones's ***Corregidora***, the names of the texts' title characters both perpetuate disturbing historical memories and contain the possibility of liberation from the conditions that provoked these memories. In Morrison's text, "Beloved" acts as a key to painful remembrance that unlocks future potential and healing. Beloved died an unnamed child, the "crawling-already? baby" (93). She takes her name from the epitaph on her gravestone, a name Sethe, impoverished and degraded, purchases with ten minutes of "rutting among the headstones with the engraver, his young son looking on" (5).

By invoking the name *Beloved*, the major characters re-experience or "rememory" the past in a way that reclaims it for them. When Beloved seduces Paul D., who was on the Sweet Home plantation with Sethe, she asks him to "'touch me on the inside part and call me my name'" (116). As he does, the tin box of memories rusted shut in his heart begins to flake and open (117). And, at the beginning of each of their rememories, Sethe, Denver, and Beloved invoke Beloved's name to conjure up their collective and individual histories. The eventual outcome of this communal recollection is the entry of Denver into the black community, the re-union of Paul D. and Sethe, and, most importantly, Sethe's re-membering of a dis-membered past and an already dead future. Henderson, in "Toni Morrison's *Beloved*: Re-Membering the Body as Historical Text," comments:

> In speaking, that is, in storytelling, Sethe is able to construct an alternate text of black womanhood. This power to fashion a counternarrative, thereby rejecting the definitions imposed by the dominant other(s), finally provides Sethe with a self—a past, present, and future.
>
> (77)

The penultimate chapter of the novel ends with Paul D.'s affirmation, "'You your best thing, Sethe. You are'" and

her incredulous, doubting, joyful response, "'Me? Me?'" (273). By calling the name of a child murdered by her own mother to protect that child from slavery, the characters in *Beloved* unleash the past, disjoint and revise it, and unlock the promise of days to come. Beloved's name, a container of uncontainable incongruities, becomes a crystal of consciousness that shatters the truth-value of Schoolteacher's method of historiography.

In Gayl Jones's ***Corregidora***, Ursa's family name perpetuates a memory that contradicts the "truth" of the past. Because slavers destroyed evidence that could later incriminate them, only the oral history surrounding Ursa's name preserves the knowledge of the indignities experienced by her foremothers. In Portuguese, *corregidore* means 'colonial magistrate,' thus implying the extent of Corregidora's power over his slaves and their descendants and underscoring the legality of his brutality. In Spanish, ***Corregidora*** translates as 'the wife of a chief magistrate,' which conveys the persistence of a psychosexual domination that continues to disable the Corregidora women well into the twentieth century; they are all effectively his wives in the novel. But the word ***Corregidora*** also incorporates the sense of its French root *corregir*—'to correct.' ***Corregidora*** manifests Ursa's reconfiguration of history through memory and the blues; she "corrects" the past by making it more comprehensible to her. Ralph Ellison's comment on the European origin of Afro-American names is relevant here:

> We take what we have and make of them what we can. And there are even those who know where the old broken connections lie, who recognize their relatives across the chasms of historical denial and the artificial barriers of society. . . . I speak here not of mere forgiveness, nor of obsequious insensitivity to the outrages symbolized by the denial and division [of slavery and racism], but of the conscious acceptance of the harsh realities of the human condition, of the ambiguities and hypocrisies of human history as they have played themselves out in the United States.
>
> Perhaps, taken as an aggregate, these European names (sometimes with irony, sometimes with pride, but always with personal investment) represent a certain triumph of the spirit, speaking to us of those who rallied, reassembled and transformed themselves and who under dismembering pressures refused to die.
>
> (149)

The name ***Corregidora*** thus simultaneously embodies the crushing memory of the past and the liberating memories of resistance and survival.

Two sets of names in Williams's *Dessa Rose* and Butler's *Kindred* present the reader with remarkably similar naming strategies. In the first text, a sustained, agonistic contest over the naming of Williams's central character embodies the struggle of the individual subject, Dessa, against the imposition of definitions by Adam Nehemiah, who by right of race, class, and gender has greater access to what Althusser would label the Ideological and the Repressive State Apparatuses of the slavocracy. From nearly the beginning of the novel through its end, Nehemiah refers to her as "Odessa," a name used only by white characters. But, as I noted at the beginning of this essay, she insists that her name is "'Dessa, Dessa Rose. Ain't no *O* to it.'" By calling Dessa out of her name, Nehemiah attempts to assert his social dominance and deny Dessa's humanity. The "O" he adds to her name is the "O" of Otherness and objectification, as well as the zero of nonbeing or worthlessness; it represents what Frederic Jameson might describe as a linguistic "strategy of containment," a method of historiographical narration that writes over Dessa and cancels out the actual conditions of her existence. Her insistence on the name *Dessa* disrupts Nehemiah's fiction and rewrites her narrative. Henderson writes:

> Her rejection of the *O* signifies her rejection of the inscription of her body by the other(s). In other words, Dessa's repudiation of the *O* (Otherness?) signifies her always already presence—what Ralph Ellison describes as the unquestioned humanity of the slave. She deletes nothing—except the white male other's inscription/ascription.
>
> ("Speaking" 32)[6]

"Edana" in *Kindred* functions in approximately the same way. Upon her second return to the past, Rufus asks Dana her name, and she replies, "'Edana. . . . Most people call me Dana'" (30). Neither Rufus nor any other white character in the text calls Dana out of her name; that is never at issue (although Dana and Rufus do have words over the use of the term *nigger*). Dana's control over her name from the outset indicates the greater extent of her authority over language. In fact, her level of literacy exceeds almost every other character's in the novel, and the onomastic struggle in her case centers on the birth of the child Hagar. Nonetheless, the prefix *E-*, like the nullity implied by the *O* in Odessa, denotes absence, negation, or exteriority, and the shortening of "Edana" contradicts this negation.

In *Dessa Rose* and *Kindred*, central white characters have homophonic "architectural" names that call attention to the foundation and collapse of slave society. When Dana first goes to the past, she learns that the young Weylin boy's name is "Rufus. Ugly name to inflict on a reasonably nice-looking little kid" (14). Instead, she calls him "Rufe" ("roof"). In *Dessa Rose*, the runaway slaves harbored at Sutton's Glen call Ruth Elizabeth "Rufel," which proves a very descriptive homophone—"roof fell." Both these acts of signification initially place the characters at the top of Big House society, but they are also reminders of that society's (*de jure*) dissolution. Upon his master's death, Nigel literally destroys Rufe's house by setting fire to it. Of course, as mentioned previously, Rufus's legacy, as promulgated by the Maryland Historical Society, continues in the twentieth century under the roof of a Georgian mansion similar to his own. His death and the end of slavery constitute only a partial victory for the black characters in *Kindred*.

Rufel contains both more destruction and construction than *Rufe*, and this name, like Dessa's, represents a locus of struggle and remembrance. Recollecting the genesis of her name, Rufel recalls her deceased personal maid, Dorcas, whom her mother renamed "Mammy," thus revising or writing over Dorcas's past. Ruth Elizabeth believed that Dorcas called her "Rufel" as an endearment, and because "the darkies could never get her name straight, slurring and garbling the syllables until the name seemed almost unrecognizable" (124). But years later, when she gives Dessa's child his names—first "Button" and then "Desmond"—Rufel, originally at odds with Dessa, "took a private pleasure in having some hand in naming Button, feeling repaid in some measure for the wench's continuing aloofness. Maybe this is what Mammy had felt when she had changed Ruth Elizabeth's name . . ." (160). What Rufel remembers as an act of love may have been a gesture of revenge, a recurrent moment of resistance that she and her family could not read. Also, as part of Williams's signification on William Styron, "roof fell" refers to her sexual love affair—her "fall"—with Nate, a slave.[7]

Finally, Rufel shatters her own representations of the past and the ideology informing it when she tells Dessa, "'My name Ruth. . . . I ain't your mistress.'" This brings me back to the beginning of my essay. Ruth never quite reaches the same insights into slavery gained by Dessa, but their mutual insistence on being called by their own names does expose the cracks and contradictions of slavery, and it opens a dialogue between the black and white female characters that had been impossible earlier in the novel:

> I wanted to hug Ruth. I didn't hold nothing against her, not "mistress," not Nathan, not skin. Maybe we couldn't speak so honest without disagreement, but that didn't change how I feel. . . . We couldn't hug each other, not on the streets, not in Acropolis, not even after dark; we both had sense enough to know that. The town could even bar us from laughing; but that night we walked the boardwalk together and we didn't hide our grins.
>
> (232–33)

In his "Theses on the Philosophy of History," Walter Benjamin describes the depiction of history as an interruption of narrative:

> Thinking involves not only the flow of thoughts, but their arrest as well. Where thinking suddenly stops in a configuration pregnant with tensions, it gives that configuration a shock, by which it crystallizes into a monad. A historical materialist approaches a historical subject only where he [or she] encounters it as a monad. In this structure [the historical materialist] recognizes the sign of a Messianic cessation of happening, or, put differently, a revolutionary chance in the fight for the oppressed past. He [or she] takes cognizance of it in order to blast a specific era out of the homogeneous course of history. . . . The nourishing fruit of the historically understood contains time as a precious but tasteless seed.
>
> (262–63)

Names in Butler's *Kindred*, Morrison's *Beloved*, Jones's **Corregidora**, and Williams's *Dessa Rose* behave much like Benjamin's monad. They are crystallizations—constant reminders—of resistance and the will to freedom. These names momentarily arrest thoughts that too often go unchallenged, and shatter the confines of hegemonic historiography. They are the precious but tasteless seeds of memory and resistance.

But, to return to the precepts of Henderson's article: The emancipatory impulses illustrated by names in these novels disrupt, delegitimize, and displace Master narratives; they do not make them or their conditions of possibility disappear. History still hurts at the ends of these books. In *Dessa Rose* and *Beloved*, the protagonists escape the South only to find racism practiced in other ways in the so-called "Free States." Dana loses her arm at the end of *Kindred*, and Ursa's rapprochement with Mutt at the end of *Corregidora* is at best a mixed blessing. This conclusion does not, however, mean that the practices of disruption, delegitimization, and displacement are ineffectual or have no value. They are the precious tools of struggle, and as long they are available, so too are resistance, healing, and transformation.

Notes

1. My thanks to J. Lee Greene and the participants of his seminar on contemporary masculinist and feminist adaptations of the slave narrative. See also McDowell 161–62.

2. Walter Benjamin describes the cultural practices of social "victors" as a "triumphal procession in which the present rulers step over those lying prostrate. According to traditional practice, the spoils are carried along in the procession. They are called cultural treasures. . . . There is no document of civilization which is not at the same time a document of barbarism" (256).

3. See Mary Kemp Davis 547–49; Henderson, "Speaking" 25–26; and McDowell 148–49 for further discussions of the name *Adam Nehemiah*.

4. More specifically, the female slave is located within a mixed mode of production characterized by the co-existence of slavery and wage-labor.

5. James Thompson and the participants of his "Marxism and Feminism" seminar in the fall of 1991 were instrumental in my understanding of the interconnections and divergences between Marxist and feminist constructions of reproduction.

6. Dessa's second name, *Rose*, also bears mentioning. She is named Rose after her mother, whose name posits a standard of black feminine beauty that defies white definitions: "'Her name was Rose,' Dessa shouted. . . . 'That's a flower so red it look black. When mammy was a girl they named her that count of her skin—smooth black. . . .'" (119). And Dessa's name carries the memories of her sisters, who died before she was born. *Rose* can also be read as a verb, as "Dessa rose against slavery" (see Henderson, "Speaking" 219n28). In this way, her name carries in it her defiance on the plantation, on the coffle, and in the various imprisonments she is forced to endure. Thus the name *Dessa Rose* acts as both predicament and solution, as the self contained by the language of dominance and as the locus of emancipation and the shattering of hegemonic discourse.

7. *Nate* signifies on Styron's "Nat" in *The Confessions of Nat Turner*. In her prefatory "Author's Note"—the title itself Signifyin(g) on Styron's opening section—Williams notes, "I admit also to being outraged by a certain, critically acclaimed novel of the early seventies [sic] that travestied the as-told-to memoir of slave revolt leader Nat Turner. Afro-Americans, having survived by word of mouth—and made of that process a high art—remain at the mercy of literature and writing; often these have betrayed us" (5). In "(W)riting *The Work* and Working the Rites," Mae Henderson suggests that "Styron's work . . . is meant to be a meditation, or reflection, on history, whereas Williams's can perhaps be more aptly understood as a meditation on historiography—in the sense that it provides the reader a guide to the contemplation of historical and literary historical works such as Styron's . . ." (636).

Works Cited

Althusser, Louis. *Lenin and Philosophy and Other Essays*. Trans. Ben Brewster. New York: Monthly Review P, 1971.

Baker, Houston. *Blues, Ideology, and Afro-American Literature: A Vernacular Theory*. Chicago: U of Chicago P, 1984.

Barrett, Michele. *women's Oppression Today*. London: Verso, 1988.

Benjamin, Walter. *Illuminations*. Ed. Hannah Arendt. Trans. Harry Zohn. New York: Shocken, 1968.

Butler, Octavia E. *Kindred*. 1979. Boston: Beacon, 1988.

"Corregidora." *The Collins Spanish Dictionary*, 1971.

"Corregidore." *Novo Michaels Dicianario Illustrado*, 1958.

Davis, Angela. "Reflections on the Black Woman's Role in the Community of Slaves." *Black Scholar*, Dec. 1971: 3–15.

Davis, Mary Kemp. "Everybody Knows Her Name: The Recovery of the Past in Sherley Anne Williams's *Dessa Rose*." *Callaloo* 12.3 (1990): 544–58.

Ellison, Ralph. *Shadow and Act*. New York: Random, 1964.

Henderson, Mae G. "Speaking in Tongues: Dialogics, Dialectics, and the Black Woman Writer's Tradition." *Changing Our Own Words: Essays on Criticism, Theory, and Writing by Black Women*. Ed. Cheryl A. Wall. New Brunswick: Rutgers UP, 1989. 16–37.

————. "Toni Morrison's *Beloved*: Re-Membering the Body as Historical Text." *Comparative American Identities: Race, Sex, and Nationality in the Modern Text.* Ed. Hortense J. Spillers. New York: Routledge, 1991. 62–86.

————. "(W)riting *The Work and Working the Rites.*" *Black American Literature Forum* 23 (1989): 631–60.

hooks, bell. *Talking Back*. Boston: South End, 1989.

Jameson, Frederic. *The Political Unconscious: Narrative as a Socially Symbolic Act*. Ithaca: Cornell UP, 1981.

Jones, Gayl. *Corregidora*. Boston: Beacon, 1975.

Marx, Karl. *The Eighteenth Brumaire of Louis Bonaparte*. New York: International, n.d.

McDowell, Deborah E. "Negotiating between Tenses: Witnessing Slavery after Freedom—*Dessa Rose.*" *Slavery and the Literary Imagination*. Ed. McDowell and Arnold Rampersad. Baltimore: Johns Hopkins UP, 1989. 144–63.

Morrison, Toni. *Beloved*. New York: Knopf, 1987.

Spivak, Gayatri Chakravorty. *In Other Worlds*. New York: Routledge, 1988.

Vogel, Lise. *Marxism and the Oppression of Women: Toward a Unitary Theory*. New Brunswick: Rutgers UP, 1983.

Williams, Sherley Anne. *Dessa Rose*. New York: Morrow, 1986.

Madhu Dubey (essay date 1994)

SOURCE: "'Don't You Explain Me': The Unreadability of *Eva's Man*," in *Black Women Novelists and the Nationalist Aesthetic*, Indiana University Press, 1994, pp. 89-105.

[*In the following excerpt, Dubey examines* Eva's Man *in light of the prescribed writing structures of the Black Aesthetics movement, arguing that Jones's focus on gender issues over racial inequality led to unfavorable reviews of the novel.*]

Unlike *Corregidora*, Gayl Jones's *Eva's Man* (1976) cannot be even partially recovered into the Black Aesthetic critical mode. Each of the novel's salient thematic and formal features, such as its treatment of castration and lesbianism, and its use of stereotypes, first-person narration, and black dialect, resists a Black Aesthetic reading. This defiance of the contemporary conditions of readability produces a visible sense of strain in the text. The most subversive moments of *Eva's Man* are shrouded in an incoherence that seriously jeopardizes the reader's interpretive function, and prevents us from distilling any clear meaning from the text. It seems almost as if the novel must disclaim its right to meaning altogether if it cannot posit the clear, didactic meaning required by the Black Aesthetic. *Eva's Man* renders itself unreadable, as it were, in order both to escape the functional reading codes of the Black Aesthetic and to obscure its own refusal of these codes.

Predictably, then, the contemporary critical reception of *Eva's Man* was almost unanimously unfavorable.[1] The rare favorable review commended the novel precisely for its divergence from Black Aesthetic literature. For example, Richard Stookey of *The Chicago Tribune Book Review* found *Eva's Man* "refreshing" because unlike Stookey's conception of the typical contemporary black novel, *Eva's Man* did not aim its anger and violence against racial oppression. Stookey went on to state that *Eva's Man* "goes about its business wholly without explicit reference to the dimension of racial oppression and in so doing elevates itself out of the supposed genre known as the 'black novel' and into the realm of universal art." Stookey's review dismisses racial oppression as a narrow, parochial concern, and explicitly states that the dynamics of sexual oppression constitute a literary theme of universal interest.[2] A reading such as Stookey's lends credence to the black nationalist argument that black feminist literature was actively promoted by the white literary establishment primarily because it deflected attention away from white racism to black sexism.[3] Loyle Hairston, a prominent Black Aesthetic critic, wrote that *Eva's Man* was accepted by white reviewers because of its critique of black men rather than of white society. While Hairston defended *Corregidora* because it was "far from being a feminist tract," he castigated *Eva's Man* for being "a study in male hostility."[4] However, the contemporary critical furor over *Eva's Man* cannot be fully accounted for by the novel's feminist focus and its emphasis on sexual rather than racial oppression. As we have already seen, *Sula*, too, was denounced by Black Aesthetic critics as a feminist novel that diverted attention away from white racism toward black sexism. But the Black Aestheticians' disapproval of *Eva's Man* was pitched considerably higher than their critique of *Sula*. While Black Aesthetic critics debated the thematics and the sexual politics of *Sula*, *Eva's Man* seemed to represent such a powerful threat to black nationalist ideology that the very legitimacy of its publication was contested. Keith Mano, writing in *Esquire*, argued that *Eva's Man* lacks any artistic merit and if it had been written by a white or a black male novelist, "it would still be in manuscript."[5] Insinuating that *Eva's Man* was published only because Toni Morrison, as the editor at Random House, agreed to publish it, Mano deplored the fact that "more and more of late, publishing has become a transaction between women, for women."[6]

Toni Morrison was fully cognizant of the ideological implications of her decision to publish *Eva's Man*. Morrison described the novel as a "considered editorial risk" because "someone might say, 'Gee, all her [Jones's] novels are about women tearing up men.'"[7] Morrison's comment points to the one feature of *Eva's Man* that drew the most extreme negative reaction from contemporary critics— Eva's castration of Davis, which constitutes the climax of the novel. Unlike the other novels considered here, *Eva's Man* does not even attempt a resolution within the heterosexual parameters of Black Aesthetic ideology. The novel presents no black male character equivalent to Ajax in *Sula*, Mutt in *Corregidora*, Grange in *The Third Life of*

Grange Copeland, or Truman in *Meridian*. While Mutt could be regarded as the liberator of a new black heterosexual femininity, the representation of black male characters in *Eva's Man* admits no possibility of a heterosexual compromise. Eva's castration of Davis and her consequent imprisonment appear to be the only logical conclusion to the novel, for each of Eva's heterosexual encounters results in violence and imprisonment. Eva's first heterosexual experience, with Freddy Smoot, initiates her into violence: after molesting her with a dirty popsicle stick (one of the many objects in the novel that stands in for the penis), Freddy presents Eva with a pocket knife. Eva threatens to use this pocket knife when Alfonso tries to molest her, and actually uses it when Moses Tripp takes her for a whore. Eva's stabbing of Moses Tripp leads to her first imprisonment in the novel, an imprisonment that is later replicated when her husband, James Hunn, keeps her locked in his home, and when Davis confines her to his apartment.

Eva's literal, physical imprisonment parallels her psychological imprisonment in the male-created stereotypes of black women as whores and bitches. These stereotypes serve the double function of constructing black women as a powerful, dangerous force, and of justifying the black masculine attempt to contain this force. The stereotype of the black woman as a whore, for example, invests black women with an excessive, disorderly sexual energy, which then becomes the object of masculine regulation. Similarly, the bitch stereotype endows the black woman with destructive power and strength; the subjugation of black women by black men is then rationalized as an attempt to curb this destructive power. However, stereotypes in the novel do not enact a simple exchange of power originating in the oppressor and directed at a helpless victim. Stereotypes are not merely imposed upon black women by black men; black women characters in the novel often appropriate the stereotype because it offers them their only means of exercising power. For example, when Eva occupies the position of greatest power over Davis, as she kills and castrates him, she is actually submitting to the images through which Davis has perceived her. Soon after they meet, Davis misnames Eva Medina as Eve and Medusa, thus remaking her in the traditional conception of women as evil corrupters and destroyers of men. Eva seems to acquiesce to Davis's naming of her even at her moment of greatest resistance. Biting Davis's penis, she casts herself in the role that Davis assigned her, of Eve biting the apple: "I bit down hard. My teeth in an apple."[8] Immediately after the castration, Eva assumes Davis's second image of her: "I'm Medusa, I was thinking. Men look at me and get hard-ons. I turn their dicks to stone. I laughed" (p. 130). Eva's laugh is only one of the many details that complicate the novel's treatment of stereotypes: Eva is both laughing the powerful laugh of the Medusa and laughing at Davis's conception of her as Medusa.

The novel's presentation of the stereotype as the site of ambivalent exchanges of power is most clearly apparent in its treatment of the Queen Bee, the community's name for a woman who takes on a series of lovers, each of whom dies soon after his encounter with her. The image of the Queen Bee, created by the black women of the community, reveals these women's internalization of the conception of black women as whores and bitches. However, this image does not merely reflect the women's passive acceptance of masculine stereotypes; the Queen Bee stereotype is manipulated by the novel's black female characters to serve a number of different uses. Miss Billie and Eva's mother turn the type into a subject, humanize the Queen Bee by looking at her from the inside rather than the outside. Eva's mother feels that "she would be more scared to be the Queen Bee than to be any of the men" (p. 41) because the Queen Bee cannot love whom she wants. Miss Billie, receptive to this entirely new perception of the Queen Bee, admits that "she hadn't never looked at it that way, but it must be hard on the Queen Bee too" (p. 41). Eva's appropriation of the Queen Bee stereotype plays yet another variation on it. While the original Queen Bee commits suicide, helplessly accepting the guilt for her involuntary destructive power over men, Eva actively exercises this power when she murders Davis. Eva's assumption of the Queen Bee stereotype transforms it into a symbol of vengeance, but even this articulation does not finally fix the type's potential meaning. The Queen Bee type continues to transform itself, accruing new and even contradictory layers of meaning with each configuration. Toward the end of the novel, Eva's madness mobilizes the stereotype beyond recognition, as Eva becomes both the Queen Bee and the victim of the bee's sting (p. 151). Eva's insane play with the stereotype finally divests it even of the gender specificity that originally motivated the type; Eva imagines herself as a feminine flower stung by a masculine Queen Bee: "He stings me between my breasts, the bud between my legs. My flower" (p. 151).

The novel's treatment of the Queen Bee and of other sexual stereotypes is markedly at odds with the theorization of the stereotype in Black Aesthetic and early black feminist criticism, both of which construed the stereotype as a false image imposed on the oppressed by the oppressor, and enjoined black writers to counter the stereotype with the authentic, actual experience of black men and women. The black writer should thus invoke the authority of realism to challenge and correct the falsity of the stereotype. In his diatribe against *Sula*, *Corregidora*, and *Eva's Man*, Addison Gayle urges readers to censure these novels' distorted, stereotypical presentation of blacks and to demand, instead, more "realistic paradigms" of black experience.[9] In a black feminist reading that only superficially differs from Gayle's, Gloria Wade-Gayles justifies *Eva's Man* on the grounds of its realism: "Jones's fictive world mirrors the real world Ladner and other sociologists have studied."[10] In their common appeal to realism, both Addison Gayle and Gloria Wade-Gayles overlook the complex status of "reality" in *Eva's Man*. The novel not only eschews the authority of narrative realism; it also thematically poses the question of the "real" in terms entirely incommensurate with Gayle's and Wade-Gayles's opposition of stereotype and reality.

Eva's Man provides no authentic black femininity against which we might measure the truth or falsity of a particular stereotype. Characters in the novel are entirely constructed by the distorted perceptions of others; the novel presents no original, essential selfhood that escapes this stereotypical structuring. Eva's character, for example, is first introduced to us through the words and images of others: the newspaper portrays Eva as a "wild woman" (p. 3), and the general public perceives her as a whore (p. 4). Nowhere in the novel are these images revised or superseded, as Eva never articulates her sense of difference from these stereotypical constructions. We are given no reason to believe that she possesses a hidden, integral self that resists or precedes the stereotype; on the contrary, Eva consistently validates the stereotypical expectations of male characters in the novel. To give one example, Moses Tripp tells Eva, "One of these days you going to meet a man, and go somewhere and sleep with him. I know a woman like you" (p. 166). Eva's encounter with Davis, to all appearances, confirms Tripp's perception of her as a whore. Even while the novel militates against the stereotypical perception of black women as whores and bitches, it does not offer any alternative, authentic definition of black femininity that exceeds these stereotypes.

The novel's exclusive reliance on stereotypical characterization refuses the realist model of character as the reflection of a knowable real subject. Not only the characters in the novel, but the novel itself relentlessly constructs identity in stereotypical terms.[11] Characterization in *Eva's Man* is a random yoking of names and attributes. Especially in the second half of the novel, traits are so arbitrarily shuffled from one name to another that the difference between names ceases to signify, and the realist notion of character—as a distinctive collection of physical and psychological traits—loses all functional value. The displacement of character traits along a chain of different names is so pervasive that it is difficult to isolate particular examples; character fragments double and triple each other in a hollow mirroring that complicates any conception of the subject as a coherent, unified entity. Eva and Elvira, Charlotte and Joanne double each other. In an imagined scene with Mr. Logan, Eva substitutes herself for Miss Billie, James Hunn substitutes for Freddy Smoot, for Eva's father, and for Davis. The prison psychiatrist (who shares Freddy Smoot's last name and reminds Eva of Tyrone) tries to fix the process of character substitution around the name of Davis, suggesting that he represents all the men who had ever abused Eva. Eva's response to the psychiatrist's suggestion—"Who?" (p. 81)—indicates that the chain of substitutions lacks any end or origin; characters ceaselessly displace and replace each other in a process of empty reflection that denies any access to the real nature of identity. Far from the authentic, self-present subject of black nationalist discourse, the novel's use of stereotypes figures the black subject as fragmented, absent,[12] and lacking any ground in reality.

The novel's failure to posit an authentic black subject is not, however, its most serious point of difference from contemporary black articulations of the stereotype. While Black Aesthetic and feminist critics invoked the authority of realism, their equally strong emphasis on positive images exposed the limits of this realism. According to these theorists, the black writer must not only contest stereotypes with the truth; more importantly, the black writer must replace negative stereotypes with positive images.[13] The contradiction between realism and positive images apparently went unnoticed; in the same essay, Addison Gayle advised black writers to present "realistic paradigms" and to "create images, symbols and metaphors of positive import from the black experience."[14] Some of the most critical contemporary reviews of *Eva's Man* focused on the novel's failure to present positive, politically functional images of blacks. June Jordan, for example, begins her review of the novel with the familiar opposition of stereotype and reality, describing *Eva's Man* as a book of "sinister misinformation" that fails to revise the existing stereotypes of black women.[15] Further in Jordan's review, however, it becomes clear that the real problem with *Eva's Man* is not that it perpetuates stereotypes, but that these stereotypes are negative and do not serve a clear moral or political function:

> I fear for the meaning of this novel. What does it mean when a young Black woman sits down to compose a universe of Black people limited to animal dynamics? And what will such testimony, such perverse ambivalence contribute to the understanding of young girls in need of rescue and protection?[16]

Jordan's comments identify the two features of the novel's use of negative stereotypes that cannot be reconciled with Black Aesthetic or early black feminist theory: the novel's presentation of blacks through time-worn sexual stereotypes ("people limited to animal dynamics"), and its refusal to offer a clear, didactic judgment of these stereotypes ("perverse ambivalence").

Eva's Man provides more than enough support for the first of Jordan's objections, in its narrow presentation of blacks as entirely sexual creatures. All of the novel's characters are driven by a sexual appetite that seems absolutely beyond the control of reason. Eva learns to view herself and other blacks as sexual animals through the education she receives from Miss Billie and her mother. Miss Billie repeatedly uses animal imagery to describe black males: Freddy Smoot is a "banny rooster" (p. 14) and the other black boys in the neighborhood are "a bunch of wild horses" (p. 20). Miss Billie's repetition of the words, "Once you open your legs, . . . it seem like you caint close them" (p. 15), impresses upon Eva her society's perception of black feminine sexuality as an uncontrollable natural urge. The rest of the novel sustains this association of sexual, natural, and animal by means of frequent metaphorical overlaps between food, sex, and defecation. When Eva rejects Elvira's sexual propositioning, Elvira describes Eva as "sitting right on a pot, but afraid to shit" (p. 40). Mustard reminds Davis of "baby's turd" (p. 8) and vinegar and egg of feminine sexuality. As the man with no thumb refers to Eva as "sweetmeat" (p.

68), Eva's gaze persistently returns to the plate of pigfeet in front of him. Alfonso mocks Eva's virginity, repeating, "Most girls your age had the meat *and* the gravy" (p. 57). After sex with Davis, Eva feels "like an egg sucked hollow and then filled with raw oysters" (p. 66). The metaphorical identification of food and sex culminates in Eva's castration of Davis: "I raised blood, slime from cabbage, blood sausage" (p. 128).

Confining its characters to this restricted orbit of food, sex, and defecation, *Eva's Man* seems to support the age-old racist stereotype of blacks as primitive and animalistic. The novel's apparent adherence to this stereotype drew the most extreme negative reactions from Black Aesthetic critics. In his caustic review of *Eva's Man*, Addison Gayle wrote that the novel remains trapped in negative myths "borrowed from a racist society." According to Gayle, *Eva's Man* envisions blacks as "a primitive people defined totally in terms of our sexuality; . . . ours is the world of instinctual gratification—where sex, not power, not humanity, reigns supreme."[17] Gayle's comment is accurate in the sense that *Eva's Man* does not overtly or thematically reject the primitive black stereotype.[18] On a formal level, however, the novel's tight enclosure of the reader as well as the characters within the sexual stereotype implicitly conveys the limitations of this stereotype. The novel's obsessive emphasis on the natural, instinctual functions paradoxically achieves the effect of denaturalizing these functions. *Eva's Man* repeats and recycles a limited number of sexual stereotypes in a stylized manner that forces us to regard black sexuality as a textual fabrication rather than a natural essence. The problem with *Eva's Man*, then, is not that it fails to critique the stereotype of the primitive black, but that this critique is not explicit enough to meet the Black Aesthetic demand for a clear, didactic literature. Gayl Jones herself was aware that her ambivalent use of stereotypes could not be reconciled with the contemporary concern with "positive race images."[19] The "perverse ambivalence" of *Eva's Man* derives from its reluctance to pass unequivocal thematic judgments on the racist and sexist stereotypes of the past, and its failure to offer a new set of positive and politically useful images of blacks.

The question of negative stereotypes versus positive images of blacks intersects with another important area of Black Aesthetic theory: its opposition of the oppressive past and the free future. Black Aestheticians optimistically relegated negative stereotypes of blacks to the historical past; Larry Neal, for example, declared that "there are no stereotypes any more. History has killed Uncle Tom."[20] Only through a repression of the oppressive historical past could Black Aesthetic writers liberate a new, revolutionary consciousness. The temporal vision of *Eva's Man* fails to respect this dichotomy between old and new, past and present. Toward the beginning of the novel, Eva states that "the past is still as hard on me as the present" (p. 5). The novel's structure insistently enacts the repetition of the past in the present. The entire narrative is a desperate act of memory: Eva obsessively remembers her past in an unsuccessful attempt to order and transcend it. Eva's conception of time as a repetitive sameness erases any difference between the past, present, and future. This sameness, however, does not constitute a vision of temporal continuity. The fragmented structure of the novel presents time as a series of shattered moments linked to each other by sheer, random repetition.

Of all the novels considered here, *Eva's Man* most radically disrupts the bildungsroman structuring of time as a medium of change, progress, and development. It is possible to detect a submerged linear strand in the first part of the novel, which presents Eva's life in a roughly chronological fashion. In chapter 1, the eight-year-old Eva has her first sexual encounter with Freddy Smoot. Chapter 2, the only chapter in the novel that preserves a clear linear focus, deals with the twelve-year-old Eva's perception of her mother, father, and Tyrone. Subsequent chapters present the key incidents in Eva's life, from her stabbing of Moses Tripp to her marriage with James Hunn. Part 1 ends with Eva's desertion of James Hunn and her decision to work at P. Lorillard Tobacco Company. The next three sections of the novel abandon linear chronology altogether; Eva's earliest memories of Freddy Smoot and her encounters with Elvira and the psychiatrist in the narrative present merge into the same meaningless cycle.

The cyclic structure of *Eva's Man* offers no possibility of redemption, unlike the spiral structure of *Sula* or the blues form of *Corregidora*. The structure of *Eva's Man* is more akin to the tightly closed circles that structure *The Bluest Eye*. In both novels, circular repetition creates a sense of suffocation for the reader; the thematic entrapment of the protagonists of the two novels is replicated by the reader's imprisonment in the novels' repetitive structures.[21] The circular repetition of both novels installs a deterministic vision of time and history that allows no possibility of change or transformation.[22] *Eva's Man*, even more so than *The Bluest Eye*, bears out Roger Rosenblatt's thesis that circular form in black American fiction frequently figures history as an overdetermined, inescapable destiny.[23] This despairing vision of history is, of course, exactly opposed to the black nationalist belief in new beginnings, in a revolutionary future that can obliterate the oppressive past.

Eva does seek an escape from her own oppressive past, but her search for temporal redemption does not direct her toward the future-oriented goal of black nationalist discourse. Eva's attempt to counter her sense of the fragmentation of time involves a recursion into her ancestral past. Contrary to the nationalist affirmation of temporal discontinuity, *Eva's Man* implies that only a recovery of ancestral continuity can redeem the senseless temporal cycle that imprisons Eva. Early in the novel, Miss Billie gives Eva one of her "ancestors bracelets," and impresses upon Eva the importance of being "true to one's ancestors. She said there were two people you had to be true to—those people who came before you and those people who came after you" (p. 22). Eva's alienation from the ancestral cycle is signaled by her loss of Miss Billie's bracelet when she is eight years old. The bracelet seems to symbolize a temporal continuity dependent upon reproduction: Miss Billie with-holds the bracelet from her daughter, Charlotte, until she decides to get married and have children. Charlotte and Eva—like Joanne Riley, who doubles Charlotte and Eva in several ways—refuse to have any children; this refusal does not seem to be liberating, as it is for Sula or Ursa. For Eva, at least, a liberation from the temporal cycle seems possible only through a recovery of generational continuity.

The redemptive possibilities of Eva's lost ancestral past are embodied in the gypsy Medina, after whom Eva and her great-grandmother are named. Medina's character is rich with inchoate possibilities that Eva (or the novel) fails to realize. Medina intersects only obliquely with Eva's ancestral past: she is a white gypsy whose incoherent promise is filtered to Eva though the memories of her great-grandmother. Medina's race is crucial to her function in the novel; as a white woman, she cannot represent a pure racial or ancestral origin for Eva. Moreover, Medina speaks deprecatingly of peckerwoods, seemingly unaware that she herself falls into this stereotypical category. When Eva's great-grandfather tries to reduce Medina to the stereotype, Eva's great-grandmother points out that Medina is not a peckerwood simply because she does not see herself as one. Medina's perception of herself provides Eva's sole glimpse of a psychological freedom that escapes the constriction of racial stereotyping.

Medina offers a possible release not only from Eva's imprisonment in stereotypes, but also from her imprisonment in time and in hetero-sexuality:

> The gypsy Medina, Great-Grandmama said, had time in the palm of her hand. She told Great-Grandfather, "She told me to look in the palm of her hand and she had time in it."
>
> Great-Grandfather said, "What did she want you to do, put a little piece of silver over top of the time."
>
> Great-Grandmother said, "No." Then she looked embarrassed. Then she said, "She wanted me to kiss her inside her hand."
>
> Great-Grandfather started laughing.
>
> (p. 48)

The image of Medina holding time in the palm of her hand exemplifies her control over time, as opposed to Eva's helpless entrapment in it. Meditating on her own sense of time as an inevitable, uncontrollable force that denies human choice, Eva repeatedly recalls Medina, and asks, "Do you think there are some things we can't help from letting happen?" (p. 49). Eva tries to recover Medina's secret power over time by kissing the palm of Davis's hand, but Eva's heterosexual variation on Medina's latently lesbian gesture robs it of all meaning. In the passage quoted above, Eva's great-grandmother's embarrassment at mentioning the kiss to her husband suggests its unspoken erotic implications. Eva's great-grandFather's laughter and his cynical interpretation of Medina as a typi-

cal gypsy who wants nothing but money, imply that Medina's mysterious promise is not accessible to men. That Medina represents a distinctly feminine possibility is confirmed in the scene when Eva tells Davis about Medina, and he, like Eva's great-grandfather, "laughed hard" and "said he didn't know what I meant" (p. 49).

Throughout the novel, Eva tries to affirm her continuity with her namesake. When Davis misnames her Medusa, Eva fiercely defends her ancestral name. Wandering from town to town, Eva attempts to recover the mobility of the gypsy, and repeatedly draws attention to her own wild hair, reminiscent of the thick hair of Medina. However, Eva's continuity with Medina does not go beyond the external details of name, appearance, and physical mobility. Eva holds only sweat in the palms of her hands, failing to recapture Medina's grasp of time. The redemptive possibility suggested by Medina becomes increasingly obscure and in-accessible as the novel progresses: "I licked the palms of my hands. I bit shadows" (p. 157). Soon after Eva kills and castrates Davis, she imagines Medina telling her to "toss his blood into the wind and it will dry" (p. 138). Medina's advice does not help to absolve Eva's sense of guilt, as is clear from the blood imagery that pervades the last two sections of the novel.

The very end of the novel, however, seems to suggest that Eva has succeeded in realizing some of the possibilities figured by Medina: Eva's acceptance of Elvira as a lover implies that Eva has escaped the heterosexual pattern of violence and imprisonment. The novel's conclusion also suggests that with Elvira, Eva has finally liberated herself from the past, as this is the only time in the novel that Eva is able to live in and affirm the present moment:

> "Tell me when it feels sweet, Eva. Tell me when it feels sweet, honey."
>
> I leaned back, squeezing her face between my legs, and told her, "*Now.*"
>
> (p. 177, emphasis mine)

It is questionable, however, whether Elvira actually represents a viable alternative to Eva's earlier imprisonment in heterosexual relationships. For one thing, the very physical setting of their relationship, a prison cell, detracts from its liberatory possibilities. Darryl Pinckney argues that the lesbian encounter of Eva and Elvira is "not prison rape, the articulation of power. It is an indication of emotional requirements still unsatisfied."[24] Eva's acceptance of Elvira, however, seems to be motivated not by emotional but by purely sexual requirements. An earlier conversation between the two women, in which Elvira complains that female prisoners are not allowed male "sex visits" (p. 149), suggests that Eva and Elvira come together only because heterosexual relationships are not permitted in prison.

Further, Elvira pursues Eva as aggressively as do the men in the novel, and her propositioning of Eva is couched in the language of heterosexual seduction. Frequently, it is impossible to distinguish between Elvira's words and the words of Eva's male lovers. For example, Elvira's "You hard, why you have to be so hard?" (p. 158) recalls Davis's "You a hard woman, too, ain't you?" (p. 8). In some passages in the novel, Elvira's words exactly echo the words of male characters who probe or violate the privacy of women:

> "How did it feel?" Elvira asked.
>
> "How did you feel?" the psychiatrist asked.
>
> "How did it feel?" Elvira asked.
>
> "How do it feel, Mizz Canada?" the man asked my mama.
>
> (p. 77)

This passage, along with many others, reduces Elvira's lesbian difference to the repetitive sameness of all the heterosexual encounters in the novel. It is not the radical difference of lesbianism from heterosexuality, but a mere fact of circumstance (the unavailability of men in prison) that leads Eva to Elvira.

However, if the lesbian encounter of Eva and Elvira is no different from Eva's heterosexual encounters, why is it made to carry the burden of resolving the novel's heterosexual conflicts? The very placing of the Eva-Elvira scene, at the end of the novel, invites us to read it with the special emphasis that fictional conclusions conventionally require. Simply through its placing at the end of the plot, lesbianism is invested with a significance that the novel otherwise refuses to develop. This ambivalent treatment of lesbianism is also evident in other details, such as the brevity of the scene, as well as its absolute lack of preparation. Immediately before Eva succumbs to Elvira, the narrative directly addresses Davis: "Last night she got in the bed with me, Davis. I knocked her out, but I don't know how long I'm going to keep knocking her out" (p. 176). This is, significantly, the only instance in the novel where Eva's narrative directly addresses another character; this address achieves the effect of reasserting Eva's heterosexual desire for Davis and diminishing the value of her lesbian encounter with Elvira. Eva's address to Davis further strips the lesbian scene of all significance by suggesting that Eva is motivated by the sheer tedium of resisting Elvira's persistent advances.

The novel's incoherent treatment of lesbianism is not surprising, given the contemporary hostility to positive portrayals of lesbian characters in black fiction.[25] As we have already seen in the chapters on *Sula* and *Corregidora*, the ambivalent presentation of lesbianism in black women's fiction of the 1970s marks these novels' adjustment to the heterosexual emphasis of black nationalist discourse. *Eva's Man* goes further than *Sula* or *Corregidora* in pushing the resolution of its protagonist's plot outside a heterosexual frame. This uncompromising refusal of heterosexuality logically leads to a consideration of lesbianism as a probable point of resolution. *Eva's Man* does admit the full implications of its critique of hetero-

sexuality, presenting lesbianism as the only remaining plot choice for its protagonist. Having gone so far, however, the novel withdraws meaning from its own conclusion, as if in a belated effort to appease its contemporary reading public. The necessity of this self-protective gesture becomes evident through even a superficial glance at contemporary reviews of *Eva's Man*; the judgment expressed in *Publishers Weekly*, that Eva "descends into the ultimate corruption in prison,"[26] is typical of the contemporary response to the novel's lesbian conclusion.

The novel's treatment of castration is even more fraught with ambivalence than its treatment of lesbianism. Lesbianism and castration are the two thematic elements of *Eva's Man* that pose the most serious threat to the heterosexual assumptions of Black Aesthetic ideology; hence, the severely strained treatment of these two elements. Like lesbianism, castration occupies a highly privileged place in the novel's plot: as the climax, the castration inevitably bears a heavy interpretive weight. The castration scene is marked by the sudden appearance of italics and by a symbolic and metaphorical overload that further encourages the reader to attach extra emphasis to the scene. The very language of the narration thickens as Eva remembers her castration of Davis. Almost as if to compensate for the castration, Eva offers a series of metaphorical substitutes for the penis, such as sausage, apple, plum, and milkweed. In later chapters, this metaphorical substitution extends to include owl, eel, cock, and lemon. The strain in the novel's presentation of the castration is apparent in that the scene seems unable to bear the burden of meaning that it is made to carry. For example, Eva's comparison of the castration to Eve's biting the apple opens up a possibly rich symbolic field. However, the immediately following comparison of the penis to another fruit, the plum, denies the symbolic potential of the apple by returning us to a literal level of meaning, where the apple is merely a fruit.

This simultaneous arousal and withdrawal of meaning exemplifies the difficult interpretive access that the castration scene provides the reader. In this scene, Eva directly addresses the reader for the first and only time in the novel: "What would you do if you bit down and your teeth raised blood from an apple? Flesh from an apple? What would you do? Flesh and blood from an apple? What would you do with the apple? How would you feel?" (p. 128). While this direct address appears to solicit the reader's active participation in the scene, Eva's questions actually deflect the reader's interpretive activity. Instead of answering the reader's question, "How did it feel?"—a question obsessively posed to Eva by the other characters in the novel—Eva simply throws this question back at the reader. She further complicates the reader's function in this scene by suggesting that she killed and castrated Davis because he did not tell her about his wife (p. 129). The reader cannot, however, accept the explanation Eva offers here, for we have been told earlier that "there were also people saying I did it because I found out about his wife. That's what they tried to say at the trial because that was the easiest answer they could get" (p. 4). Pushing us toward an interpretation that has been discredited earlier, the novel makes it impossible for us to answer the question, "How did it feel?"—the question that, in a sense, motivates the entire narrative. Michael Cooke has described *Eva's Man* as "a curt, elided whydunit."[27] The novel offers several possible reasons for Eva's castration of Davis: his silence about his wife, his physical imprisonment of Eva, his refusal to commit himself to her, his stereotypical perception of her as a whore. All these answers are true to a certain extent, but they do not seem to answer adequately the question of Eva's motivation. The novel anticipates all the explanations the reader is likely to entertain and robs them of validity by showing that they were imposed upon Eva at the trial, by the psychiatrist and by a curious, sensation-seeking press and public. Eva herself remains conspicuously silent about her motive, refusing to provide an authoritative interpretation of the castration.

The castration, then, seems to mean everything and nothing; the novel surrounds its climactic incident with an obscurity and density that discourage the reader from extracting any clear meanings or ideological messages from the incident. This incoherence, like the incoherent treatment of lesbianism, partially obscures the novel's uncompromising refusal to cater to the heterosexual expectations of its contemporary reading public. Again, a mere glance at the contemporary critical response to *Eva's Man* allows us to understand the novel's contradictory treatment of the castration as a necessary defensive gesture. Black Aesthetic criticism of *Eva's Man* rises to a shrill and almost paranoid pitch when it confronts the novel's presentation of castration. In Addison Gayle's review of the novel, for example, literary and even political judgments give way to sheer personal vilification of the author. According to Gayle, it is Jones and not Eva who seeks "a personal release from pain, a private catharsis, which could be achieved only when the Black man had been rendered impotent."[28] In a discussion with Roseann Bell, Gayle goes even further: "If Gayl Jones believes that Black men are what she says they are, she ought to get a white man."[29]

Perhaps it was precisely in order to protect herself from such criticism that Gayl Jones repeatedly tried to curtail the scope of the novel's meaning. Jones said, in an interview: "I'm sure people will ask me if That's the way I see the essential relationship between men and women. But that man and woman don't stand for men and women—they stand for themselves, really."[30] Jones partly succeeded in her attempt to restrict the meaning of *Eva's Man* to a particular story of a particular man and woman. Several critics, such as Margo Jefferson and Larry McMurtry, have read the novel as a narrow, concentrated exploration of a single life that is not representative of the lives of black men and women in general.[31] Jones also tried to delimit the political significance of *Eva's Man* by emphasizing the difference between the author and the narrator, and directly linking this difference to the absence of political messages in her work:

> There are moments in my literature, as in any literature, that have aesthetic, social, and political implications but I don't think that I can be a "responsible" writer in

the sense that those things are meant because I'm too interested in contradictory character and ambivalent character and I like to explore them without judgements entering the work—without a point of view entering.[32]

The use of first-person narration in *Eva's Man* works to distance the author from the risky ideological implications of the novel. The complete absence of authorial intervention closes us within Eva's mind, and compels us to read the novel as an effect of a particular character's restricted vision.[33] The first-person narration of *Eva's Man* thus helps to contain the novel's controversial thematic material.

This containment is facilitated by the unreliability of the novel's first-person narrator. It is impossible to assign any truth value to Eva's narration because, as the psychiatrist tells her at the beginning of the novel, she does not know how "to separate the imagined memories from the real ones" (p. 10). Eva insistently tries to convince us of the truth of her narrative at precisely those moments when the reader most seriously doubts her: "Naw, I'm not lying. He [James] said, 'Act like a whore, I'll fuck you like a whore.' *Naw, I'm not lying*" (p. 163). We know, however, that Eva is lying, for she attributes to James the exact words that her father spoke to her mother. The very exactness of the repetition here and elsewhere, robs Eva's narrative of the authority of realism.[34] Eva's unreliability permeates every detail of the novel, including her castration of Davis. The police report and the prison psychiatrist inform Eva that she did not bite off Davis's penis, as she believes; the very truth of the novel's central incident is thus thrown into doubt.

The unreliability of Eva's narration is, of course, a result of her madness. Eva's madness functions as a kind of safety valve, allowing readers to dismiss the more uncomfortable moments of the novel as the distorted fabrications of an insane mind. The use of a mad narrator serves to distance not only the reader, but also the author, from the ideological implications of the work. Keith Byerman, in fact, discounts a reading of *Eva's Man* as a feminist novel precisely on the grounds of Eva's madness, emphasizing that "the ideology, the madness are Eva's, not Gayl Jones'."[35] The peculiar ideological function performed by madness in *Eva's Man* may be better appreciated by means of a comparison with *The Bluest Eye*. Pecola's madness serves as an instrument of social satire, strengthening the novel's powerful critique of the violence, racism, and sexism of American society. The novel's relentless tracing of the causality of Pecola's madness gives this madness a social dimension, and constructs Pecola as a helpless victim of her society. That Pecola's madness is narrated by Claudia and the omniscient narrator allows the reader to place her madness in some kind of relation to a sane, "real" world. *Eva's Man* provides the reader no directions, no clues to a correct reading of Eva's madness. The novel's kaleidoscopic jumbling of time (itself an effect of Eva's madness) makes it impossible to establish a causality, an origin for Eva's madness. We have no means of judging whether the repetition of events in Eva's life caused her insanity or whether Eva's insanity is the source of the repetition of events in her narrative. All we have is Eva's madness, unmediated by a sane narrator; we are given no relatively real fictional world that might help us place Eva's madness in perspective. This unmooring of Eva's madness from any "real" narrative context greatly complicates the reader's interpretive function. We cannot identify with Eva, or take away any clear meaning from her madness. Eva's madness contributes, as it were, to the impression of self-containment conveyed by *Eva's Man*. Eva's unfiltered, insane, first-person narration serves to lock meaning inside the text, and to diminish the text's power to illuminate the reader's world.

Our sense of the self-containment of the text is intensified by the narrator's vehement denial of the very acts of reading and interpretation. The novel presents a supposedly qualified reader of Eva's madness in the prison psychiatrist, who anticipates most of the reader's possible explanations for Eva's madness. At the end, Eva effectively stalls the psychiatrist's and the reader's interpretive activity: "don't explain me. don't you explain me. don't you explain me" (p. 173). It is difficult to disregard Eva's plea, considering that all the reader surrogates in the novel (the lawyers, the police, the journalists, and the general public) assault Eva's integrity with their sexist, stereotypical readings. Eva tells the psychiatrist, "don't look at me. don't make people look at me" (p. 168). Throughout the novel, Eva is defined by male characters looking at her and interpreting her. In her attempt to explain to the prison psychiatrist why she killed Davis, Eva keeps repeating, "The way he was looking at me . . . , the way he was looking at me. . . . Every man could look at me the way he was looking. They all would" (p. 171). The acts of looking and interpretation are invariably acts of masculine power in *Eva's Man*; the novel offers no possibility of a looking, a reading that can respect the integrity of the feminine object. Any kind of interpretation appears to be a violation of the text's privacy. *Eva's Man* preserves its own integrity by refusing the reader's function, and constituting itself as an unreadable, inviolable text.

The opaque surface of *Eva's Man* works as a kind of protective device, and achieves a formal containment of the novel's subversive treatment of contemporary ideological material. This use of first-person narration also challenges the formal requirements of Black Aesthetic ideology, although the first-person voice in itself is not inimical to the collective, oral emphasis of the Black Aesthetic. As Charles Rowell points out, "the first person as a narrative device is . . . a preferred form in the oral tradition." Gayl Jones agrees that the "subjective testimony" of first-person oral storytelling establishes a continuity between the speaker and the listener.[36] In *Eva's Man*, however, the first-person mode serves the exactly opposite function of sealing off the narrator from the reader. Eva announces, "I didn't want to tell my story" (p. 77); her resistance to the act of narration, her view of interpretation as violation, and her distrust of her audience,[37] controvert the Black Aesthetic celebration of the oral artist's untroubled relation

to the community. As Jones herself pointed out, *Eva's Man* poses "a kind of challenge to the listener."[38] While the novel employs the first-person mode privileged in the oral tradition, its use of this mode achieves an effect of self-enclosure that denies the collective emphasis of Black Aesthetic ideology.

A similar contradiction characterizes the novel's presentation of black speech, another formal feature valorized in Black Aesthetic theory. *Eva's Man* seems in accord with the Black Aesthetic in its exclusive reliance on black speech (or dialect) as the medium of narration. Unlike *The Bluest Eye, Sula*, and *Corregidora*, *Eva's Man* does not use standard English to mediate the dialect spoken by its characters. In an influential essay on the development of black dialect as a literary language, John Wideman writes that in most black fiction, dialect is contained within the linguistic hierarchy implied by a standard English narrative frame. According to Wideman, Jones's novels mark a significant development in the use of black dialect, for they provide

> no privileged position from which to view [the] fictional world, no terms into which it asks to be translated. . . . A Black Woman's voice creates the only valid terms . . . ; the authority of her language is not subordinated to other codes; the frame has disappeared.[39]

It is true that the dialect in *Eva's Man*, used without a legitimizing frame, constitutes a literary language in its own right. But it is not so easy to agree with Wideman's assertion that the novel grants full authority to the black Woman's voice, for Eva does not fully possess or exercise control over the language she uses. If anything, she seems imprisoned in the dialect, which, as it is presented in the novel, is emphatically not a black Woman's language. Melvin Dixon argues that Eva is unable to achieve salvation because she is alienated from the regenerative possibilities of the black speech community.[40] In *Eva's Man*, however, the dialect is not invested with any regenerative possibilities for black women.[41] Throughout the novel, black dialect constructs black women as obscene sexual objects, as whores and bitches. In this dialect, with its profusion of derogatory terms for black women, black men possess the sole right to name women. Eva's rare attempt to usurp this masculine prerogative is promptly corrected by Tyrone: "don't you call me evil, you little evil devil bitch" (p. 35). For the most part, Eva helplessly reproduces the dialect that she recognizes is not her own language: "I didn't give a shit what his name was, I was thinking in the kind of language Alfonso would use" (p. 97). Eva's entrapment in the dialect is accentuated by the novel's repetitive play with the dialect. Gayl Jones has drawn attention to her use of ritualized as opposed to naturalistic dialogue.[42] In *Eva's Man*, stylized repetition of dialogue fragments creates a ritual effect that denaturalizes black dialect, and forces a recognition of its non-dialogic construction of black women. The very fact that, so often in *Eva's Man*, dialogues are not even attributed to particular characters emphasizes the sameness of these dialogues. One dialogue after another defines and traps Eva in the same narrow terminology of bitch and whore.

On the level of narrative voice, then, *Eva's Man* upsets all the formal priorities of Black Aesthetic theory—the authority of realism, the immediate relationship between narrator and audience, and the use of black dialect to free a unique literary voice. Eva's first-person narration partly succeeds in containing the novel's treatment of lesbianism and castration, the two thematic elements that absolutely negate the heterosexual emphasis of black nationalist ideology. However, if the first-person narrator works as a device of thematic containment, it produces fresh contradictions at a formal level. The self-enclosure of the novel's first-person voice, and its resistance to interpretation, controvert both the collective and the didactic bent of Black Aesthetic discourse. Moreover, while using the dialect that would ostensibly liberate a new, distinctly black voice, *Eva's Man* filters the dialect through a feminine narrator (or, more accurately, filters a feminine narrator through the dialect), thus exposing the restricted liberatory possibilities of this language. Unlike *Corregidora*'s use of the blues, *Eva's Man* does not explore any alternative means of representing the black feminine difference from the Black Aesthetic. The novel does, however, graphically display the difficulty of reading or writing black femininity according to the codes of Black Aesthetic ideology.

Notes

1. Clarence Major was one of the very few contemporary black critics to give *Eva's Man* a favorable review. Major's review stands virtually alone in its consideration of the novel's formal features rather than its ideology. See Major, Review of *Eva's Man, Library Journal* (March 15, 1976): 834–35.

2. Richard Stookey, Review of *Eva's Man, Chicago Tribune Book Review* (March 28, 1976): 3. The novel's exclusive emphasis on the sexual victimization of black women by black men was the feature most emphasized by contemporary reviewers. Like Stookey, Charles Larson praised *Eva's Man* for its exploration of sexual conflict, which, according to Larson, "is not exactly a Black issue." See Larson, Review of *Eva's Man, National Observer* (April 17, 1976): section 5, p. 27. Also see Jessica Harris, Review of *Eva's Man, Essence* 7 (1976): 87; and two unsigned reviews of *Eva's Man* in *Kirkus Reviews* 44 (1976): 90, and *Booklist* 72 (1976): 1164.

3. This argument is offered by Askia Toure, "Black Male/Female Relations: A Political Overview of the 1970s," *The Black Scholar* 10, nos. 8–9 (1979): 46; and Ron Karenga, "On Wallace's Myths: Wading through Troubled Waters," *The Black Scholar* 10, nos. 8–9 (1979): 36.

4. Loyle Hairston, "No Feminist Tract," *Freedomways* 15 (1975): 291; Hairston, "The Repelling World of Sex and Violence," *Freedomways* 16 (1976); 133.

5. Keith Mano, "How to Write Two First Novels with Your Knuckles," *Esquire* (December 1976): 66.

6. Ibid., p. 62.

7. Ibid.

8. Gayl Jones, *Eva's Man* (Boston: Beacon, 1976), p. 128. All further references to this work are included in the text.

9. Addison Gayle, Jr., "Blueprint for Black Criticism," *Black World* 1, no. 1 (1977): 44.

10. Gloria Wade-Gayles, *No Crystal Stair: Visions of Race and Sex in Black women's Fiction* (New York: Pilgrim Press, 1984), p. 178.

11. The novel's reliance on stereotypical characterization provoked John Updike's comment that "the characters are dehumanized as much by [Jones's] artistic vision as by their circumstances." See Updike, Review of *Eva's Man, The New Yorker* (August 9, 1976): 75.

12. In its figuration of the black feminine subject as an absence, *Eva's Man* resembles *The Bluest Eye* (New York: Simon and Schuster, 1970). Like Pecola, Eva tries to understand black feminine sexuality by observing her mother's sexual relationship with her father. Like Pecola, who cannot imagine the black woman as the subject of desire because of the "no noise at all from her mother" (p. 49), Eva perceives black feminine sexuality as a matter of silence and absence: "I didn't hear nothing from her the whole time. I didn't hear a thing from her" (p. 37). Unlike *Sula* and *Corregidora*, which explore absence as a source of power and freedom, *Eva's Man* and *The Bluest Eye* present black women who suffer from a culturally imposed negation of identity.

13. Jerilyn Fisher writes that black women writers of the 1970s "avoid the cliché of sexist—or feminist—stereotypes of Black women," and prefer to expose the contradictions of black femininity. See Fisher, "From under the Yoke of Race and Sex: Black and Chicano women's Fiction of the Seventies," *Minority Voices* 2, no. 2 (1978): 1. While seeming to differ from black feminist criticism that calls for positive images, Fisher, too, sets up a false opposition between complex, contradictory characterization and reductive, simplistic stereotypes. As *Eva's Man* illustrates, stereotypes can be the means of highly complex and contradictory explorations of black femininity.

14. Addison Gayle, Jr., "Blueprint for Black Criticism," p. 43.

15. June Jordan, Review of *Eva's Man, New York Times Book Review* (May 16, 1976): 36.

16. Ibid., p. 37.

17. Addison Gayle, Jr., "Black Women and Black Men: The Literature of Catharsis," *Black Books Bulletin* 4, no. 4 (1976): 50, 51.

18. John Leonard, in his review of *Eva's Man, New York Times* (April 30, 1976): C17, argues that the novel obliquely targets white racism as the source of the sexual black stereotype: "The whites took everything away from the Blacks but their sexuality, and the distortions of that sexuality are responsible for Eva."

19. Claudia Tate, *Black Women Writers at Work* (New York: Continuum, 1983), pp. 96–97. Six years after the publication of *Eva's Man*, Gayl Jones seemed to have capitulated to the Black Aesthetic critique of her novel. In an interview with Charles Rowell in 1982, Jones said that in her current writing, she finds herself "wanting to back away from some questions. . . . I should mention that the male characters in those early novels are unfortunate, like the sexual theme—in this society that looks for things to support stereotypes." See Rowell, "An Interview with Gayl Jones," *Callaloo* 5, no. 3 (1982): 51.

20. Larry Neal, "The Black Arts Movement," in *The Black Aesthetic*, ed. Addison Gayle, Jr. (New York: Doubleday, 1972), p. 267.

21. For a perceptive discussion of the reader's entrapment in the novel's structure, see Jerry R. Ward, "Escape from Trublem: The Fiction of Gayl Jones," in *Black Women Writers*, ed. Mari Evans (New York: Anchor, 1984), pp. 249–52.

22. See Keith Byerman, "Black Vortex: The Gothic Structure of *Eva's Man*," *MELUS* 7, no. 4 (1980): 93–101, for an extensive analysis of the sense of inevitability created by the "whirlpool" structure of the novel.

23. Roger Rosenblatt, *Black Fiction* (Cambridge, Mass.: Harvard University Press, 1974), p. 64.

24. Darryl Pinckney, Review of *Eva's Man, The New Republic* (June 19, 1976): 27.

25. Ann Allen Shockley argues that "the ideology of the sixties provided added impetus to the Black community's negative image of homosexuality"; the lesbian, in particular, posed a "threat to the projection of Black male macho." See "The Black Lesbian in American Literature: An Overview," *Conditions: Five* (1979): 85.

26. Unsigned review of *Eva's Man, Publishers Weekly* 209 (1976): 92.

27. Michael Cooke, "Recent Novels: Women Bearing Violence," *Yale Review* 66 (1976): 92.

28. Addison Gayle, Jr., "Black Women and Black Men," p. 50.

29. Roseann Bell, "Judgement: Addison Gayle," in *Sturdy Black Bridges*, ed. Roseann Bell, Bettye J. Parker, and Beverly Guy-Sheftall (New York: Anchor, 1979), p. 215.

30. Michael Harper, "Gayl Jones: An Interview," in *Chant of Saints*, ed. Michael Harper and Robert B. Stepto (Chicago: University of Chicago Press, 1979), p. 361.

31. Margo Jefferson, "A Woman Alone," *Newsweek* (April 12, 1976): 104; Larry McMurtry, Review of *Eva's Man, The Washington Post* (April 12, 1976): C5. Also see an unsigned review of the novel in *Choice* (September 1976): "The novel . . . is of interest only for its investigation into abnormal psychology. . . . It does not have the larger canvas and social perspective of her previous *Corregidora*" (p. 823).

32. Charles Rowell, "An Interview with Gayl Jones," p. 43.

33. Diane Johnson remarks that "Jones seems to record what people say and think as if it were no fault of hers. . . . Perhaps art is always subversive in this way." See "The Oppressor in the Next Room," *The New York Times Review of Books* (November 10, 1979): 7.

34. In eschewing the authority of realism, *Eva's Man* may be said to signify upon one of the founding motives of early black American narrative—the struggle to establish a credible and morally reliable black narrative voice. The narrating "I" of the slave narratives was constructed as a representative, transparent reflector of reality in order to authenticate the often surreal accounts of the horrors of slavery. Richard Yarborough, in "The First Person in Afro-American Fiction," *Afro-American Literary Study in the 1990s*, ed. Houston A. Baker, Jr., and Patricia Redmond (Chicago: University of Chicago Press, 1989), pp. 105–21, writes that this same "abiding concern . . . with establishing the credibility of their literary voices and thus of their views of reality" motivated the avoidance of first-person narration in early black fiction (p. 111). *Eva's Man*, like several black novels published in the 1970s, employs an atypical, incredible first-person narrator as a gesture of revolt against the truth-telling imperative that was imposed on black writers by Black Aesthetic theorists.

35. Keith Byerman, "Black Vortex," p. 99.

36. Charles Rowell, "An Interview with Gayl Jones," p. 37.

37. Robert Stepto argues, in "Distrust of the Reader in Afro-American Narratives," *Reconstructing American Literary History*, ed. Sacvan Bercovitch (Cambridge, Mass.: Harvard University Press, 1986), pp. 300–22, that distrust of the reader and of literacy are primary reasons for the use of the oral storytelling model in black fiction (pp. 303–305). Stepto's persuasive claim that the storytelling paradigm schools readers into the role of responsive and responsible listeners, and thereby serves a didactic function (pp. 309–10) is belied by the unusual function of the storytelling model in *Eva's Man*. Eva's distrust of the reader entails neither a

hidden didactic intention nor an absent listener who may be responsive to such an intention.

38. Claudia Tate, *Black Women Writers at Work*, p. 92.

39. John Wideman, "Defining the Black Voice in Fiction," *Black American Literature Forum* 1 (1983): 81.

40. Melvin Dixon, "Singing a Deep Song: Language as Evidence in the Novels of Gayl Jones," in *Black Women Writers*, ed. Mari Evans, p. 237.

41. My reading of black dialect in the novel diverges from Valerie Gray Lee's argument that black women novelists such as Toni Morrison and Gayl Jones use black folk talk as an effective medium for expressing the deepest feelings of their female protagonists. See "The Use of Folk Talk in Novels by Black Women Writers," *CLA Journal* 23 (1980): 266–72. *Eva's Man*, in particular, shows black folk talk to be unamenable to feminine intentions; if anything, the novel bears out Roger Abrahams's assertion that urban black dialect often displays a strong animosity toward and "rejection of the 'feminine principle.'" See *Deep Down in the Jungle* (Chicago: Aldine, 1970), p. 32.

42. Michael Harper, "Gayl Jones: An Interview," p. 359.

Madhu Dubey (essay date Winter 1995)

SOURCE: "Gayl Jones and the Matrilineal Metaphor of Tradition," in *Signs*, Vol. 20, No. 2, Winter, 1995, pp. 245-67.

[*In the essay below, Dubey analyzes Jones's use of a matrilineal structure to achieve meaning in her novels* Corregidora *and* Song of Anninho.]

Since the publication of Alice Walker's *In Search of Our Mothers' Gardens* in 1974, black feminist literary critics have recurrently used the metaphor of matrilineage to authorize their construction of a black feminine literary tradition. Essays such as Dianne Sadoff's "Black Matrilineage: The Case of Alice Walker and Zora Neale Hurston," Marjorie Pryse's "Zora Neale Hurston, Alice Walker and the 'Ancient Power' of Black Women," and Joanne Braxton's "Afra-American Culture and the Contemporary Literary Renaissance" posit the mother as the origin of the black women's literary tradition, as well as the guarantor of its temporal continuity. Apparently resuming a familial metaphor long familiar to Euro-American feminist theory—as early as 1929, Virginia Woolf declared that women writers "think back through [their] mothers" ([1929] 1957, 79)—the black feminist discourse on matrilineage seeks to unwrite a brutal history of rupture and dislocation and to write an alternative story of familial and cultural connection. While generating an empowering new critical narrative that takes Zora Neale Hurston as the mother of the black women's fictional tradition and Alice

Walker as her most dutiful daughter, the matrilineal model of tradition has implicitly relegated some compelling black women novelists to the margins of its familial circle. One such novelist, Gayl Jones, explicitly engages the matrilineal problematic in two of her works, the blues novel *Corregidora* (1975) and the lesser-known poem *Song for Anninho* (1981); her absence from the black feminist discourse on literary matrilineage thus appears especially puzzling. In the following pages, I shall read the theory of black literary matrilineage both with and against *Corregidora* and *Song for Anninho*, in the process perhaps elucidating the possibilities as well as the hazards of using the matrilineal metaphor to naturalize the black feminine literary tradition.

The black feminist appropriation of the metaphor of literary matrilineage acquires its special resonance from the peculiar history of black motherhood in America. As several historians of slavery have testified, reproduction constituted a site of oppression as well as power for black women slaves (Davis 1981, 7–10; Ladner 1981). Particularly following the 1808 law banning the importation of slaves into the United States, the slave woman was appraised primarily for her reproductive capacity, "property that reproduced itself without cost," to take a phrase from Toni Morrison's *Beloved* (1987, 228). Angela Davis's distinction between "breeder" and "mother" starkly captures the black slave Woman's contradictory experience of reproduction (1981, 7); her economic value as a breeder of slaves only reinforced the ideological devaluation of her desire to mother her children. In another contradictory twist, the law stipulating that children inherit their condition (of slavery or freedom) from the mother would seem to ensure a stronger generational line through the mother than the father. However, slave mothers had no legal claims over their children, and generational links were more often than not snapped as children were separated and sold away from their mothers. Incomplete as it is, historical evidence indicates that some slave women contested their prescribed (and often violently enforced) function as breeders by means of abortion and infanticide, thereby refusing to transmit the legacy of slavery to future generations (Hine and Wittenstein 1981).[1]

This simultaneity of oppression and resistance, generational rupture and survival, forms the "double history" of black motherhood, as Dianne Sadoff calls it (1985, 10). Sadoff goes on to draw a causal connection between this history and the contemporary construction of black feminine literary history: "The historical burden of black matrifocality and motherhood—slavery, sexual exploitation, forced loss of children, and economic marginality—also creates the special 'duty,' as Alice Walker defines it, of black literary matriliny" (11). Sadoff's move from history to literature and from biological to figurative motherhood is so common in recent black feminist theory as to appear self-evident. Tracing the missing steps of this move may help to clarify the special duty of the contemporary black woman writer and critic.

The slide from an actual to a metaphorical familial genealogy is perhaps most boldly apparent in Alice Walker's claim to being the illegitimate niece of Zora Neale Hurston (Walker 1984, 102). More frequently cast as Walker's literary mother, Hurston collaborates with Walker's actual mother in enabling Walker's creative project: Hurston's books provided Walker with the missing historical information she needed to authenticate her literary inscription of a story told to her by her mother. Biological and literary motherhood converged in the case of Walker's mother, whose storytelling offered both general inspiration and specific models for Walker's literary work.[2] What is striking about Walker's reconstruction of her literary ancestry, however, is not her naming of her mother as a literary precursor but her naming of a literary precursor as a mother. Far from being a careless slippage, this "chosen kinship," as Joanne Braxton describes the intertextual relation between black women writers, strives to overcome a history of cultural disinheritance by means of a familial fiction of origin and connection (1990a, xxii).

Moving between biology and culture, black feminist critics and novelists both reflect and resist the particular historical circumstances that forced a direct link between generational and cultural continuity for African-Americans. Because of their legal exclusion from literate culture, slave children had to depend on their mothers and other kin as their primary sources of education and cultural transmission. The disruption of the generational line could thus often literally translate into a rupture of cultural tradition. The scarcity of official historical texts documenting black experience intensifies the need for black writers to assemble an unbroken cultural tradition, simultaneously underlining the difficulty of this reconstructive project. Neither a cultural nor a familial lineage was available as a seemingly natural given for black Americans; it is precisely this lack of a naturalized tradition that motivates the impulse to naturalize tradition and that paradoxically exposes the constructed status of the natural in black feminist discourse. Patricia Williams eloquently articulates the contradiction implicit in the black feminist tracing of matrilineage: "Claiming for myself a heritage the weft of whose genesis is my own disinheritance is a profoundly troubling paradox" (1990, 21).

The movement between biological and literary lineage in black feminist discourse displays the imaginary desire that drives the work of tradition building. Keenly conscious of loss as the underside of desire, proponents of this tradition portray the mother as the medium of an alternative fictional invention of history. As a locus of the daughter's desire, the mother holds forth the promise of a pure origin, an unbroken continuity of tradition, and an authentic black feminine identity. Perhaps what distinguishes this particular fiction of tradition from others is its acute perception of tradition as a necessary fiction.[3] Black feminist critics have founded their tradition building on a dialogic exchange between unifying gestures and disruptive countergestures. For example, as Jane Gallop remarks in her review of *Conjuring*, this critical anthology "comes with its own de-

construction" (1992, 165): Marjorie Pryse's introduction identifies the commonalities between black women writers that authorize a unified literary tradition, while Hortense Spillers's afterword emphasizes the discontinuities that destabilize the very notion of tradition. Sometimes this double gesture is apparent in a single essay. Dianne Sadoff's "Black Matrilineage," for instance, simultaneously sketches the historical conditions that validate Alice Walker's celebration of black matrilineage and exposes the anxieties that are masked by the matrilineage model. Sadoff criticizes this model for its false imposition of unity on a recalcitrant and heterogeneous body of texts, specifically highlighting the disjunction between the idealized recovery of the mother in Walker's womanist prose and her ambivalent depiction in Walker's fiction (1985, 22–24).

Clarifying the totalizing aims of any tradition-building enterprise remains a valuable critical task, even given the understanding that no tradition can be adequate to the texts it organizes and represents. Theorists of black matrilineage, by bestowing an imaginary unity on a previously diffused body of texts, have created an enabling critical context in which these texts may be read and interconnected. As is inevitable, however, in any construction of tradition, the matrilineage model overtly and covertly identifies a cluster of values as essential, defining features of the black women's fictional tradition. The figure of the mother or the maternal ancestor is insistently aligned with the black oral and folk tradition (usually situated in the rural South), which is celebrated as a cultural origin, a medium of temporal synthesis and continuity, and the basis of an alternative construction of black feminine history and tradition.[4] Given this set of symbolic equivalences, it is scarcely surprising that the matrilineage model tends to install Zora Neale Hurston, Toni Morrison, and Alice Walker as the major authors of the black women's fictional tradition and to marginalize those novelists, such as Nella Larsen and Ann Petry, whose works render the experience of cultural displacement and fragmentation without harking back to an oral or maternal origin.[5]

Gayl Jones's absence from the matrilineal model of tradition is even more conspicuous than that of Larsen of Petry, considering that some of her works centrally explore the nucleus of values privileged by theorists of black literary matrilineage. Moreover, given the overwhelming critical attention recently accorded to black women novelists of the "second renaissance" of the 1970s, the neglect of Jones's work appears even more puzzling. Only one of the many critical anthologies on black women novelists contains essays on Jones.[6] Jones began publishing during the peak of the renaissance in black women's fiction; her first novel, *Corregidora*, was published in 1975, followed a year later by her second novel, *Eva's Man*. Since then, Jones has published several volumes of poetry (including *Song for Anninho*), which have not received any critical recognition. Jones's decision to turn from fiction to poetry can only remain a matter of speculation. Her two novels were published in a cultural context marked by the dominance of the nationalist Black Aesthetic movement as well as by the emergence of black feminist literary criticism. Both nationalist and early black feminist critics brought a firm set of didactic expectations to bear on fiction, expectations that prompted their harsh critiques of *Eva's Man* in particular.[7] These critiques faulted Jones's fiction primarily for its "perverse ambivalence" (Jordan 1976, 37)—its refusal to offer unequivocally positive images of black culture. Even beyond the immediate context in which Jones's work was first published, most subsequent efforts to map a black feminine literary tradition (whether centered on positive images of black culture, on a distinctive use of oral forms, or on the metaphor of matrilineage) have continued to overlook Jones, perhaps because her work consistently poses seriously disquieting questions about the very process of tradition building.

In this article, I shall concentrate on *Corregidora* and *Song for Anninho*, rather than the more widely known *Eva's Man*, for several reasons.[8] In both *Corregidora* and *Song for Anninho*, Jones seeks to clarify the ways in which the history of slavery has conditioned the project of black cultural reconstruction. Further, in both texts, she explicitly treats the issue of tradition building, and matrilineal tradition building in particular, as a central thematic concern. As I hope to show in the following pages, *Corregidora* and *Song for Anninho* articulate a daughterly language of desire that cannot be readily equated with the maternal discourse valorized by theorists of black literary matrilineage. Whereas the matrilineal paradigm affirms the daughter/writer's total identification with the prior maternal tradition, *Corregidora* and *Song for Anninho* disclose the contradictions and breaks that are as necessary to the development of a tradition as are its continuities. As a blues novel, *Corregidora* foregrounds the history of loss and dispossession that both activates and impedes the black feminist effort to reconstitute an uninterrupted matrilineal continuum. In a gesture typical of the blues mode, which is distinguished by its refusal to transcend the contingencies of time and place, the novel does not even attempt to resolve the contradictions of historical experience. In counterpoint, the lyrical mode of *Song for Anninho* effects an imaginative transcendence of history, enabling instead an empowering visionary fabrication of cultural connection and continuity. The different generic dynamics of the two texts, if read together, thus produce a doubled understanding of the historical limits as well as the visionary possibilities of the matrilineal model of tradition.

Song for Anninho takes as its point of departure the destruction of Palmares, the rebel slave settlement in Pernambuco, Brazil, which withstood countless Dutch and Portuguese raids through the better part of the seventeenth century. Almeyda, the speaker and subject of the poem, escapes with her lover Anninho during the course of the final battle for Palmares, only to be separated from him when she is caught by Portuguese soldiers who sever her breasts and leave her lying unconscious in the forests surrounding the defeated settlement. Almeyda is found by Zibatra, a conjure woman who inhabits these forests; assuming the role of surrogate mother, Zibatra strains her magical

skills to heal Almeyda's emotional and bodily scars. The entire poem consists of Almeyda's first-person lyrical lament over her loss of both Anninho and Palmares. Although, as the title of the poem indicates, Almeyda sings her love song *for* Anninho, it is in fact addressed to Zibatra, whose special powers aid not only Almeyda's attempt to recover her memories of Anninho and the lost rebel slave community but also her dreams of reuniting with her lover in a newly reconstructed Palmares.

Set two and a half centuries later in Kentucky, *Corregidora* also explores the possibilities of singing a love song in a historical context shadowed by Brazilian slavery. The novel's protagonist, a blues singer named Ursa Corregidora, finds that her love for her husband, Mutt Thomas, continues to be haunted by the complex relationships of three generations of her maternal ancestors with their Portuguese slave owner, Corregidora. Following a practice common in Brazilian slavery, Corregidora capitalizes on his female slaves' sexuality by hiring them out as prostitutes to white men.[9] Forbidding his slave women from indulging in any sexual relations with black male slaves, Corregidora incestuously fathers both Ursa's mother and grandmother. Ursa's foremothers strive to preserve their experience of slavery by giving birth to female descendants who will continue to transmit their bitter narrative about Corregidora to future generations. Ursa's own story begins soon after her husband pushes her down a flight of stairs in a fit of sexual possessiveness strongly reminiscent of CorregiDora's attempt to own and police his slave women's sexuality. Ursa's hysterectomy, a consequence of Mutt's violence, disables her from fulfilling her foremothers' mission to reproduce and precipitates her quest for a new identity that can compensate for her lack of a womb. Although the events in Ursa's life occur more than half a century after the 1888 abolition of slavery in Brazil, the novel's structure so thoroughly fuses Ursa's story with the history of her foremothers that any distinction between past and present becomes inoperative. Ursa's fragmented memories of the stories told to her by her maternal ancestors repeatedly erupt into her narrative, stalling her attempt to transcend history and to create a new story for herself. The novel ends with Ursa reuniting with Mutt after a twenty-two-year-long separation, a reunion that fails to resolve the complications of either Ursa's own sexual history or the broader history of American slavery. Nevertheless, in the concluding scene of the novel, as Ursa performs oral sex on Mutt, she is paradoxically able not only to reenact her great-grandmother's ambivalent sexual power over her slave master (a power that, as Ursa realizes in the final moments of the novel, derived from the act of fellatio) but also to exercise a feminine sexual power of her own that can exceed the reproductive terms of her maternal ancestors' ideology. Ursa's blues song, like Almeyda's love song, thus seeks to express a black feminine sexuality that can at once contain and transcend the contradictory history of American slavery.

Both *Corregidora* and *Song for Anninho* rehearse the founding gesture of matrilineage theory in presenting the mother as the medium of the daughter's access to history. In both texts, the mother's oral discourse gains its oppositional value when positioned against the misrepresentations and absences of official historiography. In *Corregidora*, the official historical text of slavery is significant in its absence. The slave owner Corregidora burns all written records of slavery; this erasure of the Corregidora women's experience occasions their oral narration of history. *Song for Anninho* compels us to read Almeyda's dream of an alternative future against an official historical text of slavery. The epigraph to the poem is an excerpt from the "Petition presented to His Majesty by Domingos Jorge Velho, 'field master' in the Campaign against Palmares, 1695" (Jones 1981, 7). This master text, which informs us of the defeat and scattering of Palmares, motivates Almeyda's visionary dream of a new, reconstituted Palmares. If the Corregidora women's story demands an obsessive remembering that can counter the amnesia of official history, the official historical document in *Song for Anninho* provides the pretext for a forgetting of history and an imaginative creation of a utopian future. Both strategies, of remembering and forgetting, are aided by the mother, who thus emerges as the double sign of historical preservation as well as imaginative transcendence.

As agents of historical preservation, the Corregidora women perform the crucial task of sustaining the past and transmitting it to future generations. Their incantatory, repetitive narrative serves as "a substitute for memory" (Jones 1975, 11), an oral ritual of remembrance that can rectify the imbalances and silences of official records.[10] Inevitably, however, in making a history for themselves, the Corregidora women become imprisoned in a history that is not of their own making, for what their possession of history gives them is nothing other than the history of their own dispossession. Their very name, Portuguese for judicial magistrate, is bequeathed to them by their slave master and attests to their mixed historical legacy. Repeatedly describing their story in legal terms—"witness" (72), "evidence" (14), and "verdict" (22)—the Corregidora women seek to exercise the official, juridical power invested in their name. Authorized by their master's name, their story usurps his powers, misappropriating the authoritative accents of official discourse.

As a paradigm of historical reconstruction and tradition building, the Corregidora women's story offers some invaluable cautionary lessons, the most obvious of them expressed in Audre Lorde's celebrated statement, "The master's tools will never dismantle the master's house" (1984, 112). The Corregidora women's attempt to fill in the gaps of the master text of American history necessarily activates the dynamics of power inscribed in this text. Their historical narrative, with its absolute truthtelling claims, replicates the masterful and repressive gestures of the dominant tradition it tries to supplant. This alternative maternal tradition commands the daughter's unqualified acceptance, as is clear in the scene where Ursa is slapped for questioning the truth of Great Gram's story (1975, 14).

Like a skeptical daughter, Gayl Jones interrogates the means by which a matrilineal or any other tradition achieves its cohesion and authority. If the matrilineage paradigm insists on an idealized consolidation of a fragmented past, *Corregidora* pluralizes the past, revealing its resistance to any homogenizing or totalizing gesture. For example, Ursa wonders whether her mother's past did not significantly differ from her grandmother's, but the Corregidora women's story erases this difference in the interests of ideological coherence. *Corregidora* not only multiplies the past in a manner that infinitely complicates the project of tradition building but also challenges the very assumption (fundamental to the matrilineage model) that the mother's past should provide the ground for the daughter's utterance. Michele Wallace has expressed her discomfort with the suggestion in Alice Walker's *In Search of Our Mothers' Gardens* that "black women writers would always 'speak' from the platform of a silenced past" (1990, 59). The very plot of *Corregidora*, characterized as it is by twenty-two years of temporal impasse, raises the possibility that an uncritical preoccupation with the mother's past might obstruct rather than assist the development of the daughter's story.

If the Corregidora women as the custodians of memory help tighten the grip of history on Ursa's narrative present, Zibatra, Almeyda's surrogate mother in *Song for Anninho*, draws upon magic rather than memory to conjure up a new future for Almeyda. Casting the mother as a "wizard woman" (Jones 1981, 11), *Song for Anninho* feeds directly into the black feminist discourse on conjuring. Marjorie Pryse argues that conjuring, a black folk art passed down from the mothers to the daughters, offers a unique metaphor of literary authority for black women writers, displacing the official "patriarchal genealogy" that invokes divine inspiration as the source of its authority (1985, 9). For black women writers, who are doubly excluded from this tradition, magic provides an alternative, unofficial basis of cultural authority, a "power to reassert . . . one's heritage in the face of overwhelming injustice" (16). Pryse's words seem to describe exactly the function of Zibatra's conjuring in *Song for Anninho*: in the face of the Portuguese soldiers' brutal conquest of the rebel slave stronghold, Zibatra's wizardry reasserts the continuing imaginative power of the heritage of resistance embodied in the lost Palmares.

Imaginative is the key word here, for Zibatra's magical powers facilitate a liberating leap from a historical to an imaginary register—liberating because history as encapsulated in Velho's petition is nothing but a record of loss and dispersal. Unlike the alternative history of the Corregidora women, Zibatra's art proffers an alternative to history; while the memory work of the Corregidora women keeps the past alive, Zibatra's magic is directed toward the unseen possibilities of the future. Early in the poem, Almeyda tells Zibatra: "The battle of Palmares / ended, we escaped; Portuguese soldiers / caught us at the river. / My memory does not go beyond that" (1981, 11). The limitations of memory, as well as the limits of the historical world to which Almeyda's memory so obsessively returns, generate the need for Zibatra's magical transcendence. Almeyda's lament, "Why can't my memory be whole?" (15), cries out for the supplementary powers of the imagination, the magical faculty that can rejoin the ruptures and fill in the gaps of Almeyda's history. Zibatra's conjuring, which recognizes "no boundaries / to the world . . . / no impossibilities" (11), effects a transcendence of the spatial and temporal coordinates of the real—the contingencies and necessities of history—so that Almeyda's fragmented memories can be assembled into the visionary dream of a new Palmares. Memory and magic coalesce in Almeyda's lyrical discourse; the past and the future, the old and the new Palmares are integrated into a seamless temporal unity.

The treatment of conjuring in *Song for Anninho* thus enacts many of the familiar moves of black matrilineage theory: the mother with her special legacy of magical powers emerges as the medium of temporal wholeness and continuity, countering the daughter's traumatic experience of historical dislocation. *Song for Anninho* vividly displays the imaginary desire that propels the black feminist discourse of the mother as conjure woman: Zibatra's magic aids Almeyda's attempt to re-create time in the crucible of desire, to "translate the past into a lover's language" (15).

Yet this compelling desire, "to translate the past into a lover's language," also signals the text's departure from matrilineage theory and begins to clarify Gayl Jones's ambivalent relation to this theory. In seeking to shape history around the contours of sexual desire, the protagonists of both *Corregidora* and *Song for Anninho* grope for a lover's language that is not readily equated with the mother's language valorized by black feminist critics who subscribe to the matrilineal paradigm. Joanne Braxton writes that "contemporary black women writers are linked to those who went before first and foremost by the 'mother tongue'" (1990a, xxv), and Temma Kaplan elaborates that "the mother tongue *is* the oral tradition" (Braxton 1990a, xxvi). On an apparent level, this definition of the mother tongue would apply both to the Corregidora women's oral storytelling and to Zibatra's speaking in tongues. These maternal languages derive their oppositional force from their emphatically oral nature, which in Karla Holloway's words "dissemble[s] Euro-American traditions that privilege writing," decentering the "scriptocentric" authority of official historical discourse (1992, 123).

Despite their strong oral accentuation, however, neither the Corregidora women's nor Zibatra's language can be properly characterized as the mother tongue. As we have already seen, the narrative of the Corregidora women does not qualify as a purely oral mother tongue, inflected and tainted as it is by their master's official accents. Similarly, Almeyda's grandmother "had lost her original [language] generations before," had "tried to piece it/back together like a crazy quilt, / but she had forgotten the old words" (47). Not even the magical powers of Zibatra can recall

this irrevocably forgotten language; her speaking in tongues, like the grandmother's crazy quilt, displaces a unitary linguistic origin in favor of a language hybridized by the history of slavery. Whereas, according to Joanne Braxton, the mother tongue conjoins the daughters and the mothers into an unbroken linguistic lineage, Zibatra's many languages (including Portuguese and Tupi) require an act of mediation and translation that the daughter is unable to perform: "She [Zibatra] speaks in tongues. / . . . And there is no translation for it" (Jones 1981, 10–11).

Not only are the daughters in Gayl Jones's work refused immediate access to an original maternal language, but this language is also distinct from the lover's language into which the daughters wish to translate the past. A lover's language is precisely what the Corregidora mothers cannot speak in their narrative. As the ideological coherence of their story derives from their absolute hatred of their oppressor, they cannot but repress the ambivalent dynamics of desire, cannot but refuse to confront the discomforting question of "how much was hate for Corregidora and how much was love" (131). The mother's language in *Corregidora* denies its own entanglement in the contradictions of sexual desire as well as prohibits any complex utterance of the daughter's desire.

Corregidora insistently directs us to the history that inhibited the development of a black lover's language, clarifying the economic logic that proscribed any relation of love, filial or sexual, among slaves. CorregiDora's profiteering drive seeks to regulate the sexual desires as well as the bodies of his female slaves. He forcibly prohibits any expression of sexual desire among his slaves, since such a desire would escape the gamut of rape and prostitution that circumscribes the sexuality of his slave women. The ramifications of CorregiDora's sexual exploitation extend far beyond the legal abolition of slavery; internalizing the slave master's creed, the Corregidora women discourage their female descendants from engaging in any heterosexual relation that does not fulfill reproductive ends. In *Song for Anninho*, the unnamed "mutilated woman" (51) resists the economic exploitation of the black slave Woman's body by sewing together the lips of her vagina, violently desexualizing her body rather than yielding to the slavemasters' economic assessment of her sexuality. If the predicament of slavery ruptured the bond between black mothers and daughters and thus gave rise to the black Woman's need to recall the mother tongue, it equally produced the urgent need for a lover's language by constricting the sexual relations between black men and women. In Almeyda's words, slavery "was not the time or place / for a man and woman" (62).

In their doubled reclamation of history from the sometimes conflicting standpoints of lover and daughter, *Corregidora* and *Song for Anninho* activate a split desire that is directed at both the mother and the lover. Ursa's and Almeyda's desires for a masculine lover exceed the mother-daughter matrix that is privileged in the matrilineal paradigm. Jane Gallop observes that Marjorie Pryse's introduction to *Conjuring*, an essay that offers perhaps the most influential articulation of matrilineal theory, "centers the anthology and its literary tradition on female connectedness" and willfully conflates various forms of female connection, such as mother-daughter bonds, friendships between women, sisterly ties, and lesbian love (1992, 154). Gallop remarks that in tracing the black feminine literary tradition from Hurston's *Their Eyes Were Watching God* to Walker's *The Color Purple*, Pryse seeks to excavate the lesbian subtext of earlier black women's novels, regarding the friendships between Janie and Phoeby and Toni Morrison's Sula and Nel as latent blueprints for the later and fuller lesbian love of Shug and Celie (154–55). A remarkably bold move, Pryse's reconstruction of the black feminine fictional tradition creates a critical nexus that can include novels, such as Ann Allen Shockley's *Loving Her*, that are absent from all previous formulations of a black narrative tradition precisely because of their lesbian content. In its celebration of a unified feminine continuum, however, Pryse's essay paradoxically erases the specificity of lesbian desire and its often fraught difference from other forms of feminine (and especially familial) connection. While powerfully disclosing a tradition driven by a hitherto concealed or disguised desire, in this essay Pryse simultaneously forecloses a conception of tradition as the scene of struggle between competing and often incommensurable desires.

Gayl Jones's works stage just such a scenario in which conflicting desires cross and displace each other, infinitely deferring any possibility of a primal or singular desire. The splintering of desire is conveyed by the mixed sources and directions of the lover's language in both *Corregidora* and *Song for Anninho*. Ursa's text is a hybrid medium that voices a host of contradictory desires: her foremothers' reproductive desire, Mutt's heterosexual desire, Cat's lesbian desire, and even CorregiDora's desire for mastery all complicate Ursa's understanding of herself as a desiring subject. As the addressee of her narrative rapidly shifts from Cat to Tad to Mutt to her maternal ancestors, her desires are mobilized and ceaselessly displaced from one object to another. *Song for Anninho*, too, unsettles any notion of a unitary subject or object of desire, as Almeyda's discourse of love negotiates the words and desires of others (including Zibatra, her grandmother, the mutilated woman, and Anninho) and equivocally addresses the absent Anninho as well as the mediating presence of Zibatra.

In both texts, even as heterosexual desire interrupts the mother-daughter relation, this desire is in turn filtered through the maternal ancestor's discourse on desire. For example, the nonreproductive configuration of Ursa's desire for Mutt at the end of *Corregidora* disrupts the generational continuity of the Corregidora women's matrilineal tradition. Yet the novel does not sustain Mutt's naming of himself as Ursa's "original Man" (Jones 1975, 100) and thus her primary object of desire, because the enactment of Mutt's and Ursa's desires at the end of the novel replays a prior ancestral scene. The act of fellatio enables Ursa not only to exercise her sexual power over Mutt but

also to recapture the source of Great Gram's mysterious sexual power over Corregidora.[11] Similarly, the two maternal figures in *Song for Anninho* at once mediate and block Almeyda's expression of her love for Anninho. Her surrogate mother Zibatra serves as a literal medium for Almeyda's desire, conjuring into being the spirit of her lost lover, while Almeyda's love song is also interspersed with her grandmother's cautionary words, her "sore prophecy" (Jones 1981, 45) about the complications of black heterosexual love during slavery. In each case, maternal discourse so fully permeates the daughter's language of heterosexual love that the daughter ultimately merges into her maternal ancestor. Ursa's statement that "it was like I didn't know how much was me and Mutt and how much was Great Gram and Corregidora" (1975, 184) is closely echoed by Almeyda's "I became my grandmother and she became me" (1981, 33).

This identification of the daughters with their maternal ancestors seems to suggest that the lover's language of both texts does after all closely echo the language of the mother. However, the daughter's merger with the mother is achieved across the body of the masculine lover; it is in her own expression of heterosexual desire that each daughter paradoxically intersects with and deviates from the prior maternal tradition. The male lover triangulates the mother-daughter dyad even as he facilitates the daughter's identification with her mother. The lover's language of *Corregidora* and *Song for Anninho* thus refuses the assumption of an original, unmediated desire that is pivotal to both heterosexual and matrilineal discourses.

Almeyda's love song, like Ursa's blues song, is catalyzed by the conviction that "desire is real" (Jones 1981, 75), yet both texts forcefully render the impossibility of black heterosexual desire. Almeyda's sense of this impossibility is deeply historical. Inspired as it is by a desire at once personal and political, her love song requires the existence of a new Palmares as its condition of possibility. Given the wreck of the old Palmares, she can only sing the kind of love song that "would set your ears / to bleeding. . . . / It would not be romantic. / It would be full of desire without / possibility" (66). The same disabling history of slavery shadows the love of Ursa and Mutt; "desire without possibility" is also what their lover's language, the blues, so tautly articulates. One of the earliest cultural forms that allowed black women to speak of themselves as "sexual subjects" (Russell 1982, 131), blues music offers an especially apt model for Ursa's discourse of love. Taking heterosexual conflict as a central concern,[12] the blues constitutes a lover's language that can voice the silences of the maternal narrative. Ursa and Mutt consummately express their desire in a dialogue that evokes the repetition-with-variation structure of a blues stanza:

"I don't want a kind of woman that hurt you."
"Then you don't want me."
"I don't want a kind of woman that hurt you."
"Then you don't want me."

He shook me till I fell against him crying. "I don't want a kind of man that'll hurt me neither." I said.

[Jones 1975, 185]

Ursa and Mutt are able to say only what they do not want in a heterosexual relationship: Mutt wants Ursa, who is exactly the hurtful woman whom he does not want, and Ursa wants Mutt, who is exactly the hurtful man she does not want. Their final blues dialogue thus underscores the impossible conditions of heterosexual desire.

As a discourse of "desire without possibility," the lover's language of *Corregidora* and *Song for Anninho* accomplishes the thorough denaturalization of desire. Both texts obsessively remember the history that foreclosed any naturalized conception of motherhood or heterosexuality for African-Americans. As we have already seen, black matrilineal critics confound and reverse this history by way of a strategic naturalization of history itself. Their rhetorical movement between cultural and biological motherhood enables them to establish an uninterrupted historical legacy legitimized by the continuity of the reproductive cycle.

In *Corregidora* and *Song for Anninho*, Jones explores with remarkable subtlety the rich ironies of this naturalizing gesture. The Corregidora women's text, like the matrilineage paradigm, metaphorically equates cultural and reproductive continuity, as the transmission of this oral narrative crucially depends on the perpetuation of the generational cycle. By thus installing reproduction as its governing principle, their alternative feminine history bears the traces of the oppressive history it seeks to replace. Tadpole, a male character in *Corregidora*, rightfully remarks that "procreation . . . could also be a slavebreeder's way of thinking" (Jones 1975, 131). But the novel fully acknowledges, as Tadpole does not, the ambivalent status—at once oppositional and complicitous—of the Corregidora women's reproductive narrative.[13] Reclaiming the power of their wombs, these women attempt to transfigure the primary site of their oppression into a locus of resistance, wresting their own liberatory story out of the very history of their enslavement.

In keeping with the inversive bent of their narrative, the Corregidora women counter the perversion of motherhood during slavery with a thoroughgoing naturalization of reproduction. The desire to procreate is so deeply instilled in Ursa's mother that she perceives it as a natural desire rooted in her body: "I know it was something my body wanted, just something my body wanted" (Jones 1975, 116). This naturalized view of reproduction provides an incontrovertible biological basis of connection between the mothers and daughters. Alice Walker proclaims the self-evident nature of this connection: "How simple a thing it seems to me that to know ourselves as we are, we must know our mothers' names" (1984, 276). What is at stake in Walker's and other black feminists' discourses on matrilineage is the definition of an authentic black feminine identity secured by the name of the mother. As a guarantor of the daughter's identity, the mother's name can only invoke a biological connection, for patriarchal social practice fixes a daughter's identity on the paternal rather than the maternal name. The natural, Edenic imagery of another of Alice Walker's famous statements—"In search of my mother's garden, I found my own" (1984, 243)—bespeaks the daughter's intense desire for an identity grounded in the mother, an identity that precedes the daughter's historical displacement from her presumably natural origin.

Song for Anninho explores black feminine identity through a route remarkably parallel to Walker's. As Walker searched for herself in her mother's garden, so Almeyda approaches the question of her identity by way of her maternal ancestors' naturalized discourse on black womanhood. The guardian of black femininity, Almeyda's grandmother possesses "truths for a woman to know" (Jones 1981, 49). When Almeyda begins menstruating, her grandmother hides an unnamed "something," perhaps the secret essence of womanhood, "deep" in Almeyda (50). Using natural imagery that conveys the elusive quality of femininity, Almeyda's grandmother urges her to catch her womanhood "like a small bird, and h[o]ld it close" (53). For Almeyda's grandmother, the womb is the prime marker of black womanhood: in her opinion, the mutilated woman "no longer had the spirit of a woman" because she had denied the reproductive possibilities of her body (53).

Even as Almeyda's contemplation of the meaning of her own womanhood is mediated by her grandmother's words, Almeyda does interrogate her grandmother's naturalized conception of femininity. Almeyda's poetic discourse destabilizes her grandmother's sign of femininity, subjecting the bird image to various mutations—from actual birds, to the Palmaristas whom Almeyda imagines transformed into birds, to her vision of Anninho as a bird. Almeyda also challenges her grandmother's equation of womanhood and reproduction in an exactly contrary view of the mutilated woman: "She did have a Woman's spirit. / To me it seemed so" (53). Almeyda agrees with the mutilated Woman's perception of her act as a means of preserving a whole womanhood, which would otherwise have been violated by the reproductive imperative of her slave owner: "They think I have mutilated myself, but I have kept myself whole" (57). Almeyda's and her grandmother's conflicting interpretations of the mutilated woman underline not only the contradictory status of the womb (the site of both violation and wholeness) but also the historical contingencies that press upon any definition of black womanhood. As Almeyda says in response to her grandmother's insistence that she firmly grasp her womanhood, "Then was a time it was not easy to catch one's womanhood and hold it close" (53).

For Almeyda, as for the mutilated woman, black womanhood is predicated on bodily loss and disfigurement. Almeyda's breasts are cut off by the Portuguese soldiers who participate in the military campaign against Palmares; the violence of history is thus literally inscribed in the scarring of her flesh. Historical mutilation and loss incite Alm- eyda's desire for an intact, natural feminine body, but this body cannot be remembered as an original plenitude that precedes the violence of history. Nothing less than the magical agency of Zibatra is needed to fill the absence of Almeyda's severed breasts. *Song for Anninho* reconstitutes an imaginary fullness of being through its lyrical, celebra- tory evocation of nature. Organically identifying herself with the earth ("the earth was me" [Jones 1981, 10]), Alm- eyda reclaims it as the natural ground that both withstands the displacements of history (39) and subtends her desire to create a new history: "This earth is my history, An- ninho, / none other than this whole earth" (11).

At first glance, *Song for Anninho* appears to participate in the "feminization of nature" that feminist critics such as Margaret Homans have ascribed to the Romantic lyric (1990, 13). Homans convincingly argues that, given this metaphorical equation of nature with a silent maternal femininity and of the masculine poet with a transcendent, articulate subjectivity, women poets who position them- selves in maternal nature risk losing not only their identi- ties but also the very possibilities of poetic voice (15–17). *Song for Anninho* both recalls and reworks the conven- tional Romantic lyric's inscription of nature. Almeyda's insistent identification with nature at times verges on a disquieting submergence of her poetic subjectivity into inchoate nature. However, the geographical territory of the poem—the forests surrounding Palmares—configures nature not as a mute biological force but, rather, as the symbolic projection of an active political imagination. In a tactical move, *Song for Anninho* textually produces nature as a locus of bodily recuperation and imaginative resis- tance, as a symbolic elsewhere that lies outside the range of history. This kind of deployment of nature against his- tory is akin to the strategic naturalization of history in black matrilineal theory. If Alice Walker discovered herself in her mother's garden, Almeyda recovers a sense of wholeness through the curative plants and herbs of her surrogate mother. Although Almeyda cannot entirely obliterate the intervening history that separates her from her grandmother (unlike Walker, who is able to affirm her total identification with her mother), *Song for Anninho* nonetheless steals a brief respite from history, its lyrical mode abetting its visionary leap beyond the limits of time and place.

No such imaginative transcendence is available in *Cor- regidora*, which as a blues novel remains embroiled in the contradictions and irresolutions of historical process.[14] If the lyrical mode of *Song for Anninho* aids Almeyda's rhetorical renaming of black womanhood as a natural plenitude, the blues mode of *Corregidora* enables Ursa's unnaming of a natural black femininity. Ursa's hysterec- tomy, her lack of what her maternal ancestors consider to be the essential sign of black womanhood, detaches her from their reproductive narrative and thus initiates her quest for a denaturalized identity. Ursa's story reverses the Corregidora women's metaphorical equation of storytell-

ing and making generations, as it is precisely her inability to make generations that generates her desire for a differ- ent story.

Ursa first glimpses her difference from her maternal ancestors' story in a conversation with her mother in chapter 2. Although her mother insistently reiterates her commitment to the Corregidora women's reproductive ideology, Ursa can sense that her mother's experience of childbirth did not exhaustively express her femininity. In Ursa's words, "There was things left, yes. It wasn't the kind of giving where There's nothing left" (Jones 1975, 102). This residual energy that escapes the act of reproduc- tion is described by Ursa on the following page as an excess that cannot be verbalized within the terms of the Corregidora women's text: "I knew she had more than their memories. . . . But she'd speak only their life" (103). Transforming her own lack (of a womb) into a surplus, however, Ursa does not try to name or specify this "something else" (102), this "more" that a reproductive definition of femininity cannot contain. She turns instead to the blues, which allows her to intimate what is unspeak- able about black femininity: "I was trying to explain it, in blues, without words, the explanation somewhere behind the words" (66).

Yet, if the blues permits an utterance of what exceeds the Corregidora women's reproductive narrative, it also firmly situates this utterance in a context structured by the history of Ursa's foremothers. The "more" of Ursa's feminine identity derives its meaning from its relational nature, its being more than something, and this something always re- inscribes the prior text of the Corregidora women's his- tory. Ursa's blues music bears a complicated relation to her ancestral past: enjoyed by her grandmother but denounced as "devil music" by her mother (146), the blues expresses a denaturalized, fractured, and nonreproductive sexuality. Prior to her hysterectomy, Ursa sang "out of [her] whole body," but later her missing womb changes the quality of her music: "The center of a Woman's being. Is it? No seeds. Is that what snaps away my music. . . . Strain in my voice" (46). This blues voice modulated by lack is anything but the unified, whole, and coherent voice that Ursa's maternal ancestors wish to transmit to future generations. Yet her blues voice allows Ursa to sound both her sameness with and her difference from the prior ancestral tradition: "a song that would touch me, touch my life *and* theirs. A Portuguese song, but not a Portuguese song. A new world song" (59). Incorporating several sets of oppositions—between Ursa's life and that of her ances- tors, between the past and the future, between the history of Portuguese slavery in the New World and a utopian vi- sion of a free new world—Ursa's song exhibits the remark- able capacity of the blues to contain contradictions in a state of unresolved yet productive tension.

In its elaboration of a blues aesthetic, *Corregidora* offers a model of tradition that is quite sharply distinct from the matrilineal model. Geared toward an expression of black feminine sexuality and identity, the blues also passionately engages with the masculine, interrupting the exclusively feminine continuum affirmed in matrilineal theory. Refusing the synthesizing, totalizing impulse of matrilineal tradition building, the blues operates on the principle of contradiction, taking Ursa's difference from her maternal ancestors as its point of departure. Accommodating difference and rupture into its system,[15] the blues model of tradition calls to mind Hortense Spillers's depiction of the black women's literary tradition as a series of breaks and discontinuities that subvert "a hierarchy of dynastic meanings that unfold in linear succession and according to our customary sense of 'influence'" (1985, 258).

However, *Corregidora* circumvents the trap of privileging sheer contradiction as the motor of tradition through its structural reliance on the blues method of repetition with variation. Always articulating contradiction within a structure of relation, this method engages the past in a manner different from both an oedipal model of tradition based on generational rivalry and the matrilineal model with its affirmation of generational unity.[16] In a complicated double move, Ursa's blues voice at least partially breaks free from the collective feminine tradition represented by the Corregidora women's narrative, but it does not thereby achieve an absolute break from the past, for the blues voice always carries the traces of prior history and tradition. The novel's structure of repetition with difference denies an exclusive privileging of either generational conflict or continuity and offers instead a model of tradition that holds the past and the present in a state of creative disequilibrium.

In *Corregidora*, then, Gayl Jones retains the prior maternal tradition as a necessary structuring frame, even as she discloses the differences and contradictions repressed by this tradition. In *Song for Anninho*, the mother as a conjure woman supplies the daughter access to a naturalized temporal continuum, yet Zibatra's status as Almeyda's surrogate mother as well as her reliance on magic foreground the mediated, artificial quality of this continuum. If *Song for Anninho* explores the redemptive potential of a strategically naturalized maternal tradition, *Corregidora* frees up different possibilities for the daughter's utterance by denaturalizing the maternal tradition. Read together, the two texts disclose the double gesture necessary for the reclamation of a black feminine cultural tradition. Some black feminist critics, notably Mae Henderson, Deborah McDowell, and Hortense Spillers, have recently called for precisely such a double strategy in order to keep alive the critical edge of black feminist theory.[17] While insisting on the necessity of tradition building, these critics caution against the construction of a homogeneous, definitive canon that might prematurely foreclose the development of the black feminine literary tradition and that might inadvertently silence the questions and differences raised by black women writers such as Gayl Jones.

Notes

1. This appears to have been as true of Brazilian slavery (which forms the context for Gayl Jones's *Corregidora* and *Song for Anninho*) as it was of slavery in the United States. Because the foreign slave trade to Brazil was not closed until 1850 (only four decades or so prior to the abolition of Brazilian slavery in 1888), slave owners had access to a continuous supply of slave labor and thus did not find it economically worthwhile to promote procreation as a means of reproducing the slave population (Degler 1971, 61–65; Toplin 1981, xv; Schwartz 1992, 41–42). Nevertheless, the children who *were* born to Brazilian slave women followed their mothers' legal status and were as subject to being sold away from their families as were slave children in the United States (Degler 1971, 37–38; Russell-Wood 1982, 181). Historians report that slave women in Brazil, like their North American counterparts, also took frequent recourse to contraception and abortion to obstruct reproduction of the slave system (Russell-Wood 1982, 184).

2. Like Alice Walker, Gayl Jones, too, cites her mother's storytelling as a strong influence on her writing (Harper 1979, 352).

3. For example, Mary Helen Washington and Valerie Smith both use the phrase "fiction of tradition." See Smith 1989, 48; Washington 1990, 32.

4. This cluster of terms is succinctly articulated in Joanne Braxton's essay, "Ancestral Presence: The Outraged Mother Figure in Contemporary Afra-American Writing": "Black women writers employ 'orality' as a literary device to speak directly to the audience and by so doing 'bear witness' to the unwritten history and wisdom preserved in the folklore and oral literature of black Americans—the body of folk knowledge commonly referred to as 'mother wit'" (1990b, 314).

5. Nella Larsen's *Passing* represents the urban experience of cultural alienation without turning to the rural South as the origin of an authentic black cultural practice, while her *Quicksand*, with its bleak closing image of the protagonist, Helga Crane, trapped in a debilitating cycle of reproduction as well as in a deeply repressive Southern black folk community, seriously problematizes each of the terms privileged by matrilineal critics. Ann Petry's *The Street* similarly conveys the acute cultural dislocation of black urban life in the wake of the Northern migration; conjuring, the only black folk practice derived from the rural South that is presented in the novel, certainly fails to offer the protagonist, Lutie Johnson, an effective means of combating her hostile urban environment.

6. *Black Women Writers*, edited by Mari Evans (1984), includes two essays on Jones's fiction. Among the critical anthologies on black women's fiction that do not contain any discussion of Jones's work are: Pryse and Spillers 1985; Wall 1989; and Gates 1990.

7. For example, see Gayle 1976, 50–51; Hairston 1976, 133; and Jordan 1976, 36–37.

8. Issues involving maternal tradition are peripheral to *Eva's Man*, which focuses on a set of verbally and physically violent relationships between black men and women. The protagonist of the novel, Eva Medina Canada, is initiated into the abusive rituals of heterosexuality by her mother and Miss Billie, her mother's closest friend. The informal sexual education that Eva receives from these two women teaches her the ways in which society invests black women with a grotesque hypersexuality, which is then used to justify their negative stereotyping as "bitches" and "whores." Eva glimpses the possibility of psychological liberation from these and other negative images of women through the gypsy Medina, after whom both Eva and her grandmother are named. Eva learns of Medina from her grandmother's stories; however, as a white woman who is not related to Eva's family, Medina contributes only indirectly to Eva's ancestral heritage. In any case, the novel does not fully develop the possibilities of resistance, that are embodied in Medina. The redemptive potential of the maternal tradition is also obliquely suggested through the "ancestors bracelets" that Miss Billie gives Eva, advising her to be "true to [her] ancestors. She said there were two people you had to be true to—those people who came before you and those people who came after you" (Jones 1976, 22). Eva fails on both of these counts: not only does she lose her ancestors' bracelets, but she also disrupts the generational line by refusing to have any children. The maternal tradition in *Eva's Man* is significant largely because of its failure to offer Eva any viable means of resisting her oppressive experience of heterosexuality.

9. The prostitution of female slaves for financial profit was far more widely practiced in Brazil than in the United States (Degler 1971, 70; Russell-Wood 1982, 37). One reason that Jones chose to set *Corregidora* and *Song for Anninho* in the context of Brazilian rather than U.S. slavery might be that the Brazilian setting, with its higher incidence of slave prostitution, allowed her the license to dramatize more graphically the economic exploitation of female slaves' sexuality.

10. In an interview with Michael Harper, Gayl Jones said that for African-American and Native American writers, "It's necessary to make connections between the oral traditions and written documentation, . . . It's necessary to document the [oral] traditions—to counteract the effects of the false documentations" (Harper 1979, 356).

11. In the novel's concluding scene, Ursa is finally able to regard her lack of a womb as a source of strength rather than a disability. Fellatio, an act that does not serve reproductive ends, allows Ursa to exercise a feminine sexual power that exceeds the terms of her ancestral narrative. Ursa experiences fellatio as "a moment of pleasure and excruciating pain at the

same time, a moment of broken skin but not sexlessness, a moment that stops just before sexlessness, a moment that stops before it breaks the skin: 'I could kill you'" (Jones 1975, 184). As these lines suggest, in this scene Ursa discovers a potentially destructive feminine power situated at the very edges of heterosexuality ("a moment that stops just before sexlessness"); this edge is perhaps the only place where a woman like Ursa, who has felt profoundly defeminized by her hysterectomy, can come to accept the ambivalence of sexual power and agency.

12. Sherley Anne Williams suggests that the blues, as "a description of interaction between equal and opposing forces," offers the most suitable form for representing black heterosexual conflict. See Williams 1979, 51.

13. The reproductive ideology of the Corregidora women is far more oppositional when set in the context of the Brazilian rather than the U.S. slave system, given that Brazilian slave owners did not actively promote natural reproduction among slaves. Carl Degler, in fact, reports some cases where in order to avoid the financial costs of raising slave children "masters deliberately restricted slave reproduction by locking up the sexes separately at night" (1971, 64). Such is precisely the case in *Corregidora*, where the slave master forcibly prohibits his slave women from reproducing with male slaves; this prohibition increases the subversive value of the Corregidora women's commitment to reproduction.

14. In her most recently published book, *Liberating Voices: Oral Tradition in African American Literature*, Gayl Jones discusses the blues as a processual form that can contain contradictions in a state of unresolved suspension (1991, 71). For a more extensive analysis of the term *blues novel* as well as of *Corregidora* as a blues novel, see Dubey 1994, 72–88.

15. I am indebted here to James Snead's discussion of the "cut" (a device common to black musical forms such as the blues and jazz), which enables a structural accommodation of differences; see Snead 1984, 67.

16. I am alluding to Ralph Ellison's famous remarks on the relation between the individual artist and the prior tradition that jazz music posits (1964, 189). Ellison's comments apply equally to the blues model of tradition.

17. See Mae Gwendolyn Henderson's call for a "dialectics/dialogics of identity and difference" (1989, 37). Also see McDowell 1989, 52–55; and Spillers 1989, 71–73. Asking black feminist theorists to confront "the convergences of differences on our commonly shared cultural practice" (Spillers 1989, 71), Spillers echoes Audre Lorde's emphasis a decade earlier on the "creative function of difference" in black feminist theory (1984, 111).

References

Braxton, Joanne M. 1990a. "Afra-American Culture and the Contemporary Literary Renaissance." In *Wild Women in the Whirlwind: Afra-American Culture and the Contemporary Literary Renaissance*, ed. Joanne M. Braxton and Andree Nicola McLaughlin, xxi-xxx. New Brunswick, N.J.: Rutgers University Press.

———. 1990b. "Ancestral Presence: The Outraged Mother Figure in Contemporary Afra-American Writing." In *Wild Women in the Whirlwind: Afra-American Culture and the Contemporary Literary Renaissance*, ed. Joanne M. Braxton and Andree Nicola McLaughlin, 299–315. New Brunswick, N.J.: Rutgers University Press.

Davis, Angela. 1981. *Women, Race and Class*. New York: Random House.

Degler, Carl N. 1971. *Neither Black nor White: Slavery and Race Relations in Brazil and the United States*. New York: Macmillan.

Dubey, Madhu. 1994. *Black Women Novelists and the Nationalist Aesthetic*. Bloomington: Indiana University Press.

Ellison, Ralph. 1964. *Shadow and Act*. New York: Random House.

Evans, Mari, ed. 1984. *Black Women Writers*. New York: Anchor.

Gallop, Jane. 1992. *Around 1981: Academic Feminist Literary Theory*. New York: Routledge.

Gates, Henry Louis, Jr., ed. 1990. *Reading Black, Reading Feminist*. New York: Meridian.

Gayle, Addison, Jr. 1976. "Black Women and Black Men: The Literature of Catharsis." *Black Books Bulletin* 4(4): 48–52.

Hairston, Loyle. 1976. "The Repelling World of Sex and Violence." *Freedomways* 16(2):133–35.

Harper, Michael. 1979. "Gayl Jones: An Interview." In *Chant of Saints: A Gathering of Afro-American Literature*, ed. Michael Harper and Robert Stepto, 352–75. Chicago: University of Chicago Press.

Henderson, Mae Gwendolyn. 1989. "Speaking in Tongues: Dialogics, Dialectics, and the Black Woman Writer's Literary Tradition." In *Changing Our Own Words*, ed. Cheryl Wall, 16–37. New Brunswick, N.J.: Rutgers University Press.

Hine, Darlene Clark, and Kate Wittenstein. 1981. "Female Slave Resistance: The Economics of Sex." In *The Black Woman Cross-Culturally*, ed. Filomina Chioma Steady, 289–300. Cambridge, Mass.: Schenkman.

Holloway, Karla F.C. 1992. *Moorings and Metaphors: Figures of Culture and Gender in Black women's Literature*. New Brunswick, N.J.: Rutgers University Press.

Homans, Margaret. 1990. *Women Writers and Poetic Identity*. Princeton, N.J.: Princeton University Press.

Jones, Gayl. 1975. *Corregidora*. Boston: Beacon.

———. 1976. *Eva's Man*. Boston: Beacon.

———. 1981. *Song for Anninho*. Detroit: Lotus.

———. 1991. *Liberating Voices: Oral Tradition in African American Literature*. Cambridge, Mass.: Harvard University Press.

Jordan, June. 1976. Review of *Eva's Man*, by Gayl Jones. *New York Times Book Review*, May 16, 36–37.

Ladner, Joyce A. 1981. "Racism and Tradition: Black Womanhood in Historical Perspective." In *The Black Woman Cross-Culturally*, ed. Filomina Chioma Steady, 269–88. Cambridge, Mass.: Schenkman.

Lorde, Audre. 1984. *Sister Outsider*. New York: Crossing.

McDowell, Deborah. 1989. "Boundaries: Or Distant Relations and Close Kin." In *Afro-American Literary Study in the 1990s*, ed. Houston Baker, Jr., and Patricia Redmond, 51–70. Chicago: University of Chicago Press.

Morrison, Toni. 1987. *Beloved*. New York: Knopf.

Pryse, Marjorie, 1985. "Zora Neale Hurston, Alice Walker and the 'Ancient Power' of Black Women." In Pryse and Spillers 1985, 1–24.

Pryse, Marjorie, and Hortense Spillers, eds. 1985. *Conjuring: Black Women, Fiction and Literary Tradition*. Bloomington: Indiana University Press.

Russell, Michele. 1982. "Slave Codes and Liner Notes." In *But Some of Us Are Brave*, ed. Gloria T. Hull, Patricia Bell Scott, and Barbara Smith, 129–40. New York: Feminist Press.

Russell-Wood, A.J.R. 1982. *The Black Man in Slavery and Freedom in Colonial Brazil*. New York: St. Martin's.

Sadoff, Dianne F. 1985. "Black Matrilineage: The Case of Alice Walker and Zora Neale Hurston." *Signs: Journal of Women in Culture and Society* 11(1):4–26.

Schwartz, Stuart B. 1992. *Slaves, Peasants, and Rebels: Reconsidering Brazilian Slavery*. Urbana: University of Illinois Press.

Smith, Valerie. 1989. "Black Feminist Theory and the Representation of the 'Other.'" In Wall 1989, 38–57.

Snead, James. 1984. "Repetition as a Figure of Black Culture." *In Black Literature and Literary Theory*, ed. Henry Louis Gates, Jr., 59–80. New York: Methuen.

Spillers, Hortense. 1985. "Cross-currents, Discontinuities: Black women's Fiction." In Pryse and Spillers 1985, 249–61.

———. 1989. "Response." In *Afro-American Literary Study in the 1990s*, ed. Houston Baker, Jr., and Patricia Redmond, 71–73. Chicago: University of Chicago Press.

Toplin, Robert Brent. 1981. *Freedom and Prejudice: The Legacy of Slavery in the United States and Brazil*. Westport, Conn.: Greenwood.

Walker, Alice. 1984. *In Search of Our Mothers' Gardens*. New York: Harcourt Brace Jovanovich.

Wall, Cheryl, ed. 1989. *Changing Our Own Words*. New Brunswick, N.J.: Rutgers University Press.

Wallace, Michele. 1990. "Variations on Negation and the Heresy of Black Feminist Creativity." In Gates 1990, 52–67.

Washington, Mary Helen. 1990. "'The Darkened Eye Restored': Notes toward a Literary History of Black Women." In Gates 1990, 30–43.

Williams, Patricia. 1990. "On Being the Object of Property." In *Black Women in America*, ed. Micheline R. Malson, Elisabeth Mudimbe-Boyi, Jean F. O'Barr, and Mary Wyer, 19–38. Chicago: University of Chicago Press.

Williams, Sherley Anne. 1979. "Comment on the Curb." *Black Scholar* 10(8–9): 49–51.

Woolf, Virginia. (1929) 1957. *A Room of one's Own.* New York: Harcourt Brace.

Biman Basu (essay date Winter 1996)

SOURCE: "Public and Private Discourses and the Black Female Subject: Gayl Jones' *Eva's Man*," in *Callaloo*, Vol. 19, No. 1, Winter, 1996, pp. 193-208.

[*In the essay below, Basu discusses the political motivations behind critical reaction to Jones's work and argues that* Eva's Man *differs from other African-American writings.*]

In the past two decades at least, we have witnessed an increasing politicization of literature in the academy. The text has been dislocated from the fixed and autonomous position it occupied in New Critical theory and made to participate in the larger machinery of cultural production. Such a move may, in general, have the effect of liberating the text from narrowly defined limits, but such critical maneuvers may generate an entirely different set of meanings in different cultural configurations. For example, unlike New Criticism which examined "literature for literature's sake," critical discourses concerning themselves with African-American literature often did not treat it as literature. African-American literature was treated as political statement. Thus the move to politicize literary texts cannot have the same consequences in the African-American literary and critical tradition as it has had on literary studies in general.

In the introductory chapters of *The Signifying Monkey*, Henry Louis Gates outlines some of the issues that concerned the African-American critical establishment in the early twentieth century. One of the major concerns then had been the question "How Shall the Negro be Portrayed?" and the discourses around this question resulted in what Gates calls "the ideology of mimesis" (179). Gates invokes the African-American critical tradition to make his point that the overwhelming emphasis in this tradition has been on content over form. This opposition between content and form generates, in different contexts, oppositions between politics and aesthetics, between materialist and formalist analyses, between ideology and ontology. Such oppositions are still firmly entrenched in the study of African-American literature today, and as a result, particular texts have received only a limited reading.

Before going on to consider the critical reception of a specific text, Gayl Jones' *Eva's Man*, we may observe some of the broader implications of such oppositions. Ideological analysis, to be sure, serves many important purposes; for example, it brings to our attention seriously neglected aspects of the text, such as the material conditions of its existence. And to that end, such analyses must be as rigorous as the best of them have been. Yet ideological analysis of race and gender in black women's fiction often restricts itself from asking questions about the very possibilities of representation and being. The result, in short, is that ideology is dislocated from ontology.

The analysis of race and gender, and of history and ideology itself, is, of course, not limited. The analysis depends on the way we construct these categories. These different constructions can be traced in the fluctuating meanings that have been assigned historically to the word "ideology" itself. At one level, ideology is understood as equivalent to politics, and in this limited sense, it concerns itself with the social, the political, and the economic. The disjunction between ideology and ontology is rigorous. Addressing the issue of a narrowly conceived form of multiculturalism, often predicated on an ideology that is restricted as a category, Gates observes that "under the sign of multiculturalism, literary readings are often guided by the desire to elicit, first and foremost, indices of ethnic particularity" ("Beyond" 8). Ethnic particularity may certainly be foregrounded productively, but when it becomes the "first and foremost," and sometimes the only index of value, literary readings are compromised. Because African-American writers have been forced to respond to a racist literary establishment, we have, in the past, seen discourses—historically necessary and necessarily compromised—surrounding "racial uplift," the "Negro problem," and the protest novel in general. More specifically, the necessity for explicit political statement has manifested itself in, for example, Wright's criticism of Hurston's *Their Eyes*.

As suggested earlier, this sort of criticism is still pervasive today and is usually aimed at texts that explore issues that the African-American critical community is, perhaps with good reason, extremely sensitive about. One of the most flagrant irruptions of such criticism is perhaps Joyce Joyce's charge that Gates and Baker, in using post-structuralist theories, have betrayed the race. Similarly, Toni Morrison's novels have repeatedly been subjected to a type of sociological criticism which claims that her characters are not representative of the black community—a claim that she has freely endorsed. We are, then, not far removed today from asking the question, "How Shall the Negro be Portrayed?"

These concerns may be crucial for historical reasons, but while we expend our energy on censure and inhibit the artist, we fail to ask larger questions about language and representation. This is particularly distressing because writers, like Toni Morrison, but not only Toni Morrison, have repeatedly stated that what marks black literature as distinctive is the language of the text. This might be a particularly apt time to remind ourselves of what Ralph Ellison said three decades ago: that "when critics confront the American as *Negro* they suddenly drop their advanced critical armament and revert . . . to quite primitive models of analysis . . . [and that] sociology-oriented critics seem to rate literature so far below politics and ideology that they would rather kill a novel than modify their presumptions concerning a given reality" (107–08, my ellipses).

If the intention to examine a text at the level of language and representation seems to naively depoliticize the text, to reinstate the text in an oppressive discourse of universalism, to facilitate the recuperation of the text into a dominant discourse, it will seem to do all this only if we insist on the rigorous disjunction between ideology and ontology and if we denigrate the ideological as only the "merely political" (Gates, "Beyond" 8).[1] A critique of a narrowly defined multiculturalism (and a narrowly defined ideological criticism sometimes associated with it) from within, offered as a corrective, in the spirit of broadening its range, may instead lead to richer readings of black women's fiction.

Gayl Jones' *Eva's Man* has suffered in the critical and political atmosphere outlined above. She is herself keenly aware of the difficulty of such a text being positively received in the African-American community. Generally, the text goes against the grain politically and is disturbing in the violence of both its language and sexuality. In an interview with Charles H. Rowell, Jones states that "some critics would probably want a greater directness of political statement. I don't like direct political statements" (42). She is aware that "conflict between aesthetic, political, and social responsibilities . . . involves dilemmas in Afro-American literary tradition" (42), and one cannot but suspect that she is reminded of Zora Neale Hurston's vitriolic responses to the criticisms of Richard Wright, who did "want a greater directness of political statement." Jones, however, adds, "I don't dwell on it [the conflict] when I'm telling a story" (42).

While Jones states, "I don't fault the early writers for being 'too preoccupied with oppression,'" and "I don't dismiss them or their preoccupations," she adds, "I do discuss how these preoccupations give problems (ironically) in terms of the works' ability to reveal the characters—oppressed people" (42). Her statement is, of course, reminiscent of James Baldwin's critique of Richard Wright's *Native Son* (Baldwin 35–36). This is a formal problem for the novelist because the demand for "a greater directness of political statement" may interfere with artistic integrity. This is an aesthetic problem that John Wideman has referred to as "a linguistic hierarchy," a phrase that Jones quotes in her interview with Rowell (32). This hierarchy is the effect of the larger phenomenon of orality which Jones addresses at length in her interview with Harper where she repeatedly invokes a paradoxical "hearing" of the text. While literature is always political in some way, both Baldwin and Jones maintain a distinction

between the two and, further, perceive that a certain type of politics can be an obstacle to literary achievement. It also seems clear that when Jones speaks about the demand for political statement, she means racial politics.

While Jones' statements about racial politics betray an uncomfortable anxiety, her comments on gender and sexuality are even more anxiety-ridden. She recognizes the problem in the African-American literary tradition:

> That subject is problematic for Afro-American writers—even more so women (and why many of our early writers scrupulously avoided it)—because when you write about anything dealing with sexuality it appears as if you're supporting the sexual stereotypes about blacks. So do you scrupulously avoid the subject as the so-called uplift writers did or do you go ahead with it?
>
> (46)

When she speaks of gender, Jones is, similarly, conscious of the strictures on African-American women's artistic freedom. She states, "I should mention that the male characters in those early novels are unfortunate, like the sexual theme—in this society that looks for things to support stereotypes. I'd like to be free of that. I used to think one could be" (51).

If *Eva's Man* suggests that Jones is politically naive, her stated awareness of these problems in the African-American literary and critical tradition and of the dichotomy between technique and moral content suggests otherwise. In an interview with Michael Harper, when asked about the influence of Latin American writers on her work, she says that

> Because of the kinds of historical things that have gone down—that continue to go down—the 'revolutions,' the kinds of perpetual change—political things (Chile, Mexico, Brazil)—you don't come across many morally and socially irresponsible Latin American writers. They are technically innovative, but the technical innovation isn't devoid of its human implications.
>
> (366)

Gayl Jones is not alone among African-American writers who find "Third World" writers particularly appealing. Toni Morrison, for example, has indicated the same interest. While these preferences do not preclude interest in certain Western writers, these "Third World" writers offer a political urgency that African-American writers recognize.

As her comments indicate, Jones is keenly aware of her responsibilities as an African-American writer, of how her work may participate in a retrograde politics. Further, she suggests that the contemporary predilection for postmodernist forms, "technical innovation," cannot be assessed in purely aesthetic terms but must be held morally and socially accountable. Yet the vocabulary and rhetoric in these statements are an index to the ambivalence and anguish she feels about how these ideological formulations can be artistically constricting. She perceives "conflict" and "dilemmas." She observes how a preoccupation with oppression may interfere with artistic achievement. Revealing her anxiety most poignantly, perhaps, is the shift in pronoun in "I used to think one could be." Gayl Jones seems torn between political accountability and artistic freedom, but she believes that the two may be fused in a "technical innovation [that] isn't devoid of its human implications."

In spite of her awareness that technical innovation can be infused with moral and political responsibility, Jones' comment (made after the publication and initial reception of her first two novels) that she "used to think" that she could escape certain constraints on the representation of sexuality and gender suggests that she has retreated in her position. This sort of withdrawal is unfortunate in that it demonstrates the censorial pressure that the critical community can bring to bear on writers. Criticism of *Eva's Man* indicates that the representation of sexuality and gender is, in fact, perceived as politically problematic. More recent criticism, which offers alternative readings of the text, is, then, put in the awkward position of "rescuing" the text not only from some of its critics but also from some pronouncements of its author.

Much criticism of *Eva's Man* simply does not do justice to the complexity of the text. Aside from these, however, criticism that is otherwise perceptive renders judgements that are ideologically limited in their response to sexuality and gender. For example, Melvin Dixon states that "Rather than acknowledging the part she played in abusing men . . . Eva persists in acting out with Davis the roles of women predators" (247, my ellipsis). *Corregidora* does present the "abuse of men" by Ursa and her maternal ancestors, but to insist that *Eva's Man* do the same is to distort the focus of the text. The text clearly invites us to understand Eva's culminating act, murder and genital mutilation, in the light of everything else it offers—among other things, the multiple instances of the abuse of women.

In general, Dixon compares *Eva's Man* unfavorably to *Corregidora*. One reason for Eva's failure is her passivity, which Dixon perceives in her sexuality and her silence. He states, "When Eva allows herself to be seduced by her cellmate, Elvira Moody, she passively enjoys cunnilingus" (246). Aside from the fact that such an act may not be passive at all, a series of deferrals sets up a consistent expectation which culminates in Elvira's question, "Tell me when . . . ," making Eva's "Now" at the end of the text far from passive or "chilling" (Dixon 247). Furthermore, the theme of lesbian sexuality, which Jones remarks has gone almost unnoticed (Tate 97), must be seen in its intertextual relation to *Corregidora*. Jones' first novel is clearly disturbed by Catherine Lawson and Jeffrene. Even if Jeffrene is partially redeemed later in the text, Ursa rejects any association with her: "whenever I saw Jeffrene, I'd cross the street" (178). Given Ursa's homophobic, even violently homophobic, response to lesbian sexuality, Eva's culminating "Now" has to be read as an affirmation, even if made in prison. Far from being passive acquiescence, Eva's participation represents affirmation.

Eva's silence, according to Dixon, is yet another sign of her passivity: "Eva remains imprisoned literally and figuratively by her silence that simply increases her passivity and her acceptance of the words and definitions of others" (246). Jones herself has commented on Eva's silence: "Eva refuses to render her story coherently. By controlling what she will and will not tell, she maintains her autonomy. Her silences are also ways of maintaining this autonomy" (Tate 97). Eva's "acceptance of the words and definitions of others" may not be passive but, in fact, according to Sally Robinson, an active, subversive form of mimicry with which she undermines the dominant discourse. Finally, we have to remind ourselves that Eva tells her own story. Jones makes a conscious, and risky, decision to write *Eva's Man* in the first person (Tate 97), and this invests Eva with a certain narrative agency, however compromised and indeterminate it may seem to be.

The text, and its reader, cannot finally evade the question of Eva's response to others' representation of, and dominion over, her subjectivity. Broadly speaking, critical views on the question may be plotted along two lines, those that see Eva as passive and paralyzed by dominant constructions of her subjectivity and those that see her as resisting, even disrupting, those constructions. This difference is embodied in the distinction Sally Robinson makes between two meanings of "representation." The first is a response to "a form of colonization, an imperial move," and the other is "*self*-representation," that is, "the processes by which subjects produce themselves as women and, thus, make 'visible' the contradictions in hegemonic discursive and political systems" (190).

Two radical readings of this process of self-representation are that Eva's self-representation is ultimately indeterminate and Sally Robinson's reading that it is a mimicry of the subjectivities that would be imposed on her. The first coincides with Gayl Jones' conception of the narrative. She says, "The main idea I wanted to communicate is Eva's unreliability as the narrator of her story" (Tate 95). Whether this comes across as the "main idea" or not, Jones' statement aligns itself to a reading of indeterminacy. While an indeterminate subjectivity may seem to be tantamount to a denial of agency, Jones asserts that Eva's resistance to all determinate subject positions is itself empowering: "By controlling what she will and will not tell, she maintains her autonomy" (Tate 97). The key words here are "controlling" and "autonomy." By rejecting the coherence of a dominant discourse, she maintains a vestigial control. While "autonomy" may seem to be an outrageous misnomer for someone in prison, silence, indeterminacy, and mimicry can be understood as resistance only if we acknowledge the prevailing structures of violence, the pervasiveness of dominant discursive formations.

The text is, of course, rife with the incoherence that renders the subject indeterminate. Briefly, then, the textual strategies that undermine determinate meaning fall into two groups. The first consists of statements that are flatly and candidly contradictory. Eva defiantly flouts the conventions of consistency demanded by realism. For example, the central act of the story, genital mutilation, is never confirmed in its details. While this first group juxtaposes contradictory statements which perhaps are finally not relevant to meanings (it does not really matter, after all, whether she "bit it all off" [167] or not), the second group undermines authorial voice and discloses the anxiety of narrative itself. This strain begins in statements like "What I'm trying to say is" (35) and "I don't remember" (170) and culminates in a stunning disavowal in what is after all an autobiographical narrative: "I don't want to tell my story" (77).

African-American literary and critical discourses in general and discourses on subjectivity specifically have vacillated between an oppositional and a celebratory rhetoric, between a rhetoric that "repudiates" as Houston Baker once put it and one that affirms. To read the formation of black female subjectivity in terms of indeterminacy is to engage an oppositional rhetoric. Eva does "repudiate" all dominant discourse, and by relinquishing the sometimes extremely seductive coherence of authoritative discourse, she maintains a vestigial control. This indeterminate position which confers a vestigial control collapses into a nihilism against which Sally Robinson's reading seems invigorating. If the indeterminate subject of the text constitutes an opposition to subject positions constructed in a dominant discourse, Robinson's reading of mimicry is an affirmation, but an excessive affirmation.

Robinson states that Eva's "refusal to explain her act (her*self*) is one of two subversive strategies Eva practices; the other is her excessive identification with mythological figures of black womanhood" (167). The two strategies, then, are silence and mimicry. The latter involves a relationship of excess to and literalization of the dominant discourses' metaphorical construction of black female subjectivity (Robinson 169). This relationship between mimic and the object of mimicry is, of course, what poses difficult questions. If indeterminacy seems to drain the subject of agency, mimicry, although it offers different subversive possibilities, does not entirely escape the ambivalence of subject-object relations. If mimicry involves "'returning the look of surveillance'" (Benita Parry, qtd. by Robinson, 172), we are still caught in a mode of "returning," that is, *self*-representation is dependent on a dominant discourse. Robinson acknowledges the historical inevitability of this dialectic between negation and affirmation: "if this power [of mimicry] is negative it is because discourses of racism and sexism only allow black women negative positions" (182).

While Robinson's is one of the more compelling readings of *Eva's Man*, she uses the term "official discourses" too broadly. This is understandable because her reading, like other readings of the novel, focuses on Eva's self-representation. Eva's representation of herself, however, is deeply implicated in the way she is represented by others.

Paying attention to these other representations of her subjectivity, we need to distinguish, for example, the psychiatric institution from that of the lawyers and police officers. Eva's decision to speak to one and not to the others marks this distinction. We need also to distinguish between institutional discourses and the discourse community represented by Davis Carter and, to a lesser extent, by Elvira. This is a distinction between the public and the private, between the institutional and the individual, between the hegemonic and the "ambiguously (non)hegemonic" (Henderson 20). We must posit this difference if only to return to the continuity that exists, in certain ways, between public and private discourses.

Despite Gayl Jones' consistent preoccupation not only with language and representation but also with sexuality and reproduction, most of the criticism of *Eva's Man* does not adequately address these issues. The novel needs a larger conceptual framework, one that addresses, for example, the privilege of heterosexual and genital sexuality, the reproductive imperative, and the phallus as "privileged signifier." While Gyatri Chakravorty Spivak warns that women cannot fully escape "a uterine social organization . . . *in favor of* a clitoral" (152), she does point out that "The clitoris escapes reproductive framing" in a way that male orgasmic pleasure "normally" cannot (151). Further, if "clitoridectomy has always been the 'normal' accession to womanhood . . . , it might be necessary to plot out the entire geography of female sexuality in terms of the imagined possibility of the dismemberment of the phallus" (151, my ellipses). Where *Corregidora* ends, *Eva's Man* begins with such an "imagined possibility." The text asks its readers to speculate on what might be the response of public and private discourses to such a "dismemberment." The proliferation of discourses in response to such a possibility is, in fact, hysterically systematic.

The text of *Eva's Man* is, in fact, everywhere concerned with language. It engages a variety of public discourses which, because of their position of dominance and privilege, are instrumental in the construction of black womanhood. The novel opens with the representation of Eva's crime in the media and its popular reception. Elvira informs Eva that "they's people that go there just so they can sleep in the same place where it happened, bring their whores up there and all. Sleep in the same bed where you killed him at" (4). In a repetition of the Trueblood episode in Ellison's *Invisible Man*, the site of violent and aberrant sexuality becomes a space for occult ritual. The crime undergoes a bizarre reenactment, or retelling. It is as if by retelling, and having it be retold, the media and other authorities hope to contain it. As if, by explaining it, by fixing it in certain authoritative discourses, an otherwise intractable and outlawed trajectory of desire may be brought within the bounds of the law. As if sheer repetition, acting like a narcotic, may make the experience manageable: "They want me to tell it over and over again" (4).

As if in response to the current academic preoccupation with "being silenced" or of "finding a voice," Jones suggests that silence itself may be empowering. Eva is not silenced; in fact, hegemonic institutions invite and encourage her loquacity. Her participation would only provide "data" which would allow her subject position to be gathered or recuperated into the different forms of institutional discourse. What we have in the text is a literary representation of institutional discourse and its deployment of various categories of containment. Rather than being "repressed,"

> Rather than the uniform concern to hide sex, rather than a general prudishness of language, what distinguishes these last three centuries is the variety, the wide dispersion of devices that were invented for speaking about it, for having it be spoken about, for inducing it to speak of itself, for listening, recording, transcribing, and redistributing what is said about it.
>
> (Foucault 34)

What Eva confronts, "Rather than a massive censorship," is "a regulated and polymorphous incitement to discourse" (Foucault 34).

The psychiatrist does provide incitement, represented as benevolent incitement: "His voice was soft. It was like cotton candy. He said he wanted to know how it felt, what I did, how did it make me feel." This is followed by his assurance, "'I want to help you, Eva'" (76) and "'Talk to me'" (77). Further, the juxtaposition of the statements "My knees were open. I closed my knees" (76) and "'you're going to have to open up sometime, woman, to somebody. I want to help you'" (77) indicates that this sort of interrogation is tantamount to a form of sexual violation that Eva has experienced all her life and that the psychiatrist ironically reenacts. Language must, in fact, penetrate the field in which the object of knowledge is constituted in order to recuperate it in an ordered textuality and epistemological coherence. We have, then, an ostensibly and insistently benevolent motivation. His voice is "soft . . . like cotton candy," and he is explicitly and obsessively repetitive: "I want to help you." In the same breath, however, his language is violent.

It is this urge to circumscribe a nomadic meaning within manageable territory that motivates the internal logic and consistency of public discourses. These are represented in the text by law enforcement officers who arrest and interrogate her, the lawyers who try her, and the psychiatrists who attempt to treat her. The officers, with whom Eva admittedly has minimal contact, begin the process through which various institutions will try to explain her crime. The captain, looking for the normal signs of domestic abuse, asks, "'She got any marks on her?'" (69). Attempting to assign a rational explanation to Eva's act, he looks for a cause and effect relationship. He is surprised that Eva does not bear such signs of abuse: "'He didn't beat her or anything?'" (69). Unable to pin it down as retaliation to domestic abuse, the police attempt to force it into another category: "'Hers was a crime of passion'" (82).[2]

Stated as a cliche, the statement underlines not only the process through which experience is forced into predictable categories, but also the process through which institutions are popularly sanctioned. The cliche and the "easy" answer, the familiar, ordered, and the rational assure a continuity between the public and the private.

The lawyers, for their part, try to consign the crime to yet another recognizable category, that of the "unfaithful/deceitful lover." The narrator tells us, "There were also people saying I did it because I found out about his wife. That's what they tried to say at the trial because that was the easiest answer they would get" (4). Here, in addition to a persistence of classificatory logic, we have another motive introduced, that of the "easiest answer." As a variant, and in some ways, as an extension of the category of the "unfaithful/deceitful lover," we have the image of "unrequited love." The image is presented in an italicized passage, suggesting a disembodied voice, but the code that is invoked identifies the voice as that of a lawyer: "*I submit the insanity of Eva Medina Canada, a woman who loved a man who did not return that love*" (150). The passage ends, "*Your honor the court recommends that . . .*" (150).

"Domestic abuse," "crime of passion," "unfaithful/deceitful lover," "unrequited love"—these are all categories, in some cases constructed by experts, but in all cases recognizable and familiar. Once formulated, these terms gain the currency through which these ideas circulate in popular culture. This is not to deny the empirical reality, for example, of domestic abuse, but to try to understand the way in which these categories are deployed in the text. The text clearly represents this deployment at the level of critique. These categories are male constructions which position the female subject in a particular, and negative, relation to the male subject. The female is the passive victim or an excessive, and therefore irrational, agent.

The text, however, does not present these categories realistically, but in a spirit which is infused with elements of grotesquerie and caricature. One cannot, for example, miss the note of derision at the confidence of the pronouncement, "Hers was a crime of passion." What is perhaps more remarkable, however, is not the force of institutional power, not the profundity of its discourse, but precisely its banality. It is the confidence and regularity with which the institution deploys its explanatory models. In addition to sharing these characteristics, the language of the psychiatrists, far from being aggressive or malevolent, insists on its benevolence.

Even though the psychiatrists in the prison are the experts who are qualified to "help," even rehabilitate, Eva, they fare no better, and the text presents a sharp critique of certain contemporary practices. Although Eva is silent during the trial, once she is in prison, she starts talking to the psychiatrists. She doesn't "even get it straight any more" (5), but they want to hear it all anyway. This, then, is what initially motivates Eva's "telling" of her story. Although this "talking" to the psychiatrists constitutes only part of the text, this "talk" resembles rather closely the production of the text in general. Thus the reader is analogously placed in the position of the psychiatrist, or that of the "listener." Through the conclusions that the psychiatrists come to, or attempt to come to, Gayl Jones anticipates the critical reception of the text. And some critics have indeed come to the conclusions that the text anticipates.

In order to make sense or assign a coherent meaning to Eva's act, the psychiatric institution has to rely on its legitimized discourses and the categories they make available. Eva's incarceration, of course, indicates that her crime has been assigned to the category of "madness," but Elvira comments more broadly on a culture that associates women and madness. She tells Eva, "'Naw, you ain't crazy. When you first come you was crazy, but you ain't crazy now. They gon keep thinking it, though. Cause It's easier for them if they keep on thinking it. A woman done what you done to a man'" (41). Like the judicial system that finds the "easiest answer" in assigning the motivation of revenge to Eva's act, the psychiatric institution finds it "easier" to assign aberrant acts a definitive category, that of madness. The last statement underlines the antagonism between "man" and "woman" and clarifies *what* the designation of madness is "easier" than. It may be easier to fix Eva's act in an explanatory category than to speculate on what may be a very real response to clitoridectomy, on the "imagined possibility" of dismemberment. The category of madness contains and averts the threat of such a possibility.

The psychiatrists go after what have become some rather predictable motivations for human behavior: "They want to hear about what happened between my mother and father as well as what happened between me and that man. One of them came in here and even wanted to know about my grandmother and grandfather" (5). The "came in here and even" suggests that Eva is somewhat derisive about this line of reasoning. The discourse being mobilized here is that which attempts to establish "parental abuse/neglect" as a cause. Eva, admittedly, is not reliable, yet her statements are often congruent with the text's general critique of certain forms of psychology and associated forms of therapy. While the psychiatrists claim to be helping her, she says, "I'm forty-three years old, and I ain't seen none of their help yet" (5). Eva refutes the insistent benevolence of psychiatry and points to its complicity with the systems of law enforcement and justice.

Turning from what has been an apparently benign enquiry into the possibility of parental abuse, the psychiatrists invoke a stereotype with a long history in the discourses on race in the United States. When Elvira asks, "'What your doctors been telling you?'", Eva says, "'They think I was trying to fuck him when he couldn't fuck back'" (159). This is the lusty counterpart of "a woman who loved a man who did not return that love." The category of "insatiable lust" is the counterpart of that of "unrequited love." This category constructs the black woman as repository of "insatiable lust."

An explanation that is more difficult to refute, and one which the text in some ways, in fact, encourages us to accept as probable is presented in a fragmented exchange between the psychiatrist and Eva:

> "You know what I think," the psychiatrist said. "I think he came to represent all the men you'd known in your life."
>
> "Who?"
>
> "I got *something* out of you," he said. He was proud of himself.
>
> (81)

Eva's Man offers a series of instances of abuse which may credibly culminate in Davis Carter's "representative" status. This credibility, however, is undermined by the way in which Davis Carter and his relationship with Eva is individualized. The textual context of the fragmented exchange, which registers Eva's derision, also destabilizes this credibility: "He was proud of himself." Most importantly, the unreliability of the narrative voice and the obdurately indeterminate quality of the text destabilize the authority of such definitive explanations. The coherence of the text, such as it is, falls apart after the description of the genital mutilation (128). In the last fragmentary exchanges, the psychiatrist still asks, "Did he do something to frighten you? He humiliated and frightened you, didn't he?" (167) and again, "Did you think Davis was Alfonso?" (169). In both questions we hear echoes of the discourses of the "abused victim" and the "representative" victimizer. The exchange culminates in her repeated cry, "don't explain me. don't you explain me. don't you explain me" (173) and in violence—"Matron? Matron! Hold her! Hold her!" (174).

This is perhaps Eva's most explicit response to the web of discursive formations in which she is ensnared. While the meanings of her other responses are implied, here she is explicit in her resistance to certain types of explanation. Further, these explanations are inadequate because although Eva certainly rebels against particular individuals, her rebellion is against a larger structure of power, the anonymity and pervasiveness of which cannot be addressed by these explanations. Where human behavior is constituted as the object of knowledge, this knowledge, on one hand, has often offered reductionist explanations and, on the other hand, certain instances of human behavior, like Eva's, are so utterly dissonant that they are either only partially susceptible to, or entirely elude, these explanations. Her silence and the inconsistency of her statements may be understood as affirmative only if we acknowledge the preponderance of the institutional apparatus in which she is held. Her violence is a response to the violence inherent in the logic of explanatory categories.

The institutional forces—law enforcement, judicial, and psychiatric—do not, then, suppress a certain type of discourse, but, in fact, encourage, even solicit it. The institutionally warranted discourse, however, has specific contours: "domestic abuse," "crime of passion," "unfaithful/deceitful lover," "unrequited love," "mad woman," "parental neglect/abuse," "insatiable lust," and "representative" criminal. The consistency with which these discourses are represented makes it clear that they are not incidental, benign, or benevolent but that they constitute a systematic deployment of strategies which, by means of a certain type of textuality, would order, organize, and make manageable a phenomenon that resists such reduction. This terminology has been disseminated effectively enough to insure its circulation in the larger culture. Institutionally sanctioned, these terms and the situations they describe are thoroughly familiar. These are not part of a scholarly recondite vocabulary, and for this very reason, they, as cliches, can all the more insidiously constitute and simultaneously sustain certain stereotypes. What they all share, moreover, is a desire for closure, and this text vigorously subverts.

These public discourses are guided by certain underlying assumptions. One such assumption is that if we can collect enough "data," we can render the unknown as surface, reduce the strange to the familiar, make the intractable manageable. We can then move from the opacity of the text to posit a transcendent essence, in this case, the essence of blackness or femaleness which then permits the proliferation of discursive formations on black sexuality and black crime. When we turn from these public discourses to the private exchanges between Eva Medina Canada and Davis Carter, we find some of these assumptions still in place.

The discontinuous, and continuous, relation of the public and the private in *Eva's Man* is suggestively caught in the Western gaze attempting to read a non-Western Other. One could understand Orientalism as a vast project in attempting to understand the Oriental Other largely by textualizing it. As Said reminds us over and over again, "the Orient studied was a textual universe by and large" (52). At the risk of simplification, one might plot the thematics of the Orientalist text in the twin impulses of the unknowable, "inscrutable," "mysterious" Easterner and the all too easily known, all too readily available East as surface, without depth.

Said's syntax simulates the systematic hysteria of the latter:

> To restore . . . ; to instruct . . . ; to subordinate . . . ; to formulate . . . ; to dignify all the knowledge . . . ; to feel oneself as a European in command . . . ; to institute . . . ; to establish . . . ; to divide, deploy, schematize, tabulate, index, and record in sight (and out of sight); . . . and, above all, to transmute living reality into the stuff of texts . . . : these are the features of Orientalist projection.
>
> (86, my ellipses)

Said observes this twin projection as a "vacillation": "The Orient at large, therefore, vacillates between the West's contempt for what is familiar and its shivers of delight in—or fear of—novelty" (59). This vacillation is caught

by Sara Suleri in the contradictory projection of ambivalent images of Indian women in Anglo-Indian women's writing: "Anglo-Indian narrative schematizes the Indian woman into two parallel images: she is either sequestered in the unknowability of the *zenana* or all too visible in the excessive availability of the professional courtesan" (92).

That post-colonial theory should be useful in studying black women's fiction should not be altogether surprising. While Said examines the construction of the Arab or Muslim in English and French colonial discourse and Suleri that of the Indian in English colonial discourse, both are focussed on one of the most profound processes of Othering in modern times, the Othering of the East. What happens when the Western gaze is turned on Africa and, on this side of the Atlantic, on African-Americans is similar. Eva is a racial, gendered, and sexual Other.

Eva's Man, moreover, may be said to "vacillate" between the twin impulses of the colonialist/Orientalist text, that between surface and depth, between the always available surface and the unbearably vertiginous depth. Institutional discourse, seeking to domesticate a disruptive phenomenon, attempts to recuperate it into a system of always available surfaces. It attempts to textualize the phenomenon in the always available categories. The private discourse of a Davis Carter, however, would penetrate the vertiginous depth of the object of knowledge and retrieve an essential meaning, would lay bare and touch the interiority of the object. The impossibility of the desire, the resulting unbearable vertigo of the desire leads to the representation of the other as unknowable, inscrutable, or unnatural. At this point, the institutional and the individual become complicitous, and it is the status of the cliche that installs the circuitry between the two poles, that assures the circulation of explanatory categories.

The text of *Eva's Man* is constituted by an obsessive repetition, sometimes a repetition of statements that are slightly altered, and sometimes a repetition of statements uttered by different characters in different contexts. A thread of continuity in Davis' exchanges with Eva is precisely his concern for her "talk." After explaining that only rich men make money at the tracks, he seeks affirmation and says, "'Say something,'" and Eva says, "'Yes, I understand'" (102). When he repeats the statement, however, in an isolated unit of conversation that is characteristic of the text, Eva responds differently:

> "Say something, Eva."
>
> "There's nothing."
>
> (121)

That the latter is isolated as a unit forces us to focus on the language itself. Eva's response suggests that there is nothing beyond or behind the language, and that she be read in terms of her self-representation. The difficulty, of course, is that she often says nothing, or reveals very little, or becoming prolix, flouts the conventions of a consistent and coherent text.

If "say something" seems innocuous, another set of questions, a little more precise, makes more clear the nature of these verbal exchanges between Eva and Davis. He repeatedly asks, "'Eva, why won't you talk?'" (116). This sort of questioning, which amounts to an interrogation, suggests that Eva's silence somehow unnerves Davis. Because textualizing an experience serves, as Said indicates, as a means of controlling it, Eva's silence or taciturnity deprives others of the very means of control. Davis senses this loss of control: "'What are you thinking? you're not talking'" (126). The repetition of these and other questions makes increasingly clear that his desire for knowledge is not altogether benign, and the pattern of questioning that emerges suggests the connection between knowledge and power.

Davis asks, "'Eva, why won't you talk about yourself?'" (67), and conversely, "'Why won't you talk to me, Eva?'" (101). The constant "Why won't you talk," the variable "about yourself" and "to me," and even the chiasmic reversal of the personal pronoun all indicate the firmly entrenched subject-object positions and the closure, or the closed circuit, which determine the direction of the discourse. He is convinced, and he never questions this assumption that language, in its transparency, will yield an inner sanctum of the self to him. Ensnared discursively, an inside will be displayed as an outside, a subject will be surveyed by the sovereign gaze as an object. When Eva simply asserts that she does not "like to talk of [her]self," and offers no explanation but a cavalier, "I just don't," Davis responds, "'You make a man wonder what's there,'" and insists that "'There's more to you than what I see'" (73). The reference of "there" is, of course, the inside that he wishes to mine, and "what's there" introduces an ominous note in that there *is* something, and more importantly, that this something, this inside, is directly accessible. He assumes that laid bare to a penetrating discursive practice, this inside shall be revealed.

He also assumes that having been penetrated by the gaze of the subject, the interiority of the object is the reality, the preferred reality over its exteriority. He says, "'By the time I get through with you, I want to know you inside out,'" and then referring to a song, "'I don't want to love you outside, I want to love you inside'" (45). In his desire to "get through *with*" Eva, he is complicitous with the discursive practices of the institutions represented in the text. This marks a moment of collusion between public and private discourses. The oxymoronic "inside out" and the antithetical "outside, . . . inside" are the self-conscious signs of the twin impulses of surface and depth, metonymic of two discourse worlds. Duplicating the collapse of the sexual and the discursive that we have noted in the representation of the psychiatrist, the text represents Davis' desire to penetrate an interiority in terms of both language and desire. It tells us in an isolated unit, "He went in like he was tearing something besides her flesh" (51). The "something besides" is of the nature of essence, on the level of ideality, something prediscursive.

A different set of questions, although formulated in slightly different terms, suggests an extension of this line of enquiry: "'Where are you from?' he asked again. He probably thought I would answer this time" (116). The last sentence indicates that the battle lines are firmly drawn between speech and silence, the antagonism established. More generally, subject-object positions are clearly apprehended, and language is recognized as instrumental to establishing these positions and therefore is itself contested territory. Davis takes this line of questioning one step further when he states, "'you're like a lost woman,'" and asks "'Who were you lost from?'" (101). The question suggests an ontological dimension. The state of being lost, that human beings do "feel lost," implies a deprivation of, a dislocation from. The question implies a nostalgia for an origin, a search for a principle of coherence, a unitary center of subjectivity.

When Davis fails to draw an answer from Eva, when he cannot get Eva to talk about herself, he says, "'You hard to get into'" (76). The quality of hardness is ascribed to Eva severally by Davis, the psychiatrist, Alfonso, and Elvira. Given the culminating "Now" of the novel, Elvira's variation on the line seems significant: "'You ain't so hard as you think you are. . . . You gon start feeling, honey'" (45, my ellipsis). The term is used variously with sexual, emotional, and psychological connotations. It also evokes the connotation of opacity, of surface, opposed in the text to transparency, which underlies Davis' assumption that language will refer directly to an inner being, to an originary self. Eva's self-representation, then, is constructed as opacity, as surface, but this is not the surface on which institutional discourse would fix her as subject. To this static schema, this charted and tabulated surface, Eva counters a mobile and elusive dynamic of shifting surfaces.

The statement "You hard" is complemented by "'you're too serene'" (118). Once again, Elvira's repetition of the statement indicates how an institutionally sanctioned discourse is all too readily appropriable by the individual: "'You too serene. When a woman done something like you done and serene like that, no wonder they think you crazy'" (155). From hardness to serenity, we witness a movement from surface to surface as impassivity and impenetrability. Eva's "serenity," her taciturnity, establishes a relationship of mimicry to institutional discourse. "Returning the look of surveillance," she mimics the supreme confidence, the serenity of a discursive project that would domesticate the Other.

The verbal exchanges between Eva and Davis are accompanied by their sexual interactions, and the two, language and desire, are implicated at different points in the text. When Davis cannot get past her "hardness" and "serenity," the opacity of her self-representation, Eva's sexuality becomes the direct target of his verbal aggression. The text makes clear that their relationship is not only sexual but also involves a power struggle. When he fails to control her as subject, he attacks her sexuality as aberrant. He says, "'I'm all fucked out,'" and expects

Eva's sexual desires to mirror his own: "'You should be all fucked out,' he said. He wasn't joking" (66). Because he expects her desire to match the ebb and flow of his, he feels threatened here by her unsatiated desire, or, in the formulation of an institutional discourse, by her "insatiable lust." Once vulnerable to this threat, he begins to construe her sexuality as abnormal. This anxiety is reinforced by another short exchange:

> When he came out of me he was sweating, but I wasn't.
>
> "Don't you ever sweat?"
>
> "No." I smiled.
>
> "You made me tired," he said.
>
> (118)

This exchange plots one point in Davis' maneuver from a vulnerable position, anxiety-ridden, threatened by Eva's sexuality, to his inevitable condemnation of her as inhuman, as irreducibly other. In a familiar move of domination, in a familiar process of othering, he says, "'You ain't natural'" (120).

Eva, then, has to answer to certain institutional forces for her crime, forces represented by a set of public discourses. Her silence or the unmanageability of her responses provokes a desire for "easy answers," for "explanation," for closure. Similarly, in her engagement with private discourse, impassivity and impenetrability drive Davis to rely on categories that have been disseminated by institutional discourses and made available to private individuals. Davis has at his disposal the category of madness, of the unnatural, in which his desire for closure can contain recalcitrant elements. We witness here another moment of collusion between public and private discourses in their representation of the other.

Eva's Man is not a pleasant novel but an extremely disturbing one. Gayl Jones, in fact, calls it a "horror story" (Harper 361). As a response to oppression, murder and mutilation may not be justifiable, may not even be the most effective strategy. The text, however, does not endorse murder and genital mutilation. Instead, it asks us to speculate on the "imagined possibility" of dismemberment. Given the preponderance of dominant structures, the text speculates on how the oppressed subject might negotiate these structures of violence, what the dismantling of a phallogocentric structure might entail, so that, if the violence is disturbing, it serves to underline the violence of the discursive formations which circulate around and circumscribe the subject. Attention to the language of the text, analysis of language and representation, far from being apolitical, unmasks the politics of language and the ideology of representation which are some of the most powerful instruments for the construction of the subject.

Notes

1. Gates is referring to Jean-Loup Amselle's critique of multiculturalism and his warning against "ethnic or cultural fundamentalism." What is useful for the purposes of this paper, however, is the opposition between the political and the ontological: "Amselle's concerns are not merely political; they are ontological as well."

2. Any reading, but particularly a reading of a text like *Eva's Man*, depends on certain reading strategies. The category "crime of passion," for example, may be thematically close to the lawyer's subsequent accusation of Eva as "a woman who loved a man who did not return that love" (150). The pattern of the novel, however, dictates that when a similar, even identical, statement occurs, we have to situate the context in order to be able to attribute the otherwise disembodied voice. Immediately following the phrase "crime of passion," the text tells us, "We were at another long table" (82). This is a direct echo of a passage in which Eva's police record is being read out. The passage begins, "There was a long table in the room" (70). While it is irrelevant for the purposes of my reading here whether the category is evoked by the police or the lawyers, I offer this as a clarification for my reading of the specific line.

Works Cited

Baldwin, James. *Notes of a Native Son*. Boston: Beacon Press, 1984.

Dixon, Melvin. "Singing a Deep Song: Language as Evidence in the Novels of Gayl Jones." In *Black Women Writers (1950–1980): A Critical Evaluation*. Garden City, NY: Anchor-Doubleday, 1984.

Ellison, Ralph. *Shadow and Act*. New York: Random House, 1964.

Foucault, Michel. *The History of Sexuality: An Introduction*. Vol. 1. New York: Vintage, 1990.

Gates, Henry Louis, Jr. "Beyond the Culture Wars: Identities in Dialogue." *Profession 93*. The Modern Language Association of America. 6–11.

———. *The Signifying Monkey: A Theory of African-American Literary Criticism*. New York: Oxford University Press, 1989.

Harper, Michael S. "Gayl Jones: An Interview." In *Chant of Saints: A Gathering of Afro-American Literature, Art, and Scholarship*. Ed. Michael S. Harper and Robert B. Stepto. Urbana: University of Illinois Press, 1978. 352–75.

Henderson, Mae Gwendolyn. "Speaking in Tongues: Dialogic, Dialectics, and the Black Woman Writer's Literary Tradition." In *Changing Our Own Words*. Ed. Cheryl A. Wall. New Brunswick: Rutgers University Press, 1989.

Jones, Gayl. *Corregidora*. Boston: Beacon Press, 1986.

———. *Eva's Man*. Boston: Beacon Press, 1987.

Robinson, Sally. *Engendering the Subject: Gender and Self-Representation in Contemporary women's Fiction*. Albany: State University of New York Press, 1991.

Rowell, Charles H. "An Interview with Gayl Jones." *Callaloo* 5.3 (16) (1982): 32–53.

Said, Edward. *Orientalism*. New York: Vintage, 1979.

Spivak, Gyatri Chakravorty. *In Other Worlds: Essays in Cultural Politics*. New York: Routledge, 1988.

Suleri, Sara. *The Rhetoric of English India*. Chicago: University of Chicago Press, 1992.

Tate, Claudia. Ed. *Black Women Writers at Work*. New York: Continuum, 1983.

Wideman, John. "Defining the Black Voice in Fiction." *Black American Literature Forum* 11 (1977): 79–82.

Willis, Susan. *Specifying: Black Women Writing the American Experience*. Madison: University of Wisconsin Press, 1987.

Naomi Morgenstern (essay date Summer 1996)

SOURCE: "Mother's Milk and Sister's Blood: Trauma and the Neoslave Narrative," in *Differences*, Vol. 8, No. 2, Summer, 1996, pp. 101-26.

[*In the following essay, Morgenstern discusses the role of trauma and repetitive accounts in Jones's* Corregidora *and Toni Morrison's* Beloved.]

In "Negotiating Between Tenses: Witnessing Slavery After Freedom—*Dessa Rose*," Deborah McDowell poses a question: "Why the compulsion to repeat the massive story of slavery, in the contemporary African-American novel, especially so long after the empirical event itself?" (144). In referring to repetition compulsion, the name given to a psychic and behavioral phenomenon that is seemingly senseless and potentially destructive, McDowell implicitly evokes the theory of trauma. She suggests that retelling manifests an attempt to gain mastery over elusive or defeating histories and their narration. This essay will pursue McDowell's lead in exploring the connections and disjunctions between trauma and the neoslave narrative, the twentieth-century novel about slavery.[1] In what follows I will examine the term "trauma" in order to argue that it can be useful for focusing a discussion of two texts by African-American women: Gayl Jones's **Corregidora** and Toni Morrison's *Beloved*.[2] I do not wish to suggest that anything as meticulously worked out and worked upon as either of these novels could simply be a manifestation of psychic trauma. In fact, these novels make possible a reading that calls into question such an understanding of psychopathology. If the neoslave narrative marks the undesirable return of an unforgettable past, it also attempts to theorize and control this very phenomenon.

I

The relationship between repetition compulsion and trauma is addressed in one of the most enigmatic of Freud's texts, *Beyond the Pleasure Principle*. In his search for a beyond, Freud encounters the traumatic neurosis ("a condition has

long been known and described which occurs after severe mechanical concussions, railway disasters, and other accidents involving a risk to life . . . the terrible war which has just ended gave rise to a great number of illnesses of this kind" [12]). The symptoms of traumatic neurosis make Freud uneasy, for the trauma sufferer dreams repeatedly of his accident ("Anyone who accepts it as something self-evident that their dreams should put them back at night into the situation that caused them to fall ill has misunderstood the nature of dreams" [13]). The important point is that these dreams cannot be read as wish-fulfilling texts. If symptoms are compromise formations that yield pleasure, how then to explain the intrusive phenomena of hallucination and nightmare, the "symptoms" of trauma? Is trauma an accident, temporarily suspending the rules that govern the psyche, or is it cause to rethink pleasure and the very possibility that self-destruction and self-interest can be thought apart? Freud develops both of these lines of thinking. *Beyond the Pleasure Principle* is a difficult text to read in a linear fashion because its own move beyond the dominance of the pleasure principle to the death drive is also a circling back. Nevertheless, Freud's text serves as a point of departure for current work on trauma and the recently acknowledged syndrome, Post-Traumatic Stress Disorder (PTSD).

Recent work on trauma suggests that to write about PTSD is to account for ghosts. The trauma sufferer is "haunt[ed]" or "possess[ed]" by an image or event that she or he has missed as experience; a trauma is violently imposed and is always reimposing itself (Caruth, "Introduction" 2–3). It is because a trauma forces psychic reorganization that it can only happen again. Trauma victims cannot simply remember what they never forgot. And it is at least in part because the trauma cannot be temporally located that it becomes strangely transmissible down through generations. As the skeleton in the closet, the ghost in the attic, the family secret is preserved in its very unutterability. "A trauma," Cathy Caruth writes, "is never . . . one's own" ("Unclaimed Experience" 192).[3] For example, Ilse Grubrich-Simitis, a psychoanalyst who works with the children of Holocaust survivors, writes of a patient who "literally lived in a double reality." She was both herself, a young painter and a college student, and her Father's past (the life she led was actually more than doubled as she identified both with surviving and with dying in a concentration camp). Grubrich-Simitis points out that in this instance what we think of as "identification" works more like "incorporation": "Namely, it was characterized both by the totality of immersion in another reality and by involvement of the body" (302–03).[4]

Trauma and repetition compulsion ask one to think about what it means to transmit a culture, to share a story, to pass it on. Repetition constitutes and consolidates identity. But what is the effect, on a culture, of repetitions that are traumatic in character? The traumatic "symptom" (hallucination, flashback, recurring nightmare, compulsively repetitive behavior) has a non-symbolic or literal quality, and, since it is what it is, it resists interpretation or cure. It is as if the thing itself returns as opposed to its representation. Grubrich-Simitis uses the term "concretism" to describe the trauma victim's experience of the world. She claims that those who have been traumatized have no sense of the figural, that nothing for them has "sign character" (302). Thus both the terms "traumatic symptom" and "traumatic memory" are at best awkward approximations. While it might sound ludicrous to say that someone who suffers from recurring nightmares or invasive and oppressive hallucinations is suffering from senselessness or meaninglessness, this is indeed what trauma reveals.[5] The most powerful writing on PTSD consistently describes trauma as a force that is not meaningfully experienced: to be traumatized is to be haunted by the literality of events.

The distinction between trauma and repression, a distinction stressed in some of the writing on trauma, is crucial for reading neoslave narratives.[6] Repression is a response to conflict: that which has been repressed returns symptomatically, in a compromised or distorted form. The traumatic past in *Corregidora* and *Beloved*, however, has not been forgotten, nor is it accessible only indirectly. It is strangely concrete, forcefully present, literally there, not past at all. Only by thinking of the history that *Corregidora* and *Beloved* depict as traumatic can we begin to give that history some specificity.

PTSD has recently received a great deal of media attention. The typical "balanced" account weights the claims of opposing parties: adults who have just recently remembered that they were abused as children are pitted against groups like the "False Memory Syndrome Foundation" who believe that "fabricated memories" can be implanted or imposed by the power of a psychotherapist's suggestion.[7] This by now familiar way of presenting PTSD to a popular audience invokes a simple opposition: memories are either fully rememberable and true, or entirely false. Trauma, in this context, seems to be synonymous with "bad experience." Therapists who participate in this construction of PTSD claim that patients have bad experiences and "repress" them. Their antagonists counter that individuals have false memories imposed upon them, and this, they warn, can have devastating consequences for the lives of others. Literary critic Frederick Crews, for example, demonizes therapeutic suggestion and psychoanalytic practice itself becomes the original site of horror ("Revenge"). The subject, he insists, is not self-divided, but weak, subject to possession. Force only comes from the outside. But these two apparently conflicting accounts (the accounts of those who seem to affirm and those who would deny the reality of trauma) both insist on the stability and locatability of the event. Psychoanalysis's discovery of the distortion of memories is thus passed over in favor of a simple causal narrative: terrible events trouble the subject. But neither an event nor an individual psyche, taken separately, can account for trauma. Trauma theory (at its best) refuses the "choice" between self-division and external force and asks us to consider the psychopathology of the historical subject. And there is no knowing in

advance that any particular kind of event will be experienced as traumatic.[8] The difficulty that trauma theory then encounters is that of articulating the specificity of violence against the psyche. This is a difficulty that can be bypassed ("trauma" or "psychoanalysis" can be posited as the answer), but it is not a difficulty that will go away (Laplanche and Pontalis, "Traumatic").[9]

In her analysis of trauma and history, Caruth is concerned with what contextualization does to trauma, with what happens when it is read and rendered significant. When trauma becomes narrative, the "precision" and "force" of traumatic recall are lost; a comprehensible trauma is traumatic no more ("Introduction" 420). Through literal repetition ("an overwhelming occurrence . . . remains in its insistent return, absolutely true to the event" ["Introduction" 4]), however, trauma preserves the past that it also renders inaccessible. What is at stake in Caruth's analysis, then, is not so much the *possibility* of history as its *preservation*.[10] If trauma endangers the subject, it would seem to keep "history" safe. "History" as a pre-text, as an event or force that is not yet meaningful, can be valued by survivors precisely in its "affront to understanding" ("Introduction" 420). Survivors often do not want what they suffered to become intelligible. "History" in Caruth's text, then, is history from the perspective of the traumatized subject.[11]

Since psychoanalysis has always thought in terms of personal narratives and that which blocks and disrupts them, it should come as no surprise to discover that recent writing on the specificity of trauma concerns itself with a form of narrative: the testimonial. Whereas neurotics need to have their free associations analyzed, trauma sufferers need to have their testimonies witnessed. A witness, unlike an analytic listener, witnesses the reality of the event in the name of justice, and, thus, in the study of psychic trauma the juridical supplements or relocates the psychoanalytic.[12] To testify, however, is always to take the risk of repeating, and indeed both therapy and testimony strive to reproduce the very past that they are designed to enable their subjects to leave behind.[13] The crucial if unstable difference between retraumatization and cure may be the difference between the unwitnessed and the witnessed repetition: a repetition addressed to and heard by another becomes testimonial.

The concept of testimony has its place both in psychoanalysis and in African-American culture. In *The Signifying Monkey*, Henry Louis Gates refers to testimony as a key "black rhetorical trope" (52), and Geneva Smitherman writes of "testifyin" as a "concept referring to a ritualized form of black communication in which the speaker gives verbal witness to the efficacy, truth, and power of some experience in which all blacks have shared" (58). She adds, "To testify is to tell the truth through 'story' . . . the content of testifying, then, is not plain and simple commentary but a dramatic narration and communal reenactment of one's feelings and experiences" (150).[14] Testimony in the form of the slave narrative could be said to have produced many of the tropes that still dominate the African-American literary tradition. Testimony offered during a trial makes available a past that it produces; it produces that which will have been. It is only effective, however, if it seems to describe what "really" happened. As *fictional* testimonial literature, neoslave narratives both stage a simple return of history and reinscribe it: "Everything said in the beginning must be said better than in the beginning" (*Corregidora* 54). In this sense they do what all testimonies do: they both return to an event and make it happen for the first time. Their status as self-conscious fictions means that they represent, as well as enact, this process. When the novel is a witness to history, it also witnesses its own act of witnessing.

The very structure of trauma—its belatedness—makes testifying possible. When the event is told, it is experienced for the first time and can be placed in a story about history. It is worth recalling here that when Freud searches for a beyond the pleasure principle, he finds that the enigma he has chosen to explore not only resides at the very boundary of psychoanalysis, but also makes itself (un)comfortable in the consulting room every day. While the analyst wants his or her patient to remember rather than repeat, years of experience, Freud claims, have shown that repetition is not only inevitable, but is the very key to therapeutic success. Thus Freud finds his "new and remarkable fact"—there is a beyond the pleasure principle, people do repeat experiences from the past which include no possibility of pleasure—in an old and familiar place (20). A traumatic neurosis and a transference neurosis have much in common. The most intriguing moment in Caruth's reading of Freud is her account of trauma in all its resistant literality as also already bound up with cure. This precarious interrelationship is established through a reading of trauma as departure: "trauma is a repeated suffering of the event, but it is also a continual leaving of its site . . . trauma is not simply an effect of destruction but also, fundamentally, an enigma of survival" ("Introduction" 10).[15]

Contradictory as it might sound, then, it is possible to explore the "uses" of trauma, and the patterns of investment in theoretical and literary texts that make the traumatic event their concern. If *Beloved* and *Corregidora* could be said to retraumatize the slave narrative, to refuse its linearity, to refuse to move on, what do they thereby accomplish?

II

Corregidora thematizes a concern with the transmission of culture and with the recording and judging of a history of violence: "*The important thing is making generations. They can burn the papers but they can't burn conscious, Ursa. And that what makes the evidence. And That's what makes the verdict*" (22).[16] History, in this articulation, needs to be preserved in the name of justice. While writing belongs to the white father and can easily be used to "forget" history's inconveniences, *Corregidora* suggests

that the body, specifically the body of the black woman, can constitute a site of resistance. The black woman can reproduce, "make generations" (there is a parthenogenetic fantasy at work here), and pass on stories of her own life and the lives of those before her; *Corregidora* is a tale about maternal telling. Yet the black Woman's body is the site of resistance even (and only) as it is the site of oppression (parthenogenesis is, of course, impossible): "Procreation. That could also be a slave breeder's way of thinking" (22). Part of the horror of *Corregidora* is that these meanings cannot be separated. To bear witness—literally, to bear witness by bearing witnesses—is to resist and to repeat a history of enslavement. In *Corregidora* the body occupies a doubled position: it both enables testimony and is itself the testifying text. Skin color and facial and bodily features can be read to tell the story of the master's sexual violence. *Corregidora*'s protagonist is troubled by the way in which she is compelled to be embodied, to be the history of her own contamination: "Stained with another's past as well as our own. Their past in my blood. I'm a blood" (45). The question of identity in this novel ("Do you know what you are?" [71]) is a question about the materialization of the past: "What all you got in you?" (72).[17]

The novel is the first-person narration of a blues singer, Ursa Corregidora. Her songs are her not entirely satisfactory alternatives to maternal telling, to testimony based on the logic of reproduction: "I'll sing as you talked it," she says, "let me give witness the only way I can" (53–54). Ursa is the descendent of a Portuguese slave-breeder who prostituted and raped his slaves. Corregidora is *his* name. Ursa's jealous husband, Mutt Thomas, comes to the cafe where she is singing; they have a fight and Ursa falls. She is taken to the hospital, and the doctors perform a hysterectomy. Ursa will not be able to make evidence, bear witness by bearing children. *Corregidora* begins, then, with Ursa's anxiety about the problem of transmissibility, an anxiety aggravated by her inability to extend the tradition of phono-and uterocentrism. But *Corregidora* is not only concerned with the impossibility of fully transmitting culture; it also confronts the fact that cultural transmission entails the burden of being compelled to repeat the past with one's own life. It is in this sense that *Corregidora* is a novel about trauma. The trauma sufferer faces a paradox: the past that is her obsession is a past that is not, strictly speaking, hers. Ursa has never been a slave, but neither can she leave enslavement behind her.

Corregidora, then, does not quite fit Bernard W. Bell's definition of the neoslave narrative. It may be a "residually oral, modern narrative" about slavery, but it does not tell the story of "escape from bondage to freedom" (289). It refuses this story to the extent that it is a traumatized text, a text about trauma. As such, it cannot be so linear, nor can it leave the past behind. There is no question of retrieving a repressed memory and putting it in its place. Jones's *Corregidora*, like Morrison's *Beloved*, pushes at the boundaries of Bell's definition. Through their preoccupation with traumatic memory, both novels rewrite an old form (the slave narrative) and testify to their own contemporary status (their "neo-ness").[18] Both take part in the contemporary discourse of memory, trauma, and survival, and in so doing reflect on the problem of what it means to speak from the present moment, to "have" a past.

Ursa is brought up on telling. "*They kept to the house, telling me things. My mother would work while my grandmother told me, then she'd come home and tell me. I'd go to school and come back and be told*" (101). Moreover, she has great difficulty distinguishing between the "epic" memory of slavery and "personal" memory. A past that she did not witness crowds out her own.[19] The problem seems to be that the Corregidora women do more than remember: they repeat even when forgetting no longer seems a real possibility. Ursa describes her great-grandmother: "*It was as if the words were helping her, as if the words, repeated again and again, could be a substitute for memory, were somehow more than the memory*" (11). Great Gram's repetition of words seems to empty them of their referential capacity. To over-remember is perhaps not to remember at all. Great Gram puts something in the place of memory, or, rather, memory becomes memorization and rote recitation. The past in *Corregidora* is not forgotten, repressed, or acted out symptomatically. It is, in this telling, inaccessible because too ritualistically repeated. Ursa's great-grandmother could be said to be cultivating a traumatic effect, that is to say, using trauma. Instead of meaninglessness being bound into meaning, we have the reverse procedure: through repetition, meaning comes undone. *Corregidora* suggests that repetition compulsion can be either a sign of trauma or a desired end of its own, a defense against significance.

In *Corregidora*, maternal telling has the force of literalization, a force which undermines representability. The past is not simply transmissible from generation to generation; it repeats itself. When Ursa visits her mother demanding to be told her mother's personal story (the story of her relationship with Ursa's father), the mother tells the tale, but she also repeats it, and the repetition has a force that dissolves the boundaries of subjecthood: "Mama kept talking until it wasn't her that was talking but Great Gram. I stared at her because she wasn't Mama now, she was Great Gram talking" (124). Mama *was* Great Gram. When Mutt tries to comfort Ursa—"don't look like that Ursa . . . whichever way you look at it, we ain't them"—she thinks her response: "I didn't answer that, because the way I'd been brought up, it was almost as if I was" (151). And in fact, it is in the context of Ursa's and Mutt's relationship that this threat of generational repetition is most dangerously evoked. Ursa tells us at the end of the book, "I didn't know how much was me and Mutt and how much was Great Gram and Corregidora" (184). At most, at best, there is the possibility that Ursa and her great grandmother, and Mutt and Corregidora, may not be identical ("I didn't know how much . . .").

Writings about trauma suggest that to testify is to find an addressable other, and that this is a form of "cure." But Ursa is told too soon ("*I am Ursa Corregidora . . . I was made to touch my past at an early age*" [77]). By the time she is five, Ursa has heard and reheard the family story. A trauma sufferer, it might be said, always knows too soon. The twist in *Corregidora* is that it is the address itself that has traumatizing power. It is not the past but scenes of being told that return in a kind of flashback. The novel is repeatedly punctuated by these italicized scenes, which might be said to mark the trauma in the text. They have an antinarrational force in that they stand outside the narrative as narrative, as a chronologically locatable record of events. If repetition compulsion is usually regarded as a symptom of trauma, here the compulsion to repeat is itself traumatizing.

In its concern with the traumatic nature of testimony, *Corregidora* forges a link between the maternal and the traumatic.[20] It is the mother's testimony that collapses structures of identification and representation. There is no place for absence; Ursa Corregidora cannot lose her mother. Readers of Freud's analysis of the *fort-da* game know that the child who can represent his mother's absence is emblematic of the untraumatized subject, of subjectivity that works. In psychoanalysis, the first experience of losing the mother comes with the "discovery" that the infant and mother together are not complete, that the mother wants something *other* than the baby. While a premature separation of mother and infant might seem to be constitutive of the truly traumatic, *Corregidora* poses the problem of the mother who never leaves, the mother whose only desire is for her daughter: Ursa's mother says that she wanted Ursa with her whole body and knew that she was to be a girl before she was born. The one part of Ursa's story that suggests that she will move forward and leave her "epic" past behind is her decision to learn about her father, her mother's "private memory" (104). The father here, as in many psychoanalytic texts, becomes the name of separation, the very possibility of substitution and of narrativization. It is important to notice, however, that *Corregidora* does not stage any simple opposition between an oral/maternal order and a phallic/paternal economy, for the oral/maternal with all of its dangers is also associated with an absolute father, the white, epical, Corregidora.[21]

To discuss *Corregidora* in terms of trauma is not to suggest that the workings of trauma can totally account for the text. The past repeats itself in the novel not only because it is traumatic, but also because forms of power endure. In other words, a traumatized Ursa might confuse Mutt and Corregidora, but Mutt is abusive all on his own. *Corregidora* is also not wholly a text about trauma in that it also is a story of conflict, a story of the fraught relationship between desire and survival. Ursa has to wonder to what extent the Corregidora narrative is a kind of tribute to a horror so stunning that it has a peculiar appeal: "How much was hate for Corregidora and how much was love?" (131). The scandal of *Corregidora* is its staging of the possibility that an enslaved woman might desire her enslaver. The novel skirts the edges of trauma theory here, in puzzling over the mystery of pleasure in unpleasure. To say that *Corregidora* is a blues novel, an exquisite rendering of suffering, is one way of naming this precarious distinction between the impasses of trauma and the conflict that generates texts.

III

In Morrison's novel a ghost-woman, Beloved, returns almost two decades later, to be with her mother, Sethe, who killed her to save her. Sethe, an escaped slave, chose death over enslavement for her children, that being the only choice: "I took and put my babies where they'd " (164). Sethe knows about the presence of the past even before her daughter returns in the flesh, even before she recognizes the daughter that she once killed. Sethe warns her other daughter, Denver:

> *Some things go. Pass on. Some things just stay. I used to think it was my rememory. You know. Some things you forget. Other things you never do. But It's not. Places, places are still there. If a house burns down, It's gone, but the place—the picture of it—stays, and not just in my rememory, but out there, in the world. What I remember is a picture floating around there outside my head. . . . Someday you be walking down the road and you hear something or see something going on. So clear. And you think It's you thinking it up. A thought picture. But no. It's when you bump into a rememory that belongs to somebody else.*
>
> (36)

Sethe seems to offer Denver an account of the experience of traumatization. The event or image imposes itself. It is extra-subjective. It has a thing-like quality (not "she remembered" but "there it was again" [4]). History as trauma belongs to no one, yet it is also shared: one can walk quite easily into someone else's past. Trauma confuses the relationship between inside and outside, the psyche and the social, the present and the past (or the "personal" and the "epic," in Gayl Jones's terms). The overly immediate character of the traumatic event leaves the sufferer strangely uncertain ("And you think It's you thinking it up . . . But no").

Sethe and Denver lead a suspended life in a haunted house in Ohio in the years following the Civil War. Sethe avoids the "inside," her inside, and Denver, the "outside"; she never leaves the yard. A baby ghost is their only company. Sethe's mother-in-law, Baby Suggs, worn out by white people ("'They don't know when to stop'" [104]), has died. Buglar and Howard, Sethe's sons, scared of their mother and her haunting child, have run off, and Halle, Sethe's husband, seems never to have successfully escaped "Sweet Home," the ironically named Kentucky plantation. The narrative begins when Paul D, another ex-slave from Sweet Home, arrives at Sethe's address: 124 Bluestone Road. If Paul D walks out of the past, he nevertheless represents the possibility of a future, of a story that can go on. He threatens to nurture Sethe, thereby disrupting a prolonged stasis, the very persistence of the past in the present that characterizes gothicized domestic space.[22] Denver is deeply hurt when her mother looks away and

chats girlishly with this "stranger," and the baby ghost is enraged. Beloved is the past that returns in the flesh to challenge Paul D's claim and Sethe's new aspirations ("[to] trust things and remember things" [18]).[23]

Beloved allegorizes, then, contending forces in Sethe's life, the relationship between narrative possibility (Paul D) and the trauma that disrupts and resists (Beloved). The traumatic return, the novel suggests, is simultaneous with the beginning of the possibility of narrative or testimony. If Sethe experiences her past as traumatic, so does the reader. Sometimes the past returns, becomes present in the text, when nobody is telling it or thinking it, or when it exceeds their telling or thinking. In a Faulkneresque scene, Denver "tells" Beloved (Beloved feeds on sugar and stories about Sethe), and the past becomes animated.

> *Now, watching Beloved's alert and hungry face, how she took in every word, asking questions about the color of things and their size, her downright craving to know, Denver began to see what she was saying and not just to hear it. . . . So she anticipated the questions by giving blood to the scraps that her mother and grandmother had told her—and a heartbeat. The monologue became, in fact, a duet as they lay down together, Denver nursing Beloved's interest like a lover whose pleasure was to overfeed the loved.*
>
> (77–78)

The scene takes on the character of flashback as it modulates into direct quotation (78).

Since it is Beloved who returns to represent a traumatic resistance to narrative, the temptation is to locate the novel's traumatic center at the site of the infanticide. Yet it is not this scene, or at least not the actual killing, that returns to haunt Sethe. The only vivid description of Beloved's death is filtered through the perspective of the white men: Schoolteacher, his nephew, the slave catcher, the sheriff. In this description, Sethe's deed is both outrageously overrationalized, made "sense" of as "testimony to the results of a little so-called freedom imposed on people who needed every care and guidance in the world to keep them from the cannibal life they preferred" (151), and depicted as the white man's trauma (the nephew, in particular, is overwhelmed and cannot bring himself to name Sethe's deed [150]). These modes of representation remind us that the experience is not Sethe's; it is too close, too immediate to be hers. They also work to undermine any "gothic" pleasure the reader might derive from shocking revelation. The novel makes it all the more difficult to look by suggesting here that to look would be to identify with Schoolteacher, the slave catcher, and the sheriff.

It is difficult to say whether this moment is overtold (it is approached more than once), undertold (by the time the white men arrive it is too late), or never adequately and justly narrated (what would it mean to narrate such an event adequately and justly?). The point is not that the infanticide is not traumatic, only that trauma in *Beloved* cannot be looked for and located in a single place. For if the infanticide does not return to haunt in the form of a flashback, it does seem to have bypassed her consciousness in its very immediacy: "if she thought anything, it was No. No. Nono. Nonono. Simple" (163). After the baby's death Sethe's life is numbed and colorless ("It was as though one day she saw red baby blood, another day the pink gravestone chips, and that was the last of it" [39]). Paul D is dizzied listening to Sethe tell her story. While he thinks, at first, that this is because she is being evasive, just "circling the subject," he realizes soon enough that she is "too near," unbearably close to Paul D and to the events themselves (161). Paul D refuses, at this point, to witness Sethe's testimony.

If the infanticide is not *the* trauma, neither is Sethe *the* traumatized subject. *Beloved* is about a traumatized, gothicized, culture ("Not a house in this country ain't packed to its rafters with some dead Negro's grief" [5]). Moreover, the story of slavery in general, insofar as it is a story of captivity, torture, and sexual violence, is also a traumatized, gothic narrative. And yet one can make the opposing case: in its very testimonial character (all testimonial requires a referential effect), the story of slavery in African-American literature explodes the concept of gothicism, of violence as fantasy. I would like to argue that much of *Beloved*'s power comes from its dual status as literary gothic text and as testimonial to history. The close and uncomfortable relationship between the conventional elements and the story that exceeds convention restores the horror to what could have been the merely sensational.[24]

If there is an "original" trauma in *Beloved*, an event that renders history gothic, it is the trauma of Middle Passage, which establishes a pattern of separation and desertion. Beloved's words make it more than apparent that this event or series of events cannot be left in the past: "All of it is now it is always now there will never be a time when I am not crouching and watching others who are crouching too I am always crouching the man on my face is dead" (210). Beloved is both Sethe's child and the representative of "Sixty Million and more." Beloved tells Denver: "In the dark my name is Beloved" (75). The dark of the womb? the tomb? the ship's belly? Beloved's speech is overdetermined, always marked by her personal past as well as by the past of a culture.

It has been suggested that the recognition of PTSD allows clinicians to take more seriously the traumatic character of events experienced by adults. Not all that has an impact on the psyche must or can be traced back to early childhood. This is one of the ways in which thinking about trauma disorients psychoanalysis, asking that psychoanalytic inquiry relocate itself. But in the case of *Beloved*, trying to separate out an account of trauma from an account of the mother-child dyad proves difficult, and for good reason. *Beloved* is about its conflation of "maternal" and "historical" thematics. Denver, we are told repeatedly, drinks her sister's blood along with her mother's milk (a stunned Sethe, having killed Beloved, goes on to nurse her youngest baby). This unhealthy mixture, mother's milk and sister's blood, is an emblem of *Beloved*'s doubled relationship to the discourse of trauma. The infant's experience is the trauma of Middle Passage and vice versa. Beloved does not haunt Sethe because Sethe killed her—the infanticide is not traumatic in this sense—but because she left her, deserted her repeatedly: the infanticide is one more desertion. If Sethe is the mother who killed her daughter to protect her from being re-enslaved, she is also *the* mother separated from *the* child in Middle Passage, and the one who left Beloved behind—or actually sent her on ahead—when she ran from Sweet Home (if Ursa's mother never leaves, Beloved is the perpetually abandoned child). *Beloved* retells the story of how mother and child lose one another, but in this particular instance, and in the culture of slavery more generally, the loss in both premature and the product of external force rather than conflict.[25]

The unspeakable secret in *Beloved*, what Sethe can never say, is that her own mother deserted her. When Sethe was a small child her mother was hanged, but Sethe has never known why. What was her mother doing when she was caught: "Running, you think? No. Not that. Because she was my ma'am and nobody's ma'am would run off and leave her daughter, would she? Would she, now?" (203). With her question Sethe simultaneously posits and negates this tale of desertion. What Sethe cannot say—my mother deserted me—Beloved returns to say incessantly. Beloved depends on Sethe for survival. She craves bodily intimacy and no degree of separation is tolerable; desire and identification are one: "her face is my own and I want to be there in the place where her face is and to be looking at it too" (210). But *Beloved* is not just a novel about an infant's need for mirroring, her oral economy, her intense ambivalence, her fantasies and fears about bodily integrity, or her experience of narcissistic woundedness (although it is also all of these things). These fears and fantasies are those of a (pre)subject in crisis, the crisis of (de)formation. While it sounds too simple to say that *Beloved* is governed by a regressive dynamic, it does seem fair to say that it is a novel about a crisis of subjectivity, a crisis inseparable from the traumatic legacy of slave culture. The infant's experience of the precariousness of self-image (Beloved's twin fears are that she will be eaten or that her body will explode [133]) resonates with the slave's experience of a fragmented body, a body that belongs to someone else (141,226). Barbara Matheison has suggested that the novel's dramatization of pre-Oedipal dynamics provides the metaphorical vehicle for its depiction of the experience of slavery. Morrison herself would seem to reverse the emphasis. In an interview with Marsha Darling in *The women's Review of Books*, she claims that slavery presented "an ideal situation" for discussing the intricacies of the mother-child relationship (Darling 6). Clearly neither assertion wholly accounts for the novel's pattern of figuration. *Beloved* is a difficult text precisely in the way that it conflates those traumas that are not "outside the range" of human experience, the traumas of subject formation (what Freud would find in his consulting room every day), and the violence of particular histories.[26] If the novel of disrupted domesticity can often be read as an allegory of political anxiety, *Beloved* troubles the family at its roots. In other words, it implicitly suggests that family harmony is never possible. The gothicized domestic space is not just symptomatic of cultural conflict.[27]

The conflation of maternal and historical thematics in *Beloved* combines two forms of resistance to representation: the resistance of the pre-Oedipal pre-subject, who exists prior to the dividing and identity-securing structures of language ("Why did you leave me who am you?" [216]), and the resistance of the traumatized subject, for whom the already expressive possibilities of language are (temporarily) overwhelmed. Although Sethe wants to share her story with Paul D, it may be impossible; there are horrors that "neither ha[s] word-shapes for" (99). Morrison renders the unrepresentable gothic by renaming it the unspeakable. After hearing of Sethe's deed, Paul D leaves 124 and Sethe shuts herself in alone with her daughters:

> *Paul D convinced me there was a world out there and that I could live in it. Should have known better. Did know better. Whatever is going on outside my door ain't for me. The world is in this room. This here's all there is and all there needs to be.*

(182–83)

When Stamp Paid, an ex-slave who has helped many others to gain their freedom, approaches Sethe's home, he hears sounds that he cannot make sense of: "something was wrong with the order of the words and he could not describe or cipher it to save his life" (172). He hears what he cannot possibly hear: "unspeakable thoughts, unspoken" (199). In his unsuccessful attempts to cross the threshold, Stamp Paid encounters both pre-Oedipal mumblings, sounds that are not yet dialogue, sounds of a woman alone or of a woman and child together, and the constant "roar" of unbearable suffering. Jean Wyatt's powerful reading of Morrison's text offers an account of these two kinds of unspeakability: "Outcast both as victim of slavery whose death is unspeakable and as preverbal infant who has not made her way into the symbolic order, Beloved remains outside language and therefore outside narrative memory" (484).

Lest we give in to an over-hasty gothicization, Wyatt also argues that Morrison is not only concerned with the unspeakable or the unrepresentable but also with the unspoken or the just plain under-represented. In other words, the task of *Beloved* is also to "break . . . the silence," to use Wyatt's phrase, to represent what has been "le[ft] out" of "Western cultural narratives" (476, 474). What one ought to question, however, is the conflation of these terms: not the conflation of the "maternal" (the trauma of subject formation) and the "historical" (the trauma of slavery) as unrepresentable or unspeakable, but the conflation of the concept of the unrepresentable and the concept of the *under*represented, the conflation of a linguistic and a political problematic. This is not to suggest that the linguistic is apolitical (not to suggest that

there is nothing at stake in what is constituted as an outside), nor that the political is not also a question of language, but to insist that there is a difference between what has not yet been said and what is constitutively excluded from the possibility of saying. To conflate the problematic of the unrepresentable or unspeakable with that of the underrepresented or not-yet-spoken is to restage, reperform, what *Beloved* itself does.[28] As a neoslave narrative, *Beloved* is both the text that has been excluded from the canon—the story that now demands its place, a place for the stories of slaves, and for the literariness of the black tradition—and the story of its own impossibility: how can there be a story of trauma? ("This is not a story to pass on" [275]).[29] In her conversation with Darling, Morrison claims that "the purpose of making [Beloved] real is making history possible, making memory real—somebody walks in the door and sits down at the table, so you have to think about it, whatever they may be" (5–6). This is the enabling fantasy of Morrison's text: the unrepresentable can be approached as if it were only a problem of not yet being represented. In this depiction, the forceful and literal return of the past is domesticated and used. If *Beloved* is about the literalization, personification and reanimation of the past, it not only shows repetition compulsion at work, but is also a fantasy realized, a wish fulfilled.[30]

This fantasy, of course, is also the fantasy of successful testimonial, and *Beloved* certainly moves in the direction of restoring the possibility of witnessing to the world it depicts. Paul D returns and promises to hear Sethe's story ("He wants to put his story next to hers" [273]), and at the end of the novel the women of the community acknowledge Sethe's trouble and banish Beloved (the ghost becomes ghost-like once again, her status uncertain, "Could be hiding in the trees waiting for another chance" [263]). But by this point Sethe and Beloved have exchanged positions: Beloved is large and pregnant, and Sethe is wasted, small, and child-like, literally eaten away by Beloved's insatiable demand. Morrison's novel is about history as trauma insofar as it is about what happens when your past wants you. Indeed, it is only in its moments of willful optimism (the sentimental ending with Sethe and Paul D is, after all, "much much happier than what really happened") that the precariousness of testimony itself seems to disappear.[31] *Beloved* stresses the importance of extra-familial community. With its depiction of testimonies that do not and cannot succeed (Sethe can testify, at first, neither to the unwilling Paul D nor to either of her too close daughters), *Beloved*, like **Corregidora**, allows for no easy cure.[32]

And this should not be surprising. Testimony inevitably troubles the opposition between a pure repetition of the past (trauma) and representation through narrative. Because it must reproduce the past it purports to represent, it always risks retraumatizing both victim and witness. As a testimony to the difficulty of testifying or witnessing, *Beloved* allegorizes the conflict between a political imperative to preserve history (to preserve it against the distortions of representation) and the political imperative to represent (to give voice to what has been kept silent). In 1986, Morrison spoke about nineteenth-century slave narratives and their relationship to her then current project, the writing of *Beloved*. Morrison claimed that these narratives had been underread—not read for their literariness—and that the writers themselves were limited, by literary and social convention, in what they could say. She expressed a desire to reveal the "interior life" of slaves and to "rip that veil drawn over 'proceedings too terrible to relate'" ("The Site of Memory" 110). But if *Beloved* addresses itself to these problems, problems of inadequate representation, it also thematizes other resistances to representation: what most needs to be said in the novel defies narrative form. Instead it is said through the unlocatability of trauma, the conflation of the maternal and the historical, and the ambivalence of an ending that repudiates Beloved ("Just weather. Certainly no clamor for a kiss." [275]) even as it conjures her once more. While *Beloved*, like **Corregidora**, repeats the story of slavery, then, it also asserts that it is only through an account of traumatic repetition that the story of slavery ever gets told.

Notes

1. Bernard W. Bell coins the term "neoslave narrative" in *The Afro-American Novel and its Tradition*. According to Bell neoslave narratives are "residually oral, modern narratives of escape from bondage to freedom" (289).

2. Much of the criticism, particularly of *Beloved*, already centers on questions of memory, history, and event, but it either appeals to the language of repression, which does not adequately or accurately account for the quality of the past in Morrison's text, as I will show, or it uses "trauma" in an underspecified sense in which it seems to mean no more than "bad event." See Ferguson; Henderson; Horvitz; Mathieson; and Mobley. It is of course difficult to reconcile the pleasure produced by literature with the fact that trauma, strictly speaking, excludes such enjoyment: unpleasurable repetition is trauma's "symptom," or rather since unpleasurable repetition signifies trauma, the logic of symptom must be reinterrogated.

3. See also Caruth, *Unclaimed Experience*. The rhetoric of ghostliness or gothicism in Caruth's account recalls Nicolas Abraham's concept of "the phantom" In "Notes on the Phantom." Abraham claims that children act out their parents' past secrets, secrets to which they would seem to have no access: "The phantom remains beyond the reach of traditional analysis. It will only vanish once we recognize its radically heterogeneous nature with respect to the subject—to whom it at no time bears any direct reference. In no way can the subject relate to it as his own repressed experience, not even as an experience by incorporation. *The phantom which returns to haunt bears witness to the existence of the dead buried within the other*" (79).

4. The deconstruction of an opposition between Identification and incorporation (between being like and literally being) has been central to more recent accounts of subjectivity, accounts in which "trauma" is either not an issue or in which the "trauma" is the trauma of subject formation. See Borch-Jacobsen ("Identification brings the desiring subject into being, and not the other way around" [47]) and Butler.

5. In *Beyond the Pleasure Principle* Freud is concerned with a force that violates the protective shield of consciousness and must be bound into meaning. For Walter Benjamin, it is specifically the modern subject who must constantly "parry the shocks" that threaten to violate this protective shield. Benjamin historicizes a line of thought already present in Freud's text: to speak of trauma or shock is not merely to consider pathology but to rethink the category of experience. See "On Some Motifs" 165.

6. Caruth sets up an opposition (trauma vs. repression) but also reads how the term "repression" divides. See, in particular, her reading of *Moses and Monotheism* and her use of the term "inherent latency" ("Unclaimed Experience" [187]). See also van der Kolk and van der Hart; and Leys.

7. See, for example, "Childhood Trauma." See also Crews, "The Unknown Freud," "The Revenge of the Repressed," and "The Revenge of the Repressed: Part II."

8. Not all slave narratives, or neoslave narratives, are necessarily testimonies to trauma. Lorene Cary's *The Price of a Child*, for example, is strikingly similar to *Beloved* both thematically and structurally: Cary spins her fictional tale of the after-effects of enslavement, and of a mother forcefully separated from her young child, out of a kernel of historical truth. Yet, unlike *Beloved* Cary's novel is not a consideration or enactment of the workings of trauma. For example, when Cary writes of Mercer Gray's scars she is more interested in problematizing the abolitionists' eagerness to read the slave's body. Cary thus takes on, in quite a different way, the risks of testimony (167). See note 9.

9. The analogy to the physiological (trauma means wound) remains precarious and is always in danger of collapse. *Corregidora* and *Beloved* call attention to this precariousness in their depiction of the scar not only as a record of the violence done to the body but also as a metaphor for the violence suffered by the psyche. Scars signify deadness, loss or lack of feeling. In *Beloved* Sethe's scars are on her back where she cannot see them, signifying the presence of an unreadable yet persistently present past. The dead flesh of the scar must be read to become meaningful; Sethe's back is read and re-read (*Beloved* 17–18). In *Corregidora* the scar becomes the testimony: *"'that scar That's left to bear*

witness. We got to keep it as visible as our blood'"
(*Corregidora* 72). The reading of scars, I want to
suggest, is a compelling figure for the process of
de-traumatizing, or making trauma mean. Sherley
Ann William's *Dessa Rose* is another neoslave
narrative that includes a scene of scar reading.

10. While Benjamin's thought is not easily assimilable
to much of the recent work on trauma, he is another
thinker who suggests that history needs to be
thought of as that which disrupts or prevents
narrative. See "Theses."

11. See also Felman and Laub; and van der Kolk and
van der Hart. Leys begins to articulate a critique of
"the redemptive authority of history" and of "the
modern recovery movement" (652, 653).

12. Laplanche and Pontalis assert that analysis is
predicated on the "absolute suspension of all reality
judgements . . . as the unconscious . . . knows no
such judgements" ("Fantasy" 7). But they also
acknowledge the difficulty of absolutely dismissing
a reality/fantasy distinction (see their discussion of
the fantasy and reality of adoption, also in "Fantasy"
20n). Felman and Laub explore the relationship
between trauma, testimony, and witnessing. Both
Felman and Laub and Grubrich-Simitis talk about
how trauma pushes at the boundaries of normal
analytic procedure: "In psychoanalytic work with
survivors . . . historical reality has to be
reconstructed and reaffirmed before any other work
can start" (Felman and Laub 69).

13. When the argument is made that the victim of
sexual abuse experiences a trial as a second rape,
this may not only be because the judicial system
adopts a masculinized point of view, but also
because a testimony to trauma can also be a
traumatized testimony. As "Andrea" says in Andrea
Dworkin's feminist testimonial novel, *Mercy*:
"There's no what happened next" (160).

14. The recent work of African-American legal scholar
Patricia J. Williams makes use of the testimonial
form.

15. The above also draws on Caruth's talk "Traumatic
Departures." For another interpretation of trauma as
departure see Christopher Bollas. Bollas describes
the case of a battered woman and ponders the
enigma of her repeated return to the abusive
relationship. He suggests that she may be staging a
return to "[her] own relational origin" (205). She is
thus returning not so much to the violence, as to its
cessation. She returns time and again to the elusive
care that the end of conflict repeatedly promises.
Abuse is seductive because it stops (203–05).

16. Corregidore means, in Portuguese, "judicial
magistrate." Melvin Dixon suggests that "by
changing the gender designation, Jones makes Ursa
Corregidora a female judge charged by the women
in her family to 'correct' (from the Portuguese verb

corrigir) the historical invisibility they have
suffered" (239).

17. See also Williams, "On Being the Object of
Property" in *Alchemy*. Williams tells the story of her
departure for law school. Her mother tries to
reassure her of her worthiness by telling her that the
law is "in [her] blood." Williams's
great-great-grand-mother Sophie was purchased and
impregnated by a white lawyer named Austin Miller
(216).

18. While Jones and Morrison revise the slave narrative,
this revision works in part to reveal what is already
there. One can read, for example, what is non-linear
in Harriet Jacobs's story: Jacobs does not want her
freedom to be purchased by a white woman.
Purchased freedom is, in a sense, no freedom.
Despite Jacobs's desires, however, this is what
happens (199–200).

18. In an interview, Jones says, "in the *Corregidora*
story I was concerned with getting across a sense of
an intimate history, particularly a personal history,
and to contrast it with the broad, impersonal telling
of the Corregidora story. Thus one reason for Ursa
telling her story and her mother's story is to contrast
them with the 'epic' almost impersonal history of
Corregidora" ('Interview' 92). Jones also claims,
however, that she did not initially include the
personal (Corregidora was all "epic"). She added a
hundred pages when her editor, Toni Morrison,
asked the question: what about Ursa's past? Notably,
critics of the blues suggest that this musical genre
conjoins shared and intimate history. See Carby 750.

20. For example, psychoanalyst André Green writes of
the paradoxes of maternal love and specifically of
what he calls "normal maternal madness" ("It is
when this 'madness' does not appear that we have
reason to suspect that the matter is disturbing"
[245]). The father in this narrative represents the
"cure" ("He is, so to speak, the guarantee of the
transformation of this madness, and of its evolution
towards inevitable separation" [247]). Green argues
that the father is mad "elsewhere—in the world, in
social life, in his preoccupation with power." In this
rendering, social reality—or being the father—is one
long and elaborate attempt at disengaging oneself
from the "delicious[ness]" of passivity (247).

21. See Kristeva. She gives an account of the imaginary
father, which also complicates any simple separating
out of maternal and paternal orders.

22. The house on 124 Bluestone Road is the novel's
main character. In addition to this haunting of
domestic space, *Beloved* is a gothic novel in that it
involves intergenerational transmission, features
scandalous sexuality and bodily mutilations, and
makes use of the trope of unspeakable horror.

23. Perhaps *Beloved* is Morrison's most aesthetically
compelling work to date because its theme, the

literal or material return of the past, echoes Morrison's style, the intimacy and corporeality of her figuration: secrets are sweet, sleep has a lip, disapproval a scent (28, 85, 138).

24. James Baldwin suggests that the temporality of trauma is also the temporality of gothicized African-American experience. "This horror . . . has so welded past and present that it is virtually impossible and certainly meaningless to speak of it as occurring, as it were, in time" (xii).

25. While there are several psychoanalytic stories of the crisis, or triumph, of infant-mother separation, *Beloved* could be said to reveal the necessarily fantastic component of most of these tales. In Lacan's mirror stage the child that "loses" or "overcomes" the mother and sees himself as whole and independent actually props himself upon her (his self-recognition is a scene of misrecognition—he fantasizes both that he has lost his mother and that he is independent and whole). See also Nicolas Abraham and Maria Torok, who suggest that a "real" loss of the mother would constitute a trauma and impede language acquisition. A loss, then, as necessary as it is for subject constitution, is only bearable (i.e. non-traumatic) when it is not a real loss.

26. The phrase "outside the range" comes from the *Diagnostic and Statistical Manual's* (DSM-III-R) definition of the traumatic event ("the person has experienced an event that is outside the range of human experience" [qtd. in Brown 120]). Laura S. Brown considers this wording in her feminist critique of the DSM's definition. She argues that politics determine what counts as traumatic. Brown describes a case in which an adult incest survivor was told that she could not possibly be traumatized since incest is fairly common, and in order to have suffered a trauma one must have suffered from something that is "outside the range of human experience." Brown's point is that the category "human," while seeming to represent all, excludes people from non-dominant groups.

27. Anticipating the conflation that characterizes *Beloved*, Morrison's *Sula* juxtaposes "too thick" mother love (is the maternal the position where excess and insufficiency inevitably meet?) and trauma, specifically war trauma. Shadrack the World War I veteran is "permanently astonished": "He knew the smell of death and was terrified of it, for he could not anticipate it. It was not death or dying that frightened him, but the unexpectedness of both" (7, 14).

28. Much of the criticism on *Beloved* celebrates the text as it retells its story as a story of cure. See Duvall, Horvitz, Mathieson, Rushdy, and Wyatt. (Rushdy's article is already a polemical response to Stanley Crouch, who argues that "*Beloved* means to prove that Afro-Americans are the result of a cruel

determinism" [42]). For Wyatt, this cure, which she names "the maternal symbolic," is not just Sethe's cure, or a cultural cure, but a cure for language itself. The process of signification needs healing, and *Beloved* does the work. Sethe may revert to materiality and refuse the process of exchange and substitution, but the world that she rejects, the world that according to Wyatt psychoanalysis describes, is a world in which materiality and the maternal must be entirely surrendered. *Beloved*, Wyatt argues, ultimately offers a middle way. It is not so much that these therapeutic or celebratory readings are wrong (the text provides plenty of support for such readings), but that it seems worth scrutinizing their investment in such a healing project. In successfully doing the work of reading *Beloved* as a progressive narrative, as a narrative that progresses, the criticism itself becomes, or is able to present itself as, a powerful antidote to the culture's ills and trauma's resistance to narrativization.

29. Morrison also addresses the question of unspeakability in "Unspeakable Things Unspoken." In this essay Morrison's concern would seem to be primarily with the political, that is, with the problem of forms of "willful oblivion," with "certain absences . . . so stressed, so ornate, so planned, they call attention to themselves; arrest us with intentionality and purpose, like neighborhoods that are defined by the population held away from them" (11). Even here, "unspeakability" takes on a variety of meanings. It also means, for example, that which can only be cited. Morrison writes, "Thus, in spite of its implicit and explicit acknowledgment, 'race' is still a virtually unspeakable thing, as can be seen in the apologies, notes of 'special use' and circumscribed definition that accompany it—not least of which is my own deference in surrounding it with quotation marks" (3).

30. Morrison has spoken of "a necessity for remembering the horror," but, she adds, "of course There's a necessity for remembering it in a manner in which it can be digested. . . . my story, my invention, is much, much happier than what really happened" (Darling 5). By opposing her version to "what really happened," Morrison exposes the willfulness of her project, its investment in the very possibility of fictional language (a power that she also acknowledges in her epigraph: "'I will call them my people/which were not my people;/and her beloved,/which was not beloved' *Romans* [9:25]"). Similarly, *Beloved* both preserves and rewrites the life of Margaret Garner, an escaped slave who did kill one of her children to prevent her from being re-enslaved. In the historical account, Margaret Garner is re-enslaved, but she falls or jumps with her baby from the boat taking her further south. The end of Garner's story, such as it is, is reinscribed in *Beloved*, but not as the end of Sethe's tale. Instead Morrison conflates Garner's story with the shared,

unlocatable account of Middle Passage. For Beloved, Sethe is the mother lost in an attempt to "escape" from a slave ship: "She was about to smile at me when the men without skin came and took us up into the sunlight with the dead and then shoved them into the sea. Sethe went into the sea. . . . When I went in, I saw her face coming to me and it was my face too" (214). Despite Morrison's avowed investment in the possibility of cure, the manageability of history, this treatment of the Garner material displays a traumatic resistance to narrative. For the Margaret Garner story see Coffin; Darling; Lerner; Morrison and Naylor; "The Cincinnati Slaves"; and "A Visit."

31. Morrison says of her relationship to sentimentality, "I want a residue of emotion in my fiction, and this means verging upon sentimentality, or being willing to let it happen and then draw back from it. Also, stories seem so old-fashioned now. But narrative remains the best way to learn anything, whether history or theology, so I continue with narrative form" (Leclair 372).

32. Although *Corregidora* is not governed by the same intensity of infantile affect that predominates in *Beloved*, in both novels there is a specifically mother-child violence associated with the force of repetition. Between mothers and daughters, it seems, the future has no chance. It is as if relationships within the family, the gothicized domestic space, are always in danger of becoming pre-objectival (particularly if they are relationships between women), and the pre-object cannot bear witness.

Works Cited

Abraham, Nicolas, "Notes on the Phantom: A Complement to Freud's Metapsychology." *The Trial(s) of Psychoanalysis*. Ed. Françoise Meltzer. Chicago: U of Chicago P, 1987, 75–80.

Abraham, Nicolas and Maria Tork, "Introjection—incorporation: *Mourning* or *Melancholia*." *Psychoanalysis in France*. Ed. Serge Lebovici and Daniel Widiocher. New York: International UP, 1980, 5–16.

Baldwin, James, *Notes of A Native Son*. 1955. London: Pluto P, 1985.

Bell, Bernard W. *The Afro-American Novel and Its Tradition*. Amherst: U of Massachusetts P, 1987.

Benjamin, Walter, "On Some Motifs in Baudelaire." *Illuminations*. Trans. Harry Zohn. Ed. Hannah Arendt. New York: Schocken, 1969. 155–200.

———. "Theses on the Philosophy of History." *Illuminations*. Trans. Harry Zohn. Ed. Hannah Arendt. New York: Schocken, 1969, 255–64.

Bollas, Christopher, *Cracking Up: The Work of Unconscious Experience*, New York: Hill and Wang, 1995.

Borch-Iacobsen, Mikkel. *The Freudlan Subject*. Trans. Catherine Porter. Standord: Stanford UP, 1988.

Brown, Laura. "Not Outside the Range: One Feminist Perspective on Psychic Trauma." *American Imago* 48 (1991): 119–34.

Butler, Judith. *Gender Trouble: Feminism and the Subversion of Identity*. New York: Routledge, 1990.

Carby, Hazel. "It Jus Be's Dat Way Sometime: The Sexual Politics of women's Blues." *Feminisms: An Anthology of Literary Theory and Criticism*. Ed. Robyn R. Warhol and Diane price Herndl. New Brunswick: Rutgers UP, 1991, 746–58.

Caruth, Cathy, "Introduction." *American Imago* 48 (1991): 1–12.

———. "Introduction." *American Imago* 48 (1991): 417–24.

———. "Traumatic Departures: Survival and History in Freud." Cornell University. 26 Feb. 1993.

———. *Unclaimed Experience: Trauma, Narrative, and History*, Baltimore: Johns Hopkins, 1995.

———. "Unclaimed Experience: Trauma and the Possibility of History." *Yale French Studies* 79 (1991): 181–92.

Cary, Lorene, *The Price of Child*. New York: Vintage 1995.

"Childhood Trauma: Memory or Invention." *New York Times* 21 July 1992: C17.

"The Cincinnati Slaves—Another Thrilling Scene in the Tragedy." *The Liberator* 21 Mar. 1856: 47.

Coffin, Levi. *Reminiscences of Levi Coffin*. Cincinnati: Western Tract Society, 1876.

Crews, Frederick. "The Revenge of the Repressed." *The New York Review of Books* 17 Nov. 1994: 54–60.

———. "The Revenge of the Repressed: Part II." *The New York Review of Books* 1 Dec. 1994: 49–58.

———. "The Unknown Freud." *The New York Review of Books*. 18 Nov. 1993: 55–66.

Crouch. Stanley, "Aunt Medea." *New Republic* 19 Oct. 1987: 38–43.

Darling, Marsha. "In the Realm of Responsibility: A Conversation with Toni Morrison." *women's Review of Books* Mar. 1988: 5–6.

Dixon, Melvin. "Singing a Deep Song: Language as Evidence in the Novels of Gayl Jones." *Black Women Writers* (1950–1980): *A Critical Evaluation*. Ed. Mari Evans. New York: Anchor, 1984. 236–48.

Duvall, John N. "Authentic Ghost Stories: *Uncle Tom's Cabin, Absalom, Absalom!* and *Beloved*." *The Faulkner Journal* 4.1–2 (1988–89): 83–98.

Dworkin, Andrea, *Mercy*. New York: Four Walls Eight Windows, 1990.

Felman, Shoshana and Dori Laub. *Testimony: Crises of Witnessing in Literature, Psychoanalysis, and History*. New York: Routledge, 1992.

Ferguson, Rebecca. "History, Memory and Language in Toni Morrison's *Beloved*." *Feminist Criticism: Theory and Practice*. Ed. Susan Sellers. Toronto: U of Toronto P, 1991. 109–27.

Freud, Sigmund, *Beyond the Pleasure Principle*, 1920. *The Standard Edition of the Complete Psychological Works of Sigmund Freud*, Trans, and ed. James Strachey, Vol. 18. London: Hogarth, 1955. 7–64. 24 vols. 1953–74.

Gates, Henry Louis, Jr. *The Signifying Monkey: A Theory of African-American Literary Criticism*. New York: Oxford UP, 1988.

Green, André *On Private Madness*, Madison, CT: International UP, 1986.

Grubrich-Simitis, Ilse, "From Concretism to Metaphor: Thoughts on Some Theoretical and Technical Aspects of the Psychoanalytic Work with Children of Holocaust Survivors." *The Psycho-analytic Study of the Child*. Vol. 39. New Haven: Yale UP, 1984. 301–19.

Henderson, Mae G. "Toni Morrison's *Beloved*: ReMembering the Body as Historical Text." *Comparative American Identities: Race, Sex, and Nationality in the Modern Text*, Ed. Hortense J. Spillers. New York: Routledge, 1991. 62–86.

Horvitz, Deborah. "Nameless Ghosts: Possession and Dispossession in *Beloved*." *Studies in American Fiction* 17 (1989): 157–67.

Jacobs, Harriet, *Incidents in the Life of a Slave Girl*, 1861. New York: New American Library, 1987.

Jones, Gayl. *Corregidora*, Boston: Beacon, 1975.

——. Interview. *Black Women Writers at Work*. Ed. Claudia Tate. New York: Continuum, 1983, 89–99.

Kristeva, Julia. "Freud and Love: Treatment and its Discontents." Trans. Léon S. Roudlez. *The Kristeva Reader*. Ed. Toril Mol. Oxford: Blackwell, 1986. 238–71.

Lacan, Jacques. "The Mirror Stage as Formative of the Function of the I." *Écrits: A Selection*. Trans. Alan Sheridan. New York: Norton, 1977. 1–7.

Laplanche, Jean and J.-B. Pontalis. "Fantasy and the Origins of Sexuality." *Formations of Fantasy*: Ed. Victor Burgin, James Donald, Cora Kaplan, London: Methuen, 1986, 5–34.

——. "Traumatic Neurosis." *The Language of Psycho-Analysis*. Trans. Jeffrey Mehiman. Baltimore: Johns Hopkins UP, 1976. 470–73.

Leclair, Thomas. "'The Language Must Not Sweat': A Conversation with Toni Morrison." *Toni Morrison: Critical Perspectives Past and Present*. Eds. Henry Louis Gates, Jr. and K.A. Appiah, New York: Amistad, 1993, 360–77.

Lerner, Gerda, ed. *Black Women in White America: A Documentary History*. New York: Pantheon, 1972.

Leys, Ruth. "Traumatic Curses: Shell Shock, Janet, and the Question of Memory." *Critical Inquiry* 20 (1994): 623–62.

Mathieson, Barbara O. "Memory and Mother Love in Morrison's *Beloved*." *American Imago* 47 (1990): 1–22.

McDowell, Deborah E. "Negotiating Between Tenses: Witnessing Slavery After Freedom—*Dessa Rose*." *Slavery and the Literary Imagination*. Ed. Deborah McDowell and Arnold Rampersad. Baltimore: Johns Hopkins UP, 1987. 144–63.

Mobley, Marilyn Sanders. "A Different Remembering: Memory, History, and Meaning in Toni Morrison's *Beloved*." *Modern Critical Views: Toni Morrison*. Ed. Harold Bloom. New York: Chelsea House, 1990. 189–99.

Morrison, Toni *Beloved*. New York: Knopf, 1987.

——. "The Site of Memory." *Inventing The Truth: The Art and Craft of Memoir*. Ed. William Zinsser. Boston: Houghton Mifflin, 1987. 101–24.

——. *Sula*. New York: Penguin, 1975.

——. "Unspeakable Things Unspoken: The Afro-American Presence In American Literature." *Michigan Quarterly Review* 28.1 (1989): 1–34.

Morrison, Toni, and Gloria Naylor. "A Conversation." *The Southern Review* 21 (1985): 567–93.

Rushdy, Ashraf H.A. "Daughter's Signifyin(g) History: The Example of Toni Morrison's *Beloved*." *American Literature* 64 (1992): 567–97.

Smitherman, Geneva. *Talkin and Testifyin: The Language of Black America*. Boston: Houghton Mifflin: 1977.

van der Kolk, Bessel A., and Onno van der Hari. "The Intrusive Past: The Flexibility of Memory and the Engraving of Trauma." *American Imago* 48 (1991): 425–54.

"A Visit to the Slae Mother who Killed Her Child." *The Liberator* 21 Mar. 1856: 43.

Williams, Patricia J. *The Alchemy of Race and Rights: Diary of a Law Professor*. Cambridge: Harvard UP, 1991.

Williams, Sherley Anne. *Dessa Rose*. New York: Berkley Books, 1987.

Wyatt, Jean. "Giving Body to the World: The Maternal Symbolle in Toni Morrison's *Beloved*." *PMLA* 108 (1995): 474–88.

Janelle Wilcox (essay date 1996)

SOURCE: "Resistant Silence, Resistant Subject: (Re)Reading Gayl Jones's *Eva's Man*," in *Bodies of Writing, Bodies in Performance*, edited by Thomas Foster, Carol Siegal, and Ellen E. Berry, New York University Press, 1996, pp. 72-96.

[*In the following essay, Wilcox, a professor at Washington State University, applies Michel Foucault's theories on discourse to analyze Jones's use of silence in* Eva's Man.]

In an interview conducted in the spring of 1975, just after the publication of Gayl Jones's first novel, ***Corregidora***, Michael S. Harper asks Jones if any of her work was autobiographical. Jones responds with an acknowledgment that despite her use of first-person narration, none of her writing was "strictly autobiographical." She names one story as a slight exception: "'The Welfare Check' is only in terms of the Woman's being like me."¹ Jones elaborates further on the function of the narrator of the story and the purpose the story served:

[T]he woman narrator, even though the details of her life were different, was me in the sense that I needed her to explain myself. There was no way I could explain who I was to myself or anybody else except that way. Particularly my silence. I had to say something about it some way. . . . And I felt that if people read the story or if I read it to them, they would feel less badly about my not talking and it usually worked that way. So I needed the woman to be me at that time.[2]

Jones's thematic exploration of silence is not limited to "The Welfare Check." Silences punctuate the narratives of her two novels, *Corregidora* (1975) and *Eva's Man* (1976), as well as several short stories in *White Rat* (1977). In fact, Mae Gwendolyn Henderson's 1991 introduction to the paperback edition of *White Rat* points to silence as the defining element of the collection: "Her stories both thematize and formalize silence as a strategem that reveals the discontinuities and breaks in the connections and bonds between individuals."[3] What interests me here is Jones's subsequent silence—her absence from textual production—what Henderson terms Jones's "rather sudden and mysterious disappearance from the public eye."[4] After only two novels and one collection of short stories, Jones has stopped publishing her fiction.

In conjunction with examining Jones's silence, both her textual exploration of silence and her subsequent absence from textual production, I want to look at the critical apparatus that affects the reception of texts. Jones's work stretches across both decades and genres from fiction published in the seventies, poetry in the eighties, and criticism in the nineties. But it is the reception of her fiction that functions as an illuminating example of the normalizing force of literary reviews and criticism. Despite early critical acclaim, she remains one of the lesser-known, lesser-read, and underappreciated contemporary African American women writers. *Corregidora* was greeted by reviewers with nearly unqualified praise. When her second novel was published the next year, however, the same reviewers who had seen the author of *Corregidora* as a promising young writer saw the author of *Eva's Man* as perpetuating stereotypes about black women[5] and promoting hostility toward black men.[6] Jones's collection of short stories was published the year after *Eva's Man*, but no other fiction has appeared since then.

In *Discourse and the Other: The Production of the Afro-American Text*, W. Lawrence Hogue contends that "criticism as practiced by editors, publishers, reviewers, and critics . . . is a preeminently political exercise that works upon and mediates the reception of literary texts."[7] Following Terry Eagleton's assertion that literature is a construction "fashioned by particular people for particular reasons,"[8] Hogue moves beyond the general field of the politics of literary theory and into an examination of the politics of racial construction in literary theory and criticism. Historically, ideological forces (using the universalizing discourse of aesthetic value) determined what African American texts were considered aesthetically compatible to texts in the (Euro) American literary canon. For example, Hogue points out that naturalist novels such as

Richard Wright's *Native Son* (1941) were admitted entrance to the canon, though still in a token position, because literary study in the United States was dominated by naturalism for the first half of the twentieth century. It is Hogue's contention that the social movements of the sixties provided space for African American writers to more effectively challenge the stereotypes and images that had dominated and disciplined the production of African American texts.

Hogue's examination of African American literary production is explicitly informed by Michel Foucault's analysis of discursive formation. As Hogue explains, discourse naturalizes itself and thus conceals its discrepancies and silences; therefore "the archaeologist's function is to demask this process of naturalization."[9] Numerous critics and theorists in American literary study have undertaken the task of unmasking the ideologies that underlie the construction of an American canon of literature, and African American critics in particular have noted the silencing of African American texts that do not conform to mainstream literary aesthetics.[10] Barbara Herrnstein Smith argues that "literary value is not the property of an object or of a subject but rather the product of the dynamics of a system."[11] Furthermore, she contends that literary critics and reviewers are within the system and view texts from a particular perspective. The perspective from which a reviewer read Gayl Jones's fiction was affected by aesthetic and political ideologies, as well as his or her social positioning.[12] The discourses of the 1970s that influenced the evaluation of literary texts included not only those informed by "universal" values of a predominantly Euro-American male perspective, but also those grounded in oppositional values—literary and political—such as black nationalism and feminism.

Many critics specifically name the social movements of the 1960s and 1970s as the major influence on the literary production of African American literature. Mary Helen Washington calls both the civil rights movement and the feminist movement the "subtexts" of the stories by black women collected in *Black-Eyed Susans/Midnight Birds*. She particularly notes the connections between the social text and the literary text of the writers, contending that "[b]oth of these movements for political change in our society have revised the lives and the art of black women."[13] W. Lawrence Hogue also points to the liberatory effects of the sixties social movements. He argues that breaking away from the dominant literary apparatus "gave Afro-American writers, perhaps for the first time in American history, the opportunity to write for black audiences of similar ideological persuasions."[14]

In contrast to Washington and Hogue, Madhu Dubey looks more closely at the contradictions and tensions between and within the dominant discourses of the 1970s. Her study of black women novelists of the 1970s focuses on works by Toni Morrison, Gayl Jones, and Alice Walker, which she says "constitute themselves as novels by carefully navigating between two influential contemporary definitions of good fiction."[15] Journals such as the *New York Times Book Review* promoted politically neutral fiction, while black nationalist journals such as *Black World* and *Freedomways* valued work that was didactic and politically useful. In addition to negotiating between two opposing standards of literature, those upheld by the white literary establishment and those valued by the Black Aesthetic, black women writers questioned and undermined the gender assumptions of black nationalist discourse. Dubey argues, "The internal gaps and contradictions of black nationalist discourse, especially visible in its construction of black womanhood, opened the space for an alternative black feminist definition of womanhood."[16] Dubey contends that the novels written in the 1970s by Morrison, Jones, and Walker strain the limits of both feminist discourse and black nationalist discourse.

As Dubey points out, the two interpretive communities that were in a position to review Jones's novels were the white literary press and the black nationalist journals. Barbara Herrnstein Smith maintains that the two kinds of texts that appear in interpretive communities appeal to either divergent or convergent tastes. Divergent tastes, Smith explains, are resistant to cultural channeling, while convergent tastes are tractable to cultural channeling. When texts that do not yield easily to cultural channeling appear in an interpretive community, "institutions of evaluative authority are called in to validate the community's established tastes and preferences."[17] As a result, texts with divergent tastes are discounted or even pathologized by the persons or institutions with evaluative authority. Although the focus of Smith's examination of the contingencies of value is on mainstream Euro-American literary study, she contends that all interpretive communities engage in normative criticism, valuing some texts and devaluing others. Black nationalist critics—male and female—who reviewed *Eva's Man* found no sociological relevance or realistic representation in a text about a criminally insane black woman. Eva's story and her mode of telling it resisted Black Aesthetic cultural channeling. Eva's story also resisted cultural channeling by critics looking for "universal" or "apolitical" literature. Although for different ideological reasons, white reviewers joined black nationalist reviewers in their condemnation of Jones's second novel.

Several interviews with Jones appeared in print between the years 1977 and 1984. The 1975 interview with Gayl Jones was conducted by African American poet Michael S. Harper, Jones's "first reader"[18] while she was at Brown University. It was first published in the *Massachusetts Review* in 1977.[19] In August 1978, black feminist critic Claudia Tate interviewed Jones at the University of Michigan; the interview was published in *Black American Literature Forum* in 1979 and reprinted in Tate's *Black Women Writers at Work* (1983). Roseann P. Bell records her conversation with Jones about *Corregidora* in *Sturdy Black Bridges* (1979), but states that the interview took place before the publication of *Eva's Man*. A brief interview/essay by Jones appeared in Marie Evans's *Black

Women Writers (1950–1980): A Critical Evaluation (1984). In 1982, Charles Rowell conducted an interview with Jones by mail, which was published later that year in *Callaloo*. The information provided in and the tone of the interviews seem to indicate that reviewers and critics, performing their role as "institutions of evaluative authority," affected Jones's public discourse. In contrast to the Harper interview, which provided biographical information and personal anecdotes, subsequent interviews are marked by a greater reserve and reticence on the part of the subject/object of the interview.

The interview with Claudia Tate is the first interview that makes explicit Jones's decision to resist biographical or psychological interpretation. In the 1978 interview, Tate provides an overview of Jones's published fiction and introduces Jones to the reader:

> Born in 1949 in Lexington, Kentucky, where she continued to reside until she first went to Connecticut College and then to Brown University, Jones is now Assistant Professor of English at the University of Michigan. She refuses to divulge additional biographical information, contending that her work must live independently of its creator, that it must sustain its own character and artistic autonomy. But while she will not discuss her private life, she did, in the interview that follows, share some insights into her artistic endeavors and about her perceptions of American literary history.[20]

In addition to establishing Jones's reluctance to provide personal details that might be used for interpretive purposes, the interviews also provide evidence of Jones's continued production of texts. In the introduction to her interview, Tate says that Jones told her she was working on another novel entitled *Palmares* and that Jones expected it to be published in the "not-too-distant future."[21] In other interviews and reviews of her novels, reference is made to work either completed or in progress. Roseann P. Bell's introduction to her interview of Jones states that Jones had already completed three novels.[22] Margo Jefferson's review of *Eva's Man* indicates that Jones had completed four novels and was working on a fifth.[23] In the Charles H. Rowell interview, Jones talks about novels and short story collections she has written, referring to them by both title and content.[24] Despite the fact that the interview took place in 1982, none of the works ever appeared in print.

The interviews with Claudia Tate and Charles H. Rowell provide evidence that Jones was affected by the overwhelmingly negative response to *Eva's Man*. Toward the end of the Tate interview, Claudia Tate asks Jones if she is influenced by reviews and criticism of her writing. Jones responds, "As I write, I imagine how certain critics will respond to various elements of the story, and I force myself to go ahead and say 'Well, you would ordinarily include this, so go ahead and do it.'"[25] In the Rowell interview, Jones refers to a "double-consciousness" evoked in her whenever she writes anything about sexuality. She also discusses the way critical reception influenced her choice of subject matter. When Rowell asks her about her decision to write on the Afro-Brazilian slave experience after having written two novels set in the United States, Jones explains that the Brazilian history and landscape helped her imagination. But she further articulates the decision in terms of a distancing strategy:

> I also wanted to write about someone and a time distant from my own. It was also a way of getting away from things that some readers consider "autobiographical" or "private obsessions" rather than literary inventions— that they don't accept as imagination from a black woman writing about black female characters in a certain American world.[26]

The sense of restriction Jones voices is not limited to one particular African American writer. Jones herself indicates her awareness that the limitations she feels stem in part from her subject-position as a black woman. The reception of Jones's second novel, however, provides a particularly apt example of the silencing and containment of counter-hegemonic writers.

RESISTANT SILENCE, RESISTANT SUBJECT

Jones's *Eva's Man* plays out textually the ways that knowledge and power are linked in discourse. Eva begins telling her story from the cell of a psychiatric prison where she has been incarcerated for five years for the crime of poisoning and castrating a man. At her arrest, at her trial, at her sentencing. Eva's silence had been her defense. Her refusal to talk, either in justification for or explanation of her crime, signifies a resistance to entering the dominant medical, juridical, and sexual discourses represented in the novel. Eva's discursive containment and simultaneous resistance function as a metaphor for the containment of the marginalized writer. In contemporary literary study, the dominant culture often mishears the marginalized writer who is resisting or revising the dominant discourse. Even more likely to be misheard is the voice different from the naturalized minority discourse. Eva's silencing within the novel textually prefigures Jones's silencing within African American literary study. Eva Medina Canada, the character in Jones's novel, exhibits a resistance to interpretation that is paralleled by Gayl Jones, the writer and creator of that character.

Despite the connection I draw between the fictionally represented silence of Eva and the literal silence of Jones, I wish to be explicit here that it is not my intention to psychoanalyze Gayl Jones's silence. In fact, I am very much arguing against interpretation that collapses the distinction between character and creator. Jones's refusal to authorially intrude in her fiction has placed her in the defensive position of being mistaken for the characters she invents. In Mari Evans's *Black Women Writers*, Jones says, "I think I have an unfortunate public image, because of the published work. People imagine you're the person you've imagined."[27] The violence of interpretation that *Eva's Man* metaphorically represents extends from readers of the text to readers of Jones herself. I am suggesting, however, that her silence can be read in two interconnected ways: as the result of the disciplinary function of

institutions, in this case the hegemonic and ambiguously (non)hegemonic[28] critical apparatus made up of publishers, reviewers, and critics, and as a silence that resists and denaturalizes the universalizing tendencies of interpretive communities. Because of my reluctance to participate in further interpretive "violation" of Jones, I have chosen to read both Jones's silence and Eva's silence as strategies of resistance. The following reading of *Eva's Man* is informed by Foucault's theories of discourse and resistant subjectivity, especially as they have been appropriated by feminist philosophers.

While other feminist theorists have examined silence as resistance, my appropriation of Foucault here foregrounds my interest in the ways that both Foucault and Jones explore how the psychoanalytic situation works as discipline. Foucault's refusal of psychoanalytic paradigms is echoed in Eva's hostile relationship with psychoanalysis in Jones's text. In the 1982 interview with Charles Rowell, Jones stresses Eva's resistance to participating in the psychoanalytic relationship: "She doesn't talk to the policemen. Ideally—and the kind of character I imagine her to be—she wouldn't have even talked to the psychiatrist either. But to tell the novel I had to have her do that."[29] Because Eva tells her story and at the same time resists telling her story, the reader is put in an uncomfortably complicitous position with the prison psychiatrist of "knowing" Eva only through her distorted narrative. Jones connects the unreliability of Eva's storytelling with the ambiguous positioning of Eva's audience: "How much of Eva's story is true and how much is deliberately not true; that is, how much of a game is she playing with her listeners/psychiatrists/others?"[30] The ambiguous designation of "listeners/psychiatrists/others" as Eva's "audience" functions to situate the reader in the position of being a knowing, thus violating, subject.

Because Jones undermines the authority of psychiatric discourse, we cannot unproblematically read Eva as the object of the text. At the same time, neither can we read Eva as a rational subject. Consequently, we must learn to read her as a resisting subject. Susan J. Hekman explains that for Foucault, "the constituted subject is the subject that resists."[31] More important, Hekman stresses the implications of Foucault's thought for feminism: "[w]omen's resistance to the constitution of their subjectivity is the essence of the feminist movement. . . . The result of resistance is the creation of a new discourse— born out of resistance to the modes of discourse that have constituted the feminine subject."[32] What Eva resists are the ways in which she is constituted by and within discourse. To subvert these constructions of sexuality, gender, and race, Eva uses silence—what Foucault would call the gaps and discrepancies in discourse. Learning to read Eva's silence means learning to read Eva's resistance.

Jones's strategy of telling the story only through Eva's subjectivity confounds the reader's attempts to read Eva as the object of the story. Throughout the text, Jones calls attention to the dynamic between a knowing subject and a known object. The knowing subjects take the form of Davis in his sexual relationship with Eva, the police in their disciplinary relationship, the court in its juridical relationship, the psychiatrist in his medical relationship, and newspapers and readers who are looking for the "truth" to be produced about Eva, the object to be known. Eva uses silence to resist violation and definition by these knowing subjects. Her words. "I said nothing," become an ironic refrain, echoing in every conversation, in every relationship.

Because Davis "knows" Eva only as a sexual object, he ties together the themes of sex and silence in one of the opening scenes of the novel. After joining Eva at her table, he says that he can tell something about her: "You ain't been getting it, have you?" Eva says nothing—to which Davis responds, "I don't expect you to say nothing. I can read your eyes."[33] He combines assertion, question, and interpretation without needing a response from Eva herself. Yet Eva's resistant silence disrupts Davis's definition of Eva, and he seeks more information from Eva in order to know/explain her. During the five days that Eva spends with Davis in his hotel room, Davis makes various attempts to break through Eva's silence: "'Eva, why won't you talk about yourself?' I said nothing" (67); "'Why won't you talk to me, Eva?' 'There's nothing to say'" (101); "'Why won't you talk?' I said nothing" (116); "'How do you feel about it, Eva?' 'It doesn't matter'" (118); "'Say something, Eva.' 'There's nothing'" (121). "'What are you thinking? you're not talking.' 'Nothing.' 'Why aren't you speaking?' 'I don't have anything to say right now'" (126). By refusing to talk, Eva avoids containment within the category of woman as defined by Davis.

"THEY SAY THAT'S ALL RIGHT, TO GO AHEAD TALKING"

The other knowing subjects in the text, the police, the court, the psychiatrist, the newspapers, likewise demand discourse from Eva. In *The History of Sexuality*, Foucault contends that "one confesses—or is forced to confess."[34] In the opening pages of the novel, Eva says,

> [P]eople come in here and ask me how it happened. They want me to tell it over and over again. I don't mean just the psychiatrists, but people from newspapers and things. They read about it or hear about it someplace and just want to keep it living. At first I wouldn't talk to anybody. All during the trial I wouldn't talk to anybody. But then, after I came in here, I started talking. I tell them so much I don't even get it straight any more. I tell them things that don't even have to do with what I did, but they say they want to hear that too. They want to hear about what happened between my mother and father as well as what happened between me and that man. One of them came in here and even wanted to know about my grandmother and grandfather. I know when I'm not getting things straight, and I tell them I'm not getting this straight, but they say That's all right, to go ahead talking.
>
> (4–5)

The relentless pressure upon Eva to talk about her crime can be illuminated through Foucault's discussion of confes-

sion in Western tradition as it moved from the church and into the scientific and medical discourses. Sex was and continues to be the privileged theme of confession, and confession in turn governs "the production of the true discourse on sex."[35] Because Eva has committed a crime of sex and violence in her murder and dental castration of Davis, she is exhorted to confess and thus produce the truth about herself. Foucault further explains the connection between power and knowledge that exists in the relation between the confessor and his/her audience:

> The confession is a ritual of discourse in which the speaking subject is also the subject of the statement; it is also a ritual that unfolds within a power relationship, for one does not confess without the presence (or virtual presence) of a partner who is not simply the interlocutor but the authority who requires the confession.[36]

For the prison psychiatrist, Eva's story, her confession, her recounting of intimate moments, are necessary for him to evaluate and judge her, but at the same time, Eva resists and challenges his knowledge of her. Though she is denied a role as a knowing subject herself, through her silence, she refuses to be a known object.

Foucault contends that "[t]here is not one but many silences, and they are an integral part of the strategies that underlie and permeate discourses."[37] Silence, as Foucault understands it, is "an element that functions alongside the things said, with them and in relation to them."[38] The "things said" work in relation to one another to form a discourse, but they are only a part of that discourse. In his adaptation of Foucauldian thought, W. Lawrence Hogue considers the text a discursive field of facts existing in relation to one another. For example, in examining the feminist discourse that informs Alice Walker's *Third Life of Grange Copeland*, Hogue calls the image of the oppressed black male a repeated discursive fact that works in relation to other discursive facts, such as the submissive and loyal black woman, to form the text's feminist enunciation.[39] In *Eva's Man*, the repeated discursive fact of the male character who reads Eva only through her gender and sexuality is a part of the discursive field of the text but only as it exists in relation to Eva's resistant silences. Each of the male characters attempts to force Eva into a discursive relation. Each engages in the discourse of sex in an attempt to "know" Eva, to produce the "truth" about Eva. What bothers Eva, Jones says, is that "men repeatedly thought she was a different kind of woman than she actually was."[40] In order to challenge and modify these discursive relationships, Eva relies on silence. Her resistance exposes the gaps in the discourse of black women's sexuality as it is defined by the male characters in the text.

"I HAD NEVER SAID JOIN ME BEFORE"

In Eva's storytelling, scenes from her days with Davis in the motel room are intercut with scenes from her childhood. The relations between Eva and Eva's man are punctuated with Davis's probing and Eva's silence, with Davis's interpretations and Eva's resistance. She tells him nothing about herself, yet Davis "knows" what kind of woman Eva is. He tells her that "most women who look like [her] wear earrings" and that she has "the kind of ass that a woman should show off" by wearing tight skirts (18, 54). Davis's reading of Eva is informed by dominant cultural representations of women that are based on both a Woman's looks and her actions. Eva retrospectively speculates on what Davis must have thought (what any man would have thought) of her because of her willingness to engage in sexual relations with him:

> What Elvira said those people think I am [a whore], Davis probably thought so too. It's funny how somebody can remind you of somebody you didn't like, or ended up not liking and fearing—fearing is a better word—but . . . I hadn't said anything to any man in a long time. And I had never said Join me before. He probably thought I was in the habit of sitting there in that dark corner just so men would . . . Yeah, they'd come where I was. "Shit, bitch. Why don't you stay in the house if you don't wont a man to say nothing to you." "Where you from, sweetheart?" "Shit, I know you got a tongue, I ain't never met a bitch that didn't have a tongue." And then when I was standing at the corner that time that man drove his car real close to the curb and opened the door. I just stood there looking at him, and then he slammed the door and went around the curb real quick. "Shit, you the coldest-ass bitch I ever seen in my life." "If you don't want a man to talk to you you ought to . . ."

> (9, ellipses in original)

The above passage illustrates the way Eva makes connections between her time with Davis and her past experiences and impressions. Eva realizes that Davis probably thought she was a whore, or at least whore-like, even though Davis expected, even demanded, a sexual response from her. Davis's understanding of Eva as woman/whore echoes the voices from Eva's past, the same demanding and inscribing voices of men who defined Eva by her sexual function while simultaneously condemning her for it.[41] Jones sets up a narrative structure that conflates Eva's memories into a flattened representation of relations between Eva and all the men she has known. Yet as Eva recollects these men, each relationship is described in terms of Eva's resistance to imposed definitions and emphasizes her strategies to effect self-definition. In her relationships with Freddy Smoot, Tyrone, Alphonso, Moses Tripp, and finally Davis, Eva's (contra)diction and her silences undermine the totalizing male definition of her. Through dissent, silence, and violence, Eva produces an alternative discourse that competes with the circumscribing male discourse in the text.

Eva's first sexual encounter is with the neighbor boy Freddy Smoot. Eva and Freddy are playmates until Freddy initiates a sexual relationship; Eva participates in the sexual encounter the first time but then rejects further contact. Eva says, "After he had that popsicle up in me I wouldn't play with him anymore" (13). Keith Byerman suggests that Eva cooperates in the sex play, but has no desire to repeat it. Freddy's subsequent meetings with Eva focus on Freddy's request to repeat the play, setting up a

demand and rejection pattern. Byerman argues that "[a]ll the other major scenes replicate this initial one. In each, a male attempts to dominate a woman through some forceful act. The woman responds with a combination of passivity and resistance."[42] I would add that Eva's silence is a combination of passivity and resistance, but that it is generally read only as a passive act by the other characters in the novel and by readers. By granting Eva agency as storyteller, in other words, by listening to her own construction of self, one can more easily read Eva's silence as a resistant act. When Freddy persistently attempts to engage Eva in sexual play again both verbally—"You let me do it once"—and physically—cornering Eva to rub up against her, Eva counters Freddy's continuation and interpretation of their play:

> "You let me do it once."

> "I ain't gon let you do it no more."

> "When you gon let me fuck you again, Eva?"

> "You didn't fuck me before."

> (14)

Although the five-year-old Eva refuses a continued relationship with Freddy, she learns that his interpretation of both his and her sexuality is the one condoned by society. When Freddy is with his friends, he initiates a sexual chase of Eva: "There's Eva, we can get some" (19). Despite this pursuit every time Eva is alone, Eva's mother's friend Miss Billie laughingly characterizes Freddy as "just a little banny rooster, all stuck out in front" (67), and Eva's mother simply calls Freddy and his friends who chase Eva "a bunch of wild horses" (20). Neither of the women questions the constructions of sexuality that generate predatory males and victimized females. Instead, they draw on animal imagery to further naturalize the relations between men and women as relations between predator and prey.

Eva's next entrapment into sexual discourse is with Tyrone, her mother's young musician boyfriend. Eva is twelve when her mother begins bringing Tyrone home, and Eva recalls, "I never would say anything to him, and he never said anything to me" (29). But Tyrone breaks the silence between the two of them with a sexual act, taking her hand and placing it on his crotch. Eva pulls away and the relations between the two lapse back into a strained silence, occasionally punctuated with Tyrone's references to the event. Eva refuses to talk to him or about his actions until Tyrone demands a response from her. Confronting her alone on the steps one day, Tyrone says, "You see me, you can speak" (34). He demands that Eva enter into a discourse that will define her through her sexuality. Eva refuses to engage with him either sexually or verbally, contradicting Tyrone's insistence that she is sexually attracted to him with her statement: "I didn't feel nothing" (34). The phrase is a modification of her "I said nothing" refrain and is used for a similarly resistant effect. Tyrone responds with a threatening gesture to Eva's rebellion against the ways that he defines her, and Eva runs to the safety of her house.

The next male character who attempts a sexual/discursive relation with Eva is her married cousin Alphonso, who begins taking Eva to bars when she is seventeen. Because they are related, Alphonso expects Eva to tell him things that she wouldn't tell other men, like whether or not she has "been getting it." Eva truthfully tells him no. Eva's response gives Alphonso the reference point he needs to define Eva as a woman, in other words, to make comparisons that inscribe her in terms of sexual activity. He tells Eva that most girls her age have had the "meat *and the gravy*" (57, emphasis in original). Alphonso repeatedly tells Eva that she is "too old . . . way too old not to had the meat" (58). Like Tyrone, Alphonso collapses the discursive and the sexual, attempting to initiate Eva into both. When his verbal suggestions are repeatedly contradicted, evaded, or ignored by Eva, Alphonso resorts to a physical discourse, grabbing Eva's hand and placing it on his exposed, erect penis. Eva again runs from a forced sexual exchange. When she goes out to the bars again with Alphonso, he tells her that she is "hard on a man" (72). Eva contradicts his interpretation of her by reminding him of their family relationship: "I told you to tell people I'm your cousin. You haven't been telling yourself, have you?" (72). The relation that Alphonso had invoked in order to engage Eva in his sexual discourse is turned against him by Eva's use of it to reject a sexual relation with him. While Eva's discursive strategy is effective in avoiding sexual relations with her cousin, she is again confronted by the inscriptions of women—sweetmeat, bitch, hussy, cunt, whore—that men use to both describe and condemn women through their sexuality.

Although Alphonso continues to insist that Eva's reasons for going out to bars is because she is looking for the meat and gravy, Eva continues to insist that she's "not looking for nobody" (72). When Alphonso leaves Eva alone in the bar one night, Moses Tripp, a man Eva says looked old enough to be her grandfather, attempts to buy a five-dollar feel from Eva. She leaves the bar, enacting the flight strategy she had used with Freddy, Tyrone, and Alphonso, but this time Eva is followed. Eva explains:

> I got up and went out. He followed me out. I was thinking I should've known he'd follow me out.
>
> "Do it for me, huh? Come on, honey. This is my last five."
>
> "Leave me alone."
>
> "Least feel on it for me. That ain't fair. Five dollars for a feel, that ain't . . . Alonso ain't got nothing I . . . Let." He reached for me down between my legs, then he screamed and pulled his hand back. He called me "bitch."
>
> (98, ellipses in original)

With this exchange, Eva makes a transition from a discourse of contradiction and denial into a discourse of violence. Rather than subject herself to the sexual violence of Moses Tripp, she stabs him with the knife that Freddy had given her. The active use of the phallic gift initiates a rejection and subversion of gender roles that Jones carries

through the rest of the novel. Eva's violence also initiates a more resistant and insistent use of silence against those who demand explanation of her actions. She refuses to enter the juridical discourse: "I didn't tell anybody. . . . I just let the man tell his side" (98). Eva's silence functions as a metaphor for the unhearing audience that confronts her. Her refrain of silence underscores the inadequacies of her contradiction: "I didn't answer . . . I said nothing. . . . Nobody knew why I knifed him because I didn't say" (99). What can a bitch-cunt-hussy-whore say that will counter what is inscribed in the dominant male discourse?

"IT WAS JUST THE THING ABOUT THE TELEPHONE"

In addition to emphasizing the pervasive sexual discourse of the male characters, Jones uses a combination of white woman and black woman stereotypes to reveal how Eva's gender identification is constructed. The woman that Eva comes to identify most overtly with is the queen bee. When she is a child, Eva overhears Miss Billie and her mother talking about a woman they call the queen bee because, as Miss Billie explains, "every man she had end up dying. I don't mean natural dying, I mean something happen to them" (17). Although Eva's mother suggests that such a curse would be harder on the woman than the man, since she would not be free to really love a man, Miss Billie and the rest of the community judge the queen bee on her destructive powers. Eva says that she "used to think the queen bee looked like a bee and went around stinging men," but when she sees her for the first time, Eva notes, "[s]he didn't look any different from Mama or Miss Billie or Freddy's mama" (44). As she gets older, Eva learns that in the universalizing discourse of the men, all women are indeed like the queen bee in their destructive capabilities. When Eva stabs Moses Tripp in the hand for reaching between her legs, she is literally enacting the sting of the queen bee. Eva's violence functions on two seemingly contradictory levels: on the one hand, she has become what the dominant discourse says she is—the castrating bitch—on the other, her action challenges the logic of a discourse that expects passivity and sexual victimization from what it fears.

Eva's transition from a discourse of denial and rejection into a discourse of violence both initiates and serves as metaphor for her overt efforts at self-construction. She assumes an active role in constructing an identity that is not imposed on her by men who demand whore-like behavior from her, and she rejects a passive role of victimization.[43] Instead Eva enters a discursive and sexual relationship based on tenderness. Eva marries James Hunn, a man three times her age, who had visited her while she was in the girls' reformatory for her knife attack. Eva moves to Kentucky with Hunn and attends Kentucky State, where their marriage is happy until Eva realizes that as a wife, too, she is limited to always already inscribed interpretations of female sexuality. She recalls, "I didn't know that anything was wrong with him until we moved in this house and there was a telephone there and he said he was going to take the telephone out" (110). When Eva says that she wants to keep the telephone, Hunn tells her no, he doesn't want her lovers calling her. Eva thinks he is joking at first; when she realizes he is not, Eva says, "I told him I didn't have any lovers. He said every woman had lovers. He said he wasn't going to have a telephone in the house so that my lovers could be calling me up and then meeting me some place" (110). Eva is again confronted by a universalizing discourse that overrides her individual identity and self-construction. Eva leaves Hunn after two years, in spite of his continued tenderness toward her. He never turned his temper on her, but "[i]t was just the thing about the telephone" (111). Eva rejects, again, a prescribed role, this time the unfaithful wife. Furthermore, Eva refuses to have her speaking self, symbolized through the importance of the telephone, restricted because of a discourse that conflates access to communication and access to sex.

"IT'S EASIER BEING A WOMAN AND ALONE IN DIFFERENT PLACES THAN IT IS IN THE SAME PLACE"

When Eva leaves Hunn, she constructs an existence for herself comprising work and travel, suggesting a play with and performance of gender roles that denaturalizes cultural codes. Eva spends all her life on the road "just like a man" (75). When Eva begins her recollections, her life is a catalogue of place-names:

> I was in Upstate New York then. I've lived in Kentucky. I've lived in New York City. I been in West Virginia, New Orleans. I just came from out in New Mexico. I just up and went down to New Mexico after I got laid off in Wheeling. they've got tobacco farms in Connecticut. I been there too. I didn't travel so much until after I was married, and that went wrong, and then I said I would just stay alone. It's easier being a woman and alone in different places than it is in the same place.
>
> (5)

Eva's point that it is easier for her to be alone in different places than in the same place indicates her unwillingness to be circumscribed by boundaries either geographic or cultural. Yet it also recalls her strategy of flight from situations in which she is physically or psychologically threatened. Despite her subversion of gender codes, Eva is never far from the material reality of male discourse and oppression. At one of the tobacco factories that she worked in, Eva is offered money for information about whether the black workers were going to vote for a union. Eva refuses the foreman but is made a counteroffer:

> I said that I didn't know how anybody else was going to vote. He asked me how I was going to vote. I said I knew how I was going to vote. He said he had some money for me if I wanted it. I said I didn't know how anybody else was going to vote. He said never mind that. He said he didn't mean that. He said he had some money for me. I said by the time the voting was over, it would be time for me to be back on the road again. He said I didn't seem like I belonged around there anyway. He said I could be on the road before the voting was over. He sent me out and called somebody else in. He said he didn't like people who didn't know how to be grateful.
>
> (75)

Racial and gender oppression intersect in this exchange—if the foreman cannot buy information about the black workers in the factory from her, he will accept sexual favors instead. Both requests stem from his reading of Eva as a black woman and from his assumption of a right to violation.[44] In Eva's telling of the story, she collapses the event with other (mis)readings of her. In this section of the narrative, Eva also refers to Davis's displeasure because she is "hard to get into" (76), to the psychiatrist's insistence that she "open up" so he can help her, to Alphonso's assertion that Eva "frustrates a man" (80). In each case, Eva's resistance is not seen as a strategy to construct a subjectivity in opposition to dominant gender roles but as an unnatural resistance to culturally condoned penetration.

Eva's subversion of gender roles is played out further in the five days she spends with Davis in his room. Jones denaturalizes and destabilizes both male and female roles. Eva and Davis share the role of sexual initiator, but the rest of their roles get mixed up, with slippage back and forth from traditional roles to a reversal of the roles.[45] In the five days Eva spends with Davis in his room, Davis does the domestic chores, refusing to allow Eva to either cook or clean the room. Yet when the landlord presses him for the rent money, Davis responds harshly to Eva's suggestion that she pay for the room. Money and control remain a male prerogative. Eva's looks, as interpreted by Davis, challenge gender codes—she doesn't wear earrings or tight skirts like other women who look like her do. And it is Davis who conflates, across gender lines, two images of destruction:

> You look like a lion, all that hair."
>
> "It's the male lions that have a lot of hair."
>
> "Then you look like a male lion," he said laughing, "Eva Medusa's a lion."
>
> (16)

As the narrative swirls into greater fragmentation, the irony of Davis's naming of Eva as a destructive force is matched by the literalness of Eva's interpretation. The images of debilitation conflate as Eva literalizes the metaphors of Eve—"I squeezed his dick in my teeth. I bit down hard. My teeth in an apple" (128), Medusa—"I'm Medusa, I was thinking. Men look at me and get hard-ons. I turn their dicks to stone" (130), and the queen bee—"The sweet milk in the queen bee's breasts has turned to blood" (132). Eva's denaturalization of the male discourse culminates in the very action that underlies the discourse. The discourse that constructs predatory males and devouring females is carried to its logical conclusion. It is consequently—and ironically—designated as madness.

"DON'T YOU EXPLAIN ME"

Keith Byerman contends that Eva's "madness" demands that we question not only the grounds upon which the judgment is made, but examine also how the designation of madness functions, particularly in the "judgment of madness as an act of domination."[46] Eva's actions, the poisoning and castration of Davis, together with her insistent silence suggest to the "rational" reader that she is insane. Byerman, however, proposes that we examine the implications of labeling Eva insane:

> Eva must be declared insane so that the meaning of her act can be evaded and suppressed. Through the symbolic significance of her violence, she threatens to expose male domination for the dehumanizing and exploitive system that it is. She has challenged, in a primal way, the right of that system to be considered natural and rational. Both her crime and her silence call into question this particular universe of discourse.[47]

Eva's madness, then, denaturalizes both the dominant male discourse that relegates her to dual roles of whore and castrator and the logic that designates her mad for performing these roles.

In addition to challenging naturalized systems of domination, Eva's silences function to refuse validation of the psychiatric monologue generated about her. In the final pages of the novel, a long "dialogue" is recorded between Eva and the prison psychiatrist. The passage is marked by Eva's refusal to speak confessionally within the discourse of psychiatry. While the psychiatrist prompts Eva to tell him about herself, Eva consistently resists his violation and interpretation of her through silence, contradiction, and violence. At one point, Eva tells the psychiatrist, "don't look at me. don't make people look at me" (168). She echoes and expands her resistance a few moments later, saying, "don't explain me. don't you explain me. don't explain me" (173). Despite her resistance, the psychiatrist continues to "explain" Eva. The passage ends with the suggestion that violence is again Eva's only recourse to resist interpretative violation:

> You thought you were a bad woman, so you went out and got you a bad man.
>
> don't explain me.
>
> And then you . . . Matron? Matron! Hold her! Hold her!
>
> (174, ellipses in original)

In *Madness and Civilization*, Foucault contends that silence is the underlying foundation for discourse about the mad: the emergence of psychiatry as a profession "thrusts into oblivion all those stammered, imperfect words without fixed syntax in which the exchange between madness and reason was made. The language of psychiatry, which is the monologue of reason *about* madness, has been established only on the basis of such a silence."[48] The silencing of Eva is necessary for the discourse on madness; her resistant silence, however, counters and delegitimizes the psychiatrist's (as well as the reader's) interpretive authority.

Foucault's genealogies of madness, prisons, and sexuality reveal how power is deployed and subjects are created through discourse. As Jana Sawicki explains, "ways of knowing are equated with ways of exercising power over individuals."[49] In a similar fashion, Jones's *Eva's Man* reveals how the subject Eva Medina Canada is created by her resistance to power exercised through discursive and disciplinary institutions. Eva's silence can be read as an act of agency that denaturalizes and subverts imposed silences. Sawicki contends that Foucault's strategy of genealogical critique is offered as an alternative to traditional—and totalizing—revolutionary theories that posit an oppressive force and a subjugated victim:

> [G]enealogy as resistance involves using history to give voice to the marginal and submerged voices which lie "a little beneath history"—the voices of the mad, the delinquent, the abnormal, the disempowered. It locates many discontinuous and regional struggles against power both in the past and present. These voices are the sources of resistance, the creative subjects of history.[50]

I would suggest that literary works such as *Eva's Man* also give voice to marginal and submerged voices.[51] Eva's voice, through its dissent, silence, and violence, is the source of resistance in the text that both constitutes her subjectivity and allows her to modify the power wielded over her. By creating a character revealed only through her resistant subjectivity, Jones refuses to allow Eva to be violated by either the knowing subjects *in* the text (other characters) or the knowing subjects *of* the text (readers). My reading of *Eva's Man* ultimately suggests that while Eva is "unknowable," the meaning of her silence is not inaudible.

(RE)READING GAYL JONES'S *EVA'S MAN*

The possibility I have been exploring here is that Jones's work and, to some extent, the writer herself, were silenced by the disciplinary function of the interpretive communities of the 1970s. Madhu Dubey's recent analysis of *Eva's Man* focuses on its utter incompatibility with the "functional reading codes" of the Black Aesthetic:

> The most subversive moments of *Eva's Man* are shrouded in an incoherence that seriously jeopardizes the reader's interpretive function, and prevents us from distilling any clear meaning from the text. It seems almost as if the novel must disclaim its right to meaning altogether if it cannot posit the clear, didactic meaning required by the Black Aesthetic. *Eva's Man* renders itself unreadable, as it were, in order both to escape the functional reading codes of the Black Aesthetic and to obscure its own refusal of these codes.[52]

The text's resistance to reading codes—of the Black Aesthetic as well as the codes required by mainstream (white) literary audiences—is mimicked throughout the text by Eva's resistance to reading codes of both the hegemonic culture and the ambiguously (non)hegemonic culture of black male domination. At the time of its publication, this narrative and thematic strategy functioned to refuse the novel entrance into either feminist or black nationalist literary study. The text strained the limits of the oppositional discourses of the 1970s—*Eva's Man* presents neither a female subject achieving self-definition nor an African American subject breaking free of stereotypes imposed by the dominant white culture.[53]

My (re)reading of *Eva's Man* is intended to suggest that, at the present cultural/critical moment, it is both useful and desirable to open the novel to new reading possibilities. Certainly, one element of the value of Jones's novel is in its exposure of the gaps and inconsistencies in both the dominant and subdominant discourses of the 1970s. I would also argue, however, that it is important to reread *Eva's Man* through its resistance to and denaturalization of the silence and essentialism imposed upon black female subjectivity by hegemonic white patriarchal discourse and the ambiguously (non)hegemonic discourses of white women and black men. In the nearly twenty years since the publication of *Eva's Man*, African American women writers have generated formally complex and thematically compelling works in black women's poetry, fiction, criticism, and political and literary theory. Resistance to dominant and subdominant constructions of black female subjectivity has resulted in the creation of new discourses, through which African American writers, as well as critics and theorists, have problematized notions of an essential black identity in literary and cultural studies. While Jones has not produced any fiction for the reading public since the 1970s, recent paperback publications suggest the possibility that new audiences exist for her fiction.[54] If *Eva's Man* can be reassessed and revalued by present interpretive communities, perhaps there can emerge a receptive audience for more of Gayl Jones's fiction.

Notes

1. Michael S. Harper, "Gayl Jones: An Interview," *Massachusetts Review* 18 (1977): 711.

2. Ibid., 712.

3. Mae Gwendolyn Henderson, foreword to *White Rat*, by Gayl Jones (Boston: Northeastern University Press, 1991), xi.

4. Ibid.

5. June Jordan accuses Jones of reinscribing the "'crazy whore'/'castrating bitch' images that long have defamed black women in our literature." "All about Eva," *New York Times Book Review*, 16 May 1976, 37.

6. Loyle Hairston calls *Eva's Man* an "awful little book" and interprets it as "a study in male hostility." "Repelling World of Sexual Violence," *Freedomways* 16 (Second Quarter 1976): 133. Though less judgmental than many reviewers, Darryl Pinckney also concludes that "Gayl Jones's novels are, finally, indictments against black men." Darryl Pinckney, review of *Eva's Man, New Republic*, 19 June 1976, 27.

7. W. Lawrence Hogue, *Discourse and the Other: The Production of the Afro-American Text* (Durham: Duke University Press, 1986), 5.

8. Ibid., 3.

9. Ibid., 6.

10. African American theorists and critics who have pointed out the exclusionary nature of American literary study and have offered alternative theories of literature include Robert Stepto, *From behind the Veil* (Urbana: University of Illinois Press, 1979); Houston A. Baker, Jr., *Blues Ideology and Afro-American Literature: A Vernacular Theory* (Chicago: University of Chicago Press, 1984); Henry Louis Gates, Jr., *The Signifying Monkey: A Theory of Afro-American Literary Criticism* (New York: Oxford University Press, 1988); and Michael Awkward, "Race, Gender, and the Politics of Reading," *Black American Literature Forum* 22, no. 1 (1988): 5–27. African American feminist theorists and critics who have pointed out the exclusionary nature of both mainstream literary study and the male bias of African American study include Barbara Christian, *Black Women Novelists: Development of a Tradition* (Westport, CT: Greenwood Press, 1980); Gloria T. Hull, Patricia Bell-Scott, and Barbara Smith, eds., *All the Women Are White, All the Blacks Are Men, But Some of Us Are Brave* (New York: Feminist Press, 1982); Deborah E. McDowell, "New Directions for Black Feminist Criticism," *Black American Literature Forum* 14, no. 4 (1980): 153–73; idem, "Boundaries: Or Distant Relations and Close Kin," in *Afro-American Literary Study in the 1990s*, ed. Houston A. Baker, Jr. and Patricia Redmond (Chicago: University of Chicago Press, 1989); and Nellie McKay, "Reflections on Black Women Writers: Revising the Literary Canon," in *Feminisms*, ed. Robyn R. Warhol and Diane Price Herndl (New Brunswick: Rutgers University Press, 1991).

11. Barbara Herrnstein Smith, *Contingencies of Value: Alternative Perspectives for Critical Theory* (Cambridge: Harvard University Press, 1988), 11.

12. By "social positioning," I am referring to how one's race, gender, class, and sexuality affect one's speaking position through degrees of privilege and/or marginality.

13. Mary Helen Washington, ed., *Black-Eyed Susans/Midnight Birds: Stories by and about Black Women* (New York: Anchor Press/Doubleday, 1990), 15.

14. Hogue, 55.

15. Madhu Dubey, *Black Women Novelists and the Nationalist Aesthetic* (Bloomington: Indiana University Press, 1994), 12.

16. Ibid., 15.

17. Smith, 40.

18. Jones uses this term while discussing her graduate study at Brown, where she had "time to write" and a "first reader" whom she admired and trusted. Charles H. Rowell, "An Interview with Gayl Jones," *Callaloo* 5, no. 3 (1982): 53.

19. The interview with Jones was conducted for inclusion in Michael S. Harper and Robert B.

Stepto, eds., *Chant of Saints: A Gathering of Afro-American Literature, Art, and Scholarship* (Chicago: University of Illinois Press, 1979). The anthology initially appeared in two issues of the *Massachusetts Review* in the fall and winter of 1977.

20. Claudia C. Tate, "An Interview with Gayl Jones," *Black American Literature Forum* 13, no. 4 (1979): 142.

21. Ibid.

22. In discussing the chronology of Jones's publications, Bell misnames one of Jones's works as a novel: "Since the interview was conducted, she has published a second novel. *Eva's Man*, and a third, *Almeyda*, as well as a collection of short stories called *White Rat*." Roseann P. Bell, "Gayl Jones Takes a Look at *Corregidora*," in *Sturdy Black Bridges: Visions of Black Women in Literature*, ed. Roseann P. Bell. Bettye J. Parker, and Beverly Guy-Sheftall (Garden City, NY: Anchor Press, 1979), 282. Excerpts from a longer work appeared in *Chant of Saints* under the title of "Almeyda." The work was an early version of *Palmares*, which Jones had told Claudia Tate in 1978 would be published soon as a novel, but which appeared in 1981 in the form of a long poem, *Song for Anninho*.

23. Jefferson's review of *Eva's Man* ends with a comment by Jefferson about Jones's writing style and personal reticence: "Gayl Jones writes rapidly and obsessively: she has completed two more novels and is at work on a fifth. She will not discuss it, which is just as well. Her imagination seems to thrive on outstripping one's expectations." Margo Jefferson, "A Woman Alone," *Newsweek*, 12 April 1976, 107.

24. Jones names five works that she had written but not published at the time of the interview: *Palmares* (a "straight dramatic novel" from which *Song for Anninho* was adapted), a collection of short stories called *The Straw Woman*, a novel in which the main character is named after the Brazilian trickster turtle Jaboti, a novel titled *The Birdcatcher*, and a work (the genre is unspecified) titled *The Stone Dragon*.

25. Tate, 148.

26. Rowell, 40.

27. Gayl Jones, "About My Work," in *Black Women Writers (1950–1980): A Critical Evaluation*, ed. Mari Evans (Garden City, NY: Anchor-Doubleday, 1984), 235.

28. Mae Gwendolyn Henderson uses the phrase "ambiguously (non)hegemonic" to describe the discursive status of both white women, a group privileged by race and oppressed by gender, and black men, a group privileged by gender, and oppressed by race. It seems an appropriate description of the status of white feminist reviewers and black nationalist reviewers of *Eva's Man* in the 1970s.

29. Rowell, 33.

30. Tate, 143.

31. Susan J. Hekman, *Gender and Knowledge: Elements of a Postmodern Feminism* (Boston: Northeastern University Press, 1990), 73.

32. Ibid.

33. Gayl Jones, *Eva's Man* (New York: Random House, 1976), 7–8. Subsequent references to this work are included parenthetically in the text.

34. Michel Foucault, *The History of Sexuality: An Introduction* (New York: Vintage Books, 1990), 59.

35. Ibid., 63.

36. Ibid., 61.

37. Ibid., 27.

38. Ibid.

39. Hogue is adapting Foucault's concept of discursive relations as developed in *The Archaeology of Knowledge*. Hogue says that in a literary text, certain discursive facts are repeated "with the intention of generating what Foucault calls an 'enunciation'—the object or statement of discourse—within the text" (67).

40. Tate, 146.

41. The sexual discourse of the men universalizes all women into whores, but Eva maintains a sense of individual female subjectivity in her descriptions of the women she has known. Even though her mother's infidelity is treated by her father as whore-like behavior—"Act like a whore, I'm gonna fuck you like a whore" (37)—and Alphonso and his wife act out a beating ritual for Jean's infidelity, Eva distinguishes between behavior and identity—she says that Freddy's mother, a prostitute, was the only whore she ever knew.

42. Keith Byerman, "Black Vortex: The Gothic Structure of *Eva's Man*," *MELUS* 7 (1980): 95.

43. The significance of Eva's action is "unheard" by her family: her mother infantilizes her—"I thought it was a play knife, Mama said . . . if she'd known it was a real knife she would have taken it away from me"; her father interprets her as passive and incapable of action—"Daddy said it all didn't sound like Eva"; and her cousin contends that Eva must have been physically violated—"Alphonso said Moses must've done something to me, but they gave me this test, and couldn't find that he'd done anything" (98—99). Eva refuses to say why she stabbed Moses Tripp, even to her family, because they too already have her limited to certain categories.

44. In "About My Work," Jones briefly discusses the theme that recurs in her writing—the complexity of the intersection of racism and sexism: "In terms of personal/private relationships I suppose I'm more

besieged as a woman. In terms of public/social relationships I suppose I'm more besieged as a Black. Being both, It's hard to sometimes distinguish the occasion for being 'besieged'" (234).

45. Jones creates an equally interesting play with gender roles and gender performance when Alphonso points out a transvestite to Eva: "You see that bitch over there? That ain't really no bitch, That's a bastard. Dress up like a woman and then come in here. Shit. He don't bother the men that knows him. Most of us know what he is. He just pick up on the men that don't. Most of the ones that hang around here don't fool with him. Sometimes she makes pickups, drunks or strangers. They find out right quick, though. They start messing around her. Naw, I don't even git drunk when I come in here, cause I know how I do when I'm drunk. I wouldn't get mixed up with that bastard for nothing. Wake up the next morning and find *his* wig in my face. Shit" (78–79). The literal cross-dressing and linguistic slippage between gender pronouns signify the instability of gender as a fixed identity. Judith Butler notes that the notion of a primary gender identity is parodied through such performative acts as drag and cross-dressing: "As much as drag creates a unified picture of 'woman' (what its [feminist] critics often oppose), it also reveals the distinctness of those aspects of gendered experience which are falsely naturalized as a unity through the regulatory fiction of heterosexual coherence. In imitating gender, drag implicitly reveals the imitative structure of gender itself." Judith Butler, "Gender Trouble, Feminist Theory, and Psychoanalytic Discourse," in *Feminism/Postmodernism*, ed. Linda Nicholson (New York: Routledge, 1990), 338.

46. Keith Byerman, *Fingering the Jagged Grain: Tradition and Form in Recent Black Fiction* (Athens: University of Georgia Press, 1985), 184.

47. Ibid.

48. Michel Foucault, *Madness and Civilization: A History of Insanity in the Age of Reason* (New York: Pantheon Books, 1965), x-xi.

49. Jana Sawicki, *Discipling Foucault: Feminism, Power, and the Body* (New York: Routledge, 1991), 32.

50. Ibid., 28.

51. In the concluding chapter of *Madness and Civilization*, Foucault suggests that our only confrontation with madness, since the rise of the psychiatric profession, comes through aesthetic representations and that "by the madness which interrupts it, a work of art opens a void, a moment of silence, a question without answer, provokes a breach without reconciliation where the world is forced to question itself" (288).

52. Dubey, 89.

53. The interpretive communities who reviewed *Eva's Man* were particularly disturbed by Jones's use of

sexual stereotypes as well as her textual representations of black men. Jones's editor at Random House, Toni Morrison, said that publishing *Eva's Man* was an "editorial risk" because of the similarities between Jones's two novels. Morrison said she considered the possibility that readers might say that all of Jones's books were "about women tearing up men" (qtd. in Keith Mano, "How to Write Two First Novels with Your Knuckles," *Esquire* [December 1976]: 66). In the 1978 interview, after the initial furor over *Eva's Man*, Claudia Tate asks Jones to explain why she used three pervasive symbols—queen bee, Medusa, and Eve biting the apple—that have been "very detrimental to men in our cultural history" (146). Jones explains that she "put those images in the story to show how myths or ways in which men perceive women actually define their characters" (146). In the 1982 interview with Charles Rowell, Jones says that she has come to see sex, as subject matter, problematic for African American writers "because when you write about anything dealing with sexuality it appears as if you're supporting the sexual stereotypes about blacks" (47). As a counter to the negative criticism about Jones's use of stereotypes, Madhu Dubey contends that attention to the formal elements of Jones's fiction reveal that rather than reinscribing the stereotype of the primitive black, Jones is deconstructing stereotypes that represent black identity: "*Eva's Man* repeats and recycles a limited number of sexual stereotypes in a stylized manner that forces us to regard black sexuality as a textual fabrication rather than a natural essence" (95).

54. Deborah E. McDowell's *Black Women Writers Series* published *Corregidora* in 1986 and *Eva's Man* in 1987 through Beacon Press, while Northeastern University Press published a paperback edition of *White Rat* in 1991.

Valerie Boyd (review date 1 March 1998)

SOURCE: "Faith in Herself," in *Washington Post Book World*, Vol. 28, No. 5, March 1, 1998, p. 9.

[*In the following review of* The Healing, *Boyd remarks favorably on the novel's characters and plot but argues that Jones fails to provide enough details.*]

Like a bright idea, Gayl Jones first beamed onto the American literary landscape in the mid-1970s, when Toni Morrison—then an editor at Random House—introduced Jones's first two novels. *Corregidora* and *Eva's Man* both earned glowing reviews.

James Baldwin called *Corregidora* "the most brutally honest and painful revelation of what has occurred, and is occurring, in the souls of Black men and women." In praise of *Eva's Man*, John Updike called Jones "an American writer with a powerful sense of vital inheritance, of history in the blood." On the heels of such high praise, Jones virtually disappeared from the American literary scene. Walking away from a tenured professorship at the University of Michigan, she retreated to Europe in the early '80s after an unspecified "incident of racial injustice," according to a statement issued by her publisher. While living in France, Jones quietly published a novel in Germany as her growing community of U.S. readers wondered if we'd ever hear from her again.

Now Gayl Jones is back, with her first U.S. novel in more than 20 years. But Jones's literary comeback has been tragically overshadowed by recent dramatic events in her life. On Feb. 24, *The Washington Post* reported that Jones's husband, Bob Jones (a k a Bob Higgins) killed himself during a standoff with Lexington, Ky., police over a 15-year-old weapons conviction. Saying she was suicidal, police committed Gayl Jones to emergency detention in a state psychiatric hospital, where she may remain for up to a year. After these latest surreal developments, readers are again left wondering if we'll ever hear from Jones again.

For now, though, we have her ironically titled new novel, *The Healing*. This book—disturbing to read in light of the recent news reports—makes it clear why *Kirkus Reviews* once wrote: "Gayl Jones is some furious, lacerating writer. You don't read her easily, and you can't forget her at all."

As *The Healing* opens, we enter the stream-of-consciousness of Harlan Jane Eagleton as she rides a bus into the small town where she is to perform a faith healing. To the working-class, churchgoing black people in this community—and in the countless other towns she's already visited—Harlan is known simply as the Healing Woman. Through a series of delightfully nonlinear flashbacks, however, Jones reveals Harlan to be much more complex than the small-town believers and skeptics imagine.

In the first two chapters, Jones prepares readers to experience Harlan's healing magic and to watch her transform the lives of the townsfolk. But by the fourth or fifth chapter, we realize that Jones has pulled a literary sleight of hand and that the novel isn't about the town's transformation at all. Instead, it is about Harlan's own transformation from manager of a minor rock star to a traveling faith healer.

This is not an evangelistic tale of great revelations or mystical messages. Harlan is, in some ways, exactly what her skeptics think she is: an ordinary woman. But she's not a charlatan, and she's not a saint Jones allows Harlan to tell her own story, to guide readers down the worldly road that led her to her "spirit gift," as she calls it.

Along the way, we meet a fascinating array of characters, including Joan, the self-indulgent rock star Harlan manages; Harlan's grandmother, who claims she used to be a

turtle; Harlan's mentally disturbed sister-in-law, Cayenne, who snaps out of her Elvis Presley reverie long enough to make some startlingly insightful observations about Harlan; and Nicholas Love, the man who witnessed Harlan's first healing—of herself.

The problem with the story is that Harlan is telling it. As a narrator, she is not as articulate, introspective or revealing as readers might wish her to be—or as we know Jones to be. The novelist has created an intriguing plot and a well-written portrait of a remarkable character, but we only get to see Harlan—and all the others—through her own limited vision. As you read Harlan's version of the story, you can't help but long for Jones to step in as an eloquent, omniscient, third-person narrator who can tell us what's really going on.

Near the end of the novel, Harlan demands of a lover. "Tell me your whole story." He wisely responds: "No one ever tells their whole story." And That's the irony—and the fundamental flaw—of this novel: We never get to hear Harlan's whole story because she's the one who's telling it.

Still, *The Healing* marks the long-awaited return—and perhaps the final how—of a major literary talent. The novel's shortcomings won't change anyone's essential view of Gayl Jones's fiction. She remains an important, graceful writer who deserves readers' attention. Reading, her inventive prose and earthy dialogue is its own reward.

Judith Grossman (review date March 1998)

SOURCE: "Love's Reward," in *Women's Review of Books*, Vol. XV, No. 6, March, 1998, pp. 15-6.

[*In the following review of* The Healing, *Grossman states that the book differs from Jones's earlier works but that her humanistic romance is as moving as her previous novels.*]

The appearance of this novel by Gayl Jones, the first since her powerful debut in the 1970s with *Corregidora* and *Eva's Man*, is a notable event indeed. As her publishers report it, by the end of that decade Jones had abandoned her successful career as a fiction writer and teacher at the University of Michigan following "an incident of racial injustice." Exiling herself to Europe for several years, she continued to write fiction, plays and poetry, occasionally publishing with small presses. Now, with *The Healing*, Jones announces a welcome return to the American scene, thematically and otherwise.

I found it hard (as many will) to read the new novel without recalling the impact of Jones' early fiction—specifically, her portrayal of lives under extreme compulsion, from both external forces and a tyrannical and violent eros within. With all their stripped-down contemporaneity, those fiercely deterministic narratives belonged to the lineage of fictional naturalism—traced back through Richard Wright, perhaps, to elements in Eugene O'Neill and Theodore Dreiser. For such a writer, whose imagination moved in closed circles of victimage, passion and revenge, the question of how to go forward must have presented a challenge. *The Healing* is Gayl Jones' answer, offering at once continuity and surprise.

what's immediately familiar is the characteristic immersion in a Woman's voice taking up a story already in progress. In *The Healing* that voice belongs to Harlan Jane Eagleton, itinerant faith healer with an adventurous past, riding a bus to the small Southern town where she's scheduled to make her next appearance. However, unlike Eva Canada of *Eva's Man*, whose notoriety is alluded to here in passing, Harlan doesn't speak in the intense, spare mode of tragic closure. As she reflects on the congregation she is scheduled to meet that evening, her spoken idiom—informally recursive, even chatty—places her closer to the world of comedy.

> Of course they's always three kinds of people there: them that believes without questioning those that believe only when It's themselves being healed, and those who could suck a cactus dry—they ain't got cactus in this region, but the region I just come from, little town name Cuba, New Mexico—and'ud still tell you it ain't got no juice in it. I'll tell y'all the truth. If I wasn't the one doing the healing, I'd be among the tough nuts.
>
> (p. 9)

Dressed as she is in blue jeans and a bomber jacket, utterly without social or spiritual pretensions, Harlan understands well the scepticism of some of her hosts. And yet experience has shown her the actuality of her gift, the first proof of which was her own self-healing in a deadly knife attack. Harlan Eagleton, we are to know, is that real, unexplainable thing: the bearer of a power to recognize the sufferers before her, and to heal them.

On this evening, a figure from Harlan's past turns up in the congregation: Josef, her former lover, whom she met at Saratoga one summer while betting on horses, and who hopes to win her back. After the healing session he speaks to her, and even though Harlan knows that her life has changed beyond his recognition, the encounter propels her into a labyrinth of memory. Through a series of flashbacks, we trace Harlan's beginnings in the Louisville beauty parlor owned by her mother and grandmother, where her grandmother tells about her years spent playing "Turtle Woman" in a carnival, until she loved a man so much that, as she puts it, "I followed him until I turned into a human being." These words become a refrain in the book, as the young Harlan marries, then leaves her much-loved husband, Norvelle, out of jealousy over his studies with an African medicine-woman, and travels the world as business manager to a minor rock singer, Joan Savage.

Joan, a flamboyant performer with a cult following, plays a complex role in Harlan's story. Part soul-sister and mentor, part temperamental genius, part demonic threat, she will ultimately become the catalyst for Harlan's spiritual accession. A tough challenge for any writer to take on, and Gayl Jones rises to her creation with nerve and a palpable enjoyment. Here is Joan's first entrance, standing in the doorway watching, while her former husband makes love to Harlan:

> She has a handful of yellow hair sticking up, looking like Don King's. She's wearing faded green gaucho trousers and a bright purple tank top and a purple bandanna, worn like the cowgirls wear. Chewing a pear, she watches us with an air of nonchalance and tepid curiosity like you'd watch reruns on an old TV.
>
> (p. 67)

For drama is Joan's element, which she not only seeks but creates—even to the perverse extent of setting up this damaging affair.

The magnetism she exerts seems credible, at first. Later, however, as Joan's sexual jealousy spins out of control, Harlan's loyalty to her friend and employer becomes a puzzling factor—except as a requirement of the plot. Especially when Harlan is cast as the meek disciple to Joan, whose intelligence her scientist ex-husband claims as "world-class," the narrative voice stumbles into awkwardness. For instance, just after the scene in which Joan has spied on her ex-husband's lovemaking, Harlan segues abruptly into an elaboration of Joan's views on a popular novel:

> That novel supposed to be about a colored cowgirl. 'Cept she say that novel ain't true popular fiction, it just satirizes the popular fiction. She say it uses the techniques of the popular novel to satirize the popular novel, but she also say this Amanda Wordlaw thinks that African-American writers oughta be able to write "the popular novel" and not just the Great African-American Novels. You know, like some book reviewers think that African-American writers are only supposed to write the Great African-American Novel.
>
> (p. 69)

Not that Joan doesn't have a commonsense point—but the break from context in this scene appears merely willed by Jones, thus putting Harlan the narrator-character in a bizarrely false position, as the surrogate speaker, it seems, for another surrogate. Again, in the middle of a scene between Harlan and Josef, Joan's reported views on race and religion intrude with minimal relevance:

> 'Cept them original Christians wasn't fair-haired, amongst the Mediterranean peoples. They mythologizes that Christianity. So them Europeans have always been kinda ambivalent about they aesthetics. I don't know whether she read that in one of them nonfiction books. . . .
>
> (p. 93)

Here, although the jarring mixture of academic and black English may be justified in the speech of a character like Harlan, positioned between disparate social worlds, the narrative logic in the passage remains a problem. So also does the author's division of the goods of this fictional universe between Joan and Harlan, allocating the domain of intellect to shared, though volatile, friendship between these two women, their dialogue of challenge-and-response, to sustain the central sections of the book. When that falters, and when Jones relies on Harlan's narrative voice alone, with its unedited veerings into garrulity and laboriousness, I found myself losing track of the writer's initial vision.

And *The Healing* does, surely, have a vision at stake. Harlan and Joan are both believers in "the one great love," embodied for each in the man she originally married. For Harlan, that man is Norvelle; and her transient affairs since leaving him only serve to convince her that she chose rightly the first time. Gayl Jones is telling us here an ultimately benign tale of love guiding a progress into humanity—as unafraid as her fictional writer Amanda Wordlaw of its frankly romantic agenda and the turn from a closed to an open destiny for her characters. Thus Harlan becomes fully human through her quietly learned and sustained commitment to Norvelle, and her loyal service and friendship to Joan. As a mark of that achievement the gift for healing emerges, canceling out Joan's irrational hatred, and setting in motion Norvelle's return.

The guiding structure of *The Healing*, as I read it, is that of classical high romance, in which lovers are separated until a series of ordeals and initiations (as in *Parzifal*, or *The Magic Flute*) has prepared them for the transcendent humanity That's celebrated in their reunion. An unexpected move, certainly, for the writer of *Corregidora*, but in its own way just as bold.

Jill Nelson (review date 25 May 1998)

SOURCE: "Hiding from Salvation," in *The Nation*, Vol. 266, No. 19, May 25, 1998, pp. 30-32.

[*In the review below, Nelson praises the language, character development, and message of* The Healing.]

There was a time, not all that long ago, when writers could choose to be private people. People who spoke through words on a page, identifiable by the way they used language, a turn of phrase, a subject often written about, more obviously by their name on a title page. There was a time, I think, when most writers preferred it that way. But those days are long gone, swallowed up by television, the grind of book tours, the gobbling up of small publishing houses by conglomerates, America's erasure of the line between celebrity and talent. Nowadays, too often the writer as personality/celebrity is either indistinguishable from or overtakes the written word. "I'm famous, therefore I'm good" might well be their mantra.

Gayl Jones, whose first novel in twenty years, *The Healing*, was published to great fanfare in February by Beacon Press—the only original novel published by that house in its 144-year history—is an extremely private writer living in an extremely public time. The fact that she had not published or been otherwise heard from in twenty years attests to this, as does the absence of even the smallest of author photos on the dust jacket and the lack of any book tour or media appearances.

In this era, the absence of hype—of either book or self—might be seen as a bold, risky move, a writer letting her work stand on its own. Then *Newsweek*, while heralding the publication of *The Healing* as "a major literary event," included in what was more profile than review information about Jones and her husband, the former Bob Higgins, who took Jones's name when they married. In 1983 Higgins had been arrested after exhibiting bizarre behavior and bringing a gun to a gay rights rally in Ann Arbor, Michigan, where Jones was a tenured professor at the university. The couple left town before the trial, and Higgins was convicted in absentia. After living for several years in Europe, they quietly returned to Lexington, Kentucky, Jones's birthplace. Apparently, Higgins had been writing threatening letters and acting strange in Lexington as well. A member of the sheriff's department read the *Newsweek* article and decided to arrest Bob Jones for the prior conviction. Surrounded by police, barricaded in their home, Gayl and Bob Jones threatened suicide after apparently filling the house with gas. The police waited three hours and rushed the front door. Bob Jones cut his throat with a butcher knife. Gayl Jones has been in a mental hospital, under suicide watch.

It is difficult not to feel that this tragedy could have been avoided had Jones's well-documented reclusiveness been respected, had her work been allowed to succeed—or fail—on its own merits. Yet at the same time, all of us, writers and readers both, understand the lure of the personal, the often prurient desire to know the private details of others' lives. Ultimately, the blame must fall on the culture of celebrity, and the concurrent disrespect for the rights of privacy that many of us cultivate and encourage. The death of Bob Jones and collapse of the supremely talented Gayl Jones should make us all examine under a harsh light the contemporary assumption that the public has a right to know everything about everyone's personal life.

The Healing is the story of Harlan Jane Eagleton, a beautician turned manager of an obnoxious female rock star who then becomes a faith healer. It is a haunting story, beautifully written, rich with humor and intelligence. Jones's first novel, *Corregidora*, published in 1975, was the story of a woman trapped by the violence of her history; her second, *Eva's Man*, plumbed the same material. While *The Healing* doesn't ignore the power of history or violence, its focus is on reconciliation and forgiveness, our ability to escape the violence that is visited upon us, to heal first ourselves and, like Harlan Jane Eagleton, those around us.

The Healing is a tale told backward, unfolding with an offhand seductiveness that leaves the reader breathless.

The command of language is spectacular, as is the breadth of knowledge and allusions casually tossed into Harlan's tale. I chuckled at Jones's literary audacity, marveling at her ability to weave together dialogue, history and references to pop culture. About that healing:

> I lay my hands on a young woman suffering from a skin rash and immediately her skin become smooth and clear as a baby's. A elderly woman suffers from a bone ailment that make her lower back painful. I lay my hands on and she strengthens, healthy, then bends forward and touches her toes. A baby's got chronic earache; I kiss both its little ears and they's made whole again. Gurgling and laughing, he don't wanna let go of my fingers. Then they's a young man who I'm unable to heal in public, 'cause it necrospermia he's suffering from, so before he comes forward I ask Nicholas to go inform him that we'll come privately to his home and heal him, and then he can expect that wife of his to have babies the very next year.

And once the healing is done:

> Must tire you out so all them healings, says Martha. Although she's made all that strawberry pie and all them sweet cakes, she's only got a little corn pudding on her plate. I healed her colitis years ago, but she still just nibbles.
>
> I don't feel it while I'm healing. While I'm healing I feel energized. It's just afterwards that I do get sort of tired out.
>
> While *He's* healing, corrects Zulinda.
>
> Yeah, That's what I meant.
>
> Martha stands in front of me like a shield, then leads me up them basement stairs. The teacher-woman looks like she wants to follow us, but she stays eating her strawberry pie. When I glance back, she's talking to Big Sal. Sane women again.
>
> Then you shouldn't be tired, you, says Zulinda, from behind.

Jones's ability to create bizarre yet believable characters is magical, requiring a subtle act of faith between writer and reader. While it may seem incongruous that the leather-jacketed, rock-music-loving, sexually liberated Harlan is a true healer, Jones offers us just the right pieces of odd his-

tory that will allow us to believe. About Harlan's grandmother she writes:

> She played the Turtle Woman. You know how them carnivals got them the Bearded Lady. Well, they's got Turtle Women and Crocodile Women and every type of freakish womanhood. They had her in one of them carnival tents and people paid their money to come and see the Turtle Woman. In those days, I think it only cost them a nickel or a dime to see the Turtle Woman or them other freakish women. . . . But that was considered good money in those days. They put a nacre shell on her back. A fake shell to pretend like she was part turtle and part woman. I don't even know if they paid her good money to be their Turtle Woman, but I guess they paid her better money than they were paying domestics in those days, but not as good money as they paid them factory workers, you know.

The Healing is so rich it is difficult to put down. The pity is that its publication, which should have been a purely joyous event, is surrounded by such tragedy. The hope is that Jones, able to write so compellingly of healing, will be able to heal herself. As for the rest of us, we should read this book and take a lesson from Harlan Jane Eagleton:

> What were her first healing? She healed herself. Aw, girl, you don't believe that! Yes, I believe it, 'cause That's the proof of a true healer. They's got to heal they-self first. You's got to work your own salvation first. . . . But ain't none of them religious books works your salvation for you. There's people that hides from they own salvation, but even they's got to work they own salvation first.

FURTHER READING

Criticism

Chambers, Veronica. "The Invisible Woman Reappears—Sort of." *Newsweek* CXXXI, No. 7 (16 February 1998): 68.

    Remarks on *The Healing* and summarizes Jones's life.

Additional coverage of Jones's life and career is contained in the following sources published by the Gale Group: *Black Literature Criticism*, Vol. 2; *Black Writers*, Vol. 2; *Contemporary Authors*, Vols. 77-80; *Contemporary Authors New Revision Series*, Vols. 27, 66; *Contemporary Literary Criticism*, Vols. 6, 9; *Dictionary of Literary Biography*, Vol. 33; *DISCovering Authors Modules: Multicultural*; and *Major 20th-Century Writers*, Vols. 1, 2.

Paul Tillich
1886-1965

German-born American philosopher, writer, essayist, and Protestant theologian.

The following entry presents an overview of Tillich's career through 1991.

INTRODUCTION

Tillich was a renowned American Protestant theologian. As a self-proclaimed philosophical theologian, Tillich saw the very nature of Christian faith expressed in religious symbols that demanded constant reinterpretation. Tillich sought to blend traditional Christianity with current modes of thinking regarding science, sociology, and ethics in order to illuminate Christianity as meaningful in modern life. He felt it necessary to create a unified Christian realism in order to meet the needs of religious people adrift in the scientific and technological universe of the 1950s. Tillich concerned himself with the lonely and alienated "contemporary" man and his pseudo-philosophical cloak "existentialism," which Tillich sought to integrate with the religious basis of human life, seeing religion as a "unifying center" for existence.

BIOGRAPHICAL INFORMATION

Tillich was born in Prussia and was the son of a Lutheran pastor. He studied theology at the Universities of Berlin, Tuebingen, and Halle, and earned his Ph.D. from the University of Breslau and the Licentiate in Theology from Halle. Tillich was ordained a minister of Germany's Evangelical Lutheran Church in 1912, and during World War I, served as a chaplain with German ground forces. Bitterly opposed to the war, it was "the dirt, the horrors and the ugliness" he found in the trenches that inspired him "systematically to study the history of art and to collect as many as possible of the cheap reproductions available." It was also the declaration of war by Germany that signaled the end of the nineteenth century for Tillich: "This moment was for my whole generation a real *kairos* [great moment]—a tremendous *kairos*. And during the war, not immediately but gradually, slowly, we began to see the world differently." Tillich's own emerging philosophy/theology was also profoundly affected by the war: "In one night all my friends were brought to me either already dead or dying; this was the moment in which something . . . broke down forever. . . . That was the second *kairos* in which the first came to fulfilment. Then a process of maturity started in which I slowly developed

the basic ideas of my own thinking." During the 1920s Tillich became one of Germany's most influential philosopher/theologians, publishing many seminal works reflecting religion as the paramount concern in all human endeavor. Teaching at various German universities, Tillich was eventually ousted by the Nazis in 1933 because of his tolerant, humanistic views. "I had the great honor and luck to be about the first non-Jewish professor dismissed from a German university," he said of his forced emigration. Tillich immigrated to the United States and served as a faculty member of the Union Theological Seminary in New York from 1933 to 1954. He also lectured throughout the United States and abroad, including engagements in Germany, where after World War II his writings became popular. In 1954 he joined the Divinity School of Harvard University and the University of Chicago in 1962. Tillich died in 1965.

MAJOR WORKS

Tillich's writings are not only concerned with theology and philosophy, but with politics, the arts, and sociology, often concentrating on the relationship between religion and psychology. *The Courage To Be* (1952) and *Dynamics Of Faith* (1956) reached a major public audience not usually concerned with religious issues. His works were welcomed by American Protestants who sought an alternative to fundamentalist interpretations of the Bible. *The Shaking of the Foundations* (1948) and *The Courage to Be*, which was considered his most accessible book, reckoned existentialism from a numinous perspective and attempted to amalgamate it with a sacrosanct world view. In the three-volume *Systematic Theology* (1951-63), considered by many to be his life's work, Tillich took contemporary philosophical and psychological concepts and related them to sociological and scientific theories. *Systematic Theology*'s main thesis held that Protestant theology can "without losing its Christian foundations, incorporate strictly scientific methods, a critical philosophy, a realistic understanding of man and society and powerful ethical principles and motives." Critic Roger Hazelton held that in *Systematic Theology* Tillich attained "the power of a synthesizing comprehension which could discover basic, relevant connections where others saw only fragmentation or contradiction." Tillich did not see theology as separate from philosophy, "for, whatever the relation of God, world, and man may be, it lies in the frame of being; and any interpretation of the meaning and structure of being as being unavoidably such has consequences for the interpretation of God, man and the world in their interrelations." He believed that for the modern person "the traditional language has become irrelevant," and that, therefore, the meaning of Christian symbols has been confused. This meaning is the ultimate message of Christianity and must now be interpreted with the language of our own culture, according to Tillich. In much of his writings, Tillich saw the task of philosophy and theology as a seeking out of the shared bond between the questions modern culture asks and the answers found in Christian symbols. Tillich found these questions to be deeply grounded in the universal human situation, and it is with Christian symbols that these eternal questions may be answered. In much of Tillich's work, it was exactly these types of questions that primarily interested him: "My work is with those who ask questions, and for them I am here." In fact, his theology was built upon "the method of correlation between questions arising out of the human predicament and the answers given in the classical symbols of religion." As Hazelton said of *Systematic Theology*, "[Tillich's] is therefore an *answering* theology, which is also to say a *listening* theology." Tillich saw American culture as quite distant from past cultures which revered God, which he defined as "the answer to the question implied in man's finitude; He is the name for that which concerns man ultimately." To Tillich, modern culture promotes self-reliance, without any manifestation of religious transcendence. He found all cultural forms to be expressions of "ultimate concern." Tillich termed this cultural lack of spirituality as autonomous—finding law in itself, and as opposed to being heteronomous—deriving law from the sublime. He proposed instead that one should become theonomous—finding law in "ultimate concern,

the divine." Like Jung's collective unconscious or Emerson's oversoul, Tillich founded his personal philosophy on a grand unifying principle: "the most intimate motions within the depths of our souls are not completely our own. For they belong also to our friends, to mankind, to the universe, and to the Ground of being, the aim of our life. Nothing can be hidden ultimately. It is always reflected in the mirror in which nothing can be concealed."

CRITICAL RECEPTION

Critics see many of Tillich's books, such as *The Shaking of the Foundation* and *The Courage to Be*, as an integration of existentialism with the religious, "unifying center" of human life. He was praised for believing in a reconciling, "New Being," which is democratically available to all who seek it. Critics have found the manifestation of this "being" in Tillich's writings to be the symbol of Christ. According to Roger Hazelton, the meaning of this universal symbol "is that human existence everywhere and always can be renewed through ecstatic participation in being-itself, which is Tillich's word for God." According to John K. Roth, "Tillich explored the uncertainties of human existence and, in spite of those conditions, helped people to discern the God who provides the courage to be." Tillich is regarded as an extremely influential figure in American religious and social life. "[Tillich] displayed to the American communities of learning and culture, the wholeness of religious philosophy and of the political and social dimensions of human existence," said colleague Reinhold Niebuhr. Many critics have found in Tillich a definite sense of the transcendent. "In short, . . . justifying faith is the transcendental condition for the possibility of the courage to be in the midst of total despair," said George Lindbeck. Most critics agree that Tillich found his ontological answer in "Being-itself" and "ultimate concern," which are synonymous with God. Tillich strove for a philosophical theology of unity that could be known through symbols he called "the most revealing creations of the human mind" and the "results of a creative encounter with reality." As Iris M. Yob noted, "[Tillich's] cosmological understanding of the world is that 'the knower and that which is known is united,' since everything is ultimately derived from the unity he calls 'Being-itself.'"

PRINCIPAL WORKS

Die religiose Lage der Gegenwart [*The Religious Situation*] (philosophy) 1926
The Interpretation of History (philosophy) 1936
The Protestant Era (philosophy) 1948
The Shaking of the Foundations (sermons) 1948
Christianity and the Problem of Existence (philosophy) 1951
Systematic Theology 3 vols. (philosophy) 1951-63
The Courage to Be (lectures) 1952

CRITICISM

Paul Tillich (essay date 1966)

SOURCE: "The Decline and the Validity of the Idea of Progress," in *Ohio University Review,* Vol. 8, 1966, pp. 5-22.

[*In the following essay, Tillich discusses the notion of progress as concept, symbol, and idea, linking it to his conception of* kairoi *or "great moments."*]

This lecture was delivered as one in the series of Edwin and Ruth Kennedy Lectures at Ohio University on May 19th, 1964. At the time, Professor Tillich granted *The Ohio University Review* the right to print the lecture after revision. A tape was made of the lecture and the transcript of it was edited by Professor Stanley Grean of the Philosophy Department of Ohio University. Tillich made some revisions of this but had not completed them at the time of his death. The lecture as it appears here is based on this text as found among his papers and first printed earlier this year in Paul Tillich, *The Future of Religions*, ed. Jerald C. Brauer (Harper & Row, Publishers, Inc., New York, 1966). Used by arrangement with the publishers. After the original lecture there was a brief period of questions and answers which was also taped. A transcript of this, as edited by Professor Grean, appears here for the first time by permission of the Executor of the Literary Estate of Paul Tillich.

My subject is the idea of progress, which I will examine from the point of view that it is valid, that it has declined very much in its importance, and that in a new form it might be revived. Therefore, my title is **"The Decline and the Validity of the Idea of Progress."**

Let us, first, examine some basic considerations about the concepts involved. This is where my semantic critics are right. Every discussion today in philosophy and theology demands a semantic clearing up of the concepts which are used, because we are living in Babylon after the tower has been destroyed and the languages of man have been disturbed and dispersed all over the world. This is the situation one faces today in reading theological and philosophical books. Therefore, I must guide you through some burdensome logical, semantic, and historical journeys.

Now, first, there is a difference between the concept of progress and the idea of progress. The concept of progress is an abstraction, based on the description of a group of facts, of objects of observation which may well be verified or falsified; but the idea of progress is an interpretation of existence as a whole, which means first of all our own existence. Thus, it is a matter of decision. It is an answer everybody has to give about the meaning of his life. Progress as an idea is a symbol for an attitude toward our existence. As so often in history, a concept open to logical and empirical description and analysis has become a symbol, and in the case of progress this is particularly true—the concept has become a symbol. What is extracted from a special realm of facts has become an expression of a general attitude toward life. Therefore, we must look at progress both as concept and as symbol. Since observation always precedes interpretation, I will give most attention to progress as a concept, because most of the confusions about progress as a symbol come from a limited and wrong analysis of progress as a concept.

Obviously progress is a universal experience which everybody has. The word is derived from *gressus* which means step, progress means stepping ahead from a less satisfactory situation to a more satisfactory situation. Imagine a lecture like this about progress, yet denying the idea of progress; someone might attempt this. But even such a person in denying the idea of progress works for progress; that is, he wants the less informed of his listeners to be better informed at the end of his lecture. In this sense, even if he speaks against the idea of progress, he accepts the concept of progress. He is implicitly progressivistic. I call this kind of thinking about progress "progressivism," which is implied in every action. Everybody who acts, acts in order to change a state of things in the direction of a better state of things. He wants to make progress. This is the most simple, the most fundamental, and actually the least contradictory way of understanding progress—the progressivism implied in every action. Nobody can get away from this. Yet this simple sense of progress is far from progress as the universal way of life and as the law of human history. Therefore, we ask how could the idea have arisen that human history and, even preceding it, the history of all life, the history of the universe, has a progressivistic character—is progress from something lower to something higher. How could this idea develop? What are the motives behind it?

Now I must first guide you on the thorny path—especially so for Americans—of historical reminder. I hope it is a reminder because I presume that all of you know what I am referring to, but if not, be patient with me because the historical question gives the basis for the understanding of what today seems natural to us. The idea of this country is that it represents a new beginning in the history of mankind. This is true in many respects. But the new beginning is never fully new. It is always a result of preceding events, and if I may comment on my experience on two continents, I would say that Europe is endangered by its past and by all the curses coming from that past. America, on the other hand, is endangered by going ahead without looking back at the creative forces which have determined the whole of Western culture. So I wish to direct your thoughts in the first part of this paper to the past. You will discover how relevent this is to our present understanding of such an idea as that of progress.

Let us first consider the religious background of the idea of progress. The fundamental factor in this respect is prophetic religion as expressed in the Old Testament and in many forms ever since in the Christian church as well as in Judaism and Islam. It involves the idea that God has elected a nation and, later on in Christianity, people from all over the world, that he has promised something related to the future, and that in spite of all resistance on the part of the people, he will fulfill his promise. There is the vision of progress toward the future in this idea. The belief of the prophets that Yahweh, the God of Israel, will establish his heavenly rule or his kingdom over all the world is the primary basis of an interpretation of history as the place where the divine reveals itself in progress toward an end. Now this idea has always been important in the development of Christianity. There was, for example, a man whose name should be remembered, Joachim De Fiore, an abbot in Southern Italy in the twelfth century, who expressed this idea of progress in the doctrine that there were three stages in history, the stage of the Father in the Old Testament, the stage of the Son (the last thousand years of church history), and the coming or third stage of the Divine Spirit in which there will be no more church since everyone will be taught directly by the spirit. In this last stage, too, there will be equality and there will be no more marriage: history will come to an end.

Now this half-fantastic, half-realistic idea had many consequences for the whole subsequent church history, and also for this country. The idea of the third stage was taken on by the radical evangelicals in the time of the Reformation, which underlies most of this country's religion, and is seen in the idea of a revolutionary or progressivistic realization of the kingdom of God in Calvinism. It became the religious basis deep-rooted in every Western man. If you don't believe it, go to Asia—to India or Japan. I had the privilege of being in Japan for ten weeks talking every day with Buddhist priests and scholars. There is nothing like this. "The religions of the East are of the past," I was told, "not of the future." For the religious people of the East, one wants to return to the Eternal from which one came directly, not caring for history, going out of history at some time of one's life into the desert, if possible. If you contrast this with the Western religious feeling of progressive activity, then you see what the difference is.

However, this was only the religious basis for the idea of progress. Now we come to the secular motives, and the secular elaboration of the idea of progress, which, of course, starts with the Renaissance. The man of the Renaissance is something new, not only as compared with the Middle Ages but also as compared with the late ancient world. The most important impact of the ancient world on Renaissance man was made by Stoic philosophy, but it was a transformed Stoicism. It was not the Stoicism of resignation, as it was under the Roman empire in the later Greek world, but it was the Stoicism of action. The Romans—some of the Roman emperors even—were partly mediators in this direction. However, the man of the Renaissance does not feel he is dependent on fate as the Stoics did. Rather, he feels—as expressed in painting—that when the destiny of man is compared with a sailboat, driven by the winds of contingency, man stands at the rudder and directs it. Of course, he knows that destiny gives the winds, but nevertheless, man directs destiny. This conception is unheard of in all Greek culture and is a presupposition of the idea of progress in the modern world. Out of this arose the great Renaissance Utopian writings, that is, the anticipation of a reality—*outopos*—which "has no place" in history, but which is nevertheless being expected. Such Utopias have been written ever since, into the twentieth century. It was the idea of the third stage of history, the stage of reason in bourgeois society, the stage of the classless society in the working-class movements. It was a secularized idea of the third stage, the religious foundations of which we saw. But it was not only ideas which produced this passion for purpose, it was also the social reality, the activities of bourgeois society at this time, such as the colonial extension of Europe in all directions; space extension, which has remained an element in the idea of progress up to the space exploration we are doing today; and technical extension—continuous progress in controlling nature and putting it into the service of man. All this has been based on the boundary lines of science which we have trespassed year by year since the beginning of the Renaissance up until today.

But there was another element of great importance in the idea of progress, namely the vision of nature as a progressive process from the atom to the molecule, to the cell, to the developed organism, and finally to man. This is evolution, progress in largeness of elements united in one being, with centeredness and, therefore, power being in the individual. And this line, then, was drawn beyond nature through humanity, from primitive to civilized man, to us as the representatives of the age of reason in which the potentialities of creation have come to their fulfillment.

When I tell you this, you yourself can feel how overwhelmingly impressive it is, and how virtually impossible it was to escape this idea as a symbol of faith. Progress became in the nineteenth century not only a conscious doctrine but also an unconscious dogma. When I came to this country in 1933 and spoke with students of theology, and criticized certain ideas of God, of Christ, of the Spirit, of the Church, or of sin or salvation, it didn't touch them very much but when I criticized the idea of progress, they said to me, "In what then can we believe? What do you do with our real faith?" And these were students of theology. It means that all the Christian dogmas had been transformed in the unconscious of these people (which my questions brought out) into a faith in progress. But then something happened! This dogma was shaken in the twentieth century, as foreseen by some prophetic minds in the nineteenth, first in Europe, then in America.

In Europe one of the greatest expressions of the shaking of this faith was Nietzsche's prophecy of—what unfortunately today has become a fashionable phrase—the death of God. This doesn't mean primitive, materialistic atheism; Nietzsche was far from this. But it meant the undercutting of the value-systems, Christian as well as secular, and the view of the human predicament as something in conflict, in destruction, in estrangement from true humanity.

Nietzsche was one of the predecessors of what today is called "existentialist" literature. The trend was further supported by the historical pessimism of men like Spengler, who wrote two important volumes on *The Decline of the West* in which much historical imagination was connected with much true prophecy. In the year 1916 he prophesied the coming of the period of the dictators, and in the early thirties the Communist and the Fascist dictators were a reality. The first World War and then the rise of what he prophesied of the totalitarian powers—this was the end of the belief in progress as an idea in Europe. In America it started somehow with the great economic crisis in the thirties. In Germany it started with the beginning of the Hitler period and the experience that history can fall back and that a rebarbarization can happen in any moment even in the highest culture. Then came the second World War, the cold war, and the atomic crises. And with all this there came in this country the end of the crusading utopianism of the first third of the century. Instead, opposite Utopias appeared in literature—negative Utopias—like Huxley's *Brave New World*, or Orwell's *1984*. In many other novels and treatises the future is painted in terms of negative utopianism, in terms not of fulfillment but of dehumanization. The same can be seen in the existentialist style in the arts—whether you call it expressionist, cubist, or abstract—wherein the expression of the demonic in the underground of the individual or the group moves away from the figures and faces of human beings toward the abstract elements in the underground of reality. In philosophy there is a withdrawal into a merely formal analysis of the possibility of thinking without going into reality itself with one's thinking. This was the end of a phase in the idea of progress, but the active motive of all our behavior cannot die, nor can the lure of future possibilities.

Today we need a new inquiry into the validity and the limits of the idea of progress. There are symptoms of reconsideration: For instance, in philosophy now there is an attempt finally to use the sharpened instruments of logical analysis to go into the real problems of human existence and in the arts at least an attempt to use the elementary forms discovered in the last fifty years to express in a new way reality as manifestly encountered. There are other elements too: the extension of national independence; the real fight about the racial problem; and the increasing awareness, even among conservative theologians, that our attitude toward the non-Christian religions has to be one of dialogue—even the present Pope used that term. But, of course, these are symptoms and not yet fulfillments, and the threat of a relapse into the predominant pessimism (if you use that word which shouldn't be used by a philosopher) is always a danger.

We must now contribute to this reappraisal by going through a serious and perhaps painstaking analysis of the concept of progress as it appears in the different realms of life. After this somewhat dramatic historical section, I ask you to follow me through an analytic section, through an analysis of all the things one does oneself, especially in academic surroundings.

II

The tremendous force of the progressivistic idea was rooted, firstly, in observations about particular instances of progress in technical and scientific matters. But this observation was inadequate, and what is needed now is to show the non-progressive elements in reality and culture, and to demonstrate in some way how they are related to the progressive elements. There is a general principle for all this which one can follow through more fully when one thinks about these ideas. The general principle is: Where there is freedom to contradict fulfillment, there the rule of progress is broken. Freedom to contradict one's fulfillment breaks the rule of the law of progress. This freedom is nothing else but another word for the moral act, which we perform every day innumerable times. There is no progress with respect to the moral act because there is no morality without free decisions, without the awareness of the power to turn with one's centered self in the one or the other direction. It means that every individual starts anew and has to make decisions for himself, whether he be on the lowest or highest level of culture or education. The German rebarbarization was looked at with great astonishment by a world which was adhering to the faith in progress. But there it was. In one of the most highly civilized nations, decisions were made by individuals and followed by many which contradicted anything we consider to be human nature and human fulfillment. This was a tremendous shock. And here is the first answer to the whole problem of progress. Every newborn infant has, when it comes to a certain point of self-awareness, the possibility of stopping progress by contradicting fulfillment in man's essential nature.

There is something else in what we usually call progress in the ethical realm, namely, coming to maturity—maturation. The child matures, and in this respect, there is progress. There is as in nature a progression from the seed to the fruit of the tree, or to the fully grown tree, but this element of maturity belongs to the individual first, and he may at any moment break out of it. We know how much this happens even in people whom we consider to be mature, and we know many who never become mature. There is something like maturing also in social groups. It means deeper understanding of man's essential nature in individual and social relations. This is not moral progress but it is cultural progress in the moral realm. It is cultural because it sees better what human nature is, but it doesn't make people better. If we had attained the full idea now of the social interrelation between the races in this country, we would be on a higher, on a more mature level; we would have deeper insight into human nature and into the content of the moral demand, but we would not have better human beings, because the goodness or not-goodness of a human being appears on all levels of culture and insight. So we can say—and this is very important for our whole consideration of this idea and for our whole culture today with respect to the free moral decisions of individuals—there are always new beginnings in the individual and sometimes in the group, but the contents can mature and can grow from one generation to another. This is the difference between civilized ethics and primitive ethics, but do not believe that on the level of primitive ethics people were worse than we are. In the smallest decisions you make in your classes, or in your homes, or wherever it may be, there is the same problem of ethical decision which is found in the crudeness of the cavemen; you are not better than they. You may be better than one of them, but one of them may be better than you. The distinction between moral decision and progress in moral content is fundamental for our judging the whole of past history.

When we look at education, we arrive at the same result. Education leads to higher cultural levels, to progress and maturity, to a production of habits of good behavior. As a consequence, education can be a kind of second nature in each of you, useful for society, but, when it comes to moral freedom, you are still able to become rebarbarized, even if not openly as it was in Germany, in your personal relation to another person, to your children, your husband, your wife, or your friends. You can again start on a level which is that of freedom to contradict what you ought to be. When we add to the ordinary educational process, as we have it in a college or university, when we add to it education in psychotherapy, psychoanalysis, counselling, and all these things which are so important, what can they do? They can heal you from disturbances, they can help you to become free, but when you have been set free, let us say by successful analysis, you still have to decide. This is not moral progress; it is progress in healing, but the moral decision remains free, and now has become really free by medical or psychoanalytical help.

Besides moral freedom, the freedom of contradicting every possible instance of progress, there is a second element where there is no progress, namely, the freedom of spiritual creativity—creation in culture.

Let us look at the different cultural functions. There are the arts. Is there progress in the arts? There is progress in the technical use of materials, in the better mixing of colors, and in things like that, but is there progress in the arts? Has Homer ever been surpassed by anyone? Has Shakespeare ever been surpassed by anyone? Is an early Greek frieze worse than a classical sculpture, or is a classical worse than a modern expressionist? No. There is maturity of styles; there are good and bad representatives of style, but you cannot compare artistic styles in terms of progress. A style starts, often very modestly and preliminarily. It grows, it becomes mature, it produces its greatest expressions, then it decays. But there is no progress from one style to another. There is no progress from the Gothic to the Classical style. (And this needs to be said against our Gothic church buildings—we shouldn't pretend that we can go back to the Gothic style, after our modern stylistic feelings and developmental possibilities have become so different.) So, creativity in the arts admits of maturity, admits of "great moments"—*kairoi*—right times, decisive times, turning points, all this, but it does not admit progress from one style to another.

The same is true in the realm of knowledge. If you look at philosophy, you see an analytic element in our great philosophers as well as a visionary element. Take Aristotle, for example, who unites both of them so clearly. In every kind of knowledge a philosophical element is present. You can also speak of a logical and empirical element in knowledge which is detached and necessary, and an existentialist and inspirational element which is involved. Both are there, and the very fact that in all great philosophers there was this visionary, involved, inspirational element makes it impossible to speak about progress in the history of philosophy except in those elements which are connected with a sharpened logical analysis or a tremendous increase in empirical knowledge. I have never found a philosopher who I could say progressed over Parmenides the Eleatic of the sixth century B.C. Of course, there is much more empirical knowledge, there is much more refined analysis, but the vision of this man, and of Heraclitus, his polar friend and opposite, cannot be surpassed. There is no qualitative progress from Heraclitus to Whitehead.

And there is no progress in humanity, that is, in the formation of the individual person. I was struck by this once when I saw a photograph of an old Sumerian sculpture, perhaps of a priestess, and looking at it said to myself, "Look at the sculptures and paintings of great representatives of humanity in the following history of three or four thousand years." I found no progress at all. I found differences, but I didn't find progress. This means that even justice as well as humanity are not matters of progress except in technical elements. If I think, for instance, of democracy there is progress in largeness of the number of people involved, and progress in maturity in some respects, but there was justice in the state of Athens, justice in old Israel, in Rome, in the Middle Ages, and there is justice in modern democracy. The progress is quantitative, but the quality of the ideas of humanity and justice has not progressed.

Now I come to the most difficult problem—progress in religion. Of course, it is simple if you follow the conservative or fundamentalist idea that there is one true religion and many false ones. Then, needless to say, there is no progress. But even if you hold this view, you have a difficulty, namely, the Old Testament—what about that? Isn't there something then like progress—progressive revelation? So the problem appears even in Christianity. There is development, there is progress. Even in church history there is supposed to be progress according to the Gospel of John where Jesus is reported to have said that the Spirit will introduce you into all truth. This is progress. Furthermore, there are Christian theologies which expect new revelations even beyond Jesus the Christ. This, of course, would be post-Christian religion. Now if we look at this, we encounter great difficulties. On the one hand, Christianity claims that there is no possible progress beyond what is given in Jesus the Christ; on the other hand, there is great progress in world history in many respects—in knowledge as well as in other areas. How shall we deal with this problem?

Here is where religion might provide the standpoint from which we might understand the whole problem better. I would say that we must replace the idea of progress by two other concepts: the concept of maturing, and the concept of "the decisive moment." What we need is an understanding of history in which there are two things, rather than a single, continuous line of progress. (I hope that what I have said about all the other realms—the ethical, the cultural, the artistic, the scientific, the philosophical, the religious—showed this clearly.) "Great moments" or, if you want to accept the term I like very much, taken from the New Testament or from classical Greek, the term *kairos*, the right time, fulfilled time, time in which something decisive happens, is not the same as *chronos*, chronological time, which is watch time, but it means the qualitative time in which "something happens." I would say, therefore, that in history we have two processes, not progress as a universal event, but the maturing of potentialities, the maturing of a style, for instance, or the maturing in the education of a human being. It is not progress beyond this human being. He or she may give something to their children, but children must decide again on their own. There is no progress; they must start anew. Two things then we can see in history. One is the process of maturing in terms of potentialities; the other is the great moments, the *kairoi*, in history in which something new happens. However, that new thing which happens is not in a progressivistic line with the other new things before and after it. This is only true in the technical and scientific realm so far as the logical elements are implied, but it is not so in the realm of spiritual creativity and of the moral act.

My description and analysis of progress has been more careful than is usual, but I believe that the service an academic lecturer can give is to show his listeners where the problems lie, and to steer them away from the popular talk about such weighty problems. This I have tried to do,

and now perhaps we will have some of the fruits of this. When progress is elevated into a symbol or an idea, as I said in the beginning, then it can take on two forms. The one is the idea of endless progress, without a limit, in which one moves further and further along, and things get better and better. The other is the Utopian form, which is historically much more important; namely, that at some point in time man's essential nature will be fulfilled. What is possible for man will then exist. Now, what happens with these two? In the first type, progress runs ahead without aim, unless progress itself is taken to be the aim, but there is no goal at the end of the progression. Thus, it is simply a matter of going ahead, and of course, if my analysis before was right, this is possible to a certain extent in the technical and scientific realms. But it is not possible in the realms where vision and inspiration play a role. The other type, the Utopian, has produced all the tremendous passions in history, for it is the principle of revolution. However, after the revolution is successful, the great disappointment follows, and this disappointment produces cynicism and sometimes complete withdrawal from history. We have it in some forms of Christianity—we have it strongly in Lutheranism and in the Greek Orthodox Church; we have it less in Calvinism and Evangelical radicalism, which underlies this country; and we have it in an anti-Christian way as a result of the terrible experiences of suffering in Asiatic religions, especially in Buddhism with its withdrawal from history.

Now the question is, is there a way of avoiding the Utopianism which sees the fulfillment of history around the corner; which says, only one step more and we will be in the classless society; only one step more and we will be an educated nation; only one step more and all our youngsters will reach full humanity, or all our social groups will stand for true justice. If only all men of good will—that means we—stand together, everything will be all right. All this is Utopianism. In contrast, I want to save you, by my criticism of the idea of progress, from the cynical consequences of disappointed Utopianism. In my long life I have experienced the breakdown of the Utopianism of the Western intelligentsia both in Europe and America and the tremendous cynicism and despair which followed it and, finally, the emptiness of not being ultimately concerned about anything. Therefore, I think that we must put something else in place of these two types of progressivism. Endless progress may be symbolized by running ahead indefinitely into an empty space. We will do that, but it is not the meaning of life; nor are better and better gadgets the meaning of life. What is the meaning of life then? Perhaps it is something else. Perhaps there are great moments in history. There is in these great moments not total fulfillment, but there is the victory over a particular power of destruction, a victory over a demonic power which was creative and now has become destructive. This is a possibility, but don't expect that it *must* happen. It might not happen; that is a continuous threat hanging over development in history. But there *may* be a *kairos*.

After the first World War in Germany, we believed, just because of the defeat of Germany, that there was a *kairos*, a great moment, in which something new could be created. In this sense we were progressive, but we did not believe that it was necessary that this would happen. Inevitable progress should not be sought by us, for there is no such thing. Of course, what we hoped for then was completely destroyed by the Hitler movement. Out of these experiences we came to see that there is a possibility of victory over a particular demonic power—a particular force of destruction—or to put it simply, there is a possibility of solving a particular problem, as for instance, the race problem in our time. But even if this does happen, it doesn't mean inevitable progress. We must fight for it, and we may be defeated, but even if not, new demonic powers will arise.

There is a wonderful symbolism in the last book of the Bible, in the idea of the thousand years' rule of Christ in history. In these thousand years, which is a symbolic number, of course, the demonic forces will be banned—put into chains in the underworld. This is all symbolism. But they are not annihilated and they may come to the surface again, as they will in the final struggle. When we thought about our problems after the first World War, we used this symbol—not in its literal sense, of course—as expressing the awareness that you can ban a particular demonic force. Hitler was banned, but the powers behind Hitler, the demonic forces in mankind and in every individual, are not definitely annihilated; they are banned for a moment and they may return again. So instead of a progressivistic, Utopian, or empty vision of history, let us think of the great moments for which we must keep ourselves open, and in which the struggle of the divine and the demonic in history may be decided for one moment for the divine against the demonic, though there is no guarantee that this will happen. On the contrary, in the view of the Bible, especially the book of Revelation, the growth of the divine powers in history is contradicted by a growth of the demonic powers.

So in every moment the fight is going on and the only thing we can say is this: If there is a new beginning, let us mature in it; if there is a new beginning in world history as we have it now in this country and beyond this country, let us follow it and develop it to its maturity. But let us not look at history in the sense of progress which will be going on and finally come to an end which is wonderful and fulfilling. There is no such thing in history, because man is free, free to contradict his own essential nature and his own fulfillment. As a Christian theologian I would say that fulfillment is going on in every moment here and now beyond history, not some time in the future, but here and now above ourselves. When I have to apply this to a meeting like this, then I would say it might well be that in such a meeting in the inner movements of some of us, something might happen which is elevated out of time into eternity. This then is a non-Utopian and a true fulfillment of the meaning of history and of our own individual life.

Discussion Following the Lecture

[Question 1:] Does the nature of the society before the "great moment" or kairos affect the quality, character, or nature of the "great moment"?

[Paul Tillich:] This is a question of the dialectics of history, of how the "new" comes into existence in the historical process. This is a very fundamental question. If we look at history both with the eyes of the sociologist and the dialectician (which we must), then we can say with certainty that nothing can happen in a situation in the present moment which was not made possible by the situation in the preceding moment. (I am using the word "situation" here in the sense in which Whitehead often used it.) But between the preceding moment and the present moment there is that category which is the category of all history—namely, the "new"—and this category of the "new" is clearly expressed in the nature of historical time. Historical time is never reversed; it never goes back. It always goes ahead towards something, and therefore, we have to say that in the preceding stage of society the tensions are prepared out of which the new stage is born.

Let me give you an example of the wrong way of using this dialectical method, and also an example of what I believe to be the right way. The wrong way was that employed by the German Social Democrats in the years before Hitler came to power. They used the dialectical method, saying, "This is the stage in industrial development which belongs to the working classes with all its associated characteristics, so we can sit looking out of the window and watch the classless society come." But it didn't come; instead, Hitler came and destroyed them all. What this means is that you cannot derive the next stage in history from the preceding stage with any kind of absolute certainty. In my interpretation of history I distinguish between "chance" and "trends." When, in Europe after the first World War, we envisaged a new society, we took account only of the element of chance. We saw a *kairos*, a great turning point, and we were ecstatic at the thought of fulfilling the task given to us at this great moment, but we failed to see the underground trends, and it was these underground trends that led directly to Hitler and fascism. So the picture is a complicated one. This "within-each-otherness" of chance and trend characterizes history. You can say rightly that the trends come from what is given, from the preceding stage of society. But there is also the chance of something "new"—a new person or a new vision—a factor from the outside which changes the trend and makes possible something new. These two elements of chance and trend mean that the dialectic of the historical process cannot be developed mechanistically leaving out the factors of contingency, of chance, and of freedom.

[Question 2:] Hasn't there been progress in medicine?

[Paul Tillich:] Yes, there is probably no place in which there is more progress than in medicine. This progress falls partly under the principle of scientific progress and partly under the principle of technical progress, both of which I mentioned. And these two forms of progress can not be denied at all. The idea of progress today is largely derived from the fact of technical progress.

But there is a problem left—the problem of the visionary element in the healing relation between the subject and object of healing. I would say that despite this tremendous increase in scientific knowledge, in technical ability, in skill in the process (for which I myself am especially thankful), this progress has not yet found expression in the relationship of the healer and the healed. I often have the feeling that our hospitals have regressed from the time of the simple family doctor in the past. When on the first day in a hospital I am treated by twenty different nurses, by half a dozen internes, and two main doctors, I don't feel that the personal relationship of healing which is essential for the healing process is fulfilled. So I would say that technical progress has not been fully balanced on the human, existential and inspirational side of the healing relationship. But, of course, on the scientific and technical side we have doubled the age-expectancy of mankind; that is certainly progress, tremendous progress. But we must look for progress in the context of all human relationships, and that is where a question sometimes rises.

[Question 3:] Is there not progress in art and literature in the sense that we learn more about what man is and what he can do?

[Paul Tillich:] In so far as art and literature give us objectifiable insights which you can extract and say, "Here is better psychology or better sociology in this novel or in this painting," then you are right; then they are communicators of progress in knowledge, but that's not what they aim to be. Every vision of man is not only a progressive enlargement of what we can say about man, but it is also a definite forgetting of what other generations have said about man. Artistic visions are not simply accumulative. Accumulation is not the decisive characteristic of vision. Accumulation can be used for this and that, but it always obscures some fundamentals if it is not put into a context in which it can be used.

Indirectly I would even agree with you. I would say that everything which is produced by art, philosophy, or religion also has an indirect effect on those things in which progress is possible. And so they contribute to progress, but that is their indirect function which, moreover, has a very ambiguous character, for it can produce a nonunderstanding of what is really meant in their creation. Let me give you an example. You in the Western World have my most beloved of all dramatic creations—Shakespeare's *Hamlet*—which is also the most existentialist. Now what can I learn in a progressivistic way from it? I could dissolve the whole vision and say that here we learn that men must make quick decisions and not hesitate too long—or such things as that. But this becomes banal. However, if you see it as a total human situation, then you can enter

into it; you can, as I did in the sixteenth and seventeenth years of my life, *become* Hamlet and live it all through—live *in* it. This affected my experience of maturing; it was even a great *kairos* for me when I first encountered *Hamlet*. However, if you extract from it some psychological insights, then every psychologist would say, "But that we know anyway"; yet they couldn't write *Hamlet,* and that's quite a difference!

[Question 4:] Is the protest against the idea of progress, itself progress? Is it a kairos? Is it a sign of maturity?

[Paul Tillich:] Now, this is a very good dialectical question, and I would like to escape it. But let me try to answer it. First, it certainly was a *kairos*. This we all experienced who came from the nineteenth century—I started with one leg or at least big toe still in the nineteenth century. I was fourteen years old when the twentieth came, so I can still breathe the air of the nineteenth century—smell it in memory. The end was the first of August 1914; then the nineteenth century came to an end, and not before—not on some first of January. But the declaration of war against Russia by Germany on the first of August 1914 (or second of August, but I call it first of August symbolically) was really the end of the nineteenth century, and, therefore, I would say that this moment was for my whole generation a real *kairos*—a tremendous *kairos*. And during the war, not immediately but gradually, slowly, we began to see the world differently. I can give you a particular moment in the battle of the Champagne which was the worst at least in my experience—probably the worst in the whole war. My division was in the midst of it, and I was Chaplain there. In one night all my friends were brought to me either already dead or dying; this was the moment in which something which has to do with progressivism broke down forever, namely a kind of idealism which I had interpreted in terms of classical German philosophy and liberal Christianity—this simply broke down. That was the second *kairos* in which the first came to fulfilment. Then a process of maturity started in which I slowly developed the basic ideas of my own thinking. So at least for me I would say the breakdown of the idea of progress was a *kairos* and was a beginning of maturity. It was not *the* end—I would emphasize this very strongly; *a kairos* is not *the kairos*.

[Question 5:] You say that freedom to contradict one's fulfilment breaks the law of progress, but if we were not allowed our freedom of decision how could we have a free and democratic society?

[Paul Tillich:] If we didn't have the freedom to contradict our own essential natures—former generations of Christians called it "sin"—if we didn't have the freedom to sin, how could we experience freedom as in a democratic situation? We couldn't. Yet freedom is at the same time both the basis of human dignity and of human tragedy. But freedom should be defended. God preferred to have sinners rather than saints without freedom—though they would not have really been saints, they would simply have been natural phenomena. Freedom is decisive, but freedom has in itself something which makes the law of the continuing progress of humanity impossible. However, this is not a criticism of freedom but a description of the implication of the greatness of man—his ability to contradict himself.

[Question 6:] What do you say to those who deny that there is any freedom to act?

[Paul Tillich:] I ask them whether they have asked me this question in freedom or not. If they have not asked it in freedom, then it's irrelevant; it's like a formation of their nose for which they are not responsible. If they have asked it in freedom, so that it is more than a product of the particular structure of their brain, then we can discuss it. And I also am free to discuss it; otherwise they could say I only argue as I do because this morning I had tea and not coffee for breakfast. Now this kind of discussion is impossible. When I use the word "freedom," I don't mean the obsolete term "freedom of the will." We shouldn't use that anymore; but I mean the total reaction of the centered self—this is freedom, and not the compulsory reaction of a part of us, which is a subject for the psychoanalyst.

Roger Hazelton (review date 5-12 August 1967)

SOURCE: "Tillich's Questions and Answers," in *The New Republic*, Vol. 157, August 5-12, 1967, pp. 36-38.

[In the following review, Hazelton favorably treats Systematic Theology *as a summing up of Tillich's reflections on the significance of modern culture and the Christian faith.]*

Those who knew Paul Tillich even slightly were quick to recognize in him a seldom encountered intellectual greatness. His mind had a style of its own: gravely lucid, wide-ranging, refreshingly different from the ingrown dogmatism of so many of his theological contemporaries. At two points especially he seemed to stand above them. He was able to penetrate with remarkable agility and accuracy into viewpoints and issues taking shape within the general culture, whether in politics, psychotherapy or in the plastic arts. And to this gift he added another—the power of a synthesizing comprehension which could discover basic, relevant connections where others saw only fragmentation or contradiction.

Tillich's exceptional intellectual qualities found their most ample outlet in his *Systematic Theology*, now published as a whole and containing the three volumes brought out at seven-year intervals between 1951 and 1963. Tillich was determined to get his *Systematics* finished despite an exhausting schedule of other writing, changes in academic appointment (he "retired" at least three times), travel and engagements of many sorts, not to mention his continual participation in conferences and his promotion of worthy social causes.

In Tillich the *Herr Professor* took on a new, Americanized dimension. By no means a recondite or withdrawn scholar (he loved the world too much for that), he greatly enhanced the prestige of his profession by demonstrating that ardent rationality and critical responsibility belong together. One of his favorite teaching words was "tension," and he knew its meaning intimately. He was a far more dialectical thinker than most of the theologians who claimed to be so; and although he preferred the word "systematic" to characterize his own work, the thought that went into it was very far from being as much of a monologue or package as this term suggests.

Systematic Theology makes Tillich's life work available in the form in which he himself envisaged it, a summing up of his reflections on the significance of modern culture and the Christian faith for one another. It is a quite uneven work, undeniably great in its conception but redundant or inconclusive at some crucial points, which Tillich himself would probably have been the first to grant.

What gives the *Systematic Theology* its decisive signature and texture? More than anything else, it is what Tillich called the question-answer correlation. Once toward the very end of his career he said to some students at Santa Barbara: "I presuppose in my theological thinking the entire history of Christian thought up until now, and I consider the attitude of those people who are in doubt or estrangement or opposition to everything ecclesiastical and religious, including Christianity. And I have to speak to them. My work is with those who ask questions, and for them I am here." That remark explains why topics like Ambiguity, Anxiety and Estrangement figure as prominently in the common index as Faith, Kingdom and Spirit. What gave body and drive to Tillich's monumental effort was his unshakable conviction that cultural questions could be met and satisfied by Christian answers. His is therefore an *answering* theology, which is also to say a *listening* theology. In the *Systematics* there are several variations of this question-answer scheme: situation and message, world and church, "existential" and "essential" being, among others. His confidence that theology can establish meaningful correlations between these polarities is fundamental to his entire enterprise; it is a working *a priori* which cannot itself be questioned if the questions dealt with in the system are to find theological answers.

Still another sort of confidence that shines through the pages of this epochal work, particularly in its new format, is closely related to what Tillich called his "ontology." Almost alone among the significant theological minds of his time, Tillich never despaired of knowing Being. In this respect he belonged to the classical Christian past rather than to its troubled present. By "ontology," to be sure, he meant something quite unlike traditional conceptions stemming from neo-Platonic or idealistic sources; and he tried to overcome the conflicts between rationalists and pragmatists, absolutists and positivists, in his own thought. Yet he did not waver in his view that human thinking lies open to and is based upon "that which is"; indeed, radical skepticism was to him strictly unthinkable. This confidence kept him from setting philosophy and theology against each other, as was the current fashion; it also kept the lines between them fluctuating and indistinct, especially when he came to discuss the central Christian matter of "Jesus as the Christ."

The dominant tone is always affirmative. The text is made up mainly of declarative sentences, generally of quite simple construction, with a noticeable absence of inter-rogations and imperatives. The lingering Germanism of his writing style shows itself chiefly in his preference for large, loose-jointed abstract nouns, and an almost total avoidance of concrete illustrations. Tillich is very sparing in his use of neologisms, although he can burnish familiar terms until they shine with unexpected brilliance. The density of his thought consists in its very abstractness, which imparts the sense of "depth" he prized so greatly and wanted to communicate. In Tillich's writing, just as in his speaking, the concept remains in control, even when he is referring to such symbols for God as "Lord" and "Father," for example.

What does Tillich *teach*? The system consists of five parts, each divided into two sections, one expressing the human situation or question, the other setting forth the theological answer. There is a rhythm of thought which yields not so much an argument in the classical sense as a theme with variations.

Man, says Tillich, experiences his present situation chiefly "in terms of disruption, conflict, self-destruction, meaning-lessness and despair in all realms of life." This may be documented by looking at his arts, philosophy (particularly existentialism), political and social tensions, and attempts to analyze and treat the lesions of the unconscious. The question that emerges is whether there is a reality in which our self-estrangement can be overcome, through rapport with which man can discover for himself a reconciling, reuniting "New Being." Tillich believed with all his mind and heart that such a reality is accessible and available to every man in his need, and that this assurance is the crux of the Christian message.

If we ask where this New Being is disclosed, the theological answer is "in Jesus as the Christ." For Tillich this is not a claim to be defended against other religious options, but a confession to be given with "ultimate concern" for everything that makes man human. The symbol of Christ, concrete, historic, and traditional as it is, is nevertheless also a universally valid one. Its meaning is that human existence everywhere and always can be renewed through ecstatic participation in being-itself, which is Tillich's word for God.

This involves of course considering the place and worth of Bible and Church in addressing the human situation with the Christian message—a task which Tillich accomplishes with rare learning and critical insight. Every theologian finds it necessary to reinterpret the handed-down images and formulations of his faith in order to show that they mean more than they seem to say, or can be made to say

what they really mean. Tillich is no exception. In the reinterpreting process as he carries it on, some traditional concepts and symbols come off rather badly, and those who are still wedded to them naturally take offense. But the remarkable thing is that, given Tillich's unwavering al-legiance to the question-answer scheme, so much of the tradition can be retrieved and enhanced.

Just how well Tillich commends and conveys the Christian message in this or that respect is a matter which has already been widely, earnestly discussed. But there is abundant evidence of general and continued admiration for the spaciousness, vitality, and rich elaboration of Tillich's vision, in which truth and faith are fused with incomparable appeal and power.

John C. Cooper (review date 16 October 1968)

SOURCE: "Master Teacher," in *The Christian Century,* Vol. LXXXV, No. 42, October 16, 1968, pp. 1305-06.

[*In the following review, Cooper recommends* A History of Christian Thought *to readers both familiar with and new to Tillich, stating that the book introduces Tillich's main theological interests.*]

This is the second posthumous work of Paul Tillich to be edited by his former student, Carl E. Braaten of the Luth-eran School of Theology at Chicago. Its substance was originally given as lectures during Tillich's tenure at Union Theological Seminary, but he had neither the time nor the inclination to put those lectures into book form. The "first edition" of Tillich's lectures on the history of Christian thought was produced in 1953 by Peter H. John, who stenographically recorded, transcribed and mimeographed them. Braaten's text is based on John's "second edition," produced in 1956.

Like **Perspectives on 19th and 20th Century Protestant Theology**, Braaten's first effort at editing Tillich's lectures, **A History of Christian Thought** is a vital contribution to the present generation of theological students and teachers. In a sense it constitutes the first part of the great story of the Christian intellectual tradition as interpreted by Tillich, the latter part having been presented in **Perspectives**.

The over-all schema of Tillich's **History of Christian Thought** is straightforward and clear. He begins with a general introduction to "The Concept of Dogma," in which he deals with the element of thought in human religious experience. Next he discusses "The Preparation for Christianity," stressing the concept of *kairos* and the importance of the Roman Empire, Hellenistic philosophy and the mystery religions as well as developments within Judaism. Next Tillich describes "Theological Develop-ments in the Ancient Church," discussing in his character-istic manner the importance of philosophy for the develop-ment of the Christian creedal formulas. Tillich's favorites, Origen and Pseudo-Dionysius, receive special attention here.

Tillich further develops the history of Christian thought by recounting "Trends in the Middle Ages," which he identifies as "scholasticism, mysticism, and Biblicism," a trinity of interests which often occurred together. Tillich buffs will enjoy his discussion of "Pantheism and Church Doctrine" and his accounts of Joachim of Floris and the meaning of German mysticism. All of Tillich's pet interests receive thorough treatment: mysticism, the Holy Spirit, philosophy, the conquest of demonic anxiety.

Tillich is helpful, as always, in his examination of "Roman Catholicism from Trent to the Present" (Section IV) and "The Theology of the Protestant Reformers" (Section V). Reading Tillich's relatively lengthy discussions of Martin Luther and John Calvin should be instructive to those who may wonder why Tillich often declared himself to be a "Lutheran" theologian. Section VI, "The Development of Protestant Theology," covers Protestant Orthodoxy, the phenomenon of pietism and the coming and development of the Enlightenment. For further interpretation of the Enlightenment the reader should turn to *Perspectives on 19th and 20th Century Protestant Theology*, which begins approximately where *A History of Christian Thought* ends.

For those who know their Tillich, reading this book will be a refreshing experience—like the memory of a happy event now forever past. For those who are new to Tillich's thought, it is a good place to begin, for in the history of Christian thought Tillich was a master teacher—and in its dialectic of Catholic substance and Protestant principle he lived and moved and had his being.

George Lindbeck (essay date October 1983)

SOURCE: "An Assessment Reassessed: Paul Tillich on the Reformation," in *Journal of Religion,* Vol. 63, No. 4, October, 1983, pp. 376-393.

[*In the essay below, Lindbeck discusses Tillich's conception of the Reformation and how it applies to modern theories of thought such as existentialism and psychology.*]

Forty-six years ago Paul Tillich wrote an article for the *American Journal of Sociology* on the question of whether the Reformation has a future.[1] It was later republished in *The Protestant Era,*[2] where generations of theology students have since encountered it. Together with various other of Tillich's writings, it will serve well as a starting point for reflections on the Reformation in this celebratory decade of the 1980s which began with the 450th anniversary of the Augsburg Confession and now continues with the 500th anniversary of Martin Luther's birth.

One reason for using Tillich as a stimulus for thinking about the future of the Reformation is that his view of the human prospect is by no means wholly outdated. What he foresaw in 1937 on the eve of the Second World War, in the midst of the depression, and at the height of Nazism

and Stalinism was no less grim than our present projections, and not altogether dissimilar in outline. We shall say more about this later. In the second place, some of his attempts to interpret Reformation insights in contemporary terms have probably been more influential than any other similar efforts, especially in North America. They have become standard fare in academic theology, not to mention pastoral counseling or CPE (Clinical Pastoral Education) courses where his name may never be mentioned. In our present context, however, the most important consideration is that the Reformation of which Tillich approved was structurally very much like that proposed by the *Confessio Augustana*. His assessment of the Reformation is from a perspective strikingly similar to that of the Confession.

This may seem surprising. Tillich was Lutheran in background, but he was anything but a confessionalist. I have found only one specific reference to the Confessions in his writings. That happens to be a passing, though favorable, mention of the *Augustana* which I shall note in due course, but it provides no grounds for postulating any special affinity. Tillich thought of himself as close to Luther, not Melanchthon. Yet Tillich's Luther is clearly the Luther who approved of the Augsburg Confession. I shall, as a matter of fact, often be thinking of this Luther—the Luther who provides background and support for the Confession—when I refer in what follows to Augsburg and the Reformation as defined by Augsburg.

The major similarity between Tillich and Augsburg is on the structural interrelationship of the reformatory principle—justification by faith—and the catholic heritage. For both Tillich and Augsburg, these two elements are interdependent. The message of justification needs what Tillich calls Catholic substance as its source of energy and effectiveness, while the Catholic substance, in turn, needs the message in order to keep it or make it a source of justifying faith. The relation could be compared to that of a pruning knife and a fruit tree, especially if one stresses that those who wield the pruning knife are themselves nourished by the fruit of the tree. As we shall see, Tillich and Augsburg differ in their descriptions of justification and catholicity, but on the structure of the interaction they are in agreement.

Thus, in the case of Augsburg, justification by faith—that is, trust in God alone for salvation—operates as a rule in terms of which abuses in church teaching, worship, discipline, and governance are to be corrected (articles 22-28). The elimination of abuses, however, is not meant to abolish use. The basic doctrines, liturgy, church discipline, and ecclesiastical structures of the past are to be retained, except that they are now to be employed to console consciences rather than terrify them, and to promote the new obedience (article 6) which is the offshoot of faith rather than the vain works by which human beings seek to save or justify themselves. The contention of Augsburg is that it is a catholic document. It proposes to purify the catholic heritage rather than to jettison it. Its claim, one might say, is that it does not throw out the baby with the bathwater.

If one asks why Catholic substance is so important, the fundamental theological (as contrasted with practical or political) argument is that it serves as means of grace. It is through the sacraments properly administered and the Word purely preached in accordance with the ancient trinitarian and christological creeds that God gives his Spirit and evokes the response of faith. Usages which promote faith are to be retained even when they are post-biblical developments. This is the major argument for the continuation of private confession on which both Augsburg (article 25) and Luther laid much stress. Similarly, the historic ministerial and episcopal polity should be maintained (articles 5, 14, 28) because they are needed for the sake of preaching, sacraments, church discipline, and unity. The only condition, expressed in the vivid language of the times, is that the bishops stop raging against the gospel. If they do this, their authority must be affirmed, because that authority can be used to promote the trust in God and new obedience for whose sake authority should be reshaped. Thus the reciprocity between Catholic substance and justification by faith is everywhere in evidence.

Tillich, no less than Augsburg, thinks of Catholic substance as means of grace, although he does not use that terminology. He does not speak in sixteenth-century Aristotelian fashion of the sacraments, for example, as tools or instrumental causes (article 5). Instead his concepts are derived from nineteenth-century existentialism. Thus for him the phrase "Catholic substance" refers to a total milieu rich in symbolism, mystery, sacraments, and liturgical celebration with a strong sense of tradition and of the wider church community and its authority. It is not to be narrowly identified with Roman Catholicism, although it is certainly to be found there.[3] He suggests that it is present in a less authoritarian and therefore potentially more available form in Eastern Orthodoxy, and to a smaller extent in Anglicanism.[4] Nor, for that matter, is it totally lacking in older Lutheran and other Protestant traditions, and in Protestant liberalism.[5] It is easier in such settings for human beings to become aware of the depth dimension of human existence in both its sacral and demonic power. The conscious and unconscious levels interact. It becomes possible to be more open to transcendent reality or, as he prefers to say, the ground of being. Vitalities inaccessible to conscious control flow upward through the Catholic substance and transform the person for good or for ill. As the reference to "ill" indicates, the substance in itself is ambiguous or ambivalent. It is for this reason that the Protestant principle, the message of justification by faith, is critically important. Its purpose is to make sure that the catholic heritage is rightly used rather than abused.

Tillich's name for the corruption of Catholic substance is heteronomy.[6] Instead of being theonomous—that is, porous or transparent to the divine ground—the substance can become hardened and opaque. It ceases to be a means, and

becomes an end in itself. The ecclesiastical system becomes tyrannical, the source of alienating and oppressive laws. The sacraments become automatic guarantees operating with magical power rather than tangible promises through which God awakens and communicates faith. Relative goods are absolutized, and conditional truths are treated as unconditional. Thus, idolatry proliferates: finite things are made into objects of trust and used for self-justification. The catholic heritage, in short, can become a substitute for and obstacle to God rather than the medium through which comes grace, freedom, and faith.

Such corruptions, it should be noted, can be the source either of false anxiety or of false security. Terror results when the false gods fail, or when their demands are impossible or alienating. This very fear, however, may be used to enforce dependence on the ecclesiastical system. When capitulation is complete, peace of mind may be the reward, but at the cost of personal development and creativity. Tillich is at times exceedingly harsh in his criticisms of authoritarian Catholicism.

Against these corruptions, the Protestant principle proclaims the priority of justifying faith, of basic confidence. This confidence is grounded in the God beyond all gods and therefore does not rely unconditionally on anything finite no matter how good, true, precious, or powerful it may be. It is double-edged. It opposes false absolutes, on the one hand, and confers true assurance, on the other. It is the source of the prophetic critique of all idolatry, self-salvation, and injustice, but also the source of the consoling word of the gospel, the promise of unconditional forgiveness and acceptance. Prophetic iconoclasm destroys false security, while gospel promises confer true assurance. The prophet frees from fear of idols until the only fear remaining is the fear of God, while the gospel preacher makes clear that God's mercy is greater than his wrath.

Thus prophetic criticism and gospel comfort spring from and serve the same justifying faith. They are in their unity generally referred to by Tillich as the Protestant principle, while, like Augsburg, he tends to reserve "justification by faith" for the consolatory aspect, for the proclamation that God accepts the unacceptable. But the Protestant principle itself combines, one might say, this Lutheran stress on the consolation of consciences with the more typically Calvinistic abhorrence of idols.[7]

The conceptualization is different, but the conclusion is the same as Augsburg's. Tillich agrees that Protestant principle and Catholic substance depend on each other. Both hold that the substance has more independence than the principle. The absolutization and rigidification of the tradition at its idolatrous worst cannot prevent a few droplets of grace from seeping through, while a Protestantism emptied of the heritage cannot transmit anything at all. No saving confidence is generated by prophetically destroying the false securities of the past and then failing to use the words, sacraments, and symbols which mediate the presence of the Unconditionally Reliable. That is rather like driving out one demon and leaving the souls of men and women open to seven devils worse than the first (Luke 11:24-27). This is why the papal church, even if ruled by the Antichrist, was not condemned by Augsburg as was the systematic anticatholicism of the left-wing Reformation. Rome, at least, was not swept and garnished, but retained the substance.[8] For comparable reasons, Tillich, with all his dislike for the authoritarianism of pre-Vatican II Roman Catholicism, expresses much more respect for its staying power and social and religious significance than for traditionless, up-to-date, middle-class Protestant liberalism. In short, to use a contrast Tillich once employs, the Protestant principle is corrective rather than constitutive of the church.[9] To make it constitutive leads ultimately to the evisceration of Protestantism.

The story of later Protestantism from this perspective is that of protracted and progressive disaster. Because of the schism, the continuing polemic with Rome, and internal divisions, the Protestant principle has become constitutive rather than corrective. Gradually the Catholic substance has drained away.

Yet, as Tillich emphasizes, the achievements of Protestantism during the centuries when it still retained much of the heritage were enormous. Protestants were stripped of external security, unsure of themselves, burdened with an immense sense of guilt, and yet because what confidence they had was grounded in the Ultimate, they were capable, as Luther paradigmatically illustrates, of great courage, energy, and creativity. We have here a historically unique combination of self-abasement and self-affirmation. As has been said of the Puritans, they groveled in the dust before God and trod on the neck of kings. Thus Protestants were often to a remarkable degree critical without being nihilists, iconoclastic without being anarchists, and individualistic without being socially irresponsible. They forged new and powerful types of personality, culture, political and social organization, and theology and philosophy.

Not only liberal democracy, but also movements as diverse as Enlightenment humanism, Marxism, existentialism, and depth psychology are, according to Tillich, largely secular outworkings of the Protestant principle in its critical aspect. In its anti-ideological thrust, for example, Marxism carries out the eminently Protestant task of unmasking the gods of tradition,[10] and Freudianism struggles against the illusory gods of the psyche. Each of these movements, to be sure, has its own tendency toward self-absolutization and stands in constant need of the Protestant critique. Thus, in conclusion, Protestantism has deeply influenced modern Western culture which, with all its strengths and weaknesses, has produced the closest thing to a universal civilization the world has ever seen.

Yet it must be remembered that aberrant interpretations of justifying faith developed even during the period when Protestantism was at the height of its power. Tillich criticizes two developments in particular. One of these—

starting with Melanchthon, according to Tillich—intellectualized faith.[11] The element of trust, of *fiducia*, was shortchanged in favor of *assensus*, of assent or belief in correct doctrine. This led to the blight of Protestant orthodoxy which lives on in fundamentalistic biblicism. Nothing has done more to alienate modern men and women from religion. To make justification by faith inseparable from correct beliefs is to require the sacrifice of the critical faculties on the altar of an absolutized bible or doctrinal system. But the prophetic element in Protestantism has resisted such idolatry. One manifestation of this prophetic resistance is the flourishing of biblical criticism on Protestant soil. Biblical criticism, Tillich claims, is the most daringly and creatively self-critical enterprise which any religion has ever had the courage to undertake.[12] And yet there were losses as well as gains. The fight against absolutizing belief was admirable because it was inspired by faith, but this same battle also contributed to the loss of the understanding of justification by faith.

This loss is no less apparent in another development which opposed the orthodox absolutizing of intellectual beliefs by emphasizing, not critical intelligence, but religious experience. Here again the proper understanding of faith was impaired. Pietism, revivalism, and experience-centered liberalism all tended, though in different ways, to confuse faith with conversion experiences, or pious feelings, or decisions for Christ. Faith, however, is none of these things, but may or may not be accompanied by them. When faith is thought of as a higher or better state of feeling or consciousness, it is likely to be made into a self-induced human act which, so to speak, merits salvation. Tillich warns against this danger in his **Systematic Theology**. We must always, he says, remember that justification is *"by grace through faith"* (italics added).[13] The *sola gratia* (as, of course, Augsburg also insists) is necessary to the *sola fide*. The emphasis on grace makes clear that God is the cause of faith. Faith is receptivity. It accepts God's acceptance of us and is thus independent of any particular experience. To suppose otherwise is for both Augsburg and Tillich to fall into the *Schwärmerei*, the enthusiasm, of the left-wing Reformation, which was then revived in new forms by pietism, revivalism, and experience-centered liberalism.

Given these distortions, it is not surprising that Protestantism has lost its creative power. The distortions in the understanding of faith have, as we have already noted, been accompanied by the progressive dissipation of the traditional heritage. "The loss of spiritual substance," to quote Tillich, "has been tremendous. . . . Few are the springs of life which are left. . . . The springs of the past are almost exhausted—the substance has almost wasted away."[14] The historic Protestant churches can no doubt maintain their organizational existence for an indefinitely extended time, but their pallid religiosity is no longer a potent force in the lives of their members or in the wider society. If Tillich were writing now, forty years later, he would probably add that what power remains is largely found in the dangerously uncatholic and unprotestant—

that is uncritical and idolatrous—Protestant folk piety exploited by the so-called conservative and electronic churches. Even a half century ago he concluded that the Protestant era had come to an end.

In this post-Protestant age, he goes on to say, the doctrine of justification has become unintelligible "even to Protestant people in the churches; indeed, as I [i.e., Tillich] have over and over again had the opportunity to learn, it is so strange to the modern man that there is scarcely any way of making it intelligible to him. And yet this doctrine . . . has torn asunder Europe . . . has made innumerable martyrs; has kindled the bloodiest and most terrible wars of the past; and has deeply affected European history and with it the history of humanity. This whole complex of ideas which for more than a century—not so very long ago—was discussed in every household and workshop, in every market and country inn . . . is now scarcely understandable even to our most intelligent scholars. We have here a breaking down of tradition which has few parallels."[15]

Tillich believed that even in the absence of traditional substance, justification by faith could at least in part be made intelligible to the modern mind. His efforts to do so, however, for the first time move him and us beyond the perspectives of the *Confessio Augustana*. Up until now his opponents have been the Confession's opponents, and his friends, its friends. Even his attack on orthodox and biblicist distortions of faith can, in the version I have presented, be construed as consistent with the Reformers' denunciations of the dead intellectualism of the scholastics. His language, to be sure, is often alien to Melanchthon, but this by itself is no indication of disagreement. The imagery which Luther freely borrowed from the German mystics, for example, is at least as luxuriantly non-Melanchthonian (nonbiblical, nonhumanistic, and nonscholastic) as Tillich's idealistic, romantic and existentialist conceptuality. What counts in these matters is use, and Tillich's usage in the form so far expounded can, like Luther's, be considered as well within the Augsburg guidelines. Doubts arise, however, when we turn to his translation of justification by faith into a modern idiom.

He does this by extending the meanings of the concepts of sin and of faith in order to make them intelligible in our day. This is the most widely known part of his analysis. All of us are to some extent familiar with it, even if not under Tillich's name. The Reformation understanding of sin, he claims, includes insights which have been more fully developed in modern existentialism; or, to put it the other way around, philosophical existentialism gives us a picture of the human being which is a secularized version of the Reformation understanding of man as sinner. In the one citation of the Augsburg Confession which I earlier mentioned, Tillich approvingly notes that its definition of original sin, in contrast to traditional ones, incorporates the notion of unbelief, that is, anxiety or lack of trust.[16] Anxiety, however, is what existentialism sees as fundamental to human existence. The centrality of anxiety, in turn,

implies a whole anthropology. Human beings are precarious centers of finite freedom who, just because they are both finite and free, are permeated to the very core of their beings by the anxious search for security. This search takes three forms: the quest for ontic assurance against threat of death, for spiritual assurance against the threat of meaninglessness or emptiness, and for moral assurance against the threat of sinful guilt and condemnation.[17]

In the light of this analysis, the great difference between the Reformation and the present is that the anxiety of sin then predominated, whereas now the anxiety of meaninglessness reigns supreme. It is because of this that the Reformers do not speak to our situation. They address the problem of sin, not of meaninglessness. But modern men and women both inside and outside the church no longer ask Luther's question, "How do I get a gracious God?" They are not troubled by the divine demand for righteousness nor consumed by the search for a merciful God. They do not live in apprehension of the Last Judgment, purgatorial fires, or the horrors of hell. They may be burdened by what we generally call "guilt feelings" or a sense of worthlessness, but these are quite different from fear and trembling before God's wrath. It thus makes no sense to tell them—to tell us—that God forgives unconditionally. That is not our problem.

Our problem is meaninglessness. The pluralism of the modern world and the relativization of all religious, moral, political, and even scientific absolutes (which has in part resulted from the Protestant critique) has produced a state of pervasive uncertainty and doubt. Most people feel that they do not really believe or know anything, not even their own identity, although they may make vigorous protestations to the contrary. When they are forced to be honest with themselves, the underlying meaninglessness breaks through, and they are plunged into a despair and hopelessness similar to Luther's *Anfechtungen*.

Luther countered his despair with the thought that limitless self-accusation—the experience of being absolutely unforgivable—can itself be a sign of grace. He affirms, in effect, that the courage honestly to confront our total sinfulness is possible only if we are sustained at a deeper level of our being by basic confidence or justifying faith in God's goodness.

Tillich translates this teaching into the statement that illusionless and nonescapist acknowledgment of despair, whether over sin or meaninglessness, presupposes meaning or forgiveness.[18] This goes beyond the Reformers in three ways. It includes, as we would expect, the anxiety of meaninglessness, and not only of sin, in the despair which is unto life rather than death. Second, however, Tillich argues from hopelessness to prior grace as to a logically necessary presupposition, while for Luther the connection is contingent, that is, dependent on God's free decision. God is under no necessity to save the despairing. We know that utter despair can be a work of God's grace only because that is the kind of God the Bible tells us about. A third difference is that for Tillich justifying faith or basic confidence need not involve any conscious recognition of God or his mercy. Considered in itself, faith is preconceptual and may exist without any conscious object. It is what Tillich calls "absolute faith" which exists "without the safety of words and concepts . . . without a name, a church, a cult, a theology. But it is moving in the depth of all of them."[19] In short, to use technical philosophical language, justifying faith is the transcendental condition for the possibility of the courage to be in the midst of total despair, of total meaninglessness.

On this third point, the difference from the Reformers is most striking. They never thought of faith as preconceptual—except, perhaps, in the case of infants. For them it includes some kind of conscious reference to the God of Abraham, Isaac, Jacob, and Jesus Christ. To sum up, the message of justification *sola fide* is not an argument that despair presupposes faith, but is rather the good news that God forgives the unforgivable for Christ's sake.

Yet, despite these radical differences, it is not self-evident that Tillich's reformulation contradicts the Reformers. They never envisioned anything like his proposal and therefore never directly said either "yea" or "nay." Further, the question of contradiction or compatibility involves at least three distinct issues. One may ask whether the conclusion is true, whether the argument is valid or, third, whether the reformulation as a whole effectively communicates, and the answer might be different in each case. Thus on the issue of truth, it would be possible to conclude with Tillich that justifying faith is present in the authentically despairing who, like infants, know nothing of God's existence or mercy, yet, on the issue of validity, reject his argument for this conclusion. One might instead try to adduce biblical grounds. One might say, for example, that the God of Scripture works also through and in the midst of despair, and given the unboundedness of his love, we cannot limit his gift of faith, of basic confidence, to those who explicitly acknowledge his existence and grace. It is not clear that Luther would have condemned such an argument, and the Augsburg Confession never had occasion to do so. Further, Luther and the Confession might have been neutral on the question of the validity or invalidity of the philosophical argument that despair presupposes faith, just as they were on the arguments of reason for the existence of God. Their major problem, one suspects, would be that Tillich's reformulation could not effectively communicate the message of justification in a fully secularized situation (not to mention other contexts).

This doubt, interestingly enough, can be supported from Tillich's own work. On his own account, the communicative power of his reformulation seems to depend on a situation in which "the effects of the [church's] previous power are latently present"[20] under the secularized surface of Western culture. He makes his case by appealing to philosophical existentialisms whose insights are anticipated by the Reformation understanding of the human condition.[21] These insights, however, cannot be expected to have much persuasiveness for those uninfluenced by historically Christian cultures. Non-Christians or largely de-christianized westerners are not likely to see their own experience reflected in existentialist descriptions of meaninglessness;[22] and, even if they do, they will be likely to interpret this experience of meaninglessness in psychological or sociological terms rather than existentially.

In the second place, the message, meaninglessness presupposes meaning, is not particularly helpful even if accepted. There is little or no transforming power in the recognition that authentic self-acceptance depends on accepting one's unconditional acceptance by something or somebody, one knows not what. In order for God's acceptance to be effective, as we recall from the discussion of Catholic substance, it must be concretely mediated through something or somebody. Where religious symbols have lost their force, however, it is difficult to specify what this might be.

At this point Tillich draws on depth psychology in what is perhaps the best-known of all his proposals. The self-acceptance which a person learns in psychoanalysis on the basis of the acceptance which he receives from the therapist is both an analogue and a possible occasion for the more fundamental self-acceptance which is rooted in the Ground of Being.[23] Under the impulse of this Tillichian suggestion, it is now commonplace to say that God's grace can be mediated wherever one person genuinely accepts another. If Erik Erikson is right, the most fundamental instance of this takes place in earliest infancy through the acceptance which the child receives from its mother. It is this which is the first and deepest source of the basic confidence necessary to healthy human development. In short, interpersonal relations of the right kind are a means of justifying grace.

As we all know, this psychotherapeutic analogue of Reformation doctrine has become the major theological rationale for much contemporary pastoral counseling and CPE work. It has even resulted in some church circles in the use of a book like *I'm O.K., You're O.K.*[24] as an exposition of the contemporary meaning of justification by faith.

It would seem, however, that from Tillich's perspective—not to mention others—such a book is a complete vulgarization of the doctrine. Those who have experienced the reality of justification in their lives do not say, "I'm O.K.," but rather, "I am not O.K." They accuse themselves. They rightly recognize that they are not acceptable. The unconditional acceptance which justifies is not uncritical acceptance. Rather it includes the element of judgment, as Tillich's treatment of the Protestant principle makes evident. The self-acceptance which basic confidence makes possible is not a matter of feeling good about oneself, but rather is strong enough to embrace the realistic recognition of guilt and meaninglessness. Only the neurotic varieties are excluded, and so also is complacency.

In view of the neglect of this judgmental element in much contemporary psychotherapy, it is doubtful that the popularity of depth psychology has made the Reformation view of justification more easily intelligible. Perhaps, indeed, it has done the opposite. According to its critics, it fosters a self-acceptance which discourages self-condemnation and encourages a kind of adjustment to society which has little room for the prophetic protest against idolatry and injustice. In so far as Tillich's discussion of the relation of psychoanalysis to justification by faith has failed to guard against these distortions, so it could be argued, it has contributed to the bastardization rather than the revitalization of the Reformation teaching.

Actually Tillich's analysis would lead one to expect this to happen. In an autonomous culture unredeemed by theonomy and unthreatened by heteronomy, the self is both absolutized and empty. Like Christopher Lasch's infantile narcissistic self,[25] the absolutized autonomous self demands uncritical approval from others. Permissiveness becomes a fundamental human right. Such a self is concerned with human relations only as a means to self-satisfaction or self-realization, and seeks to fill its emptiness with whatever gives it pleasure or peace of mind whether this be material goods or higher states of consciousness. In a society dominated by such attitudes justification by faith is inevitably misinterpreted. Quite another context is needed in order to understand it rightly.

That other context, we recall, has already been described by Tillich. In the light of what we have earlier heard him say about Catholic substance, it would seem that reinterpretations of justification by faith in an autonomous secularized culture can never be more than stopgap measures. No reformulations of the doctrine are likely to have·major impact apart from the symbols, rites, and disciplines transmitted by concrete religious communities. Such means of grace are necessary if the message of justification is to help significantly in transforming individuals, groups, or cultures.

Even if one grants this point, however, it does not mean for Tillich that the Reformation principles have no future. In the essay which I first cited,[26] he argues that the modern Western world which finds them unintelligible is itself coming to an end. It cannot indefinitely survive the disappearance of its substrata of Christian ideals and values. Without the support which these provide, the autonomous individualism of Western modernity degenerates into atomistic anarchy. New collectivism will inevitably arise in which something like the sacred worlds of the past will be necessary for social integration. All the pressures in such a situation would be toward the re-catholicizing of the church.

The collectivist part of this forecast has become more rather than less plausible in the intervening years. New and by now familiar arguments have been added. A futurist such as Robert Heilbronner in his *An Inquiry into the Human Prospect*,[27] for example, thinks that the threat of atomic destruction and the crises provoked by the environmental limits on growth will force great changes

for the sake of human survival (which, as we are all aware, has become vastly more problematic in the last four decades). The typically modern Western attitudes which have developed during centuries of accelerated and uncontrolled growth will have to be reversed, and respect for restraint, stability, and tradition reestablished. Re-catholicization would seem to be part of this package. The church will have to regain the religious substance of the heritage in order to be relevant. Even if Christians are everywhere a small minority amid non-Christian majorities, the more catholic portions of the Christian movement may well have a competitive advantage just as they did in the first centuries under the pagan Roman empire.

If the revival of Catholic substance is to be healthy, however, it will need the pruning knife of the Protestant principle. This, obviously, is a self-evident or analytic conclusion from Tillich's premises. The question, however, is the form which the Protestant principle will take. Will it, in fact, have much continuity with the formulation which it received in the Reformation era?

Tillich never discussed this question in detail, but we can make some projections on the basis of his principles. First, we must note that the culturally dominant form of anxiety may well be very different. It will not be anxiety over individual sin or guilt, as in the sixteenth century, nor over personal meaninglessness, as in the twentieth. Rather, fear of collective death, over the extinction of the human race, will predominate. Unless this anxiety drives us to develop radically different social and cultural patterns, *Homo sapiens* has very little chance of surviving the next thousand years. A change in the culturally dominant form of anxiety, however, is equivalent to a transformation in the experience of sin or evil. Sin and evil will be experienced, so to speak, as outer rather than inner. The new patterns will be closer in some respects to those of the New Testament than to those of the Reformation period. Collectivist regimentation, to be sure, is not the same as the demons and implacable fate which bedeviled late classical antiquity, but it is equally external and equally oppressive. In short, so one could argue, evil will be experienced once again as basically captivity to forces outside the self, to the principalities and powers of which Saint Paul speaks, rather than as inward corruption or meaningless. This would amount to a radical weakening of what Krister Stendahl has called the "Introspective Conscience of the West."[28] That conscience, according to Stendahl, has developed over the course of over 1,500 years. It was articulated by Saint Augustine, deepened by medieval penitentialism, reformed by Luther, and secularized by Freud, but despite the appeals which have been made to Saint Paul on its behalf, it is not a necessary or inevitable part of the biblical message. The fallenness of the human condition can also be experienced and understood, as it largely was in New Testament days, not as inborn or original sin within the individual, but as communal or cosmic entrapment in the old age.

If such a transformation were to take place in the experience of evil, a corresponding shift in the message of salvation could be expected. Something like the futuristic and cosmic eschatology of biblical times would presumably become central. If so, the vivifying message which communicates justifying faith would center on the communal vision of God's coming kingdom rather than on individualistic concern with unconditional forgiveness or on the meaning presupposed by authentic despair.

The critical function of the Protestant principle, furthermore, could be expected to operate in favor of Catholic substance as in the first centuries, rather than against it as in most later periods. In the first centuries it was the more catholic part of the professedly Christian movement which was the chief bearer of the protest against Gnostic absolutization of the spiritual realm over against the material, on the one hand, and the apocalyptic and millennialist reifications of eschatological hope, on the other. Above all it was the catholic center which most effectively struggled against the major idolatry of the time, that of the empire and of emperor worship. It was the Catholics not the Gnostics who produced the martyrs who refused to place a pinch of incense on the emperor's altar. Parallels to all these struggles would seem inevitable in a regimented and collectivist future. The Gnostic spiritualizers who view the world as irremediably evil and therefore withdraw from it into higher states of consciousness are already with us, and so also are the apocalyptic millennialists who set dates for the end of the age. As far as the imperial assumption of divine honors is concerned, this will be a major temptation of any political and cultural order strong enough to rescue humanity from self-destruction. In order to do its job effectively, it will almost be obligated to represent itself as sacrosanct. Thus something like the catholicism of the first centuries would be needed in this hypothetical future as the bearer of both prophetic protest and gospel consolation.

Would this not be, however, the end of the Reformation? A futuristic analogue of early catholicism is not what most Protestants have thought of as a continuation of Luther's work or that of the *Confessio Augustana*. Justification by faith in the sense of confidence in God's forgiving mercy *pro me* would no longer be primary. The chief task of the church would not be seen as that of consoling the terrified consciences of individuals. It would not even be the proclamation of a modern form of this teaching (e.g., despair presupposes meaning). It could perhaps still be described as the message of the acceptance of the unacceptable, but this message would now take a new shape. In the context of a communal and cosmic eschatology, it is entire peoples and humanity as a whole, not primarily individuals considered one by one, which are the locus of unacceptability, and the acceptance of God's acceptance of the self, while by no means abolished, is subsumed under hope for the coming kingdom.

Oddly enough, the sixteenth-century Reformers might have found it easier than Tillich to think of this transformation as a continuation of their work. It would have been easier for them because—as is particularly clear in the case of

Luther—it was Christ as the one to which we should cling rather than the particular form of the clinging which was of decisive importance. The essence of the *sola fide*, in other words, is the *solus Christus* or the *propter Christum solum*.[29] As long as salvation is through Christ alone, it is of secondary importance whether he is trusted for personal forgiveness or relied upon as the coming Messiah.[30] When the problem is that of *Heilsgewissheit*, of assurance of salvation, the answer is in terms of faith in forgiveness for Christ's sake alone, but if the question is, for example, that of the future of humankind, it is hope which responds, but once again, *propter Christum solum*.[31] In the latter case, as long as Christians hope for a future stamped with the lineaments of the crucified and risen one, and not someone else, they are in agreement with the chief article of the Augsburg Confession quite apart from their use or nonuse of the specifically Reformation understandings of sin, faith, and forgiveness *pro me*.

Tillich sometimes seems to affirm something very near to the *solus Christus*. He says, for example, that the message of Christ is "the ultimate expression of the divine,"[32] and protests against all attempts to dissolve that message into a complex of religious experiences, ethical requirements, and philosophical teachings. The message of Christ combines concrete universality with absolute validity because it can embrace every religious possibility and yet, as we see in Jesus' cry of God-forsakenness on the cross, it also prophetically negates every religious reality including itself. Thus, only where the New Being as expressed in the biblical picture of Jesus the Christ is both the center and circumference of life can religious substance and Protestant principle be fully united.

Yet this *solus Christus*, unlike that of the Reformation, is relative to faith rather than independent of it. Christ is "sole" in the sense that only the message of Christ is the absolute symbol of absolute faith. This would appear to mean, however, that one can talk in religiously significant ways about Christ only as a function of the faith which he symbolizes, whereas the logic of the Reformers' position allows them to talk of Christ as savior independently of the faith which he inspires or represents. It would seem, therefore, that Tillich has relativized Jesus Christ and instead made absolute that pattern of human responsiveness implied in justification by faith. He has formulated an anthropological theory—a picture of human existence—suggested by Luther's emphasis on despair as the way to faith, and made this central. This enables him to abstract the "being accepted even though unacceptable" from any explicit reference to Jesus Christ or even to God. It makes it possible for him to speak of justifying (or absolute) faith as operative among all religions and among all peoples whether religious or irreligious. It warrants the formulation of a version of justification by faith which is meaningful to secularists, who are alienated from traditional religious substance or symbolism.

This is, from one point of view, a notable achievement. It constitutes a great increase in the range of the Reformation teaching. On the other hand, however, it is a limitation of that teaching. It would seem that where the introspective conscience of the West disappears, where the human problem is experienced neither as terror over sin nor as existentialist angst, there the Tillichian version of justification by faith is no longer relevant. The Reformation version, in contrast, can survive, although in transmuted form, because the *solus Christus*, rather than a particular form of the experience of the *sola fide*, is crucial.

It would thus seem, in conclusion, that Tillich's reinterpretation of the Reformation is at least at this point at odds with the Reformers' own theology. From their point of view, his mistake is to make a pattern of human existence which was correlated with the proclamation of the *solus Christus* in the late medieval setting into a general norm for that proclamation (as well as for Christianity and for religion as a whole). For him, the Reformers came closer than had ever been done before to describing the essential features of human authenticity, and that is why their message is enduringly valid. Thus anthropology is the constant, and religious symbols the variable for Tillich, as for most contemporary philosophers of religion. For the Reformers, in contrast, the particular religious symbolism represented by the Christian story was the constant, and anthropologies could—at least in principle—vary from one time and place to another. As they put it in their sixteenth-century language, it is not the *verbum internum*, but the *verbum externum* of the gospel which is normative (Augsburg Confession, article 5). It is for this reason that one can relativize their experiences, even their experience of justification by faith, without abandoning allegiance to their doctrine, to the doctrine of Augsburg Confession. It is for this reason also that for Augsburg a re-catholicized Christianity somewhat analogous to that of the first centuries might very well be the triumph, not the end, of the Reformation.

Notes

1. Paul Tillich, "Protestantism in the Present World Situation," *American Journal of Sociology* 43, no. 2 (1937): 236- 48.

2. Paul Tillich, *The Protestant Era*, trans, and ed. James Luther Adams (Chicago: University of Chicago Press, 1948).

3. See esp. Paul Tillich, "The Permanent Significance of the Catholic Church for Protestantism," *Protestant Digest* 3, no. 10 (1941): 23-31. Reprinted in German translation in *Gesammelte Werke*, 14 vols. (Stuttgart: Evangelisches Verlagswerk, 1959-75), 7:124-32 (henceforth cited in the form: *GW*, vol. no., p. no.).

4. E.g., *PE*, p. 248.

5. "Protestantism also has a strong line of thought in which the reality of participation is expressed, from the mystical elements of the early Luther on, to the doctrine of the *unio mystica* in Protestant Orthodoxy, to Pietism, Schleiermacher, Rudolph

Otto and the liturgical reform movements. In these cases 'Catholic substance' reappeared under the control of the 'Protestant principle.'" From an "Afterword" by Paul Tillich in *Paul Tillich in Catholic Thought*, ed. T.F. O'Meara and D.M. Weisser (New York: Doubleday & Co., Image Book ed., 1969), p. 372.

6. *PE*, p. xvi, and "Religionsphilosophic," in *GW*, 1.

7. This double aspect of the Protestant principle is well presented in Tillich's untranslated article, "Der Protestantismus als kritisches und gestaltendes Prinzip," in *GW*, 7: 29-53, and is summarized by James Luther Adams, "Paul Tillich on Luther," in *Interpreters of Luther: Essays in Honor of Wilhelm Pauck*, ed. J. Pelikan (Philadelphia: Fortress Press, 1968), esp. pp. 309-15.

8. This was also Luther's position, as is indicated with particular vividness in his *Concerning Rebaptism* of 1528: "The Christendom which now is under the papacy is truly the body of Christ and a member of it. If it is his body, then it has the true spirit, gospel, faith, baptism, sacrament, keys, the office of the ministry, prayer, holy scripture, and everything that pertains to Christendom. So we are all still under the papacy and therefrom have received our Christian treasures" (*Luther's Works*, American edition, ed. Jaroslav Pelikan and Helmut T. Lehmann [St. Louis: Concordia Publishing House; Philadelphia: Fortress Press, 1958], 40:232).

9. Paul Tillich, "The End of the Protestant Era," *Student World* 30 (1937): 49-51, esp. 57, and, in a more accessible form, *GW*, 7:157.

10. "Religiöser Sozialismus I," *GW*, 2:156, 164.

11. Paul Tillich, *Systematic Theology*, 3 vols. (Chicago: University of Chicago Press, 1957), 2:178.

12. *PE*, p. xliii.

13. Tillich, *Systematic Theology*, 2:179. Tillich comments that "the abbreviated form of 'justification by faith' . . . is extremely misleading" (2:179).

14. *PE*, p. 194.

15. Ibid., p. 196.

16. Tillich, *Systematic Theology*, 2:47.

17. Here I follow Tillich's analysis in *The Courage to Be* (New Haven, Conn.: Yale University Press, 1952), pp. 32-63.

18. *PE*, pp. xiv-xv; but see esp. Paul Tillich, "Rechtfertigung und Zweifel," *Vorträge der theologischen Konferenz zu Giessen*, ser. 39 (Giessen: Alfred Töpelmann, 1924), pp. 19-32.

19. Tillich, *The Courage to Be*, p. 189.

20. Tillich, *Systematic Theology* (1963), 3:246.

21. Tillich, *The Courage to Be*, p. 170.

22. There are, to be sure, exceptions, such as the interest some Japanese Buddhists have in the thought of Heidegger.

23. Tillich, *The Courage to Be*, pp. 164 ff.

24. Thomas A. Harris, *I'm O.K., You're O.K.* (New York: Harper & Row, 1969).

25. Christopher Lasch, *The Culture of Narcissism* (New York: Warner Books, 1979).

26. See n. 1 above.

27. Robert Heilbronner, *An Inquiry into the Human Prospect* (New York: W.W. Norton & Co., 1974).

28. Krister Stendahl, "The Apostle Paul and the Introspective Conscience of the West," reprinted in *Paul among Gentiles and Jews* (Philadelphia: Fortress Press, 1976), pp. 78-96.

29. Often cited as evidence of these assertions are the *Smalcald Articles*, pt. 2, article 1, and Luther's explanation of the second article of the creed in the *Small Catechism*. The texts are in T.G. Tappart, ed., *The Book of Concord* (Philadelphia: Fortress Press, 1959), pp. 292, 345.

30. As Philip Melanchthon puts it in the *Apology* to the Augsburg Confession (article 4:312) faith and hope "cannot be divided as they are in the idle scholastic speculations" (See Tappert, ed., p. 155).

31. This view that justification by faith is the "chief article" only in correlation to a particular type of threat to the gospel is now increasingly widespread even in Lutheran circles. E.g., the report of the international Lutheran/Roman Catholicism Joint Study Commission on "The Gospel and the Church" (commonly called the "Malta Report") says: "As the message of justification is the foundation of Christian freedom in opposition to legalistic conditions for the reception of salvation, it must be articulated ever anew as an important interpretation of the center of the gospel. But . . . the event of salvation to which the gospel testifies can also be expressed comprehensively in other representations derived from the New Testament, such as reconciliation, freedom, redemption, new life and new creation" (See "Das Evangelium und die Kirche, 1967-1971," *Evangelium—Well—Kirche: Schlussbericht und Referate der römisch-katholisch/evangelisch-lutherischen Studien-kommission*, ed. H. Meyer [Frankfurt am Main: Verlag Otto Lembeck, 1975], p. 41).

32. *GW*, 7:137 (my translation).

John K. Roth (review date 22 November 1987)

SOURCE: "A Review of *The Essential Tillich: An Anthology of the Writings of Paul Tillich*," in *Los Angeles Times Book Review*, November 22, 1987, p. 4.

[*In the brief review below, Roth asserts that* The Essential Tillich's *"judicious selections allow Tillich to explain, interpret, and amplify his own themes."*]

Opposed to Nazism, Paul Tillich (1886-1965) left his native Germany for the United States in 1933. His philosophical theology decisively influenced mainline American Protestantism during its heyday in the middle third of this century.

"God," wrote Tillich, "is the answer to the question implied in man's finitude; He is the name for that which concerns man ultimately." Tillich explored the uncertainties of human existence and, in spite of those conditions, helped people to discern the God who provides the courage to be.

This book's editor, F. Forrester Church, senior minister at the Unitarian Church of All Souls in New York City correctly observes that "the religious situation has changed dramatically" since Tillich's death. Impatience with ambiguity and skepticism pushed his approach "into the shadows," but therefore, Church argues, Tillich's insights are needed more than ever "to liberate us from the tyrannies of our times."

Finding Tillich essential, Church offers the essential Tillich. The anthology's eight chapters draw from his sermons as well as from his major books. Its judicious selections allow Tillich to explain, interpret, and amplify his own themes.

In the book's forward, Tillich's daughter, Mutie Tillich Farris, provides an apt evaluation when she commends Church for making her father's thought newly accessible to "any serious reader who has ever asked an existential question."

Iris M. Yob (essay date Fall 1991)

SOURCE: "The Arts as Ways of Understanding: Reflections on the Ideas of Paul Tillich," in *Journal of Aesthetic Education*, Vol. 25, No. 3, Fall, 1991, pp. 5-20.

[*In the following essay, Yob presents Tillich's conception of aesthetic symbols as the most revealing, genuine, and powerful creations of the human mind, and explains how they relate to the visual and aural arts.*]

One may wonder how it is that the German-American Paul Johannes Tillich (1886-1965), theologian primarily and philosopher by training, comes to be included in a discussion of research and teaching for music educators. The wonder may be exacerbated when one also discovers that music is an aesthetic endeavor to which he gave little or no attention. He seldom mentions it, or dance and drama, in his voluminous writings and innumerable papers, and often when he does, they appear in parentheses as though he sensed they somehow belonged to the arts but did not quite know what to do with them once they were admitted for consideration.

His father was an amateur performer and composer, but the son's artistic desires drew him first to literature and then to painting, sculpture, and architecture which, under the disapproving eye of his minister-parent, became a constant source of inspiration and reflection throughout his long professional career. Even then, he laid claim to being "neither an artist, an art historian, an art critic, nor even a philosopher whose special subject is art"—but simply to being "a philosophical theologian."[1]

However, I believe that Tillich warrants our attention because he struggled with many of the same issues, confronted the same challenges, and sensed many of the same possibilities in the study of the visual arts as those who are engaged in the study of the aural arts. He reflected, among other things, on the kinds of understandings paintings, sculptures, and architecture could impart as distinct from those of science and mathematics. And he analyzed the elements of artworks to discover how they function to produce their own distinct understandings. A study of Tillich, therefore, may lead music educators effectively into a search for answers to their own similar questions: Can music be regarded as a way of understanding? If so, how do the elements of music function to impart understandings?

In pursuing his version of these questions, Tillich alerts us to promising ways of thinking about the arts, although his answers are limited by the assumptions of German idealism and the predominance of expressionistic artworks in his analysis. Our critique will build on and offer alternative perspectives to his original contribution.

Are the Arts Ways of Understanding?

As a young man, Tillich served as a German army chaplain during the First World War. It was, he declares, "the dirt, the horrors and the ugliness" he experienced in the trenches more than anything else that induced him "systematically to study the history of art and to collect as many as possible of the cheap reproductions available" to him on the battlefield. On furlough, he visited a Berlin museum where he discovered Botticelli's *Madonna and Child with Singing Angels*, an experience for which he reports he had no better name than "revelatory ecstasy."[2]

To describe the experience as one of ecstasy indicates that it was an intensely emotional one, still memorable over thirty years later and a whole continent removed. But the qualifier "revelatory" suggests its significance had to do with more than feelings, powerful as these may have been. It suggests he also learned something from the experience, and in fact he indicates that in this "one moment of beauty," as he later called it,[3] he gained a new understanding, a decisive insight, which remained with him from that time. It gave him, he declares, "the keys for the interpretation of human existence" and along with "vital joy" brought him "spiritual truth."[4]

From his analysis of the human situation, Tillich identifies certain inescapables: awareness of our own finitude and the anxiety and fear that this produces. He describes anxiety as "the state in which a being is aware of its possible nonbeing" or "the existential awareness of nonbeing."[5] The threat of nonbeing may have been sharpened by the trauma of some of his early experiences, but on continuing reflection he came to understand it not only as the anxiety of having to die, but also, in a preliminary way, as any experience of meaninglessness, guilt, or condemnation in our daily lives.[6] And when being is threatened with nonbeing, he reasons, human beings are driven to ask "the ontological question," "the question of being." This, he claims, is the universal question—the central question of philosophy as well as of myth and the arts.[7]

Although the question of being arises first in the personal experience of existential anxiety, Tillich argues that it is pursued through a number of levels, including inquiry into the nature of being as a part of everything that human beings encounter, evolving eventually into a search for what he calls "the ground of being," "the power of being," or "Being-itself."[8] Between his first formulation of the question and the last lies a vast distance, moving as it does from personal experience (concern about our own mortality) to philosophy (inquiry into the nature of being) and ultimately to religion (the search for Being-itself), but he regards Being-itself as the ultimate answer to the original question of our being. The search for this answer he describes as "ultimate concern,"[9] the driving, shaping, integrating feature of individuals and societies.

It is in this setting that he finds the arts have an indispensable role. They are an active expression of ultimate concern. They explore the nature of being and at some level reveal to us in our existential *angst* how we may find "the courage to be."

As a way of understanding these things, art performs three interrelated functions, according to Tillich. First, it expresses. That is, it expresses humankind's fear of the reality it discovers, the finitude, meaninglessness, and isolation in human experience. But in its expression, art transcends both "mere objectivity," for it gives more than a camera record of reality and also "mere subjectivity," for it is more than just an "outcry"—it may also express a level of being or reality beyond the immediate.

Art also transforms. It transforms ordinary reality "in order to give it the power of expressing something which is not itself." That is, art takes givens and makes them into symbols. So the gold ground of Byzantine or early Gothic pictures is not merely decorative but is symbolic of the heavenly spheres beyond, and the landscapes in Dutch paintings are not the landscapes we meet in an ordinary encounter with trees, fields, roads, and wide horizons.

Finally, art anticipates. It anticipates the possibilities that transcend the given in both its portrayal of perfection and also of distortion. It is able to find a kind of harmony in the disharmonious or, in effect, courage in the experience of anxiety, finitude, meaninglessness, and estrangement. In other words, art anticipates salvation.[10]

When science examines something, he explains, it discovers the thing's structure and appearance but, he indicates, this does not show what the thing means for itself. The tree registered and explained by Linnaeus does not give us the kind of knowledge that a Van Gogh painting of the same tree would give. In art, he says, we experience "the dynamic power of being which is effective in the life and struggle of the tree." We can "discover its inner meaning, the way in which it expresses the power of being which is present in everything that is."

Of course, he recognizes the arts and the sciences have much in common. They both transform elements of the perceived world around us into images so they may become objects for our reception. Both art and science are rightly labelled *theoria*. But, he adds, in its "cognitive" or scientific capacity, *theoria* gives an analysis of what things are in their relation to each other; in its "aesthetic" capacity, *theoria* gives the vision of what things are in their very being.

He continues, the kind of knowledge that science gives depends on a degree of distance and detachment from the object, but art unites us with and relates us to its objects. Consequently, "intuitive participation in works of art liberates us from the loneliness of our separated existence in a much more radical way than cognitive participation can."[11] That is, art can do what science cannot. By means of scientific transformation and reception, we can learn nothing more about an object, a tree, an animal, or whatever, than "its calculable internal and external relations";[12] but art "uses pieces of the ordinarily encountered reality in order to show a meaning which is mediated by the given object but transcends it."[13]

Apparently Tillich recognizes that the arts no less than the sciences contribute to what we know of the world we live in and who we are, and yet they contribute different kinds of knowledge. While he reserves the expression "cognitive function" for the activity of the sciences and related disciplines and "aesthetic awareness" for the arts, he nevertheless prefers to call the products of both "knowledge."[14] Art, like science, he proposes, "discovers reality. It is theoretical in the genuine sense of *theoria* but it is not cognitive."[15]

It produces knowledge, it brings awareness, it is theoretical, but it is not cognitive. What is Tillich saying here? We inhabit a world we have constructed largely on scientific assumptions, by means of scientific method, and according to scientific findings. Science has criticized and often overturned the old myths about who we are and what we know—thankfully, irreversibly. But Tillich is reminding us here that all that can be known is not the result of scientific activity alone. He is reclaiming "knowledge" from the

exclusive use of science and sharing it among all the activities of searching, thinking, theorizing, expressing, meaning-making human beings. He is reminding us that all we can know is mediated not only by the scientific enterprise but also by aesthetic, philosophical, and religious endeavors.

It seems that Tillich has the same problem with the term "cognition" that he believes others may have with the term "knowledge," although neither "knowledge" nor "cognition" need exclude "aesthetic awareness." We may prefer, however, to regard music as a "way of understanding" or a "form of thought."[16] But whatever music may be called, the important point is that some knowledge may not be propositional in character—it may be "awareness" (to adopt Tillich's term) that is mediated by means of the intuited, the expressive, the allusive, the imaginative, the emotional, or the spiritual.

While we may applaud Tillich's pointing us in the direction of regarding the arts as serious makers of meaning, we may not be satisfied with his description of the meaning that they make. His moment of "revelatory ecstasy" in contemplation of *Madonna and Child with Singing Angels* may have found best expression for him in an exploration of the themes of finitude, being, and the ground of being, themes that he could pursue with vigor in theology and philosophy. However, in his enthusiasm for these ideas, he sometimes lost clarity. Being-itself is said to "embrace" not only being but also nonbeing.[17] It is the "ground," "power," and "structure of being" and "the really real," but is not a thing.[18] It is something we are at once separated from yet participate in. It is God and it is beyond God and secularized. It is our ultimate concern, but it is nonpersonal and amoral. Ontologically speaking, it is "Being-itself," psychologically speaking, it is "ultimate concern," theologically speaking, it is "God," but this blurring of distinctions gives rise to many questions.

Leaving aside the difficulties raised by the notions of being, nonbeing and Being-itself, the significant feature of aesthetic productions, according to Tillich, is that the realities they refer to have to do with who we are, what we fear, and wherein we may find hope and courage. That is, they provide cognitive access to fundamental issues lying at the heart of human experience, some of which, it is possible, cannot be empirically explored.

Scientific knowledge too is frequently of transcendent realities, if by "transcendent" we mean outside the reach of observation, measurement, and other means of experimental verification, for science deals with putative entities such as black holes, electrical charges, quanta, and subatomic structures. However, art has always had a particular affinity with religion because it is often the most adequate means, if not the only means, of representing or expressing the transcendent realities that religion is attentive to.

Whatever it may be that art productions reveal, it is, Tillich proposes, something that without art otherwise "would be covered forever." This suggests that the arts are both indispensable and irreplaceable in the sum total of human knowledge and also that they are irreducible. Their revelations are not always accessible by any other means and cannot be expressed in any other medium without loss. This does not mean that talk about the meanings of artworks is impossible or pointless, but simply that, for great art at least, such talk is not exhaustive for something will always be lost in the translation. Tillich's work testifies to this fact when one peruses the voluminous works in which he continues to explore the insight he gained originally from the Botticelli. Maybe the most adequate and meaningful response to art is more art.

Although he has collapsed together existential, ontological, aesthetic, and religious notions, and although his own argument is sometimes more bewildering than enlightening, Tillich is at least attempting to indicate that aesthetic productions have meaning that is arguably important in our understanding of ourselves, of the world, and of the transcendent. This meaning is, he suggests, not accessible to other ways of understanding. Others agree and on these grounds, a substantial body of literature proposes that the arts are an essential part of a well-rounded liberal education.[19] As an irreplaceable, indispensable, irreducible way of understanding, they belong in the curriculum. The task of teachers and their students is to discover the revelations and insights of particular art productions and communicate these discoveries in ways that faithfully reflect the medium that embodies them. And this leads us into our next consideration.

How Do the Arts Impart and Shape Our Understandings?

That which sets human beings apart from the nonhuman, Tillich maintains, is their capacity for language. In encountering a particular tree, he explains, we experience more than just the tree—we experience at the same time "treehood, the universal, that which makes a tree a tree." And, through language, we give this universal a name, liberating ourselves from the particular. But language, he notes, is not bound to the spoken word. It may be written or read. And more than that, "It is present in silence as well as in talk. It is effective in the visual arts, in the creative as well as the receptive act." As he observes, "Only that being which can speak can also paint." In a painting, he proposes, meaning is expressed through the choice of colors, grades of light and darkness, forms of balance, and structural features[20]—all of which may be symbolic elements.

Tillich heartily welcomed the renewed philosophical interest in symbols, believing that only with more profound understandings of symbolic functioning can we comprehend without distortion the meaning of alternative "languages" (that is, verbal and nonverbal symbol systems). He is particularly anxious to avoid the derogative "Only a symbol!" For him, it is instead a matter of "Not less than a symbol!" because he regards symbols as

"the most revealing creations of the human mind."[21] While his approach to symbols can only loosely be called a theory, he nevertheless identifies with those who recognize that different kinds of understandings "demand different approaches and different languages."[22] As an introduction to the specific languages of religion in which he was primarily interested, he variously specifies six characteristic of symbols in general[23] which he believes are foundational for any understanding of symbolic languages.

First, he indicates that symbols point beyond themselves to something else. The implication is that not the symbol itself but that to which it points is the focus of interest. In this way, he proposes, symbols are like signs: just as the sign of the red traffic light does not point to itself but "to the necessity of stopping,"[24] so we employ some "symbolic material" to point to something else. This "material" need not be verbal, he notes, but can be pictorial, dramatic, concrete, or abstract. And just as colors, shapes, shades, and balance may be visual symbols, so, this suggests, rhythm, pitch, tone, volume, and the other elements of musical works are potentially aural symbols. Whatever the symbolic material may be, Tillich has identified here a basic "pointing" function of symbols—a symbol is something that stands for, refers to, points to, denotes, or represents.

In elaborating this first characteristic, Tillich goes on to indicate to what a symbol may refer: a symbol is anything which refers to the transcendent, extraordinary, and ultimate. That is, a symbol "points to something which cannot be directly grasped but must be expressed indirectly"—to that which transcends empirical reality or to "a dimension of reality which is not open to an ordinary encounter" or to "ultimate reality."[25]

The second characteristic of symbols he identifies is that while many things may "point," symbols are able to point or refer because they "participate in the reality and power" and "the meaning" of that to which they point. Nonsymbolic pointers are such things as mathematical signs; the letters of the alphabet because they do not participate in the sound to which they point; a word such as "desk" because the desk itself has essentially nothing to do with the four letters d-e-s-k; and the red light which summons the driver to stop but which bears no intrinsic relationship to stopping.

In contrast, he identifies as symbols the representatives of a person or institution because they "participate in the honor of those they are called on to represent"; liturgical and poetical languages because they have built up over time "connotations in situations in which they appear so that they cannot be replaced"; and the flag because it "participates in the power of the king or nation for which it stands."[26] Because they participate in what they symbolize, he adds, symbols have a certain irreplaceableness and an "organic connection" with that to which they point. Nonsymbolic pointers, on the other hand, are arbitrarily chosen, merely conventional, and readily replaced if ever it is expedient to do so.[27]

Participation, developed within idealist and romantic traditions, has been a rather indeterminate notion.[28] In one respect it is too narrow, in another too broad, to explain clearly how symbols work. It is too limited in that it depends on metaphysical considerations and assumptions that are inherently problematic. Primarily, it assumes that if there is a symbol, then there is something which is symbolized and in which it participates. As Peter Fingesten points out, however, this is particularly open to question when one recalls the symbols of prehistoric and forgotten religious art. The Egyptian term *Ka* and its bird symbol, for instance, are no guarantee that the shadow soul which they symbolized actually existed. "One can make a symbol of anything," he warns, "but only at the expense of its objective reality or by inventing a symbol like the Ka which may have no reality at all."[29]

Further, since Tillich regards participation in ontological terms, he implies that a symbol participates in several realities, each dependent on what it is a symbol of. But what is the real nature of a rising crescendo if in various musical pieces it may symbolize power, triumph, mounting excitement, deepening agony, or simply a change of intensity in whatever mood is being portrayed? If it participates in the being of all the realities it points to, how are these various beings interrelated within the ontological structure of the symbol itself? These troublesome questions can be eliminated only if participation is redescribed in terms that avoid narrowly defined ontological claims, as we shall see.

In another sense, the notion of participation fails as an explanation of how symbols work because it claims more than it can deliver. Primarily, it does not distinguish symbols from nonsymbols. As William Rowe rightly points out,[30] our response to a ringing fire alarm, which in Tillich's analysis is not a symbol, is the same fear and flight that would accompany our response to an actual fire. As he enumerates other instances, the distinction between nonsymbol and symbol on the grounds that nonsymbols are conventional, arbitrary, and replaceable begins to break down, for these signs also come to be inextricably related to what they signify.

Moreover, some things Tillich identifies as symbols, Rowe points out, are not as organically connected with their referent as he may suggest. A nation's flag is such a symbol—it is accepted through a process that typically begins with a number of artists' designs, which are deliberated over and evaluated at many levels, until eventual agreement and final approval is reached by vote or general consensus. Such a selection process would be unnecessary if in its very being the symbol "radiated the power of being and meaning of that for which it stands,"[31] as Tillich claims.

And yet, to describe symbols as participating in another reality does seem at times to coincide with our experience of them: we treat sacramental wine and bread differently from other wine and bread, the flag differently form other pieces of fabric, a king's representatives differently from other people. We tend to regard these things with the same reverence, care, and even awe that would apply to what they symbolize; we develop elaborate procedures for properly handling them; and should we ever see one of our highly regarded symbols being treated without proper respect, we would become duly upset, as Tillich indicates.[32] Similarly, the symbolic elements of a musical performance may induce in us an imaginative experience of hope, fear, the joy of victory, grief, awe, or relief that rivals the actual experience of such moments. If the relationship between a symbol and its referent cannot be adequately explained as ontological participation, how can it be explained?

I suggest a fruitful line of exploration is to attend to the observable rather than the supposed differences in *modus operandi* of the things Tillich identifies as symbols and nonsymbols. That is, if we look at how the symbols actually work, we may avoid problematic metaphysical assumptions and implications, and we may find a way of describing the relationship between symbol and symbolized that does not depend on speculation about covert symbol properties. Clearly, red stoplights, the letters of the alphabet, words used in what he calls their "ordinary" sense, and mathematical notation function differently as pointers from the way the flag, the king's designate, and a great deal of poetic, liturgical, artistic, and musical languages do. The former, or what Tillich regards as nonsymbols, are nothing more than labels or indicators to be read literally. They simply name, indicate, predicate, or describe, and once learned, they involve no cognitive strain or insight but are taken as referring in a direct, straightforward, and uncomplicated way.

The latter, or what he calls "symbols," make different cognitive demands. They refer indirectly and require some imaginative effort on the part of the symbol maker and symbol user because they employ figurative processes. For example, when a symphony expresses feelings of tragic loss, it does not literally have those feelings, nor are the feelings expressed literally those of the composer, the performers, or the listeners. Rather, they are feelings perceived to be present in the work itself, and since a work does not literally possess feelings, they must be present figuratively.

In *Death Set to Music*, Paul Minear examines how four masterworks express various meanings of death in human experience. As he takes each of the works apart movement by movement, it is apparent that the message of the music depends significantly on nonliteral symbols. To illustrate, we can look at his discussion of the statement in the second movement of Brahms's *A German Requiem*:

> the grass withers and the flower falls
> but
> the word of the Lord abides forever.

Central in this statement is what he calls "one of the most decisive 'buts' in all music." From the mournful words of the first phrase there is an abrupt change to the positive affirmation of the second phrase, a transition that is expressed equally in the musical qualities as in the words. The first phrase is sung as a dirge—slowly, in the lower voices—but at the "but" there is a marked acceleration in tempo and a brighter mood. He attributes the "brightness" of mood to the more animated and exuberant voices of the higher ranges taking over from the somber tones of the voices in the lower pitches, by the coming into play of the whole orchestra, and by the interplay of musical lines in a fugue. The combined effect of words and music in this context is the sober recognition of the transience of life even in the course of one summer's wait for "the latter rains" contrasted with the endless patience and permanence of God.[33]

Seen in this light, participation is less dependent on a symbol's literal embodiment of what is symbolized than on figurative embodiment. When a musical symbol expresses a feeling, an idea, or a state of affairs, it points to what it expresses through the characteristics it possesses, characteristics that are understood metaphorically. In the context of Brahms's *Requiem*, we hear the slow rhythm and low voices of the first line as mournful and the interplay of exuberant, high, accelerated voices in the second line as bright because we have learned how to interpret the figurative qualities of the music. In both lines, the music directs our thought to particular notions and emotions because it metaphorically embodies them.

In recasting the idea of participation this way, however, we are not countering some of Tillich's valuable insights. He has rightly recognized that not all "languages" can be reduced to the equivalent of literal labels or pointers,[34] but may in fact "participate" in the meanings they refer to, if not in what they are, then at least in how they represent and express. That is, aesthetic symbols must be evaluated by standards different from those of literal pointers—they must be seen appropriately to embody that which they symbolize for those who have learned the "language." Because aesthetic symbols figuratively incorporate or embody what they express, their interpretation requires attention to their nuances, their possible overlays of meanings, their subtlety, in general, their suggestiveness.

The third characteristic of symbols he identifies is that they open up levels of reality that otherwise are closed to us. Artistic symbols, he suggests, are particularly apt in this function—an artwork "expresses a level of reality to which only the artistic creation has an approach";[35] a painting "mediates" something that "cannot be expressed in any other way than through the painting itself."[36] In fact, the "ecstatic," "expressionistic," and "spiritual" elements are the very features that enable art most effectively to refer to the ultimate, the transcendent, or the extraordinary[37] which are otherwise beyond the descriptive capacity of ordinary, literal, direct language. In referring to the transcendent, the symbols of art and music are most effective pointers simply because they suggest without delineating and describe without circumscribing.

Again, he believes this mediation is made possible by the participation of the symbols in that which they symbolize. Here too, however, the participation need not be literal; it can be nonliteral, providing aural figures to point beyond the ordinary to the extraordinary. Reference is none the less powerful for being nonliteral, for the capacity of musical symbolic language to be as sad, triumphal, excited, fearful, militant, and so on, at the figurative level as its referents are at the literal level makes it an especially appropriate accompaniment to patriotic occasions, celebrations of various kinds, funerals, and religious ceremonies.

The third characteristic of symbols is intimately tied to the fourth; namely, symbols also open up dimensions and elements of our soul that correspond to the dimensions and elements of reality. At the least, in their cognitive capacity symbols are not always employed detachedly or neutrally. They have an impact on the symbol maker and symbol user, either by way of cognitive surprise or affective response. More than this, in making symbols we make ourselves, for our reality is that meaning which through our symbol systems we have imposed on the world around us.

Of course, Tillich intends more than this when he speaks of a correspondence between our soul and the dimensions and elements of reality. His cosmological understanding of the world is that "the knower and that which is known is united," since everything is ultimately derived from the unity he calls "Being-itself."[38] One does not have to go as far as this, however, to appreciate that the central symbols of our various discourses make our self-understanding and in so doing touch us profoundly and determine us personally. This is as true of aesthetic symbolisms as of scientific symbolism.

The fifth characteristic of symbols in Tillich's summary is that they cannot be invented—rather, they grow out of the collective unconscious and function only when they are accepted by the unconscious dimension of our being. The term "collective unconscious" is borrowed from Jungian psychology, but Tillich uses it somewhat hesitantly. He qualifies it by admitting, "I would say out of the womb which is usually called today the 'group unconscious' or 'collective unconscious,' or whatever you want to call it—out of a group which acknowledges, in this thing, this word, this flag, or whatever it may be, its own thing."[39]

This implies that symbols are not a private matter but are socially rooted and socially accepted. They are not a matter of individual preference but arise in a community of users. Although he also expects they are best understood within that community, it should be noted that their meanings should not be regarded as forever exclusively accessible only to the group in which they originated even if others reject those meanings. In dialogue, a wider public may be persuaded by or can bring pertinent critique to the discourse of a particular group.

Tillich leaves open the question of how, if symbols are not invented, they might grow out of the collective unconscious. Artists, scientists, philosophers, religious thinkers, and other symbol makers are certainly embedded in a cultural milieu by which they are influenced, but against which they must sometimes react if they hold a place at the cutting edge of thought or artistic expression. But whether they are reflecting or rejecting current cultural understandings, there is no reason to insist that they do not invent any new symbols. Tillich shows some confusion on this very point when he speaks of symbols as the "results of a creative encounter with reality."[40] What is "creative" about the encounter, as he puts it, if nothing is created?

Anybody, it seems, could invent a symbol, but as Tillich explains,[41] invention does not guarantee general acceptance. The artist at work, although a responsive member of a larger community, creates or invents the symbols of an artwork, but these may or may not be accepted by the public at large. Here the "collective unconscious" makes a determination,[42] if by that we mean the group decides on the work's appropriateness, insightfulness, usefulness, or simply its "goodness of fit."

As the sixth and final characteristic, Tillich proposes that symbols, like human beings, pass through a life cycle of birth, growth, and death. In their development, they are dependent on their environment—they grow "when the situation is ripe for them and they die when the situation changes." Their existence depends on their ability to "produce a response" in the group where they originally find expression.[43] He holds that symbols cannot be destroyed by criticism, but they will cease to be effective as symbols only if the relationship between the group and the symbol significantly changes. "In the moment in which this inner situation of the human group to a symbol has ceased to exist, then the symbol dies. The symbol does not 'say' anything any more."[44]

It is not clear, however, what he means when he speaks of an "inner situation." If it refers to an emotional commitment to a symbol, he could be noting the psychological attachment people may have which maintains the symbol even after good reasons for its continuation have ceased. Many Australians, for instance, are loyal to their flag with its Union Jack, although the country's increasing independence from Britain was signalled by Federation at the turn of the century. But emotional attachment to a symbol does not insulate the symbol from historical, scientific, aesthetic, or philosophical criticism. And sooner or later, such criticism can affect what is considered acceptable as a symbol or schema. Again, Tillich has tended to fall back on an obscure notion like the "death" of a symbol and one's "inner situation," and to speculate about covert processes and situations. Alternatively, and more straightforwardly, it could be said that at times accepted symbols prove to be inappropriate, and favored explanations no longer "fit" changing situations. At that point, they fall into disuse, without there being anything particularly occult about it. But certainly he is right in noting that new times abandon old symbols in favor of new ones, and in fact, new times are ushered in by new symbols.

Tillich's theory of symbols depends on a number of indeterminate or unclarified terms such as "participation," "organic connection," "mediation," "levels of reality," "opening up the soul," "inner situation," and "collective unconscious." Many of his claims about symbols and symbolic functioning are based on assumptions that, rather than clarifying the nature of symbols, raise a number of new questions. Nevertheless, he describes well our existential involvement with significant symbols when he illuminates their role, tenacity, and influence in social groups. His theory of symbols is also more convincing when it recognizes the complexity of symbols, especially in figurative modes and changing interpretations to meet changes in context. And he alerts modern thinkers to the challenge of dealing with symbols that no longer vitalize and energize us.

By way of practical application, he advises that the role of educators in respect of symbols is threefold: conceptualization, explanation, and criticism.[45] That is to say, their task involves the presentation and exploration of symbols as symbols; the interpretation and exegesis of them; and in understanding how symbols relate to each other and to that which they symbolize, the discovery of adequate symbols and the rejection of inadequate ones. In consequence, he believes symbols will be protected from profanation and valued for their capacity to disclose at some level the mystery of life and the meaning of human experience.

CRITICAL QUESTIONS FOR MUSIC EDUCATORS

From our conversation with the ideas of Tillich, a number of questions and implications emerge for music educators. In the interests of simplicity, I would like to suggest two sets of questions, one revolving around the concept of musical understanding and the other around the related notion of musical symbolic language.

Is music legitimately regarded as a way of understanding? If it is not, then music may be nothing more than the enjoyable experience of sound, a disembodied and ungrounded emotional event, or a display of technical skill with an instrument—in which case it no more belongs in the liberal arts curriculum than eating ice cream, recreational napping, or mowing lawns.

If it is a way of understanding, then the experience of its sounds, its emotional events, and the technical skills that produce it combine to provide cognitive access to notions, ideas, structures, and relationships that may not be accessible in other ways; in giving form, it may also give meaning to the emotional and spiritual moments in our experience; and it may contribute to our perception of ourselves, our society, and possibly something beyond.

If music is a way of understanding, then educators may seriously consider their role in the "conceptualization, explanation and criticism" of music. At the least, the study of music will involve them and the learner in an experience of music as music, symbolic element as symbolic—an immersion in the musical sounds, forms, nuances, moods, voices, and shapes of a musical work. It will also involve them in an analysis of that musical experience, an interpretation that articulates in words or re-expresses in related aesthetic forms its insights in search of its distinctive and multilayered meanings. And to complete the learning, it will involve them in an assessment and evaluation of those expressions and meanings for their existential relevance and veracity. Beyond these minimal considerations, it may also encourage students of music to look for and even contribute to musical meaning making on the growing edge of our cultural understandings.

Is the nature of music properly understood as a symbolic language? If not, then one may overlook the relationships among its elements and neglect the coherence within an individual work and its interdependence with other aesthetic products. If music is not a symbolic "language," then it may very well not have a "message" or be a way of understanding.

If music is regarded as a "language," we have a schematic organization for approaching the phenomenon of music which can be insightful and productive in a number of ways. The term "language" brings with it a particularly rich network of associated notions such as "words," "sentences," "grammar," "figures of speech," "punctuation," "mood," "tone," "idioms," and so on, which in turn suggest two possible lines of study in music: semantics and syntax. Where the "semantics" of music refers to *what* meanings or understandings music may afford, "syntax" refers to *how* music makes its meanings. Students who are "fluent" in music will have a working knowledge of both.

If music is a symbolic language, its syntactical structure may be analyzed and learned. The question is, How does music function as a symbol system? Our discussion of Tillich's ideas suggests that music may express meaning because its combined elements are figurative embodiments of the notions and emotions it refers to. This kind of expression may very well be a significant syntactical feature of musical functioning, but other possibilities should not be overlooked. If sounds and sound qualities are to musical language what words are to verbal language, and if words and combinations of words may function in a variety of ways, both literal and nonliteral, music may also exhibit a similar variety of syntactical forms and functions. In fact, Peter Kivy has recognized various degrees of literal depiction in what he identifies as musical pictures or musical representations: the simulation of the cuckoo call in Beethoven's Sixth Symphony, the clash and whir of machinery in Mossolov's *Iron Foundry*, the chugging of the train engine in Honegger's *Pacific 231*, and the buzz of flies in Handel's Israel in Egypt.[46] An exploration of possible, even simultaneous, literal and figurative levels of expression may contribute to our understanding of how music makes its meanings.

Tillich may have speculated on how aesthetic symbols achieve results in ways that prove problematic, but there

may be something the music teacher will find worth exploring in his claim that these symbols are the "most revealing creations of the human mind, the most genuine ones, the most powerful ones."[47]

Notes

1. From an address given at the Minneapolis Institute of Arts in 1952. Entitled "Art and Society," this three-part address now appears in the collection edited by John Dillenberger and Jane Dillenberger, *Paul Tillich: On Art and Architecture* (New York: Crossroad, 1987), pp. 11-41.

2. Ibid., p. 12.

3. Tillich, "One Moment of Beauty," in *On Art and Architecture*, pp. 234-35.

4. Ibid., p. 235.

5. Tillich, *The Courage to Be* (New Haven, Conn.: Yale University Press, 1952), pp. 35, 36.

6. Ibid., p. 41.

7. Tillich, *Biblical Religion and the Search for Ultimate Reality* (Chicago: University of Chicago Press, 1955), p. 9.

8. Ibid., pp. 6-13.

9. Tillich, *Systematic Theology*, three volumes in one (Chicago: University of Chicago Press, 1967), vol. 1, p. 14.

10. Tillich, "Art and Society," pp. 18-21.

11. Ibid., pp. 15, 16.

12. Ibid., p. 27.

13. Tillich, *Systematic Theology*, vol. 3, p. 71.

14. Tillich, "Art and Society," p. 26.

15. Ibid., p. 27.

16. Nelson Goodman and Catherine Elgin, *Reconstructions in Philosophy and Other Arts and Sciences* (Indianapolis: Hackett, 1988), pp. 3-5, propose "understanding," suggesting that it comprehends cognition in all of its modes: perception, depiction, and emotion as well as description and that it can be imparted in verbal and nonverbal, literal and metaphorical, descriptive and normative systems of understandings. Israel Scheffler, *Reason and Teaching* (Indianapolis: Bobbs-Merrill, 1963), p. 37, adopts the expression "forms of thought" because it may involve, among other things, inferring, categorizing, perceiving, evaluating, deciding, attitude forming, and expecting.

17. Tillich, *The Courage to Be,* p. 34.

18. Tillich, *Systematic Theology*, vol. 1, p. 189.

19. For instance, Paul H. Hirst, *Knowledge and the Curriculum: A Collection of Philosophical Papers*, International Library of the Philosophy of Education, gen. ed. R. S. Peters (London: Routledge

and Kegan Paul, 1974); Elliot Eisner, ed. *Learning and Teaching the Ways of Knowing*, Eighty-fourth Yearbook of the National Society for the Study of Education (Chicago: University of Chicago Press, 1985).

20. Tillich, "Art and Society" p. 23.

21. Tillich, "Religious Symbols and Our Knowledge of God," *Christian Scholar* 38 (September 1955): 193.

22. Ibid., p. 189.

23. Tillich, *Dynamics of Faith* (New York: Harper and Row, 1957), pp. 41-43; "The Meaning and Justification of Religious Symbols," in *Religious Experience and Truth*, ed. Sidney Hook (New York: New York University Press, 1961), pp. 3-5; "Theology and Symbolism," in *Religious Symbolism*, ed. F.E. Johnson (New York: Institute for Religion and Social Studies, 1955), pp. 75-77, 108-16; "Religious Symbols and Our Knowledge of God," pp. 189-92; "The Religious Symbol," *Journal of Liberal Religion* 11 (1940): 13-15; "Art and Society," pp. 36-37.

24. Tillich, "Religious Symbols and Our Knowledge of God," p. 189.

25. Tillich, "Meaning and Justification of Religious Symbols," p. 4.

26. Tillich, "Religious Symbols and Our Knowledge of God," p. 190.

27. Tillich, "Theology and Symbolism," pp. 108, 109.

28. Plato, adopting the term from the Pythagoreans, first applies participation to the relationship between ideal forms and their instances, suggesting it has to do with cause, essence, and naming. (*Phaedo*, 100d.ff., Jowett translation.) S. T. Coleridge uses the notion of participation to distinguish symbols from other forms of figurative representation. Where other figures are merely translations of abstract notions into picture language, he sees symbols being characteristically "translucent": by participating in the reality to which it points, a symbol "abides itself as a living part in that unity of which it is the representative." (*The Statesman's Manual* [New York: Harper & Row, 1853], pp. 437-38.)

29. Peter Fingesten, *The Eclipse of Symbolism* (Columbia: University of South Carolina Press, 1970), pp. 126, 127.

30. William L. Rowe, *Religious Symbols and God: A Philosophical Study of Paul Tillich's Theology* (Chicago: University of Chicago Press, 1968), pp. 108-26.

31. Tillich, "Meaning and Justification of Religious Symbols," p. 4.

32. Tillich, *Dynamics of Faith*, p. 42.

33. Paul S. Minear, *Death Set to Music* (Atlanta: John Knox Press, 1987), pp. 70-71.

34. Tillich, "Religious Symbols and Our Knowledge of God," p. 190.

35. Tillich, "Theology and Symbolism," p. 109.

36. Tillich, "Religious Symbols and Our Knowledge of God," p. 191.

37. Tillich, "Art and Ultimate Reality," in *Art, Creativity and the Sacred*, ed. Diane Apostolos-Cappadona (New York: Crossroads, 1986), pp. 217-35.

38. Tillich, *Systematic Theology*, vol. 1, p. 94.

39. Tillich, "Religious Symbols and Our Knowledge of God," p. 192.

40. Tillich, "Theology and Symbolism," p. 109.

41. Tillich, "The Religious Symbol," p. 14.

42. Tillich, "Religious Symbols and Our Knowledge of God," p. 192.

43. Tillich, *Dynamics of Faith*, p. 43.

44. Tillich, "Religious Symbols and Our Knowledge of God," p. 192.

45. Tillich, "Theology and Symbolism," pp. 111-13.

46. Peter Kivy, *Sound and Semblance: Reflections on Musical Representation* (Princeton, N.J.: Princeton University Press, 1984), p. 59.

47. Tillich, "Religious Symbols and Our Knowledge of God," p. 193.

FURTHER READING

Criticism

Bahr, Ehrhard. "Paul Tillich and the Problem of a German Exile Government in the United States." *Yearbook of German American Studies* 21 (1986): 1–12.

Discusses Tillich's relationship to government after he left Germany.

Bulman, Raymond F. "Paul Tillich and the Millennialist Heritage." *Theology Today* 53 (January 1997): 464–76.

Examines the biblical origins of Christian millennialism, its role in the early church, the various resurgences of millennialism throughout history and modern times, and specifically, the millennialism of Tillich.

Byrd, Max. "Johnson's Spiritual Anxiety." *Modern Philology: A Journal Devoted to Research in Medieval and Modern Literature* 78, No. 4 (May 1981): 368–78.

Applies Tillich's theories to the prose of Samuel Johnson.

Cobb, Kelton. "Reconsidering the Status of Popular Culture in Tillich's *Theology of Culture*." *Journal of the American Academy of Religion* 63 (Spring 1995): 53–84.

Argues that Tillich's *Theology of Culture* is biased greatly toward high culture over that of material culture.

Cremer, Douglas J. "Protestant Theology in Early Weimar Germany: Barth, Tillich, and Bultmann." *Journal of the History of Ideas* 56 (April 1995): 289–307.

Analysis of Tillich and other German Protestant theologians, Karl Barth and Rudolph Bultmann, after World War I.

Dourly, John P. "Jacob Boehme and Paul Tillich on Trinity and God: Similarities and Differences." *Religious Studies* 31 (December 1995): 429–45.

Explores Tillich's use of central motifs taken from the seventeenth-century German mystic, Jacob Boehme.

Dreisbach, Donald F. *Symbols and Salvation: Paul Tillich's Doctrine of Religious Symbols and his Interpretation of the Symbols of the Christian Tradition.* Lanham, MA: University Press of America, 1993.

Book-length study dedicated to Tillich's analysis of religious symbolism.

Grube, Dirk-Martin. "A Critical Reconstruction of Paul Tillich's Epistemology." *Religious Studies* 33 (March 1997): 67–80.

Provides a critical evaluation of Tillich's notion of epistemology.

Matteson, John T. "The Little Lower Layer: Anxiety and *The Courage To Be* in *Moby Dick*." *Harvard Theological Review* 81, No. 1 (January 1988): 97–116.

Analyzes the influence of *Moby Dick* on Tillich's writings.

McCandless, David. "Beckett and Tillich: Courage and Existence in *Waiting for Godot*." *Philosophy and Literature* 12, No. 1 (April 1988): 48–57.

Discussion of Irish writer Samuel Beckett's play *Waiting for Godot* as compared to Tillich's *The Courage To Be*.

Need, Stephen W. "Holiness and Idolatry: Coleridge and Tillich on the Nature of Symbols." *Theology* 99 (January/February 1996): 45–52.

Explores the views of Samuel Taylor Coleridge and Tillich on the nature of symbols.

Niebuhr, Reinhold. "A Window into the Heart of a Giant." *New York Times Book Review,* 72 (10 May 1970): 6, 34.

Offers mixed analysis of *My Travel Diary, 1936: Between Two Worlds,* praising Tillich as "so much of a giant that even an insignificant travel diary may be regarded as a 'window to the heart of a creative influence in American life.'"

Novak, David. "Buber and Tillich." *Journal of Ecumenical Studies* 29 (Spring 1992): 159–74.

Compares the varied religious dialogues of German Jewish theologian Martin Buber and Tillich.

Nuovo, Victor. "Tillich and Emerson." *Journal of the American Academy of Religion* 52 (December 1984): 709–22.

Discussion of the writings of Ralph Waldo Emerson in relation to Tillich.

Scharlemann, Robert P. "Can Religion Be Understood Philosophically?" *International Journal for Philosophy of Religion* 38 (December (1995): 93–101.

Adresses the question of whether religion can be understood philosophically.

Stackhouse, Max L. "Humanism After Tillich." *First Things* No. 72 (April 1997): 24–8.

Discussion of Tillich's combination of religion and humanism and the relevance of his ideas to a global society.

Additional coverage of Tillich's life and career is contained in the following sources published by the Gale Group: *Contemporary Authors,* **Vols. 5-8, 25-28;** *Contemporary Authors New Revision Series,* **Vol. 33; and** *Major 20th-Century Writers,* **Vols. 1, 2.**

How to Use This Index

The main references

Calvino, Italo
1923-1985 .... CLC 5, 8, 11, 22, 33, 39,
73; SSC 3

list all author entries in the following Gale Literary Criticism series:

BLC = *Black Literature Criticism*
CLC = *Contemporary Literary Criticism*
CLR = *Children's Literature Review*
CMLC = *Classical and Medieval Literature Criticism*
DA = *DISCovering Authors*
DAB = *DISCovering Authors: British*
DAC = *DISCovering Authors: Canadian*
DAM = *DISCovering Authors: Modules*
   DRAM: *Dramatists Module;* *MST:* *Most-Studied Authors Module;*
   MULT: *Multicultural Authors Module;* *NOV:* *Novelists Module;*
   POET: *Poets Module;* *POP:* *Popular Fiction and Genre Authors Module*
DC = *Drama Criticism*
HLC = *Hispanic Literature Criticism*
LC = *Literature Criticism from 1400 to 1800*
NCLC = *Nineteenth-Century Literature Criticism*
NNAL = *Native North American Literature*
PC = *Poetry Criticism*
SSC = *Short Story Criticism*
TCLC = *Twentieth-Century Literary Criticism*
WLC = *World Literature Criticism, 1500 to the Present*

The cross-references

See also CANR 23; CA 85-88;
obituary CA116

list all author entries in the following Gale biographical and literary sources:

AAYA = *Authors & Artists for Young Adults*
AITN = *Authors in the News*
BEST = *Bestsellers*
BW = *Black Writers*
CA = *Contemporary Authors*
CAAS = *Contemporary Authors Autobiography Series*
CABS = *Contemporary Authors Bibliographical Series*
CANR = *Contemporary Authors New Revision Series*
CAP = *Contemporary Authors Permanent Series*
CDALB = *Concise Dictionary of American Literary Biography*
CDBLB = *Concise Dictionary of British Literary Biography*
DLB = *Dictionary of Literary Biography*
DLBD = *Dictionary of Literary Biography Documentary Series*
DLBY = *Dictionary of Literary Biography Yearbook*
HW = *Hispanic Writers*
JRDA = *Junior DISCovering Authors*
MAICYA = *Major Authors and Illustrators for Children and Young Adults*
MTCW = *Major 20th-Century Writers*
SAAS = *Something about the Author Autobiography Series*
SATA = *Something about the Author*
YABC = *Yesterday's Authors of Books for Children*

Literary Criticism Series
Cumulative Author Index

Andersen, Hans Christian
1805-1875 .... **NCLC 7, 79; DA; DAB; DAC; DAM MST, POP; SSC 6; WLC**
See also CLR 6; DA3; MAICYA; SATA 100; YABC 1

Anderson, C. Farley
See Mencken, H(enry) L(ouis); Nathan, George Jean

Anderson, Jessica (Margaret) Queale 1916- **CLC 37**
See also CA 9-12R; CANR 4, 62

Anderson, Jon (Victor) 1940- . **CLC 9; DAM POET**
See also CA 25-28R; CANR 20

Anderson, Lindsay (Gordon)
1923-1994 .... **CLC 20**
See also CA 125; 128; 146; CANR 77

Anderson, Maxwell 1888-1959 .... **TCLC 2; DAM DRAM**
See also CA 105; 152; DLB 7; MTCW 2

Anderson, Poul (William) 1926- .... **CLC 15**
See also AAYA 5, 34; CA 1-4R, 181; CAAE 181; CAAS 2; CANR 2, 15, 34, 64; CLR 58; DLB 8; INT CANR-15; MTCW 1, 2; SATA 90; SATA-Brief 39; SATA-Essay 106

Anderson, Robert (Woodruff)
1917- .... **CLC 23; DAM DRAM**
See also AITN 1; CA 21-24R; CANR 32; DLB 7

Anderson, Sherwood 1876-1941 ..... **TCLC 1, 10, 24; DA; DAB; DAC; DAM MST, NOV; SSC 1; WLC**
See also AAYA 30; CA 104; 121; CANR 61; CDALB 1917-1929; DA3; DLB 4, 9, 86; DLBD 1; MTCW 1, 2

Andier, Pierre
See Desnos, Robert

Andouard
See Giraudoux, (Hippolyte) Jean

Andrade, Carlos Drummond de ...... **CLC 18**
See also Drummond de Andrade, Carlos

Andrade, Mario de 1893-1945 .... **TCLC 43**

Andreae, Johann V(alentin)
1586-1654 .... **LC 32**
See also DLB 164

Andreas-Salome, Lou 1861-1937 ... **TCLC 56**
See also CA 178; DLB 66

Andress, Lesley
See Sanders, Lawrence

Andrewes, Lancelot 1555-1626 .... **LC 5**
See also DLB 151, 172

Andrews, Cicily Fairfield
See West, Rebecca

Andrews, Elton V.
See Pohl, Frederik

Andreyev, Leonid (Nikolaevich) 1871-1919 **TCLC 3**
See also CA 104; 185

Andric, Ivo 1892-1975 .... **CLC 8; SSC 36**
See also CA 81-84; 57-60; CANR 43, 60; DLB 147; MTCW 1

Androvar
See Prado (Calvo), Pedro

Angelique, Pierre
See Bataille, Georges

Angell, Roger 1920- .... **CLC 26**
See also CA 57-60; CANR 13, 44, 70; DLB 171, 185

Angelou, Maya 1928- .... **CLC 12, 35, 64, 77; BLC 1; DA; DAB; DAC; DAM MST, MULT, POET, POP; WLCS**
See also AAYA 7, 20; BW 2, 3; CA 65-68; CANR 19, 42, 65; CDALBS; CLR 53; DA3; DLB 38; MTCW 1, 2; SATA 49

Anna Comnena 1083-1153 .... **CMLC 25**

Annensky, Innokenty (Fyodorovich)
1856-1909 .... **TCLC 14**
See also CA 110; 155

Annunzio, Gabriele d'
See D'Annunzio, Gabriele

Anodos
See Coleridge, Mary E(lizabeth)

Anon, Charles Robert
See Pessoa, Fernando (Antonio Nogueira)

Anouilh, Jean (Marie Lucien Pierre)
1910-1987 .... **CLC 1, 3, 8, 13, 40, 50; DAM DRAM; DC 8**
See also CA 17-20R; 123; CANR 32; MTCW 1, 2

Anthony, Florence
See Ai

Anthony, John
See Ciardi, John (Anthony)

Anthony, Peter
See Shaffer, Anthony (Joshua); Shaffer, Peter (Levin)

Anthony, Piers 1934- .... **CLC 35; DAM POP**
See also AAYA 11; CA 21-24R; CANR 28, 56, 73; DLB 8; MTCW 1, 2; SAAS 22; SATA 84

Anthony, Susan B(rownell)
1916-1991 .... **TCLC 84**
See also CA 89-92; 134

Antoine, Marc
See Proust, (Valentin-Louis-George-Eugene-) Marcel

Antoninus, Brother
See Everson, William (Oliver)

Antonioni, Michelangelo 1912- .... **CLC 20**
See also CA 73-76; CANR 45, 77

Antschel, Paul 1920-1970
See Celan, Paul
See also CA 85-88; CANR 33, 61; MTCW 1

Anwar, Chairil 1922-1949 .... **TCLC 22**
See also CA 121

Anzaldua, Gloria 1942-
See also CA 175; DLB 122; HLCS 1

Apess, William 1798-1839(?) .... **NCLC 73; DAM MULT**
See also DLB 175; NNAL

Apollinaire, Guillaume 1880-1918 .. **TCLC 3, 8, 51; DAM POET; PC 7**
See also Kostrowitzki, Wilhelm Apollinaris de
See also CA 152; MTCW 1

Appelfeld, Aharon 1932- .... **CLC 23, 47**
See also CA 112; 133; CANR 86

Apple, Max (Isaac) 1941- .... **CLC 9, 33**
See also CA 81-84; CANR 19, 54; DLB 130

Appleman, Philip (Dean) 1926- .... **CLC 51**
See also CA 13-16R; CAAS 18; CANR 6, 29, 56

Appleton, Lawrence
See Lovecraft, H(oward) P(hillips)

Apteryx
See Eliot, T(homas) S(tearns)

Apuleius, (Lucius Madaurensis)
125(?)-175(?) .... **CMLC 1**
See also DLB 211

Aquin, Hubert 1929-1977 .... **CLC 15**
See also CA 105; DLB 53

Aquinas, Thomas 1224(?)-1274 ..... **CMLC 33**
See also DLB 115

Aragon, Louis 1897-1982 .. **CLC 3, 22; DAM NOV, POET**
See also CA 69-72; 108; CANR 28, 71; DLB 72; MTCW 1, 2

Arany, Janos 1817-1882 .... **NCLC 34**

Aranyos, Kakay
See Mikszath, Kalman

Arbuthnot, John 1667-1735 .... **LC 1**
See also DLB 101

Archer, Herbert Winslow
See Mencken, H(enry) L(ouis)

Archer, Jeffrey (Howard) 1940- ...... **CLC 28; DAM POP**
See also AAYA 16; BEST 89:3; CA 77-80; CANR 22, 52; DA3; INT CANR-22

Archer, Jules 1915- .... **CLC 12**
See also CA 9-12R; CANR 6, 69; SAAS 5; SATA 4, 85

Archer, Lee
See Ellison, Harlan (Jay)

Arden, John 1930- .... **CLC 6, 13, 15; DAM DRAM**
See also CA 13-16R; CAAS 4; CANR 31, 65, 67; DLB 13; MTCW 1

Arenas, Reinaldo 1943-1990 . **CLC 41; DAM MULT; HLC 1**
See also CA 124; 128; 133; CANR 73; DLB 145; HW 1; MTCW 1

Arendt, Hannah 1906-1975 .... **CLC 66, 98**
See also CA 17-20R; 61-64; CANR 26, 60; MTCW 1, 2

Aretino, Pietro 1492-1556 .... **LC 12**

Arghezi, Tudor 1880-1967 .... **CLC 80**
See also Theodorescu, Ion N.
See also CA 167

Arguedas, Jose Maria 1911-1969 .... **CLC 10, 18; HLCS 1**
See also CA 89-92; CANR 73; DLB 113; HW 1

Argueta, Manlio 1936- .... **CLC 31**
See also CA 131; CANR 73; DLB 145; HW 1

Arias, Ron(ald Francis) 1941-
See also CA 131; CANR 81; DAM MULT; DLB 82; HLC 1; HW 1, 2; MTCW 2

Ariosto, Ludovico 1474-1533 .... **LC 6**

Aristides
See Epstein, Joseph

Aristophanes 450B.C.-385B.C. .... **CMLC 4; DA; DAB; DAC; DAM DRAM, MST; DC 2; WLCS**
See also DA3; DLB 176

Aristotle 384B.C.-322B.C. .... **CMLC 31; DA; DAB; DAC; DAM MST; WLCS**
See also DA3; DLB 176

Arlt, Roberto (Godofredo Christophersen)
1900-1942 .... **TCLC 29; DAM MULT; HLC 1**
See also CA 123; 131; CANR 67; HW 1, 2

Armah, Ayi Kwei 1939- . **CLC 5, 33; BLC 1; DAM MULT, POET**
See also BW 1; CA 61-64; CANR 21, 64; DLB 117; MTCW 1

Armatrading, Joan 1950- .... **CLC 17**
See also CA 114; 186

Arnette, Robert
See Silverberg, Robert

Arnim, Achim von (Ludwig Joachim von Arnim) 1781-1831 ..... **NCLC 5; SSC 29**
See also DLB 90

Arnim, Bettina von 1785-1859 .... **NCLC 38**
See also DLB 90

Arnold, Matthew 1822-1888 ..... **NCLC 6, 29; DA; DAB; DAC; DAM MST, POET; PC 5; WLC**
See also CDBLB 1832-1890; DLB 32, 57

Arnold, Thomas 1795-1842 .... **NCLC 18**
See also DLB 55

Arnow, Harriette (Louisa) Simpson
1908-1986 .... **CLC 2, 7, 18**
See also CA 9-12R; 118; CANR 14; DLB 6; MTCW 1, 2; SATA 42; SATA-Obit 47

Arouet, Francois-Marie
See Voltaire

Arp, Hans
See Arp, Jean

Arp, Jean 1887-1966 .... **CLC 5**
See also CA 81-84; 25-28R; CANR 42, 77

Arrabal
See Arrabal, Fernando

Baudrillard, Jean 1929- .... **CLC 60**

Baum, L(yman) Frank 1856-1919 ... **TCLC 7**
See also CA 108; 133; CLR 15; DLB 22;
JRDA; MAICYA; MTCW 1, 2; SATA 18,
100

Baum, Louis F.
See Baum, L(yman) Frank

Baumbach, Jonathan 1933- .... **CLC 6, 23**
See also CA 13-16R; CAAS 5; CANR 12,
66; DLBY 80; INT CANR-12; MTCW 1

Bausch, Richard (Carl) 1945- .... **CLC 51**
See also CA 101; CAAS 14; CANR 43, 61,
87; DLB 130

Baxter, Charles (Morley) 1947- .... **CLC 45,
78; DAM POP**
See also CA 57-60; CANR 40, 64; DLB
130; MTCW 2

Baxter, George Owen
See Faust, Frederick (Schiller)

Baxter, James K(eir) 1926-1972 .... **CLC 14**
See also CA 77-80

Baxter, John
See Hunt, E(verette) Howard, (Jr.)

Bayer, Sylvia
See Glassco, John

Baynton, Barbara 1857-1929 .... **TCLC 57**

Beagle, Peter S(oyer) 1939- .... **CLC 7, 104**
See also CA 9-12R; CANR 4, 51, 73; DA3;
DLBY 80; INT CANR-4; MTCW 1;
SATA 60

Bean, Normal
See Burroughs, Edgar Rice

Beard, Charles A(ustin)
1874-1948 .... **TCLC 15**
See also CA 115; DLB 17; SATA 18

Beardsley, Aubrey 1872-1898 .... **NCLC 6**

Beattie, Ann 1947- ..... **CLC 8, 13, 18, 40, 63;
DAM NOV, POP; SSC 11**
See also BEST 90:2; CA 81-84; CANR 53,
73; DA3; DLBY 82; MTCW 1, 2

Beattie, James 1735-1803 .... **NCLC 25**
See also DLB 109

Beauchamp, Kathleen Mansfield 1888-1923
See Mansfield, Katherine
See also CA 104; 134; DA; DAC; DAM
MST; DA3; MTCW 2

Beaumarchais, Pierre-Augustin Caron de
1732-1799 .... **DC 4**
See also DAM DRAM

Beaumont, Francis 1584(?)-1616 .... **LC 33;
DC 6**
See also CDBLB Before 1660; DLB 58, 121

**Beauvoir, Simone (Lucie Ernestine Marie
Bertrand) de** 1908-1986 .... **CLC 1, 2, 4,
8, 14, 31, 44, 50, 71, 124; DA; DAB;
DAC; DAM MST, NOV; SSC 35; WLC**
See also CA 9-12R; 118; CANR 28, 61;
DA3; DLB 72; DLBY 86; MTCW 1, 2

Becker, Carl (Lotus) 1873-1945 ..... **TCLC 63**
See also CA 157; DLB 17

Becker, Jurek 1937-1997 .... **CLC 7, 19**
See also CA 85-88; 157; CANR 60; DLB
75

Becker, Walter 1950- .... **CLC 26**

Beckett, Samuel (Barclay)
1906-1989 .. **CLC 1, 2, 3, 4, 6, 9, 10, 11,
14, 18, 29, 57, 59, 83; DA; DAB; DAC;
DAM DRAM, MST, NOV; SSC 16;
WLC**
See also CA 5-8R; 130; CANR 33, 61; CD-
BLB 1945-1960; DA3; DLB 13, 15;
DLBY 90; MTCW 1, 2

Beckford, William 1760-1844 .... **NCLC 16**
See also DLB 39

Beckman, Gunnel 1910- .... **CLC 26**
See also CA 33-36R; CANR 15; CLR 25;
MAICYA; SAAS 9; SATA 6

Becque, Henri 1837-1899 .... **NCLC 3**
See also DLB 192

Becquer, Gustavo Adolfo 1836-1870
See also DAM MULT; HLCS 1

Beddoes, Thomas Lovell
1803-1849 .... **NCLC 3**
See also DLB 96

Bede c. 673-735 .... **CMLC 20**
See also DLB 146

Bedford, Donald F.
See Fearing, Kenneth (Flexner)

Beecher, Catharine Esther
1800-1878 .... **NCLC 30**
See also DLB 1

Beecher, John 1904-1980 .... **CLC 6**
See also AITN 1; CA 5-8R; 105; CANR 8

Beer, Johann 1655-1700 .... **LC 5**
See also DLB 168

Beer, Patricia 1924-1999 .... **CLC 58**
See also CA 61-64; 183; CANR 13, 46;
DLB 40

Beerbohm, Max
See Beerbohm, (Henry) Max(imilian)

Beerbohm, (Henry) Max(imilian) 1872-1956
TCLC 1, 24
See also CA 104; 154; CANR 79; DLB 34,
100

Beer-Hofmann, Richard
1866-1945 .... **TCLC 60**
See also CA 160; DLB 81

Begiebing, Robert J(ohn) 1946- .... **CLC 70**
See also CA 122; CANR 40, 88

Behan, Brendan 1923-1964 ...... **CLC 1, 8, 11,
15, 79; DAM DRAM**
See also CA 73-76; CANR 33; CDBLB
1945-1960; DLB 13; MTCW 1, 2

Behn, Aphra 1640(?)-1689 .... **LC 1, 30, 42;
DA; DAB; DAC; DAM DRAM, MST,
NOV, POET; DC 4; PC 13; WLC**
See also DA3; DLB 39, 80, 131

Behrman, S(amuel) N(athaniel) 1893-1973
CLC 40
See also CA 13-16; 45-48; CAP 1; DLB 7,
44

Belasco, David 1853-1931 .... **TCLC 3**
See also CA 104; 168; DLB 7

Belcheva, Elisaveta 1893- .... **CLC 10**
See also Bagryana, Elisaveta

Beldone, Phil "Cheech"
See Ellison, Harlan (Jay)

Beleno
See Azuela, Mariano

Belinski, Vissarion Grigoryevich 1811-1848
NCLC 5
See also DLB 198

Belitt, Ben 1911- .... **CLC 22**
See also CA 13-16R; CAAS 4; CANR 7,
77; DLB 5

Bell, Gertrude (Margaret Lowthian)
1868-1926 .... **TCLC 67**
See also CA 167; DLB 174

Bell, J. Freeman
See Zangwill, Israel

Bell, James Madison 1826-1902 ... **TCLC 43;
BLC 1; DAM MULT**
See also BW 1; CA 122; 124; DLB 50

Bell, Madison Smartt 1957- ...... **CLC 41, 102**
See also CA 111, 183; CAAE 183; CANR
28, 54, 73; MTCW 1

Bell, Marvin (Hartley) 1937- ...... **CLC 8, 31;
DAM POET**
See also CA 21-24R; CAAS 14; CANR 59;
DLB 5; MTCW 1

Bell, W. L. D.
See Mencken, H(enry) L(ouis)

Bellamy, Atwood C.
See Mencken, H(enry) L(ouis)

Bellamy, Edward 1850-1898 ...... **NCLC 4, 86**
See also DLB 12

Belli, Gioconda 1949-
See also CA 152; HLCS 1

Bellin, Edward J.
See Kuttner, Henry

**Belloc, (Joseph) Hilaire (Pierre Sebastien
Rene Swanton)** 1870- .... **TCLC 7, 18;
DAM POET; PC 24**
See also CA 106; 152; DLB 19, 100, 141,
174; MTCW 1; SATA 112; YABC 1

Belloc, Joseph Peter Rene Hilaire
See Belloc, (Joseph) Hilaire (Pierre Sebastien Rene Swanton)

Belloc, Joseph Pierre Hilaire
See Belloc, (Joseph) Hilaire (Pierre Sebastien Rene Swanton)

Belloc, M. A.
See Lowndes, Marie Adelaide (Belloc)

Bellow, Saul 1915- . **CLC 1, 2, 3, 6, 8, 10, 13,
15, 25, 33, 34, 63, 79; DA; DAB; DAC;
DAM MST, NOV, POP; SSC 14; WLC**
See also AITN 2; BEST 89:3; CA 5-8R;
CABS 1; CANR 29, 53; CDALB 1941-
1968; DA3; DLB 2, 28; DLBD 3; DLBY
82; MTCW 1, 2

Belser, Reimond Karel Maria de 1929-
See Ruyslinck, Ward
See also CA 152

Bely, Andrey .... **TCLC 7; PC 11**
See also Bugayev, Boris Nikolayevich
See also MTCW 1

Belyi, Andrei
See Bugayev, Boris Nikolayevich

Benary, Margot
See Benary-Isbert, Margot

Benary-Isbert, Margot 1889-1979 .... **CLC 12**
See also CA 5-8R; 89-92; CANR 4, 72;
CLR 12; MAICYA; SATA 2; SATA-Obit
21

Benavente (y Martinez), Jacinto 1866-1954
**TCLC 3; DAM DRAM, MULT; HLCS
1**
See also CA 106; 131; CANR 81; HW 1, 2;
MTCW 1, 2

Benchley, Peter (Bradford) 1940- . **CLC 4, 8;
DAM NOV, POP**
See also AAYA 14; AITN 2; CA 17-20R;
CANR 12, 35, 66; MTCW 1, 2; SATA 3,
89

Benchley, Robert (Charles)
1889-1945 .... **TCLC 1, 55**
See also CA 105; 153; DLB 11

Benda, Julien 1867-1956 .... **TCLC 60**
See also CA 120; 154

Benedict, Ruth (Fulton)
1887-1948 .... **TCLC 60**
See also CA 158

Benedict, Saint c. 480-c. 547 .... **CMLC 29**

Benedikt, Michael 1935- .... **CLC 4, 14**
See also CA 13-16R; CANR 7; DLB 5

Benet, Juan 1927- .... **CLC 28**
See also CA 143

Benet, Stephen Vincent 1898-1943 . **TCLC 7;
DAM POET; SSC 10**
See also CA 104; 152; DA3; DLB 4, 48,
102; DLBY 97; MTCW 1; YABC 1

Benet, William Rose 1886-1950 .... **TCLC 28;
DAM POET**
See also CA 118; 152; DLB 45

Benford, Gregory (Albert) 1941- ..... **CLC 52**
See also CA 69-72, 175; CAAE 175; CAAS
27; CANR 12, 24, 49; DLBY 82

Bengtsson, Frans (Gunnar)
1894-1954 .... **TCLC 48**
See also CA 170

Benjamin, David
See Slavitt, David R(ytman)

Benjamin, Lois
See Gould, Lois

Bourjaily, Vance (Nye) 1922- .... **CLC 8, 62**
   See also CA 1-4R; CAAS 1; CANR 2, 72;
   DLB 2, 143

Bourne, Randolph S(illiman) 1886-1918
   TCLC 16
   See also CA 117; 155; DLB 63

Bova, Ben(jamin William) 1932- ...... **CLC 45**
   See also AAYA 16; CA 5-8R; CAAS 18;
   CANR 11, 56; CLR 3; DLBY 81; INT
   CANR-11; MAICYA; MTCW 1; SATA 6,
   68

Bowen, Elizabeth (Dorothea Cole) 1899-1973
   CLC 1, 3, 6, 11, 15, 22, 118; DAM NOV;
   SSC 3, 28
   See also CA 17-18; 41-44R; CANR 35;
   CAP 2; CDBLB 1945-1960; DA3; DLB
   15, 162; MTCW 1, 2

Bowering, George 1935- .... **CLC 15, 47**
   See also CA 21-24R; CAAS 16; CANR 10;
   DLB 53

Bowering, Marilyn R(uthe) 1949- .... **CLC 32**
   See also CA 101; CANR 49

Bowers, Edgar 1924- .... **CLC 9**
   See also CA 5-8R; CANR 24; DLB 5

Bowie, David .... **CLC 17**
   See also Jones, David Robert

Bowles, Jane (Sydney) 1917-1973 ..... **CLC 3,**
   68
   See also CA 19-20; 41-44R; CAP 2

Bowles, Paul (Frederick) 1910-1999 . **CLC 1,**
   2, 19, 53; SSC 3
   See also CA 1-4R; 186; CAAS 1; CANR 1,
   19, 50, 75; DA3; DLB 5, 6; MTCW 1, 2

Box, Edgar
   See Vidal, Gore

Boyd, Nancy
   See Millay, Edna St. Vincent

Boyd, William 1952- .... **CLC 28, 53, 70**
   See also CA 114; 120; CANR 51, 71

Boyle, Kay 1902-1992 .... **CLC 1, 5, 19, 58,**
   121; SSC 5
   See also CA 13-16R; 140; CAAS 1; CANR
   29, 61; DLB 4, 9, 48, 86; DLBY 93;
   MTCW 1, 2

Boyle, Mark
   See Kienzle, William X(avier)

Boyle, Patrick 1905-1982 .... **CLC 19**
   See also CA 127

Boyle, T. C. 1948-
   See Boyle, T(homas) Coraghessan

Boyle, T(homas) Coraghessan
   1948- .... **CLC 36, 55, 90; DAM POP;**
   SSC 16
   See also BEST 90:4; CA 120; CANR 44,
   76, 89; DA3; DLBY 86; MTCW 2

Boz
   See Dickens, Charles (John Huffam)

Brackenridge, Hugh Henry
   1748-1816 .... **NCLC 7**
   See also DLB 11, 37

Bradbury, Edward P.
   See Moorcock, Michael (John)
   See also MTCW 2

Bradbury, Malcolm (Stanley)
   1932- .... **CLC 32, 61; DAM NOV**
   See also CA 1-4R; CANR 1, 33, 91; DA3;
   DLB 14, 207; MTCW 1, 2

Bradbury, Ray (Douglas) 1920- .... **CLC 1, 3,**
   10, 15, 42, 98; DA; DAB; DAC; DAM
   MST, NOV, POP; SSC 29; WLC
   See also AAYA 15; AITN 1, 2; CA 1-4R;
   CANR 2, 30, 75; CDALB 1968-1988;
   DA3; DLB 2, 8; MTCW 1, 2; SATA 11,
   64

Bradford, Gamaliel 1863-1932 .... **TCLC 36**
   See also CA 160; DLB 17

Bradley, David (Henry), Jr. 1950- ... **CLC 23,**
   118; BLC 1; DAM MULT
   See also BW 1, 3; CA 104; CANR 26, 81;
   DLB 33

Bradley, John Ed(mund, Jr.) 1958- . **CLC 55**
   See also CA 139

Bradley, Marion Zimmer
   1930-1999 .... **CLC 30; DAM POP**
   See also AAYA 9; CA 57-60; 185; CAAS
   10; CANR 7, 31, 51, 75; DA3; DLB 8;
   MTCW 1, 2; SATA 90; SATA-Obit 116

Bradstreet, Anne 1612(?)-1672 ...... **LC 4, 30;**
   DA; DAC; DAM MST, POET; PC 10
   See also CDALB 1640-1865; DA3; DLB
   24

Brady, Joan 1939- .... **CLC 86**
   See also CA 141

Bragg, Melvyn 1939- .... **CLC 10**
   See also BEST 89:3; CA 57-60; CANR 10,
   48, 89; DLB 14

Brahe, Tycho 1546-1601 .... **LC 45**

Braine, John (Gerard) 1922-1986 . **CLC 1, 3,**
   41
   See also CA 1-4R; 120; CANR 1, 33; CD-
   BLB 1945-1960; DLB 15; DLBY 86;
   MTCW 1

Bramah, Ernest 1868-1942 .... **TCLC 72**
   See also CA 156; DLB 70

Brammer, William 1930(?)-1978 ...... **CLC 31**
   See also CA 77-80

Brancati, Vitaliano 1907-1954 .... **TCLC 12**
   See also CA 109

Brancato, Robin F(idler) 1936- .... **CLC 35**
   See also AAYA 9; CA 69-72; CANR 11,
   45; CLR 32; JRDA; SAAS 9; SATA 97

Brand, Max
   See Faust, Frederick (Schiller)

Brand, Millen 1906-1980 .... **CLC 7**
   See also CA 21-24R; 97-100; CANR 72

Branden, Barbara .... **CLC 44**
   See also CA 148

Brandes, Georg (Morris Cohen) 1842-1927
   TCLC 10
   See also CA 105

Brandys, Kazimierz 1916- .... **CLC 62**

Branley, Franklyn M(ansfield)
   1915- .... **CLC 21**
   See also CA 33-36R; CANR 14, 39; CLR
   13; MAICYA; SAAS 16; SATA 4, 68

Brathwaite, Edward (Kamau)
   1930- ...... **CLC 11; BLCS; DAM POET**
   See also BW 2, 3; CA 25-28R; CANR 11,
   26, 47; DLB 125

Brautigan, Richard (Gary)
   1935-1984 .... **CLC 1, 3, 5, 9, 12, 34, 42;**
   DAM NOV
   See also CA 53-56; 113; CANR 34; DA3;
   DLB 2, 5, 206; DLBY 80, 84; MTCW 1;
   SATA 56

Brave Bird, Mary 1953-
   See Crow Dog, Mary (Ellen)
   See also NNAL

Braverman, Kate 1950- .... **CLC 67**
   See also CA 89-92

Brecht, (Eugen) Bertolt (Friedrich)
   1898-1956 .... **TCLC 1, 6, 13, 35; DA;**
   DAB; DAC; DAM DRAM, MST; DC
   3; WLC
   See also CA 104; 133; CANR 62; DA3;
   DLB 56, 124; MTCW 1, 2

Brecht, Eugen Berthold Friedrich
   See Brecht, (Eugen) Bertolt (Friedrich)

Bremer, Fredrika 1801-1865 .... **NCLC 11**

Brennan, Christopher John
   1870-1932 .... **TCLC 17**
   See also CA 117

Brennan, Maeve 1917-1993 .... **CLC 5**
   See also CA 81-84; CANR 72

Brent, Linda
   See Jacobs, Harriet A(nn)

Brentano, Clemens (Maria)
   1778-1842 .... **NCLC 1**
   See also DLB 90

Brent of Bin Bin
   See Franklin, (Stella Maria Sarah) Miles
   (Lampe)

Brenton, Howard 1942- .... **CLC 31**
   See also CA 69-72; CANR 33, 67; DLB 13;
   MTCW 1

Breslin, James 1930-1996
   See Breslin, Jimmy
   See also CA 73-76; CANR 31, 75; DAM
   NOV; MTCW 1, 2

Breslin, Jimmy .... **CLC 4, 43**
   See also Breslin, James
   See also AITN 1; DLB 185; MTCW 2

Bresson, Robert 1901- .... **CLC 16**
   See also CA 110; CANR 49

Breton, Andre 1896-1966 .. **CLC 2, 9, 15, 54;**
   PC 15
   See also CA 19-20; 25-28R; CANR 40, 60;
   CAP 2; DLB 65; MTCW 1, 2

Breytenbach, Breyten 1939(?)- .. **CLC 23, 37,**
   126; DAM POET
   See also CA 113; 129; CANR 61

Bridgers, Sue Ellen 1942- .... **CLC 26**
   See also AAYA 8; CA 65-68; CANR 11,
   36; CLR 18; DLB 52; JRDA; MAICYA;
   SAAS 1; SATA 22, 90; SATA-Essay 109

Bridges, Robert (Seymour)
   1844-1930 ... **TCLC 1; DAM POET; PC**
   28
   See also CA 104; 152; CDBLB 1890-1914;
   DLB 19, 98

Bridie, James .... **TCLC 3**
   See also Mavor, Osborne Henry
   See also DLB 10

Brin, David 1950- .... **CLC 34**
   See also AAYA 21; CA 102; CANR 24, 70;
   INT CANR-24; SATA 65

Brink, Andre (Philippus) 1935- . **CLC 18, 36,**
   106
   See also CA 104; CANR 39, 62; INT 103;
   MTCW 1, 2

Brinsmead, H(esba) F(ay) 1922- ...... **CLC 21**
   See also CA 21-24R; CANR 10; CLR 47;
   MAICYA; SAAS 5; SATA 18, 78

Brittain, Vera (Mary) 1893(?)-1970 . **CLC 23**
   See also CA 13-16; 25-28R; CANR 58;
   CAP 1; DLB 191; MTCW 1, 2

Broch, Hermann 1886-1951 .... **TCLC 20**
   See also CA 117; DLB 85, 124

Brock, Rose
   See Hansen, Joseph

Brodkey, Harold (Roy) 1930-1996 ... **CLC 56**
   See also CA 111; 151; CANR 71; DLB 130

Brodskii, Iosif
   See Brodsky, Joseph

Brodsky, Iosif Alexandrovich 1940-1996
   See Brodsky, Joseph
   See also AITN 1; CA 41-44R; 151; CANR
   37; DAM POET; DA3; MTCW 1, 2

Brodsky, Joseph 1940-1996 ..... **CLC 4, 6, 13,**
   36, 100; PC 9
   See also Brodskii, Iosif; Brodsky, Iosif Alexandrovich
   See also MTCW 1

Brodsky, Michael (Mark) 1948- .... **CLC 19**
   See also CA 102; CANR 18, 41, 58

Bromell, Henry 1947- .... **CLC 5**
   See also CA 53-56; CANR 9

Bromfield, Louis (Brucker)
   1896-1956 .... **TCLC 11**
   See also CA 107; 155; DLB 4, 9, 86

The Coen Brothers
See Coen, Ethan; Coen, Joel

Coetzee, J(ohn) M(ichael) 1940- ...... **CLC 23, 33, 66, 117; DAM NOV**
See also CA 77-80; CANR 41, 54, 74; DA3; MTCW 1, 2

Coffey, Brian
See Koontz, Dean R(ay)

Coffin, Robert P(eter) Tristram 1892-1955 **TCLC 95**
See also CA 123; 169; DLB 45

Cohan, George M(ichael)
1878-1942 .... **TCLC 60**
See also CA 157

Cohen, Arthur A(llen) 1928-1986 ...... **CLC 7, 31**
See also CA 1-4R; 120; CANR 1, 17, 42; DLB 28

Cohen, Leonard (Norman) 1934- ...... **CLC 3, 38; DAC; DAM MST**
See also CA 21-24R; CANR 14, 69; DLB 53; MTCW 1

Cohen, Matt 1942- .... **CLC 19; DAC**
See also CA 61-64; CAAS 18; CANR 40; DLB 53

Cohen-Solal, Annie 19(?)- .... **CLC 50**

Colegate, Isabel 1931- .... **CLC 36**
See also CA 17-20R; CANR 8, 22, 74; DLB 14; INT CANR-22; MTCW 1

Coleman, Emmett
See Reed, Ishmael

Coleridge, M. E.
See Coleridge, Mary E(lizabeth)

Coleridge, Mary E(lizabeth) 1861-1907 **TCLC 73**
See also CA 116; 166; DLB 19, 98

Coleridge, Samuel Taylor
1772-1834 .... **NCLC 9, 54; DA; DAB; DAC; DAM MST, POET; PC 11; WLC**
See also CDBLB 1789-1832; DA3; DLB 93, 107

Coleridge, Sara 1802-1852 .... **NCLC 31**
See also DLB 199

Coles, Don 1928- .... **CLC 46**
See also CA 115; CANR 38

Coles, Robert (Martin) 1929- .... **CLC 108**
See also CA 45-48; CANR 3, 32, 66, 70; INT CANR-32; SATA 23

Colette, (Sidonie-Gabrielle)
1873-1954 . **TCLC 1, 5, 16; DAM NOV; SSC 10**
See also CA 104; 131; DA3; DLB 65; MTCW 1, 2

Collett, (Jacobine) Camilla (Wergeland)
1813-1895 .... **NCLC 22**

Collier, Christopher 1930- .... **CLC 30**
See also AAYA 13; CA 33-36R; CANR 13, 33; JRDA; MAICYA; SATA 16, 70

Collier, James L(incoln) 1928- .... **CLC 30; DAM POP**
See also AAYA 13; CA 9-12R; CANR 4, 33, 60; CLR 3; JRDA; MAICYA; SAAS 21; SATA 8, 70

Collier, Jeremy 1650-1726 .... **LC 6**

Collier, John 1901-1980 .... **SSC 19**
See also CA 65-68; 97-100; CANR 10; DLB 77

Collingwood, R(obin) G(eorge) 1889(?)-1943 **TCLC 67**
See also CA 117; 155

Collins, Hunt
See Hunter, Evan

Collins, Linda 1931- .... **CLC 44**
See also CA 125

Collins, (William) Wilkie
1824-1889 .... **NCLC 1, 18**
See also CDBLB 1832-1890; DLB 18, 70, 159

Collins, William 1721-1759 . **LC 4, 40; DAM POET**
See also DLB 109

Collodi, Carlo 1826-1890 .... **NCLC 54**
See also Lorenzini, Carlo
See also CLR 5

Colman, George 1732-1794
See Glassco, John

Colt, Winchester Remington
See Hubbard, L(afayette) Ron(ald)

Colter, Cyrus 1910- .... **CLC 58**
See also BW 1; CA 65-68; CANR 10, 66; DLB 33

Colton, James
See Hansen, Joseph

Colum, Padraic 1881-1972 .... **CLC 28**
See also CA 73-76; 33-36R; CANR 35; CLR 36; MAICYA; MTCW 1; SATA 15

Colvin, James
See Moorcock, Michael (John)

Colwin, Laurie (E.) 1944-1992 .... **CLC 5, 13, 23, 84**
See also CA 89-92; 139; CANR 20, 46; DLBY 80; MTCW 1

Comfort, Alex(ander) 1920- .... **CLC 7; DAM POP**
See also CA 1-4R; CANR 1, 45; MTCW 1

Comfort, Montgomery
See Campbell, (John) Ramsey

Compton-Burnett, I(vy)
1884(?)-1969 .... **CLC 1, 3, 10, 15, 34; DAM NOV**
See also CA 1-4R; 25-28R; CANR 4; DLB 36; MTCW 1

Comstock, Anthony 1844-1915 ...... **TCLC 13**
See also CA 110; 169

Comte, Auguste 1798-1857 .... **NCLC 54**

Conan Doyle, Arthur
See Doyle, Arthur Conan

Conde (Abellan), Carmen 1901-
See also CA 177; DLB 108; HLCS 1; HW 2

Conde, Maryse 1937- .... **CLC 52, 92; BLCS; DAM MULT**
See also BW 2, 3; CA 110; CANR 30, 53, 76; MTCW 1

Condillac, Etienne Bonnot de
1714-1780 .... **LC 26**

Condon, Richard (Thomas)
1915-1996 ...... **CLC 4, 6, 8, 10, 45, 100; DAM NOV**
See also BEST 90:3; CA 1-4R; 151; CAAS 1; CANR 2, 23; INT CANR-23; MTCW 1, 2

Confucius 551B.C.-479B.C. .. **CMLC 19; DA; DAB; DAC; DAM MST; WLCS**
See also DA3

Congreve, William 1670-1729 .... **LC 5, 21; DA; DAB; DAC; DAM DRAM, MST, POET; DC 2; WLC**
See also CDBLB 1660-1789; DLB 39, 84

Connell, Evan S(helby), Jr. 1924- . **CLC 4, 6, 45; DAM NOV**
See also AAYA 7; CA 1-4R; CAAS 2; CANR 2, 39, 76; DLB 2; DLBY 81; MTCW 1, 2

Connelly, Marc(us Cook) 1890-1980 . **CLC 7**
See also CA 85-88; 102; CANR 30; DLB 7; DLBY 80; SATA-Obit 25

Connor, Ralph .... **TCLC 31**
See also Gordon, Charles William
See also DLB 92

Conrad, Joseph 1857-1924 .... **TCLC 1, 6, 13, 25, 43, 57; DA; DAB; DAC; DAM MST, NOV; SSC 9; WLC**
See also AAYA 26; CA 104; 131; CANR 60; CDBLB 1890-1914; DA3; DLB 10, 34, 98, 156; MTCW 1, 2; SATA 27

Conrad, Robert Arnold
See Hart, Moss

Conroy, Pat
See Conroy, (Donald) Pat(rick)
See also MTCW 2

Conroy, (Donald) Pat(rick) 1945- ... **CLC 30, 74; DAM NOV, POP**
See also Conroy, Pat
See also AAYA 8; AITN 1; CA 85-88; CANR 24, 53; DA3; DLB 6; MTCW 1

Constant (de Rebecque), (Henri) Benjamin
1767-1830 .... **NCLC 6**
See also DLB 119

Conybeare, Charles Augustus
See Eliot, T(homas) S(tearns)

Cook, Michael 1933- .... **CLC 58**
See also CA 93-96; CANR 68; DLB 53

Cook, Robin 1940- .... **CLC 14; DAM POP**
See also AAYA 32; BEST 90:2; CA 108; 111; CANR 41, 90; DA3; INT 111

Cook, Roy
See Silverberg, Robert

Cooke, Elizabeth 1948- .... **CLC 55**
See also CA 129

Cooke, John Esten 1830-1886 .... **NCLC 5**
See also DLB 3

Cooke, John Estes
See Baum, L(yman) Frank

Cooke, M. E.
See Creasey, John

Cooke, Margaret
See Creasey, John

Cook-Lynn, Elizabeth 1930- . **CLC 93; DAM MULT**
See also CA 133; DLB 175; NNAL

Cooney, Ray .... **CLC 62**

Cooper, Douglas 1960- .... **CLC 86**

Cooper, Henry St. John
See Creasey, John

Cooper, J(oan) California (?)- .... **CLC 56; DAM MULT**
See also AAYA 12; BW 1; CA 125; CANR 55; DLB 212

Cooper, James Fenimore
1789-1851 .... **NCLC 1, 27, 54**
See also AAYA 22; CDALB 1640-1865; DA3; DLB 3; SATA 19

Coover, Robert (Lowell) 1932- ...... **CLC 3, 7, 15, 32, 46, 87; DAM NOV; SSC 15**
See also CA 45-48; CANR 3, 37, 58; DLB 2; DLBY 81; MTCW 1, 2

Copeland, Stewart (Armstrong)
1952- .... **CLC 26**

Copernicus, Nicolaus 1473-1543 .... **LC 45**

Coppard, A(lfred) E(dgar)
1878-1957 .... **TCLC 5; SSC 21**
See also CA 114; 167; DLB 162; YABC 1

Coppee, Francois 1842-1908 .... **TCLC 25**
See also CA 170

Coppola, Francis Ford 1939- ... **CLC 16, 126**
See also CA 77-80; CANR 40, 78; DLB 44

Corbiere, Tristan 1845-1875 .... **NCLC 43**

Corcoran, Barbara 1911- .... **CLC 17**
See also AAYA 14; CA 21-24R; CAAS 2; CANR 11, 28, 48; CLR 50; DLB 52; JRDA; SAAS 20; SATA 3, 77

Cordelier, Maurice
See Giraudoux, (Hippolyte) Jean

Corelli, Marie 1855-1924 .... **TCLC 51**
See also Mackay, Mary
See also DLB 34, 156

Corman, Cid 1924- .... **CLC 9**
See also Corman, Sidney
See also CAAS 2; DLB 5, 193

Corman, Sidney 1924-
See Corman, Cid
See also CA 85-88; CANR 44; DAM POET

DAB; DAC; DAM MST, NOV; SSC 17;
WLC
See also AAYA 23; CDBLB 1832-1890;
DA3; DLB 21, 55, 70, 159, 166; JRDA;
MAICYA; SATA 15

Dickey, James (Lafayette)
1923-1997 .... **CLC 1, 2, 4, 7, 10, 15, 47,
109; DAM NOV, POET, POP**
See also AITN 1, 2; CA 9-12R; 156; CABS
2; CANR 10, 48, 61; CDALB 1968-1988;
DA3; DLB 5, 193; DLBD 7; DLBY 82,
93, 96, 97, 98; INT CANR-10; MTCW 1,
2

Dickey, William 1928-1994 .... **CLC 3, 28**
See also CA 9-12R; 145; CANR 24, 79;
DLB 5

Dickinson, Charles 1951- .... **CLC 49**
See also CA 128

Dickinson, Emily (Elizabeth) 1830-1886
**NCLC 21, 77; DA; DAB; DAC; DAM
MST, POET; PC 1; WLC**
See also AAYA 22; CDALB 1865-1917;
DA3; DLB 1; SATA 29

Dickinson, Peter (Malcolm) 1927- .. **CLC 12,
35**
See also AAYA 9; CA 41-44R; CANR 31,
58, 88; CLR 29; DLB 87, 161; JRDA;
MAICYA; SATA 5, 62, 95

Dickson, Carr
See Carr, John Dickson

Dickson, Carter
See Carr, John Dickson

Diderot, Denis 1713-1784 .... **LC 26**

Didion, Joan 1934- .... **CLC 1, 3, 8, 14, 32,
129; DAM NOV**
See also AITN 1; CA 5-8R; CANR 14, 52,
76; CDALB 1968-1988; DA3; DLB 2,
173, 185; DLBY 81, 86; MTCW 1, 2

Dietrich, Robert
See Hunt, E(verette) Howard, (Jr.)

Difusa, Pati
See Almodovar, Pedro

Dillard, Annie 1945- .. **CLC 9, 60, 115; DAM
NOV**
See also AAYA 6; CA 49-52; CANR 3, 43,
62, 90; DA3; DLBY 80; MTCW 1, 2;
SATA 10

Dillard, R(ichard) H(enry) W(ilde) 1937-
CLC 5
See also CA 21-24R; CAAS 7; CANR 10;
DLB 5

Dillon, Eilis 1920-1994 .... **CLC 17**
See also CA 9-12R, 182; 147; CAAE 182;
CAAS 3; CANR 4, 38, 78; CLR 26; MAI-
CYA; SATA 2, 74; SATA-Essay 105;
SATA-Obit 83

Dimont, Penelope
See Mortimer, Penelope (Ruth)

Dinesen, Isak .... **CLC 10, 29, 95; SSC 7**
See also Blixen, Karen (Christentze
Dinesen)
See also MTCW 1

Ding Ling .... **CLC 68**
See also Chiang, Pin-chin

Diphusa, Patty
See Almodovar, Pedro

Disch, Thomas M(ichael) 1940- ... **CLC 7, 36**
See also AAYA 17; CA 21-24R; CAAS 4;
CANR 17, 36, 54, 89; CLR 18; DA3;
DLB 8; MAICYA; MTCW 1, 2; SAAS
15; SATA 92

Disch, Tom
See Disch, Thomas M(ichael)

d'Isly, Georges
See Simenon, Georges (Jacques Christian)

Disraeli, Benjamin 1804-1881 ... **NCLC 2, 39,
79**
See also DLB 21, 55

Ditcum, Steve
See Crumb, R(obert)

Dixon, Paige
See Corcoran, Barbara

Dixon, Stephen 1936- .... **CLC 52; SSC 16**
See also CA 89-92; CANR 17, 40, 54, 91;
DLB 130

Doak, Annie
See Dillard, Annie

Dobell, Sydney Thompson
1824-1874 .... **NCLC 43**
See also DLB 32

Doblin, Alfred .... **TCLC 13**
See also Doeblin, Alfred

Dobrolyubov, Nikolai Alexandrovich
1836-1861 .... **NCLC 5**

Dobson, Austin 1840-1921 .... **TCLC 79**
See also DLB 35; 144

Dobyns, Stephen 1941- .... **CLC 37**
See also CA 45-48; CANR 2, 18

Doctorow, E(dgar) L(aurence)
1931- .... **CLC 6, 11, 15, 18, 37, 44, 65,
113; DAM NOV, POP**
See also AAYA 22; AITN 2; BEST 89:3;
CA 45-48; CANR 2, 33, 51, 76; CDALB
1968-1988; DA3; DLB 2, 28, 173; DLBY
80; MTCW 1, 2

Dodgson, Charles Lutwidge 1832-1898
See Carroll, Lewis
See also CLR 2; DA; DAB; DAC; DAM
MST, NOV, POET; DA3; MAICYA;
SATA 100; YABC 2

Dodson, Owen (Vincent)
1914-1983 .... **CLC 79; BLC 1; DAM
MULT**
See also BW 1; CA 65-68; 110; CANR 24;
DLB 76

Doeblin, Alfred 1878-1957 .... **TCLC 13**
See also Doblin, Alfred
See also CA 110; 141; DLB 66

Doerr, Harriet 1910- .... **CLC 34**
See also CA 117; 122; CANR 47; INT 122

Domecq, H(onorio Bustos)
See Bioy Casares, Adolfo

Domecq, H(onorio) Bustos
See Bioy Casares, Adolfo; Borges, Jorge
Luis

Domini, Rey
See Lorde, Audre (Geraldine)

Dominique
See Proust, (Valentin-Louis-George-
Eugene-) Marcel

Don, A
See Stephen, SirLeslie

Donaldson, Stephen R. 1947- .... **CLC 46;
DAM POP**
See also CA 89-92; CANR 13, 55; INT
CANR-13

Donleavy, J(ames) P(atrick) 1926- .... **CLC 1,
4, 6, 10, 45**
See also AITN 2; CA 9-12R; CANR 24, 49,
62, 80; DLB 6, 173; INT CANR-24;
MTCW 1, 2

Donne, John 1572-1631 .... **LC 10, 24; DA;
DAB; DAC; DAM MST, POET; PC 1;
WLC**
See also CDBLB Before 1660; DLB 121,
151

Donnell, David 1939(?)- .... **CLC 34**

Donoghue, P. S.
See Hunt, E(verette) Howard, (Jr.)

Donoso (Yanez), Jose 1924-1996 ... **CLC 4, 8,
11, 32, 99; DAM MULT; HLC 1; SSC
34**
See also CA 81-84; 155; CANR 32, 73;
DLB 113; HW 1, 2; MTCW 1, 2

Donovan, John 1928-1992 .... **CLC 35**
See also AAYA 20; CA 97-100; 137; CLR
3; MAICYA; SATA 72; SATA-Brief 29

Don Roberto
See Cunninghame Graham, Robert
(Gallnigad) Bontine

Doolittle, Hilda 1886-1961 . **CLC 3, 8, 14, 31,
34, 73; DA; DAC; DAM MST, POET;
PC 5; WLC**
See also H. D.
See also CA 97-100; CANR 35; DLB 4, 45;
MTCW 1, 2

Dorfman, Ariel 1942- ...... **CLC 48, 77; DAM
MULT; HLC 1**
See also CA 124; 130; CANR 67, 70; HW
1, 2; INT 130

Dorn, Edward (Merton) 1929- ... **CLC 10, 18**
See also CA 93-96; CANR 42, 79; DLB 5;
INT 93-96

Dorris, Michael (Anthony)
1945-1997 .... **CLC 109; DAM MULT,
NOV**
See also AAYA 20; BEST 90:1; CA 102;
157; CANR 19, 46, 75; CLR 58; DA3;
DLB 175; MTCW 2; NNAL; SATA 75;
SATA-Obit 94

Dorris, Michael A.
See Dorris, Michael (Anthony)

Dorsan, Luc
See Simenon, Georges (Jacques Christian)

Dorsange, Jean
See Simenon, Georges (Jacques Christian)

Dos Passos, John (Roderigo)
1896-1970 ... **CLC 1, 4, 8, 11, 15, 25, 34,
82; DA; DAB; DAC; DAM MST, NOV;
WLC**
See also CA 1-4R; 29-32R; CANR 3;
CDALB 1929-1941; DA3; DLB 4, 9;
DLBD 1, 15; DLBY 96; MTCW 1, 2

Dossage, Jean
See Simenon, Georges (Jacques Christian)

Dostoevsky, Fedor Mikhailovich 1821-1881
**NCLC 2, 7, 21, 33, 43; DA; DAB; DAC;
DAM MST, NOV; SSC 2, 33; WLC**
See also DA3

Doughty, Charles M(ontagu) 1843-1926
TCLC 27
See also CA 115; 178; DLB 19, 57, 174

Douglas, Ellen .... **CLC 73**
See also Haxton, Josephine Ayres; William-
son, Ellen Douglas

Douglas, Gavin 1475(?)-1522 .... **LC 20**
See also DLB 132

Douglas, George
See Brown, George Douglas

Douglas, Keith (Castellain)
1920-1944 .... **TCLC 40**
See also CA 160; DLB 27

Douglas, Leonard
See Bradbury, Ray (Douglas)

Douglas, Michael
See Crichton, (John) Michael

Douglas, (George) Norman
1868-1952 .... **TCLC 68**
See also CA 119; 157; DLB 34, 195

Douglas, William
See Brown, George Douglas

Douglass, Frederick 1817(?)-1895 .. **NCLC 7,
55; BLC 1; DA; DAC; DAM MST,
MULT; WLC**
See also CDALB 1640-1865; DA3; DLB 1,
43, 50, 79; SATA 29

Dourado, (Waldomiro Freitas) Autran 1926-
CLC 23, 60
See also CA 25-28R; 179; CANR 34, 81;
DLB 145; HW 2

Dourado, Waldomiro Autran 1926-
See Dourado, (Waldomiro Freitas) Autran
See also CA 179

Dove, Rita (Frances) 1952- .... **CLC 50, 81;
    BLCS; DAM MULT, POET; PC 6**
    See also BW 2; CA 109; CAAS 19; CANR
    27, 42, 68, 76; CDALBS; DA3; DLB 120;
    MTCW 1
Doveglion
    See Villa, Jose Garcia
Dowell, Coleman 1925-1985 .... **CLC 60**
    See also CA 25-28R; 117; CANR 10; DLB
    130
Dowson, Ernest (Christopher) 1867-1900
    TCLC 4
    See also CA 105; 150; DLB 19, 135
Doyle, A. Conan
    See Doyle, Arthur Conan
Doyle, Arthur Conan 1859-1930 .... **TCLC 7;
    DA; DAB; DAC; DAM MST, NOV;
    SSC 12; WLC**
    See also AAYA 14; CA 104; 122; CDBLB
    1890-1914; DA3; DLB 18, 70, 156, 178;
    MTCW 1, 2; SATA 24
Doyle, Conan
    See Doyle, Arthur Conan
Doyle, John
    See Graves, Robert (von Ranke)
Doyle, Roddy 1958(?)- .... **CLC 81**
    See also AAYA 14; CA 143; CANR 73;
    DA3; DLB 194
Doyle, Sir A. Conan
    See Doyle, Arthur Conan
Doyle, Sir Arthur Conan
    See Doyle, Arthur Conan
Dr. A
    See Asimov, Isaac; Silverstein, Alvin
Drabble, Margaret 1939- ...... **CLC 2, 3, 5, 8,
    10, 22, 53, 129; DAB; DAC; DAM
    MST, NOV, POP**
    See also CA 13-16R; CANR 18, 35, 63;
    CDBLB 1960 to Present; DA3; DLB 14,
    155; MTCW 1, 2; SATA 48
Drapier, M. B.
    See Swift, Jonathan
Drayham, James
    See Mencken, H(enry) L(ouis)
Drayton, Michael 1563-1631 ..... **LC 8; DAM
    POET**
    See also DLB 121
Dreadstone, Carl
    See Campbell, (John) Ramsey
Dreiser, Theodore (Herman Albert)
    1871-1945 .... **TCLC 10, 18, 35, 83; DA;
    DAC; DAM MST, NOV; SSC 30; WLC**
    See also CA 106; 132; CDALB 1865-1917;
    DA3; DLB 9, 12, 102, 137; DLBD 1;
    MTCW 1, 2
Drexler, Rosalyn 1926- .... **CLC 2, 6**
    See also CA 81-84; CANR 68
Dreyer, Carl Theodor 1889-1968 ...... **CLC 16**
    See also CA 116
Drieu la Rochelle, Pierre(-Eugene)
    1893-1945 .... **TCLC 21**
    See also CA 117; DLB 72
Drinkwater, John 1882-1937 .... **TCLC 57**
    See also CA 109; 149; DLB 10, 19, 149
Drop Shot
    See Cable, George Washington
Droste-Hulshoff, Annette Freiin von
    1797-1848 .... **NCLC 3**
    See also DLB 133
Drummond, Walter
    See Silverberg, Robert
Drummond, William Henry
    1854-1907 .... **TCLC 25**
    See also CA 160; DLB 92
Drummond de Andrade, Carlos 1902-1987
    CLC 18
    See also Andrade, Carlos Drummond de
    See also CA 132; 123

Drury, Allen (Stuart) 1918-1998 .... **CLC 37**
    See also CA 57-60; 170; CANR 18, 52; INT
    CANR-18
Dryden, John 1631-1700 .... **LC 3, 21; DA;
    DAB; DAC; DAM DRAM, MST,
    POET; DC 3; PC 25; WLC**
    See also CDBLB 1660-1789; DLB 80, 101,
    131
Duberman, Martin (Bauml) 1930- ..... **CLC 8**
    See also CA 1-4R; CANR 2, 63
Dubie, Norman (Evans) 1945- .... **CLC 36**
    See also CA 69-72; CANR 12; DLB 120
Du Bois, W(illiam) E(dward) B(urghardt)
    1868-1963 ... **CLC 1, 2, 13, 64, 96; BLC
    1; DA; DAC; DAM MST, MULT,
    NOV; WLC**
    See also BW 1, 3; CA 85-88; CANR 34,
    82; CDALB 1865-1917; DA3; DLB 47,
    50, 91; MTCW 1, 2; SATA 42
Dubus, Andre 1936-1999 ..... **CLC 13, 36, 97;
    SSC 15**
    See also CA 21-24R; 177; CANR 17; DLB
    130; INT CANR-17
Duca Minimo
    See D'Annunzio, Gabriele
Ducharme, Rejean 1941- .... **CLC 74**
    See also CA 165; DLB 60
Duclos, Charles Pinot 1704-1772 .... **LC 1**
Dudek, Louis 1918- .... **CLC 11, 19**
    See also CA 45-48; CAAS 14; CANR 1;
    DLB 88
Duerrenmatt, Friedrich 1921-1990 ... **CLC 1,
    4, 8, 11, 15, 43, 102; DAM DRAM**
    See also CA 17-20R; CANR 33; DLB 69,
    124; MTCW 1, 2
Duffy, Bruce 1953(?)- .... **CLC 50**
    See also CA 172
Duffy, Maureen 1933- .... **CLC 37**
    See also CA 25-28R; CANR 33, 68; DLB
    14; MTCW 1
Dugan, Alan 1923- .... **CLC 2, 6**
    See also CA 81-84; DLB 5
du Gard, Roger Martin
    See Martin du Gard, Roger
Duhamel, Georges 1884-1966 .... **CLC 8**
    See also CA 81-84; 25-28R; CANR 35;
    DLB 65; MTCW 1
Dujardin, Edouard (Emile Louis) 1861-1949
    TCLC 13
    See also CA 109; DLB 123
Dulles, John Foster 1888-1959 .... **TCLC 72**
    See also CA 115; 149
Dumas, Alexandre (pere)
    See Dumas, Alexandre (Davy de la
    Pailleterie)
Dumas, Alexandre (Davy de la Pailleterie)
    1802-1870 ...... **NCLC 11, 71; DA; DAB;
    DAC; DAM MST, NOV; WLC**
    See also DA3; DLB 119, 192; SATA 18
Dumas, Alexandre (fils)
    1824-1895 .... **NCLC 71; DC 1**
    See also AAYA 22; DLB 192
Dumas, Claudine
    See Malzberg, Barry N(athaniel)
Dumas, Henry L. 1934-1968 .... **CLC 6, 62**
    See also BW 1; CA 85-88; DLB 41
du Maurier, Daphne 1907-1989 .. **CLC 6, 11,
    59; DAB; DAC; DAM MST, POP; SSC
    18**
    See also CA 5-8R; 128; CANR 6, 55; DA3;
    DLB 191; MTCW 1, 2; SATA 27; SATA-
    Obit 60
Du Maurier, George 1834-1896 ..... **NCLC 86**
    See also DLB 153, 178

Dunbar, Paul Laurence 1872-1906 . **TCLC 2,
    12; BLC 1; DA; DAC; DAM MST,
    MULT, POET; PC 5; SSC 8; WLC**
    See also BW 1, 3; CA 104; 124; CANR 79;
    CDALB 1865-1917; DA3; DLB 50, 54,
    78; SATA 34
Dunbar, William 1460(?)-1530(?) .... **LC 20**
    See also DLB 132, 146
Duncan, Dora Angela
    See Duncan, Isadora
Duncan, Isadora 1877(?)-1927 .... **TCLC 68**
    See also CA 118; 149
Duncan, Lois 1934- .... **CLC 26**
    See also AAYA 4, 34; CA 1-4R; CANR 2,
    23, 36; CLR 29; JRDA; MAICYA; SAAS
    2; SATA 1, 36, 75
Duncan, Robert (Edward)
    1919-1988 .... **CLC 1, 2, 4, 7, 15, 41, 55;
    DAM POET; PC 2**
    See also CA 9-12R; 124; CANR 28, 62;
    DLB 5, 16, 193; MTCW 1, 2
Duncan, Sara Jeannette
    1861-1922 .... **TCLC 60**
    See also CA 157; DLB 92
Dunlap, William 1766-1839 .... **NCLC 2**
    See also DLB 30, 37, 59
Dunn, Douglas (Eaglesham) 1942- .... **CLC 6,
    40**
    See also CA 45-48; CANR 2, 33; DLB 40;
    MTCW 1
Dunn, Katherine (Karen) 1945- .... **CLC 71**
    See also CA 33-36R; CANR 72; MTCW 1
Dunn, Stephen 1939- .... **CLC 36**
    See also CA 33-36R; CANR 12, 48, 53;
    DLB 105
Dunne, Finley Peter 1867-1936 ...... **TCLC 28**
    See also CA 108; 178; DLB 11, 23
Dunne, John Gregory 1932- .... **CLC 28**
    See also CA 25-28R; CANR 14, 50; DLBY
    80
**Dunsany, Edward John Moreton Drax
    Plunkett** 1878-1957
    See Dunsany, Lord
    See also CA 104; 148; DLB 10; MTCW 1
Dunsany, Lord .... **TCLC 2, 59**
    See also Dunsany, Edward John Moreton
    Drax Plunkett
    See also DLB 77, 153, 156
du Perry, Jean
    See Simenon, Georges (Jacques Christian)
Durang, Christopher (Ferdinand)
    1949- .... **CLC 27, 38**
    See also CA 105; CANR 50, 76; MTCW 1
Duras, Marguerite 1914-1996 . **CLC 3, 6, 11,
    20, 34, 40, 68, 100; SSC 40**
    See also CA 25-28R; 151; CANR 50; DLB
    83; MTCW 1, 2
Durban, (Rosa) Pam 1947- .... **CLC 39**
    See also CA 123
Durcan, Paul 1944- .... **CLC 43, 70; DAM
    POET**
    See also CA 134
Durkheim, Emile 1858-1917 .... **TCLC 55**
Durrell, Lawrence (George)
    1912-1990 .... **CLC 1, 4, 6, 8, 13, 27, 41;
    DAM NOV**
    See also CA 9-12R; 132; CANR 40, 77;
    CDBLB 1945-1960; DLB 15, 27, 204;
    DLBY 90; MTCW 1, 2
Durrenmatt, Friedrich
    See Duerrenmatt, Friedrich
Dutt, Toru 1856-1877 .... **NCLC 29**
Dwight, Timothy 1752-1817 .... **NCLC 13**
    See also DLB 37
Dworkin, Andrea 1946- .... **CLC 43**
    See also CA 77-80; CAAS 21; CANR 16,
    39, 76; INT CANR-16; MTCW 1, 2
Dwyer, Deanna
    See Koontz, Dean R(ay)

Farquhar, George 1677-1707 ... **LC 21; DAM DRAM**
See also DLB 84

Farrell, J(ames) G(ordon)
1935-1979 .... **CLC 6**
See also CA 73-76; 89-92; CANR 36; DLB 14; MTCW 1

Farrell, James T(homas) 1904-1979 . **CLC 1, 4, 8, 11, 66; SSC 28**
See also CA 5-8R; 89-92; CANR 9, 61; DLB 4, 9, 86; DLBD 2; MTCW 1, 2

Farren, Richard J.
See Betjeman, John

Farren, Richard M.
See Betjeman, John

Fassbinder, Rainer Werner
1946-1982 .... **CLC 20**
See also CA 93-96; 106; CANR 31

Fast, Howard (Melvin) 1914- .. **CLC 23, 131; DAM NOV**
See also AAYA 16; CA 1-4R, 181; CAAE 181; CAAS 18; CANR 1, 33, 54, 75; DLB 9; INT CANR-33; MTCW 1; SATA 7; SATA-Essay 107

Faulcon, Robert
See Holdstock, Robert P.

Faulkner, William (Cuthbert) 1897-1962 **CLC 1, 3, 6, 8, 9, 11, 14, 18, 28, 52, 68; DA; DAB; DAC; DAM MST, NOV; SSC 1, 35; WLC**
See also AAYA 7; CA 81-84; CANR 33; CDALB 1929-1941; DA3; DLB 9, 11, 44, 102; DLBD 2; DLBY 86, 97; MTCW 1, 2

Fauset, Jessie Redmon
1884(?)-1961 .... **CLC 19, 54; BLC 2; DAM MULT**
See also BW 1; CA 109; CANR 83; DLB 51

Faust, Frederick (Schiller) 1892-1944(?) **TCLC 49; DAM POP**
See also CA 108; 152

Faust, Irvin 1924- .... **CLC 8**
See also CA 33-36R; CANR 28, 67; DLB 2, 28; DLBY 80

Fawkes, Guy
See Benchley, Robert (Charles)

Fearing, Kenneth (Flexner)
1902-1961 .... **CLC 51**
See also CA 93-96; CANR 59; DLB 9

Fecamps, Elise
See Creasey, John

Federman, Raymond 1928- .... **CLC 6, 47**
See also CA 17-20R; CAAS 8; CANR 10, 43, 83; DLBY 80

Federspiel, J(uerg) F. 1931- .... **CLC 42**
See also CA 146

Feiffer, Jules (Ralph) 1929- ..... **CLC 2, 8, 64; DAM DRAM**
See also AAYA 3; CA 17-20R; CANR 30, 59; DLB 7, 44; INT CANR-30; MTCW 1; SATA 8, 61, 111

Feige, Hermann Albert Otto Maximilian
See Traven, B.

Feinberg, David B. 1956-1994 .... **CLC 59**
See also CA 135; 147

Feinstein, Elaine 1930- .... **CLC 36**
See also CA 69-72; CAAS 1; CANR 31, 68; DLB 14, 40; MTCW 1

Feldman, Irving (Mordecai) 1928- ..... **CLC 7**
See also CA 1-4R; CANR 1; DLB 169

Felix-Tchicaya, Gerald
See Tchicaya, Gerald Felix

Fellini, Federico 1920-1993 .... **CLC 16, 85**
See also CA 65-68; 143; CANR 33

Felsen, Henry Gregor 1916-1995 ..... **CLC 17**
See also CA 1-4R; 180; CANR 1; SAAS 2; SATA 1

Fenno, Jack
See Calisher, Hortense

Fenollosa, Ernest (Francisco) 1853-1908 **TCLC 91**

Fenton, James Martin 1949- .... **CLC 32**
See also CA 102; DLB 40

Ferber, Edna 1887-1968 .... **CLC 18, 93**
See also AITN 1; CA 5-8R; 25-28R; CANR 68; DLB 9, 28, 86; MTCW 1, 2; SATA 7

Ferguson, Helen
See Kavan, Anna

Ferguson, Samuel 1810-1886 .... **NCLC 33**
See also DLB 32

Fergusson, Robert 1750-1774 .... **LC 29**
See also DLB 109

Ferling, Lawrence
See Ferlinghetti, Lawrence (Monsanto)

Ferlinghetti, Lawrence (Monsanto) 1919(?)- **CLC 2, 6, 10, 27, 111; DAM POET; PC 1**
See also CA 5-8R; CANR 3, 41, 73; CDALB 1941-1968; DA3; DLB 5, 16; MTCW 1, 2

Fern, Fanny 1811-1872
See Parton, Sara Payson Willis

Fernandez, Vicente Garcia Huidobro
See Huidobro Fernandez, Vicente Garcia

Ferre, Rosario 1942- .... **SSC 36; HLCS 1**
See also CA 131; CANR 55, 81; DLB 145; HW 1, 2; MTCW 1

Ferrer, Gabriel (Francisco Victor) Miro
See Miro (Ferrer), Gabriel (Francisco Victor)

Ferrier, Susan (Edmonstone) 1782-1854 **NCLC 8**
See also DLB 116

Ferrigno, Robert 1948(?)- .... **CLC 65**
See also CA 140

Ferron, Jacques 1921-1985 .... **CLC 94; DAC**
See also CA 117; 129; DLB 60

Feuchtwanger, Lion 1884-1958 .... **TCLC 3**
See also CA 104; DLB 66

Feuillet, Octave 1821-1890 .... **NCLC 45**
See also DLB 192

Feydeau, Georges (Leon Jules Marie)
1862-1921 .... **TCLC 22; DAM DRAM**
See also CA 113; 152; CANR 84; DLB 192

Fichte, Johann Gottlieb
1762-1814 .... **NCLC 62**
See also DLB 90

Ficino, Marsilio 1433-1499 .... **LC 12**

Fiedeler, Hans
See Doeblin, Alfred

Fiedler, Leslie A(aron) 1917- .. **CLC 4, 13, 24**
See also CA 9-12R; CANR 7, 63; DLB 28, 67; MTCW 1, 2

Field, Andrew 1938- .... **CLC 44**
See also CA 97-100; CANR 25

Field, Eugene 1850-1895 .... **NCLC 3**
See also DLB 23, 42, 140; DLBD 13; MAICYA; SATA 16

Field, Gans T.
See Wellman, Manly Wade

Field, Michael 1915-1971 .... **TCLC 43**
See also CA 29-32R

Field, Peter
See Hobson, Laura Z(ametkin)

Fielding, Henry 1707-1754 ..... **LC 1, 46; DA; DAB; DAC; DAM DRAM, MST, NOV; WLC**
See also CDBLB 1660-1789; DA3; DLB 39, 84, 101

Fielding, Sarah 1710-1768 .... **LC 1, 44**
See also DLB 39

Fields, W. C. 1880-1946 .... **TCLC 80**
See also DLB 44

Fierstein, Harvey (Forbes) 1954- .... **CLC 33; DAM DRAM, POP**
See also CA 123; 129; DA3

Figes, Eva 1932- .... **CLC 31**
See also CA 53-56; CANR 4, 44, 83; DLB 14

Finch, Anne 1661-1720 .... **LC 3; PC 21**
See also DLB 95

Finch, Robert (Duer Claydon)
1900- .... **CLC 18**
See also CA 57-60; CANR 9, 24, 49; DLB 88

Findley, Timothy 1930- . **CLC 27, 102; DAC; DAM MST**
See also CA 25-28R; CANR 12, 42, 69; DLB 53

Fink, William
See Mencken, H(enry) L(ouis)

Firbank, Louis 1942-
See Reed, Lou
See also CA 117

Firbank, (Arthur Annesley) Ronald
1886-1926 .... **TCLC 1**
See also CA 104; 177; DLB 36

Fisher, Dorothy (Frances) Canfield
1879-1958 .... **TCLC 87**
See also CA 114; 136; CANR 80; DLB 9, 102; MAICYA; YABC 1

Fisher, M(ary) F(rances) K(ennedy)
1908-1992 .... **CLC 76, 87**
See also CA 77-80; 138; CANR 44; MTCW 1

Fisher, Roy 1930- .... **CLC 25**
See also CA 81-84; CAAS 10; CANR 16; DLB 40

Fisher, Rudolph 1897-1934 .. **TCLC 11; BLC 2; DAM MULT; SSC 25**
See also BW 1, 3; CA 107; 124; CANR 80; DLB 51, 102

Fisher, Vardis (Alvero) 1895-1968 ...... **CLC 7**
See also CA 5-8R; 25-28R; CANR 68; DLB 9, 206

Fiske, Tarleton
See Bloch, Robert (Albert)

Fitch, Clarke
See Sinclair, Upton (Beall)

Fitch, John IV
See Cormier, Robert (Edmund)

Fitzgerald, Captain Hugh
See Baum, L(yman) Frank

FitzGerald, Edward 1809-1883 .... **NCLC 9**
See also DLB 32

Fitzgerald, F(rancis) Scott (Key) 1896-1940 **TCLC 1, 6, 14, 28, 55; DA; DAB; DAC; DAM MST, NOV; SSC 6, 31; WLC**
See also AAYA 24; AITN 1; CA 110; 123; CDALB 1917-1929; DA3; DLB 4, 9, 86; DLBD 1, 15, 16; DLBY 81, 96; MTCW 1, 2

Fitzgerald, Penelope 1916-2000 . **CLC 19, 51, 61**
See also CA 85-88; CAAS 10; CANR 56, 86; DLB 14, 194; MTCW 2

Fitzgerald, Robert (Stuart)
1910-1985 .... **CLC 39**
See also CA 1-4R; 114; CANR 1; DLBY 80

FitzGerald, Robert D(avid)
1902-1987 .... **CLC 19**
See also CA 17-20R

Fitzgerald, Zelda (Sayre)
1900-1948 .... **TCLC 52**
See also CA 117; 126; DLBY 84

Flanagan, Thomas (James Bonner) 1923- **CLC 25, 52**
See also CA 108; CANR 55; DLBY 80; INT 108; MTCW 1

Flaubert, Gustave 1821-1880 .... **NCLC 2, 10, 19, 62, 66; DA; DAB; DAC; DAM MST, NOV; SSC 11; WLC**
See also DA3; DLB 119

Freud, Sigmund 1856-1939 .... **TCLC 52**
  See also CA 115; 133; CANR 69; MTCW
  1, 2
Friedan, Betty (Naomi) 1921- .... **CLC 74**
  See also CA 65-68; CANR 18, 45, 74;
  MTCW 1, 2
Friedlander, Saul 1932- .... **CLC 90**
  See also CA 117; 130; CANR 72
Friedman, B(ernard) H(arper)
  1926- .... **CLC 7**
  See also CA 1-4R; CANR 3, 48
Friedman, Bruce Jay 1930- ...... **CLC 3, 5, 56**
  See also CA 9-12R; CANR 25, 52; DLB 2,
  28; INT CANR-25
Friel, Brian 1929- .... **CLC 5, 42, 59, 115; DC
  8**
  See also CA 21-24R; CANR 33, 69; DLB
  13; MTCW 1
Friis-Baastad, Babbis Ellinor
  1921-1970 .... **CLC 12**
  See also CA 17-20R; 134; SATA 7
Frisch, Max (Rudolf) 1911-1991 ... **CLC 3, 9,
  14, 18, 32, 44; DAM DRAM, NOV**
  See also CA 85-88; 134; CANR 32, 74;
  DLB 69, 124; MTCW 1, 2
Fromentin, Eugene (Samuel Auguste)
  1820-1876 .... **NCLC 10**
  See also DLB 123
Frost, Frederick
  See Faust, Frederick (Schiller)
Frost, Robert (Lee) 1874-1963 .. **CLC 1, 3, 4,
  9, 10, 13, 15, 26, 34, 44; DA; DAB;
  DAC; DAM MST, POET; PC 1; WLC**
  See also AAYA 21; CA 89-92; CANR 33;
  CDALB 1917-1929; DA3; DLB 54;
  DLBD 7; MTCW 1, 2; SATA 14
Froude, James Anthony
  1818-1894 .... **NCLC 43**
  See also DLB 18, 57, 144
Froy, Herald
  See Waterhouse, Keith (Spencer)
Fry, Christopher 1907- .... **CLC 2, 10, 14;
  DAM DRAM**
  See also CA 17-20R; CAAS 23; CANR 9,
  30, 74; DLB 13; MTCW 1, 2; SATA 66
Frye, (Herman) Northrop
  1912-1991 .... **CLC 24, 70**
  See also CA 5-8R; 133; CANR 8, 37; DLB
  67, 68; MTCW 1, 2
Fuchs, Daniel 1909-1993 .... **CLC 8, 22**
  See also CA 81-84; 142; CAAS 5; CANR
  40; DLB 9, 26, 28; DLBY 93
Fuchs, Daniel 1934- .... **CLC 34**
  See also CA 37-40R; CANR 14, 48
Fuentes, Carlos 1928- .. **CLC 3, 8, 10, 13, 22,
  41, 60, 113; DA; DAB; DAC; DAM
  MST, MULT, NOV; HLC 1; SSC 24;
  WLC**
  See also AAYA 4; AITN 2; CA 69-72;
  CANR 10, 32, 68; DA3; DLB 113; HW
  1, 2; MTCW 1, 2
Fuentes, Gregorio Lopez y
  See Lopez y Fuentes, Gregorio
Fuertes, Gloria 1918- .... **PC 27**
  See also CA 178; 180; DLB 108; HW 2;
  SATA 115
Fugard, (Harold) Athol 1932- . **CLC 5, 9, 14,
  25, 40, 80; DAM DRAM; DC 3**
  See also AAYA 17; CA 85-88; CANR 32,
  54; MTCW 1
Fugard, Sheila 1932- .... **CLC 48**
  See also CA 125
Fukuyama, Francis 1952- .... **CLC 131**
  See also CA 140; CANR 72
Fuller, Charles (H., Jr.) 1939- .... **CLC 25;
  BLC 2; DAM DRAM, MULT; DC 1**
  See also BW 2; CA 108; 112; CANR 87;
  DLB 38; INT 112; MTCW 1

Fuller, John (Leopold) 1937- .... **CLC 62**
  See also CA 21-24R; CANR 9, 44; DLB 40
Fuller, Margaret .... **NCLC 5, 50**
  See also Fuller, Sarah Margaret
Fuller, Roy (Broadbent) 1912-1991 ... **CLC 4,
  28**
  See also CA 5-8R; 135; CAAS 10; CANR
  53, 83; DLB 15, 20; SATA 87
Fuller, Sarah Margaret 1810-1850
  See Fuller, Margaret
  See also CDALB 1640-1865; DLB 1, 59,
  73, 83, 223
Fulton, Alice 1952- .... **CLC 52**
  See also CA 116; CANR 57, 88; DLB 193
Furphy, Joseph 1843-1912 .... **TCLC 25**
  See also CA 163
Fussell, Paul 1924- .... **CLC 74**
  See also BEST 90:1; CA 17-20R; CANR 8,
  21, 35, 69; INT CANR-21; MTCW 1, 2
Futabatei, Shimei 1864-1909 .... **TCLC 44**
  See also CA 162; DLB 180
Futrelle, Jacques 1875-1912 .... **TCLC 19**
  See also CA 113; 155
Gaboriau, Emile 1835-1873 .... **NCLC 14**
Gadda, Carlo Emilio 1893-1973 .... **CLC 11**
  See also CA 89-92; DLB 177
Gaddis, William 1922-1998 ... **CLC 1, 3, 6, 8,
  10, 19, 43, 86**
  See also CA 17-20R; 172; CANR 21, 48;
  DLB 2; MTCW 1, 2
Gage, Walter
  See Inge, William (Motter)
Gaines, Ernest J(ames) 1933- ...... **CLC 3, 11,
  18, 86; BLC 2; DAM MULT**
  See also AAYA 18; AITN 1; BW 2, 3; CA
  9-12R; CANR 6, 24, 42, 75; CDALB
  1968-1988; CLR 62; DA3; DLB 2, 33,
  152; DLBY 80; MTCW 1, 2; SATA 86
Gaitskill, Mary 1954- .... **CLC 69**
  See also CA 128; CANR 61
Galdos, Benito Perez
  See Perez Galdos, Benito
Gale, Zona 1874-1938 .... **TCLC 7; DAM
  DRAM**
  See also CA 105; 153; CANR 84; DLB 9,
  78
Galeano, Eduardo (Hughes) 1940- . **CLC 72;
  HLCS 1**
  See also CA 29-32R; CANR 13, 32; HW 1
Galiano, Juan Valera y Alcala
  See Valera y Alcala-Galiano, Juan
Galilei, Galileo 1546-1642 .... **LC 45**
Gallagher, Tess 1943- ...... **CLC 18, 63; DAM
  POET; PC 9**
  See also CA 106; DLB 212
Gallant, Mavis 1922- .. **CLC 7, 18, 38; DAC;
  DAM MST; SSC 5**
  See also CA 69-72; CANR 29, 69; DLB 53;
  MTCW 1, 2
Gallant, Roy A(rthur) 1924- .... **CLC 17**
  See also CA 5-8R; CANR 4, 29, 54; CLR
  30; MAICYA; SATA 4, 68, 110
Gallico, Paul (William) 1897-1976 ..... **CLC 2**
  See also AITN 1; CA 5-8R; 69-72; CANR
  23; DLB 9, 171; MAICYA; SATA 13
Gallo, Max Louis 1932- .... **CLC 95**
  See also CA 85-88
Gallois, Lucien
  See Desnos, Robert
Gallup, Ralph
  See Whitemore, Hugh (John)
Galsworthy, John 1867-1933 .... **TCLC 1, 45;
  DA; DAB; DAC; DAM DRAM, MST,
  NOV; SSC 22; WLC**
  See also CA 104; 141; CANR 75; CDBLB
  1890-1914; DA3; DLB 10, 34, 98, 162;
  DLBD 16; MTCW 1
Galt, John 1779-1839 .... **NCLC 1**
  See also DLB 99, 116, 159

Galvin, James 1951- .... **CLC 38**
  See also CA 108; CANR 26
Gamboa, Federico 1864-1939 .... **TCLC 36**
  See also CA 167; HW 2
Gandhi, M. K.
  See Gandhi, Mohandas Karamchand
Gandhi, Mahatma
  See Gandhi, Mohandas Karamchand
Gandhi, Mohandas Karamchand 1869-1948
  TCLC 59; DAM MULT
  See also CA 121; 132; DA3; MTCW 1, 2
Gann, Ernest Kellogg 1910-1991 ..... **CLC 23**
  See also AITN 1; CA 1-4R; 136; CANR 1,
  83
Garber, Eric 1943(?)-
  See Holleran, Andrew
  See also CANR 89
Garcia, Cristina 1958- .... **CLC 76**
  See also CA 141; CANR 73; HW 2
Garcia Lorca, Federico 1898-1936 . **TCLC 1,
  7, 49; DA; DAB; DAC; DAM DRAM,
  MST, MULT, POET; DC 2; HLC 2;
  PC 3; WLC**
  See also Lorca, Federico Garcia
  See also CA 104; 131; CANR 81; DA3;
  DLB 108; HW 1, 2; MTCW 1, 2
Garcia Marquez, Gabriel (Jose)
  1928- .... **CLC 2, 3, 8, 10, 15, 27, 47, 55,
  68; DA; DAB; DAC; DAM MST,
  MULT, NOV, POP; HLC 1; SSC 8;
  WLC**
  See also Marquez, Gabriel (Jose) Garcia
  See also AAYA 3, 33; BEST 89:1, 90:4; CA
  33-36R; CANR 10, 28, 50, 75, 82; DA3;
  DLB 113; HW 1, 2; MTCW 1, 2
Garcilaso de la Vega, El Inca 1503-1536
  See also HLCS 1
Gard, Janice
  See Latham, Jean Lee
Gard, Roger Martin du
  See Martin du Gard, Roger
Gardam, Jane 1928- .... **CLC 43**
  See also CA 49-52; CANR 2, 18, 33, 54;
  CLR 12; DLB 14, 161; MAICYA; MTCW
  1; SAAS 9; SATA 39, 76; SATA-Brief 28
Gardner, Herb(ert) 1934- .... **CLC 44**
  See also CA 149
Gardner, John (Champlin), Jr. 1933-1982
  **CLC 2, 3, 5, 7, 8, 10, 18, 28, 34; DAM
  NOV, POP; SSC 7**
  See also AITN 1; CA 65-68; 107; CANR
  33, 73; CDALBS; DA3; DLB 2; DLBY
  82; MTCW 1; SATA 40; SATA-Obit 31
Gardner, John (Edmund) 1926- ...... **CLC 30;
  DAM POP**
  See also CA 103; CANR 15, 69; MTCW 1
Gardner, Miriam
  See Bradley, Marion Zimmer
Gardner, Noel
  See Kuttner, Henry
Gardons, S. S.
  See Snodgrass, W(illiam) D(e Witt)
Garfield, Leon 1921-1996 .... **CLC 12**
  See also AAYA 8; CA 17-20R; 152; CANR
  38, 41, 78; CLR 21; DLB 161; JRDA;
  MAICYA; SATA 1, 32, 76; SATA-Obit 90
Garland, (Hannibal) Hamlin 1860-1940
  TCLC 3; SSC 18
  See also CA 104; DLB 12, 71, 78, 186
Garneau, (Hector de) Saint-Denys 1912-1943
  TCLC 13
  See also CA 111; DLB 88
Garner, Alan 1934- ..... **CLC 17; DAB; DAM
  POP**
  See also AAYA 18; CA 73-76, 178; CAAE
  178; CANR 15, 64; CLR 20; DLB 161;
  MAICYA; MTCW 1, 2; SATA 18, 69;
  SATA-Essay 108

Garner, Hugh 1913-1979 .... **CLC 13**
See also CA 69-72; CANR 31; DLB 68

Garnett, David 1892-1981 .... **CLC 3**
See also CA 5-8R; 103; CANR 17, 79; DLB 34; MTCW 2

Garos, Stephanie
See Katz, Steve

Garrett, George (Palmer) 1929- .. **CLC 3, 11, 51; SSC 30**
See also CA 1-4R; CAAS 5; CANR 1, 42, 67; DLB 2, 5, 130, 152; DLBY 83

Garrick, David 1717-1779 .... **LC 15; DAM DRAM**
See also DLB 84

Garrigue, Jean 1914-1972 .... **CLC 2, 8**
See also CA 5-8R; 37-40R; CANR 20

Garrison, Frederick
See Sinclair, Upton (Beall)

Garro, Elena 1920(?)-1998
See also CA 131; 169; DLB 145; HLCS 1; HW 1

Garth, Will
See Hamilton, Edmond; Kuttner, Henry

Garvey, Marcus (Moziah, Jr.) 1887-1940
TCLC 41; BLC 2; DAM MULT
See also BW 1; CA 120; 124; CANR 79

Gary, Romain .... **CLC 25**
See Kacew, Romain
See also DLB 83

Gascar, Pierre .... **CLC 11**
See also Fournier, Pierre

Gascoyne, David (Emery) 1916- .... **CLC 45**
See also CA 65-68; CANR 10, 28, 54; DLB 20; MTCW 1

Gaskell, Elizabeth Cleghorn 1810-1865
NCLC 70; DAB; DAM MST; SSC 25
See also CDBLB 1832-1890; DLB 21, 144, 159

Gass, William H(oward) 1924- . **CLC 1, 2, 8, 11, 15, 39, 132; SSC 12**
See also CA 17-20R; CANR 30, 71; DLB 2; MTCW 1, 2

Gassendi, Pierre 1592-1655 .... **LC 54**

Gasset, Jose Ortega y
See Ortega y Gasset, Jose

Gates, Henry Louis, Jr. 1950- .... **CLC 65; BLCS; DAM MULT**
See also BW 2, 3; CA 109; CANR 25, 53, 75; DA3; DLB 67; MTCW 1

Gautier, Theophile 1811-1872 .. **NCLC 1, 59; DAM POET; PC 18; SSC 20**
See also DLB 119

Gawsworth, John
See Bates, H(erbert) E(rnest)

Gay, John 1685-1732 .. **LC 49; DAM DRAM**
See also DLB 84, 95

Gay, Oliver
See Gogarty, Oliver St. John

Gaye, Marvin (Penze) 1939-1984 ..... **CLC 26**
See also CA 112

Gebler, Carlo (Ernest) 1954- .... **CLC 39**
See also CA 119; 133

Gee, Maggie (Mary) 1948- .... **CLC 57**
See also CA 130; DLB 207

Gee, Maurice (Gough) 1931- .... **CLC 29**
See also CA 97-100; CANR 67; CLR 56; SATA 46, 101

Gelbart, Larry (Simon) 1923- .... **CLC 21, 61**
See also CA 73-76; CANR 45

Gelber, Jack 1932- .... **CLC 1, 6, 14, 79**
See also CA 1-4R; CANR 2; DLB 7

Gellhorn, Martha (Ellis)
1908-1998 .... **CLC 14, 60**
See also CA 77-80; 164; CANR 44; DLBY 82, 98

Genet, Jean 1910-1986 .. **CLC 1, 2, 5, 10, 14, 44, 46; DAM DRAM**
See also CA 13-16R; CANR 18; DA3; DLB 72; DLBY 86; MTCW 1, 2

Gent, Peter 1942- .... **CLC 29**
See also AITN 1; CA 89-92; DLBY 82

Gentile, Giovanni 1875-1944 .... **TCLC 96**
See also CA 119

Gentlewoman in New England, A
See Bradstreet, Anne

Gentlewoman in Those Parts, A
See Bradstreet, Anne

George, Jean Craighead 1919- .... **CLC 35**
See also AAYA 8; CA 5-8R; CANR 25; CLR 1; DLB 52; JRDA; MAICYA; SATA 2, 68

George, Stefan (Anton) 1868-1933 . **TCLC 2, 14**
See also CA 104

Georges, Georges Martin
See Simenon, Georges (Jacques Christian)

Gerhardi, William Alexander
See Gerhardie, William Alexander

Gerhardie, William Alexander 1895-1977
CLC 5
See also CA 25-28R; 73-76; CANR 18; DLB 36

Gerstler, Amy 1956- .... **CLC 70**
See also CA 146

Gertler, T. .... **CLC 34**
See also CA 116; 121; INT 121

Ghalib .... **NCLC 39, 78**
See also Ghalib, Hsadullah Khan

Ghalib, Hsadullah Khan 1797-1869
See Ghalib
See also DAM POET

Ghelderode, Michel de 1898-1962 ..... **CLC 6, 11; DAM DRAM**
See also CA 85-88; CANR 40, 77

Ghiselin, Brewster 1903- .... **CLC 23**
See also CA 13-16R; CAAS 10; CANR 13

Ghose, Aurabinda 1872-1950 .... **TCLC 63**
See also CA 163

Ghose, Zulfikar 1935- .... **CLC 42**
See also CA 65-68; CANR 67

Ghosh, Amitav 1956- .... **CLC 44**
See also CA 147; CANR 80

Giacosa, Giuseppe 1847-1906 .... **TCLC 7**
See also CA 104

Gibb, Lee
See Waterhouse, Keith (Spencer)

Gibbon, Lewis Grassic .... **TCLC 4**
See also Mitchell, James Leslie

Gibbons, Kaye 1960- .... **CLC 50, 88; DAM POP**
See also AAYA 34; CA 151; CANR 75; DA3; MTCW 1; SATA 117

Gibran, Kahlil 1883-1931 .... **TCLC 1, 9; DAM POET, POP; PC 9**
See also CA 104; 150; DA3; MTCW 2

Gibran, Khalil
See Gibran, Kahlil

Gibson, William 1914- .. **CLC 23; DA; DAB; DAC; DAM DRAM, MST**
See also CA 9-12R; CANR 9, 42, 75; DLB 7; MTCW 1; SATA 66

Gibson, William (Ford) 1948- ... **CLC 39, 63; DAM POP**
See also AAYA 12; CA 126; 133; CANR 52, 90; DA3; MTCW 1

Gide, Andre (Paul Guillaume) 1869-1951
TCLC 5, 12, 36; DA; DAB; DAC; DAM MST, NOV; SSC 13; WLC
See also CA 104; 124; DA3; DLB 65; MTCW 1, 2

Gifford, Barry (Colby) 1946- .... **CLC 34**
See also CA 65-68; CANR 9, 30, 40, 90

Gilbert, Frank
See De Voto, Bernard (Augustine)

Gilbert, W(illiam) S(chwenck) 1836-1911
TCLC 3; DAM DRAM, POET
See also CA 104; 173; SATA 36

Gilbreth, Frank B., Jr. 1911- .... **CLC 17**
See also CA 9-12R; SATA 2

Gilchrist, Ellen 1935- ...... **CLC 34, 48; DAM POP; SSC 14**
See also CA 113; 116; CANR 41, 61; DLB 130; MTCW 1, 2

Giles, Molly 1942- .... **CLC 39**
See also CA 126

Gill, Eric 1882-1940 .... **TCLC 85**

Gill, Patrick
See Creasey, John

Gilliam, Terry (Vance) 1940- .... **CLC 21**
See also Monty Python
See also AAYA 19; CA 108; 113; CANR 35; INT 113

Gillian, Jerry
See Gilliam, Terry (Vance)

Gilliatt, Penelope (Ann Douglass) 1932-1993
CLC 2, 10, 13, 53
See also AITN 2; CA 13-16R; 141; CANR 49; DLB 14

Gilman, Charlotte (Anna) Perkins (Stetson)
1860-1935 .... **TCLC 9, 37; SSC 13**
See also CA 106; 150; DLB 221; MTCW 1

Gilmour, David 1949- .... **CLC 35**
See also CA 138, 147

Gilpin, William 1724-1804 .... **NCLC 30**

Gilray, J. D.
See Mencken, H(enry) L(ouis)

Gilroy, Frank D(aniel) 1925- .... **CLC 2**
See also CA 81-84; CANR 32, 64, 86; DLB 7

Gilstrap, John 1957(?)- .... **CLC 99**
See also CA 160

Ginsberg, Allen 1926-1997 .... **CLC 1, 2, 3, 4, 6, 13, 36, 69, 109; DA; DAB; DAC; DAM MST, POET; PC 4; WLC**
See also AAYA 33; AITN 1; CA 1-4R; 157; CANR 2, 41, 63; CDALB 1941-1968; DA3; DLB 5, 16, 169; MTCW 1, 2

Ginzburg, Natalia 1916-1991 .... **CLC 5, 11, 54, 70**
See also CA 85-88; 135; CANR 33; DLB 177; MTCW 1, 2

Giono, Jean 1895-1970 .... **CLC 4, 11**
See also CA 45-48; 29-32R; CANR 2, 35; DLB 72; MTCW 1

Giovanni, Nikki 1943- .... **CLC 2, 4, 19, 64, 117; BLC 2; DA; DAB; DAC; DAM MST, MULT, POET; PC 19; WLCS**
See also AAYA 22; AITN 1; BW 2, 3; CA 29-32R; CAAS 6; CANR 18, 41, 60, 91; CDALBS; CLR 6; DA3; DLB 5, 41; INT CANR-18; MAICYA; MTCW 1, 2; SATA 24, 107

Giovene, Andrea 1904- .... **CLC 7**
See also CA 85-88

Gippius, Zinaida (Nikolayevna) 1869-1945
See Hippius, Zinaida
See also CA 106

Giraudoux, (Hippolyte) Jean 1882-1944
TCLC 2, 7; DAM DRAM
See also CA 104; DLB 65

Gironella, Jose Maria 1917- .... **CLC 11**
See also CA 101

Gissing, George (Robert)
1857-1903 .... **TCLC 3, 24, 47; SSC 37**
See also CA 105; 167; DLB 18, 135, 184

Giurlani, Aldo
See Palazzeschi, Aldo

Gladkov, Fyodor (Vasilyevich) 1883-1958
TCLC 27
See also CA 170

Glanville, Brian (Lester) 1931- .... **CLC 6**
  See also CA 5-8R; CAAS 9; CANR 3, 70; DLB 15, 139; SATA 42

Glasgow, Ellen (Anderson Gholson)
  1873-1945 .... **TCLC 2, 7; SSC 34**
  See also CA 104; 164; DLB 9, 12; MTCW 2

Glaspell, Susan 1882(?)-1948 . **TCLC 55; DC 10**
  See also CA 110; 154; DLB 7, 9, 78; YABC 2

Glassco, John 1909-1981 .... **CLC 9**
  See also CA 13-16R; 102; CANR 15; DLB 68

Glasscock, Amnesia
  See Steinbeck, John (Ernst)

Glasser, Ronald J. 1940(?)- .... **CLC 37**

Glassman, Joyce
  See Johnson, Joyce

Glendinning, Victoria 1937- .... **CLC 50**
  See also CA 120; 127; CANR 59, 89; DLB 155

Glissant, Edouard 1928- . **CLC 10, 68; DAM MULT**
  See also CA 153

Gloag, Julian 1930- .... **CLC 40**
  See also AITN 1; CA 65-68; CANR 10, 70

Glowacki, Aleksander
  See Prus, Boleslaw

Gluck, Louise (Elisabeth) 1943- .. **CLC 7, 22, 44, 81; DAM POET; PC 16**
  See also CA 33-36R; CANR 40, 69; DA3; DLB 5; MTCW 2

Glyn, Elinor 1864-1943 .... **TCLC 72**
  See also DLB 153

Gobineau, Joseph Arthur (Comte) de
  1816-1882 .... **NCLC 17**
  See also DLB 123

Godard, Jean-Luc 1930- .... **CLC 20**
  See also CA 93-96

Godden, (Margaret) Rumer
  1907-1998 .... **CLC 53**
  See also AAYA 6; CA 5-8R; 172; CANR 4, 27, 36, 55, 80; CLR 20; DLB 161; MAI-CYA; SAAS 12; SATA 3, 36; SATA-Obit 109

Godoy Alcayaga, Lucila 1889-1957
  See Mistral, Gabriela
  See also BW 2; CA 104; 131; CANR 81; DAM MULT; HW 1, 2; MTCW 1, 2

Godwin, Gail (Kathleen) 1937- ..... **CLC 5, 8, 22, 31, 69, 125; DAM POP**
  See also CA 29-32R; CANR 15, 43, 69; DA3; DLB 6; INT CANR-15; MTCW 1, 2

Godwin, William 1756-1836 .... **NCLC 14**
  See also CDBLB 1789-1832; DLB 39, 104, 142, 158, 163

Goebbels, Josef
  See Goebbels, (Paul) Joseph

Goebbels, (Paul) Joseph
  1897-1945 .... **TCLC 68**
  See also CA 115; 148

Goebbels, Joseph Paul
  See Goebbels, (Paul) Joseph

Goethe, Johann Wolfgang von 1749-1832
  NCLC 4, 22, 34; DA; DAB; DAC; DAM DRAM, MST, POET; PC 5; SSC 38; WLC
  See also DA3; DLB 94

Gogarty, Oliver St. John
  1878-1957 .... **TCLC 15**
  See also CA 109; 150; DLB 15, 19

Gogol, Nikolai (Vasilyevich) 1809-1852
  NCLC 5, 15, 31; DA; DAB; DAC; DAM DRAM, MST; DC 1; SSC 4, 29; WLC
  See also DLB 198

Goines, Donald 1937(?)-1974 . **CLC 80; BLC 2; DAM MULT, POP**
  See also AITN 1; BW 1, 3; CA 124; 114; CANR 82; DA3; DLB 33

Gold, Herbert 1924- .... **CLC 4, 7, 14, 42**
  See also CA 9-12R; CANR 17, 45; DLB 2; DLBY 81

Goldbarth, Albert 1948- .... **CLC 5, 38**
  See also CA 53-56; CANR 6, 40; DLB 120

Goldberg, Anatol 1910-1982 .... **CLC 34**
  See also CA 131; 117

Goldemberg, Isaac 1945- .... **CLC 52**
  See also CA 69-72; CAAS 12; CANR 11, 32; HW 1

Golding, William (Gerald)
  1911-1993 ..... **CLC 1, 2, 3, 8, 10, 17, 27, 58, 81; DA; DAB; DAC; DAM MST, NOV; WLC**
  See also AAYA 5; CA 5-8R; 141; CANR 13, 33, 54; CDBLB 1945-1960; DA3; DLB 15, 100; MTCW 1, 2

Goldman, Emma 1869-1940 .... **TCLC 13**
  See also CA 110; 150; DLB 221

Goldman, Francisco 1954- .... **CLC 76**
  See also CA 162

Goldman, William (W.) 1931- ...... **CLC 1, 48**
  See also CA 9-12R; CANR 29, 69; DLB 44

Goldmann, Lucien 1913-1970 .... **CLC 24**
  See also CA 25-28; CAP 2

Goldoni, Carlo 1707-1793 .... **LC 4; DAM DRAM**

Goldsberry, Steven 1949- .... **CLC 34**
  See also CA 131

Goldsmith, Oliver 1728-1774 . **LC 2, 48; DA; DAB; DAC; DAM DRAM, MST, NOV, POET; DC 8; WLC**
  See also CDBLB 1660-1789; DLB 39, 89, 104, 109, 142; SATA 26

Goldsmith, Peter
  See Priestley, J(ohn) B(oynton)

Gombrowicz, Witold 1904-1969 .... **CLC 4, 7, 11, 49; DAM DRAM**
  See also CA 19-20; 25-28R; CAP 2

Gomez de la Serna, Ramon
  1888-1963 .... **CLC 9**
  See also CA 153; 116; CANR 79; HW 1, 2

Goncharov, Ivan Alexandrovich 1812-1891
  NCLC 1, 63

Goncourt, Edmond (Louis Antoine Huot) de
  1822-1896 .... **NCLC 7**
  See also DLB 123

Goncourt, Jules (Alfred Huot) de 1830-1870
  NCLC 7
  See also DLB 123

Gontier, Fernande 19(?)- .... **CLC 50**

Gonzalez Martinez, Enrique 1871-1952
  TCLC 72
  See also CA 166; CANR 81; HW 1, 2

Goodman, Paul 1911-1972 ..... **CLC 1, 2, 4, 7**
  See also CA 19-20; 37-40R; CANR 34; CAP 2; DLB 130; MTCW 1

Gordimer, Nadine 1923- ...... **CLC 3, 5, 7, 10, 18, 33, 51, 70; DA; DAB; DAC; DAM MST, NOV; SSC 17; WLCS**
  See also CA 5-8R; CANR 3, 28, 56, 88; DA3; INT CANR-28; MTCW 1, 2

Gordon, Adam Lindsay
  1833-1870 .... **NCLC 21**

Gordon, Caroline 1895-1981 . **CLC 6, 13, 29, 83; SSC 15**
  See also CA 11-12; 103; CANR 36; CAP 1; DLB 4, 9, 102; DLBD 17; DLBY 81; MTCW 1, 2

Gordon, Charles William 1860-1937
  See Connor, Ralph
  See also CA 109

Gordon, Mary (Catherine) 1949- .... **CLC 13, 22, 128**
  See also CA 102; CANR 44; DLB 6; DLBY 81; INT 102; MTCW 1

Gordon, N. J.
  See Bosman, Herman Charles

Gordon, Sol 1923- .... **CLC 26**
  See also CA 53-56; CANR 4; SATA 11

Gordone, Charles 1925-1995 .... **CLC 1, 4; DAM DRAM; DC 8**
  See also BW 1, 3; CA 93-96; 180; 150; CAAE 180; CANR 55; DLB 7; INT 93-96; MTCW 1

Gore, Catherine 1800-1861 .... **NCLC 65**
  See also DLB 116

Gorenko, Anna Andreevna
  See Akhmatova, Anna

Gorky, Maxim 1868-1936 ..... **TCLC 8; DAB; SSC 28; WLC**
  See also Peshkov, Alexei Maximovich
  See also MTCW 2

Goryan, Sirak
  See Saroyan, William

Gosse, Edmund (William)
  1849-1928 .... **TCLC 28**
  See also CA 117; DLB 57, 144, 184

Gotlieb, Phyllis Fay (Bloom) 1926- .. **CLC 18**
  See also CA 13-16R; CANR 7; DLB 88

Gottesman, S. D.
  See Kornbluth, C(yril) M.; Pohl, Frederik

Gottfried von Strassburg fl. c.
  1210- .... **CMLC 10**
  See also DLB 138

Gould, Lois .... **CLC 4, 10**
  See also CA 77-80; CANR 29; MTCW 1

Gourmont, Remy (-Marie-Charles) de
  1858-1915 .... **TCLC 17**
  See also CA 109; 150; MTCW 2

Govier, Katherine 1948- .... **CLC 51**
  See also CA 101; CANR 18, 40

Goyen, (Charles) William
  1915-1983 .... **CLC 5, 8, 14, 40**
  See also AITN 2; CA 5-8R; 110; CANR 6, 71; DLB 2; DLBY 83; INT CANR-6

Goytisolo, Juan 1931- . **CLC 5, 10, 23; DAM MULT; HLC 1**
  See also CA 85-88; CANR 32, 61; HW 1, 2; MTCW 1, 2

Gozzano, Guido 1883-1916 .... **PC 10**
  See also CA 154; DLB 114

Gozzi, (Conte) Carlo 1720-1806 .... **NCLC 23**

Grabbe, Christian Dietrich
  1801-1836 .... **NCLC 2**
  See also DLB 133

Grace, Patricia Frances 1937- .... **CLC 56**
  See also CA 176

Gracian y Morales, Baltasar
  1601-1658 .... **LC 15**

Gracq, Julien .... **CLC 11, 48**
  See also Poirier, Louis
  See also DLB 83

Grade, Chaim 1910-1982 .... **CLC 10**
  See also CA 93-96; 107

Graduate of Oxford, A
  See Ruskin, John

Grafton, Garth
  See Duncan, Sara Jeannette

Graham, John
  See Phillips, David Graham

Graham, Jorie 1951- .... **CLC 48, 118**
  See also CA 111; CANR 63; DLB 120

Graham, R(obert) B(ontine) Cunninghame
  See Cunninghame Graham, Robert (Gallnigad) Bontine
  See also DLB 98, 135, 174

Graham, Robert
  See Haldeman, Joe (William)

Graham, Tom
See Lewis, (Harry) Sinclair
Graham, W(illiam) S(ydney)
1918-1986 .... **CLC 29**
See also CA 73-76; 118; DLB 20
Graham, Winston (Mawdsley)
1910- .... **CLC 23**
See also CA 49-52; CANR 2, 22, 45, 66;
DLB 77
Grahame, Kenneth 1859-1932 ...... **TCLC 64;**
DAB
See also CA 108; 136; CANR 80; CLR 5;
DA3; DLB 34, 141, 178; MAICYA;
MTCW 2; SATA 100; YABC 1
Granovsky, Timofei Nikolaevich 1813-1855
NCLC 75
See also DLB 198
Grant, Skeeter
See Spiegelman, Art
Granville-Barker, Harley
1877-1946 .... **TCLC 2; DAM DRAM**
See also Barker, Harley Granville
See also CA 104
Grass, Guenter (Wilhelm) 1927- ... **CLC 1, 2,**
4, 6, 11, 15, 22, 32, 49, 88; DA; DAB;
DAC; DAM MST, NOV; WLC
See also CA 13-16R; CANR 20, 75; DA3;
DLB 75, 124; MTCW 1, 2
Gratton, Thomas
See Hulme, T(homas) E(rnest)
Grau, Shirley Ann 1929- . **CLC 4, 9; SSC 15**
See also CA 89-92; CANR 22, 69; DLB 2;
INT CANR-22; MTCW 1
Gravel, Fern
See Hall, James Norman
Graver, Elizabeth 1964- .... **CLC 70**
See also CA 135; CANR 71
Graves, Richard Perceval 1945- .... **CLC 44**
See also CA 65-68; CANR 9, 26, 51
Graves, Robert (von Ranke)
1895-1985 .. **CLC 1, 2, 6, 11, 39, 44, 45;**
DAB; DAC; DAM MST, POET; PC 6
See also CA 5-8R; 117; CANR 5, 36; CD-
BLB 1914-1945; DA3; DLB 20, 100, 191;
DLBD 18; DLBY 85; MTCW 1, 2; SATA
45
Graves, Valerie
See Bradley, Marion Zimmer
Gray, Alasdair (James) 1934- .... **CLC 41**
See also CA 126; CANR 47, 69; DLB 194;
INT 126; MTCW 1, 2
Gray, Amlin 1946- .... **CLC 29**
See also CA 138
Gray, Francine du Plessix 1930- ..... **CLC 22;**
DAM NOV
See also BEST 90:3; CA 61-64; CAAS 2;
CANR 11, 33, 75, 81; INT CANR-11;
MTCW 1, 2
Gray, John (Henry) 1866-1934 ...... **TCLC 19**
See also CA 119; 162
Gray, Simon (James Holliday)
1936- .... **CLC 9, 14, 36**
See also AITN 1; CA 21-24R; CAAS 3;
CANR 32, 69; DLB 13; MTCW 1
Gray, Spalding 1941- ..... **CLC 49, 112; DAM**
POP; DC 7
See also CA 128; CANR 74; MTCW 2
Gray, Thomas 1716-1771 .... **LC 4, 40; DA;**
DAB; DAC; DAM MST; PC 2; WLC
See also CDBLB 1660-1789; DA3; DLB
109
Grayson, David
See Baker, Ray Stannard
Grayson, Richard (A.) 1951- .... **CLC 38**
See also CA 85-88; CANR 14, 31, 57
Greeley, Andrew M(oran) 1928- ..... **CLC 28;**
DAM POP
See also CA 5-8R; CAAS 7; CANR 7, 43,
69; DA3; MTCW 1, 2

Green, Anna Katharine
1846-1935 .... **TCLC 63**
See also CA 112; 159; DLB 202, 221
Green, Brian
See Card, Orson Scott
Green, Hannah
See Greenberg, Joanne (Goldenberg)
Green, Hannah 1927(?)-1996 .... **CLC 3**
See also CA 73-76; CANR 59
Green, Henry 1905-1973 .... **CLC 2, 13, 97**
See also Yorke, Henry Vincent
See also CA 175; DLB 15
Green, Julian (Hartridge) 1900-1998
See Green, Julien
See also CA 21-24R; 169; CANR 33, 87;
DLB 4, 72; MTCW 1
Green, Julien .... **CLC 3, 11, 77**
See also Green, Julian (Hartridge)
See also MTCW 2
Green, Paul (Eliot) 1894-1981 .... **CLC 25;**
DAM DRAM
See also AITN 1; CA 5-8R; 103; CANR 3;
DLB 7, 9; DLBY 81
Greenberg, Ivan 1908-1973
See Rahv, Philip
See also CA 85-88
Greenberg, Joanne (Goldenberg)
1932- .... **CLC 7, 30**
See also AAYA 12; CA 5-8R; CANR 14,
32, 69; SATA 25
Greenberg, Richard 1959(?)- .... **CLC 57**
See also CA 138
Greene, Bette 1934- .... **CLC 30**
See also AAYA 7; CA 53-56; CANR 4; CLR
2; JRDA; MAICYA; SAAS 16; SATA 8,
102
Greene, Gael .... **CLC 8**
See also CA 13-16R; CANR 10
Greene, Graham (Henry)
1904-1991 ... **CLC 1, 3, 6, 9, 14, 18, 27,**
37, 70, 72, 125; DA; DAB; DAC; DAM
MST, NOV; SSC 29; WLC
See also AITN 2; CA 13-16R; 133; CANR
35, 61; CDBLB 1945-1960; DA3; DLB
13, 15, 77, 100, 162, 201, 204; DLBY 91;
MTCW 1, 2; SATA 20
Greene, Robert 1558-1592 .... **LC 41**
See also DLB 62, 167
Greer, Germaine 1939- .... **CLC 131**
See also AITN 1; CA 81-84; CANR 33, 70;
MTCW 1, 2
Greer, Richard
See Silverberg, Robert
Gregor, Arthur 1923- .... **CLC 9**
See also CA 25-28R; CAAS 10; CANR 11;
SATA 36
Gregor, Lee
See Pohl, Frederik
Gregory, Isabella Augusta (Persse)
1852-1932 .... **TCLC 1**
See also CA 104; 184; DLB 10
Gregory, J. Dennis
See Williams, John A(lfred)
Grendon, Stephen
See Derleth, August (William)
Grenville, Kate 1950- .... **CLC 61**
See also CA 118; CANR 53
Grenville, Pelham
See Wodehouse, P(elham) G(renville)
Greve, Felix Paul (Berthold Friedrich)
1879-1948
See Grove, Frederick Philip
See also CA 104; 141, 175; CANR 79;
DAC; DAM MST
Grey, Zane 1872-1939 . **TCLC 6; DAM POP**
See also CA 104; 132; DA3; DLB 212;
MTCW 1, 2

Grieg, (Johan) Nordahl (Brun) 1902-1943
TCLC 10
See also CA 107
Grieve, C(hristopher) M(urray) 1892-1978
CLC 11, 19; DAM POET
See also MacDiarmid, Hugh; Pteleon
See also CA 5-8R; 85-88; CANR 33;
MTCW 1
Griffin, Gerald 1803-1840 .... **NCLC 7**
See also DLB 159
Griffin, John Howard 1920-1980 ..... **CLC 68**
See also AITN 1; CA 1-4R; 101; CANR 2
Griffin, Peter 1942- .... **CLC 39**
See also CA 136
Griffith, D(avid Lewelyn) W(ark)
1875(?)-1948 .... **TCLC 68**
See also CA 119; 150; CANR 80
Griffith, Lawrence
See Griffith, D(avid Lewelyn) W(ark)
Griffiths, Trevor 1935- .... **CLC 13, 52**
See also CA 97-100; CANR 45; DLB 13
Griggs, Sutton (Elbert)
1872-1930 .... **TCLC 77**
See also CA 123; 186; DLB 50
Grigson, Geoffrey (Edward Harvey)
1905-1985 .... **CLC 7, 39**
See also CA 25-28R; 118; CANR 20, 33;
DLB 27; MTCW 1, 2
Grillparzer, Franz 1791-1872 .... **NCLC 1;**
SSC 37
See also DLB 133
Grimble, Reverend Charles James
See Eliot, T(homas) S(tearns)
Grimke, Charlotte L(ottie) Forten
1837(?)-1914
See Forten, Charlotte L.
See also BW 1; CA 117; 124; DAM MULT,
POET
Grimm, Jacob Ludwig Karl 1785-1863
NCLC 3, 77; SSC 36
See also DLB 90; MAICYA; SATA 22
Grimm, Wilhelm Karl 1786-1859 .. **NCLC 3,**
77; SSC 36
See also DLB 90; MAICYA; SATA 22
Grimmelshausen, Johann Jakob Christoffel
von 1621-1676 .... **LC 6**
See also DLB 168
Grindel, Eugene 1895-1952
See Eluard, Paul
See also CA 104
Grisham, John 1955- .... **CLC 84; DAM POP**
See also AAYA 14; CA 138; CANR 47, 69;
DA3; MTCW 2
Grossman, David 1954- .... **CLC 67**
See also CA 138
Grossman, Vasily (Semenovich) 1905-1964
CLC 41
See also CA 124; 130; MTCW 1
Grove, Frederick Philip .... **TCLC 4**
See also Greve, Felix Paul (Berthold
Friedrich)
See also DLB 92
Grubb
See Crumb, R(obert)
Grumbach, Doris (Isaac) 1918- . **CLC 13, 22,**
64
See also CA 5-8R; CAAS 2; CANR 9, 42,
70; INT CANR-9; MTCW 2
Grundtvig, Nicolai Frederik Severin
1783-1872 .... **NCLC 1**
Grunge
See Crumb, R(obert)
Grunwald, Lisa 1959- .... **CLC 44**
See also CA 120
Guare, John 1938- .... **CLC 8, 14, 29, 67;**
DAM DRAM
See also CA 73-76; CANR 21, 69; DLB 7;
MTCW 1, 2

Hayford, J(oseph) E(phraim) Casely
See Casely-Hayford, J(oseph) E(phraim)

Hayman, Ronald 1932- .... **CLC 44**
See also CA 25-28R; CANR 18, 50, 88;
DLB 155

Haywood, Eliza (Fowler)
1693(?)-1756 .... **LC 1, 44**
See also DLB 39

Hazlitt, William 1778-1830 ...... **NCLC 29, 82**
See also DLB 110, 158

Hazzard, Shirley 1931- .... **CLC 18**
See also CA 9-12R; CANR 4, 70; DLBY
82; MTCW 1

Head, Bessie 1937-1986 .... **CLC 25, 67; BLC
2; DAM MULT**
See also BW 2, 3; CA 29-32R; 119; CANR
25, 82; DA3; DLB 117; MTCW 1, 2

Headon, (Nicky) Topper 1956(?)- ..... **CLC 30**

Heaney, Seamus (Justin) 1939- ..... **CLC 5, 7,
14, 25, 37, 74, 91; DAB; DAM POET;
PC 18; WLCS**
See also CA 85-88; CANR 25, 48, 75, 91;
CDBLB 1960 to Present; DA3; DLB 40;
DLBY 95; MTCW 1, 2

Hearn, (Patricio) Lafcadio (Tessima Carlos)
1850-1904 .... **TCLC 9**
See also CA 105; 166; DLB 12, 78, 189

Hearne, Vicki 1946- .... **CLC 56**
See also CA 139

Hearon, Shelby 1931- .... **CLC 63**
See also AITN 2; CA 25-28R; CANR 18,
48

Heat-Moon, William Least .... **CLC 29**
See also Trogdon, William (Lewis)
See also AAYA 9

Hebbel, Friedrich 1813-1863 .... **NCLC 43;
DAM DRAM**
See also DLB 129

Hebert, Anne 1916- ..... **CLC 4, 13, 29; DAC;
DAM MST, POET**
See also CA 85-88; CANR 69; DA3; DLB
68; MTCW 1, 2

Hecht, Anthony (Evan) 1923- ...... **CLC 8, 13,
19; DAM POET**
See also CA 9-12R; CANR 6; DLB 5, 169

Hecht, Ben 1894-1964 .... **CLC 8**
See also CA 85-88; DLB 7, 9, 25, 26, 28,
86

Hedayat, Sadeq 1903-1951 .... **TCLC 21**
See also CA 120

Hegel, Georg Wilhelm Friedrich 1770-1831
NCLC 46
See also DLB 90

Heidegger, Martin 1889-1976 .... **CLC 24**
See also CA 81-84; 65-68; CANR 34;
MTCW 1, 2

Heidenstam, (Carl Gustaf) Verner von
1859-1940 .... **TCLC 5**
See also CA 104

Heifner, Jack 1946- .... **CLC 11**
See also CA 105; CANR 47

Heijermans, Herman 1864-1924 .... **TCLC 24**
See also CA 123

Heilbrun, Carolyn G(old) 1926- .... **CLC 25**
See also CA 45-48; CANR 1, 28, 58

Heine, Heinrich 1797-1856 .... **NCLC 4, 54;
PC 25**
See also DLB 90

Heinemann, Larry (Curtiss) 1944- .. **CLC 50**
See also CA 110; CAAS 21; CANR 31, 81;
DLBD 9; INT CANR-31

Heiney, Donald (William) 1921-1993
See Harris, MacDonald
See also CA 1-4R; 142; CANR 3, 58

Heinlein, Robert A(nson) 1907-1988 . **CLC 1,
3, 8, 14, 26, 55; DAM POP**
See also AAYA 17; CA 1-4R; 125; CANR
1, 20, 53; DA3; DLB 8; JRDA; MAICYA;
MTCW 1, 2; SATA 9, 69; SATA-Obit 56

Helforth, John
See Doolittle, Hilda

Hellenhofferu, Vojtech Kapristian z
See Hasek, Jaroslav (Matej Frantisek)

Heller, Joseph 1923- .. **CLC 1, 3, 5, 8, 11, 36,
63; DA; DAB; DAC; DAM MST, NOV,
POP; WLC**
See also AAYA 24; AITN 1; CA 5-8R;
CABS 1; CANR 8, 42, 66; DA3; DLB 2,
28; DLBY 80; INT CANR-8; MTCW 1, 2

Hellman, Lillian (Florence)
1906-1984 .. **CLC 2, 4, 8, 14, 18, 34, 44,
52; DAM DRAM; DC 1**
See also AITN 1, 2; CA 13-16R; 112;
CANR 33; DA3; DLB 7; DLBY 84;
MTCW 1, 2

Helprin, Mark 1947- .... **CLC 7, 10, 22, 32;
DAM NOV, POP**
See also CA 81-84; CANR 47, 64;
CDALBS; DA3; DLBY 85; MTCW 1, 2

Helvetius, Claude-Adrien 1715-1771 .. **LC 26**

Helyar, Jane Penelope Josephine 1933-
See Poole, Josephine
See also CA 21-24R; CANR 10, 26; SATA
82

Hemans, Felicia 1793-1835 .... **NCLC 71**
See also DLB 96

Hemingway, Ernest (Miller)
1899-1961 .... **CLC 1, 3, 6, 8, 10, 13, 19,
30, 34, 39, 41, 44, 50, 61, 80; DA;
DAB; DAC; DAM MST, NOV; SSC 1,
25, 36, 40; WLC**
See also AAYA 19; CA 77-80; CANR 34;
CDALB 1917-1929; DA3; DLB 4, 9, 102,
210; DLBD 1, 15, 16; DLBY 81, 87, 96,
98; MTCW 1, 2

Hempel, Amy 1951- .... **CLC 39**
See also CA 118; 137; CANR 70; DA3;
MTCW 2

Henderson, F. C.
See Mencken, H(enry) L(ouis)

Henderson, Sylvia
See Ashton-Warner, Sylvia (Constance)

Henderson, Zenna (Chlarson)
1917-1983 .... **SSC 29**
See also CA 1-4R; 133; CANR 1, 84; DLB
8; SATA 5

Henkin, Joshua .... **CLC 119**
See also CA 161

Henley, Beth .... **CLC 23; DC 6**
See also Henley, Elizabeth Becker
See also CABS 3; DLBY 86

Henley, Elizabeth Becker 1952-
See Henley, Beth
See also CA 107; CANR 32, 73; DAM
DRAM, MST; DA3; MTCW 1, 2

Henley, William Ernest 1849-1903 .. **TCLC 8**
See also CA 105; DLB 19

Hennissart, Martha
See Lathen, Emma
See also CA 85-88; CANR 64

Henry, O. .... **TCLC 1, 19; SSC 5; WLC**
See also Porter, William Sydney

Henry, Patrick 1736-1799 .... **LC 25**

Henryson, Robert 1430(?)-1506(?) ...... **LC 20**
See also DLB 146

Henry VIII 1491-1547 .... **LC 10**
See also DLB 132

Henschke, Alfred
See Klabund

Hentoff, Nat(han Irving) 1925- .... **CLC 26**
See also AAYA 4; CA 1-4R; CAAS 6;
CANR 5, 25, 77; CLR 1, 52; INT CANR-
25; JRDA; MAICYA; SATA 42, 69;
SATA-Brief 27

Heppenstall, (John) Rayner
1911-1981 .... **CLC 10**
See also CA 1-4R; 103; CANR 29

Heraclitus c. 540B.C.-c. 450B.C. ... **CMLC 22**
See also DLB 176

Herbert, Frank (Patrick)
1920-1986 .... **CLC 12, 23, 35, 44, 85;
DAM POP**
See also AAYA 21; CA 53-56; 118; CANR
5, 43; CDALBS; DLB 8; INT CANR-5;
MTCW 1, 2; SATA 9, 37; SATA-Obit 47

Herbert, George 1593-1633 ..... **LC 24; DAB;
DAM POET; PC 4**
See also CDBLB Before 1660; DLB 126

Herbert, Zbigniew 1924-1998 ..... **CLC 9, 43;
DAM POET**
See also CA 89-92; 169; CANR 36, 74;
MTCW 1

Herbst, Josephine (Frey)
1897-1969 .... **CLC 34**
See also CA 5-8R; 25-28R; DLB 9

Heredia, Jose Maria 1803-1839
See also HLCS 2

Hergesheimer, Joseph 1880-1954 ... **TCLC 11**
See also CA 109; DLB 102, 9

Herlihy, James Leo 1927-1993 .... **CLC 6**
See also CA 1-4R; 143; CANR 2

Hermogenes fl. c. 175- .... **CMLC 6**

Hernandez, Jose 1834-1886 .... **NCLC 17**

Herodotus c. 484B.C.-429B.C. .... **CMLC 17**
See also DLB 176

Herrick, Robert 1591-1674 .... **LC 13; DA;
DAB; DAC; DAM MST, POP; PC 9**
See also DLB 126

Herring, Guilles
See Somerville, Edith

Herriot, James 1916-1995 ..... **CLC 12; DAM
POP**
See also Wight, James Alfred
See also AAYA 1; CA 148; CANR 40;
MTCW 2; SATA 86

Herris, Violet
See Hunt, Violet

Herrmann, Dorothy 1941- .... **CLC 44**
See also CA 107

Herrmann, Taffy
See Herrmann, Dorothy

Hersey, John (Richard) 1914-1993 .... **CLC 1,
2, 7, 9, 40, 81, 97; DAM POP**
See also AAYA 29; CA 17-20R; 140; CANR
33; CDALBS; DLB 6, 185; MTCW 1, 2;
SATA 25; SATA-Obit 76

Herzen, Aleksandr Ivanovich 1812-1870
NCLC 10, 61

Herzl, Theodor 1860-1904 .... **TCLC 36**
See also CA 168

Herzog, Werner 1942- .... **CLC 16**
See also CA 89-92

Hesiod c. 8th cent. B.C.- .... **CMLC 5**
See also DLB 176

Hesse, Hermann 1877-1962 ... **CLC 1, 2, 3, 6,
11, 17, 25, 69; DA; DAB; DAC; DAM
MST, NOV; SSC 9; WLC**
See also CA 17-18; CAP 2; DA3; DLB 66;
MTCW 1, 2; SATA 50

Hewes, Cady
See De Voto, Bernard (Augustine)

Heyen, William 1940- .... **CLC 13, 18**
See also CA 33-36R; CAAS 9; DLB 5

Heyerdahl, Thor 1914- .... **CLC 26**
See also CA 5-8R; CANR 5, 22, 66, 73;
MTCW 1, 2; SATA 2, 52

Heym, Georg (Theodor Franz Arthur)
1887-1912 .... **TCLC 9**
See also CA 106; 181

Heym, Stefan 1913- .... **CLC 41**
See also CA 9-12R; CANR 4; DLB 69

Heyse, Paul (Johann Ludwig von) 1830-1914
TCLC 8
See also CA 104; DLB 129

Holub, Miroslav 1923-1998 .... **CLC 4**
　See also CA 21-24R; 169; CANR 10
Homer c. 8th cent. B.C.- ... **CMLC 1, 16; DA;**
　DAB; DAC; DAM MST, POET; PC
　23; WLCS
　See also DA3; DLB 176
Hongo, Garrett Kaoru 1951- .... **PC 23**
　See also CA 133; CAAS 22; DLB 120
Honig, Edwin 1919- .... **CLC 33**
　See also CA 5-8R; CAAS 8; CANR 4, 45;
　DLB 5
Hood, Hugh (John Blagdon) 1928- . **CLC 15,**
　28
　　See also CA 49-52; CAAS 17; CANR 1,
　　33, 87; DLB 53
Hood, Thomas 1799-1845 .... **NCLC 16**
　See also DLB 96
Hooker, (Peter) Jeremy 1941- .... **CLC 43**
　See also CA 77-80; CANR 22; DLB 40
hooks, bell .... **CLC 94; BLCS**
　See also Watkins, Gloria Jean
　See also MTCW 2
Hope, A(lec) D(erwent) 1907- .... **CLC 3, 51**
　See also CA 21-24R; CANR 33, 74; MTCW
　1, 2
Hope, Anthony 1863-1933 .... **TCLC 83**
　See also CA 157; DLB 153, 156
Hope, Brian
　See Creasey, John
Hope, Christopher (David Tully)
　1944- .... **CLC 52**
　See also CA 106; CANR 47; SATA 62
Hopkins, Gerard Manley
　1844-1889 ..... **NCLC 17; DA; DAB;**
　DAC; DAM MST, POET; PC 15; WLC
　See also CDBLB 1890-1914; DA3; DLB
　35, 57
Hopkins, John (Richard) 1931-1998 .. **CLC 4**
　See also CA 85-88; 169
Hopkins, Pauline Elizabeth
　1859-1930 ...... **TCLC 28; BLC 2; DAM**
　MULT
　　See also BW 2, 3; CA 141; CANR 82; DLB
　　50
Hopkinson, Francis 1737-1791 .... **LC 25**
　See also DLB 31
Hopley-Woolrich, Cornell George 1903-1968
　See Woolrich, Cornell
　　See also CA 13-14; CANR 58; CAP 1;
　　MTCW 2
Horace 65B.C.-8B.C. .... **CMLC 39**
　See also DLB 211
Horatio
　See Proust, (Valentin-Louis-George-
　Eugene-) Marcel
Horgan, Paul (George Vincent
　O'Shaughnessy) 1903-1995 . **CLC 9, 53;**
　DAM NOV
　　See also CA 13-16R; 147; CANR 9, 35;
　　DLB 212; DLBY 85; INT CANR-9;
　　MTCW 1, 2; SATA 13; SATA-Obit 84
Horn, Peter
　See Kuttner, Henry
Hornem, Horace Esq.
　See Byron, George Gordon (Noel)
Horney, Karen (Clementine Theodore
　Danielsen) 1885-1952 .... **TCLC 71**
　See also CA 114; 165
Hornung, E(rnest) W(illiam) 1866-1921
　TCLC 59
　See also CA 108; 160; DLB 70
Horovitz, Israel (Arthur) 1939- ...... **CLC 56;**
　DAM DRAM
　　See also CA 33-36R; CANR 46, 59; DLB 7
Horton, George Moses 1797(?)-1883(?)
　NCLC 87
　See also DLB 50

Horvath, Odon von
　See Horvath, Oedoen von
　See also DLB 85, 124
Horvath, Oedoen von 1901-1938 ... **TCLC 45**
　See also Horvath, Odon von; von Horvath,
　Oedoen
　See also CA 118
Horwitz, Julius 1920-1986 .... **CLC 14**
　See also CA 9-12R; 119; CANR 12
Hospital, Janette Turner 1942- .... **CLC 42**
　See also CA 108; CANR 48
Hostos, E. M. de
　See Hostos (y Bonilla), Eugenio Maria de
Hostos, Eugenio M. de
　See Hostos (y Bonilla), Eugenio Maria de
Hostos, Eugenio Maria
　See Hostos (y Bonilla), Eugenio Maria de
Hostos (y Bonilla), Eugenio Maria de
　1839-1903 .... **TCLC 24**
　See also CA 123; 131; HW 1
Houdini
　See Lovecraft, H(oward) P(hillips)
Hougan, Carolyn 1943- .... **CLC 34**
　See also CA 139
Household, Geoffrey (Edward West)
　1900-1988 .... **CLC 11**
　　See also CA 77-80; 126; CANR 58; DLB
　　87; SATA 14; SATA-Obit 59
Housman, A(lfred) E(dward) 1859-1936
　TCLC 1, 10; DA; DAB; DAC; DAM
　MST, POET; PC 2; WLCS
　See also CA 104; 125; DA3; DLB 19;
　MTCW 1, 2
Housman, Laurence 1865-1959 .... **TCLC 7**
　See also CA 106; 155; DLB 10; SATA 25
Howard, Elizabeth Jane 1923- ..... **CLC 7, 29**
　See also CA 5-8R; CANR 8, 62
Howard, Maureen 1930- .... **CLC 5, 14, 46**
　See also CA 53-56; CANR 31, 75; DLBY
　83; INT CANR-31; MTCW 1, 2
Howard, Richard 1929- .... **CLC 7, 10, 47**
　See also AITN 1; CA 85-88; CANR 25, 80;
　DLB 5; INT CANR-25
Howard, Robert E(rvin)
　1906-1936 .... **TCLC 8**
　See also CA 105; 157
Howard, Warren F.
　See Pohl, Frederik
Howe, Fanny (Quincy) 1940- .... **CLC 47**
　See also CA 117; CAAS 27; CANR 70;
　SATA-Brief 52
Howe, Irving 1920-1993 .... **CLC 85**
　See also CA 9-12R; 141; CANR 21, 50;
　DLB 67; MTCW 1, 2
Howe, Julia Ward 1819-1910 .... **TCLC 21**
　See also CA 117; DLB 1, 189
Howe, Susan 1937- .... **CLC 72**
　See also CA 160; DLB 120
Howe, Tina 1937- .... **CLC 48**
　See also CA 109
Howell, James 1594(?)-1666 .... **LC 13**
　See also DLB 151
Howells, W. D.
　See Howells, William Dean
Howells, William D.
　See Howells, William Dean
Howells, William Dean 1837-1920 .. **TCLC 7,**
　17, 41; SSC 36
　See also CA 104; 134; CDALB 1865-1917;
　DLB 12, 64, 74, 79, 189; MTCW 2
Howes, Barbara 1914-1996 .... **CLC 15**
　See also CA 9-12R; 151; CAAS 3; CANR
　53; SATA 5
Hrabal, Bohumil 1914-1997 .... **CLC 13, 67**
　See also CA 106; 156; CAAS 12; CANR
　57

Hroswitha of Gandersheim c. 935-c. 1002
　CMLC 29
　See also DLB 148
Hsun, Lu
　See Lu Hsun
Hubbard, L(afayette) Ron(ald) 1911-1986
　CLC 43; DAM POP
　See also CA 77-80; 118; CANR 52; DA3;
　MTCW 2
Huch, Ricarda (Octavia)
　1864-1947 .... **TCLC 13**
　See also CA 111; DLB 66
Huddle, David 1942- .... **CLC 49**
　See also CA 57-60; CAAS 20; CANR 89;
　DLB 130
Hudson, Jeffrey
　See Crichton, (John) Michael
Hudson, W(illiam) H(enry)
　1841-1922 .... **TCLC 29**
　See also CA 115; DLB 98, 153, 174; SATA
　35
Hueffer, Ford Madox
　See Ford, Ford Madox
Hughart, Barry 1934- .... **CLC 39**
　See also CA 137
Hughes, Colin
　See Creasey, John
Hughes, David (John) 1930- .... **CLC 48**
　See also CA 116; 129; DLB 14
Hughes, Edward James
　See Hughes, Ted
　See also DAM MST, POET; DA3
Hughes, (James) Langston
　1902-1967 .... **CLC 1, 5, 10, 15, 35, 44,**
　108; BLC 2; DA; DAB; DAC; DAM
　DRAM, MST, MULT, POET; DC 3;
　PC 1; SSC 6; WLC
　　See also AAYA 12; BW 1, 3; CA 1-4R; 25-
　　28R; CANR 1, 34, 82; CDALB 1929-
　　1941; CLR 17; DA3; DLB 4, 7, 48, 51,
　　86; JRDA; MAICYA; MTCW 1, 2; SATA
　　4, 33
Hughes, Richard (Arthur Warren)
　1900-1976 .... **CLC 1, 11; DAM NOV**
　　See also CA 5-8R; 65-68; CANR 4; DLB
　　15, 161; MTCW 1; SATA 8; SATA-Obit
　　25
Hughes, Ted 1930-1998 . **CLC 2, 4, 9, 14, 37,**
　119; DAB; DAC; PC 7
　See also Hughes, Edward James
　　See also CA 1-4R; 171; CANR 1, 33, 66;
　　CLR 3; DLB 40, 161; MAICYA; MTCW
　　1, 2; SATA 49; SATA-Brief 27; SATA-
　　Obit 107
Hugo, Richard F(ranklin)
　1923-1982 .... **CLC 6, 18, 32; DAM**
　POET
　　See also CA 49-52; 108; CANR 3; DLB 5,
　　206
Hugo, Victor (Marie) 1802-1885 .... **NCLC 3,**
　10, 21; DA; DAB; DAC; DAM DRAM,
　MST, NOV, POET; PC 17; WLC
　See also AAYA 28; DA3; DLB 119, 192;
　SATA 47
Huidobro, Vicente
　See Huidobro Fernandez, Vicente Garcia
Huidobro Fernandez, Vicente Garcia
　1893-1948 .... **TCLC 31**
　See also CA 131; HW 1
Hulme, Keri 1947- .... **CLC 39, 130**
　See also CA 125; CANR 69; INT 125
Hulme, T(homas) E(rnest)
　1883-1917 .... **TCLC 21**
　See also CA 117; DLB 19
Hume, David 1711-1776 .... **LC 7, 56**
　See also DLB 104
Humphrey, William 1924-1997 .... **CLC 45**
　See also CA 77-80; 160; CANR 68; DLB
　212

Kinnell, Galway 1927- ..... **CLC 1, 2, 3, 5, 13, 29, 129; PC 26**
See also CA 9-12R; CANR 10, 34, 66; DLB 5; DLBY 87; INT CANR-34; MTCW 1, 2

Kinsella, Thomas 1928- .... **CLC 4, 19**
See also CA 17-20R; CANR 15; DLB 27; MTCW 1, 2

Kinsella, W(illiam) P(atrick) 1935- . **CLC 27, 43; DAC; DAM NOV, POP**
See also AAYA 7; CA 97-100; CAAS 7; CANR 21, 35, 66, 75; INT CANR-21; MTCW 1, 2

Kinsey, Alfred C(harles) 1894-1956 .... **TCLC 91**
See also CA 115; 170; MTCW 2

Kipling, (Joseph) Rudyard 1865-1936 .... **TCLC 8, 17; DA; DAB; DAC; DAM MST, POET; PC 3; SSC 5; WLC**
See also AAYA 32; CA 105; 120; CANR 33; CDBLB 1890-1914; CLR 39, 65; DA3; DLB 19, 34, 141, 156; MAICYA; MTCW 1, 2; SATA 100; YABC 2

Kirkland, Caroline M. 1801-1864 . **NCLC 85**
See also DLB 3, 73, 74; DLBD 13

Kirkup, James 1918- .... **CLC 1**
See also CA 1-4R; CAAS 4; CANR 2; DLB 27; SATA 12

Kirkwood, James 1930(?)-1989 .... **CLC 9**
See also AITN 2; CA 1-4R; 128; CANR 6, 40

Kirshner, Sidney
See Kingsley, Sidney

Kis, Danilo 1935-1989 .... **CLC 57**
See also CA 109; 118; 129; CANR 61; DLB 181; MTCW 1

Kivi, Aleksis 1834-1872 .... **NCLC 30**

Kizer, Carolyn (Ashley) 1925- ... **CLC 15, 39, 80; DAM POET**
See also CA 65-68; CAAS 5; CANR 24, 70; DLB 5, 169; MTCW 2

Klabund 1890-1928 .... **TCLC 44**
See also CA 162; DLB 66

Klappert, Peter 1942- .... **CLC 57**
See also CA 33-36R; DLB 5

Klein, A(braham) M(oses) 1909-1972 . **CLC 19; DAB; DAC; DAM MST**
See also CA 101; 37-40R; DLB 68

Klein, Norma 1938-1989 .... **CLC 30**
See also AAYA 2; CA 41-44R; 128; CANR 15, 37; CLR 2, 19; INT CANR-15; JRDA; MAICYA; SAAS 1; SATA 7, 57

Klein, T(heodore) E(ibon) D(onald) 1947- **CLC 34**
See also CA 119; CANR 44, 75

Kleist, Heinrich von 1777-1811 ...... **NCLC 2, 37; DAM DRAM; SSC 22**
See also DLB 90

Klima, Ivan 1931- .... **CLC 56; DAM NOV**
See also CA 25-28R; CANR 17, 50, 91

Klimentov, Andrei Platonovich 1899-1951
See Platonov, Andrei
See also CA 108

Klinger, Friedrich Maximilian von 1752-1831 .... **NCLC 1**
See also DLB 94

Klingsor the Magician
See Hartmann, Sadakichi

Klopstock, Friedrich Gottlieb 1724-1803 **NCLC 11**
See also DLB 97

Knapp, Caroline 1959- .... **CLC 99**
See also CA 154

Knebel, Fletcher 1911-1993 .... **CLC 14**
See also AITN 1; CA 1-4R; 140; CAAS 3; CANR 1, 36; SATA 36; SATA-Obit 75

Knickerbocker, Diedrich
See Irving, Washington

Knight, Etheridge 1931-1991 . **CLC 40; BLC 2; DAM POET; PC 14**
See also BW 1, 3; CA 21-24R; 133; CANR 23, 82; DLB 41; MTCW 2

Knight, Sarah Kemble 1666-1727 .... **LC 7**
See also DLB 24, 200

Knister, Raymond 1899-1932 .... **TCLC 56**
See also CA 186; DLB 68

Knowles, John 1926- . **CLC 1, 4, 10, 26; DA; DAC; DAM MST, NOV**
See also AAYA 10; CA 17-20R; CANR 40, 74, 76; CDALB 1968-1988; DLB 6; MTCW 1, 2; SATA 8, 89

Knox, Calvin M.
See Silverberg, Robert

Knox, John c. 1505-1572 .... **LC 37**
See also DLB 132

Knye, Cassandra
See Disch, Thomas M(ichael)

Koch, C(hristopher) J(ohn) 1932- .... **CLC 42**
See also CA 127; CANR 84

Koch, Christopher
See Koch, C(hristopher) J(ohn)

Koch, Kenneth 1925- .... **CLC 5, 8, 44; DAM POET**
See also CA 1-4R; CANR 6, 36, 57; DLB 5; INT CANR-36; MTCW 2; SATA 65

Kochanowski, Jan 1530-1584 .... **LC 10**

Kock, Charles Paul de 1794-1871 . **NCLC 16**

Koda Rohan 1867-
See Koda Shigeyuki

Koda Shigeyuki 1867-1947 .... **TCLC 22**
See also CA 121; 183; DLB 180

Koestler, Arthur 1905-1983 ... **CLC 1, 3, 6, 8, 15, 33**
See also CA 1-4R; 109; CANR 1, 33; CD-BLB 1945-1960; DLBY 83; MTCW 1, 2

Kogawa, Joy Nozomi 1935- ..... **CLC 78, 129; DAC; DAM MST, MULT**
See also CA 101; CANR 19, 62; MTCW 2; SATA 99

Kohout, Pavel 1928- .... **CLC 13**
See also CA 45-48; CANR 3

Koizumi, Yakumo
See Hearn, (Patricio) Lafcadio (Tessima Carlos)

Kolmar, Gertrud 1894-1943 .... **TCLC 40**
See also CA 167

Komunyakaa, Yusef 1947- .... **CLC 86, 94; BLCS**
See also CA 147; CANR 83; DLB 120

Konrad, George
See Konrad, Gyoergy

Konrad, Gyoergy 1933- .... **CLC 4, 10, 73**
See also CA 85-88

Konwicki, Tadeusz 1926- .... **CLC 8, 28, 54, 117**
See also CA 101; CAAS 9; CANR 39, 59; MTCW 1

Koontz, Dean R(ay) 1945- .... **CLC 78; DAM NOV, POP**
See also AAYA 9, 31; BEST 89:3, 90:2; CA 108; CANR 19, 36, 52; DA3; MTCW 1; SATA 92

Kopernik, Mikolaj
See Copernicus, Nicolaus

Kopit, Arthur (Lee) 1937- ..... **CLC 1, 18, 33; DAM DRAM**
See also AITN 1; CA 81-84; CABS 3; DLB 7; MTCW 1

Kops, Bernard 1926- .... **CLC 4**
See also CA 5-8R; CANR 84; DLB 13

Kornbluth, C(yril) M. 1923-1958 .... **TCLC 8**
See also CA 105; 160; DLB 8

Korolenko, V. G.
See Korolenko, Vladimir Galaktionovich

Korolenko, Vladimir
See Korolenko, Vladimir Galaktionovich

Korolenko, Vladimir G.
See Korolenko, Vladimir Galaktionovich

Korolenko, Vladimir Galaktionovich 1853-1921 .... **TCLC 22**
See also CA 121

Korzybski, Alfred (Habdank Skarbek) 1879-1950 .... **TCLC 61**
See also CA 123; 160

Kosinski, Jerzy (Nikodem) 1933-1991 ... **CLC 1, 2, 3, 6, 10, 15, 53, 70; DAM NOV**
See also CA 17-20R; 134; CANR 9, 46; DA3; DLB 2; DLBY 82; MTCW 1, 2

Kostelanetz, Richard (Cory) 1940- .. **CLC 28**
See also CA 13-16R; CAAS 8; CANR 38, 77

Kostrowitzki, Wilhelm Apollinaris de 1880-1918
See Apollinaire, Guillaume
See also CA 104

Kotlowitz, Robert 1924- .... **CLC 4**
See also CA 33-36R; CANR 36

Kotzebue, August (Friedrich Ferdinand) von 1761-1819 .... **NCLC 25**
See also DLB 94

Kotzwinkle, William 1938- ..... **CLC 5, 14, 35**
See also CA 45-48; CANR 3, 44, 84; CLR 6; DLB 173; MAICYA; SATA 24, 70

Kowna, Stancy
See Szymborska, Wislawa

Kozol, Jonathan 1936- .... **CLC 17**
See also CA 61-64; CANR 16, 45

Kozoll, Michael 1940(?)- .... **CLC 35**

Kramer, Kathryn 19(?)- .... **CLC 34**

Kramer, Larry 1935- .. **CLC 42; DAM POP; DC 8**
See also CA 124; 126; CANR 60

Krasicki, Ignacy 1735-1801 .... **NCLC 8**

Krasinski, Zygmunt 1812-1859 .... **NCLC 4**

Kraus, Karl 1874-1936 .... **TCLC 5**
See also CA 104; DLB 118

Kreve (Mickevicius), Vincas 1882-1954 **TCLC 27**
See also CA 170; DLB 220

Kristeva, Julia 1941- .... **CLC 77**
See also CA 154

Kristofferson, Kris 1936- .... **CLC 26**
See also CA 104

Krizanc, John 1956- .... **CLC 57**

Krleza, Miroslav 1893-1981 .... **CLC 8, 114**
See also CA 97-100; 105; CANR 50; DLB 147

Kroetsch, Robert 1927- . **CLC 5, 23, 57, 132; DAC; DAM POET**
See also CA 17-20R; CANR 8, 38; DLB 53; MTCW 1

Kroetz, Franz
See Kroetz, Franz Xaver

Kroetz, Franz Xaver 1946- .... **CLC 41**
See also CA 130

Kroker, Arthur (W.) 1945- .... **CLC 77**
See also CA 161

Kropotkin, Peter (Aleksieevich) 1842-1921 **TCLC 36**
See also CA 119

Krotkov, Yuri 1917- .... **CLC 19**
See also CA 102

Krumb
See Crumb, R(obert)

Krumgold, Joseph (Quincy) 1908-1980 .... **CLC 12**
See also CA 9-12R; 101; CANR 7; MAI-CYA; SATA 1, 48; SATA-Obit 23

Krumwitz
See Crumb, R(obert)

Krutch, Joseph Wood 1893-1970 ..... **CLC 24**
See also CA 1-4R; 25-28R; CANR 4; DLB 63, 206

Latsis, Mary J(ane) 1927(?)-1997
See Lathen, Emma
See also CA 85-88; 162

Lattimore, Richmond (Alexander) 1906-1984
CLC 3
See also CA 1-4R; 112; CANR 1

Laughlin, James 1914-1997 .... **CLC 49**
See also CA 21-24R; 162; CAAS 22; CANR
9, 47; DLB 48; DLBY 96, 97

Laurence, (Jean) Margaret (Wemyss)
1926-1987 . CLC 3, 6, 13, 50, 62; DAC;
DAM MST; SSC 7
See also CA 5-8R; 121; CANR 33; DLB
53; MTCW 1, 2; SATA-Obit 50

Laurent, Antoine 1952- .... **CLC 50**

Lauscher, Hermann
See Hesse, Hermann

Lautreamont, Comte de
1846-1870 .... **NCLC 12; SSC 14**

Laverty, Donald
See Blish, James (Benjamin)

Lavin, Mary 1912-1996 . CLC 4, 18, 99; SSC
4
See also CA 9-12R; 151; CANR 33; DLB
15; MTCW 1

Lavond, Paul Dennis
See Kornbluth, C(yril) M.; Pohl, Frederik

Lawler, Raymond Evenor 1922- .... **CLC 58**
See also CA 103

Lawrence, D(avid) H(erbert Richards)
1885-1930 .... TCLC 2, 9, 16, 33, 48, 61,
93; DA; DAB; DAC; DAM MST, NOV,
POET; SSC 4, 19; WLC
See also CA 104; 121; CDBLB 1914-1945;
DA3; DLB 10, 19, 36, 98, 162, 195;
MTCW 1, 2

Lawrence, T(homas) E(dward) 1888-1935
TCLC 18
See also Dale, Colin
See also CA 115; 167; DLB 195

Lawrence of Arabia
See Lawrence, T(homas) E(dward)

Lawson, Henry (Archibald Hertzberg)
1867-1922 .... **TCLC 27; SSC 18**
See also CA 120; 181

Lawton, Dennis
See Faust, Frederick (Schiller)

Laxness, Halldor .... **CLC 25**
See also Gudjonsson, Halldor Kiljan

Layamon fl. c. 1200- .... **CMLC 10**
See also DLB 146

Laye, Camara 1928-1980 ... CLC 4, 38; BLC
2; DAM MULT
See also BW 1; CA 85-88; 97-100; CANR
25; MTCW 1, 2

Layton, Irving (Peter) 1912- .... CLC 2, 15;
DAC; DAM MST, POET
See also CA 1-4R; CANR 2, 33, 43, 66;
DLB 88; MTCW 1, 2

Lazarus, Emma 1849-1887 .... **NCLC 8**

Lazarus, Felix
See Cable, George Washington

Lazarus, Henry
See Slavitt, David R(ytman)

Lea, Joan
See Neufeld, John (Arthur)

Leacock, Stephen (Butler)
1869-1944 .... TCLC 2; DAC; DAM
MST; SSC 39
See also CA 104; 141; CANR 80; DLB 92;
MTCW 2

Lear, Edward 1812-1888 .... **NCLC 3**
See also CLR 1; DLB 32, 163, 166; MAI-
CYA; SATA 18, 100

Lear, Norman (Milton) 1922- .... **CLC 12**
See also CA 73-76

Leautaud, Paul 1872-1956 .... **TCLC 83**
See also DLB 65

Leavis, F(rank) R(aymond)
1895-1978 .... **CLC 24**
See also CA 21-24R; 77-80; CANR 44;
MTCW 1, 2

Leavitt, David 1961- ..... **CLC 34; DAM POP**
See also CA 116; 122; CANR 50, 62; DA3;
DLB 130; INT 122; MTCW 2

Leblanc, Maurice (Marie Emile) 1864-1941
TCLC 49
See also CA 110

Lebowitz, Fran(ces Ann) 1951(?)- ... CLC 11,
36
See also CA 81-84; CANR 14, 60, 70; INT
CANR-14; MTCW 1

Lebrecht, Peter
See Tieck, (Johann) Ludwig

le Carre, John .... CLC 3, 5, 9, 15, 28
See also Cornwell, David (John Moore)
See also BEST 89:4; CDBLB 1960 to
Present; DLB 87; MTCW 2

Le Clezio, J(ean) M(arie) G(ustave) 1940-
CLC 31
See also CA 116; 128; DLB 83

Leconte de Lisle, Charles-Marie-Rene
1818-1894 .... **NCLC 29**

Le Coq, Monsieur
See Simenon, Georges (Jacques Christian)

Leduc, Violette 1907-1972 .... **CLC 22**
See also CA 13-14; 33-36R; CANR 69;
CAP 1

Ledwidge, Francis 1887(?)-1917 .... **TCLC 23**
See also CA 123; DLB 20

Lee, Andrea 1953- ... CLC 36; BLC 2; DAM
MULT
See also BW 1, 3; CA 125; CANR 82

Lee, Andrew
See Auchincloss, Louis (Stanton)

Lee, Chang-rae 1965- .... **CLC 91**
See also CA 148; CANR 89

Lee, Don L. .... **CLC 2**
See also Madhubuti, Haki R.

Lee, George W(ashington)
1894-1976 .... CLC 52; BLC 2; DAM
MULT
See also BW 1; CA 125; CANR 83; DLB
51

Lee, (Nelle) Harper 1926- . CLC 12, 60; DA;
DAB; DAC; DAM MST, NOV; WLC
See also AAYA 13; CA 13-16R; CANR 51;
CDALB 1941-1968; DA3; DLB 6;
MTCW 1, 2; SATA 11

Lee, Helen Elaine 1959(?)- .... **CLC 86**
See also CA 148

Lee, Julian
See Latham, Jean Lee

Lee, Larry
See Lee, Lawrence

Lee, Laurie 1914-1997 .... CLC 90; DAB;
DAM POP
See also CA 77-80; 158; CANR 33, 73;
DLB 27; MTCW 1

Lee, Lawrence 1941-1990 .... **CLC 34**
See also CA 131; CANR 43

Lee, Li-Young 1957- .... **PC 24**
See also CA 153; DLB 165

Lee, Manfred B(ennington)
1905-1971 .... **CLC 11**
See also Queen, Ellery
See also CA 1-4R; 29-32R; CANR 2; DLB
137

Lee, Shelton Jackson 1957(?)- .... CLC 105;
BLCS; DAM MULT
See also Lee, Spike
See also BW 2, 3; CA 125; CANR 42

Lee, Spike
See Lee, Shelton Jackson
See also AAYA 4, 29

Lee, Stan 1922- .... **CLC 17**
See also AAYA 5; CA 108; 111; INT 111

Lee, Tanith 1947- .... **CLC 46**
See also AAYA 15; CA 37-40R; CANR 53;
SATA 8, 88

Lee, Vernon .... **TCLC 5; SSC 33**
See also Paget, Violet
See also DLB 57, 153, 156, 174, 178

Lee, William
See Burroughs, William S(eward)

Lee, Willy
See Burroughs, William S(eward)

Lee-Hamilton, Eugene (Jacob) 1845-1907
TCLC 22
See also CA 117

Leet, Judith 1935- .... **CLC 11**

Le Fanu, Joseph Sheridan
1814-1873 ..... NCLC 9, 58; DAM POP;
SSC 14
See also DA3; DLB 21, 70, 159, 178

Leffland, Ella 1931- .... **CLC 19**
See also CA 29-32R; CANR 35, 78, 82;
DLBY 84; INT CANR-35; SATA 65

Leger, Alexis
See Leger, (Marie-Rene Auguste) Alexis
Saint-Leger

Leger, (Marie-Rene Auguste) Alexis
Saint-Leger 1887-1975 .. CLC 4, 11, 46;
DAM POET; PC 23
See also CA 13-16R; 61-64; CANR 43;
MTCW 1

Leger, Saintleger
See Leger, (Marie-Rene Auguste) Alexis
Saint-Leger

Le Guin, Ursula K(roeber) 1929- ..... CLC 8,
13, 22, 45, 71; DAB; DAC; DAM MST,
POP; SSC 12
See also AAYA 9, 27; AITN 1; CA 21-24R;
CANR 9, 32, 52, 74; CDALB 1968-1988;
CLR 3, 28; DA3; DLB 8, 52; INT CANR-
32; JRDA; MAICYA; MTCW 1, 2; SATA
4, 52, 99

Lehmann, Rosamond (Nina)
1901-1990 .... **CLC 5**
See also CA 77-80; 131; CANR 8, 73; DLB
15; MTCW 2

Leiber, Fritz (Reuter, Jr.)
1910-1992 .... **CLC 25**
See also CA 45-48; 139; CANR 2, 40, 86;
DLB 8; MTCW 1, 2; SATA 45; SATA-
Obit 73

Leibniz, Gottfried Wilhelm von 1646-1716
LC 35
See also DLB 168

Leimbach, Martha 1963-
See Leimbach, Marti
See also CA 130

Leimbach, Marti .... **CLC 65**
See also Leimbach, Martha

Leino, Eino .... **TCLC 24**
See also Loennbohm, Armas Eino Leopold

Leiris, Michel (Julien) 1901-1990 ..... **CLC 61**
See also CA 119; 128; 132

Leithauser, Brad 1953- .... **CLC 27**
See also CA 107; CANR 27, 81; DLB 120

Lelchuk, Alan 1938- .... **CLC 5**
See also CA 45-48; CAAS 20; CANR 1, 70

Lem, Stanislaw 1921- .... CLC 8, 15, 40
See also CA 105; CAAS 1; CANR 32;
MTCW 1

Lemann, Nancy 1956- .... **CLC 39**
See also CA 118; 136

Lemonnier, (Antoine Louis) Camille
1844-1913 .... **TCLC 22**
See also CA 121

Lenau, Nikolaus 1802-1850 .... **NCLC 16**

L'Engle, Madeleine (Camp Franklin) 1918-
CLC 12; DAM POP
See also AAYA 28; AITN 2; CA 1-4R;
CANR 3, 21, 39, 66; CLR 1, 14, 57; DA3;

Luxemburg, Rosa 1870(?)-1919 ..... **TCLC 63**
See also CA 118

Luzi, Mario 1914- .... **CLC 13**
See also CA 61-64; CANR 9, 70; DLB 128

Lyly, John 1554(?)-1606 .... **LC 41; DAM DRAM; DC 7**
See also DLB 62, 167

L'Ymagier
See Gourmont, Remy (-Marie-Charles) de

Lynch, B. Suarez
See Bioy Casares, Adolfo; Borges, Jorge Luis

Lynch, B. Suarez
See Bioy Casares, Adolfo

Lynch, David (K.) 1946- .... **CLC 66**
See also CA 124; 129

Lynch, James
See Andreyev, Leonid (Nikolaevich)

Lynch Davis, B.
See Bioy Casares, Adolfo; Borges, Jorge Luis

Lyndsay, Sir David 1490-1555 .... **LC 20**

Lynn, Kenneth S(chuyler) 1923- ...... **CLC 50**
See also CA 1-4R; CANR 3, 27, 65

Lynx
See West, Rebecca

Lyons, Marcus
See Blish, James (Benjamin)

Lyre, Pinchbeck
See Sassoon, Siegfried (Lorraine)

Lytle, Andrew (Nelson) 1902-1995 ... **CLC 22**
See also CA 9-12R; 150; CANR 70; DLB 6; DLBY 95

Lyttelton, George 1709-1773 .... **LC 10**

Maas, Peter 1929- .... **CLC 29**
See also CA 93-96; INT 93-96; MTCW 2

Macaulay, Rose 1881-1958 .... **TCLC 7, 44**
See also CA 104; DLB 36

Macaulay, Thomas Babington 1800-1859
NCLC 42
See also CDBLB 1832-1890; DLB 32, 55

MacBeth, George (Mann)
1932-1992 .... **CLC 2, 5, 9**
See also CA 25-28R; 136; CANR 61, 66; DLB 40; MTCW 1; SATA 4; SATA-Obit 70

MacCaig, Norman (Alexander)
1910- .... **CLC 36; DAB; DAM POET**
See also CA 9-12R; CANR 3, 34; DLB 27

MacCarthy, Sir(Charles Otto) Desmond
1877-1952 .... **TCLC 36**
See also CA 167

MacDiarmid, Hugh ..... **CLC 2, 4, 11, 19, 63; PC 9**
See also Grieve, C(hristopher) M(urray)
See also CDBLB 1945-1960; DLB 20

MacDonald, Anson
See Heinlein, Robert A(nson)

Macdonald, Cynthia 1928- .... **CLC 13, 19**
See also CA 49-52; CANR 4, 44; DLB 105

MacDonald, George 1824-1905 .... **TCLC 9**
See also CA 106; 137; CANR 80; DLB 18, 163, 178; MAICYA; SATA 33, 100

Macdonald, John
See Millar, Kenneth

MacDonald, John D(ann)
1916-1986 .. **CLC 3, 27, 44; DAM NOV, POP**
See also CA 1-4R; 121; CANR 1, 19, 60; DLB 8; DLBY 86; MTCW 1, 2

Macdonald, John Ross
See Millar, Kenneth

Macdonald, Ross ...... **CLC 1, 2, 3, 14, 34, 41**
See also Millar, Kenneth
See also DLBD 6

MacDougal, John
See Blish, James (Benjamin)

MacDougal, John
See Blish, James (Benjamin)

MacEwen, Gwendolyn (Margaret)
1941-1987 .... **CLC 13, 55**
See also CA 9-12R; 124; CANR 7, 22; DLB 53; SATA 50; SATA-Obit 55

Macha, Karel Hynek 1810-1846 .... **NCLC 46**

Machado (y Ruiz), Antonio
1875-1939 .... **TCLC 3**
See also CA 104; 174; DLB 108; HW 2

Machado de Assis, Joaquim Maria
1839-1908 ..... **TCLC 10; BLC 2; HLCS 2; SSC 24**
See also CA 107; 153; CANR 91

Machen, Arthur .... **TCLC 4; SSC 20**
See also Jones, Arthur Llewellyn
See also CA 179; DLB 36, 156, 178

Machiavelli, Niccolo 1469-1527 ..... **LC 8, 36; DA; DAB; DAC; DAM MST; WLCS**

MacInnes, Colin 1914-1976 .... **CLC 4, 23**
See also CA 69-72; 65-68; CANR 21; DLB 14; MTCW 1, 2

MacInnes, Helen (Clark)
1907-1985 .... **CLC 27, 39; DAM POP**
See also CA 1-4R; 117; CANR 1, 28, 58; DLB 87; MTCW 1, 2; SATA 22; SATA-Obit 44

Mackenzie, Compton (Edward Montague)
1883-1972 .... **CLC 18**
See also CA 21-22; 37-40R; CAP 2; DLB 34, 100

Mackenzie, Henry 1745-1831 .... **NCLC 41**
See also DLB 39

Mackintosh, Elizabeth 1896(?)-1952
See Tey, Josephine
See also CA 110

MacLaren, James
See Grieve, C(hristopher) M(urray)

Mac Laverty, Bernard 1942- .... **CLC 31**
See also CA 116; 118; CANR 43, 88; INT 118

MacLean, Alistair (Stuart)
1922(?)-1987 .. **CLC 3, 13, 50, 63; DAM POP**
See also CA 57-60; 121; CANR 28, 61; MTCW 1; SATA 23; SATA-Obit 50

Maclean, Norman (Fitzroy)
1902-1990 .... **CLC 78; DAM POP; SSC 13**
See also CA 102; 132; CANR 49; DLB 206

MacLeish, Archibald 1892-1982 ... **CLC 3, 8, 14, 68; DAM POET**
See also CA 9-12R; 106; CANR 33, 63; CDALBS; DLB 4, 7, 45; DLBY 82; MTCW 1, 2

MacLennan, (John) Hugh
1907-1990 . **CLC 2, 14, 92; DAC; DAM MST**
See also CA 5-8R; 142; CANR 33; DLB 68; MTCW 1, 2

MacLeod, Alistair 1936- .... **CLC 56; DAC; DAM MST**
See also CA 123; DLB 60; MTCW 2

Macleod, Fiona
See Sharp, William

MacNeice, (Frederick) Louis
1907-1963 .... **CLC 1, 4, 10, 53; DAB; DAM POET**
See also CA 85-88; CANR 61; DLB 10, 20; MTCW 1, 2

MacNeill, Dand
See Fraser, George MacDonald

Macpherson, James 1736-1796 .... **LC 29**
See also Ossian
See also DLB 109

Macpherson, (Jean) Jay 1931- .... **CLC 14**
See also CA 5-8R; CANR 90; DLB 53

MacShane, Frank 1927-1999 .... **CLC 39**
See also CA 9-12R; 186; CANR 3, 33; DLB 111

Macumber, Mari
See Sandoz, Mari(e Susette)

Madach, Imre 1823-1864 .... **NCLC 19**

Madden, (Jerry) David 1933- .... **CLC 5, 15**
See also CA 1-4R; CAAS 3; CANR 4, 45; DLB 6; MTCW 1

Maddern, Al(an)
See Ellison, Harlan (Jay)

Madhubuti, Haki R. 1942- . **CLC 6, 73; BLC 2; DAM MULT, POET; PC 5**
See also Lee, Don L.
See also BW 2, 3; CA 73-76; CANR 24, 51, 73; DLB 5, 41; DLBD 8; MTCW 2

Maepenn, Hugh
See Kuttner, Henry

Maepenn, K. H.
See Kuttner, Henry

Maeterlinck, Maurice 1862-1949 ... **TCLC 3; DAM DRAM**
See also CA 104; 136; CANR 80; DLB 192; SATA 66

Maginn, William 1794-1842 .... **NCLC 8**
See also DLB 110, 159

Mahapatra, Jayanta 1928- .... **CLC 33; DAM MULT**
See also CA 73-76; CAAS 9; CANR 15, 33, 66, 87

Mahfouz, Naguib (Abdel Aziz Al-Sabilgi)
1911(?)-
See Mahfuz, Najib
See also BEST 89:2; CA 128; CANR 55; DAM NOV; DA3; MTCW 1, 2

Mahfuz, Najib .... **CLC 52, 55**
See also Mahfouz, Naguib (Abdel Aziz Al-Sabilgi)
See also DLBY 88

Mahon, Derek 1941- .... **CLC 27**
See also CA 113; 128; CANR 88; DLB 40

Mailer, Norman 1923- ... **CLC 1, 2, 3, 4, 5, 8, 11, 14, 28, 39, 74, 111; DA; DAB; DAC; DAM MST, NOV, POP**
See also AAYA 31; AITN 2; CA 9-12R; CABS 1; CANR 28, 74, 77; CDALB 1968-1988; DA3; DLB 2, 16, 28, 185; DLBD 3; DLBY 80, 83; MTCW 1, 2

Maillet, Antonine 1929- .. **CLC 54, 118; DAC**
See also CA 115; 120; CANR 46, 74, 77; DLB 60; INT 120; MTCW 2

Mais, Roger 1905-1955 .... **TCLC 8**
See also BW 1, 3; CA 105; 124; CANR 82; DLB 125; MTCW 1

Maistre, Joseph de 1753-1821 .... **NCLC 37**

Maitland, Frederic 1850-1906 .... **TCLC 65**

Maitland, Sara (Louise) 1950- .... **CLC 49**
See also CA 69-72; CANR 13, 59

Major, Clarence 1936- . **CLC 3, 19, 48; BLC 2; DAM MULT**
See also BW 2, 3; CA 21-24R; CAAS 6; CANR 13, 25, 53, 82; DLB 33

Major, Kevin (Gerald) 1949- . **CLC 26; DAC**
See also AAYA 16; CA 97-100; CANR 21, 38; CLR 11; DLB 60; INT CANR-21; JRDA; MAICYA; SATA 32, 82

Maki, James
See Ozu, Yasujiro

Malabaila, Damiano
See Levi, Primo

Malamud, Bernard 1914-1986 .. **CLC 1, 2, 3, 5, 8, 9, 11, 18, 27, 44, 78, 85; DA; DAB; DAC; DAM MST, NOV, POP; SSC 15; WLC**
See also AAYA 16; CA 5-8R; 118; CABS 1; CANR 28, 62; CDALB 1941-1968; DA3; DLB 2, 28, 152; DLBY 80, 86; MTCW 1, 2

McCullers, (Lula) Carson (Smith) 1917-1967 **CLC 1, 4, 10, 12, 48, 100; DA; DAB; DAC; DAM MST, NOV; SSC 9, 24; WLC**
See also AAYA 21; CA 5-8R; 25-28R; CABS 1, 3; CANR 18; CDALB 1941-1968; DA3; DLB 2, 7, 173; MTCW 1, 2; SATA 27

McCulloch, John Tyler
See Burroughs, Edgar Rice

McCullough, Colleen 1938(?)- .... **CLC 27, 107; DAM NOV, POP**
See also CA 81-84; CANR 17, 46, 67; DA3; MTCW 1, 2

McDermott, Alice 1953- .... **CLC 90**
See also CA 109; CANR 40, 90

McElroy, Joseph 1930- .... **CLC 5, 47**
See also CA 17-20R

McEwan, Ian (Russell) 1948- .... **CLC 13, 66; DAM NOV**
See also BEST 90:4; CA 61-64; CANR 14, 41, 69, 87; DLB 14, 194; MTCW 1, 2

McFadden, David 1940- .... **CLC 48**
See also CA 104; DLB 60; INT 104

McFarland, Dennis 1950- .... **CLC 65**
See also CA 165

McGahern, John 1934- ... **CLC 5, 9, 48; SSC 17**
See also CA 17-20R; CANR 29, 68; DLB 14; MTCW 1

McGinley, Patrick (Anthony) 1937- . **CLC 41**
See also CA 120; 127; CANR 56; INT 127

McGinley, Phyllis 1905-1978 .... **CLC 14**
See also CA 9-12R; 77-80; CANR 19; DLB 11, 48; SATA 2, 44; SATA-Obit 24

McGinniss, Joe 1942- .... **CLC 32**
See also AITN 2; BEST 89:2; CA 25-28R; CANR 26, 70; DLB 185; INT CANR-26

McGivern, Maureen Daly
See Daly, Maureen

McGrath, Patrick 1950- .... **CLC 55**
See also CA 136; CANR 65

McGrath, Thomas (Matthew) 1916-1990 **CLC 28, 59; DAM POET**
See also CA 9-12R; 132; CANR 6, 33; MTCW 1; SATA 41; SATA-Obit 66

McGuane, Thomas (Francis III) 1939- .... **CLC 3, 7, 18, 45, 127**
See also AITN 2; CA 49-52; CANR 5, 24, 49; DLB 2, 212; DLBY 80; INT CANR-24; MTCW 1

McGuckian, Medbh 1950- .... **CLC 48; DAM POET; PC 27**
See also CA 143; DLB 40

McHale, Tom 1942(?)-1982 .... **CLC 3, 5**
See also AITN 1; CA 77-80; 106

McIlvanney, William 1936- .... **CLC 42**
See also CA 25-28R; CANR 61; DLB 14, 207

McIlwraith, Maureen Mollie Hunter
See Hunter, Mollie
See also SATA 2

McInerney, Jay 1955- .... **CLC 34, 112; DAM POP**
See also AAYA 18; CA 116; 123; CANR 45, 68; DA3; INT 123; MTCW 2

McIntyre, Vonda N(eel) 1948- .... **CLC 18**
See also CA 81-84; CANR 17, 34, 69; MTCW 1

McKay, Claude . **TCLC 7, 41; BLC 3; DAB; PC 2**
See also McKay, Festus Claudius
See also DLB 4, 45, 51, 117

McKay, Festus Claudius 1889-1948
See McKay, Claude
See also BW 1, 3; CA 104; 124; CANR 73; DA; DAC; DAM MST, MULT, NOV, POET; MTCW 1, 2; WLC

McKuen, Rod 1933- .... **CLC 1, 3**
See also AITN 1; CA 41-44R; CANR 40

McLoughlin, R. B.
See Mencken, H(enry) L(ouis)

McLuhan, (Herbert) Marshall 1911-1980 **CLC 37, 83**
See also CA 9-12R; 102; CANR 12, 34, 61; DLB 88; INT CANR-12; MTCW 1, 2

McMillan, Terry (L.) 1951- .... **CLC 50, 61, 112; BLCS; DAM MULT, NOV, POP**
See also AAYA 21; BW 2, 3; CA 140; CANR 60; DA3; MTCW 2

McMurtry, Larry (Jeff) 1936- .. **CLC 2, 3, 7, 11, 27, 44, 127; DAM NOV, POP**
See also AAYA 15; AITN 2; BEST 89:2; CA 5-8R; CANR 19, 43, 64; CDALB 1968-1988; DA3; DLB 2, 143; DLBY 80, 87; MTCW 1, 2

McNally, T. M. 1961- .... **CLC 82**

McNally, Terrence 1939- ... **CLC 4, 7, 41, 91; DAM DRAM**
See also CA 45-48; CANR 2, 56; DA3; DLB 7; MTCW 2

McNamer, Deirdre 1950- .... **CLC 70**

McNeal, Tom .... **CLC 119**

McNeile, Herman Cyril 1888-1937
See Sapper
See also CA 184; DLB 77

McNickle, (William) D'Arcy 1904-1977 .... **CLC 89; DAM MULT**
See also CA 9-12R; 85-88; CANR 5, 45; DLB 175, 212; NNAL; SATA-Obit 22

McPhee, John (Angus) 1931- .... **CLC 36**
See also BEST 90:1; CA 65-68; CANR 20, 46, 64, 69; DLB 185; MTCW 1, 2

McPherson, James Alan 1943- .. **CLC 19, 77; BLCS**
See also BW 1, 3; CA 25-28R; CAAS 17; CANR 24, 74; DLB 38; MTCW 1, 2

McPherson, William (Alexander) 1933- .... **CLC 34**
See also CA 69-72; CANR 28; INT CANR-28

Mead, George Herbert 1873-1958 . **TCLC 89**

Mead, Margaret 1901-1978 .... **CLC 37**
See also AITN 1; CA 1-4R; 81-84; CANR 4; DA3; MTCW 1, 2; SATA-Obit 20

Meaker, Marijane (Agnes) 1927-
See Kerr, M. E.
See also CA 107; CANR 37, 63; INT 107; JRDA; MAICYA; MTCW 1; SATA 20, 61, 99; SATA-Essay 111

Medoff, Mark (Howard) 1940- ... **CLC 6, 23; DAM DRAM**
See also AITN 1; CA 53-56; CANR 5; DLB 7; INT CANR-5

Medvedev, P. N.
See Bakhtin, Mikhail Mikhailovich

Meged, Aharon
See Megged, Aharon

Meged, Aron
See Megged, Aharon

Megged, Aharon 1920- .... **CLC 9**
See also CA 49-52; CAAS 13; CANR 1

Mehta, Ved (Parkash) 1934- .... **CLC 37**
See also CA 1-4R; CANR 2, 23, 69; MTCW 1

Melanter
See Blackmore, R(ichard) D(oddridge)

Melies, Georges 1861-1938 .... **TCLC 81**

Melikow, Loris
See Hofmannsthal, Hugo von

Melmoth, Sebastian
See Wilde, Oscar (Fingal O'Flahertie Wills)

Meltzer, Milton 1915- .... **CLC 26**
See also AAYA 8; CA 13-16R; CANR 38; CLR 13; DLB 61; JRDA; MAICYA; SAAS 1; SATA 1, 50, 80

Melville, Herman 1819-1891 ..... **NCLC 3, 12, 29, 45, 49; DA; DAB; DAC; DAM MST, NOV; SSC 1, 17; WLC**
See also AAYA 25; CDALB 1640-1865; DA3; DLB 3, 74; SATA 59

Menander c. 342B.C.-c. 292B.C. ... **CMLC 9; DAM DRAM; DC 3**
See also DLB 176

Menchu, Rigoberta 1959-
See also HLCS 2

Menchu, Rigoberta 1959-
See also CA 175; HLCS 2

Mencken, H(enry) L(ouis) 1880-1956 .... **TCLC 13**
See also CA 105; 125; CDALB 1917-1929; DLB 11, 29, 63, 137; MTCW 1, 2

Mendelsohn, Jane 1965(?)- .... **CLC 99**
See also CA 154

Mercer, David 1928-1980 .... **CLC 5; DAM DRAM**
See also CA 9-12R; 102; CANR 23; DLB 13; MTCW 1

Merchant, Paul
See Ellison, Harlan (Jay)

Meredith, George 1828-1909 .. **TCLC 17, 43; DAM POET**
See also CA 117; 153; CANR 80; CDBLB 1832-1890; DLB 18, 35, 57, 159

Meredith, William (Morris) 1919- .... **CLC 4, 13, 22, 55; DAM POET; PC 28**
See also CA 9-12R; CAAS 14; CANR 6, 40; DLB 5

Merezhkovsky, Dmitry Sergeyevich 1865-1941 .... **TCLC 29**
See also CA 169

Merimee, Prosper 1803-1870 ... **NCLC 6, 65; SSC 7**
See also DLB 119, 192

Merkin, Daphne 1954- .... **CLC 44**
See also CA 123

Merlin, Arthur
See Blish, James (Benjamin)

Merrill, James (Ingram) 1926-1995 .. **CLC 2, 3, 6, 8, 13, 18, 34, 91; DAM POET; PC 28**
See also CA 13-16R; 147; CANR 10, 49, 63; DA3; DLB 5, 165; DLBY 85; INT CANR-10; MTCW 1, 2

Merriman, Alex
See Silverberg, Robert

Merriman, Brian 1747-1805 .... **NCLC 70**

Merritt, E. B.
See Waddington, Miriam

Merton, Thomas 1915-1968 ..... **CLC 1, 3, 11, 34, 83; PC 10**
See also CA 5-8R; 25-28R; CANR 22, 53; DA3; DLB 48; DLBY 81; MTCW 1, 2

Merwin, W(illiam) S(tanley) 1927- ... **CLC 1, 2, 3, 5, 8, 13, 18, 45, 88; DAM POET**
See also CA 13-16R; CANR 15, 51; DA3; DLB 5, 169; INT CANR-15; MTCW 1, 2

Metcalf, John 1938- .... **CLC 37**
See also CA 113; DLB 60

Metcalf, Suzanne
See Baum, L(yman) Frank

Mew, Charlotte (Mary) 1870-1928 .. **TCLC 8**
See also CA 105; DLB 19, 135

Mewshaw, Michael 1943- .... **CLC 9**
See also CA 53-56; CANR 7, 47; DLBY 80

Meyer, Conrad Ferdinand 1825-1905 .... **NCLC 81**
See also DLB 129

Meyer, June
See Jordan, June

Meyer, Lynn
See Slavitt, David R(ytman)

Meyer-Meyrink, Gustav 1868-1932
See Meyrink, Gustav
See also CA 117

Palamas, Kostes 1859-1943 .... **TCLC 5**
See also CA 105

Palazzeschi, Aldo 1885-1974 .... **CLC 11**
See also CA 89-92; 53-56; DLB 114

Pales Matos, Luis 1898-1959
See also HLCS 2; HW 1

Paley, Grace 1922- .... **CLC 4, 6, 37; DAM POP; SSC 8**
See also CA 25-28R; CANR 13, 46, 74; DA3; DLB 28; INT CANR-13; MTCW 1, 2

Palin, Michael (Edward) 1943- .... **CLC 21**
See also Monty Python
See also CA 107; CANR 35; SATA 67

Palliser, Charles 1947- .... **CLC 65**
See also CA 136; CANR 76

Palma, Ricardo 1833-1919 .... **TCLC 29**
See also CA 168

Pancake, Breece Dexter 1952-1979
See Pancake, Breece D'J
See also CA 123; 109

Pancake, Breece D'J .... **CLC 29**
See also Pancake, Breece Dexter
See also DLB 130

Panko, Rudy
See Gogol, Nikolai (Vasilyevich)

Papadiamantis, Alexandros
1851-1911 .... **TCLC 29**
See also CA 168

Papadiamantopoulos, Johannes 1856-1910
See Moreas, Jean
See also CA 117

Papini, Giovanni 1881-1956 .... **TCLC 22**
See also CA 121; 180

Paracelsus 1493-1541 .... **LC 14**
See also DLB 179

Parasol, Peter
See Stevens, Wallace

Pardo Bazan, Emilia 1851-1921 .... **SSC 30**

Pareto, Vilfredo 1848-1923 .... **TCLC 69**
See also CA 175

Parfenie, Maria
See Codrescu, Andrei

Parini, Jay (Lee) 1948- .... **CLC 54**
See also CA 97-100; CAAS 16; CANR 32, 87

Park, Jordan
See Kornbluth, C(yril) M.; Pohl, Frederik

Park, Robert E(zra) 1864-1944 ..... **TCLC 73**
See also CA 122; 165

Parker, Bert
See Ellison, Harlan (Jay)

Parker, Dorothy (Rothschild)
1893-1967 .... **CLC 15, 68; DAM POET; PC 28; SSC 2**
See also CA 19-20; 25-28R; CAP 2; DA3; DLB 11, 45, 86; MTCW 1, 2

Parker, Robert B(rown) 1932- .... **CLC 27; DAM NOV, POP**
See also AAYA 28; BEST 89:4; CA 49-52; CANR 1, 26, 52, 89; INT CANR-26; MTCW 1

Parkin, Frank 1940- .... **CLC 43**
See also CA 147

Parkman, Francis Jr., Jr.
1823-1893 .... **NCLC 12**
See also DLB 1, 30, 186

Parks, Gordon (Alexander Buchanan) 1912-
CLC 1, 16; BLC 3; DAM MULT
See also AITN 2; BW 2, 3; CA 41-44R; CANR 26, 66; DA3; DLB 33; MTCW 2; SATA 8, 108

Parmenides c. 515B.C.-c.
450B.C. .... **CMLC 22**
See also DLB 176

Parnell, Thomas 1679-1718 .... **LC 3**
See also DLB 94

Parra, Nicanor 1914- ...... **CLC 2, 102; DAM MULT; HLC 2**
See also CA 85-88; CANR 32; HW 1; MTCW 1

Parra Sanojo, Ana Teresa de la 1890-1936
See also HLCS 2

Parrish, Mary Frances
See Fisher, M(ary) F(rances) K(ennedy)

Parson
See Coleridge, Samuel Taylor

Parson Lot
See Kingsley, Charles

Parton, Sara Payson Willis
1811-1872 .... **NCLC 86**
See also DLB 43, 74

Partridge, Anthony
See Oppenheim, E(dward) Phillips

Pascal, Blaise 1623-1662 .... **LC 35**

Pascoli, Giovanni 1855-1912 .... **TCLC 45**
See also CA 170

Pasolini, Pier Paolo 1922-1975 .. **CLC 20, 37, 106; PC 17**
See also CA 93-96; 61-64; CANR 63; DLB 128, 177; MTCW 1

Pasquini
See Silone, Ignazio

Pastan, Linda (Olenik) 1932- .... **CLC 27; DAM POET**
See also CA 61-64; CANR 18, 40, 61; DLB 5

Pasternak, Boris (Leonidovich) 1890-1960
CLC 7, 10, 18, 63; DA; DAB; DAC; DAM MST, NOV, POET; PC 6; SSC 31; WLC
See also CA 127; 116; DA3; MTCW 1, 2

Patchen, Kenneth 1911-1972 .. **CLC 1, 2, 18; DAM POET**
See also CA 1-4R; 33-36R; CANR 3, 35; DLB 16, 48; MTCW 1

Pater, Walter (Horatio) 1839-1894 .. **NCLC 7**
See also CDBLB 1832-1890; DLB 57, 156

Paterson, A(ndrew) B(arton) 1864-1941
TCLC 32
See also CA 155; SATA 97

Paterson, Katherine (Womeldorf)
1932- .... **CLC 12, 30**
See also AAYA 1, 31; CA 21-24R; CANR 28, 59; CLR 7, 50; DLB 52; JRDA; MAICYA; MTCW 1; SATA 13, 53, 92

Patmore, Coventry Kersey Dighton
1823-1896 .... **NCLC 9**
See also DLB 35, 98

Paton, Alan (Stewart) 1903-1988 ...... **CLC 4, 10, 25, 55, 106; DA; DAB; DAC; DAM MST, NOV; WLC**
See also AAYA 26; CA 13-16; 125; CANR 22; CAP 1; DA3; DLBD 17; MTCW 1, 2; SATA 11; SATA-Obit 56

Paton Walsh, Gillian 1937-
See Walsh, Jill Paton
See also AAYA 11; CANR 38, 83; DLB 161; JRDA; MAICYA; SAAS 3; SATA 4, 72, 109

Patton, George S. 1885-1945 .... **TCLC 79**

Paulding, James Kirke 1778-1860 ... **NCLC 2**
See also DLB 3, 59, 74

Paulin, Thomas Neilson 1949-
See Paulin, Tom
See also CA 123; 128

Paulin, Tom .... **CLC 37**
See also Paulin, Thomas Neilson
See also DLB 40

Pausanias c. 1st cent. - .... **CMLC 36**

Paustovsky, Konstantin (Georgievich)
1892-1968 .... **CLC 40**
See also CA 93-96; 25-28R

Pavese, Cesare 1908-1950 .. **TCLC 3; PC 13; SSC 19**
See also CA 104; 169; DLB 128, 177

Pavic, Milorad 1929- .... **CLC 60**
See also CA 136; DLB 181

Pavlov, Ivan Petrovich 1849-1936 . **TCLC 91**
See also CA 118; 180

Payne, Alan
See Jakes, John (William)

Paz, Gil
See Lugones, Leopoldo

Paz, Octavio 1914-1998 . **CLC 3, 4, 6, 10, 19, 51, 65, 119; DA; DAB; DAC; DAM MST, MULT, POET; HLC 2; PC 1; WLC**
See also CA 73-76; 165; CANR 32, 65; DA3; DLBY 90, 98; HW 1, 2; MTCW 1, 2

p'Bitek, Okot 1931-1982 .... **CLC 96; BLC 3; DAM MULT**
See also BW 2, 3; CA 124; 107; CANR 82; DLB 125; MTCW 1, 2

Peacock, Molly 1947- .... **CLC 60**
See also CA 103; CAAS 21; CANR 52, 84; DLB 120

Peacock, Thomas Love
1785-1866 .... **NCLC 22**
See also DLB 96, 116

Peake, Mervyn 1911-1968 .... **CLC 7, 54**
See also CA 5-8R; 25-28R; CANR 3; DLB 15, 160; MTCW 1; SATA 23

Pearce, Philippa .... **CLC 21**
See also Christie, (Ann) Philippa
See also CLR 9; DLB 161; MAICYA; SATA 1, 67

Pearl, Eric
See Elman, Richard (Martin)

Pearson, T(homas) R(eid) 1956- .... **CLC 39**
See also CA 120; 130; INT 130

Peck, Dale 1967- .... **CLC 81**
See also CA 146; CANR 72

Peck, John 1941- .... **CLC 3**
See also CA 49-52; CANR 3

Peck, Richard (Wayne) 1934- .... **CLC 21**
See also AAYA 1, 24; CA 85-88; CANR 19, 38; CLR 15; INT CANR-19; JRDA; MAICYA; SAAS 2; SATA 18, 55, 97; SATA-Essay 110

Peck, Robert Newton 1928- .... **CLC 17; DA; DAC; DAM MST**
See also AAYA 3; CA 81-84, 182; CAAE 182; CANR 31, 63; CLR 45; JRDA; MAICYA; SAAS 1; SATA 21, 62, 111; SATA-Essay 108

Peckinpah, (David) Sam(uel)
1925-1984 .... **CLC 20**
See also CA 109; 114; CANR 82

Pedersen, Knut 1859-1952
See Hamsun, Knut
See also CA 104; 119; CANR 63; MTCW 1, 2

Peeslake, Gaffer
See Durrell, Lawrence (George)

Peguy, Charles Pierre 1873-1914 ... **TCLC 10**
See also CA 107

Peirce, Charles Sanders
1839-1914 .... **TCLC 81**

Pellicer, Carlos 1900(?)-1977
See also CA 153; 69-72; HLCS 2; HW 1

Pena, Ramon del Valle y
See Valle-Inclan, Ramon (Maria) del

Pendennis, Arthur Esquir
See Thackeray, William Makepeace

Penn, William 1644-1718 .... **LC 25**
See also DLB 24

PEPECE
See Prado (Calvo), Pedro

Pepys, Samuel 1633-1703 ..... **LC 11, 58; DA; DAB; DAC; DAM MST; WLC**
See also CDBLB 1660-1789; DA3; DLB 101

Percy, Walker 1916-1990 .... **CLC 2, 3, 6, 8, 14, 18, 47, 65; DAM NOV, POP**
See also CA 1-4R; 131; CANR 1, 23, 64; DA3; DLB 2; DLBY 80, 90; MTCW 1, 2

Percy, William Alexander 1885-1942 .... **TCLC 84**
See also CA 163; MTCW 2

Perec, Georges 1936-1982 .... **CLC 56, 116**
See also CA 141; DLB 83

Pereda (y Sanchez de Porrua), Jose Maria de 1833-1906 .... **TCLC 16**
See also CA 117

Pereda y Porrua, Jose Maria de
See Pereda (y Sanchez de Porrua), Jose Maria de

Peregoy, George Weems
See Mencken, H(enry) L(ouis)

Perelman, S(idney) J(oseph) 1904-1979 .. **CLC 3, 5, 9, 15, 23, 44, 49; DAM DRAM; SSC 32**
See also AITN 1, 2; CA 73-76; 89-92; CANR 18; DLB 11, 44; MTCW 1, 2

Peret, Benjamin 1899-1959 .... **TCLC 20**
See also CA 117; 186

Peretz, Isaac Loeb 1851(?)-1915 ... **TCLC 16; SSC 26**
See also CA 109

Peretz, Yitzkhok Leibush
See Peretz, Isaac Loeb

Perez Galdos, Benito 1843-1920 ... **TCLC 27; HLCS 2**
See also CA 125; 153; HW 1

Peri Rossi, Cristina 1941-
See also CA 131; CANR 59, 81; DLB 145; HLCS 2; HW 1, 2

Perlata
See Peret, Benjamin

Perrault, Charles 1628-1703 ... **LC 3, 52; DC 12**
See also MAICYA; SATA 25

Perry, Anne 1938- .... **CLC 126**
See also CA 101; CANR 22, 50, 84

Perry, Brighton
See Sherwood, Robert E(mmet)

Perse, St.-John
See Leger, (Marie-Rene Auguste) Alexis Saint-Leger

Perutz, Leo(pold) 1882-1957 .... **TCLC 60**
See also CA 147; DLB 81

Peseenz, Tulio F.
See Lopez y Fuentes, Gregorio

Pesetsky, Bette 1932- .... **CLC 28**
See also CA 133; DLB 130

Peshkov, Alexei Maximovich 1868-1936
See Gorky, Maxim
See also CA 105; 141; CANR 83; DA; DAC; DAM DRAM, MST, NOV; MTCW 2

Pessoa, Fernando (Antonio Nogueira) 1888-1935 .... **TCLC 27; DAM MULT; HLC 2; PC 20**
See also CA 125; 183

Peterkin, Julia Mood 1880-1961 ...... **CLC 31**
See also CA 102; DLB 9

Peters, Joan K(aren) 1945- .... **CLC 39**
See also CA 158

Peters, Robert L(ouis) 1924- .... **CLC 7**
See also CA 13-16R; CAAS 8; DLB 105

Petofi, Sandor 1823-1849 .... **NCLC 21**

Petrakis, Harry Mark 1923- .... **CLC 3**
See also CA 9-12R; CANR 4, 30, 85

Petrarch 1304-1374 .... **CMLC 20; DAM POET; PC 8**
See also DA3

Petronius c. 20-66 .... **CMLC 34**
See also DLB 211

Petrov, Evgeny .... **TCLC 21**
See also Kataev, Evgeny Petrovich

Petry, Ann (Lane) 1908-1997 ... **CLC 1, 7, 18**
See also BW 1, 3; CA 5-8R; 157; CAAS 6; CANR 4, 46; CLR 12; DLB 76; JRDA; MAICYA; MTCW 1; SATA 5; SATA-Obit 94

Petursson, Halligrimur 1614-1674 .... **LC 8**

Peychinovich
See Vazov, Ivan (Minchov)

Phaedrus c. 18B.C.-c. 50 .... **CMLC 25**
See also DLB 211

Philips, Katherine 1632-1664 .... **LC 30**
See also DLB 131

Philipson, Morris H. 1926- .... **CLC 53**
See also CA 1-4R; CANR 4

Phillips, Caryl 1958- . **CLC 96; BLCS; DAM MULT**
See also BW 2; CA 141; CANR 63; DA3; DLB 157; MTCW 2

Phillips, David Graham 1867-1911 .... **TCLC 44**
See also CA 108; 176; DLB 9, 12

Phillips, Jack
See Sandburg, Carl (August)

Phillips, Jayne Anne 1952- .... **CLC 15, 33; SSC 16**
See also CA 101; CANR 24, 50; DLBY 80; INT CANR-24; MTCW 1, 2

Phillips, Richard
See Dick, Philip K(indred)

Phillips, Robert (Schaeffer) 1938- .... **CLC 28**
See also CA 17-20R; CAAS 13; CANR 8; DLB 105

Phillips, Ward
See Lovecraft, H(oward) P(hillips)

Piccolo, Lucio 1901-1969 .... **CLC 13**
See also CA 97-100; DLB 114

Pickthall, Marjorie L(owry) C(hristie) 1883-1922 .... **TCLC 21**
See also CA 107; DLB 92

Pico della Mirandola, Giovanni 1463-1494 **LC 15**

Piercy, Marge 1936- .... **CLC 3, 6, 14, 18, 27, 62, 128; PC 29**
See also CA 21-24R; CAAS 1; CANR 13, 43, 66; DLB 120; MTCW 1, 2

Piers, Robert
See Anthony, Piers

Pieyre de Mandiargues, Andre 1909-1991
See Mandiargues, Andre Pieyre de
See also CA 103; 136; CANR 22, 82

Pilnyak, Boris .... **TCLC 23**
See also Vogau, Boris Andreyevich

Pincherle, Alberto 1907-1990 .... **CLC 11, 18; DAM NOV**
See also Moravia, Alberto
See also CA 25-28R; 132; CANR 33, 63; MTCW 1

Pinckney, Darryl 1953- .... **CLC 76**
See also BW 2, 3; CA 143; CANR 79

Pindar 518B.C.-446B.C. .... **CMLC 12; PC 19**
See also DLB 176

Pineda, Cecile 1942- .... **CLC 39**
See also CA 118

Pinero, Arthur Wing 1855-1934 ... **TCLC 32; DAM DRAM**
See also CA 110; 153; DLB 10

Pinero, Miguel (Antonio Gomez) 1946-1988 **CLC 4, 55**
See also CA 61-64; 125; CANR 29, 90; HW 1

Pinget, Robert 1919-1997 .... **CLC 7, 13, 37**
See also CA 85-88; 160; DLB 83

Pink Floyd
See Barrett, (Roger) Syd; Gilmour, David; Mason, Nick; Waters, Roger; Wright, Rick

Pinkney, Edward 1802-1828 .... **NCLC 31**

Pinkwater, Daniel Manus 1941- .... **CLC 35**
See also Pinkwater, Manus
See also AAYA 1; CA 29-32R; CANR 12, 38, 89; CLR 4; JRDA; MAICYA; SAAS 3; SATA 46, 76, 114

Pinkwater, Manus
See Pinkwater, Daniel Manus
See also SATA 8

Pinsky, Robert 1940- .... **CLC 9, 19, 38, 94, 121; DAM POET; PC 27**
See also CA 29-32R; CAAS 4; CANR 58; DA3; DLBY 82, 98; MTCW 2

Pinta, Harold
See Pinter, Harold

Pinter, Harold 1930- .. **CLC 1, 3, 6, 9, 11, 15, 27, 58, 73; DA; DAB; DAC; DAM DRAM, MST; WLC**
See also CA 5-8R; CANR 33, 65; CDBLB 1960 to Present; DA3; DLB 13; MTCW 1, 2

Piozzi, Hester Lynch (Thrale) 1741-1821 **NCLC 57**
See also DLB 104, 142

Pirandello, Luigi 1867-1936 ...... **TCLC 4, 29; DA; DAB; DAC; DAM DRAM, MST; DC 5; SSC 22; WLC**
See also CA 104; 153; DA3; MTCW 2

Pirsig, Robert M(aynard) 1928- ... **CLC 4, 6, 73; DAM POP**
See also CA 53-56; CANR 42, 74; DA3; MTCW 1, 2; SATA 39

Pisarev, Dmitry Ivanovich 1840-1868 .... **NCLC 25**

Pix, Mary (Griffith) 1666-1709 .... **LC 8**
See also DLB 80

Pixerecourt, (Rene Charles) Guilbert de 1773-1844 .... **NCLC 39**
See also DLB 192

Plaatje, Sol(omon) T(shekisho) 1876-1932 **TCLC 73; BLCS**
See also BW 2, 3; CA 141; CANR 79

Plaidy, Jean
See Hibbert, Eleanor Alice Burford

Planche, James Robinson 1796-1880 .... **NCLC 42**

Plant, Robert 1948- .... **CLC 12**

Plante, David (Robert) 1940- ...... **CLC 7, 23, 38; DAM NOV**
See also CA 37-40R; CANR 12, 36, 58, 82; DLBY 83; INT CANR-12; MTCW 1

Plath, Sylvia 1932-1963 ..... **CLC 1, 2, 3, 5, 9, 11, 14, 17, 50, 51, 62, 111; DA; DAB; DAC; DAM MST, POET; PC 1; WLC**
See also AAYA 13; CA 19-20; CANR 34; CAP 2; CDALB 1941-1968; DA3; DLB 5, 6, 152; MTCW 1, 2; SATA 96

Plato 428(?)B.C.-348(?)B.C. ... **CMLC 8; DA; DAB; DAC; DAM MST; WLCS**
See also DA3; DLB 176

Platonov, Andrei .... **TCLC 14; SSC 38**
See also Klimentov, Andrei Platonovich

Platt, Kin 1911- .... **CLC 26**
See also AAYA 11; CA 17-20R; CANR 11; JRDA; SAAS 17; SATA 21, 86

Plautus c. 251B.C.-184B.C. ... **CMLC 24; DC 6**
See also DLB 211

Plick et Plock
See Simenon, Georges (Jacques Christian)

Plimpton, George (Ames) 1927- .... **CLC 36**
See also AITN 1; CA 21-24R; CANR 32, 70; DLB 185; MTCW 1, 2; SATA 10

Pliny the Elder c. 23-79 .... **CMLC 23**
See also DLB 211

Plomer, William Charles Franklin 1903-1973 **CLC 4, 8**
See also CA 21-22; CANR 34; CAP 2; DLB 20, 162, 191; MTCW 1; SATA 24

Prowler, Harley
   See Masters, Edgar Lee
Prus, Boleslaw 1845-1912 .... **TCLC 48**
Pryor, Richard (Franklin Lenox Thomas)
   1940- .... **CLC 26**
   See also CA 122; 152
Przybyszewski, Stanislaw
   1868-1927 .... **TCLC 36**
   See also CA 160; DLB 66
Pteleon
   See Grieve, C(hristopher) M(urray)
   See also DAM POET
Puckett, Lute
   See Masters, Edgar Lee
Puig, Manuel 1932-1990 .... **CLC 3, 5, 10, 28,**
   65; DAM MULT; HLC 2
   See also CA 45-48; CANR 2, 32, 63; DA3;
   DLB 113; HW 1, 2; MTCW 1, 2
Pulitzer, Joseph 1847-1911 .... **TCLC 76**
   See also CA 114; DLB 23
Purdy, A(lfred) W(ellington) 1918- ... **CLC 3,**
   6, 14, 50; DAC; DAM MST, POET
   See also CA 81-84; CAAS 17; CANR 42,
   66; DLB 88
Purdy, James (Amos) 1923- .... **CLC 2, 4, 10,**
   28, 52
   See also CA 33-36R; CAAS 1; CANR 19,
   51; DLB 2; INT CANR-19; MTCW 1
Pure, Simon
   See Swinnerton, Frank Arthur
Pushkin, Alexander (Sergeyevich) 1799-1837
   NCLC 3, 27, 83; DA; DAB; DAC; DAM
   DRAM, MST, POET; PC 10; SSC 27;
   WLC
   See also DA3; DLB 205; SATA 61
P'u Sung-ling 1640-1715 .... **LC 49; SSC 31**
Putnam, Arthur Lee
   See Alger, Horatio Jr., Jr.
Puzo, Mario 1920-1999 .... **CLC 1, 2, 6, 36,**
   107; DAM NOV, POP
   See also CA 65-68; 185; CANR 4, 42, 65;
   DA3; DLB 6; MTCW 1, 2
Pygge, Edward
   See Barnes, Julian (Patrick)
Pyle, Ernest Taylor 1900-1945
   See Pyle, Ernie
   See also CA 115; 160
Pyle, Ernie 1900-1945 .... **TCLC 75**
   See also Pyle, Ernest Taylor
   See also DLB 29; MTCW 2
Pyle, Howard 1853-1911 .... **TCLC 81**
   See also CA 109; 137; CLR 22; DLB 42,
   188; DLBD 13; MAICYA; SATA 16, 100
Pym, Barbara (Mary Crampton) 1913-1980
   CLC 13, 19, 37, 111
   See also CA 13-14; 97-100; CANR 13, 34;
   CAP 1; DLB 14, 207; DLBY 87; MTCW
   1, 2
Pynchon, Thomas (Ruggles, Jr.)
   1937- ...... **CLC 2, 3, 6, 9, 11, 18, 33, 62,**
   72; DA; DAB; DAC; DAM MST, NOV,
   POP; SSC 14; WLC
   See also BEST 90:2; CA 17-20R; CANR
   22, 46, 73; DA3; DLB 2, 173; MTCW 1,
   2
Pythagoras c. 570B.C.-c. 500B.C. . **CMLC 22**
   See also DLB 176

Q
   See Quiller-Couch, SirArthur (Thomas)
Qian Zhongshu
   See Ch'ien Chung-shu
Qroll
   See Dagerman, Stig (Halvard)
Quarrington, Paul (Lewis) 1953- ..... **CLC 65**
   See also CA 129; CANR 62
Quasimodo, Salvatore 1901-1968 ..... **CLC 10**
   See also CA 13-16; 25-28R; CAP 1; DLB
   114; MTCW 1

Quay, Stephen 1947- .... **CLC 95**
Quay, Timothy 1947- .... **CLC 95**
Queen, Ellery .... **CLC 3, 11**
   See also Dannay, Frederic; Davidson,
   Avram (James); Lee, Manfred
   B(ennington); Marlowe, Stephen; Stur-
   geon, Theodore (Hamilton); Vance, John
   Holbrook
Queen, Ellery, Jr.
   See Dannay, Frederic; Lee, Manfred
   B(ennington)
Queneau, Raymond 1903-1976 ..... **CLC 2, 5,**
   10, 42
   See also CA 77-80; 69-72; CANR 32; DLB
   72; MTCW 1, 2
Quevedo, Francisco de 1580-1645 .... **LC 23**
Quiller-Couch, SirArthur (Thomas)
   1863-1944 .... **TCLC 53**
   See also CA 118; 166; DLB 135, 153, 190
Quin, Ann (Marie) 1936-1973 .... **CLC 6**
   See also CA 9-12R; 45-48; DLB 14
Quinn, Martin
   See Smith, Martin Cruz
Quinn, Peter 1947- .... **CLC 91**
Quinn, Simon
   See Smith, Martin Cruz
Quintana, Leroy V. 1944-
   See also CA 131; CANR 65; DAM MULT;
   DLB 82; HLC 2; HW 1, 2
Quiroga, Horacio (Sylvestre) 1878-1937
   TCLC 20; DAM MULT; HLC 2
   See also CA 117; 131; HW 1; MTCW 1
Quoirez, Francoise 1935- .... **CLC 9**
   See also Sagan, Francoise
   See also CA 49-52; CANR 6, 39, 73;
   MTCW 1, 2
Raabe, Wilhelm (Karl) 1831-1910 . **TCLC 45**
   See also CA 167; DLB 129
Rabe, David (William) 1940- .. **CLC 4, 8, 33;**
   DAM DRAM
   See also CA 85-88; CABS 3; CANR 59;
   DLB 7
Rabelais, Francois 1483-1553 ...... **LC 5; DA;**
   DAB; DAC; DAM MST; WLC
Rabinovitch, Sholem 1859-1916
   See Aleichem, Sholom
   See also CA 104
Rabinyan, Dorit 1972- .... **CLC 119**
   See also CA 170
Rachilde
   See Vallette, Marguerite Eymery
Racine, Jean 1639-1699 . **LC 28; DAB; DAM**
   MST
   See also DA3
Radcliffe, Ann (Ward) 1764-1823 ... **NCLC 6,**
   55
   See also DLB 39, 178
Radiguet, Raymond 1903-1923 ...... **TCLC 29**
   See also CA 162; DLB 65
Radnoti, Miklos 1909-1944 .... **TCLC 16**
   See also CA 118
Rado, James 1939- .... **CLC 17**
   See also CA 105
Radvanyi, Netty 1900-1983
   See Seghers, Anna
   See also CA 85-88; 110; CANR 82
Rae, Ben
   See Griffiths, Trevor
Raeburn, John (Hay) 1941- .... **CLC 34**
   See also CA 57-60
Ragni, Gerome 1942-1991 .... **CLC 17**
   See also CA 105; 134
Rahv, Philip 1908-1973 .... **CLC 24**
   See also Greenberg, Ivan
   See also DLB 137
Raimund, Ferdinand Jakob 1790-1836
   NCLC 69
   See also DLB 90

Raine, Craig 1944- .... **CLC 32, 103**
   See also CA 108; CANR 29, 51; DLB 40
Raine, Kathleen (Jessie) 1908- ..... **CLC 7, 45**
   See also CA 85-88; CANR 46; DLB 20;
   MTCW 1
Rainis, Janis 1865-1929 .... **TCLC 29**
   See also CA 170; DLB 220
Rakosi, Carl 1903- .... **CLC 47**
   See also Rawley, Callman
   See also CAAS 5; DLB 193
Raleigh, Richard
   See Lovecraft, H(oward) P(hillips)
Raleigh, Sir Walter 1554(?)-1618 .... **LC 31,**
   39; PC 30
   See also CDBLB Before 1660; DLB 172
Rallentando, H. P.
   See Sayers, Dorothy L(eigh)
Ramal, Walter
   See de la Mare, Walter (John)
Ramana Maharshi 1879-1950 .... **TCLC 84**
Ramoacn y Cajal, Santiago
   1852-1934 .... **TCLC 93**
Ramon, Juan
   See Jimenez (Mantecon), Juan Ramon
Ramos, Graciliano 1892-1953 .... **TCLC 32**
   See also CA 167; HW 2
Rampersad, Arnold 1941- .... **CLC 44**
   See also BW 2, 3; CA 127; 133; CANR 81;
   DLB 111; INT 133
Rampling, Anne
   See Rice, Anne
Ramsay, Allan 1684(?)-1758 .... **LC 29**
   See also DLB 95
Ramuz, Charles-Ferdinand
   1878-1947 .... **TCLC 33**
   See also CA 165
Rand, Ayn 1905-1982 ...... **CLC 3, 30, 44, 79;**
   DA; DAC; DAM MST, NOV, POP;
   WLC
   See also AAYA 10; CA 13-16R; 105; CANR
   27, 73; CDALBS; DA3; MTCW 1, 2
Randall, Dudley (Felker) 1914- .... **CLC 1;**
   BLC 3; DAM MULT
   See also BW 1, 3; CA 25-28R; CANR 23,
   82; DLB 41
Randall, Robert
   See Silverberg, Robert
Ranger, Ken
   See Creasey, John
Ransom, John Crowe 1888-1974 .. **CLC 2, 4,**
   5, 11, 24; DAM POET
   See also CA 5-8R; 49-52; CANR 6, 34;
   CDALBS; DA3; DLB 45, 63; MTCW 1,
   2
Rao, Raja 1909- ..... **CLC 25, 56; DAM NOV**
   See also CA 73-76; CANR 51; MTCW 1, 2
Raphael, Frederic (Michael) 1931- ... **CLC 2,**
   14
   See also CA 1-4R; CANR 1, 86; DLB 14
Ratcliffe, James P.
   See Mencken, H(enry) L(ouis)
Rathbone, Julian 1935- .... **CLC 41**
   See also CA 101; CANR 34, 73
Rattigan, Terence (Mervyn)
   1911-1977 .... **CLC 7; DAM DRAM**
   See also CA 85-88; 73-76; CDBLB 1945-
   1960; DLB 13; MTCW 1, 2
Ratushinskaya, Irina 1954- .... **CLC 54**
   See also CA 129; CANR 68
Raven, Simon (Arthur Noel) 1927- .. **CLC 14**
   See also CA 81-84; CANR 86
Ravenna, Michael
   See Welty, Eudora
Rawley, Callman 1903-
   See Rakosi, Carl
   See also CA 21-24R; CANR 12, 32, 91

Riis, Jacob A(ugust) 1849-1914 ..... **TCLC 80**
See also CA 113; 168; DLB 23

Riley, James Whitcomb
1849-1916 .... **TCLC 51; DAM POET**
See also CA 118; 137; MAICYA; SATA 17

Riley, Tex
See Creasey, John

Rilke, Rainer Maria 1875-1926 .. **TCLC 1, 6,
19; DAM POET; PC 2**
See also CA 104; 132; CANR 62; DA3;
DLB 81; MTCW 1, 2

Rimbaud, (Jean Nicolas) Arthur 1854-1891
**NCLC 4, 35, 82; DA; DAB; DAC; DAM
MST, POET; PC 3; WLC**
See also DA3

Rinehart, Mary Roberts
1876-1958 .... **TCLC 52**
See also CA 108; 166

Ringmaster, The
See Mencken, H(enry) L(ouis)

Ringwood, Gwen(dolyn Margaret) Pharis
1910-1984 .... **CLC 48**
See also CA 148; 112; DLB 88

Rio, Michel 19(?)- .... **CLC 43**

Ritsos, Giannes
See Ritsos, Yannis

Ritsos, Yannis 1909-1990 .... **CLC 6, 13, 31**
See also CA 77-80; 133; CANR 39, 61;
MTCW 1

Ritter, Erika 1948(?)- .... **CLC 52**

Rivera, Jose Eustasio 1889-1928 ... **TCLC 35**
See also CA 162; HW 1, 2

Rivera, Tomas 1935-1984
See also CA 49-52; CANR 32; DLB 82;
HLCS 2; HW 1

Rivers, Conrad Kent 1933-1968 .... **CLC 1**
See also BW 1; CA 85-88; DLB 41

Rivers, Elfrida
See Bradley, Marion Zimmer

Riverside, John
See Heinlein, Robert A(nson)

Rizal, Jose 1861-1896 .... **NCLC 27**

Roa Bastos, Augusto (Antonio)
1917- .... **CLC 45; DAM MULT; HLC 2**
See also CA 131; DLB 113; HW 1

Robbe-Grillet, Alain 1922- .... **CLC 1, 2, 4, 6,
8, 10, 14, 43, 128**
See also CA 9-12R; CANR 33, 65; DLB
83; MTCW 1, 2

Robbins, Harold 1916-1997 .... **CLC 5; DAM
NOV**
See also CA 73-76; 162; CANR 26, 54;
DA3; MTCW 1, 2

Robbins, Thomas Eugene 1936-
See Robbins, Tom
See also CA 81-84; CANR 29, 59; DAM
NOV, POP; DA3; MTCW 1, 2

Robbins, Tom .... **CLC 9, 32, 64**
See also Robbins, Thomas Eugene
See also AAYA 32; BEST 90:3; DLBY 80;
MTCW 2

Robbins, Trina 1938- .... **CLC 21**
See also CA 128

Roberts, Charles G(eorge) D(ouglas)
1860-1943 .... **TCLC 8**
See also CA 105; CLR 33; DLB 92; SATA
88; SATA-Brief 29

Roberts, Elizabeth Madox
1886-1941 .... **TCLC 68**
See also CA 111; 166; DLB 9, 54, 102;
SATA 33; SATA-Brief 27

Roberts, Kate 1891-1985 .... **CLC 15**
See also CA 107; 116

Roberts, Keith (John Kingston)
1935- .... **CLC 14**
See also CA 25-28R; CANR 46

Roberts, Kenneth (Lewis)
1885-1957 .... **TCLC 23**
See also CA 109; DLB 9

Roberts, Michele (B.) 1949- .... **CLC 48**
See also CA 115; CANR 58

Robertson, Ellis
See Ellison, Harlan (Jay); Silverberg, Robert

Robertson, Thomas William 1829-1871
NCLC 35; DAM DRAM

Robeson, Kenneth
See Dent, Lester

Robinson, Edwin Arlington
1869-1935 ... **TCLC 5; DA; DAC; DAM
MST, POET; PC 1**
See also CA 104; 133; CDALB 1865-1917;
DLB 54; MTCW 1, 2

Robinson, Henry Crabb
1775-1867 .... **NCLC 15**
See also DLB 107

Robinson, Jill 1936- .... **CLC 10**
See also CA 102; INT 102

Robinson, Kim Stanley 1952- .... **CLC 34**
See also AAYA 26; CA 126; SATA 109

Robinson, Lloyd
See Silverberg, Robert

Robinson, Marilynne 1944- .... **CLC 25**
See also CA 116; CANR 80; DLB 206

Robinson, Smokey .... **CLC 21**
See also Robinson, William, Jr.

Robinson, William, Jr. 1940-
See Robinson, Smokey
See also CA 116

Robison, Mary 1949- .... **CLC 42, 98**
See also CA 113; 116; CANR 87; DLB 130;
INT 116

Rod, Edouard 1857-1910 .... **TCLC 52**

Roddenberry, Eugene Wesley 1921-1991
See Roddenberry, Gene
See also CA 110; 135; CANR 37; SATA 45;
SATA-Obit 69

Roddenberry, Gene .... **CLC 17**
See also Roddenberry, Eugene Wesley
See also AAYA 5; SATA-Obit 69

Rodgers, Mary 1931- .... **CLC 12**
See also CA 49-52; CANR 8, 55, 90; CLR
20; INT CANR-8; JRDA; MAICYA;
SATA 8

Rodgers, W(illiam) R(obert)
1909-1969 .... **CLC 7**
See also CA 85-88; DLB 20

Rodman, Eric
See Silverberg, Robert

Rodman, Howard 1920(?)-1985 .... **CLC 65**
See also CA 118

Rodman, Maia
See Wojciechowska, Maia (Teresa)

Rodo, Jose Enrique 1872(?)-1917
See also CA 178; HLCS 2; HW 2

Rodriguez, Claudio 1934- .... **CLC 10**
See also DLB 134

Rodriguez, Richard 1944-
See also CA 110; CANR 66; DAM MULT;
DLB 82; HLC 2; HW 1, 2

Roelvaag, O(le) E(dvart)
1876-1931 .... **TCLC 17**
See also Rolvaag, O(le) E(dvart)
See also CA 117; 171; DLB 9

Roethke, Theodore (Huebner) 1908-1963
**CLC 1, 3, 8, 11, 19, 46, 101; DAM
POET; PC 15**
See also CA 81-84; CABS 2; CDALB 1941-
1968; DA3; DLB 5, 206; MTCW 1, 2

Rogers, Samuel 1763-1855 .... **NCLC 69**
See also DLB 93

Rogers, Thomas Hunton 1927- .... **CLC 57**
See also CA 89-92; INT 89-92

Rogers, Will(iam Penn Adair) 1879-1935
TCLC 8, 71; DAM MULT
See also CA 105; 144; DA3; DLB 11;
MTCW 2; NNAL

Rogin, Gilbert 1929- .... **CLC 18**
See also CA 65-68; CANR 15

Rohan, Koda
See Koda Shigeyuki

Rohlfs, Anna Katharine Green
See Green, Anna Katharine

Rohmer, Eric .... **CLC 16**
See also Scherer, Jean-Marie Maurice

Rohmer, Sax .... **TCLC 28**
See also Ward, Arthur Henry Sarsfield
See also DLB 70

Roiphe, Anne (Richardson) 1935- .. **CLC 3, 9**
See also CA 89-92; CANR 45, 73; DLBY
80; INT 89-92

Rojas, Fernando de 1465-1541 .... **LC 23;
HLCS 1**

Rojas, Gonzalo 1917-
See also HLCS 2; HW 2

Rojas, Gonzalo 1917-
See also CA 178; HLCS 2

**Rolfe, Frederick (William Serafino Austin
Lewis Mary)** 1860-1913 .... **TCLC 12**
See also CA 107; DLB 34, 156

Rolland, Romain 1866-1944 .... **TCLC 23**
See also CA 118; DLB 65

Rolle, Richard c. 1300-c. 1349 ...... **CMLC 21**
See also DLB 146

Rolvaag, O(le) E(dvart)
See Roelvaag, O(le) E(dvart)

Romain Arnaud, Saint
See Aragon, Louis

Romains, Jules 1885-1972 .... **CLC 7**
See also CA 85-88; CANR 34; DLB 65;
MTCW 1

Romero, Jose Ruben 1890-1952 .... **TCLC 14**
See also CA 114; 131; HW 1

Ronsard, Pierre de 1524-1585 . **LC 6, 54; PC
11**

Rooke, Leon 1934- . **CLC 25, 34; DAM POP**
See also CA 25-28R; CANR 23, 53

Roosevelt, Franklin Delano
1882-1945 .... **TCLC 93**
See also CA 116; 173

Roosevelt, Theodore 1858-1919 ..... **TCLC 69**
See also CA 115; 170; DLB 47, 186

Roper, William 1498-1578 .... **LC 10**

Roquelaure, A. N.
See Rice, Anne

Rosa, Joao Guimaraes 1908-1967 ... **CLC 23;
HLCS 1**
See also CA 89-92; DLB 113

Rose, Wendy 1948- .. **CLC 85; DAM MULT;
PC 13**
See also CA 53-56; CANR 5, 51; DLB 175;
NNAL; SATA 12

Rosen, R. D.
See Rosen, Richard (Dean)

Rosen, Richard (Dean) 1949- .... **CLC 39**
See also CA 77-80; CANR 62; INT
CANR-30

Rosenberg, Isaac 1890-1918 .... **TCLC 12**
See also CA 107; DLB 20

Rosenblatt, Joe .... **CLC 15**
See also Rosenblatt, Joseph

Rosenblatt, Joseph 1933-
See Rosenblatt, Joe
See also CA 89-92; INT 89-92

Rosenfeld, Samuel
See Tzara, Tristan

Rosenstock, Sami
See Tzara, Tristan

Rosenstock, Samuel
See Tzara, Tristan

Rosenthal, M(acha) L(ouis)
1917-1996 .... **CLC 28**
See also CA 1-4R; 152; CAAS 6; CANR 4,
51; DLB 5; SATA 59

Ross, Barnaby
  See Dannay, Frederic
Ross, Bernard L.
  See Follett, Ken(neth Martin)
Ross, J. H.
  See Lawrence, T(homas) E(dward)
Ross, John Hume
  See Lawrence, T(homas) E(dward)
Ross, Martin
  See Martin, Violet Florence
  See also DLB 135
Ross, (James) Sinclair 1908-1996 ... CLC 13;
  DAC; DAM MST; SSC 24
  See also CA 73-76; CANR 81; DLB 88
Rossetti, Christina (Georgina) 1830-1894
  **NCLC 2, 50, 66; DA; DAB; DAC; DAM
  MST, POET; PC 7; WLC**
  See also DA3; DLB 35, 163; MAICYA;
  SATA 20
Rossetti, Dante Gabriel 1828-1882 . NCLC 4,
  77; DA; DAB; DAC; DAM MST,
  POET; WLC**
  See also CDBLB 1832-1890; DLB 35
Rossner, Judith (Perelman) 1935- . CLC 6, 9,
  29
  See also AITN 2; BEST 90:3; CA 17-20R;
  CANR 18, 51, 73; DLB 6; INT CANR-
  18; MTCW 1, 2
Rostand, Edmond (Eugene Alexis)
  1868-1918 .... TCLC 6, 37; DA; DAB;
  DAC; DAM DRAM, MST; DC 10
  See also CA 104; 126; DA3; DLB 192;
  MTCW 1
Roth, Henry 1906-1995 ..... CLC 2, 6, 11, 104
  See also CA 11-12; 149; CANR 38, 63;
  CAP 1; DA3; DLB 28; MTCW 1, 2
Roth, Philip (Milton) 1933- .... CLC 1, 2, 3, 4,
  6, 9, 15, 22, 31, 47, 66, 86, 119; DA;
  DAB; DAC; DAM MST, NOV, POP;
  SSC 26; WLC**
  See also BEST 90:3; CA 1-4R; CANR 1,
  22, 36, 55, 89; CDALB 1968-1988; DA3;
  DLB 2, 28, 173; DLBY 82; MTCW 1, 2
Rothenberg, Jerome 1931- .... CLC 6, 57
  See also CA 45-48; CANR 1; DLB 5, 193
Roumain, Jacques (Jean Baptiste) 1907-1944
  TCLC 19; BLC 3; DAM MULT**
  See also BW 1; CA 117; 125
Rourke, Constance (Mayfield) 1885-1941
  TCLC 12
  See also CA 107; YABC 1
Rousseau, Jean-Baptiste 1671-1741 ...... LC 9
Rousseau, Jean-Jacques 1712-1778 .... LC 14,
  36; DA; DAB; DAC; DAM MST; WLC**
  See also DA3
Roussel, Raymond 1877-1933 .... TCLC 20
  See also CA 117
Rovit, Earl (Herbert) 1927- .... CLC 7
  See also CA 5-8R; CANR 12
Rowe, Elizabeth Singer 1674-1737 ..... LC 44
  See also DLB 39, 95
Rowe, Nicholas 1674-1718 .... LC 8
  See also DLB 84
Rowley, Ames Dorrance
  See Lovecraft, H(oward) P(hillips)
Rowson, Susanna Haswell 1762(?)-1824
  NCLC 5, 69**
  See also DLB 37, 200
Roy, Arundhati 1960(?)- .... CLC 109
  See also CA 163; CANR 90; DLBY 97
Roy, Gabrielle 1909-1983 .... CLC 10, 14;
  DAB; DAC; DAM MST**
  See also CA 53-56; 110; CANR 5, 61; DLB
  68; MTCW 1; SATA 104
Royko, Mike 1932-1997 .... CLC 109
  See also CA 89-92; 157; CANR 26

Rozewicz, Tadeusz 1921- .. CLC 9, 23; DAM
  POET
  See also CA 108; CANR 36, 66; DA3;
  MTCW 1, 2
Ruark, Gibbons 1941- .... CLC 3
  See also CA 33-36R; CAAS 23; CANR 14,
  31, 57; DLB 120
Rubens, Bernice (Ruth) 1923- .... CLC 19, 31
  See also CA 25-28R; CANR 33, 65; DLB
  14, 207; MTCW 1
Rubin, Harold
  See Robbins, Harold
Rudkin, (James) David 1936- .... CLC 14
  See also CA 89-92; DLB 13
Rudnik, Raphael 1933- .... CLC 7
  See also CA 29-32R
Ruffian, M.
  See Hasek, Jaroslav (Matej Frantisek)
Ruiz, Jose Martinez .... CLC 11
  See also Martinez Ruiz, Jose
Rukeyser, Muriel 1913-1980 . CLC 6, 10, 15,
  27; DAM POET; PC 12**
  See also CA 5-8R; 93-96; CANR 26, 60;
  DA3; DLB 48; MTCW 1, 2; SATA-Obit
  22
Rule, Jane (Vance) 1931- .... CLC 27
  See also CA 25-28R; CAAS 18; CANR 12,
  87; DLB 60
Rulfo, Juan 1918-1986 ...... CLC 8, 80; DAM
  MULT; HLC 2; SSC 25**
  See also CA 85-88; 118; CANR 26; DLB
  113; HW 1, 2; MTCW 1, 2
Rumi, Jalal al-Din 1297-1373 .... CMLC 20
Runeberg, Johan 1804-1877 .... NCLC 41
Runyon, (Alfred) Damon
  1884(?)-1946 .... TCLC 10
  See also CA 107; 165; DLB 11, 86, 171;
  MTCW 2
Rush, Norman 1933- .... CLC 44
  See also CA 121; 126; INT 126
Rushdie, (Ahmed) Salman 1947- .... CLC 23,
  31, 55, 100; DAB; DAC; DAM MST,
  NOV, POP; WLCS**
  See also BEST 89:3; CA 108; 111; CANR
  33, 56; DA3; DLB 194; INT 111; MTCW
  1, 2
Rushforth, Peter (Scott) 1945- .... CLC 19
  See also CA 101
Ruskin, John 1819-1900 .... TCLC 63
  See also CA 114; 129; CDBLB 1832-1890;
  DLB 55, 163, 190; SATA 24
Russ, Joanna 1937- .... CLC 15
  See also CA 5-28R; CANR 11, 31, 65; DLB
  8; MTCW 1
Russell, George William 1867-1935
  See Baker, Jean H.
  See also CA 104; 153; CDBLB 1890-1914;
  DAM POET
Russell, (Henry) Ken(neth Alfred)
  1927- .... CLC 16
  See also CA 105
Russell, William Martin 1947- .... CLC 60
  See also CA 164
Rutherford, Mark .... TCLC 25
  See also White, William Hale
  See also DLB 18
Ruyslinck, Ward 1929- .... CLC 14
  See also Belser, Reimond Karel Maria de
Ryan, Cornelius (John) 1920-1974 ..... CLC 7
  See also CA 69-72; 53-56; CANR 38
Ryan, Michael 1946- .... CLC 65
  See also CA 49-52; DLBY 82
Ryan, Tim
  See Dent, Lester
Rybakov, Anatoli (Naumovich) 1911-1998
  CLC 23, 53**
  See also CA 126; 135; 172; SATA 79;
  SATA-Obit 108

Ryder, Jonathan
  See Ludlum, Robert
Ryga, George 1932-1987 .... CLC 14; DAC;
  DAM MST**
  See also CA 101; 124; CANR 43, 90; DLB
  60
S. H.
  See Hartmann, Sadakichi
S. S.
  See Sassoon, Siegfried (Lorraine)
Saba, Umberto 1883-1957 .... TCLC 33
  See also CA 144; CANR 79; DLB 114
Sabatini, Rafael 1875-1950 .... TCLC 47
  See also CA 162
Sabato, Ernesto (R.) 1911- .... CLC 10, 23;
  DAM MULT; HLC 2**
  See also CA 97-100; CANR 32, 65; DLB
  145; HW 1, 2; MTCW 1, 2
Sa-Carniero, Mario de 1890-1916 . TCLC 83
Sacastru, Martin
  See Bioy Casares, Adolfo
Sacastru, Martin
  See Bioy Casares, Adolfo
Sacher-Masoch, Leopold von 1836(?)-1895
  NCLC 31**
Sachs, Marilyn (Stickle) 1927- .... CLC 35
  See also AAYA 2; CA 17-20R; CANR 13,
  47; CLR 2; JRDA; MAICYA; SAAS 2;
  SATA 3, 68; SATA-Essay 110
Sachs, Nelly 1891-1970 .... CLC 14, 98
  See also CA 17-18; 25-28R; CANR 87;
  CAP 2; MTCW 2
Sackler, Howard (Oliver)
  1929-1982 .... CLC 14
  See also CA 61-64; 108; CANR 30; DLB 7
Sacks, Oliver (Wolf) 1933- .... CLC 67
  See also CA 53-56; CANR 28, 50, 76; DA3;
  INT CANR-28; MTCW 1, 2
Sadakichi
  See Hartmann, Sadakichi
**Sade, Donatien Alphonse Francois, Comte
  de** 1740-1814 .... NCLC 47
Sadoff, Ira 1945- .... CLC 9
  See also CA 53-56; CANR 5, 21; DLB 120
Saetone
  See Camus, Albert
Safire, William 1929- .... CLC 10
  See also CA 17-20R; CANR 31, 54, 91
Sagan, Carl (Edward) 1934-1996 .... CLC 30,
  112
  See also AAYA 2; CA 25-28R; 155; CANR
  11, 36, 74; DA3; MTCW 1, 2; SATA 58;
  SATA-Obit 94
Sagan, Francoise .... CLC 3, 6, 9, 17, 36
  See also Quoirez, Francoise
  See also DLB 83; MTCW 2
Sahgal, Nayantara (Pandit) 1927- .... CLC 41
  See also CA 9-12R; CANR 11, 88
Saint, H(arry) F. 1941- .... CLC 50
  See also CA 127
St. Aubin de Teran, Lisa 1953-
  See Teran, Lisa St. Aubin de
  See also CA 118; 126; INT 126
Saint Birgitta of Sweden c.
  1303-1373 .... CMLC 24
Sainte-Beuve, Charles Augustin 1804-1869
  NCLC 5**
**Saint-Exupery, Antoine (Jean Baptiste
  Marie Roger) de** 1900-1944 .... TCLC 2,
  56; DAM NOV; WLC**
  See also CA 108; 132; CLR 10; DA3; DLB
  72; MAICYA; MTCW 1, 2; SATA 20
St. John, David
  See Hunt, E(verette) Howard, (Jr.)
Saint-John Perse
  See Leger, (Marie-Rene Auguste) Alexis
  Saint-Leger

Shacochis, Robert G. 1951-
See Shacochis, Bob
See also CA 119; 124; INT 124

Shaffer, Anthony (Joshua) 1926- ..... **CLC 19; DAM DRAM**
See also CA 110; 116; DLB 13

Shaffer, Peter (Levin) 1926- .. **CLC 5, 14, 18, 37, 60; DAB; DAM DRAM, MST; DC 7**
See also CA 25-28R; CANR 25, 47, 74; CDBLB 1960 to Present; DA3; DLB 13; MTCW 1, 2

Shakey, Bernard
See Young, Neil

Shalamov, Varlam (Tikhonovich) 1907(?)-1982 .... **CLC 18**
See also CA 129; 105

Shamlu, Ahmad 1925- .... **CLC 10**

Shammas, Anton 1951- .... **CLC 55**

Shandling, Arline
See Berriault, Gina

Shange, Ntozake 1948- .... **CLC 8, 25, 38, 74, 126; BLC 3; DAM DRAM, MULT; DC 3**
See also AAYA 9; BW 2; CA 85-88; CABS 3; CANR 27, 48, 74; DA3; DLB 38; MTCW 1, 2

Shanley, John Patrick 1950- .... **CLC 75**
See also CA 128; 133; CANR 83

Shapcott, Thomas W(illiam) 1935- .. **CLC 38**
See also CA 69-72; CANR 49, 83

Shapiro, Jane .... **CLC 76**

Shapiro, Karl (Jay) 1913- . **CLC 4, 8, 15, 53; PC 25**
See also CA 1-4R; CAAS 6; CANR 1, 36, 66; DLB 48; MTCW 1, 2

Sharp, William 1855-1905 .... **TCLC 39**
See also CA 160; DLB 156

Sharpe, Thomas Ridley 1928-
See Sharpe, Tom
See also CA 114; 122; CANR 85; INT 122

Sharpe, Tom .... **CLC 36**
See also Sharpe, Thomas Ridley
See also DLB 14

Shaw, Bernard .... **TCLC 45**
See also Shaw, George Bernard
See also BW 1; MTCW 2

Shaw, G. Bernard
See Shaw, George Bernard

Shaw, George Bernard 1856-1950 .. **TCLC 3, 9, 21; DA; DAB; DAC; DAM DRAM, MST; WLC**
See also Shaw, Bernard
See also CA 104; 128; CDBLB 1914-1945; DA3; DLB 10, 57, 190; MTCW 1, 2

Shaw, Henry Wheeler 1818-1885 .. **NCLC 15**
See also DLB 11

Shaw, Irwin 1913-1984 .... **CLC 7, 23, 34; DAM DRAM, POP**
See also AITN 1; CA 13-16R; 112; CANR 21; CDALB 1941-1968; DLB 6, 102; DLBY 84; MTCW 1, 21

Shaw, Robert 1927-1978 .... **CLC 5**
See also AITN 1; CA 1-4R; 81-84; CANR 4; DLB 13, 14

Shaw, T. E.
See Lawrence, T(homas) E(dward)

Shawn, Wallace 1943- .... **CLC 41**
See also CA 112

Shea, Lisa 1953- .... **CLC 86**
See also CA 147

Sheed, Wilfrid (John Joseph) 1930- . **CLC 2, 4, 10, 53**
See also CA 65-68; CANR 30, 66; DLB 6; MTCW 1, 2

Sheldon, Alice Hastings Bradley 1915(?)-1987
See Tiptree, James, Jr.
See also CA 108; 122; CANR 34; INT 108; MTCW 1

Sheldon, John
See Bloch, Robert (Albert)

Shelley, Mary Wollstonecraft (Godwin) 1797-1851 ..... **NCLC 14, 59; DA; DAB; DAC; DAM MST, NOV; WLC**
See also AAYA 20; CDBLB 1789-1832; DA3; DLB 110, 116, 159, 178; SATA 29

Shelley, Percy Bysshe 1792-1822 .. **NCLC 18; DA; DAB; DAC; DAM MST, POET; PC 14; WLC**
See also CDBLB 1789-1832; DA3; DLB 96, 110, 158

Shepard, Jim 1956- .... **CLC 36**
See also CA 137; CANR 59; SATA 90

Shepard, Lucius 1947- .... **CLC 34**
See also CA 128; 141; CANR 81

Shepard, Sam 1943- ... **CLC 4, 6, 17, 34, 41, 44; DAM DRAM; DC 5**
See also AAYA 1; CA 69-72; CABS 3; CANR 22; DA3; DLB 7, 212; MTCW 1, 2

Shepherd, Michael
See Ludlum, Robert

Sherburne, Zoa (Lillian Morin) 1912-1995 **CLC 30**
See also AAYA 13; CA 1-4R; 176; CANR 3, 37; MAICYA; SAAS 18; SATA 3

Sheridan, Frances 1724-1766 .... **LC 7**
See also DLB 39, 84

Sheridan, Richard Brinsley 1751-1816 .. **NCLC 5; DA; DAB; DAC; DAM DRAM, MST; DC 1; WLC**
See also CDBLB 1660-1789; DLB 89

Sherman, Jonathan Marc .... **CLC 55**

Sherman, Martin 1941(?)- .... **CLC 19**
See also CA 116; 123; CANR 86

Sherwin, Judith Johnson 1936-
See Johnson, Judith (Emlyn)
See also CANR 85

Sherwood, Frances 1940- .... **CLC 81**
See also CA 146

Sherwood, Robert E(mmet) 1896-1955 .... **TCLC 3; DAM DRAM**
See also CA 104; 153; CANR 86; DLB 7, 26

Shestov, Lev 1866-1938 .... **TCLC 56**

Shevchenko, Taras 1814-1861 .... **NCLC 54**

Shiel, M(atthew) P(hipps) 1865-1947 .... **TCLC 8**
See also Holmes, Gordon
See also CA 106; 160; DLB 153; MTCW 2

Shields, Carol 1935- .... **CLC 91, 113; DAC**
See also CA 81-84; CANR 51, 74; DA3; MTCW 2

Shields, David 1956- .... **CLC 97**
See also CA 124; CANR 48

Shiga, Naoya 1883-1971 ..... **CLC 33; SSC 23**
See also CA 101; 33-36R; DLB 180

Shikibu, Murasaki c. 978-c. 1014 ... **CMLC 1**

Shilts, Randy 1951-1994 .... **CLC 85**
See also AAYA 19; CA 115; 127; 144; CANR 45; DA3; INT 127; MTCW 2

Shimazaki, Haruki 1872-1943
See Shimazaki Toson
See also CA 105; 134; CANR 84

Shimazaki Toson 1872-1943 .... **TCLC 5**
See also Shimazaki, Haruki
See also DLB 180

Sholokhov, Mikhail (Aleksandrovich) 1905-1984 .... **CLC 7, 15**
See also CA 101; 112; MTCW 1, 2; SATA-Obit 36

Shone, Patric
See Hanley, James

Shreve, Susan Richards 1939- .... **CLC 23**
See also CA 49-52; CAAS 5; CANR 5, 38, 69; MAICYA; SATA 46, 95; SATA-Brief 41

Shue, Larry 1946-1985 .... **CLC 52; DAM DRAM**
See also CA 145; 117

Shu-Jen, Chou 1881-1936
See Lu Hsun
See also CA 104

Shulman, Alix Kates 1932- .... **CLC 2, 10**
See also CA 29-32R; CANR 43; SATA 7

Shuster, Joe 1914- .... **CLC 21**

Shute, Nevil .... **CLC 30**
See also Norway, Nevil Shute
See also MTCW 2

Shuttle, Penelope (Diane) 1947- .... **CLC 7**
See also CA 93-96; CANR 39, 84; DLB 14, 40

Sidney, Mary 1561-1621 .... **LC 19, 39**

Sidney, Sir Philip 1554-1586 . **LC 19, 39; DA; DAB; DAC; DAM MST, POET**
See also CDBLB Before 1660; DA3; DLB 167

Siegel, Jerome 1914-1996 .... **CLC 21**
See also CA 116; 169; 151

Siegel, Jerry
See Siegel, Jerome

Sienkiewicz, Henryk (Adam Alexander Pius) 1846-1916 .... **TCLC 3**
See also CA 104; 134; CANR 84

Sierra, Gregorio Martinez
See Martinez Sierra, Gregorio

Sierra, Maria (de la O'LeJarraga) Martinez
See Martinez Sierra, Maria (de la O'LeJarraga)

Sigal, Clancy 1926- .... **CLC 7**
See also CA 1-4R; CANR 85

Sigourney, Lydia Howard (Huntley) 1791-1865 .... **NCLC 21, 87**
See also DLB 1, 42, 73

Siguenza y Gongora, Carlos de 1645-1700 **LC 8; HLCS 2**

Sigurjonsson, Johann 1880-1919 ... **TCLC 27**
See also CA 170

Sikelianos, Angelos 1884-1951 ...... **TCLC 39; PC 29**

Silkin, Jon 1930-1997 .... **CLC 2, 6, 43**
See also CA 5-8R; CAAS 5; CANR 89; DLB 27

Silko, Leslie (Marmon) 1948- .... **CLC 23, 74, 114; DA; DAC; DAM MST, MULT, POP; SSC 37; WLCS**
See also AAYA 14; CA 115; 122; CANR 45, 65; DA3; DLB 143, 175; MTCW 2; NNAL

Sillanpaa, Frans Eemil 1888-1964 ... **CLC 19**
See also CA 129; 93-96; MTCW 1

Sillitoe, Alan 1928- ... **CLC 1, 3, 6, 10, 19, 57**
See also AITN 1; CA 9-12R; CAAS 2; CANR 8, 26, 55; CDBLB 1960 to Present; DLB 14, 139; MTCW 1, 2; SATA 61

Silone, Ignazio 1900-1978 .... **CLC 4**
See also CA 25-28; 81-84; CANR 34; CAP 2; MTCW 1

Silver, Joan Micklin 1935- .... **CLC 20**
See also CA 114; 121; INT 121

Silver, Nicholas
See Faust, Frederick (Schiller)

Silverberg, Robert 1935- .... **CLC 7; DAM POP**
See also AAYA 24; CA 1-4R, 186; CAAE 186; CAAS 3; CANR 1, 20, 36, 85; CLR 59; DLB 8; INT CANR-20; MAICYA; MTCW 1, 2; SATA 13, 91; SATA-Essay 104

Silverstein, Alvin 1933- .... **CLC 17**
See also CA 49-52; CANR 2; CLR 25; JRDA; MAICYA; SATA 8, 69

Staunton, Schuyler
  See Baum, L(yman) Frank
Stead, Christina (Ellen) 1902-1983 ... **CLC 2, 5, 8, 32, 80**
  See also CA 13-16R; 109; CANR 33, 40; MTCW 1, 2
Stead, William Thomas 1849-1912 .... **TCLC 48**
  See also CA 167
Steele, Richard 1672-1729 .... **LC 18**
  See also CDBLB 1660-1789; DLB 84, 101
Steele, Timothy (Reid) 1948- .... **CLC 45**
  See also CA 93-96; CANR 16, 50; DLB 120
Steffens, (Joseph) Lincoln 1866-1936 .... **TCLC 20**
  See also CA 117
Stegner, Wallace (Earle) 1909-1993 .. **CLC 9, 49, 81; DAM NOV; SSC 27**
  See also AITN 1; BEST 90:3; CA 1-4R; 141; CAAS 9; CANR 1, 21, 46; DLB 9, 206; DLBY 93; MTCW 1, 2
Stein, Gertrude 1874-1946 .... **TCLC 1, 6, 28, 48; DA; DAB; DAC; DAM MST, NOV, POET; PC 18; WLC**
  See also CA 104; 132; CDALB 1917-1929; DA3; DLB 4, 54, 86; DLBD 15; MTCW 1, 2
Steinbeck, John (Ernst) 1902-1968 ... **CLC 1, 5, 9, 13, 21, 34, 45, 75, 124; DA; DAB; DAC; DAM DRAM, MST, NOV; SSC 11, 37; WLC**
  See also AAYA 12; CA 1-4R; 25-28R; CANR 1, 35; CDALB 1929-1941; DA3; DLB 7, 9, 212; DLBD 2; MTCW 1, 2; SATA 9
Steinem, Gloria 1934- .... **CLC 63**
  See also CA 53-56; CANR 28, 51; MTCW 1, 2
Steiner, George 1929- .. **CLC 24; DAM NOV**
  See also CA 73-76; CANR 31, 67; DLB 67; MTCW 1, 2; SATA 62
Steiner, K. Leslie
  See Delany, Samuel R(ay, Jr.)
Steiner, Rudolf 1861-1925 .... **TCLC 13**
  See also CA 107
Stendhal 1783-1842 .... **NCLC 23, 46; DA; DAB; DAC; DAM MST, NOV; SSC 27; WLC**
  See also DA3; DLB 119
Stephen, Adeline Virginia
  See Woolf, (Adeline) Virginia
Stephen, SirLeslie 1832-1904 .... **TCLC 23**
  See also CA 123; DLB 57, 144, 190
Stephen, Sir Leslie
  See Stephen, SirLeslie
Stephen, Virginia
  See Woolf, (Adeline) Virginia
Stephens, James 1882(?)-1950 .... **TCLC 4**
  See also CA 104; DLB 19, 153, 162
Stephens, Reed
  See Donaldson, Stephen R.
Steptoe, Lydia
  See Barnes, Djuna
Sterchi, Beat 1949- .... **CLC 65**
Sterling, Brett
  See Bradbury, Ray (Douglas); Hamilton, Edmond
Sterling, Bruce 1954- .... **CLC 72**
  See also CA 119; CANR 44
Sterling, George 1869-1926 .... **TCLC 20**
  See also CA 117; 165; DLB 54
Stern, Gerald 1925- .... **CLC 40, 100**
  See also CA 81-84; CANR 28; DLB 105
Stern, Richard (Gustave) 1928- ... **CLC 4, 39**
  See also CA 1-4R; CANR 1, 25, 52; DLBY 87; INT CANR-25
Sternberg, Josef von 1894-1969 .... **CLC 20**
  See also CA 81-84

Sterne, Laurence 1713-1768 .. **LC 2, 48; DA; DAB; DAC; DAM MST, NOV; WLC**
  See also CDBLB 1660-1789; DLB 39
Sternheim, (William Adolf) Carl 1878-1942 **TCLC 8**
  See also CA 105; DLB 56, 118
Stevens, Mark 1951- .... **CLC 34**
  See also CA 122
Stevens, Wallace 1879-1955 ...... **TCLC 3, 12, 45; DA; DAB; DAC; DAM MST, POET; PC 6; WLC**
  See also CA 104; 124; CDALB 1929-1941; DA3; DLB 54; MTCW 1, 2
Stevenson, Anne (Katharine) 1933- .. **CLC 7, 33**
  See also CA 17-20R; CAAS 9; CANR 9, 33; DLB 40; MTCW 1
Stevenson, Robert Louis (Balfour) 1850-1894 . **NCLC 5, 14, 63; DA; DAB; DAC; DAM MST, NOV; SSC 11; WLC**
  See also AAYA 24; CDBLB 1890-1914; CLR 10, 11; DA3; DLB 18, 57, 141, 156, 174; DLBD 13; JRDA; MAICYA; SATA 100; YABC 2
Stewart, J(ohn) I(nnes) M(ackintosh) 1906-1994 .... **CLC 7, 14, 32**
  See also CA 85-88; 147; CAAS 3; CANR 47; MTCW 1, 2
Stewart, Mary (Florence Elinor) 1916- .... **CLC 7, 35, 117; DAB**
  See also AAYA 29; CA 1-4R; CANR 1, 59; SATA 12
Stewart, Mary Rainbow
  See Stewart, Mary (Florence Elinor)
Stifle, June
  See Campbell, Maria
Stifter, Adalbert 1805-1868 .. **NCLC 41; SSC 28**
  See also DLB 133
Still, James 1906- .... **CLC 49**
  See also CA 65-68; CAAS 17; CANR 10, 26; DLB 9; SATA 29
Sting 1951-
  See Sumner, Gordon Matthew
  See also CA 167
Stirling, Arthur
  See Sinclair, Upton (Beall)
Stitt, Milan 1941- .... **CLC 29**
  See also CA 69-72
Stockton, Francis Richard 1834-1902
  See Stockton, Frank R.
  See also CA 108; 137; MAICYA; SATA 44
Stockton, Frank R. .... **TCLC 47**
  See also Stockton, Francis Richard
  See also DLB 42, 74; DLBD 13; SATA-Brief 32
Stoddard, Charles
  See Kuttner, Henry
Stoker, Abraham 1847-1912
  See Stoker, Bram
  See also CA 105; 150; DA; DAC; DAM MST, NOV; DA3; SATA 29
Stoker, Bram 1847-1912 .... **TCLC 8; DAB; WLC**
  See also Stoker, Abraham
  See also AAYA 23; CDBLB 1890-1914; DLB 36, 70, 178
Stolz, Mary (Slattery) 1920- .... **CLC 12**
  See also AAYA 8; AITN 1; CA 5-8R; CANR 13, 41; JRDA; MAICYA; SAAS 3; SATA 10, 71
Stone, Irving 1903-1989 . **CLC 7; DAM POP**
  See also AITN 1; CA 1-4R; 129; CAAS 3; CANR 1, 23; DA3; INT CANR-23; MTCW 1, 2; SATA 3; SATA-Obit 64
Stone, Oliver (William) 1946- .... **CLC 73**
  See also AAYA 15; CA 110; CANR 55

Stone, Robert (Anthony) 1937- ... **CLC 5, 23, 42**
  See also CA 85-88; CANR 23, 66; DLB 152; INT CANR-23; MTCW 1
Stone, Zachary
  See Follett, Ken(neth Martin)
Stoppard, Tom 1937- ... **CLC 1, 3, 4, 5, 8, 15, 29, 34, 63, 91; DA; DAB; DAC; DAM DRAM, MST; DC 6; WLC**
  See also CA 81-84; CANR 39, 67; CDBLB 1960 to Present; DA3; DLB 13; DLBY 85; MTCW 1, 2
Storey, David (Malcolm) 1933- . **CLC 2, 4, 5, 8; DAM DRAM**
  See also CA 81-84; CANR 36; DLB 13, 14, 207; MTCW 1
Storm, Hyemeyohsts 1935- ..... **CLC 3; DAM MULT**
  See also CA 81-84; CANR 45; NNAL
Storm, Theodor 1817-1888 .... **SSC 27**
Storm, (Hans) Theodor (Woldsen) 1817-1888 **NCLC 1; SSC 27**
  See also DLB 129
Storni, Alfonsina 1892-1938 . **TCLC 5; DAM MULT; HLC 2**
  See also CA 104; 131; HW 1
Stoughton, William 1631-1701 .... **LC 38**
  See also DLB 24
Stout, Rex (Todhunter) 1886-1975 ..... **CLC 3**
  See also AITN 2; CA 61-64; CANR 71
Stow, (Julian) Randolph 1935- ... **CLC 23, 48**
  See also CA 13-16R; CANR 33; MTCW 1
Stowe, Harriet (Elizabeth) Beecher 1811-1896 .... **NCLC 3, 50; DA; DAB; DAC; DAM MST, NOV; WLC**
  See also CDALB 1865-1917; DA3; DLB 1, 12, 42, 74, 189; JRDA; MAICYA; YABC 1
Strabo c. 64B.C.-c. 25 .... **CMLC 37**
  See also DLB 176
Strachey, (Giles) Lytton 1880-1932 .... **TCLC 12**
  See also CA 110; 178; DLB 149; DLBD 10; MTCW 2
Strand, Mark 1934- .... **CLC 6, 18, 41, 71; DAM POET**
  See also CA 21-24R; CANR 40, 65; DLB 5; SATA 41
Straub, Peter (Francis) 1943- . **CLC 28, 107; DAM POP**
  See also BEST 89:1; CA 85-88; CANR 28, 65; DLBY 84; MTCW 1, 2
Strauss, Botho 1944- .... **CLC 22**
  See also CA 157; DLB 124
Streatfeild, (Mary) Noel 1895(?)-1986 .... **CLC 21**
  See also CA 81-84; 120; CANR 31; CLR 17; DLB 160; MAICYA; SATA 20; SATA-Obit 48
Stribling, T(homas) S(igismund) 1881-1965 **CLC 23**
  See also CA 107; DLB 9
Strindberg, (Johan) August 1849-1912 .... **TCLC 1, 8, 21, 47; DA; DAB; DAC; DAM DRAM, MST; WLC**
  See also CA 104; 135; DA3; MTCW 2
Stringer, Arthur 1874-1950 .... **TCLC 37**
  See also CA 161; DLB 92
Stringer, David
  See Roberts, Keith (John Kingston)
Stroheim, Erich von 1885-1957 ..... **TCLC 71**
Strugatskii, Arkadii (Natanovich) 1925-1991 **CLC 27**
  See also CA 106; 135
Strugatskii, Boris (Natanovich) 1933- .... **CLC 27**
  See also CA 106

Strummer, Joe 1953(?)- .... **CLC 30**

Strunk, William, Jr. 1869-1946 ...... **TCLC 92**
See also CA 118; 164

Stryk, Lucien 1924- .... **PC 27**
See also CA 13-16R; CANR 10, 28, 55

Stuart, Don A.
See Campbell, John W(ood, Jr.)

Stuart, Ian
See MacLean, Alistair (Stuart)

Stuart, Jesse (Hilton) 1906-1984 ... **CLC 1, 8, 11, 14, 34; SSC 31**
See also CA 5-8R; 112; CANR 31; DLB 9, 48, 102; DLBY 84; SATA 2; SATA-Obit 36

Sturgeon, Theodore (Hamilton) 1918-1985 **CLC 22, 39**
See also Queen, Ellery
See also CA 81-84; 116; CANR 32; DLB 8; DLBY 85; MTCW 1, 2

Sturges, Preston 1898-1959 .... **TCLC 48**
See also CA 114; 149; DLB 26

Styron, William 1925- .... **CLC 1, 3, 5, 11, 15, 60; DAM NOV, POP; SSC 25**
See also BEST 90:4; CA 5-8R; CANR 6, 33, 74; CDALB 1968-1988; DA3; DLB 2, 143; DLBY 80; INT CANR-6; MTCW 1, 2

Su, Chien 1884-1918
See Su Man-shu
See also CA 123

Suarez Lynch, B.
See Bioy Casares, Adolfo; Borges, Jorge Luis

Suassuna, Ariano Vilar 1927-
See also CA 178; HLCS 1; HW 2

Suckling, John 1609-1641 .... **PC 30**
See also DAM POET; DLB 58, 126

Suckow, Ruth 1892-1960 .... **SSC 18**
See also CA 113; DLB 9, 102

Sudermann, Hermann 1857-1928 .. **TCLC 15**
See also CA 107; DLB 118

Sue, Eugene 1804-1857 .... **NCLC 1**
See also DLB 119

Sueskind, Patrick 1949- .... **CLC 44**
See also Suskind, Patrick

Sukenick, Ronald 1932- .... **CLC 3, 4, 6, 48**
See also CA 25-28R; CAAS 8; CANR 32, 89; DLB 173; DLBY 81

Suknaski, Andrew 1942- .... **CLC 19**
See also CA 101; DLB 53

Sullivan, Vernon
See Vian, Boris

Sully Prudhomme 1839-1907 .... **TCLC 31**

Su Man-shu .... **TCLC 24**
See also Su, Chien

Summerforest, Ivy B.
See Kirkup, James

Summers, Andrew James 1942- .... **CLC 26**

Summers, Andy
See Summers, Andrew James

Summers, Hollis (Spurgeon, Jr.) 1916- .... **CLC 10**
See also CA 5-8R; CANR 3; DLB 6

Summers, (Alphonsus Joseph-Mary Augustus) Montague 1880-1948 .... **TCLC 16**
See also CA 118; 163

Sumner, Gordon Matthew .... **CLC 26**
See also Sting

Surtees, Robert Smith 1803-1864 .. **NCLC 14**
See also DLB 21

Susann, Jacqueline 1921-1974 .... **CLC 3**
See also AITN 1; CA 65-68; 53-56; MTCW 1, 2

Su Shih 1036-1101 .... **CMLC 15**

Suskind, Patrick
See Sueskind, Patrick
See also CA 145

Sutcliff, Rosemary 1920-1992 .... **CLC 26; DAB; DAC; DAM MST, POP**
See also AAYA 10; CA 5-8R; 139; CANR 37; CLR 1, 37; JRDA; MAICYA; SATA 6, 44, 78; SATA-Obit 73

Sutro, Alfred 1863-1933 .... **TCLC 6**
See also CA 105; 185; DLB 10

Sutton, Henry
See Slavitt, David R(ytman)

Svevo, Italo 1861-1928 ...... **TCLC 2, 35; SSC 25**
See also Schmitz, Aron Hector

Swados, Elizabeth (A.) 1951- .... **CLC 12**
See also CA 97-100; CANR 49; INT 97-100

Swados, Harvey 1920-1972 .... **CLC 5**
See also CA 5-8R; 37-40R; CANR 6; DLB 2

Swan, Gladys 1934- .... **CLC 69**
See also CA 101; CANR 17, 39

Swanson, Logan
See Matheson, Richard Burton

Swarthout, Glendon (Fred) 1918-1992 .... **CLC 35**
See also CA 1-4R; 139; CANR 1, 47; SATA 26

Sweet, Sarah C.
See Jewett, (Theodora) Sarah Orne

Swenson, May 1919-1989 ...... **CLC 4, 14, 61, 106; DA; DAB; DAC; DAM MST, POET; PC 14**
See also CA 5-8R; 130; CANR 36, 61; DLB 5; MTCW 1, 2; SATA 15

Swift, Augustus
See Lovecraft, H(oward) P(hillips)

Swift, Graham (Colin) 1949- ...... **CLC 41, 88**
See also CA 117; 122; CANR 46, 71; DLB 194; MTCW 2

Swift, Jonathan 1667-1745 ..... **LC 1, 42; DA; DAB; DAC; DAM MST, NOV, POET; PC 9; WLC**
See also CDBLB 1660-1789; CLR 53; DA3; DLB 39, 95, 101; SATA 19

Swinburne, Algernon Charles 1837-1909 **TCLC 8, 36; DA; DAB; DAC; DAM MST, POET; PC 24; WLC**
See also CA 105; 140; CDBLB 1832-1890; DA3; DLB 35, 57

Swinfen, Ann .... **CLC 34**

Swinnerton, Frank Arthur 1884-1982 .... **CLC 31**
See also CA 108; DLB 34

Swithen, John
See King, Stephen (Edwin)

Sylvia
See Ashton-Warner, Sylvia (Constance)

Symmes, Robert Edward
See Duncan, Robert (Edward)

Symonds, John Addington 1840-1893 .... **NCLC 34**
See also DLB 57, 144

Symons, Arthur 1865-1945 .... **TCLC 11**
See also CA 107; DLB 19, 57, 149

Symons, Julian (Gustave) 1912-1994 .... **CLC 2, 14, 32**
See also CA 49-52; 147; CAAS 3; CANR 3, 33, 59; DLB 87, 155; DLBY 92; MTCW 1

Synge, (Edmund) J(ohn) M(illington) 1871-1909 . **TCLC 6, 37; DAM DRAM; DC 2**
See also CA 104; 141; CDBLB 1890-1914; DLB 10, 19

Syruc, J.
See Milosz, Czeslaw

Szirtes, George 1948- .... **CLC 46**
See also CA 109; CANR 27, 61

Szymborska, Wislawa 1923- .... **CLC 99**
See also CA 154; CANR 91; DA3; DLBY 96; MTCW 2

T. O., Nik
See Annensky, Innokenty (Fyodorovich)

Tabori, George 1914- .... **CLC 19**
See also CA 49-52; CANR 4, 69

Tagore, Rabindranath 1861-1941 ... **TCLC 3, 53; DAM DRAM, POET; PC 8**
See also CA 104; 120; DA3; MTCW 1, 2

Taine, Hippolyte Adolphe 1828-1893 .... **NCLC 15**

Talese, Gay 1932- .... **CLC 37**
See also AITN 1; CA 1-4R; CANR 9, 58; DLB 185; INT CANR-9; MTCW 1, 2

Tallent, Elizabeth (Ann) 1954- .... **CLC 45**
See also CA 117; CANR 72; DLB 130

Tally, Ted 1952- .... **CLC 42**
See also CA 120; 124; INT 124

Talvik, Heiti 1904-1947 .... **TCLC 87**

Tamayo y Baus, Manuel 1829-1898 .... **NCLC 1**

Tammsaare, A(nton) H(ansen) 1878-1940 **TCLC 27**
See also CA 164; DLB 220

Tam'si, Tchicaya U
See Tchicaya, Gerald Felix

Tan, Amy (Ruth) 1952- . **CLC 59, 120; DAM MULT, NOV, POP**
See also AAYA 9; BEST 89:3; CA 136; CANR 54; CDALBS; DA3; DLB 173; MTCW 2; SATA 75

Tandem, Felix
See Spitteler, Carl (Friedrich Georg)

Tanizaki, Jun'ichiro 1886-1965 ... **CLC 8, 14, 28; SSC 21**
See also CA 93-96; 25-28R; DLB 180; MTCW 2

Tanner, William
See Amis, Kingsley (William)

Tao Lao
See Storni, Alfonsina

Tarantino, Quentin (Jerome) 1963- .... **CLC 125**
See also CA 171

Tarassoff, Lev
See Troyat, Henri

Tarbell, Ida M(inerva) 1857-1944 . **TCLC 40**
See also CA 122; 181; DLB 47

Tarkington, (Newton) Booth 1869-1946 **TCLC 9**
See also CA 110; 143; DLB 9, 102; MTCW 2; SATA 17

Tarkovsky, Andrei (Arsenyevich) 1932-1986 **CLC 75**
See also CA 127

Tartt, Donna 1964(?)- .... **CLC 76**
See also CA 142

Tasso, Torquato 1544-1595 .... **LC 5**

Tate, (John Orley) Allen 1899-1979 .. **CLC 2, 4, 6, 9, 11, 14, 24**
See also CA 5-8R; 85-88; CANR 32; DLB 4, 45, 63; DLBD 17; MTCW 1, 2

Tate, Ellalice
See Hibbert, Eleanor Alice Burford

Tate, James (Vincent) 1943- ..... **CLC 2, 6, 25**
See also CA 21-24R; CANR 29, 57; DLB 5, 169

Tauler, Johannes c. 1300-1361 ...... **CMLC 37**
See also DLB 179

Tavel, Ronald 1940- .... **CLC 6**
See also CA 21-24R; CANR 33

Taylor, C(ecil) P(hilip) 1929-1981 .... **CLC 27**
See also CA 25-28R; 105; CANR 47

Taylor, Edward 1642(?)-1729 ..... **LC 11; DA; DAB; DAC; DAM MST, POET**
See also DLB 24

Titmarsh, Michael Angelo
See Thackeray, William Makepeace

Tocqueville, Alexis (Charles Henri Maurice Clerel, Comte) de 1805-1859 . **NCLC 7, 63**

Tolkien, J(ohn) R(onald) R(euel) 1892-1973 **CLC 1, 2, 3, 8, 12, 38; DA; DAB; DAC; DAM MST, NOV, POP; WLC**
See also AAYA 10; AITN 1; CA 17-18; 45-48; CANR 36; CAP 2; CDBLB 1914-1945; CLR 56; DA3; DLB 15, 160; JRDA; MAICYA; MTCW 1, 2; SATA 2, 32, 100; SATA-Obit 24

Toller, Ernst 1893-1939 .... **TCLC 10**
See also CA 107; 186; DLB 124

Tolson, M. B.
See Tolson, Melvin B(eaunorus)

Tolson, Melvin B(eaunorus) 1898(?)-1966 **CLC 36, 105; BLC 3; DAM MULT, POET**
See also BW 1, 3; CA 124; 89-92; CANR 80; DLB 48, 76

Tolstoi, Aleksei Nikolaevich
See Tolstoy, Alexey Nikolaevich

Tolstoy, Alexey Nikolaevich 1882-1945 .... **TCLC 18**
See also CA 107; 158

Tolstoy, Count Leo
See Tolstoy, Leo (Nikolaevich)

Tolstoy, Leo (Nikolaevich) 1828-1910 .. **TCLC 4, 11, 17, 28, 44, 79; DA; DAB; DAC; DAM MST, NOV; SSC 9, 30; WLC**
See also CA 104; 123; DA3; SATA 26

Tomasi di Lampedusa, Giuseppe 1896-1957
See Lampedusa, Giuseppe (Tomasi) di
See also CA 111

Tomlin, Lily .... **CLC 17**
See also Tomlin, Mary Jean

Tomlin, Mary Jean 1939(?)-
See Tomlin, Lily
See also CA 117

Tomlinson, (Alfred) Charles 1927- .... **CLC 2, 4, 6, 13, 45; DAM POET; PC 17**
See also CA 5-8R; CANR 33; DLB 40

Tomlinson, H(enry) M(ajor) 1873-1958 **TCLC 71**
See also CA 118; 161; DLB 36, 100, 195

Tonson, Jacob
See Bennett, (Enoch) Arnold

Toole, John Kennedy 1937-1969 ..... **CLC 19, 64**
See also CA 104; DLBY 81; MTCW 2

Toomer, Jean 1894-1967 .... **CLC 1, 4, 13, 22; BLC 3; DAM MULT; PC 7; SSC 1; WLCS**
See also BW 1; CA 85-88; CDALB 1917-1929; DA3; DLB 45, 51; MTCW 1, 2

Torley, Luke
See Blish, James (Benjamin)

Tornimparte, Alessandra
See Ginzburg, Natalia

Torre, Raoul della
See Mencken, H(enry) L(ouis)

Torrence, Ridgely 1874-1950 .... **TCLC 97**
See also DLB 54

Torrey, E(dwin) Fuller 1937- .... **CLC 34**
See also CA 119; CANR 71

Torsvan, Ben Traven
See Traven, B.

Torsvan, Benno Traven
See Traven, B.

Torsvan, Berick Traven
See Traven, B.

Torsvan, Berwick Traven
See Traven, B.

Torsvan, Bruno Traven
See Traven, B.

Torsvan, Traven
See Traven, B.

Tournier, Michel (Edouard) 1924- .... **CLC 6, 23, 36, 95**
See also CA 49-52; CANR 3, 36, 74; DLB 83; MTCW 1, 2; SATA 23

Tournimparte, Alessandra
See Ginzburg, Natalia

Towers, Ivar
See Kornbluth, C(yril) M.

Towne, Robert (Burton) 1936(?)- ..... **CLC 87**
See also CA 108; DLB 44

Townsend, Sue .... **CLC 61**
See also Townsend, Susan Elaine
See also AAYA 28; SATA 55, 93; SATA-Brief 48

Townsend, Susan Elaine 1946-
See Townsend, Sue
See also CA 119; 127; CANR 65; DAB; DAC; DAM MST

Townshend, Peter (Dennis Blandford) 1945- **CLC 17, 42**
See also CA 107

Tozzi, Federigo 1883-1920 .... **TCLC 31**
See also CA 160

Traill, Catharine Parr 1802-1899 .. **NCLC 31**
See also DLB 99

Trakl, Georg 1887-1914 .... **TCLC 5; PC 20**
See also CA 104; 165; MTCW 2

Transtroemer, Tomas (Goesta) 1931- .... **CLC 52, 65; DAM POET**
See also CA 117; 129; CAAS 17

Transtromer, Tomas Gosta
See Transtroemer, Tomas (Goesta)

Traven, B. (?)-1969 .... **CLC 8, 11**
See also CA 19-20; 25-28R; CAP 2; DLB 9, 56; MTCW 1

Treitel, Jonathan 1959- .... **CLC 70**

Trelawny, Edward John 1792-1881 .... **NCLC 85**
See also DLB 110, 116, 144

Tremain, Rose 1943- .... **CLC 42**
See also CA 97-100; CANR 44; DLB 14

Tremblay, Michel 1942- .... **CLC 29, 102; DAC; DAM MST**
See also CA 116; 128; DLB 60; MTCW 1, 2

Trevanian .... **CLC 29**
See also Whitaker, Rod(ney)

Trevor, Glen
See Hilton, James

Trevor, William 1928- .. **CLC 7, 9, 14, 25, 71, 116; SSC 21**
See also Cox, William Trevor
See also DLB 14, 139; MTCW 2

Trifonov, Yuri (Valentinovich) 1925-1981 **CLC 45**
See also CA 126; 103; MTCW 1

Trilling, Diana (Rubin) 1905-1996 . **CLC 129**
See also CA 5-8R; 154; CANR 10, 46; INT CANR-10; MTCW 1, 2

Trilling, Lionel 1905-1975 .... **CLC 9, 11, 24**
See also CA 9-12R; 61-64; CANR 10; DLB 28, 63; INT CANR-10; MTCW 1, 2

Trimball, W. H.
See Mencken, H(enry) L(ouis)

Tristan
See Gomez de la Serna, Ramon

Tristram
See Housman, A(lfred) E(dward)

Trogdon, William (Lewis) 1939-
See Heat-Moon, William Least
See also CA 115; 119; CANR 47, 89; INT 119

Trollope, Anthony 1815-1882 ... **NCLC 6, 33; DA; DAB; DAC; DAM MST, NOV; SSC 28; WLC**
See also CDBLB 1832-1890; DA3; DLB 21, 57, 159; SATA 22

Trollope, Frances 1779-1863 .... **NCLC 30**
See also DLB 21, 166

Trotsky, Leon 1879-1940 .... **TCLC 22**
See also CA 118; 167

Trotter (Cockburn), Catharine 1679-1749 .... **LC 8**
See also DLB 84

Trotter, Wilfred 1872-1939 .... **TCLC 97**

Trout, Kilgore
See Farmer, Philip Jose

Trow, George W. S. 1943- .... **CLC 52**
See also CA 126; CANR 91

Troyat, Henri 1911- .... **CLC 23**
See also CA 45-48; CANR 2, 33, 67; MTCW 1

Trudeau, G(arretson) B(eekman) 1948-
See Trudeau, Garry B.
See also CA 81-84; CANR 31; SATA 35

Trudeau, Garry B. .... **CLC 12**
See also Trudeau, G(arretson) B(eekman)
See also AAYA 10; AITN 2

Truffaut, Francois 1932-1984 ... **CLC 20, 101**
See also CA 81-84; 113; CANR 34

Trumbo, Dalton 1905-1976 .... **CLC 19**
See also CA 21-24R; 69-72; CANR 10; DLB 26

Trumbull, John 1750-1831 .... **NCLC 30**
See also DLB 31

Trundlett, Helen B.
See Eliot, T(homas) S(tearns)

Tryon, Thomas 1926-1991 .... **CLC 3, 11; DAM POP**
See also AITN 1; CA 29-32R; 135; CANR 32, 77; DA3; MTCW 1

Tryon, Tom
See Tryon, Thomas

Ts'ao Hsueh-ch'in 1715(?)-1763 .... **LC 1**

Tsushima, Shuji 1909-1948
See Dazai Osamu
See also CA 107

Tsvetaeva (Efron), Marina (Ivanovna) 1892-1941 .... **TCLC 7, 35; PC 14**
See also CA 104; 128; CANR 73; MTCW 1, 2

Tuck, Lily 1938- .... **CLC 70**
See also CA 139; CANR 90

Tu Fu 712-770 .... **PC 9**
See also DAM MULT

Tunis, John R(oberts) 1889-1975 ..... **CLC 12**
See also CA 61-64; CANR 62; DLB 22, 171; JRDA; MAICYA; SATA 37; SATA-Brief 30

Tuohy, Frank .... **CLC 37**
See also Tuohy, John Francis
See also DLB 14, 139

Tuohy, John Francis 1925-1999
See Tuohy, Frank
See also CA 5-8R; 178; CANR 3, 47

Turco, Lewis (Putnam) 1934- ..... **CLC 11, 63**
See also CA 13-16R; CAAS 22; CANR 24, 51; DLBY 84

Turgenev, Ivan 1818-1883 .... **NCLC 21; DA; DAB; DAC; DAM MST, NOV; DC 7; SSC 7; WLC**

Turgot, Anne-Robert-Jacques 1727-1781 .... **LC 26**

Turner, Frederick 1943- .... **CLC 48**
See also CA 73-76; CAAS 10; CANR 12, 30, 56; DLB 40

Tutu, Desmond M(pilo) 1931- .... **CLC 80; BLC 3; DAM MULT**
See also BW 1, 3; CA 125; CANR 67, 81

Tutuola, Amos 1920-1997 ...... **CLC 5, 14, 29; BLC 3; DAM MULT**
See also BW 2, 3; CA 9-12R; 159; CANR 27, 66; DA3; DLB 125; MTCW 1, 2

Wallace, David Foster 1962- ..... CLC 50, 114
See also CA 132; CANR 59; DA3; MTCW 2

Wallace, Dexter
See Masters, Edgar Lee

Wallace, (Richard Horatio) Edgar 1875-1932
TCLC 57
See also CA 115; DLB 70

Wallace, Irving 1916-1990 .... CLC 7, 13; DAM NOV, POP
See also AITN 1; CA 1-4R; 132; CAAS 1; CANR 1, 27; INT CANR-27; MTCW 1, 2

Wallant, Edward Lewis 1926-1962 ... CLC 5, 10
See also CA 1-4R; CANR 22; DLB 2, 28, 143; MTCW 1, 2

Wallas, Graham 1858-1932 .... TCLC 91

Walley, Byron
See Card, Orson Scott

Walpole, Horace 1717-1797 .... LC 49
See also DLB 39, 104

Walpole, Hugh (Seymour) 1884-1941 .... TCLC 5
See also CA 104; 165; DLB 34; MTCW 2

Walser, Martin 1927- .... CLC 27
See also CA 57-60; CANR 8, 46; DLB 75, 124

Walser, Robert 1878-1956 .... TCLC 18; SSC 20
See also CA 118; 165; DLB 66

Walsh, Jill Paton .... CLC 35
See also Paton Walsh, Gillian
See also CLR 2, 65

Walter, Villiam Christian
See Andersen, Hans Christian

Wambaugh, Joseph (Aloysius, Jr.) 1937- .... CLC 3, 18; DAM NOV, POP
See also AITN 1; BEST 89:3; CA 33-36R; CANR 42, 65; DA3; DLB 6; DLBY 83; MTCW 1, 2

Wang Wei 699(?)-761(?) .... PC 18

Ward, Arthur Henry Sarsfield 1883-1959
See Rohmer, Sax
See also CA 108; 173

Ward, Douglas Turner 1930- .... CLC 19
See also BW 1; CA 81-84; CANR 27; DLB 7, 38

Ward, E. D.
See Lucas, E(dward) V(errall)

Ward, Mary Augusta
See Ward, Mrs. Humphry

Ward, Mrs. Humphry 1851-1920 .. TCLC 55
See also DLB 18

Ward, Peter
See Faust, Frederick (Schiller)

Warhol, Andy 1928(?)-1987 .... CLC 20
See also AAYA 12; BEST 89:4; CA 89-92; 121; CANR 34

Warner, Francis (Robert le Plastrier) 1937-
CLC 14
See also CA 53-56; CANR 11

Warner, Marina 1946- .... CLC 59
See also CA 65-68; CANR 21, 55; DLB 194

Warner, Rex (Ernest) 1905-1986 ...... CLC 45
See also CA 89-92; 119; DLB 15

Warner, Susan (Bogert) 1819-1885 .... NCLC 31
See also DLB 3, 42

Warner, Sylvia (Constance) Ashton
See Ashton-Warner, Sylvia (Constance)

Warner, Sylvia Townsend 1893-1978 .... CLC 7, 19; SSC 23
See also CA 61-64; 77-80; CANR 16, 60; DLB 34, 139; MTCW 1, 2

Warren, Mercy Otis 1728-1814 ..... NCLC 13
See also DLB 31, 200

Warren, Robert Penn 1905-1989 .. CLC 1, 4, 6, 8, 10, 13, 18, 39, 53, 59; DA; DAB; DAC; DAM MST, NOV, POET; SSC 4; WLC
See also AITN 1; CA 13-16R; 129; CANR 10, 47; CDALB 1968-1988; DA3; DLB 2, 48, 152; DLBY 80, 89; INT CANR-10; MTCW 1, 2; SATA 46; SATA-Obit 63

Warshofsky, Isaac
See Singer, Isaac Bashevis

Warton, Thomas 1728-1790 ..... LC 15; DAM POET
See also DLB 104, 109

Waruk, Kona
See Harris, (Theodore) Wilson

Warung, Price 1855-1911 .... TCLC 45

Warwick, Jarvis
See Garner, Hugh

Washington, Alex
See Harris, Mark

Washington, Booker T(aliaferro) 1856-1915
TCLC 10; BLC 3; DAM MULT
See also BW 1; CA 114; 125; DA3; SATA 28

Washington, George 1732-1799 .... LC 25
See also DLB 31

Wassermann, (Karl) Jakob 1873-1934 .... TCLC 6
See also CA 104; 163; DLB 66

Wasserstein, Wendy 1950- .. CLC 32, 59, 90; DAM DRAM; DC 4
See also CA 121; 129; CABS 3; CANR 53, 75; DA3; INT 129; MTCW 2; SATA 94

Waterhouse, Keith (Spencer) 1929- . CLC 47
See also CA 5-8R; CANR 38, 67; DLB 13, 15; MTCW 1, 2

Waters, Frank (Joseph) 1902-1995 .. CLC 88
See also CA 5-8R; 149; CAAS 13; CANR 3, 18, 63; DLB 212; DLBY 86

Waters, Roger 1944- .... CLC 35

Watkins, Frances Ellen
See Harper, Frances Ellen Watkins

Watkins, Gerrold
See Malzberg, Barry N(athaniel)

Watkins, Gloria Jean 1952(?)-
See hooks, bell
See also BW 2; CA 143; CANR 87; MTCW 2; SATA 115

Watkins, Paul 1964- .... CLC 55
See also CA 132; CANR 62

Watkins, Vernon Phillips 1906-1967 .... CLC 43
See also CA 9-10; 25-28R; CAP 1; DLB 20

Watson, Irving S.
See Mencken, H(enry) L(ouis)

Watson, John H.
See Farmer, Philip Jose

Watson, Richard F.
See Silverberg, Robert

Waugh, Auberon (Alexander) 1939- .. CLC 7
See also CA 45-48; CANR 6, 22; DLB 14, 194

Waugh, Evelyn (Arthur St. John) 1903-1966
CLC 1, 3, 8, 13, 19, 27, 44, 107; DA; DAB; DAC; DAM MST, NOV, POP; WLC
See also CA 85-88; 25-28R; CANR 22; CD-BLB 1914-1945; DA3; DLB 15, 162, 195; MTCW 1, 2

Waugh, Harriet 1944- .... CLC 6
See also CA 85-88; CANR 22

Ways, C. R.
See Blount, Roy (Alton), Jr.

Waystaff, Simon
See Swift, Jonathan

Webb, Beatrice (Martha Potter) 1858-1943
TCLC 22
See also CA 117; 162; DLB 190

Webb, Charles (Richard) 1939- .... CLC 7
See also CA 25-28R

Webb, James H(enry), Jr. 1946- ...... CLC 22
See also CA 81-84

Webb, Mary Gladys (Meredith) 1881-1927
TCLC 24
See also CA 182; 123; DLB 34

Webb, Mrs. Sidney
See Webb, Beatrice (Martha Potter)

Webb, Phyllis 1927- .... CLC 18
See also CA 104; CANR 23; DLB 53

Webb, Sidney (James) 1859-1947 .. TCLC 22
See also CA 117; 163; DLB 190

Webber, Andrew Lloyd .... CLC 21
See also Lloyd Webber, Andrew

Weber, Lenora Mattingly 1895-1971 .... CLC 12
See also CA 19-20; 29-32R; CAP 1; SATA 2; SATA-Obit 26

Weber, Max 1864-1920 .... TCLC 69
See also CA 109

Webster, John 1579(?)-1634(?) ... LC 33; DA; DAB; DAC; DAM DRAM, MST; DC 2; WLC
See also CDBLB Before 1660; DLB 58

Webster, Noah 1758-1843 .... NCLC 30
See also DLB 1, 37, 42, 43, 73

Wedekind, (Benjamin) Frank(lin) 1864-1918
TCLC 7; DAM DRAM
See also CA 104; 153; DLB 118

Weidman, Jerome 1913-1998 .... CLC 7
See also AITN 2; CA 1-4R; 171; CANR 1; DLB 28

Weil, Simone (Adolphine) 1909-1943 .... TCLC 23
See also CA 117; 159; MTCW 2

Weininger, Otto 1880-1903 .... TCLC 84

Weinstein, Nathan
See West, Nathanael

Weinstein, Nathan von Wallenstein
See West, Nathanael

Weir, Peter (Lindsay) 1944- .... CLC 20
See also CA 113; 123

Weiss, Peter (Ulrich) 1916-1982 .. CLC 3, 15, 51; DAM DRAM
See also CA 45-48; 106; CANR 3; DLB 69, 124

Weiss, Theodore (Russell) 1916- ... CLC 3, 8, 14
See also CA 9-12R; CAAS 2; CANR 46; DLB 5

Welch, (Maurice) Denton 1915-1948 .... TCLC 22
See also CA 121; 148

Welch, James 1940- ..... CLC 6, 14, 52; DAM MULT, POP
See also CA 85-88; CANR 42, 66; DLB 175; NNAL

Weldon, Fay 1931- . CLC 6, 9, 11, 19, 36, 59, 122; DAM POP
See also CA 21-24R; CANR 16, 46, 63; CDBLB 1960 to Present; DLB 14, 194; INT CANR-16; MTCW 1, 2

Wellek, Rene 1903-1995 .... CLC 28
See also CA 5-8R; 150; CAAS 7; CANR 8; DLB 63; INT CANR-8

Weller, Michael 1942- .... CLC 10, 53
See also CA 85-88

Weller, Paul 1958- .... CLC 26

Wellershoff, Dieter 1925- .... CLC 46
See also CA 89-92; CANR 16, 37

Welles, (George) Orson 1915-1985 .. CLC 20, 80
See also CA 93-96; 117

Wellman, John McDowell 1945-
See Wellman, Mac
See also CA 166

Wellman, Mac 1945- .... **CLC 65**
  See also Wellman, John McDowell; Well-
  man, John McDowell
Wellman, Manly Wade 1903-1986 ... **CLC 49**
  See also CA 1-4R; 118; CANR 6, 16, 44;
  SATA 6; SATA-Obit 47
Wells, Carolyn 1869(?)-1942 .... **TCLC 35**
  See also CA 113; 185; DLB 11
Wells, H(erbert) G(eorge)
  1866-1946 . **TCLC 6, 12, 19; DA; DAB;**
  DAC; DAM MST, NOV; SSC 6; WLC
  See also AAYA 18; CA 110; 121; CDBLB
  1914-1945; CLR 64; DA3; DLB 34, 70,
  156, 178; MTCW 1, 2; SATA 20
Wells, Rosemary 1943- .... **CLC 12**
  See also AAYA 13; CA 85-88; CANR 48;
  CLR 16; MAICYA; SAAS 1; SATA 18,
  69, 114
Welty, Eudora 1909- ...... **CLC 1, 2, 5, 14, 22,**
  33, 105; DA; DAB; DAC; DAM MST,
  NOV; SSC 1, 27; WLC
  See also CA 9-12R; CABS 1; CANR 32,
  65; CDALB 1941-1968; DA3; DLB 2,
  102, 143; DLBD 12; DLBY 87; MTCW
  1, 2
Wen I-to 1899-1946 .... **TCLC 28**
Wentworth, Robert
  See Hamilton, Edmond
Werfel, Franz (Viktor) 1890-1945 ... **TCLC 8**
  See also CA 104; 161; DLB 81, 124
Wergeland, Henrik Arnold
  1808-1845 .... **NCLC 5**
Wersba, Barbara 1932- .... **CLC 30**
  See also AAYA 2, 30; CA 29-32R, 182;
  CAAE 182; CANR 16, 38; CLR 3; DLB
  52; JRDA; MAICYA; SAAS 2; SATA 1,
  58; SATA-Essay 103
Wertmueller, Lina 1928- .... **CLC 16**
  See also CA 97-100; CANR 39, 78
Wescott, Glenway 1901-1987 .. **CLC 13; SSC**
  35
  See also CA 13-16R; 121; CANR 23, 70;
  DLB 4, 9, 102
Wesker, Arnold 1932- ... **CLC 3, 5, 42; DAB;**
  DAM DRAM
  See also CA 1-4R; CAAS 7; CANR 1, 33;
  CDBLB 1960 to Present; DLB 13; MTCW
  1
Wesley, Richard (Errol) 1945- .... **CLC 7**
  See also BW 1; CA 57-60; CANR 27; DLB
  38
Wessel, Johan Herman 1742-1785 .... **LC 7**
West, Anthony (Panther)
  1914-1987 .... **CLC 50**
  See also CA 45-48; 124; CANR 3, 19; DLB
  15
West, C. P.
  See Wodehouse, P(elham) G(renville)
West, (Mary) Jessamyn 1902-1984 ... **CLC 7,**
  17
  See also CA 9-12R; 112; CANR 27; DLB
  6; DLBY 84; MTCW 1, 2; SATA-Obit 37
West, Morris L(anglo) 1916- .... **CLC 6, 33**
  See also CA 5-8R; CANR 24, 49, 64;
  MTCW 1, 2
West, Nathanael 1903-1940 .... **TCLC 1, 14,**
  44; SSC 16
  See also CA 104; 125; CDALB 1929-1941;
  DA3; DLB 4, 9, 28; MTCW 1, 2
West, Owen
  See Koontz, Dean R(ay)
West, Paul 1930- .... **CLC 7, 14, 96**
  See also CA 13-16R; CAAS 7; CANR 22,
  53, 76, 89; DLB 14; INT CANR-22;
  MTCW 2
West, Rebecca 1892-1983 ... **CLC 7, 9, 31, 50**
  See also CA 5-8R; 109; CANR 19; DLB
  36; DLBY 83; MTCW 1, 2

Westall, Robert (Atkinson)
  1929-1993 .... **CLC 17**
  See also AAYA 12; CA 69-72; 141; CANR
  18, 68; CLR 13; JRDA; MAICYA; SAAS
  2; SATA 23, 69; SATA-Obit 75
Westermarck, Edward 1862-1939 . **TCLC 87**
Westlake, Donald E(dwin) 1933- .... **CLC 7,**
  33; DAM POP
  See also CA 17-20R; CAAS 13; CANR 16,
  44, 65; INT CANR-16; MTCW 2
Westmacott, Mary
  See Christie, Agatha (Mary Clarissa)
Weston, Allen
  See Norton, Andre
Wetcheek, J. L.
  See Feuchtwanger, Lion
Wetering, Janwillem van de
  See van de Wetering, Janwillem
Wetherald, Agnes Ethelwyn
  1857-1940 .... **TCLC 81**
  See also DLB 99
Wetherell, Elizabeth
  See Warner, Susan (Bogert)
Whale, James 1889-1957 .... **TCLC 63**
Whalen, Philip 1923- .... **CLC 6, 29**
  See also CA 9-12R; CANR 5, 39; DLB 16
Wharton, Edith (Newbold Jones) 1862-1937
  TCLC 3, 9, 27, 53; DA; DAB; DAC;
  DAM MST, NOV; SSC 6; WLC
  See also AAYA 25; CA 104; 132; CDALB
  1865-1917; DA3; DLB 4, 9, 12, 78, 189;
  DLBD 13; MTCW 1, 2
Wharton, James
  See Mencken, H(enry) L(ouis)
Wharton, William (a pseudonym) .. **CLC 18,**
  37
  See also CA 93-96; DLBY 80; INT 93-96
Wheatley (Peters), Phillis
  1754(?)-1784 ...... **LC 3, 50; BLC 3; DA;**
  DAC; DAM MST, MULT, POET; PC
  3; WLC
  See also CDALB 1640-1865; DA3; DLB
  31, 50
Wheelock, John Hall 1886-1978 .... **CLC 14**
  See also CA 13-16R; 77-80; CANR 14;
  DLB 45
White, E(lwyn) B(rooks)
  1899-1985 . **CLC 10, 34, 39; DAM POP**
  See also AITN 2; CA 13-16R; 116; CANR
  16, 37; CDALBS; CLR 1, 21; DA3; DLB
  11, 22; MAICYA; MTCW 1, 2; SATA 2,
  29, 100; SATA-Obit 44
White, Edmund (Valentine III)
  1940- .... **CLC 27, 110; DAM POP**
  See also AAYA 7; CA 45-48; CANR 3, 19,
  36, 62; DA3; MTCW 1, 2
White, Patrick (Victor Martindale)
  1912-1990 ...... **CLC 3, 4, 5, 7, 9, 18, 65,**
  69; SSC 39
  See also CA 81-84; 132; CANR 43; MTCW
  1
White, Phyllis Dorothy James 1920-
  See James, P. D.
  See also CA 21-24R; CANR 17, 43, 65;
  DAM POP; DA3; MTCW 1, 2
White, T(erence) H(anbury)
  1906-1964 .... **CLC 30**
  See also AAYA 22; CA 73-76; CANR 37;
  DLB 160; JRDA; MAICYA; SATA 12
White, Terence de Vere 1912-1994 ... **CLC 49**
  See also CA 49-52; 145; CANR 3
White, Walter
  See White, Walter F(rancis)
  See also BLC; DAM MULT
White, Walter F(rancis)
  1893-1955 .... **TCLC 15**
  See also White, Walter
  See also BW 1; CA 115; 124; DLB 51

White, William Hale 1831-1913
  See Rutherford, Mark
  See also CA 121
Whitehead, Alfred North
  1861-1947 .... **TCLC 97**
  See also CA 117; 165; DLB 100
Whitehead, E(dward) A(nthony)
  1933- .... **CLC 5**
  See also CA 65-68; CANR 58
Whitemore, Hugh (John) 1936- .... **CLC 37**
  See also CA 132; CANR 77; INT 132
Whitman, Sarah Helen (Power) 1803-1878
  NCLC 19
  See also DLB 1
Whitman, Walt(er) 1819-1892 .. **NCLC 4, 31,**
  81; DA; DAB; DAC; DAM MST,
  POET; PC 3; WLC
  See also CDALB 1640-1865; DA3; DLB 3,
  64; SATA 20
Whitney, Phyllis A(yame) 1903- ...... **CLC 42;**
  DAM POP
  See also AITN 2; BEST 90:3; CA 1-4R;
  CANR 3, 25, 38, 60; CLR 59; DA3;
  JRDA; MAICYA; MTCW 2; SATA 1, 30
Whittemore, (Edward) Reed (Jr.)
  1919- .... **CLC 4**
  See also CA 9-12R; CAAS 8; CANR 4;
  DLB 5
Whittier, John Greenleaf
  1807-1892 .... **NCLC 8, 59**
  See also DLB 1
Whittlebot, Hernia
  See Coward, Noel (Peirce)
Wicker, Thomas Grey 1926-
  See Wicker, Tom
  See also CA 65-68; CANR 21, 46
Wicker, Tom .... **CLC 7**
  See also Wicker, Thomas Grey
Wideman, John Edgar 1941- ...... **CLC 5, 34,**
  36, 67, 122; BLC 3; DAM MULT
  See also BW 2, 3; CA 85-88; CANR 14,
  42, 67; DLB 33, 143; MTCW 2
Wiebe, Rudy (Henry) 1934- .. **CLC 6, 11, 14;**
  DAC; DAM MST
  See also CA 37-40R; CANR 42, 67; DLB
  60
Wieland, Christoph Martin
  1733-1813 .... **NCLC 17**
  See also DLB 97
Wiene, Robert 1881-1938 .... **TCLC 56**
Wieners, John 1934- .... **CLC 7**
  See also CA 13-16R; DLB 16
Wiesel, Elie(zer) 1928- .... **CLC 3, 5, 11, 37;**
  DA; DAB; DAC; DAM MST, NOV;
  WLCS
  See also AAYA 7; AITN 1; CA 5-8R; CAAS
  4; CANR 8, 40, 65; CDALBS; DA3; DLB
  83; DLBY 87; INT CANR-8; MTCW 1,
  2; SATA 56
Wiggins, Marianne 1947- .... **CLC 57**
  See also BEST 89:3; CA 130; CANR 60
Wight, James Alfred 1916-1995
  See Herriot, James
  See also CA 77-80; SATA 55; SATA-Brief
  44
Wilbur, Richard (Purdy) 1921- ..... **CLC 3, 6,**
  9, 14, 53, 110; DA; DAB; DAC; DAM
  MST, POET
  See also CA 1-4R; CABS 2; CANR 2, 29,
  76; CDALBS; DLB 5, 169; INT CANR-
  29; MTCW 1, 2; SATA 9, 108
Wild, Peter 1940- .... **CLC 14**
  See also CA 37-40R; DLB 5
Wilde, Oscar (Fingal O'Flahertie Wills)
  1854(?)-1900 .... **TCLC 1, 8, 23, 41; DA;**
  DAB; DAC; DAM DRAM, MST, NOV;
  SSC 11; WLC
  See also CA 104; 119; CDBLB 1890-1914;
  DA3; DLB 10, 19, 34, 57, 141, 156, 190;
  SATA 24

Wolfe, Thomas (Clayton)
1900-1938 ...... **TCLC 4, 13, 29, 61; DA; DAB; DAC; DAM MST, NOV; SSC 33; WLC**
See also CA 104; 132; CDALB 1929-1941; DA3; DLB 9, 102; DLBD 2, 16; DLBY 85, 97; MTCW 1, 2

Wolfe, Thomas Kennerly, Jr. 1930-
See Wolfe, Tom
See also CA 13-16R; CANR 9, 33, 70; DAM POP; DA3; DLB 185; INT CANR-9; MTCW 1, 2

Wolfe, Tom .... **CLC 1, 2, 9, 15, 35, 51**
See also Wolfe, Thomas Kennerly, Jr.
See also AAYA 8; AITN 2; BEST 89:1; DLB 152

Wolff, Geoffrey (Ansell) 1937- .... **CLC 41**
See also CA 29-32R; CANR 29, 43, 78

Wolff, Sonia
See Levitin, Sonia (Wolff)

Wolff, Tobias (Jonathan Ansell)
1945- .... **CLC 39, 64**
See also AAYA 16; BEST 90:2; CA 114; 117; CAAS 22; CANR 54, 76; DA3; DLB 130; INT 117; MTCW 2

Wolfram von Eschenbach c. 1170-c. 1220
CMLC 5
See also DLB 138

Wolitzer, Hilma 1930- .... **CLC 17**
See also CA 65-68; CANR 18, 40; INT CANR-18; SATA 31

Wollstonecraft, Mary 1759-1797 ..... **LC 5, 50**
See also CDBLB 1789-1832; DLB 39, 104, 158

Wonder, Stevie .... **CLC 12**
See also Morris, Steveland Judkins

Wong, Jade Snow 1922- .... **CLC 17**
See also CA 109; CANR 91; SATA 112

Woodberry, George Edward 1855-1930
TCLC 73
See also CA 165; DLB 71, 103

Woodcott, Keith
See Brunner, John (Kilian Houston)

Woodruff, Robert W.
See Mencken, H(enry) L(ouis)

Woolf, (Adeline) Virginia
1882-1941 .. **TCLC 1, 5, 20, 43, 56; DA; DAB; DAC; DAM MST, NOV; SSC 7; WLC**
See also Woolf, Virginia Adeline
See also CA 104; 130; CANR 64; CDBLB 1914-1945; DA3; DLB 36, 100, 162; DLBD 10; MTCW 1

Woolf, Virginia Adeline
See Woolf, (Adeline) Virginia
See also MTCW 2

Woollcott, Alexander (Humphreys)
1887-1943 .... **TCLC 5**
See also CA 105; 161; DLB 29

Woolrich, Cornell 1903-1968 .... **CLC 77**
See also Hopley-Woolrich, Cornell George

Woolson, Constance Fenimore 1840-1894
NCLC 82
See also DLB 12, 74, 189, 221

Wordsworth, Dorothy 1771-1855 .. **NCLC 25**
See also DLB 107

Wordsworth, William 1770-1850 .. **NCLC 12, 38; DA; DAB; DAC; DAM MST, POET; PC 4; WLC**
See also CDBLB 1789-1832; DA3; DLB 93, 107

Wouk, Herman 1915- ... **CLC 1, 9, 38; DAM NOV, POP**
See also CA 5-8R; CANR 6, 33, 67; CDALBS; DA3; DLBY 82; INT CANR-6; MTCW 1, 2

Wright, Charles (Penzel, Jr.) 1935- .. **CLC 6, 13, 28, 119**
See also CA 29-32R; CAAS 7; CANR 23, 36, 62, 88; DLB 165; DLBY 82; MTCW 1, 2

Wright, Charles Stevenson 1932- ... **CLC 49; BLC 3; DAM MULT, POET**
See also BW 1; CA 9-12R; CANR 26; DLB 33

Wright, Frances 1795-1852 .... **NCLC 74**
See also DLB 73

Wright, Frank Lloyd 1867-1959 .... **TCLC 95**
See also AAYA 33; CA 174

Wright, Jack R.
See Harris, Mark

Wright, James (Arlington)
1927-1980 .... **CLC 3, 5, 10, 28; DAM POET**
See also AITN 2; CA 49-52; 97-100; CANR 4, 34, 64; CDALBS; DLB 5, 169; MTCW 1, 2

Wright, Judith (Arandell) 1915- ..... **CLC 11, 53; PC 14**
See also CA 13-16R; CANR 31, 76; MTCW 1, 2; SATA 14

Wright, L(aurali) R. 1939- .... **CLC 44**
See also CA 138

Wright, Richard (Nathaniel)
1908-1960 .... **CLC 1, 3, 4, 9, 14, 21, 48, 74; BLC 3; DA; DAB; DAC; DAM MST, MULT, NOV; SSC 2; WLC**
See also AAYA 5; BW 1; CA 108; CANR 64; CDALB 1929-1941; DA3; DLB 76, 102; DLBD 2; MTCW 1, 2

Wright, Richard B(ruce) 1937- .... **CLC 6**
See also CA 85-88; DLB 53

Wright, Rick 1945- .... **CLC 35**

Wright, Rowland
See Wells, Carolyn

Wright, Stephen 1946- .... **CLC 33**

Wright, Willard Huntington 1888-1939
See Van Dine, S. S.
See also CA 115; DLBD 16

Wright, William 1930- .... **CLC 44**
See also CA 53-56; CANR 7, 23

Wroth, LadyMary 1587-1653(?) .... **LC 30**
See also DLB 121

Wu Ch'eng-en 1500(?)-1582(?) .... **LC 7**

Wu Ching-tzu 1701-1754 .... **LC 2**

Wurlitzer, Rudolph 1938(?)- .... **CLC 2, 4, 15**
See also CA 85-88; DLB 173

Wyatt, Thomas c. 1503-1542 .... **PC 27**
See also DLB 132

Wycherley, William 1641-1715 ...... **LC 8, 21; DAM DRAM**
See also CDBLB 1660-1789; DLB 80

Wylie, Elinor (Morton Hoyt) 1885-1928
TCLC 8; PC 23
See also CA 105; 162; DLB 9, 45

Wylie, Philip (Gordon) 1902-1971 ... **CLC 43**
See also CA 21-22; 33-36R; CAP 2; DLB 9

Wyndham, John .... **CLC 19**
See also Harris, John (Wyndham Parkes Lucas) Beynon

Wyss, Johann David Von
1743-1818 .... **NCLC 10**
See also JRDA; MAICYA; SATA 29; SATA-Brief 27

Xenophon c. 430B.C.-c. 354B.C. ... **CMLC 17**
See also DLB 176

Yakumo Koizumi
See Hearn, (Patricio) Lafcadio (Tessima Carlos)

Yamamoto, Hisaye 1921- .... **SSC 34; DAM MULT**

Yanez, Jose Donoso
See Donoso (Yanez), Jose

Yanovsky, Basile S.
See Yanovsky, V(assily) S(emenovich)

Yanovsky, V(assily) S(emenovich) 1906-1989
CLC 2, 18
See also CA 97-100; 129

Yates, Richard 1926-1992 .... **CLC 7, 8, 23**
See also CA 5-8R; 139; CANR 10, 43; DLB 2; DLBY 81, 92; INT CANR-10

Yeats, W. B.
See Yeats, William Butler

Yeats, William Butler 1865-1939 .... **TCLC 1, 11, 18, 31, 93; DA; DAB; DAC; DAM DRAM, MST, POET; PC 20; WLC**
See also CA 104; 127; CANR 45; CDBLB 1890-1914; DA3; DLB 10, 19, 98, 156; MTCW 1, 2

Yehoshua, A(braham) B. 1936- .. **CLC 13, 31**
See also CA 33-36R; CANR 43, 90

Yellow Bird
See Ridge, John Rollin

Yep, Laurence Michael 1948- .... **CLC 35**
See also AAYA 5, 31; CA 49-52; CANR 1, 46; CLR 3, 17, 54; DLB 52; JRDA; MAICYA; SATA 7, 69

Yerby, Frank G(arvin) 1916-1991 . **CLC 1, 7, 22; BLC 3; DAM MULT**
See also BW 1, 3; CA 9-12R; 136; CANR 16, 52; DLB 76; INT CANR-16; MTCW 1

Yesenin, Sergei Alexandrovich
See Esenin, Sergei (Alexandrovich)

Yevtushenko, Yevgeny (Alexandrovich) 1933- **CLC 1, 3, 13, 26, 51, 126; DAM POET**
See also CA 81-84; CANR 33, 54; MTCW 1

Yezierska, Anzia 1885(?)-1970 .... **CLC 46**
See also CA 126; 89-92; DLB 28, 221; MTCW 1

Yglesias, Helen 1915- .... **CLC 7, 22**
See also CA 37-40R; CAAS 20; CANR 15, 65; INT CANR-15; MTCW 1

Yokomitsu, Riichi 1898-1947 .... **TCLC 47**
See also CA 170

Yonge, Charlotte (Mary)
1823-1901 .... **TCLC 48**
See also CA 109; 163; DLB 18, 163; SATA 17

York, Jeremy
See Creasey, John

York, Simon
See Heinlein, Robert A(nson)

Yorke, Henry Vincent 1905-1974 ..... **CLC 13**
See also Green, Henry
See also CA 85-88; 49-52

Yosano Akiko 1878-1942 .... **TCLC 59; PC 11**
See also CA 161

Yoshimoto, Banana .... **CLC 84**
See also Yoshimoto, Mahoko

Yoshimoto, Mahoko 1964-
See Yoshimoto, Banana
See also CA 144

Young, Al(bert James) 1939- . **CLC 19; BLC 3; DAM MULT**
See also BW 2, 3; CA 29-32R; CANR 26, 65; DLB 33

Young, Andrew (John) 1885-1971 ...... **CLC 5**
See also CA 5-8R; CANR 7, 29

Young, Collier
See Bloch, Robert (Albert)

Young, Edward 1683-1765 .... **LC 3, 40**
See also DLB 95

Young, Marguerite (Vivian)
1909-1995 .... **CLC 82**
See also CA 13-16; 150; CAP 1

Young, Neil 1945- .... **CLC 17**
See also CA 110

Young Bear, Ray A. 1950- ..... **CLC 94; DAM MULT**
See also CA 146; DLB 175; NNAL

Literary Criticism Series
Cumulative Topic Index

This index lists all topic entries in Gale's *Classical and Medieval Literature Criticism, Contemporary Literary Criticism, Literature Criticism from 1400 to 1800, Nineteenth-Century Literature Criticism,* and *Twentieth-Century Literary Criticism.*

Topic Index

Topic Index

CLC Cumulative Nationality Index

Nationality Index

Nationality Index

CLC-131 **Title Index**

ISBN 0-7876-3206-6

90000